W9-CLQ-844

EARLY OHIO SETTLERS

State of Ohio
YEAR COUNTY ORGANIZED

Although a county may have been established earlier, it did not function as a county until it was organized. The year shown on this map represents the year of organization and the records of the County Recorder should begin in that year. Since many counties were formed from existing counties, earlier records may exist in the parent county or surrounding counties. It is possible for a land-owner never to have moved, yet various records may show four different counties of residence.

From *Ohio Lands, A Short History* (Auditor of State, Columbus, Ohio, n.d.)

EARLY OHIO SETTLERS

Purchasers of Land in East and East Central Ohio, 1800-1840

Compiled by

Ellen Thomas Berry & David A. Berry

Genealogical Publishing Co., Inc.

Dedicated

to the memory of

Arlene J. Peterson
who was so interested in this project and gave us
encouragement when we most needed it

and

to our Grandchildren, Jason and Julie

PURCHASERS OF LAND IN EAST AND EAST CENTRAL OHIO,
1800-1840 is the third of a series of books listing original
purchasers of Ohio lands.   The two earlier volumes in the series
covered purchases in the southeastern and the southwestern areas
of Ohio, specifically land sold from the Marietta and the
Cincinnati Land Offices. In this present volume, in tabular
format, the names of the purchasers are arranged in alphabetical
order, after which is given the date on which a person first
entered his or her name on the record, the residence of the buyer
at that time, and the location of the land recorded as the range,
township and section. The original data were taken from records
of the State Auditor's Office, Columbus, Ohio, Steubenville
Series No. 428 and Zanesville Series Nos. 259 and 2686.

The actual record books are housed in the
Archives/Library of The Ohio Historical Society, Columbus, Ohio.
They are neither alphabetized nor indexed, so the contents are
virtually inaccessible unless the researcher has unlimited time
in the Columbus area. The present volume is a listing of the
sales of the Zanesville Land Office during the years 1804 to
1840. Zanesville was on a direct route westward from
Pennsylvania, a trail later known as the Cumberland, or National,
Road. The land records contain many instances of purchasers
coming from as far away as Rhode Island, Massachusetts, Maryland,
Virginia, New York, Vermont, New Jersey, Delaware and, of course,
Pennsylvania, and they are therefore of particular value to
genealogists searching for ancestors who lived in Ohio, either
for a short while or for a lifetime.

Included in this volume are purchases from the Steubenville, Ohio, Land Office from 1820 to 1840. This was one of the
four original .land offices and was open until 1840. The years
1800 to 1820 are not included because data for this time span can
be found in a book compiled by Carol Willsey Bell entitled
Steubenville Land Office, 1800-1820, and repeating Mrs. Bell's
work would be pointless.

The counties covered in this volume, whole or in part,
are: Belmont, Carroll, Harrison, Jefferson, Guernsey, Muskingum,
Licking, Knox, Holmes, Delaware, Franklin, and Tuscarawas.
The frontispiece shows this area.

A brief history of the division and sale of Ohio land
is given here as an explanation of how to use this data. After
the Revolutionary War the country had what appeared to be almost
limitless land resources. At the same time cash was in short
supply. What could be more natural than to sell acreage to land-
hungry and restless settlers who wanted to possess land almost
above all else. At the same time the money-supply problem could
be solved. The first step was to have Virginia cede claims to
ownership of lands north of the Ohio River. This was finally
accomplished March 1, 1784 when Congress accepted Virginia's
cession of her western lands - with the exception of a large area
of southern Ohio now known as the Virginia Military District, the
only portion of Ohio where the archaic "metes and bounds"
surveying method was, and remains, in use. Virginia reserved
this tract of approximately 4,200,000 acres for her Revolutionary
soldiers.

It was apparent that a new way to survey land had to be
developed if the remainder of the Northwest Territory was to be
divided in a rational and precise manner. The new government's
proposal was the "grid" system which divided land into thirty-six
square mile portions by using north-south lines six miles wide.
This resulted in long strips called ranges. These ranges are
always designated on maps in roman numerals. East-west lines
were surveyed dividing the ranges at six-mile intervals. Each
block of thirty-six square miles was to be called a township (not
a political designation) and each township was divided into

thirty-six equal portions of 640 acres, or one square mile called a section.

At first it was believed that entire townships would be sold, but this was an overly optimistic projection. At $4.00 per acre only a few prospective purchasers had this much money. Even the smaller sections could not be sold. Eventually, most of the land was sold on the credit system in parcels of eighty acres, and even then much of it was relinquished for non-payment in spite of the willingness on the part of the United States Government to permit the purchaser to spread the total payments over a period of four years. In addition, during the first five years of ownership all taxes on the land were cancelled. Any reader who plans to search tax records should keep this in mind. The credit system was revoked in 1820 and from that time all purchases were on a cash basis.

In spite of rough terrain, Indians, poor instruments, and other difficulties, the surveys were made and were reasonably accurate. The Seven Ranges started at a point where the Ohio River comes out of Pennsylvania and first touches the present State of Ohio. A line known as the Geographer's Line was drawn forty-two miles into Ohio - hence, Seven Ranges. The Line was the northern boundary of this first survey. The township lines were drawn using the Ohio River as the eastern, and downstream the southern, boundary. The natural contours of the river caused problems because in most instances full thirty-six square mile townships could not be made along the river. But it was a beginning. The Seven Ranges Survey was made under the Ordinance of 1785. Sales began in 1787.

In the same year land was sold to The Ohio Company of Associates, a group of Revolutionary War veterans from New England. The group purchased approximately 1.2 million acres in southeastern Ohio at a price not exceeding $0.10 per acre. This was the first of what could rightfully be called land specula-tion. Although it brought settlers to the area beginning in April 1788, overall the Ohio Company venture was not a huge success and at least one-half of the acreage was released by the Company and it was then sold by the United States.

An Act of May 10, 1800 established land offices at Chillicothe, Cincinnati, Marietta and Steubenville and really opened up the Northwest Territory. The boundaries for each office were well described in the legislation, those of t'.. Cincinnati office extending into the east-central and southeastern corner of (now) Indiana, a narrow section usually referred to as the "Gore." The boundaries for each of the four offices are shown on the map designated as Figure 1. As the surveys progressed, the land was sold at $1.25 per acre. The new grid system worked well and was later used across the entire country. Ohio was the original testing ground for this surveying method and, ultimately, it opened the West to settlement more quickly than any other single development.

There are seven major surveys in Ohio and a researcher must know the survey name for any land for which original papers are desired. These surveys are shown in Figure 2. While the United States Military District (also referred to as the United States Tract, Lands or Survey) was set aside by Congress on June 1, 1796 for Continental Line veterans, soldiers' warrants could not be redeemed at the Zanesville Land Office until March of 1805 under an Act of 1803 (W. E. Peters, Laws of the United States: 554) due to surveying problems. When writing to the Bureau of Land Management, Eastern States Office, 350 S. Pickett Street, Alexandria, Virginia 22304, for possible extant documents, or to the Land Office, Auditor of State, 1272 South Front Street, P. O. Box 1140, Columbus, Ohio 43266-0040, for additional information, it is necessary to list the survey name, the range, township and section numbers, along with the purchaser's name and the date of purchase.

Surveying mistakes were made and errors in judgment

occurred because of the new grid system. But the experience gained in Ohio kept the mistakes from being repeated as the land craze swept the country. A study of the surveys and sales of Ohio lands should be a prerequisite for anyone interested in the development of western land.

It soon became evident that offices secondary to the four listed above were necessary in order to place land agents within the areas being sold. As a result, land offices were established in Zanesville, Canton, Wooster, Wapakoneta, Delaware, Bucyrus, Lima, Tiffin, Defiance, Upper Sandusky, and an Ashland branch of the Chillicothe office - all open for three, four or five years to accommodate purchasers of newly surveyed land. The Zanesville office was an exception as it was in business from 1804 to 1840. For this reason, plus other important genealogical considerations, Zanesville land records were chosen for the third volume of this series. And it was also decided to include the final twenty years of land records from the Steubenville office.

We have mentioned that the four original offices had well-defined boundaries. However, the Zanesville office sold land eastward to the Ohio River which included tracts originally reserved for the Marietta and Steubenville offices. Of even greater importance, part of the land in the area reserved by Congress for Revolutionary soldiers, known as the United States Military District, was sold out of the Zanesville office (the western portion of the District was sold from the Chillicothe Land Office). The Act of 3 March 1803, Sec. 6, defined the United States Military District boundaries as: "...lands within the said eleventh range, and east of it, within the said military tract, and all the lands north of the Ohio Company's purchase, west of the seven first ranges, and east of the district of Chillicothe, shall be offered for sale at Zanesville...." This land was south of the Geographer's Line mentioned above. In spite of the limitation of the western boundary as Range 11, the Zanesville records include sales as far west as Range 18. This area is shown in Figure 3, which depicts the entire United States Military District. The land was first divided into townships five miles square rather than the usual six miles. These were later divided into quarter-townships of 4,000 acres each to accommodate warrants in multiples of 50 and 100 acres, the usual amounts awarded to Revolutionary soldiers. This even division cannot be made with six-mile townships. The surveyors also ignored the fact that the lines of longitude diminished in width as they traversed northward, much as the sections in an orange diminish. Internal corrections were made but were never completely satisfactory. The northern boundary of the Military District is the Greenville Treaty line which, as shown in Figure 3, slants from southwest to northeast. This makes sections bordering the line partial sections rather than whole ones. In addition, the numbering along the Geographer's Line was not continued as an extension of the Seven Ranges' numbering as would be the natural way to proceed. The surveyors assigned an entire new set of range numbers for the Military Lands. As a result, the reader must take care in reading the range numbers in this volume.

Each name in the book is followed by a letter or letters in parenthesis. These are not middle initials nor are they guesses about letters of the names. They designate from which office the purchases were made as well as the location of the land. For example: (Y) means it was sold out of the Steubenville office while (Z) indicates the transaction was made in the Zanesville office. (Z-M) after a name designates that the purchase was completed in the Zanesville office for land located in the United States Military District. (Z) following a name indicates the range numbers are those along the original Geographer's Line and the purchase was made at Zanesville. This nomenclature must be used by the researcher or the location of the purchased acreage cannot be determined. As mentioned earlier, to obtain additional information from the National Archives in Washington, D. C. the survey names must be used; in this volume the survey is

either the U. S. Military District or the Ohio River Survey. We
would like to emphasize the importance of knowing the survey name
for any parcel of land, plus the range, township and section
numbers.

About The Names

Transcription of names from the original records is
literal. In many cases it was obvious that the names were misspelled, but the original entry has been given and in some cases
variant spellings are also given. The reader will also find
multiple listings which appear with great frequency. At first
glance this seems redundant, but these multiple entries represent
separate purchases by one person - not mistakes on the part of
the compilers - indicating wealth or land speculation, either of
which could be important information for a researcher.

In some instances the handwriting in the original records was difficult to read, most often because of the poor
penmanship, sometimes because the ink had faded almost to illegi-
bility. We have endeavored to make this present volume as
accurate as possible, but we take full responsibility for any
inaccuracies. The Zanesville volumes, particularly, represent a
very poor level of record-keeping by the land agents or their
clerks. On the other hand, we as genealogists must all be
grateful to these men because they did leave these records about
the land sales.

The Zanesville land records are typical in showing the
numerous places from which settlers set out in pursuit of the
dream of owning their own land. In this volume the abbreviations
used for the place of residence are, in most cases, self-evident.
However, sometimes place names entered in the records are
misspelled or even appear to be incorrect. The following list
explains some of these apparent errors in spelling and will
clarify any confusing entries. As heretofore explained, all
transcriptions are literal.

Place of Residence	Explanation
AleghnaCo,Pa	Allegheny County, Penna.
Barnes'l.Ohio	Barnesville, Ohio
BerklyCoVir	Berkeley County, West Virginia
BrisleCoMass	Bristol County, Massachusetts
BristlCoMass	do do do
CambrayCo,Pa	Cambria County, Penna.
CharllonMass	Charlton, Massachusetts
CoyahogaCoOh	Cuyahoga County, Ohio
FayetteCoVir	Fayette County, West Virginia
GeorgeTownPa	Georgetown ? Virginia/Kentucky
HampshreCoVa	Hampshire County, West Vir.
HardyCo.,Vir	Hardy County, West Virginia
HartfordCoMd	Harford County, Maryland
HuntingtonPa	Huntingdon County,? Penna.
HuntngtnCoPa	Huntingdon County, Penna.
JeffersnCoVir	Jefferson County, West Vir.
KendlStkCoOh	Kendal, Stark County, Ohio
KnoxCo.,Penn	Knox County, Ohio ?
LoudenCo,Vir	Loudoun County, Virginia
LoudonCo,Vir	do do do
MarshallCoVa	Marshall County, West Vir.
MongahlaCoVa	Monongalia County, West Vir.
MonongahlaVa	Monongalia County, West Vir. ?
MordganCoOh	Morgan County, Ohio
MunroeCoOhio	Monroe County, Ohio
Newark ?	Newark - Ohio or New Jersey ?
OhioCo.,Ohio	Ohio County, West Virginia
WarwickCoRI	Warwick, Rhode Island
WindronCo,Vt	Windham, Vermont ?
WindronCo,Vt	Windsor County, Vermont ?
Wooster,Mass	Worcester, Massachusetts

Three listings in this volume are followed by an asterisk - " * ". The entry in the original record reads as follows:

"John Miller & Francis Devera, Trustees for
Sundry persons of colour (sic) emancipated by Ruth
Davis of the same place [Rockingham County, Vir-
ginia.]"

As always with such undertakings many persons have made
this volume possible. We would like to thank Thomas E. Ferguson,
Auditor of State for Ohio; McCullough Williams III, Deputy
Auditor, Administration; Thomas Aquinas Burke, Auditor of State's
Records Officer; Richard H. Schorr of the Land Office, Auditor's
office, Columbus, Ohio. Without their complete cooperation this
book would not have been possible. At The Ohio Historical
Society we are particularly indebted to Thomas J. Rieder and Mrs.
Arlene J. Peterson. On the technical side the talents of Harvey
G. Shulman and James Edgar have kept us going through difficult
periods. We owe each one our most sincere gratitude. Lastly,
our appreciation goes to our editors at the Genealogical
Publishing Company.

                          Ellen Thomas Berry, M. A., C. G.
                          David Allen Berry, B. S., C. G.

Columbus, Ohio
15 June 1989

xi

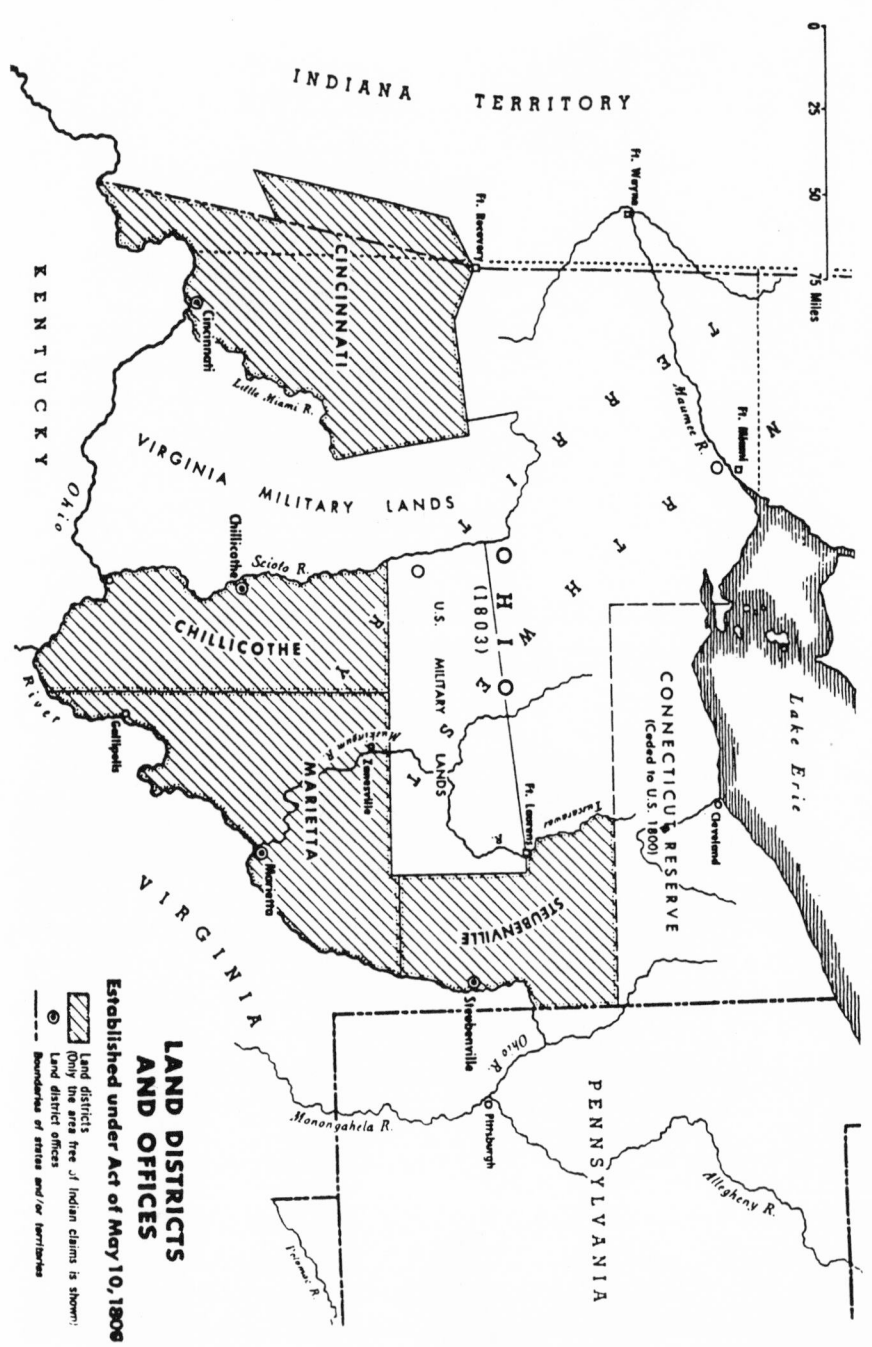

Fig. 1 BOUNDARIES OF FOUR LAND OFFICES ESTABLISHED IN OHIO.

From Malcomb J. Rohrbough, *The Land Office Business* (New York: Oxford University Press, 1968), p. 24.

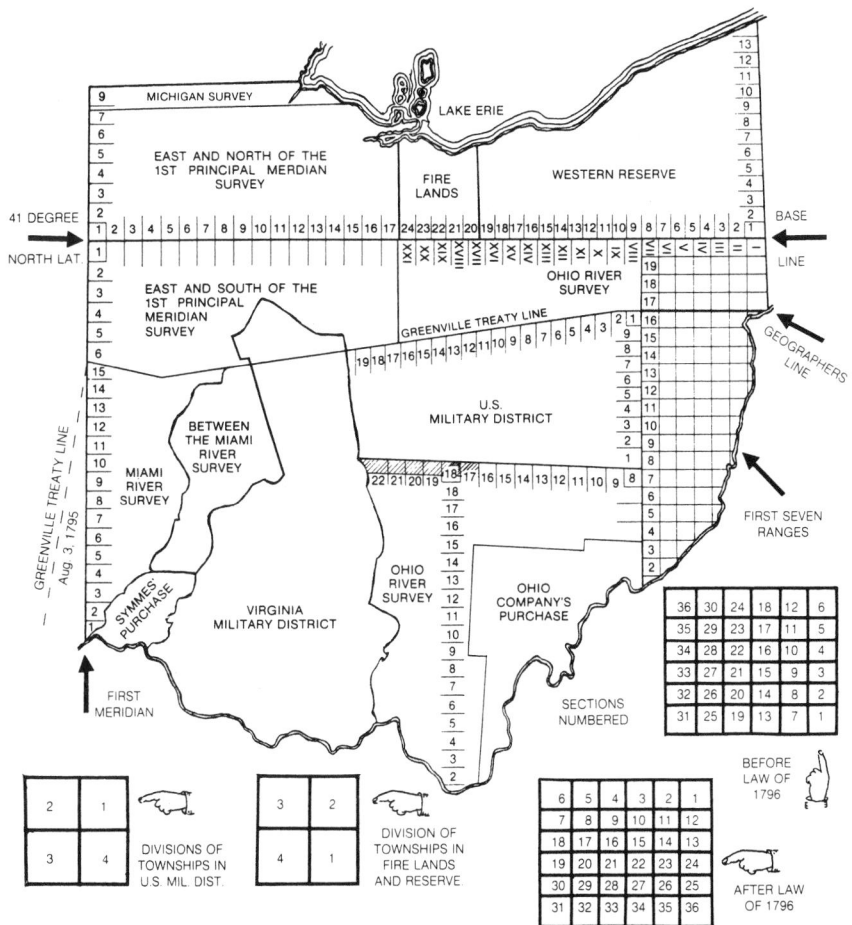

(The "Geographers Line" From which point the survey of the Seven Ranges began is indicated by the arrow.)

Fig. 2. MAJOR LAND SURVEYS OF OHIO.

From *Ohio Lands, A Short History* (Auditor of State, Columbus, Ohio, n.d.)

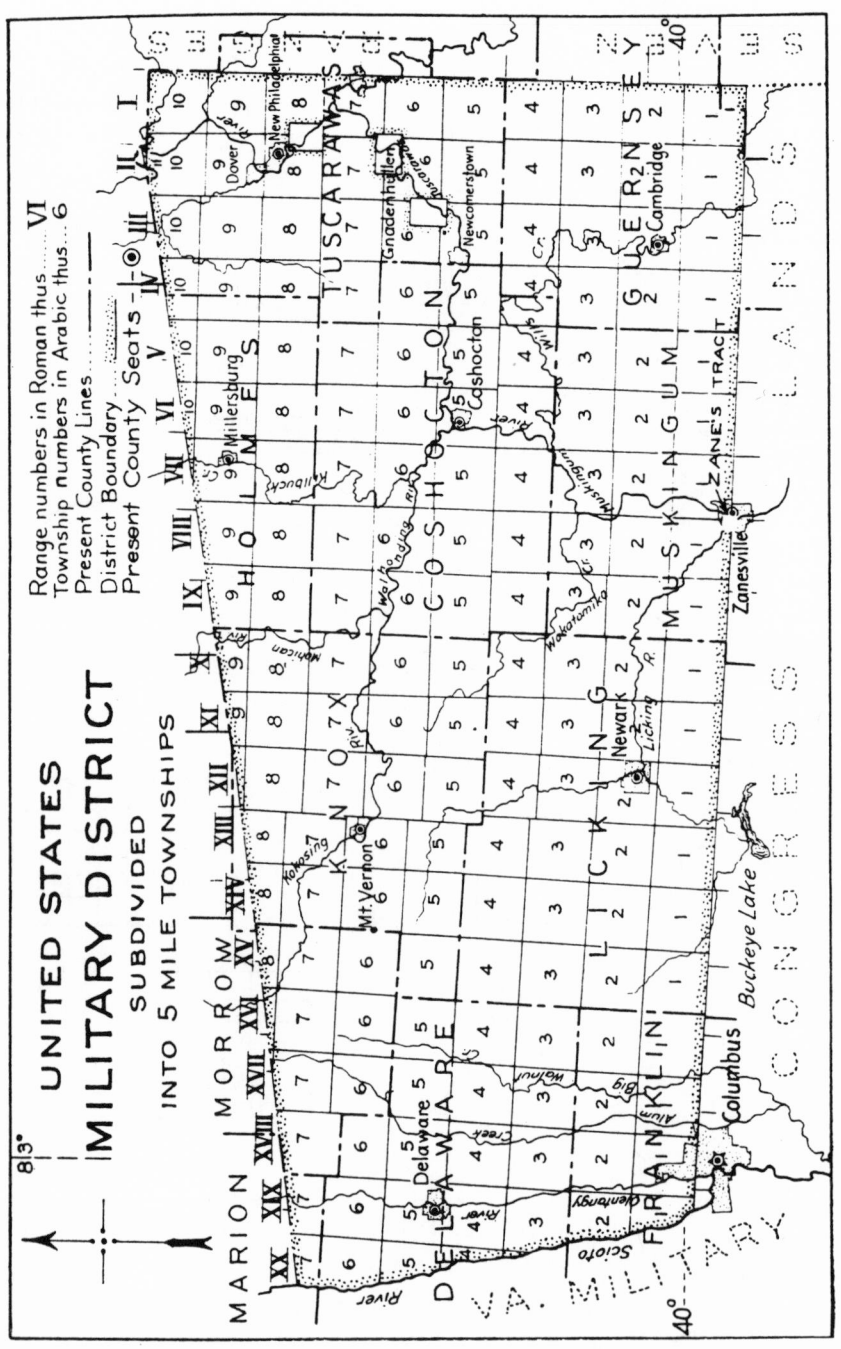

Fig. 3. UNITED STATES MILITARY DISTRICT, State of Ohio.

From C. E. Sherman, *Original Ohio Land Subdivisions*, Vol. III of the Final Report (1925; repr. Columbus, Ohio, State of Ohio, Dept. of Natural Resources, Division of Geological Survey, 1976), p. 91.

PURCHASER	YEAR	DATE	RESIDENCE	R	T	S
Aarner, Samuel(Z-M)	1835	Aug. 08	LickingCo,Oh	10	04	13
Abbahl, David(Z-M)	1836	April 19	TuscarwsCoOh	03	08	16
Abbet, Curtiss(Z)	1808	Jan. 12	MuskingmCoOh	14	15	03
Abboohl, John(Z-M)	1834	Nov. 04	TuscarwsCoOh	03	08	17
Abbot, Curtis(Z)	1811	Oct. 26	TuscarwsCoOh	11	13	12
Abbot, Nicholas(Z-M)	1831	July 08	CoshoctnCoOh	04	07	07
Abbuhll, David(Z-M)	1836	Dec. 10	TuscarwsCoOh	03	07	02
Abbuhll, Jacob(Z-M)	1836	Dec. 10	TuscarwsCoOh	04	07	10
Abel, Adam(Y)	1831	March 10	Jeff.Co.,Oh.	05	13	03
Abel, Conrad(Y)	1827	March 08	HarrisonCoOh	05	12	10
Abel, Conrad(Y)	1827	Sept. 24	HarrisonCoOh	05	12	11
Abel, Conrad(Y)	1827	Nov. 03	HarrisonCoOh	05	13	13
Abel, Conrad(Y)	1829	March 16	HarrisonCoOh	05	12	11
Abel, George(Z)	1835	Nov. 16	HarrisonCoOh	10	08	35
Abel, George(Z)	1835	Nov. 16	HarrisonCoOh	10	08	36
Abeless, John(Z)	1816	Dec. 30	GuernseyCoOh	01	03	21
Abinger, Fred'k.(Z-M)	1835	Dec. 30	WayneCo.,Oh.	09	09	14
Abrahims, Michael(Y)	1821	Jan. 18	Jeff.Co.,Oh.	05	14	19
Abrahims, Michael(Y)	1822	June 25	ColumbanCoOh	05	13	21
Acbaugh, John(Y)	1830	Aug. 31	HarrisonCoOh	05	12	34
Achauer, Jacob(Z)	1835	Aug. 05	MuskingmCoOh	13	10	10
Achauer, Jacob(Z)	1835	Dec. 11	MuskingmCoOh	13	10	03
Acheson, D. R.(Z-M)	1831	Oct. 05	MuskingmCoOh	04	03	25
Acheson, David R.(Z-M)	1832	June 20	GuernseyCoOh	04	03	25
Acheson, Humphrey(Z)	1815	Nov. 23	GuernseyCoOh	01	03	12
Acheson, Humphrey(Z-M)	1836	Aug. 31	CoshoctnCoOh	06	04	23
Acheson, Humphry(Z)	1825	May 03	MuskingmCoOh	05	03	22
Acheson, James(Z-M)	1832	May 23	GuernseyCoOh	04	03	25
Acheson, James(Z-M)	1832	May 23	GuernseyCoOh	05	03	20
Acheson, John R.(Z-M)	1837	June 27	GuernseyCoOh	04	03	05
Acheson, John R.(Z-M)	1837	June 27	GuernseyCoOh	04	03	05
Acheson, John(Z)	1815	Nov. 22	WashCo.,Penn	05	03	21
Acheson, John(Z)	1816	Jan. 01	WashCo.,Penn	05	03	22
Acheson, John(Z-M)	1831	April 01	MuskingmCoOh	04	03	18
Acheson, John(Z-M)	1834	Aug. 22	MuskingmCoOh	04	03	25
Acheson, John(Z-M)	1835	Dec. 19	MuskingmCoOh	04	03	05
Acheson, John(Z-M)	1836	Dec. 13	MuskingmCoOh	04	03	05
Acheson, Robert(Z-M)	1835	March 20	MuskingmCoOh	04	03	05
Acheson, William(Z-M)	1835	April 22	MuskingmCoOh	05	03	15
Achison, David R.(Z-M)	1824	Aug. 26	MuskingmCoOh	05	03	11
Achley, Obed(Z)	1832	July 04	MonroeCo.,Oh	08	06	06
Ackerman, John(Y)	1827	Nov. 30	Stark Co.,Oh	06	19	32
Ackerman, Wm.(Z)	1831	Feb. 04	Morgan Co,Oh	13	08	01
Ackley, Calvin(Z-M)	1833	March 19	LickingCo,Oh	11	03	24
Ackley, Calvin(Z-M)	1833	March 29	LickingCo,Oh	11	03	24
Ackley, Daniel(Z)	1836	Feb. 10	MonroeCo.,Oh	08	06	06
Ackley, Daniel(Z)	1836	April 22	MonroeCo.,Oh	08	07	31
Ackley, Levi(Z-M)	1831	Sept. 14	LickingCo,Oh	11	04	24
Ackley, Lewis(Z)	1835	Dec. 26	Morgan Co,Oh	09	06	11
Ackley, Philander(Z)	1836	Sept. 08	MonroeCo.,Oh	08	06	06
Ackley, Samuel(Z)	1833	Aug. 07	Morgan Co,Oh	09	06	09
Ackley, Samuel(Z)	1835	Dec. 03	Morgan Co,Oh	09	06	35
Ackord, Joseph(Z)	1833	Jan. 05	Perry Co.,Oh	14	12	18
Acord, Absalom(Z-M)	1835	Aug. 22	MuskingmCoOh	09	03	06
Acord, James(Z)	1820	Aug. 22	PerryCo,Ohio	14	12	30
Acord, John Jr.(Z)	1820	Aug. 22	PerryCo,Ohio	15	14	25
Acord, John(Z-M)	1833	March 18	MuskingmCoOh	09	03	06
Acord, Michael(Z-M)	1835	Nov. 17	MuskingmCoOh	09	03	06
Adair, Arthur(Z)	1806	Aug. 16	MuskingmCoOh	01	02	04
Adair, George(Z)	1827	Nov. 05	KnoxCo.,Ohio	10	06	07
Adair, George(Z)	1806	Aug. 16	MuskingmCoOh	01	03	24

PURCHASER	YEAR	DATE	RESIDENCE	R	T	S
Adair, John(Z)	1804	Nov. 09	HuntngtnCoPa	01	03	05
Adair, John(Z)	1806	Aug. 16	MuskingmCoOh	02	04	21
Adair, John(Z)	1815	Sept. 19	GuernseyCoOh	01	03	13
Adair, Rebecca(Z-M)	1836	June 04	GuernseyCoOh	02	04	15
Adair, Robert(Z-M)	1836	May 30	GuernseyCoOh	02	04	05
Adair, Robert(Z-M)	1836	June 04	GuernseyCoOh	02	04	05
Adam, Jacob(Z)	1815	March 11	ZanesvilleOh	15	17	01
Adam, John W.(Z)	1814	Oct. 19	BelmontCo,Oh	10	01	09
Adam, Schnided(Z)	1807	July 27	WashngtnCoOh	03	09	21
Adams, Abraham(Z-M)	1837	March 20	MuskingmCoOh	09	03	17
Adams, Baldwin(Y)	1831	March 19	TuscarwsCoOh	07	14	31
Adams, Beal(Z)	1807	June 22	MuskingmCoOh	07	04	25
Adams, David(Z-M)	1836	Nov. 07	TuscarwsCoOh	02	07	03
Adams, Edmond(Z)	1835	Jan. 06	Morgan Co,Oh	13	09	31
Adams, Elijah(Z)	1836	April 30	Perry Co.,Oh	14	12	15
Adams, Elijah(Z)	1837	Jan. 10	Perry Co.,Oh	14	12	15
Adams, Elizabeth(Z-M)	1836	May 26	TuscarwsCoOh	02	07	03
Adams, Francis(Y)	1833	March 18	Jeff.Co.,Oh.	03	12	10
Adams, Francis(Y)	1833	Nov. 18	ColumbanCoOh	03	12	28
Adams, Francis(Z)	1834	Nov. 03	Morgan Co,Oh	11	11	13
Adams, Geo. W.(Z-M)	1830	June 21	MuskingmCoOh	05	03	07
Adams, George W.(Z-M)	1825	Nov. 28	MuskingmCoOh	07	03	13
Adams, George W.(Z-M)	1828	May 13	MuskingmCoOh	07	03	12
Adams, George(Z)	1809	Oct. 14	MuskingmCoOh	07	03	18
Adams, George(Z)	1816	July 30	MuskingmCoOh	05	02	07
Adams, Jacob(Y)	1836	Dec. 10	Jeff.co.,Oh.	03	12	28
Adams, Jacob(Z)	1829	Jan. 12	Morgan Co,Oh	12	11	34
Adams, Jacob(Z)	1816	April 06	ZanesvilleOh	12	13	09
Adams, James(Y)	1833	March 18	ColumbanCoOh	03	12	14
Adams, Jas.(Z)	1817	Oct. 04	HarrisonCoOh	06	06	10
Adams, John Junr.(Y)	1834	Feb. 04	Jeff.Co.,Oh.	03	12	22
Adams, John(Y)	1828	June 21	ColumbanCoOh	04	13	25
Adams, John(Z)	1832	March 27	Morgan Co,Oh	14	12	01
Adams, John(Z)	1831	Aug. 10	Morgan Co,Oh	14	12	01
Adams, John(Z)	1807	Oct. 26	FauquierCoVa	08	02	14
Adams, John(Z)	1807	Oct. 26	FauquierCoVa	08	02	14
Adams, John(Z)	1807	Oct. 26	FauquierCoVa	07	04	14
Adams, John(Z)	1809	July 05	MuskingmCoOh	08	04	12
Adams, John(Z)	1809	July 05	MuskingmCoOh	08	04	12
Adams, John(Z)	1810	June 15	MuskingmCoOh	08	04	12
Adams, John(Z)	1810	Aug. 14	MuskingmCoOh	08	04	04
Adams, John(Z)	1810	Nov. 19	MuskingmCoOh	08	04	04
Adams, John(Z-M)	1823	Dec. 03	GuernseyCoOh	02	03	05
Adams, John(Z-M)	1829	Nov. 28	GuernseyCoOh	02	03	04
Adams, Johnathan(Z)	1832	Oct. 15	Morgan Co,Oh	14	13	26
Adams, Jonathan(Z)	1832	June 26	Morgan Co,Oh	14	13	36
Adams, Jonathan(Z)	1832	June 26	Morgan Co,Oh	14	13	36
Adams, Jonathan(Z)	1832	June 26	Morgan Co,Oh	13	08	06
Adams, Jonathan(Z)	1832	June 30	Morgan Co,Oh	14	12	15
Adams, Jonathan(Z)	1832	June 30	Morgan Co,Oh	14	12	22
Adams, Jonathan(Z)	1832	June 30	Morgan Co,Oh	14	12	22
Adams, Jonathan(Z)	1834	Aug. 29	Perry Co.,Oh	14	13	36
Adams, Jonathan(Z)	1816	Dec. 16	CoshoctnCoOh	13	09	05
Adams, Jonathan(Z-M)	1836	Nov. 07	TuscarwsCoOh	02	07	03
Adams, Josiah(Z)	1809	May 30	FauquierCoVa	10	03	01
Adams, Josiah(Z)	1809	May 30	FauquierCoVa	10	03	01
Adams, Josiah(Z)	1809	May 30	FauquierCoVa	10	04	21
Adams, Josiah(Z)	1809	May 30	FauquierCoVa	10	03	10
Adams, Josiah(Z)	1811	Feb. 25	FauquierCoVa	10	04	21
Adams, Josiah(Z)	1811	Feb. 25	FauquierCoVa	10	03	10
Adams, Martin(Y)	1831	Aug. 31	ColumbanCoOh	03	12	25
Adams, Martin(Y)	1832	Oct. 06	ColumbanCoOh	03	12	02
Adams, Mordecai(Z-M)	1823	Jan. 25	GuernseyCoOh	04	04	22
Adams, Philip(Z)	1833	Jan. 04	Morgan Co,Oh	14	13	36
Adams, Richard(Z)	1817	July 19	FauquierCoVa	10	04	21
Adams, Robert(Z)	1829	March 25	Morgan Co,Oh	13	09	05
Adams, Robert(Z)	1832	March 03	Morgan Co,Oh	13	09	04
Adams, Robert(Z)	1830	June 12	Morgan Co,Oh	13	09	04
Adams, Robert(Z)	1836	Dec. 21	Morgan Co,Oh	14	13	36

PURCHASER	YEAR	DATE	RESIDENCE	R	T	S
Adams, Samuel(Z)	1811	Aug. 08	FauquierCoVa	13	08	01
Adams, Samuel(Z)	1811	Aug. 08	FauquierCoVa	13	08	01
Adams, Thomas(Y)	1825	March 14	Ohio Co.,Vir	03	12	01
Adams, Thomas(Y)	1832	June 22	ColumbanCoOh	03	12	28
Adams, Thomas(Y)	1833	March 30	Jeff.Co.,Oh.	03	12	01
Adams, Thomas(Y)	1835	Dec. 22	Jeff.Co.,Oh.	03	12	22
Adams, Thompson(Z-M)	1833	Nov. 27	MuskingmCoOh	09	04	25
Adams, Thompson(Z-M)	1835	June 17	MuskingmCoOh	09	04	25
Adams, William(Z)	1808	Aug. 23	MuskingmCoOh	10	03	01
Adams, William(Z)	1811	Feb. 25	FauquierCoVa	10	03	10
Adams, William(Z)	1811	Feb. 25	FauquierCoVa	10	03	10
Adams, William(Z-M)	1829	Jan. 08	Jeff.Co.,Oh.	06	06	09
Adams, William(Z-M)	1829	April 03	Jeff.Co.,Oh.	05	06	06
Adamson, Frederick(Z)	1833	July 24	MuskingmCoOh	14	14	13
Adas, James(Y)	1835	Dec. 22	CarrollCo,Oh	04	13	17
Adcock, Michael(Z)	1836	Feb. 12	MuskingmCoOh	09	05	25
Adcock, William(Z)	1836	Jan. 09	MuskingmCoOh	09	05	21
Adcock, William(Z)	1836	June 09	Morgan Co,Oh	09	05	27
Addis, Josiah(Z)	1833	Oct. 05	GuernseyCoOh	09	06	29
Addis, Josiah(Z-M)	1835	Aug. 19	Morgan Co,Oh	09	06	29
Addison, Jacob(Z)	1815	Jan. 03	FairfeldCoOh	13	11	15
Addison, Jonathan(Z)	1804	Nov. 24	MuskingmCoOh	14	15	02
Addison, Jonathan(Z)	1812	Feb. 08	MuskingmCoOh	13	11	14
Addy, Hugh(Z)	1806	Dec. 25	MuskingmCoOh	04	04	04
Addy, Hugh(Z)	1812	June 16	CoshoctnCoOh	05	04	20
Addy, James(Z)	1816	Oct. 25	GuernseyCoOh	04	03	06
Addy, Thomas(Z)	1812	June 16	CoshoctnCoOh	05	04	20
Addy, William(Z)	1806	Dec. 25	MuskingmCoOh	04	04	04
Ades, James(Y)	1821	June 19	ColumbanCoOh	05	15	05
Ades, James(Y)	1825	July 05	ColumbanCoOh	05	15	05
Adkins, Isaac(Z)	1837	April 11	BelmontCo,Oh	13	08	18
Aduddell, Cornelius(Z)	1834	Aug. 27	GuernseyCoOh	10	07	26
Aduddell, Cornelius(Z)	1834	Aug. 27	GuernseyCoOh	10	07	26
Aduddill, George(Y)	1824	Dec. 27	BelmontCo,Oh	05	07	25
Ady, James T.(Z-M)	1827	June 05	HarrisonCoOh	03	06	17
Agar, Samuel H.(Z-M)	1837	May 17	BelmontCo,Oh	04	07	11
Agy, Mathias(Z)	1833	March 16	GuernseyCoOh	09	08	14
Ahahims, Michael(Y)	1821	July 03	ColumbanCoOh	05	14	19
Aikin, John(Z)	1824	Jan. 10	GuernseyCoOh	03	01	14
Aikins, J.(Z)	1816	Nov. 11	CoshoctnCoOh	09	05	13
Aikins, Robert(Z)	1833	Aug. 10	MuskingmCoOh	11	12	23
Aikins, Robert(Z)	1836	Feb. 16	MuskingmCoOh	10	09	03
Aikins, Robert(Z)	1836	Oct. 22	MuskingmCoOh	10	09	25
Aikins, Robert(Z)	1815	Oct. 26	BelmontCo,Oh	13	09	36
Aikins, Samuel(Z)	1829	Dec. 21	Morgan Co,Oh	13	09	34
Aimes, Wm.(Y)	1828	Dec. 11	HarrisonCoOh	05	13	21
Aimstrong, Lewis(Z)	1836	Feb. 17	WashngtnCoOh	08	05	27
Aisch, Christian(Z-M)	1831	July 27	HolmesCoOhio	05	08	07
Aitkinson, George(Z)	1810	July 03	Ohio Co.,Vir	04	04	21
Akin, George(Z-M)	1821	Oct. 02	GuernseyCoOh	03	01	16
Alban, Abraham(Z)	1835	June 30	GuernseyCoOh	09	08	14
Albaugh, Ezra(Y)	1832	Aug. 29	TuscarwsCoOh	07	16	19
Albaugh, Morris(Y)	1827	March 13	HarrisonCoOh	05	12	23
Albaugh, Peter(Y)	1828	Dec. 24	HarrisonCoOh	05	13	08
Albaugh, Peter(Y)	1830	Nov. 22	HarrisonCoOh	05	13	08
Albaugh, Solomon(Y)	1827	May 17	HarrisonCoOh	05	12	11
Albert, Jacob(Z-M)	1829	March 28	TuscarwsCoOh	01	08	02
Albert, John(Z)	1815	June 05	Jeff.Co.,Oh.	05	07	22
Albert, Nicholas(Z-M)	1828	March 17	TuscarwsCoOh	05	06	05
Albertson, John(Z-M)	1826	Oct. 28	HolmesCoOhio	06	09	06
Albin, Abraham(Z)	1836	Jan. 05	GuernseyCoOh	09	08	15
Albin, James(Z)	1807	April 18	BelmontCo,Oh	09	08	05
Albrecht, Henry(Z)	1808	March 22	TuscarwsCoOh	05	08	10
Albright, Henry Jr.(Z-M)	1822	Sept. 02	TuscarwsCoOh	05	07	05
Albright, Henry(Z)	1816	June 07	TuscarwsCoOh	05	07	05
Albright, Henry(Z-M)	1829	March 26	CoshoctnCoOh	05	07	06
Albright, Jacob(Z)	1810	Jan. 12	CentreCoPenn	04	08	06
Albright, Thomas(Z-M)	1824	Oct. 08	TuscarwsCoOh	06	08	19
Albright, Thomas(Z-M)	1836	Feb. 20	TuscarwsCoOh	05	07	06

PURCHASER	YEAR	DATE	RESIDENCE	R	T	S
Aldrich, Martin(Z)	1836	Aug. 13	GuernseyCoOh	09	05	31
Aldrich, Martin(Z)	1836	Aug. 13	GuernseyCoOh	09	05	31
Aldrich, Martin(Z)	1836	Aug. 13	GuernseyCoOh	09	05	32
Aldrich, Martin(Z)	1836	Aug. 13	GuernseyCoOh	09	05	32
Aldrich, Martin(Z-M)	1835	Aug. 15	GuernseyCoOh	01	01	20
Aldridge, Abraham(Z)	1807	Sept. 20	MuskingmCoOh	05	01	03
Aldridge, Nicholas(Y)	1826	Feb. 16	TuscarwsCoOh	07	15	25
Alexander, Betsy(Y)	1835	Aug. 26	TuscarwsCoOh	07	14	23
Alexander, Esther(Y)	1831	March 09	HarrisonCoOh	06	11	36
Alexander, James Jr.(Y)	1823	Sept. 01	BelmontCo,Oh	03	05	21
Alexander, James Jr.(Y)	1823	Sept. 01	BelmontCo,Oh	03	05	22
Alexander, James(Y)	1822	March 08	BelmontCo,Oh	03	05	21
Alexander, James(Y)	1824	Oct. 09	Jeff.Co.,Oh.	05	13	27
Alexander, James(Z)	1817	Sept. 12	Brooke CoVir	12	12	36
Alexander, John L.(Z)	1828	June 25	MuskingmCoOh	12	12	04
Alexander, John(Y)	1825	July 27	BelmontCo,Oh	06	18	27
Alexander, John(Y)	1825	July 27	BelmontCo,Oh	06	18	27
Alexander, John(Y)	1829	July 02	HarrisonCoOh	06	12	24
Alexander, John(Z)	1827	June 29	Morgan Co,Oh	13	09	22
Alexander, Mathew(Z)	1824	May 25	MuskingmCoOh	11	12	21
Alexander, Robert B.(Z)	1833	June 25	HarrisonCoOh	11	12	33
Alexander, Robert(Y)	1825	Aug. 04	Stark Co.,Oh	06	17	10
Alexander, Robt.(Y)	1823	Jan. 18	Stark Co.,Oh	06	16	17
Alexander, Samuel(Z-M)	1836	Nov. 08	KnoxCo.,Ohio	10	08	09
Alexander, Thomas(Y)	1825	July 27	BelmontCo,Oh	06	18	27
Alexander, Thos.(Z)	1833	May 20	HarrisonCoOh	11	12	33
Alexander, Thos.(Z-M)	1837	Feb. 24	CoshoctnCoOh	08	07	11
Alexander, William(Z-M)	1833	Dec. 06	TuscarwsCoOh	01	06	23
Alexander, Wm.(Z)	1826	April 20	Perry Co.,Oh	13	09	22
Alfred, Gurdon(Z-M)	1835	Nov. 30	HolmesCoOhio	08	08	11
Alfred, Gurdon(Z-M)	1836	Oct. 06	HolmesCoOhio	08	08	11
Algeo, Charles(Y)	1826	Dec. 13	WashCo.,Penn	04	12	25
Algeo, John(Y)	1828	Feb. 15	Jeff.Co.,Oh.	05	13	18
Allaback, Samuel(Y)	1832	March 22	Jeff.Co.,Oh.	02	09	20
Allard, Reuben(Z)	1825	Sept. 20	Morgan Co,Oh	13	09	15
Allard, Shadrach(Z)	1826	Dec. 19	Morgan Co,Oh	13	09	15
Allbaugh, Eli(Y)	1825	Oct. 21	Jeff.Co.,Oh.	04	12	19
Allbaugh, Peter(Y)	1829	March 18	HarrisonCoOh	05	13	08
Allebaugh, George(Z-M)	1826	Oct. 28	WashCo.,Penn	05	07	20
Allebaugh, Sam'l.(Z-M)	1827	May 22	TuscarwsCoOh	04	07	07
Allebaugh, Samuel(Z-M)	1832	Nov. 17	TuscarwsCoOh	04	07	07
Allen, Christopher(Z-M)	1832	Oct. 16	LickingCo,Oh	10	04	18
Allen, Christopher(Z-M)	1836	Nov. 05	KnoxCo.,Ohio	10	05	24
Allen, Elias(Z-M)	1831	Oct. 24	KnoxCo.,Ohio	10	06	19
Allen, F. B.(Z-M)	1833	July 22	GuernseyCoOh	02	03	04
Allen, Francis Baldwin(Z-M)	1833	July 22	GuernseyCoOh	02	03	04
Allen, Joseph(Y)	1821	Oct. 22	OtsegoCoNYrk	05	12	22
Allen, Joseph(Y)	1821	Dec. 28	OtsegoCoNYrk	05	12	22
Allen, Joseph(Y)	1823	Aug. 13	HarrisonCoOh	05	12	22
Allen, Joseph(Y)	1828	Dec. 08	HarrisonCoOh	05	12	22
Allen, Joseph(Z)	1812	May 07	MuskingmCoOh	11	13	36
Allen, Joseph(Z-M)	1839	Feb. 01	MuskingmCoOh	08	06	07
Allen, Samuel(Z)	1810	Aug. 25	WashngtnCoOh	09	06	10
Allen, Samuel(Z)	1814	March 07	GuernseyCoOh	09	06	10
Allen, Samuel(Z-M)	1832	April 10	GuernseyCoOh	03	01	22
Allen, Samuel(Z-M)	1833	Aug. 21	CoshoctnCoOh	07	05	08
Allen, Samuel(Z-M)	1837	May 16	CoshoctnCoOh	08	07	19
Allen, Wm. C.(Z-M)	1839	Jan. 29	MuskingmCoOh	08	06	07
Allen, Wm. C.(Z-M)	1839	Jan. 29	MuskingmCoOh	08	06	14
Allen, Zephaniah(Z)	1832	June 25	Perry Co.,Oh	15	14	19
Allen, Zephaniah(Z)	1832	Aug. 03	Perry Co.,Oh	15	14	19
Allender, John(Z-M)	1823	Aug. 04	FayetteCo,Pa	04	07	02
Allender, Thomas(Z)	1833	Dec. 14	GuernseyCoOh	08	08	35
Allender, Wm. Jr.(Z)	1830	Jan. 22	BelmontCo,Oh	08	08	26
Allerton, Amos Senr.(Y)	1827	Aug. 27	ColumbanCoOh	05	18	06
Allerton, Amos(Y)	1822	Feb. 20	PortageCo,Oh	05	18	06
Allerton, James(Y)	1824	Aug. 20	Stark Co.,Oh	05	18	05
Allerton, James(Y)	1825	Jan. 03	Stark Co.,Oh	07	17	06
Allerton, John(Y)	1824	Aug. 20	Stark Co.,Oh	05	18	05

4

PURCHASER	YEAR	DATE	RESIDENCE	R	T	S
Allertos, Amos R.(Y)	1820	Dec. 16	Stark Co.,Oh	05	18	05
Alleshouse, David(Z-M)	1829	May 27	TuscarwsCoOh	03	08	15
Alleshouse, David(Z-M)	1832	Aug. 18	TuscarwsCoOh	03	08	15
Allis, Oliver(Y)	1821	Sept. 14	HarrisonCoOh	06	10	22
Allis, Oliver(Y)	1821	Sept. 14	HarrisonCoOh	06	10	22
Allis, Oliver(Y)	1822	Sept. 28	JeffersnCoNY	06	10	22
Allison, Archibald(Z)	1806	May 23	WashngtnCoOh	12	13	18
Allison, David(Z-M)	1838	Oct. 30	MuskingmCoOh	05	03	02
Allison, Hugh(Z)	1835	Feb. 23	WashngtnCoOh	09	05	33
Allison, Hugh(Z)	1836	Jan. 08	Morgan Co,Oh	09	05	33
Allison, James(Z)	1815	May 08	WashngtnCoOh	04	02	01
Allison, James(Z-M)	1821	Oct. 03	GuernseyCoOh	05	03	18
Allison, William(Z)	1820	Nov. 15	Morgan Co,Oh	10	07	32
Allison, William(Z)	1828	March 27	Morgan Co,Oh	09	05	33
Allison, Zachariah(Z)	1836	June 04	Perry Co.,Oh	14	13	34
Allison, Zachariah(Z)	1836	June 04	Perry Co.,Oh	14	12	03
Allman, John(Y)	1829	March 16	Jeff.Co.,Oh.	04	12	24
Allman, John(Y)	1833	Dec. 20	CarrollCo,Oh	04	12	18
Allman, John(Z)	1807	June 01	WestmrldCoPa	04	08	10
Allman, Thomas(Y)	1836	Aug. 16	CarrollCo,Oh	04	12	18
Allmon, John(Y)	1832	June 15	Jeff.Co.,Oh.	04	12	18
Allmon, William(Y)	1824	May 24	ColumbanCoOh	07	20	22
Allmong, John(Y)	1825	April 08	ColumbanCoOh	05	17	15
Alloway, William(Z)	1832	Aug. 18	Morgan Co,Oh	12	09	02
Alltop, Geo.(Z)	1833	June 24	Morgan Co,Oh	08	06	06
Allwine, Barnhard(Z)	1832	Oct. 24	Perry Co.,Oh	14	12	05
Almon, William(Y)	1830	April 23	Jeff.Co.,Oh.	04	12	35
Alt, James(Z)	1816	Dec. 11	MuskingmCoOh	14	13	20
Altman, John(Z)	1815	May 31	TuscarwsCoOh	03	09	10
Amann, Peter(Z-M)	1836	July 06	PittsburghPa	05	04	14
Ambler, Samuel(Y)	1826	May 03	BelmontCo,Oh	03	05	17
Ambler, William(Y)	1826	May 03	BelmontCo,Oh	03	05	17
Ambury, Joseph(Z)	1815	Dec. 18	BedfordCo,Pa	10	08	04
Amend, Anthony(Y)	1827	April 02	ColumbanCoOh	05	17	22
Amends, Joshua(Y)	1827	June 23	HarrisonCoOh	05	13	13
Ames, Dorsey P.(Z)	1834	March 19	Morgan Co,Oh	13	08	17
Amiot, Francis(Z-M)	1836	May 17	CoshoctnCoOh	06	04	19
Ammon, Joseph(Z-M)	1836	Oct. 01	CoshoctnCoOh	07	08	24
Ammow, Jacob(Z-M)	1835	March 26	CoshoctnCoOh	07	07	11
Amon, Alexander(Z)	1835	Aug. 27	MuskingmCoOh	11	12	35
Anderson, Absalom(Z-M)	1828	May 07	CoshoctnCoOh	09	04	16
Anderson, Anarew(Y)	1830	Feb. 08	ColumbanCoOh	02	09	34
Anderson, Andrew(Y)	1830	March 02	ColumbanCoOh	02	09	34
Anderson, Daniel(Z-M)	1838	June 16	TuscarwsCoOh	03	05	01
Anderson, David(Z)	1833	Nov. 12	ZanesvilleOh	09	07	26
Anderson, David(Z)	1836	Jan. 01	Morgan Co,Oh	09	07	27
Anderson, Ducan(Z)	1836	Jan. 01	Morgan Co,Oh	10	07	26
Anderson, Duncan(Z)	1835	Sept. 22	Morgan Co,Oh	10	06	02
Anderson, Elizabeth(Z)	1837	Jan. 02	GuernseyCoOh	09	05	34
Anderson, Ezekiel(Z)	1836	Feb. 18	MonroeCo.,Oh	08	07	20
Anderson, George(Z)	1815	March 01	GuernseyCoOh	01	04	14
Anderson, George(Z-M)	1832	Dec. 05	GuernseyCoOh	03	04	09
Anderson, George(Z-M)	1832	Dec. 05	GuernseyCoOh	03	04	02
Anderson, Grafton(Z-M)	1836	Oct. 11	GuernseyCoOh	02	04	17
Anderson, Henry Harrison(Z)	1836	Jan. 04	MuskingmCoOh	12	12	18
Anderson, Hump'y.(Y)	1822	Sept. 09	BelmontCo,Oh	07	09	22
Anderson, Isaac(Y)	1833	June 01	Jeff.Co.,Oh.	06	12	22
Anderson, Isaac(Y)	1833	June 01	Jeff.Co.,Oh.	06	12	22
Anderson, Isaac(Z)	1832	Aug. 23	GuernseyCoOh	09	08	36
Anderson, Isaac(Z)	1835	Nov. 16	Morgan Co,Oh	09	06	30
Anderson, Isaac(Z)	1837	Jan. 02	Morgan Co,Oh	09	06	09
Anderson, James(Y)	1828	Jan. 17	ColumbanCoOh	02	09	34
Anderson, James(Y)	1828	Feb. 08	ColumbanCoOh	02	09	34
Anderson, James(Y)	1833	Oct. 12	Stark Co.,Oh	09	11	02
Anderson, James(Z)	1832	May 22	Morgan Co,Oh	10	06	23
Anderson, James(Z)	1832	Dec. 07	Morgan Co,Oh	10	06	24
Anderson, James(Z)	1804	Oct. 16	BelmontCo,Oh	01	04	24
Anderson, James(Z-M)	1836	Oct. 15	CoshoctnCoOh	08	07	14
Anderson, Jas.(Z)	1830	Dec. 08	Morgan Co,Oh	10	06	24

5

PURCHASER	YEAR	DATE	RESIDENCE	R	T	S
Anderson, Jas.(Z)	1830	Dec. 08	Morgan Co,Oh	10	06	24
Anderson, Jno. P.(Z)	1817	Oct. 20	GuernseyCoOh	10	06	13
Anderson, John(Y)	1824	May 20	Stark Co.,Oh	06	17	26
Anderson, John(Y)	1836	March 10	ColumbanCoOh	03	12	03
Anderson, John(Z)	1829	July 06	Perry Co.,Oh	15	14	14
Anderson, John(Z)	1836	July 07	Morgan Co,Oh	09	07	01
Anderson, John(Z)	1836	Sept. 06	Morgan Co,Oh	09	07	01
Anderson, John(Z)	1811	Jan. 26	BelmontCo,Oh	08	05	24
Anderson, John(Z)	1814	Dec. 06	FairfeldCoOh	15	16	33
Anderson, John(Z)	1817	May 03	MuskingmCoOh	14	13	08
Anderson, John(Z-M)	1828	Sept. 06	GuernseyCoOh	02	01	08
Anderson, John(Z-M)	1834	Oct. 14	TuscarwsCoOh	03	05	19
Anderson, John(Z-M)	1836	Dec. 30	TuscarwsCoOh	03	05	11
Anderson, Joseph Junr.(Z)	1816	Jan. 08	PutnamCoOhio	13	09	26
Anderson, Joseph(Z)	1822	March 19	GuernseyCoOh	09	07	10
Anderson, Joseph(Z)	1829	July 03	Perry Co.,Oh	15	14	13
Anderson, Joseph(Z-M)	1836	Jan. 14	KnoxCo.,Ohio	10	05	22
Anderson, Joshua(Z-M)	1829	June 12	CoshoctnCoOh	09	04	25
Anderson, Joshua(Z-M)	1833	Dec. 06	MuskingmCoOh	09	03	04
Anderson, Lewis(Z-M)	1835	Jan. 15	LickingCo,Oh	10	05	22
Anderson, Mathew(Z-M)	1836	Aug. 25	TuscarwsCoOh	03	05	19
Anderson, Nancy(Z)	1837	Jan. 02	Morgan Co,Oh	09	05	36
Anderson, Nathan'l.(Y)	1827	June 19	Stark Co.,Oh	06	16	01
Anderson, Rob't.(Y)	1828	April 10	ColumbanCoOh	03	13	24
Anderson, Robert(Y)	1830	Feb. 23	ColumbanCoOh	03	13	24
Anderson, Robert(Z-M)	1833	July 05	TuscarwsCoOh	02	07	08
Anderson, Robert(Z-M)	1833	Oct. 29	GuernseyCoOh	04	06	12
Anderson, Samuel(Z)	1829	Oct. 13	MonroeCo.,Oh	08	07	17
Anderson, Simon(Z-M)	1832	Sept. 06	Perry Co.,Oh	10	05	22
Anderson, Simon(Z-M)	1832	Sept. 06	Perry Co.,Oh	10	04	02
Anderson, Thomas(Z)	1827	Nov. 19	GreeneCo.,Pa	01	06	21
Anderson, Thomas(Z)	1827	Nov. 19	GreeneCo.,Pa	01	06	21
Anderson, William(Z)	1832	Dec. 15	Morgan Co,Oh	09	06	30
Anderson, William(Z-M)	1828	May 02	GuernseyCoOh	02	04	15
Anderson, William(Z-M)	1828	May 07	CoshoctnCoOh	10	03	07
Anderson, Wm. Junr.(Z)	1816	Jan. 20	BelmontCo,Oh	09	05	18
Anderson, Wm.(Z)	1826	June 30	Morgan Co,Oh	10	06	11
Anderson, Wm.(Z)	1830	March 10	Morgan Co,Oh	10	06	22
Anderson, Wm.(Z)	1835	Dec. 14	Morgan Co,Oh	09	05	21
Andress, William(Z-M)	1835	Dec. 11	TuscarwsCoOh	03	07	21
Andrews, Alexander H.(Y)	1830	July 17	SteubenvleOh	04	13	33
Andrews, Jacob(Y)	1832	June 18	Stark Co.,Oh	07	17	23
Andrews, Jared(Z)	1816	Jan. 31	WashngtnCoOh	11	11	27
Andrews, Martin(Y)	1828	July 24	SteubenvleOh	02	08	18
Andrews, Martin(Z)	1829	Dec. 23	Morgan Co,Oh	11	11	11
Andrews, Perry(Z-M)	1827	Jan. 11	TuscarwsCoOh	02	06	20
Andrews, Perry(Z-M)	1832	Dec. 13	TuscarwsCoOh	02	06	21
Andrews, Perry(Z-M)	1833	April 02	TuscarwsCoOh	02	06	21
Andrews, Robert(Z)	1811	Jan. 07	WashngtnCoOh	10	06	30
Andrews, Samuel(Y)	1833	June 17	Jeff.Co.,Oh.	02	08	34
Andrews, Seth(Z)	1811	Jan. 07	WashngtnCoOh	10	06	30
Andrews, Seth(Z)	1816	March 19	WashngtnCoOh	10	06	30
Andrews, William(Z-M)	1833	Sept. 11	TuscarwsCoOh	04	07	10
Andrews, William(Z-M)	1833	Sept. 11	TuscarwsCoOh	04	07	11
Andrews, Wm. Augustus(Z-M)	1837	Nov. 15	CoshoctnCoOh	10	05	20
Andrews, Wm. Augustus(Z-M)	1837	Nov. 15	CoshoctnCoOh	10	05	20
Andrey, Robert(Z)	1810	Nov. 10	Jeff.Co.,Oh.	11	13	13
Angel, Israel(Z-M)	1835	Dec. 22	HarrisonCoOh	03	07	01
Ankany, George(Z)	1815	Oct. 19	SomersetCoPa	02	07	07
Ankany, George(Z)	1815	Oct. 19	SomersetCoPa	02	07	06
Ankeny, Christian Jr.(Z-M)	1833	April 15	TuscarwsCoOh	02	08	24
Ankeny, Christian(Z-M)	1832	Nov. 30	TuscarwsCoOh	03	07	11
Ankeny, Christian(Z-M)	1832	Dec. 28	TuscarwsCoOh	03	07	20
Ankeny, Geo.(Z-M)	1831	June 08	TuscarwsCoOh	02	08	24
Ankeny, Henry(Z-M)	1833	July 02	TuscarwsCoOh	02	08	24
Ankeny, Jos.(Z-M)	1836	Aug. 06	HolmesCoOhio	07	07	16
Ankrum, David(Z)	1835	April 13	BelmontCo,Oh	15	14	01
Annet, Archibald(Z)	1817	June 11	GuernseyCoOh	09	06	31
Annett, Arthur(Z-M)	1821	Dec. 14	GuernseyCoOh	04	02	20

PURCHASER	YEAR	DATE	RESIDENCE	R	T	S
Annett, Arthur(Z-M)	1833	Feb. 05	GuernseyCoOh	04	02	20
Anspack, John(Z)	1807	May 25	FranklinCoPa	07	01	03
Anstatt, Jacob(Z)	1814	Nov. 30	AlleghnyCoPa	11	12	19
Anstott, Jacob(Z)	1814	Nov. 30	AlleghnyCoPa	11	12	19
Anthony, George(Z)	1835	March 23	Morgan Co,Oh	10	06	14
Anthony, S.(Z)	1830	Sept. 24	Morgan Co,Oh	10	07	22
Anthony, Samuel(Z)	1832	March 15	Morgan Co,Oh	10	07	14
Apleman, John(Z)	1832	April 10	Morgan Co,Oh	13	09	19
Appel, John(Y)	1828	Nov. 10	ColumbanCoOh	03	13	20
Appel, John(Y)	1830	Dec. 06	ColumbanCoOh	04	14	36
Appleby, Benj.(Z)	1830	Dec. 20	MuskingmCoOh	11	12	21
Applegate, Daniel(Z-M)	1837	March 03	ZanesvilleOh	07	08	08
Appleman, George A.(Z)	1835	Aug. 14	Morgan Co,Oh	13	09	19
Appleman, George(Z)	1826	Jan. 24	Perry Co.,Oh	13	09	18
Appleman, Jacob(Z)	1830	Feb. 02	Morgan Co,Oh	13	09	21
Appleman, Jacob(Z)	1833	Feb. 18	Morgan Co,Oh	13	09	19
Appleman, James(Z)	1836	Dec. 07	Perry Co.,Oh	14	13	27
Appleman, Jesse(Z)	1836	Jan. 18	Morgan Co,Oh	13	09	30
Appleman, Levi(Z)	1833	Feb. 18	Perry Co.,Oh	14	12	02
Appleman, Levi(Z)	1834	Aug. 30	Morgan Co,Oh	13	09	30
Appleton, George(Z)	1815	Dec. 08	MuskingmCoOh	14	14	35
Arb, David(Z-M)	1836	Jan. 13	TuscarwsCoOh	04	07	04
Arb, David(Z-M)	1836	Jan. 13	TuscarwsCoOh	04	07	04
Arb, David(Z-M)	1836	Jan. 22	TuscarwsCoOh	04	07	03
Arbaugh, Daniel(Y)	1827	April 21	HarrisonCoOh	06	13	03
Arbuckle, James(Z)	1827	Oct. 25	MuskingmCoOh	03	01	25
Arbuckle, James(Z-M)	1834	Feb. 18	GuernseyCoOh	03	01	13
Arbuckle, John(Z)	1812	May 21	CoshoctnCoOh	05	04	12
Arbuckle, John(Z)	1814	Nov. 18	CoshoctnCoOh	11	05	06
Arbuckle, Rebecca(Z)	1812	May 21	CoshoctnCoOh	05	04	12
Arbuckle, Samuel(Z)	1812	Feb. 25	KnoxCo.,Ohio	11	05	15
Archbald, David(Z)	1834	Dec. 09	Morgan Co,Oh	10	07	25
Archbold, Thos. Jr.(Z-M)	1828	Aug. 20	TuscarwsCoOh	01	05	16
Archer, Abram(Z)	1836	March 22	MonroeCo.,Oh	08	07	20
Archer, Elijah(Z)	1836	Sept. 26	MonroeCo.,Oh	08	06	03
Archer, Enoch(Z)	1836	Jan. 16	MonroeCo.,Oh	08	05	02
Archer, George(Z)	1832	Sept. 10	GuernseyCoOh	10	09	24
Archer, George(Z)	1835	July 29	GuernseyCoOh	10	09	23
Archer, Henry(Z)	1832	Sept. 27	GuernseyCoOh	10	09	24
Archer, Henry(Z)	1835	March 16	GuernseyCoOh	10	09	24
Archer, Jacob Jr.(Z)	1836	Jan. 29	MonroeCo.,Oh	08	07	32
Archer, Jacob(Z)	1831	March 10	Morgan Co,Oh	08	07	26
Archer, Jacob(Z)	1835	Nov. 23	MonroeCo.,Oh	08	06	11
Archer, Jacob(Z)	1835	Nov. 23	MonroeCo.,Oh	08	06	11
Archer, Jacob(Z)	1836	Sept. 09	MonroeCo.,Oh	08	06	11
Archer, Jacob(Z)	1836	Sept. 09	MonroeCo.,Oh	08	06	11
Archer, James Jnr.(Z)	1836	April 07	MonroeCo.,Oh	08	07	34
Archer, James Jr.(Z)	1833	Oct. 18	MonroeCo.,Oh	08	07	28
Archer, James Jr.(Z)	1833	Oct. 18	MonroeCo.,Oh	08	07	27
Archer, James Jr.(Z)	1836	Aug. 31	MonroeCo.,Oh	08	07	28
Archer, James Junr.(Z)	1836	Sept. 02	MonroeCo.,Oh	08	07	28
Archer, James Senr.(Z)	1833	Oct. 24	MonroeCo.,Oh	08	06	05
Archer, James Senr.(Z)	1833	Oct. 24	MonroeCo.,Oh	08	07	32
Archer, James(Z)	1822	Dec. 31	MonroeCo.,Oh	08	07	27
Archer, James(Z)	1829	May 11	MonroeCo.,Oh	08	05	12
Archer, James(Z)	1835	Aug. 17	MonroeCo.,Oh	08	07	22
Archer, James(Z)	1836	April 07	MonroeCo.,Oh	08	07	22
Archer, James(Z)	1815	March 20	GuernseyCoOh	08	07	35
Archer, Joseph(Z)	1824	May 19	MonroeCo.,Oh	08	07	22
Archer, Joseph(Z)	1836	Jan. 16	MonroeCo.,Oh	08	06	23
Archer, Joseph(Z)	1836	Sept. 09	MonroeCo.,Oh	08	07	33
Archer, Joseph(Z)	1836	Sept. 09	MonroeCo.,Oh	08	07	33
Archer, Joseph(Z)	1809	March 29	MuskingmCoOh	09	08	05
Archer, Joseph(Z)	1814	July 13	GuernseyCoOh	08	07	26
Archer, Joseph(Z)	1816	Feb. 17	GuernseyCoOh	09	08	06
Archer, Michael Jr.(Z)	1833	Nov. 26	MonroeCo.,Oh	08	07	34
Archer, Michael(Z)	1820	Dec. 06	Monroe Co,Oh	08	07	35
Archer, Michael(Z)	1831	Oct. 20	MonroeCo.,Oh	08	07	34
Archer, Michael(Z)	1831	March 10	Morgan Co,Oh	08	07	28

PURCHASER	YEAR	DATE	RESIDENCE	R	T	S
Archer, Michael(Z)	1833	Nov. 20	MonroeCo.,Oh	08	07	28
Archer, Michael(Z)	1833	Nov. 20	MonroeCo.,Oh	08	07	34
Archer, Michael(Z)	1835	Nov. 30	MonroeCo.,Oh	08	07	34
Archer, Michael(Z)	1835	Dec. 12	MonroeCo.,Oh	08	07	22
Archer, Michael(Z)	1836	Sept. 09	MonroeCo.,Oh	08	06	03
Archer, Michael(Z)	1836	Sept. 09	MonroeCo.,Oh	08	07	21
Archer, Michael(Z)	1836	Sept. 26	MonroeCo.,Oh	08	06	03
Archer, Michael(Z)	1816	July 31	GuernseyCoOh	08	07	35
Archer, Nathan(Z)	1827	Aug. 22	MonroeCo.,Oh	08	06	02
Archer, Nathan(Z)	1836	Aug. 12	MunroeCo.,Oh	08	06	14
Archer, Nathan(Z)	1836	Aug. 12	MonroeCo.,Oh	08	06	14
Archer, Siman(Z)	1833	Oct. 10	MonroeCo.,Oh	08	06	02
Archer, Siman(Z)	1833	Oct. 10	MonroeCo.,Oh	08	06	02
Archer, Simon Jun.(Z)	1836	Sept. 09	MonroeCo.,Oh	08	07	28
Archer, Simon(Z)	1836	Aug. 29	MonroeCo.,Oh	08	06	02
Archer, Stephen(Z)	1835	Aug. 17	MonroeCo.,Oh	08	07	22
Archer, Wm.(Z)	1836	Sept. 09	MonroeCo.,Oh	08	07	34
Archibald, David(Z)	1822	Nov. 29	Morgan Co,Oh	10	06	05
Archibald, David(Z)	1828	Aug. 21	Morgan Co,Oh	10	07	28
Archibald, David(Z)	1835	Nov. 19	Morgan Co,Oh	10	07	26
Archibald, James(Z)	1826	Dec. 21	Morgan Co,Oh	10	07	13
Archibald, James(Z)	1834	Nov. 25	Morgan Co,Oh	09	06	19
Archibald, James(Z)	1814	June 13	BelmontCo,Oh	09	06	18
Archibald, Jas.(Z)	1835	Nov. 20	Morgan Co,Oh	09	06	19
Archibald, John(Z)	1832	May 23	Morgan Co,Oh	09	06	19
Archibald, John(Z)	1835	Nov. 20	Morgan Co,Oh	09	06	19
Archibald, John(Z)	1836	Jan. 02	Morgan Co,Oh	09	06	19
Archibald, Robert(Z)	1828	June 03	MuskingmCoOh	13	10	14
Archie, Jacob(Z)	1816	Sept. 04	GuernseyCoOh	08	07	35
Archur, Hugh(Y)	1829	March 17	ColumbanCoOh	04	14	25
Areon, Philip Jnr.(Z-M)	1835	April 01	GreenCo.,Pa.	05	07	08
Areon, Philip Jnr.(Z-M)	1835	April 01	GreenCo.,Pa.	05	07	13
Arlewine, John(Z)	1812	Feb. 13	KnoxCo.,Ohio	10	05	03
Arment, Levi(Z)	1832	Oct. 01	MuskingmCoOh	12	12	28
Armstrong, Abraham(Z)	1814	April 21	GuernseyCoOh	02	03	16
Armstrong, Abraham(Z)	1814	April 21	GuernseyCoOh	03	03	20
Armstrong, Alexander(Z)	1809	Nov. 15	AlleghnyCoPa	06	01	13
Armstrong, Alexander(Z)	1815	April 11	MuskingmCoOh	06	02	12
Armstrong, Archibald(Z)	1816	Dec. 16	Jeff.Co.,Oh.	04	06	02
Armstrong, Archibald(Z-M)	1832	April 02	HolmesCoOhio	04	09	08
Armstrong, Geo.(Z-M)	1833	July 22	HolmesCoOhio	07	10	04
Armstrong, George(Z-M)	1836	April 22	BeaverCo.,Pa	03	07	19
Armstrong, James Jr.(Z-M)	1831	Aug. 13	MuskingmCoOh	05	03	07
Armstrong, James Jr.(Z-M)	1831	Aug. 13	MuskingmCoOh	05	03	06
Armstrong, James(Z)	1832	Oct. 04	MonroeCo.,Oh	08	06	07
Armstrong, James(Z)	1836	March 08	MonroeCo.,Oh	08	06	07
Armstrong, James(Z)	1836	March 08	MonroeCo.,Oh	08	06	06
Armstrong, James(Z)	1815	Jan. 14	MuskingmCoOh	06	02	20
Armstrong, James(Z-M)	1833	Oct. 10	BelmontCo,Oh	11	08	08
Armstrong, James(Z-M)	1833	Oct. 10	BelmontCo,Oh	11	08	07
Armstrong, John(Z)	1813	Dec. 30	GuernseyCoOh	02	03	24
Armstrong, John(Z-M)	1833	March 11	LickingCo,Oh	11	04	13
Armstrong, Joseph(Z-M)	1828	Aug. 07	GuernseyCoOh	02	03	16
Armstrong, Joseph(Z-M)	1828	Sept. 12	GuernseyCoOh	02	03	16
Armstrong, Joseph(Z-M)	1831	July 09	GuernseyCoOh	02	03	16
Armstrong, Lessly(Z-M)	1838	Nov. 26	MuskingmCoOh	05	03	19
Armstrong, Robert(Z)	1811	Aug. 19	FayetteCo,Pa	12	13	25
Armstrong, Thomas(Y)	1821	June 11	ColumbanCoOh	04	13	18
Armstrong, Thomas(Y)	1825	Jan. 21	ColumbanCoOh	04	13	18
Armstrong, William(Z)	1833	April 13	Morgan Co,Oh	09	06	11
Armstrong, Wm.(Y)	1826	June 29	ColumbanCoOh	05	18	12
Armstrong, Wm.(Z-M)	1827	June 29	BelmontCo,Oh	11	08	07
Arnell, John(Z)	1814	Oct. 15	BelmontCo,Oh	01	04	24
Arnell, John(Z)	1815	July 04	GuernseyCoOh	01	04	22
Arner, Peter(Y)	1827	Aug. 29	TrumbullCoOh	06	19	02
Arner, Philip(Y)	1826	Aug. 22	TrumbullCoOh	06	19	02
Arnold, Charles(Z-M)	1831	Oct. 11	HarrisonCoOh	09	05	25
Arnold, David(Z-M)	1832	Nov. 05	HolmesCoOhio	08	08	14
Arnold, David(Z-M)	1835	Sept. 14	HolmesCoOhio	08	08	07

PURCHASER	YEAR	DATE	RESIDENCE	R	T	S
Arnold, George(Z)	1814	May 30	SomersetCoPa	04	08	16
Arnold, Jacob(Z-M)	1831	July 18	MuskingmCoOh	06	02	05
Arnold, James(Z)	1808	Aug. 29	Jeff.Co.,Oh.	13	12	11
Arnold, James(Z)	1810	Sept. 22	MuskingmCoOh	14	15	05
Arnold, John H.(Z-M)	1835	Dec. 05	LickingCo,Oh	10	03	09
Arnold, John(Z)	1829	Aug. 17	HolmesCoOhio	08	08	02
Arnold, John(Z-M)	1831	March 17	LickingCo,Oh	10	04	13
Arnold, John(Z-M)	1833	Sept. 23	TuscarwsCoOh	03	08	18
Arnold, John(Z-M)	1835	Aug. 27	TuscarwsCoOh	03	08	17
Arnold, Martin(Z)	1832	Nov. 09	Perry Co.,Oh	14	14	18
Arnold, Solomon(Y)	1821	Nov. 26	HarrisonCoOh	07	14	27
Arnold, Solomon(Y)	1823	June 16	Jeff.Co.,Oh.	07	14	27
Arnold, Thomas(Z-M)	1832	Sept. 04	HolmesCoOhio	08	08	08
Arnold, Thomas(Z-M)	1832	Sept. 04	HolmesCoOhio	08	08	09
Arnold, William(Z-M)	1832	July 13	HolmesCoOhio	08	08	07
Arnold, William(Z-M)	1832	July 13	HolmesCoOhio	08	08	14
Arthur, Elias(Z-M)	1833	Jan. 19	CoshoctnCoOh	08	06	10
Arthur, Elias(Z-M)	1833	Jan. 19	CoshoctnCoOh	08	06	10
Ashbrook, John(Y)	1829	Dec. 08	ColumbanCoOh	05	15	29
Ashbrooke, Jno.(Y)	1827	April 17	WashCo.,Penn	05	15	20
Ashbrooke, John(Y)	1832	Feb. 23	ColumbanCoOh	05	15	33
Ashburn, William(Z-M)	1824	Dec. 18	GreeneCo.,Pa	11	06	19
Ashcraft, Daniel(Z)	1808	June 03	MuskingmCoOh	09	04	22
Ashcraft, Jacob(Z)	1817	Jan. 15	MuskingmCoOh	09	04	18
Ashcraft, Jesse(Z-M)	1840	April 08	KnoxCo.,Ohio	10	06	23
Ashcraft, Jonathan(Z)	1816	Oct. 23	CoshoctnCoOh	09	04	32
Ashe, John(Z-M)	1833	Feb. 09	TuscarwsCoOh	03	08	04
Asher, Abraham(Z)	1832	Dec. 01	MuskingmCoOh	10	09	02
Asher, Henry(Z)	1817	Aug. 08	MuskingmCoOh	13	09	05
Ashercraft, Daniel(Z)	1814	Jan. 01	CoshoctnCoOh	10	07	23
Ashpaw, Jacob(Z)	1824	June 03	FairfeldCoOh	15	15	15
Ashpaw, Jacob(Z)	1825	Oct. 01	Perry Co.,Oh	15	15	15
Ashton, John(Z)	1816	Nov. 13	MuskingmCoOh	14	15	36
Ashton, Joseph(Z)	1816	Oct. 11	Ohio Co.,Vir	14	15	36
Asire, Henry(Z-M)	1833	Sept. 02	HolmesCoOhio	06	08	10
Askins, John(Z-M)	1832	June 09	GuernseyCoOh	03	02	11
Askins, William(Z)	1815	April 17	WashCo.,Penn	01	02	17
Askren, David(Z)	1836	March 21	MonroeCo.,Oh	08	07	09
Askren, Thomas(Z-M)	1834	Feb. 08	CoshoctnCoOh	07	05	12
Asper, Martin(Y)	1835	Nov. 12	Stark Co.,Oh	10	02	12
Assington, James(Z)	1811	April 26	FayetteCo,Pa	15	17	02
Atchason, John L.(Z-M)	1832	Aug. 02	CoshoctnCoOh	06	04	23
Atchbacher, John(Z-M)	1836	Nov. 16	CoshoctnCoOh	05	04	14
Atchbacher, John(Z-M)	1836	Nov. 16	CoshoctnCoOh	05	04	15
Atcheson, Reuben(Z)	1816	April 05	MuskingmCoOh	11	13	35
Atchinson, Reubon(Z)	1824	May 10	MuskingmCoOh	11	13	35
Atchison, David(Z-M)	1836	May 10	MuskingmCoOh	04	03	05
Atchison, David(Z-M)	1836	May 10	MuskingmCoOh	04	03	04
Aten, Aaron(Y)	1828	Aug. 29	BeaverCo.,Pa	04	13	21
Aten, Aaron(Y)	1828	Sept. 06	BeaverCo.,Pa	03	12	26
Aten, Aaron(Y)	1832	Sept. 20	ColumbanCoOh	05	12	26
Aten, Charles Morgan(Y)	1836	March 09	ColumbanCoOh	01	07	35
Atherton, Boaz(Z)	1836	Feb. 22	Morgan Co,Oh	09	07	23
Atherton, Daniel(Z)	1826	Oct. 11	Jeff.Co.,Oh.	12	09	09
Atkins, William(Z)	1815	Feb. 11	MuskingmCoOh	12	13	08
Atkinson, John(Z-M)	1833	May 25	GuernseyCoOh	03	04	05
Atkinson, John(Z-M)	1836	Nov. 01	GuernseyCoOh	03	04	07
Atkinson, Joseph B.(Z)	1834	Feb. 14	MuskingmCoOh	13	10	04
Atkinson, Robert(Z-M)	1836	Nov. 21	GuernseyCoOh	04	03	02
Atkinson, Sam'l.(Z)	1828	Sept. 26	MuskingmCoOh	13	10	04
Atkinson, Sam'l.(Z)	1833	June 10	MuskingmCoOh	13	10	04
Atkinson, Warner(Y)	1822	June 04	ColumbanCoOh	04	17	18
Atkison, James(Z-M)	1838	Sept. 06	MuskingmCoOh	04	03	08
Atkison, Jno.(Y)	1822	Feb. 20	HarrisonCoOh	06	12	21
Atkison, Joseph(Z)	1832	Dec. 08	BelmontCo,Oh	11	10	14
Atkison, Joseph(Z)	1832	Dec. 08	BelmontCo,Oh	11	10	02
Atkison, Joseph(Z)	1836	April 27	Perry Co.,Oh	14	13	29
Aton, Aaron(Y)	1833	Feb. 14	ColumbanCoOh	03	12	26
Aton, Aaron(Y)	1833	Feb. 14	ColumbanCoOh	03	12	27

9

PURCHASER	YEAR	DATE	RESIDENCE	R	T	S
Attinkruger, Henry(Z)	1834	Sept. 17	FairfeldCoOh	15	14	03
Atwater, Sam'l.(Z-M)	1831	July 01	CoshoctnCoOh	06	08	12
Atwood, Cornelius(Z-M)	1837	March 16	MuskingmCoOh	04	03	13
Atwood, Cornelius(Z-M)	1837	May 10	MuskingmCoOh	04	03	08
Atwood, James(Z-M)	1835	Nov. 09	LickingCo,Oh	10	04	22
Atwood, William(Z-M)	1833	Jan. 08	MuskingmCoOh	09	03	15
August, Anthony(Y)	1832	Dec. 03	Stark Co.,Oh	09	11	24
Augustin, Henry(Y)	1829	March 16	Stark Co.,Oh	06	16	22
Augustine, John(Y)	1824	May 17	ColumbanCoOh	01	08	21
Augustine, John(Y)	1824	May 17	ColumbanCoOh	01	08	21
Auker, George(Z)	1834	Jan. 20	Perry Co.,Oh	15	14	20
Auker, George(Z)	1836	Jan. 26	Perry Co.,Oh	15	14	20
Auld, J.(Z)	1814	Nov. 03	IndianaCo,Pa	11	13	31
Auld, Sam'l. Jr.(Y)	1827	March 23	HarrisonCoOh	07	12	06
Auld, Sam'l. Jr.(Y)	1827	March 23	HarrisonCoOh	07	12	05
Auld, Samuel(Y)	1832	Oct. 04	HarrisonCoOh	07	12	04
Ault, Jacob(Z)	1815	Dec. 19	BelmontCo,Oh	09	05	11
Ault, John(Z)	1815	Feb. 21	BelmontCo,Oh	09	04	01
Ault, John(Z)	1815	Feb. 21	BelmontCo,Oh	09	05	21
Ault, Oliver(Y)	1827	July 16	Jeff.Co.,Oh.	01	03	29
Ault, Peter(Z)	1815	Feb. 21	BelmontCo,Oh	09	05	23
Ault, Philip(Y)	1825	Jan. 29	BelmontCo,Oh	04	06	31
Ault, Valentine(Y)	1828	Aug. 1	BelmontCo,Oh	03	05	33
Aultman, Peter(Z-M)	1824	Nov. 06	CoshoctnCoOh	06	08	12
Austin, James W.(Z-M)	1835	July 31	MuskingmCoOh	07	04	23
Austin, James W.(Z-M)	1835	July 31	MuskingmCoOh	07	04	24
Awnwiler, Nicholas(Z-M)	1836	Oct. 24	Stark Co.,Oh	10	08	01
Ayer, Henry(Z)	1810	March 03	BelmontCo,Oh	05	01	07
Ayer, Jacob(Z)	1811	Jan. 26	MuskingmCoOh	12	11	17
Ayer, Jacob(Z)	1811	Jan. 26	MuskingmCoOh	03	01	21
Ayer, Jacob(Z)	1811	Jan. 26	MuskingmCoOh	13	11	01
Ayers, David(Z)	1810	June 20	WashngtnCo ?	11	06	14
Ayers, Jac.(Z)	1804	June 08	MuskingmCoOh	13	11	05
Ayers, Jacob(Z)	1804	June 08	MuskingmCoOh	12	12	08
Ayers, Jacob(Z)	1804	Dec. 04	MuskingmCoOh	13	11	10
Ayers, Jacob(Z)	1805	Aug. 06	MuskingmCoOh	13	11	01
Ayers, Jacob(Z)	1805	Oct. 30	MuskingmCoOh	12	11	17
Ayers, Jacob(Z)	1805	Dec. 14	MuskingmCoOh	12	13	18
Ayers, Jacob(Z)	1810	Jan. 06	MuskingmCoOh	12	13	20
Ayers, Jacob(Z)	1812	Feb. 25	ZanesvilleOh	13	11	27
Ayers, James(Z-M)	1833	June 04	CoshoctnCoOh	08	06	02
Ayers, James(Z-M)	1833	June 04	CoshoctnCoOh	08	06	01
Ayers, Moses(Z)	1825	July 09	MuskingmCoOh	13	11	11
Ayers, Moses(Z)	1825	Aug. 13	MuskingmCoOh	13	11	13
Ayers, Moses(Z)	1825	Oct. 11	MuskingmCoOh	13	11	12
Ayers, Moses(Z)	1832	June 25	MuskingmCoOh	13	11	11
Ayers, Moses(Z)	1817	July 10	MuskingmCoOh	12	13	32
Ayers, Thomas(Z-M)	1833	March 27	GuernseyCoOh	02	03	09
Ayers, Thos. Rich'd.(Z)	1833	April 10	Perry Co.,Oh	15	14	01
Ayers, Wm. H.(Z-M)	1837	June 26	MuskingmCoOh	08	07	21
Ayers, Wm. H.(Z-M)	1837	June 26	MuskingmCoOh	08	07	22
Ayle, James(Z)	1814	Nov. 19	WashngtnCoOh	08	05	24
Ayles, Patan(Z)	1817	Oct. 10	WashngtnCoOh	08	05	23
Ayles, Payton(Z)	1835	Aug. 15	WashngtnCoOh	08	05	26
Ayles, Payton(Z)	1835	Aug. 22	WashngtnCoOh	08	05	13
Ayres, Moses(Z)	1829	April 09	MuskingmCoOh	13	11	19
Ayres, Moses(Z)	1831	Oct. 10	MuskingmCoOh	13	11	12
Ayres, Moses(Z)	1815	July 28	MuskingmCoOh	13	11	02
Ayres, Moses(Z)	1816	June 07	MuskingmCoOh	13	11	13
Ayres, Nath'l.(Z)	1830	Aug. 02	MuskingmCoOh	12	12	18
Ayres, Nath'l.(Z)	1815	July 28	MuskingmCoOh	13	11	02
Ayres, Nath.(Z)	1830	Aug. 03	MuskingmCoOh	12	12	07
Ayres, Nathaniel(Z)	1828	March 11	MuskingmCoOh	12	12	18
Ayres, Thomas R.(Z)	1836	May 28	Perry Co.,Oh	15	14	01
Ayres, Thomas(Z)	1816	Feb. 13	MuskingmCoOh	10	03	14
Ayres, William(Z)	1817	Feb. 19	MuskingmCoOh	06	02	07
Azbill, David(Z-M)	1834	Jan. 21	KnoxCo.,Ohio	03	01	17
Azbill, David(Z-M)	1834	Feb. 10	KnoxCo.,Ohio	03	01	18
B_?___, Jacob(Z)	1809	Oct. 18	?	06	01	07

PURCHASER	YEAR	DATE	RESIDENCE	R	T	S
Babb, Jackson(Z)	1832	Feb. 10	Perry Co.,Oh	14	13	06
Babb, Joseph(Z)	1831	May 16	Perry Co.,Oh	14	13	33
Babb, Joseph(Z)	1808	June 13	FairfeldCoOh	15	15	03
Babb, Joseph(Z)	1808	Dec. 29	FairfeldCoOh	15	15	03
Babb, Joseph(Z)	1813	Sept. 02	FairfeldCoOh	15	15	03
Babb, Joseph(Z)	1815	May 16	MuskingmCoOh	15	15	02
Babb, Joseph(Z)	1815	July 14	MuskingmCoOh	15	15	29
Babcock, Abel S.(Z-M)	1834	July 25	MuskingmCoOh	06	04	01
Babcock, Abel S.(Z-M)	1836	April 01	CoshoctnCoOh	06	04	01
Babcock, Abel(Z-M)	1834	Oct. 07	CoshoctnCoOh	06	04	01
Babcock, Richard(Z)	1814	Jan. 01	HarrisonCoOh	06	07	18
Baby, Joab(Z)	1833	Nov. 04	Morgan Co,Oh	10	07	25
Bacchler, David(Z-M)	1837	April 11	TuscarwsCoOh	03	08	18
Bachtal, Geo.(Z-M)	1831	Dec. 20	HolmesCoOhio	04	09	05
Backer, John(Z)	1817	Oct. 24	LancastrCoPa	01	06	10
Backman, Christian(Z)	1804	Sept. 24	MuskingmCoOh	03	09	01
Backus, Andrew(Z)	1817	May 10	PlymouthMass	11	03	24
Backuss, John(Z)	1816	Aug. 13	AlleghnyCoMd	10	08	10
Bacon, Linus(Z)	1817	April 19	CharltonMass	10	08	05
Bader, Christopher(Z-M)	1835	Sept. 09	TuscarwsCoOh	03	10	17
Badger, Adam(Z)	1836	Jan. 12	ZanesvilleOh	14	14	20
Badger, Geo.(Y)	1834	May 22	WashCo.,Penn	07	12	28
Baechler, David(Z-M)	1836	Sept. 13	Stark Co.,Oh	03	08	24
Baechler, David(Z-M)	1838	Jan. 30	CoshoctnCoOh	09	07	21
Baelsford, Brown(Z-M)	1833	Jan. 05	MuskingmCoOh	06	03	01
Baelsford, Phebe(Z)	1834	Oct. 21	MuskingmCoOh	13	10	02
Baer, Abm. Senr.(Y)	1827	June 18	Stark Co.,Oh	06	19	31
Baer, Abm. Senr.(Y)	1827	June 18	Stark Co.,Oh	06	18	06
Baer, Abraham Jr.(Y)	1826	June 27	Stark Co.,Oh	06	17	15
Baer, Abraham Jr.(Y)	1829	March 14	Stark Co.,Oh	06	17	29
Baer, Abraham Senr.(Y)	1827	May 05	Stark Co.,Oh	06	18	05
Baer, David(Y)	1822	July 29	Stark Co.,Oh	07	18	21
Baer, Ephraim(Y)	1831	July 09	Stark Co.,Oh	06	17	29
Baer, Joel(Y)	1835	Sept. 08	Stark Co.,Oh	07	20	17
Baer, John(Z)	1810	Aug. 07	MuskingmCoOh	09	06	23
Baetchi, Rudolph(Y)	1826	Sept. 08	Stark Co.,Oh	06	18	08
Bagh, William(Z)	1814	Nov. 17	FairfeldCoOh	15	15	10
Baghman, Henry(Y)	1828	April 24	Stark Co.,Oh	06	16	15
Bahler, John(Z-M)	1833	Oct. 05	TuscarwsCoOh	03	08	15
Baid, John(Z)	1805	Dec. 05	FairfeldCoOh	15	18	16
Baid, John(Z)	1805	Dec. 06	FairfeldCoOh	15	17	04
Baile, John(Y)	1831	July 15	WashCo.,Penn	06	13	29
Bailey, Benj.(Z)	1828	Oct. 01	BelmontCo,Oh	12	10	25
Bailey, Benjamin(Z)	1828	Dec. 18	BelmontCo,Oh	12	10	25
Bailey, David(Z)	1816	Oct. 15	BelmontCo,Oh	09	04	24
Bailey, Frederick(Z-M)	1835	July 18	HolmesCoOhio	05	07	07
Bailey, Frederick(Z-M)	1835	July 18	HolmesCoOhio	05	07	07
Bailey, George(Z)	1812	July 15	CoshoctnCoOh	09	06	21
Bailey, Ira(Z)	1814	Nov. 11	WashngtnCoOh	11	11	28
Bailey, James(Z)	1828	June 03	MuskingmCoOh	13	10	14
Bailey, Mathew(Z)	1832	Oct. 02	Perry Co.,Oh	15	15	33
Bailey, Matthew(Z)	1834	Jan. 06	Perry Co.,Oh	13	15	33
Bailey, Wiate(Y)	1826	March 15	BelmontCo,Oh	06	08	19
Bailey, William(Z)	1805	Nov. 08	CentreCoPenn	13	12	14
Bailey, William(Z)	1817	June 09	FairfeldCoOh	15	14	05
Baily, John(Z)	1810	Oct. 18	WashngtnCoOh	04	08	14
Baily, Peter(Z)	1834	Feb. 27	Perry Co.,Oh	15	14	09
Baily, William(Z)	1836	March 21	Perry Co.,Oh	14	13	32
Baily, William(Z-M)	1834	Feb. 18	HolmesCoOhio	08	08	24
Bains, John(Z)	1831	Dec. 27	Morgan Co,Oh	10	08	17
Bainter, George(Z)	1816	March 05	MuskingmCoOh	05	03	12
Bainter, Jacob(Z-M)	1833	Sept. 24	MuskingmCoOh	05	03	15
Bainter, James(Z-M)	1832	April 30	MuskingmCoOh	05	04	09
Bainter, James(Z-M)	1835	Sept. 10	CoshoctnCoOh	05	04	23
Bainter, James(Z-M)	1837	Jan. 30	CoshoctnCoOh	05	04	22
Bainter, John(Z-M)	1836	May 07	TuscarwsCoOh	03	07	25
Bainter, Sprague(Z-M)	1833	Sept. 17	CoshoctnCoOh	05	04	23
Bainter, Sprague(Z-M)	1835	Sept. 07	CoshoctnCoOh	05	04	24
Bair, Andrew(Z)	1828	Aug. 07	MuskingmCoOh	13	10	33

PURCHASER	YEAR	DATE	RESIDENCE	R	T	S
Bair, Daniel(Y)	1824	Jan. 13	BelmontCo,Oh	04	06	15
Bair, Samuel(Y)	1826	Aug. 02	HarrisonCoOh	05	12	30
Baird, Hugh(Z)	1806	Aug. 16	MuskingmCoOh	15	17	04
Baird, James(Z)	1805	July 10	FairfeldCoOh	15	17	05
Baird, James(Z)	1805	Oct. 02	FairfeldCoOh	15	18	15
Baird, James(Z)	1806	June 04	FairfeldCoOh	15	18	15
Baird, James(Z)	1807	June 15	MuskingmCoOh	15	18	17
Baird, James(Z)	1812	May 26	MuskingmCoOh	15	18	17
Baird, James(Z)	1813	March 22	?	15	17	06
Baird, James(Z)	1813	Aug. 23	MuskingmCoOh	15	17	08
Baird, Jane(Z)	1806	June 04	FairfeldCoOh	15	18	17
Baird, Jane(Z)	1809	June 15	MuskingmCoOh	15	17	06
Baird, John C.(Z)	1813	March 22	?	15	17	06
Baird, John H.(Z-M)	1832	May 23	CoshoctnCoOh	07	05	10
Baird, John Hamilton(Z-M)	1832	Jan. 17	CoshoctnCoOh	07	05	01
Baird, John(Z)	1805	July 10	FairfeldCoOh	15	17	08
Baird, John(Z)	1805	Sept. 04	FairfeldCoOh	15	17	08
Baird, John(Z)	1805	Oct. 03	FairfeldCoOh	15	18	10
Baird, John(Z)	1810	June 30	FayetteCo,Pa	02	03	24
Baird, John(Z)	1811	Jan. 23	MuskingmCoOh	15	18	10
Baird, John(Z)	1814	Sept. 26	MuskingmCoOh	14	14	04
Baird, John(Z)	1816	Feb. 17	MuskingmCoOh	14	14	01
Baird, John(Z-M)	1832	Feb. 03	GuernseyCoOh	02	03	15
Baird, John(Z-M)	1836	Jan. 02	GuernseyCoOh	03	04	11
Baird, John(Z-M)	1836	Jan. 02	GuernseyCoOh	03	04	11
Baird, John(Z-M)	1836	Nov. 18	GuernseyCoOh	03	04	11
Baird, John(Z-M)	1839	April 03	GuernseyCoOh	05	03	20
Baird, Josiah(Z)	1831	July 26	GuernseyCoOh	08	08	18
Baird, Moses(Z)	1814	Nov. 24	GuernseyCoOh	02	01	03
Baird, Philip(Z-M)	1833	Nov. 21	KnoxCo.,Ohio	10	07	18
Baird, Sam'l.(Z)	1811	Aug. 19	MuskingmCoOh	15	17	06
Baird, Samuel(Y)	1828	Feb. 18	Stark Co.,Oh	07	20	17
Baird, Samuel(Z)	1812	April 11	MuskingmCoOh	15	18	02
Baird, Sarah(Z)	1812	May 15	MuskingmCoOh	15	18	03
Baird, Sarah(Z)	1813	Aug. 23	MuskingmCoOh	15	17	08
Baird, William(Z)	1811	Aug. 19	MuskingmCoOh	15	17	06
Baird, William(Z)	1815	Dec. 22	Jeff.Co.,Oh.	06	07	13
Baker, Aaron Jr.(Z)	1835	Nov. 13	Jeff.Co.,Oh.	10	08	35
Baker, Aaron(Z)	1814	Dec. 02	LickingCo,Oh	11	03	24
Baker, Aaron(Z)	1817	March 19	LickingCo,Oh	11	04	11
Baker, Anthony(Z)	1815	Jan. 25	MuskingmCoOh	06	02	18
Baker, Archibald S.(Z)	1835	Nov. 13	CarrollCo,Oh	10	08	35
Baker, Archibald S.(Z)	1835	Nov. 13	CarrollCo,Oh	10	08	35
Baker, Bazel(Z)	1811	May 27	MuskingmCoOh	05	04	10
Baker, Catharine(Z-M)	1829	May 04	KnoxCo.,Ohio	10	08	19
Baker, Charles(Z)	1806	Dec. 17	MuskingmCoOh	05	04	01
Baker, Charles(Z)	1812	April 21	MuskingmCoOh	05	04	01
Baker, Charles(Z-M)	1821	July 06	CoshoctnCoOh	09	05	16
Baker, David(Z)	1809	Nov. 08	WashngtnCo ?	05	08	20
Baker, Esaias(Z)	1810	Feb. 16	MuskingmCoOh	05	04	01
Baker, Isaiah(Z)	1807	Dec. 26	MuskingmCoOh	05	04	10
Baker, Jacob(Z)	1806	May 01	LoudonCo,Vir	14	15	31
Baker, Jacob(Z)	1807	March 02	BelmontCo,Oh	10	09	28
Baker, Jacob(Z)	1808	Jan. 19	MuskingmCoOh	11	12	01
Baker, Jacob(Z)	1813	Sept. 09	MuskingmCoOh	13	11	20
Baker, Jacob(Z)	1814	Nov. 23	KnoxCo.,Ohio	11	06	20
Baker, Jacob(Z-M)	1829	Aug. 18	KnoxCo.,Ohio	11	04	11
Baker, Jacob(Z-M)	1833	Nov. 06	LickingCo,Oh	11	04	11
Baker, James(Z)	1825	Dec. 22	Morgan Co,Oh	12	10	15
Baker, James(Z-M)	1830	Dec. 03	MuskingmCoOh	09	03	14
Baker, John(Y)	1824	Aug. 20	HarrisonCoOh	06	14	06
Baker, John(Y)	1826	March 17	ColumbanCoOh	05	17	09
Baker, John(Z)	1827	May 07	CoshoctnCoOh	04	06	02
Baker, John(Z)	1836	April 07	MuskingmCoOh	15	14	28
Baker, John(Z)	1837	Feb. 04	Perry CoOhio	15	14	27
Baker, John(Z)	1813	April 02	KnoxCo.,Ohio	10	06	22
Baker, John(Z-M)	1823	Feb. 28	GuernseyCoOh	01	01	12
Baker, John(Z-M)	1829	July 04	CoshoctnCoOh	04	06	12
Baker, John(Z-M)	1831	Oct. 24	CoshoctnCoOh	04	06	02

PURCHASER	YEAR	DATE	RESIDENCE	R	T	S
Baker, John(Z-M)	1832	Nov. 23	CoshoctnCoOh	03	06	04
Baker, John(Z-M)	1835	Oct. 03	CoshoctnCoOh	04	06	09
Baker, John(Z-M)	1836	May 31	CoshoctnCoOh	06	04	02
Baker, Michael(Z-M)	1839	Feb. 15	TuscarwsCoOh	02	07	01
Baker, Nathan(Z)	1805	Nov. 18	HarrisonCoVa	10	03	23
Baker, Nathan(Z)	1806	Nov. 19	MuskingmCoOh	09	03	23
Baker, Otho(Y)	1829	April 04	HarrisonCoOh	06	12	36
Baker, Otho(Y)	1829	Oct. 03	HarrisonCoOh	06	13	25
Baker, Philip(Z)	1809	Dec. 25	MuskingmCoOh	06	01	02
Baker, Philip(Z)	1810	Nov. 13	MuskingmCoOh	06	01	01
Baker, Philip(Z)	1812	Sept. 21	MuskingmCoOh	06	02	19
Baker, Philip(Z)	1812	Oct. 29	MuskingmCoOh	06	02	12
Baker, Philip(Z)	1815	Feb. 16	MuskingmCoOh	07	01	01
Baker, Philip(Z)	1815	July 07	KnoxCo.,Ohio	11	06	19
Baker, Philip(Z-M)	1822	Aug. 27	KnoxCo.,Ohio	10	08	01
Baker, Philip(Z-M)	1832	June 30	CoshoctnCoOh	07	08	16
Baker, Philip(Z-M)	1837	April 07	KnoxCo.,Ohio	10	09	22
Baker, Reson(Z)	1807	Sept. 07	MuskingmCoOh	04	04	05
Baker, Rich'd.(Y)	1823	Oct. 27	Stark Co.,Oh	07	17	15
Baker, Sam. C.(Z)	1830	March 23	Morgan Co,Oh	12	10	23
Baker, Sam. C.(Z)	1830	April 19	Morgan Co,Oh	12	10	23
Baker, Thomas(Z-M)	1833	Aug. 22	TuscarwsCoOh	01	05	09
Baker, William(Z)	1816	April 27	MuskingmCoOh	09	01	07
Balderston, Jacob(Z)	1827	June 28	MuskingmCoOh	12	10	25
Balderston, Jacob(Z)	1831	June 10	Morgan Co,Oh	12	09	01
Baldwin, David(Z)	1834	Dec. 16	WashngtnCoOh	10	06	34
Baldwin, David(Z)	1835	March 27	WashngtnCoOh	09	05	22
Baldwin, David(Z)	1836	Jan. 11	WashngtnCoOh	09	05	23
Baldwin, David(Z)	1836	Jan. 11	WashngtnCoOh	09	05	20
Baldwin, David(Z)	1836	Feb. 01	WashngtnCoOh	09	05	23
Baldwin, David(Z)	1836	May 13	WashngtnCoOh	09	05	20
Baldwin, David(Z)	1836	May 13	WashngtnCoOh	09	05	20
Baldwin, David(Z)	1836	May 13	WashngtnCoOh	09	05	15
Baldwin, David(Z)	1836	May 13	WashngtnCoOh	10	06	15
Baldwin, David(Z)	1836	May 13	WashngtnCoOh	10	06	24
Baldwin, David(Z)	1836	Oct. 27	WashngtnCoOh	09	05	30
Baldwin, John(Z-M)	1833	June 11	CoshoctnCoOh	07	07	20
Baldwin, John(Z-M)	1834	Aug. 18	CoshoctnCoOh	07	07	20
Baldwin, Reed(Y)	1831	Sept. 16	Jeff.Co.,Oh.	07	14	29
Baldwin, William(Z)	1817	June 20	MuskingmCoOh	06	02	15
Balentine, Alexander(Z-M)	1832	May 22	MuskingmCoOh	05	04	21
Balentine, Hugh Senr.(Z)	1814	June 28	MuskingmCoOh	06	03	01
Balentine, Hugh(Z)	1813	Aug. 09	CoshoctnCoOh	06	03	01
Baley, Joab(Z)	1833	April 05	Morgan Co,Oh	10	07	25
Baley, Joab(Z)	1835	Nov. 16	Morgan Co,Oh	10	07	25
Baley, John(Z-M)	1832	Aug. 14	HolmesCoOhio	09	07	02
Baley, John(Z-M)	1834	Sept. 11	CoshoctnCoOh	09	07	02
Baley, John(Z-M)	1836	Aug. 04	CoshoctnCoOh	09	07	02
Balinger, Leroy(Z)	1834	Jan. 10	MuskingmCoOh	13	10	03
Balis, Thomas Junr.(Z)	1833	Dec. 12	MonroeCo.,Oh	08	07	30
Ball, Ann(Z)	1831	May 09	Morgan Co,Oh	09	07	14
Ball, Anna(Z)	1835	Dec. 14	Perry Co.,Oh	15	14	20
Ball, Asa(Z)	1836	April 12	Perry Co.,Oh	15	14	32
Ball, Daniel(Z)	1831	May 09	Morgan Co,Oh	09	07	11
Ball, Daniel(Z)	1831	May 09	Morgan Co,Oh	09	07	11
Ball, Daniel(Z)	1831	May 09	Morgan Co,Oh	09	07	02
Ball, Daniel(Z)	1832	Oct. 27	Morgan Co,Oh	09	07	13
Ball, Daniel(Z)	1836	Jan. 29	MonroeCo.,Oh	08	07	32
Ball, Daniel(Z)	1836	Oct. 08	MonroeCo.,Oh	08	07	32
Ball, Elijah(Z)	1816	Sept. 21	MuskingmCoOh	13	09	33
Ball, James(Z)	1833	June 13	Perry Co.,Oh	15	14	20
Ball, James(Z)	1836	May 30	Perry Co.,Oh	15	14	20
Ball, James(Z)	1811	April 20	FairfeldCoOh	15	17	35
Ball, John(Z-M)	1831	June 04	MuskingmCoOh	06	03	20
Ball, Jonas(Z)	1822	Dec. 27	Morgan Co,Oh	09	07	11
Ball, Jonas(Z)	1830	Aug. 26	Morgan Co,Oh	08	07	17
Ball, Jonas(Z)	1831	May 09	Morgan Co,Oh	09	07	11
Ball, Jonas(Z)	1831	May 09	Morgan Co,Oh	09	07	11
Ball, Jonas(Z)	1831	May 09	Morgan Co,Oh	09	07	02

PURCHASER	YEAR	DATE	RESIDENCE	R	T	S
Ball, Jonas(Z)	1831	June 30	Morgan Co,Oh	08	07	06
Ball, Jonas(Z)	1832	Dec. 22	Morgan Co,Oh	09	07	01
Ball, Jonas(Z)	1833	Jan. 22	Morgan Co,Oh	08	07	06
Ball, Jonas(Z)	1833	April 29	Morgan Co,Oh	08	06	10
Ball, Joseph J.(Z)	1831	May 16	Morgan Co,Oh	13	09	32
Ball, M.(Z)	1829	Dec. 21	MonroeCo.,Oh	08	07	05
Ball, Mathew(Z)	1816	Aug. 22	AlleghnyCoMd	08	07	05
Ball, Mathew(Z)	1816	Aug. 22	AlleghnyCoMd	09	07	12
Ball, Mathew(Z)	1816	Aug. 22	AlleghnyCoMd	08	07	18
Ball, Mathew(Z)	1816	Aug. 22	AlleghnyCoMd	08	07	07
Ball, Matthew(Z)	1831	Nov. 03	MonroeCo.,Oh	08	08	32
Ball, Matthew(Z)	1833	May 31	GuernseyCoOh	08	08	32
Ball, Matthew(Y)	1836	Oct. 28	WashngtnCoOh	08	05	15
Ball, Nathan(Y)	1835	June 18	CarrollCo,Oh	07	14	09
Ball, Oliver C.(Z)	1832	Nov. 30	Perry Co.,Oh	15	14	29
Ball, Oliver C.(Z)	1833	April 20	Perry Co.,Oh	15	14	29
Ball, Samuel(Z)	1833	Nov. 12	MonroeCo.,Oh	08	07	13
Ball, Samuel(Z)	1833	Nov. 12	MonroeCo.,Oh	08	07	13
Ball, Samuel(Z)	1836	April 08	Perry Co.,Oh	15	14	20
Ball, Samuel(Z)	1836	April 08	Perry Co.,Oh	15	14	20
Ball, William(Z)	1814	Aug. 15	Brooke CoVir	11	05	23
Ballard, Stephen(Z)	1805	Nov. 25	MuskingmCoOh	01	01	09
Ballard, Stephen(Z)	1816	Dec. 16	GuernseyCoOh	01	01	08
Ballentine, A.(Z-M)	1836	June 16	MuskingmCoOh	06	04	21
Ballentine, Alex'r.(Z-M)	1835	Oct. 31	MuskingmCoOh	06	04	11
Ballentine, Alex'r.(Z-M)	1835	Oct. 31	MuskingmCoOh	05	04	15
Ballentine, Alex'r.(Z-M)	1835	Oct. 31	MuskingmCoOh	06	04	11
Ballentine, Alex'r.(Z-M)	1835	Oct. 31	MuskingmCoOh	05	04	15
Ballentine, Alex'r.(Z-M)	1835	Nov. 07	MuskingmCoOh	06	04	11
Ballentine, Alex'r.(Z-M)	1835	Nov. 07	MuskingmCoOh	06	04	22
Ballentine, Alex'r.(Z-M)	1837	July 21	MuskingmCoOh	06	04	20
Ballentine, Alex.(Z-M)	1836	Feb. 06	MuskingmCoOh	06	04	21
Ballentine, Alex.(Z-M)	1836	Feb. 06	MuskingmCoOh	06	04	21
Ballentine, Alex.(Z-M)	1836	Feb. 08	MuskingmCoOh	06	04	11
Ballentine, Alexander(Z-M)	1835	Sept. 10	MuskingmCoOh	06	04	21
Ballentine, Alexander(Z-M)	1836	Sept. 19	MuskingmCoOh	05	04	25
Ballentine, Hugh(Z-M)	1836	Jan. 12	MuskingmCoOh	06	04	22
Ballentine, Hugh(Z-M)	1836	Feb. 06	MuskingmCoOh	06	04	20
Balmer, Jacob C.(Y)	1823	March 27	Stark Co.,Oh	09	11	02
Balmer, Jacob Christian(Y)	1832	June 11	Stark Co.,Oh	09	11	02
Baltzley, David(Z-M)	1836	Feb. 12	TuscarwsCoOh	01	08	02
Baltzley, Jacob(Z)	1817	April 01	TuscarwsCoOh	04	08	04
Baltzley, Jacob(Z-M)	1826	Aug. 29	HolmesCoOhio	04	08	05
Bamhouse, Elizabeth J.(Z)	1834	Feb. 18	Morgan Co,Oh	09	07	29
Bance, John Masterson(Y)	1832	May 28	Jeff.Co.,Oh.	04	13	13
Bane, Thomas(Z)	1830	July 14	Morgan Co,Oh	12	09	13
Banel, Andrew(Z-M)	1830	May 12	CoshoctnCoOh	06	07	11
Banks, Benjamin(Z)	1813	Oct. 15	MuskingmCoOh	15	16	28
Banks, Samuel(Z-M)	1838	April 16	GuernseyCoOh	04	04	09
Banning, Nathan'l.(Z)	1813	March 29	MuskingmCoOh	14	15	07
Bany, Henry(Z-M)	1839	June 14	ZanesvilleOh	09	08	06
Barber, Condiey(Y)	1831	July 25	HarrisonCoOh	07	11	04
Barber, Isaac(Y)	1824	Feb. 07	ColumbanCoOh	05	18	12
Barber, Jacob(Y)	1821	Oct. 06	ColumbanCoOh	04	17	22
Barber, Jacob(Y)	1822	Jan. 01	ColumbanCoOh	04	17	22
Barber, James(Z)	1827	Nov. 21	MuskingmCoOh	06	02	07
Barber, Robert(Y)	1835	Dec. 02	ColumbanCoOh	03	12	10
Barclay, James(Y)	1827	Nov. 23	Jeff.Co.,Oh.	03	11	05
Barclay, John(Z)	1835	Dec. 23	Morgan Co,Oh	09	07	27
Barclay, John(Z)	1837	July 17	Morgan Co,Oh	09	07	27
Barclay, Joseph(Y)	1821	April 27	ColumbanCoOh	04	13	09
Barclay, Joseph(Y)	1822	Sept. 11	ColumbanCoOh	04	13	03
Barclay, Joseph(Y)	1828	Aug. 22	ColumbanCoOh	04	13	09
Barclay, Joseph(Y)	1829	Oct. 09	ColumbanCoOh	04	13	15
Barcroft, Anna(Z-M)	1833	Aug. 08	Jeff.Co.,Oh.	07	07	11
Barcroft, John(Z)	1817	Feb. 17	MuskingmCoOh	14	14	08
Barcroft, John(Z-M)	1825	Sept. 25	Jeff.Co.,Oh.	07	07	11
Barcroft, John(Z-M)	1836	Jan. 13	Jeff.Co.,Oh.	07	07	11

PURCHASER	YEAR	DATE	RESIDENCE	R	T	S
Barcus, Samuel(Z)	1816	Oct. 23	KnoxCo.,Ohio	10	05	10
Barcus, Thomas(Y)	1836	April 04	Jeff.Co.,Oh.	02	09	25
Barcus, Thomas(Z-M)	1832	Nov. 03	KnoxCo.,Ohio	10	05	11
Barcus, William(Z-M)	1835	Nov. 09	KnoxCo.,Ohio	10	05	20
Barcus, William(Z-M)	1835	Nov. 17	KnoxCo.,Ohio	10	05	20
Barcus, Wm.(Z-M)	1828	June 16	CoshoctnCoOh	07	05	11
Barcus, Wm.(Z-M)	1828	June 16	CoshoctnCoOh	07	05	11
Bareas, William(Z-M)	1834	Feb. 10	Jeff.Co.,Oh.	02	05	02
Barens, John(Z-M)	1838	May 05	MuskingmCoOh	11	03	08
Barens, Thomas(Z-M)	1833	Feb. 26	KnoxCo.,Ohio	10	05	11
Barens, William(Z)	1815	June 10	SteubenvleOh	01	05	14
Bareurt, ? (Z)	1814	April 27	BelmontCo,Oh	10	05	02
Barge, Joseph(Z-M)	1837	Aug. 17	BelmontCo,Oh	03	08	18
Barge, Robert(Z-M)	1836	Nov. 11	BelmontCo,Oh	03	08	18
Barger, John(Z-M)	1823	Dec. 03	HarrisonCoOh	07	05	09
Barkdull, Joseph(Z-M)	1828	Sept. 02	ColumbanCoOh	04	08	23
Barkelaw, Corne's.(Z)	1814	Oct. 24	KnoxCo.,Ohio	11	05	15
Barker, Jacob(Z-M)	1836	Aug. 11	TuscarwsCoOh	04	07	08
Barker, Jacob(Z-M)	1836	Aug. 11	TuscarwsCoOh	04	07	09
Barker, James(Z)	1838	April 30	MonroeCo.,Oh	08	06	36
Barker, James(Z-M)	1835	Sept. 14	GuernseyCoOh	03	06	14
Barker, S. A.(Z)	1835	Oct. 10	ZanesvilleOh	11	10	28
Barker, S. A.(Z)	1836	Feb. 02	ZanesvilleOh	09	05	31
Barker, S. A.(Z)	1836	Feb. 02	ZanesvilleOh	09	05	12
Barker, S. A.(Z)	1836	Feb. 02	ZanesvilleOh	09	05	14
Barker, Sam'l. A.(Z)	1828	May 12	Morgan Co,Oh	12	10	12
Barker, Sam'l. Augustus(Z-M)	1837	Feb. 25	ZanesvilleOh	08	07	05
Barker, Sam'l. Augustus(Z-M)	1837	Feb. 25	ZanesvilleOh	09	07	01
Barker, Sam'l. Augustus(Z-M)	1837	Feb. 25	ZanesvilleOh	09	07	01
Barker, Samuel A.(Z)	1835	Sept. 18	ZanesvilleOh	11	10	28
Barker, Samuel A.(Z)	1835	Sept. 18	ZanesvilleOh	11	10	28
Barker, Samuel A.(Z)	1836	Jan. 11	ZanesvilleOh	09	05	20
Barker, Samuel A.(Z)	1836	Jan. 22	ZanesvilleOh	09	05	29
Barker, Samuel A.(Z)	1836	April 22	ZanesvilleOh	09	05	29
Barker, Samuel A.(Z)	1836	Sept. 24	ZanesvilleOh	10	06	35
Barker, Thos. Sen.(Z)	1830	Dec. 10	MonroeCo.,Oh	08	07	11
Barkey, Catharine(Z-M)	1836	June 15	HolmesCoOhio	05	07	07
Barkhurst, Eb.(Z)	1831	March 07	Morgan Co,Oh	11	10	11
Barkhurst, John(Y)	1832	May 29	Jeff.Co.,Oh.	07	12	33
Barkhurst, John(Z)	1825	Aug. 27	HarrisonCoOh	12	11	22
Barkhurst, Joshua(Y)	1822	May 20	Jeff.Co.,Oh.	07	10	22
Barkhurst, Joshua(Y)	1822	May 20	Jeff.Co.,Oh.	07	10	22
Barklett, Peter W.(Z-M)	1832	Dec. 04	TuscarwsCoOh	03	10	17
Barkley, Andrew(Z-M)	1832	May 15	TuscarwsCoOh	01	06	11
Barkley, David(Z-M)	1834	Jan. 07	HarrisonCoOh	04	06	20
Barkley, David(Z-M)	1835	April 09	HarrisonCoOh	04	06	20
Barkman, Jacob(Z)	1806	Nov. 28	BaltimreCoMd	08	04	07
Barkman, Jacob(Z)	1806	Nov. 28	BaltimreCoMd	08	04	07
Barkman, Jacob(Z)	1806	Nov. 28	BaltimreCoMd	08	04	04
Barkshere, Robt.(Z-M)	1829	April 14	BelmontCo,Oh	01	05	06
Barkus, James(Z)	1816	Dec. 09	KnoxCo.,Ohio	11	08	17
Barkus, Jefferson B.(Z-M)	1826	Oct. 28	KnoxCo.,Ohio	11	08	16
Barkus, Obadiah(Z-M)	1826	Oct. 28	KnoxCo.,Ohio	11	08	16
Barkuss, Daniel(Z)	1816	Aug. 13	AlleghnyCoMd	10	08	24
Barky, Samuel(Z-M)	1834	Nov. 14	TuscarwsCoOh	05	07	07
Barlin, Abn.(Y)	1825	May 25	TuscarwsCoOh	06	14	24
Barnard, Christian(Z)	1812	Feb. 18	MuskingmCoOh	15	16	36
Barnard, Jason(Z-M)	1838	Oct. 26	MuskingmCoOh	05	03	09
Barnes, Alexander(Z)	1817	May 08	Jeff.Co.,Oh.	06	06	11
Barnes, Alexander(Z)	1817	May 08	Jeff.Co.,Oh.	06	06	11
Barnes, Charles(Z-M)	1832	Nov. 13	LickingCo,Oh	11	03	16
Barnes, Chas.(Z-M)	1830	Oct. 30	LickingCo,Oh	11	03	16
Barnes, Daniel(Z-M)	1836	Sept. 09	MuskingmCoOh	09	07	05
Barnes, Dorsey Hall(Y)	1825	Jan. 18	BelmontCo,Oh	04	06	31
Barnes, Henry(Z)	1816	Oct. 21	FranklinCoPa	06	06	09
Barnes, Isaac(Z)	1815	May 05	MuskingmCoOh	15	15	06
Barnes, Isaac(Z)	1815	May 05	MuskingmCoOh	15	15	06
Barnes, Jacob(Z)	1835	May 30	GuernseyCoOh	08	07	14
Barnes, James(Z-M)	1836	March 24	CoshoctnCoOh	09	08	24

PURCHASER	YEAR	DATE	RESIDENCE	R	T	S
Barnes, Joseph(Z)	1817	Feb. 18	LickingCo,Oh	14	14	34
Barnes, Leonard(Z-M)	1832	July 11	HolmesCoOhio	09	08	09
Barnes, Leonard(Z-M)	1832	July 11	HolmesCoOhio	09	08	09
Barnes, Lorenzo(Z-M)	1837	Feb. 25	HolmesCoOhio	09	08	22
Barnes, Matilda(Z-M)	1833	Nov. 22	HarrisonCoOh	01	06	13
Barnes, Nathan(Z-M)	1835	Aug. 31	GuernseyCoOh	02	03	01
Barnes, Otho(Y)	1824	May 18	ColumbanCoOh	04	13	08
Barnes, Otho(Z)	1816	Sept. 27	Barnes'lOhio	15	15	28
Barnes, Parmanas(Z-M)	1836	Jan. 09	HolmesCoOhio	08	09	03
Barnes, Philemon(Z)	1834	Jan. 09	Perry Co.,Oh	15	14	14
Barnes, Philemon(Z)	1836	May 27	Perry Co.,Oh	15	14	14
Barnes, Reuben(Z-M)	1833	April 24	GuernseyCoOh	02	03	14
Barnes, Richard(Z-M)	1836	May 21	HarrisonCoOh	09	08	17
Barnes, Richard(Z-M)	1837	March 08	HolmesCoOhio	09	08	08
Barnes, Robert(Z)	1817	Aug. 25	FranklinCoPa	06	06	02
Barnes, Robt.(Z)	1836	Aug. 23	BelmontCo,Oh	08	07	23
Barnes, Sam'l.(Z-M)	1835	Dec. 25	HolmesCoOhio	09	08	12
Barnes, Sarah(Z)	1837	April 14	ColumbanCoOh	15	14	35
Barnes, Thomas(Z)	1837	April 14	ColumbanCoOh	15	14	35
Barnes, Thos. Jnr.(Z)	1837	April 14	ColumbanCoOh	15	14	32
Barnes, Thos. Jnr.(Z)	1837	April 14	ColumbanCoOh	15	14	32
Barnes, Thos. Jnr.(Z)	1837	April 14	ColumbanCoOh	15	14	33
Barnes, Wm.(Y)	1824	Aug. 26	BelmontCo,Oh	06	08	27
Barnes, Wm.(Z)	1816	Nov. 30	Barnes'lOhio	15	15	20
Barnet, Joseph(Z)	1838	Feb. 06	GuernseyCoOh	08	06	25
Barnet, Mark(Z)	1807	Jan. 26	Jeff.Co.,Oh.	02	01	02
Barnet, William(Y)	1826	Oct. 16	ColumbanCoOh	02	11	36
Barnet, William(Y)	1830	Jan. 15	PittsburghPa	04	06	25
Barney, Sennet(Z)	1830	July 26	Morgan Co,Oh	13	10	36
Barnhart, Joseph(Y)	1832	Oct. 03	Stark Co.,Oh	07	16	27
Barnhart, Peter(Y)	1821	Nov. 19	ColumbanCoOh	05	16	21
Barnhill, George(Y)	1832	Nov. 22	ColumbanCoOh	04	13	07
Barnhill, George(Y)	1836	March 24	CarrollCo,Oh	04	13	07
Barnhill, Robert Junr.(Y)	1836	April 05	CarrollCo,Oh	04	13	01
Barnhill, Robert(Y)	1826	Dec. 07	HarrisonCoOh	05	12	30
Barnhill, Robert(Y)	1834	Sept. 09	CarrollCo,Oh	04	13	08
Barnhill, William(Y)	1825	Aug. 26	HarrisonCoOh	06	12	29
Barnhouse, Benjamin(Z)	1832	Oct. 29	Morgan Co,Oh	09	07	29
Barnhouse, Benjamin(Z)	1832	Oct. 29	Morgan Co,Oh	09	07	32
Barnhouse, Elizabeth J.(Z)	1834	Feb. 18	Morgan Co,Oh	09	07	29
Barnhouse, George(Z)	1835	Dec. 10	Jeff.Co.,Oh.	09	07	32
Barnhouse, John(Y)	1828	Nov. 17	HarrisonCoOh	06	14	02
Barnhouse, Peter(Z)	1835	Nov. 16	HarrisonCoOh	09	07	29
Barnhouse, Peter(Z)	1835	Nov. 16	HarrisonCoOh	09	07	29
Barnhouse, Wm.(Y)	1828	Jan. 09	HarrisonCoOh	05	13	33
Barnhouse, Wm.(Y)	1829	Sept. 07	HarrisonCoOh	05	13	33
Barns, Andrew(Y)	1821	Nov. 20	ColumbanCoOh	05	16	22
Barns, Chas. S.(Z-M)	1831	Dec. 01	Jeff.Co.,Oh.	01	08	02
Barns, Ford(Z)	1812	March 17	GreeneCoPenn	10	09	17
Barns, Ford(Z)	1815	June 19	GuernseyCoOh	10	09	18
Baroff, Henry(Z)	1816	June 05	StClrsvlOhio	05	01	04
Baron, John(Z)	1814	Oct. 20	TuscarwsCoOh	05	09	05
Barr, Daniel(Z-M)	1833	Jan. 30	BelmontCo,Oh	03	06	13
Barr, Eleazer(Z-M)	1836	Oct. 26	KnoxCo.,Ohio	10	06	13
Barr, Eli(Z)	1831	March 29	Morgan Co,Oh	11	10	29
Barr, Eli(Z)	1831	April 18	MuskingmCoOh	12	12	33
Barr, Mathew(Y)	1835	Sept. 05	Jeff.Co.,Oh.	03	11	23
Barr, Matthew(Y)	1824	March 23	WashCo.,Penn	05	07	18
Barr, Matthew(Y)	1825	Nov. 07	WashCo.,Penn	03	11	21
Barr, Matthew(Y)	1831	March 16	Jeff.Co.,Oh.	03	11	21
Barr, Nathan(Z)	1830	Feb. 22	MuskingmCoOh	11	10	28
Barrat, Wyllis(Y)	1832	June 16	ColumbanCoOh	03	12	28
Barrell, William(Z)	1828	May 28	Morgan Co,Oh	12	10	04
Barret, Harman(Z)	1810	Aug. 17	?	06	01	13
Barrett, Daniel(Z)	1836	March 22	GuernseyCoOh	08	07	10
Barrett, Hugh(Z)	1815	Dec. 02	SteubenvleOh	08	05	04
Barrett, Hugh(Z)	1815	Dec. 02	SteubenvleOh	08	05	15
Barrett, Hugh(Z-M)	1837	Jan. 31	CoshoctnCoOh	07	05	02
Barrett, Hugh(Z-M)	1837	Jan. 31	CoshoctnCoOh	07	05	02

PURCHASER	YEAR	DATE	RESIDENCE	R	T	S
Barrett, John(Z-M)	1820	Aug. 29	MuskingmCoOh	06	03	19
Barrett, Joseph(Z)	1816	May 07	CoshoctnCoOh	08	05	04
Barrett, Peter(Z)	1815	May 27	MuskingmCoOh	15	17	15
Barrett, Peter(Z)	1815	May 29	MuskingmCoOh	15	17	15
Barrett, William(Z-M)	1825	March 21	CoshoctnCoOh	07	07	18
Barrick, Ann Mary(Z-M)	1835	May 02	CarrolCo.,Oh	03	06	04
Barrick, Eve(Z-M)	1835	June 02	CarrolCo.,Oh	03	07	24
Barrick, Eve(Z-M)	1837	April 22	CarrollCo,Oh	03	06	01
Barrick, Frederick(Z-M)	1836	Feb. 29	CoshoctnCoOh	05	07	17
Barrick, George(Y)	1822	April 10	TuscarwsCoOh	07	15	15
Barrick, Jacob(Z-M)	1835	May 02	TuscarwsCoOh	03	06	05
Barrick, Jacob(Z-M)	1837	Feb. 15	TuscarwsCoOh	03	07	22
Barrick, Jacob(Z-M)	1837	March 03	TuscarwsCoOh	03	06	01
Barrick, Jacob(Z-M)	1837	April 22	TuscarwsCoOh	03	07	14
Barrick, Lewis(Z-M)	1836	Feb. 29	CoshoctnCoOh	05	07	17
Barrick, Lewis(Z-M)	1837	May 23	CoshoctnCoOh	05	07	17
Barrick, Philip(Z-M)	1828	Feb. 04	LickingCo,Oh	10	03	17
Barrick, Wm.(Y)	1826	April 24	ColumbanCoOh	05	17	15
Barrit, John(Z)	1815	Sept. 13	SteubenvleOh	08	05	05
Barron, Thomas(Z)	1834	July 28	Morgan Co,Oh	13	09	30
Barrow, Jane(Z)	1835	March 06	Morgan Co,Oh	14	13	36
Barrows, Elisha(Z)	1815	Feb. 08	CoshoctnCoOh	08	04	19
Barry, Benj.(Z)	1836	Aug. 02	Morgan Co,Oh	09	07	23
Barry, Benjamin(Z)	1822	April 11	Morgan Co,Oh	09	07	23
Barry, Benjamin(Z)	1835	Oct. 20	Morgan Co,Oh	09	07	23
Barry, Benjamin(Z)	1816	Nov. 25	BaltimreCoMd	01	03	18
Barry, James(Z)	1825	Aug. 11	Morgan Co,Oh	09	07	23
Barry, John(Z)	1836	Oct. 06	BelmontCo,Oh	08	06	17
Barry, John(Z)	1837	March 25	HarrisonCoOh	08	06	08
Barry, Robert Jr.(Z)	1827	March 30	Morgan Co,Oh	09	07	26
Barry, Thomas(Z)	1835	Dec. 07	Morgan Co,Oh	09	07	27
Barry, Thomas(Z)	1835	Dec. 07	Morgan Co,Oh	09	07	22
Barry, Willson(Z)	1836	Oct. 08	Morgan Co,Oh	08	06	29
Barry, Wilson(Z)	1833	Oct. 26	Morgan Co,Oh	09	07	22
Barshing, Christian(Z-M)	1823	Jan. 31	TuscarwsCoOh	03	08	15
Bart, Ebenezer(Z)	1833	Jan. 25	GuernseyCoOh	10	09	23
Barten, William(Z)	1817	March 15	MariettaOhio	09	05	12
Barten, William(Z)	1817	March 15	MariettaOhio	09	05	01
Barthelemew(Y)	1831	April 12	Jeff.Co.,Oh.	04	13	27
Bartholome, Hopherius(Y)	1835	May 16	HarrisonCoOh	07	14	14
Bartholomew, George(Y)	1831	May 16	ColumbanCoOh	04	13	27
Bartholomew, Henry(Y)	1830	Oct. 20	Jeff.Co.,Oh.	05	12	18
Bartholomew, Jere'h.(Z)	1815	Feb. 14	LickingCo,Oh	10	01	11
Bartholomew, John(Z)	1807	Jan. 21	FairfeldCoOh	10	01	21
Bartlet, Jacob(Z)	1807	April 24	MuskingmCoOh	03	10	25
Bartlett, James(Z)	1837	Sept. 13	WashngtnCoOh	08	05	04
Bartlett, John(Z)	1836	March 04	Morgan Co,Oh	08	05	09
Bartley, John(Z)	1834	March 24	Morgan Co,Oh	09	07	27
Barton, Andrew(Z)	1833	April 09	Perry Co.,Oh	14	13	31
Barton, Elizabeth(Z)	1815	April 08	MuskingmCoOh	13	12	12
Barton, Isaac(Z)	1828	June 21	MuskingmCoOh	13	11	02
Barton, John(Z)	1832	April 12	MuskingmCoOh	14	12	06
Barton, John(Z)	1834	Jan. 10	Perry Co.,Oh	15	14	01
Barton, John(Z)	1807	April 15	BelmontCo,Oh	02	01	01
Barton, John(Z)	1810	Nov. 05	GuernseyCoOh	02	02	20
Barton, John(Z)	1811	Nov. 22	GuernseyCoOh	02	02	20
Barton, Richard(Z)	1833	Jan. 08	GuernseyCoOh	10	09	01
Barton, Richard(Z)	1834	Jan. 01	GuernseyCoOh	10	09	01
Barton, Sam'l.(Z-M)	1836	June 09	HolmesCoOhio	06	09	18
Barton, Samuel(Z-M)	1835	Aug. 08	HolmesCoOhio	07	08	01
Barton, Wm. Roberts(Z-M)	1835	May 23	TuscarwsCoOh	02	07	02
Barton, Wm.(Z-M)	1828	Oct. 31	GuernseyCoOh	02	04	04
Bartow, George(Y)	1829	April 04	HarrisonCoOh	06	12	06
Bartow, George(Y)	1831	Oct. 03	HarrisonCoOh	06	12	18
Bartow, John(Y)	1832	Aug. 10	ColumbanCoOh	03	12	34
Bartow, Samuel(Z)	1837	March 24	HarrisonCoOh	08	06	25
Bash, Henry(Z)	1810	Oct. 15	MuskingmCoOh	14	15	22
Bash, John(Z)	1817	Sept. 01	StarkeCo.,Oh	03	10	17
Basil, J.(Z)	1814	March 29	FayetteCo,Pa	10	01	23

17

PURCHASER	YEAR	DATE	RESIDENCE	R	T	S
Bass, Elias(Z)	1831	Dec. 14	Morgan Co,Oh	09	07	26
Bass, Elias(Z)	1836	Feb. 01	MonroeCo.,Oh	08	07	31
Bass, Elias(Z)	1836	Feb. 20	MonroeCo.,Oh	08	07	32
Bastian, George(Y)	1827	Sept. 03	Stark Co.,Oh	09	11	36
Bates, Ama(Z)	1814	Nov. 25	GuernseyCoOh	10	08	08
Bates, Amos(Z)	1817	April 24	GuernseyCoOh	09	07	17
Bates, Barzillai(Y)	1822	May 01	ColumbanCoOh	05	16	31
Bates, D.(Z)	1829	Dec. 21	MonroeCo.,Oh	08	07	05
Bates, D.(Z)	1829	Dec. 21	Morgan Co,Oh	08	07	08
Bates, Daniel Jnr.(Z)	1835	Nov. 13	MonroeCo.,Oh	08	06	03
Bates, Daniel Junr.(Z)	1835	Nov. 10	MonroeCo.,Oh	08	07	34
Bates, Daniel(Z)	1824	Feb. 25	GuernseyCoOh	09	07	11
Bates, Daniel(Z)	1831	Nov. 29	MonroeCo.,Oh	08	08	34
Bates, Daniel(Z)	1833	March 22	MonroeCo.,Oh	08	08	34
Bates, Daniel(Z)	1833	March 22	MonroeCo.,Oh	08	07	08
Bates, Daniel(Z)	1836	March 01	MonroeCo.,Oh	08	07	08
Bates, Daniel(Z)	1836	March 30	MonroeCo.,Oh	08	07	09
Bates, Daniel(Z)	1836	Oct. 24	MonroeCo.,Oh	09	07	29
Bates, Daniel(Z)	1810	Dec. 12	GuernseyCoOh	09	07	12
Bates, Daniel(Z)	1814	March 30	GuernseyCoOh	08	07	08
Bates, Ephraim(Z)	1831	March 07	GuernseyCoOh	08	08	23
Bates, Ephraim(Z)	1832	Sept. 06	GuernseyCoOh	08	08	23
Bates, Ephriam(Z)	1810	Dec. 12	GuernseyCoOh	09	07	12
Bates, Ezekiel(Z)	1833	Jan. 12	Morgan Co,Oh	09	07	13
Bates, Ezekiel(Z)	1815	Feb. 24	GuernseyCoOh	09	07	13
Bates, Isaac(Z)	1836	Jan. 29	Morgan Co,Oh	08	07	20
Bates, Isaac(Z)	1836	March 15	Morgan Co,Oh	08	07	20
Bates, Isaac(Z)	1806	June 25	BelmontCo,Oh	08	08	24
Bates, Isaac(Z)	1814	Aug. 23	GuernseyCoOh	08	07	07
Bates, Isaac(Z)	1816	Nov. 14	GuernseyCoOh	08	07	08
Bates, J.(Z)	1829	Dec. 21	Morgan Co,Oh	08	07	08
Bates, Jacob(Z)	1836	Jan. 07	Morgan Co,Oh	08	06	04
Bates, Jacob(Z)	1836	Jan. 07	Morgan Co,Oh	08	07	33
Bates, John(Z)	1834	Dec. 01	MonroeCo.,Oh	08	07	08
Bates, John(Z)	1835	Dec. 11	MonroeCo.,Oh	08	07	08
Bates, John(Z)	1814	Nov. 25	GuernseyCoOh	10	08	08
Bates, Richard(Z)	1836	Aug. 04	MonroeCo.,Oh	08	06	03
Bates, Sam'l.(Z)	1834	Feb. 14	MonroeCo.,Oh	09	07	14
Bates, Samuel(Z)	1836	April 26	MonroeCo.,Oh	08	07	20
Bates, Timothy(Z)	1831	Sept. 21	GuernseyCoOh	08	08	24
Bates, Timothy(Z)	1835	Aug. 18	GuernseyCoOh	08	08	25
Bates, Timothy(Z)	1836	April 01	GuernseyCoOh	08	08	23
Bates, Timothy(Z)	1806	June 25	BelmontCo,Oh	08	08	24
Bates, Timothy(Z)	1816	Sept. 23	GuernseyCoOh	08	08	23
Bates, Timothy(Z)	1816	Nov. 09	GuernseyCoOh	08	08	14
Bates, Usel(Z)	1837	Jan. 11	MonroeCo.,Oh	08	07	33
Bates, William(Z)	1836	March 01	MonroeCo.,Oh	08	07	33
Bates, William(Z)	1811	Jan. 19	GuernseyCoOh	10	08	05
Battan, John(Z)	1836	June 02	Perry Co.,Oh	15	14	29
Batton, John(Z)	1834	March 07	Perry Co.,Oh	15	14	28
Bauack, Philip(Z)	1812	Dec. 28	LickingCo,Oh	10	03	25
Bauer, Jacob(Z-M)	1835	Jan. 06	TuscarwsCoOh	04	07	14
Bauer, Jacob(Z-M)	1836	July 15	TuscarwsCoOh	04	07	15
Bauer, Jacob(Z-M)	1838	April 03	CoshoctnCoOh	09	07	19
Bauer, John(Z-M)	1838	April 03	CoshoctnCoOh	09	07	20
Baug, Jacob(Z-M)	1828	Dec. 05	BelmontCo,Oh	11	08	06
Baughman, Chris'n.(Z)	1816	Dec. 07	KnoxCo.,Ohio	10	05	03
Baughman, Chris(Z)	1830	Feb. 20	MuskingmCoOh	13	10	34
Baughman, Christ(Z)	1832	Feb. 18	MuskingmCoOh	14	15	24
Baughman, Christian(Z-M)	1836	Jan. 04	LickingCo,Oh	10	04	23
Baughman, Daniel(Z-M)	1828	March 31	MuskingmCoOh	06	02	06
Baughman, Geo.(Z-M)	1829	March 07	CoshoctnCoOh	10	04	10
Baughman, George(Z-M)	1836	Feb. 29	LickingCo,Oh	10	04	11
Baughman, Henry(Z-M)	1836	Aug. 03	MuskingmCoOh	09	03	16
Baughman, Jacob(Z)	1829	Dec. 24	MuskingmCoOh	13	10	18
Baughman, Jacob(Z)	1830	Jan. 30	MuskingmCoOh	13	10	34
Baughman, Jacob(Z)	1811	Feb. 14	KnoxCo.,Ohio	10	07	14
Baughman, Jacob(Z-M)	1829	Dec. 21	KnoxCo.,Ohio	10	05	13
Baughman, Jacob(Z-M)	1832	June 25	KnoxCo.,Ohio	10	05	18

PURCHASER	YEAR	DATE	RESIDENCE	R	T	S
Baughman, Jno.(Z-M)	1831	Dec. 29	LickingCo,Oh	10	04	13
Baughman, John(Z-M)	1833	March 26	LickingCo,Oh	10	04	13
Baughman, John(Z-M)	1833	March 26	LickingCo,Oh	10	04	18
Baum, George Senr.(Y)	1823	Jan. 14	ColumbanCoOh	05	18	13
Baum, George Senr.(Y)	1823	Jan. 14	ColumbanCoOh	05	18	12
Baum, George(Y)	1821	April 14	ColumbanCoOh	04	17	09
Baum, George(Y)	1821	April 14	ColumbanCoOh	04	17	10
Baum, George(Y)	1827	June 26	ColumbanCoOh	05	18	01
Baum, George(Y)	1827	Sept. 12	ColumbanCoOh	05	18	01
Baum, Thomas(Y)	1822	July 31	ColumbanCoOh	04	17	04
Baumberger, Jacob(Z-M)	1832	Nov. 08	TuscarwsCoOh	02	07	14
Baur, Charles(Z-M)	1838	July 05	CoshoctnCoOh	09	07	22
Baur, Jacob(Z-M)	1838	June 28	CoshoctnCoOh	09	07	22
Baur, John(Z-M)	1838	June 28	CoshoctnCoOh	09	07	22
Bavington, Jno.(Y)	1827	May 26	ColumbanCoOh	05	18	30
Bawman, Adam(Z)	1815	Oct. 30	MuskingmCoOh	06	02	21
Baxter, Benjamin(Y)	1829	June 09	Stark Co.,Oh	07	16	04
Baxter, Benjamin(Y)	1831	April 30	Stark Co.,Oh	06	15	34
Baxter, Cornelius(Y)	1821	Oct. 15	Stark Co.,Oh	06	15	21
Baxter, George(Z)	1815	Nov. 04	PutnamCoOhio	06	02	21
Baxter, James(Y)	1826	April 26	Stark Co.,Oh	06	15	32
Baxter, James(Y)	1829	April 24	Stark Co.,Oh	06	15	27
Baxter, James(Y)	1830	Nov. 06	Stark Co.,Oh	07	16	06
Baxter, Robert(Y)	1825	Nov. 29	GuernseyCoOh	07	11	15
Baxter, Samuel(Y)	1829	Sept. 26	ColumbanCoOh	05	15	06
Baxter, William(Z-M)	1836	Jan. 06	KnoxCo.,Ohio	10	05	12
Bay, Andrew(Y)	1824	Aug. 10	GuernseyCoOh	07	09	35
Bay, Andrew(Y)	1827	Sept. 24	GuernseyCoOh	07	09	34
Bay, Archibald(Z)	1816	Dec. 11	GuernseyCoOh	10	09	30
Bay, Benjamin(Z)	1814	May 23	GuernseyCoOh	10	09	23
Bay, Benjamin(Z)	1814	July 08	GuernseyCoOh	10	09	27
Bay, Benjamin(Z)	1816	Nov. 13	GuernseyCoOh	10	09	27
Bay, John(Z)	1812	Feb. 11	WashCo.,Penn	10	09	28
Bay, John(Z)	1816	Nov. 26	GuernseyCoOh	10	09	28
Bay, Robert(Z)	1814	March 23	TuscarwsCoOh	10	09	30
Bay, Robert(Z)	1817	April 25	GuernseyCoOh	10	09	30
Bay, Samuel(Z)	1812	June 19	GuernseyCoOh	10	09	31
Bay, Thomas Junr.(Z)	1816	Aug. 09	GuernseyCoOh	10	09	33
Bay, Thomas Senr.(Z)	1813	Aug. 17	GuernseyCoOh	10	09	33
Bay, Thomas Senr.(Z)	1816	April 27	GuernseyCoOh	10	09	29
Bay, Thomas Senr.(Z)	1816	April 27	GuernseyCoOh	10	09	30
Bay, Thomas(Z)	1812	Feb. 11	WashCo.,Penn	10	09	33
Bay, Thomas(Z)	1814	April 30	GuernseyCoOh	10	09	29
Bay, Thomas(Z)	1817	April 25	GuernseyCoOh	10	09	29
Bay, William C.(Z)	1832	Sept. 28	GuernseyCoOh	10	09	21
Bay, William(Z)	1810	April 05	WashCo.,Penn	10	09	28
Bay, Wm. C.(Z)	1831	Feb. 17	GuernseyCoOh	10	09	21
Bay, Wm.(Y)	1825	April 16	GuernseyCoOh	07	09	35
Bayer, Adam(Z)	1815	Oct. 27	MontgmryCoMd	01	05	21
Bayer, Adam(Z)	1815	Oct. 27	MontgmryCoMd	01	04	10
Bayer, Adam(Z)	1815	Oct. 27	MontgmryCoMd	01	04	10
Bayer, Adam(Z)	1815	Oct. 27	MontgmryCoMd	01	04	01
Bazey, Wm. Jr.(Z-M)	1831	Nov. 30	TuscarwsCoOh	03	10	23
Beaber, Abraham(Z-M)	1836	July 07	TuscarwsCoOh	03	08	04
Beaber, Jacob(Z-M)	1835	May 07	TuscarwsCoOh	02	08	24
Beackley, John(Y)	1827	March 14	WashCo.,Penn	06	16	33
Beadenhead, Coonrad(Z-M)	1838	Dec. 07	ZanesvilleOh	04	04	10
Beader, Ezekiel(Z)	1810	June 08	GuernseyCoOh	02	02	22
Beadle, Frederick(Z)	1815	Dec. 15	TuscarwsCoOh	04	09	21
Beal, Asa(Z)	1826	Feb. 13	Jeff.Co.,Oh.	11	10	21
Beal, Asa(Z)	1826	Aug. 31	Jeff.Co.,Oh.	11	10	21
Beal, Elias(Z-M)	1830	April 10	GuernseyCoOh	02	04	06
Beal, George Jnr.(Z-M)	1837	April 19	GuernseyCoOh	03	04	11
Beal, George Jnr.(Z-M)	1837	April 19	GuernseyCoOh	03	04	11
Beal, George(Z)	1816	Jan. 24	GuernseyCoOh	02	04	20
Beal, George(Z-M)	1829	April 28	GuernseyCoOh	02	04	06
Beal, George(Z-M)	1832	May 22	GuernseyCoOh	02	04	18
Beal, George(Z-M)	1832	May 24	GuernseyCoOh	03	04	11
Beal, George(Z-M)	1831	March 25	GuernseyCoOh	03	04	08

19

PURCHASER	YEAR	DATE	RESIDENCE	R	T	S
Beal, Isaac(Z-M)	1825	Jan. 14	GuernseyCoOh	02	05	22
Beal, Isaac(Z-M)	1825	Jan. 14	GuernseyCoOh	02	04	02
Beal, Isaac(Z-M)	1831	Aug. 09	GuernseyCoOh	03	04	08
Beal, Jeremiah(Z-M)	1832	Aug. 20	GuernseyCoOh	03	04	08
Beal, John(Z-M)	1828	June 06	GuernseyCoOh	02	04	13
Beal, John(Z-M)	1831	April 14	HolmesCoOhio	03	04	10
Beal, John(Z-M)	1831	April 14	HolmesCoOhio	02	04	06
Beal, Nicholas(Z-M)	1831	June 02	GuernseyCoOh	02	04	03
Beal, Wm.(Z-M)	1833	June 13	GuernseyCoOh	02	04	15
Beale, Jacob(Z-M)	1833	March 16	KnoxCo.,Ohio	10	06	13
Beale, Jacob(Z-M)	1836	May 17	KnoxCo.,Ohio	10	06	12
Bealer, Fred'k.(Y)	1826	Aug. 07	ColumbanCoOh	05	17	15
Beall, Alexander(Y)	1828	Feb. 27	HarrisonCoOh	06	11	21
Beall, Colmore(Y)	1829	March 17	WashCo.,Penn	06	11	21
Beall, Dory(Y)	1820	Dec. 18	HarrisonCoOh	06	12	04
Beall, Elijah(Y)	1821	June 06	GuernseyCoOh	07	09	25
Beall, George(Z)	1814	Nov. 24	BeaverCo.,Pa	02	04	11
Beall, Jacob(Z-M)	1831	March 10	KnoxCo.,Ohio	10	06	19
Beall, James P.(Y)	1827	Oct. 02	HarrisonCoOh	06	11	22
Beall, John(Y)	1827	Oct. 25	HarrisonCoOh	06	11	21
Beall, John(Z)	1826	Nov. 13	HarrisonCoOh	11	10	27
Beaman, George(Z)	1833	July 17	Morgan Co,Oh	11	12	25
Bean, Christian(Z-M)	1830	Jan. 27	HolmesCoOhio	04	08	05
Bean, David(Z)	1824	Nov. 26	MuskingmCoOh	12	12	15
Bean, David(Z)	1826	March 31	MuskingmCoOh	12	12	09
Bean, Jacob(Y)	1827	Nov. 22	HarrisonCoOh	05	12	29
Bean, Jacob(Z)	1830	Jan. 30	MuskingmCoOh	13	10	33
Bean, Jas.(Z)	1830	Dec. 09	MuskingmCoOh	13	11	29
Bean, Silas(Z)	1823	Oct. 03	Morgan Co,Oh	11	12	25
Bean, Vincent(Z)	1829	March 03	MuskingmCoOh	13	10	15
Beanes, James(Z)	1826	April 19	MuskingmCoOh	13	11	29
Beanes, James(Z)	1826	July 26	MuskingmCoOh	13	11	29
Beans, Harman(Z-M)	1833	Sept. 28	HarrisonCoOh	01	06	24
Beans, James(Z)	1832	Dec. 06	MuskingmCoOh	13	11	29
Beans, James(Z)	1832	Dec. 06	MuskingmCoOh	13	11	30
Bear, Adam(Z)	1811	Sept. 23	MuskingmCoOh	14	15	23
Bear, Christian(Z-M)	1829	May 27	HolmesCoOhio	06	08	19
Bear, Jacob(Y)	1825	Nov. 28	HarrisonCoOh	05	12	29
Beard, Alexander(Y)	1831	March 21	BelmontCo,Oh	07	12	26
Beard, Alexander(Z-M)	1833	Jan. 26	BelmontCo,Oh	03	06	02
Beard, Edward(Z-M)	1832	Nov. 19	BelmontCo,Oh	03	06	03
Beard, Jesse(Z)	1836	Feb. 01	MuskingmCoOh	13	11	30
Beard, John(Y)	1821	Oct. 16	ColumbanCoOh	04	16	21
Beard, John(Z)	1813	Aug. 16	MuskingmCoOh	13	11	17
Beard, Joseph(Z)	1805	Feb. 09	MuskingmCoOh	15	17	27
Beard, William(Z-M)	1836	Nov. 15	TuscarwsCoOh	03	06	07
Beard, Wm. H.(Z)	1813	March 10	MuskingmCoOh	15	17	21
Bearinger, Frederick(Z)	1835	Sept. 23	MuskingmCoOh	13	10	11
Bearinger, Gotlob(Z)	1835	Aug. 10	MuskingmCoOh	13	10	03
Beary, Joseph(Y)	1828	Jan. 07	Stark Co.,Oh	06	17	27
Beary, Joseph(Y)	1828	Jan. 07	Stark Co.,Oh	06	17	31
Beatten, James(Z)	1812	May 14	MifflinCo,Pa	01	03	15
Beattey, Martin(Z)	1835	Aug. 21	Belmontco,Oh	08	08	33
Beattey, Martin(Z)	1835	Aug. 21	BelmontCo,Oh	08	08	33
Beattey, Martin(Z)	1835	Aug. 21	BelmontCo,Oh	08	08	26
Beattey, Martin(Z)	1836	March 28	BelmontCo,Oh	08	08	33
Beattey, Martin(Z)	1836	March 28	BelmontCo,Oh	08	07	10
Beatty, Abraham(Z)	1815	March 20	KnoxCo.,Ohio	11	04	04
Beatty, Cyrus P.(Z)	1811	Aug. 20	GuernseyCoOh	03	02	03
Beatty, Cyrus P.(Z)	1814	May 07	Cambridge,Oh	03	02	04
Beatty, Cyrus P.(Z)	1814	May 07	Cambridge,Oh	03	02	05
Beatty, Cyrus P.(Z)	1815	June 02	Cambridge,Oh	04	02	10
Beatty, Isaac(Z-M)	1836	Sept. 27	CoshoctnCoOh	08	08	23
Beatty, Jane(Z)	1813	May 07	KnoxCo.,Ohio	10	06	23
Beatty, Jeremiah(Z)	1813	May 07	KnoxCo.,Ohio	10	06	23
Beatty, John(Z)	1806	Jan. 07	MuskingmCoOh	03	01	05
Beatty, John(Z)	1806	June 16	MuskingmCoOh	03	02	03
Beatty, John(Z)	1806	July 07	MuskingmCoOh	03	02	03
Beatty, John(Z)	1815	Oct. 26	FairfeldCoOh	15	16	15

PURCHASER	YEAR	DATE	RESIDENCE	R	T	S
Beatty, Sampon(Y)	1832	Sept. 22	HarrisonCoOh	07	12	30
Beatty, Sarah(Z)	1813	May 07	KnoxCo.,Ohio	10	06	23
Beatty, Stephen(Z)	1815	Oct. 09	KnoxCo.,Ohio	10	08	25
Beatty, William D.(Z)	1813	Sept. 13	FairfeldCoOh	10	05	03
Beatty, Wm. D.(Z)	1813	May 07	KnoxCo.,Ohio	10	06	23
Beatty, Wm.(Y)	1823	Oct. 14	HarrisonCoOh	05	12	21
Beaty, James(Y)	1824	Nov. 24	Stark Co.,Oh	10	01	25
Beaty, James(Y)	1824	Nov. 24	Stark Co.,Oh	10	01	26
Beaty, Joseph(Z-M)	1836	Oct. 28	ColumbanCoOh	10	08	01
Beaty, Joseph(Z-M)	1836	Oct. 28	ColumbanCoOh	09	08	05
Beaty, Robert(Z-M)	1832	Oct. 29	CoshoctnCoOh	09	07	23
Beaty, Robert(Z-M)	1837	Jan. 11	CoshoctnCoOh	09	07	23
Beaty, William(Y)	1832	Sept. 29	ColumbanCoOh	01	07	36
Bebout, Ebenezer(Z-M)	1834	Jan. 27	LickingCo,Oh	10	04	13
Bebout, Elisha(Z-M)	1833	May 03	LickingCo,Oh	11	04	01
Bebout, Enoch(Z-M)	1831	Nov. 30	WashCo.,Penn	11	06	21
Bebout, Enoch(Z-M)	1831	Nov. 30	WashCo.,Penn	10	06	25
Bechdel, Martin(Z-M)	1831	Nov. 14	TuscarwsCoOh	04	07	10
Bechtel, John(Z-M)	1837	April 13	Wayne Co.,Oh	08	08	10
Bechtel, John(Z-M)	1837	April 13	Wayne Co.,Oh	08	08	11
Beck, Michael(Z-M)	1821	Nov. 02	WestmrldCoPa	06	08	10
Beck, Michael(Z-M)	1824	Nov. 06	CoshoctnCoOh	06	08	11
Beckel, Thomas Junr.(Z)	1816	May 04	CoshoctnCoOh	06	07	01
Becker, Henry(Z-M)	1835	Nov. 26	Stark Co.,Oh	02	10	23
Becker, Israel H.(Z-M)	1831	July 18	CoshoctnCoOh	06	04	08
Becker, Israel H.(Z-M)	1831	July 18	CoshoctnCoOh	06	04	03
Becket, Martin(Y)	1827	Sept. 03	TrumbullCoOh	05	18	06
Beckford, James(Z-M)	1836	Dec. 27	LickingCo,Oh	10	03	06
Beckford, John(Z-M)	1836	March 14	LickingCo,Oh	10	03	06
Beckford, John(Z-M)	1836	Dec. 27	LickingCo,Oh	10	03	06
Beckham, Robt.(Z-M)	1832	Feb. 11	LickingCo,Oh	10	03	08
Beckham, William(Z-M)	1833	Jan. 25	LickingCo,Oh	10	03	02
Beckle, David Jr.(Z-M)	1836	Sept. 14	HolmesCoOhio	05	07	14
Beckle, David(Z-M)	1836	July 11	HolmesCoOhio	05	07	14
Beckley, George(Y)	1829	March 13	HarrisonCoOh	07	16	03
Beckwith, David(Z)	1805	April 17	MuskingmCoOh	13	12	15
Beckwith, David(Z)	1805	Nov. 16	MuskingmCoOh	12	13	20
Beckwith, George(Z)	1812	April 21	FairfeldCoOh	01	02	06
Beckwith, Tobias(Z)	1816	May 07	MuskingmCoOh	13	08	02
Becom, John(Y)	1832	June 08	Jeff.Co.,Oh.	03	11	11
Becom, John(Y)	1836	Sept. 01	Jeff.Co.,Oh.	03	11	11
Becom, Robert(Y)	1825	Jan. 24	WashCo.,Penn	03	11	17
Bedall, Moses(Y)	1822	May 29	WashCo.,Penn	05	13	22
Bedall, Moses(Y)	1822	Nov. 21	WashCo.,Penn	05	13	22
Bedford, Benjamin(Z)	1827	Aug. 28	BelmontCo,Oh	12	11	01
Beebe, Waltor Butler(Y)	1832	Feb. 11	HarrisonCoOh	06	12	04
Beebout, Jonah(Z-M)	1837	April 19	TuscarwsCoOh	03	08	25
Beebout, Jonah(Z-M)	1837	April 19	TuscarwsCoOh	03	08	17
Beebout, Jonah(Z-M)	1837	April 19	TuscarwsCoOh	03	08	17
Beecher, Henry(Z-M)	1833	Aug. 23	TuscarwsCoOh	02	10	23
Beechey, Moses(Z-M)	1828	June 25	HolmesCoOhio	05	08	01
Beektel, George(Z)	1815	July 13	ShanandhCoVa	11	01	19
Beem, John(Z)	1814	Dec. 21	MuskingmCoOh	14	15	29
Beeman, Thomas(Z-M)	1836	Oct. 10	HolmesCoOhio	10	09	12
Beemer, H.(Z)	1804	Nov. 29	MuskingmCoOh	02	02	11
Been, John(Z)	1828	Feb. 22	MuskingmCoOh	13	10	14
Beens, Harvey(Y)	1829	Nov. 28	WashCo.,Penn	07	11	34
Beer, James(Y)	1828	May 07	Stark Co.,Oh	06	16	29
Beer, James(Y)	1831	May 21	Stark Co.,Oh	06	16	20
Beeringer, Baltas(Y)	1825	Sept. 19	Stark Co.,Oh	07	19	27
Beeringer, Baltus(Y)	1828	June 30	Stark Co.,Oh	07	20	28
Beeringer, Baltus(Y)	1828	June 30	Stark Co.,Oh	07	20	27
Beers, Vincent(Z)	1830	July 07	Morgan Co,Oh	13	10	15
Beeson, Hermon(Z-M)	1836	Dec. 16	TuscarwsCoOh	03	07	16
Beggs, Thomas(Z)	1813	July 08	MuskingmCoOh	15	16	04
Begley, Michael(Z-M)	1829	Feb. 19	WayneCo.,Oh.	04	09	05
Belch, John(Y)	1828	Dec. 20	Jeff.Co.,Oh.	07	15	26
Belch, John(Y)	1830	Dec. 11	TuscarwsCoOh	07	15	32
Belford, Daniel(Z)	1832	Sept. 03	Morgan Co,Oh	09	07	31

PURCHASER	YEAR	DATE	RESIDENCE	R	T	S
Belford, Jefferson(Z-M)	1837	June 19	CoshoctnCoOh	08	06	12
Belknap, Thomas(Z-M)	1825	Dec. 01	HarrisonCoOh	01	08	10
Bell, Alexander(Z-M)	1836	Nov. 08	HolmesCoOhio	09	09	04
Bell, Anarew(Z-M)	1833	May 06	GuernseyCoOh	03	01	07
Bell, Andrew(Z)	1825	Nov. 21	MuskingmCoOh	11	10	09
Bell, Andrew(Z)	1809	Sept. 27	WashngtnCoOh	05	01	24
Bell, Andrew(Z)	1812	Feb. 17	MuskingmCoOh	05	01	24
Bell, Andrew(Z)	1814	Dec. 15	MuskingmCoOh	05	01	25
Bell, Andrew(Z)	1815	Aug. 29	MuskingmCoOh	06	01	21
Bell, Andrew(Z-M)	1828	Aug. 11	MuskingmCoOh	05	03	21
Bell, Andrew(Z-M)	1829	Sept. 22	MuskingmCoOh	05	03	21
Bell, Benjamin(Z)	1814	April 23	KnoxCo.,Ohio	11	05	25
Bell, Benjamin(Z)	1815	March 11	KnoxCo.,Ohio	11	05	18
Bell, Benjamin(Z)	1815	March 22	KnoxCo.,Ohio	11	04	06
Bell, Daniel(Z-M)	1824	Oct. 11	MadisonCoInd	07	09	21
Bell, Francis(Z-M)	1829	Jan. 30	Jeff.Co.,Oh.	04	02	02
Bell, George(Z)	1827	Nov. 06	Morgan Co,Oh	09	06	28
Bell, George(Z)	1835	Feb. 19	Morgan Co,Oh	09	06	07
Bell, George(Z)	1817	June 18	WashCo.,Penn	02	03	04
Bell, George(Z-M)	1822	March 19	MuskingmCoOh	04	02	13
Bell, Graft(Z)	1837	April 20	HarrisonCoOh	08	05	14
Bell, Hamilton(Z-M)	1838	Oct. 27	GuernseyCoOh	03	03	17
Bell, Henry(Z)	1833	Nov. 12	Perry Co.,Oh	15	15	14
Bell, Isaac(Z)	1814	Oct. 29	GreeneCo.,Pa	11	05	16
Bell, James(Z)	1809	Oct. 24	Ohio Co.,Vir	03	03	18
Bell, James(Z)	1814	Oct. 29	GreeneCo.,Pa	11	05	15
Bell, James(Z)	1815	Feb. 24	GuernseyCoOh	03	03	18
Bell, James(Z-M)	1836	Dec. 07	GuernseyCoOh	03	03	13
Bell, John Jr.(Z-M)	1832	June 02	MuskingmCoOh	06	03	11
Bell, John Jr.(Z-M)	1830	Oct. 02	ZanesvilleOh	06	03	11
Bell, John(Z)	1832	Sept. 18	Morgan Co,Oh	11	10	20
Bell, John(Z)	1817	Oct. 16	MuskingmCoOh	13	10	26
Bell, John(Z-M)	1833	May 06	GuernseyCoOh	03	01	07
Bell, John(Z-M)	1833	Dec. 05	LickingCo,Oh	11	04	22
Bell, John(Z-M)	1837	Jan. 10	GuernseyCoOh	03	01	07
Bell, Joseph(Y)	1835	Aug. 25	BeaverCo.,Pa	03	12	19
Bell, Joseph(Y)	1836	March 08	BeaverCo.,Pa	03	12	19
Bell, Joseph(Z)	1831	Jan. 28	Morgan Co,Oh	10	08	17
Bell, Joseph(Z)	1806	Nov. 08	Ohio Co.,Vir	03	03	12
Bell, Joseph(Z)	1814	Jan. 19	GuernseyCoOh	03	03	09
Bell, Joseph(Z-M)	1823	April 14	GuernseyCoOh	03	04	19
Bell, Joseph(Z-M)	1832	June 28	GuernseyCoOh	03	03	12
Bell, Joseph(Z-M)	1836	Dec. 07	GuernseyCoOh	02	01	15
Bell, Joseph(Z-M)	1837	Feb. 24	GuernseyCoOh	03	04	20
Bell, Joseph(Z-M)	1837	Feb. 27	GuernseyCoOh	03	03	10
Bell, Nancy(Y)	1830	July 29	ColumbanCoOh	05	15	22
Bell, Robert(Z)	1832	Aug. 01	Morgan Co,Oh	11	10	20
Bell, Robert(Z-M)	1831	Dec. 06	GuernseyCoOh	01	04	21
Bell, Robert(Z-M)	1830	Nov. 24	GuernseyCoOh	01	04	22
Bell, Robert(Z-M)	1836	Jan. 01	GuernseyCoOh	03	03	14
Bell, Robert(Z-M)	1836	Oct. 22	GuernseyCoOh	03	03	14
Bell, Robert(Z-M)	1836	Dec. 13	GuernseyCoOh	03	03	14
Bell, Robt.(Z)	1830	Jan. 11	Morgan Co,Oh	11	10	20
Bell, Robt.(Z)	1806	Feb. 24	BelmontCo,Oh	10	09	17
Bell, Walter(Z)	1824	May 10	Perry Co.,Oh	14	14	21
Bell, William Senr.(Z)	1832	May 23	Morgan Co,Oh	09	06	20
Bell, William(Z)	1810	Dec. 01	MuskingmCoOh	13	11	02
Bell, William(Z)	1815	Nov. 20	BelmontCo,Oh	09	06	04
Bell, William(Z-M)	1835	Sept. 15	HolmesCoOhio	09	09	02
Bellangee, Aaron(Y)	1821	Dec. 10	BurlngtnCoNJ	04	17	15
Bellangee, Aaron(Y)	1821	Dec. 10	BurlngtnCoNJ	04	17	15
Bellangee, Aaron(Y)	1821	Dec. 10	BurlngtnCoNJ	04	17	15
Bellangee, Thomas(Y)	1821	Dec. 10	BurlngtnCoNJ	04	17	15
Bellangee, Thos.(Y)	1821	Dec. 10	BurlngtnCoNJ	04	17	15
Bellew, Joseph(Z)	1833	May 21	GuernseyCoOh	10	09	10
Bellman, Andrew(Z)	1810	June 09	CumberldCo ?	09	05	20
Bellman, David(Z)	1811	March 19	WashCo.,Penn	09	05	22
Bellman, George(Z-M)	1832	May 23	TuscarwsCoOh	04	07	03
Bellman, Henry(Z)	1815	July 05	BelmontCo,Oh	09	05	13

PURCHASER	YEAR	DATE	RESIDENCE	R	T	S
Bellman, Henry(Z)	1815	July 05	BelmontCo,Oh	09	05	21
Belout, Wm.(Z-M)	1831	March 05	KnoxCo.,Ohio	11	04	01
Belout, Wm.(Z-M)	1831	March 05	KnoxCo.,Ohio	11	06	19
Belvel, Henry(Z)	1833	April 05	GuernseyCoOh	08	08	32
Bemis, Jonas(Z)	1824	Nov. 10	Morgan Co,Oh	10	08	21
Bemis, Jonas(Z)	1831	Dec. 09	Morgan Co,Oh	10	08	21
Bemis, Wm.(Z)	1816	Oct. 15	Wooster,Mass	10	06	17
Bender, Frederick(Z-M)	1833	March 18	TuscarwsCoOh	03	07	25
Bender, Frederick(Z-M)	1833	March 18	TuscarwsCoOh	03	07	25
Bender, Henry(Z-M)	1839	Oct. 07	CoshoctnCoOh	08	08	14
Benel, James(Z-M)	1835	Oct. 20	CoshoctnCoOh	05	07	01
Benel, William(Z)	1816	Feb. 17	TuscarwsCoOh	03	08	16
Benel, William(Z-M)	1831	July 04	TuscarwsCoOh	03	08	16
Benell, William(Z-M)	1832	May 29	TuscarwsCoOh	03	08	17
Benell, William(Z-M)	1834	Oct. 29	TuscarwsCoOh	03	08	16
Beney, Charles(Z-M)	1836	Jan. 25	LickingCo,Oh	11	04	18
Benfer, Henry(Z-M)	1833	March 11	TuscarwsCoOh	03	09	02
Benfer, Henry(Z-M)	1836	June 16	TuscarwsCoOh	03	09	03
Benfer, John Jr.(Z-M)	1831	May 16	TuscarwsCoOh	03	07	23
Benfer, John(Z)	1831	April 07	TuscarwsCoOh	03	07	23
Benfer, John(Z-M)	1832	Aug. 06	TuscarwsCoOh	03	07	18
Benfer, John(Z-M)	1833	March 11	TuscarwsCoOh	03	07	18
Benfer, John(Z-M)	1833	March 11	TuscarwsCoOh	03	07	23
Benifield, William(Z)	1805	Dec. 30	MuskingmCoOh	09	01	12
Beninger, John(Z-M)	1833	July 26	TuscarwsCoOh	03	08	14
Benjamin, James(Z-M)	1838	Oct. 08	CoshoctnCoOh	04	04	23
Benjamin, Nathan(Z)	1836	Sept. 06	Perry Co.,Oh	14	13	35
Bennell, John(Z-M)	1831	March 19	ZanesvilleOh	06	03	11
Benner, Adam(Y)	1825	March 02	ColumbanCoOh	05	18	33
Benner, John(Y)	1821	April 19	ColumbanCoOh	03	13	18
Benner, Michael(Y)	1831	March 23	Stark Co.,Oh	10	02	13
Bennet, Abraham(Z)	1825	Dec. 16	Perry Co.,Oh	15	15	21
Bennet, Abraham(Z)	1813	Sept. 01	LickingCo,Oh	10	01	18
Bennet, Daniel(Z)	1817	March 10	GuernseyCoOh	01	03	18
Bennet, Isaac(Z-M)	1825	June 29	CoshoctnCoOh	06	07	07
Bennet, Michael(Z-M)	1836	March 07	TuscarwsCoOh	01	06	08
Bennet, William(Z)	1816	Sept. 19	GuernseyCoOh	01	01	18
Bennett, J. V.(Z-M)	1830	March 02	TuscarwsCoOh	01	06	19
Bennett, James Cummings(Y)	1831	July 26	TuscarwsCoOh	07	14	07
Bennett, Jared(Z-M)	1827	March 12	AllenhnyCoPa	03	08	07
Bennett, John(Z)	1814	Sept. 27	BedfordCo,Pa	14	14	26
Benning, Nathaniel(Z-M)	1836	Jan. 06	KnoxCo.,Ohio	10	05	18
Benninger, John(Z-M)	1832	July 07	TuscarwsCoOh	04	06	09
Bensley, John(Y)	1833	Feb. 19	ColumbanCoOh	03	13	17
Benson, James(Y)	1831	May 30	ColumbanCoOh	02	10	19
Benton, E. O.(Z)	1831	Jan. 27	Morgan Co,Oh	10	08	12
Bentz, Jacob(Z-M)	1833	May 27	TuscarwsCoOh	02	08	24
Bentz, Jacob(Z-M)	1838	March 31	LickingCo,Oh	10	04	08
Bentz, Nicholas(Z-M)	1835	June 12	TuscarwsCoOh	02	07	01
Benzenhafer, Lorenzo(Z-M)	1833	Aug. 31	MuskingmCoOh	06	03	09
Beort, William S.(Z)	1812	Feb. 07	MuskingmCoOh	15	16	01
Berger, David(Y)	1821	Sept. 15	Stark Co.,Oh	06	17	22
Berger, John(Z)	1814	Oct. 15	TuscarwsCoOh	04	08	25
Berkdoll, Christian(Y)	1835	June 13	CarrollCo,Oh	06	15	35
Berkholder, Peter(Z-M)	1836	Jan. 21	TuscarwsCoOh	05	07	07
Berkshire, Otho(Z-M)	1832	June 02	TuscarwsCoOh	02	05	19
Berlin, Abraham(Y)	1826	March 11	TuscarwsCoOh	06	14	24
Bernard, Henry Jacob(Z)	1811	Sept. 28	New York, NY	15	17	34
Berry, Aaron(Z)	1833	Sept. 24	Perry Co.,Oh	14	13	32
Berry, Aaron(Z)	1833	Nov. 21	Perry Co.,Oh	14	13	32
Berry, James(Z)	1823	May 28	MuskingmCoOh	13	11	28
Berry, James(Z)	1823	Nov. 24	MuskingmCoOh	13	11	28
Berry, James(Z)	1835	Jan. 29	MuskingmCoOh	13	10	03
Berry, James(Z)	1835	Nov. 14	MuskingmCoOh	13	10	03
Berry, James(Z)	1835	Dec. 02	MuskingmCoOh	13	11	30
Berry, James(Z)	1835	Dec. 07	Morgan Co,Oh	09	07	01
Berry, John(Z)	1816	April 09	BelmontCo,Oh	09	05	08
Berry, John(Z)	1816	June 04	WashCo.,Penn	10	09	20
Berry, John(Z)	1816	June 04	WashCo.,Penn	10	09	20

PURCHASER	YEAR	DATE	RESIDENCE	R	T	S
Berry, Joseph(Z-M)	1838	April 07	HolmesCoOhio	08	09	03
Berry, Robert(Z)	1831	Jan. 31	Morgan Co,Oh	09	07	14
Berry, Robert(Z-M)	1833	Feb. 28	KnoxCo.,Ohio	11	08	17
Berry, Thomas(Z)	1807	Nov. 20	MuskingmCoOh	03	13	13
Berry, Thomas(Z)	1814	July 04	GuernseyCoOh	03	03	02
Besst, John(Z-M)	1834	March 05	CoshoctnCoOh	05	06	23
Best, Christian(Z-M)	1833	Sept. 14	CarrollCo,Oh	09	08	12
Best, Henry(Z)	1822	Nov. 04	WashCo.,Ohio	13	10	35
Best, John(Y)	1829	March 17	Stark Co.,Oh	07	16	03
Bethel, James(Z-M)	1835	Sept. 04	BelmontCo,Oh	04	06	20
Bethel, James(Z-M)	1835	Sept. 04	BelmontCo,Oh	04	06	21
Bethel, James(Z-M)	1835	Sept. 04	BelmontCo,Oh	04	06	21
Bethel, James(Z-M)	1835	Sept. 04	BelmontCo,Oh	04	06	21
Bethel, James(Z-M)	1835	Sept. 12	BelmontCo,Oh	04	06	10
Bethel, James(Z-M)	1835	Sept. 12	BelmontCo,Oh	04	06	20
Bethel, James(Z-M)	1835	Sept. 12	BelmontCo,Oh	04	06	21
Bethel, James(Z-M)	1835	Sept. 12	BelmontCo,Oh	04	06	10
Bethel, James(Z-M)	1835	Nov. 06	BelmontCo,Oh	04	06	11
Bethel, Thompson(Y)	1825	Aug. 16	HarrisonCoOh	06	10	35
Bethell, Richard(Z)	1835	Jan. 13	GuernseyCoOh	09	08	23
Bethell, Richard(Z)	1836	May 20	GuernseyCoOh	09	08	23
Betts, Jordan(Z)	1831	Sept. 20	Morgan Co,Oh	11	11	11
Betts, William(Z-M)	1837	Sept. 11	CoshoctnCoOh	03	05	19
Betz, Frederick(Z)	1825	Jan. 11	MuskingmCoOh	12	12	15
Betz, Frederick(Z)	1815	Aug. 26	MuskingmCoOh	12	13	26
Betz, Frederick(Z)	1816	Sept. 24	MuskingmCoOh	12	13	34
Betz, J.(Z)	1815	Aug. 26	MuskingmCoOh	12	13	26
Bevan, William(Z)	1835	Oct. 17	MonroeCo.,Oh	08	07	14
Bevard, Charles(Z-M)	1824	May 11	GuernseyCoOh	01	02	14
Bevard, Jonathan(Z-M)	1834	Dec. 16	GuernseyCoOh	03	04	18
Bevard, Samuel(Z-M)	1825	May 25	GuernseyCoOh	01	03	19
Bevard, Samuel(Z-M)	1836	Jan. 12	GuernseyCoOh	03	04	18
Bevard, Samuel(Z-M)	1836	Dec. 12	GuernseyCoOh	03	04	17
Bever, John(Y)	1822	April 02	GeorgeTownPa	06	16	15
Bever, John(Y)	1822	May 04	BeaverCo,Pa.	06	16	15
Bever, John(Y)	1824	Sept. 02	BeaverCo,Pa.	01	06	35
Bever, Sampson C.(Z-M)	1839	Feb. 23	CoshoctnCoOh	07	07	02
Bever, Sampson Cicero(Z-M)	1836	Feb. 22	CoshoctnCoOh	07	08	17
Bever, Sampson Cicero(Z-M)	1836	Feb. 22	CoshoctnCoOh	07	08	17
Bevor, Daniel(Z-M)	1835	April 13	TuscarwsCoOh	03	06	13
Beyher, Simon(Z)	1806	Dec. 27	MuskingmCoOh	01	02	06
Beymer, G.(Z)	1804	June 06	MuskingmCoOh	01	02	11
Beymer, George(Z)	1804	Dec. 25	MuskingmCoOh	01	02	05
Beymer, George(Z)	1805	Feb. 15	MuskingmCoOh	01	02	03
Beymer, George(Z)	1805	June 14	MuskingmCoOh	02	02	11
Beymer, George(Z)	1805	July 03	MuskingmCoOh	01	02	25
Beymer, George(Z)	1805	Nov. 25	MuskingmCoOh	02	02	10
Beymer, George(Z)	1805	Dec. 14	MuskingmCoOh	01	02	07
Beymer, George(Z)	1805	Dec. 14	MuskingmCoOh	01	02	17
Beymer, George(Z)	1806	April 09	MuskingmCoOh	02	02	11
Beymer, George(Z)	1806	June 21	MuskingmCoOh	05	01	16
Beymer, George(Z)	1807	March 07	MuskingmCoOh	05	01	16
Beymer, Philip(Z-M)	1820	Nov. 22	GuernseyCoOh	02	02	13
Beymer, Simon(Z)	1815	June 20	WashngtnCoOh	02	02	10
Beysang, Joseph(Z-M)	1837	July 12	KnoxCo.,Ohio	10	09	23
Bezant, William(Z)	1805	Dec. 18	MuskingmCoOh	14	13	02
Bicharce, James(Z-M)	1822	April 24	GuernseyCoOh	03	01	24
Bickel, David(Z)	1816	May 04	CoshoctnCoOh	06	08	21
Bickel, Henry(Z-M)	1823	May 12	CoshoctnCoOh	05	08	24
Bickel, Thomas Senr.(Z)	1807	Sept. 01	MuskingmCoOh	04	08	07
Bickel, Thomas Senr.(Z)	1807	Sept. 01	MuskingmCoOh	04	08	07
Bickel, Thomas(Z)	1825	Nov. 03	HolmesCoOhio	05	08	24
Bickel, Thomas(Z-M)	1825	June 15	HolmesCoOhio	06	08	21
Bickel, Thomas(Z-M)	1827	May 08	HolmesCoOhio	05	07	04
Bickel, Thos.(Z-M)	1830	July 05	HolmesCoOhio	06	08	21
Bickerstaff, Augustin(Y)	1824	Sept. 13	Jeff.Co.,Oh.	06	14	27
Bickerstaff, Samuel(Y)	1833	March 11	Jeff.Co.,Oh.	05	13	03
Bickerstaff, William(Y)	1832	Aug. 08	Jeff.Co.,Oh.	05	13	03
Bickey, Moses(Z-M)	1825	June 14	TuscarwsCoOh	05	08	01

PURCHASER	YEAR	DATE	RESIDENCE	R	T	S
Bickle, David(Z)	1815	Nov. 23	TuscarwsCoOh	06	08	21
Bickle, Henry(Z)	1815	Nov. 23	TuscarwsCoOh	05	08	16
Bickle, Jacob(Z)	1817	Feb. 08	LickingCo,Oh	11	01	22
Bickle, Thomas(Z)	1812	Feb. 25	TuscarwsCoOh	04	08	06
Bickle, Thomas(Z)	1815	Nov. 23	TuscarwsCoOh	06	08	21
Biddison, William Jr.(Z)	1832	Nov. 06	Perry Co.,Oh	15	15	25
Biddison, William V.(Z)	1833	Aug. 06	Perry Co.,Oh	15	15	25
Biddison, William(Z)	1833	April 16	Perry Co.,Oh	15	15	25
Biddison, William(Z)	1816	Nov. 25	MuskingmCoOh	14	13	30
Biddle, Frederick(Z)	1814	June 23	TuscarwsCoOh	04	09	21
Bigger, Samuel(Z)	1824	May 26	MuskingmCoOh	11	13	15
Bigger, Samuel(Z)	1827	Oct. 01	MuskingmCoOh	12	12	06
Bigger, Samuel(Z)	1816	July 31	MuskingmCoOh	04	01	18
Biggs, Eleazar(Z)	1808	March 23	FairfeldCoOh	11	06	15
Biggs, Ephraim(Z)	1814	Nov. 02	KnoxCo.,Ohio	11	06	17
Biggs, Jeremiah(Z)	1808	Oct. 26	MuskingmCoOh	11	06	16
Biggs, Jeremiah(Z)	1814	Jan. 05	KnoxCo.,Ohio	11	06	24
Biggs, Noah(Z)	1814	Oct. 28	MuskingmCoOh	11	06	24
Biggs, Zacheus(Z)	1804	Oct. 15	SteubenvleOh	03	02	13
Biggs, Zacheus(Z)	1804	Oct. 15	SteubenvleOh	03	02	14
Biggs, Zacheus(Z)	1804	Oct. 15	SteubenvleOh	03	02	14
Biggs, Zacheus(Z)	1804	Oct. 15	SteubenvleOh	03	02	15
Biggs, Zacheus(Z)	1804	Oct. 15	SteubenvleOh	03	02	08
Biggs, Zacheus(Z)	1804	Oct. 15	SteubenvleOh	03	02	07
Bigham, James(Z-M)	1828	Nov. 21	GuernseyCoOh	02	01	02
Bigham, James(Z-M)	1833	Nov. 27	GuernseyCoOh	04	02	11
Bigham, William(Z)	1810	Oct. 13	MuskingmCoOh	02	01	12
Bigley, James(Z)	1815	Oct. 20	BelmontCo,Oh	10	07	24
Bigley, Margaret(Z)	1835	Aug. 29	Morgan Co,Oh	09	06	19
Bigley, Thomas W.(Z-M)	1837	March 07	CoshoctnCoOh	03	04	15
Bigley, Thomas W.(Z-M)	1837	March 07	CoshoctnCoOh	03	04	06
Billingsley, William(Y)	1826	Feb. 01	BelmontCo,Oh	07	12	11
Billman, David(Y)	1822	Dec. 07	WarrenCo.,Pa	05	15	19
Billman, David(Y)	1823	May 30	WarrenCo.,Pa	05	15	19
Billman, Henry(Z)	1816	June 04	CoshoctnCoOh	09	04	01
Billman, Henry(Z)	1816	June 04	CoshoctnCoOh	09	05	22
Bills, William(Z-M)	1838	March 17	BelmontCo,Oh	07	07	23
Bingham, David(Z)	1805	Dec. 12	MuskingmCoOh	12	13	28
Bingham, David(Z)	1805	Dec. 12	MuskingmCoOh	12	13	12
Bingham, David(Z)	1807	Aug. 31	MuskingmCoOh	10	09	33
Bingham, Eli(Z)	1813	Aug. 17	GuernseyCoOh	10	09	32
Bingham, Eli(Z)	1807	Aug. 31	MuskingmCoOh	10	09	32
Bingham, Wm.(Z)	1809	Aug. 19	FayetteCo,Pa	02	02	21
Bingman, Seth S.(Z)	1830	March 01	HarrisonCoOh	12	09	17
Bintruet, J., Agt.((Z-M)	1820	Sept. 12	BedfordCo,Pa	04	01	21
Bintruet, J., Agt.(Z)	1820	Sept. 12	Morgan Co,Oh	09	06	03
Birch, Jonathan(Z)	1811	Dec. 26	MuskingmCoOh	05	03	05
Birch, William(Z)	1812	Feb. 06	AthensCoOhio	08	03	07
Bird, Andrew A.(Z)	1813	Dec. 15	MuskingmCoOh	15	17	10
Bird, Isaac(Z-M)	1832	Sept. 01	HolmesCoOhio	07	08	08
Bird, John(Y)	1822	Dec. 13	ColumbanCoOh	05	15	21
Bird, John(Z)	1832	April 13	MuskingmCoOh	11	12	30
Bird, John(Z-M)	1837	March 01	TuscarwsCoOh	03	04	05
Bird, John(Z-M)	1837	March 01	TuscarwsCoOh	03	05	25
Bird, Joseph(Z)	1828	Aug. 19	MuskingmCoOh	13	10	02
Bird, Joseph(Z)	1833	Nov. 28	MuskingmCoOh	09	08	18
Bird, Thomas B.(Z-M)	1835	Nov. 13	HolmesCoOhio	08	09	03
Bird, Thomas B.(Z-M)	1835	Nov. 13	HolmesCoOhio	08	09	03
Bird, Thomas(Z)	1812	April 14	CoshoctnCoOh	07	08	03
Bird, W.(Z)	1815	Dec. 02	CoshoctnCoOh	06	09	15
Bird, William(Z-M)	1831	Nov. 23	HolmesCoOhio	08	08	07
Bird, William(Z-M)	1831	Sept. 27	HolmesCoOhio	08	08	04
Birkhimer, Philip(Z-M)	1833	June 14	MuskingmCoOh	05	04	23
Birney, Hugh Jnr.(Y)	1825	Nov. 16	HarrisonCoOh	06	12	36
Birney, Hugh Junr.(Y)	1825	Dec. 06	HarrisonCoOh	06	12	36
Birney, Jno.(Y)	1824	May 28	HarrisonCoOh	04	10	17
Birney, Jno.(Y)	1824	May 28	HarrisonCoOh	04	10	17
Birney, Wm.(Y)	1824	May 28	HarrisonCoOh	04	10	17
Birney, Wm.(Y)	1824	May 28	HarrisonCoOh	04	10	17

PURCHASER	YEAR	DATE	RESIDENCE	R	T	S
Birney, Wm.(Y)	1826	Aug. 17	HarrisonCoOh	06	12	36
Birney, Wm.(Y)	1827	March 09	HarrisonCoOh	07	12	30
Birtwell, Thomas(Z-M)	1834	Sept. 23	NewportRdIsl	09	07	12
Birtwell, Thomas(Z-M)	1834	Sept. 23	NewportRdIsl	09	07	12
Birtwell, Thomas(Z-M)	1834	Sept. 23	NewportRdIsl	09	07	12
Bisant, W.(Z)	1816	July 02	MuskingmCoOh	13	09	10
Bise, John(Z-M)	1826	Aug. 09	MuskingmCoOh	07	07	23
Bisel, Joseph(Z-M)	1832	Feb. 13	Stark Co.,Oh	01	09	14
Bisel, Joseph(Z-M)	1834	Nov. 06	TuscarwsCoOh	01	09	14
Bishop, Edward(Z-M)	1839	Jan. 31	KnoxCo.,Ohio	04	04	01
Bishop, Eli(Z)	1833	Sept. 21	GuernseyCoOh	10	09	24
Bishop, Eli(Z)	1833	Sept. 25	GuernseyCoOh	10	09	24
Bishop, Henry(Z)	1832	May 26	Morgan Co,Oh	12	10	20
Bishop, John(Y)	1822	Sept. 21	HarrisonCoOh	04	10	18
Bishop, John(Y)	1829	April 22	HarrisonCoOh	05	12	35
Bishop, Lovett(Z)	1815	Jan. 19	WashngtnCoOh	11	11	20
Bishop, Stephen(Z-M)	1835	Dec. 28	MuskingmCoOh	10	05	22
Bishop, Stephen(Z-M)	1835	Dec. 28	MuskingmCoOh	10	05	21
Bitchey, Moses(Z)	1815	June 06	CoshoctnCoOh	05	08	07
Bitler, Geo. J.(Z)	1833	Feb. 16	BelmontCo,Oh	08	07	23
Bitner, Mathias(Z)	1812	June 01	SomersetCoPa	04	08	17
Bitting, Joseph(Z-M)	1835	April 15	LickingCo,Oh	11	03	05
Bixler, John(Z-M)	1832	March 26	BelmontCo,Oh	01	03	22
Black, David(Z)	1831	Jan. 27	MuskingmCoOh	14	13	09
Black, David(Z)	1816	Nov. 25	GuernseyCoOh	04	02	14
Black, George(Z-M)	1832	Dec. 01	KnoxCo.,Ohio	10	08	23
Black, Isaac(Y)	1831	May 30	WashCo.,Penn	06	14	20
Black, Jacob(Z)	1813	Sept. 15	KnoxCo.,Ohio	10	07	03
Black, Jacob(Z)	1815	Jan. 14	KnoxCo.,Ohio	10	08	14
Black, Jacob(Z-M)	1822	Oct. 25	KnoxCo.,Ohio	10	07	03
Black, Jacob(Z-M)	1832	June 09	KnoxCo.,Ohio	10	07	03
Black, Jacob(Z-M)	1834	Nov. 08	KnoxCo.,Ohio	10	07	03
Black, James(Z)	1815	Oct. 10	MuskingmCoOh	14	13	14
Black, James(Z)	1816	Oct. 22	WashngtnCoOh	14	12	20
Black, Jos.(Z)	1816	Nov. 25	GuernseyCoOh	04	02	14
Black, Matthew(Y)	1828	Nov. 22	ColumbanCoOh	03	13	19
Black, Matthew(Y)	1828	Dec. 11	ColumbanCoOh	03	13	22
Black, Matthew(Y)	1832	Oct. 06	ColumbanCoOh	03	13	28
Black, Robert(Y)	1827	Nov. 10	BelmontCo,Oh	04	06	27
Black, Samuel(Z-M)	1831	March 22	GuernseyCoOh	02	02	07
Black, William(Y)	1835	March 16	BeaverCo.,Pa	03	12	34
Black, William(Z)	1828	March 25	Perry Co.,Oh	15	16	22
Black, William(Z)	1815	Jan. 03	MuskingmCoOh	15	16	32
Blackbrurn, Zecheriah(Z)	1835	Dec. 02	Morgan Co,Oh	11	12	36
Blackbrurn, Zecheriah(Z)	1835	Dec. 02	Morgan Co,Oh	11	11	02
Blackbun, Anthony(Z-M)	1835	Jan. 20	GuernseyCoOh	03	06	23
Blackburn, Anthony(Z)	1816	Nov. 18	Jeff.Co.,Oh.	05	02	23
Blackburn, David(Z)	1832	July 24	Morgan Co,Oh	10	08	18
Blackburn, Joseph Jr.(Z)	1833	April 02	Morgan Co,Oh	10	08	19
Blackburn, Joseph(Z)	1835	Feb. 17	MuskingmCoOh	10	08	19
Blackburn, L.(Z)	1835	March 12	Morgan Co,Oh	10	08	30
Blackburn, Wm.(Z)	1806	April 29	WestmrldCoPa	10	07	08
Blackburn, Zachariah Jr.(Z)	1833	Oct. 12	MuskingmCoOh	11	11	12
Blackledge, Abraham(Y)	1821	Oct. 03	ColumbanCoOh	03	15	21
Blackledge, Robert(Z)	1824	Oct. 06	Morgan Co,Oh	10	06	22
Blackmer, Jesse(Z)	1837	Feb. 18	Morgan Co,Oh	09	05	19
Blackston, James(Z)	1814	Sept. 07	FayetteCo,Pa	10	09	05
Blackston, James(Z)	1817	Feb. 18	GuernseyCoOh	10	09	07
Blackwood, Isaac(Z)	1835	July 28	AthensCoOhio	14	12	29
Blackwood, Jno.(Y)	1822	Nov. 28	SteubenvleOh	03	05	21
Blackwood, Jno.(Y)	1822	Nov. 28	SteubenvleOh	03	05	21
Blair, Alexander Jr.(Z-M)	1828	Sept. 04	LickingCo,Oh	04	02	12
Blair, Alexander Jr.(Z-M)	1836	Jan. 08	GuernseyCoOh	03	02	05
Blair, Alexander Sr.(Z-M)	1836	Jan. 14	GuernseyCoOh	03	02	07
Blair, James(Y)	1831	May 03	BeaverCo.,Pa	04	13	20
Blair, James(Z)	1817	Jan. 25	FayetteCo,Pa	11	04	11
Blair, James(Z-M)	1824	Feb. 17	GuernseyCoOh	03	02	11
Blair, James(Z-M)	1835	Nov. 20	LickingCo,Oh	11	04	09
Blair, John(Z)	1816	Oct. 05	FayetteCo,Pa	10	04	06

PURCHASER	YEAR	DATE	RESIDENCE	R	T	S
Blair, John(Z-M)	1823	March 01	GuernseyCoOh	02	02	06
Blair, John(Z-M)	1826	Nov. 16	GuernseyCoOh	02	02	06
Blair, John(Z-M)	1828	Nov. 03	GuernseyCoOh	02	02	15
Blair, John(Z-M)	1829	June 27	GuernseyCoOh	02	02	15
Blair, John(Z-M)	1832	May 23	GuernseyCoOh	02	02	06
Blair, John(Z-M)	1834	Feb. 24	GuernseyCoOh	02	02	06
Blair, Joseph(Z)	1836	Oct. 29	MuskingmCoOh	15	14	36
Blair, William(Z-M)	1836	Jan. 08	GuernseyCoOh	04	02	12
Blake, George(Z)	1836	May 05	MonroeCo.,Oh	08	06	23
Blake, Israel(Z)	1833	July 09	Morgan Co,Oh	09	06	23
Blake, James(Z)	1824	Dec. 20	Morgan Co,Oh	09	06	21
Blake, James(Z)	1810	Oct. 25	Ohio Co.,Vir	09	05	03
Blake, Joseph(Z)	1836	May 05	MonroeCo.,Oh	08	06	23
Blake, Simeon(Z)	1836	Feb. 02	Morgan Co,Oh	09	06	22
Blake, Simeon, Jr.(Z)	1831	Jan. 27	Morgan Co,Oh	09	06	22
Blake, Walter M.(Z-M)	1837	Aug. 15	TuscarwsCoOh	03	05	11
Blakely, James(Y)	1834	Oct. 31	ColumbanCoOh	02	09	27
Blakely, James(Y)	1834	Oct. 31	ColumbanCoOh	02	09	27
Blakley, John(Y)	1834	Dec. 30	ColumbanCoOh	02	09	27
Blakley, John(Y)	1835	Nov. 04	ColumbanCoOh	02	09	27
Blanchard, Horace(Z)	1832	June 29	Morgan Co,Oh	10	08	29
Blanchard, Horace(Z)	1834	Jan. 21	Morgan Co,Oh	10	08	30
Bland, Joel(Z-M)	1836	Feb. 17	KnoxCo.,Ohio	10	04	08
Bland, John(Z)	1804	Nov. 29	MuskingmCoOh	08	02	13
Bland, John(Z)	1805	July 15	MuskingmCoOh	08	02	06
Bland, John(Z)	1805	Nov. 27	MuskingmCoOh	08	02	04
Bland, John(Z)	1805	Dec. 17	MuskingmCoOh	08	02	04
Bland, Silas(Z-M)	1827	Dec. 26	LickingCo,Oh	10	04	08
Bland, Silas(Z-M)	1832	Aug. 04	LickingCo,Oh	10	04	08
Bland, Silas(Z-M)	1836	Jan. 12	LickingCo,Oh	10	04	08
Bland, Silas(Z-M)	1838	April 04	LickingCo,Oh	10	04	08
Blane, Wm. Henry(Z)	1835	Jan. 22	WashngtnCoOh	08	05	32
Blank, John(Z)	1814	Feb. 09	SomersetCoPa	05	09	12
Blasor, Joseph(Z-M)	1832	April 16	BelmontCo,Oh	01	03	22
Blassens, Valentine(Z-M)	1836	June 03	TuscarwsCoOh	04	07	18
Blasseus, Valentine(Z-M)	1834	July 25	TuscarwsCoOh	04	07	13
Blazer, Abram(Z)	1836	Aug. 23	Morgan Co,Oh	13	08	09
Blazer, George(Y)	1829	Oct. 17	ColumbanCoOh	03	11	35
Blazer, George(Y)	1832	Oct. 31	ColumbanCoOh	03	12	34
Blazer, Jacob(Z)	1836	Feb. 17	GuernseyCoOh	13	08	09
Blazer, Philip(Z-M)	1836	May 04	GuernseyCoOh	03	06	13
Bleakley, Hugh(Z-M)	1836	April 06	KnoxCo.,Ohio	10	08	05
Bleakney, Edward(Y)	1831	Nov. 17	HarrisonCoOh	06	12	18
Blickensdorfer, J.(Z)	1816	Oct. 03	TuscarwsCoOh	05	08	24
Blickenstorffer, Christian(Z)	1812	July 07	TuscarwsCoOh	01	06	03
Blickundorfer, Wm.(Z)	1817	Feb. 13	LancastrCoPa	02	07	10
Bliss, J.(Z)	1817	Feb. 15	MuskingmCoOh	12	10	09
Bliss, Sam.(Z)	1817	Feb. 15	MuskingmCoOh	12	10	09
Bliss, Washington(Z-M)	1836	Jan. 12	GuernseyCoOh	03	01	07
Bliss, Washington(Z-M)	1837	Dec. 12	GuernseyCoOh	04	03	13
Bliss, Zadok(Y)	1831	March 07	HarrisonCoOh	06	12	32
Blizard, Solomon L.(Z)	1833	Oct. 18	Perry Co.,Oh	15	16	24
Blizzard, John(Z)	1806	Oct. 17	MuskingmCoOh	09	03	23
Blizzard, John(Z)	1805	Nov. 18	HarrisonCoVa	10	03	23
Blizzard, Thomas(Z)	1806	Oct. 13	MuskingmCoOh	09	03	23
Blizzard, Thomas(Z)	1806	Nov. 06	MuskingmCoOh	09	03	18
Blizzard, Thomas(Z)	1806	Nov. 06	MuskingmCoOh	09	03	22
Blizzard, Thomas(Z)	1808	April 01	MuskingmCoOh	09	03	12
Blocksom, Fusker A.(Y)	1828	Dec. 27	NewLisbon,Oh	04	12	23
Blotz, Daniel(Z-M)	1832	May 22	HolmesCoOhio	06	09	07
Blubaugh, Benjamin(Z-M)	1826	March 11	AlleghnyCoPa	11	08	18
Blubaugh, Benjamin(Z-M)	1837	April 03	KnoxCo.,Ohio	10	08	12
Blubaugh, Jacob(Z-M)	1828	Dec. 24	KnoxCo.,Ohio	11	08	18
Blubaugh, John(Z-M)	1837	April 03	KnoxCo.,Ohio	10	08	19
Blubaugh, John(Z-M)	1837	April 03	KnoxCo.,Ohio	10	08	19
Blubaugh, Stephen(Z-M)	1832	Dec. 15	KnoxCo.,Ohio	11	08	18
Blucker, F.(Z)	1816	May 17	FairfeldCoOh	12	12	26
Blucker, John(Z)	1816	May 17	FairfeldCoOh	12	12	26
Blue, Daniel(Z-M)	1833	Feb. 25	KnoxCo.,Ohio	10	05	12

PURCHASER	YEAR	DATE	RESIDENCE	R	T	S
Blue, Gilbert(Z)	1833	April 22	MuskingmCoOh	14	13	22
Blum, George(Z-M)	1834	July 25	TuscarwsCoOh	04	07	15
Blum, George(Z-M)	1836	July 18	TuscarwsCoOh	04	07	15
Blum, Jacob(Z-M)	1834	July 30	TuscarwsCoOh	03	09	22
Blunt, Hezekiah(Z)	1815	April 14	MuskingmCoOh	10	04	02
Blunt, Hezekiah(Z-M)	1827	July 09	LickingCo,Oh	10	05	17
Blunt, William(Z)	1806	Jan. 27	MuskingmCoOh	08	02	07
Blunt, William(Z)	1806	Jan. 27	MuskingmCoOh	08	02	03
Blunt, William(Z)	1806	Jan. 27	MuskingmCoOh	08	02	04
Blunt, William(Z)	1815	Jan. 17	MuskingmCoOh	09	05	22
Blunt, William(Z-M)	1831	Oct. 21	KnoxCo.,Ohio	10	05	16
Blunt, William(Z-M)	1831	Oct. 21	KnoxCo.,Ohio	10	05	23
Blunt, William(Z-M)	1832	July 18	KnoxCo.,Ohio	10	05	18
Blunt, Wilson(Z-M)	1836	Jan. 22	LickingCo,Oh	10	04	09
Blunt, Wilson(Z-M)	1836	Jan. 22	LickingCo,Oh	10	04	12
Blyth, Henry(Y)	1828	Aug. 22	Jeff.Co.,Oh.	04	12	12
Blythe, Henry(Y)	1829	June 15	Jeff.Co.,Oh.	03	11	29
Blythe, Henry(Y)	1831	June 02	Jeff.co.,Oh.	04	12	05
Boal, James(Z)	1815	March 24	MuskingmCoOh	11	12	19
Boal, John(Z)	1837	March 27	MuskingmCoOh	15	14	34
Boal, John(Z)	1837	March 27	MuskingmCoOh	15	14	34
Boal, John(Z)	1837	April 03	MuskingmCoOh	15	14	34
Boale, Archibald(Z)	1806	April 15	Jeff.Co.,Oh.	11	12	32
Boale, Archibald(Z)	1806	April 15	Jeff.Co.,Oh.	11	12	29
Boardman, Jacob(Z)	1813	June 18	MuskingmCoOh	15	16	10
Boatman, Henry(Y)	1822	Dec. 14	Stark Co.,Oh	07	20	26
Bobb, Joseph(Z)	1810	Dec. 06	MuskingmCoOh	15	16	34
Bobb, Joseph(Z)	1810	Dec. 13	MuskingmCoOh	15	16	34
Bochstetler, Gabriel(Z)	1827	Sept. 26	HolmesCoOhio	05	09	08
Boda, John Craft(Z-M)	1834	Sept. 23	HolmesCoOhio	08	08	15
Boda, John Craft(Z-M)	1834	Sept. 23	HolmesCoOhio	08	08	14
Boda, Joseph(Z-M)	1834	Sept. 23	HolmesCoOhio	08	08	14
Boda, Joseph(Z-M)	1834	Sept. 23	HolmesCoOhio	08	08	15
Bodle, Michael(Z)	1815	Sept. 29	KnoxCo.,Ohio	10	05	13
Bodle, Michael(Z)	1817	May 16	LickingCo,Oh	11	04	14
Bodle, Michael(Z-M)	1832	Nov. 30	LickingCo,Oh	11	04	18
Bodle, Michael(Z-M)	1832	Nov. 30	LickingCo,Oh	11	04	18
Bodle, Michael(Z-M)	1832	Nov. 30	LickingCo,Oh	11	04	17
Bodle, Michael(Z-M)	1832	Dec. 13	LickingCo,Oh	11	04	18
Boehmer, Jacob(Z-M)	1836	Aug. 31	TuscarwsCoOh	04	07	07
Boeshertz, Jacob(Z-M)	1838	March 02	MuskingmCoOh	09	08	08
Boeshutz, Ferdinand(Z-M)	1838	May 24	HolmesCoOhio	09	08	09
Boettler, Frederick(Z-M)	1836	Nov. 21	Stark Co.,Oh	03	07	02
Boettler, Frederick(Z-M)	1836	Nov. 21	Stark Co.,Oh	03	07	02
Boettler, Frederick(Z-M)	1836	Nov. 21	Stark Co.,Oh	03	07	02
Boettler, Frederick(Z-M)	1836	Nov. 21	Stark Co.,Oh	03	07	01
Bogan, Martin(Y)	1822	April 16	Stark Co.,Oh	06	17	21
Boggs, Francis(Z)	1815	June 16	Ohio Co.,Vir	06	03	18
Boggs, Francis(Z)	1815	June 16	Ohio Co.,Vir	06	03	18
Boggs, Jas.(Z-M)	1822	Oct. 11	GuernseyCoOh	03	03	19
Boggs, Rice(Z)	1807	Jan. 26	BelmontCo,Oh	10	09	06
Bogle, John(Z-M)	1821	Jan. 26	GuernseyCoOh	03	03	25
Bogle, John(Z-M)	1821	Feb. 02	GuernseyCoOh	03	03	25
Bogle, John(Z-M)	1825	April 21	GuernseyCoOh	03	03	25
Bogle, John(Z-M)	1828	March 01	GuernseyCoOh	03	03	25
Bogle, John(Z-M)	1830	April 19	GuernseyCoOh	03	03	25
Bogle, Joseph(Z-M)	1822	Aug. 28	GuernseyCoOh	03	03	24
Bogle, Joseph(Z-M)	1824	Feb. 14	GuernseyCoOh	03	03	16
Bogle, Joseph(Z-M)	1830	Jan. 15	GuernseyCoOh	03	03	16
Bogle, Samuel(Z)	1827	Sept. 04	GuernseyCoOh	04	03	20
Bogle, Samuel(Z-M)	1826	April 27	GuernseyCoOh	04	03	20
Bohinger, Frederick(Z)	1833	Nov. 19	MuskingmCoOh	13	10	15
Bohon,Slingluff & Deardorff(Z)	1806	Sept. 08	MuskingmCoOh	03	08	01
Bohon,Slingluff & Deardorff(Z)	1806	Sept. 08	MuskingmCoOh	03	08	01
Bohon,Slingluff & Deardorff(Z)	1806	Sept. 22	MuskingmCoOh	03	08	03
Bohon,Slingluff & Deardorff(Z)	1806	Sept. 08	MuskingmCoOh	03	08	02
Boland, Samuel(Y)	1832	April 18	HarrisonCoOh	06	14	30
Bolander, David(Y)	1822	May 11	Stark Co.,Oh	08	09	29
Bolder, Elijah(Z)	1810	April 14	KnoxCo.,Ohio	10	07	04

28

PURCHASER	YEAR	DATE	RESIDENCE	R	T	S
Bolder, John(Z)	1810	April 14	KnoxCo.,Ohio	10	07	04
Bole, Henry(Z)	1826	June 30	Morgan Co,Oh	13	08	15
Bole, Henry(Z)	1831	June 07	Morgan Co,Oh	13	08	15
Bolebur, Jacob(Z-M)	1825	April 23	TuscarwsCoOh	04	08	05
Bolen, Sam'l.(Y)	1829	Aug. 06	HarrisonCoOh	06	11	22
Boles, James(Y)	1828	March 24	HarrisonCoOh	07	12	21
Boles, James(Y)	1829	Aug. 17	HarrisonCoOh	07	12	21
Bolinger, Nicholas(Y)	1825	Jan. 06	Stark Co.,Oh	07	20	21
Bolinger, Peter(Z)	1836	May 10	Morgan Co,Oh	10	06	14
Bollingar, Abraham(Z)	1835	Nov. 12	AlleghnyCoPa	10	06	02
Bollinger, John(Z-M)	1838	March 17	ZanesvilleOh	09	08	06
Bollman, Christian(Z-M)	1833	April 01	TuscarwsCoOh	03	08	15
Bollman, George(Z)	1806	Dec. 15	BedfordCo,Pa	04	08	10
Bollman, George(Z-M)	1822	Dec. 18	TuscarwsCoOh	03	08	15
Bollman, George(Z-M)	1834	Feb. 22	TuscarwsCoOh	04	07	03
Bollman, John(Z-M)	1833	Dec. 30	TuscarwsCoOh	03	08	15
Bolt, Jeremiah D.(Z)	1834	March 18	MonroeCo.,Oh	08	07	04
Bolton, James(Z)	1811	April 04	KnoxCo.,Ohio	11	05	04
Bonars, Henry(Z-M)	1829	June 20	WashCo.,Penn	07	08	02
Bonars, Henry(Z-M)	1829	June 20	WashCo.,Penn	07	08	02
Bonce, Mathew(Z)	1814	March 28	CoshactnCoOh	07	07	25
Bond, Joshua(Z)	1835	Dec. 14	Jeff.Co.,Oh.	09	07	08
Bond, Larkin(Y)	1824	Dec. 01	GuernseyCoOh	07	10	12
Bond, Peter(Z)	1831	March 14	MuskingmCoOh	10	08	02
Bond, Peter(Z)	1833	Nov. 14	HockingCo,Oh	14	13	15
Bond, Peter(Z)	1835	Nov. 14	MuskingmCoOh	09	05	26
Bond, Peter(Z)	1814	Dec. 22	BaltimreCoMd	05	02	12
Bond, Peter(Z)	1814	Dec. 22	BaltimreCoMd	05	02	13
Bond, Richard(Z)	1831	Aug. 24	Morgan Co,Oh	09	07	15
Bond, Richard(Z)	1835	Dec. 09	Morgan Co,Oh	09	07	15
Bond, William(Z)	1831	Aug. 29	GuernseyCoOh	10	09	26
Bond, William(Z)	1831	Aug. 29	GuernseyCoOh	10	09	36
Bond, William(Z)	1814	Dec. 22	HarrisonCoOh	05	02	12
Bone, Peter(Z-M)	1828	Dec. 05	LickingCo,Oh	11	03	05
Bone, Peter(Z-M)	1829	Dec. 14	LickingCo,Oh	11	03	05
Boner, John(Z)	1805	May 07	BelmontCo,Oh	01	01	03
Bonham, Evan(Z-M)	1833	Jan. 05	HarrisonCoOh	01	06	14
Bonham, Evan(Z-M)	1833	Jan. 05	HarrisonCoOh	01	06	14
Bonham, Philip(Z)	1833	Jan. 04	Morgan Co,Oh	11	11	05
Bonham, Smith(Z-M)	1833	Aug. 09	TuscarwsCoOh	01	06	13
Bonham, Wm.(Z-M)	1833	Oct. 19	TuscarwsCoOh	01	06	18
Bonham, Zacharah(Z)	1814	April 18	AlleghnyCoPa	09	03	22
Bonham, Zachariah(Z)	1814	Jan. 11	?	09	03	23
Bonifield, Samuel(Z)	1816	April 19	MuskingmCoOh	09	04	15
Bonifield, Samuel(Z)	1817	July 10	MuskingmCoOh	09	01	08
Bontz, Jacob(Z)	1807	Sept. 01	Alexandria ?	18	01	21
Booker, Joseph(Y)	1832	Sept. 11	Stark Co.,Oh	10	02	33
Books, Anthony(Y)	1832	July 12	Stark Co.,Oh	07	16	10
Boon, Margaret(Z)	1837	Feb. 02	Morgan Co,Oh	08	05	04
Boon, Thomas(Z)	1835	Nov. 09	Morgan Co,Oh	09	06	34
Boon, Thomas(Z)	1835	Dec. 03	Morgan Co,Oh	09	06	34
Boon, William(Z)	1831	Sept. 13	Morgan Co,Oh	09	06	34
Boon, William(Z)	1837	Feb. 02	Morgan Co,Oh	08	05	04
Boone, Richard(Y)	1825	July 05	Ohio Co.,Vir	07	11	20
Boone, Richard(Y)	1826	Aug. 14	Ohio Co.,Vir	07	11	13
Boop, Jacob(Y)	1827	May 08	HarrisonCoOh	07	16	03
Boose, Henry(Z)	1816	Oct. 09	P.GeorgeCoMd	15	16	23
Booth, Daniel(Z)	1815	Nov. 08	CoshoctnCoOh	03	06	18
Booth, Daniel(Z)	1815	Nov. 08	CoshoctnCoOh	03	05	22
Booth, Eli(Z-M)	1836	May 27	TuscarwsCoOh	04	06	10
Booth, John(Z-M)	1836	April 13	TuscarwsCoOh	03	05	22
Booth, John(Z-M)	1837	March 06	TuscarwsCoOh	03	05	22
Booth, Sarah(Z-M)	1834	Dec. 08	TuscarwsCoOh	03	05	19
Booth, Sarah(Z-M)	1835	Nov. 09	TuscarwsCoOh	03	05	22
Booth, Sarah(Z-M)	1832	May 23	TuscarwsCoOh	03	05	22
Booth, Sarah(Z-M)	1838	May 14	TuscarwsCoOh	03	05	22
Borden, Bradford(Z-M)	1836	Dec. 30	CoshoctnCoOh	09	07	09
Borden, George(Z-M)	1831	June 07	MuskingmCoOh	06	03	09
Borden, Sam'l. S.(Z-M)	1837	Feb. 23	HolmesCoOhio	09	08	15

PURCHASER	YEAR	DATE	RESIDENCE	R	T	S
Borden, Thomas(Z-M)	1837	May 03	CoshoctnCoOh	09	07	09
Borden, Thos.(Z-M)	1831	Dec. 22	CoshoctnCoOh	09	07	03
Bordenkercher, David(Z-M)	1836	Oct. 29	CoshoctnCoOh	05	04	06
Bordenkercher, David(Z-M)	1836	Nov. 08	CoshoctnCoOh	05	04	06
Bordenkercher, David(Z-M)	1836	Nov. 16	CoshoctnCoOh	05	04	15
Bordenkercher, David(Z-M)	1836	Dec. 02	CoshoctnCoOh	05	04	08
Bordenkercher, David(Z-M)	1836	Dec. 02	CoshoctnCoOh	05	04	08
Bordenkercher, David(Z-M)	1836	Dec. 02	CoshoctnCoOh	05	04	03
Bordenkercher, David(Z-M)	1838	Sept. 06	CoshoctnCoOh	05	04	13
Border, Geo.(Z-M)	1830	Jan. 13	MuskingmCoOh	06	03	08
Border, George(Z)	1829	Sept. 21	MuskingmCoOh	06	03	09
Border, George(Z-M)	1829	Nov. 24	MuskingmCoOh	06	03	25
Border, Jacob(Z-M)	1833	Aug. 03	TuscarwsCoOh	03	07	16
Border, Jacob(Z-M)	1833	Aug. 03	TuscarwsCoOh	03	07	25
Border, Nicholas(Z)	1804	June 11	MuskingmCoOh	13	12	28
Border, Nicholas(Z)	1805	Dec. 20	MuskingmCoOh	13	12	01
Border, Nicholas(Z)	1805	Dec. 20	MuskingmCoOh	13	12	01
Border, Nicholas(Z)	1815	Feb. 11	MuskingmCoOh	12	12	14
Border, Nicholas(Z)	1816	Nov. 29	MuskingmCoOh	12	11	23
Border, Nicholas(Z-M)	1831	Sept. 07	MuskingmCoOh	06	03	13
Boren, Daniel(Y)	1833	April 08	CarrollCo,Oh	07	16	05
Boring, George(Y)	1831	July 20	ColumbanCoOh	04	13	11
Boring, George(Y)	1834	Dec. 19	CarrollCo,Oh	04	13	17
Boring, James(Z-M)	1833	Feb. 09	CoshoctnCoOh	09	06	11
Boring, Kinsey(Z-M)	1832	April 28	CoshoctnCoOh	07	05	07
Borland, John(Z-M)	1833	July 22	TuscarwsCoOh	01	08	02
Borland, Mathew(Z-M)	1821	Dec. 22	WashCo.,Penn	08	08	06
Borland, Samuel(Y)	1831	Aug. 26	HarrisonCoOh	06	12	20
Borland, Samuel(Y)	1832	April 24	HarrisonCoOh	06	14	24
Borozer, Jacob(Z)	1807	Dec. 02	WashngtnCoOh	08	05	17
Borring, James(Z-M)	1833	Feb. 21	CoshoctnCoOh	09	06	20
Borthwick, John(Z-M)	1832	Aug. 04	HolmesCoOhio	09	08	18
Borton, Daniel(Y)	1825	Nov. 23	ColumbanCoOh	05	17	09
Borton, Reuben(Z-M)	1833	March 30	GuernseyCoOh	02	03	12
Bortz, Daniel(Y)	1822	March 04	Stark Co.,Oh	07	18	26
Bortz, Daniel(Y)	1825	Oct. 21	Stark Co.,Oh	07	17	02
Bortz, Daniel(Y)	1825	Oct. 21	Stark Co.,Oh	07	17	02
Bose, Michael(Z-M)	1833	July 22	TuscarwsCoOh	03	10	02
Bosinburg, John(Z-M)	1834	Sept. 25	KnoxCo.,Ohio	10	06	11
Boslen, Joseph(Y)	1822	April 17	HarrisonCoOh	05	13	27
Boslen, Wm.(Y)	1822	April 17	HarrisonCoOh	05	13	27
Bosler, Joseph(Y)	1823	May 09	HarrisonCoOh	05	13	27
Bosler, Wm.(Y)	1823	May 09	HarrisonCoOh	05	13	27
Bost, Michael(Z)	1835	Dec. 07	Perry Co.,Oh	14	12	14
Bost, Peter(Y)	1826	Nov. 29	ColumbanCoOh	04	13	24
Bost, Peter(Y)	1827	June 29	ColumbanCoOh	04	13	29
Bosville, Benjamin(Y)	1825	Aug. 12	BelmontCo,Oh	06	08	25
Botaw, Thomas(Y)	1829	March 13	ColumbanCoOh	05	10	22
Bothwell, James(Z-M)	1833	April 29	CoshoctnCoOh	05	07	24
Botkin, Richard(Z)	1836	April 25	BelmontCo,Oh	14	13	21
Bottman, George(Z)	1806	Dec. 15	BedfordCo,Pa	04	08	10
Botts, Jno.(Z-M)	1831	Dec. 29	GuernseyCoOh	02	01	08
Botts, John(Z-M)	1823	June 10	GuernseyCoOh	02	01	08
Boumer, Benjamin(Z-M)	1836	Nov. 14	LickingCo,Oh	11	04	18
Bounds, Thomas(Z)	1813	Oct. 23	MuskingmCoOh	09	01	05
Bovard, George(Y)	1835	Nov. 17	TuscarwsCoOh	07	14	28
Bowden, John(Z)	1827	Dec. 14	BelmontCo,Oh	04	10	28
Bowen, Benjamin(Y)	1825	Nov. 26	BelmontCo,Oh	06	08	25
Bowen, Francis(Z)	1806	Nov. 28	BelmontCo,Oh	02	01	03
Bowen, James(Z)	1836	June 18	WashngtnCoOh	10	06	26
Bowen, James(Z)	1836	Oct. 01	WashngtnCoOh	10	06	14
Bower, Benjamin(Z-M)	1835	Aug. 13	HolmesCoOhio	09	08	09
Bower, Bernard(Y)	1827	May 29	TuscarwsCoOh	06	13	32
Bower, Bernard(Y)	1830	Aug. 20	TuscarwsCoOh	06	13	18
Bower, Bernard(Y)	1830	Sept. 13	TuscarwsCoOh	07	14	01
Bower, Christian(Z-M)	1836	Nov. 11	HolmesCoOhio	08	07	21
Bower, David Senr.(Y)	1827	May 29	TuscarwsCoOh	06	13	32
Bower, David(Y)	1829	Dec. 14	TuscarwsCoOh	06	13	13
Bower, David(Y)	1830	Aug. 20	TuscarwsCoOh	06	13	26

PURCHASER	YEAR	DATE	RESIDENCE	R	T	S
Bower, David(Y)	1831	Nov. 11	TuscarwsCoOh	06	13	19
Bower, George(Z)	1810	Dec. 14	MuskingmCoOh	06	01	04
Bower, Henry(Y)	1830	Aug. 20	TuscarwsCoOh	06	13	32
Bower, Jacob(Y)	1827	March 13	Stark Co.,Oh	09	11	02
Bower, John Jr.(Y)	1828	Dec. 19	TuscarwsCoOh	06	13	17
Bower, John(Y)	1825	Dec. 24	Jeff.Co.,Oh.	07	16	15
Bower, John(Y)	1826	June 10	Stark Co.,Oh	07	16	21
Bower, John(Y)	1827	June 12	HarrisonCoOh	06	12	24
Bower, John(Y)	1828	March 28	HarrisonCoOh	06	12	30
Bower, John(Z)	1807	June 09	WashCo.,Penn	06	01	06
Bower, Madelena(Y)	1830	Aug. 20	TuscarwsCoOh	06	13	26
Bower, Michael(Z)	1829	Oct. 21	BelmontCo,Oh	12	10	15
Bower, William(Z)	1815	Oct. 14	HarrisonCoOh	01	04	01
Bowers, George(Z)	1815	Jan. 14	MuskingmCoOh	06	02	16
Bowers, Jacob(Y)	1829	Aug. 13	TuscarwsCoOh	06	13	31
Bowers, Jacob(Y)	1829	Aug. 13	TuscarwsCoOh	07	14	01
Bowers, Jacob(Z)	1804	Dec. 04	MuskingmCoOh	14	15	17
Bowers, Jacob(Z)	1809	Oct. 18	GreeneCo.,Pa	06	01	08
Bowers, Jacob(Z)	1810	Sept. 09	MuskingmCoOh	12	13	09
Bowers, John(Z)	1832	Sept. 18	MuskingmCoOh	12	12	07
Bowers, John(Z)	1810	March 09	GuernseyCoOh	02	01	26
Bowers, John(Z)	1811	May 04	MuskingmCoOh	06	01	08
Bowers, John(Z)	1811	Dec. 11	MuskingmCoOh	02	06	25
Bowers, John(Z)	1815	Feb. 18	MuskingmCoOh	06	01	04
Bowers, Joseph(Z)	1810	Sept. 09	MuskingmCoOh	12	13	09
Bowers, Joseph(Z)	1814	Dec. 19	MuskingmCoOh	06	02	13
Bowers, Joseph(Z)	1816	May 28	MuskingmCoOh	06	01	03
Bowers, Josiah(Z)	1815	Oct. 14	GuernseyCoOh	01	02	22
Bowers, Martin(Z-M)	1837	March 06	CarrollCo,Oh	04	04	03
Bowers, William(Z)	1816	Aug. 17	?	01	04	08
Bowersacks, David(Y)	1827	June 25	HarrisonCoOh	05	13	13
Bowie, William(Z)	1832	April 09	Morgan Co,Oh	09	06	12
Bowie, William(Z)	1833	June 18	Morgan Co,Oh	09	06	01
Bowie, William(Z)	1835	Dec. 29	Morgan Co,Oh	09	06	12
Bowlands, William(Z)	1834	Aug. 08	MonroeCo.,Oh	08	05	19
Bowlby, J.(Z-M)	1836	Feb. 19	LickingCo,Oh	11	04	08
Bowlby, Joseph(Z-M)	1836	July 16	LickingCo,Oh	11	04	13
Bowman, D.(Z)	1814	March 29	FayetteCo,Pa	10	01	23
Bowman, Henry(Y)	1827	Oct. 26	Stark Co.,Oh	08	09	13
Bowman, Henry(Z)	1816	Dec. 14	Brooke CoVir	01	09	20
Bowman, Jacob(Z-M)	1835	Dec. 12	MuskingmCoOh	05	03	04
Bowman, John(Y)	1822	Aug. 12	Stark Co.,Oh	09	12	15
Bowman, Leonard(Z-M)	1831	Oct. 22	MuskingmCoOh	05	03	04
Bowman, Sarah S.(Z-M)	1833	Dec. 02	MuskingmCoOh	06	03	02
Bowzer, Jacob(Z)	1809	June 21	WashngtnCo ?	08	05	18
Boyce, Robert(Y)	1828	Jan. 12	ColumbanCoOh	02	09	11
Boyce, Robert(Z-M)	1837	March 02	MuskingmCoOh	05	04	22
Boyce, Robert(Z-M)	1837	March 02	MuskingmCoOh	05	04	22
Boyce, Robert(Z-M)	1837	March 02	MuskingmCoOh	05	04	22
Boyd, Adam(Z-M)	1824	Sept. 18	Jeff.Co.,Oh.	04	01	13
Boyd, Alex'd.(Z-M)	1836	Aug. 26	HolmesCoOhio	09	08	20
Boyd, Alexander(Y)	1830	March 09	ColumbanCoOh	04	13	22
Boyd, Alexander(Y)	1830	March 09	ColumbanCoOh	04	13	22
Boyd, Alexander(Z-M)	1837	Feb. 02	HolmesCoOhio	09	08	20
Boyd, Andrew(Y)	1829	April 22	ColumbanCoOh	04	13	29
Boyd, Andrew(Z-M)	1835	Jan. 08	GuernseyCoOh	02	03	12
Boyd, Benj.(Z-M)	1833	Aug. 20	TuscarwsCoOh	01	05	13
Boyd, Cyrus(Z)	1826	Nov. 11	BelmontCo,Oh	13	08	22
Boyd, Cyrus(Z)	1826	Nov. 11	BelmontCo,Oh	13	08	07
Boyd, Cyrus(Z)	1831	June 02	BelmontCo,Oh	13	08	27
Boyd, Daniel(Z-M)	1824	Sept. 08	Jeff.Co.,Oh.	05	06	15
Boyd, James(Y)	1821	Sept. 25	Jeff.Co.,Oh.	07	14	21
Boyd, James(Y)	1831	March 23	TuscarwsCoOh	07	14	27
Boyd, James(Y)	1831	March 31	TuscarwsCoOh	07	14	27
Boyd, James(Y)	1831	June 30	TuscarwsCoOh	07	14	28
Boyd, James(Y)	1831	July 02	TuscarwsCoOh	07	14	27
Boyd, James(Z)	1832	Oct. 15	Morgan Co,Oh	13	08	22
Boyd, James(Z-M)	1832	Sept. 22	GuernseyCoOh	02	02	15
Boyd, James(Z-M)	1835	July 27	TuscarwsCoOh	01	08	09

31

PURCHASER	YEAR	DATE	RESIDENCE	R	T	S
Boyd, James(Z-M)	1835	Aug. 01	TuscarwsCoOh	05	04	06
Boyd, James(Z-M)	1838	Jan. 02	GuernseyCoOh	03	04	16
Boyd, John(Y)	1822	Aug. 10	AlleghnyCoPa	05	15	28
Boyd, John(Z)	1827	Jan. 26	MuskingmCoOh	13	10	04
Boyd, John(Z)	1829	March 13	MuskingmCoOh	14	14	13
Boyd, John(Z)	1829	Dec. 21	MuskingmCoOh	13	10	05
Boyd, John(Z-M)	1830	Sept. 24	CoshoctnCoOh	05	06	05
Boyd, John(Z-M)	1824	May 11	AlleghnyCoPa	04	03	22
Boyd, Jon.(Z-M)	1831	Feb. 28	GuernseyCoOh	01	03	19
Boyd, Jonathan(Z-M)	1837	Nov. 13	GuernseyCoOh	02	03	12
Boyd, Joseph(Z-M)	1820	Aug. 08	GuernseyCoOh	02	03	08
Boyd, Joseph(Z-M)	1835	Dec. 29	GuernseyCoOh	03	01	05
Boyd, Philip(Z)	1833	Feb. 06	MuskingmCoOh	13	10	08
Boyd, Robert(Y)	1827	Sept. 01	TuscarwsCoOh	07	14	26
Boyd, Robert(Y)	1832	March 05	TuscarwsCoOh	07	14	33
Boyd, Robert(Y)	1832	March 05	TuscarwsCoOh	07	14	27
Boyd, Robert(Z)	1816	June 06	Jeff.Co.,Oh.	06	06	09
Boyd, Robert(Z)	1816	June 06	Jeff.Co.,Oh.	06	06	12
Boyd, Robert(Z-M)	1833	Feb. 20	Brooke CoVir	05	06	14
Boyd, Robert(Z-M)	1834	March 22	CoshoctnCoOh	05	06	15
Boyd, Robert(Z-M)	1834	Nov. 21	CoshoctnCoOh	05	06	15
Boyd, Samuel(Z-M)	1824	May 11	AlleghnyCoPa	01	04	20
Boyd, Samuel(Z-M)	1835	Aug. 17	CoshoctnCoOh	05	06	24
Boyd, Thomas(Z)	1814	June 13	BelmontCo,Oh	09	06	17
Boyd, Thomas(Z-M)	1829	Sept. 01	GuernseyCoOh	01	03	22
Boyd, Thomas(Z-M)	1831	Jan. 27	GuernseyCoOh	01	03	22
Boyd, Thos.(Z)	1815	Sept. 28	BelmontCo,Oh	09	06	08
Boyd, Volney(Z)	1832	Jan. 11	Morgan Co,Oh	11	11	35
Boyd, William(Z-M)	1832	Sept. 28	CoshoctnCoOh	05	07	25
Boyd, William(Z-M)	1837	Feb. 07	CoshoctnCoOh	05	07	25
Boyd, Wm.(Z)	1835	March 13	GuernseyCoOh	09	07	14
Boyd, Wm.(Z)	1835	March 13	GuernseyCoOh	09	07	14
Boyd, Wm.(Z)	1815	Sept. 28	BelmontCo,Oh	09	06	08
Boyd, Wm.(Z-M)	1833	Oct. 19	CoshoctnCoOh	05	07	25
Boyer, Daniel(Z)	1831	Nov. 14	MuskingmCoOh	12	13	11
Boyer, Jacob(Y)	1826	June 09	Stark Co.,Oh	07	18	25
Boyer, Peter(Z)	1827	May 01	MuskingmCoOh	09	01	06
Boyer, Peter(Z)	1827	May 01	MuskingmCoOh	09	01	07
Boyer, William(Z-M)	1826	Feb. 14	GuernseyCoOh	01	06	18
Boyers, John(Y)	1829	March 18	Stark Co.,Oh	06	17	30
Boylan, George(Z)	1833	Dec. 06	Perry Co.,Oh	14	13	31
Boyle, Edward(Y)	1834	Nov. 28	ColumbanCoOh	03	13	33
Boyle, Hugh(Y)	1834	Dec. 29	ColumbanCoOh	03	12	30
Boyle, Hugh(Z)	1816	Oct. 03	Lancaster,Oh	15	14	17
Boyle, Hugh(Z)	1817	Feb. 17	Lancaster,Oh	15	15	20
Boyle, Hugh(Z-M)	1831	April 29	TuscarwsCoOh	01	05	02
Boyle, John(Y)	1832	Oct. 12	ColumbanCoOh	03	13	28
Boyle, Pat.(Z-M)	1831	March 12	LickingCo,Oh	11	01	20
Boyle, William(Z)	1815	Dec. 11	FairfeldCoOh	15	17	15
Bozman, Benj'm.(Z)	1824	June 16	MuskingmCoOh	11	12	21
Bozman, James(Z)	1837	Jan. 23	Morgan Co,Oh	08	05	04
Bozman, W. S.(Z)	1829	Nov. 20	Brooke CoVir	11	10	25
Bozman, Wilkes(Z)	1824	May 17	Morgan Co,Oh	11	10	06
Bozman, William(Z)	1836	Oct. 22	Morgan Co,Oh	08	05	10
Bozman, William(Z)	1836	Oct. 22	Morgan Co,Oh	08	05	09
Bracken, Cornelius(Y)	1827	Sept. 10	Jeff.Co.,Oh.	05	13	29
Brackin, Cornelius(Y)	1826	April 15	Jeff.Co.,Oh.	05	13	29
Brackin, John(Z-M)	1835	Nov. 06	GuernseyCoOh	02	03	09
Braddock, Michael(Z)	1823	Sept. 13	Morgan Co,Oh	13	09	03
Braddock, William(Z)	1814	June 15	Greene Co,Pa	10	05	04
Braden, E.(Z)	1815	Nov. 21	GuernseyCoOh	02	02	22
Braden, Samuel(Z-M)	1835	Sept. 15	GuernseyCoOh	04	02	20
Bradford, Gasper(Z-M)	1830	March 10	MuskingmCoOh	05	03	14
Bradford, James(Z-M)	1833	Jan. 16	GuernseyCoOh	04	02	12
Bradford, John(Z-M)	1828	April 08	MuskingmCoOh	05	02	09
Bradford, Peter(Z)	1816	June 29	MuskingmCoOh	05	02	07
Brading, John(Z-M)	1830	Jan. 09	GuernseyCoOh	04	02	13
Brading, John(Z-M)	1835	Aug. 28	GuernseyCoOh	04	02	12
Bradley, John W.(Z)	1828	Aug. 12	Morgan Co,Oh	13	08	08

PURCHASER	YEAR	DATE	RESIDENCE	R	T	S
Bradley, John W.(Z)	1835	Dec. 07	Morgan Co,Oh	13	08	08
Bradley, John William(Z)	1832	Sept. 18	Morgan Co,Oh	13	08	08
Bradley, John(Z)	1828	Aug. 01	Brooke CoVir	11	11	32
Bradock, John(Z)	1817	June 21	MuskingmCoOh	13	09	04
Bradrick, Abraham(Z)	1815	Nov. 20	BelmontCo,Oh	13	08	02
Bradshaw, James(Z-M)	1836	Nov. 30	GuernseyCoOh	03	03	10
Bradshaw, James(Z-M)	1837	Feb. 01	GuernseyCoOh	03	03	10
Brady, James W.(Z)	1833	Oct. 02	Morgan Co,Oh	10	07	30
Brady, James W.(Z)	1833	Oct. 24	Morgan Co,Oh	10	07	31
Brady, James(Z)	1810	May 28	BrookCo.,Vir	11	13	30
Brady, Levi(Z)	1815	Feb. 03	MuskingmCoOh	11	13	31
Brady, William(Z)	1836	Dec. 31	MuskingmCoOh	15	14	26
Braemer, John(Z-M)	1830	Aug. 09	TuscarwsCoOh	03	06	09
Bran, Alexander(Y)	1828	Nov. 10	TuscarwsCoOh	06	13	23
Brand, Lewis(Z-M)	1833	Sept. 27	TuscarwsCoOh	03	08	24
Brand, Peter(Z)	1835	Nov. 23	BelmontCo,Oh	08	07	04
Brand, Peter(Z)	1835	Nov. 23	BelmontCo,Oh	08	08	33
Brand, Philip(Z)	1836	Jan. 18	BelmontCo,Oh	08	08	33
Brandeberry, Ab'm.(Y)	1828	Aug. 15	Stark Co.,Oh	06	16	08
Branqla, Casper(Y)	1831	March 09	ColumbanCoOh	07	16	04
Brannan, George(Z)	1835	July 08	Morgan Co,Oh	10	08	19
Branneman, Dan'l.(Z-M)	1822	Oct. 30	KnoxCo.,Ohio	10	07	18
Brannon, Henry(Z-M)	1829	Jan. 16	MuskingmCoOh	06	03	10
Brannon, Henry(Z-M)	1829	Jan. 16	MuskingmCoOh	05	03	06
Brannon, James(Y)	1831	Aug. 30	AlleghnyCoPa	03	13	20
Brannon, John(Y)	1828	Dec. 29	ColumbanCoOh	03	13	20
Brannon, John(Z)	1834	Dec. 20	CoshoctnCoOh	10	05	11
Brannon, John(Z-M)	1834	Dec. 20	CoshoctnCoOh	09	05	15
Brant, Henry(Z-M)	1832	May 17	TuscarwsCoOh	04	07	04
Brashear, Otho(Z)	1817	April 04	FayetteCo,Pa	01	04	05
Brashears, Otho(Z-M)	1831	Jan. 27	TuscarwsCoOh	01	04	05
Brathan, James(Z)	1804	Dec. 06	BelmontCo,Oh	01	03	15
Bratshaw, Joseph B. H.(Z-M)	1838	April 07	MuskingmCoOh	03	04	06
Brattan, Wm.(Z)	1815	Aug. 09	GuernseyCoOh	02	03	25
Bratton, Edward(Z)	1812	May 14	GuernseyCoOh	03	03	11
Bratton, Edward(Z-M)	1825	Sept. 19	GuernseyCoOh	02	04	24
Bratton, James(Z)	1812	June 06	GuernseyCoOh	02	02	05
Bratton, James(Z-M)	1823	July 04	GuernseyCoOh	02	04	18
Bratton, William(Z-M)	1822	June 07	BelmontCo,Oh	06	03	17
Bratton, William(Z-M)	1836	Jan. 16	GuernseyCoOh	02	04	18
Brawn, Wm.(Z-M)	1839	March 04	CoshoctnCoOh	10	04	09
Bray, John(Z)	1835	Dec. 02	Perry Co.,Oh	14	14	19
Breem, J.(Z)	1814	Dec. 26	MuskingmCoOh	11	05	14
Breese, Joshua(Z)	1816	Dec. 17	FrederkCoVir	13	09	20
Brehmer, Conrad(Z-M)	1833	July 22	TuscarwsCoOh	02	05	02
Breithaupt, Charles(Z-M)	1836	Dec. 26	HolmesCoOhio	04	07	07
Breithaupt, Chas.(Z-M)	1836	Aug. 11	TuscarwsCoOh	04	07	06
Brelsford, Abraham(Z)	1836	Feb. 08	MuskingmCoOh	13	10	11
Brelsford, David(Z-M)	1836	March 12	MuskingmCoOh	06	03	02
Breninger, Jno.(Z-M)	1831	Nov. 24	TuscarwsCoOh	03	10	18
Brennstuhl, Jacob(Z-M)	1836	July 26	HolmesCoOhio	09	09	24
Brennstuhl, Jacob(Z-M)	1836	July 27	HolmesCoOhio	09	09	24
Brent, William S.(Z)	1812	Feb. 07	MuskingmCoOh	15	16	01
Brewer, Isaac(Z-M)	1831	Feb. 28	GuernseyCoOh	02	04	04
Brewster, J.(Z)	1817	Aug. 21	MuskingmCoOh	13	09	06
Brewster, Johnson(Z)	1824	Aug. 11	MuskingmCoOh	13	10	22
Brewster, Johnson(Z)	1828	Dec. 29	MuskingmCoOh	12	13	09
Brewster, Johnson(Z)	1806	March 28	MuskingmCoOh	12	13	03
Brewster, Johnson(Z)	1806	April 02	MuskingmCoOh	12	13	09
Brewster, Johnston(Z)	1811	Sept. 28	?	12	11	09
Brewster, Nathaniel(Y)	1835	March 25	CarrollCo,Oh	05	13	04
Brewster, William(Z)	1826	Feb. 02	WashCo.,Ohio	11	11	30
Breymoier, Mathias(Z-M)	1831	May 27	TuscarwsCoOh	02	10	25
Brian, Terence(Y)	1827	March 06	ColumbanCoOh	05	15	10
Brice, Benjamin W.(Z-M)	1838	Nov. 07	LickingCo,Oh	10	03	06
Brice, Benjamin W.(Z-M)	1838	Nov. 08	LickingCo,Oh	10	04	24
Brice, Benjamin W.(Z-M)	1838	Nov. 08	LickingCo,Oh	10	03	04
Brice, Ephraim(Z-M)	1837	April 29	Brooke CoVir	03	07	19
Bricker, Geo.(Z-M)	1831	March 26	HolmesCoOhio	04	08	05

PURCHASER	YEAR	DATE	RESIDENCE	R	T	S
Bricker, George(Z-M)	1821	Sept. 29	Jeff.Co.,Oh.	04	08	05
Briggle, Joseph(Y)	1828	March 07	Stark Co.,Oh	07	20	09
Briggs, Andrew(Z)	1828	Dec. 23	MuskingmCoOh	12	13	15
Briggs, Andrew(Z)	1836	March 29	Morgan Co,Oh	09	05	12
Briggs, Gordon(Z)	1823	Dec. 29	WashCo.,Ohio	10	08	13
Briggs, John(Z)	1828	Oct. 29	Morgan Co,Oh	12	11	29
Briggs, John(Z)	1828	Dec. 03	Morgan Co,Oh	12	11	29
Briggs, John(Z)	1835	Aug. 14	Morgan Co,Oh	13	09	12
Briggs, John(Z)	1805	Feb. 27	MuskingmCoOh	12	12	29
Briggs, John(Z)	1810	Sept. 26	MuskingmCoOh	13	09	19
Briggs, John(Z-M)	1829	May 27	Morgan Co,Oh	12	11	29
Briggs, William(Z)	1828	Oct. 29	Morgan Co,Oh	12	12	28
Bright, David(Z)	1816	Oct. 01	MuskingmCoOh	10	04	20
Bright, George(Z)	1814	March 17	GuernseyCoOh	01	03	20
Bright, Nicholas(Z)	1816	Oct. 30	MuskingmCoOh	10	05	21
Brightwell, John(Z-M)	1836	Sept. 14	HolmesCoOhio	09	08	21
Brill, George(Y)	1830	Nov. 26	GuernseyCoOh	07	09	26
Brill, George(Y)	1832	Oct. 20	GuernseyCoOh	07	09	32
Brill, Jacob L.(Z)	1832	Nov. 02	GuernseyCoOh	10	07	21
Brill, Jacob L.(Z)	1832	Dec. 20	GuernseyCoOh	10	07	21
Brill, John L.(Z-M)	1831	June 02	GuernseyCoOh	03	04	09
Brill, John(Y)	1828	Aug. 27	GuernseyCoOh	07	09	25
Brill, John(Z)	1806	Oct. 30	BedfordCo,Pa	01	02	07
Brill, Michael(Z)	1814	Dec. 16	GuernseyCoOh	01	01	01
Brill, Samuel(Z)	1814	June 01	LoudonCo,Vir	01	01	01
Brillhart, David(Z-M)	1836	Dec. 10	CoshoctnCoOh	08	07	12
Brillhart, David(Z-M)	1837	April 11	CoshoctnCoOh	08	07	19
Brillhart, Samuel(Z-M)	1832	Oct. 27	CoshoctnCoOh	08	07	18
Brillhart, Samuel(Z-M)	1836	Dec. 10	CoshoctnCoOh	08	07	03
Briltaur, Horace(Z-M)	1835	Sept. 23	CoshoctnCoOh	07	05	10
Brindley, Henry(Z)	1816	April 29	Jeff.Co.,Oh.	10	08	09
Brindley, Henry(Z)	1817	April 28	Jeff.Co.,Oh.	10	08	17
Brink, Abraham(Z-M)	1832	Oct. 03	HolmesCoOhio	08	08	13
Brink, Abraham(Z-M)	1836	Oct. 06	HolmesCoOhio	08	08	18
Brink, Abraham(Z-M)	1837	March 29	HolmesCoOhio	08	08	13
Brink, George(Z-M)	1836	Nov. 04	HolmesCoOhio	08	08	13
Brink, Jesse Runnels(Z-M)	1838	Dec. 05	HolmesCoOhio	08	08	17
Brink, Mordacai R.(Z-M)	1836	Oct. 31	HolmesCoOhio	08	08	13
Brink, Mordicai R.(Z-M)	1834	July 29	HolmesCoOhio	08	08	13
Brittaur, Horace(Z-M)	1835	Sept. 23	CoshoctnCoOh	07	05	10
Britthart, Sam'l.(Z-M)	1836	Aug. 17	CoshoctnCoOh	08	07	23
Britton, James(Z-M)	1835	Dec. 31	GuernseyCoOh	03	04	18
Britton, John(Z-M)	1833	Jan. 11	GuernseyCoOh	03	03	07
Britton, John(Z-M)	1836	Aug. 25	GuernseyCoOh	03	03	16
Britton, Robert(Z-M)	1833	Jan. 09	GuernseyCoOh	03	04	18
Britton, Robert(Z-M)	1836	Oct. 04	GuernseyCoOh	03	04	12
Broadebooks, George(Z-M)	1835	Nov. 07	HolmesCoOhio	09	09	14
Broadebooks, George(Z-M)	1835	Nov. 07	HolmesCoOhio	09	09	15
Broadelook, Jacob(Z-M)	1835	Sept. 10	MonroeCo.,NY	09	09	02
Broadibook, Jacob(Z-M)	1835	Sept. 05	MonroeCo.,NY	09	09	02
Brock, Casper(Z)	1820	July 17	MuskingmCoOh	13	10	35
Brock, Conrad(Z)	1820	July 05	MuskingmCoOh	13	10	34
Brock, Geo. S.(Z-M)	1835	Oct. 21	BelmontCo,Oh	03	06	06
Brock, Geo. S.(Z-M)	1835	Oct. 21	BelmontCo,Oh	03	06	06
Brock, Geo. S.(Z-M)	1835	Oct. 21	Belmontco,Oh	03	06	06
Brock, George S.(Z-M)	1832	Jan. 04	BelmontCo,Oh	02	06	21
Brock, George S.(Z-M)	1832	Jan. 04	BelmontCo,Oh	02	06	21
Brock, William(Y)	1831	June 25	TuscarwsCoOh	07	14	34
Brocker, John G.(Z)	1833	Nov. 26	MuskingmCoOh	13	10	21
Brodrick, James(Z-M)	1839	Nov. 20	Jeff.Co.,Oh.	09	08	17
Broegler, Francis(Z-M)	1836	Oct. 03	Stark Co.,Oh	10	08	12
Brombaugh, Conrad(Y)	1827	Dec. 28	Stark Co.,Oh	06	12	12
Brombaugh, Conrad(Y)	1828	Jan. 26	Stark Co.,Oh	07	20	06
Brombaugh, Conrad(Y)	1828	May 21	Stark Co.,Oh	08	12	01
Brombaugh, Conrad(Y)	1828	Dec. 20	Stark Co.,Oh	07	20	17
Brombaugh, Conrad(Y)	1830	March 30	Stark Co.,Oh	07	20	18
Brombaugh, Conrad(Y)	1832	Jan. 10	Stark Co.,Oh	08	12	12
Bronner, Bennett(Z-M)	1833	March 21	CoshoctnCoOh	09	06	21
Bronner, Bennett(Z-M)	1833	March 21	CoshoctnCoOh	09	06	21

PURCHASER	YEAR	DATE	RESIDENCE	R	T	S
Bront, Lewis(Z-M)	1837	Nov. 01	TuscarwsCoOh	03	07	15
Brooke, James(Y)	1822	Nov. 06	ColumbanCoOh	04	17	04
Brooke, Wm. Jr.(Z)	1827	Sept. 18	BelmontCo,Oh	08	04	11
Brooken, Jacob(Z)	1831	Nov. 30	Morgan Co,Oh	13	10	27
Brooks, Elisha(Y)	1831	Sept. 09	Jeff.Co.,Oh.	04	12	03
Brooks, Ezra(Z)	1834	Feb. 13	Morgan Co,Oh	10	08	21
Brooks, Henry(Y)	1829	July 15	HarrisonCoOh	06	14	04
Brooks, Isaac(Y)	1828	Dec. 02	Brooke CoVir	03	12	31
Brooks, John(Y)	1827	Nov. 22	HarrisonCoOh	05	13	33
Brooks, John(Y)	1828	Oct. 18	HarrisonCoOh	05	13	33
Brooks, John(Z)	1808	Jan. 30	FairfeldCoOh	10	01	19
Brooks, John(Z-M)	1836	Oct. 31	MuskingmCoOh	10	05	22
Brooks, Johnsey(Z)	1835	March 17	GuernseyCoOh	08	08	23
Brooks, Philip(Z)	1824	May 25	LoudenCo,Vir	10	07	07
Brooks, Philip(Z)	1826	Nov. 06	Morgan Co,Oh	10	07	07
Brooks, Thomas(Y)	1826	Aug. 19	HarrisonCoOh	06	14	03
Brooks, William(Z)	1830	March 11	ZanesvilleOh	11	11	33
Broom, Hugh(Z)	1836	Feb. 19	GuernseyCoOh	09	06	24
Broom, Hugh(Z)	1836	Feb. 23	GuernseyCoOh	08	06	19
Broom, Hugh(Z)	1836	Feb. 23	GuernseyCoOh	08	06	18
Broom, Hugh(Z)	1836	Oct. 03	GuernseyCoOh	08	06	13
Broom, Hugh(Z-M)	1836	Oct. 03	GuernseyCoOh	04	03	08
Broom, James(Z)	1836	Feb. 13	GuernseyCoOh	10	07	36
Broom, James(Z)	1836	Feb. 19	GuernseyCoOh	10	07	36
Brosnahan, Thos.(Z-M)	1831	Sept. 03	CoshoctnCoOh	08	06	12
Brothers, Abraham(Y)	1826	Nov. 25	Stark Co.,Oh	06	16	28
Brothers, Charles(Z)	1828	Dec. 10	HarrisonCoOh	11	10	26
Brothers, Charles(Z)	1829	Jan. 06	HarrisonCoOh	12	10	26
Brothers, Francis(Y)	1831	May 13	Stark Co.,Oh	06	15	06
Brothers, Francis(Y)	1832	April 27	Stark Co.,Oh	06	16	01
Brothers, Jacob(Y)	1829	Aug. 05	Stark Co.,Oh	06	16	30
Brothers, John(Z)	1832	Oct. 31	MonroeCo.,Oh	08	07	20
Brothers, John(Z)	1833	Oct. 15	MonroeCo.,Oh	08	07	20
Broton, Andrew(Z)	1833	May 17	Morgan Co,Oh	09	07	29
Broton, Andrew(Z)	1834	Feb. 28	Morgan Co,Oh	09	07	15
Broton, Solomon(Z)	1825	Nov. 23	Morgan Co,Oh	10	08	27
Broton, Solomon(Z)	1827	Jan. 04	Morgan Co,Oh	09	07	21
Broton, Solomon(Z)	1828	Nov. 11	Morgan Co,Oh	10	01	27
Brounsberger, Moses(Y)	1828	June 26	Stark Co.,Oh	09	10	11
Brous, Jonathan(Y)	1824	June 01	Stark Co.,Oh	09	11	11
Brous, Jonathan(Y)	1825	April 21	Stark Co.,Oh	09	11	11
Brout, Elias(Z-M)	1836	Oct. 15	TuscarwsCoOh	03	07	02
Brout, John(Z-M)	1833	June 28	TuscarwsCoOh	04	07	06
Brower, David(Y)	1831	Sept. 12	TuscarwsCoOh	06	13	30
Brown, Aaron(Z)	1814	April 22	LickingCo,Oh	11	05	25
Brown, Aaron(Z)	1815	June 20	KnoxCo.,Ohio	11	04	08
Brown, Adam Junr.(Z)	1806	Nov. 25	FayetteCo,Pa	11	01	12
Brown, Adam(Z-M)	1823	Dec. 17	LickingCo,Oh	11	01	10
Brown, Admiral N.(Z)	1836	Feb. 29	MonroeCo.,Oh	08	07	04
Brown, Alexander(Y)	1832	Feb. 01	Jeff.Co.,Oh.	04	12	21
Brown, Alexander(Z)	1833	July 26	Perry Co.,Oh	14	12	02
Brown, Alexander(Z)	1835	Jan. 07	CarrolCo.,Oh	10	08	26
Brown, Alexander(Z-M)	1833	Jan. 01	Morgan Co,Oh	07	07	11
Brown, Alexander(Z-M)	1835	Sept. 16	HolmesCoOhio	07	07	11
Brown, Andrew(Y)	1824	Aug. 17	TuscarwsCoOh	06	13	29
Brown, Archibald(Z)	1833	May 28	AlleghnyCoPa	10	06	03
Brown, Benj. Sen.(Z)	1830	Jan. 15	TuscarwsCoOh	02	10	25
Brown, Benjamin Jr.(Z-M)	1832	Sept. 21	TuscarwsCoOh	03	10	17
Brown, Benjamin S.(Z-M)	1836	March 21	Mt.Vernon,Oh	11	08	16
Brown, Benjamin(Z)	1831	Oct. 18	MuskingmCoOh	14	14	22
Brown, Benjamin(Z)	1815	May 30	LickingCo,Oh	11	05	19
Brown, Benjamin(Z)	1815	Dec. 02	KnoxCo.,Ohio	10	05	24
Brown, Charles(Z)	1826	March 10	Morgan Co,Oh	10	08	07
Brown, Charles(Z)	1832	Jan. 28	MuskingmCoOh	11	12	14
Brown, David(Y)	1823	June 18	TuscarwsCoOh	07	15	31
Brown, David(Z)	1815	Oct. 30	N.Phila.Penn	01	08	11
Brown, Dexter(Z)	1831	July 18	Morgan Co,Oh	09	07	19
Brown, Elias(Y)	1826	May 25	Stark Co.,Oh	06	18	21
Brown, George(Y)	1827	Oct. 16	Stark Co.,Oh	06	16	33

PURCHASER	YEAR	DATE	RESIDENCE	R	T	S
Brown, George(Z)	1835	Dec. 28	MonroeCo.,Oh	08	07	15
Brown, George(Z)	1835	Dec. 28	MonroeCo.,Oh	08	07	10
Brown, George(Z)	1837	Jan. 13	MonroeCo.,Oh	08	06	23
Brown, George(Z)	1817	June 13	BelmontCo,Oh	08	07	24
Brown, George(Z)	1817	June 13	BelmontCo,Oh	08	07	25
Brown, George(Z-M)	1826	May 01	HarrisonCoOh	02	06	20
Brown, George(Z-M)	1826	May 01	HarrisonCoOh	02	06	20
Brown, George(Z-M)	1833	Aug. 13	HarrisonCoOh	01	06	16
Brown, Henry(Y)	1825	Feb. 07	Stark Co.,Oh	08	12	21
Brown, Henry(Z)	1836	June 13	Perry Co.,Oh	14	12	05
Brown, Isaac(Z)	1807	May 19	MuskingmCoOh	15	16	19
Brown, J. B.(Z)	1834	Dec. 08	MonroeCo.,Oh	08	07	04
Brown, Jacob De(Z)	1810	April 06	Jeff.Co.,Oh.	02	02	02
Brown, Jacob(Y)	1831	July 23	Stark Co.,Oh	08	12	23
Brown, Jacob(Z)	1816	April 27	BedfordCo,Pa	08	04	06
Brown, James Jr.(Z)	1810	May 28	MuskingmCoOh	10	06	30
Brown, James Jr.(Z)	1813	Dec. 24	MuskingmCoOh	06	01	11
Brown, James Junr.(Z)	1804	Dec. 07	WashngtnCoOh	10	06	32
Brown, James Junr.(Z)	1805	Feb. 27	WashngtnCoOh	10	06	30
Brown, James L.(Z-M)	1836	Oct. 31	HolmesCoOhio	08	08	22
Brown, James Linzy(Z-M)	1836	Nov. 29	HolmesCoOhio	08	08	20
Brown, James(Z)	1830	Jan. 27	Perry Co.,Oh	13	08	09
Brown, James(Z)	1832	Sept. 07	Perry Co.,Oh	13	08	05
Brown, James(Z)	1836	Jan. 09	Morgan Co,Oh	13	08	05
Brown, James(Z)	1804	June 28	MuskingmCoOh	06	01	19
Brown, James(Z)	1806	May 13	MuskingmCoOh	06	01	11
Brown, James(Z)	1814	April 23	HarrisonCoOh	13	11	26
Brown, James(Z-M)	1829	March 27	LickingCo,Oh	11	01	21
Brown, Jer'h.(Z)	1814	Dec. 26	MuskingmCoOh	11	05	14
Brown, Jeremiah B.(Z)	1829	Aug. 08	FayetteCo,Pa	08	07	05
Brown, Jeremiah B.(Z)	1833	Jan. 12	MonroeCo.,Oh	08	07	05
Brown, Jeremiah B.(Z)	1836	Oct. 19	MonroeCo.,Oh	08	07	04
Brown, Jesse(Z)	1811	Oct. 23	MuskingmCoOh	10	06	12
Brown, Jesse(Z)	1815	June 06	FayetteCo,Pa	08	08	08
Brown, Jno. Senr.(Y)	1822	June 12	Stark Co.,Oh	06	15	22
Brown, John F.(Z)	1831	Sept. 10	BelmontCo,Oh	11	11	36
Brown, John G.(Z)	1824	Sept. 29	Morgan Co,Oh	13	08	17
Brown, John H.(Z)	1831	June 24	MuskingmCoOh	10	07	21
Brown, John M.(Z)	1834	July 28	Perry Co.,Oh	14	13	25
Brown, John M.(Z)	1836	March 17	Perry Co.,Oh	14	13	25
Brown, John M.(Z-M)	1836	Feb. 24	HarrisonCoOh	01	05	12
Brown, John M.(Z-M)	1836	Feb. 24	HarrisonCoOh	01	05	12
Brown, John R.(Z-M)	1833	Nov. 23	TuscarwsCoOh	02	07	01
Brown, John Senr.(Y)	1821	July 09	Stark Co.,Oh	06	15	19
Brown, John(Y)	1820	Nov. 14	WashCo.,Penn	07	11	13
Brown, John(Y)	1824	June 22	Stark Co.,Oh	06	18	22
Brown, John(Y)	1826	May 25	Stark Co.,Oh	06	18	17
Brown, John(Y)	1831	July 05	HarrisonCoOh	07	12	33
Brown, John(Z)	1829	Feb. 11	Morgan Co,Oh	11	10	19
Brown, John(Z)	1833	May 08	Morgan Co,Oh	10	08	20
Brown, John(Z)	1833	Aug. 06	Perry Co.,Oh	15	14	04
Brown, John(Z)	1833	Dec. 13	Morgan Co,Oh	10	08	20
Brown, John(Z)	1810	Nov. 01	WashngtnCo ?	14	15	29
Brown, John(Z)	1814	Oct. 19	Brooke CoVir	07	08	21
Brown, John(Z)	1814	Nov. 19	GuernseyCoOh	01	05	19
Brown, John(Z)	1815	Feb. 04	Brooke CoVir	07	09	18
Brown, John(Z)	1815	Feb. 04	Brooke CoVir	07	09	19
Brown, John(Z)	1815	Feb. 04	Brooke CoVir	07	09	22
Brown, John(Z)	1815	March 09	Brooke CoVir	07	09	21
Brown, John(Z-M)	1820	Nov. 08	WashCo.,Penn	01	04	21
Brown, John(Z-M)	1828	Jan. 16	GuernseyCoOh	04	02	02
Brown, John(Z-M)	1833	March 14	GuernseyCoOh	04	02	01
Brown, John(Z-M)	1835	March 17	GuernseyCoOh	04	03	03
Brown, John(Z-M)	1836	Jan. 16	GuernseyCoOh	04	03	03
Brown, John(Z-M)	1836	Feb. 24	HolmesCoOhio	03	07	02
Brown, John(Z-M)	1836	Feb. 24	HolmesCoOhio	03	07	02
Brown, John(Z-M)	1836	Sept. 07	ColumbanCoOh	09	08	17
Brown, John(Z-M)	1836	Nov. 10	ColumbanCoOh	09	08	17
Brown, John(Z-M)	1838	April 06	HolmesCoOhio	09	08	17

PURCHASER	YEAR	DATE	RESIDENCE	R	T	S
Brown, Joseph(Y)	1824	June 22	Stark Co.,Oh	06	18	17
Brown, Joseph(Z)	1836	March 10	MonroeCo.,Oh	08	06	07
Brown, Joseph(Z)	1810	Jan. 12	MuskingmCoOh	14	16	04
Brown, Joseph(Z)	1811	Jan. 26	MuskingmCoOh	03	10	24
Brown, Joseph(Z-M)	1822	March 24	CoshoctnCoOh	07	08	24
Brown, Josephus(Z)	1836	Aug. 05	MonroeCo.,Oh	08	07	29
Brown, Joshua(Z-M)	1833	Nov. 11	ColumbanCoOh	09	08	09
Brown, Joshua(Z-M)	1833	Nov. 11	ColumbanCoOh	09	08	12
Brown, Mason(Z)	1824	Feb. 20	GuernseyCoOh	10	09	19
Brown, Mason(Z)	1830	March 11	MuskingmCoOh	11	12	11
Brown, Mathew(Z)	1829	Jan. 20	Perry Co.,Oh	15	15	15
Brown, Michael(Y)	1822	June 24	HarrisonCoOh	07	12	22
Brown, Michael(Z-M)	1826	Aug. 08	HarrisonCoOh	01	06	21
Brown, Moses(Y)	1826	May 25	Stark Co.,Oh	06	18	21
Brown, Obadiah(Z-M)	1836	Dec. 16	HolmesCoOhio	08	08	21
Brown, Obadiah(Z-M)	1838	March 31	HolmesCoOhio	09	08	22
Brown, Parley(Z)	1806	Dec. 24	MuskingmCoOh	06	01	19
Brown, Parley(Z)	1816	May 04	MuskingmCoOh	06	01	19
Brown, Patrick(Z)	1835	Dec. 15	Perry Co.,Oh	15	15	30
Brown, Penley(Z-M)	1830	Jan. 13	MuskingmCoOh	06	01	19
Brown, Ralph(Z-M)	1831	March 03	CoshoctnCoOh	06	07	09
Brown, Rebecca(Z-M)	1836	Dec. 08	HolmesCoOhio	07	08	18
Brown, Richard(Z-M)	1821	Aug. 01	GuernseyCoOh	06	03	13
Brown, Robert(Z)	1825	Feb. 03	MuskingmCoOh	11	10	22
Brown, Robert(Z)	1811	April 11	GuernseyCoOh	04	02	23
Brown, Robert(Z-M)	1831	Dec. 01	Jeff.Co.,Oh.	01	09	22
Brown, Sam'l.(Y)	1828	June 20	ColumbanCoOh	03	13	31
Brown, Sam'l.(Y)	1828	June 20	ColumbanCoOh	04	14	25
Brown, Sam'l.(Z)	1832	June 02	Morgan Co,Oh	10	06	09
Brown, Samuel(Y)	1826	May 01	ColumbanCoOh	03	13	18
Brown, Samuel(Y)	1826	May 01	ColumbanCoOh	04	14	13
Brown, Samuel(Y)	1828	Sept. 30	ColumbanCoOh	03	13	30
Brown, Samuel(Y)	1829	Sept. 05	ColumbanCoOh	03	13	31
Brown, Samuel(Y)	1831	Aug. 29	ColumbanCoOh	03	13	30
Brown, Samuel(Y)	1832	Jan. 31	ColumbanCoOh	03	13	30
Brown, Samuel(Y)	1832	Dec. 22	ColumbanCoOh	03	13	31
Brown, Samuel(Y)	1832	Dec. 22	ColumbanCoOh	04	13	06
Brown, Samuel(Y)	1833	Oct. 12	ColumbanCoOh	03	13	31
Brown, Samuel(Y)	1833	Oct. 12	ColumbanCoOh	03	13	31
Brown, Samuel(Z)	1835	Aug. 26	Morgan Co,Oh	10	06	09
Brown, Samuel(Z-M)	1833	Sept. 14	CoshoctnCoOh	04	06	22
Brown, Solomon(Z)	1815	Dec. 08	?	09	07	33
Brown, T. G.(Z)	1816	March 20	FayetteCo,Pa	01	05	20
Brown, Uriah(Z)	1834	Feb. 26	MuskingmCoOh	11	12	10
Brown, Van S.(Z)	1826	Oct. 26	BelmontCo,Oh	13	08	09
Brown, William(Y)	1828	Oct. 03	WashCo.,Penn	05	11	29
Brown, William(Y)	1831	July 05	HarrisonCoOh	07	12	29
Brown, William(Z)	1826	June 28	MuskingmCoOh	10	09	19
Brown, William(Z)	1834	March 05	Morgan Co,Oh	10	07	19
Brown, William(Z)	1806	April 28	GreeneCo.,Pa	07	01	01
Brown, William(Z)	1811	April 02	MuskingmCoOh	11	13	07
Brown, William(Z)	1811	Dec. 11	GreeneCo.,Pa	11	13	05
Brown, William(Z)	1814	April 04	MuskingmCoOh	11	05	04
Brown, William(Z)	1815	Nov. 22	LickingCo,Oh	10	01	08
Brown, William(Z-M)	1824	Sept. 06	CoshoctnCoOh	09	04	13
Brown, William(Z-M)	1836	March 01	CoshoctnCoOh	09	04	15
Brown, William(Z-M)	1836	April 26	CoshoctnCoOh	09	04	16
Brown, William(Z-M)	1836	May 16	CoshoctnCoOh	09	04	15
Brown, William(Z-M)	1837	Feb. :6	TuscarwsCoOh	02	06	18
Brown, William(Z-M)	1837	Feb. 16	TuscarwsCoOh	02	06	19
Brown, Wm.(Y)	1822	Oct. 31	WashCo.,Penn	05	12	15
Brown, Wm.(Y)	1828	March 31	AlleghnyCoPa	03	05	14
Brown, Wm.(Y)	1829	March 13	Stark Co.,Oh	07	16	28
Brown, Wm.(Z-M)	1831	Aug. 29	BelmontCo,Oh	07	03	21
Brown, Wm.(Z-M)	1831	Sept. 22	MuskingmCoOh	03	01	06
Browning, L.(Y)	1825	Jan. 20	Brooke CoVir	02	07	11
Browning, William(Z-M)	1832	Aug. 13	CoshoctnCoOh	06	04	09
Browning, William(Z-M)	1837	Jan. 12	CoshoctnCoOh	06	04	01
Browning, Wm. R.(Z)	1816	March 18	WashngtnCoOh	14	15	20

PURCHASER	YEAR	DATE	RESIDENCE	R	T	S
Brownlee, James(Y)	1831	June 06	HarrisonCoPa	06	13	18
Brownley, John(Y)	1832	Oct. 23	ColumbanCoOh	03	12	03
Brownrigg, John(Z)	1831	Aug. 10	Morgan Co,Oh	10	07	11
Brubaker, Jacob(Z-M)	1839	Feb. 12	HolmesCoOhio	10	06	05
Bruce, Adam(Z-M)	1835	June 03	KnoxCo.,Ohio	10	05	19
Bruce, John Masterson(Y)	1835	May 12	CarrollCo,Oh	04	13	07
Bruff, Charles(Y)	1823	April 07	PhladlphiaPa	05	18	13
Bruff, James B.(Y)	1823	April 28	ColumbanCoOh	05	18	25
Bruff, James B.(Y)	1826	March 13	ColumbanCoOh	05	18	11
Brumbaugh, Geo.(Y)	1826	Dec. 15	Stark Co.,Oh	07	20	36
Brumbaugh, Jacob(Y)	1826	June 09	Stark Co.,Oh	08	12	02
Brumbaugh, Jacob(Y)	1832	Aug. 23	Stark Co.,Oh	08	12	02
Brumbaugh, John(Y)	1824	May 20	Stark Co.,Oh	08	12	15
Brumley, Peter(Z-M)	1831	June 16	GuernseyCoOh	01	05	09
Bruner, Jacob(Z)	1816	March 07	BedfordCo,Pa	09	04	10
Bruner, James(Z-M)	1832	Jan. 30	TuscarwsCoOh	03	08	14
Brush, Daniel(Z)	1836	Jan. 28	ZanesvilleOh	08	08	28
Brush, Daniel(Z)	1836	Feb. 02	ZanesvilleOh	10	06	35
Brush, Daniel(Z)	1836	Feb. 26	ZanesvilleOh	08	07	05
Brush, Daniel(Z)	1836	Jan. 21	ZanesvilleOh	14	12	24
Brush, Daniel(Z)	1836	Jan. 21	ZanesvilleOh	14	12	08
Brush, Daniel(Z)	1836	Jan. 21	ZanesvilleOh	09	08	18
Brush, Daniel(Z)	1836	Jan. 21	ZanesvilleOh	09	08	27
Brush, Daniel(Z)	1836	Oct. 15	ZanesvilleOh	14	12	17
Brush, Daniel(Z)	1836	Oct. 15	ZanesvilleOh	08	06	26
Brush, Daniel(Z)	1836	Dec. 17	ZanesvilleOh	09	08	30
Brush, Daniel(Z)	1837	Jan. 12	ZanesvilleOh	08	06	09
Brush, Daniel(Z)	1837	Jan. 21	ZanesvilleOh	09	08	23
Brush, Daniel(Z)	1837	March 27	ZanesvilleOh	15	14	35
Brush, Daniel(Z)	1837	June 12	ZanesvilleOh	14	12	34
Brush, Daniel(Z)	1837	June 12	ZanesvilleOh	14	12	34
Brush, Daniel(Z)	1837	Aug. 09	ZanesvilleOh	14	12	34
Brush, Daniel(Z)	1837	Nov. 06	ZanesvilleOh	15	14	34
Brush, Daniel(Z)	1838	June 11	ZanesvilleOh	10	04	09
Brush, Daniel(Z)	1838	June 15	ZanesvilleOh	08	05	02
Brush, Daniel(Z)	1815	July 13	CoshoctnCoOh	05	04	02
Brush, Daniel(Z-M)	1835	Dec. 28	ZanesvilleOh	10	05	23
Brush, Daniel(Z-M)	1835	Dec. 28	ZanesvilleOh	10	05	23
Brush, Daniel(Z-M)	1836	Jan. 23	ZanesvilleOh	10	05	12
Brush, Daniel(Z-M)	1836	Jan. 25	ZanesvilleOh	04	04	21
Brush, Daniel(Z-M)	1836	Jan. 25	ZanesvilleOh	04	06	22
Brush, Daniel(Z-M)	1836	Jan. 28	ZanesvilleOh	03	07	24
Brush, Daniel(Z-M)	1836	Feb. 04	ZanesvilleOh	10	04	08
Brush, Daniel(Z-M)	1836	Jan. 21	ZanesvilleOh	03	05	20
Brush, Daniel(Z-M)	1836	Jan. 22	ZanesvilleOh	04	04	02
Brush, Daniel(Z-M)	1836	Jan. 22	ZanesvilleOh	04	04	01
Brush, Daniel(Z-M)	1836	May 04	ZanesvilleOh	10	03	02
Brush, Daniel(Z-M)	1836	July 29	ZanesvilleOh	08	09	03
Brush, Daniel(Z-M)	1836	Aug. 01	ZanesvilleOh	08	06	02
Brush, Daniel(Z-M)	1836	Oct. 03	ZanesvilleOh	04	04	20
Brush, Daniel(Z-M)	1836	Nov. 30	ZanesvilleOh	03	06	02
Brush, Daniel(Z-M)	1836	Nov. 30	ZanesvilleOh	03	06	02
Brush, Daniel(Z-M)	1836	Dec. 03	ZanesvilleOh	03	08	17
Brush, Daniel(Z-M)	1837	Jan. 02	ZanesvilleOh	10	05	22
Brush, Daniel(Z-M)	1837	Jan. 10	ZanesvilleOh	04	03	02
Brush, Daniel(Z-M)	1837	Jan. 14	ZanesvilleOh	10	04	06
Brush, Daniel(Z-M)	1837	Feb. 09	ZanesvilleOh	10	08	22
Brush, Daniel(Z-M)	1837	Feb. 20	ZanesvilleOh	08	08	25
Brush, Daniel(Z-M)	1837	Feb. 23	ZanesvilleOh	04	05	19
Brush, Daniel(Z-M)	1837	March 06	ZanesvilleOh	10	06	04
Brush, Daniel(Z-M)	1837	March 06	ZanesvilleOh	10	02	25
Brush, Daniel(Z-M)	1837	March 14	ZanesvilleOh	10	08	18
Brush, Daniel(Z-M)	1837	March 14	ZanesvilleOh	10	08	23
Brush, Daniel(Z-M)	1837	March 14	ZanesvilleOh	10	08	19
Brush, Daniel(Z-M)	1837	April 03	ZanesvilleOh	03	08	25
Brush, Daniel(Z-M)	1837	Oct. 09	ZanesvilleOh	04	04	01
Brush, Daniel(Z-M)	1838	Jan. 29	ZanesvilleOh	07	08	16
Brush, Daniel(Z-M)	1838	Aug. 07	ZanesvilleOh	09	07	05
Brush, Daniel(Z-M)	1838	Aug. 15	ZanesvilleOh	04	03	04

PURCHASER	YEAR	DATE	RESIDENCE	R	T	S
Brush, Daniel(Z-M)	1838	Sept. 17	ZanesvilleOh	03	03	14
Brush, Daniel(Z-M)	1838	Nov. 21	MuskingmCoOh	04	03	03
Brush, Daniel(Z-M)	1838	Nov. 21	MuskingmCoOh	04	03	03
Brush, Daniel(Z-M)	1838	Nov. 21	MuskingmCoOh	04	03	04
Brush, Daniel(Z-M)	1838	Nov. 26	ZanesvilleOh	09	08	21
Brush, Daniel(Z-M)	1838	Nov. 26	ZanesvilleOh	08	08	25
Brush, Daniel(Z-M)	1838	Dec. 06	ZanesvilleOh	05	03	11
Brush, Daniel(Z-M)	1838	Dec. 06	ZanesvilleOh	05	03	08
Brush, Daniel(Z-M)	1838	Dec. 06	ZanesvilleOh	05	03	09
Brush, Daniel(Z-M)	1838	Dec. 06	ZanesvilleOh	04	03	06
Brush, Daniel(Z-M)	1838	Dec. 14	ZanesvilleOh	08	07	19
Brush, Daniel(Z-M)	1839	Jan. 24	ZanesvilleOh	08	06	07
Brush, Daniel(Z-M)	1839	Jan. 25	ZanesvilleOh	04	03	19
Brushal, John Frederick(Z-M)	1838	Nov. 17	MuskingmCoOh	04	04	09
Bryan, Cornelius(Z)	1835	Jan. 26	MonroeCo.,Oh	09	06	31
Bryan, David(Z-M)	1831	Jan. 28	CoshoctnCoOh	07	05	24
Bryan, David(Z-M)	1832	Sept. 06	CoshoctnCoOh	07	05	24
Bryan, James(Z)	1813	Aug. 20	FayetteCo,Oh	09	04	12
Bryan, Jno.(Z)	1813	Aug. 20	FayetteCo,Pa	09	04	12
Bryan, John(Z)	1829	April 03	MonroeCo.,Oh	08	07	03
Bryan, John(Z)	1833	Dec. 30	MonroeCo.,Oh	08	07	03
Bryan, Peter(Z)	1835	Jan. 26	MonroeCo.,Oh	09	05	07
Bryan, Peter(Z)	1835	Jan. 26	MonroeCo.,Oh	09	05	06
Bryan, Peter(Z)	1836	Feb. 12	Morgan Co,Oh	09	05	07
Bryant, J.(Z)	1817	May 03	CoshoctnCoOh	09	04	07
Bryant, William S.(Z)	1815	Oct. 03	MuskingmCoOh	14	14	06
Bryemoir, Mathias(Z-M)	1834	Nov. 20	TuscarwsCoOh	02	10	24
Bryson, Abraham(Z-M)	1835	June 02	GuernseyCoOh	03	01	05
Bubler, John Jr.(Z)	1827	Oct. 19	KnoxCo.,Ohio	10	08	11
Buchanan, Ar.(Z)	1813	Dec. 13	Ohio Co.,Vir	13	11	25
Buchanan, David(Z-M)	1831	May 30	WashCo.,Penn	02	04	20
Buchanan, George(Z)	1835	April 13	Morgan Co,Oh	11	10	13
Buchanan, John(Z-M)	1835	March 31	WashCo.,Penn	04	03	25
Buchanan, John(Z-M)	1835	Nov. 17	WashCo.,Penn	04	03	25
Buchanan, John(Z-M)	1835	Nov. 20	WashCo.,Penn	04	03	25
Buchanan, John(Z-M)	1837	April 04	GuernseyCoOh	04	03	05
Buchanan, Thomas(Z-M)	1834	Nov. 25	WashCo.,Penn	02	04	15
Buchel, John W.(Z-M)	1836	March 04	MuskingmCoOh	06	04	20
Bucher, Abraham(Z)	1834	Dec. 12	GuernseyCoOh	09	08	26
Bucher, Frederick(Y)	1826	Nov. 13	Stark Co.,Oh	06	19	32
Buck, Abraham(Z-M)	1835	March 18	GuernseyCoOh	02	06	01
Buck, John(Y)	1826	May 22	WashCo.,Penn	06	14	15
Buck, Kraft(Y)	1827	June 06	ColumbanCoOh	06	19	02
Buck, Rose(Z)	1814	Oct. 10	LickingCo,Oh	10	03	17
Buck, Thomas(Y)	1825	Oct. 03	WashCo.,Penn	06	14	14
Buck, Thomas(Y)	1826	May 22	HarrisonCoOh	06	14	15
Buck, William(Z)	1825	July 18	LickingCo,Oh	10	04	22
Buck, Wm.(Y)	1825	May 27	TrumbullCoOh	05	18	06
Buckanan, Joseph(Z)	1833	Sept. 30	MuskingmCoOh	12	13	34
Buckeloo, John(Z-M)	1839	Feb. 14	MuskingmCoOh	08	07	09
Buckey, George(Z)	1836	Dec. 10	Brooke CoVir	08	05	09
Buckey, George(Z)	1836	Dec. 10	Brooke CoVir	08	05	10
Buckhort, Venibles(Z-M)	1835	Feb. 27	CoshoctnCoOh	05	07	15
Buckingham, A.(Z)	1830	March 10	MuskingmCoOh	13	10	35
Buckingham, A.(Z)	1830	March 29	PutnamCoOhio	14	14	27
Buckingham, A.(Z)	1834	Dec. 06	PutnamCoOhio	13	10	03
Buckingham, A.(Z)	1835	Jan. 31	PutnamCoOhio	11	12	36
Buckingham, A.(Z)	1835	Dec. 19	PutnamCoOhio	15	14	02
Buckingham, A.(Z)	1835	Dec. 22	PutnamCoOhio	14	14	19
Buckingham, A.(Z)	1835	Dec. 24	PutnamCoOhio	09	07	27
Buckingham, A.(Z)	1835	Dec. 26	PutnamCoOhio	15	15	35
Buckingham, A.(Z)	1835	Dec. 28	PutnamCoOhio	13	08	20
Buckingham, A.(Z)	1835	Dec. 28	PutnamCoOhio	13	08	19
Buckingham, A.(Z)	1835	Dec. 28	PutnamCoOhio	13	08	17
Buckingham, A.(Z)	1835	Dec. 28	PutnamCoOhio	13	08	29
Buckingham, A.(Z)	1835	Dec. 28	PutnamCoOhio	13	10	02
Buckingham, A.(Z)	1835	Dec. 28	PutnamCoOhio	14	12	08
Buckingham, A.(Z)	1835	Dec. 29	PutnamCoOhio	15	14	01
Buckingham, A.(Z)	1835	Dec. 30	PutnamCoOhio	10	08	19

PURCHASER	YEAR	DATE	RESIDENCE	R	T	S
Buckingham, A.(Z)	1836	Jan. 28	PutnamCoOhio	08	07	04
Buckingham, A.(Z)	1836	Feb. 01	PutnamCoOhio	09	05	24
Buckingham, A.(Z)	1836	Feb. 03	PutnamCoOhio	10	07	23
Buckingham, A.(Z)	1836	Feb. 04	PutnamCoOhio	14	13	07
Buckingham, A.(Z)	1836	Feb. 09	PutnamCoOhio	15	14	05
Buckingham, A.(Z)	1836	Feb. 10	PutnamCoOhio	13	08	24
Buckingham, A.(Z)	1836	Feb. 10	PutnamCoOhio	13	08	06
Buckingham, A.(Z)	1836	Feb. 17	PutnamCoOhio	15	14	12
Buckingham, A.(Z)	1836	Feb. 20	PutnamCoOhio	13	10	02
Buckingham, A.(Z)	1836	Feb. 22	PutnamCoOhio	14	12	08
Buckingham, A.(Z)	1836	Feb. 22	PutnamCoOhio	13	08	33
Buckingham, A.(Z)	1836	Feb. 24	PutnamCoOhio	15	14	09
Buckingham, A.(Z)	1836	Feb. 29	PutnamCoOhio	09	05	23
Buckingham, A.(Z)	1836	Feb. 29	PutnamCoOhio	10	06	03
Buckingham, A.(Z)	1836	March 02	PutnamCoOhio	14	13	20
Buckingham, A.(Z)	1836	March 02	PutnamCoOhio	08	07	03
Buckingham, A.(Z)	1836	March 03	PutnamCoOhio	13	10	15
Buckingham, A.(Z)	1836	March 05	PutnamCoOhio	09	06	19
Buckingham, A.(Z)	1836	March 07	PutnamCoOhio	14	13	26
Buckingham, A.(Z)	1836	March 11	PutnamCoOhio	09	07	36
Buckingham, A.(Z)	1836	March 12	PutnamCoOhio	13	10	04
Buckingham, A.(Z)	1836	March 15	PutnamCoOhio	14	12	22
Buckingham, A.(Z)	1836	March 17	PutnamCoOhio	14	13	25
Buckingham, A.(Z)	1836	March 17	PutnamCoOhio	14	12	25
Buckingham, A.(Z)	1836	March 17	PutnamCoOhio	15	14	04
Buckingham, A.(Z)	1836	March 21	PutnamCoOhio	09	06	28
Buckingham, A.(Z)	1836	March 21	PutnamCoOhio	09	05	13
Buckingham, A.(Z)	1836	March 22	PutnamCoOhio	09	06	15
Buckingham, A.(Z)	1836	March 24	PutnamCoOhio	13	10	15
Buckingham, A.(Z)	1836	March 25	PutnamCoOhio	09	06	28
Buckingham, A.(Z)	1836	March 25	PutnamCoOhio	09	06	22
Buckingham, A.(Z)	1836	March 28	PutnamCoOhio	09	05	31
Buckingham, A.(Z)	1836	April 02	PutnamCoOhio	13	09	30
Buckingham, A.(Z)	1836	April 05	PutnamCoOhio	13	10	15
Buckingham, A.(Z)	1836	April '05	PutnamCoOhio	09	05	27
Buckingham, A.(Z)	1836	April 05	PutnamCoOhio	14	12	36
Buckingham, A.(Z)	1836	April 06	PutnamCoOhio	15	14	22
Buckingham, A.(Z)	1836	April 06	PutnamCoOhio	15	14	23
Buckingham, A.(Z)	1836	April 07	PutnamCoOhio	13	09	30
Buckingham, A.(Z)	1836	April 07	PutnamCoOhio	15	14	28
Buckingham, A.(Z)	1836	April 07	PutnamCoOhio	08	06	02
Buckingham, A.(Z)	1836	April 13	PutnamCoOhio	14	12	06
Buckingham, A.(Z)	1836	April 16	PutnamCoOhio	14	13	24
Buckingham, A.(Z)	1836	April 19	PutnamCoOhio	13	10	26
Buckingham, A.(Z)	1836	April 22	PutnamCoOhio	15	14	04
Buckingham, A.(Z)	1836	April 25	PutnamCoOhio	14	13	21
Buckingham, A.(Z)	1836	April 28	PutnamCoOhio	14	13	28
Buckingham, A.(Z)	1836	April 28	PutnamCoOhio	14	13	28
Buckingham, A.(Z)	1837	Jan. 06	PutnamCoOhio	13	08	06
Buckingham, A.(Z)	1837	Jan. 06	PutnamCoOhio	13	08	06
Buckingham, A.(Z)	1837	Jan. 06	PutnamCoOhio	13	08	06
Buckingham, A.(Z)	1837	Jan. 06	PutnamCoOhio	13	08	05
Buckingham, A.(Z)	1837	Jan. 19	PutnamCoOhio	13	08	34
Buckingham, A.(Z)	1937	Jan. 25	PutnamCoOhio	14	12	12
Buckingham, A.(Z)	1837	Jan. 25	PutnamCoOhio	14	12	12
Buckingham, A.(Z)	1837	Jan. 26	PutnamCoOhio	14	12	02
Buckingham, A.(Z)	1837	Jan. 26	PutnamCoOhio	14	12	03
Buckingham, A.(Z)	1837	Feb. 03	PutnamCoOhio	14	12	08
Buckingham, A.(Z)	1837	Feb. 03	PutnamCoOhio	14	12	13
Buckingham, A.(Z)	1837	Feb. 04	PutnamCoOhio	15	15	28
Buckingham, A.(Z)	1837	Feb. 08	PutnamCoOhio	14	12	36
Buckingham, A.(Z)	1837	Feb. 08	PutnamCoOhio	08	05	15
Buckingham, A.(Z)	1837	Feb. 08	PutnamCoOhio	08	05	15
Buckingham, A.(Z)	1837	Feb. 08	PutnamCoOhio	08	05	28
Buckingham, A.(Z)	1837	Feb. 10	PutnamCoOhio	15	14	25
Buckingham, A.(Z)	1937	Feb. 13	PutnamCoOhio	14	12	23
Buckingham, A.(Z)	1837	Feb. 14	PutnamCoOhio	14	12	03
Buckingham, A.(Z)	1837	Feb. 15	PutnamCoOhio	15	15	36
Buckingham, A.(Z)	1837	Feb. 16	PutnamCoOhio	14	12	23

PURCHASER	YEAR	DATE	RESIDENCE	R	T	S
Buckingham, A.(Z)	1837	Feb. 16	PutnamCoOhio	14	12	24
Buckingham, A.(Z)	1837	Feb. 16	PutnamCoOhio	14	13	35
Buckingham, A.(Z)	1837	Feb. 16	PutnamCoOhio	14	13	26
Buckingham, A.(Z)	1837	Feb. 17	PutnamCoOhio	15	14	02
Buckingham, A.(Z)	1837	Feb. 17	PutnamCoOhio	15	15	34
Buckingham, A.(Z)	1837	Feb. 18	PutnamCoOhio	14	13	22
Buckingham, A.(Z)	1837	Feb. 21	PutnamCoOhio	14	12	31
Buckingham, A.(Z)	1837	Feb. 21	PutnamCoOhio	14	12	31
Buckingham, A.(Z)	1837	Feb. 21	PutnamCoOhio	14	13	27
Buckingham, A.(Z)	1837	Feb. 28	PutnamCoOhio	15	14	31
Buckingham, A.(Z)	1837	March 04	PutnamCoOhio	15	15	25
Buckingham, A.(Z)	1837	March 07	PutnamCoOhio	15	14	03
Buckingham, A.(Z)	1837	March 07	PutnamCoOhio	13	08	30
Buckingham, A.(Z)	1837	March 08	PutnamCoOhio	13	10	10
Buckingham, A.(Z)	1837	March 08	PutnamCoOhio	13	10	10
Buckingham, A.(Z)	1837	March 09	PutnamCoOhio	08	05	28
Buckingham, A.(Z)	1837	March 14	PutnamCoOhio	15	14	34
Buckingham, A.(Z)	1837	March 15	PutnamCoOhio	14	13	22
Buckingham, A.(Z)	1837	March 15	PutnamCoOhio	14	13	27
Buckingham, A.(Z)	1837	March 17	PutnamCoOhio	15	14	32
Buckingham, A.(Z)	1837	March 20	PutnamCoOhio	15	15	23
Buckingham, A.(Z)	1837	March 20	PutnamCoOhio	15	15	24
Buckingham, A.(Z)	1837	March 23	PutnamCoOhio	14	12	36
Buckingham, A.(Z)	1837	April 10	PutnamCoOhio	08	05	29
Buckingham, A.(Z)	1837	June 12	PutnamCoOhio	14	13	35
Buckingham, A.(Z)	1837	July 01	PutnamCoOhio	14	13	34
Buckingham, A.(Z)	1837	July 01	PutnamCoOhio	14	13	34
Buckingham, A.(Z)	1837	Nov. 09	PutnamCoOhio	08	05	11
Buckingham, A.(Z)	1837	Nov. 09	PutnamCoOhio	08	05	12
Buckingham, A.(Z)	1837	Nov. 10	PutnamCoOhio	14	12	34
Buckingham, A.(Z)	1837	Nov. 10	PutnamCoOhio	14	12	10
Buckingham, A.(Z)	1837	Nov. 11	PutnamCoOhio	08	05	11
Buckingham, A.(Z)	1837	Nov. 11	PutnamCoOhio	08	05	03
Buckingham, A.(Z)	1837	Nov. 11	PutnamCoOhio	08	05	27
Buckingham, A.(Z-M)	1830	June 24	PutnamCo.,Oh	08	07	11
Buckingham, A.(Z-M)	1835	Jan. 23	PutnamCoOhio	10	03	05
Buckingham, A.(Z-M)	1835	Jan. 23	PutnamCoOhio	10	04	25
Buckingham, A.(Z-M)	1835	Feb. 18	PutnamCoOhio	11	08	18
Buckingham, A.(Z-M)	1835	Dec. 21	PutnamCoOhio	04	03	02
Buckingham, A.(Z-M)	1835	Dec. 30	PutnamCoOhio	03	06	07
Buckingham, A.(Z-M)	1836	Feb. 04	PutnamCoOhio	08	06	01
Buckingham, A.(Z-M)	1836	Feb. 10	PutnamCoOhio	06	09	25
Buckingham, A.(Z-M)	1836	Feb. 11	PutnamCoOhio	08	07	09
Buckingham, A.(Z-M)	1836	Feb. 11	PutnamCoOhio	07	05	08
Buckingham, A.(Z-M)	1836	Feb. 12	PutnamCoOhio	03	06	09
Buckingham, A.(Z-M)	1836	Feb. 13	PutnamCoOhio	10	04	03
Buckingham, A.(Z-M)	1836	Feb. 13	PutnamCoOhio	10	04	13
Buckingham, A.(Z-M)	1836	Feb. 17	PutnamCoOhio	03	04	01
Buckingham, A.(Z-M)	1836	Feb. 23	PutnamCoOhio	08	09	03
Buckingham, A.(Z-M)	1836	Feb. 23	PutnamCoOhio	08	09	03
Buckingham, A.(Z-M)	1836	Feb. 24	PutnamCoOhio	01	06	23
Buckingham, A.(Z-M)	1836	Feb. 24	PutnamCoOhio	01	06	22
Buckingham, A.(Z-M)	1836	March 05	PutnamCoOhio	08	07	20
Buckingham, A.(Z-M)	1836	March 11	PutnamCoOhio	03	04	07
Buckingham, A.(Z-M)	1836	March 15	PutnamCoOhio	02	03	18
Buckingham, A.(Z-M)	1836	Feb. 01	PutnamCoOhio	10	04	09
Buckingham, A.(Z-M)	1836	April 02	PutnamCoOhio	06	04	23
Buckingham, A.(Z-M)	1836	April 07	PutnamCoOhio	05	03	15
Buckingham, A.(Z-M)	1836	April 07	PutnamCoOhio	03	07	23
Buckingham, A.(Z-M)	1836	April 07	PutnamCoOhio	04	06	09
Buckingham, A.(Z-M)	1836	April 13	PutnamCoOhio	07	05	08
Buckingham, A.(Z-M)	1836	April 20	PutnamCoOhio	09	09	04
Buckingham, A.(Z-M)	1836	April 29	PutnamCoOhio	07	05	03
Buckingham, A.(Z-M)	1837	Jan. 28	PutnamCoOhio	03	05	21
Buckingham, A.(Z-M)	1837	Feb. 17	PutnamCoOhio	10	09	03
Buckingham, A.(Z-M)	1837	Feb. 17	PutnamCoOhio	10	08	12
Buckingham, A.(Z-M)	1837	Feb. 24	PutnamCoOhio	08	07	11
Buckingham, A.(Z-M)	1837	March 01	PutnamCoOhio	09	09	17
Buckingham, A.(Z-M)	1837	March 07	PutnamCoOhio	04	07	15

PURCHASER	YEAR	DATE	RESIDENCE	R	T	S
Buckingham, A.(Z-M)	1837	March 07	PutnamCoOhio	10	07	23
Buckingham, A.(Z-M)	1837	March 10	PutnamCoOhio	09	07	01
Buckingham, A.(Z-M)	1837	March 10	PutnamCoOhio	09	07	10
Buckingham, A.(Z-M)	1837	March 10	PutnamCoOhio	09	07	10
Buckingham, A.(Z-M)	1837	March 10	PutnamCoOhio	09	07	12
Buckingham, A.(Z-M)	1837	March 10	PutnamCoOhio	09	07	22
Buckingham, A.(Z-M)	1837	March 10	PutnamCoOhio	09	07	22
Buckingham, A.(Z-M)	1837	March 10	PutnamCoOhio	09	07	23
Buckingham, A.(Z-M)	1837	March 10	PutnamCoOhio	09	07	03
Buckingham, A.(Z-M)	1837	March 15	PutnamCoOhio	10	09	03
Buckingham, A.(Z-M)	1837	March 15	PutnamCoOhio	10	09	21
Buckingham, A.(Z-M)	1837	March 15	PutnamCoOhio	10	08	01
Buckingham, A.(Z-M)	1837	April 08	PutnamCoOhio	09	08	25
Buckingham, A.(Z-M)	1837	April 28	PutnamCoOhio	08	07	09
Buckingham, A.(Z-M)	1837	June 17	PutnamCoOhio	08	06	13
Buckingham, A.(Z-M)	1837	June 17	PutnamCoOhio	10	09	03
Buckingham, A.(Z-M)	1837	Sept. 30	PutnamCoOhio	04	04	02
Buckingham, A.(Z-M)	1837	Sept. 30	PutnamCoOhio	09	09	18
Buckingham, A.(Z-M)	1837	Nov. 04	PutnamCoOhio	09	09	17
Buckingham, A.(Z-M)	1837	Dec. 13	PutnamCoOhio	07	07	15
Buckingham, A.(Z-M)	1837	Dec. 28	PutnamCoOhio	08	09	03
Buckingham, A.(Z-M)	1837	Dec. 28	PutnamCoOhio	08	06	09
Buckingham, Alva(Z)	1823	Aug. 15	PutnamCoOhio	13	09	01
Buckingham, Alvah(Z)	1827	Sept. 11	MuskingmCoOh	10	01	03
Buckingham, Alvah(Z)	1828	May 13	MuskingmCoOh	12	12	31
Buckingham, Alvah(Z)	1828	July 23	MuskingmCoOh	12	11	32
Buckingham, Alvah(Z)	1829	Feb. 21	PutnamCoOhio	13	10	14
Buckingham, Alvah(Z)	1830	Jan. 20	PutnamCoOhio	12	12	19
Buckingham, Alvah(Z)	1830	Jan. 30	MuskingmCoOh	13	09	06
Buckingham, Alvah(Z)	1834	Jan. 10	PutnamCoOhio	15	15	28
Buckingham, Alvah(Z)	1834	Jan. 11	PutnamCoOhio	14	13	18
Buckingham, Alvah(Z)	1834	Jan. 14	PutnamCoOhio	15	14	36
Buckingham, Alvah(Z)	1834	Jan. 24	PutnamCoOhio	11	12	22
Buckingham, Alvah(Z)	1834	Jan. 28	PutnamCoOhio	13	08	34
Buckingham, Alvah(Z)	1834	Feb. 21	PutnamCoOhio	11	10	13
Buckingham, Alvah(Z)	1834	Feb. 22	PutnamCoOhio	15	14	04
Buckingham, Alvah(Z)	1834	Feb. 28	PutnamCoOhio	15	15	27
Buckingham, Alvah(Z)	1834	March 03	PutnamCoOhio	10	07	12
Buckingham, Alvah(Z)	1834	March 06	PutnamCoOhio	11	10	32
Buckingham, Alvah(Z)	1834	March 10	PutnamCoOhio	13	08	19
Buckingham, Alvah(Z)	1834	Aug. 12	PutnamCoOhio	10	06	15
Buckingham, Alvah(Z)	1834	Aug. 22	PutnamCoOhio	11	12	25
Buckingham, Alvah(Z)	1834	Oct. 09	PutnamCoOhio	15	14	22
Buckingham, Alvah(Z)	1835	Jan. 06	PutnamCoOhio	11	10	35
Buckingham, Alvah(Z)	1835	Feb. 07	PutnamCoOhio	11	11	15
Buckingham, Alvah(Z)	1835	March 02	PutnamCoOhio	11	11	02
Buckingham, Alvah(Z)	1835	March 02	PutnamCoOhio	11	11	01
Buckingham, Alvah(Z)	1835	May 25	PutnamCoOhio	11	12	24
Buckingham, Alvah(Z)	1835	May 26	PutnamCoOhio	11	12	24
Buckingham, Alvah(Z)	1835	July 08	PutnamCoOhio	13	08	26
Buckingham, Alvah(Z)	1835	July 30	PutnamCoOhio	15	14	22
Buckingham, Alvah(Z)	1835	Aug. 15	PutnamCoOhio	14	14	31
Buckingham, Alvah(Z)	1835	Aug. 19	PutnamCoOhio	15	14	01
Buckingham, Alvah(Z)	1835	Sept. 02	PutnamCoOhio	13	08	30
Buckingham, Alvah(Z)	1835	Sept. 15	PutnamCoOhio	13	09	02
Buckingham, Alvah(Z)	1835	Sept. 23	PutnamCoOhio	09	07	03
Buckingham, Alvah(Z)	1835	Nov. 11	PutnamCoOhio	08	07	14
Buckingham, Alvah(Z)	1835	Nov. 28	PutnamCoOhio	13	09	30
Buckingham, Alvah(Z)	1835	Nov. 28	PutnamCoOhio	13	08	05
Buckingham, Alvah(Z)	1835	Dec. 07	PutnamCoOhio	13	08	08
Buckingham, Alvah(Z)	1835	Dec. 08	PutnamCoOhio	08	07	30
Buckingham, Alvah(Z)	1835	Dec. 12	PutnamCoOhio	14	13	18
Buckingham, Alvah(Z)	1835	Dec. 12	PutnamCoOhio	10	08	37
Buckingham, Alvah(Z)	1836	Jan. 07	PutnamCoOhio	09	07	24
Buckingham, Alvah(Z)	1836	Jan. 13	PutnamCoOhio	15	14	04
Buckingham, Alvah(Z)	1836	Jan. 14	PutnamCoOhio	14	13	25
Buckingham, Alvah(Z)	1836	Jan. 16	PutnamCoOhio	08	05	02
Buckingham, Alvah(Z)	1836	Jan. 20	PutnamCoOhio	14	13	29
Buckingham, Alvah(Z)	1836	Jan. 25	PutnamCoOhio	13	09	30

PURCHASER	YEAR	DATE	RESIDENCE	R	T	S
Buckingham, Alvah(Z)	1836	Jan. 25	PutnamCoOhio	14	12	12
Buckingham, Alvah(Z)	1836	Jan. 25	PutnamCoOhio	14	14	12
Buckingham, Alvah(Z)	1836	Jan. 25	PutnamCoOhio	11	12	25
Buckingham, Alvah(Z)	1836	Jan. 28	PutnamCoOhio	14	14	19
Buckingham, Alvah(Z)	1834	Jan. 10	PutnamCoOhio	15	15	33
Buckingham, Alvah(Z)	1834	Feb. 11	PutnamCoOhio	15	14	09
Buckingham, Alvah(Z)	1836	Nov. 19	PutnamCoOhio	14	12	06
Buckingham, Alvah(Z)	1836	Nov. 19	PutnamCoOhio	14	13	26
Buckingham, Alvah(Z)	1836	Dec. 01	PutnamCoOhio	14	12	26
Buckingham, Alvah(Z)	1836	Dec. 03	PutnamCoOhio	14	13	21
Buckingham, Alvah(Z)	1836	Dec. 03	PutnamCoOhio	14	13	32
Buckingham, Alvah(Z)	1836	Dec. 03	PutnamCoOhio	14	13	33
Buckingham, Alvah(Z)	1836	Dec. 03	PutnamCoOhio	14	13	27
Buckingham, Alvah(Z)	1837	Jan. 03	PutnamCoOhio	08	05	28
Buckingham, Alvah(Z)	1837	Jan. 16	PutnamCoOhio	14	12	12
Buckingham, Alvah(Z)	1837	Jan. 16	PutnamCoOhio	14	12	02
Buckingham, Alvah(Z)	1837	Jan. 17	PutnamCoOhio	14	12	10
Buckingham, Alvah(Z)	1837	Jan. 17	PutnamCoOhio	15	14	29
Buckingham, Alvah(Z)	1837	Jan. 17	PutnamCoOhio	14	12	15
Buckingham, Alvah(Z)	1837	Jan. 17	PutnamCoOhio	15	14	29
Buckingham, Alvah(Z)	1837	Jan. 18	PutnamCoOhio	15	14	22
Buckingham, Alvah(Z)	1837	Jan. 18	PutnamCoOhio	09	08	24
Buckingham, Alvah(Z)	1837	Jan. 18	PutnamCoOhio	08	05	20
Buckingham, Alvah(Z)	1837	Jan. 18	PutnamCoOhio	08	05	29
Buckingham, Alvah(Z)	1837	Feb. 02	PutnamCoOhio	14	12	13
Buckingham, Alvah(Z)	1837	Feb. 02	PutnamCoOhio	14	13	27
Buckingham, Alvah(Z)	1837	March 18	PutnamCoOhio	08	06	19
Buckingham, Alvah(Z)	1837	March 24	PutnamCoOhio	14	12	27
Buckingham, Alvah(Z)	1837	March 24	PutnamCoOhio	08	06	12
Buckingham, Alvah(Z)	1837	March 28	PutnamCoOhio	14	12	26
Buckingham, Alvah(Z)	1837	April 24	PutnamCoOhio	14	13	36
Buckingham, Alvah(Z)	1837	May 05	PutnamCoOhio	08	06	10
Buckingham, Alvah(Z)	1837	May 10	PutnamCoOhio	15	14	35
Buckingham, Alvah(Z)	1837	Aug. 21	PutnamCoOhio	08	06	30
Buckingham, Alvah(Z)	1837	Sept. 08	PutnamCoOhio	08	06	02
Buckingham, Alvah(Z)	1837	Oct. 06	PutnamCoOhio	14	12	24
Buckingham, Alvah(Z)	1837	Oct. 14	PutnamCoOhio	14	12	13
Buckingham, Alvah(Z)	1837	Oct. 14	PutnamCoOhio	14	12	14
Buckingham, Alvah(Z)	1837	Oct. 30	PutnamCoOhio	08	05	26
Buckingham, Alvah(Z)	1837	March 18	PutnamCoOhio	08	06	19
Buckingham, Alvah(Z)	1837	Oct. 02	PutnamCoOhio	08	06	28
Buckingham, Alvah(Z)	1837	Oct. 02	PutnamCoOhio	08	06	28
Buckingham, Alvah(Z-M)	1826	April 10	PutnamCoOhio	10	02	18
Buckingham, Alvah(Z-M)	1829	Feb. 16	PutnamCoOhio	09	01	07
Buckingham, Alvah(Z-M)	1834	Jan. 08	PutnamCoOhio	10	02	18
Buckingham, Alvah(Z-M)	1834	March 21	PutnamCoOhio	07	08	21
Buckingham, Alvah(Z-M)	1835	Aug. 22	PutnamCoOhio	11	04	12
Buckingham, Alvah(Z-M)	1835	Aug. 22	PutnamCoOhio	11	04	12
Buckingham, Alvah(Z-M)	1835	Sept. 01	PutnamCoOhio	07	05	10
Buckingham, Alvah(Z-M)	1835	Sept. 05	PutnamCoOhio	10	09	03
Buckingham, Alvah(Z-M)	1836	Jan. 04	PutnamCoOhio	10	09	03
Buckingham, Alvah(Z-M)	1836	Jan. 13	PutnamCoOhio	02	06	03
Buckingham, Alvah(Z-M)	1836	Jan. 13	PutnamCoOhio	02	06	03
Buckingham, Alvah(Z-M)	1836	Jan. 13	PutnamCoOhio	09	09	04
Buckingham, Alvah(Z-M)	1836	Jan. 14	PutnamCoOhio	10	04	04
Buckingham, Alvah(Z)	1834	March 19	PutnamCoOhio	13	08	31
Buckingham, Alvah(Z)	1835	July 18	PutnamCoOhio	08	07	06
Buckingham, Alvah(Z)	1835	Nov. 06	PutnamCoOhio	13	10	03
Buckingham, A.(Z)	1836	Jan. 30	PutnamCoOhio	14	13	33
Buckingham, Alvan(Z-M)	1835	July 09	PutnamCoOhio	11	03	24
Buckingham, Alvah(Z-M)	1836	Jan. 04	PutnamCoOhio	10	09	03
Buckingham, Alvah(Z-M)	1836	Jan. 07	PutnamCoOhio	03	04	04
Buckingham, Alvah(Z-M)	1836	Jan. 25	PutnamCoOhio	07	04	10
Buckingham, Eben'r. Jr.(Z)	1824	June 09	PutnamCoOhio	13	11	13
Buckingham, Evan(Z)	1833	Feb. 11	MuskingmCoOh	12	12	21
Bucklew, A.(Z-M)	1831	Feb. 17	CoshoctnCoOh	08	06	01
Buckingham, Alvah(Z-M)	1835	July 09	PutnamCoOhio	11	03	24
Buckingham, Alvah(Z-M)	1837	March 13	PutnamCoOhio	09	08	22
Buckingham, Alvah(Z-M)	1837	March 13	PutnamCoOhio	02	01	15

PURCHASER	YEAR	DATE	RESIDENCE	R	T	S
Buckingham, Alvah(Z-M)	1837	April 05	PutnamCoOhio	09	03	17
Buckingham, Alvah(Z-M)	1837	Oct. 02	PutnamCoOhio	03	05	17
Buckingham, Alvah(Z-M)	1837	Oct. 02	PutnamCoOhio	03	05	17
Buckingham, Alvah(Z-M)	1837	Oct. 02	PutnamCoOhio	03	05	17
Buckingham, Alvah(Z-M)	1837	Dec. 11	PutnamCoOhio	03	06	01
Buckingham, Alvah(Z-M)	1839	April 06	PutnamCoOhio	10	06	13
Buckingham, Alvah(Z-M)	1839	April 08	PutnamCoOhio	10	06	07
Buckingham, Alvah(Z-M)	1837	March 13	PutnamCoOhio	09	08	25
Buckingham, Milton(Z)	1836	Dec. 09	PutnamCoOhio	15	14	21
Buckingham, Milton(Z)	1836	Dec. 12	PutnamCoOhio	08	06	26
Buckingham, Milton(Z)	1836	Dec. 13	PutnamCoOhio	14	12	04
Buckingham, Milton(Z)	1836	Dec. 14	PutnamCoOhio	14	12	14
Buckingham, Milton(Z)	1836	Dec. 14	PutnamCoOhio	14	12	03
Buckingham, Milton(Z)	1836	Dec. 14	PutnamCoOhio	14	12	14
Buckingham, Nich.(Z)	1816	Dec. 21	BaltimreCoMd	09	05	14
Buckingham, Walter(Z)	1836	Dec. 14	PutnamCoOhio	14	12	03
Buckleloo, John(Z-M)	1838	Oct. 17	CoshoctnCoOh	08	07	08
Bucklew, Andrew(Z-M)	1832	March 19	CoshoctnCoOh	08	06	10
Bucklew, Andrew(Z-M)	1836	Sept. 12	CoshoctnCoOh	08	07	20
Bucklew, John(Z-M)	1832	Sept. 15	HolmesCoOhio	07	08	17
Bucklew, John(Z-M)	1833	Sept. 07	HolmesCoOhio	07	08	23
Bucklew, John(Z-M)	1836	Sept. 12	CoshoctnCoOh	07	07	02
Bucklew, John(Z-M)	1837	March 30	CoshoctnCoOh	08	07	20
Bucklew, Nathan(Z-M)	1836	Oct. 07	CoshoctnCoOh	08	07	20
Bucklew, Samuel(Z-M)	1833	Feb. 01	CoshoctnCoOh	08	07	20
Bucklew, Wm. H.(Z-M)	1836	June 17	CoshoctnCoOh	08	07	20
Buckley, Samuel(Z)	1816	June 25	MuskingmCoOh	13	09	33
Buckley, Thomas(Z)	1836	April 20	Morgan Co,Oh	09	07	08
Bucklin, Jno. Jr.(Z-M)	1834	Feb. 06	HolmesCoOhio	07	08	16
Buckmaster, Corbin W.(Z-M)	1835	Nov. 03	ZanesvilleOh	04	06	13
Buckmaster, John(Z-M)	1833	Sept. 07	CoshoctnCoOh	06	07	06
Buckmaster, John(Z-M)	1837	April 21	HolmesCoOhio	08	07	02
Buckmaster, John(Z-M)	1840	April 10	CoshoctnCoOh	08	07	14
Buckmaster, Peter(Z-M)	1838	June 14	CoshoctnCoOh	08	07	10
Buckmaster, Peter(Z-M)	1838	June 14	CoshoctnCoOh	08	07	11
Buckmaster, Richard(Z-M)	1837	April 07	Wayne Co.,Oh	08	08	17
Budd, William(Z)	1807	Jan. 03	SomersetCoPa	03	08	06
Budd, William(Z)	1807	Sept. 07	MuskingmCoOh	03	09	21
Buffington, Ann(Z-M)	1821	Jan. 15	TuscarwsCoOh	01	05	06
Buffington, Ann(Z-M)	1821	April 08	TuscarwsCoOh	01	05	03
Buffington, Ann(Z-M)	1822	Sept. 05	TuscarwsCoOh	01	05	03
Buffington, Isaac(Z-M)	1821	April 08	TuscarwsCoOh	01	05	03
Buford, Daniel(Z)	1827	April 13	Morgan Co,Oh	09	07	31
Bugh, Barnhart W.(Z)	1834	Jan. 24	Perry Co.,Oh	15	15	34
Bugh, William(Z)	1816	Feb. 16	FairfeldCoOh	15	16	14
Bugher, Isaac(Z)	1828	Oct. 08	Morgan Co,Oh	09	07	09
Bullen, Alex.(Z)	1830	May 03	Morgan Co,Oh	11	10	27
Buller, James(Z)	1821	Jan. 13	Morgan Co,Oh	11	10	14
Buller, James(Z)	1822	Nov. 04	Morgan Co,Oh	11	10	23
Bumbgardner, Jacob(Z)	1816	Oct. 03	GuernseyCoOh	01	02	06
Bumgardner, Jacob(Z)	1828	July 16	MuskingmCoOh	14	14	12
Bumgardner, Jacob(Z)	1829	March 13	MuskingmCoOh	14	14	13
Bumgardner, Jacob(Z)	1832	May 01	MuskingmCoOh	14	14	12
Bumgardner, Jacob(Z)	1833	March 13	MuskingmCoOh	14	14	12
Bumgardner, Jacob(Z)	1808	April 15	MuskingmCoOh	14	16	15
Bumgardner, Jacob(Z)	1813	Aug. 17	MuskingmCoOh	14	16	15
Bumgardner, Jas.(Z)	1830	Dec. 20	MuskingmCoOh	13	11	30
Bumgardner, Rudolph(Z-M)	1836	Dec. 03	Stark Co.,Oh	05	04	08
Bumtrager, Abraham(Z-M)	1824	Aug. 18	TuscarwsCoOh	04	07	20
Bunfil, Alpheus R.(Z-M)	1837	Feb. 23	MuskingmCoOh	09	03	15
Bunnel, Jesse(Z-M)	1836	March 15	GuernseyCoOh	02	03	13
Bunnell, Richard(Z)	1827	Sept. 06	TuscarwsCoOh	03	09	10
Bunsen, Henry(Z)	1811	Oct. 23	WestmrldCoPa	04	09	20
Burch, William(Z-M)	1832	Feb. 14	MuskingmCoOh	08	03	14
Burchfield, Chas.(Y)	1829	July 14	Jeff.Co.,Oh.	06	14	11
Burchfield, Mathias(Z)	1810	Aug. 20	FredrickCo ?	03	09	11
Burden, David(Y)	1827	April 13	ColumbanCoOh	05	18	06
Burden, Reuben(Z)	1813	Feb. 19	GuernseyCoOh	01	03	22
Burden, Sam'l. S.(Z-M)	1833	Nov. 12	CoshoctnCoOh	09	07	03

PURCHASER	YEAR	DATE	RESIDENCE	R	T	S
Burden, Samuel J.(Z-M)	1835	Dec. 01	HolmesCoOhio	09	08	14
Burden, Stephen T.(Z-M)	1834	Sept. 25	CoshoctnCoOh	09	08	14
Burden, Stephen T.(Z-M)	1834	Sept. 25	CoshoctnCoOh	09	08	17
Burdin, T.(Z)	1815	Nov. 09	CoshoctnCoOh	09	07	08
Burg, Wm.(Z)	1810	Oct. 15	GreenCo.,Pa.	10	01	02
Burger, Christian(Z-M)	1832	May 08	TuscarwsCoOh	04	07	05
Burger, Christian(Z-M)	1833	March 21	TuscarwsCoOh	04	07	04
Burger, Daniel(Z-M)	1829	May 25	HolmesCoOhio	04	08	24
Burger, David(Y)	1822	June 28	Stark Co.,Oh	06	17	15
Burger, John(Z)	1811	Oct. 03	SomersetCoPa	04	08	25
Burger, John(Z)	1814	June 01	TuscarwsCoOh	04	08	25
Burger, John(Z)	1815	Feb. 27	TuscarwsCoOh	04	08	24
Burger, John(Z)	1815	Feb. 27	TuscarwsCoOh	04	08	17
Burger, John(Z-M)	1823	Aug. 13	TuscarwsCoOh	04	07	04
Burger, John(Z-M)	1829	June 16	CoshoctnCoOh	06	07	09
Burger, Sam'l.(Z-M)	1828	Feb. 08	HolmesCoOhio	04	08	15
Burges, John Junr.(Z)	1810	Oct. 25	SomersetCoPa	04	08	17
Burges, John Senr.(Z)	1810	Oct. 25	SomersetCoPa	04	08	16
Burges, Joseph(Z)	1808	May 16	MuskingmCoOh	15	17	18
Burgess, David(Z)	1817	Oct. 28	TuscarwsCoOh	01	05	16
Burgess, David(Z-M)	1829	March 20	TuscarwsCoOh	01	05	23
Burgess, James(Z)	1816	Nov. 09	FayetteCo,Pa	02	04	32
Burgess, Richard(Z)	1816	July 26	MuskingmCoOh	14	13	10
Burget, George(Y)	1828	Dec. 22	ColumbanCoOh	04	13	05
Burget, George(Y)	1835	Dec. 24	CarrollCo,Oh	04	12	05
Burgett, William T.(Y)	1829	Dec. 07	Jeff.Co.,Oh.	03	11	35
Burgoon, James(Z)	1815	Oct. 03	CambrayCo,Pa	13	10	32
Burgoon, Peter(Z)	1816	April 30	MuskingmCoOh	13	10	32
Burgoon, Peter(Z)	1816	July 30	MuskingmCoOh	13	10	31
Burk, David Junr.(Z)	1833	Sept. 19	GuernseyCoOh	09	08	09
Burk, James(Z)	1810	Sept. 22	MuskingmCoOh	15	16	09
Burk, John(Z)	1815	May 06	Jeff.Co.,Oh.	01	10	03
Burkhalter, Adam(Z)	1833	Aug. 26	MuskingmCoOh	13	11	12
Burkhalter, Adam(Z)	1833	Aug. 26	MuskingmCoOh	13	11	04
Burkhart, John(Z-M)	1827	Nov. 27	HolmesCoOhio	05	08	10
Burkhart, John(Z-M)	1831	April 15	HolmesCoOhio	05	08	10
Burkhart, Jos.(Z-M)	1830	July 05	CoshoctnCoOh	05	07	16
Burkhart, Venible(Z-M)	1821	Nov. 28	CoshoctnCoOh	05	07	16
Burkholder, John(Z-M)	1824	Aug. 28	TuscarwsCoOh	03	09	23
Burley, J.(Z)	1815	March 27	MuskingmCoOh	14	14	17
Burley, L.(Z)	1815	March 27	MuskingmCoOh	14	14	17
Burlingame, Asa(Z)	1835	Nov. 26	Morgan Co,Oh	10	08	13
Burlingame, Asa(Z)	1831	May 31	Morgan Co,Oh	10	08	13
Burlingame, Josiah(Z)	1833	June 22	Morgan Co,Oh	09	07	19
Burlingame, Rich'd.(Z)	1826	Nov. 14	Morgan Co,Oh	10	08	36
Burnhouse, Christopher(Y)	1821	Oct. 03	Jeff.Co.,Oh.	04	11	22
Burns, Daniel(Y)	1821	Oct. 04	ColumbanCoOh	04	16	15
Burns, Jacob(Z)	1836	Oct. 20	Morgan Co,Oh	13	08	19
Burns, James(Z)	1832	Dec. 03	Perry Co.,Oh	14	14	17
Burns, John(Z)	1816	May 24	AlleghnyCoPa	07	05	14
Burns, John(Z)	1816	May 24	AlleghnyCoPa	07	05	06
Burns, Joseph(Z-M)	1833	May 30	CoshoctnCoOh	07	05	11
Burns, Michael(Z)	1822	March 15	Morgan Co,Oh	12	11	27
Burns, Michael(Z)	1817	April 23	WashngtnCoOh	11	10	06
Burns, William(Y)	1831	March 05	HarrisonCoOh	06	12	30
Burnside, Wm.(Y)	1822	Oct. 01	HarrisonCoOh	07	11	21
Burnside, Wm.(Y)	1822	Oct. 01	HarrisonCoOh	07	11	15
Burntrager, Jos.(Z-M)	1828	Dec. 24	TuscarwsCoOh	01	08	02
Burr, Jacob(Z)	1833	Feb. 14	BelmontCo,Oh	11	12	35
Burr, William(Z)	1822	June 22	Jeff.Co.,Oh.	11	11	02
Burr, William(Z)	1833	March 20	BelmontCo,Oh	11	12	34
Burrall, Benjamin(Z)	1815	Feb. 04	CoshoctnCoOh	06	08	12
Burrall, Benjamin(Z)	1815	Feb. 04	CoshoctnCoOh	06	08	18
Burrea, John(Z-M)	1836	Dec. 10	TuscarwsCoOh	02	07	09
Burrel, Richard(Z)	1808	Nov. 30	TuscarwsCoOh	03	10	16
Burrel, Richard(Z)	1808	Nov. 30	TuscarwsCoOh	03	10	25
Burrel, William(Z-M)	1821	Jan. 11	CoshoctnCoOh	07	07	18
Burrell, Charles(Z-M)	1837	Feb. 02	LickingCo,Oh	11	04	22
Burrier, Andrew(Z-M)	1835	Nov. 17	CarrollCo,Oh	03	07	12

PURCHASER	YEAR	DATE	RESIDENCE	R	T	S
Burrier, Daniel(Y)	1827	Nov. 29	HarrisonCoOh	05	13	08
Burrier, Philip(Z-M)	1836	June 23	HarrisonCoOh	03	07	19
Burris, Benjamin(Z)	1834	Nov. 21	BelmontCo,Oh	13	08	26
Burris, Nelson(Z-M)	1836	Aug. 30	KnoxCo.,Ohio	10	08	06
Burris, William(Z)	1837	March 28	Morgan Co,Oh	10	07	33
Burrow, Richard(Z-M)	1832	Nov. 14	HarrisonCoOh	01	06	25
Burrows, James(Z)	1816	April 26	WashCo.,Penn	01	04	19
Burrows, Jesse(Z)	1836	April 12	GreenCo.,Pa.	08	07	32
Burrows, John(Z)	1829	Jan. 17	LickingCo,Oh	10	06	27
Burrows, John(Z)	1836	June 16	WashngtnCoOh	10	06	36
Burrows, John(Z)	1836	June 20	WashngtnCoOh	10	06	36
Burrows, Richard(Z-M)	1836	Feb. 01	HarrisonCoOh	02	06	23
Burrows, Thomas(Z)	1816	April 26	WashCo.,Penn	01	04	22
Burson, James C.(Y)	1828	Feb. 19	ColumbanCoOh	04	13	10
Burson, Silas(Z)	1831	Oct. 05	ColumbanCoOh	14	12	09
Burt, Daniel(Z-M)	1835	July 24	GuernseyCoOh	03	01	12
Burt, David Jr.(Z-M)	1833	Oct. 03	GuernseyCoOh	03	01	16
Burt, James(Z)	1810	Sept. 21	MuskingmCoOh	15	16	09
Burt, John(Z-M)	1824	March 02	GuernseyCoOh	02	01	05
Burt, Joseph(Z)	1831	April 13	GuernseyCoOh	10	09	23
Burtch, Thomas(Z-M)	1836	March 04	GuernseyCoOh	03	07	22
Burtnell, John(Z)	1816	Dec. 27	GreeneCo.,Pa	09	05	14
Burton, Edmund(Z)	1825	Nov. 23	Morgan Co,Oh	10	08	13
Burton, Edmund(Z)	1835	Dec. 02	Morgan Co,Oh	10	08	13
Burton, Edmund(Z)	1836	Dec. 24	Morgan Co,Oh	09	05	35
Burton, Lee S.(Z-M)	1833	Oct. 19	HarrisonCoOh	01	08	04
Burton, Shadrach(Z)	1836	Jan. 19	MonroeCo.,Oh	08	07	09
Burton, Thomas(Z)	1817	Oct. 27	FairfeldCoOh	09	06	23
Busby, Abraham(Y)	1822	Dec. 10	HarrisonCoOh	05	11	05
Busenberg, Peter(Z)	1810	Nov. 07	SomersetCoPa	10	06	21
Busenburg, Hugh Junr.(Z)	1816	Feb. 21	KnoxCo.,Ohio	10	06	20
Busenburgh, John(Z-M)	1828	May 22	KnoxCo.,Ohio	10	08	18
Buser, Wernhart(Z-M)	1833	Aug. 13	HolmesCoOhio	05	07	19
Bush, Daniel(Z-M)	1836	Jan. 19	ZanesvilleOh	05	04	16
Bush, George(Y)	1829	Oct. 06	ColumbanCoOh	06	19	30
Bush, George(Y)	1829	Oct. 06	ColumbanCoOh	06	19	30
Bush, George(Z)	1832	May 05	Morgan Co,Oh	13	10	33
Bush, John(Z)	1828	Aug. 22	Morgan Co,Oh	13	10	28
Bush, John(Z)	1805	Oct. 11	FairfeldCoOh	14	15	09
Bush, John(Z)	1805	Oct. 11	FairfeldCoOh	15	17	23
Bush, John(Z)	1805	Oct. 24	MuskingmCoOh	15	17	24
Bush, John(Z)	1805	Nov. 23	MuskingmCoOh	15	17	25
Bush, John(Z)	1806	March 08	FairfeldCoOh	15	17	35
Bush, John(Z)	1806	June 17	FairfeldCoOh	15	17	24
Bush, John(Z)	1812	Feb. 01	FairfeldCoOh	15	16	10
Bush, Leonard(Z)	1828	Aug. 22	Morgan Co,Oh	13	10	28
Bush, Nicholas(Z)	1806	Jan. 20	FairfeldCoOh	15	17	36
Bush, Nicholas(Z)	1806	Jan. 20	FairfeldCoOh	15	16	02
Bush, Richard(Z)	1825	Sept. 06	MuskingmCoOh	11	12	21
Bush, Shadrach(Z-M)	1825	Jan. 04	Baltimore,Md	09	05	14
Bush, Thomas(Z)	1825	Aug. 13	MuskingmCoOh	11	12	21
Bushholder, John(Z)	1809	Sept. 20	TuscarwsCoOh	03	09	22
Bushong, John(Y)	1825	June 24	Stark Co.,Oh	06	16	31
Butler, Benj. Senr.(Z-M)	1828	Feb. 01	KnoxCo.,Ohio	10	07	23
Butler, Benjamin(Z)	1813	May 26	KnoxCo.,Ohio	10	07	23
Butler, Caleb(Z)	1836	March 02	MuskingmCoOh	12	12	28
Butler, Elisha(Y)	1824	Sept. 20	Stark Co.,Oh	07	20	14
Butler, Isaac(Z-M)	1833	Feb. 13	CoshoctnCoOh	08	06	03
Butler, Isaac(Z-M)	1836	Sept. 23	RichlandCoOh	08	06	04
Butler, James(Z)	1830	April 12	Morgan Co,Oh	11	10	25
Butler, James(Z)	1806	Sept. 08	MuskingmCoOh	10	08	10
Butler, James(Z)	1807	May 04	MuskingmCoOh	10	08	20
Butler, James(Z)	1813	Dec. 24	KnoxCo.,Ohio	10	08	10
Butler, James(Z)	1815	Jan. 05	KnoxCo.,Ohio	09	08	06
Butler, James(Z)	1816	April 04	KnoxCo.,Ohio	10	08	10
Butler, James(Z)	1807	Oct. 24	MuskingmCoOh	15	18	12
Butler, Jefferson(Z-M)	1832	Nov. 06	CoshoctnCoOh	08	06	09
Butler, Jesse(Z-M)	1831	Dec. 30	HolmesCoOhio	08	08	20
Butler, Jesse(Z-M)	1832	June 30	CoshoctnCoOh	07	08	16

PURCHASER	YEAR	DATE	RESIDENCE	R	T	S
Butler, Jesse(Z-M)	1832	Oct. 11	HolmesCoOhio	08	08	11
Butler, John Jr.(Z-M)	1828	Sept. 04	HolmesCoOhio	08	08	20
Butler, John(Z)	1806	Sept. 08	MuskingmCoOh	10	09	19
Butler, John(Z)	1806	Oct. 04	MuskingmCoOh	10	07	20
Butler, John(Z)	1807	Oct. 05	MuskingmCoOh	10	09	22
Butler, John(Z)	1813	April 09	KnoxCo.,Ohio	07	08	25
Butler, John(Z)	1813	Sept. 10	KnoxCo.,Ohio	07	08	16
Butler, John(Z)	1816	Jan. 23	KnoxCo.,Ohio	10	07	20
Butler, John(Z-M)	1837	March 18	HolmesCoOhio	08	08	20
Butler, Joseph(Z)	1805	March 02	MuskingmCoOh	08	06	15
Butler, Joseph(Z)	1807	Jan. 20	MuskingmCoOh	10	09	19
Butler, Laurence W.(Y)	1828	Sept. 08	ColumbanCoOh	06	16	13
Butler, Lawrence W.(Y)	1824	Feb. 07	ColumbanCoOh	05	18	11
Butler, Levi L.(Z-M)	1832	Nov. 21	HolmesCoOhio	09	08	01
Butler, Noah(Z-M)	1836	March 26	CoshoctnCoOh	09	07	21
Butler, Noah(Z-M)	1836	Sept. 06	CoshoctnCoOh	09	07	22
Butler, Stephen(Z)	1806	Aug. 01	MuskingmCoOh	10	09	22
Butler, Thomas(Z)	1804	Dec. 01	MuskingmCoOh	08	06	15
Butler, Thomas(Z)	1804	Dec. 01	MuskingmCoOh	08	06	06
Butler, Thos.(Z)	1804	Nov. 30	MuskingmCoOh	07	05	01
Butler, Thos.(Z)	1804	Dec. 01	MuskingmCoOh	07	05	01
Butler,Thos.byPeterCaseyEx(Z-M	1833	Jan. 07	HolmesCoOhio	07	08	02
Butt, Benjamin(Z)	1817	Feb. 06	TuscarwsCoOh	03	09	10
Butt, Edward(Z)	1827	Jan. 02	MuskingmCoOh	13	09	18
Butt, Geo. W.(Z)	1833	Aug. 30	Morgan Co,Oh	09	06	33
Butt, Hazael(Z)	1836	April 16	Morgan Co,Oh	13	09	32
Butt, Hazel(Z)	1824	Nov. 19	MuskingmCoOh	13	11	19
Butt, Jacob(Z-M)	1835	Feb. 18	TuscarwsCoOh	02	08	13
Butt, Jacob(Z-M)	1834	Jan. 11	TuscarwsCoOh	02	08	14
Butt, Jacob(Z-M)	1837	Jan. 25	TuscarwsCoOh	02	07	05
Butt, Jacob(Z-M)	1837	Jan. 25	TuscarwsCoOh	02	07	05
Butt, James(Z-M)	1827	April 09	TuscarwsCoOh	02	07	08
Butt, William Junr.(Z)	1811	April 04	TuscarwsCoOh	02	08	18
Butt, William(Z-M)	1833	Dec. 10	TuscarwsCoOh	02	08	14
Butt, Zach'h.(Z)	1815	Jan. 05	MuskingmCoOh	13	11	15
Butter, James(Z)	1827	Sept. 03	CoshoctnCoOh	08	06	06
Butter, John(Z-M)	1835	Dec. 07	HolmesCoOhio	07	08	16
Butter, Thomas Senr.(Z-M)	1822	April 17	WayneCo.,Oh.	07	08	02
Butterfield, Jno.(Y)	1827	Jan. 23	HarrisonCoOh	06	13	12
Butterfield, John(Y)	1830	Jan. 07	HarrisonCoOh	06	13	11
Butterfield, Thos.(Y)	1827	July 16	HarrisonCoOh	06	13	11
Buttes, Jno.(Z)	1832	Oct. 27	Morgan Co,Oh	13	08	19
Buy, Archibald(Z)	1816	Dec. 11	GuernseyCoOh	10	09	30
Buy, Benjamin(Z)	1817	Jan. 02	GuernseyCoOh	10	09	27
Buyen, Caleb(Z)	1816	Dec. 02	LickingCo,Oh	10	03	25
Buyen, Jno.(Z)	1816	Dec. 02	LickingCo,Oh	10	03	25
Buzzard, Peter(Z-M)	1827	Jan. 25	HolmesCoOhio	04	08	06
Bye, Godleib(Z-M)	1832	Oct. 11	HolmesCoOhio	03	10	15
Bye, J.(Z-M)	1820	Sept. 16	GuernseyCoOh	02	01	06
Bye, Jonathan(Z-M)	1832	March 03	GuernseyCoOh	02	01	06
Bye, Jonathan(Z-M)	1836	March 18	GuernseyCoOh	02	01	06
Bye, Jonathan(Z-M)	1836	Oct. 25	GuernseyCoOh	02	01	06
Byer, John(Y)	1826	June 29	Stark Co.,Oh	06	18	26
Byers, Andrew(Z)	1815	Oct. 21	BelmontCo,Oh	09	07	30
Byers, Andrew(Z)	1815	Oct. 23	BelmontCo,Oh	10	08	25
Byers, Andrew(Z)	1815	Nov. 27	BelmontCo,Oh	13	09	34
Byers, James(Z)	1833	Oct. 21	Morgan Co,Oh	10	06	03
Byers, John(Y)	1832	Dec. 18	Stark Co.,Oh	06	17	34
Byers, John(Z)	1835	Sept. 17	Morgan Co,Oh	10	06	29
Byers, Samuel(Z)	1835	Nov. 21	Morgan Co,Oh	10	08	26
Byers, Thos.(Z)	1833	Nov. 22	Morgan Co,Oh	09	07	30
Byers, Wm.(Z)	1832	Jan. 19	Morgan Co,Oh	09	07	19
Byrnes, Thomas(Z)	1835	Dec. 02	MonroeCo.,Oh	08	07	14
Cabbison, Andrew McC.(Z)	1834	Sept. 29	Perry Co.,Oh	15	14	06
Cabeem, Thomas(Z)	1809	Sept. 27	WashngtnCoOh	11	13	06
Cable, Jonathan(Z-M)	1830	May 04	TuscarwsCoOh	01	10	07
Cable, Jonathan(Z-M)	1831	Jan. 24	Stark Co.,Oh	01	10	04
Cables, Benjamin(Z)	1817	Jan. 04	SomersetCoPa	01	10	04
Cackler, Abraham(Z)	1816	April 05	TrumbullCoOh	10	05	09

PURCHASER	YEAR	DATE	RESIDENCE	R	T	S
Cadwalader, John(Z)	1812	Sept. 21	TuscarwsCoOh	01	05	20
Cadwalader, John(Z)	1812	Sept. 21	TuscarwsCoOh	01	05	20
Cadwallader, Jno. Junr.(Z)	1817	Jan. 16	TuscarwsCoOh	01	05	12
Cadwell, Mary(Z)	1817	Aug. 01	MariettaOhio	09	05	15
Cadwell, Mary(Z)	1817	Aug. 01	MariettaOhio	09	05	14
Cady, Peter(Z)	1816	Feb. 02	WashngtnCoOh	11	11	20
Caeims, James S.(Z)	1834	Feb. 19	MuskinqmCoOh	10	09	23
Cahill, David(Z-M)	1835	April 25	CarrolCo.,Oh	03	07	19
Cahill, Griffith(Z-M)	1831	Aug. 03	TuscarwsCoOh	01	06	10
Cain, Abel(Z)	1815	Oct. 20	CoshoctnCoOh	07	05	15
Cain, Aron(Z-M)	1835	Feb. 10	CoshoctnCoOh	07	05	03
Calahan, Marg't.(Z)	1826	July 19	Morgan Co,Oh	12	10	36
Calden, James(Z)	1814	Jan. 10	CoshoctnCoOh	07	05	17
Calder, James(Z)	1814	Feb. 14	CoshoctnCoOh	05	05	24
Calder, Jno.(Y)	1825	April 11	ColumbanCoOh	02	09	32
Calder, John Senr.(Y)	1829	March 17	ColumbanCoOh	02	09	31
Caldwell, David(Z)	1833	Nov. 07	Morgan Co,Oh	09	06	09
Caldwell, Ebenezer(Z)	1816	May 28	WestmrldCoPa	11	13	21
Caldwell, James(Z)	1826	Aug. 07	BelmontCo,Oh	09	06	07
Caldwell, James(Z)	1805	Sept. 12	BelmontCo,Oh	01	03	14
Caldwell, James(Z)	1807	Nov. 25	MuskingmCoOh	11	13	14
Caldwell, James(Z)	1812	April 07	BelmontCo,Oh	15	17	22
Caldwell, James(Z)	1815	Nov. 01	MuskingmCoOh	07	05	18
Caldwell, John(Z)	1835	Dec. 28	Morgan Co,Oh	09	06	09
Caldwell, John(Z)	1808	Jan. 22	FayetteCo,Pa	02	01	01
Caldwell, Levi(Z-M)	1837	June 27	SenecaCoOhio	03	05	24
Caldwell, Levi(Z-M)	1838	Dec. 15	TuscarwsCoOh	03	04	04
Caldwell, Robert(Z)	1820	Sept. 12	Morgan Co,Oh	09	06	03
Caldwell, Robert(Z)	1834	Aug. 23	Morgan Co,Oh	09	07	31
Caldwell, Robert(Z)	1805	Dec. 05	WashngtnCoOh	09	06	03
Caldwell, Robert(Z)	1811	Nov. 08	GuernseyCoOh	09	06	03
Caldwell, Robert(Z)	1815	Oct. 23	GuernseyCoOh	09	07	34
Caldwell, Sam'l.(Z)	1825	April 06	Morgan Co,Oh	09	06	04
Caldwell, Sam'l.(Z)	1832	June 07	Morgan Co,Oh	09	07	35
Caldwell, Sam'l.(Z)	1830	Jan. 11	Morgan Co,Oh	09	08	34
Caldwell, Samuel Jnr.(Z-M)	1836	Dec. 14	TuscarwsCoOh	03	05	24
Caldwell, Samuel Jr.(Z-M)	1837	March 11	TuscarwsCoOh	03	05	24
Caldwell, Samuel Jr.(Z-M)	1839	Feb. 28	TuscarwsCoOh	03	05	15
Caldwell, Samuel Sr.(Z-M)	1838	Dec. 15	TuscarwsCoOh	03	05	16
Calhon, John(Z)	1811	Nov. 12	SomersetCoPa	15	15	04
Calhoon, David(Z)	1807	June 12	AlleghnyCoPa	05	01	23
Calhoon, David(Z)	1807	June 26	AlleghnyCoPa	10	09	06
Calhoon, David(Z)	1808	May 23	AlleghnyCoPa	11	13	03
Calhoon, David(Z)	1816	Dec. 02	BeaverCo.,Pa	07	09	11
Calhoon, David(Z-M)	1828	Dec. 25	HolmesCoOhio	06	09	15
Calhoon, James(Z-M)	1833	March 19	HolmesCoOhio	06	09	24
Calhoon, James(Z-M)	1833	March 19	HolmesCoOhio	06	09	24
Calhoon, Jane(Z-M)	1836	May 09	MuskingmCoOh	06	03	01
Calhoon, John(Z)	1807	Oct. 16	MuskingmCoOh	10	01	20
Calhoon, Milton(Z-M)	1826	June 10	HolmesCoOhio	07	08	11
Calhoon, Milton(Z-M)	1833	Jan. 18	HolmesCoOhio	06	09	24
Calhoon, Milton(Z-M)	1835	Sept. 28	HolmesCoOhio	06	09	24
Calhoun, Adley(Y)	1830	Jan. 13	Jeff.Co.,Oh.	04	12	08
Calhoun, Sam'l.(Z-M)	1823	July 02	CoshoctnCoOh	07	09	21
Caliman, Benjamin(Z)	1829	May 27	MuskingmCoOh	11	12	26
Caliman, Benjamin(Z)	1833	Nov. 13	MuskinqmCoOh	11	12	26
Caliman, John(Z)	1835	Sept. 07	MuskinqmCoOh	11	12	34
Call, David(Y)	1826	Sept. 07	Jeff.Co.,Oh.	03	12	35
Call, David(Y)	1828	Aug. 16	Jeff.Co.,Oh.	03	11	30
Call, David(Y)	1828	Aug. 25	Jeff.Co.,Oh.	03	11	29
Call, David(Y)	1828	Oct. 04	Jeff.Co.,Oh.	03	11	30
Call, David(Y)	1833	Oct. 02	Jeff.Co.,Oh.	03	11	11
Call, Henry(Y)	1825	Oct. 13	Jeff.Co.,Oh.	02	08	35
Call, Henry(Y)	1828	Jan. 23	Jeff.Co.,Oh.	03	11	18
Call, Jas.(Z)	1823	June 21	Perry Co.,Oh	15	16	36
Callaghan, Thomas(Z)	1835	April 13	Morgan Co,Oh	10	06	18
Callantine, Henry(Z-M)	1836	Dec. 31	TuscarwsCoOh	03	05	23
Callantine, Henry(Z-M)	1836	Dec. 31	CoshoctnCoOh	03	04	03
Callender, Thomas(Z-M)	1832	March 27	TuscarwsCoOh	01	09	21

PURCHASER	YEAR	DATE	RESIDENCE	R	T	S
Callendine, Henry(Z-M)	1828	June 16	GuernseyCoOh	01	03	24
Callihan, Elias(Y)	1826	Nov. 18	ColumbanCoOh	06	19	14
Calvert, Hiram(Z)	1835	Nov. 13	Morgan Co,Oh	10	08	12
Calvert, John Junr.(Y)	1831	July 05	BelmontCo,Oh	04	06	13
Camble, William(Z)	1817	Sept. 04	GuernseyCoOh	08	07	25
Camblit, Andrew(Z)	1829	Dec. 21	Morgan Co,Oh	09	07	07
Cameron, Absalom(Y)	1827	May 25	ColumbanCoOh	06	18	23
Cameron, Alex'r.(Y)	1826	Aug. 25	Stark Co.,Oh	07	16	29
Cameron, Alex'r.(Y)	1829	March 13	Stark Co.,Oh	07	16	36
Cameron, Alexander(Y)	1823	Nov. 24	Stark Co.,Oh	07	16	36
Cameron, Alexander(Y)	1831	May 11	Stark Co.,Oh	07	16	34
Cameron, Alexander(Y)	1831	May 11	Stark Co.,Oh	07	16	34
Cameron, Eliel(Y)	1826	April 28	ColumbanCoOh	05	17	06
Cameron, John(Y)	1827	June 06	ColumbanCoOh	06	16	36
Cameron, Nancy(Y)	1830	Nov. 16	PittsburghPa	03	13	23
Cameron, Robert(Y)	1828	Feb. 01	ColumbanCoOh	05	15	09
Cameron, Sam'l.(Y)	1828	Aug. 18	Stark Co.,Oh	07	16	29
Cameron, William(Y)	1825	July 13	PittsburghPa	03	13	28
Camerson, Samuel(Y)	1829	June 30	Stark Co.,Oh	07	16	29
Camp, Robert(Z-M)	1827	June 26	GuernseyCoOh	04	01	12
Camp, Thomas(Z-M)	1827	Aug. 03	GuernseyCoOh	04	01	11
Campbell, Alexander(Z)	1815	Feb. 04	Brooke CoVir	07	09	22
Campbell, Andrew(Z-M)	1837	Jan. 18	KnoxCo.,Ohio	10	09	23
Campbell, Archibald(Z)	1809	April 18	WashngtnCo ?	05	01	24
Campbell, Archibald(Z)	1814	April 20	MuskingmCoOh	11	13	29
Campbell, Arh'd.(Z)	1809	April 18	WashngtnCo ?	05	01	24
Campbell, Dan'l.(Z-M)	1832	Jan. 16	KnoxCo.,Ohio	10	06	15
Campbell, Daniel(Z-M)	1832	Jan. 30	KnoxCo.,Ohio	10	06	17
Campbell, Daniel(Z-M)	1830	Feb. 09	KnoxCo.,Ohio	10	06	15
Campbell, Daniel(Z-M)	1833	Jan. 24	KnoxCo.,Ohio	10	06	14
Campbell, Daniel(Z-M)	1835	Jan. 06	KnoxCo.,Ohio	10	06	14
Campbell, David(Z)	1813	June 03	MuskingmCoOh	15	18	11
Campbell, David(Z)	1816	June 11	Ohio Co.,Vir	10	06	14
Campbell, Hannah(Z)	1833	March 11	MuskingmCoOh	14	14	18
Campbell, James(Y)	1823	April 29	Jeff.Co.,Oh.	06	15	22
Campbell, James(Y)	1827	July 20	SteubenvleOh	07	10	27
Campbell, James(Z)	1815	Oct. 03	Jeff.Co.,Oh.	08	08	24
Campbell, James(Z-M)	1832	Sept. 17	GuernseyCoOh	02	03	02
Campbell, Jas.(Z)	1831	Dec. 15	Morgan Co,Oh	13	08	24
Campbell, Jesse(Z)	1814	April 27	CoshoctnCoOh	09	03	03
Campbell, John(Z)	1815	Aug. 29	MuskingmCoOh	06	03	18
Campbell, Josias(Z)	1816	Dec. 11	MercerCoPenn	05	02	19
Campbell, Moses(Z)	1822	Sept. 04	GuernseyCoOh	08	08	24
Campbell, Moses(Z)	1830	Dec. 20	GuernseyCoOh	08	08	25
Campbell, Moses(Z-M)	1825	Nov. 17	GuernseyCoOh	02	01	12
Campbell, Rich'd. Junr.(Z-M)	1833	June 14	KnoxCo.,Ohio	10	06	14
Campbell, Richard(Z-M)	1832	June 22	KnoxCo.,Ohio	11	08	19
Campbell, Robert(Z)	1823	Nov. 01	Morgan Co,Oh	09	08	32
Campbell, Robert(Z)	1836	Feb. 09	Morgan Co,Oh	14	12	12
Campbell, Sam'l.(Z)	1827	Sept. 10	Morgan Co,Oh	11	11	06
Campbell, Thomas(Z)	1829	May 11	Morgan Co,Oh	13	09	02
Campbell, Thomas(Z)	1836	Jan. 25	Morgan Co,Oh	13	09	03
Campbell, Thos.(Z)	1830	Feb. 24	Morgan Co,Oh	11	10	24
Campbell, Thos.(Z)	1831	July 29	Morgan Co,Oh	13	09	14
Campbell, William(Y)	1830	Oct. 06	HarrisonCoOh	06	14	25
Campbell, William(Y)	1833	Oct. 18	CarrollCo,Oh	06	14	27
Campbell, Wm.(Z-M)	1826	Dec. 23	GuernseyCoOh	02	02	07
Cane, Benjamin(Z)	1835	Dec. 28	MonroeCo.,Oh	08	07	15
Cane, Benjamin(Z)	1836	May 10	MonroeCo.,Oh	08	06	22
Cane, Benjamin(Z)	1836	May 10	MonroeCo.,Oh	08	06	23
Cannady, David(Z-M)	1832	May 07	HolmesCoOhio	06	09	14
Cannon, Dennis(Y)	1834	Aug. 07	ColumbanCoOh	04	13	14
Cantwell, Martin(Z)	1833	Oct. 26	ZanesvilleOh	15	15	26
Capel, Wm.(Z)	1827	Sept. 13	Monroe Co,Oh	08	07	17
Capes, John(Y)	1831	Aug. 15	TuscarwsCoOh	07	15	27
Capins, Benjamin(Z)	1833	Oct. 23	Morgan Co,Oh	13	08	32
Capler, Charles(Z-M)	1827	Dec. 05	TuscarwsCoOh	01	06	01
Capler, William(Z)	1807	March 23	MuskingmCoOh	01	06	01
Caples, Charles(Z-M)	1829	July 02	TuscarwsCoOh	01	06	01

49

PURCHASER	YEAR	DATE	RESIDENCE	R	T	S
Caples, Charles(Z-M)	1829	July 02	TuscarwsCoOh	01	06	02
Caples, Charles(Z-M)	1836	Feb. 06	TuscarwsCoOh	01	06	09
Capper, David(Y)	1829	June 20	HarrisonCoOh	06	14	01
Capper, David(Y)	1829	Dec. 24	HarrisonCoOh	06	13	06
Car, Daniel(Z-M)	1836	Jan. 18	CoshoctnCoOh	09	06	11
Car, Daniel(Z-M)	1838	April 07	CoshoctnCoOh	08	06	05
Carell, Charles(Z-M)	1836	March 21	MuskingmCoOh	03	01	25
Carens, John(Z-M)	1837	March 27	HolmesCoOhio	09	08	17
Carens, Joshua(Y)	1830	June 03	HarrisonCoOh	06	12	20
Carey, Richard(Y)	1829	July 30	ColumbanCoOh	03	13	30
Carhartt, William(Z-M)	1833	May 16	CoshoctnCoOh	08	06	11
Cariens, R.(Z)	1817	Jan. 14	MuskingmCoOh	11	13	26
Cariens, R.(Z)	1817	May 03	MuskingmCoOh	11	13	25
Cariens, William(Z)	1816	June 22	HartfordCoMd	11	13	27
Cariens, William(Z)	1816	June 22	HartfordCoMd	11	13	27
Carins, Christopher(Z)	1833	March 19	MuskingmCoOh	11	12	23
Carle, Richard(Y)	1822	Jan. 15	ColumbanCoOh	04	16	15
Carlile, James Jr.(Z-M)	1836	Jan. 08	TuscarwsCoOh	01	08	04
Carlile, Jas.(Z-M)	1835	Oct. 10	TuscarwsCoOh	01	08	02
Carlile, Jas.(Z-M)	1835	Oct. 10	TuscarwsCoOh	01	08	04
Carlile, John(Z-M)	1832	May 15	GuernseyCoOh	01	03	06
Carlile, William(Z-M)	1832	June 02	GuernseyCoOh	01	03	06
Carlin, James(Z)	1834	Sept. 24	Morgan Co,Oh	10	07	01
Carlin, Mary(Z)	1832	Dec. 27	Morgan Co,Oh	11	11	05
Carlin, Thomas(Z)	1827	Aug. 10	Morgan Co,Oh	11	11	08
Carlin, Thomas(Z)	1832	May 26	Morgan Co,Oh	11	12	33
Carlisle, David(Z)	1814	Dec. 24	MuskingmCoOh	10	03	14
Carlisle, David(Z)	1815	Jan. 26	MuskingmCoOh	10	03	17
Carlisle, David(Z)	1815	March 25	MuskingmCoOh	10	03	13
Carlisle, George(Z)	1817	April 19	GuernseyCoOh	01	03	22
Carlisle, Jacob(Y)	1827	Dec. 13	ColumbanCoOh	03	12	11
Carlisle, John(Z)	1815	Oct. 17	GuernseyCoOh	01	03	17
Carlisle, John(Z)	1817	May 10	GuernseyCoOh	01	03	17
Carlisle, Jonathan Jr.(Z)	1807	July 13	MuskingmCoOh	14	16	08
Carlisle, Jonathan Jr.(Z)	1810	Feb. 01	MuskingmCoOh	13	11	14
Carlisle, William(Z)	1812	May 14	MifflinCo,Pa	01	03	07
Carlyle, William(Z)	1832	Aug. 24	GuernseyCoOh	08	08	07
Carman, James(Y)	1825	July 26	ColumbanCoOh	05	15	03
Carmichael, Eman(Z)	1834	Dec. 17	Perry Co.,Oh	13	09	30
Carmichael, Eman(Z)	1834	Dec. 17	Perry Co.,Oh	14	13	25
Carmichael, Emanuel(Z)	1833	March 13	Morgan Co,Oh	14	13	24
Carmichael, Emanuel(Z)	1836	Dec. 13	Perry Co.,Oh	13	09	31
Carmichael, John Jr.(Z)	1836	Oct. 19	WashngtnCoOh	08	05	12
Carmichael, John Jr.(Z)	1836	Nov. 11	WashngtnCoOh	08	05	12
Carmichael, John Junr.(Z)	1833	March 01	WashngtnCoOh	08	05	12
Carmichael, John(Z)	1815	March 16	KnoxCo.,Ohio	11	05	22
Carmichael, John(Z)	1815	March 16	KnoxCo.,Ohio	11	05	15
Carnaham, James(Z-M)	1834	Feb. 17	CoshoctnCoOh	05	06	23
Carnahan, Andrew(Z-M)	1833	Feb. 23	CoshoctnCoOh	05	06	14
Carnahan, Andrew(Z-M)	1833	Feb. 23	CoshoctnCoOh	05	06	14
Carnahan, James(Z-M)	1826	May 01	Jeff.Co.,Oh.	05	06	14
Carnahan, James(Z-M)	1827	Aug. 29	Jeff.Co.,Oh.	05	06	14
Carnahan, John(Z-M)	1826	April 13	Jeff.Co.,Oh.	05	06	14
Carnahan, John(Z-M)	1831	July 02	CoshoctnCoOh	05	06	14
Carnahan, Kenedy(Z)	1829	April 11	BelmontCo,Oh	13	08	18
Carnahan, Wm.(Z-M)	1832	Sept. 14	WestmrldCoPa	07	08	09
Carnehen, Kennedy(Z)	1836	Dec. 05	Morgan Co,Oh	13	08	07
Carner, Seth(Z)	1816	Feb. 27	LickingCo,Oh	11	03	15
Carnes, Adam(Z-M)	1836	June 28	LoudonCo,Vir	06	04	09
Carnes, James(Z)	1831	March 05	MuskingmCoOh	11	10	22
Carnes, John(Z)	1814	Feb. 09	MuskingmCoOh	13	12	11
Carnes, Samuel(Z-M)	1835	Jan. 08	CarrolCo.,Oh	04	06	10
Carney, John(Z-M)	1832	Oct. 08	GuernseyCoOh	01	05	18
Carney, John(Z-M)	1832	Dec. 11	GuernseyCoOh	01	05	18
Carns, Jacob(Z)	1817	Oct. 04	LoudonCo,Vir	13	10	29
Carns, John(Y)	1822	March 25	TuscarwsCoOh	07	15	20
Carns, Manasseh Jr.(Y)	1832	Feb. 21	TuscarwsCoOh	07	14	35
Carns, Nathaniel(Y)	1826	May 29	TuscarwsCoOh	07	14	24
Carns, Nathaniel(Y)	1831	April 04	TuscarwsCoOh	07	15	19

PURCHASER	YEAR	DATE	RESIDENCE	R	T	S
Carns, Robert(Z)	1812	Jan. 21	GuernseyCoOh	01	04	25
Carns, Robert(Z)	1814	Nov. 05	GuernseyCoOh	02	02	08
Carothers, Christopher(Y)	1823	May 10	GuernseyCoOh	07	10	22
Carothers, George(Z-M)	1833	Sept. 03	HarrisonCoOh	03	06	08
Carothers, John(Z-M)	1831	March 08	HarrisonCoOh	01	06	12
Carpenter, Abraham(Z)	1833	Sept. 25	GuernseyCoOh	08	08	27
Carpenter, George W.(Z-M)	1835	Dec. 09	BelmontCo,Oh	03	04	02
Carpenter, George(Z)	1815	March 06	Jeff.Co.,Oh.	06	08	19
Carpenter, George(Z)	1815	March 06	Jeff.Co.,Oh.	06	08	12
Carpenter, John(Z)	1815	Feb. 04	GuernseyCoOh	07	08	15
Carpenter, John(Z-M)	1833	Feb. 04	HolmesCoOhio	07	08	07
Carpenter, John(Z-M)	1835	Nov. 11	HolmesCoOhio	07	08	07
Carpenter, John(Z-M)	1836	Jan. 04	HolmesCoOhio	07	08	15
Carpenter, John(Z-M)	1836	April 30	KnoxCo.,Ohio	10	07	22
Carpenter, Thomas(Z)	1815	Feb. 24	GuernseyCoOh	09	07	07
Carpenter, William(Z-M)	1833	April 30	TuscarwsCoOh	01	05	09
Carpenter, William(Z-M)	1833	Dec. 14	KnoxCo.,Ohio	10	06	08
Carpenter, William(Z-M)	1833	Dec. 14	KnoxCo.,Ohio	10	06	08
Carr, Abr'hm.(Z-M)	1838	Feb. 27	TuscarwsCoOh	08	06	06
Carr, Aquilla(Z-M)	1838	Feb. 27	TuscarwsCoOh	08	06	06
Carr, Elizabeth(Y)	1823	Jan. 10	WashCo.,Penn	05	12	15
Carr, Elizabeth(Y)	1829	Sept. 17	HarrisonCoOh	05	12	15
Carr, James(Y)	1831	May 31	Jeff.Co.,Oh.	07	12	27
Carr, John W.(Z-M)	1828	Dec. 04	HarrisonCoOh	07	07	20
Carr, John(Z)	1821	Sept. 12	YorkCo.,Penn	15	16	24
Carr, John(Z-M)	1837	April 10	GuernseyCoOh	03	04	13
Carr, Joseph(Z)	1833	Nov. 30	Brooke CoVir	11	11	13
Carr, Joseph(Z)	1833	Nov. 30	Brooke CoVir	11	11	13
Carr, Joseph(Z)	1834	Jan. 22	Brooke CoVir	11	11	24
Carr, Joseph(Z)	1836	March 18	Morgan Co,Oh	09	05	24
Carr, Joseph(Z)	1836	Dec. 10	Morgan Co,Oh	08	05	03
Carr, Joseph(Z)	1836	Dec. 10	Morgan Co,Oh	08	05	04
Carr, Rich'd. B.(Z-M)	1829	June 23	TuscarwsCoOh	03	06	08
Carr, Rich'd. B.(Z-M)	1829	June 23	TuscarwsCoOh	03	06	03
Carr, Richard(Z-M)	1833	March 16	TuscarwsCoOh	03	06	10
Carr, Robert(Z-M)	1828	Dec. 04	HarrisonCoOh	07	07	20
Carr, Robert(Z-M)	1832	April 23	CoshoctnCoOh	07	05	05
Carr, Robert(Z-M)	1834	Jan. 21	CoshoctnCoOh	08	06	11
Carr, Thomas(Z-M)	1833	March 16	TuscarwsCoOh	03	06	10
Carr, Thos.(Z-M)	1829	June 23	TuscarwsCoOh	03	06	08
Carr, Thos.(Z-M)	1829	June 23	TuscarwsCoOh	03	06	03
Carr, William(Z-M)	1832	March 30	CoshoctnCoOh	08	06	09
Carr, William(Z-M)	1832	March 30	CoshoctnCoOh	08	06	10
Carr, William(Z-M)	1833	Feb. 28	CoshoctnCoOh	08	06	11
Carr, William(Z-M)	1836	Sept. 21	CoshoctnCoOh	08	06	04
Carr, Wm.(Z-M)	1828	July 25	TuscarwsCoOh	03	06	12
Carrel, Aaron(Z)	1835	March 27	Morgan Co,Oh	09	05	20
Carrel, Aaron(Z)	1836	Jan. 11	Morgan Co,Oh	09	05	19
Carrel, George(Z)	1810	April 30	GuernseyCoOh	09	08	08
Carrel, Jonathan(Z)	1806	June 23	?	15	16	06
Carrel, Joseph(Z)	1832	Sept. 29	Morgan Co,Oh	09	05	20
Carrel, Joseph(Z)	1836	Jan. 11	Morgan Co,Oh	09	05	19
Carrel, Joseph(Z)	1836	Jan. 11	Morgan Co,Oh	09	05	19
Carrel, Philip(Z-M)	1833	March 20	CarrollCo,Oh	07	05	03
Carrel, William(Z)	1826	Aug. 23	Morgan Co,Oh	09	05	18
Carrel, William(Z)	1835	Nov. 09	Morgan Co,Oh	09	05	21
Carrel, William(Z)	1836	Feb. 01	Morgan Co,Oh	10	06	24
Carrel, William(Z)	1836	Feb. 01	Morgan Co,Oh	10	06	24
Carrell, George(Z)	1815	Jan. 26	GuernseyCoOh	09	05	17
Carrell, James(Z)	1834	July 29	Morgan Co,Oh	11	11	03
Carrell, John(Z)	1835	Oct. 07	MuskingmCoOh	11	11	03
Carrick, Jacob(Z)	1826	Feb. 07	GuernseyCoOh	09	08	22
Carrol, Jonathan(Z)	1811	Dec. 17	MuskingmCoOh	15	15	05
Carrol, Thomas(Z)	1811	Nov. 13	MuskingmCoOh	15	15	04
Carroll, Andrew(Z-M)	1836	April 25	CoshoctnCoOh	05	04	06
Carroll, Francis(Z-M)	1832	Oct. 05	CoshoctnCoOh	05	04	07
Carrothers, C.(Z-M)	1831	Feb. 04	CoshoctnCoOh	09	04	10
Carrothers, James(Y)	1821	Oct. 01	GuernseyCoOh	07	10	22
Carrothers, John(Z-M)	1832	Sept. 15	TuscarwsCoOh	01	06	12

PURCHASER	YEAR	DATE	RESIDENCE	R	T	S
Carruthers, James(Z)	1833	Sept. 09	PittsburghPa	08	07	02
Carruthers, James(Z)	1833	Sept. 09	PittsburghPa	08	07	11
Carruthers, John(Z)	1836	Jan. 09	Morgan Co,Oh	10	06	22
Carry, Wm.(Z-M)	1833	Nov. 14	MuskingmCoOh	03	01	06
Carson, Andrew(Z)	1815	Dec. 08	Jeff.Co.,Oh.	01	04	14
Carson, John(Y)	1823	Aug. 15	HarrisonCoOh	06	12	15
Carson, John(Y)	1829	July 08	Brooke CoVir	04	13	08
Carson, Robert(Y)	1832	Oct. 05	ColumbanCoOh	04	13	13
Carter, Andrew(Z-M)	1838	Nov. 10	GuernseyCoOh	03	04	19
Carter, Evan(Y)	1836	March 21	Jeff.Co.,Oh.	07	12	26
Carter, Henry(Y)	1827	Aug. 23	TuscarwsCoOh	07	14	15
Carter, Henry(Z-M)	1832	April 09	TuscarwsCoOh	01	08	01
Carter, Isaac(Z)	1822	Feb. 28	MuskingmCoOh	11	12	11
Carter, John W.(Z-M)	1836	May 11	LickingCo,Oh	10	03	02
Carter, John(Z)	1837	Feb. 14	BrookeCo,Vir	08	05	08
Carter, John(Z)	1837	Feb. 14	BrookeCo,Vir	08	05	05
Carter, Lewis(Z)	1837	Feb. 14	BrookeCo,Vir	08	05	05
Carter, Lewis(Z)	1837	Feb. 14	BrookeCo,Vir	08	05	05
Carter, Richard(Z)	1834	Feb. 08	BelmontCo,Oh	10	09	01
Carter, Wm. A.(Z-M)	1831	April 07	Jeff.Co.,Oh.	03	04	02
Cartlick, Jesse(Z)	1810	April 12	MuskingmCoOh	15	16	19
Cartlick, Jesse(Z)	1816	Aug. 24	MadisonCo,Oh	15	14	18
Cartlick, Jesse(Z)	1816	Aug. 28	MadisonCo,Oh	14	13	04
Cartmill, James(Z-M)	1835	Sept. 26	TuscarwsCoOh	05	04	13
Caruthers, Hugh(Z-M)	1832	July 24	TuscarwsCoOh	01	06	19
Caruthers, James(Y)	1832	Oct. 23	HarrisonCoOh	07	12	05
Caruthers, James(Z)	1805	March 25	WestmrldCoPa	14	15	20
Caruthers, Jesse(Y)	1832	Oct. 20	HarrisonCoOh	07	12	06
Caruthers, John(Y)	1832	Oct. 23	HarrisonCoOh	06	11	35
Carver, Abraham(Z)	1809	Nov. 01	SomersetCoOh	03	08	04
Carver, Abraham(Z)	1812	July 28	TuscarwsCoOh	04	09	17
Carver, Meller(Z-M)	1825	May 25	MuskingmCoOh	06	03	12
Carver, Seth(Z-M)	1836	Feb. 05	LickingCo,Oh	11	03	06
Carver, Seth(Z-M)	1834	Jan. 10	LickingCo,Oh	11	03	06
Cary, John(Z-M)	1837	March 30	HolmesCoOhio	07	08	07
Cary, Richard(Y)	1826	May 16	ColumbanCoOh	03	13	30
Casacy, James(Y)	1829	Aug. 05	Stark Co.,Oh	06	16	30
Casebear, James(Z-M)	1837	April 17	CoshoctnCoOh	09	07	19
Casebear, William(Z-M)	1835	Dec. 02	CoshoctnCoOh	07	07	13
Casebeer, James(Z-M)	1832	Dec. 15	HolmesCoOhio	07	08	23
Casebeer, Solomon(Z-M)	1832	Oct. 05	HolmesCoOhio	07	08	20
Casebier, William(Z-M)	1833	Oct. 08	HolmesCoOhio	07	08	20
Casebier, John(Z)	1811	June 10	WashCo.,Penn	03	09	12
Casey, John(Z)	1815	Dec. 19	Jeff.Co.,Oh.	07	08	23
Casey, P.(Z)	1824	May 11	HolmesCoOhio	07	09	20
Casey, Peter(Z)	1810	Feb. 19	MuskingmCoOh	07	09	13
Casey, Peter(Z)	1815	Dec. 02	CoshoctnCoOh	06	09	15
Casey, William(Z-M)	1838	March 31	HolmesCoOhio	08	08	21
Casey,Peter,Ex.Thos.Butler(Z-M	1833	Jan. 07	HolmesCoOhio	07	08	02
Cash, Rezen(Z-M)	1836	Nov. 16	GuernseyCoOh	03	06	02
Cash, Vinian(Y)	1822	June 01	HarrisonCoOh	06	11	21
Caskey, Samuel(Y)	1822	May 15	Canton, Ohio	06	17	15
Casner, Jno.(Z)	1831	Dec. 10	GuernseyCoOh	08	08	14
Casner, John(Z)	1824	June 07	GuernseyCoOh	08	08	14
Casner, John(Z)	1825	Oct. 03	GuernseyCoOh	08	08	14
Casner, John(Z)	1833	March 22	GuernseyCoOh	08	08	23
Casner, John(Z)	1836	Jan. 12	GuernseyCoOh	08	08	15
Casner, John(Z)	1836	April 04	GuernseyCoOh	08	08	23
Casner, Vandel(Z)	1827	Jan. 13	GuernseyCoOh	08	08	21
Casner, Vendal(Z)	1826	April 07	GuernseyCoOh	08	08	14
Casner, Vendel(Z)	1825	Oct. 03	GuernseyCoOh	08	08	21
Casner, William(Z)	1832	Aug. 29	GuernseyCoOh	08	08	22
Casner, William(Z)	1832	Aug. 29	GuernseyCoOh	08	08	22
Casner, William(Z)	1836	April 04	GuernseyCoOh	08	08	22
Cass, Lasis(Z)	1808	June 15	MuskingmCoOh	08	04	25
Cass, Lewis(Z)	1806	March 19	MuskingmCoOh	07	04	16
Cass, Lewis(Z)	1806	March 29	MuskingmCoOh	08	03	07
Cass, Lewis(Z)	1806	April 07	MuskingmCoOh	13	12	01
Cass, Lewis(Z)	1806	May 17	MuskingmCoOh	08	03	07

PURCHASER	YEAR	DATE	RESIDENCE	R	T	S
Cass, Lewis(Z)	1806	June 02	MuskingmCoOh	07	01	02
Cass, Lewis(Z)	1806	July 08	MuskingmCoOh	07	01	12
Cass, Lewis(Z)	1806	Oct. 24	MuskingmCoOh	06	01	06
Cass, Lewis(Z)	1807	June 16	MuskingmCoOh	07	01	02
Cass, Lewis(Z)	1807	Oct. 30	MuskingmCoOh	08	02	21
Cassaday, James(Y)	1828	June 21	Stark Co.,Oh	06	16	29
Cassady, James(Y)	1830	Oct. 07	Stark Co.,Oh	06	16	13
Cassatt, Dennis(Z)	1804	Nov. 29	Ohio Co.,Vir	01	02	20
Cassatt, Dennis(Z)	1806	May 16	Wheeling,Vir	06	01	22
Cassatt, Dennis(Z)	1806	Oct. 17	Ohio Co.,Vir	02	02	01
Cassert, Dennis(Z)	1805	April 08	Ohio Co.,Vir	01	01	02
Cassidy, Asa R.(Z-M)	1837	Jan. 11	ZanesvilleOh	02	03	05
Cassidy, Asa R.(Z-M)	1837	Jan. 11	ZanesvilleOh	06	03	03
Cassidy, Asa Richards(Z-M)	1837	Feb. 10	ZanesvilleOh	03	06	10
Cassidy, Hugh(Z-M)	1829	Sept. 01	WashCo.,Penn	05	06	17
Cassidy, Hugh(Z-M)	1829	Sept. 01	WashCo.,Penn	05	06	18
Cassidy, John(Z)	1836	Feb. 27	ClarkCo,Ohio	14	12	02
Cassner, John(Z)	1827	July 02	GuernseyCoOh	08	08	15
Cassner, Vendal(Z)	1825	May 10	RandolphCoVa	08	08	14
Cassner, Vendal(Z)	1825	May 10	RandolphCoVa	08	08	22
Casteel, Amos(Z-M)	1833	March 15	LickingCo,Oh	11	04	21
Casteel, Archibald Jr.(Z-M)	1835	Nov. 21	LickingCo,Oh	11	03	08
Casteel, Archibald Jr.(Z-M)	1836	Feb. 23	LickingCo,Oh	11	03	08
Casteel, Jesse(Z-M)	1836	Feb. 29	KnoxCo.,Ohio	10	08	11
Casteel, Jesse(Z-M)	1836	Feb. 29	KnoxCo.,Ohio	09	08	06
Casteel, Sarah(Z-M)	1831	Nov. 29	CoshoctnCoOh	09	05	25
Castell, John Jr.(Y)	1829	Aug. 06	HarrisonCoOh	06	12	19
Castell, John Junr.(Y)	1829	July 29	HarrisonCoOh	06	12	19
Castelow, James(Z)	1820	Sept. 16	Morgan Co,Oh	14	14	01
Caster, Noah(Z-M)	1835	Dec. 30	HolmesCoOhio	07	08	07
Casto, Andrew(Z)	1812	March 16	KnoxCo.,Ohio	11	06	17
Casto, Andrew(Z)	1813	Oct. 21	KnoxCo.,Ohio	11	06	17
Casto, David(Z)	1816	Dec. 09	KnoxCo.,Ohio	10	05	18
Caston, John(Y)	1838	July 12	Stark Co.,Oh	10	02	12
Cathar, Wm.(Z)	1835	Jan. 23	GuernseyCoOh	09	08	23
Cather, William(Z)	1827	Nov. 22	GuernseyCoOh	09	08	23
Cathon, Wm.(Y)	1825	May 02	Stark Co.,Oh	06	19	15
Caton, Charles(Z-M)	1833	Feb. 25	CoshoctnCoOh	05	06	04
Caton, Daniel(Z-M)	1833	Feb. 25	CoshoctnCoOh	05	06	04
Caton, Daniel(Z-M)	1835	Dec. 15	CoshoctnCoOh	05	06	04
Caton, Gabriel(Z-M)	1832	Nov. 12	WashCo.,Penn	05	06	04
Caton, Gabriel(Z-M)	1834	Aug. 27	CoshoctnCoOh	05	06	04
Cattell, David(Y)	1825	Oct. 01	FayetteCo,Pa	09	11	20
Caughey, Patrick(Z)	1815	Nov. 04	MuskingmCoOh	05	02	03
Caughey, William(Z)	1815	March 10	WashCo.,Penn	05	02	22
Causland, Lindsey M.(Y)	1829	Sept. 24	HarrisonCoOh	05	14	02
Cavene, Edward(Z)	1834	Jan. 09	Perry Co.,Oh	15	15	33
Cavene, Jacob(Z)	1834	Jan. 09	Perry Co.,Oh	15	14	10
Cavene, Jacob(Z)	1836	May 27	Perry Co.,Oh	15	14	11
Cavene, John(Z)	1834	Jan. 09	Perry Co.,Oh	15	14	11
Cavene, John(Z)	1835	July 28	Perry Co.,Oh	15	14	11
Cavene, Patric(Z)	1834	Jan. 09	Perry Co.,Oh	15	14	14
Cavene, Patrick(Z)	1836	July 02	Perry Co.,Oh	15	14	14
Cavene, William(Z)	1836	May 13	Perry Co.,Oh	15	14	11
Cavener, Garret(Z)	1817	July 12	BelmontCo,Oh	13	08	10
Cazier, Sam'l. Junr.(Z-M)	1833	Nov. 05	CoshoctnCoOh	10	04	11
Cazier, Samuel Jnr.(Z-M)	1836	Oct. 03	CoshoctnCoOh	10	04	11
Ceasar, John(Z-M)	1832	Dec. 22	TuscarwsCoOh	02	10	24
Cecil, Elizabeth(Z)	1837	March 18	MonroeCo.,Oh	08	06	25
Cecil, Harriet(Z)	1837	March 04	MonroeCo.,Oh	08	06	11
Cecil, Levi(Z)	1836	Nov. 28	MonroeCo.,Oh	08	06	35
Cecil, Levi(Z)	1836	Nov. 28	MonroeCo.,Oh	08	06	36
Cecil, Levi(Z)	1836	Dec. 03	MonroeCo.,Oh	08	06	27
Cecil, Levi(Z)	1836	Dec. 21	MonroeCo.,Oh	08	06	10
Cecil, Levi(Z)	1837	Feb. 10	MonroeCo.,Oh	08	06	11
Cecil, Levi(Z)	1837	Feb. 10	MonroeCo.,Oh	08	06	12
Cecil, Levi(Z)	1837	March 18	MonroeCo.,Oh	08	06	12
Cecil, Levi(Z)	1837	March 24	MonroeCo.,Oh	08	06	21
Cecil, Levi(Z)	1837	Oct. 28	MonroeCo.,Oh	08	06	11

PURCHASER	YEAR	DATE	RESIDENCE	R	T	S
Cecil, Martha(Z)	1836	Dec. 21	MonroeCo.,Oh	08	06	26
Cecil, Martha(Z)	1837	Feb. 10	MonroeCo.,Oh	08	06	11
Cecill, Adam(Z-M)	1830	July 01	HarrisonCoOh	01	05	15
Cenbaugh, Simon B.(Z)	1809	April 22	MuskingmCoOh	05	09	21
Cenoweth, Elias(Z)	1836	Feb. 16	Perry Co.,Oh	15	14	03
Ceon, Noah(Y)	1821	Feb. 13	GuernseyCoOh	07	11	32
Cer, William(Z)	1813	Aug. 27	WashCo.,Penn	04	02	21
Cer, William(Z)	1813	Aug. 27	WashCo.,Penn	01	03	16
Cerbaugh, Simon B.(Z)	1809	April 22	MuskingmCoOh	05	09	21
Cessna, John(Z)	1815	Dec. 25	BedfordCo,Pa	09	04	11
Cessner, John(Z-M)	1831	Aug. 23	CoshoctnCoOh	09	04	04
Chalfant, Chads(Z)	1817	July 23	FayetteCo,Pa	14	13	08
Chalfant, James(Z)	1807	Dec. 05	MuskingmCoOh	07	04	15
Chalfant, Jesse(Y)	1820	Nov. 27	BelmontCo,Oh	07	09	19
Chalfant, Mordecai(Z)	1807	Jan. 31	MuskingmCoOh	10	01	21
Chalfant, Mordecai(Z)	1807	Sept. 28	FairfeldCoOh	08	04	21
Chalfant, Mordecai(Z)	1807	Sept. 28	FairfeldCoOh	08	04	20
Chalfant, Mordecai(Z)	1813	Aug. 17	CoshoctnCoOh	08	04	21
Chalfant, Mordecai(Z)	1813	Sept. 17	CoshoctnCoOh	08	04	13
Chalk, Joseph(Z)	1834	Feb. 17	Morgan Co,Oh	10	07	28
Chamberlain, Isaac(Y)	1822	April 01	ColumbanCoOh	02	10	15
Chamberlain, J. M.(Z)	1836	June 13	WashngtnCoOh	08	05	18
Chamberlain, J. M.(Z)	1836	Aug. 11	WashngtnCoOh	08	05	18
Chamberlain, Stout(Y)	1823	Dec. 02	ColumbanCoOh	02	10	15
Chamberlin, Orison(Z-M)	1836	Oct. 12	KnoxCo.,Ohio	10	09	03
Chambers, James(Z-M)	1821	Oct. 30	LickingCo,Oh	11	04	17
Chambers, James(Z-M)	1833	July 11	LickingCo,Oh	11	04	17
Chambers, Samuel(Z-M)	1837	Oct. 18	LickingCo,Oh	11	04	08
Chambers, W.(Z)	1817	Jan. 15	Jeff.Co.,Oh.	03	02	06
Chambers, W.(Z)	1817	Jan. 20	Jeff.Co.,Oh.	03	02	12
Chance, Joshua(Z-M)	1835	Dec. 07	CoshoctnCoOh	04	06	22
Chance, Peter(Y)	1827	June 23	Stark Co.,Oh	06	18	14
Chance, Peter(Y)	1827	June 23	Stark Co.,Oh	06	18	03
Chandler, A. D.(Z)	1831	March 28	MuskingmCoOh	13	09	01
Chandler, Aaron(Y)	1822	Nov. 16	FayetteCo,Pa	06	10	21
Chandler, Benj'm.(Z-M)	1831	Dec. 26	LickingCo,Oh	10	03	09
Chandler, Benjamin(Z-M)	1833	Nov. 27	LickingCo,Oh	09	03	06
Chandler, Benjamin(Z-M)	1833	Dec. 31	LickingCo,Oh	09	03	06
Chandler, Daniel(Z)	1810	July 13	MuskingmCoOh	14	14	25
Chandler, Daniel(Z)	1816	Nov. 06	MuskingmCoOh	12	11	36
Chandler, Enoch Senr.(Y)	1831	Sept. 02	BelmontCo,Oh	06	10	33
Chandler, Enoch(Y)	1831	April 18	BelmontCo,Oh	06	10	34
Chandler, Isaac H.(Z-M)	1836	Oct. 31	BelmontCo,Oh	03	05	24
Chandler, Isaac H.(Z-M)	1836	Oct. 31	BelmontCo,Oh	03	04	04
Chandler, Isaac H.(Z-M)	1836	Oct. 31	Belmontco,Oh	03	04	04
Chandler, Jason(Z-M)	1832	Feb. 08	BelmontCo,Oh	01	05	23
Chandler, John(Z-M)	1833	April 08	LickingCo,Oh	10	04	22
Chandler, Martin(Z)	1810	Dec. 22	MuskingmCoOh	12	13	03
Chandler, Martin(Z)	1815	Nov. 06	MuskingmCoOh	12	13	29
Chandler, Martin(Z)	1815	Nov. 06	MuskingmCoOh	12	10	13
Chandler, Martin(Z)	1815	Nov. 06	MuskingmCoOh	12	10	14
Chandler, Sam'l.(Z)	1829	Jan. 17	MuskingmCoOh	12	13	23
Chandler, Spencer(Z)	1817	April 28	FayetteCo,Pa	01	04	04
Chandler, Spencer(Z-M)	1829	Dec. 21	GuernseyCoOh	01	04	04
Chandler, Zachariah(Z)	1805	Nov. 23	MuskingmCoOh	06	01	22
Chandler, Zachariah(Z)	1805	Nov. 23	MuskingmCoOh	12	13	03
Chandler, Zachariah(Z)	1805	Nov. 23	MuskingmCoOh	12	13	20
Chandler, Zachariah(Z)	1808	June 07	MuskingmCoOh	12	13	11
Chaney, Ezekiel(Z)	1836	July 15	AthensCoOhio	15	14	35
Chaney, Ezekiel(Z)	1837	May 10	Perry Co.,Oh	15	14	35
Chaney, William(Z-M)	1833	Oct. 26	HarrisonCoOh	07	05	03
Chaney, William(Z-M)	1837	Nov. 17	HarrisonCoOh	03	04	04
Chaney, William(Z-M)	1837	Nov. 17	HarrisonCoOh	03	05	24
Channel, Jeremiah(Y)	1830	May 24	HarrisonCoOh	06	13	18
Chany, Joseph(Z)	1811	Dec. 05	MuskingmCoOh	09	04	22
Chapin, James(Z-M)	1822	March 04	CoshoctnCoOh	09	05	24
Chapin, James(Z-M)	1833	Feb. 06	CoshoctnCoOh	09	05	24
Chapin, James(Z-M)	1837	Jan. 30	CoshoctnCoOh	09	05	24
Chaplean, Hedgman(Z)	1832	Oct. 26	MuskingmCoOh	13	08	33

PURCHASER	YEAR	DATE	RESIDENCE	R	T	S
Chapman, Abrose(Y)	1825	May 02	Stark Co.,Oh	10	01	03
Chapman, Ambrose(Y)	1825	March 11	Stark Co.,Oh	09	11	26
Chapman, Ambrose(Y)	1825	March 11	Stark Co.,Oh	10	01	24
Chapman, Ambrose(Y)	1825	March 11	Stark Co.,Oh	10	02	36
Chapman, Andrew(Z)	1836	May 10	Morgan Co,Oh	13	08	26
Chapman, John(Z-M)	1835	Jan. 06	GuernseyCoOh	03	01	03
Chapman, Linus(Z-M)	1833	Jan. 17	HolmesCoOhio	07	08	15
Chapman, Linus(Z-M)	1836	Jan. 13	HolmesCoOhio	08	08	09
Chapman, Linus(Z-M)	1836	Jan. 13	HolmesCoOhio	08	08	09
Chapman, Moses(Z-M)	1822	Oct. 24	FranklinCoOh	07	08	15
Chapman, Moses(Z-M)	1824	Jan. 31	CoshoctnCoOh	07	08	14
Chapman, Moses(Z-M)	1824	Jan. 31	CoshoctnCoOh	07	08	15
Chapman, Moses(Z-M)	1830	Sept. 23	HolmesCoOhio	07	08	14
Chapman, Moses(Z-M)	1833	Jan. 17	HolmesCoOhio	07	08	15
Chapman, Silas(Z-M)	1836	Dec. 07	MuskingmCoOh	05	03	11
Chapman, William(Z-M)	1834	Jan. 10	CoshoctnCoOh	07	04	13
Chapman, Wm.(Z)	1821	Aug. 22	Morgan Co,Oh	13	08	25
Chapman, Wm.(Z)	1822	Jan. 17	Morgan Co,Oh	13	08	25
Chappelear, Aylett W.(Z)	1834	March 08	Morgan Co,Oh	13	08	33
Chappelear, Hedgman(Z)	1833	Oct. 23	Morgan Co,Oh	13	08	28
Chappelear, William A.(Z)	1832	Dec. 13	Morgan Co,Oh	13	08	29
Chappelear, William A.(Z)	1835	May 30	Morgan Co,Oh	13	08	29
Chappelear, William A.(Z)	1836	April 06	Morgan Co,Oh	13	08	29
Charlesworth, Rich'd.(Y)	1824	Nov. 08	BelmontCo,Oh	04	06	21
Charlton, Sarah(Y)	1827	April 04	ColumbanCoOh	06	19	24
Chase, Benj'n.(Y)	1823	Aug. 02	HarrisonCoOh	05	13	07
Chase, Benjamin(Y)	1825	June 04	HarrisonCoOh	05	13	07
Chavey, William(Z)	1817	Aug. 09	GuernseyCoOh	11	11	13
Cheek, Amelia(Z-M)	1833	March 02	LickingCo,Oh	10	04	16
Cheffy, Jesse S.(Z)	1831	Feb. 19	Jeff.Co.,Oh.	11	11	21
Cheffy, Jesse S.(Z)	1829	Nov. 28	Jeff.Co.,Oh.	11	11	21
Cheney, Aza(Z)	1835	Dec. 10	Perry Co.,Oh	14	13	26
Cheney, Jesse(Z-M)	1835	Nov. 13	HolmesCoOhio	09	08	10
Cheney, Jesse(Z-M)	1835	Nov. 13	HolmesCoOhio	09	08	11
Cheney, John(Z-M)	1832	Sept. 19	HolmesCoOhio	09	08	11
Cheney, John(Z-M)	1835	Nov. 14	HolmesCoOhio	09	08	11
Cheney, John(Z-M)	1835	Nov. 14	HolmesCoOhio	09	08	11
Cheney, John(Z-M)	1837	Sept. 14	HolmesCoOhio	08	08	14
Cheniweth, James(Z)	1813	Dec. 27	FairfeldCoOh	15	15	18
Chenoweth, Absalom(Z)	1833	Oct. 28	Perry Co.,Oh	15	15	27
Chenoweth, Elias(Z)	1827	Feb. 14	Perry Co.,Oh	15	16	22
Chenoweth, Elias(Z)	1835	Nov. 10	Perry Co.,Oh	15	14	03
Chenoweth, Elias(Z)	1814	Aug. 30	MuskingmCoOh	15	16	20
Chenoweth, James(Z)	1813	Dec. 27	FairfeldCoOh	15	15	18
Chenoweth, Wm.(Z)	1833	Nov. 19	Perry Co.,Oh	15	15	22
Cheny, Thos.(Z-M)	1830	Nov. 16	MuskingmCoOh	06	03	09
Cherry, Ralph(Z)	1816	May 11	FairfeldCoOh	14	13	01
Chess, Noble(Z)	1816	Dec. 14	MuskingmCoOh	11	13	35
Chesshir, William(Z)	1836	March 31	GuernseyCoOh	09	06	34
Cheurront, Joseph(Z-M)	1833	Nov. 19	MuskingmCoOh	05	03	10
Chidester, James(Z)	1815	Dec. 21	FairfeldCoOh	15	16	23
Chigage, James(Z)	1813	Feb. 19	KnoxCo.,Ohio	10	05	06
Chilcote, Richard(Z)	1826	Aug. 15	Morgan Co,Oh	09	07	11
Childs, James(Z-M)	1838	March 21	CoshoctnCoOh	10	05	11
Chisnal, George(Y)	1825	March 16	LancastrCoPa	09	12	04
Chrisman, Jacob(Y)	1820	Nov. 23	WashCo.,Penn	07	18	25
Christ, Daniel(Z-M)	1835	Oct. 30	HolmesCoOhio	09	09	04
Christ, Thomas(Y)	1832	June 11	ColumbanCoOh	03	12	02
Christie, G.(Z)	1817	Oct. 24	MuskingmCoOh	14	14	02
Christie, George(Z)	1817	Aug. 23	ZanesvilleOh	14	14	02
Christler, Samuel(Z)	1810	Nov. 02	WashCo.,Penn	02	02	22
Christmas, Gabriel(Z-M)	1832	April 23	HolmesCoOhio	06	09	17
Christmas, William(Y)	1826	March 17	Stark Co.,Oh	09	10	01
Christmas, William(Z-M)	1831	April 09	StarkeCo.,Oh	01	09	07
Christmas, Wm.(Y)	1826	Sept. 09	Canton, Ohio	09	10	01
Christmas, Wm.(Z-M)	1832	Jan. 06	TuscarwsCoOh	01	09	06
Christmas, Wm.(Z-M)	1832	Jan. 06	TuscarwsCoOh	01	09	06
Christmas, Wm.(Z-M)	1832	May 12	TuscarwsCoOh	01	09	15
Christmas, Wm.(Z-M)	1832	May 12	TuscarwsCoOh	01	09	04

PURCHASER	YEAR	DATE	RESIDENCE	R	T	S
Christmas, Wm.(Z-M)	1832	Dec. 07	TuscarwsCoOh	01	09	08
Christmas, Wm.(Z-M)	1833	Dec. 16	StarkeCoOhio	01	09	05
Christmay, Wm.(Y)	1822	Aug. 01	Stark Co.,Oh	07	19	15
Christy, Henry(Z-M)	1828	Aug. 14	CoshoctnCoOh	05	06	23
Chritz, Andrew(Z-M)	1832	Nov. 26	TuscarwsCoOh	03	07	11
Church, George(Z)	1832	June 25	MonroeCo.,Oh	08	07	13
Church, George(Z)	1835	Nov. 11	MonroeCo.,Oh	08	07	14
Church, Sarah(Z)	1833	Aug. 08	MonroeCo.,Oh	08	07	13
Churchhill, Eben'r.(Y)	1825	Jan. 13	ColumbanCoOh	01	07	15
Churchill, Branch(Y)	1825	Dec. 12	ColumbanCoOh	01	07	15
Cisna, Charles(Z)	1814	Aug. 09	CoshoctnCoOh	08	05	17
Cissna, Thomas(Z)	1806	Jan. 07	FairfeldCoOh	06	04	18
Clabaugh, Henry(Z)	1806	Feb. 28	FairfeldCoOh	15	18	07
Clabaugh, Nicholas(Z-M)	1833	Jan. 26	MuskingmCoOh	10	03	03
Clabaugh, Nicholas(Z-M)	1833	Jan. 26	MuskingmCoOh	10	03	08
Clabaugh, Nicholas(Z-M)	1836	Jan. 02	LickingCo,Oh	10	11	17
Clabaugh, Thos.(Z-M)	1836	Feb. 06	LickingCo,Oh	10	04	17
Clancey, Charles(Z)	1828	June 23	Morgan Co,Oh	12	11	34
Clancy, Charles(Z)	1826	Dec. 01	Jeff.Co.,Oh.	12	11	34
Clantz, Charles(Z)	1827	April 26	FredrickCoMd	01	05	11
Clappen, Philip(Z)	1829	June 01	MuskingmCoOh	12	13	22
Clapper, George(Z)	1808	Aug. 08	MuskingmCoOh	12	13	05
Clapper, George(Z)	1815	Jan. 07	MuskingmCoOh	12	13	23
Clapper, George(Z)	1815	Feb. 25	MuskingmCoOh	12	12	11
Clapper, John(Z)	1828	June 17	MuskingmCoOh	12	13	22
Clapper, John(Z)	1832	June 30	MuskingmCoOh	13	11	30
Clapper, John(Z)	1833	Aug. 16	MuskingmCoOh	12	13	22
Clapper, Joseph(Z)	1826	Oct. 16	MuskingmCoOh	12	12	09
Clapper, Joseph(Z)	1828	Feb. 23	MuskingmCoOh	12	12	10
Clapper, Joseph(Z)	1829	July 04	MuskingmCoOh	12	12	10
Clapper, Peter(Z)	1833	March 06	MuskingmCoOh	13	10	02
Clapper, Peter(Z)	1833	Oct. 05	MuskingmCoOh	13	11	30
Clapper, Peter(Z)	1831	July 02	MuskingmCoOh	12	13	22
Clapper, Philip(Z)	1829	Dec. 28	MuskingmCoOh	13	11	21
Clapper, Philip(Z)	1830	Dec. 18	MuskingmCoOh	13	11	30
Clapper, Philip(Z)	1832	Sept. 05	MuskingmCoOh	13	11	21
Clapper, Philip(Z)	1833	Sept. 25	MuskingmCoOh	13	11	21
Clark, Abel(Z-M)	1835	March 20	KnoxCo.,Ohio	10	09	23
Clark, Abel(Z-M)	1837	March 28	KnoxCo.,Ohio	10	09	23
Clark, Abner(Z-M)	1836	Dec. 05	Jeff.Co.,Oh.	10	09	18
Clark, Abner(Z-M)	1836	Dec. 05	Jeff.Co.,Oh.	10	09	13
Clark, Alex'r.(Z-M)	1831	Oct. 21	HarrisonCoOh	01	04	03
Clark, Alexander(Y)	1821	Aug. 07	GuernseyCoOh	07	11	34
Clark, Alva(Z)	1814	Dec. 17	MuskingmCoOh	06	02	19
Clark, Andrew(Z)	1810	Nov. 01	WashngtnCo ?	03	04	24
Clark, Andrew(Z)	1814	June 29	WashCo.,Penn	02	03	06
Clark, Aurelius(Z)	1836	Feb. 12	Morgan Co,Oh	09	06	27
Clark, Charles(Z)	1832	Oct. 20	Morgan Co,Oh	11	11	24
Clark, Conolly(Z)	1833	March 22	Morgan Co,Oh	10	07	20
Clark, Esau(Z-M)	1833	Sept. 20	CarrollCo,Oh	10	08	01
Clark, Esau(Z-M)	1837	March 20	KnoxCo.,Ohio	10	09	21
Clark, George(Y)	1824	Sept. 18	ColumbanCoOh	03	12	04
Clark, George(Z)	1811	March 11	LickingCo,Oh	11	01	22
Clark, Hazelett(Z)	1836	April 20	Morgan Co,Oh	10	06	13
Clark, Hazlett(Z)	1833	Nov. 07	Morgan Co,Oh	10	07	31
Clark, Hugh(Y)	1831	March 15	ColumbanCoOh	03	12	07
Clark, Hugh(Y)	1835	Jan. 05	Jeff.Co.,Oh.	03	12	07
Clark, Hugh(Y)	1838	July 02	Jeff.Co.,Oh.	03	12	07
Clark, Hugh(Z-M)	1833	Sept. 13	CoshoctnCoOh	05	04	25
Clark, J.(Z)	1816	Nov. 28	ZanesvilleOh	09	03	02
Clark, J.(Z)	1816	Dec. 02	ZanesvilleOh	14	15	12
Clark, J.(Z)	1816	Dec. 02	ZanesvilleOh	14	15	13
Clark, J.(Z)	1816	Dec. 02	ZanesvilleOh	14	15	13
Clark, Jacob(Z)	1827	Sept. 22	GuernseyCoOh	10	09	01
Clark, Jacob(Z)	1816	Nov. 08	GuernseyCoOh	09	08	32
Clark, James(Y)	1829	March 16	ColumbanCoOh	03	12	22
Clark, James(Z)	1813	Oct. 13	MuskingmCoOh	14	14	05
Clark, James(Z)	1815	Oct. 30	TuscarwsCoOh	03	06	11
Clark, James(Z-M)	1829	Sept. 04	CoshoctnCoOh	05	04	17

PURCHASER	YEAR	DATE	RESIDENCE	R	T	S
Clark, James(Z-M)	1832	May 03	CoshoctnCoOh	05	04	17
Clark, James(Z-M)	1832	June 15	CoshoctnCoOh	05	04	25
Clark, James(Z-M)	1830	March 13	CoshoctnCoOh	05	04	17
Clark, James(Z-M)	1832	Aug. 15	CoshoctnCoOh	05	04	25
Clark, James(Z-M)	1835	Nov. 11	MuskingmCoOh	05	04	16
Clark, James(Z-M)	1835	Nov. 20	CoshoctnCoOh	10	04	12
Clark, Jeremiah(Z)	1832	Feb. 13	Perry Co.,Oh	14	13	18
Clark, Jeremiah(Z)	1833	Feb. 25	Perry Co.,Oh	15	15	12
Clark, John C.(Z)	1835	Aug. 06	Morgan Co,Oh	10	07	20
Clark, John S.(Z)	1815	June 20	MariettaOhio	10	06	27
Clark, John S.(Z)	1817	Jan. 15	MariettaOhio	10	06	34
Clark, John(Z-M)	1822	Sept. 25	AlleghnyCoPa	04	03	13
Clark, John(Z-M)	1832	March 02	CoshoctnCoOh	09	03	06
Clark, John(Z-M)	1832	June 13	GuernseyCoOh	04	03	13
Clark, John(Z-M)	1832	June 13	GuernseyCoOh	04	03	13
Clark, John(Z-M)	1829	Dec. 21	CoshoctnCoOh	11	05	19
Clark, John(Z-M)	1835	Sept. 07	CoshoctnCoOh	05	04	15
Clark, John(Z-M)	1836	Jan. 18	CoshoctnCoOh	10	04	12
Clark, John(Z-M)	1836	Jan. 18	CoshoctnCoOh	10	04	19
Clark, John(Z-M)	1836	Oct. 28	ColumbanCoOh	09	08	06
Clark, John(Z-M)	1836	Oct. 28	ColumbanCoOh	09	08	06
Clark, John(Z-M)	1836	Nov. 02	ColumbanCoOh	09	08	06
Clark, Jonathan(Z)	1816	Dec. 09	ZanesvilleOh	09	04	21
Clark, Jonathan(Z)	1816	Dec. 09	ZanesvilleOh	09	04	21
Clark, Jonathan(Z)	1817	Jan. 21	ZanesvilleOh	09	04	24
Clark, Jonathan(Z)	1817	Feb. 19	ZanesvilleOh	09	04	23
Clark, Joseph(Z)	1809	Sept. 19	AlleghnyCoPa	12	13	05
Clark, Joseph(Z)	1815	April 14	AlleghnyCoPa	11	11	15
Clark, Joseph(Z-M)	1826	Jan. 20	GuernseyCoOh	03	01	22
Clark, Joshua(Y)	1832	June 25	ColumbanCoOh	03	12	08
Clark, Joshua(Z)	1833	Aug. 31	Morgan Co,Oh	09	07	31
Clark, Joshua(Z)	1813	April 16	CoshoctnCoOh	09	04	12
Clark, Joshua(Z)	1813	April 16	CoshoctnCoOh	09	04	12
Clark, Lambert(Y)	1825	April 20	TuscarwsCoOh	07	15	14
Clark, Lambert(Y)	1827	Feb. 15	TuscarwsCoOh	07	15	07
Clark, Mathew(Y)	1833	March 13	HarrisonCoOh	07	12	30
Clark, Nathan'l.(Z)	1817	Feb. 19	MuskingmCoOh	11	11	07
Clark, Nathaniel(Z)	1816	Sept. 27	WashngtnCoOh	12	11	13
Clark, Payne(Z)	1813	April 16	CoshoctnCoOh	09	04	12
Clark, S.(Y)	1825	Jan. 20	Brooke CoVir	02	07	11
Clark, Samuel Junr.(Y)	1833	March 12	Jeff.Co.,Oh.	03	12	08
Clark, Samuel(Z)	1837	Jan. 31	GuernseyCoOh	02	01	04
Clark, Samuel(Z-M)	1835	May 15	GuernseyCoOh	02	01	04
Clark, Samuel(Z-M)	1837	Feb. 28	GuernseyCoOh	02	01	04
Clark, Sanford(Z-M)	1836	Sept. 03	CoshoctnCoOh	08	06	08
Clark, Shirebiah(Z)	1817	Sept. 11	WashngtnCoOh	09	06	26
Clark, Shirebiah(Z)	1817	Sept. 11	WashngtnCoOh	09	06	14
Clark, Solomon(Y)	1823	Dec. 05	HarrisonCoOh	05	12	24
Clark, Thomas(Y)	1833	March 13	HarrisonCoOh	07	12	30
Clark, Thomas(Z-M)	1832	April 28	CoshoctnCoOh	06	04	01
Clark, William R.(Z-M)	1835	Sept. 26	CoshoctnCoOh	05	04	13
Clark, William R.(Z-M)	1837	April 05	CoshoctnCoOh	05	04	14
Clark, William(Z)	1813	Oct. 20	MuskingmCoOh	09	01	05
Clark, William(Z-M)	1833	Feb. 05	GuernseyCoOh	04	03	12
Clark, William(Z-M)	1833	April 16	CoshoctnCoOh	05	04	14
Clark, William(Z-M)	1836	May 11	CoshoctnCoOh	05	04	25
Clark, Wm. H.(Z-M)	1835	Feb. 14	GuernseyCoOh	04	03	13
Clark, Wm. R.(Z-M)	1837	Dec. 14	CoshoctnCoOh	05	04	13
Clark, Zachariah(Z-M)	1826	June 13	BelmontCo,Oh	06	03	15
Clarke, Alexander(Y)	1831	Jan. 14	HarrisonCoOh	07	11	05
Clarke, Andrew(Z-M)	1832	Oct. 04	GuernseyCoOh	02	03	07
Clarke, Andrew(Z-M)	1835	Dec. 14	GuernseyCoOh	02	03	07
Clarke, John(Y)	1821	Aug. 06	BelmontCo,Oh	04	06	27
Clarke, Matthew(Y)	1826	Sept. 05	Jeff.Co.,Oh.	07	12	35
Clarke, Robert(Y)	1826	Sept. 05	Jeff.Co.,Oh.	07	12	29
Clarke, Th's.(Y)	1826	Sept. 05	Jeff.Co.,Oh.	07	12	35
Clary, Enoch(Y)	1831	Oct. 10	Jeff.Co.,Oh.	09	07	21
Clary, Henry(Z)	1812	Feb. 21	GuernseyCoOh	01	03	21
Clary, Nathaniel(Y)	1826	Feb. 18	GuernseyCoOh	07	09	09

PURCHASER	YEAR	DATE	RESIDENCE	R	T	S
Clary, Nathaniel(Y)	1827	July 18	Guernsey	07	09	15
Clary, Nathaniel(Y)	1831	July 18	GuernseyCoOh	07	09	15
Clary, Samuel Jr.(Y)	1831	Oct. 10	Jeff.Co.,Oh.	07	09	21
Clary, Turner(Z)	1836	Oct. 18	GuernseyCoOh	08	06	10
Clay, Isaac(Y)	1824	Dec. 06	Stark Co.,Oh	09	11	21
Clay, William(Z-M)	1833	Sept. 07	TuscarwsCoOh	01	05	14
Clay, William(Z-M)	1834	Feb. 21	TuscarwsCoOh	01	05	05
Clay, William(Z-M)	1837	June 30	TuscarwsCoOh	02	06	03
Claypool, James(Z)	1808	Jan. 01	MuskingmCoOh	14	15	30
Claypool, James(Z)	1813	Nov. 12	MuskingmCoOh	14	15	30
Claypool, Joseph H.(Z)	1813	Nov. 03	?	15	17	34
Claypool, William(Z)	1808	Jan. 05	FairfeldCoOh	09	03	24
Clayton, George(Z)	1832	Sept. 17	Morgan Co,Oh	11	11	23
Clayton, George(Z-M)	1832	June 16	GuernseyCoOh	11	11	26
Clayton, Jno.(Z)	1814	Aug. 13	MuskingmCoOh	15	16	29
Clayton, John(Z)	1813	Nov. 15	FairfeldCoOh	15	16	20
Clayton, Joseph(Z)	1814	Aug. 13	MuskingmCoOh	15	16	29
Clayton, Samuel(Z)	1813	July 27	MuskingmCoOh	15	15	09
Clayton, Samuel(Z)	1816	June 18	FairfeldCoOh	15	15	15
Clayton, Samuel(Z)	1816	June 18	FairfeldCoOh	15	15	14
Clayton, Thomas(Z)	1805	Dec. 28	MuskingmCoOh	15	16	07
Clayton, Thomas(Z)	1805	Dec. 28	MuskingmCoOh	15	16	18
Clegg, Alexander(Z-M)	1829	Feb. 06	GuernseyCoOh	02	02	05
Clegg, Matthew(Z-M)	1829	Nov. 12	GuernseyCoOh	02	02	04
Clegg, Matthew(Z-M)	1831	May 04	GuernseyCoOh	02	02	05
Clements, Abraham(Z)	1810	Feb. 26	MuskingmCoOh	02	02	08
Clements, Henry H.(Z)	1833	Nov. 12	Perry Co.,Oh	15	15	14
Clements, Jacob(Z-M)	1833	Dec. 11	Brooke CoVir	03	08	07
Clements, Jacob(Z-M)	1833	Dec. 11	Brooke CoVir	03	08	08
Clements, James(Z-M),	1828	Oct. 15	GuernseyCoOh	04	02	19
Clements, Margaret(Z-M)	1834	Jan. 22	Brooke CoVir	03	08	08
Clements, Robt. S.(Z-M)	1826	May 24	KnoxCo.,Ohio	10	08	07
Clendenen, James(Z)	1833	Nov. 20	Morgan Co,Oh	09	07	30
Clendennan, James(Y)	1836	April 09	Jeff.Co.,Oh.	03	11	24
Cless, Henry(Y)	1827	Dec. 21	ColumbanCoOh	06	19	29
Clevinger, Eli(Y)	1827	March 24	BelmontCo,Oh	06	10	33
Clevinger, John(Z)	1827	March 06	BelmontCo,Oh	08	07	19
Clevinger, John(Z)	1836	Feb. 11	MonroeCo.,Oh	08	07	19
Clifford, Edward(Z)	1830	Aug. 13	HarrisonCoOh	11	11	11
Clifton, Josiah(Z)	1827	Dec. 19	Morgan Co,Oh	13	09	25
Cline, Adam(Z-M)	1828	May 03	TuscarwsCoOh	03	08	08
Cline, Daniel J.(Z)	1831	May 17	MuskingmCoOh	11	12	20
Cline, Jacob(Z)	1814	March 03	TuscarwsCoOh	01	10	05
Cline, Michael(Z)	1811	July 23	MuskingmCoOh	06	01	02
Cline, Michael(Z)	1816	May 25	MuskingmCoOh	05	01	05
Cline, Newberry(Y)	1831	June 04	Stark Co.,Oh	09	10	12
Clinger, John(Z)	1809	April 22	MuskingmCoOh	05	09	20
Clinis, David(Z)	1834	Feb. 24	MuskingmCoOh	11	12	34
Close, Charles(Y)	1822	Sept. 18	ColumbanCoOh	03	13	21
Close, Jesse(Z-M)	1830	Jan. 06	HolmesCoOhio	07	08	11
Close, John(Y)	1829	July 01	TuscarwsCoOh	07	15	04
Close, Peter(Y)	1829	May 25	TuscarwsCoOh	07	15	05
Clouse, Jacob(Z-M)	1835	Sept. 03	CoshoctnCoOh	07	05	04
Clouser, John(Z)	1821	Dec. 28	Morgan Co,Oh	09	07	10
Clover, Thomas C.(Y)	1830	May 31	BelmontCo,Oh	04	06	25
Clow, Abraham(Z-M)	1833	April 04	HolmesCoOhio	08	08	12
Clow, Alfred(Z-M)	1836	Oct. 31	HolmesCoOhio	08	08	03
Clow, Chaney(Z-M)	1832	Sept. 07	HolmesCoOhio	08	08	08
Clow, Chaney(Z-M)	1836	June 09	HolmesCoOhio	08	08	08
Clow, Chaney(Z-M)	1836	June 09	HolmesCoOhio	08	08	08
Clow, Chaney(Z-M)	1837	Dec. 26	HolmesCoOhio	08	08	04
Clow, Edward(Z-M)	1832	Oct. 15	HolmesCoOhio	08	08	05
Clow, Jackson(Z-M)	1833	Aug. 10	HolmesCoOhio	08	08	?
Clow, Malachi(Z-M)	1833	April 04	HolmesCoOhio	08	08	09
Clow, Malachi(Z-M)	1833	April 04	HolmesCoOhio	08	08	09
Clunes, John(Z-M)	1834	Dec. 03	LickingCo,Oh	11	04	13
Cly, George(Z-M)	1838	July 05	CoshoctnCoOh	09	07	21
Coalman, Colly(Z)	1830	Dec. 09	Morgan Co,Oh	11	11	03
Coalman, Wm.(Z-M)	1831	June 25	HarrisonCoOh	01	05	11

PURCHASER	YEAR	DATE	RESIDENCE	R	T	S
Coalson, David(Z)	1830	March 08	BelmontCo,Oh	12	09	13
Coalson, David(Z)	1830	May 10	Morgan Co,Oh	12	09	13
Coarts, Charles(Z)	1838	Oct. 29	GuernseyCoOh	08	05	22
Coarts, Charles(Z-M)	1829	Dec. 02	GuernseyCoOh	02	02	04
Coates, John(Z)	1816	Dec. 12	Boston, Mass	08	04	23
Coates, Josiah(Z)	1827	June 04	Ohio Co.,Vir	13	10	08
Coates, Lewis(Z-M)	1828	Sept. 10	GuernseyCoOh	01	04	15
Cobb, William(Z-M)	1832	May 22	CoshoctnCoOh	05	07	06
Cobb, Wm.(Z)	1809	Oct. 19	WashCo.,Penn	07	20	02
Cobbs, Pleasant Jr.(Y)	1828	June 07	Jeff.Co.,Oh.	05	18	31
Cobbs, Pleasant(Y)	1824	July 24	ColumbanCoOh	05	18	36
Cobbs, Pleasant(Y)	1828	Oct. 16	ColumbanCoOh	05	17	04
Coble, Philip(Y)	1830	June 14	TuscarwsCoOh	06	14	27
Coblentz, Jacob(Z)	1815	March 14	TuscarwsCoOh	03	08	05
Cobourn, Benjamin Junr.(Y)	1825	Dec. 21	ColumbanCoOh	05	14	02
Cobourz, Benjamin Jr.(Y)	1832	Jan. 10	ColumbanCoOh	04	12	29
Coburn, James(Y)	1831	Jan. 14	ColumbanCoOh	03	13	24
Cocher, George(Z-M)	1832	July 18	TuscarwsCoOh	02	10	24
Cochram, Joseph(Z-M)	1832	Oct. 02	CoshoctnCoOh	10	05	11
Cochran, Elijah(Z-M)	1835	Aug. 01	CoshoctnCoOh	09	04	15
Cochran, James(Z)	1831	July 18	ZanesvilleOh	11	01	19
Cochran, James(Z)	1836	Jan. 23	ZanesvilleOh	10	06	23
Cochran, James(Z-M)	1837	Jan. 11	ZanesvilleOh	01	06	11
Cochran, James(Z-M)	1837	Nov. 17	ZanesvilleOh	05	03	12
Cochran, John(Z)	1814	Dec. 08	MuskingmCoOh	15	15	10
Cochran, Joseph(Y)	1823	March 15	Jeff.Co.,Oh.	01	04	31
Cochran, William(Z-M)	1820	Nov. 01	GuernseyCoOh	04	03	21
Cochrane, Alex.(Z-M)	1831	April 16	GuernseyCoOh	04	02	01
Cock, John S.(Y)	1828	July 29	Jeff.Co.,Oh.	03	11	34
Cockram, Joseph(Z-M)	1833	March 15	CoshoctnCoOh	10	05	11
Cockram, Joshua(Z)	1816	Feb. 01	CoshoctnCoOh	09	05	04
Cockram, William(Z)	1816	Jan. 06	CoshoctnCoOh	09	05	07
Cockran, Joshua(Z)	1816	May 02	CoshoctnCoOh	09	05	14
Cockran, William(Z-M)	1833	March 26	GuernseyCoOh	04	03	21
Cockrell, Gabriel(Z)	1806	May 12	LoudonCo,Vir	13	12	03
Cockrell, John(Z)	1826	Jan. 12	Perry Co.,Oh	14	14	07
Coddington, Aza(Z)	1835	Jan. 06	Perry Co.,Oh	15	15	35
Coddington, Benjamin(Z)	1832	April 23	Perry Co.,Oh	15	15	35
Coddington, David(Z-M)	1835	Feb. 28	TompkinsCoNY	07	08	16
Coddington, David(Z-M)	1834	Sept. 27	TompkinsCoNY	08	08	17
Coddington, Zach'h.(Z)	1815	Jan. 05	WashngtnCoOh	12	11	24
Coe, Harvey(Z-M)	1825	March 09	FranklinCoOh	07	08	17
Coen, Isaac(Z)	1814	Feb. 18	KnoxCo.,Ohio	11	06	16
Coen, Jacob(Z)	1835	Feb. 20	GuernseyCoOh	08	08	09
Coen, William(Z)	1833	Sept. 02	Morgan Co,Oh	10	06	27
Coen, William(Z)	1815	June 21	KnoxCo.,Ohio	11	06	18
Coen, William(Z-M)	1832	May 22	Morgan Co,Oh	10	06	27
Coffee, John(Z)	1834	Jan. 16	Morgan Co,Oh	09	05	13
Coffee, William(Z)	1832	Sept. 03	Morgan Co,Oh	09	06	17
Coffield, Lawrence(Z)	1816	Nov. 18	WashCo.,Penn	10	05	13
Coffman, Christian(Z-M)	1824	July 06	MuskingmCoOh	09	03	15
Coffman, William(Z)	1825	Aug. 06	MuskingmCoOh	15	17	02
Coffman, William(Z)	1825	Nov. 04	MuskingmCoOh	15	17	02
Coffman, William(Z)	1805	Dec. 21	MuskingmCoOh	15	17	12
Coffy, John(Z-M)	1836	March 03	CarrollCo,Oh	03	07	02
Cohagen, Aquilla(Z)	1824	Nov. 27	FrederkCoVir	11	10	18
Colborn, John(Z)	1836	Feb. 02	Perry Co.,Oh	15	14	21
Colburn, R.(Z)	1815	April 01	MuskingmCoOh	15	16	26
Coldarer, Fred'k.(Y)	1827	Dec. 24	AlleghnyCoPa	06	13	10
Coldwell, John(Z)	1832	May 22	Morgan Co,Oh	09	06	03
Cole, Albert(Z)	1817	Jan. 14	MuskingmCoOh	12	10	02
Cole, Charles(Y)	1826	Jan. 12	Jeff.Co.,Oh.	04	10	18
Cole, Daniel(Z-M)	1837	March 30	HolmesCoOhio	09	08	23
Cole, Daniel(Z-M)	1837	April 08	HolmesCoOhio	09	08	23
Cole, Ezekiel(Z)	1820	July 03	Morgan Co,Oh	09	07	09
Cole, Peter(Y)	1824	May 26	HarrisonCoOh	05	12	05
Cole, Thomas(Y)	1827	Jan. 04	Jeff.Co.,Oh.	03	10	22
Cole, Thomas(Z)	1813	Oct. 09	Baltimore,Md	15	16	28
Coleman, E.(Z)	1816	Jan. 09	W.ZanesvleOh	13	09	27

PURCHASER	YEAR	DATE	RESIDENCE	R	T	S
Coleman, J.(Z)	1829	Nov. 23	Morgan Co,Oh	13	10	36
Coleman, Jacob(Y)	1824	July 03	Stark Co.,Oh	09	12	08
Coleman, John(Y)	1828	Sept. 03	HarrisonCoOh	06	11	28
Coleman, N.(Z)	1816	Jan. 09	W.ZanesvleOh	13	09	27
Coleman, Nathan(Z)	1832	Sept. 14	MuskingmCoOh	11	12	34
Coleman, Thomas(Z)	1836	Jan. 26	Perry Co.,Oh	14	12	25
Colepy, Jacob(Z-M)	1825	March 02	KnoxCo.,Ohio	10	08	22
Coler, George(Z)	1830	Nov. 08	Morgan Co,Oh	13	08	22
Coles, Isaac(Y)	1831	Sept. 28	GuernseyCoOh	07	09	09
Coles, John(Z)	1827	Dec. 29	GuernseyCoOh	13	08	36
Coles, Thomas(Z)	1835	March 05	GuernseyCoOh	08	07	10
Collantine, Henry(Z-M)	1835	Sept. 18	GuernseyCoOh	03	05	21
Collet, William(Z)	1815	May 30	TuscarwsCoOh	03	10	16
Collinge, Nancy(Z)	1829	May 23	MuskingmCoOh	14	14	14
Collins, Elijah(Z)	1831	Dec. 10	Morgan Co,Oh	10	08	06
Collins, Elijah(Z-M)	1833	Aug. 05	HolmesCoOhio	07	08	18
Collins, Elisha(Z)	1813	Dec. 08	GuernseyCoOh	10	08	05
Collins, Elisha(Z)	1815	Jan. 05	GuernseyCoOh	11	13	36
Collins, Fenley(Z)	1827	Nov. 19	Morgan Co,Oh	10	08	06
Collins, Findley(Z)	1816	April 03	GuernseyCoOh	10	09	31
Collins, Finley(Z)	1831	Dec. 27	Morgan Co,Oh	10	08	06
Collins, John(Y)	1835	Aug. 17	ColumbanCoOh	03	13	30
Collins, John(Z-M)	1832	Dec. 08	GuernseyCoOh	03	01	22
Collins, John(Z-M)	1835	July 06	GuernseyCoOh	03	01	22
Collins, Sam'l.(Z)	1835	Oct. 23	CarrollCo,Oh	09	06	19
Collins, Sam'l.(Z)	1835	Oct. 23	CarrollCo,Oh	09	06	19
Collins, Thomas(Y)	1831	Sept. 16	ColumbanCoOh	03	13	30
Collins, Thomas(Y)	1832	Nov. 08	ColumbanCoOh	03	13	30
Collins, Thomas(Z)	1815	Dec. 18	MuskingmCoOh	06	02	13
Collins, William K.(Z)	1833	Jan. 04	GuernseyCoOh	08	08	05
Collins, William(Y)	1831	Sept. 16	ColumbanCoOh	03	13	29
Collopy, Jacob(Z-M)	1832	Nov. 22	KnoxCo.,Ohio	10	08	23
Collopy, Jacob(Z-M)	1832	Dec. 15	KnoxCo.,Ohio	10	08	22
Collopy, Timothy W.(Z-M)	1833	Nov. 18	KnoxCo.,Ohio	10	08	22
Colopy, Jacob(Z-M)	1831	June 16	KnoxCo.,Ohio	10	08	22
Colopy, Jacob(Z-M)	1835	May 04	KnoxCo.,Ohio	10	08	22
Colopy, Thomas(Z-M)	1835	Nov. 19	CoshoctnCoOh	05	04	05
Colp, Jacob(Z-M)	1831	Aug. 31	HolmesCoOhio	04	09	05
Colp, Jacob(Z-M)	1831	Aug. 31	HolmesCoOhio	04	09	05
Colshear, Mathias(Z)	1816	May 16	MuskingmCoOh	07	03	20
Colson, James C.(Z-M)	1833	March 14	CoshoctnCoOh	04	06	03
Colvig, Wm.(Z)	1835	Dec. 17	MonroeCo.,Oh	08	06	21
Colvin, William(Z-M)	1836	Oct. 29	BeaverCo.,Pa	03	05	16
Colwell, William(Y)	1826	March 29	Stark Co.,Oh	06	16	31
Colwell, William(Z-M)	1833	Jan. 09	MuskingmCoOh	06	03	20
Combs, John(Z)	1835	Sept. 15	Morgan Co,Oh	10	07	18
Combs, Mathew(Z)	1831	Jan. 27	Perry Co.,Oh	14	14	07
Combs, Robert(Z)	1833	March 25	Morgan Co,Oh	10	06	20
Comly, Jas.(Z)	1823	May 21	Perry Co.,Oh	15	14	19
Compton, Rich'd.(Z-M)	1835	March 13	CoshoctnCoOh	07	05	09
Comstock, David(Z)	1804	Nov. 29	Ohio Co.,Vir	06	01	18
Conaghan, Dennis H.(Y)	1822	July 20	Stark Co.,Oh	07	19	22
Conan, Caleb(Z-M)	1833	Sept. 07	GuernseyCoOh	02	03	13
Conann, Caleb(Z-M)	1836	Feb. 10	GuernseyCoOh	02	03	13
Conaway, Basil(Z)	1832	Sept. 10	Perry Co.,Oh	14	14	29
Conaway, Isaiah(Z)	1833	Dec. 05	Perry Co.,Oh	14	13	32
Conaway, Isaiah(Z)	1836	April 27	Perry Co.,Oh	14	13	29
Conaway, Jesse(Z)	1826	Feb. 11	Morgan Co,Oh	13	09	22
Concle, John(Z)	1807	Sept. 12	MuskingmCoOh	10	07	13
Condon, Perry(Y)	1830	Oct. 08	BelmontCo,Oh	07	09	26
Condon, William(Z-M)	1835	May 18	BelmontCo,Oh	02	01	04
Cone, Jared Jr.(Z-M)	1831	June 15	CoshoctnCoOh	10	03	09
Cone, Jared Jr.(Z-M)	1831	July 18	CoshoctnCoOh	10	03	09
Cone, Jared(Z)	1816	Oct. 02	HarrisonCoOh	09	04	13
Cone, Jared(Z)	1816	Oct. 02	HarrisonCoOh	09	04	14
Cone, Jared(Z)	1816	Oct. 02	HarrisonCoOh	09	04	14
Cone, Jared(Z)	1816	Oct. 02	HarrisonCoOh	09	04	18
Cone, Jared(Z)	1816	Oct. 02	HarrisonCoOh	09	04	11
Cone, Jared(Z)	1816	Oct. 02	HarrisonCoOh	09	04	10

PURCHASER	YEAR	DATE	RESIDENCE	R	T	S
Cone, Jered(Z)	1816	Sept. 27	HarrisonCoOh	01	05	18
Cone, Michael(Z)	1814	March 29	TuscarwsCoOh	03	09	08
Cone, Michael(Z)	1814	March 29	TuscarwsCoOh	03	09	02
Coneal, George(Z)	1815	Feb. 11	GuernseyCoOh	10	07	08
Coneal, John(Z)	1807	Sept. 12	MuskingmCoOh	10	07	13
Conqar, Aaron(Z-M)	1826	Oct. 06	KnoxCo.,Ohio	11	04	01
Conley, Samuel(Y)	1832	Sept. 03	ColumbanCoOh	04	13	19
Conlin, John(Y)	1833	Feb. 14	ColumbanCoOh	05	15	05
Conlin, John(Z)	1831	March 15	MuskingmCoOh	11	12	30
Conn, Alexander(Z)	1828	Jan. 09	Morgan Co,Oh	10	06	04
Conn, Alexander(Z)	1833	March 29	Morgan Co,Oh	10	06	05
Conn, Alexander(Z)	1834	Oct. 01	Morgan Co,Oh	10	06	05
Conn, Alexander(Z)	1835	Sept. 01	Morgan Co,Oh	10	06	05
Conn, James(Z)	1820	Nov. 21	Morgan Co,Oh	10	07	30
Conn, James(Z)	1827	June 22	Morgan Co,Oh	10	06	17
Conn, James(Z)	1831	Oct. 14	Morgan Co,Oh	10	06	17
Conn, James(Z)	1836	Jan. 19	Morgan Co,Oh	10	06	08
Conn, John(Z)	1831	June 18	Morgan Co,Oh	10	06	17
Conn, Robert(Z)	1836	Jan. 19	Morgan Co,Oh	10	06	20
Connelly, B.(Y)	1823	March 07	AlleghnyCoPa	04	14	22
Connelly, Charles(Z)	1815	Sept. 14	PittsburghPa	02	04	10
Connelly, David(Y)	1830	April 29	HarrisonCoOh	05	12	28
Connelly, R. H.(Y)	1823	March 07	AlleghnyCoPa	04	14	22
Connelly, Th's.(Y)	1823	March 07	AlleghnyCoPa	05	15	21
Connelly, Thos.(Y)	1822	Aug. 06	AlleghnyCoPa	05	15	21
Connelly, Ths.(Y)	1822	June 26	AlleghnyCoPa	05	15	21
Connelly, Wm.(Y)	1822	Aug. 06	AlleghnyCoPa	05	15	21
Connelly, Wm.(Y)	1823	March 07	AlleghnyCoPa	05	15	21
Connelly, Wm.(Y)	1825	April 06	AlleghnyCoPa	05	15	21
Connely, Wm.(Y)	1822	June 26	AlleghnyCoPa	05	15	21
Conner, Daniel(Z-M)	1826	Dec. 08	CoshoctnCoOh	09	07	02
Conner, Edw'd.(Z)	1828	Dec. 16	Morgan Co,Oh	12	10	02
Conner, James(Z)	1816	Dec. 06	BeaverCo.,Pa	09	07	13
Conner, James(Z-M)	1827	Nov. 30	CoshoctnCoOh	09	09	16
Conner, James(Z-M)	1831	Nov. 07	CoshoctnCoOh	09	07	08
Conner, James(Z-M)	1832	May 22	HolmesCoOhio	09	09	16
Conner, James(Z-M)	1836	Jan. 08	HolmesCoOhio	09	09	17
Conner, James(Z-M)	1836	April 02	CoshoctnCoOh	09	07	09
Conner, James(Z-M)	1837	Feb. 16	CoshoctnCoOh	08	07	05
Conner, John Junr.(Z)	1816	June 04	GuernseyCoOh	10	09	34
Conner, John Senr.(Z)	1815	Aug. 09	GuernseyCoOh	10	09	34
Conner, John(Z)	1833	Sept. 03	GuernseyCoOh	10	09	27
Conner, John(Z)	1808	April 22	MuskingmCoOh	04	01	23
Conner, John(Z)	1815	May 02	Brooke CoVir	09	05	07
Conner, John(Z)	1817	Sept. 15	BeaverCo.,Pa	09	07	06
Conner, John(Z-M)	1835	July 10	CoshoctnCoOh	09	08	23
Conner, John(Z-M)	1836	Aug. 18	HolmesCoOhio	09	08	23
Conner, Patrick(Y)	1827	July 26	PortageCo,Oh	05	15	11
Conner, Robert(Z-M)	1822	Nov. 29	CoshoctnCoOh	09	07	03
Conner, Robert(Z-M)	1828	Dec. 22	HolmesCoOhio	09	08	12
Conner, Robert(Z-M)	1834	Sept. 13	HolmesCoOhio	09	07	18
Conner, Robt.(Z-M)	1830	Dec. 03	HolmesCoOhio	08	08	23
Conner, William(Z)	1816	Nov. 13	WashngtnCoOh	13	08	12
Conner, William(Z-M)	1832	May 22	CoshoctnCoOh	09	07	04
Conner, William(Z-M)	1834	Nov. 08	CoshoctnCoOh	09	08	25
Conner, Wm.(Z-M)	1835	Dec. 16	CoshoctnCoOh	09	08	25
Connon, Richard(Z)	1806	Aug. 02	MuskingmCoOh	14	16	02
Conoway, Eli(Y)	1832	March 07	HarrisonCoOh	05	11	34
Conoway, Jeremiah(Z)	1807	Sept. 07	FairfeldCoOh	13	09	36
Conoway, John(Y)	1832	May 30	HarrisonCoOh	06	12	17
Conoway, Mich'l.(Y)	1829	April 13	HarrisonCoOh	06	11	33
Conrad, Elizabeth(Z)	1806	July 23	FairfeldCoOh	11	05	06
Conrad, Jacob(Z)	1816	Sept. 24	WestmrldCoPa	06	07	03
Conrad, Jacob(Z)	1816	Sept. 24	WestmrldCoPa	06	07	03
Conrad, Jacob(Z)	1816	Sept. 24	WestmrldCoPa	06	07	08
Conrad, Joseph(Z-M)	1837	March 11	CarrollCo,Oh	03	07	23
Conrad, Nathan(Z)	1806	July 23	FairfeldCoOh	11	05	07
Conrow, Jacob(Z-M)	1832	Oct. 13	BelmontCo,Oh	01	06	15
Conser, David(Z)	1814	May 30	CoshoctnCoOh	05	08	21

PURCHASER	YEAR	DATE	RESIDENCE	R	T	S
Conser, Henry(Z)	1810	Oct. 30	TuscarwsCoOh	05	08	20
Conser, Henry(Z)	1810	Oct. 30	TuscarwsCoOh	05	08	20
Conser, Henry(Z)	1814	May 30	CoshoctnCoOh	05	08	21
Conser, Jacob(Z)	1811	Nov. 26	CentreCoPenn	04	07	05
Convers, Daniel(Z)	1814	May 16	ZanesvilleOh	12	13	36
Convers, Daniel(Z)	1814	Oct. 13	ZanesvilleOh	06	04	03
Converse & Munro(Z)	1811	Aug. 20	ZanesvilleOh	03	02	08
Converse, Daniel(Z)	1806	Nov. 25	ZanesvilleOh	13	12	10
Converse, Daniel(Z)	1812	May 19	ZanesvilleOh	13	11	24
Converse, Daniel(Z)	1814	Feb. 25	?	10	04	11
Conway, Isaah(Z)	1833	Dec. 07	Perry Co.,Oh	14	13	29
Conway, Jeremiah(Z)	1815	June 13	MuskingmCoOh	14	15	15
Conway, Jeremiah(Z)	1815	June 24	MuskingmCoOh	12	11	21
Conway, William(Z)	1830	April 19	MuskingmCoOh	14	14	18
Conway, Wm.(Z)	1817	Oct. 24	MuskingmCoOh	14	14	02
Conwell, Pretyman(Z-M)	1827	June 02	FayetteCo,Pa	01	06	21
Conwell, Pretyman(Z-M)	1827	June 02	FayetteCo,Pa	01	06	22
Conwell, Thos.(Z-M)	1831	Nov. 02	TuscarwsCoOh	01	06	20
Conwell, William(Z)	1811	Nov. 27	MuskingmCoOh	13	10	05
Conyinghan, Henry(Z)	1811	June 25	MuskingmCoOh	15	17	10
Cook, Daniel(Y)	1822	April 30	ColumbanCoOh	04	17	02
Cook, Daniel(Y)	1825	Sept. 03	BelmontCo,Oh	06	08	26
Cook, Daniel(Y)	1826	Dec. 22	ColumbanCoOh	05	17	17
Cook, Daniel(Y)	1826	Dec. 22	ColumbanCoOh	05	17	17
Cook, Ellis(Z-M)	1832	Sept. 07	BelmontCo,Oh	03	04	03
Cook, Ellis(Z-M)	1834	Nov. 22	BelmontCo,Oh	03	04	02
Cook, John(Z)	1836	Feb. 18	Perry Co.,Oh	14	13	06
Cook, John(Z)	1836	Feb. 19	Perry Co.,Oh	14	13	05
Cook, Joseph(Y)	1836	Jan. 09	SteubenvleOh	03	12	02
Cook, Joshua(Z-M)	1835	Nov. 04	CarrollCo,Oh	03	08	04
Cook, Peter(Y)	1823	May 30	Stark Co.,Oh	06	16	15
Cook, Peter(Y)	1824	April 01	Stark Co.,Oh	06	16	22
Cook, Peter(Y)	1825	June 10	Stark Co.,Oh	06	16	22
Cook, Robert(Z)	1815	July 10	HarrisonCoOh	10	05	13
Cook, Robert(Z-M)	1838	March 22	HarrisonCoOh	04	03	01
Cook, Robert(Z-M)	1838	March 22	HarrisonCoOh	03	04	25
Cook, Robert(Z-M)	1837	Nov. 29	HarrisonCoOh	04	04	11
Cook, Stacey(Y)	1822	April 30	ColumbanCoOh	04	17	13
Cook, Stephen(Z)	1814	July 28	KnoxCo.,Ohio	11	05	17
Cook, Thomas(Y)	1822	Oct. 31	WashCo.,Penn	06	15	12
Cook, William John(Y)	1836	May 19	HarrisonCoOh	07	11	17
Cookerly, Henry(Z)	1834	March 25	Perry Co.,Oh	14	12	29
Cooks, Charles(Z-M)	1829	Dec. 02	GuernseyCoOh	02	02	04
Cooksey, Samuel(Z-M)	1831	Oct. 15	CoshoctnCoOh	07	04	17
Cooksey, William(Z)	1815	April 01	MuskingmCoOh	08	03	13
Cooley, Francis(Z-M)	1824	Nov. 25	TuscarwsCoOh	04	09	05
Coomes, John(Z)	1815	Nov. 18	LickingCo,Oh	10	01	01
Coomes, John(Z)	1816	Feb. 16	LickingCo,Oh	10	01	10
Coomes, William(Z)	1815	March 20	LickingCo,Oh	01	07	08
Coomes, William(Z)	1816	Aug. 16	LickingCo,Oh	09	01	06
Coon, Nathaniel(Z-M)	1838	Oct. 25	RichlandCoOh	10	08	08
Coon, William Junr.(Z)	1832	July 09	GuernseyCoOh	08	08	15
Cooney, George(Z-M)	1835	July 31	HolmesCoOhio	06	03	10
Cooper, Caleb(Y)	1825	Nov. 23	HarrisonCoOh	07	11	15
Cooper, Caleb(Y)	1827	May 11	HarrisonCoOh	07	12	15
Cooper, Caleb(Y)	1827	May 11	HarrisonCoOh	07	12	15
Cooper, Cunningham S.(Y)	1829	March 18	Brooke CoVir	02	09	15
Cooper, George(Z)	1815	Feb. 28	KnoxCo.,Ohio	11	04	05
Cooper, Isaac(Z)	1811	April 03	FayetteCo,Pa	15	16	09
Cooper, Jacob(Z)	1805	June 07	FairfeldCoOh	14	15	17
Cooper, Jacob(Z)	1811	April 03	FayetteCo,Pa	15	16	08
Cooper, Jacob(Z)	1811	April 29	LoudonCo,Vir	14	15	31
Cooper, Jacob(Z)	1816	March 05	MuskingmCoOh	14	14	08
Cooper, James(Y)	1831	May 30	ColumbanCoOh	02	10	19
Cooper, James(Z)	1811	June 15	MuskingmCoOh	15	16	08
Cooper, James(Z)	1814	Nov. 22	MuskingmCoOh	15	16	10
Cooper, Joseph(Y)	1824	July 31	ColumbanCoOh	05	17	09
Cooper, Joseph(Z)	1832	Aug. 07	Morgan Co,Oh	10	08	22
Cooper, Levi(Z)	1805	Oct. 18	FrederkCoVir	08	02	07

PURCHASER	YEAR	DATE	RESIDENCE	R	T	S
Cooper, Marmaduke(Z)	1831	Aug. 23	HolmesCoOhio	08	08	25
Cooper, Meshach(Z-M)	1833	May 24	HolmesCoOhio	09	08	13
Cooper, Philip(Y)	1821	Sept. 26	ColumbanCoOh	02	10	15
Cooper, Robert(Z)	1806	Jan. 06	WestmrldCoPa	11	13	28
Cooper, Robert(Z)	1806	Jan. 06	WestmrldCoPa	11	13	17
Cooper, Samuel(Z)	1835	Jan. 09	MonroeCo.,Oh	08	07	08
Cooper, Stephen Senr.(Z)	1811	Oct. 30	MuskingmCoOh	10	03	11
Cope, Abiah Junr.(Z)	1820	Oct. 23	ChesterCo,Pa	12	11	13
Cope, Edmund(Z)	1838	Dec. 03	MonroeCo.,Oh	08	06	15
Cope, Henry(Y)	1830	Jan. 04	ColumbanCoOh	02	09	33
Cope, James(Z)	1821	June 11	MuskingmCoOh	12	12	14
Copeland, David(Y)	1832	Feb. 08	Jeff.Co.,Oh.	06	12	23
Copeland, James(Y)	1829	March 18	Jeff.Co.,Co.	07	12	34
Copeland, John(Z-M)	1828	March 11	HarrisonCoOh	01	03	20
Copeland, Josiah S.(Z)	1832	April 04	ZanesvilleOh	11	12	28
Copeland, Josiah S.(Z)	1832	Aug. 31	MuskingmCoOh	11	12	28
Coplen, Elijah(Z-M)	1833	Feb. 21	LickingCo,Oh	09	06	19
Coppock, John(Y)	1821	Nov. 15	ColumbanCoOh	04	16	15
Coppock, John(Y)	1826	Nov. 29	ColumbanCoOh	06	18	13
Coppock, Sam'l. Jr.(Y)	1823	June 10	ColumbanCoOh	05	18	26
Coppock, Samuel Jr.(Y)	1821	June 06	ColumbanCoOh	05	18	35
Coppock, Samuel Junr.(Y)	1826	Jan. 24	ColumbanCoOh	05	18	35
Corbal, John(Z)	1816	May 20	ChesterCo,Pa	07	05	15
Corbet, Peter(Z)	1807	Feb. 02	MuskingmCoOh	03	01	20
Corbet, Peter(Z-M)	1836	Aug. 06	GuernseyCoOh	04	03	22
Corbet, Peter(Z-M)	1836	Aug. 08	GuernseyCoOh	04	03	19
Corbet, Robert(Z)	1813	May 04	CoshoctnCoOh	04	06	19
Corbin, Joseph(Z-M)	1829	Jan. 08	CoshoctnCoOh	03	06	04
Corbin, Joseph(Z-M)	1832	Nov. 20	CoshoctnCoOh	06	04	12
Corbin, Joshua(Z-M)	1825	Oct. 14	KnoxCo.,Ohio	10	05	14
Corbin, Thomas(Z-M)	1835	Sept. 09	CoshoctnCoOh	06	04	09
Corbin, William K.(Z-M)	1829	Dec. 24	KnoxCo.,Ohio	10	05	17
Corbman, Geo.(Z)	1809	May 04	TuscarwsCoOh	02	07	12
Corder, William(Z-M)	1836	Oct. 27	CoshoctnCoOh	07	04	17
Cordery, Thomas Senr.(Z)	1814	Feb. 10	?	01	09	20
Cordray, John(Z-M)	1833	March 18	MuskingmCoOh	03	06	16
Cordreey, Thomas Senr.(Z)	1814	Feb. 10	?	01	09	20
Cordrey, Thomas Senr.(Z)	1814	Jan. 22	TuscarwsCoOh	01	09	19
Cordry, Nathan(Z-M)	1834	Feb. 10	TuscarwsCoOh	01	09	06
Corier, Jacob(Z)	1811	Nov. 26	CentreCoPenn	04	07	05
Corl, Neil(Z)	1836	Sept. 27	PittsburghPa	15	15	13
Corm, Robt.(Z)	1821	June 08	Morgan Co,Oh	10	06	08
Corn, Hardman T.(Z-M)	1829	May 27	KnoxCo.,Ohio	10	05	23
Corn, Isaac(Z)	1810	April 13	Jeff.Co.,Oh.	11	06	16
Cornel, Richard(Z)	1817	Aug. 21	GuernseyCoOh	02	03	25
Cornelius, Christp'r.(Z-M)	1837	Feb. 09	MuskingmCoOh	05	03	10
Cornelius, Christp'r.(Z-M)	1837	Feb. 09	MuskingmCoOh	05	03	11
Cornelius, Isaac(Z)	1814	Feb. 22	?	05	02	04
Cornelius, William(Z-M)	1835	Nov. 28	MuskingmCoOh	05	03	03
Cornelius, William(Z-M)	1838	Dec. 15	MuskingmCoOh	04	03	14
Cornell, Ralph(Z-M)	1831	Nov. 23	HolmesCoOhio	07	08	10
Cornell, Thomas(Z)	1835	Sept. 12	GuernseyCoOh	10	06	01
Cornell, William(Z)	1835	Oct. 26	GuernseyCoOh	10	07	36
Cornell, William(Z-M)	1837	March 15	KnoxCo.,Ohio	10	08	05
Corner, Geo. L.(Z)	1830	June 09	Morgan Co,Oh	13	08	23
Corner, William(Z)	1829	Aug. 10	Morgan Co,Oh	12	10	29
Corner, William(Z)	1816	Nov. 13	WashngtnCoOh	13	08	12
Corns, William(Z)	1830	March 18	MuskingmCoOh	12	12	09
Cornwell, Benjamin(Y)	1830	May 21	ColumbanCoOh	03	13	21
Cornwell, William(Z)	1806	June 23	ZanesvilleOh	13	12	11
Corp, Benjamin(Z)	1827	Nov. 12	WashCo.,Penn	08	05	06
Corp, John S.(Z)	1836	Aug. 17	WashngtnCoOh	09	05	13
Corp, John Squire(Z)	1832	May 22	Morgan Co,Oh	09	05	12
Corran, Isabella(Y)	1827	March 29	ColumbanCoOh	06	18	23
Cortright, William(Z-M)	1836	Jan. 21	GuernseyCoOh	02	04	15
Corvin, Morris(Z-M)	1837	Dec. 30	Wayne Co.,Oh	08	07	10
Coryel, Andrew(Z)	1811	Oct. 28	FredrickCo ?	15	18	17
Cosgrove, Elliott(Z-M)	1833	July 05	TuscarwsCoOh	01	05	22
Cotter, James(Y)	1834	Feb. 14	ColumbanCoOh	03	13	33

PURCHASER	YEAR	DATE	RESIDENCE	R	T	S
Cotter, Richard(Y)	1829	March 30	WashCo.,Penn	06	14	19
Couden, John(Z)	1806	Aug. 13	HampshreCoVa	14	15	34
Couden, John(Z)	1812	Feb. 13	MuskingmCoOh	15	16	01
Coughenour, Jos.(Z-M)	1830	May 30	TuscarwsCoOh	04	07	14
Coughenoure, Joseph(Z-M)	1833	Jan. 22	TuscarwsCoOh	04	07	14
Coulson, Jabez(Y)	1822	Aug. 15	ColumbanCoOh	04	14	06
Coulter, E.(Z-M)	1820	Sept. 12	BedfordCo,Pa	04	01	21
Coulter, Eliz. & Heirs(Z-M)	1821	Dec. 17	GuernseyCoOh	04	01	21
Coulter, Eliz. & Heirs(Z-M)	1821	Dec. 17	GuernseyCoOh	04	01	22
Coulter, James(Z-M)	1836	Oct. 12	GuernseyCoOh	04	03	16
Coulter, James(Z-M)	1836	Oct. 12	GuernseyCoOh	04	03	17
Coulter, James(Z-M)	1837	May 12	GuernseyCoOh	04	03	17
Coulter, Jenny(Y)	1823	March 24	Jeff.Co.,Oh.	06	17	34
Coulter, John(Y)	1832	Oct. 03	HarrisonCoOh	07	14	33
Coulter, John(Y)	1832	Oct. 03	HarrisonCoOh	07	14	32
Coulter, John(Y)	1832	Oct. 10	HarrisonCoOh	07	14	29
Coulter, John(Z)	1827	May 03	LickingCo,Oh	11	01	11
Coulter, Joseph(Z-M)	1839	June 25	WestmrldCoPa	11	04	11
Coulter, Joseph(Z-M)	1839	June 25	WestmrldCoPa	07	08	07
Coulter, Thomas(Z-M)	1837	Aug. 07	CoshoctnCoOh	04	05	23
Coulter, William(Z)	1815	Dec. 26	CoshoctnCoOh	09	05	12
Coumbe, Thos.(Z-M)	1831	Sept. 28	KnoxCo.,Ohio	10	08	24
Coumbe, William(Z-M)	1833	Jan. 04	KnoxCo.,Ohio	10	08	21
Coumbie, John(Z-M)	1832	July 20	KnoxCo.,Ohio	10	08	24
Counover, John(Y)	1833	April 25	ColumbanCoOh	03	12	24
Counsil, Isaac(Z)	1832	April 10	Morgan Co,Oh	11	10	01
Countryman, David(Z-M)	1830	Oct. 19	TuscarwsCoOh	02	08	23
Courson, Richard(Z)	1806	March 24	MuskingmCoOh	15	18	09
Courtney, David(Z-M)	1835	Jan. 23	MuskingmCoOh	10	04	25
Courtney, David(Z-M)	1835	Sept. 01	MuskingmCoOh	10	04	16
Courtney, David(Z-M)	1835	Sept. 05	MuskingmCoOh	10	04	25
Courtney, Edw'd.(Y)	1822	Nov. 11	ColumbanCoOh	05	18	22
Courtney, Geo.(Z)	1830	Jan. 25	BelmontCo,Oh	11	10	11
Courtney, J.(Z)	1814	May 23	MuskingmCoOh	09	01	20
Courtney, W.(Z)	1814	May 23	MuskingmCoOh	09	01	20
Coury, Louis(Y)	1826	Aug. 12	Stark Co.,Oh	07	19	15
Cousins, John(Y)	1833	June 18	Jeff.Co.,Oh.	06	12	23
Couts, William(Z)	1817	Aug. 14	GuernseyCoOh	02	05	22
Couts, William(Z-M)	1827	May 24	GuernseyCoOh	02	05	22
Couts, William(Z-M)	1830	June 12	GuernseyCoOh	02	05	21
Covington, Elijah(Y)	1832	June 02	HarrisonCoOh	07	12	26
Covnel, Richard(Z)	1817	Aug. 21	GuernseyCoOh	02	03	25
Covner, William(Z)	1816	Nov. 13	WashngtnCoOh	13	08	12
Cowan, Henry(Z)	1836	Feb. 19	MonroeCo.,Oh	08	06	05
Cowan, Henry(Z)	1836	Feb. 19	MonroeCo.,Oh	08	06	05
Cowan, Henry(Z)	1836	Feb. 19	MonroeCo.,Oh	08	06	06
Cowan, Henry(Z)	1836	Feb. 19	MonroeCo.,Oh	08	06	06
Cowan, Isabella(Y)	1827	March 09	ColumbanCoOh	06	18	23
Cowan, William(Z-M)	1836	Feb. 19	GuernseyCoOh	03	03	15
Cowan, Wm.(Z)	1827	Sept. 04	GuernseyCoOh	03	03	15
Cowden, David(Z)	1836	Jan. 06	MuskingmCoOh	05	03	03
Cowden, John(Z)	1831	March 29	MuskingmCoOh	10	09	26
Cowden, John(Z)	1831	March 29	MuskingmCoOh	10	09	26
Cowden, John(Z-M)	1828	April 18	MuskingmCoOh	05	02	01
Cowden, Joseph(Z-M)	1831	Oct. 10	MuskingmCoOh	06	03	11
Cowden, Robert(Z-M)	1833	March 27	MuskingmCoOh	05	03	04
Cowden, Robert(Z-M)	1835	Nov. 20	MuskingmCoOh	05	03	04
Cowden, Robert(Z-M)	1836	Jan. 26	MuskingmCoOh	05	03	03
Cowder, William N.(Z-M)	1835	Oct. 01	TuscarwsCoOh	01	05	04
Cowel, Christopher(Z-M)	1837	Nov. 29	GuernseyCoOh	04	03	14
Cowen, Robert(Z)	1816	Nov. 25	MuskingmCoOh	06	02	17
Cowgill, Isaac(Z)	1809	Aug. 28	BelmontCo,Oh	04	04	22
Cowgill, Isaac(Z)	1809	Oct. 14	BelmontCo,Oh	04	04	21
Cowgill, James Simpson(Y)	1827	July 04	ColumbanCoOh	05	17	03
Cowgill, Joseph(Z-M)	1837	April 13	GuernseyCoOh	04	04	23
Cox, Benjamin(Z)	1825	May 16	Morgan Co,Oh	09	07	21
Cox, Benjamin(Z)	1835	Dec. 11	Morgan Co,Oh	09	07	15
Cox, Church(Z-M)	1823	Dec. 23	GuernseyCoOh	01	03	05
Cox, Church(Z-M)	1823	Dec. 23	GuernseyCoOh	02	03	10

PURCHASER	YEAR	DATE	RESIDENCE	R	T	S
Cox, Elijah(Z-M)	1836	Jan. 12	CoshoctnCoOh	05	07	01
Cox, Elijah(Z-M)	1836	Jan. 12	CoshoctnCoOh	05	07	15
Cox, Israel(Z)	1828	April 10	Brooke CoVir	12	11	34
Cox, Israel(Z)	1830	Feb. 06	Brooke CoVir	11	12	28
Cox, Jacob(Z-M)	1835	Dec. 09	TuscarwsCoOh	03	05	21
Cox, Jaret(Z)	1834	March 05	Morgan Co,Oh	10	08	26
Cox, John(Z)	1824	May 19	MuskingmCoOh	11	13	15
Cox, Joseph(Z-M)	1833	Sept. 30	MuskingmCoOh	03	01	07
Cox, Joseph(Z-M)	1834	Sept. 08	GuernseyCoOh	03	01	14
Cox, Nicholas(Z-M)	1835	Dec. 09	TuscarwsCoOh	03	05	19
Cox, Tunis(Z)	1832	Oct. 06	FairfeldCoOh	15	14	08
Coy, Benjamin(Z)	1804	Dec. 07	BelmontCo,Oh	14	15	30
Coyl, Neal(Z)	1835	Aug. 22	PittsburghPa	14	13	07
Coyle, Peter(Z)	1836	Feb. 23	Morgan Co,Oh	14	12	12
Coyle, Peter(Z)	1836	Oct. 22	Morgan Co,Oh	14	12	12
Cozad, Elias(Z)	1833	Aug. 27	Morgan Co,Oh	09	06	09
Cozad, Elias(Z)	1835	Nov. 17	Morgan Co,Oh	09	06	09
Cozens, Hezekiah(Z)	1832	May 11	MonroeCo.,Oh	08	05	13
Crabs, Henry(Y)	1822	Dec. 17	Jeff.Co.,Oh.	03	11	21
Crabtree, James(Z-M)	1833	March 09	TuscarwsCoOh	01	06	18
Crabtree, John(Z-M)	1834	Feb. 18	LickingCo,Oh	11	03	23
Crabtree, John(Z-M)	1834	Feb. 18	LickingCo,Oh	11	03	23
Crabtree, John(Z-M)	1838	Aug. 20	LickingCo,Oh	11	04	24
Crabtree, Lewis(Z-M)	1832	Aug. 20	HarrisonCoOh	01	06	12
Crabtree, Thomas L.(Z-M)	1829	May 08	HarrisonCoOh	01	06	12
Craft, David S.(Z)	1824	June 09	FayetteCo,Pa	08	08	29
Craft, George B.(Z)	1824	June 09	FayetteCo,Pa	08	08	13
Craft, George B.(Z)	1825	May 20	FayetteCo,Pa	08	08	29
Craft, George B.(Z)	1825	May 20	FayetteCo,Pa	08	08	30
Craft, George B.(Z)	1825	May 20	FayetteCo,Pa	08	08	29
Craft, George B.(Z)	1826	Aug. 07	FayetteCo,Pa	08	08	29
Craft, Jesse(Z-M)	1831	Nov. 17	LickingCo,Oh	10	04	05
Craft, John(Z-M)	1832	Oct. 03	KnoxCo.,Ohio	10	05	24
Craig, Abraham(Z)	1812	Feb. 04	FairfeldCoOh	15	17	09
Craig, Abraham(Z)	1812	Dec. 18	MuskingmCoOh	15	17	09
Craig, Absalom(Y)	1824	Aug. 09	ColumbanCoOh	06	17	26
Craig, And'w.(Z-M)	1837	Feb. 23	MuskingmCoOh	03	01	07
Craig, And'w.(Z-M)	1837	Feb. 23	MuskingmCoOh	03	01	07
Craig, Fawcet(Z)	1835	May 04	MonroeCo.,Oh	08	07	02
Craig, Fawcett(Z)	1832	Aug. 03	MonroeCo.,Oh	08	07	03
Craig, Fawcett(Z)	1832	Aug. 03	MonroeCo.,Oh	08	07	03
Craig, Fawcett(Z)	1836	Aug. 31	MonroeCo.,Oh	08	07	10
Craig, Fawcett(Z)	1836	Dec. 07	MonroeCo.,Oh	08	07	14
Craig, George(Z-M)	1832	Jan. 16	TuscarwsCoOh	01	07	18
Craig, George(Z-M)	1832	Feb. 13	TuscarwsCoOh	01	09	18
Craig, Henry(Z)	1831	Sept. 08	MonroeCo.,Oh	08	07	02
Craig, Isaac(Y)	1822	April 24	ColumbanCoOh	05	16	21
Craig, James(Z)	1832	May 30	Morgan Co,Oh	11	10	14
Craig, James(Z)	1832	Dec. 20	MonroeCo.,Oh	08	06	22
Craig, James(Z)	1836	Jan. 01	MonroeCo.,Oh	08	06	22
Craig, James(Z)	1829	Jan. 20	Brooke CoVir	11	10	13
Craig, John(Y)	1830	Aug. 14	TuscarwsCoOh	07	15	21
Craig, John(Z)	1832	Oct. 22	MonroeCo.,Oh	08	06	27
Craig, John(Z)	1835	Dec. 18	MonroeCo.,Oh	08	06	26
Craig, John(Z)	1836	July 07	MonroeCo.,Oh	08	05	03
Craig, Joshua Jr.(Z)	1827	Aug. 16	MonroeCo.,Oh	08	07	01
Craig, Joshua Jr.(Z)	1835	Aug. 27	MonroeCo.,Oh	08	07	02
Craig, Joshua Jur.(Z)	1832	Oct. 13	MonroeCo.,Oh	08	07	02
Craig, Joshua Jur.(Z)	1832	Oct. 13	MonroeCo.,Oh	08	07	02
Craig, Joshua(Z)	1834	Nov. 11	MonroeCo.,Oh	08	08	35
Craig, Joshua(Z)	1835	Nov. 16	MonroeCo.,Oh	08	07	10
Craig, Joshua(Z)	1817	Sept. 08	PittsburghPa	08	07	13
Craig, Philip(Z)	1835	Dec. 10	MonroeCo.,Oh	08	06	34
Craig, Philip(Z)	1837	April 27	MonroeCo.,Oh	08	06	34
Craig, Philip(Z)	1837	April 27	MonroeCo.,Oh	08	06	26
Craig, Sam'l.(Z)	1836	Aug. 31	MonroeCo.,Oh	08	07	10
Craig, Samuel(Z)	1828	Jan. 24	MonroeCo.,Oh	08	07	13
Craig, Samuel(Z)	1834	Oct. 16	MonroeCo.,Oh	08	07	13
Craig, Samuel(Z)	1835	Nov. 16	MonroeCo.,Oh	08	07	02

PURCHASER	YEAR	DATE	RESIDENCE	R	T	S
Craig, Stokely(Y)	1822	Nov. 15	GreeneCo.,Pa	07	12	35
Craig, Stokely(Y)	1822	Nov. 15	GreeneCo.,Pa	07	12	35
Craig, William(Z)	1835	Dec. 10	MonroeCo.,Oh	08	06	27
Craig, William(Z)	1836	April 05	MonroeCo.,Oh	08	06	27
Craig, William(Z)	1817	May 20	ZanesvilleOh	09	06	04
Cramblet, John(Y)	1830	Jan. 04	Jeff.Co.,Oh.	06	12	22
Cramblet, Perry Green(Z)	1834	Nov. 03	GuernseyCoOh	08	08	26
Cramblit, Andrew Junr.(Z)	1833	Feb. 12	GuernseyCoOh	10	08	01
Cramblit, Andrew Junr.(Z)	1833	Feb. 23	Morgan Co,Oh	10	08	01
Cramblit, Andrew(Z)	1833	Jan. 25	GuernseyCoOh	08	08	27
Cramer, Henry(Z)	1816	Dec. 17	GuernseyCoOh	01	03	16
Cranan, Timothy(Z-M)	1838	July 05	ZanesvilleOh	05	04	13
Crane, George(Z)	1808	April 26	MuskingmCoOh	12	13	05
Crane, James(Z)	1828	April 17	MuskingmCoOh	12	13	23
Crane, Robert(Z)	1828	March 12	MuskingmCoOh	12	13	11
Cranston, John(Z)	1836	Aug. 18	GuernseyCoOh	08	06	17
Cranston, Thos.(Z)	1838	March 12	GuernseyCoOh	08	06	20
Cranston, William(Z)	1837	Jan. 24	GuernseyCoOh	08	06	17
Crapo, Reuben(Z-M)	1820	Oct. 27	CoshoctnCoOh	09	08	22
Crapo, Reuben(Z-M)	1831	Nov. 12	HolmesCoOhio	09	08	22
Crapo, Reuben(Z-M)	1835	Sept. 04	HolmesCoOhio	09	08	22
Crass, Hohm W.(Z)	1807	Dec. 15	MuskingmCoOh	09	01	21
Craven, Robert(Y)	1827	Aug. 21	HarrisonCoOh	05	12	10
Craw, George(Z)	1838	Dec. 05	MonroeCo.,Oh	08	06	24
Crawford, Alex'r.(Z-M)	1825	Nov. 24	CoshoctnCoOh	09	04	17
Crawford, Armour(Y)	1836	Jan. 31	Jeff.Co.,Oh.	03	12	19
Crawford, Augustus(Z)	1831	Nov. 03	Perry Co.,Oh	15	14	29
Crawford, Edward(Z)	1817	Feb. 19	MuskingmCoOh	11	13	34
Crawford, Elisha(Z)	1833	April 22	Perry Co.,Oh	15	14	30
Crawford, Elisha(Z)	1833	Dec. 09	Perry Co.,Oh	15	14	30
Crawford, Geo.(Z)	1833	Oct. 19	Perry Co.,Oh	15	14	29
Crawford, George(Z)	1816	Oct. 08	FayetteCo,Pa	09	04	21
Crawford, George(Z)	1816	Oct. 08	FayetteCo,Pa	09	04	23
Crawford, George(Z-M)	1825	Nov. 24	Jeff.Co.,Oh.	09	04	13
Crawford, Hugh(Z-M)	1835	Jan. 17	GuernseyCoOh	03	04	14
Crawford, James(Y)	1826	Aug. 04	ColumbanCoOh	02	11	36
Crawford, James(Y)	1829	Oct. 24	Stark Co.,Oh	07	16	06
Crawford, James(Z-M)	1832	July 30	CoshoctnCoOh	05	07	25
Crawford, Jno.(Y)	1824	May 17	Jeff.Co.,Oh.	03	08	15
Crawford, John(Y)	1829	Sept. 17	HarrisonCoOh	06	12	17
Crawford, John(Y)	1832	Aug. 17	ColumbanCoOh	05	15	14
Crawford, John(Z)	1826	June 22	MuskingmCoOh	11	12	08
Crawford, John(Z)	1831	Nov. 08	MuskingmCoOh	11	12	15
Crawford, John(Z)	1810	May 03	MuskingmCoOh	11	13	01
Crawford, John(Z)	1814	Dec. 05	WashCo.,Penn	11	13	13
Crawford, John(Z)	1817	June 19	WashCo.,Penn	11	13	26
Crawford, John(Z-M)	1832	March 28	GuernseyCoOh	02	03	14
Crawford, John(Z-M)	1832	April 09	CoshoctnCoOh	09	03	03
Crawford, John(Z-M)	1833	April 22	GuernseyCoOh	02	03	13
Crawford, John(Z-M)	1833	April 22	GuernseyCoOh	02	03	14
Crawford, John(Z-M)	1833	April 22	GuernseyCoOh	02	03	18
Crawford, Johnston(Z-M)	1832	Oct. 29	LickingCo,Oh	10	04	23
Crawford, Lewis(Y)	1827	July 06	ColumbanCoOh	05	14	22
Crawford, Lewis(Y)	1833	Aug. 22	CarrollCo,Oh	05	14	12
Crawford, Lewis(Y)	1833	Sept. 06	CarrollCo,Oh	05	14	12
Crawford, Rich'd.(Y)	1822	Oct. 31	WashCo.,Penn	04	06	31
Crawford, Robert(Z)	1835	Nov. 11	MonroeCo.,Oh	08	06	14
Crawford, Robert(Z-M)	1829	July 31	CoshoctnCoOh	06	07	11
Crawford, Robert(Z-M)	1836	Jan. 06	CoshoctnCoOh	05	07	25
Crawford, Robt.(Z-M)	1830	Aug. 02	CoshoctnCoOh	06	07	20
Crawford, Thomas(Z)	1817	Oct. 25	Jeff.Co.,Oh.	09	04	08
Crawford, Thomas(Z)	1817	Oct. 25	Jeff.Co.,Oh.	09	04	08
Crawford, Thomas(Z-M)	1820	Sept. 09	CoshoctnCoOh	06	07	11
Crawford, Thomas(Z-M)	1837	Jan. 11	HarrisonCoOh	04	07	16
Crawford, Thomas(Z-M)	1837	Jan. 11	HarrisonCoOh	08	07	10
Crawford, William(Z)	1824	Feb. 03	Morgan Co,Oh	11	12	05
Crawford, William(Z)	1832	June 19	MuskingmCoOh	11	12	15
Crawford, William(Z)	1816	April 24	MuskingmCoOh	11	13	25
Crawford, William(Z)	1817	Feb. 19	WashCo.,Penn	11	13	34

PURCHASER	YEAR	DATE	RESIDENCE	R	T	S
Crawford, William(Z-M)	1835	May 13	Jeff.Co.,Oh.	08	09	03
Crayton, Thomas(Y)	1830	Dec. 13	HarrisonCoOh	05	13	09
Crebs, Peter(Z)	1815	Oct. 28	TuscarwsCoOh	02	07	02
Creder, John(Z)	1810	March 26	BaltimreCoMd	01	09	10
Credner, Morris M.(Y)	1829	Sept. 28	ColumbanCoOh	04	13	29
Cree, James(Z)	1827	Oct. 12	GreeneCo.,Pa	01	06	20
Cree, James(Z-M)	1836	May 17	HarrisonCoOh	03	05	18
Cree, James(Z-M)	1836	May 17	HarrisonCoOh	03	05	18
Creekfield, Joseph(Z)	1813	June 25	KnoxCo.,Ohio	10	07	16
Creger, Jacob(Y)	1829	Oct. 02	TuscarwsCoOh	07	14	27
Creger, Peter(Y)	1828	Aug. 05	TuscarwsCoOh	07	14	26
Creighton, John(Z)	1816	Nov. 11	Ohio Co.,Vir	12	11	23
Creighton, John(Z)	1816	Nov. 11	Ohio Co.,Vir	12	11	23
Creighton, Mich'l.(Y)	1823	Sept. 06	BelmontCo,Oh	06	08	32
Creighton, Robert(Y)	1823	Nov. 24	Stark Co.,Oh	07	17	15
Creighton, William(Z-M)	1830	Jan. 05	GuernseyCoOh	04	03	04
Creighton, Wm.(Z-M)	1826	June 02	GuernseyCoOh	04	03	07
Cremer, Henry(Z-M)	1836	Jan. 11	CoshoctnCoOh	06	04	10
Cremer, Henry(Z-M)	1836	Nov. 28	CoshoctnCoOh	06	04	10
Cren, Obadiah(Y)	1828	Oct. 16	ColumbanCoOh	05	17	03
Cress, George(Y)	1832	Oct. 24	Jeff.Co.,Oh.	04	12	03
Cress, John(Y)	1828	Feb. 05	TuscarwsCoOh	06	14	35
Cress, Michael(Z)	1814	Sept. 14	FayetteCo,Pa	02	01	10
Cressly, Edward(Z)	1833	March 11	Perry Co.,Oh	14	13	19
Cressly, Edward(Z)	1833	March 11	Perry Co.,Oh	14	13	19
Creswell, John(Z-M)	1833	Feb. 08	KnoxCo.,Ohio	10	06	07
Crews,H.T.&Benj'n.W.Ladd,Tr(Y)	1821	Sept. 24	ColumbanCoOh	06	12	21
Cribs, Peter(Z)	1814	Sept. 22	TuscarwsCoOh	03	08	03
Cribs, Peter(Z)	1815	Oct. 28	TuscarwsCoOh	02	07	08
Crichfield, Isaac(Z)	1817	June 11	KnoxCo.,Ohio	11	08	24
Crichfield, Joseph(Z)	1816	Oct. 21	KnoxCo.,Ohio	11	08	21
Crichfield, Joseph(Z)	1817	Jan. 07	KnoxCo.,Ohio	11	08	21
Cricklaum, Jacob(Z)	1832	Oct. 18	Morgan Co,Oh	13	09	04
Crider, John(Z-M)	1828	May 22	TuscarwsCoOh	01	09	19
Crider, Philip(Z)	1816	Nov. 28	TuscarwsCoOh	04	09	13
Criss, Wm.(Z-M)	1830	Dec. 13	TuscarwsCoOh	01	09	06
Criswell, Jehu(Z-M)	1833	April 15	KnoxCo.,Ohio	10	06	06
Critchfield, Abran.(Z)	1831	June 10	KnoxCo.,Ohio	10	08	17
Critchfield, Albert G.(Z-M)	1833	Sept. 04	HolmesCoOhio	09	08	01
Critchfield, Alvan(Z-M)	1829	April 13	KnoxCo.,Ohio	10	08	23
Critchfield, Alvan(Z-M)	1829	May 04	KnoxCo.,Ohio	10	08	18
Critchfield, Alvin(Z-M)	1832	Oct. 20	KnoxCo.,Ohio	10	08	18
Critchfield, Asa(Z-M)	1831	Jan. 27	HolmesCoOhio	09	08	01
Critchfield, Elza S.(Z-M)	1828	April 23	HolmesCoOhio	09	08	03
Critchfield, Jas.(Z-M)	1831	March 04	KnoxCo.,Ohio	10	08	24
Critchfield, Wm. Jr.(Z-M)	1823	June 05	KnoxCo.,Ohio	10	08	23
Critchfield, Wm.(Z-M)	1831	Jan. 27	KnoxCo.,Ohio	10	08	24
Crits, Andrew(Z)	1815	June 03	WashCo.,Penn	01	04	23
Crits, Daniel(Z-M)	1836	Jan. 26	TuscarwsCoOh	03	07	11
Crittes, Nicholas(Z)	1816	April 03	TuscarwsCoOh	02	07	08
Croasbey, John(Z)	1816	Nov. 14	MuskingmCoOh	12	11	29
Croasbey, John(Z)	1816	Nov. 14	MuskingmCoOh	12	11	29
Croasby, John(Z)	1835	Oct. 15	Perry Co.,Oh	14	12	07
Crochet, Thomas(Y)	1825	Oct. 29	ColumbanCoOh	07	20	05
Crocket, Thomas(Y)	1829	March 14	Stark Co.,Oh	07	20	05
Crocking, William(Y)	1825	Nov. 29	HarrisonCoOh	06	14	14
Croft, Matthew(Z-M)	1836	Feb. 24	TuscarwsCoOh	01	09	12
Crom, Thomas(Z-M)	1835	Jan. 07	TuscarwsCoOh	01	06	08
Crom, William(Z-M)	1833	Aug. 22	TuscarwsCoOh	01	06	08
Cronbaugh, Barbara(Y)	1825	March 02	Stark Co.,Oh	07	20	20
Crooch, Robert(Z)	1834	March 25	Morgan Co,Oh	10	07	34
Crooks, Henry(Y)	1820	April 20	TuscarwsCoOh	07	15	20
Crooks, Henry(Z)	1804	June 07	MuskingmCoOh	14	16	11
Crooks, Henry(Z)	1804	Dec. 01	MuskingmCoOh	14	16	13
Crooks, Henry(Z)	1804	Dec. 01	MuskingmCoOh	14	16	13
Crooks, Henry(Z)	1805	Sept. 03	MuskingmCoOh	14	16	13
Crooks, Henry(Z)	1816	Dec. 16	WestmrldCoPa	04	02	07
Crooks, Jacob(Z)	1810	Nov. 02	ZanesvilleOh	12	13	04
Crooks, Jacob(Z)	1811	July 23	MuskingmCoOh	05	03	05

PURCHASER	YEAR	DATE	RESIDENCE	R	T	S
Crooks, Jacob(Z)	1811	Oct. 22	ZanesvilleOh	14	13	02
Crooks, Jacob(Z)	1811	Nov. 21	MuskingmCoOh	02	02	11
Crooks, Jacob(Z)	1812	May 25	ZanesvilleOh	14	14	04
Crooks, Jacob(Z)	1814	Aug. 31	ZanesvilleOh	06	04	13
Crooks, Jacob(Z)	1815	June 22	ZanesvilleOh	14	15	09
Crooks, Jacob(Z)	1815	Aug. 16	ZanesvilleOh	12	11	21
Crooks, John(Z)	1835	Dec. 15	BelmontCo,Oh	09	06	20
Crooks, Robert E.(Y)	1825	May 04	TuscarwsCoOh	07	15	32
Crooks, Robert(Z)	1823	May 19	MuskingmCoOh	13	11	22
Crooks, William(Z-M)	1834	Jan. 28	CarrollCo,Oh	01	08	04
Crop, Samuel(Z-M)	1832	Dec. 11	WashCo.,Penn	03	06	17
Crosbay, Isaac(Z)	1836	Dec. 01	Morgan Co,Oh	15	14	33
Crosby, Edward(Z)	1833	May 25	Perry Co.,Oh	14	13	19
Crosby, Edward(Z)	1814	Aug. 17	FairfeldCoOh	15	16	27
Crosby, Eliakem(Y)	1833	Dec. 12	PortageCo,Oh	10	02	01
Crosby, John(Z)	1815	Aug. 19	WashCo.,Penn	07	07	24
Cross, Daniel(Z-M)	1833	April 28	TuscarwsCoOh	06	09	23
Cross, Geo. H.(Z-M)	1833	May 30	Jeff.Co.,Oh.	02	04	07
Cross, Isaac(Z-M)	1830	Nov. 05	CoshoctnCoOh	08	07	12
Cross, Isaac(Z-M)	1836	Sept. 12	CoshoctnCoOh	08	07	12
Cross, James(Z-M)	1835	Jan. 22	WashCo.,Penn	03	06	17
Cross, John(Y)	1821	Oct. 30	ColumbanCoOh	06	16	15
Cross, John(Z)	1811	March 08	MuskingmCoOh	08	02	20
Cross, Levi(Z-M)	1828	May 29	TuscarwsCoOh	01	10	14
Cross, Richard(Z-M)	1834	Aug. 04	BelmontCo,Oh	03	06	03
Cross, Richard(Z-M)	1835	June 03	TuscarwsCoOh	03	06	03
Cross, Uriah T.(Z-M)	1836	Feb. 02	TuscarwsCoOh	03	06	02
Cross, William(Z)	1811	March 08	MuskingmCoOh	08	02	20
Cross, William(Z-M)	1836	June 25	CoshoctnCoOh	08	07	11
Cross, William(Z-M)	1837	April 28	CoshoctnCoOh	08	07	10
Crossland, Luke G.(Z)	1831	Oct. 19	Morgan Co,Oh	13	10	31
Crossland, Luke G.(Z)	1829	Dec. 21	MuskingmCoOh	13	10	17
Croul, Jacob(Y)	1822	May 11	FredrickCoMd	06	17	22
Crow, George(Z)	1826	May 26	Morgan Co,Oh	12	11	22
Crow, George(Z)	1836	May 05	MonroeCo.,Oh	08	06	24
Crow, George(Z)	1836	May 10	MonroeCo.,Oh	08	06	24
Crow, George(Z)	1836	May 10	MonroeCo.,Oh	08	06	24
Crow, George(Z)	1836	May 10	MonroeCo.,Oh	08	06	24
Crow, George(Z)	1837	April 21	MonroeCo.,Oh	08	06	24
Crow, Isaac(Z-M)	1835	Nov. 12	GuernseyCoOh	03	03	06
Crow, Isaac(Z-M)	1837	April 17	GuernseyCoOh	03	03	06
Crow, Joseph(Y)	1823	Oct. 08	ColumbanCoOh	03	16	09
Crow, Martin(Z)	1811	Sept. 25	GreeneCo.,Pa	08	07	36
Crow, Martin(Z)	1816	Aug. 02	GuernseyCoOh	08	07	36
Crow, William J.(Z)	1833	April 27	GuernseyCoOh	09	08	30
Crow, William J.(Z)	1835	Sept. 22	GuernseyCoOh	09	08	30
Crow, Wm. J.(Z)	1831	Dec. 22	GuernseyCoOh	10	09	24
Crow, Wm. J.(Z)	1836	Jan. 28	GuernseyCoOh	09	08	30
Crow, Wm. J.(Z)	1836	Jan. 28	GuernseyCoOh	09	08	30
Crow, Wm.(Y)	1829	Aug. 18	HarrisonCoOh	05	13	33
Crowley, Patrick(Z-M)	1837	Nov. 27	CoshoctnCoOh	05	04	14
Crown, John W.(Z-M)	1836	June 03	LickingCo,Oh	10	03	04
Crown, John W.(Z-M)	1836	June 03	LickingCo,Oh	10	04	24
Croxton, Abraham(Y)	1833	Sept. 25	Jeff.Co.,Oh.	03	12	34
Croy, Andrew(Y)	1828	Sept. 22	Stark Co.,Oh	07	16	17
Croy, Mathias Jr.(Z)	1807	Jan. 07	BelmontCo,Oh	08	04	21
Croy, Mathias(Z)	1806	Jan. 04	Ohio Co.,Vir	06	04	19
Croy, Mathias(Z)	1806	March 12	BelmontCo,Oh	08	04	21
Crubaugh, Geo.(Z)	1833	Nov. 12	ColumbanCoOh	14	12	23
Crum, George(Z)	1837	March 18	ColumbanCoOh	08	06	15
Crum, John(Z)	1837	March 17	ColumbanCoOh	08	06	14
Crum, John(Z)	1837	March 17	ColumbanCoOh	08	06	14
Crumbakes, John(Z-M)	1828	Nov. 13	MuskingmCoOh	06	03	11
Crumrine, Jno.(Y)	1822	Sept. 27	TuscarwsCoOh	07	14	02
Crumrine, John(Y)	1830	July 22	TuscarwsCoOh	07	14	01
Crumrine, John(Y)	1830	Sept. 13	TuscarwsCoOh	07	14	02
Culbertson, Alex'r.(Z)	1809	Feb. 13	MuskingmCoOh	07	01	03
Culbertson, Alexander(Z)	1810	June 11	MuskingmCoOh	07	01	01
Culbertson, Alexander(Z)	1810	June 13	NrthmbldCo ?	06	01	14

PURCHASER	YEAR	DATE	RESIDENCE	R	T	S
Culbertson, Alexander(Z)	1810	June 13	NrthmbldCo ?	06	01	14
Culbertson, Alexander(Z)	1813	June 03	MuskingmCoOh	14	16	09
Culbertson, Benjamin(Z-M)	1836	Oct. 29	HarrisonCoOh	02	04	14
Culbertson, Benjamin(Z-M)	1836	Oct. 29	HarrisonCoOh	02	04	14
Culbertson, Ezekiel(Z)	1833	Nov. 19	Morgan Co,Oh	10	08	28
Culbertson, J. W.(Z)	1814	Oct. 14	ZanesvilleOh	12	12	30
Culbertson, James(Z)	1814	June 21	ZanesvilleOh	14	16	03
Culbertson, James(Z)	1816	April 19	ZanesvilleOh	12	12	19
Culbertson, Joseph(Z)	1814	Dec. 16	BelmontCo,Oh	10	01	09
Culbertson, Robert(Z)	1811	April 26	WestmrldCoPa	05	06	25
Culbertson, Robt.(Z)	1831	Aug. 18	Morgan Co,Oh	10	08	08
Culbertson, Sam'l. W.(Z)	1827	Dec. 27	ZanesvilleOh	12	12	09
Culbertson, Sam'l. W.(Z)	1827	Dec. 27	ZanesvilleOh	12	12	09
Culbertson, Sam'l. W.(Z)	1828	Jan. 26	ZanesvilleOh	12	12	09
Culbertson, Sam'l. W.(Z)	1815	July 12	ZanesvilleOh	12	12	29
Culbertson, William(Z-M)	1824	Jan. 19	GuernseyCoOh	04	03	23
Culbertson, Wm.(Z)	1832	June 11	Morgan Co,Oh	10	08	29
Culbitson, Ezekiel(Z-M)	1835	Feb. 14	Morgan Co,Oh	10	08	28
Cullen, James(Z)	1827	Nov. 12	AlleghnyCoPa	04	03	20
Cullen, James(Z-M)	1830	March 29	GuernseyCoOh	04	03	20
Cullen, Richard(Z-M)	1837	March 23	HolmesCoOhio	07	08	05
Cullen, William(Z-M)	1834	Feb. 26	GuernseyCoOh	04	03	19
Culler, John(Y)	1828	March 25	ColumbanCoOh	06	19	29
Culler, John(Y)	1828	Aug. 20	ColumbanCoOh	06	19	30
Cullison, Elijah(Z)	1817	Oct. 28	CoshoctnCoOh	09	05	01
Cullison, Elijah(Z-M)	1825	March 04	CoshoctnCoOh	08	05	16
Cullison, James(Z)	1817	May 29	LickingCo,Oh	09	05	09
Cullison, John(Z)	1815	Dec. 11	CoshoctnCoOh	09	05	11
Cullison, John(Z)	1816	April 09	CoshoctnCoOh	09	05	11
Cullison, William(Z)	1815	Dec. 16	Baltimore,Md	09	05	02
Cully, Daniel(Z-M)	1837	Aug. 26	AlleghnyCoPa	03	03	04
Culver, Asa(Z)	1812	May 12	MuskingmCoOh	10	09	06
Culver, Isaiah(Z)	1815	April 26	MuskingmCoOh	10	09	09
Culver, Levi(Z)	1826	March 10	GuernseyCoOh	10	09	10
Cummings, George(Y)	1832	May 01	Jeff.Co.,Oh.	02	08	35
Cummings, James(Y)	1829	March 14	TuscarwsCoOh	06	14	31
Cummings, James(Y)	1831	Aug. 12	TuscarwsCoOh	06	14	31
Cummings, James(Y)	1831	Aug. 12	TuscarwsCoOh	06	14	31
Cummings, Sam'l.(Z)	1835	Dec. 31	BelmontCo,Oh	08	08	27
Cummings, Thomas(Y)	1830	Feb. 04	TuscarwsCoOh	06	13	11
Cummings, Thomas(Y)	1831	May 28	TuscarwsCoOh	07	14	14
Cummings, Thomas(Y)	1831	Aug. 12	TuscarwsCoOh	07	14	10
Cummings, Thomas(Y)	1831	Oct. 04	TuscarwsCoOh	07	14	36
Cummings, Thomas(Y)	1831	Dec. 03	TuscarwsCoOh	07	14	15
Cummins, James(Z)	1806	Nov. 14	Jeff.Co.,Oh.	05	01	09
Cummins, Jno.(Z)	1831	Dec. 31	GuernseyCoOh	11	12	25
Cummins, John S.(Z-M)	1838	July 26	TuscarwsCoOh	07	07	13
Cummins, John(Y)	1836	June 20	TuscarwsCoOh	07	15	31
Cummins, John(Z)	1831	Feb. 17	GuernseyCoOh	10	09	21
Cummins, John(Z)	1837	Feb. 15	MuskingmCoOh	15	14	31
Cummins, John(Z)	1837	Feb. 15	MuskingmCoOh	15	14	31
Cummins, Paul(Z)	1833	Dec. 14	Perry Co.,Oh	15	14	15
Cummins, Paul(Z)	1836	June 20	Perry Co.,Oh	15	14	10
Cummins, Samuel(Z)	1836	Nov. 05	GuernseyCoOh	08	06	17
Cummins, William(Z-M)	1838	May 14	IndianaCo,Pa	08	08	25
Cummins, William(Z-M)	1838	May 14	IndianaCo,Pa	08	08	25
Cummins, Wm.(Z)	1817	June 12	MuskingmCoOh	11	10	17
Cummins, Wm.(Z)	1817	June 12	MuskingmCoOh	11	10	20
Cummins, Wm.(Z)	1817	Aug. 30	MuskingmCoOh	11	10	07
Cummins, Wm.(Z)	1817	Aug. 30	MuskingmCoOh	11	10	07
Cummins, Wm.(Z)	1817	Aug. 30	MuskingmCoOh	12	10	12
Cuningham, Jas.(Z)	1832	Feb. 16	MuskingmCoOh	13	10	07
Cunnan, Peter(Z)	1838	Feb. 20	Perry Co.,Oh	14	12	23
Cunningham, A.(Z)	1830	Oct. 02	Morgan Co,Oh	10	08	21
Cunningham, Francis(Z-M)	1829	Nov. 14	WashCo.,Penn	05	06	16
Cunningham, Geo. W.(Z)	1833	Jan. 21	MonroeCo.,Oh	08	06	32
Cunningham, Geo. W.(Z)	1836	Aug. 29	MonroeCo.,Oh	08	06	32
Cunningham, J.(Z)	1833	May 03	MonroeCo.,Oh	08	06	31
Cunningham, James(Z)	1811	Dec. 11	GuernseyCoOh	02	02	20

PURCHASER	YEAR	DATE	RESIDENCE	R	T	S
Cunningham, James(Z)	1813	Aug. 25	GuernseyCoOh	01	02	20
Cunningham, James(Z)	1817	Jan. 31	MuskingmCoOh	11	04	24
Cunningham, Jas.(Z)	1835	Jan. 20	MuskingmCoOh	14	14	12
Cunningham, Jefferson(Z)	1835	Dec. 14	MonroeCo.,Oh	08	06	31
Cunningham, Jesse(Z)	1817	Oct. 29	CoshoctnCoOh	07	08	12
Cunningham, Jesse(Z)	1817	Oct. 29	CoshoctnCoOh	07	08	23
Cunningham, John(Z)	1836	Sept. 30	Morgan Co,Oh	13	08	05
Cunningham, Mary(Z)	1833	July 24	Perry Co.,Oh	15	15	12
Cunningham, Robert(Z)	1829	Aug. 04	Morgan Co,Oh	11	11	21
Cunningham, Thomas J.(Z)	1833	Jan. 21	MonroeCo.,Oh	08	05	06
Cunningham, William(Z)	1835	Aug. 31	Morgan Co,Oh	09	06	25
Cunningham, William(Z)	1835	Oct. 27	Morgan Co,Oh	09	06	24
Cunningham, Wm.(Y)	1820	Dec. 04	TuscarwsCoOh	07	14	32
Cunningham, Wm.(Z-M)	1829	Nov. 14	WashCo.,Penn	05	06	08
Curran, John(Z)	1834	July 25	Perry Co.,Oh	14	12	22
Curran, John(Z)	1834	July 25	Perry Co.,Oh	14	12	22
Curran, Michael(Z)	1831	Sept. 09	MuskingmCoOh	14	12	24
Curran, Michael(Z)	1837	Feb. 07	Perry Co.,Oh	14	12	24
Curran, Peter(Z)	1834	March 08	Perry Co.,Oh	14	12	24
Curran, Peter(Z)	1836	March 07	Perry Co.,Oh	14	12	24
Currie, David(Z-M)	1836	Oct. 29	ColumbanCoOh	05	04	17
Currie, Robert(Z-M)	1836	Oct. 29	ColumbanCoOh	05	04	13
Curry, Agnes(Z-M)	1835	May 28	TuscarwsCoOh	04	07	23
Curry, Thomas(Z)	1812	April 21	MuskingmCoOh	11	13	03
Curry, William(Z-M)	1825	Nov. 17	HarrisonCoOh	03	06	13
Curry, William(Z-M)	1830	Feb. 25	CoshoctnCoOh	04	06	08
Curtis, Eli(Z)	1824	Aug. 17	MonroeCo.,Oh	08	07	18
Curtis, Eli(Z)	1825	Nov. 21	MonroeCo.,Oh	08	07	07
Curtis, Eli(Z)	1836	April 26	MonroeCo.,Oh	08	06	15
Curtis, James(Z)	1817	Jan. 10	Ohio Co.,Vir	10	05	01
Curtis, James(Z-M)	1821	June 04	CoshoctnCoOh	09	05	09
Curtis, John W.(Y)	1830	March 06	HarrisonCoOh	06	11	24
Curtis, Samuel(Z-M)	1837	May 11	BelmontCo,Oh	04	07	10
Curtis, Samuel(Z-M)	1837	May 11	BelmontCo,Oh	04	07	10
Curtis, Samuel(Z-M)	1837	May 17	BelmontCo,Oh	04	07	11
Curtiss, Eli(Z)	1823	Dec. 31	MonroeCo.,Oh	08	06	01
Cusac, Andrew(Z)	1810	June 25	FairfeldCoOh	15	16	14
Cusac, Dan'l.(Z)	1824	Dec. 16	Perry Co.,Oh	15	16	21
Cussens, Thomas(Z)	1815	March 27	GuernseyCoOh	11	13	27
Cussins, Thomas(Z)	1815	March 27	GuernseyCoOh	11	13	27
Custard, Daniel(Z)	1807	May 06	FayetteCo,Oh	01	09	10
Custard, George(Z)	1807	May 06	FayetteCo,Oh	01	09	19
Custer, Isaac(Z-M)	1832	Feb. 22	TuscarwsCoOh	02	10	23
Custerd, George(Z)	1808	May 02	FayetteCo,Pa	01	09	13
Cutshall, Jacob(Y)	1823	Aug. 22	Stark Co.,Oh	08	12	22
Cutshall, John(Y)	1829	May 01	HarrisonCoOh	05	13	14
Cuzzens, Elizabeth(Z)	1829	Jan. 17	MuskingmCoOh	13	08	32
Cyphers, Sarah(Z)	1814	Aug. 11	GuernseyCoOh	01	03	17
Daab, Conrad(Z-M)	1838	June 26	KnoxCo.,Ohio	10	07	22
Dabb, Conrad(Z-M)	1833	Oct. 19	KnoxCo.,Ohio	10	07	01
Dahy, John B.(Z-M)	1833	July 19	CoshoctnCoOh	06	04	12
Dailey, Chas.(Z)	1831	March 01	Perry Co.,Oh	14	12	28
Dailey, Jacob(Z)	1816	July 06	GuernseyCoOh	08	08	25
Dailey, John(Z-M)	1829	March 27	MuskingmCoOh	07	03	21
Dailey, John(Z-M)	1837	March 27	CoshoctnCoOh	08	07	06
Daily, Eli(Y)	1836	Sept. 23	Jeff.Co.,Oh.	04	13	07
Daily, Eli(Y)	1837	July 21	Jeff.Co.,Oh.	04	12	03
Daily, Jacob(Z-M)	1823	Jan. 21	GuernseyCoOh	08	07	05
Dain, Levi(Z)	1808	Jan. 15	WashngtnCoOh	08	05	17
Dains, Levi(Z)	1817	Oct. 21	WashngtnCoOh	09	06	36
Dair, John(Y)	1835	Sept. 14	Jeff.Co.,Oh.	07	14	28
Dalbey, Joel Junr.(Z-M)	1835	April 09	MuskingmCoOh	04	05	19
Dallas, Alexander(Y)	1835	April 14	ColumbanCoOh	03	13	33
Dallas, James A.(Z-M)	1833	April 10	TuscarwsCoOh	03	06	10
Dallas, James A.(Z-M)	1833	April 10	TuscarwsCoOh	03	06	11
Dallas, James A.(Z-M)	1834	Jan. 15	BelmontCo,Oh	03	06	09
Dallas, James(Y)	1825	March 12	ColumbanCoOh	03	12	03
Dallas, Jas. Alex'r.(Z-M)	1836	Dec. 12	TuscarwsCoOh	03	06	02
Dallas, Peter(Y)	1830	Aug. 31	ColumbanCoOh	03	12	24

PURCHASER	YEAR	DATE	RESIDENCE	R	T	S
Dallis, Robert A.(Y)	1822	April 18	BelmontCo,Oh	06	09	15
Danaghey, Jesse(Z-M)	1835	April 02	HarrisonCoOh	02	06	21
Danaker, Jacob(Z-M)	1833	Dec. 06	MuskingmCoOh	01	03	14
Dandy, Richard(Y)	1828	March 04	Stark Co.,Oh	06	15	19
Danford, Ab.(Z)	1831	March 07	GuernseyCoOh	08	08	13
Danford, Hiram(Z)	1829	Dec. 21	GuernseyCoOh	08	08	25
Danford, Hiram(Z)	1832	July 16	GuernseyCoOh	08	08	25
Danford, Hiram(Z)	1835	Dec. 08	GuernseyCoOh	08	08	36
Danford, Hiram(Z)	1835	Dec. 08	GuernseyCoOh	08	08	25
Danford, Hiram(Z)	1835	Dec. 08	GuernseyCoOh	08	08	36
Danford, Hiram(Z)	1832	Oct. 06	GuernseyCoOh	08	08	36
Danford, Michael(Z)	1826	March 17	MonroeCo.,Oh	08	07	01
Danford, Michael(Z)	1832	July 02	MonroeCo.,Oh	08	08	36
Danford, Michael(Z)	1833	Dec. 30	MonroeCo.,Oh	08	08	35
Danford, Michael(Z)	1836	March 02	MonroeCo.,Oh	08	07	03
Danford, Michael(Z)	1837	Jan. 11	MonroeCo.,Oh	08	08	36
Danford, Samuel(Z)	1835	March 24	MonroeCo.,Oh	08	07	01
Danford, Samuel(Z)	1835	March 24	MonroeCo.,Oh	08	07	01
Dangan, John(Z-M)	1831	Sept. 24	MuskingmCoOh	06	02	06
Danhauer, Chas.(Z)	1809	Nov. 03	PhladlhaCoPa	13	11	17
Daniel, Lee(Z)	1830	Jan. 16	Morgan Co,Oh	12	10	32
Daniel, William(Z-M)	1833	Aug. 17	HolmesCoOhio	06	09	24
Daniels, John(Z-M)	1839	Jan. 24	CoshoctnCoOh	08	06	07
Daniels, John(Z-M)	1839	Jan. 24	CoshoctnCoOh	08	06	07
Dannell, Samuel(Y)	1829	June 30	Jeff.Co.,Oh.	04	12	22
Dannison, Asahee(Z-M)	1831	Nov. 24	TuscarwsCoOh	02	06	22
Dannison, Asahee(Z-M)	1831	Nov. 24	TuscarwsCoOh	02	06	22
Daraugh, William(Z)	1836	March 29	HarrisonCoOh	09	05	24
Darby, Ephraim J.(Z-M)	1832	Dec. 22	HolmesCoOhio	09	08	01
Darby, Ephraim J.(Z-M)	1832	Dec. 22	HolmesCoOhio	09	08	02
Darling, Abm.(Z)	1811	March 28	KnoxCo.,Ohio	10	05	07
Darling, Abr'm.(Z)	1814	April 13	KnoxCo.,Ohio	10	05	07
Darling, Abraham(Z-M)	1834	Oct. 25	KnoxCo.,Ohio	09	08	21
Darling, Jacob(Z-M)	1836	Oct. 10	CoshoctnCoOh	08	06	14
Darling, Robert Jr.(Z-M)	1836	April 13	CoshoctnCoOh	08	06	14
Darling, Robert Jr.(Z-M)	1836	April 13	CoshoctnCoOh	08	06	07
Darling, Robert(Z)	1814	June 29	CoshoctnCoOh	08	06	13
Darling, Thomas(Z-M)	1836	Sept. 12	CoshoctnCoOh	08	06	07
Darling, Thomas(Z-M)	1836	Dec. 01	CoshoctnCoOh	08	07	03
Darling, Thomas(Z-M)	1837	Oct. 09	CoshoctnCoOh	08	07	03
Darling, Thomas(Z-M)	1838	June 25	CoshoctnCoOh	08	07	03
Darling, Thomas(Z-M)	1838	June 25	CoshoctnCoOh	09	07	11
Darling, William(Z)	1813	Sept. 13	KnoxCo.,Ohio	10	05	03
Darling, Wm.(Z)	1811	March 28	KnoxCo.,Ohio	10	05	07
Darling, Wm.(Z)	1814	April 13	KnoxCo.,Ohio	10	05	07
Darner, And'w.(Z)	1814	July 30	MuskingmCoOh	06	02	21
Darner, Jacob(Z)	1819	Feb. 08	?	06	02	21
Darough, William(Z)	1836	April 04	HarrisonCoOh	09	05	24
Darough, Wm.(Z)	1835	Dec. 26	HarrisonCoOh	09	05	24
Darough, Wm.(Z)	1835	Dec. 26	HarrisonCoOh	09	05	24
Darraugh, Arthur(Z)	1816	Oct. 23	WashCo.,Penn	05	02	11
Darraugh, Wm.(Z-M)	1828	March 08	MuskingmCoOh	04	02	13
Darrnan, Hathaway(Z)	1814	Nov. 28	LickingCo,Oh	10	03	14
Darrnem, Hathaway(Z)	1814	Nov. 28	LickingCo,Oh	10	03	14
Darrow, William(Z-M)	1832	July 10	TuscarwsCoOh	01	05	01
Darrow, William(Z-M)	1832	July 10	TuscarwsCoOh	01	05	02
Darrow, Wm.(Z-M)	1831	Aug. 06	TuscarwsCoOh	01	06	25
Darst, Abraham(Z)	1825	Nov. 11	Perry Co.,Oh	14	12	21
Darst, Abraham(Z)	1825	Nov. 11	Perry Co.,Oh	14	12	21
Darst, Abraham(Z)	1825	Nov. 11	Perry Co.,Oh	14	12	28
Darst, Wm. P.(Z)	1827	Oct. 12	Perry Co.,Oh	14	12	20
Daub, Frederick D.(Z-M)	1836	Feb. 11	KnoxCo.,Ohio	10	07	18
Davenport, John(Y)	1825	Nov. 01	BelmontCo,Oh	06	08	25
Davere, John(Z-M)	1829	May 16	TuscarwsCoOh	04	07	19
DaviSimerl, Samuel(Z)	1835	May 26	Morgan Co,Oh	13	08	27
David, Benjamin(Z)	1834	Nov. 05	Morgan Co,Oh	10	08	01
David, Thomas(Z)	1832	Jan. 18	Morgan Co,Oh	10	08	01
David, Thomas(Z)	1834	Oct. 09	Morgan Co,Oh	10	08	01
David, William(Z)	1832	Oct. 29	Morgan Co,Oh	09	07	06

PURCHASER	YEAR	DATE	RESIDENCE	R	T	S
Davidson, Donald(Y)	1821	Oct. 02	ColumbanCoOh	02	10	22
Davidson, Donald(Y)	1821	Oct. 02	ColumbanCoOh	02	10	21
Davidson, Duncan(Y)	1825	Feb. 18	ColumbanCoOh	02	10	21
Davidson, Elizabeth((Z-M)	1830	March 01	CoshoctnCoOh	09	05	17
Davidson, Enye(Z-M)	1838	July 28	KnoxCo.,Ohio	10	08	21
Davidson, George(Z)	1815	Oct. 21	MuskingmCoOh	13	10	20
Davidson, Jesse(Y)	1827	March 15	HarrisonCoOh	07	11	28
Davidson, Jno.(Y)	1827	May 01	HarrisonCoOh	07	12	34
Davidson, John(Z-M)	1827	June 15	FayetteCo,Pa	01	05	01
Davidson, Lewis(Y)	1831	Nov. 26	HarrisonCoOh	07	12	27
Davidson, Mathew(Z)	1816	Dec. 27	KnoxCo.,Ohio	10	08	21
Davidson, Rich'd.(Z-M)	1831	March 02	LickingCo,Oh	10	02	16
Davidson, Robert(Y)	1832	Jan. 30	TuscarwsCoOh	07	14	34
Davidson, Sam'l.(Z-M)	1835	Dec. 30	KnoxCo.,Ohio	10	05	22
Davidson, Samuel(Z-M)	1830	March 01	CoshoctnCoOh	10	05	21
Davidson, Samuel(Z-M)	1836	Dec. 21	KnoxCo.,Ohio	10	05	20
Davidson, Susanna(Z-M)	1821	Aug. 23	Jeff.Co.,Oh.	05	08	09
Davidson, Thomas(Y)	1831	April 20	HarrisonCoOh	07	11	29
Davidson, Thomas(Z)	1812	Oct. 15	BrookCo.,Vir	13	10	06
Davidson, William(Z)	1836	Jan. 12	MarshallCoVa	08	05	30
Davidson, William(Z)	1836	Jan. 12	MarshallCoVa	08	05	30
Davidson, Wm.(Z-M)	1831	March 21	TuscarwsCoOh	02	06	22
Davies, David(Z)	1831	Feb. 04	Morgan Co,Oh	09	07	14
Davies, Zadock(Z-M)	1836	March 22	GuernseyCoOh	02	01	05
Davis, Abner(Z)	1816	Oct. 26	HarrisonCoOh	01	04	03
Davis, Abner(Z-M)	1830	Jan. 20	GuernseyCoOh	01	04	04
Davis, Abraham(Z)	1815	April 28	BeaverCo.,Pa	11	11	13
Davis, Absalom(Z)	1833	Sept. 23	Morgan Co,Oh	09	07	24
Davis, Absalom(Z)	1835	April 09	Morgan Co,Oh	09	07	24
Davis, Absalom(Z)	1835	Nov. 12	Morgan Co,Oh	09	07	25
Davis, Alexander(Y)	1827	June 30	ColumbanCoOh	05	18	20
Davis, Alexander(Z-M)	1827	Aug. 17	BelmontCo,Oh	03	02	06
Davis, Amasa(Z)	1805	Jan. 07	MuskingmCoOh	06	01	23
Davis, Charles(Y)	1820	Oct. 27	Morgan Co,Oh	11	11	12
Davis, Charles(Z)	1833	April 20	Perry Co.,Oh	15	15	35
Davis, Daniel(Y)	1828	Sept. 30	ColumbanCoOh	01	06	23
Davis, Daniel(Z)	1826	April 20	BelmontCo,Oh	13	08	15
Davis, Daniel(Z)	1831	Oct. 15	Morgan Co,Oh	13	08	22
Davis, Daniel(Z)	1815	Nov. 14	GuernseyCoOh	03	01	16
Davis, David(Y)	1824	May 19	ColumbanCoOh	05	16	22
Davis, David(Z)	1826	Dec. 21	GuernseyCoOh	08	07	20
Davis, David(Z-M)	1832	Nov. 17	CoshoctnCoOh	05	04	02
Davis, Dudley(Z)	1813	Aug. 17	WashngtnCoOh	08	05	06
Davis, Dudly(Z)	1807	April 07	WashCo.,Penn	08	05	06
Davis, Edward(Z)	1836	March 29	Morgan Co,Oh	09	05	11
Davis, Edward(Z-M)	1827	Feb. 17	MuskingmCoOh	06	03	19
Davis, Edward(Z-M)	1832	June 29	MuskingmCoOh	06	03	19
Davis, Edward(Z-M)	1832	Oct. 10	MuskingmCoOh	06	03	20
Davis, Elias(Z)	1833	April 06	Perry Co.,Oh	15	15	36
Davis, Elijah(Z)	1832	May 23	Morgan Co,Oh	09	07	03
Davis, Enoch(Z)	1836	Oct. 15	WashngtnCoOh	08	05	08
Davis, Ezekiel(Y)	1826	April 03	Stark Co.,Oh	06	15	19
Davis, George(Y)	1828	Aug. 16	TuscarwsCoOh	06	14	17
Davis, Henry(Z)	1807	Nov. 30	MuskingmCoOh	10	09	06
Davis, Henry(Z)	1810	May 09	FrederkCoVir	01	09	02
Davis, Henry(Z)	1815	Feb. 15	GuernseyCoOh	10	09	07
Davis, Hezekiah(Z)	1812	May 29	WashngtnCoOh	10	06	12
Davis, Isaac 2d(Z-M)	1835	July 20	CoshoctnCoOh	05	04	02
Davis, Isaac(Z)	1816	March 14	LickingCo,Oh	12	10	28
Davis, Isaac(Z)	1816	May 31	LickingCo,Oh	12	09	10
Davis, J. W.(Z)	1836	June 16	Morgan Co,Oh	09	05	11
Davis, J.(Z)	1817	May 03	MuskingmCoOh	11	13	25
Davis, Jabez(Z-M)	1838	May 08	GuernseyCoOh	04	03	19
Davis, Jabez(Z-M)	1838	May 11	GuernseyCoOh	04	03	19
Davis, Jacob G.(Z)	1838	May 12	GuernseyCoOh	08	06	29
Davis, Jacob G.(Z)	1838	May 12	GuernseyCoOh	08	06	20
Davis, Jacob(Z)	1835	June 29	BelmontCo,Oh	08	08	35
Davis, James(Y)	1827	Oct. 15	SteubenvleOh	06	13	24
Davis, James(Y)	1829	Nov. 27	SteubenvleOh	06	14	32

PURCHASER	YEAR	DATE	RESIDENCE	R	T	S
Davis, James(Z)	1832	Jan. 24	Morgan Co,Oh	09	06	11
Davis, James(Z)	1832	May 23	Morgan Co,Oh	09	06	12
Davis, James(Z)	1831	Jan. 27	Morgan Co,Oh	12	09	03
Davis, Jesse(Y)	1827	Jan. 12	ColumbanCoOh	06	18	04
Davis, Jno. the 2nd(Z)	1835	Jan. 16	Morgan Co,Oh	09	07	14
Davis, Jno.(Z)	1817	Jan. 14	MuskingmCoOh	11	13	26
Davis, Joel(Z-M)	1830	March 05	TuscarwsCoOh	01	06	09
Davis, Joel(Z-M)	1832	June 23	TuscarwsCoOh	01	06	08
Davis, John Jnr.(Z)	1834	Feb. 18	Morgan Co,Oh	09	07	22
Davis, John Renick(Z-M)	1836	Jan. 18	LickingCo,Oh	10	04	15
Davis, John W.(Z)	1836	June 09	Morgan Co,Oh	09	05	02
Davis, John W.(Z)	1814	Oct. 29	MuskingmCoOh	05	02	08
Davis, John(Y)	1824	April 06	TrumbullCoOh	05	18	10
Davis, John(Y)	1827	July 20	ColumbanCoOh	05	13	18
Davis, John(Z)	1831	Jan. 31	Morgan Co,Oh	11	11	10
Davis, John(Z)	1814	June 10	FairfeldCoOh	15	15	09
Davis, John(Z-M)	1838	Nov. 10	CoshoctnCoOh	04	03	10
Davis, John(Z-M)	1838	Nov. 10	CoshoctnCoOh	04	03	10
Davis, Josep(Z-M)	1832	Oct. 06	CoshoctnCoOh	05	04	04
Davis, Joseph W.(Z)	1832	May 31	Morgan Co,Oh	09	03	11
Davis, Joseph(Z)	1833	March 20	Morgan Co,Oh	09	05	01
Davis, Joseph(Z)	1836	Feb. 03	GuernseyCoOh	09	08	36
Davis, Joseph(Z)	1836	Feb. 29	Morgan Co,Oh	09	05	02
Davis, Joseph(Z-M)	1832	May 22	CoshoctnCoOh	05	04	04
Davis, Joseph(Z-M)	1831	June 15	CoshoctnCoOh	05	04	03
Davis, Joshua(Y)	1825	Nov. 28	Brooke CoVir	06	14	14
Davis, Joshua(Y)	1825	Nov. 28	Brooke CoVir	06	14	14
Davis, Joshua(Z-M)	1822	March 28	TuscarwsCoOh	01	06	09
Davis, Joshua(Z-M)	1832	April 16	TuscarwsCoOh	01	06	09
Davis, Levi(Z)	1836	Feb. 12	Morgan Co,Oh	08	06	31
Davis, Lot(Z)	1829	July 28	MuskingmCoOh	11	12	35
Davis, Lott(Z)	1808	March 03	FayetteCo,Pa	15	15	08
Davis, Mahlon(Z)	1816	Jan. 19	PutnamCoOhio	13	09	34
Davis, Mary G.(Z)	1835	Sept. 08	Morgan Co,Oh	13	08	29
Davis, Nehemiah(Z)	1833	Dec. 14	GuernseyCoOh	10	08	20
Davis, Nehemiah(Z)	1833	Dec. 14	GuernseyCoOh	10	08	29
Davis, Noah(Z)	1833	April 11	Morgan Co,Oh	09	06	28
Davis, Richard(Y)	1821	Oct. 02	ColumbanCoOh	03	13	22
Davis, Robert(Z)	1826	Dec. 06	MonongahlaVa	10	08	15
Davis, Ruth(Y)*	1826	July 08	RcknghmCoVir	05	11	36
Davis, Sam'l.(Z)	1829	May 25	BelmontCo,Oh	13	08	28
Davis, Sam'l.(Z)	1829	May 25	BelmontCo,Oh	13	08	29
Davis, Samuel(Z)	1815	Feb. 15	AlleghnyCoPa	11	12	18
Davis, Samuel(Z-M)	1836	Nov. 18	CoshoctnCoOh	09	07	12
Davis, Thomas 2nd(Z)	1835	Oct. 12	Morgan Co,Oh	09	07	15
Davis, Thomas Junr.(Z)	1833	Nov. 14	Morgan Co,Oh	09	07	15
Davis, Thos. 2d(Z)	1837	July 05	Morgan Co,Oh	08	06	29
Davis, Thos.(Z)	1831	March 29	Morgan Co,Oh	11	10	19
Davis, Wesley(Y)	1830	March 02	BelmontCo,Oh	04	06	31
Davis, William(Y)	1830	Dec. 16	HarrisonCoOh	06	13	31
Davis, William(Z)	1831	May 27	MuskingmCoOh	12	12	21
Davis, William(Z)	1834	Nov. 07	Morgan Co,Oh	13	08	21
Davis, William(Z)	1834	Dec. 16	Morgan Co,Oh	13	08	21
Davis, William(Z-M)	1822	June 03	MuskingmCoOh	05	02	07
Davis, William(Z-M)	1832	Feb. 20	MuskingmCoOh	06	03	11
Davis, William(Z-M)	1832	March 10	MuskingmCoOh	05	03	15
Davison, A.(Z)	1815	April 22	?	11	04	06
Davison, George(Z-M)	1832	April 17	KnoxCo.,Ohio	11	08	04
Davison, William(Z)	1815	Dec. 15	CoshoctnCoOh	06	04	12
Davoreet, William(Z-M)	1832	May 30	GuernseyCoOh	02	04	05
Davorett, William(Z-M)	1832	May 30	GuernseyCoOh	02	04	04
Davy, John(Z)	1808	May 17	FredrickCoMd	01	09	01
Dawson, Benjamin(Z-M)	1836	Nov. 12	CoshoctnCoOh	07	04	10
Dawson, John L.(Z)	1816	March 06	Wayne Co.,Oh	06	09	03
Dawson, Levi(Z-M)	1838	March 27	GuernseyCoOh	03	04	13
Dawson, Marcus(Z-M)	1834	Nov. 18	CoshoctnCoOh	07	04	09
Dawson, Marcus(Z-M)	1836	Sept. 22	CoshoctnCoOh	07	04	09
Dawson, Moses(Z)	1832	Nov. 05	BelmontCo,Oh	13	08	30
Dawson, Moses(Z)	1832	Nov. 05	BelmontCo,Oh	13	08	19

PURCHASER	YEAR	DATE	RESIDENCE	R	T	S
Dawson, Susan(Z)	1833	Feb. 15	BelmontCo,Oh	13	08	19
Dawson, Thomas(Z)	1835	Aug. 07	Morgan Co,Oh	13	08	19
Dawson, William Jr.(Z-M)	1836	Nov. 23	CoshoctnCoOh	07	04	11
Dawson, William(Z-M)	1834	Nov. 18	CoshoctnCoOh	07	04	12
Dawson, William(Z-M)	1836	March 16	CoshoctnCoOh	07	04	12
Dawson, Wm.(Y)	1825	Jan. 21	BelmontCo,Oh	04	06	14
Day, A.(Z-M)	1831	March 03	KnoxCo.,Ohio	11	05	21
Day, Abraham(Z)	1817	Jan. 31	LickingCo,Oh	11	05	21
Day, Abraham(Z)	1817	April 15	LickingCo,Oh	11	05	22
Day, Abraham(Z-M)	1832	June 01	KnoxCo.,Ohio	11	04	09
Day, Abraham(Z-M)	1836	May 12	KnoxCo.,Ohio	10	04	03
Day, David(Y)	1823	May 28	Stark Co.,Oh	06	19	24
Day, Ezekiel(Z)	1806	April 29	WestmrldCoPa	10	08	32
Day, Israel(Y)	1832	March 26	BelmontCo,Oh	03	05	01
Day, James(Z-M)	1836	Feb. 22	MuskingmCoOh	11	04	20
Day, John Jr.(Z-M)	1836	Feb. 20	MuskingmCoOh	11	04	19
Day, John(Y)	1823	Nov. 07	BelmontCo,Oh	06	09	06
Day, John(Y)	1824	July 26	BelmontCo,Oh	06	09	22
Day, John(Z-M)	1836	April 19	LickingCo,Oh	11	04	19
Day, Josephus(Z-M)	1833	Feb. 04	BelmontCo,Oh	07	05	23
Day, Josephus(Z-M)	1837	Dec. 04	CoshoctnCoOh	08	07	08
Day, Josephus(Z-M)	1837	Dec. 04	CoshoctnCoOh	08	07	09
Day, Lewis(Z-M)	1836	Nov. 30	GuernseyCoOh	02	03	12
Day, Solomon(Y)	1823	May 28	Stark Co.,Oh	06	19	22
Dayhoff, Abraham(Y)	1827	July 02	Stark Co.,Oh	06	15	32
Dayton, Garret(Z-M)	1828	Sept. 08	GuernseyCoOh	01	03	24
DeLance, John(Z-M)	1833	Feb. 12	GuernseyCoOh	03	01	07
DeLarue, John(Z-M)	1833	Nov. 05	GuernseyCoOh	03	01	14
DeLarue, John(Z-M)	1836	Jan. 18	GuernseyCoOh	03	01	14
DeLong, David(Z)	1836	Aug. 27	WashngtnCoOh	08	05	27
Deakins, Rich'd.(Z)	1831	Oct. 19	BelmontCo,Oh	11	08	04
Deakins, Richard(Z)	1831	July 06	BelmontCo,Oh	11	08	03
Deal, Henry(Z-M)	1833	July 26	CoshoctnCoOh	10	04	04
Dealor, George(Z)	1816	May 07	TuscarwsCoOh	03	09	23
Deamude, Daniel(Z-M)	1833	June 24	LickingCo,Oh	10	03	25
Deamude, Samuel(Z-M)	1833	June 06	LickingCo,Oh	10	03	16
Dean, Barton(Y)	1835	Jan. 23	CarrollCo,Oh	05	15	04
Dean, Calvin(Z-M)	1839	Nov. 20	HolmesCoOhio	08	08	13
Dean, Henry(Z)	1825	Feb. 07	GuernseyCoOh	10	09	21
Dean, Levi(Z)	1808	Jan. 15	WashngtnCoOh	08	05	17
Dean, Samuel(Z)	1816	Nov. 27	Jeff.Co.,Oh.	08	05	22
Dearberger, Michael(Y)	1828	July 12	Stark Co.,Oh	09	11	26
Deardorff, Isaac(Z)	1806	Sept. 08	MuskingmCoOh	03	08	02
Deardorff, Isaac(Z)	1809	Feb. 25	TuscarwsCoOh	03	10	19
Deardorff, Isaac(Z)	1816	May 07	TuscarwsCoOh	03	10	18
Deardorff, Sam'l.(Z-M)	1831	March 09	TuscarwsCoOh	02	07	05
Deardorff,Bohon & Slingluff(Z)	1806	Sept. 08	MuskingmCoOh	03	08	01
Deardorff,Bohon & Slingluff(Z)	1806	Sept. 22	MuskingmCoOh	03	08	03
Deardorff,Bohon & Slingluff(Z)	1806	Sept. 08	MuskingmCoOh	03	08	01
Deardorff,Bohon & Slingluff(Z)	1806	Sept. 08	MuskingmCoOh	03	08	02
Dearholt, Henry(Y)	1823	May 05	BelmontCo,Oh	03	05	03
Dearman, Sam'l.(Y)	1826	Oct. 18	ColumbanCoOh	07	12	22
Dearstine, John(Z)	1836	Sept. 26	MuskingmCoOh	14	13	36
Dearth, John(Z-M)	1830	Sept. 11	TuscarwsCoOh	01	05	04
Deater, Lewis(Y)	1823	March 15	Jeff.Co.,Oh.	03	10	22
Deatz, Adam(Z-M)	1829	Aug. 31	HolmesCoOhio	05	08	14
Deatz, Daniel(Z-M)	1829	Aug. 29	HolmesCoOhio	05	08	10
Deatz, Henry J.(Z-M)	1829	Sept. 01	HolmesCoOhio	05	08	01
Deaver, Abraham E.(Z)	1832	Dec. 31	Perry Co.,Oh	14	13	03
Deaver, Abraham(Z)	1826	Feb. 06	Morgan Co,Oh	13	09	15
Deaver, Abraham(Z)	1826	Feb. 06	Morgan Co,Oh	14	13	03
Deaver, Jonas(Z)	1826	Dec. 22	Perry Co.,Oh	13	09	18
Deaver, Levi(Z)	1810	Sept. 22	MuskingmCoOh	14	14	36
Deaver, Levi(Z)	1817	Jan. 28	MuskingmCoOh	14	13	12
Debery, Samuel(Z-M)	1830	June 14	WayneCo.,Oh.	05	07	20
Deck, John Vandel(Y)	1831	June 07	Stark Co.,Oh	06	15	33
Decker, Aaron(Z-M)	1835	April 16	GuernseyCoOh	10	04	23
Decker, Aaron(Z-M)	1835	Nov. 02	GuernseyCoOh	10	04	23
Decker, Joseph(Z)	1807	July 11	MuskingmCoOh	06	01	10

PURCHASER	YEAR	DATE	RESIDENCE	R	T	S
Decker, Joseph(Z)	1810	June 07	MuskingmCoOh	06	01	10
Decker, Moses(Z)	1815	May 27	MuskingmCoOh	06	01	01
Decker, Moses(Z)	1817	May 24	MuskingmCoOh	05	02	14
Decker, Moses(Z)	1817	Aug. 25	MuskingmCoOh	05	02	14
Deeds, Jacob Jr.(Z-M)	1831	June 14	HolmesCoOhio	05	07	19
Deeds, Jacob(Z)	1816	June 11	TuscarwsCoOh	05	08	13
Deeds, James W.(Z)	1822	Sept. 02	MuskingmCoOh	11	12	11
Deeds, John J.(Z-M)	1831	April 18	CoshoctnCoOh	05	06	25
Deeds, John(Z)	1814	Nov. 17	SomersetCoPa	05	08	13
Deeds, John(Z-M)	1823	Feb. 27	WestmrldCoPa	05	08	24
Deems, George(Z-M)	1833	Dec. 10	HolmesCoOhio	07	08	09
Deen, Benj.(Z)	1828	July 17	Morgan Co,Oh	10	07	33
Deen, Enoch(Z)	1836	Jan. 21	Morgan Co,Oh	10	06	25
Deen, Enoch(Z)	1836	June 17	Morgan Co,Oh	10	06	25
Deen, Enos(Z)	1826	Nov. 22	Morgan Co,Oh	10	07	33
Deen, Samuel(Z)	1816	June 11	Jeff.Co.,Oh.	08	05	22
Deeren, Thomas(Z)	1832	July 13	GuernseyCoOh	10	09	01
Deeren, Thomas(Z-M)	1832	July 13	GuernseyCoOh	03	01	23
Deetz, Daniel(Z-M)	1833	April 20	CoshoctnCoOh	05	07	06
Deetz, Daniel(Z-M)	1836	April 14	CoshoctnCoOh	06	09	24
Deetz, Jacob(Z-M)	1833	March 16	HolmesCoOhio	05	08	13
Deford, John Senr.(Y)	1824	July 22	FayetteCo,Pa	05	14	12
Deford, John Sr.(Y)	1824	June 26	FayetteCo,Pa	05	14	11
Dehaven, Jacob(Z-M)	1835	Feb. 28	HolmesCoOhio	05	07	04
Deisz, John G.(Z-M)	1831	March 19	TuscarwsCoOh	03	08	03
Deitz, George(Z-M)	1832	Oct. 06	TuscarwsCoOh	03	08	15
Deitz, Jacob Senr.(Z-M)	1831	Dec. 28	TuscarwsCoOh	05	07	19
Deitz, Jacob(Z-M)	1832	May 18	CoshoctnCoOh	05	07	11
Deitz, Jacob(Z-M)	1832	May 18	CoshoctnCoOh	05	07	12
Deitz, Jacob(Z-M)	1832	July 07	CoshoctnCoOh	05	07	11
Delancey, John(Z)	1835	April 30	MonroeCo.,Oh	10	07	36
Delancey, John(Z)	1835	April 30	MonroeCo.,Oh	09	06	31
Delany, John(Z)	1833	May 06	MonroeCo.,Oh	08	08	35
Delong, Abraham(Y)	1830	Sept. 03	TuscarwsCoOh	07	14	14
Delong, Abraham(Z-M)	1835	July 07	HarrisonCoOh	01	06	02
Delong, Chauncey H.(Z)	1836	Jan. 11	MuskingmCoOh	11	12	24
Delong, David(Z)	1831	April 18	Perry Co.,Oh	14	14	27
Delong, David(Z)	1832	Sept. 24	WashngtnCoOh	08	05	27
Delong, David(Z)	1811	March 30	GuernseyCoOh	09	08	02
Delong, David(Z)	1813	Dec. 25	MuskingmCoOh	14	14	28
Delong, Edward(Z)	1833	March 23	Perry Co.,Oh	15	16	24
Delong, Edward(Z)	1833	Oct. 14	Perry Co.,Oh	15	16	24
Delong, Edward(Z)	1816	March 15	CoshoctnCoOh	09	05	19
Delong, Ephraim(Y)	1835	Sept. 15	TuscarwsCoOh	07	14	34
Delong, George S.(Z)	1833	Feb. 08	GuernseyCoOh	08	08	01
Delong, George(Z)	1806	Sept. 19	BelmontCo,Oh	01	01	11
Delong, George(Z)	1807	Sept. 14	MuskingmCoOh	08	08	05
Delong, George(Z)	1811	Dec. 17	GuernseyCoOh	01	01	11
Delong, Henry(Z-M)	1826	July 31	Brooke CoVir	04	06	18
Delong, Henry(Z-M)	1831	Oct. 21	CoshoctnCoOh	04	06	21
Delong, Isaac(Y)	1830	Nov. 08	Jeff.Co.,Oh.	07	14	27
Delong, Isaac(Z)	1814	Dec. 29	GuernseyCoOh	15	16	15
Delong, James Junr.(Z)	1833	Feb. 11	GuernseyCoOh	08	08	02
Delong, James D.(Z)	1833	Jan. 16	MuskingmCoOh	10	08	20
Delong, James Lairs(Z)	1832	June 29	MuskingmCoOh	10	08	20
Delong, James(Z)	1807	June 17	MuskingmCoOh	01	01	22
Delong, Jesse(Y)	1825	Nov. 07	TuscarwsCoOh	07	14	31
Delong, Jesse(Y)	1835	Sept. 19	TuscarwsCoOh	07	14	35
Delong, Joseph(Z)	1807	Sept. 14	MuskingmCoOh	08	08	05
Delong, Solomen(Y)	1835	July 10	TuscarwsCoOh	07	14	23
Delong, Solomon(Y)	1835	Sept. 14	TuscarwsCoOh	07	14	23
Delts, William(Z)	1817	June 04	MuskingmCoOh	13	10	18
Deming, Lot(Y)	1820	Dec. 11	TuscarwsCoOh	06	13	29
Demoss, John(Z-M)	1836	Sept. 03	CoshoctnCoOh	08	06	08
Demoss, John(Z-M)	1836	Sept. 03	CoshoctnCoOh	08	06	09
Dempster, Noah(Z)	1832	Aug. 15	Morgan Co,Oh	11	11	22
Dempster, Noah(Z)	1835	Jan. 10	Morgan Co,Oh	11	10	36
Dempster, Noah(Z)	1835	April 29	Morgan Co,Oh	11	10	36
Dempster, Rezin(Z)	1831	March 03	Morgan Co,Oh	12	12	06

PURCHASER	YEAR	DATE	RESIDENCE	R	T	S
Dempster, William(Z)	1832	July 03	Morgan Co,Oh	11	11	05
Demster, Thomas(Z)	1832	April 09	Morgan Co,Oh	13	09	09
Denbow, Basil(Y)	1832	Sept. 17	HarrisonCoOh	05	13	03
Denbow, Henry(Y)	1822	June 19	HarfordCo,Md	05	12	23
Denman, Alpheus(Z-M)	1832	Sept. 17	WashCo.,Penn	05	07	20
Denman, M.(Z)	1815	Sept. 07	CoshoctnCoOh	08	05	05
Denman, Philip(Z)	1812	Nov. 11	LickingCo,Oh	10	03	24
Denman, S.(Z)	1815	Sept. 07	CoshoctnCoOh	08	05	05
Denman, Wm.(Z)	1812	Nov. 11	LickingCo,Oh	10	03	24
Denman, Zenas H.(Z-M)	1833	Jan. 12	LickingCo,Oh	10	03	08
Denman, Zenas H.(Z-M)	1833	Jan. 12	LickingCo,Oh	10	03	07
Denner, Andrew(Z)	1811	June 22	MuskingmCoOh	06	01	02
Denner, Jacob(Z)	1811	July 01	MuskingmCoOh	06	02	22
Dennis, Aaron(Z)	1828	Nov. 14	Perry Co.,Oh	14	14	29
Dennis, Conrad(Z)	1833	Jan. 28	Perry Co.,Oh	14	14	29
Dennis, Conrad(Z)	1833	Jan. 28	Perry Co.,Oh	14	14	29
Dennis, Darid(Z)	1832	Nov. 26	GuernseyCoOh	10	09	09
Dennis, Henry(Z-M)	1835	Nov. 07	GuernseyCoOh	03	01	06
Dennis, Henry(Z-M)	1836	Jan. 19	GuernseyCoOh	03	01	06
Dennis, James(Y)	1832	Dec. 18	ColumbanCoOh	03	12	36
Dennis, Joseph(Z-M)	1833	Dec. 09	GuernseyCoOh	03	01	15
Dennis, Martin(Z-M)	1835	Dec. 31	KnoxCo.,Ohio	10	06	07
Dennis, Michael(Z)	1816	Nov. 13	WashCo.,Penn	10	06	20
Dennis, Samuel(Z-M)	1833	Oct. 11	GuernseyCoOh	03	01	16
Dennis, William(Z)	1827	Nov. 27	MuskingmCoOh	12	10	05
Dennison, Gurden(Z)	1810	Sept. 19	MuskingmCoOh	06	02	15
Dennison, Henry(Z-M)	1832	Oct. 25	GuernseyCoOh	03	01	15
Dennison, Henry(Z-M)	1833	Feb. 07	GuernseyCoOh	03	01	15
Dennison, W. S.(Z)	1815	June 30	MuskingmCoOh	06	02	14
Dennison, W.(Z)	1815	June 30	MuskingmCoOh	06	02	14
Dennison, Warren(Z)	1811	Aug. 05	MuskingmCoOh	06	02	07
Dennison, William S.(Z)	1815	June 24	MuskingmCoOh	06	02	17
Dennison, William(Z)	1810	Sept. 19	MuskingmCoOh	06	02	15
Dennison, William(Z)	1810	Dec. 19	MuskingmCoOh	06	02	06
Dennison, William(Z)	1814	July 23	MuskingmCoOh	06	02	14
Denny, Andrew(Z)	1832	Feb. 22	Morgan Co,Oh	10	08	22
Denny, Anne(Z)	1826	March 27	MuskingmCoOh	14	13	13
Denny, Christ'n.(Z)	1832	Jan. 23	Morgan Co,Oh	10	08	22
Denny, Christopher(Z)	1833	Feb. 27	Morgan Co,Oh	10	08	21
Denraster, John(Z)	1805	Sept. 24	MuskingmCoOh	13	11	04
Depew, Isaac(Z-M)	1826	March 27	GuernseyCoOh	01	01	10
Depew, James(Z)	1826	June 01	GuernseyCoOh	08	08	02
Depew, James(Z)	1829	Nov. 13	GuernseyCoOh	08	08	01
Depew, James(Z)	1831	Aug. 31	GuernseyCoOh	08	08	01
Depew, James(Z-M)	1823	Feb. 03	GuernseyCoOh	01	01	19
Depew, James(Z-M)	1827	May 25	GuernseyCoOh	01	01	23
Depew, James(Z-M)	1832	April 05	GuernseyCoOh	01	01	23
Depew, James(Z-M)	1831	March 04	GuernseyCoOh	01	01	19
Derner, Andrew(Z)	1810	June 30	MuskingmCoOh	06	01	02
Deroch, David Servis(Y)	1831	Nov. 26	Stark Co.,Oh	05	14	24
Derrah, Joseph(Z)	1804	Dec. 06	MuskingmCoOh	14	15	03
Derrah, Joseph(Z)	1805	Nov. 11	MuskingmCoOh	14	15	04
Derry, James(Y)	1829	June 11	HarrisonCoOh	06	12	07
Derwater, Jacob(Z)	1828	Aug. 08	MuskingmCoOh	12	12	10
Derwater, Jacob(Z)	1830	Aug. 23	MuskingmCoOh	13	11	28
Derwater, Jacob(Z)	1811	Dec. 11	MuskingmCoOh	01	12	01
Derwater, Jacob(Z)	1816	April 15	MuskingmCoOh	12	12	02
Derwater, Jacob(Z)	1817	Aug. 12	MuskingmCoOh	12	12	02
Desellem, Jacob Short(Y)	1836	Jan. 15	ColumbanCoOh	03	12	11
Deshonq, Adam(Z)	1832	Sept. 21	Perry Co.,Oh	15	14	05
Deshonq, Adam(Z)	1832	Nov. 24	Perry Co.,Oh	15	14	05
Detchon, Elijah(Y)	1824	Nov. 05	TrumbullCoOh	05	18	10
Detchon, George(Y)	1824	April 15	TrumbullCoOh	05	18	15
Detchon, John(Y)	1824	April 06	TrumbullCoOh	05	18	10
Detchon, Solomon(Y)	1827	April 28	TrumbullCoOh	05	18	22
Dettenheffer, Paul(Z)	1812	Dec. 12	MuskingmCoOh	14	16	05
Devany, Henry(Y)	1822	June 10	HarrisonCoOh	07	19	21
Dever, Benjamin(Z)	1810	Oct. 15	MuskingmCoOh	14	14	25
Dever, Jonas(Z)	1831	June 08	Perry Co.,Oh	13	09	06

PURCHASER	YEAR	DATE	RESIDENCE	R	T	S
Dever, Jonas(Z)	1810	Oct. 15	MuskingmCoOh	14	14	25
Deveraux, Joseph(Z)	1807	Jan. 03	WashngtnCoOh	11	11	27
Devereaux, Joseph(Z)	1811	July 25	WashngtnCoOh	11	10	13
Devereaux, Joseph(Z)	1814	Sept. 07	WashngtnCoOh	11	11	29
Devers, Francis(Y)*	1826	July 08	RcknghmCoVir	05	11	36
Deviby, John E.(Z-M)	1837	March 31	HolmesCoOhio	09	09	04
Devin, Michael(Z)	1830	May 20	Morgan Co,Oh	11	10	20
Devin, Michael(Z)	1830	May 27	Morgan Co,Oh	11	10	19
Devin, Thomas(Z)	1829	Oct. 29	Morgan Co,Oh	11	10	29
Devin, Thomas(Z)	1829	Nov. 27	Morgan Co,Oh	11	10	29
Devin, Thomas(Z)	1830	Jan. 15	Morgan Co,Oh	04	10	29
Devin, Thos.(Z)	1830	March 11	Morgan Co,Oh	11	10	19
Devin, Thos.(Z)	1831	March 19	Morgan Co,Oh	11	10	19
Devit, Alex'r.(Z)	1829	April 08	Jeff.Co.,Oh.	11	10	11
Devlin, William(Y)	1830	July 08	AlleghnyCoPa	03	12	18
Devlin, William(Y)	1831	Nov. 15	ColumbanCoOh	03	12	24
Devol, John(Z)	1817	Oct. 09	MonroeCo.,Oh	09	07	35
Devold, Levi(Z)	1835	Jan. 06	Morgan Co,Oh	09	07	25
Devoll, Richard(Z)	1827	Dec. 25	Morgan Co,Oh	09	07	25
Devolla, Daniel(Z)	1836	May 27	Morgan Co,Oh	08	07	31
Devolld, Daniel(Z)	1836	May 27	Morgan Co,Oh	08	07	31
Devolld, Richard(Z)	1834	Nov. 10	Morgan Co,Oh	09	07	25
Devore, Aaron(Y)	1832	Oct. 15	Jeff.Co.,Oh.	04	12	12
Devore, Allison(Z-M)	1836	May 25	MuskingmCoOh	10	08	17
Devore, Edward(Y)	1829	June 04	ColumbanCoOh	06	19	23
Devore, Isaac(Z)	1830	March 01	Morgan Co,Oh	09	05	04
Devore, Jacob(Y)	1831	June 28	HarrisonCoOh	06	14	26
Devore, John Jr.(Z-M)	1836	Nov. 08	TuscarwsCoOh	04	07	12
Devore, William(Z-M)	1837	Jan. 02	KnoxCo.,Ohio	10	06	06
Devos, Ellen(Z)	1827	April 13	CoshoctnCoOh	06	07	06
Devry, James(Z)	1835	June 05	HarrisonCoOh	10	08	36
Devry, James(Z)	1835	June 05	HarrisonCoOh	08	07	31
Devry, William(Z)	1835	June 05	HarrisonCoOh	10	08	36
Dew, Andrew(Z)	1836	April 19	Perry Co.,Oh	14	13	23
Dew, Andrew(Z)	1836	Dec. 06	Perry Co.,Oh	14	13	24
Dew, Andrew(Z)	1836	Dec. 06	Perry Co.,Oh	14	13	23
Dew, David(Z-M)	1836	June 18	MuskingmCoOh	04	03	04
Dew, David(Z-M)	1838	Feb. 27	GuernseyCoOh	04	03	07
Dew, James(Z)	1824	Oct. 18	Perry Co.,Oh	14	12	35
Dew, James(Z)	1836	March 21	Perry Co.,Oh	14	12	36
Dew, James(Z)	1814	Feb. 26	AthensCoOhio	14	12	35
Dew, Thomas Jr.(Z)	1805	Nov. 07	MuskingmCoOh	13	12	07
Dew, Thomas Jr.(Z)	1815	Dec. 22	MuskingmCoOh	14	12	20
Dewees, Owon Jun.(Z)	1832	March 05	AthensCoOhio	12	09	01
Dewees, Samuel(Z-M)	1832	March 28	LickingCo,Oh	10	02	25
Dewees, Samuel(Z-M)	1832	April 10	LickingCo,Oh	10	02	25
Dewile, John(Z)	1833	Aug. 24	Morgan Co,Oh	10	07	34
Dewit, Barnard(Z-M)	1825	Sept. 26	HolmesCoOhio	09	09	24
Dewit, Barney Senr.(Z-M)	1827	May 22	KnoxCo.,Ohio	11	08	08
Dewit, Paul(Z)	1810	March 24	BelmontCo,Oh	04	04	19
Dewitt, Barney Sr.(Z-M)	1828	June 16	KnoxCo.,Ohio	11	08	08
Dewitt, Barney(Z)	1813	Sept. 20	KnoxCo.,Ohio	10	07	04
Dewitt, Barney(Z)	1816	Dec. 03	GuernseyCoOh	09	08	04
Dewitt, Barney(Z-M)	1835	Aug. 04	HolmesCoOhio	09	08	07
Dewitt, Barney(Z-M)	1836	Jan. 02	HolmesCoOhio	09	08	08
Dewitt, Barney(Z-M)	1837	July 31	HolmesCoOhio	08	08	05
Dewitt, Barny(Z-M)	1834	Feb. 22	KnoxCo.,Ohio	11	08	08
Dewitt, Bernard(Z-M)	1832	March 08	HolmesCoOhio	09	09	25
Dewitt, David L.(Z-M)	1829	Jan. 02	HolmesCoOhio	09	08	03
Dewitt, David L.(Z-M)	1829	April 08	HolmesCoOhio	09	09	23
Dewitt, David Linn(Z-M)	1832	Oct. 11	HolmesCoOhio	09	08	03
Dewitt, David(Z-M)	1832	May 29	HolmesCoOhio	09	08	04
Dewitt, David(Z-M)	1836	Oct. 31	HolmesCoOhio	09	08	04
Dewitt, Elijah F.(Z-M)	1832	May 05	KnoxCo.,Ohio	11	08	13
Dewitt, Francis(Z-M)	1836	April 06	KnoxCo.,Ohio	10	08	05
Dewitt, George W.(Z-M)	1836	Oct. 31	HolmesCoOhio	09	08	09
Dewitt, Henry(Z)	1815	May 26	KnoxCo.,Ohio	09	08	04
Dewitt, Henry(Z)	1815	May 26	KnoxCo.,Ohio	09	08	04
Dewitt, Henry(Z-M)	1832	Dec. 07	HolmesCoOhio	09	08	04

PURCHASER	YEAR	DATE	RESIDENCE	R	T	S
Dewitt, John(Y)	1827	Dec. 01	HarrisonCoOh	06	11	26
Dewitt, John(Z)	1833	Aug. 24	Morgan Co,Oh	10	07	34
Dewitt, Simon P.(Z-M)	1836	Oct. 31	HolmesCoOhio	09	08	09
Dewitt, Spencer(Z-M)	1836	Oct. 03	BelmontCo,Oh	03	06	24
Dewitt, Vincent(Z-M)	1831	Oct. 13	CoshoctnCoOh	04	06	13
Dewitt, William(Z)	1816	Dec. 03	GuernseyCoOh	09	08	03
Dewitt, William(Z-M)	1832	Nov. 13	HolmesCoOhio	09	09	23
Dexter, Wm.(Y)	1822	Oct. 31	ColumbanCoOh	05	14	12
Deybert, Frederick(Z)	1805	April 23	MuskingmCoOh	03	10	21
Dhiele, Francis(Z-M)	1838	June 07	CoshoctnCoOh	10	07	22
Dial, Hiram(Z-M)	1837	June 19	AlleghnyCoPa	09	07	02
Dial, Isaac(Z-M)	1832	Oct. 10	HolmesCoOhio	08	08	05
Dial, Isaac(Z-M)	1833	June 15	KnoxCo.,Ohio	10	07	22
Dial, Isaac(Z-M)	1833	June 19	KnoxCo.,Ohio	10	07	22
Dial, John(Z-M)	1833	Jan. 25	TuscarwsCoOh	04	07	16
Dial, Joshua(Z)	1832	Nov. 12	Perry Co.,Oh	15	15	25
Dial, Vallentine(Z-M)	1828	Dec. 25	HolmesCoOhio	08	08	02
Dial, William(Z-M)	1825	Aug. 12	HolmesCoOhio	08	08	09
Dial, William(Z-M)	1832	Oct. 06	HolmesCoOhio	08	08	05
Dial, William(Z-M)	1832	Oct. 06	HolmesCoOhio	08	08	04
Dibert, Charles(Z-M)	1825	Nov. 30	BedfordCo,Pa	07	08	03
Dibert, Charles(Z-M)	1828	Sept. 20	BedfordCo,Pa	07	08	03
Dicken, Isaac(Z)	1815	April 28	CoshoctnCoOh	09	05	21
Dickerhoof, John(ofAndrewSr(Y)	1829	Dec. 07	Stark Co.,Oh	07	20	18
Dickerson, Baruch(Z)	1816	Dec. 07	HarrisonCoOh	07	05	14
Dickerson, Frederick(Z)	1815	May 11	GuernseyCoOh	01	02	11
Dickerson, Levi(Z)	1816	March 29	HarrisonCoOh	08	04	03
Dickerson, Willard(Z)	1826	Jan. 11	HardwickMass	09	06	25
Dickerson, Zadock Jn.(Z)	1837	March 09	Morgan Co,Oh	08	06	29
Dickerson, Zadock Jr.(Z)	1836	June 24	Morgan Co,Oh	08	06	32
Dickerson, Zadock(Z)	1815	Feb. 15	AlleghnyCoPa	11	11	31
Dickess, Isaac(Z-M)	1827	Jan. 30	CoshoctnCoOh	08	05	22
Dickey, Abraham(Z-M)	1832	July 10	CoshoctnCoOh	04	07	04
Dickey, Abraham(Z-M)	1833	Nov. 25	CoshoctnCoOh	05	07	15
Dickey, John(Z)	1814	Aug. 11	Jeff.Co.,Oh.	05	06	25
Dickey, John(Z-M)	1833	July 22	CoshoctnCoOh	06	07	03
Dickey, John(Z-M)	1837	Jan. 10	TuscarwsCoOh	04	07	04
Dickey, Richard(Y)	1832	Nov. 24	Brooke CoVir	03	12	19
Dickey, Richard(Y)	1833	Jan. 03	Brooke CoVir	03	12	19
Dickey, Samuel(Z-M)	1832	Aug. 07	TuscarwsCoOh	03	07	24
Dickinson, Benj'n.(Y)	1827	July 09	ColumbanCoOh	04	13	35
Dickinson, Geo.(Z-M)	1833	March 13	TuscarwsCoOh	01	05	12
Dickinson, George(Z-M)	1833	Dec. 05	TuscarwsCoOh	01	05	11
Dickinson, George(Z-M)	1835	May 29	TuscarwsCoOh	01	05	11
Dickinson, William R.(Y)	1825	July 13	SteubenvleOh	09	11	21
Dickinson, William R.(Y)	1828	Aug. 19	SteubenvleOh	09	11	22
Dickinson, Wm. R.(Y)	1824	May 21	SteubenvleOh	09	10	29
Dickinson, Wm. R.(Y)	1824	May 21	SteubenvleOh	09	10	29
Dickinson, Wm. R.(Y)	1824	May 21	SteubenvleOh	09	10	29
Dickinson, Wm. R.(Y)	1824	May 21	SteubenvleOh	09	10	29
Dickinson, Wm. R.(Y)	1824	May 22	SteubenvleOh	09	10	21
Dickinson, Wm. R.(Y)	1824	May 22	SteubenvleOh	09	11	17
Dickison, Levi(Z)	1817	April 05	HarrisonCoOh	08	04	03
Dicks, John Jr.(Z-M)	1824	Aug. 10	TuscarwsCoOh	01	05	01
Dicks, John Senr.(Z-M)	1825	Dec. 13	TuscarwsCoOh	01	05	02
Dicks, John Senr.(Z-M)	1825	Dec. 13	TuscarwsCoOh	01	05	10
Dicks, John(Y)	1824	Dec. 11	HarrisonCoPa	07	12	34
Dicks, John(Z)	1826	Oct. 10	Jeff.Co.,Oh.	01	05	01
Dicks, John(Z-M)	1824	Nov. 15	HarrisonCoOh	01	05	02
Dicks, John(Z-M)	1824	Nov. 15	HarrisonCoOh	01	05	02
Dicks, John(Z-M)	1826	Oct. 10	Jeff.Co.,Oh.	01	05	01
Dickson, Geo.(Z)	1833	Feb. 28	Morgan Co,Oh	09	07	14
Dickson, George(Z)	1835	April 02	Morgan Co,Oh	09	07	14
Dickson, George(Z)	1835	Dec. 07	Morgan Co,Oh	09	07	01
Dickson, George(Z-M)	1832	Dec. 31	Morgan Co,Oh	09	08	14
Dickson, Henry(Z-M)	1833	April 12	TuscarwsCoOh	01	05	09
Dickson, Henry(Z-M)	1833	April 12	TuscarwsCoOh	01	05	12
Dickson, James(Z)	1811	Feb. 27	MuskingmCoOh	11	13	18
Dickson, James(Z)	1815	Feb. 03	MuskingmCoOh	12	13	24

PURCHASER	YEAR	DATE	RESIDENCE	R	T	S
Dickson, Joseph(Z-M)	1821	Feb. 12	KnoxCo.,Ohio	11	04	23
Dickson, Patrick(Y)	1821	June 23	ColumbanCoOh	04	14	19
Dicus, Lemuel(Z-M)	1828	Nov. 26	CoshoctnCoOh	08	04	02
Dieters, George(Z)	1815	June 23	TuscarwsCoOh	03	10	23
Dike, N'l.(Y)	1825	Feb. 19	Ohio	10	01	11
Dike, Nathaniel(Y)	1833	Aug. 26	SteubenvleOh	09	10	02
Dildine, Harmon(Z-M)	1836	Oct. 06	TuscarwsCoOh	03	05	22
Dildine, Harmon(Z-M)	1837	Sept. 18	TuscarwsCoOh	03	04	18
Dildine, John(Y)	1826	April 08	ColumbanCoOh	03	13	22
Dildine, John(Y)	1826	April 08	ColumbanCoOh	03	13	22
Dill, James(Z)	1835	Jan. 06	Perry Co.,Oh	15	15	14
Dill, John(Z)	1836	Dec. 09	Perry Co.,Oh	15	15	14
Dille, Aaran(Z)	1833	March 06	Morgan Co,Oh	10	08	31
Dille, Ezekiel(Z)	1832	March 13	Morgan Co,Oh	10	08	10
Dillehay, Cornelius(Z)	1838	Nov. 28	GuernseyCoOh	08	06	23
Diller, John Jnr.(Z)	1835	Aug. 21	Perry Co.,Oh	15	15	31
Dilley, Abm.(Z)	1812	May 01	GuernseyCoOh	08	08	05
Dilley, Abraham(Z)	1815	Sept. 13	GuernseyCoOh	02	01	11
Dilley, Ephriam(Z)	1813	Sept. 13	FayetteCo,Pa	02	01	20
Dilley, Joseph(Z)	1813	Sept. 13	FayetteCo,Pa	02	01	20
Dilley, Robert(Z)	1815	Dec. 26	GuernseyCoOh	02	01	19
Dillin, Christopher(Z)	1825	May 28	GuernseyCoOh	11	10	21
Dillin, Christopher(Z)	1825	May 28	GuernseyCoOh	11	10	22
Dillin, James(Y)	1826	April 27	HarrisonCoOh	06	13	18
Dillman, Michael(Y)	1826	Dec. 26	Stark Co.,Oh	09	12	20
Dillon, Christopher(Z)	1826	Dec. 01	GuernseyCoOh	11	10	21
Dillon, John(Z)	1815	Nov. 04	MuskingmCoOh	10	03	09
Dillon, John(Z)	1817	March 07	MuskingmCoOh	10	03	12
Dillon, John(Z)	1817	May 05	MuskingmCoOh	10	03	09
Dillon, Jonathan(Y)	1831	May 06	Stark Co.,Oh	07	20	06
Dillon, Moses(Z)	1815	May 18	PutnamCoOhio	09	01	12
Dillon, Moses(Z)	1815	May 18	PutnamCoOhio	09	01	11
Dillon, Moses(Z)	1815	June 26	PutnamCoOhio	09	01	18
Dillon, Moses(Z)	1815	June 26	PutnamCoOhio	09	01	19
Dillon, Moses(Z)	1815	June 26	PutnamCoOhio	09	01	21
Dillon, Moses(Z)	1815	June 26	PutnamCoOhio	09	01	22
Dillon, Nehemiah(Z)	1827	Sept. 21	MuskingmCoOh	12	12	31
Dillon, Peter(Z)	1815	Aug. 29	CoshoctnCoOh	09	05	08
Dillon, Robert(Z-M)	1825	Aug. 30	KnoxCo.,Ohio	08	04	09
Dillon, Thomas(Z)	1814	Jan. 04	GreeneCo.,Pa	11	06	25
Dillon, William(Y)	1827	June 21	TrumbullCoOh	07	20	27
Dillon, William(Z)	1815	Dec. 26	GreeneCo.,Pa	09	05	08
Dills, Peter(Z)	1812	June 18	MuskingmCoOh	15	17	11
Dilly, Moses(Z)	1832	Feb. 07	MuskingmCoOh	11	12	24
Dilly, Moses(Z)	1834	Aug. 06	MuskingmCoOh	10	08	30
Dils, George(Z)	1810	June 15	MuskingmCoOh	15	17	04
Dils, John(Z)	1810	Feb. 23	MuskingmCoOh	14	15	22
Dils, John(Z)	1810	July 13	MuskingmCoOh	14	14	25
Dils, John(Z)	1814	July 08	MuskingmCoOh	13	10	06
Dils, John(Z)	1817	Jan. 15	MuskingmCoOh	14	15	23
Dilts, William(Z)	1817	June 04	MuskingmCoOh	13	10	18
Dimmick, Mathew(Z)	1824	June 04	Morgan Co,Oh	11	07	21
Dimmick, Samuel(Z)	1832	June 23	Morgan Co,Oh	10	07	22
Dimmick, Samuel(Z)	1832	Oct. 06	Morgan Co,Oh	10	07	22
Dimmock, Jos.(Z)	1830	March 29	Morgan Co,Oh	10	07	22
Dingey, Joseph(Z)	1833	Feb. 20	MuskingmCoOh	11	12	27
Dirck, Jacob(Z-M)	1837	Feb. 10	Wayne Co.,Oh	09	09	25
Dirin, Thomas(Z-M)	1832	July 19	TuscarwsCoOh	03	09	23
Disallums, John(Z-M)	1832	May 01	GuernseyCoOh	04	03	12
Disallums, John(Z-M)	1833	June 19	GuernseyCoOh	04	03	12
Disallums, John(Z-M)	1837	June 14	GuernseyCoOh	04	03	09
Disallums, Thos.(Z-M)	1832	May 01	GuernseyCoOh	04	03	12
Dishong, John(Z)	1834	Jan. 01	Perry Co.,Oh	15	14	05
Dishong, Morris(Z)	1836	Dec. 14	Perry Co.,Oh	15	14	28
Dishong, Morris(Z)	1836	Dec. 14	Perry Co.,Oh	15	14	33
Disler, Henry(Y)	1824	Aug. 20	Stark Co.,Oh	09	11	12
Dissinger, Henry(Y)	1824	Sept. 24	LancastrCoPa	10	02	22
Dissinger, Jno.(Y)	1824	June 25	Stark Co.,Oh	10	02	15
Ditz, Jacob(Z-M)	1836	Sept. 17	CoshoctnCoOh	05	07	19

PURCHASER	YEAR	DATE	RESIDENCE	R	T	S
Divan, Henry(Z)	1814	Sept. 07	BelmontCo,Oh	09	05	22
Diveny, Dan'l.(Y)	1829	Oct. 02	NrthmptnCoPa	04	13	24
Diveny, James(Y)	1829	Oct. 02	NrthmptnCoPa	04	13	24
Divit, James(Z)	1828	Nov. 12	Jeff.Co.,Oh.	11	10	02
Divit, James(Z)	1828	Nov. 12	Jeff.Co.,Oh.	11	10	03
Dixon, James(Z-M)	1826	May 17	Ohio Co.,Vir	11	05	20
Dixon, John(Z)	1835	Dec. 10	Morgan Co,Oh	09	05	36
Dixon, John(Z)	1836	Jan. 12	MarshallCoVa	08	05	30
Dixon, John(Z)	1810	Dec. 01	AlleghnyCoPa	06	01	08
Dixon, John(Z-M)	1827	March 22	HarrisonCoOh	01	05	04
Dixon, John(Z-M)	1827	March 22	HarrisonCoOh	01	05	04
Dixon, John(Z-M)	1827	March 22	HarrisonCoOh	01	05	03
Dixon, Joseph(Z)	1814	Jan. 25	Baltimore,Md	13	12	12
Dixon, Joseph(Z-M)	1825	Jan. 04	TuscarwsCoOh	02	05	21
Dixon, Thomas(Z)	1815	Nov. 27	MuskingmCoOh	04	02	24
Dixson, James(Y)	1822	Dec. 19	BelmontCo,Oh	03	05	15
Dixson, James(Z-M)	1832	March 28	OhioCo.,Ohio	10	04	05
Dixson, James(Z-M)	1832	March 28	OhioCo.,Ohio	11	05	21
Doan, Benajah(Z)	1822	July 31	Jeff.Co.,Oh.	11	12	28
Doan, Bennajah(Z)	1832	May 22	MuskingmCoOh	11	12	33
Doan, Cegillous(Z)	1813	Feb. 02	WashngtnCoOh	08	05	06
Doan, Daniel(Z)	1822	May 10	Jeff.Co.,Oh.	11	12	33
Doan, David(Z)	1822	May 23	Morgan Co,Oh	11	11	07
Doan, Israel(Z)	1832	Feb. 22	MuskingmCoOh	11	12	33
Doan, John(Z)	1833	Dec. 03	MuskingmCoOh	11	12	33
Doan, Orgillious(Z)	1813	April 19	WashngtnCoOh	09	06	36
Doan, Orgillious(Z)	1811	Sept. 25	WashngtnCoOh	09	06	23
Doane, Crgillious(Z)	1813	April 19	WashngtnCoOh	09	06	36
Dobbin, Solomon(Z)	1835	Nov. 18	MonroeCo.,Oh	08	06	20
Dobbins, Hugh(Y)	1827	Jan. 29	TrumbullCoOh	05	18	15
Dobbs, John(Y)	1828	Jan. 16	Jeff.Co.,Oh.	04	12	21
Dobler, Christian(Y)	1828	Dec. 27	Stark Co.,Oh	06	19	29
Dobson, Joseph(Y)	1833	March 04	ColumbanCoOh	03	12	36
Dobson, Joseph(Y)	1834	Oct. 27	CarrollCo,Oh	03	13	31
Dodd, John(Z)	1810	Aug. 08	MuskingmCoOh	14	14	25
Dodd, Samuel(Y)	1827	Aug. 27	ColumbanCoOh	05	14	15
Dodds, William(Z)	1804	Nov. 19	WestmrldCoPa	14	15	27
Dodson, Thomas D.(Z)	1832	June 12	Perry Co.,Oh	14	12	11
Dodson, Thos. D.(Z)	1836	Dec. 14	Perry Co.,Oh	14	12	10
Doherty, A.(Z)	1814	Nov. 28	GuernseyCoOh	02	02	02
Doherty, A.(Z)	1815	Nov. 23	GuernseyCoOh	11	10	25
Doherty, A.(Z)	1815	Nov. 23	GuernseyCoOh	11	10	25
Doherty, D.(Z)	1814	Nov. 28	GuernseyCoOh	02	02	02
Dolan, Mary A.(Z)	1833	Aug. 22	Perry Co.,Oh	14	14	31
Dolan, Patric(Z)	1832	Oct. 22	Perry Co.,Oh	14	14	31
Dolan, Patrick(Z)	1832	Oct. 16	Perry Co.,Oh	14	14	31
Dole, Daniel(Y)	1822	Aug. 19	ColumbanCoOh	04	17	10
Doll, Henry(Y)	1830	Dec. 29	Stark Co.,Oh	06	17	32
Doll, John Junr.(Y)	1825	June 21	Stark Co.,Oh	07	18	21
Doll, John(Y)	1824	May 20	Stark Co.,Oh	07	18	21
Dolls, William(Z-M)	1836	June 21	CarrollCo,Oh	03	07	21
Dolman, George(Z)	1816	Nov. 16	WashCo.,Penn	11	13	25
Dolson, T.(Z)	1815	June 12	MuskingmCoOh	14	15	15
Dolts, William(Z-M)	1836	June 21	CarrollCo,Oh	03	07	21
Doma, Elizabeth(Z)	1814	May 30	TuscarwsCoOh	04	08	08
Doman, Hugh(Z)	1811	April 27	LickingCo,Oh	11	03	14
Domer, Fred.(Z-M)	1830	Oct. 18	TuscarwsCoOh	05	08	01
Domer, Frederick(Z)	1812	April 15	TuscarwsCoOh	04	08	09
Domer, George(Z)	1806	Dec. 15	SomersetCoPa	04	08	13
Domer, Joseph(Z-M)	1833	Aug. 07	TuscarwsCoOh	03	08	15
Domer, Michael(Z)	1806	Dec. 15	SomersetCoPa	04	08	14
Donaghey, James(Z-M)	1828	Aug. 20	HarrisonCoOh	01	05	16
Donaghey, John(Y)	1827	March 07	HarrisonCoOh	07	12	18
Donaho, Gilbert(Z-M)	1830	Dec. 13	BelmontCo,Oh	05	06	08
Donahoo, Gilbert(Z-M)	1832	July 23	BelmontCo,Oh	03	06	03
Donahoo, Gilbert(Z-M)	1835	Dec. 01	BelmontCo,Oh	03	07	24
Donaker, J.(Z)	1816	Dec. 05	MuskingmCoOh	06	01	01
Donaldson, David(Y)	1829	July 28	Jeff.Co.,Oh.	04	13	21
Donaldson, David(Y)	1832	Feb. 08	ColumbanCoOh	04	13	21

PURCHASER	YEAR	DATE	RESIDENCE	R	T	S
Donaldson, James(Y)	1835	July 21	CarrollCo,Oh	05	15	10
Donaldson, John(Z-M)	1833	Jan. 23	KnoxCo.,Ohio	11	08	14
Donaldson, Thos. T.(Z-M)	1832	Sept. 18	MuskingmCoOh	11	08	17
Donaldson, Thos. T.(Z-M)	1832	Sept. 18	MuskingmCoOh	11	08	17
Donaldson, William(Z-M)	1833	Sept. 27	LickingCo,Oh	11	04	09
Donaughey, B.(Z)	1836	Aug. 11	Perry Co.,Oh	15	15	24
Donaway, Mathew(Z-M)	1828	May 31	HarrisonCoOh	01	05	13
Donley, James(Z-M)	1837	March 21	CoshoctnCoOh	09	07	19
Donley, James(Z-M)	1837	March 21	CoshoctnCoOh	09	07	18
Donley, Stephen(Z-M)	1824	Feb. 09	CoshoctnCoOh	08	05	22
Donley, Stephen(Z-M)	1824	Nov. 30	CoshoctnCoOh	08	05	04
Donnelly, Arthur(Z)	1817	Jan. 07	WashCo.,Penn	04	02	06
Donough, Barney O.(Y)	1835	March 05	ColumbanCoOh	04	13	13
Donovan, Daniel(Z)	1836	Jan. 20	Morgan Co,Oh	10	08	31
Doonigam, John(Z)	1836	Jan. 21	MonroeCo.,Oh	08	07	33
Doris, James Jr.(Y)	1826	Nov. 24	ColumbanCoOh	05	14	12
Doris, James Jr.(Y)	1826	Nov. 27	ColumbanCoOh	05	14	05
Dormen, Michael(Z-M)	1830	June 08	HolmesCoOhio	04	08	15
Dornan, James(Y)	1827	May 22	ColumbanCoOh	03	13	15
Dorrance, Samuel(Y)	1832	April 27	Jeff.Co.,Oh.	03	11	35
Dorris, James(Z)	1833	Dec. 10	Perry Co.,Oh	14	13	21
Dorris, Robert(Z)	1829	April 27	Morgan Co,Oh	13	08	32
Dorsey, Aquila(Z-M)	1831	March 21	Jeff.Co.,Oh.	01	06	25
Doser, Geo.(Z)	1831	April 27	Morgan Co,Oh	13	10	09
Doser, George(Z)	1830	Feb. 17	MuskingmCoOh	13	10	09
Doser, Henry(Z)	1831	April 16	MuskingmCoOh	13	10	10
Doser, John(Z)	1830	April 09	MuskingmCoOh	13	10	10
Doser, John(Z)	1831	April 16	MuskingmCoOh	13	10	10
Doser, John(Z)	1832	Aug. 15	MuskingmCoOh	13	10	09
Doson, John(Y)	1826	Sept. 14	Jeff.Co.,Oh.	05	12	29
Dossey, John(Z)	1836	Nov. 12	MonroeCo.,Oh	08	07	34
Doster, James(Z)	1816	Dec. 20	ZanesvilleOh	10	09	27
Doster, Smith(Z-M)	1838	Dec. 17	TuscarwsCoOh	04	05	22
Dostman, John(Y)	1823	Sept. 03	TrumbullCoOh	07	20	22
Dotts, William(Z-M)	1836	June 21	CarrollCo,Oh	03	07	21
Doty, Frazy(Z)	1813	Oct. 05	KnoxCo.,Ohio	11	06	25
Douden, Thomas(Z)	1805	Dec. 09	MuskingmCoOh	15	17	24
Doudna, John(Y)	1824	March 16	BelmontCo,Oh	06	08	25
Dougan, James(Z-M)	1824	Oct. 23	HolmesCoOhio	07	08	13
Dougan, Robert Junr.(Z-M)	1833	Feb. 28	FayetteCo,Pa	07	08	18
Dougan, Robert Senr.(Z-M)	1826	Feb. 20	FayetteCo,Pa	07	08	13
Dougherty, James Jr.(Y)	1829	Dec. 09	SteubenvleOh	05	14	17
Dougherty, James Jr.(Y)	1829	Dec. 11	SteubenvleOh	08	11	09
Dougherty, James Jr.(Y)	1829	Dec. 11	SteubenvleOh	08	11	09
Dougherty, James(Y)	1831	March 18	WashCo.,Penn	07	11	22
Dougherty, John(Y)	1831	May 10	Jeff.Co.,Oh.	07	14	22
Dougherty, John(Z-M)	1829	March 16	CoshoctnCoOh	06	06	12
Dougherty, John(Z-M)	1833	Oct. 05	HolmesCoOhio	07	08	09
Dougherty, Thos.(Z-M)	1834	Feb. 04	CoshoctnCoOh	07	05	16
Doughty, Conrad(Z)	1816	April 17	WashCo.,Penn	01	04	18
Doughty, Daniel(Z)	1806	June 16	MuskingmCoOh	13	12	02
Doughty, Daniel(Z)	1806	June 23	?	13	12	02
Douglass, David Senr.(Z-M)	1835	Nov. 03	GuernseyCoOh	03	04	25
Douglass, David Senr.(Z-M)	1835	Nov. 03	GuernseyCoOh	03	03	05
Douglass, David(Z-M)	1833	Nov. 15	GuernseyCoOh	03	03	03
Douglass, David(Z-M)	1835	Dec. 18	GuernseyCoOh	03	03	04
Douglass, George(Y)	1823	Sept. 06	BelmontCo,Oh	06	08	32
Douglass, George(Y)	1825	Nov. 25	BelmontCo,Oh	06	08	32
Douglass, Jno.(Z-M)	1831	Nov. 30	BelmontCo,Oh	07	05	07
Douglass, John Wiones(Z)	1836	Jan. 04	MuskingmCoOh	10	06	05
Douglass, John(Z-M)	1834	Oct. 22	HolmesCoOhio	07	08	10
Douglass, Joseph(Z-M)	1835	Nov. 10	GuernseyCoOh	03	03	10
Douglass, Sam'l.(Z)	1827	Oct. 03	GuernseyCoOh	03	04	12
Douglass, Sam'l.(Z)	1833	Nov. 30	GuernseyCoOh	03	05	25
Douglass, Samuel(Z-M)	1836	Jan. 04	GuernseyCoOh	03	04	25
Douney, Bazil(Z)	1824	July 02	Morgan Co,Oh	10	08	11
Dow, Joseph(Z)	1817	July 03	WashngtnCoOh	11	10	30
Dowall, Daniel(Z)	1815	Feb. 20	BelmontCo,Oh	09	07	36
Dowden, Thos.(Z)	1805	Oct. 18	MuskingmCoOh	14	15	14

PURCHASER	YEAR	DATE	RESIDENCE	R	T	S
Dowell, Benj'n.(Y)	1821	Nov. 21	Jeff.Co.,Oh.	04	11	24
Dowell, Samuel(Y)	1829	Nov. 16	Jeff.Co.,Oh.	04	12	25
Downard, David(Y)	1833	April 12	ColumbanCoOh	03	12	03
Downard, Jacob(Y)	1832	Nov. 05	ColumbanCoOh	03	12	03
Downard, James(Y)	1823	Aug. 23	ColumbanCoOh	04	12	18
Downard, James(Y)	1828	March 25	Jeff.Co.,Oh.	04	12	11
Downard, James(Y)	1832	Sept. 22	Jeff.Co.,Oh.	04	13	07
Downard, James(Y)	1833	Aug. 24	Jeff.Co.,Oh.	04	12	17
Downard, James(Y)	1836	Sept. 21	Jeff.Co.,Oh.	04	12	10
Downard, John(Y)	1827	March 24	ColumbanCoOh	03	12	03
Downard, Joseph(Y)	1824	June 08	ColumbanCoOh	03	12	09
Downard, Joseph(Y)	1832	Oct. 11	ColumbanCoOh	03	12	09
Downard, Joshua(Y)	1827	March 24	ColumbanCoOh	03	12	03
Downay, James(Z)	1814	June 28	FairfeldCoOh	15	16	09
Downerd, Jacob(Z-M)	1836	Jan. 02	MuskingmCoOh	01	05	05
Downerd, Jacob(Z-M)	1836	Jan. 02	MuskingmCoOh	01	05	05
Downes, George(Y)	1822	Aug. 27	Stark Co.,Oh	07	16	22
Downes, George(Y)	1826	Oct. 18	Stark Co.,Oh	07	16	22
Downes, Josiah(Y)	1828	Oct. 23	Stark Co.,Oh	07	16	28
Downes, Josiah(Y)	1829	April 14	Stark Co.,Oh	07	16	28
Downey, Alvey(Y)	1833	March 28	CarrollCo,Oh	04	13	13
Downey, Alvey(Y)	1833	March 28	CarrollCo,Oh	04	13	13
Downey, Charles(Z)	1820	Oct. 27	Morgan Co,Oh	10	08	02
Downey, Doctor(Z)	1829	Sept. 22	Morgan Co,Oh	09	07	09
Downey, Doctor(Z)	1831	Feb. 04	Morgan Co,Oh	09	07	04
Downey, Doctor(Z)	1835	Sept. 30	Morgan Co,Oh	09	07	04
Downey, Ephraim(Z)	1834	Dec. 03	Morgan Co,Oh	09	07	10
Downey, Joseph(Z)	1828	Nov. 19	Morgan Co,Oh	10	09	35
Downey, Meriman(Z)	1826	June 29	HarrisonCoOh	10	08	02
Downey, Thomas(Z)	1820	Oct. 27	Morgan Co,Oh	10	08	11
Downey, Walter(Z)	1825	April 15	GuernseyCoOh	09	08	31
Downey, Walter(Z)	1833	Jan. 02	GuernseyCoOh	09	08	31
Downey, Walter(Z)	1833	Jan. 02	GuernseyCoOh	09	08	31
Downing, Adam(Y)	1832	May 16	Stark Co.,Oh	07	16	21
Downing, Edward(Z)	1821	Oct. 01	Morgan Co,Oh	10	06	19
Downing, James(Y)	1829	March 18	Stark Co.,Oh	07	16	06
Downs, George(Z-M)	1832	April 13	KnoxCo.,Ohio	11	08	07
Downs, Josephus(Z-M)	1827	March 19	KnoxCo.,Ohio	11	08	25
Downy, Epraim(Z)	1829	Aug. 20	Morgan Co,Oh	09	07	10
Doyle, Mathew(Z)	1814	May 24	GuernseyCoOh	01	02	20
Doyle, Mathew(Z)	1814	Sept. 10	GuernseyCoOh	01	02	13
Dozer, John(Z)	1834	Jan. 29	MuskingmCoOh	13	10	09
Dozer, Michael(Z)	1828	June 23	MuskingmCoOh	13	10	04
Dozer, Rebecca(Z)	1833	Dec. 23	MuskingmCoOh	13	10	10
Dozer, Sam'l.(Z)	1833	Dec. 23	MuskingmCoOh	13	10	10
Dozer, Samuel(Z)	1832	April 30	MuskingmCoOh	13	10	07
Dozor, Samuel(Z)	1833	March 28	MuskingmCoOh	13	10	10
Draher, Isaac(Z-M)	1834	Feb. 06	CoshoctnCoOh	09	07	14
Draine, Francis(Z)	1815	April 17	MuskingmCoOh	15	17	11
Drake, Abner(Z-M)	1832	May 21	LickingCo,Oh	10	04	10
Drake, Abner(Z-M)	1836	Feb. 03	LickingCo,Oh	10	04	02
Drake, Abner(Z-M)	1836	Oct. 26	LickingCo,Oh	10	04	09
Drake, Abner(Z-M)	1836	Oct. 26	LickingCo,Oh	10	04	12
Drake, Clinton D.(Z)	1824	Aug. 24	BelmontCo,Oh	12	09	05
Drake, Clinton D.(Z)	1825	Jan. 17	BelmontCo,Oh	12	09	05
Drake, Dan'l. D.(Z)	1824	Aug. 24	BelmontCo,Oh	12	09	05
Drake, David(Z)	1833	Nov. 26	BelmontCo,Oh	08	08	26
Drake, David(Z-M)	1836	Oct. 07	GuernseyCoOh	03	03	01
Drake, David(Z-M)	1836	Oct. 07	GuernseyCoOh	03	03	01
Drake, James W.(Z)	1824	Aug. 24	BelmontCo,Oh	12	09	05
Drake, Jefferson(Y)	1828	Nov. 07	WashCo.,Penn	07	11	29
Drake, Joel(Z)	1836	Jan. 22	Morgan Co,Oh	09	05	30
Drake, Joel(Z)	1836	Jan. 22	Morgan Co,Oh	09	05	32
Drake, John(Z)	1815	Jan. 16	GuernseyCoOh	09	08	34
Drake, Ralph(Z)	1836	Jan. 08	Perry Co.,Oh	14	12	17
Drake, Ralph(Z)	1836	March 21	Perry Co.,Oh	14	12	09
Drake, Robert(Z-M)	1829	July 06	LickingCo,Oh	10	05	21
Drake, Robert(Z-M)	1829	July 31	LickingCo,Oh	10	05	20
Drake, Robert(Z-M)	1832	May 21	LickingCo,Oh	10	04	22

PURCHASER	YEAR	DATE	RESIDENCE	R	T	S
Drake, Robert(Z-M)	1832	May 21	LickingCo,Oh	10	04	22
Drake, Simeon(Y)	1835	Aug. 22	CarrollCo,Oh	05	13	04
Drake, Thomas(Z)	1816	July 15	MuskingmCoOh	10	04	20
Drake, William(Y)	1831	Nov. 18	ColumbanCoOh	03	12	36
Drake, William(Y)	1833	May 04	ColumbanCoOh	03	12	36
Drake, Wm.(Z-M)	1835	Jan. 28	HarrisonCoOh	03	04	21
Drake, Wm.(Z-M)	1835	Dec. 17	GuernseyCoOh	03	04	21
Draper, Isaac(Z)	1806	Dec. 02	MuskingmCoOh	09	07	15
Draper, Isaac(Z)	1815	Nov. 09	CoshoctnCoOh	09	07	06
Draper, J.(Z)	1815	Nov. 09	CoshoctnCoOh	09	07	08
Draper, Jacob(Z)	1815	Nov. 09	CoshoctnCoOh	09	07	06
Draper, Jacob(Z-M)	1835	March 07	KnoxCo.,Ohio	09	07	06
Draper, Jno.(Z)	1831	Dec. 15	Morgan Co,Oh	10	08	06
Draper, Levi(Z)	1810	April 09	MuskingmCoOh	14	14	36
Draper, Samuel(Z-M)	1832	Dec. 17	CoshoctnCoOh	09	07	05
Draper, Samuel(Z-M)	1835	Sept. 29	CoshoctnCoOh	09	07	03
Dressel, George(Z-M)	1837	Sept. 14	CoshoctnCoOh	04	05	22
Drips, William(Y)	1822	March 18	WashCo.,Penn	06	09	21
Druckamiller, John(Y)	1829	May 14	HarrisonCoOh	05	13	20
Druckemiller, Jacob(Y)	1828	Dec. 19	HarrisonCoOh	05	13	14
Drum, Samuel(Z)	1808	Oct. 10	MuskingmCoOh	09	01	15
Drum, Samuel(Z)	1817	Feb. 15	MuskingmCoOh	09	01	14
Drum, Wm.(Z-M)	1831	Oct. 05	LickingCo,Oh	10	02	24
Drummond, Hereford(Z-M)	1836	Aug. 15	CoshoctnCoOh	07	04	09
Drury, Elmer(Z)	1829	Jan. 17	LickingCo,Oh	10	06	27
Drury, Jesse(Z)	1833	Oct. 22	Perry Co.,Oh	15	15	33
Drury, John(Z)	1817	Jan. 16	SomersetCoPa	10	06	18
Drury, Jonathan(Z)	1832	Sept. 05	Perry Co.,Oh	15	15	14
Drury, Jonathan(Z)	1833	Oct. 22	Perry Co.,Oh	15	15	33
Drury, Michael(Z)	1833	Oct. 22	Perry Co.,Oh	15	15	32
Dryden, Sam'l.(Y)	1823	Sept. 30	WashCo.,Penn	07	11	15
Dryden, Samuel(Y)	1825	Dec. 20	GuernseyCoOh	07	11	15
Dryer, Jacob(Z)	1813	April 14	SomersetCoPa	05	09	06
Dryer, Jacob(Z)	1814	Feb. 09	TuscarwsCoOh	05	09	18
Dubois, John(Y)	1832	Jan. 23	Jeff.Co.,Oh.	04	12	02
Dubois, John(Y)	1832	Feb. 06	Jeff.Co.,Oh.	04	12	14
Dubois, John(Y)	1832	Feb. 07	Jeff.Co.,Oh.	04	12	27
Dubois, John(Y)	1832	Feb. 10	Jeff.Co.,Oh.	05	13	04
Dubro, David(Z)	1825	June 09	Morgan Co,Oh	11	11	21
Duclas, Matthias(Y)	1832	Dec. 14	Pittsburg,Pa	04	14	25
Ducomb, Vincent(Y)	1832	Sept. 24	Stark Co.,Oh	06	17	34
Dudgeon, Jno.(Y)	1821	Nov. 20	Brooke CoVir	04	12	19
Dudgeon, Simon(Z)	1810	Aug. 13	DelawareCoNY	11	06	18
Dudgeon, Simon(Z)	1810	Aug. 13	DelawareCoNY	11	06	13
Dudgeon, Simon(Z)	1810	Aug. 13	DelawareCoNY	11	06	13
Dudgeon, Thomas(Z)	1814	July 07	DelawareCoNY	11	05	11
Dudgeon, Thomas(Z-M)	1833	Oct. 12	Jeff.Co.,Oh.	05	07	07
Dudgeon, Thomas(Z-M)	1833	Oct. 12	Jeff.Co.,Oh.	05	07	14
Dudgeon, Thos.(Y)	1821	Nov. 20	Brooke CoVir	04	12	19
Dudgun, Richard(Y)	1829	Nov. 11	Jeff.Co.,Oh.	04	12	25
Dudley, Henry(Z)	1836	Jan. 14	GuernseyCoOh	09	08	26
Dudley, Joseph(Z)	1836	June 20	GuernseyCoOh	09	08	13
Duff, Alex'r. Jnr.(Z-M)	1837	April 21	GuernseyCoOh	04	03	14
Duff, Alex'r. Junr.(Z-M)	1836	Sept. 02	MuskingmCoOh	04	03	13
Duff, Alex. Jr.(Z-M)	1830	April 16	GuernseyCoOh	05	03	21
Duff, Alexander(Z)	1817	Aug. 22	WestmrldCoPa	05	03	20
Duff, Alexander(Z-M)	1833	Dec. 23	GuernseyCoOh	04	03	07
Duff, Andrew(Z-M)	1833	Nov. 01	GuernseyCoOh	04	03	03
Duff, Andrew(Z-M)	1836	June 30	GuernseyCoOh	04	03	07
Duff, David Jnr.(Z-M)	1838	March 03	GuernseyCoOh	04	03	07
Duff, David(Z)	1815	Jan. 11	GuernseyCoOh	05	02	03
Duff, David(Z)	1816	Nov. 15	MuskingmCoOh	04	02	16
Duff, George(Z)	1816	May 25	AlleghnyCoPa	04	02	05
Duff, George(Z-M)	1837	Feb. 25	GuernseyCoOh	04	03	17
Duff, James(Z)	1815	Nov. 30	BelmontCo,Oh	05	02	02
Duff, James(Z-M)	1832	Sept. 20	GuernseyCoOh	04	03	05
Duff, James(Z-M)	1834	Aug. 22	GuernseyCoOh	04	03	06
Duff, John(Z)	1816	Sept. 07	BelmontCo,Oh	05	02	01
Duff, John(Z-M)	1831	May 17	GuernseyCoOh	04	03	18

PURCHASER	YEAR	DATE	RESIDENCE	R	T	S
Duff, John(Z-M)	1832	Oct. 09	GuernseyCoOh	04	03	07
Duff, John(Z-M)	1836	Aug. 09	GuernseyCoOh	04	03	17
Duff, Oliver C.(Z-M)	1838	June 13	GuernseyCoOh	04	03	08
Duff, Oliver E.(Z-M)	1836	Feb. 16	WashCo.,Penn	04	03	08
Duff, Oliver E.(Z-M)	1838	June 13	GuernseyCoOh	04	03	08
Duff, Oliver(Z-M)	1828	March 22	GuernseyCoOh	04	03	18
Duff, Oliver(Z-M)	1836	June 28	GuernseyCoOh	04	03	18
Duff, Robert(Z-M)	1832	June 18	GuernseyCoOh	04	03	03
Duff, Robert(Z-M)	1835	May 28	GuernseyCoOh	04	03	08
Duff, William(Z-M)	1831	April 16	GuernseyCoOh	04	03	24
Duffey, James Jr.(Z-M)	1832	May 23	GuernseyCoOh	02	04	15
Duffey, James(Z)	1814	Sept. 19	GuernseyCoOh	01	04	24
Duffey, James(Z-M)	1828	Nov. 20	GuernseyCoOh	02	04	22
Duffey, William(Z-M)	1837	Feb. 07	GuernseyCoOh	03	04	16
Duffey, William(Z-M)	1837	Feb. 07	GuernseyCoOh	03	04	18
Duffey, Wm.(Z-M)	1828	Nov. 20	GuernseyCoOh	02	03	02
Duffy, James(Z)	1815	March 30	GuernseyCoOh	01	03	04
Duffy, James(Z-M)	1823	Aug. 22	GuernseyCoOh	02	03	03
Duffy, Patrick(Z)	1807	Dec. 30	ChesterCo,Pa	08	04	13
Dugan, Andrew(Z)	1816	Aug. 02	MuskingmCoOh	13	11	25
Dugan, David(Z-M)	1825	Feb. 22	AlleghnyCoPa	02	04	20
Dugan, James(Z)	1836	Nov. 30	HarrisonCoOh	08	05	03
Dugan, James(Z)	1836	Nov. 30	HarrisonCoOh	08	05	03
Dugan, James(Z)	1816	Dec. 18	Jeff.Co.,Oh.	02	02	02
Dugan, James(Z-M)	1822	Sept. 06	FayetteCo,Pa	07	08	08
Dugan, James(Z-M)	1822	Sept. 06	FayetteCo,Pa	07	08	09
Dugan, James(Z-M)	1826	Nov. 23	Jeff.Co.,Oh.	09	05	15
Dugan, James(Z-M)	1826	Nov. 23	Jeff.Co.,Oh.	09	05	15
Dugan, John(Z-M)	1826	Nov. 23	MuskingmCoOh	06	02	06
Dugan, John(Z-M)	1831	Jan. 27	MuskingmCoOh	06	02	06
Dugan, John(Z-M)	1835	Aug. 03	MuskingmCoOh	05	04	21
Dugan, Joseph(Z-M)	1834	Jan. 07	HarrisonCoOh	03	06	25
Dugan, Samuel(Z)	1836	Nov. 30	HarrisonCoOh	08	05	03
Dugan, Samuel(Z)	1836	Nov. 30	HarrisonCoOh	08	06	34
Dugan, Samuel(Z)	1837	Feb. 18	GuernseyCoOh	08	05	03
Dugan, William(Z)	1836	Feb. 24	Perry Co.,Oh	15	14	09
Duke, James(Z-M)	1833	Aug. 03	MuskingmCoOh	03	01	05
Duke, John(Y)	1836	June 01	Jeff.Co.,Oh.	04	12	12
Duke, Mark(Y)	1835	Sept. 07	Jeff.Co.,Oh.	04	12	17
Duker, Moses(Z)	1817	May 24	MuskingmCoOh	05	02	14
Dukes, Benedict(Z)	1832	July 17	LickingCo,Oh	10	03	09
Dule, David(Z-M)	1839	Jan. 24	GuernseyCoOh	03	03	05
Duling, C. C.(Z-M)	1837	April 22	TuscarwsCoOh	03	06	01
Duling, Collin C.(Z-M)	1834	Feb. 21	TuscarwsCoOh	03	06	04
Duling, Collin C.(Z-M)	1835	June 20	TuscarwsCoOh	03	06	04
Duling, Edmond(Z)	1813	Oct. 11	HampshreCoVa	05	04	03
Duling, Edmond(Z-M)	1835	Oct. 23	CoshoctnCoOh	05	04	03
Duling, Edmund(Z-M)	1832	May 22	CoshoctnCoOh	05	04	03
Duling, William(Z-M)	1832	June 04	CoshoctnCoOh	04	06	11
Duling, William(Z-M)	1836	Feb. 06	TuscarwsCoOh	03	06	14
Dulty, John(Z)	1815	March 23	Ohio Co.,Vir	13	11	03
Dumond, John H.(Z-M)	1836	Jan. 25	TuscarwsCoOh	01	05	03
Dums, John(Y)	1830	Jan. 13	Jeff.Co.,Oh.	05	13	34
Dun, George(Z-M)	1836	Jan. 08	LickingCo,Oh	10	04	09
Dunbar, James(Y)	1825	Nov. 09	ColumbanCoOh	04	13	03
Dunbar, James(Y)	1828	April 03	ColumbanCoOh	03	12	31
Dunbar, James(Y)	1829	May 19	ColumbanCoOh	03	12	32
Dunbar, Josiah(Z)	1835	Sept. 08	Morgan Co,Oh	10	08	21
Dunbar, Nicholas(Y)	1829	April 23	ColumbanCoOh	04	13	14
Dunbar, Nicholas(Y)	1832	Jan. 14	ColumbanCoOh	04	10	18
Duncan, James(Y)	1823	Nov. 11	GuernseyCoOh	07	11	15
Duncan, James(Y)	1824	May 21	Stark Co.,Oh	09	10	21
Duncan, James(Y)	1824	May 21	Stark Co.,Oh	09	10	21
Duncan, James(Y)	1824	Dec. 09	Stark Co.,Oh	09	10	21
Duncan, James(Y)	1825	Jan. 01	Stark Co.,Oh	09	10	29
Duncan, James(Y)	1825	April 06	Stark Co.,Oh	09	10	02
Duncan, James(Y)	1832	Nov. 10	Stark Co.,Oh	09	11	35
Duncan, James(Y)	1832	Nov. 10	Stark Co.,Oh	09	11	26
Duncan, James(Y)	1833	April 08	Stark Co.,Oh	09	10	01

PURCHASER	YEAR	DATE	RESIDENCE	R	T	S
Duncan, James(Z-M)	1828	Feb. 07	BelmontCo,Oh	02	05	11
Duncan, Jas.(Y)	1825	Feb. 19	Ohio	10	01	11
Duncan, William(Z-M)	1829	April 23	HolmesCoOhio	07	08	12
Dunfee, Benedict(Z-M)	1825	Dec. 06	CoshoctnCoOh	07	05	22
Dunfee, Benedict(Z-M)	1830	June 30	CoshoctnCoOh	07	05	22
Dunfee, Jesse(Z-M)	1835	Feb. 20	CoshoctnCoOh	07	04	10
Dunfee, Jno.(Z-M)	1831	Dec. 02	CoshoctnCoOh	07	05	21
Dunfee, John(Y)	1821	Sept. 22	BelmontCo,Oh	03	05	15
Dunhum, Nathaniel(Y)	1821	April 11	HarrisonCoOh	06	12	26
Dunlap, Adam(Z)	1817	April 05	HarrisonCoOh	08	05	21
Dunlap, Israel(Z)	1829	March 19	MuskingmCoOh	11	12	29
Dunlap, James(Y)	1830	Dec. 02	TuscarwsCoOh	07	15	01
Dunlap, John(Y)	1824	May 24	TuscarwsCoOh	06	14	21
Dunlap, Josiah(Z)	1835	Oct. 31	MuskingmCoOh	11	11	03
Dunlap, Josiah(Z)	1817	Jan. 09	Brooke CoVir	11	12	29
Dunlap, Robert(Z-M)	1833	Jan. 03	LickingCo,Oh	10	03	15
Dunlap, Wm.(Z-M)	1835	April 07	CoshoctnCoOh	09	06	20
Dunlavy, Francis(Y)	1828	Sept. 02	ColumbanCoOh	04	14	26
Dunlevy, Daniel(Z)	1824	May 11	Jeff.Co.,Oh.	11	13	21
Dunlevy, Daniel(Z-M)	1824	April 30	Jeff.Co.,Oh.	06	09	17
Dunlevy, Daniel(Z-M)	1824	May 11	Jeff.Co.,Oh.	06	06	09
Dunn, Alfred(Z-M)	1836	March 31	MuskingmCoOh	09	03	05
Dunn, Caleb(Z)	1805	Feb. 12	MuskingmCoOh	12	13	06
Dunn, Caleb(Z)	1806	Jan. 13	MuskingmCoOh	12	13	06
Dunn, James(Z-M)	1826	Aug. 02	TuscarwsCoOh	02	05	22
Dunn, Jos.(Z-M)	1831	Oct. 03	CoshoctnCoOh	08	05	22
Dunn, Richard(Z-M)	1832	Jan. 10	MuskingmCoOh	09	03	04
Dunn, Robert(Z-M)	1826	Sept. 27	TuscarwsCoOh	01	05	07
Dunsten, Eleanor(Y)	1824	Aug. 16	TuscarwsCoOh	06	14	31
Duprey, Francis(Z-M)	1833	Sept. 16	CoshoctnCoOh	05	04	16
Duprez, Mathew(Z-M)	1832	March 19	FayetteCo,Pa	05	04	25
Duprez, Mathew(Z-M)	1832	March 19	FayetteCo,Pa	05	04	25
Durbin, Bazil(Z-M)	1831	Nov. 18	KnoxCo.,Ohio	11	08	18
Durbin, David(Z-M)	1835	Dec. 16	HolmesCoOhio	08	07	02
Durbin, Jas. Junr.(Y)	1825	May 13	BelmontCo,Oh	03	05	23
Durbin, Larrance(Z-M)	1833	Dec. 13	HolmesCoOhio	08	08	23
Durbin, Larrence Jr.(Z-M)	1834	Jan. 17	HolmesCoOhio	08	08	23
Durnal, Israel B.(Z)	1836	Aug. 26	Morgan Co,Oh	08	07	32
Durrant, Nathan(Z)	1817	Feb. 19	Jeff.Co.,Oh.	06	08	19
Dusenberry, John(Z)	1810	April 18	MuskingmCoOh	14	14	20
Dusenbery, Henry(Z-M)	1831	July 02	HarrisonCoOh	08	05	12
Dusenbery, John(Z)	1831	Feb. 26	Perry Co.,Oh	14	13	15
Dush, Adam(Z)	1816	Nov. 18	MuskingmCoOh	11	04	21
Dush, Elzey(Z-M)	1833	Feb. 12	LickingCo,Oh	11	04	12
Dush, Jno.(Z)	1816	Nov. 18	MuskingmCoOh	11	04	21
Dush, John(Z)	1817	May 27	MuskingmCoOh	11	04	20
Dush, John(Z-M)	1835	Jan. 14	LickingCo,Oh	11	04	22
Dush, Rachel(Z-M)	1833	Jan. 25	LickingCo,Oh	11	04	20
Dusinberry, Wm.(Z)	1809	Nov. 15	MuskingmCoOh	14	13	02
Dusinbery, Henry(Z)	1804	Nov. 23	MuskingmCoOh	15	17	32
Dusinbery, William(Z)	1833	Oct. 22	Perry Co.,Oh	15	15	14
Dusinbery, William(Z)	1804	June 16	MuskingmCoOh	15	17	28
Dusthaemor, John(Z-M)	1829	Oct. 15	LickingCo,Oh	11	01	23
Dutro, David(Z)	1831	July 18	MuskingmCoOh	12	12	04
Dutro, David(Z)	1805	Dec. 31	MuskingmCoOh	12	12	05
Dutro, George Jr.(Z)	1825	May 31	MuskingmCoOh	12	13	22
Dutro, William(Z)	1814	Aug. 02	WashngtnCoOh	13	09	01
Dutro, William(Z)	1814	Nov. 10	MuskingmCoOh	12	13	33
Dutro, William(Z)	1815	Jan. 12	MuskingmCoOh	12	13	28
Dutton, D.(Z)	1815	Feb. 02	WashngtnCoOh	12	11	34
Dutton, Hanson(Z)	1832	Sept. 18	WashngtnCoOh	08	05	27
Dutton, Hanson(Z)	1832	Sept. 18	WashngtnCoOh	08	05	22
Dutton, Hanson(Z)	1836	Feb. 02	WashngtnCoOh	08	05	22
Dutton, Hanson(Z)	1836	Aug. 19	WashngtnCoOh	08	05	28
Dutton, Hanson(Z)	1836	Aug. 26	WashngtnCoOh	08	05	22
Dutton, James(Z)	1824	Jan. 13	WashCo.,Ohio	08	05	30
Dutton, James(Z)	1834	March 12	WashngtnCoOh	08	05	22
Dutton, James(Z)	1836	June 25	WashngtnCoOh	08	05	20
Dutton, James(Z)	1837	March 27	WashngtnCoOh	08	05	04

PURCHASER	YEAR	DATE	RESIDENCE	R	T	S
Dutton, Joseph(Z)	1831	Jan. 27	WashCo.,Ohio	08	05	30
Dutton, Joseph(Z)	1836	Aug. 09	WashngtnCoOh	08	05	19
Dutton, Joseph(Z)	1836	Sept. 09	WashngtnCoOh	08	05	20
Dutty, John(Z)	1809	Oct. 06	Wheeling,Vir	02	02	09
Duval, Charles(Z)	1805	June 18	MuskingmCoOh	14	15	01
Duval, Charles(Z)	1810	Oct. 13	MuskingmCoOh	14	15	22
Duval, Grafton(Z)	1816	Sept. 17	FrederkCoVir	14	15	36
Duval, Grafton(Z)	1816	Oct. 22	FrederkCoVir	13	11	26
Duval, Ormond(Z-M)	1833	Feb. 06	BelmontCo,Oh	11	08	07
Duvall, Eliza(Z)	1826	Oct. 18	MuskingmCoOh	12	12	19
Duvees, Samuel(Z-M)	1832	March 28	LickingCo,Oh	10	02	25
Dwan, Leonard(Z)	1815	July 05	BelmontCo,Oh	09	05	18
Dwan, Leonard(Z)	1815	July 05	BelmontCo,Oh	09	05	23
Dwiggins, James(Z)	1814	Oct. 30	WashCo.,Penn	01	04	18
Dyal, John(Z-M)	1835	Sept. 10	CoshoctnCoOh	05	07	20
Dyal, Joshua(Z)	1825	Dec. 06	FairfeldCoOh	15	15	23
Dyal, Joshua(Z)	1826	March 11	FairfeldCoOh	15	15	14
Dye, Benjamin(Z)	1831	Sept. 01	Morgan Co,Oh	09	07	02
Dye, Benjamin(Z)	1834	Sept. 15	Morgan Co,Oh	10	08	31
Dye, Benjamin(Z)	1834	Dec. 10	Morgan Co,Oh	10	08	30
Dye, Benjamin(Z)	1835	Nov. 21	Morgan Co,Oh	10	08	31
Dye, Ezekiel Senr.(Z)	1816	Feb. 29	GuernseyCoOh	10	08	33
Dye, George(Z)	1811	April 20	GuernseyCoOh	09	07	12
Dye, James(Z)	1810	Oct. 02	GuernseyCoOh	09	07	02
Dye, James(Z)	1811	April 20	GuernseyCoOh	09	07	12
Dye, James(Z)	1816	Dec. 30	GuernseyCoOh	09	07	02
Dye, James(Z)	1817	Feb. 20	GuernseyCoOh	09	07	01
Dye, John(Z)	1829	March 11	Morgan Co,Oh	08	08	32
Dye, John(Z)	1829	Oct. 10	MonroeCo.,Oh	08	06	35
Dye, Joseph(Z)	1834	Feb. 19	Morgan Co,Oh	10	08	31
Dye, Lewis(Z)	1834	Dec. 12	Morgan Co,Oh	10	08	33
Dye, Lewis(Z)	1835	Dec. 28	Morgan Co,Oh	10	08	33
Dye, Vinson(Z)	1833	April 26	Morgan Co,Oh	10	08	31
Dye, William(Z)	1833	Nov. 12	MuskingmCoOh	10	08	31
Dye, William(Z)	1816	Oct. 17	GuernseyCoOh	11	12	35
Dye, Wilson(Z)	1830	Aug. 24	Morgan Co,Oh	10	08	31
Dye, Wm.(Z)	1833	Oct. 11	MuskingmCoOh	11	12	36
Dyer, Hepburn(Z)	1833	Aug. 22	Morgan Co,Oh	09	06	24
Dyer, Hepburn(Z)	1835	Nov. 17	Morgan Co,Oh	09	06	24
Dyson, Aquila(Z)	1836	Jan. 02	GuernseyCoOh	09	08	29
Dyson, John B.(Z)	1834	March 03	GuernseyCoOh	09	08	29
Dyson, Joseph(Z)	1820	Oct. 18	GuernseyCoOh	09	08	32
Dyson, Lucy(Z)	1836	Jan. 02	GuernseyCoOh	09	08	29
Dyson, M. B.(Z)	1836	Jan. 02	GuernseyCoOh	09	08	29
Dyson, T.(Z)	1815	Nov. 21	GuernseyCoOh	02	02	22
Dyson, Thomas(Z)	1805	April 04	MuskingmCoOh	02	01	03
Dyson, Thomas(Z-M)	1828	Sept. 29	GuernseyCoOh	02	02	09
EaKman, Ephraim(Z)	1832	Oct. 05	MuskingmCoOh	12	13	34
Eaberhartt, Gottlieb(Z-M)	1836	Feb. 29	HolmesCoOhio	06	08	20
Eagler, John(Z)	1835	Dec. 28	Morgan Co,Oh	09	06	09
Eagler, John(Z)	1836	Dec. 23	Morgan Co,Oh	08	05	20
Eagleson, Alex'r.(Z)	1837	Feb. 07	GuernseyCoOh	08	05	15
Eagleton, John(Z-M)	1832	Oct. 01	GuernseyCoOh	02	02	14
Eakin, David(Y)	1827	May 08	Stark Co.,Oh	06	16	15
Ealy, John(Z-M)	1834	Jan. 25	CoshoctnCoOh	09	05	15
Earl, Benjamin(Y)	1829	March 17	ColumbanCoOh	04	13	10
Earley, Jonathan(Z-M)	1833	Aug. 30	HarrisonCoOh	01	06	13
Earley, Jonathan(Z-M)	1833	Nov. 13	HarrisonCoOh	01	06	13
Early, Alexander(Z)	1833	April 04	Morgan Co,Oh	10	07	10
Early, Andrew McGuire(Z)	1837	March 16	MuskingmCoOh	14	12	36
Early, John(Y)	1825	April 07	Stark Co.,Oh	09	12	20
Early, John(Y)	1829	March 16	Stark Co.,Oh	09	12	20
Early, Peter(Z)	1823	June 21	Perry Co.,Oh	15	16	36
Earlywine, Adam(Z-M)	1831	June 28	KnoxCo.,Ohio	10	05	11
Earlywine, Adam(Z-M)	1832	Nov. 29	KnoxCo.,Ohio	10	05	11
Earlywine, John(Z-M)	1828	March 06	KnoxCo.,Ohio	10	05	18
Earns, Samuel(Z-M)	1833	June 10	HarrisonCoOh	05	07	13
Earns, Samuel(Z-M)	1833	June 10	HarrisonCoOh	05	07	14
Earp, William(Y)	1825	Jan. 12	ColumbanCoOh	05	14	12

PURCHASER	YEAR	DATE	RESIDENCE	R	T	S
Easterday, Christ'n.(Y)	1823	June 04	Jeff.Co.,Oh.	05	14	21
Easterday, Christ'n.(Y)	1824	Dec. 03	ColumbanCoOh	05	14	21
Easterday, Jacob(Y)	1824	April 17	Jeff.Co.,Oh.	05	14	15
Eaton, Robert(Z-M)	1827	Jan. 29	TuscarwsCoOh	01	05	07
Eaton, Robert(Z-M)	1829	Sept. 23	TuscarwsCoOh	01	05	24
Ebert, Edward(Z)	1831	April 21	Morgan Co,Oh	14	14	22
Ebert, Edward(Z)	1835	March 21	Morgan Co,Oh	14	14	21
Ebert, Elias(Z)	1831	Oct. 11	Perry Co.,Oh	14	14	32
Ebert, Jacob(Z)	1832	Feb. 01	Morgan Co,Oh	14	14	33
Ebert, Jacob(Z)	1811	March 27	Jeff.Co.,Oh.	14	14	10
Ebert, Jacob(Z)	1814	June 29	MuskingmCoOh	14	14	27
Echard, Michael(Z)	1817	June 07	MuskingmCoOh	14	12	28
Echelberry, Abraham(Z)	1836	Oct. 31	MuskingmCoOh	15	14	36
Eckard, John(Z)	1820	July 01	MuskingmCoOh	14	12	20
Eckart, Henry(Z-M)	1834	Sept. 09	HolmesCoOhio	04	07	17
Eckart, Henry(Z-M)	1834	Oct. 22	TuscarwsCoOh	04	07	14
Eckart, Henry(Z-M)	1836	June 06	TuscarwsCoOh	04	07	17
Eckelbery, George(Z-M)	1837	Feb. 22	MuskingmCoOh	04	03	04
Eckelbery, George(Z-M)	1837	June 28	GuernseyCoOh	04	04	03
Eckelbury, William(Z)	1814	Jan. 06	MuskingmCoOh	12	12	01
Eckert, Andrew(Z-M)	1833	Aug. 12	HolmesCoOhio	04	07	13
Eckert, Andrew(Z-M)	1837	Feb. 02	TuscarwsCoOh	04	07	13
Eckleberry, Henry(Z)	1805	April 19	GreeneCo.,Pa	07	01	10
Eckleberry, John(Z)	1806	Oct. 14	MuskingmCoOh	06	01	06
Eckleberry, John(Z)	1810	April 09	MuskingmCoOh	06	01	06
Ecklebury, George(Z-M)	1829	Dec. 14	MuskingmCoOh	06	03	25
Ecklebury, Henry(Z-M)	1829	July 01	MuskingmCoOh	06	03	24
Ecklebury, N.(Z)	1830	June 26	MuskingmCoOh	12	12	10
Eckles, Armstrong(Z-M)	1831	Nov. 04	Brooke CoVir	04	06	11
Eckles, William(Z)	1816	April 12	WashCo.,Penn	01	04	23
Eckley, Thomas(Y)	1829	July 01	ColumbanCoOh	06	13	03
Eckley, Thomas(Y)	1829	July 01	ColumbanCoOh	03	12	33
Eckman, John(Z-M)	1836	Nov. 12	CoshoctnCoOh	08	06	14
Eckord, John(Z)	1831	Nov. 09	Perry Co.,Oh	14	12	19
Eddington, Jonothan(Z)	1832	Nov. 29	Morgan Co,Oh	13	09	05
Eddy, Arch'd. G.(Z)	1833	Oct. 21	Morgan Co,Oh	10	07	33
Eddy, John(Z)	1832	March 20	Morgan Co,Oh	10	07	29
Eddy, John(Z)	1832	Aug. 24	Morgan Co,Oh	10	07	32
Eddy, John(Z)	1832	Aug. 24	Morgan Co,Oh	10	07	33
Edelston, Jarvis(Z)	1829	March 07	Morgan Co,Oh	09	05	09
Edenburn, Benjamin(Z-M)	1836	April 05	GuernseyCoOh	03	05	18
Edenburn, Peter(Z-M)	1836	April 05	GuernseyCoOh	03	05	13
Edgar, Eliphaz(Z-M)	1836	Jan. 19	CoshoctnCoOh	09	04	05
Edgar, James(Z)	1815	May 09	CoshoctnCoOh	04	02	02
Edgington, Brice(Y)	1826	Feb. 25	Jeff.Co.,Oh.	07	15	21
Edgington, James(Y)	1825	Dec. 03	Jeff.Co.,Oh.	07	14	24
Edgington, Price(Y)	1824	Nov. 01	Jeff.Co.,Oh.	02	07	11
Edie, John(Z-M)	1836	Sept. 19	TuscarwsCoOh	02	07	09
Edie, Rosanna(Z-M)	1833	Aug. 16	GuernseyCoOh	03	04	03
Edie, Rosanna(Z-M)	1833	Aug. 16	GuernseyCoOh	03	04	04
Edmonds, Edward(Z-M)	1833	Dec. 10	TuscarwsCoOh	02	07	02
Edmundson, Eli(Y)	1824	Sept. 03	ColumbanCoOh	01	07	21
Edward, Isaac(Z)	1817	Jan. 21	FayetteCo,Pa	01	04	20
Edwards, David(Y)	1825	Jan. 29	Stark Co.,Oh	07	18	31
Edwards, David(Z)	1828	Sept. 27	Morgan Co,Oh	13	10	26
Edwards, Forster(Z)	1817	June 03	WashngtnCoOh	13	09	10
Edwards, James(Y)	1826	Sept. 01	BelmontCo,Oh	06	11	26
Edwards, John(Y)	1823	April 01	Stark Co.,Oh	06	16	27
Edwards, John(Y)	1823	April 01	Stark Co.,Oh	06	16	27
Edwards, John(Y)	1825	May 03	TuscarwsCoOh	07	14	07
Edwards, John(Y)	1833	June 04	CarrollCo,Oh	06	16	27
Edwards, John(Z)	1829	March 03	Morgan Co,Oh	13	10	36
Edwards, Mordecai(Z-M)	1821	Aug. 08	MuskingmCoOh	06	03	22
Edwards, Russell(Y)	1834	Nov. 04	Stark Co.,Oh	05	15	06
Egan, Patrick(Z-M)	1837	March 11	CoshoctnCoOh	10	07	18
Egbert, Joseph(Y)	1832	March 13	Stark Co.,Oh	09	12	06
Eichelberg, John(Z)	1828	Feb. 18	MuskingmCoOh	12	12	13
Eichenlaub, Michael(Z-M)	1836	Dec. 03	AlleghnyCoPa	05	04	07
Eichenlaub, Michael(Z-M)	1836	Dec. 03	AlleghnyCoPa	05	04	07

PURCHASER	YEAR	DATE	RESIDENCE	R	T	S
Eichmoyer, And'w.(Z-M)	1831	Dec. 30	CoshoctnCoOh	05	07	19
Eick, Anthony(Y)	1827	Sept. 04	TuscarwsCoOh	06	14	31
Eidenier, Henry(Y)	1831	March 23	ColumbanCoOh	03	12	34
Eifert, Michael(Z-M)	1838	March 22	KnoxCo.,Ohio	10	09	13
Eiglehart, Reuben(Z)	1832	Nov. 27	Perry Co.,Oh	14	12	06
Eiglehart, Reuben(Z)	1832	Nov. 27	Perry Co.,Oh	14	12	06
Eigler, Peter(Z-M)	1838	March 22	Stark Co.,Oh	04	07	11
Eirvin, Thomas(Z)	1835	Nov. 28	Morgan Co,Oh	13	08	20
Eisiminger, Conrad(Z-M)	1832	Oct. 27	CoshoctnCoOh	10	05	18
Eisiminger, Coonrod(Z-M)	1835	Jan. 20	KnoxCo.,Ohio	10	05	22
Eisiminger, John(Z-M)	1832	Oct. 27	CoshoctnCoOh	10	05	22
Eisiminger, John(Z-M)	1832	Oct. 27	CoshoctnCoOh	10	05	22
Elben, Reuben(Z-M)	1834	Jan. 14	LickingCo,Oh	10	03	06
Elbeson, Sam'l.(Y)	1826	Aug. 12	ColumbanCoOh	05	18	21
Elbin, John(Z-M)	1834	Sept. 03	CoshoctnCoOh	10	03	05
Elbin, John(Z-M)	1835	Dec. 30	CoshoctnCoOh	10	03	05
Elder, Ely(Z)	1806	March 22	MuskingmCoOh	15	18	06
Elder, Robert(Z)	1816	Nov. 06	CoshoctnCoOh	08	05	23
Elder, Robert(Z)	1817	Feb. 20	CoshoctnCoOh	08	05	23
Elder, William(Z)	1834	Jan. 04	Perry Co.,Oh	14	12	33
Elder, William(Z)	1834	Jan. 04	Perry Co.,Oh	14	12	33
Elliot, Charles(Z)	1814	Jan. 04	KnoxCo.,Ohio	11	05	14
Elliot, Charles(Z)	1814	Jan. 04	KnoxCo.,Ohio	11	06	12
Elliot, Hugh(Z)	1829	Dec. 21	MuskingmCoOh	11	13	15
Elliot, John(Y)	1832	June 16	ColumbanCoOh	04	13	09
Elliot, Thomas(Z)	1812	Feb. 25	WashCo.,Penn	11	13	07
Elliot, Thos.(Z)	1830	Nov. 26	MuskingmCoOh	07	05	16
Elliot, Thos.(Z-M)	1830	Dec. 07	MuskingmCoOh	08	05	21
Elliott, Ambrose(Z)	1822	Jan. 01	Morgan Co,Oh	10	06	13
Elliott, Ambrose(Z)	1836	Feb. 02	Morgan Co,Oh	10	06	26
Elliott, Arthur(Z-M)	1830	Nov. 20	KnoxCo.,Ohio	11	05	21
Elliott, Benj'n.(Y)	1822	April 29	Stark Co.,Oh	07	20	15
Elliott, Benj'n.(Y)	1824	April 02	Stark Co.,Oh	07	20	15
Elliott, Charles(Z)	1815	May 03	Brooke CoVir	06	06	02
Elliott, Charles(Z-M)	1835	Oct. 31	CoshoctnCoOh	07	07	22
Elliott, D. A.(Z)	1831	Aug. 10	Morgan Co,Oh	10	06	26
Elliott, Elisha(Y)	1829	Sept. 30	Jeff.Co.,Oh.	04	14	25
Elliott, Finley(Z)	1815	Nov. 16	Jeff.Co.,Oh.	06	06	02
Elliott, Francis(Z)	1824	Aug. 26	MuskingmCoOh	11	13	21
Elliott, George(Z-M)	1835	Dec. 30	HolmesCoOhio	07	08	10
Elliott, George(Z-M)	1830	Nov. 20	KnoxCo.,Ohio	11	05	21
Elliott, Isaac(of Joseph)(Y)	1832	Nov. 12	Stark Co.,Oh	06	19	21
Elliott, J. B.(Z)	1831	Aug. 10	Morgan Co,Oh	10	06	25
Elliott, James(Y)	1829	May 22	ColumbanCoOh	04	13	15
Elliott, John(Y)	1829	March 18	Jeff.Co.,Co.	03	12	31
Elliott, John(Y)	1829	May 16	ColumbanCoOh	04	13	09
Elliott, John(Z)	1824	June 10	MuskingmCoOh	11	12	03
Elliott, John(Z)	1824	July 07	MuskingmCoOh	10	09	22
Elliott, John(Z)	1831	Feb. 03	MuskingmCoOh	11	13	34
Elliott, John(Z)	1833	July 20	Morgan Co,Oh	11	11	14
Elliott, John(Z)	1833	Aug. 19	Morgan Co,Oh	10	07	19
Elliott, John(Z)	1834	Nov. 22	Jeff.Co.,Oh.	10	08	36
Elliott, John(Z)	1835	Nov. 26	Jeff.Co.,Oh.	09	05	29
Elliott, John(Z)	1835	Nov. 26	Jeff.Co.,Oh.	09	05	29
Elliott, John(Z)	1816	March 18	Brooke CoVir	09	05	06
Elliott, John(Z)	1816	March 18	Brooke CoVir	11	04	03
Elliott, John(Z-M)	1833	March 08	CoshoctnCoOh	05	06	15
Elliott, John(Z-M)	1836	Jan. 08	CoshoctnCoOh	05	06	15
Elliott, Joseph(Z)	1834	Nov. 22	Jeff.Co.,Oh.	10	08	24
Elliott, Patrick(Z)	1814	April 20	?	11	05	24
Elliott, Rezen(Z)	1835	Nov. 26	Jeff.Co.,Oh.	09	05	32
Elliott, Robert(Z-M)	1824	Sept. 07	MuskingmCoOh	05	02	10
Elliott, Robert(Z-M)	1832	May 22	CoshoctnCoOh	06	07	20
Elliott, Robert(Z-M)	1833	April 03	TuscarwsCoOh	06	07	20
Elliott, Simeon(Z)	1816	Sept. 21	Brooke CoVir	07	08	23
Elliott, Simeon(Z)	1816	Sept. 21	Brooke CoVir	07	08	19
Elliott, Simon(Z)	1828	Aug. 23	MuskingmCoOh	11	11	02
Elliott, Thomas(Y)	1826	March 31	Jeff.Co.,Oh.	03	12	31
Elliott, Thomas(Z)	1836	Feb. 17	WashCo.,Penn	10	08	36

PURCHASER	YEAR	DATE	RESIDENCE	R	T	S
Elliott, Thomas(Z)	1817	July 10	WashCo.,Penn	06	01	21
Elliott, Thomas(Z-M)	1833	Nov. 21	MuskingmCoOh	08	05	21
Elliott, Thos.(Z-M)	1831	Feb. 26	Brooke CoVir	07	07	22
Elliott, Thos.(Z-M)	1831	Feb. 26	Brooke CoVir	07	07	22
Elliott, William(Z)	1805	Dec. 12	FayetteCo,Pa	12	13	33
Elliott, William(Z)	1805	Dec. 12	FayetteCo,Pa	12	13	28
Elliott, William(Z)	1815	May 13	Jeff.Co.,Oh.	06	06	03
Elliott, William(Z-M)	1832	June 23	TuscarwsCoOh	01	05	15
Elliott, William(Z-M)	1833	March 05	TuscarwsCoOh	01	05	15
Ellis, Elias(Z)	1805	Dec. 05	BelmontCo,Oh	08	02	05
Ellis, L.(Z)	1816	Oct. 29	ZanesvilleOh	11	11	26
Ellis, Michael(Z)	1815	Dec. 06	HarrisonCoOh	15	16	33
Ellison, George(Z)	1837	March 11	Morgan Co,Oh	08	05	28
Ellisor, Thomas(Z)	1810	April 09	MuskingmCoOh	14	14	36
Ellwood, Mark(Z-M)	1836	May 31	HarrisonCoOh	03	07	17
Elroy, Archibald W.(Z)	1814	Jan. 17	PittsburghPa	14	16	17
Elsen, Archibald(Z-M)	1835	Nov. 19	CoshoctnCoOh	04	05	23
Elser, George(Y)	1824	Nov. 17	ColumbanCoOh	06	18	03
Elser, Jacob(Y)	1824	Nov. 17	ColumbanCoOh	06	18	11
Elser, John(Y)	1822	Nov. 08	ColumbanCoOh	05	17	21
Elser, John(Y)	1822	Nov. 08	ColumbanCoOh	05	17	21
Elson, Edward(Y)	1823	Feb. 21	Booke Co,Vir	07	18	25
Elson, Henry(Z-M)	1836	Jan. 09	CoshoctnCoOh	05	04	21
Elson, Jacob(Z)	1829	Nov. 24	Morgan Co,Oh	13	10	27
Elson, John(Y)	1828	Dec. 31	Stark Co.,Oh	07	17	27
Elson, John(Y)	1833	May 28	Stark Co.,Oh	07	16	05
Elson, Peter(Z)	1830	Aug. 31	Morgan Co,Oh	13	10	27
Elson, Rich'd.(Y)	1826	July 26	Stark Co.,Oh	07	17	15
Elson, Richard(Y)	1826	June 06	Stark Co.,Oh	07	18	33
Elson, Tunis(Z)	1814	July 29	CrawfordCoPa	05	03	02
Elson, Tunis(Z-M)	1833	Nov. 23	CoshoctnCoOh	05	04	21
Elson, Tunis(Z-M)	1836	Jan. 09	CoshoctnCoOh	05	04	21
Elwell, William(Z)	1823	Nov. 19	Morgan Co,Oh	13	09	06
Ely, Peter(Z)	1811	Oct. 19	WashCo.,Penn	10	06	20
Emans, Jacob(Y)	1830	Sept. 07	TuscarwsCoOh	06	14	31
Emerick, And'w.(Z)	1831	Dec. 10	HolmesCoOhio	08	08	01
Emerson, Ezekiel Jnr.(Z)	1835	Aug. 15	GuernseyCoOh	09	05	19
Emerson, Ezekiel Jnr.(Z)	1835	Aug. 15	GuernseyCoOh	09	05	19
Emerson, Ezekiel Jnr.(Z)	1835	Nov. 27	GuernseyCoOh	09	05	19
Emerson, Ezekiel Jnr.(Z)	1836	June 15	GuernseyCoOh	09	05	28
Emerson, Ezekiel Jnr.(Z)	1836	June 15	GuernseyCoOh	09	05	32
Emerson, Jno.(Z-M)	1831	Dec. 16	GuernseyCoOh	01	01	19
Emerson, John(Z-M)	1822	Nov. 19	GuernseyCoOh	01	01	12
Emerson, John(Z-M)	1824	Nov. 18	GuernseyCoOh	01	01	12
Emerson, John(Z-M)	1830	April 12	GuernseyCoOh	01	01	11
Emerson, John(Z-M)	1833	July 05	TuscarwsCoOh	02	07	05
Emery, Conrad(Z)	1811	May 16	MuskingmCoOh	14	15	04
Emler, Abraham(Z-M)	1831	Oct. 03	MuskingmCoOh	05	03	06
Emler, Abraham(Z-M)	1831	July 07	MuskingmCoOh	05	03	06
Emmons, Matilda(Z-M)	1832	Oct. 02	MuskingmCoOh	06	03	03
Emrel, Daniel(Z)	1810	Nov. 07	WestmrldCoPa	04	08	11
Emrick, Andrew(Z-M)	1833	Jan. 16	HolmesCoOhio	08	08	18
Emry, John(Z-M)	1835	Aug. 27	CoshoctnCoOh	09	04	16
Endsley, James(Z-M)	1829	Aug. 08	HarrisonCoOh	07	07	20
Endsley, James(Z-M)	1829	Aug. 08	HarrisonCoOh	07	07	20
Endsley, Thomas(Z)	1827	April 18	HarrisonCoOh	07	07	21
Endsley, Thomas(Z-M)	1826	Dec. 28	HarrisonCoOh	07	07	21
Engelskincher, John(Z-M)	1833	Sept. 21	TuscarwsCoOh	04	07	18
England, David Jr.(Y)	1828	April 28	Stark Co.,Oh	07	20	20
England, John(Z)	1813	May 04	MuskingmCoOh	15	16	17
England, Samuel(Z)	1806	Dec. 23	MuskingmCoOh	15	16	06
Engle, Asa(Z)	1814	Oct. 20	GuernseyCoOh	03	02	01
Engle, Asa(Z)	1816	Dec. 12	HarrisonCoOh	01	04	08
Engle, John(Z)	1833	Nov. 14	Jeff.Co.,Oh.	09	07	30
Engle, Levi(Z)	1816	Oct. 14	HarrisonCoOh	01	04	03
Engle, Levi(Z)	1816	Dec. 12	HarrisonCoOh	03	02	09
Engle, Levi(Z-M)	1829	Dec. 23	GuernseyCoOh	01	04	03
Engle, Samuel(Z)	1835	Nov. 03	Morgan Co,Oh	09	07	32
English & Sargent(Z-M)	1837	Oct. 10	TuscarwsCoOh	04	05	20

PURCHASER	YEAR	DATE	RESIDENCE	R	T	S
English, James W.(Z-M)	1833	Nov. 27	TuscarwsCoOh	01	08	04
English, James W.(Z-M)	1833	Nov. 27	TuscarwsCoOh	01	08	02
English, James W.(Z-M)	1834	Jan. 16	TuscarwsCoOh	03	09	10
English, James W.(Z-M)	1834	Jan. 16	TuscarwsCoOh	01	08	04
English, James W.(Z-M)	1834	Aug. 16	TuscarwsCoOh	01	08	02
English, James(Y)	1826	June 07	Stark Co.,Oh	06	18	03
English, James(Y)	1827	May 19	HarrisonCoOh	06	12	05
English, James(Y)	1829	Aug. 05	HarrisonCoOh	06	12	12
English, James(Z-M)	1825	Nov. 12	CoshoctnCoOh	08	03	22
English, Nath'l.(Y)	1822	Sept. 03	ColumbanCoOh	06	19	34
Enlow, Isaac Jr.(Z-M)	1836	Sept. 28	KnoxCo.,Ohio	10	08	01
Enlow, Isaac Jr.(Z-M)	1836	Sept. 28	KnoxCo.,Ohio	10	08	02
Enlow, Neulson(Z-M)	1836	March 28	HolmesCoOhio	10	09	12
Enochs, Cornelius(Z)	1836	March 28	MonroeCo.,Oh	08	06	14
Enochs, David(Z)	1836	April 12	MonroeCo.,Oh	08	06	12
Enochs, E.(Z)	1814	Aug. 19	GuernseyCoOh	08	06	01
Enochs, Elisha(Z)	1836	May 12	MonroeCo.,Oh	08	05	02
Enochs, Enock(Z)	1817	April 04	GuernseyCoOh	08	05	13
Enochs, Henry(Z)	1829	Feb. 13	MonroeCo.,Oh	08	06	36
Enochs, Henry(Z)	1836	May 12	MonroeCo.,Oh	08	06	36
Enochs, Henry(Z)	1836	May 12	MonroeCo.,Oh	08	05	11
Enochs, Sam'l.(Z)	1836	Aug. 27	MonroeCo.,Oh	08	06	10
Enochs, Simon(Z)	1836	Aug. 27	MonroeCo.,Oh	08	05	11
Enocks, Elisha(Z)	1835	Nov. 20	MonroeCo.,Oh	08	06	14
Enocks, Elisha(Z)	1811	June 13	GuernseyCoOh	08	06	01
Enocks, Henry(Z)	1837	May 06	MonroeCo.,Oh	08	05	01
Enos, Robert King(Z-M)	1834	Sept. 01	HolmesCoOhio	06	08	02
Enslow, David(Z)	1814	Oct. 25	GuernseyCoOh	04	02	15
Enslow, Isaac Senr.(Z)	1813	Dec. 24	KnoxCo.,Ohio	10	08	01
Enterline, Thomas(Z-M)	1832	June 13	TuscarwsCoOh	01	06	08
Epley, Godleip(Z)	1832	Oct. 26	Morgan Co,Oh	13	10	15
Epley, Jacob Jr.(Z)	1835	Dec. 26	MuskingmCoOh	13	10	15
Epley, Jacob(Z)	1832	Oct. 26	Morgan Co,Oh	13	10	15
Erllwine, Adam(Z)	1814	Nov. 28	KnoxCo.,Ohio	10	05	09
Ernst, Jacob(Z-M)	1837	Sept. 15	ZanesvilleOh	09	08	06
Ernst, Jacob(Z-M)	1837	Sept. 15	ZanesvilleOh	09	08	06
Ernst, Jacob(Z-M)	1838	Feb. 01	ZanesvilleOh	09	08	06
Ernst, Joseph(Z-M)	1838	Feb. 01	ZanesvilleOh	09	08	06
Erskine, David(Y)	1831	March 05	ColumbanCoOh	04	12	24
Erskine, David(Y)	1832	Oct. 06	Jeff.Co.,Oh.	04	12	17
Ervin, George(Z-M)	1836	April 02	HarrisonCoOh	08	08	08
Ervin, George(Z-M)	1836	April 02	HarrisonCoOh	08	08	04
Erwin, Andrew(Y)	1831	June 17	HarrisonCoOh	06	12	33
Erwin, David(Z-M)	1833	April 30	CoshoctnCoOh	07	04	17
Erwin, Jane(Y)	1825	April 19	HarrisonCoOh	06	12	14
Erwin, John(Y)	1831	July 05	Jeff.Co.,Oh.	07	14	29
Erwin, Joshua(Z)	1835	March 26	HarrisonCoOh	11	11	05
Erwin, Robert(Y)	1832	Dec. 20	HarrisonCoOh	06	12	32
Erwin, Robert(Y)	1833	Nov. 12	HarrisonCoOh	06	12	32
Erwin, Robert(Z-M)	1834	July 28	MuskingmCoOh	08	03	05
Esiminger, Conrad(Z-M)	1832	Oct. 27	CoshoctnCoOh	10	05	18
Esmamon, John A.(Z)	1831	Aug. 02	Perry Co.,Oh	14	14	22
Espech, Christian(Z)	1814	May 16	TuscarwsCoOh	01	08	09
Essex, N.(Z)	1815	Feb. 20	MuskingmCoOh	11	13	02
Essex, Nathan(Z)	1826	Nov. 15	Morgan Co,Oh	10	07	36
Essex, Nathan(Z)	1836	Jan. 06	Morgan Co,Oh	10	07	35
Essex, Philip(Z)	1829	Dec. 21	Morgan Co,Oh	12	09	17
Essex, Philip(Z)	1829	Dec. 26	Morgan Co,Oh	12	09	17
Estep, James(Z-M)	1837	Jan. 10	HolmesCoOhio	08	08	22
Estep, James(Z-M)	1837	April 14	HolmesCoOhio	08	07	03
Estep, William(Z)	1817	April 30	CoshoctnCoOh	07	08	19
Estinghausen, Asa(Z-M)	1833	July 06	CoshoctnCoOh	07	05	11
Estinghausen, Garwood(Z-M)	1834	Jan. 10	CoshoctnCoOh	07	04	13
Ettleman, Henry(Y)	1826	July 04	Stark Co.,Oh	09	12	33
Eulis, William(Y)	1833	Feb. 14	Stark Co.,Oh	07	16	25
Evans, Amos(Z)	1815	Nov. 18	MontgmryCoPa	06	07	05
Evans, Asahel(Z)	1833	Jan. 09	MuskingmCoOh	13	10	02
Evans, Asahel(Z)	1834	Nov. 22	GuernseyCoOh	10	09	09
Evans, Asher(Y)	1830	March 03	HarrisonCoOh	07	12	15

PURCHASER	YEAR	DATE	RESIDENCE	R	T	S
Evans, Asher(Z-M)	1837	April 11	HarrisonCoOh	03	05	16
Evans, Asher(Z-M)	1837	April 11	HarrisonCoOh	03	05	25
Evans, Benjamin(Z-M)	1836	March 03	GuernseyCoOh	03	04	01
Evans, David(Y)	1824	June 21	Stark Co.,Oh	10	02	15
Evans, David(Z)	1807	May 09	BelmontCo,Oh	09	03	04
Evans, David(Z-M)	1835	Jan. 15	MuskingmCoOh	09	03	16
Evans, David(Z-M)	1839	Jan. 24	ZanesvilleOh	04	03	07
Evans, David(Z-M)	1839	Jan. 24	ZanesvilleOh	04	03	08
Evans, David(Z-M)	1839	Feb. 09	ZanesvilleOh	03	03	16
Evans, Evan(Z)	1830	Aug. 26	BelmontCo,Oh	12	10	33
Evans, Evan(Z-M)	1836	Oct. 24	HolmesCoOhio	09	08	05
Evans, Hance(Z)	1832	Jan. 21	MuskingmCoOh	13	09	32
Evans, Henry H.(Z-M)	1824	Sept. 29	GuernseyCoOh	02	02	01
Evans, Henry H.(Z-M)	1825	May 21	GuernseyCoOh	02	02	01
Evans, Isaac(Y)	1829	April 16	ColumbanCoOh	05	16	32
Evans, J. R.(Z-M)	1836	Aug. 08	TuscarwsCoOh	03	05	13
Evans, James(Y)	1830	Feb. 20	HarrisonCoOh	06	12	05
Evans, James(Z)	1816	Dec. 12	LickingCo,Oh	10	03	17
Evans, James(Z-M)	1832	May 22	HarrisonCoOh	01	06	13
Evans, Job. Jr.(Y)	1828	Dec. 12	ColumbanCoOh	05	16	32
Evans, John C.(Z-M)	1835	Aug. 18	GuernseyCoOh	03	04	01
Evans, John W.(Z)	1833	Jan. 09	MuskingmCoOh	13	11	29
Evans, John W.(Z)	1833	Jan. 09	MuskingmCoOh	13	10	03
Evans, John(Z)	1813	Oct. 22	HuntngdnCoPa	04	08	01
Evans, John(Z)	1814	Nov. 07	MuskingmCoOh	14	15	13
Evans, John(Z-M)	1833	April 10	TuscarwsCoOh	03	06	24
Evans, Jonathan(Y)	1821	Sept. 24	ColumbanCoOh	04	17	22
Evans, Jonathan(Y)	1821	Sept. 25	ColumbanCoOh	04	17	22
Evans, Jonathan(Z-M)	1833	April 10	TuscarwsCoOh	03	06	25
Evans, Joseph(Z)	1805	July 25	WashngtnCoOh	12	12	20
Evans, Joseph(Z)	1814	April 09	ZanesvilleOh	14	16	09
Evans, Joseph(Z)	1814	Dec. 14	ZanesvilleOh	14	15	10
Evans, Joseph(Z)	1816	Oct. 12	Newark, Ohio	09	03	04
Evans, Joseph(Z)	1817	May 10	LickingCo,Oh	11	04	03
Evans, Joseph(Z-M)	1832	June 16	LickingCo,Oh	11	03	06
Evans, L.(Z)	1816	Dec. 12	LickingCo,Oh	10	03	17
Evans, Thomas(Z-M)	1833	Oct. 24	TuscarwsCoOh	03	06	25
Evans, William J.(Z)	1836	Jan. 29	MonongahlaVa	10	09	36
Evans, William(Y)	1832	Feb. 28	HarrisonCoOh	06	12	04
Evans, William(Z)	1807	Jan. 17	Ohio Co.,Vir	05	04	02
Evans, William(Z)	1814	Oct. 26	LickingCo,Oh	10	03	24
Evans, William(Z-M)	1832	Nov. 02	LickingCo,Oh	10	03	24
Evans, William(Z-M)	1833	April 26	BelmontCo,Oh	03	06	25
Evans, Zadoc(Z-M)	1835	Sept. 05	CoshoctnCoOh	05	04	05
Evansdant, John(Z)	1808	Aug. 29	MuskingmCoOh	15	18	03
Evehart, John K.(Z-M)	1832	Nov. 24	Jeff.Co.,Oh.	03	06	05
Evehart, John K.(Z-M)	1832	Nov. 24	Jeff.Co.,Oh.	03	06	05
Eveland, Daniel(Z)	1836	May 23	Morgan Co,Oh	13	09	01
Eveland, Jas.(Z)	1830	Jan. 09	Morgan Co,Oh	13	09	01
Eveland, John(Z)	1806	March 22	WashngtnCoOh	12	11	33
Eveland, John(Z)	1810	Jan. 06	WashngtnCoOh	12	10	11
Eveland, John(Z)	1810	Jan. 06	WashngtnCoOh	12	10	10
Eveland, William(Z)	1826	March 20	Morgan Co,Oh	13	10	36
Eveland, William(Z)	1829	July 18	Morgan Co,Oh	13	10	36
Eveland, William(Z)	1832	Oct. 20	Morgan Co,Oh	13	09	01
Eveland, William(Z)	1832	Oct. 20	Morgan Co,Oh	13	09	02
Everhart, David Jr.(Z-M)	1832	Nov. 20	CoshoctnCoOh	03	06	05
Everhart, David(Z-M)	1833	March 16	TuscarwsCoOh	03	06	06
Everhart, David(Z-M)	1833	March 16	TuscarwsCoOh	03	06	05
Everhart, David(Z-M)	1834	March 25	CoshoctnCoOh	03	06	07
Everhart, David(Z-M)	1836	Jan. 12	TuscarwsCoOh	03	06	05
Everhart, Peter Junr.(Z-M)	1833	Feb. 06	CoshoctnCoOh	03	06	05
Everhart, Peter Junr.(Z-M)	1833	May 23	CoshoctnCoOh	03	06	05
Everhart, Peter(Z-M)	1833	March 09	TuscarwsCoOh	04	06	10
Everhart, Peter(Z-M)	1833	March 09	TuscarwsCoOh	03	06	05
Everhart, Philip(Y)	1832	April 13	HarrisonCoOh	07	14	30
Everhart, Thomas(Y)	1829	April 07	HarrisonCoOh	05	13	07
Everhart, Thomas(Z-M)	1834	March 07	CarrollCo,Oh	03	06	05
Everhart, Thomas(Z-M)	1834	March 07	CarrollCo,Oh	03	06	05

PURCHASER	YEAR	DATE	RESIDENCE	R	T	S
Everherst, John(Z-M)	1829	Dec. 29	TuscarwsCoOh	04	07	24
Everston, Jeremiah(Z)	1813	Dec. 29	MuskingmCoOh	14	14	28
Ewing, Daniel H.(Z-M)	1837	April 29	CoshoctnCoOh	05	07	17
Ewing, David(Y)	1823	Oct. 31	WashCo.,Penn	05	14	08
Ewing, Henry(Y)	1829	May 04	HuntngtnCoPa	04	13	27
Ewing, James(Y)	1829	March 27	ColumbanCoOh	02	09	32
Ewing, James(Y)	1833	April 30	ColumbanCoOh	02	09	32
Ewing, Jas.(Y)	1823	Oct. 31	WashCo.,Penn	05	14	08
Ewing, Joshua(Y)	1834	Feb. 13	Jeff.Co.,Oh.	02	09	32
Ewing, Sam'l.(Y)	1823	Aug. 01	Jeff.Co.,Oh.	03	10	18
Ewings, Robt.(Z-M)	1822	June 29	GuernseyCoOh	02	02	12
Eykine, David(Y)	1831	June 09	Jeff.Co.,Oh.	04	12	23
Fab, Jeremiah(Z)	1815	Sept. 29	WashngtnCoOh	13	09	08
Fackler, Samuel(Z-M)	1835	July 02	TuscarwsCoOh	02	07	08
Faearbaugh, Barbare(Z-M)	1836	Oct. 03	CoshoctnCoOh	05	07	24
Fagan, Patrick(Z)	1833	Sept. 26	Perry Co.,Oh	14	12	13
Fagan, Patrick(Z)	1836	Oct. 17	Perry Co.,Oh	14	12	13
Fagg, Henderson(Z-M)	1837	March 18	HolmesCoOhio	09	07	02
Faick, John(Z)	1809	Nov. 09	AlleghnyCoPa	03	08	06
Fainbrother, Henry(Z)	1830	Nov. 05	Jeff.Co.,Oh.	08	05	13
Fainbrother, Henry(Z)	1830	Nov. 05	Jeff.Co.,Oh.	08	05	13
Fair, Matthias(Z-M)	1835	Nov. 26	TuscarwsCoOh	02	10	23
Fairall, Horace(Z-M)	1836	Jan. 11	MuskingmCoOh	09	03	06
Fairall, Horatio(Z-M)	1835	Jan. 20	MuskingmCoOh	09	03	15
Fairall, Levi(Z-M)	1833	March 30	MuskingmCoOh	09	03	07
Fairall, Levi(Z-M)	1836	Feb. 22	MuskingmCoOh	09	03	15
Fairall, William(Z)	1817	Feb. 08	MuskingmCoOh	09	03	14
Fairall, William(Z)	1817	Feb. 08	MuskingmCoOh	09	03	07
Fairleigh, John(Z-M)	1834	Aug. 16	BelmontCo,Oh	03	06	17
Fairleigh, John(Z-M)	1836	Nov. 14	TuscarwsCoOh	03	06	17
Fairley, David(Z)	1832	Oct. 06	MonroeCo.,Oh	08	08	34
Fairley, David(Z)	1832	Oct. 06	MonroeCo.,Oh	08	08	34
Fairley, David(Z)	1832	Oct. 06	MonroeCo.,Oh	08	08	34
Faisley, David(Z)	1832	Oct. 06	MonroeCo.,Oh	08	08	34
Faisley, David(Z)	1832	Oct. 06	MonroeCo.,Oh	08	08	34
Faisley, David(Z)	1832	Oct. 06	MonroeCo.,Oh	08	08	34
Fale, Jeremiah(Z)	1814	Jan. 24	MuskingmCoOh	15	16	31
Fale, Martin(Z)	1814	Feb. 12	FairfeldCoOh	10	01	18
Fale, Martin(Z)	1815	Oct. 06	FairfeldCoOh	13	09	19
Faler, John(Z-M)	1831	May 23	TuscarwsCoOh	02	10	24
Faler, John(Z-M)	1831	May 23	TuscarwsCoOh	02	10	25
Faler, Samuel(Z-M)	1831	May 17	TuscarwsCoOh	02	10	16
Falley, John T.(Z)	1820	Nov. 22	Morgan Co,Oh	12	11	12
Fansell, John(Z-M)	1832	Nov. 08	TuscarwsCoOh	03	10	20
Farguson, Richard(Z)	1812	June 23	TuscarwsCoOh	01	10	04
Farley, James(Z)	1834	Dec. 03	Morgan Co,Oh	10	06	26
Farmer, Benjamin(Y)	1834	Jan. 25	ColumbanCoOh	03	12	24
Farmer, Isaac(Z)	1812	Feb. 08	BelmontCo,Oh	10	01	02
Farmer, Isaac(Z-M)	1832	Aug. 14	LickingCo,Oh	10	04	23
Farmer, James(Y)	1826	Jan. 30	ColumbanCoOh	03	12	30
Farmer, James(Y)	1826	Feb. 23	ColumbanCoOh	03	12	24
Farmer, James(Y)	1832	Oct. 22	ColumbanCoOh	03	12	29
Farmer, James(Y)	1833	March 11	ColumbanCoOh	03	12	36
Farmer, John(Y)	1827	April 05	ColumbanCoOh	02	09	32
Farmer, John(Y)	1828	Aug. 27	ColumbanCoOh	03	12	30
Farmer, John(Y)	1830	Feb. 19	HarrisonCoOh	02	09	32
Farmer, John(Y)	1833	Feb. 15	ColumbanCoOh	03	12	26
Farmer, John(Z-M)	1830	Dec. 06	HolmesCoOhio	06	09	18
Farmer, Samuel(Z)	1812	Feb. 08	BelmontCo,Oh	10	01	02
Farmer, Samuel(Z-M)	1832	Oct. 25	LickingCo,Oh	10	01	03
Farney, Jacob(Z)	1815	Jan. 07	CoshoctnCoOh	04	07	05
Farnslee, Philip(Z)	1815	March 13	Jeff.Co.,Oh.	05	07	22
Farnslee, Philip(Z)	1815	March 13	Jeff.Co.,Oh.	05	07	23
Farquhar, Samuel(Z)	1808	Aug. 06	KnoxCo.,Penn	09	03	05
Farquhar, Samuel(Z)	1808	Aug. 06	KnoxCo.,Penn	09	05	04
Farquhar, Samuel(Z)	1808	Aug. 06	KnoxCo.,Penn	10	06	21
Farquhar, Samuel(Z)	1811	July 16	?	09	05	04
Farquher, Atten(Y)	1822	Dec. 06	ColumbanCoOh	04	17	10
Farra, Rees(Y)	1820	Nov. 27	BelmontCo,Oh	07	09	19

PURCHASER	YEAR	DATE	RESIDENCE	R	T	S
Farra, Rees(Y)	1825	Oct. 29	GuernseyCoOh	07	09	13
Farrell, Joseph(Z)	1815	June 16	Ohio Co.,Vir	06	03	23
Farrell, Joseph(Z)	1815	June 16	Ohio Co.,Vir	06	03	23
Farrer, Solomon W.(Z-M)	1835	Oct. 29	HolmesCoOhio	06	08	20
Farson, Ezikiel(Z-M)	1832	Oct. 02	CoshoctnCoOh	07	05	11
Farson, William(Z-M)	1826	May 09	CoshoctnCoOh	07	05	11
Farson, William(Z-M)	1826	May 12	CoshoctnCoOh	07	05	11
Farvee, Abraham(Z)	1814	April 02	TuscarwsCoOh	03	10	22
Farver, John(Z)	1815	May 31	CoshoctnCoOh	06	08	11
Farver, Solomon W.(Z-M)	1831	Nov. 07	HolmesCoOhio	05	08	23
Farver, William(Z)	1827	Nov. 22	HolmesCoOhio	06	08	11
Farver, William(Z)	1815	May 31	CoshoctnCoOh	06	08	11
Farver, William(Z)	1815	May 31	CoshoctnCoOh	05	07	21
Farver, William(Z-M)	1829	Oct. 26	HolmesCoOhio	06	08	20
Farver, William(Z-M)	1832	June 04	HolmesCoOhio	06	08	20
Farver, William(Z-M)	1834	Jan. 15	HolmesCoOhio	06	08	20
Farvor, John(Z-M)	1832	June 04	HolmesCoOhio	06	09	18
Fase, Francis L.(Z-M)	1837	Sept. 15	ZanesvilleOh	09	08	06
Fashbaugh, John Jr.(Z-M)	1832	May 31	TuscarwsCoOh	01	10	15
Fashbaugh, John(Z-M)	1832	July 27	TuscarwsCoOh	02	10	15
Fassett, Elias(Z-M)	1825	Oct. 08	LickingCo,Oh	11	03	18
Fate, Thomas(Z)	1821	Oct. 19	Perry Co.,Oh	13	08	04
Faucet, Arthur(Z)	1810	Oct. 29	KnoxCo.,Penn	11	06	12
Fauley, Peter(Z)	1806	May 01	LoudonCo,Vir	14	15	30
Fauley, Peter(Z)	1806	May 01	LoudonCo,Vir	15	16	11
Fauley, Peter(Z)	1814	Sept. 13	MuskingmCoOh	14	15	30
Faulk, John Andrew(Y)	1831	Oct. 05	Stark Co.,Oh	07	17	17
Fauman, Hartwell(Z-M)	1839	March 07	Jeff.Co.,Oh.	09	08	24
Fauts, J.(Z)	1816	Feb. 17	Ohio Co.,Vir	12	11	25
Fauur, John(Z)	1813	Oct. 11	SomersetCoPa	05	08	18
Fauw, John(Z)	1813	Oct. 11	SomersetCoPa	05	08	18
Fawcett, John(Y)	1828	Sept. 20	HarrisonCoOh	06	14	05
Fawney, Abraham(Z)	1810	April 23	TuscarwsCoOh	03	08	11
Fawney, Abraham(Z)	1811	May 04	TuscarwsCoOh	03	08	12
Fealty, Michael(Z)	1834	Feb. 07	Perry Co.,Oh	15	15	11
Fearnley, Peter(Z)	1825	April 06	Morgan Co,Oh	09	05	11
Feickert, Frederick(Z-M)	1837	July 12	TuscarwsCoOh	03	07	15
Feickert, Peter(Z-M)	1837	July 01	TuscarwsCoOh	03	07	19
Feigheley, David(Z)	1836	Dec. 17	Perry Co.,Oh	14	12	27
Feighner, John(Y)	1827	Feb. 05	Stark Co.,Oh	07	20	06
Fell, Amos(Z)	1816	Dec. 31	MuskingmCoOh	05	02	14
Feller, Jacob(Z-M)	1837	April 14	HolmesCoOhio	09	08	20
Felter, Frederick(Z)	1810	May 04	WestmrldCoPa	03	08	06
Felter, Jacob(Y)	1831	June 03	Stark Co.,Oh	07	16	11
Felton, Richard(Z-M)	1831	March 18	CoshoctnCoOh	07	04	18
Felty, John(Y)	1828	June 10	HarrisonCoOh	04	12	31
Felty, Peter(Z)	1833	July 29	Perry Co.,Oh	14	13	06
Femple, Michael(Y)	1822	Dec. 07	WarrenCo.,Pa	05	15	19
Fenar, Andrew(Z)	1808	Sept. 24	Jeff.Co.,Oh.	04	04	06
Fengstag, Frederick(Z-M)	1835	July 02	TuscarwsCoOh	03	10	11
Fenner, Oliver H.(Z-M)	1836	May 09	HolmesCoOhio	09	09	17
Fenner, Oliver H.(Z-M)	1836	May 09	HolmesCoOhio	09	09	02
Fenner, Oliver Harris(Z-M)	1836	Nov. 09	HolmesCoOhio	09	09	01
Fenny, Thomas(Z)	1813	March 29	MuskingmCoOh	06	01	22
Fenton, James(Z-M)	1827	July 04	TuscarwsCoOh	01	09	07
Fenton, Jesse(Z)	1828	March 11	MuskingmCoOh	11	12	05
Fenton, Jesse(Z)	1836	Feb. 06	MuskingmCoOh	10	06	15
Fenton, Jesse(Z)	1816	Feb. 01	WashCo.,Penn	11	12	06
Feogles, George(Z)	1813	Nov. 20	FayetteCo,Pa	02	02	02
Feoller, David(Z-M)	1836	Jan. 06	WilliamsCoOh	08	07	10
Ferbrach, Thomas(Z-M)	1828	Dec. 15	GuernseyCoOh	03	02	02
Ferbrache, Daniel(Z)	1812	Feb. 29	GuernseyCoOh	03	02	02
Ferbrache, Jacob N.(Z-M)	1836	Feb. 17	GuernseyCoOh	04	03	12
Ferbrache, Jacob N.(Z-M)	1836	Feb. 17	GuernseyCoOh	04	03	12
Ferbrache, James(Z)	1836	April 01	GuernseyCoOh	08	05	09
Ferbrache, James(Z)	1836	April 01	GuernseyCoOh	08	05	09
Ferbrache, James(Z)	1836	April 06	GuernseyCoOh	08	05	04
Ferbrache, John S.(Z-M)	1837	June 16	GuernseyCoOh	04	03	09
Ferbrache, John(Z-M)	1837	June 16	GuernseyCoOh	04	03	09

PURCHASER	YEAR	DATE	RESIDENCE	R	T	S
Ferbrache, John(Z-M)	1837	June 16	GuernseyCoOh	04	03	08
Ferbrache, Thomas(Z-M)	1836	Dec. 31	GuernseyCoOh	04	03	20
Ferbrack, Thomas(Z-M)	1824	May 11	GuernseyCoOh	03	02	09
Ferguson, An'w.(Z-M)	1830	Jan. 13	CoshoctnCoOh	05	04	03
Ferguson, Anthony(Y)	1831	May 28	ColumbanCoOh	04	13	18
Ferguson, James(Z)	1811	Oct. 30	MuskingmCoOh	09	03	17
Ferguson, Stephen(Y)	1830	Nov. 24	Jeff.Co.,Oh.	04	13	15
Ferguson, William(Z-M)	1836	Feb. 02	GuernseyCoOh	03	02	11
Ferison, John(Z-M)	1836	April 21	TuscarwsCoOh	05	07	18
Ferral, Zelek Virgil(Z-M)	1837	May 01	TuscarwsCoOh	03	06	09
Ferral, Zelek(Z-M)	1834	Aug. 04	BelmontCo,Oh	03	06	03
Ferree, Thos.(Z)	1811	Aug. 20	ZanesvilleOh	03	02	07
Ferree, Thos.(Z)	1811	Aug. 20	ZanesvilleOh	03	02	07
Ferrel, Henson(Z-M)	1837	Dec. 05	HolmesCoOhio	08	08	07
Ferrel, Henson(Z-M)	1837	Dec. 05	HolmesCoOhio	08	08	04
Ferrel, James(Y)	1822	Jan. 11	HarrisonCoOh	05	11	15
Ferrel, John P.(Z)	1832	Nov. 30	MuskingmCoOh	11	12	27
Ferrel, John P.(Z)	1833	Nov. 16	MuskingmCoOh	11	12	27
Ferrel, William(Z-M)	1833	June 10	HarrisonCoOh	03	07	17
Ferrell, James(Y)	1821	Oct. 31	HarrisonCoOh	05	11	15
Ferrell, James(Y)	1824	May 19	HarrisonCoOh	05	11	22
Ferrell, Joseph(Z)	1821	Sept. 11	BelmontCo,Oh	12	11	27
Ferrell, Margaret(Z-M)	1828	May 31	MuskingmCoOh	02	04	06
Ferrier, Andrew Jr.(Y)	1827	April 20	HarrisonCoOh	06	14	19
Ferrier, Andrew(Y)	1826	Aug. 11	HarrisonCoOh	06	14	20
Ferrier, Andrew(Y)	1826	Dec. 19	HarrisonCoOh	06	13	05
Ferrier, David(Y)	1826	Sept. 08	HarrisonCoOh	06	13	11
Ferrier, David(Y)	1826	Nov. 28	HarrisonCoOh	06	13	11
Fersen, Robert(Z)	1805	Sept. 25	SomersetCoPa	15	16	18
Fesbush, Daniel(Z)	1812	Feb. 29	GuernseyCoOh	03	02	02
Fesser, Frorentz(Z-M)	1838	March 17	ZanesvilleOh	09	08	15
Fetch, Walter(Z)	1815	Aug. 05	ColumbiaCoNY	13	09	36
Fetro, Andrew(Z)	1812	May 12	TuscarwsCoOh	01	09	03
Fetter, Frederick(Z)	1810	May 04	Westmr1dCoOh	03	08	06
Fetter, Henry(Z-M)	1833	Dec. 04	TuscarwsCoOh	03	08	07
Fetter, Michael(Z-M)	1832	Nov. 26	TuscarwsCoOh	03	08	07
Fetzer, Joannah(Z)	1833	Dec. 02	MuskingmCoOh	13	10	21
Feuar, Andrew(Z)	1808	Sept. 24	Jeff.Co.,Oh.	04	04	06
Fibzer, Peter Junr.(Z)	1815	Nov. 27	ZanesvilleOh	09	05	07
Fickel, Benjamin(Z)	1835	Oct. 23	Perry Co.,Oh	14	13	33
Fickel, William(Z)	1834	Jan. 24	Perry Co.,Oh	14	13	33
Fickel, William(Z)	1835	July 27	Perry Co.,Oh	14	13	33
Fickel, William(Z)	1836	Dec. 03	Perry Co.,Oh	14	13	34
Fickel, William(Z)	1836	Dec. 03	Perry Co.,Oh	14	13	34
Fickel, William(Z)	1836	Dec. 03	Perry Co.,Oh	14	13	34
Fickle, Benjamin Junr.(Z)	1804	Nov. 21	MuskingmCoOh	15	17	10
Fickle, Benjamin(Z)	1804	Dec. 06	FairfeldCoOh	15	17	31
Fickle, Joseph(Z)	1836	May 03	Perry Co.,Oh	14	13	21
Fickle, Joseph(Z)	1805	April 29	MuskingmCoOh	15	17	30
Fickle, Joseph(Z)	1808	June 28	MuskingmCoOh	15	17	28
Fickle, Joseph(Z)	1813	June 05	MuskingmCoOh	15	17	20
Fickle, Michael(Z-M)	1829	Dec. 05	KnoxCo.,Ohio	10	05	16
Fickle, William(Z)	1808	May 04	MuskingmCoOh	15	17	19
Fiekil, John(Z)	1826	Sept. 16	Morgan Co,Oh	11	10	15
Field, David(Z)	1806	Aug. 14	BedfordCo,Pa	08	03	08
Fields, David(Z)	1806	Nov. 21	BedfordCo,Pa	08	03	08
Fife, William(Y)	1831	July 05	ColumbanCoOh	02	10	17
Fifu, Abraham(Y)	1826	April 24	ColumbanCoOh	05	17	15
Figgins, John(Y)	1828	Dec. 02	ColumbanCoOh	03	13	21
Figley, Samuel(Y)	1826	Sept. 30	ColumbanCoOh	06	16	26
Filkel, Henry(Z)	1828	Aug. 13	Morgan Co,Oh	11	10	15
Filson, Archibald(Y)	1826	April 25	WashCo.,Penn	05	17	06
Filton, William(Z)	1816	Dec. 30	BelmontCo,Oh	06	08	08
Finch, Dawson(Y)	1834	Jan. 13	Jeff.Co.,Oh.	03	12	18
Finch, Mandeville(Y)	1834	March 17	CarrollCo,Oh	05	15	05
Finch, William(Z)	1816	June 13	LoudonCo,Vir	06	08	11
Findley, David(Z)	1829	Dec. 22	Morgan Co,Oh	13	09	21
Findley, David(Z)	1805	Nov. 07	AlleghnyCoPa	12	13	02
Findley, David(Z)	1805	Nov. 07	AlleghnyCoPa	12	13	10

94

PURCHASER	YEAR	DATE	RESIDENCE	R	T	S
Findley, David(Z)	1805	Nov. 15	AlleghnyCoPa	04	02	22
Findley, David(Z)	1805	Nov. 15	AlleghnyCoPa	12	13	01
Findley, David(Z)	1806	March 03	AlleghnyCoPa	05	01	01
Findley, David(Z)	1811	Feb. 16	MuskingmCoOh	04	02	22
Findley, David(Z)	1814	Nov. 19	MuskingmCoOh	05	02	21
Findley, James(Z)	1810	Oct. 24	FayetteCo,Pa	08	08	18
Findley, James(Z)	1810	Oct. 24	FayetteCo,Pa	08	08	17
Fink, Dan'l.(Y)	1824	May 17	ColumbanCoOh	02	13	07
Finlay, Waitman(Z-M)	1830	Oct. 15	HarrisonCoOh	01	06	24
Finley, Ebenezer(Z)	1810	May 26	FayetteCo,Pa	08	08	07
Finley, Ebenezer(Z)	1810	May 26	FayetteCo,Pa	09	08	12
Finley, Ebenezer(Z)	1811	Jan. 18	FayetteCo,Pa	09	08	20
Finley, James(Z)	1805	Sept. 04	MuskingmCoOh	12	13	10
Finley, James(Z)	1805	Dec. 31	MuskingmCoOh	12	12	05
Finley, James(Z)	1812	April 02	FayetteCo,Pa	08	08	17
Finley, John(Z)	1830	May 27	WashCo.,Penn	13	09	22
Finley, John(Z)	1836	Jan. 08	GuernseyCoOh	09	08	12
Finley, Joseph(Z)	1833	March 20	GuernseyCoOh	09	08	12
Finley, Joseph(Z)	1833	March 20	GuernseyCoOh	09	08	12
Finley, Robt.(Z)	1830	March 12	Jeff.Co.,Oh.	08	08	24
Finley, Robt.(Z-M)	1829	Feb. 16	KnoxCo.,Ohio	11	08	13
Finley, Sam'l.(Z)	1835	Dec. 29	GuernseyCoOh	09	08	20
Finley, Samuel(Z)	1836	Jan. 08	GuernseyCoOh	09	08	12
Finley, Samuel(Z)	1836	Jan. 08	GuernseyCoOh	09	08	12
Finley, William(Z)	1835	Oct. 15	MonroeCo.,Oh	08	08	32
Finley, William(Z)	1835	Dec. 02	MonroeCo.,Oh	08	08	32
Finnell, Thomas(Z-M)	1832	March 01	CoshoctnCoOh	07	05	10
Finney, Abraham(Z-M)	1837	Feb. 11	GuernseyCoOh	03	04	14
Finney, Andrew(Z-M)	1835	Jan. 09	HarrisonCoOh	03	05	20
Finney, Andrew(Z-M)	1836	Jan. 16	TuscarwsCoOh	03	05	20
Finney, James(Z)	1817	Jan. 01	AlleghnyCoPa	12	11	02
Finney, John(Z)	1824	May 11	MuskingmCoOh	12	13	21
Finney, John(Z)	1827	June 28	MuskingmCoOh	12	13	22
Finney, Walter B.(Z-M)	1833	April 12	HarrisonCoOh	11	04	12
Finney, William(Z)	1816	April 11	AlleghnyCoPa	12	12	33
Finton, John(Z-M)	1830	March 29	TuscarwsCoOh	01	09	07
Fippin, William(Z-M)	1836	Jan. 28	HolmesCoOhio	09	09	13
Fippin, William(Z-M)	1837	Jan. 26	HolmesCoOhio	09	09	14
Firebauqh, Daniel(Z-M)	1833	Sept. 26	CoshoctnCoOh	05	07	24
Fishel, Philip(Z)	1827	June 08	GuernseyCoOh	10	09	12
Fisher, Abraham(Z)	1837	Feb. 14	BrookeCo,Vir	08	05	04
Fisher, Adam(Y)	1831	March 09	ColumbanCoOh	07	16	04
Fisher, Buonaparte(Y)	1834	April 07	HarrisonCoOh	04	12	17
Fisher, David(Z-M)	1835	June 20	GuernseyCoOh	02	04	05
Fisher, George(Y)	1831	Feb. 12	HarrisonCoOh	05	11	24
Fisher, Henry(Z)	1834	Aug. 01	MuskingmCoOh	11	12	34
Fisher, Jacob(Z-M)	1836	Feb. 12	TuscarwsCoOh	02	07	01
Fisher, James(Y)	1823	Jan. 30	TuscarwsCoOh	07	14	02
Fisher, James(Y)	1826	Jan. 14	TuscarwsCoOh	07	14	07
Fisher, James(Y)	1832	Sept. 08	TuscarwsCoOh	07	14	08
Fisher, Joel(Y)	1829	Aug. 18	HarrisonCoOh	05	13	33
Fisher, John(Y)	1831	March 03	HarrisonCoOh	06	12	06
Fisher, John(Y)	1832	March 15	HarrisonCoOh	06	13	01
Fisher, John(Z-M)	1833	May 06	TuscarwsCoOh	04	08	19
Fisher, Perry G.(Y)	1828	Feb. 28	BelmontCo,Oh	06	10	25
Fisher, Perry G.(Z-M)	1835	Oct. 21	BelmontCo,Oh	03	06	25
Fisher, Peter(Z)	1827	May 05	TuscarwsCoOh	04	08	19
Fisher, Philip(Z)	1828	Aug. 20	GuernseyCoOh	10	09	13
Fisher, Philip(Z-M)	1830	March 01	GuernseyCoOh	03	01	22
Fisher, Reuben(Y)	1825	May 02	Stark Co.,Oh	06	19	15
Fisher, Simon(Y)	1834	Sept. 12	CarrollCo,Oh	07	16	05
Fisher, Thomas(Z)	1836	Sept. 07	CincinnatiOh	08	05	13
Fisher, Thomas(Z)	1807	June 08	Reading,Penn	15	16	12
Fisher, Thomas(Z)	1811	July 30	MuskingmCoOh	15	17	12
Fisher, Thomas(Z)	1811	Sept. 26	MuskingmCoOh	15	17	13
Fisher, Thomas(Z)	1813	July 26	MuskingmCoOh	15	17	12
Fisher, Thomas(Z)	1815	April 26	MuskingmCoOh	15	17	11
Fisher, Thomas(Z-M)	1835	Nov. 12	CarrollCo,Oh	03	06	03
Fisher, Thomas(Z-M)	1837	June 12	CarrollCo,Oh	03	07	12

PURCHASER	YEAR	DATE	RESIDENCE	R	T	S
Fiskett, Daniel(Y)	1829	April 08	ColumbanCoOh	05	14	24
Fitch, Sam'l.(Z-M)	1830	Sept. 14	CoshoctnCoOh	07	05	23
Fitchpatrick, James(Z)	1817	Jan. 07	WashCo.,Penn	04	02	15
Fitsimons, Stephen(Z)	1825	April 13	BelmontCo,Oh	12	09	13
Fitz, Christian(Z-M)	1836	Aug. 26	HolmesCoOhio	08	08	16
Fitz, Christin(Z-M)	1834	July 25	Stark Co.,Oh	09	08	09
Fitz, John(Z-M)	1834	Sept. 10	HolmesCoOhio	09	08	12
Fitzgerald, Thomas(Y)	1834	Oct. 03	HarrisonCoOh	06	11	35
Fitzpatrick, Bernard(Z-M)	1838	June 02	CoshoctnCoOh	04	04	03
Fitzpatrick, John(Y)	1829	Oct. 16	ColumbanCoOh	04	13	10
Flaharty, Jas.(Z)	1805	July 20	MuskingmCoOh	14	16	13
Flaharty, Jas.(Z)	1805	July 20	MuskingmCoOh	14	15	01
Flanner, Eliza(Z)	1836	Nov. 30	ZanesvilleOh	08	07	33
Flanner, Eliza(Z-M)	1836	Nov. 21	ZanesvilleOh	03	07	22
Flanner, Eliza(Z-M)	1836	Dec. 10	ZanesvilleOh	09	08	12
Flaugherty, James(Z)	1827	April 09	BelmontCo,Oh	11	10	22
Fleeckenger, Jacob(Z-M)	1834	Sept. 27	TuscarwsCoOh	03	08	07
Fleming, A.(Z)	1816	Aug. 23	DelawareCoOh	08	02	20
Fleming, Alexander(Z-M)	1824	Aug. 10	GuernseyCoOh	02	02	07
Fleming, Hugh(Z-M)	1824	March 27	LickingCo,Oh	09	04	25
Fleming, Thos.(Z-M)	1824	March 27	LickingCo,Oh	09	04	25
Flemming, William(Z-M)	1836	Nov. 08	KnoxCo.,Ohio	10	08	12
Fletcher, David(Z-M)	1839	June 25	WestmrldCoPa	07	08	16
Fletcher, Robert(Z-M)	1832	April 04	HarrisonCoOh	07	08	12
Fletcher, Wm. B.(Z-M)	1836	Sept. 27	LickingCo,Oh	10	05	22
Flickinge, Andrew(Y)	1825	Aug. 17	HarrisonCoOh	06	14	09
Flickinger, Michael(Z)	1808	July 12	TuscarwsCoOh	01	10	06
Flickinger, Michael(Z)	1811	May 27	TuscarwsCoOh	01	10	06
Flinkenger, Michael(Z)	1809	Nov. 02	TuscarwsCoOh	01	10	06
Floid, Obadiah Jr.(Z)	1833	Nov. 05	Perry Co.,Oh	15	15	27
Floid, Obadiah Jr.(Z)	1836	Feb. 27	Perry Co.,Oh	15	15	26
Floid, Obadiah(Z)	1833	Jan. 22	Perry Co.,Oh	15	15	11
Flood, Robert(Z)	1814	Dec. 06	Brooke CoVir	01	01	20
Flood, Thomas(Z)	1817	Oct. 16	ZanesvilleOh	08	06	11
Flora, David(Z-M)	1831	Jan. 27	Stark Co.,Oh	02	10	14
Flory, Abraham(Y)	1829	Aug. 06	HarrisonCoOh	05	12	36
Flory, Joseph(Y)	1829	Sept. 07	HarrisonCoOh	06	13	10
Flory, Mich'l.(Y)	1824	June 26	Stark Co.,Oh	07	19	27
Flory, Michael(Y)	1823	Nov. 11	Stark Co.,Oh	07	19	34
Flowers, Christopher(Z)	1833	Nov. 14	Perry Co.,Oh	14	14	29
Flowers, Henry(Z)	1810	Oct. 18	MuskingmCoOh	15	17	28
Flowers, Richard(Z)	1807	July 01	MuskingmCoOh	14	16	08
Flowers, Samuel(Z-M)	1835	Nov. 27	KnoxCo.,Ohio	10	07	17
Floyd, Obadiah Jr.(Z)	1835	Oct. 19	Perry Co.,Oh	15	15	26
Floyd, Obadiah(Z)	1831	April 01	Perry Co.,Oh	15	14	01
Fluck, Henry(Z)	1814	July 28	MuskingmCoOh	15	07	03
Fofo, Wallace(Y)	1833	Dec. 28	ColumbanCoOh	03	12	11
Fogle, Elijah(Z)	1836	Feb. 26	Morgan Co,Oh	09	07	22
Fogle, Elijah(Z)	1836	Feb. 26	Morgan Co,Oh	09	07	22
Fogle, Elijah(Z)	1837	March 29	Morgan Co,Oh	09	07	22
Fogle, Elisha(Z)	1826	June 30	Morgan Co,Oh	09	07	26
Fogle, Elisha(Z)	1832	Oct. 03	Morgan Co,Oh	09	07	26
Fogle, George(Z)	1816	July 13	GuernseyCoOh	02	01	13
Fogle, John(Z)	1834	Feb. 26	Morgan Co,Oh	09	07	22
Fogle, John(Z)	1836	Feb. 29	Morgan Co,Oh	09	07	27
Fogle, Michael(Z)	1822	Dec. 11	Morgan Co,Oh	09	07	23
Fogle, Michael(Z)	1835	Dec. 24	Morgan Co,Oh	09	07	22
Fogle, Peter(Z)	1834	March 13	Morgan Co,Oh	09	07	27
Fogle, Peter(Z)	1815	Oct. 26	FayetteCo,Pa	09	07	28
Fogle, William(Z)	1835	May 13	Morgan Co,Oh	08	06	04
Fogle, William(Z)	1836	July 21	MonroeCo.,Oh	08	06	04
Fogo, John(Y)	1831	Nov. 16	ColumbanCoOh	03	12	10
Folbre, Charles(Z)	1815	Sept. 30	PutnamCoOhio	06	02	24
Folk, Peter(Z)	1809	Nov. 02	TuscarwsCoOh	01	10	06
Folk, Peter(Z)	1809	Nov. 02	TuscarwsCoOh	01	10	05
Folk, Peter(Z)	1810	March 27	TuscarwsCoOh	01	10	05
Folk, Peter(Z)	1810	March 27	TuscarwsCoOh	01	10	07
Folwell, J.(Z)	1816	March 20	WashCo.,Penn	07	09	20
Folwell, J.(Z)	1816	March 20	WashCo.,Penn	08	08	01

PURCHASER	YEAR	DATE	RESIDENCE	R	T	S
Forbes, James(Y)	1822	April 11	WestmrldCoPa	06	13	22
Forbes, James(Y)	1822	April 11	WestmrldCoPa	06	13	22
Forbes, James(Z-M)	1836	Nov. 25	CarrollCo,Oh	01	08	04
Ford, Benj'm.(Z-M)	1831	Dec. 23	CoshoctnCoOh	07	05	21
Ford, Chauncy(Z)	1804	Oct. 15	WashngtnCoOh	14	15	34
Ford, Chauney(Z)	1823	Jan. 16	MuskingmCoOh	14	14	03
Ford, George(Z)	1816	June 06	Jeff.Co.,Oh	06	06	10
Ford, George(Z-M)	1824	Feb. 19	GuernseyCoOh	02	03	08
Ford, George(Z-M)	1831	May 02	GuernseyCoOh	02	03	08
Ford, Henry(Y)	1829	March 16	HarrisonCoOh	05	11	36
Ford, John(Y)	1827	June 20	HarrisonCoOh	06	11	35
Ford, Joshua Junr.(Z)	1812	March 21	Jeff.Co.,Oh.	08	02	11
Ford, Robert(Z)	1816	June 06	Jeff.Co.,Oh.	06	06	10
Ford, Robert(Z-M)	1835	Aug. 26	GuernseyCoOh	04	02	11
Ford, Thomas(Y)	1829	April 20	HarrisonCoOh	05	12	32
Ford, Thomas(Z-M)	1831	Dec. 23	CoshoctnCoOh	07	05	21
Ford, William(Z)	1804	Sept. 19	WashngtnCoOh	14	15	33
Ford, William(Z)	1804	Sept. 19	WashngtnCoOh	14	15	27
Ford, William(Z)	1805	July 22	MuskingmCoOh	14	15	34
Fordice, W.(Z)	1814	Nov. 11	WashngtnCoOh	11	11	28
Fordice, Wm.(Z)	1831	June 08	Morgan Co,Oh	11	11	11
Fordyce, David D.(Z-M)	1831	March 14	HarrisonCoOh	01	05	02
Fordyce, John(Y)	1831	May 10	TuscarwsCoOh	07	12	33
Fordyce, John(Z)	1827	April 21	GreeneCo.,Pa	04	01	21
Fordyce, John(Z-M)	1826	Oct. 12	HarrisonCoOh	01	05	01
Fordyce, Lebbens(Z)	1835	Nov. 30	Morgan Co,Oh	09	07	25
Fordyce, Lebbens(Z)	1837	Sept. 11	Morgan Co,Oh	08	06	09
Fordyce, Lebbens(Z)	1837	Sept. 11	Morgan Co,Oh	08	06	09
Fordyce, Lebbens(Z)	1837	Sept. 11	Morgan Co,Oh	08	06	17
Fordyce, Lebbens(Z)	1837	Sept. 11	Morgan Co,Oh	08	06	22
Fordyce, Sam'l.(Z-M)	1829	May 26	Morgan Co,Oh	09	07	31
Fordyce, Samuel(Y)	1825	Nov. 23	FayetteCo,Pa	07	12	35
Foreacre, James(Z)	1805	Dec. 17	BelmontCo,Oh	01	01	02
Foreacre, John(Z)	1813	July 01	MuskingmCoOh	14	14	01
Foreacre, William(Z)	1813	Oct. 30	MuskingmCoOh	14	14	25
Foreacre, William(Z)	1817	July 31	MuskingmCoOh	14	14	35
Foreacre, William(Z)	1817	Oct. 10	MuskingmCoOh	14	14	24
Foreman, Charles Junr.(Y)	1831	July 06	AlleghnyCoPa	05	15	33
Foreman, H. L.(Z-M)	1835	March 23	TuscarwsCoOh	03	06	15
Foreman, Henry Lee(Z-M)	1835	Aug. 31	TuscarwsCoOh	03	06	15
Foreman, Henry(Z-M)	1833	June 13	TuscarwsCoOh	03	07	16
Foreman, Jacob(Z-M)	1834	Sept. 30	TuscarwsCoOh	01	08	04
Forguson, James(Z-M)	1822	Oct. 29	GuernseyCoOh	04	03	18
Forguson, James(Z-M)	1836	Feb. 25	GuernseyCoOh	04	03	19
Forkey, Thomas(Z)	1815	April 22	WashngtnCoOh	08	07	36
Fornay, Christian(Z-M)	1835	May 18	TuscarwsCoOh	03	07	20
Forney, Christain(Z-M)	1832	Dec. 22	TuscarwsCoOh	03	07	20
Forney, Jacob(Z)	1814	Sept. 07	TuscarwsCoOh	05	09	05
Forney, Joseph(Z-M)	1830	March 13	TuscarwsCoOh	04	07	05
Forney, Samuel(Z-M)	1836	May 21	TuscarwsCoOh	03	07	19
Forney, Samuel(Z-M)	1836	Nov. 21	TuscarwsCoOh	03	07	12
Fornwald, John(Z-M)	1828	June 04	HolmesCoOhio	05	08	07
Forquar, John J.(Z)	1833	Aug. 03	Perry Co.,Oh	15	15	25
Forrest, John(Z-M)	1831	June 27	BelmontCo,Oh	01	01	20
Forrest, Thos. Sands(Z-M)	1837	April 08	GuernseyCoOh	04	03	08
Forry, Henry(Z-M)	1836	June 29	TuscarwsCoOh	03	08	24
Forse, John(Z)	1808	March 07	MuskingmCoOh	14	15	17
Forshey, Thomas Jr.(Z)	1836	April 28	MonroeCo.,Oh	08	06	24
Forshey, Thos.(Z)	1837	April 25	MonroeCo.,Oh	08	06	24
Forster, George(Y)	1825	Nov. 07	HarrisonCoOh	05	13	28
Forster, George(Y)	1828	May 05	Jeff.Co.,Oh.	05	13	28
Forsyth, John(Z)	1806	July 01	WashngtnCoOh	15	16	17
Forsyth, Robert(Z)	1816	June 04	WashCo.,Penn	10	09	19
Forsythe, David(Z)	1814	March 17	?	11	13	04
Forsythe, E.(Z)	1815	Dec. 06	MuskingmCoOh	11	13	30
Forsythe, Elijah(Z)	1815	May 31	IndianaCo,Pa	04	02	25
Forsythe, John(Z-M)	1830	Jan. 15	WashCo.,Penn	04	03	24
Forsythe, John(Z-M)	1830	Feb. 02	WashCo.,Penn	04	03	24
Forsythe, Robert(Z)	1815	Jan. 04	GuernseyCoOh	03	03	09

PURCHASER	YEAR	DATE	RESIDENCE	R	T	S
Forsythe, Thomas(Z-M)	1834	Nov. 05	MuskingmCoOh	04	03	24
Forsythe, W.(Z)	1815	Nov. 23	WashCo.,Penn	05	02	11
Forsythe, W.(Z)	1815	Dec. 06	MuskingmCoOh	11	13	30
Forsythe, Wm.(Z)	1814	Nov. 03	IndianaCo,Pa	11	13	31
Fortune, Andrew(Z-M)	1836	Nov. 23	CoshoctnCoOh	07	05	04
Fortune, Jacob(Z-M)	1837	March 17	CoshoctnCoOh	08	07	02
Fortune, Peter(Z-M)	1837	March 17	CoshoctnCoOh	08	07	03
Fose, Henry(Z-M)	1839	March 16	CoshoctnCoOh	09	07	20
Foster, Andrew(Z)	1829	March 03	Morgan Co,Oh	13	10	36
Foster, Andrew(Z)	1814	Feb. 19	Brooke CoVir	11	13	29
Foster, Archibald Jr.(Z)	1832	Sept. 18	Morgan Co,Oh	10	07	04
Foster, Archibald(Z)	1835	Feb. 26	Morgan Co,Oh	10	08	35
Foster, Benjamin(Z)	1813	Nov. 22	SomersetCoOh	08	04	01
Foster, Benjamin(Z)	1814	Feb. 19	Brooke CoVir	11	13	32
Foster, Charles(Z-M)	1836	Jan. 21	MuskingmCoOh	05	03	03
Foster, Charles(Z-M)	1836	Nov. 14	FayetteCo,Pa	05	03	03
Foster, Christ'n.(Z-M)	1831	Oct. 07	Jeff.Co.,Oh.	03	04	08
Foster, Daniel(Z)	1833	Feb. 16	Morgan Co,Oh	10	08	35
Foster, Daniel(Z-M)	1830	Sept. 18	TuscarwsCoOh	04	09	15
Foster, David(Z-M)	1825	June 20	GuernseyCoOh	01	01	10
Foster, Frederick(Y)	1831	Sept. 16	ColumbanCoOh	07	16	06
Foster, George(Y)	1822	Aug. 20	TrumbullCoOh	06	19	17
Foster, Greer(Z-M)	1824	Nov. 11	CoshoctnCoOh	07	08	04
Foster, James(Z)	1817	June 03	Jeff.Co.,Oh.	06	06	01
Foster, John(Y)	1824	Nov. 10	WashCo.,Penn	05	14	10
Foster, John(Y)	1828	Nov. 29	HarrisonCoOh	05	14	21
Foster, John(Z)	1825	Oct. 17	GuernseyCoOh	11	12	01
Foster, Jonathan(Z-M)	1838	Jan. 04	MuskingmCoOh	04	03	08
Foster, Sam'l.(Z)	1829	March 03	Morgan Co,Oh	13	10	36
Foster, Sarah(Z-M)	1835	Sept. 19	CoshoctnCoOh	05	08	24
Foster, Thomas(Z)	1816	Aug. 05	CoshoctnCoOh	05	04	04
Foster, Thos. Wiles(Z-M)	1834	Oct. 29	LickingCo,Oh	10	03	16
Foster, Thos. Wiles(Z-M)	1834	Oct. 29	LickingCo,Oh	10	03	16
Foster, William(Z)	1814	Nov. 29	HarrisonCoOh	07	05	06
Foster, Wilson Lee(Z)	1834	March 25	GuernseyCoOh	10	09	25
Fouck, John(Z)	1811	Sept. 20	Wood Co.,Vir	11	11	34
Foulke, Sam'l. M.(Y)	1825	May 30	Bucks Co.,Pa	07	09	26
Fourdice, Stanton(Z)	1807	Jan. 03	WashngtnCoOh	11	11	27
Fourdice, Stanton(Z)	1812	June 03	WashngtnCoOh	11	07	27
Fouse, Wm.(Y)	1822	Oct. 31	HuntngdnCoPa	08	12	22
Foust, John(Y)	1822	March 20	Stark Co.,Oh	09	12	21
Fout, John(Z)	1823	Nov. 01	Morgan Co,Oh	13	10	26
Fouts, Absalom(Z)	1817	May 26	Brooke CoVir	11	11	19
Fouts, Allen(Z)	1814	Jan. 12	BrookeCo,Vir	11	11	18
Fouts, Andrew(Z)	1814	Jan. 12	Brooke CoVir	11	11	19
Fouts, J.(Z)	1815	April 17	Brooke CoVir	12	11	24
Fouts, J.(Z)	1815	May 12	Brooke CoVir	11	11	19
Fouts, Jacob(Z)	1815	April 28	LickingCo,Oh	11	04	15
Fouts, Jacob(Z)	1813	Oct. 25	BrookCo.,Vir	11	11	29
Fouts, John(Z)	1830	Feb. 04	MuskingmCoOh	13	10	36
Fouts, Lamen(Z)	1814	Jan. 17	Brooke CoVir	11	11	27
Fouts, Lemmon(Z)	1817	June 20	WashngtnCoOh	11	11	20
Fouts, W.(Z)	1815	April 17	Brooke CoVir	12	11	24
Fovedieu, Libbens(Z)	1838	Oct. 17	MonroeCo.,Oh	08	06	21
Fowler, Andrew W.(Z-M)	1835	March 25	CarrolCo.,Oh	01	08	04
Fowler, Andrew(Y)	1830	Sept. 04	TuscarwsCoOh	07	15	02
Fowler, Benj'm.(Z)	1826	Jan. 04	Morgan Co,Oh	10	08	13
Fowler, Cherry(Z)	1832	May 30	Morgan Co,Oh	09	07	08
Fowler, Dan'l.(Z)	1835	March 20	Brooke CoVir	10	07	18
Fowler, Dan'l.(Z)	1835	April 04	Brooke CoVir	10	07	07
Fowler, John Jr.(Y)	1829	June 25	HarrisonCoOh	06	12	30
Fowler, John Junr.(Z-M)	1833	Dec. 16	LickingCo,Oh	10	04	13
Fowler, John(Y)	1825	May 09	HarrisonCoPa	06	12	23
Fowler, John(Y)	1831	Feb. 03	HarrisonCoOh	06	12	29
Fowler, John(Y)	1831	June 21	Stark Co.,Oh	06	15	33
Fowler, John(Z)	1836	July 29	HolmesCoOhio	10	06	06
Fowler, John(Z)	1811	Dec. 12	MuskingmCoOh	15	15	09
Fowler, John(Z-M)	1832	Sept. 15	LickingCo,Oh	10	04	18
Fowler, John(Z-M)	1833	Oct. 10	HolmesCoOhio	09	08	02

PURCHASER	YEAR	DATE	RESIDENCE	R	T	S
Fowler, John(Z-M)	1836	March 23	HolmesCoOhio	09	08	02
Fowler, John(Z-M)	1840	April 09	CoshoctnCoOh	10	07	22
Fowler, Manlove(Z-M)	1833	Jan. 25	LickingCo,Oh	11	04	12
Fowler, Manlove(Z)	1833	Feb. 08	LickingCo,Oh	11	04	13
Fowler, Memlov.(Z-M)	1831	March 01	LickingCo,Oh	11	04	12
Fowler, Richard(Z-M)	1835	Sept. 07	CoshoctnCoOH	05	04	04
Fowler, Royal(Z)	1832	Oct. 08	Morgan Co,Oh	09	07	08
Fowler, Royal(Z)	1832	Oct. 10	Morgan Co,Oh	09	07	08
Fowler, Thomas(Z)	1826	Feb. 21	MuskingmCoOH	14	13	09
Fowler, William M.(Z)	1832	July 07	Morgan Co,Oh	08	06	30
Fowler, William(Z)	1815	Oct. 16	MuskingmCoOH	14	13	30
Fowler, Zachariah(Z)	1814	April 09	MuskingmCoOH	08	03	07
Fowls, Wm.(Z-M)	1833	Oct. 21	KnoxCo.,Ohio	11	05	20
Fox, Amos(Z-M)	1836	June 04	CoshoctnCoOh	07	07	19
Fox, Eli(Z-M)	1822	Dec. 25	CoshoctnCoOH	07	07	13
Fox, Ely(Z-M)	1820	July 01	MuskingmCoOH	07	07	18
Fox, Ely(Z-M)	1820	Nov. 29	MuskingmCoOH	07	07	18
Fox, Ely(Z-M)	1827	March 19	CoshoctnCoOh	07	07	23
Fox, Ely(Z-M)	1831	Aug. 29	CoshoctnCoOH	07	07	19
Fox, Ely(Z-M)	1833	Jan. 24	CoshoctnCoOh	07	07	19
Fox, Ely(Z-M)	1833	Feb. 05	CoshoctnCoOh	07	07	18
Fox, Ely(Z-M)	1826	March 22	CoshoctnCoOh	07	07	18
Fox, Ely(Z-M)	1836	Feb. 05	CoshoctnCoOh	07	07	18
Fox, Ely(Z-M)	1837	Feb. 04	CoshoctnCoOh	07	07	18
Fox, Ely(Z-M)	1837	Feb. 04	CoshoctnCoOh	07	07	18
Fox, Ely(Z-M)	1837	March 04	CoshoctnCoOh	07	07	17
Fox, Ira(Z-M)	1836	Feb. 02	CoshoctnCoOh	07	07	14
Fox, Isaac(Z-M)	1833	Jan. 28	GuernseyCoOh	03	01	18
Fox, Isaac(Z-M)	1833	Oct. 19	GuernseyCoOh	03	01	18
Fox, Nathaniel(Z)	1834	Jan. 16	Morgan Co,Oh	11	11	15
Foy, William(Z-M)	1832	Sept. 17	GuernseyCoOh	03	02	10
Foy, Wm. Senr.(Z)	1809	Nov. 15	FranklinCoVa	02	02	20
Frail, Patrick O.(Z)	1834	Sept. 03	Perry Co.,Oh	14	13	06
Fraim, David(Z)	1806	Nov. 05	MuskingmCoOh	01	01	23
Fraim, James(Z)	1807	Nov. 23	FayetteCo,Pa	09	04	23
Fraim, James(Z)	1807	Nov. 23	FayetteCo,Pa	03	03	08
Fraim, Thomas(Z)	1807	Oct. 22	FayetteCo,Pa	01	02	19
Fraim, Thomas(Z)	1807	Oct. 22	FayetteCo,Pa	01	02	18
Frakes, David(Z)	1831	June 06	Morgan Co,Oh	10	08	23
Frakes, George(Z)	1823	Dec. 04	Morgan Co,Oh	10	08	11
Frakes, George(Z)	1831	Dec. 30	Morgan Co,Oh	10	08	12
Frakes, Henry(Z)	1832	Sept. 19	Morgan Co,Oh	10	08	23
Frakes, Henry(Z)	1832	Sept. 19	Morgan Co,Oh	10	08	22
Frame, Amos(Z)	1836	Nov. 15	MuskingmCoOH	13	10	14
Frame, Christopher(Z-M)	1837	March 04	HarrisonCoOh	01	05	12
Frame, David Junr.(Z)	1816	July 26	GuernseyCoOh	01	02	06
Frame, David(Z)	1807	March 14	MuskingmCoOh	02	01	01
Frame, David(Z)	1808	Jan. 29	MuskingmCoOh	01	02	23
Frame, David(Z)	1816	Dec. 19	GuernseyCoOh	02	01	07
Frame, Daviee(Z)	1808	Jan. 29	MuskingmCoOh	01	02	23
Frame, Hugh(Z-M)	1837	Feb. 16	TuscarwsCoOh	02	06	01
Frame, Jacob(Z)	1832	Aug. 29	GuernseyCoOh	10	07	13
Frame, Jacob(Z)	1832	Aug. 29	GuernseyCoOh	10	07	13
Frame, Jacob(Z)	1833	March 08	GuernseyCoOh	13	10	02
Frame, James(Z)	1807	March 14	FayetteCo,Pa	01	02	24
Frame, James(Z)	1813	Dec. 29	GuernseyCoOh	01	02	22
Frame, James(Z)	1815	Oct. 02	GuernseyCoOh	01	02	23
Frame, James(Z)	1815	Nov. 25	GuernseyCoOh	10	07	23
Frame, James(Z-M)	1832	June 11	GuernseyCoOh	10	07	23
Frame, John(Z)	1808	April 02	FayetteCo,Pa	02	01	20
Frame, John(Z)	1808	April 02	FayetteCo,Pa	02	01	19
Frame, John(Z-M)	1825	Nov. 19	GuernseyCoOh	03	04	24
Frame, John(Z-M)	1832	March 06	GuernseyCoOh	02	01	14
Frame, John(Z-M)	1833	Jan. 09	GuernseyCoOh	03	04	18
Frame, Mifflin S.(Z)	1836	April 25	Morgan Co,Oh	13	08	27
Frame, Mifflin Sandors(Z)	1835	June 01	Morgan Co,Oh	14	13	35
Frame, Thomas(Z)	1815	July 26	GuernseyCoOh	01	02	18
Frame, Thos.(Z)	1815	Oct. 02	GuernseyCoOh	01	02	23
Frame, William Jr.(Z)	1813	March 26	GuernseyCoOh	01	02	24

PURCHASER	YEAR	DATE	RESIDENCE	R	T	S
Frame, William(Z)	1807	March 14	FayetteCo,Pa	01	02	24
Frame, William(Z)	1807	Sept. 09	MuskingmCoOh	01	02	24
Frame, William(Z)	1816	Dec. 19	GuernseyCoOh	02	01	07
Frame, William(Z-M)	1836	Jan. 09	GuernseyCoOh	03	04	17
France, John(Y)	1822	June 05	Jeff.Co.,Oh.	07	15	05
France, John(Z)	1833	April 22	Perry Co.,Oh	15	15	31
France, Susannah(Z)	1806	Dec. 10	MuskingmCoOh	06	01	20
Francis, James(Z)	1813	April 27	MuskingmCoOh	11	11	10
Francis, James(Z)	1815	June 03	MuskingmCoOh	11	11	31
Francis, James(Z)	1816	March 09	MuskingmCoOh	11	11	31
Franey, William(Z-M)	1829	Sept. 24	GuernseyCoOh	02	03	25
Franklin, Alex'r.(Z)	1821	April 25	MonroeCo.,Oh	08	07	12
Franklin, Alex'r.(Z)	1835	Dec. 02	MonroeCo.,Oh	08	07	13
Franklin, Alex'r.(Z)	1835	Dec. 02	MonroeCo.,Oh	08	07	14
Franklin, Calvin(Z)	1815	Oct. 23	BelmontCo,Pa	09	07	23
Franklin, Carey(Z)	1833	April 27	MonroeCo.,Oh	08	06	20
Franklin, Carey(Z)	1837	Jan. 28	MonroeCo.,Oh	08	06	33
Franklin, Charles(Z)	1807	June 23	Ohio Co.,Vir	15	18	15
Franklin, Jackson(Z)	1837	Jan. 12	MonroeCo.,Oh	08	06	33
Franklin, John(Z)	1820	Nov. 06	MonroeCo.,Oh	08	07	11
Franklin, Joseph(Z)	1815	Aug. 21	BelmontCo,Oh	09	07	36
Franklin, Nathan(Z)	1832	May 23	Morgan Co,Oh	09	06	21
Franklin, Nathan(Z)	1832	May 23	Morgan Co,Oh	09	06	28
Franklin, Nathun(Z)	1822	April 01	MonroeCo.,Oh	08	06	08
Franklin, Wilson(Z)	1833	April 27	MonroeCo.,Oh	08	06	20
Franz, Isaac(Z)	1806	Dec. 15	WestmrldCoPa	04	08	08
Frasey, Basil Junr.(Z)	1811	Oct. 04	FayetteCo,Pa	11	01	12
Fraunce, Adam(Z)	1805	May 09	MuskingmCoOh	14	16	15
Fraunce, Susanna(Z)	1806	Jan. 11	MuskingmCoOh	06	01	12
Fraunce, Susanna(Z)	1809	April 21	MuskingmCoOh	06	01	10
Fravel, Jacob(Z-M)	1835	Jan. 20	CoshoctnCoOh	09	04	05
Frazee, Nathan(Z)	1829	Sept. 12	MuskingmCoOh	12	13	11
Frazer, Davis(Z-M)	1830	Sept. 09	HolmesCoOhio	05	08	06
Frazer, Wm.(Z)	1809	May 30	MuskingmCoOh	12	13	27
Frazey, Samuel(Z-M)	1837	March 25	MuskingmCoOh	09	03	15
Frazey, Samuel(Z-M)	1837	March 25	MuskingmCoOh	09	03	15
Frazey, Samuel(Z-M)	1837	April 01	MuskingmCoOh	09	03	17
Frazier, Daniel(Z)	1816	May 29	MuskingmCoOh	12	12	35
Frazier, David(Z-M)	1829	Dec. 21	GuernseyCoOh	04	02	13
Frazier, James(Z)	1835	May 27	HarrisonCoOh	11	12	34
Frazier, James(Z-M)	1835	Dec. 11	GuernseyCoOh	03	03	04
Frazier, John(Z)	1831	Jan. 27	MuskingmCoOh	11	12	14
Frazier, John(Z)	1831	May 04	MuskingmCoOh	11	12	14
Frazier, John(Z)	1832	Dec. 28	MuskingmCoOh	11	12	14
Frazier, Rezin(Z-M)	1832	April 30	CoshoctnCoOh	05	04	09
Frazier, William(Z)	1830	Feb. 15	BelmontCo,Oh	12	13	34
Frazier, William(Z)	1836	March 05	BelmontCo,Oh	09	07	25
Frazy, Sam(Z)	1810	Feb. 14	MuskingmCoOh	13	12	14
Frebilcock, Frank(Z)	1833	March 15	Morgan Co,Oh	10	06	20
Frebilcock, Frank(Z)	1836	Jan. 19	Morgan Co,Oh	10	06	20
Frederick, David(Z-M)	1835	Dec. 28	HolmesCoOhio	08	07	20
Frederick, J. C.(Z-M)	1832	Sept. 14	CoshoctnCoOh	08	06	01
Frederick, Jacob(Z-M)	1836	Feb. 04	CoshoctnCoOh	08	07	21
Frederick, Jacob(Z-M)	1837	Oct. 23	CoshoctnCoOh	08	07	21
Frederick, Jno. Peter(Z)	1817	June 11	TuscarwsCoOh	01	06	01
Frederick, John C.(Z-M)	1834	March 17	CoshoctnCoOh	08	06	01
Frederick, John(Y)	1825	Nov. 14	ColumbanCoOh	06	18	22
Frederick, John(Z-M)	1836	Feb. 04	CoshoctnCoOh	08	06	01
Frederick, Mich'l.(Y)	1828	May 28	ColumbanCoOh	06	19	32
Frederick, Samuel(Y)	1828	May 26	Stark Co.,Oh	07	16	06
Freebey, George(Y)	1821	Sept. 18	Stark Co.,Oh	09	12	15
Freebey, George(Y)	1821	Sept. 18	Stark Co.,Oh	09	12	15
Freed, Peter(Y)	1826	Oct. 10	ColumbanCoOh	06	17	10
Freeman, Isaac(Z)	1810	May 10	BrookCo.,Vir	12	13	02
Freeman, James(Z-M)	1823	Nov. 28	GuernseyCoOh	03	01	13
Freeman, Jonathan(Z)	1834	Nov. 12	GuernseyCoOh	14	13	33
Freeman, Jonathan(Z)	1836	Dec. 10	Perry Co.,Oh	14	12	03
Freese, John Jr.(Z-M)	1836	March 08	CoshoctnCoOh	08	06	10
Freese, John Jr.(Z-M)	1836	March 08	CoshoctnCoOh	08	06	10

PURCHASER	YEAR	DATE	RESIDENCE	R	T	S
Freese, Joseph(Z-M)	1833	Jan. 19	CoshoctnCoOh	08	06	01
Freezell, Charles(Z)	1814	Feb. 16	FairfeldCoOh	15	16	03
Freidline, Henry(Z)	1809	Nov. 01	SomersetCoPa	03	09	22
Freil, James O.(Z)	1834	Oct. 11	Perry Co.,Oh	14	13	06
Frell, Amos(Z)	1812	Feb. 04	WestmrldCoPa	05	01	05
Frell, Francis(Z)	1832	Oct. 27	Perry Co.,Oh	15	15	12
Fremm, William(Z)	1817	Oct. 31	MuskingmCoOh	11	12	13
French, Jas. B.(Z)	1831	April 25	MuskingmCoOh	13	11	23
French, Samuel(Z-M)	1834	Dec. 17	TuscarwsCoOh	03	06	09
French, William(Y)	1825	Oct. 14	BelmontCo,Oh	06	10	31
Freshsraten, Reuben(Y)	1821	Sept. 21	Brooke CoVir	06	14	22
Freshsraten, Reuben(Y)	1821	Sept. 21	Brooke CoVir	06	14	22
Freshwater, Reuben(Y)	1822	June 15	Brooke CoVir	06	14	22
Freshwater, Reuben(Y)	1822	Oct. 31	Brooke CoVir	06	14	09
Freshwater, Reuben(Y)	1823	Nov. 29	BrookeCo,Vir	06	14	15
Freshwater, Reuben(Y)	1825	July 27	Brooke CoVir	06	14	10
Freshwater, Reuben(Y)	1829	March 17	Brooke CoVir	06	14	09
Freshwater, Reuben(Y)	1829	March 17	Brooke CoVir	06	14	10
Freshwater, Wm. Jr.(Z-M)	1833	Nov. 30	HolmesCoOhio	08	08	20
Freshwater, Wm. Junr.(Z-M)	1832	Aug. 14	HolmesCoOhio	08	07	01
Freshwater, Wm.(Z-M)	1835	Dec. 17	HolmesCoOhio	08	08	21
Freshwater, Wm.(Z-M)	1835	Dec. 18	HolmesCoOhio	08	08	21
Fresize, Francis(Z-M)	1833	Dec. 30	LickingCo,Oh	11	04	21
Freswater, George(Z-M)	1836	Jan. 26	HolmesCoOhio	08	07	01
Freswater, George(Z-M)	1836	Jan. 26	HolmesCoOhio	08	08	22
Fretz, Andrew(Z-M)	1831	Oct. 17	TuscarwsCoOh	04	06	03
Frew, David(Z-M)	1831	Oct. 10	CoshoctnCoOh	07	07	24
Frew, David(Z-M)	1837	Feb. 11	CoshoctnCoOh	06	04	22
Frew, John(Z-M)	1826	Oct. 06	CoshoctnCoOh	07	05	21
Frew, John(Z-M)	1836	July 13	CoshoctnCoOh	08	06	11
Frew, John(Z-M)	1836	Dec. 05	CoshoctnCoOh	08	06	14
Frew, John(Z-M)	1837	March 18	CoshoctnCoOh	06	04	09
Frew, John(Z-M)	1837	Nov. 22	CoshoctnCoOh	10	07	21
Frew, John(Z-M)	1836	June 27	CoshoctnCoOh	06	03	03
Frew, Thomas(Z-M)	1833	Oct. 29	TuscarwsCoOh	03	06	24
Frey, Henry F.(Z-M)	1828	May 14	GuernseyCoOh	03	01	23
Frey, James(Z-M)	1826	Feb. 22	KnoxCo.,Ohio	11	05	11
Frey, Jesse(Z-M)	1828	May 10	MuskingmCoOh	10	04	05
Frey, Sam'l. Senr.(Z-M)	1826	May 02	MuskingmCoOh	11	05	20
Frey, Sam'l.(Z-M)	1831	May 06	KnoxCo.,Ohio	11	05	20
Frick, Jacob(Z)	1816	June 05	FayetteCo,Pa	03	09	11
Friebely, Daniel(Z-M)	1835	Oct. 27	TuscarwsCoOh	02	07	04
Friebley, John(Z-M)	1832	July 03	TuscarwsCoOh	02	07	03
Friebly, Jacob(Z-M)	1833	June 26	TuscarwsCoOh	02	07	03
Friebly, William B.(Z-M)	1833	June 26	TuscarwsCoOh	02	07	02
Friel, James O.(Z)	1836	Sept. 27	Perry Co.,Oh	15	15	13
Friend, Corneilus(Y)	1830	Jan. 12	AlleghnyCoMd	04	13	26
Fright, Wm. W.(Y)	1821	Nov. 08	HarrisonCoOh	06	12	21
Frigs, Henry(Y)	1824	Oct. 13	WestmrldCoPa	06	17	31
Frint, Hiram(Z)	1835	Nov. 16	MonroeCo.,Oh	08	08	25
Frint, Hiram(Z)	1835	Aug. 27	MonroeCo.,Oh	08	08	35
Fritch, L.(Z-M)	1832	April 06	HarrisonCoOh	05	08	11
Frits, John(Y)	1826	Sept. 01	ColumbanCoOh	06	15	20
Fritz, John(Y)	1831	April 26	ColumbanCoOh	03	12	28
Frizzel, Chas.(Z)	1835	Dec. 24	Perry Co.,Oh	14	12	21
Frock, Jacob(Z-M)	1834	Aug. 26	TuscarwsCoOh	04	07	17
Frock, Michael(Z)	1827	April 17	CoshoctnCoOh	05	06	04
Frock, Michael(Z)	1814	May 30	TuscarwsCoOh	01	08	18
Frock, Michael(Z-M)	1833	April 11	CoshoctnCoOh	05	06	04
Frome, Jacob(Z-M)	1826	June 19	GuernseyCoOh	01	01	19
Frosch, Frederick(Z)	1835	March 24	Morgan Co,Oh	13	09	12
Frost, Enoch(Z-M)	1837	April 07	KnoxCo.,Ohio	10	07	19
Frost, Enoch(Z-M)	1837	April 07	KnoxCo.,Ohio	10	07	22
Frost, Isaiah(Z)	1814	Jan. 04	KnoxCo.,Ohio	11	08	21
Frost, Isaiah(Z)	1814	Jan. 04	KnoxCo.,Ohio	11	08	20
Frost, Isaiah(Z)	1814	Jan. 04	KnoxCo.,Ohio	11	08	11
Frost, Isaiah(Z)	1814	Jan. 04	KnoxCo.,Ohio	10	08	16
Frost, John(Z)	1811	Nov. 10	MuskingmCoOh	10	03	12
Frost, John(Z)	1815	Nov. 08	LickingCo,Oh	10	03	02

PURCHASER	YEAR	DATE	RESIDENCE	R	T	S
Frost, John(Z-M)	1834	Nov. 11	LickingCo,Oh	11	04	19
Frost, Joseph(Z-M)	1836	Jan. 07	LickingCo,Oh	10	04	07
Frost, Josiah(Z)	1831	May 13	KnoxCo.,Ohio	10	08	04
Frost, Josiah(Z-M)	1828	Nov. 21	KnoxCo.,Ohio	10	08	07
Frost, Josiah(Z-M)	1829	June 23	KnoxCo.,Ohio	10	08	07
Frost, Josiah(Z-M)	1831	Nov. 01	KnoxCo.,Ohio	10	08	06
Frost, Josiah(Z-M)	1832	June 08	KnoxCo.,Ohio	10	08	04
Frost, Josiah(Z-M)	1836	Aug. 30	KnoxCo.,Ohio	10	08	17
Frost, Josiah(Z-M)	1836	Aug. 30	KnoxCo.,Ohio	10	08	17
Frost, Josiah(Z-M)	1836	Aug. 30	KnoxCo.,Ohio	10	08	14
Frost, Josiah(Z-M)	1837	April 07	KnoxCo.,Ohio	10	07	22
Frueshwater, Geo.(Z-M)	1839	Feb. 20	HolmesCoOhio	08	07	01
Frusel, Solomon(Z-M)	1837	May 03	HarrisonCoOh	03	07	02
Fry, Abraham(Z)	1815	Nov. 03	KnoxCo.,Ohio	10	05	12
Fry, Abram(Z-M)	1825	Dec. 30	KnoxCo.,Ohio	10	05	08
Fry, And'w.(Z-M)	1821	June 14	CoshoctnCoOh	09	05	25
Fry, Enoch(Z)	1814	Nov. 02	CoshoctnCoOh	08	05	25
Fry, George C.(Z-M)	1835	Dec. 17	HolmesCoOhio	08	08	12
Fry, Henry Forgason(Z-M)	1832	March 21	GuernseyCoOh	03	01	22
Fry, Jacob(Z-M)	1827	March 21	HolmesCoOhio	07	08	11
Fry, John(Z)	1815	April 25	BedfordCo,Pa	09	05	20
Fry, John(Z-M)	1836	June 08	HolmesCoOhio	07	08	12
Fry, John(Z-M)	1837	April 21	HolmesCoOhio	08	08	13
Fry, John(Z-M)	1837	April 21	HolmesCoOhio	08	08	13
Fry, Marg't.(Z-M)	1821	June 14	CoshoctnCoOh	09	05	25
Fry, Noah Spears(Z-M)	1835	July 27	GuernseyCoOh	03	01	19
Fry, Peter(Z)	1817	Oct. 04	LoudonCo,Vir	13	10	29
Fry, Peter(Z)	1817	Oct. 04	LoudonCo,Vir	13	10	32
Fry, Spencer H.(Z-M)	1832	Aug. 22	CoshoctnCoOh	09	05	25
Fry, Thomas(Z-M)	1828	Jan. 16	TuscarwsCoOh	07	08	01
Fry, Thomas(Z-M)	1832	Sept. 10	HolmesCoOhio	07	08	01
Fry, Thomas(Z-M)	1835	Oct. 31	LickingCo,Oh	11	03	06
Fry, Thomas(Z-M)	1836	Jan. 26	LickingCo,Oh	11	03	06
Fry, William(Z)	1832	Feb. 03	CoshoctnCoOh	09	05	16
Fry, William(Z)	1830	Jan. 20	GuernseyCoOh	09	08	29
Fry, William(Z)	1835	Dec. 29	GuernseyCoOh	09	08	29
Fry, William(Z)	1816	Feb. 01	FrederkCoVir	09	08	29
Fuell, Jesse(Z)	1836	April 08	Perry Co.,Oh	14	13	21
Fukill, Joseph(Z)	1830	Aug. 31	Morgan Co,Oh	10	08	23
Fulkison, N. B.(Z)	1836	Feb. 05	GuernseyCoOh	08	07	21
Fulks, Joseph(Z)	1836	March 18	WashngtnCoOh	10	06	14
Fullar, Elias(Z-M)	1837	Oct. 09	GuernseyCoOh	04	05	22
Fullen, Hugh S. E.(Y)	1822	June 19	ColumbanCoOh	05	18	13
Fuller, Abel(Z-M)	1836	Sept. 01	GuernseyCoOh	04	04	11
Fuller, David(Z)	1813	Dec. 13	HampshreCoVa	02	01	23
Fuller, Elijah(Z-M)	1836	Jan. 05	CoshoctnCoOh	04	05	21
Fuller, Elijah(Z-M)	1837	July 12	CoshoctnCoOh	04	04	10
Fuller, Ellet(Z-M)	1832	Oct. 08	GuernseyCoOh	03	04	10
Fuller, Jacob(Z-M)	1836	Oct. 24	GuernseyCoOh	02	04	16
Fuller, Johiel(Z-M)	1833	Aug. 08	GuernseyCoOh	03	04	10
Fuller, Johiel(Z-M)	1833	Aug. 08	GuernseyCoOh	03	04	10
Fuller, Alvan(Z)	1814	March 28	WashngtnCo ?	11	11	30
Fuller, Joseph(Z-M)	1835	Dec. 31	GuernseyCoOh	04	04	22
Fuller, Joseph(Z-M)	1836	Jan. 25	GuernseyCoOh	04	04	18
Fuller, Thomas R.(Z-M)	1834	Aug. 15	GuernseyCoOh	04	04	23
Fuller, Thomas R.(Z-M)	1836	Jan. 25	GuernseyCoOh	04	04	18
Fuller, Thomas(Z)	1807	Dec. 28	MuskingmCoOh	04	04	18
Fuller, Thomas(Z)	1807	Dec. 28	MuskingmCoOh	04	04	19
Fuller, Thomas(Z)	1812	Dec. 18	GuernseyCoOh	04	04	13
Fuller, William(Z-M)	1836	Jan. 22	GuernseyCoOh	03	03	12
Fulton & Kirker(Z)	1809	Dec. 23	MuskingmCoOh	08	02	23
Fulton, David(Y)	1832	Nov. 27	ColumbanCoOh	04	13	14
Fulton, David(Z)	1826	May 11	HarrisonCoOh	12	11	22
Fulton, Hugh(Z)	1825	Aug. 27	HarrisonCoOh	12	11	22
Fulton, Jos.(Z-M)	1824	Dec. 02	CoshoctnCoOh	05	04	17
Fulton, Levi(Z)	1832	April 11	Perry Co.,Oh	15	15	33
Fulton, Marius(Z-M)	1824	Dec. 02	CoshoctnCoOh	05	04	17
Fulton, Rob't.(Z)	1811	Aug. 20	ZanesvilleOh	03	02	07
Fulton, Rob't.(Z)	1811	Aug. 20	ZanesvilleOh	03	02	07

102

PURCHASER	YEAR	DATE	RESIDENCE	R	T	S
Fulton, Robert Junr.(Z)	1824	Aug. 03	Morgan Co,Oh	10	07	19
Fulton, Robert(Z)	1834	July 29	Morgan Co,Oh	10	07	19
Fulton, Robert(Z)	1835	May 04	LoudonCo,Vir	10	07	19
Fulton, Robert(Z)	1811	Aug. 05	MuskingmCoOh	02	02	11
Fulton, Robt.(Z)	1810	Jan. 06	MuskingmCoOh	12	13	20
Fulton, Samuel(Z)	1816	Dec. 11	FairfeldCoOh	11	01	09
Fulton, William(Z-M)	1831	March 03	HarrisonCoOh	04	02	03
Fulton, Wm.(Y)	1825	March 23	Huron Co.,Oh	07	12	23
Funck, Jacob(Y)	1832	April 14	Stark Co.,Oh	09	11	13
Funk, Jacob(Y)	1828	July 07	Stark Co.,Oh	09	11	13
Funk, Jacob(Z)	1806	Jan. 20	FairfeldCoOh	15	17	23
Funk, Jacob(Z-M)	1821	June 25	TuscarwsCoOh	04	09	24
Funk, Jacob(Z-M)	1835	May 04	CoshoctnCoOh	05	06	04
Funston, Robert(Z-M)	1820	Sept. 21	CoshoctnCoOh	06	07	20
Fuoney, John(Z-M)	1838	Nov. 14	GuernseyCoOh	03	04	06
Furbay, James(Z-M)	1831	April 07	TuscarwsCoOh	01	06	23
Furbay, James(Z-M)	1832	Aug. 14	TuscarwsCoOh	01	06	24
Furney, Abraham(Z)	1810	March 27	Jeff.Co.,Oh.	03	04	14
Furney, Abraham(Z-M)	1825	April 02	GuernseyCoOh	03	04	17
Furney, Abraham(Z-M)	1827	March 20	GuernseyCoOh	03	04	14
Furney, Abraham(Z-M)	1836	March 07	GuernseyCoOh	03	04	17
Furney, Frederick(Z-M)	1835	May 21	GuernseyCoOh	03	04	05
Furney, Frederick(Z-M)	1835	May 21	GuernseyCoOh	04	04	01
Furney, Frederick(Z-M)	1836	Feb. 23	GuernseyCoOh	04	04	01
Furney, Frederick(Z-M)	1838	April 23	GuernseyCoOh	03	05	25
Furney, John(Z-M)	1838	Feb. 02	GuernseyCoOh	03	04	06
Furney, John(Z-M)	1838	Feb. 02	GuernseyCoOh	03	04	15
Furney, Solomon(Z-M)	1838	Sept. 14	GuernseyCoOh	03	04	17
Fussel, William(Z)	1836	June 29	AthensCoOhio	15	14	27
Gaber, John(Z)	1832	Nov. 16	Perry Co.,Oh	14	12	20
Gad, Ignatus(Z)	1811	Feb. 25	Ohio Co.,Vir	08	02	11
Gadd, George(Z)	1834	Jan. 10	Morgan Co,Oh	13	08	22
Gadd, Ignatus(Z)	1811	Feb. 25	Ohio Co.,Vir	08	02	11
Gaddis, Jacob(Z)	1805	Nov. 14	FayetteCo,Pa	14	14	32
Gaddis, Jacob(Z)	1805	Nov. 14	FayetteCo,Pa	14	14	09
Gaddis, Jacob(Z)	1805	Nov. 14	FayetteCo,Pa	13	12	08
Gain, John Senr.(Z)	1815	Dec. 18	CoshoctnCoOh	06	09	04
Galagher, Hugh(Z-M)	1835	Nov. 26	GuernseyCoOh	04	03	21
Galagher, Hugh(Z-M)	1836	Jan. 15	GuernseyCoOh	04	03	21
Galbreath, Robert(Z-M)	1832	June 05	Jeff.Co.,Oh.	01	05	13
Galbreath, Robert(Z-M)	1832	July 30	Jeff.Co.,Oh.	01	05	13
Galbrith, James(Z-M)	1836	Feb. 17	TuscarwsCoOh	01	05	17
Gale, John(Z)	1836	Nov. 29	AthensCoOhio	14	12	29
Gale, Joseph(Z)	1815	March 08	MuskingmCoOh	10	03	09
Galehar, Peter(Z)	1816	March 23	MuskingmCoOh	05	01	05
Gales, Stephen(Z)	1815	Dec. 19	WashngtnCoOh	12	11	25
Galey, Robert(Y)	1824	May 19	BelmontCo,Oh	06	09	15
Galihar, Peter(Z)	1810	April 24	WestmrldCoPa	05	01	04
Gall, George(Y)	1829	Aug. 10	Stark Co.,Oh	07	17	28
Gallaher, Dominick(Y)	1833	Nov. 04	ColumbanCoOh	03	13	31
Gallaher, Francis(Y)	1834	April 26	PittsburghPa	03	12	36
Galland, Mathew(Z)	1806	May 05	WashngtnCoOh	11	11	36
Gallatin, Jeremiah(Z-M)	1828	Dec. 06	GuernseyCoOh	02	03	04
Gallentine, Jeremiah(Z-M)	1833	June 04	GuernseyCoOh	02	04	17
Galliway, William(Z-M)	1825	Dec. 30	GuernseyCoOh	07	05	14
Galliway, William(Z-M)	1836	March 21	CoshoctnCoOh	07	05	07
Galliway, William(Z-M)	1836	March 21	CoshoctnCoOh	07	05	13
Galliway, William(Z-M)	1836	July 04	CoshoctnCoOh	07	05	13
Galliway, Wm.(Z-M)	1836	Aug. 08	CoshoctnCoOh	07	05	13
Gallougher, Sam'l.(Z-M)	1833	May 31	GuernseyCoOh	03	05	20
Gallougher, Sam'l.(Z-M)	1833	May 31	GuernseyCoOh	03	05	19
Galloway & Harris(Z-M)	1830	July 06	GuernseyCoOh	03	01	24
Galloway & Haws(Z-M)	1830	July 06	GuernseyCoOh	03	01	24
Galloway, Benj.(Z-M)	1829	June 12	BelmontCo,Oh	03	01	25
Galloway, Enoch(Y)	1825	Feb. 09	GuernseyCoOh	07	09	15
Galloway, William(Z-M)	1832	April 28	CoshoctnCoOh	07	05	07
Galloway, William(Z-M)	1832	July 31	CoshoctnCoOh	07	05	07
Galloway, Wm.(Z-M)	1832	Feb. 08	CoshoctnCoOh	07	05	08
Galloway, Wm.(Z-M)	1832	June 09	CoshoctnCoOh	07	05	07

PURCHASER	YEAR	DATE	RESIDENCE	R	T	S
Gallwitz, Charles(Y)	1826	Aug. 07	Stark Co.,Oh	09	10	01
Galoway, Elijah(Z-M)	1822	March 19	GuernseyCoOh	04	01	12
Gamble, George(Y)	1822	Sept. 30	TuscarwsCoOh	07	14	12
Gamble, George(Y)	1829	Nov. 12	TuscarwsCoOh	07	14	09
Gamble, George(Y)	1829	Nov. 12	TuscarwsCoOh	07	14	09
Gamble, George(Y)	1830	March 10	TuscarwsCoOh	07	14	18
Gamble, George(Y)	1830	Sept. 15	TuscarwsCoOh	07	14	30
Gamble, George(Y)	1831	March 30	TuscarwsCoOh	07	14	18
Gamble, Jno. Robinson(Z-M)	1836	Jan. 19	KnoxCo.,Ohio	10	07	21
Gamble, John Robinson(Z-M)	1838	Dec. 08	CoshoctnCoOh	10	07	22
Gamble, Robert(Y)	1821	Sept. 24	RuscarwsCoOh	06	14	22
Gamble, William(Y)	1829	Dec. 10	TuscarwsCoOh	06	13	32
Gamble, William(Z)	1836	Nov. 08	GuernseyCoOh	08	05	05
Gamble, Wm.(Y)	1824	May 20	TuscarwsCoOh	06	13	23
Gament, Francis(Z-M)	1834	Jan. 06	TuscarwsCoOh	02	08	24
Gamertsfeldor, John(Z-M)	1837	Dec. 09	CoshoctnCoOh	08	07	02
Gamertsfeldor, John(Z-M)	1838	Jan. 05	CoshoctnCoOh	08	07	02
Gander, David(Z-M)	1835	April 01	MuskingmCoOh	07	05	18
Gander, George(Z)	1828	June 28	MuskingmCoOh	12	12	04
Gander, George(Z)	1828	July 04	MuskingmCoOh	12	12	04
Gandows, Archibald(Z-M)	1832	June 02	CoshoctnCoOh	09	04	07
Gandy, Isaiah(Z-M)	1829	May 18	LickingCo,Oh	10	02	18
Gandy, James(Z)	1828	Nov. 26	BelmontCo,Oh	13	08	09
Gandy, John(Z)	1826	Oct. 26	BelmontCo,Oh	13	08	09
Gang, Wm.(Z)	1824	Aug. 14	Morgan Co,Oh	13	10	35
Gans, Jonathan(Y)	1826	May 29	Stark Co.,Oh	06	19	28
Ganson, Philip(Z-M)	1835	April 23	MuskingmCoOh	04	04	03
Ganson, Philip(Z-M)	1836	March 09	CoshoctnCoOh	04	04	03
Gant, Richard(Z-M)	1836	Sept. 15	AlleghnyCoPa	04	03	20
Gant, Richard(Z-M)	1837	Jan. 10	GuernseyCoOh	04	03	20
Ganter, Frederick(Z)	1813	Nov. 12	SomersetCoPa	03	08	25
Ganter, Frederick(Z)	1813	Nov. 12	SomersetCoOh	03	08	16
Ganter, George(Z)	1813	Nov. 13	SomersetCoPa	04	07	08
Ganter, Jacob(Z)	1813	Nov. 12	SomersetCoPa	04	07	02
Ganter, Peter(Z)	1815	May 30	SomersetCoPa	05	08	17
Gantrell, John(Y)	1831	July 05	TuscarwsCoOh	07	14	17
Garaghty, Michael(Z)	1816	Nov. 19	Lancester,Oh	15	15	32
Garbe, Peter(Z-M)	1838	Jan. 30	CoshoctnCoOh	09	07	21
Garber, Christian(Z-M)	1833	April 20	TuscarwsCoOh	04	08	24
Garbey, Christian(Z-M)	1835	Sept. 08	CoshoctnCoOh	06	04	21
Gard, John(Z)	1809	Oct. 27	FayetteCo,Pa	04	08	03
Gard, John(Z)	1814	April 05	TuscarwsCoOh	04	08	04
Gard, John(Z)	1814	May 30	TuscarwsCoOh	04	08	05
Gard, John(Z)	1814	Oct. 10	TuscarwsCoOh	04	09	24
Gard, Lot(Z)	1813	June 09	WashngtnCoOh	11	10	13
Gard, Lott(Z)	1825	March 08	Morgan Co,Oh	10	06	21
Gard, T.(Z)	1816	March 30	LickingCo,Oh	12	09	17
Gard, Timothy(Z)	1810	March 13	LickingCo,Oh	10	06	11
Gardener, Jacob(Z)	1816	Oct. 28	WestmrldCoPa	06	08	23
Gardiner, Alonza(Z-M)	1838	Oct. 06	ColumbanCoOh	09	08	25
Gardiner, James(Y)	1825	Oct. 22	GuernseyCoOh	07	10	22
Gardner, Amos(Z)	1811	March 02	WashngtnCoOh	13	09	35
Gardner, Arch'd.(Z)	1817	April 07	AlleghnyCoPa	09	04	07
Gardner, Archibald(Z)	1816	Nov. 23	AlleghnyCoPa	09	04	18
Gardner, Archibald(Z-M)	1837	Feb. 17	CoshoctnCoOh	03	05	01
Gardner, David(Z-M)	1833	March 18	GreenCo.,Pa.	01	05	13
Gardner, David(Z-M)	1833	March 18	GreenCo.,Pa.	01	05	13
Gardner, David(Z-M)	1833	March 18	GreenCo.,Pa.	01	05	18
Gardner, David(Z-M)	1833	Sept. 07	TuscarwsCoOh	01	05	13
Gardner, Garret(Z)	1831	June 14	Morgan Co,Oh	13	08	10
Gardner, George(Z)	1811	Nov. 07	MuskingmCoOh	15	16	33
Gardner, Isaac Senr.(Z)	1817	Jan. 16	HarrisonCoOh	01	04	03
Gardner, James(Z)	1832	March 27	Perry Co.,Oh	15	15	23
Gardner, John Dorsey(Z)	1832	March 21	Perry Co.,Oh	15	15	23
Gardner, John S.(Z-M)	1836	Jan. 27	TuscarwsCoOh	01	05	12
Gardner, John(Z)	1806	Oct. 01	MuskingmCoOh	14	14	04
Gardner, John(Z-M)	1831	Jan. 27	CoshoctnCoOh	05	07	21
Gardner, Leonard(Z)	1831	Nov. 22	Morgan Co,Oh	11	10	14
Gardner, Leonard(Z)	1831	March 05	BelmontCo,Oh	11	10	14

PURCHASER	YEAR	DATE	RESIDENCE	R	T	S
Gardner, William(Z)	1806	Jan. 30	MuskingmCoOh	13	12	07
Gardner, William(Z-M)	1833	Jan. 25	LickingCo,Oh	10	04	17
Garlington, Conaway(Z)	1835	June 27	GuernseyCoOh	09	06	06
Garlington, Thomas(Z)	1835	June 20	GuernseyCoOh	09	06	08
Garman, Moses(Z)	1833	Feb. 23	Morgan Co,Oh	11	11	25
Garman, Moses(Z)	1807	June 05	Ohio Co.,Vir	15	18	09
Garnent, Francis(Z-M)	1834	Jan. 06	TuscarwsCoOh	02	08	24
Garner, James D.(Z)	1827	Nov. 09	MuskingmCoOh	09	01	08
Garner, John(Z-M)	1830	May 10	TuscarwsCoOh	04	08	22
Garner, Sarah(Z-M)	1833	Nov. 20	LickingCo,Oh	10	04	06
Garrett, Edward B.(Z)	1833	Dec. 23	HarrisonCoOh	11	11	12
Garrett, Ezra(Y)	1831	Dec. 15	BelmontCo,Oh	04	06	13
Garrett, Pennell(Z)	1829	Jan. 22	Morgan Co,Oh	13	10	34
Garrison, David(Z)	1832	April 14	Perry Co.,Oh	15	15	34
Garritson, Joel(Z)	1829	Jan. 06	BelmontCo,Oh	12	09	03
Garst, Frederick(Y)	1822	Oct. 02	LancastrCoPa	09	12	22
Garst, John(Z)	1836	Aug. 12	Wheeling,Vir	08	06	08
Gartner, John(Y)	1828	April 09	TuscarwsCoOh	06	16	31
Garver, Christian(Z-M)	1833	May 21	TuscarwsCoOh	04	08	24
Garver, James(Z-M)	1824	June 21	TuscarwsCoOh	04	07	01
Garver, John(Z)	1816	Nov. 05	FayetteCo,Pa	04	08	22
Garver, John(Z-M)	1829	Oct. 23	TuscarwsCoOh	02	10	17
Garver, John(Z-M)	1829	Oct. 23	TuscarwsCoOh	02	10	17
Garver, John(Z-M)	1831	June 02	TuscarwsCoOh	03	09	03
Garver, John(Z-M)	1833	Feb. 28	TuscarwsCoOh	03	10	23
Garver, Martin(Z-M)	1827	May 22	FayetteCo,Pa	04	07	13
Garvin, James(Z)	1827	Sept. 21	Morgan Co,Oh	09	06	20
Garvin, James(Z)	1836	June 01	Ohio Co.,Vir	15	14	12
Garvin, Matthew(Z)	1836	April 27	Morgan Co,Oh	08	05	30
Garvin, Matthew(Z)	1836	April 27	Morgan Co,Oh	08	05	29
Gaskell, Charles(Z-M)	1832	Oct. 20	GuernseyCoOh	03	04	03
Gaskell, Israel(Y)	1829	Oct. 03	ColumbanCoOh	06	19	21
Gaskell, James(Y)	1827	March 24	ColumbanCoOh	06	19	23
Gaskell, James(Y)	1827	Aug. 25	ColumbanCoOh	06	19	23
Gaskill, Abraham(Z-M)	1837	July 05	CoshoctnCoOh	04	05	19
Gaskill, Chas.(Z-M)	1835	Nov. 18	CoshoctnCoOh	04	04	15
Gaskill, John(Z)	1816	June 20	TuscarwsCoOh	03	06	24
Gaskill, John(Z-M)	1828	Feb. 02	TuscarwsCoOh	03	06	18
Gaskill, Nathan(Y)	1826	Nov. 08	Stark Co.,Oh	07	20	22
Gaskill, William(Z-M)	1835	June 26	CoshoctnCoOh	03	06	24
Gaskill, William(Z-M)	1835	Aug. 27	CoshoctnCoOh	03	06	24
Gassel, J. J.(Z)	1835	Dec. 22	Jeff.Co.,Oh.	09	05	22
Gaston, John P.(Z-M)	1833	July 01	KnoxCo.,Ohio	10	08	05
Gaston, Robert(Z)	1827	Nov. 05	BelmontCo,Oh	12	11	25
Gatchell, Hannah(Z)	1838	May 22	GuernseyCoOh	08	06	30
Gates, Gabriel(Z)	1832	July 27	Perry Co.,Oh	15	15	22
Gates, Rector(Z)	1814	April 13	AlleghnyCoPa	14	15	20
Gates, Stephen Junr.(Z)	1812	Oct. 24	WashngtnCoOh	11	10	31
Gates, Stephen Junr.(Z)	1812	Oct. 24	WashngtnCoOh	11	10	32
Gates, Timothy M.(Z)	1809	Sept. 11	MariettaOhio	12	11	33
Gates, Victor(Z)	1820	March 02	?	14	15	20
Gatshall, William(Z)	1815	June 05	Jeff.Co.,Oh.	05	07	22
Gatshull, Daniel(Z)	1816	June 25	HarrisonCoOh	05	07	21
Gatten, Richard(Z)	1833	Nov. 15	BelmontCo,Oh	11	12	34
Gatten, Sam'l.(Z)	1833	Nov. 15	BelmontCo,Oh	11	12	35
Gatwood, William(Z)	1837	March 30	Morgan Co,Oh	08	05	27
Gault, Adam(Z)	1815	Aug. 07	MercerCoPenn	09	04	02
Gaumer, Jacob(Z)	1815	Aug. 05	MuskingmCoOh	06	03	23
Gaumer, John(Z-M)	1836	July 16	MuskingmCoOh	04	04	03
Gause, Jesse(Z)	1817	June 14	ZanesvilleOh	10	04	23
Gause, Jesse(Z)	1817	June 30	ZanesvilleOh	12	10	09
Gay, Asa Junr.(Z-M)	1832	Aug. 31	KnoxCo.,Ohio	10	07	17
Gay, Asa(Z)	1832	July 06	MuskingmCoOh	12	12	19
Gay, Asa(Z)	1832	Sept. 17	MuskingmCoOh	13	09	12
Gay, Asa(Z)	1832	Sept. 17	MuskingmCoOh	12	12	18
Gay, Asa(Z)	1832	Sept. 17	MuskingmCoOh	12	12	18
Gay, John(Z)	1834	Jan. 24	MuskingmCoOh	11	12	22
Gearhart, Henry(Z-M)	1836	Jan. 05	CoshoctnCoOh	10	04	21
Geddes, Joseph(Z-M)	1836	Nov. 29	ColumbanCoOh	03	08	18

PURCHASER	YEAR	DATE	RESIDENCE	R	T	S
Geddis, Wm.(Z)	1829	Jan. 03	HarrisonCoOh	12	10	25
Geiger, Henry(Z-M)	1835	Dec. 10	HolmesCoOhio	08	08	09
Geiger, Jno.(Z)	1831	Dec. 02	Morgan Co,Oh	13	10	14
Gemand, Franz(Z)	1810	Jan. 06	TuscarwsCoOh	02	08	25
Gember, Jacob(Z)	1806	July 07	MuskingmCoOh	03	02	08
Gember, Jacob(Z)	1806	July 07	MuskingmCoOh	03	02	03
Gember, Jacob(Z)	1806	July 07	MuskingmCoOh	03	02	08
Gember, Jacob(Z)	1806	July 07	MuskingmCoOh	03	02	07
Gember, Jacob(Z)	1806	July 07	MuskingmCoOh	03	02	07
Gender, George(Z)	1830	March 09	MuskingmCoOh	12	13	33
Gentzler, John(Z-M)	1837	May 02	GuernseyCoOh	03	03	05
Gentzler, John(Z-M)	1837	May 02	GuernseyCoOh	03	03	05
Gentzler, Joseph(Z-M)	1837	May 02	GuernseyCoOh	03	03	06
George, Alex'r.(Z)	1815	Oct. 28	WashCo.,Penn	05	02	10
George, Catherine(Z)	1834	Jan. 25	Perry Co.,Oh	14	13	25
George, Isaac(Z)	1831	July 27	Morgan Co,Oh	14	13	09
George, Isaac(Z)	1833	April 11	Morgan Co,Oh	13	09	30
George, Isaac(Z)	1833	April 11	Morgan Co,Oh	13	09	30
George, Jacob(Z)	1815	Nov. 22	WashCo.,Penn	05	03	23
George, James(Y)	1827	July 18	GuernseyCoOh	07	09	33
George, Jesse(Z)	1820	Dec. 13	Morgan Co,Oh	10	08	34
George, Jesse(Z-M)	1834	Aug. 04	LickingCo,Oh	10	01	03
George, John(Y)	1828	March 06	ColumbanCoOh	03	13	20
George, John(Z)	1822	June 04	Morgan Co,Oh	10	08	28
George, John(Z)	1832	June 26	Morgan Co,Oh	14	14	22
George, John(Z)	1833	April 11	Morgan Co,Oh	14	14	26
George, John(Z)	1811	Sept. 14	MuskingmCoOh	14	16	17
George, John(Z)	1814	Nov. 25	?	09	01	19
George, John(Z)	1815	July 05	MuskingmCoOh	15	18	13
George, Lewis(Z)	1826	March 22	Morgan Co,Oh	10	08	27
George, Paul(Z)	1832	May 22	MuskingmCoOh	14	14	13
George, Presley(Z)	1829	June 08	Morgan Co,Oh	10	08	28
George, Presley(Z)	1835	Nov. 21	Morgan Co,Oh	10	08	33
George, Robert(Z-M)	1826	June 30	MuskingmCoOh	08	03	04
George, Robert(Z-M)	1827	May 10	MuskingmCoOh	08	03	04
George, Samuel(Z)	1834	Feb. 03	WashngtnCoOh	09	05	30
George, Thomas(Y)	1831	Aug. 04	Jeff.Co.,Oh.	04	13	15
George, Thomas(Y)	1839	April 15	Jeff.Co.,Oh.	03	11	29
George, William Senr.(Z)	1812	July 13	Pittsburg,Pa	15	18	12
George, William(Z)	1825	Sept. 15	MuskingmCoOh	13	11	12
George, William(Z)	1811	Sept. 14	MuskingmCoOh	14	16	17
George, William(Z-M)	1826	June 21	MuskingmCoOh	09	03	21
George, Wm.(Z)	1810	April 25	MuskingmCoOh	14	16	09
George, Wm.(Z)	1814	Nov. 25	?	09	01	19
Gepson, H.(Z)	1815	Dec. 25	BelmontCo,Oh	13	08	03
Gerber, Abraham(Z)	1807	July 13	SomersetCoPa	04	09	16
Gerber, Abraham(Z)	1810	Nov. 26	SomersetCoPa	04	09	17
Gerber, Abraham(Z)	1813	Sept. 13	TuscarwsCoOh	03	10	22
Gerber, Abraham(Z)	1813	Nov. 05	TuscarwsCoOh	03	10	22
German, Joel(Z)	1814	Feb. 15	MuskingmCoOh	15	18	01
Gernand, F.(Z)	1816	Aug. 20	?	02	08	16
Gernard, Franz(Z)	1810	Jan. 06	TuscarwsCoOh	02	08	25
Gerred, John(Z-M)	1837	Aug. 01	HolmesCoOhio	09	08	10
Gervis, Wm.(Y)	1821	Dec. 04	HarrisonCoOh	05	11	23
Gettel, Valentine(Z-M)	1835	April 23	TuscarwsCoOh	01	09	12
Gettle, Jacob(Y)	1823	Oct. 31	Stark Co.,Oh	07	19	22
Getzschia, Bernard(Y)	1834	Nov. 24	Jeff.Co.,Oh.	03	12	26
Gevin, John(Z-M)	1837	Sept. 09	HolmesCoOhio	08	08	20
Gevin, Rees(Z-M)	1828	July 16	MuskingmCoOh	05	02	06
Gevrez, Theodore(Z)	1836	Sept. 05	WashngtnCoOh	08	05	20
Geyer, Dan'l.(Z)	1831	March 14	MuskingmCoOh	10	08	02
Geyer, Daniel(Z)	1835	Nov. 14	MuskingmCoOh	09	05	26
Geyer, Daniel(Z)	1835	Nov. 14	MuskingmCoOh	09	05	27
Geyer, John(Z)	1816	Aug. 10	MuskingmCoOh	05	02	18
Gharky, Philip(Z)	1827	Oct. 10	TuscarwsCoOh	03	10	11
Gharky, Philip(Z-M)	1835	Jan. 06	TuscarwsCoOh	03	10	11
Gharp, Ethelbert(Y)	1831	March 28	ColumbanCoOh	03	12	18
Ghenky, Philip(Z-M)	1830	April 05	TuscarwsCoOh	03	10	20
Ghrist, John(Y)	1822	Sept. 24	SteubenvleOh	05	18	13

PURCHASER	YEAR	DATE	RESIDENCE	R	T	S
Gibbons, Geo. W.(Z)	1816	Sept. 25	MuskingmCoOh	12	12	35
Gibbons, George W.(Z)	1805	Aug. 15	Ohio Co.,Vir	13	12	07
Gibbons, George W.(Z)	1805	Sept. 10	Ohio Co.,Vir	12	13	07
Gibbons, George W.(Z)	1810	April 05	MuskingmCoOh	13	12	13
Gibbons, George W.(Z)	1810	Sept. 29	MuskingmCoOh	13	11	03
Gibbons, George(Y)	1826	May 30	ColumbanCoOh	02	09	11
Gibbons, John(Y)	1836	June 30	Jeff.Co.,Oh.	04	12	18
Gibbs, Dennis(Z)	1831	Nov. 24	Morgan Co,Oh	09	06	13
Gibbs, Dennis(Z)	1831	Nov. 24	Morgan Co,Oh	09	06	21
Gibbs, Dennis(Z)	1832	June 27	Morgan Co,Oh	09	06	13
Gibbs, Dennis(Z)	1832	June 27	Morgan Co,Oh	09	06	13
Gibbs, Dennis(Z)	1836	April 16	Morgan Co,Oh	09	06	13
Gibbs, Dennis(Z)	1817	Feb. 08	GuernseyCoOh	09	06	15
Gibbs, Johnathan Dudley(Z)	1832	Oct. 26	Morgan Co,Oh	09	06	22
Gibbs, Johnathan Dudley(Z)	1832	Oct. 26	Morgan Co,Oh	09	06	13
Gibbs, Levi(Z)	1832	July 25	Morgan Co,Oh	11	11	12
Gibeaut, Charles J. Jr.(Z)	1832	Dec. 19	MuskingmCoOh	11	12	15
Gibeaut, Charles J. Jr.(Z)	1832	Dec. 19	MuskingmCoOh	11	12	15
Gibs, Jesse(Z)	1816	Feb. 12	WashngtnCoOh	11	11	34
Gibson, Asa(Y)	1826	Sept. 08	ColumbanCoOh	04	17	06
Gibson, David(Y)	1822	Sept. 29	WarrenCo.,Pa	06	14	15
Gibson, Geo. Senr.(Z-M)	1833	Nov. 11	GuernseyCoOh	03	04	19
Gibson, George Jr.(Z-M)	1832	Oct. 12	GuernseyCoOh	03	03	03
Gibson, George(Z-M)	1828	Sept. 27	GuernseyCoOh	03	04	22
Gibson, James(Y)	1831	Dec. 22	Jeff.Co.,Oh.	04	12	32
Gibson, James(Z)	1826	Oct. 05	MonroeCo.,Oh	08	07	18
Gibson, James(Z)	1826	Oct. 05	MonroeCo.,Oh	08	07	18
Gibson, James(Z)	1833	Sept. 13	MonroeCo.,Oh	08	07	14
Gibson, James(Z)	1834	Dec. 20	MonroeCo.,Oh	08	07	18
Gibson, James(Z-M)	1835	Sept. 21	GuernseyCoOh	03	04	23
Gibson, John Jr.(Z-M)	1833	Nov. 26	GuernseyCoOh	03	04	22
Gibson, John N.(Z)	1814	Feb. 09	MuskingmCoOh	12	13	08
Gibson, John N.(Z)	1816	Feb. 02	MuskingmCoOh	12	11	09
Gibson, John(Z-M)	1832	June 15	GuernseyCoOh	03	04	22
Gibson, John(Z-M)	1832	June 15	GuernseyCoOh	03	04	23
Gibson, Joseph(Z)	1837	Jan. 20	MonroeCo.,Oh	08	07	33
Gibson, Joseph(Z)	1837	Jan. 20	MonroeCo.,Oh	08	07	34
Gibson, Robert(Y)	1830	Jan. 08	HarrisonCoOh	05	12	30
Gibson, Robert(Z-M)	1835	March 16	CarrolCo.,Oh	03	07	02
Gibson, Thomas(Y)	1831	April 28	Stark Co.,Oh	06	15	35
Gibson, Thomas(Z-M)	1836	Jan. 11	TuscarwsCoOh	01	06	24
Gibson, William(Z)	1807	April 06	BelmontCo,Oh	03	04	22
Gibson, William(Z-M)	1822	March 14	GuernseyCoOh	03	04	23
Gibson, William(Z-M)	1833	May 20	TuscarwsCoOh	03	07	16
Gibson, William(Z-M)	1833	Sept. 12	GuernseyCoOh	02	03	10
Gibson, William(Z-M)	1833	Sept. 12	GuernseyCoOh	02	03	11
Gibson, William(Z-M)	1833	Nov. 15	GuernseyCoOh	03	03	04
Gibson, William(Z-M)	1835	Nov. 11	GuernseyCoOh	03	03	04
Gibson, William(Z-M)	1836	Jan. 16	GuernseyCoOh	03	04	22
Gibson, Wm. Jr.(Z-M)	1828	Dec. 10	GuernseyCoOh	04	04	21
Gibson, Wm. Jr.(Z-M)	1835	Dec. 25	GuernseyCoOh	04	04	20
Gibson, Wm. Junr.(Z-M)	1827	Feb. 15	GuernseyCoOh	03	04	11
Gibson, Wm. Senr.(Z)	1807	May 16	BelmontCo,Oh	03	04	23
Giddes, William(Z)	1828	Sept. 27	HarrisonCoOh	12	10	25
Gier, John(Z)	1809	Dec. 05	KnoxCo.,Ohio	10	07	04
Giffen, Kelly(Z-M)	1836	Nov. 11	KnoxCo.,Ohio	10	06	05
Giffen, Robert(Z-M)	1836	Jan. 06	KnoxCo.,Ohio	10	06	04
Giffen, Robert(Z-M)	1836	Jan. 06	KnoxCo.,Ohio	10	06	07
Giffin, Hetty(Z-M)	1825	April 25	KnoxCo.,Ohio	10	07	24
Giffin, James(Z)	1815	Feb. 11	LickingCo,Oh	11	03	13
Giffin, John(Z)	1815	Aug. 25	LickingCo,Oh	11	03	14
Giffin, Robert(Z)	1813	April 05	CoshoctnCoOh	10	07	25
Giffin, Robert(Z-M)	1835	May 20	KnoxCo.,Ohio	10	06	05
Giffin, Robert(Z-M)	1837	April 26	KnoxCo.,Ohio	10	06	05
Giffin, William(Z-M)	1829	Oct. 31	TuscarwsCoOh	10	05	18
Giffin, William(Z-M)	1831	July 04	CoshoctnCoOh	08	07	18
Giffin, William(Z-M)	1832	Oct. 08	CoshoctnCoOh	10	06	18
Giffin, William(Z-M)	1832	Oct. 08	CoshoctnCoOh	10	06	18
Gifford, Marvin(Z)	1826	Aug. 18	Morgan Co,Oh	12	10	36

PURCHASER	YEAR	DATE	RESIDENCE	R	T	S
Gifford, William(Z-M)	1833	July 03	TuscarwsCoOh	01	08	02
Gilbert, Charles C.(Z)	1832	Nov. 20	ZanesvilleOh	10	07	33
Gilbert, Charles C.(Z)	1832	Nov. 20	ZanesvilleOh	11	10	01
Gilbert, Charles C.(Z)	1833	Dec. 02	ZanesvilleOh	08	07	31
Gilbert, Charles C.(Z)	1833	Dec. 03	ZanesvilleOh	10	07	34
Gilbert, Charles Jr.(Z)	1833	Dec. 07	MuskingmCoOh	11	12	15
Gilbert, Chas. C.(Z)	1833	Oct. 29	ZanesvilleOh	09	07	26
Gilbert, Chas. C.(Z-M)	1833	April 13	ZanesvilleOh	06	04	20
Gilbert, Chasl.(Z-M)	1831	July 19	ZanesvilleOh	11	06	15
Gilbert, Chasl.(Z-M)	1831	July 19	ZanesvilleOh	11	06	15
Gilbert, David Junr.(Z)	1835	Nov. 10	WashngtnCoOh	09	05	36
Gilbert, Isaac(Y)	1823	March 29	Stark Co.,Oh	07	20	03
Gilbert, Isaac(Y)	1826	June 24	Stark Co.,Oh	07	20	05
Gilbert, Jonas(Z-M)	1835	Dec. 05	HolmesCoOhio	06	08	20
Gilbert, Jonas(Z-M)	1837	June 10	HolmesCoOhio	08	07	14
Gilbert, Jonas(Z-M)	1837	June 10	HolmesCoOhio	08	07	15
Gilbert, Joseph(Y)	1829	April 02	HarrisonCoOh	06	11	11
Gilbreath, Fortunatus(Z)	1833	Sept. 13	Morgan Co,Oh	10	08	12
Giler, William(Z)	1834	Oct. 06	MonroeCo.,Oh	08	07	11
Giler, Wm.(Z)	1833	Nov. 14	MonroeCo.,Oh	08	07	11
Gilkason, Thomas C.(Z)	1833	May 10	Morgan Co,Oh	09	06	03
Gilkason, Thomas(Z)	1817	July 07	WashngtnCoOh	11	12	12
Gill, Elijah(Z)	1834	July 25	GuernseyCoOh	10	09	13
Gill, James(Z-M)	1836	Dec. 17	GuernseyCoOh	03	03	10
Gill, John(Z)	1835	Oct. 31	GuernseyCoOh	09	08	10
Gillam, Nancy(Z)	1833	Aug. 26	MuskingmCoOh	13	10	07
Gillam, Nancy(Z)	1833	Aug. 26	MuskingmCoOh	13	10	18
Gillaspie, James A.(Z)	1816	Aug. 16	MuskingmCoOh	12	10	05
Gillaspie, Jas.(Z-M)	1831	Aug. 31	GuernseyCoOh	02	03	07
Gillaspie, William(Z)	1814	Nov. 29	Jeff.Co.,Oh.	01	04	06
Gillehurst, William(Z-M)	1838	April 12	CoshoctnCoOh	05	04	21
Gillespie, George(Z)	1837	Feb. 18	GuernseyCoOh	08	05	03
Gillespie, James(Z-M)	1831	Oct. 22	GuernseyCoOh	02	03	08
Gillespie, James(Z-M)	1831	Feb. 04	GuernseyCoOh	02	04	24
Gillespie, James(Z-M)	1832	Dec. 20	GuernseyCoOh	02	03	07
Gillespie, John(Z-M)	1833	Aug. 23	GuernseyCoOh	02	03	13
Gillet, Wheeler(Z-M)	1834	Dec. 17	GuernseyCoOh	01	03	07
Gilliland, James(Z-M)	1833	Jan. 30	TuscarwsCoOh	04	07	23
Gilliland, James(Z-M)	1834	March 03	TuscarwsCoOh	04	07	23
Gilliland, James(Z-M)	1835	Sept. 02	TuscarwsCoOh	05	07	18
Gilliland, James(Z-M)	1835	Sept. 02	TuscarwsCoOh	04	07	24
Gillingham, Jon'n.(Z)	1817	May 12	BucksCo,Penn	01	04	05
Gillis, John(Z-M)	1836	Dec. 05	HolmesCoOhio	09	09	01
Gillispie, James(Y)	1825	Jan. 25	Stark Co.,Oh	06	17	26
Gillmer, Wm.(Y)	1823	Oct. 28	TrumbullCoOh	05	18	10
Gillogely, Wm.(Z)	1829	March 06	MuskingmCoOh	11	12	09
Gillogly, Franey(Z)	1835	Oct. 27	MuskingmCoOh	11	12	15
Gillogly, Henry(Z)	1833	Feb. 21	MuskingmCoOh	11	12	15
Gillogly, John(Z)	1835	Oct. 12	MuskingmCoOh	11	12	02
Gillum, Mary(Z-M)	1835	May 04	CoshoctnCoOh	07	05	03
Gilmer, John(Z)	1808	Sept. 29	FranklinCoPa	07	01	13
Gilmore, Francis(Z-M)	1835	Sept. 17	HarrisonCoOh	01	06	22
Gilmore, Francis(Z-M)	1836	Jan. 01	HarrisonCoOh	01	06	22
Gilmore, Nath.(Z-M)	1830	June 28	HarrisonCoOh	01	06	24
Gilmore, Nath.(Z-M)	1831	Jan. 27	HarrisonCoOh	01	05	07
Gilmore, Nathaniel(Z-M)	1834	March 22	HarrisonCoOh	02	06	21
Gilmore, Nathaniel(Z-M)	1835	Sept. 26	TuscarwsCoOh	02	06	21
Gilmore, Nathaniel(Z-M)	1836	Jan. 16	TuscarwsCoOh	01	06	25
Gilpen, Jonathan(Z-M)	1835	Nov. 13	TuscarwsCoOh	03	05	23
Gilpin, Elijah(Z-M)	1832	May 22	TuscarwsCoOh	03	04	01
Gilpin, Elijah(Z-M)	1832	May 22	TuscarwsCoOh	03	04	01
Gilpin, John(Z-M)	1832	Dec. 13	GuernseyCoOh	02	01	04
Gilpin, Samuel(Z)	1815	Feb. 10	HarrisonCoOh	01	05	17
Gilpin, Samuel(Z-M)	1836	March 22	GuernseyCoOh	02	01	04
Gilpin, William(Z-M)	1832	June 13	BelmontCo,Oh	03	04	13
Gilpon, William(Z-M)	1833	Dec. 23	BelmontCo,Oh	02	01	05
Gimlens, George(Z)	1807	Dec. 15	WashCo.,Penn	02	08	14
Gimlens, George(Z)	1807	Dec. 15	WashCo.,Penn	02	08	15
Gimlins, George(Z)	1815	Nov. 16	TuscarwsCoOh	02	07	15

PURCHASER	YEAR	DATE	RESIDENCE	R	T	S
Gimlins, Jacob(Z)	1815	July 18	TuscarwsCoOh	02	07	06
Gimmeson, John(Z-M)	1833	Jan. 16	HolmesCoOhio	06	09	24
Ginder, George(Z-M)	1836	Jan. 15	TuscarwsCoOh	02	07	10
Ginder, Joseph(Z-M)	1836	March 17	PittsburghPa	05	04	14
Gingary, John(Z-M)	1832	March 08	HolmesCoOhio	05	08	14
Gingary, John(Z-M)	1832	March 10	HolmesCoOhio	05	08	14
Gingere, Peter(Z-M)	1822	Dec. 05	CoshoctnCoOh	05	08	08
Ginn, James(Z)	1823	Dec. 01	HarrisonCoOh	10	08	18
Ginn, James(Z)	1832	Feb. 15	Morgan Co,Oh	11	12	24
Ginn, John(Z)	1823	Jan. 27	WashCo.,Penn	10	08	07
Ginn, John(Z)	1826	June 16	Morgan Co,Oh	10	08	07
Ginn, John(Z)	1815	May 20	GuernseyCoOh	09	07	17
Ginnicks, Clemont(Y)	1834	April 11	CarrollCo,Oh	04	13	13
Girby, Abraham(Z)	1816	May 07	TuscarwsCoOh	04	09	25
Giring, John(Z)	1816	April 18	LehighCo.,Pa	01	06	09
Gist, Thos.(Z-M)	1829	Feb. 06	GuernseyCoOh	04	02	02
Gittings, James(Z-M)	1833	March 01	MuskingmCoOh	09	03	16
Gittings, James(Z-M)	1833	March 01	MuskingmCoOh	09	03	17
Given, David(Z)	1810	July 03	WashngtnCo ?	11	13	05
Gladden, Frederick(Z)	1834	March 19	Morgan Co,Oh	13	08	19
Gladden, Jacob(Y)	1828	July 19	Stark Co.,Oh	05	12	29
Gladden, William(Z)	1806	May 22	WashngtnCoOh	05	01	18
Gladden, William(Z)	1806	May 22	WashngtnCoOh	05	01	13
Gladden, William(Z)	1811	April 16	WashCo.,Penn	08	08	11
Gladdin, William(Z)	1805	Nov. 18	WashCo.,Penn	08	08	11
Gladdin, William(Z)	1805	Nov. 18	WashCo.,Penn	08	08	11
Gladman, Thomas(Z)	1817	Jan. 18	LickingCo,Oh	09	01	04
Glancy, David M.(Z-M)	1836	Feb. 01	LickingCo,Oh	11	03	08
Glans, Jacob(Y)	1831	Aug. 11	Stark Co.,Oh	10	02	33
Glasgow, James(Z)	1806	May 12	GreeneCo.,Pa	11	01	22
Glass, James(Z)	1825	Dec. 02	BelmontCo,Oh	13	08	23
Glass, James(Z)	1827	Nov. 12	Morgan Co,Oh	13	08	23
Glass, James(Z)	1833	June 21	Perry Co.,Oh	14	13	31
Glass, James(Z)	1835	Dec. 15	Morgan Co,Oh	13	08	22
Glass, James(Z-M)	1829	Jan. 13	CoshoctnCoOh	09	05	15
Glass, John(Y)	1822	Feb. 09	Jeff.Co.,Oh.	03	11	22
Glass, John(Z)	1816	Jan. 18	PutnamCoOhio	13	11	20
Glass, Mathias(Y)	1832	June 14	TuscarwsCoOh	07	14	09
Glass, Mathias(Y)	1835	Nov. 02	HarrisonCoOh	07	14	29
Glass, Morgan(Z)	1833	Jan. 24	Perry Co.,Oh	14	13	32
Glass, Morgan(Z)	1833	Nov. 16	Perry Co.,Oh	14	13	31
Glass, Peter(Y)	1823	July 07	ColumbanCoOh	04	17	02
Glass, Samuel(Z)	1826	June 16	WashCo.,Penn	13	08	23
Glass, Thomas(Z)	1815	April 04	Jeff.Co.,Oh.	02	04	11
Glassener, John(Z)	1831	Sept. 07	HarrisonCoOh	11	08	04
Glassine, Absalom(Z-M)	1829	June 09	HarrisonCoOh	11	08	07
Gleason, Aaron(Z-M)	1836	Nov. 15	HolmesCoOhio	08	08	12
Gleason, Alonzo(Z-M)	1833	June 01	HolmesCoOhio	08	08	12
Gleason, Erastus(Z-M)	1836	Jan. 26	HolmesCoOhio	08	08	12
Gleason, Erastus(Z-M)	1837	Feb. 03	HolmesCoOhio	08	08	18
Gleason, Jonathan W.(Z-M)	1835	Nov. 14	HolmesCoOhio	08	08	18
Glen, James(Z)	1836	July 22	Morgan Co,Oh	09	05	36
Glen, James(Z)	1836	Dec. 12	Morgan Co,Oh	09	05	36
Glen, John(Z)	1834	Oct. 08	GuernseyCoOh	10	07	01
Glen, Joseph(Z)	1835	Nov. 18	Morgan Co,Oh	10	07	01
Glick, Jacob(Y)	1824	June 03	Stark Co.,Oh	09	11	23
Glick, Jacob(Y)	1824	June 03	Stark Co.,Oh	09	11	36
Glidden, Jefferson(Z)	1831	April 19	Morgan Co,Oh	09	06	14
Glidden, Jefferson(Z)	1833	April 12	Morgan Co,Oh	09	06	13
Glidden, Jefferson(Z)	1833	April 12	Morgan Co,Oh	09	06	14
Glidden, John(Z)	1814	Nov. 22	GuernseyCoOh	09	06	10
Glines, William(Z)	1832	July 27	Morgan Co,Oh	10	06	28
Glines, William(Z)	1835	Aug. 28	Morgan Co,Oh	10	06	28
Glohr, Paul(Z)	1833	Dec. 16	MuskingmCoOh	13	10	21
Glover, Alfred(Z-M)	1833	Jan. 26	LickingCo,Oh	11	03	06
Glover, Alfred(Z-M)	1836	Jan. 22	LickingCo,Oh	11	03	06
Glover, Joel(Z-M)	1829	Aug. 21	CoshoctnCoOh	07	07	23
Glover, Joel(Z-M)	1835	Dec. 25	CoshoctnCoOh	07	07	23
Glover, Levi(Z)	1835	Jan. 23	GuernseyCoOh	08	08	30

PURCHASER	YEAR	DATE	RESIDENCE	R	T	S
Glover, Levi(Z)	1835	March 13	GuernseyCoOh	08	08	32
Glover, Minor(Z-M)	1833	May 18	LickingCo,Oh	11	03	13
Glover, Samuel(Z)	1836	March 10	GuernseyCoOh	08	08	31
Glows, Jacob(Y)	1831	Sept. 17	Stark Co.,Oh	09	11	24
Goad, Peter(Z)	1816	March 08	TuscarwsCoOh	03	06	12
Goddard, Charles B.(Z-M)	1833	July 29	ZanesvilleOh	12	09	04
Godden, Lewis(Z)	1815	July 15	Sussex, N.J.	07	03	11
Godderd, Reuben(Y)	1828	March 07	ColumbanCoOh	03	13	15
Godfrey, Samuel(Z)	1816	Jan. 23	WashngtnCoOh	08	05	07
Godlib, Cline(Z)	1830	Feb. 17	Morgan Co,Oh	13	10	35
Godlove, Adam(Z)	1836	Feb. 12	Perry Co.,Oh	14	13	28
Goin, John Senr.(Z)	1815	Dec. 18	CoshoctnCoOh	06	09	04
Going, George(Z)	1833	Nov. 30	GuernseyCoOh	10	09	23
Goings, Wesley(Z)	1833	Oct. 03	GuernseyCoOh	10	09	15
Goldden, John(Z)	1826	Oct. 06	Jeff.Co.,Oh.	11	10	04
Golding, Wm.(Y)	1824	Dec. 01	Jeff.Co.,Oh.	04	12	35
Golliher, Davis(Z)	1836	Dec. 09	MuskingmCoOh	15	14	26
Gombar, Jacob(Z)	1811	Aug. 20	GuernseyCoOh	03	02	08
Gombar, Jacob(Z)	1815	April 22	GuernseyCoOh	03	02	15
Gonser, David(Z-M)	1833	Sept. 18	CoshoctnCoOh	05	07	05
Gonser, David(Z-M)	1834	Aug. 14	CoshoctnCoOh	05	07	05
Gonser, Henry(Z-M)	1836	March 22	CoshoctnCoOh	05	07	05
Gonser, John(Z-M)	1823	June 17	CoshoctnCoOh	05	07	03
Gonser, William(Z-M)	1837	March 10	TuscarwsCoOh	04	07	06
Good, Abraham(Z-M)	1828	March 14	TuscarwsCoOh	03	06	12
Good, Isaac(Z-M)	1833	Feb. 05	CoshoctnCoOh	07	07	23
Good, Isaac(Z-M)	1833	April 10	TuscarwsCoOh	03	06	23
Good, Isaac(Z-M)	1833	April 29	TuscarwsCoOh	03	06	11
Good, Isaac(Z-M)	1833	April 29	TuscarwsCoOh	03	06	18
Good, Jacob(Z)	1815	June 23	MuskingmCoOh	14	15	25
Good, Peter Jr.(Z-M)	1836	Feb. 01	TuscarwsCoOh	03	06	09
Goodde, Joseph(Z-M)	1840	May 27	GuernseyCoOh	03	03	15
Gooden, Asa(Z)	1814	Oct. 31	MuskingmCoOh	15	16	31
Goodere, George(Z-M)	1829	Dec. 21	GuernseyCoOh	01	01	12
Gooderl, Bailey(Z)	1836	April 19	GuernseyCoOh	09	07	13
Goodge, John(Z)	1827	Sept. 05	FayetteCo,Pa	01	09	06
Goodin, Henry(Z)	1835	Dec. 14	Morgan Co,Oh	09	05	28
Goodin, Henry(Z)	1836	Feb. 29	Morgan Co,Oh	09	05	28
Goodin, John(Z)	1835	Nov. 09	Perry Co.,Oh	14	12	05
Goodin, Moses(Z)	1810	Oct. 09	MuskingmCoOh	15	16	30
Goodin, Moses(Z)	1814	Jan. 11	MuskingmCoOh	15	16	19
Goodline, Jacob(Z)	1830	Feb. 03	Morgan Co,Oh	13	10	33
Goodman, George(Y)	1826	June 16	Stark Co.,Oh	06	18	10
Goodman, Peter(Y)	1822	June 05	WashCo.,Penn	07	11	22
Goodman, Wm.(Z-M)	1835	March 09	BelmontCo,Oh	02	05	02
Goodwin, John(Z-M)	1833	March 22	LickingCo,Oh	11	04	22
Goodwin, John(Z-M)	1833	Sept. 13	BelmontCo,Oh	07	05	13
Gookin, Madison(Z)	1832	May 25	Morgan Co,Oh	09	07	08
Gookin, Madison(Z)	1832	Oct. 08	Morgan Co,Oh	09	07	08
Gorby, Eli(Z)	1832	Aug. 25	Morgan Co,Oh	10	08	12
Gorby, Jonathan(Y)	1826	Dec. 06	ColumbanCoOh	06	18	26
Gorby, Levi(Z)	1833	March 02	Morgan Co,Oh	09	07	08
Gorby, Thomas(Z)	1833	April 08	Morgan Co,Oh	09	06	09
Gorden, John(Y)	1826	Aug. 19	WashCo.,Penn	05	11	29
Gordon, Abraham(Y)	1828	March 26	Jeff.Co.,Oh.	04	12	21
Gordon, George(Z-M)	1829	May 01	CoshoctnCoOh	07	05	16
Gordon, Henry(Z)	1813	Jan. 13	FairfeldCoOh	15	17	19
Gordon, James(Z)	1836	July 08	Morgan Co,Oh	15	14	27
Gordon, James(Z)	1836	July 08	Morgan Co,Oh	15	14	26
Gordon, James(Z)	1836	July 09	Morgan Co,Oh	15	14	27
Gordon, James(Z)	1811	Sept. 30	FayetteCo,Pa	02	01	20
Gordon, James(Z)	1815	June 02	GuernseyCoOh	02	01	10
Gordon, John(Z)	1810	Oct. 13	FayetteCo,Pa	02	01	08
Gordon, Joseph Junr.(Y)	1826	April 15	Jeff.Co.,Oh.	04	12	15
Gordon, Joseph(Y)	1831	July 25	Jeff.Co.,Oh.	04	12	15
Gordon, Joshua(Z)	1833	Feb. 05	GuernseyCoOh	10	09	04
Gordon, Joshua(Z)	1833	Feb. 05	GuernseyCoOh	10	09	04
Gordon, Joshua(Z)	1833	Feb. 05	GuernseyCoOh	10	09	04
Gordon, Robert(Y)	1828	Feb. 29	Jeff.Co.,Oh.	04	12	21

PURCHASER	YEAR	DATE	RESIDENCE	R	T	S
Gordon, Robert(Z)	1810	Oct. 13	FayetteCo,Pa	02	01	09
Gordon, William(Z)	1831	Sept. 08	Morgan Co,Oh	10	07	35
Gordon, William(Z)	1833	Jan. 03	Morgan Co,Oh	10	06	02
Gordon, William(Z)	1835	Oct. 31	Morgan Co,Oh	10	07	26
Gordon, Wm.(Z)	1830	Sept. 10	Morgan Co,Oh	10	06	10
Gore, Henry(Z)	1833	April 11	Morgan Co,Oh	09	05	10
Gore, Mary(Z)	1820	Nov. 16	Morgan Co,Oh	09	05	09
Gore, Peter(Z)	1820	Nov. 16	Morgan Co,Oh	09	05	09
Gore, Peter(Z)	1817	Aug. 01	MariettaOhio	09	05	09
Gorelon, Robert(Z)	1816	Jan. 04	GuernseyCoOh	05	02	03
Gorrell, James(Z-M)	1837	May 02	HolmesCoOhio	09	08	07
Gorsuch, Benj.(Z-M)	1828	June 09	TuscarwsCoOh	03	09	10
Gorsuch, David(Z)	1814	Oct. 10	Ohio Co.,Vir	10	06	16
Gorsuch, David(Z)	1814	Oct. 10	Ohio Co.,Vir	10	06	16
Gorsuch, Norman(Z)	1817	March 03	MuskingmCoOh	10	04	16
Gosage, Benjamin(Z)	1815	Feb. 10	TuscarwsCoOh	03	09	10
Goset, Jacob(Z)	1824	June 26	Morgan Co,Oh	10	08	34
Gosman, Andrew(Z)	1831	Aug. 02	Perry Co.,Oh	14	14	22
Gosset, Jacob(Y)	1831	June 07	GuernseyCoOh	07	09	26
Gossman, Andrew(Z)	1820	July 05	Morgan Co,Oh	14	14	23
Gossman, Frederick(Z)	1834	July 28	Morgan Co,Oh	14	13	15
Gossman, Frederick(Z)	1834	July 28	Morgan Co,Oh	14	13	15
Gotschall, Jacob(Y)	1831	July 01	HarrisonCoOh	05	13	15
Gotshall, Jonas(Y)	1823	May 19	PerryCo,Penn	05	12	21
Gotshall, Joseph(Y)	1823	May 13	HarrisonCoOh	05	12	15
Gottshall, Nicholas(Z-M)	1837	April 06	CoshoctnCoOh	08	07	01
Gottshall, William(Z-M)	1836	Sept. 24	CoshoctnCoOh	08	07	03
Gouchnour, Wm.(Z-M)	1832	Aug. 28	Morgan Co,Oh	09	06	21
Gough, Joseph(Y)	1830	Feb. 23	HarrisonCoOh	05	12	24
Gould, Benjamin(Z)	1825	Oct. 13	WashCo.,Ohio	08	05	26
Gould, Benjamin(Z)	1814	Nov. 04	WashCo.,Penn	08	05	25
Gould, Daniel(Z)	1837	April 07	WashngtnCoOh	08	05	25
Gowens, George(Z)	1831	April 01	GuernseyCoOh	10	09	21
Gowens, Joel(Z)	1825	Jan. 06	GuernseyCoOh	10	09	21
Grable, Joseph(Y)	1822	Aug. 13	Jeff.Co.,Oh.	04	13	25
Grace, Francis(Y)	1824	July 17	HarrisonCoOh	06	12	11
Grace, Francis(Y)	1830	Feb. 16	HarrisonCoOh	06	12	17
Grace, Francis(Y)	1832	June 07	HarrisonCoOh	06	12	11
Grace, John(Y)	1828	Nov. 07	HarrisonCoOh	06	12	36
Grace, John(Y)	1829	June 04	HarrisonCoOh	06	12	36
Grace, Matthew(Y)	1832	Jan. 23	HarrisonCoOh	07	14	28
Grace, William(Y)	1825	July 13	ColumbanCoOh	05	17	06
Gracey, Jackson(Y)	1823	Feb. 27	BelmontCo,Oh	07	10	15
Gracey, James(Y)	1830	Jan. 01	Jeff.Co.,Oh.	04	06	25
Graff, Fred.(Z-M)	1831	June 04	CoshoctnCoOh	06	07	01
Graff, Frederick(Z-M)	1832	March 26	CoshoctnCoOh	06	07	02
Graft, Fred.(Z-M)	1830	April 30	CoshoctnCoOh	06	07	02
Graft, Frederick(Z-M)	1820	Oct. 14	CoshoctnCoOh	06	07	01
Graft, Frederick(Z-M)	1821	April 17	CoshoctnCoOh	06	07	02
Grafton, Isaac(Y)	1824	June 16	Jeff.Co.,Oh.	02	07	11
Grafton, Samuel(Y)	1831	March 31	ColumbanCoOh	03	12	17
Graham, Alexander(Z)	1816	Nov. 23	AlleghnyCoPa	09	04	20
Graham, Alexander(Z)	1816	Dec. 30	AlleghnyCoPa	09	04	20
Graham, Alexander(Z-M)	1824	May 11	CoshoctnCoOh	09	04	20
Graham, Benj'm.(Z)	1837	July 11	Morgan Co,Oh	15	14	33
Graham, Benj.(Z-M)	1820	July 01	CoshoctnCoOh	05	06	05
Graham, Benj.(Z-M)	1828	Dec. 20	CoshoctnCoOh	06	06	01
Graham, Benj.(Z-M)	1830	June 24	CoshoctnCoOh	06	07	11
Graham, Benj.(Z-M)	1831	June 11	CoshoctnCoOh	05	07	25
Graham, Benjamin(Z-M)	1833	March 18	CoshoctnCoOh	05	07	25
Graham, Charles(Y)	1828	Dec. 09	ColumbanCoOh	06	16	23
Graham, Charles(Y)	1828	Dec. 09	ColumbanCoOh	06	16	26
Graham, Charles(Z-M)	1828	Oct. 16	GuernseyCoOh	02	04	15
Graham, Christopher(Z-M)	1826	May 16	GuernseyCoOh	02	04	06
Graham, Geo.(Z)	1816	July 02	MuskingmCoOh	13	09	10
Graham, George(Z)	1820	July 26	Morgan Co,Oh	03	09	12
Graham, George(Z)	1817	May 02	WashngtnCoOh	12	11	17
Graham, Hannah(Y)	1834	April 14	HarrisonCoOh	07	14	21
Graham, Hugh(Z)	1807	May 25	DauphinCo,Pa	02	01	02

PURCHASER	YEAR	DATE	RESIDENCE	R	T	S
Graham, Israel(Z)	1833	Nov. 14	Perry Co.,Oh	14	14	19
Graham, Israel(Z)	1833	Nov. 14	Perry Co.,Oh	14	14	30
Graham, James(Y)	1833	Nov. 28	CarrollCo,Oh	04	13	19
Graham, James(Z-M)	1825	May 03	GuernseyCoOh	03	04	20
Graham, James(Z-M)	1836	Jan. 15	GuernseyCoOh	03	04	11
Graham, John S.(Y)	1829	June 17	Jeff.Co.,Oh.	03	11	09
Graham, John Sen.(Z-M)	1830	Jan. 08	CoshoctnCoOh	05	06	15
Graham, John Senr.(Z-M)	1829	March 12	CoshoctnCoOh	05	06	16
Graham, John(Y)	1827	Aug. 07	Stark Co.,Oh	09	11	26
Graham, John(Y)	1827	Aug. 07	Stark Co.,Oh	09	11	25
Graham, John(Y)	1830	Dec. 13	PittsburghPa	03	13	19
Graham, John(Y)	1831	June 04	HuntngtnCoPa	06	13	17
Graham, John(Y)	1832	Sept. 07	HarrisonCoOh	07	14	21
Graham, John(Z-M)	1832	Oct. 31	MifflinCo,Pa	11	08	08
Graham, John(Z-M)	1839	June 13	HolmesCoOhio	08	08	21
Graham, Joseph(Y)	1831	June 03	HuntngtnCoPa	06	13	24
Graham, Joseph(Z)	1833	July 18	GuernseyCoOh	08	08	29
Graham, Nathaniel(Y)	1833	April 18	ColumbanCoOh	03	13	20
Graham, Robert(Z)	1815	Feb. 14	GuernseyCoOh	14	16	18
Graham, Sam'l.(Z-M)	1827	Aug. 28	CoshoctnCoOh	05	06	17
Graham, Samuel(Z-M)	1827	June 27	CoshoctnCoOh	05	06	16
Graham, Thomas(Z)	1821	Dec. 26	ZanesvilleOh	13	09	17
Graham, Thomas(Z-M)	1833	Aug. 01	CoshoctnCoOh	05	07	24
Graham, William(Y)	1827	Sept. 01	GuernseyCoOh	07	09	31
Graham, William(Z)	1824	May 11	GuernseyCoOh	11	10	15
Graham, William(Z)	1824	Sept. 13	GuernseyCoOh	11	10	15
Graham, William(Z-M)	1822	April 22	GuernseyCoOh	03	04	20
Graham, William(Z-M)	1825	Sept. 15	GuernseyCoOh	02	04	05
Graham, William(Z-M)	1827	March 10	HarrisonCoOh	03	01	25
Graham, Wm.(Y)	1828	July 25	GuernseyCoOh	07	09	25
Graham, Wm.(Z-M)	1828	Dec. 10	GuernseyCoOh	03	01	25
Graman, Moses(Z)	1807	June 05	Ohio Co.,Vir	15	18	09
Grandon, Bernard(Z)	1814	April 12	GuernseyCoOh	08	06	13
Grandon, Wm.(Z)	1836	Aug. 29	MonroeCo.,Oh	08	06	13
Grandon, Wm.(Z)	1836	Aug. 29	MonroeCo.,Oh	08	06	13
Grandstaff, Adam(Z)	1826	April 01	Ohio Co.,Vir	11	12	04
Grandstaff, Jacob(Z)	1816	Feb. 03	MuskingmCoOh	11	13	35
Grandstaff, John(Z)	1815	June 07	MuskingmCoOh	10	03	14
Grandstaff, John(Z)	1816	Sept. 16	Ohio Co.,Vir	11	12	13
Granger, Ebenezer(Z)	1812	Nov. 17	ZanesvilleOh	14	16	05
Granger, James(Z)	1825	Sept. 03	ZanesvilleOh	12	10	04
Grant, Joshua(Z)	1838	Aug. 16	WashngtnCoOh	08	06	33
Grant, Joshua(Z)	1838	Aug. 24	WashngtnCoOh	08	06	33
Grant, Samuel(Z)	1834	Dec. 15	MuskingmCoOh	15	14	02
Grant, Samuel(Z)	1838	Jan. 27	Morgan Co,Oh	08	05	05
Grant, Samuel(Z)	1838	Jan. 27	Morgan Co,Oh	08	05	05
Grant, Thomas(Y)	1826	May 03	Stark Co.,Oh	06	18	11
Grapes, Jacob(Z)	1811	Dec. 07	?	14	15	21
Grapes, Jacob(Z)	1817	July 11	MuskingmCoOh	14	15	24
Graryer, Ebenezer(Z)	1812	Nov. 17	ZanesvilleOh	14	16	05
Grass, Elijah(Z-M)	1831	April 13	CoshoctnCoOh	07	05	23
Grave, John George(Z-M)	1835	Aug. 14	TuscarwsCoOh	04	07	03
Graves, James Jnr.(Z-M)	1837	Feb. 03	CoshoctnCoOh	07	04	11
Graves, James(Z-M)	1834	Nov. 10	CoshoctnCoOh	07	04	09
Gray, Alexander(Y)	1830	July 29	TuscarwsCoOh	07	14	36
Gray, Barton(Y)	1831	July 02	Jeff.Co.,Oh.	04	12	20
Gray, Daniel(Z)	1835	Aug. 24	GuernseyCoOh	09	05	02
Gray, Daniel(Z)	1835	Aug. 24	GuernseyCoOh	09	06	34
Gray, David(Z)	1831	Dec. 31	Morgan Co,Oh	09	07	22
Gray, Ebenezer Atherton(Y)	1833	Feb. 27	HarrisonCoOh	07	12	34
Gray, Ebenzer A.(Z-M)	1836	May 17	HarrisonCoOh	03	05	01
Gray, Edw'd.(Z)	1811	Nov. 25	ZanesvilleOh	10	02	14
Gray, Edw'd.(Z)	1811	Nov. 25	ZanesvilleOh	09	03	08
Gray, Edw'd.(Z)	1811	Dec. 09	ZanesvilleOh	10	02	13
Gray, Edward(Z)	1811	Dec. 31	MuskingmCoOh	09	03	07
Gray, Edward(Z)	1811	Dec. 31	MuskingmCoOh	09	03	14
Gray, Israel(Z)	1836	Feb. 27	GuernseyCoOh	09	05	02
Gray, James B.(Z-M)	1831	July 02	GuernseyCoOh	03	06	17
Gray, James B.(Z-M)	1831	July 02	GuernseyCoOh	03	06	17

PURCHASER	YEAR	DATE	RESIDENCE	R	T	S
Gray, James(Z-M)	1831	Aug. 17	TuscarwsCoOh	01	08	10
Gray, James(Z-M)	1831	Aug. 17	TuscarwsCoOh	01	08	10
Gray, John Jr.(Z-M)	1833	Aug. 20	TuscarwsCoOh	01	05	13
Gray, John Junr.(Z-M)	1833	Aug. 20	TuscarwsCoOh	01	05	13
Gray, John(Z)	1815	Dec. 18	BedfordCo,Pa	15	15	11
Gray, John(Z)	1815	Dec. 18	BedfordCo,Pa	15	15	11
Gray, John(Z-M)	1834	Feb. 05	TuscarwsCoOh	01	08	02
Gray, John(Z-M)	1835	July 16	GuernseyCoOh	01	05	05
Gray, Ligget(Z)	1812	Sept. 12	ZanesvilleOh	14	16	05
Gray, Peter(Z)	1836	Sept. 24	WashngtnCoOh	08	05	11
Gray, R. K.(Y)	1827	Sept. 03	SteubenvleOh	07	17	21
Gray, Rich'd. K.(Y)	1827	Aug. 02	SteubenvleOh	07	17	21
Gray, Samuel(Z)	1814	Nov. 19	MuskingmCoOh	14	16	04
Gray, Wilders Bivins(Y)	1833	April 22	ColumbanCoOh	01	07	25
Gray, William(Z)	1835	Dec. 16	Morgan Co,Oh	09	07	27
Gray, William(Z)	1813	Dec. 09	LickingCo,Oh	11	03	25
Gray, William(Z-M)	1833	Feb. 04	TuscarwsCoOh	01	05	12
Gray, William(Z-M)	1836	March 19	TuscarwsCoOh	01	05	13
Gray, Wm. Junr.(Z-M)	1833	Oct. 23	HarrisonCoOh	01	06	25
Gray, Wm.(Z)	1836	Aug. 03	Morgan Co,Oh	09	07	27
Grechbach, Mathias(Z-M)	1836	March 12	CoshoctnCoOh	08	06	01
Greegor, George(Z)	1813	Nov. 24	TuscarwsCoOh	05	08	12
Green, Caleb(Z)	1815	Jan. 07	MuskingmCoOh	11	12	12
Green, Clark E.(Z)	1815	Dec. 18	GuernseyCoOh	09	08	03
Green, David(Z)	1822	April 10	Morgan Co,Oh	10	08	29
Green, David(Z)	1823	Oct. 03	Morgan Co,Oh	10	08	29
Green, David(Z)	1833	Nov. 05	Morgan Co,Oh	10	08	29
Green, David(Z)	1834	Jan. 21	Morgan Co,Oh	10	08	29
Green, George(Y)	1827	Sept. 11	HarrisonCoOh	05	13	22
Green, Henry(Y)	1827	March 08	HarrisonCoOh	06	12	27
Green, J.(Z)	1817	Jan. 15	ZanesvilleOh	12	12	35
Green, Jacob(Z-M)	1833	May 30	GuernseyCoOh	02	01	05
Green, John(Z)	1829	Jan. 10	Perry Co.,Oh	15	16	14
Green, John(Z)	1815	Nov. 22	KnoxCo.,Ohio	11	04	02
Green, Joseph(Z)	1815	Sept. 29	GuernseyCoOh	02	01	12
Green, Nathaniel(Z)	1831	Aug. 11	Morgan Co,Oh	13	08	31
Green, Robert(Z)	1833	Nov. 09	Perry Co.,Oh	14	12	08
Green, Sophia(Z-M)	1821	Sept. 11	LickingCo,Oh	11	01	11
Green, Thos. Asbury(Z)	1834	Oct. 09	GuernseyCoOh	08	08	36
Greene, David(Z)	1826	Nov. 06	Morgan Co,Oh	10	08	29
Greene, Jane(Y)	1825	June 25	Stark Co.,Oh	07	18	30
Greene, Joseph(Z)	1815	July 05	GuernseyCoOh	02	01	11
Greene, Thomas(Z)	1816	June 25	MuskingmCoOh	11	12	12
Greenland, Dan'l.(Z)	1827	April 20	HarrisonCoOh	06	07	10
Greenland, Thomas(Z-M)	1828	Dec. 17	HarrisonCoOh	05	07	06
Greenlee, Alexander(Z)	1835	Nov. 24	Morgan Co,Oh	09	06	07
Greer, Alex.(Z-M)	1822	Nov. 01	KnoxCo.,Ohio	10	08	24
Greer, Alex.(Z-M)	1830	Dec. 07	KnoxCo.,Ohio	10	08	24
Greer, Alex.(Z-M)	1830	Dec. 13	KnoxCo.,Ohio	10	08	23
Greer, Alexander(Z-M)	1836	Jan. 13	KnoxCo.,Ohio	09	08	24
Greer, Anne(Z-M)	1827	July 24	CharlesCo,Md	10	08	09
Greer, Anne(Z-M)	1827	July 24	CharlesCo,Md	10	08	09
Greer, Asa(Z-M)	1822	April 25	KnoxCo.,Ohio	10	08	18
Greer, George(Z-M)	1829	April 04	BelmontCo,Oh	10	08	08
Greer, George(Z-M)	1832	Oct. 26	KnoxCo.,Ohio	10	08	13
Greer, Henry(Z)	1826	Nov. 18	BelmontCo,Oh	13	08	26
Greer, Henry(Z)	1829	Jan. 12	Morgan Co,Oh	13	08	35
Greer, Henry(Z)	1829	Jan. 12	Morgan Co,Oh	13	08	34
Greer, Henry(Z)	1834	Jan. 28	Perry Co.,Oh	13	08	34
Greer, Henry(Z)·	1835	Nov. 21	Morgan Co,Oh	13	08	23
Greer, James(Z-M)	1833	Oct. 23	KnoxCo.,Ohio	10	08	13
Greer, James(Z-M)	1836	March 24	KnoxCo.,Ohio	10	08	12
Greer, James(Z-M)	1836	Nov. 23	KnoxCo.,Ohio	10	08	09
Greer, James(Z-M)	1836	Nov. 23	KnoxCo.,Ohio	10	08	13
Greer, Jas.(Z-M)	1822	Nov. 01	KnoxCo.,Ohio	10	08	24
Greer, John(Z)	1826	March 07	GuernseyCoOh	13	08	34
Greer, John(Z)	1828	Aug. 06	Morgan Co,Oh	13	08	35
Greer, John(Z)	1830	Dec. 07	KnoxCo.,Ohio	10	08	18
Greer, John(Z-M)	1824	Sept. 23	KnoxCo.,Ohio	10	09	11

PURCHASER	YEAR	DATE	RESIDENCE	R	T	S
Greer, John(Z-M)	1836	March 24	KnoxCo.,Ohio	10	08	09
Greer, John(Z-M)	1836	March 24	KnoxCo.,Ohio	10	09	12
Greer, John(Z-M)	1836	June 30	KnoxCo.,Ohio	10	08	23
Greer, John(Z-M)	1837	April 25	KnoxCo.,Ohio	10	09	20
Greer, John(Z-M)	1836	May 20	KnoxCo.,Ohio	10	08	18
Greer, Redman(Z-M)	1833	Nov. 02	KnoxCo.,Ohio	10	08	08
Greer, Richard(Z-M)	1835	Sept. 03	KnoxCo.,Ohio	10	08	02
Greer, Richard(Z-M)	1836	Sept. 26	KnoxCo.,Ohio	10	08	09
Greer, Robert(Z-M)	1833	Oct. 23	KnoxCo.,Ohio	10	08	09
Greer, Robert(Z-M)	1833	Oct. 23	KnoxCo.,Ohio	10	08	02
Greer, Samuel(Y)	1833	Dec. 04	AlleghnyCoPa	03	12	36
Gregg, Archibald(Z)	1829	Dec. 21	Morgan Co,Oh	10	07	28
Gregg, Cornelius(Z)	1835	April 14	Morgan Co,Oh	10	07	32
Gregg, Henry(Y)	1822	March 26	Jeff.Co.,Oh.	03	11	21
Gregg, Henry(Y)	1824	May 12	Jeff.Co.,Oh.	03	11	15
Gregg, Jacob H.(Z)	1831	Sept. 23	GuernseyCoOh	09	08	24
Gregg, Jacob H.(Z)	1836	Dec. 16	GuernseyCoOh	09	08	23
Gregg, Samuel(Z-M)	1833	Aug. 28	CoshoctnCoOh	06	04	23
Gregg, Stephen(Z)	1834	Dec. 17	BelmontCo,Oh	13	08	34
Gregg, Thomas(Z)	1832	Oct. 22	Morgan Co,Oh	10	07	28
Gregg, Uriah(Z)	1836	Jan. 11	GuernseyCoOh	09	08	14
Gregg, Uriah(Z)	1833	Dec. 09	GuernseyCoOh	09	08	15
Gregory, David N.(Z-M)	1832	Nov. 22	TuscarwsCoOh	01	05	05
Gregory, John(Z-M)	1836	July 07	HarrisonCoOh	03	04	10
Gregory, Nobel(Z)	1812	March 18	GuernseyCoOh	11	13	02
Grenawalt, Abraham(Z-M)	1835	Nov. 05	TuscarwsCoOh	04	07	11
Grenawalt, John(Z-M)	1832	Nov. 22	CoshoctnCoOh	09	05	25
Gress, Abraham(Y)	1829	May 21	ColumbanCoOh	04	13	29
Grewell, John(Z)	1816	Nov. 16	HarrisonCoOh	01	04	08
Grewell, Jonathan(Y)	1831	July 05	HarrisonCoOh	07	12	27
Grey, M.(Z)	1814	Aug. 19	GuernseyCoOh	08	06	01
Grier, John Jr.(Y)	1822	June 26	GuernseyCoOh	07	09	15
Grier, John(Z)	1809	Dec. 05	KnoxCo.,Ohio	10	07	04
Griffin, Asahel(Z)	1807	July 11	MuskingmCoOh	14	16	02
Griffin, Geo. Goss(Z-M)	1832	May 30	GuernseyCoOh	03	01	15
Griffin, George(Z)	1837	Feb. 09	HarrisonCoOh	15	14	32
Griffin, Henry(Z)	1833	Feb. 28	HarrisonCoOh	15	14	19
Griffin, Henry(Z)	1833	Feb. 28	HarrisonCoOh	15	14	18
Griffin, James(Z-M)	1832	June 19	BelmontCo,Oh	03	03	10
Griffin, James(Z-M)	1832	June 19	BelmontCo,Oh	03	03	11
Griffin, Robert(Z)	1812	June 06	CoshoctnCoOh	10	06	04
Griffin, Robert(Z-M)	1824	May 11	KnoxCo.,Ohio	10	06	04
Griffin, Samuel R.(Y)	1826	May 11	TuscarwsCoOh	07	15	20
Griffin, Samuel R.(Z-M)	1832	July 10	TuscarwsCoOh	01	08	01
Griffin, Samuel R.(Z-M)	1832	July 10	TuscarwsCoOh	01	09	22
Griffin, Samuel R.(Z-M)	1832	July 10	TuscarwsCoOh	01	09	22
Griffin, Thos. W.(Z-M)	1836	Aug. 31	CarrollCo,Oh	03	04	03
Griffin, Wm.(Y)	1827	Nov. 29	BelmontCo,Oh	06	10	25
Griffith, Abraham(Z)	1824	Dec. 21	Jeff.Co.,Oh.	12	12	22
Griffith, Benj'n.(Y)	1826	Aug. 24	WashCo.,Penn	06	14	15
Griffith, Charles(Z-M)	1832	June 01	Lickingco,Oh	10	03	03
Griffith, David(Y)	1824	Dec. 11	WestmrldCoPa	07	17	01
Griffith, David(Y)	1831	Aug. 18	Stark Co.,Oh	06	16	17
Griffith, Eli(Z)	1821	April 13	Morgan Co,Oh	12	10	27
Griffith, Eli(Z)	1834	Feb. 15	Morgan Co,Oh	12	10	20
Griffith, George(Z)	1808	March 03	FayetteCo,Pa	15	15	03
Griffith, George(Z)	1808	March 03	FayetteCo,Pa	15	15	04
Griffith, Isaac(Z-M)	1833	Oct. 21	KnoxCo.,Ohio	10	05	25
Griffith, James(Y)	1832	Sept. 01	Jeff.Co.,Oh.	04	12	17
Griffith, James(Y)	1834	Feb. 08	Jeff.Co.,Oh.	03	11	36
Griffith, James(Z-M)	1838	March 22	HolmesCoOhio	08	07	01
Griffith, Mahlon(Z-M)	1832	Oct. 06	KnoxCo.,Ohio	10	05	25
Griffith, Milton(Z)	1834	Feb. 15	Morgan Co,Oh	12	10	32
Griffith, Robert(Z-M)	1836	May 06	Jeff.Co.,Oh.	03	06	13
Griffith, Robert(Z-M)	1836	May 06	Jeff.Co.,Oh.	03	06	13
Griffith, Thomas(Y)	1824	Aug. 20	BelmontCo,Oh	07	10	12
Griffith, Thomas(Y)	1827	Jan. 03	BelmontCo,Oh	07	10	12
Griffith, William(Z-M)	1831	March 21	ChesterCo,Pa	01	04	09
Griffith, Wm.(Y)	1829	June 23	HarrisonCoOh	07	12	06

PURCHASER	YEAR	DATE	RESIDENCE	R	T	S
Griffith, Wm.(Z-M)	1831	July 25	CoshoctnCoOh	08	06	04
Griffith, Wm.(Z-M)	1836	Sept. 12	CoshoctnCoOh	08	06	07
Griffith, Wm.(Z-M)	1836	Sept. 12	CoshoctnCoOh	08	06	07
Grigg, Uriah(Z)	1833	Aug. 13	GuernseyCoOh	09	08	15
Griggs, Benjamin(Z)	1834	Jan. 10	Perry Co.,Oh	15	15	33
Grigsby, Harrison(Z)	1835	Sept. 03	Perry Co.,Oh	14	12	09
Grigsby, Harrison(Z)	1835	Dec. 19	Perry Co.,Oh	14	12	09
Grigsby, Moses(Z)	1833	Oct. 02	Perry Co.,Oh	14	12	08
Grigsly, Moses(Z)	1833	Nov. 05	Perry Co.,Oh	14	12	05
Grim, Abner(Z-M)	1831	March 26	CoshoctnCoOh	02	10	25
Grim, Daniel(Z-M)	1829	Sept. 02	TuscarwsCoOh	02	07	08
Grim, Henry(Z)	1810	March 22	KnoxCo.,Ohio	09	05	20
Grim, Henry(Z)	1815	Dec. 16	Jeff.Co.,Oh.	06	07	21
Grim, Jacob(Z-M)	1829	April 15	HolmesCoOhio	06	07	06
Grim, Joseph(Z-M)	1834	Jan. 18	HolmesCoOhio	09	09	25
Grim, Joseph(Z-M)	1836	Aug. 10	HolmesCoOhio	09	09	25
Grim, Onton(Z-M)	1838	July 05	CoshoctnCoOh	09	07	19
Grimbar, Jacob(Z)	1805	Oct. 21	MuskingmCoOh	03	02	13
Grimber, Jacob(Z)	1806	Jan. 07	MuskingmCoOh	03	02	08
Grimes, David(Z)	1836	Feb. 12	Perry Co.,Oh	14	12	07
Grimes, Geo.(Z-M)	1828	Dec. 10	GuernseyCoOh	02	04	24
Grimes, Geo.(Z-M)	1832	Feb. 24	GuernseyCoOh	02	04	16
Grimes, George(Z-M)	1834	Jan. 13	GuernseyCoOh	02	04	15
Grimes, Isaac(Z-M)	1832	Feb. 24	GuernseyCoOh	03	04	11
Grimes, Isaac(Z-M)	1830	April 19	GuernseyCoOh	02	04	25
Grimes, Isaac(Z-M)	1833	March 27	GuernseyCoOh	02	04	16
Grimes, Jas.(Z)	1836	Aug. 10	GuernseyCoOh	08	06	05
Grimes, Jas.(Z)	1836	Aug. 10	GuernseyCoOh	08	06	05
Grimes, John(Z)	1833	March 20	Perry Co.,Oh	14	12	07
Grimes, John(Z)	1833	March 20	Perry Co.,Oh	14	12	07
Grimes, John(Z)	1834	Jan. 31	HarrisonCoOh	10	09	35
Grimes, John(Z)	1835	May 12	GuernseyCoOh	10	09	35
Grimes, John(Z)	1815	June 20	BelmontCo,Oh	15	15	07
Grimes, Lemuel(Z)	1834	Oct. 10	Morgan Co,Oh	09	06	06
Grimes, Lewis(Z)	1817	July 19	BedfordCo,Pa	13	10	20
Grimes, Mary E.(Z-M)	1833	June 26	GuernseyCoOh	02	04	14
Grimes, Richard(Z)	1816	Nov. 09	Jeff.Co.,Oh.	02	04	22
Grimes, William(Y)	1821	April 23	ColumbanCoOh	06	16	13
Grimes, William(Z-M)	1835	June 19	BelmontCo,Oh	01	05	01
Grimlance, George(Z)	1812	June 03	TuscarwsCoOh	02	08	24
Grindle, Christena(Z)	1834	Oct. 22	Perry Co.,Oh	15	14	28
Grindle, Christian(Z)	1836	March 21	Perry Co.,Oh	15	14	28
Grines, Isaac(Z-M)	1832	Nov. 24	GuernseyCoOh	02	04	16
Grinisvelt, John(Y)	1828	Feb. 08	ColumbanCoOh	03	13	21
Griniwalt, Jno.(Y)	1828	Sept. 22	ColumbanCoOh	03	13	21
Grise, George(Y)	1824	June 21	Stark Co.,Oh	06	18	17
Groos, Peter(Z-M)	1834	Oct. 22	TuscarwsCoOh	04	07	15
Grose, Peter(Z-M)	1837	July 11	TuscarwsCoOh	03	05	18
Grosher, James(Z)	1811	Dec. 25	TuscarwsCoOh	01	09	03
Gross, Christian(Y)	1827	June 06	ColumbanCoOh	06	19	02
Grosz, Jacob(Y)	1827	July 03	Stark Co.,Oh	07	17	18
Grosz, Jacob(Y)	1827	Aug. 01	Stark Co.,Oh	08	09	24
Grove, David(Z-M)	1826	Dec. 08	CoshoctnCoOh	08	07	13
Grove, George(Z-M)	1833	Dec. 14	TuscarwsCoOh	02	10	18
Grove, Joseph(Y)	1823	March 03	ColumbanCoOh	04	13	12
Grove, Joseph(Y)	1826	May 13	ColumbanCoOh	04	13	12
Grove, Samuel(Y)	1828	Nov. 20	ColumbanCoOh	04	13	12
Grove, Samuel(Y)	1830	Feb. 23	ColumbanCoOh	04	13	12
Groves, Abraham(Y)	1823	Nov. 28	GreeneCo.,Pa	07	12	35
Groves, Christopher(Z)	1835	Oct. 10	Morgan Co,Oh	10	06	01
Groves, Henry(Y)	1826	Feb. 16	Jeff.Co.,Oh.	02	08	33
Groves, Henry(Z)	1834	Feb. 04	Morgan Co,Oh	10	06	13
Groves, Jeremiah(Z-M)	1837	March 30	BelmontCo,Oh	04	07	12
Groves, John(Z)	1806	Aug. 30	MuskingmCoOh	13	11	24
Groves, Joseph(Z-M)	1838	April 20	CarrollCo,Oh	04	04	13
Groves, Joseph(Z-M)	1838	April 20	CarrollCo,Oh	04	04	13
Groves, William(Z-M)	1835	Oct. 31	BelmontCo,Oh	03	06	09
Groves, William(Z-M)	1837	Oct. 31	BelmontCo,Oh	03	07	24
Grubb, W. W.(Z)	1830	March 12	Morgan Co,Oh	11	11	07

PURCHASER	YEAR	DATE	RESIDENCE	R	T	S
Grubb, Walter W.(Z)	1822	May 07	Morgan Co,Oh	11	11	06
Grubb, Walter W.(Z)	1822	July 01	Morgan Co,Oh	11	11	09
Grubs, David(Z-M)	1836	Jan. 04	CoshoctnCoOh	05	06	17
Grunden, Jacob(Y)	1821	Sept. 15	Stark Co.,Oh	06	16	26
Grunder, Jacob Senr.(Y)	1828	Jan. 24	Stark Co.,Oh	06	16	25
Grunder, Jacob(Y)	1828	Jan. 24	Stark Co.,Oh	06	16	25
Grundstaff, John(Z)	1817	Oct. 21	MuskingmCoOh	12	12	11
Grundy, Joseph(Z)	1817	July 10	TuscarwsCoOh	03	10	21
Gruyton, Elisha(Y)	1826	Aug. 19	TuscarwsCoOh	07	12	04
Gruyton, Elisha(Y)	1826	Aug. 19	TuscarwsCoOh	06	11	34
Gryer, John(Z)	1816	Aug. 10	MuskingmCoOh	05	02	18
Guess, John(Y)	1826	Oct. 21	Jeff.Co.,Oh.	04	12	29
Guest, Petney(Y)	1828	Dec. 23	Stark Co.,Oh	07	16	23
Guiler, William Jnr.(Z)	1836	Sept. 14	MonroeCo.,Oh	08	07	15
Guiler, William Jr.(Z)	1836	Nov. 01	MonroeCo.,Oh	08	07	22
Guiler, William Jr.(Z)	1836	Nov. 11	MonroeCo.,Oh	08	07	15
Guilinger, Martin(Y)	1824	June 16	HarrisonCoOh	05	12	30
Guilinger, Martin(Y)	1827	Jan. 12	HarrisonCoOh	05	12	30
Guilinger, Martin(Y)	1827	Jan. 25	HarrisonCoOh	05	12	30
Guin, Jacob(Z)	1816	Jan. 24	CoshoctnCoOh	06	09	04
Guist, Jacob(Z)	1822	June 22	MuskingmCoOh	11	12	18
Guist, John C.(Z)	1833	Dec. 30	MuskingmCoOh	11	12	22
Gullough, William(Z)	1836	Sept. 26	MuskingmCoOh	10	09	24
Gullough, William(Z)	1836	Sept. 26	MuskingmCoOh	10	09	24
Gultry, Josiah(Y)	1832	Oct. 06	HarrisonCoOh	07	12	05
Gum, Albert(Z-M)	1832	June 08	KnoxCo.,Ohio	10	08	06
Gum, John(Z-M)	1831	Oct. 12	KnoxCo.,Ohio	10	08	14
Gundy, Joseph(Y)	1825	Oct. 03	HarrisonCoOh	06	13	01
Gundy, Joseph(Z-M)	1832	Jan. 31	HarrisonCoOh	01	08	03
Gunkel, George(Z-M)	1833	Oct. 18	WestmrldCoPa	06	08	09
Gunn, John(Z-M)	1823	Aug. 22	GuernseyCoOh	02	03	08
Gunther, Nicholas(Z-M)	1837	Aug. 24	ZanesvilleOh	09	08	08
Gunther, Peter(Z-M)	1837	Aug. 24	ZanesvilleOh	09	08	08
Gurge, Thomas(Y)	1827	Dec. 12	Jeff.Co.,Oh.	04	13	20
Gushwa, Philip(Z-M)	1828	Aug. 14	HolmesCoOhio	05	08	15
Gusinger, John(Z)	1812	March 18	MuskingmCoOh	15	17	19
Gusinger, John(Z)	1813	Jan. 13	FairfeldCoOh	15	17	19
Gutburth, John(Y)	1821	Sept. 27	ColumbanCoOh	04	16	15
Gutchell, Hannah(Z)	1838	May 22	GuernseyCoOh	08	06	30
Guthrie, Thomas(Z-M)	1829	Dec. 14	WashCo.,Penn	06	07	05
Guthrie, Thomas(Z-M)	1836	Jan. 14	CoshoctnCoOh	06	07	15
Guthrie, Thos.(Z-M)	1831	March 19	WashCo.,Penn	06	07	15
Guthrie, William(Z-M)	1832	Aug. 22	GuernseyCoOh	04	02	14
Gutschall, George(Y)	1828	Dec. 17	HarrisonCoOh	05	13	08
Gutshall, George(Z-M)	1831	Nov. 05	TuscarwsCoOh	04	07	14
Guttery, Susannah(Z-M)	1835	June 10	HarrisonCoOh	03	07	13
Guy, Anderson(Z)	1834	Dec. 01	Morgan Co,Oh	11	12	24
Guy, James Junr.(Z)	1833	Dec. 30	Morgan Co,Oh	11	12	24
Guy, James(Z)	1831	Jan. 27	Morgan Co,Oh	10	08	07
Guy, Jesse(Z)	1824	May 10	WashCo.,Penn	14	14	21
Guy, Jesse(Z)	1824	Nov. 27	WashCo.,Penn	15	16	22
Guy, Lloyd E.(Z)	1833	July 11	Morgan Co,Oh	10	08	19
Gyer, Daniel(Z)	1810	March 27	WestmrldCoPa	05	01	03
Gyer, George(Z)	1812	Feb. 04	WestmrldCoPa	05	02	16
Gyer, George(Z)	1812	Feb. 04	WestmrldCoPa	05	02	17
Gyer, John(Z)	1811	April 15	MuskingmCoOh	?	01	01
Gyer, John(Z)	1814	July 30	MuskingmCoOh	05	02	23
Gyer, Joseph(Z)	1810	March 08	WestmrldCoPa	05	01	07
Haag, George(Z-M)	1836	Nov. 25	CoshoctnCoOh	05	04	15
Haag, John(Z-M)	1836	Oct. 28	CoshoctnCoOh	06	04	20
Haag, Michael(Z-M)	1836	Nov. 25	CoshoctnCoOh	06	04	22
Haag, Philip Michael(Z-M)	1836	Nov. 19	Stark Co.,Oh	03	07	02
Haag, Philip Michael(Z-M)	1836	Nov. 19	Stark Co.,Oh	03	07	01
Haas, Balsar(Z-M)	1833	Jan. 18	KnoxCo.,Ohio	10	07	19
Haas, Balser(Z-M)	1837	Oct. 23	KnoxCo.,Ohio	10	07	19
Haas, Daniel(Z-M)	1836	Aug. 27	TuscarwsCoOh	04	07	07
Habo, Randel(Y)	1833	April 17	Jeff.Co.,Oh.	02	08	35
Hackley, George(Z)	1835	Oct. 27	GuernseyCoOh	09	08	33
Hackstetler, Sam'l.(Z-M)	1827	March 12	HolmesCoOhio	04	09	15

PURCHASER	YEAR	DATE	RESIDENCE	R	T	S
Hadden, John(Z)	1806	May 16	BelmontCo,Oh	05	01	08
Hadden, William(Z)	1817	Feb. 20	MuskingmCoOh	06	01	20
Hadley, Jane(Z)	1836	July 02	Morgan Co,Oh	15	14	14
Hadley, Jane(Z)	1836	July 02	Morgan Co,Oh	15	14	15
Hadley, Jane(Z)	1836	July 02	Morgan Co,Oh	15	14	23
Hadley, Jane(Z)	1836	July 02	Morgan Co,Oh	15	14	22
Hadley, Jane(Z)	1836	July 02	Morgan Co,Oh	15	14	15
Hadley, William(Z)	1828	April 04	PutnamCoOhio	13	10	02
Hadley, William(Z)	1829	Aug. 25	PutnamCoOhio	13	10	11
Hadley, William(Z)	1831	April 08	MuskingmCoOh	13	09	13
Haeqny, George(Z-M)	1837	March 20	CoshoctnCoOh	05	04	07
Haeney, Daniel(Y)	1827	March 23	ColumbanCoOh	05	17	09
Haenny, Daniel(Y)	1827	Sept. 21	ColumbanCoOh	05	17	10
Hafner, Barnard(Z-M)	1836	Sept. 03	TuscarwsCoOh	03	07	14
Haqa, Adam(Z)	1835	July 18	Morgan Co,Oh	09	06	22
Haqa, John(Z)	1833	Feb. 14	Morgan Co,Oh	09	06	32
Haqa, Susannah(Z)	1833	June 18	Morgan Co,Oh	09	06	32
Haqaman, John(Y)	1832	Dec. 29	Jeff.Co.,Oh.	04	12	21
Hagaman, John(Y)	1833	Feb. 25	Jeff.Co.,Oh.	04	12	21
Hagan, John(Z)	1817	April 26	GuernseyCoOh	01	03	08
Hagan, John(Z-M)	1830	Jan. 15	GuernseyCoOh	02	05	19
Haqan, Joseph(Z-M)	1832	Aug. 09	GuernseyCoOh	02	03	11
Haqan, William(Z-M)	1837	Oct. 25	GuernseyCoOh	04	04	10
Hagen, Charles(Z-M)	1823	Dec. 15	GuernseyCoOh	01	03	06
Hagen, John(Z)	1816	May 02	FayetteCo,Pa	08	08	12
Hager, Kelion(Y)	1826	Feb. 16	BelmontCo,Oh	07	09	01
Haqey, Abraham(Y)	1824	Dec. 18	HarrisonCoPa	05	12	30
Hagey, John(Y)	1829	Aug. 06	HarrisonCoPa	05	12	35
Haque, John(Z)	1832	Oct. 24	GuernseyCoOh	08	08	01
Hague, Jonah Jnr.(Z-M)	1837	Feb. 20	MuskingmCoOh	04	05	18
Hahn, George(Z-M)	1836	June 23	ZanesvilleOh	09	03	15
Hahn, George(Z-M)	1837	April 05	MuskingmCoOh	09	03	16
Hahn, John(Y)	1830	Sept. 01	Jeff.Co.,Oh.	05	13	21
Hahn, Peter(Z-M)	1834	July 31	TuscarwsCoOh	04	07	17
Hain, Jacob(Z)	1830	May 04	Morgan Co,Oh	13	10	23
Hainelin, Sam'l.(Y)	1823	April 25	Stark Co.,Oh	08	09	29
Haines, Ab'm. K.(Y)	1823	June 23	AlleghnyCoPa	05	18	14
Haines, Charles(Y)	1826	May 22	ColumbanCoOh	05	18	11
Haines, Ephraim(Y)	1823	June 23	AlleghnyCoPa	05	18	14
Haines, John(Z-M)	1831	Jan. 29	KnoxCo.,Ohio	11	04	23
Haines, Jonathan(Y)	1823	June 23	AlleghnyCoPa	05	18	14
Haines, Jonathan(Y)	1825	July 06	ColumbanCoOh	05	18	11
Haines, Jonathan(Y)	1826	June 09	ColumbanCoOh	05	18	14
Haines, Levi(Y)	1830	Sept. 20	Stark Co.,Oh	07	20	09
Haines, Richard(Y)	1824	April 27	AlleghnyCoPa	05	18	14
Haines, Richard(Y)	1824	April 27	AlleghnyCoPa	05	18	14
Hainline, Martin(Z)	1816	Nov. 07	StarkeCo.,Oh	01	10	03
Hains, Henry Junr.(Z-M)	1833	March 29	CoshoctnCoOh	08	05	11
Hains, Henry(Z)	1811	March 11	LickingCo,Oh	08	05	18
Hains, Henry(Z)	1816	Dec. 03	CoshoctnCoOh	08	05	13
Hains, Isaac(Y)	1822	May 11	HuntngdnCoPa	06	17	21
Hains, Isaac(Z)	1815	March 29	LickingCo,Oh	11	01	19
Hains, Jacob(Z-M)	1836	April 02	GuernseyCoOh	04	02	11
Hains, Joel(Z)	1832	April 26	BelmontCo,Oh	10	09	03
Hains, John(Y)	1822	Feb. 15	Stark Co.,Oh	06	16	03
Hains, John(Y)	1822	Feb. 15	Stark Co.,Oh	06	16	03
Hains, John(Y)	1831	April 20	ColumbanCoOh	05	14	09
Hains, John(Z)	1812	Aug. 12	CoshoctnCoOh	08	05	17
Hains, John(Z)	1816	March 07	CoshoctnCoOh	08	05	14
Hains, John(Z-M)	1836	March 09	CoshoctnCoOh	07	05	08
Hainsworth, Aaron(Z)	1816	Jan. 02	MuskingmCoOh	13	09	35
Hainsworth, Robert(Z)	1816	May 15	MuskingmCoOh	13	08	04
Haius, Daniel(Z-M)	1832	March 31	CoshoctnCoOh	07	05	03
Halcomb, James(Z-M)	1838	Nov. 21	MuskingmCoOh	04	03	15
Halcomb, James(Z-M)	1838	Nov. 01	MuskingmCoOh	04	03	12
Halcomb, Joseph(Z)	1815	Nov. 03	MuskingmCoOh	13	09	09
Hale, Benjamin(Z)	1828	Oct. 25	Jeff.Co.,Oh.	12	10	28
Hale, David(Z-M)	1836	Jan. 06	KnoxCo.,Ohio	10	06	07
Hale, John(Z-M)	1826	Jan. 04	HolmesCoOhio	06	09	07

117

PURCHASER	YEAR	DATE	RESIDENCE	R	T	S
Hale, Sam'l.(Z)	1836	June 18	WashngtnCoOh	08	05	19
Hale, Thomas(Z)	1828	Oct. 25	Jeff.Co.,Oh.	11	11	21
Haley, Joel(Z)	1834	Jan. 01	Perry Co.,Oh	15	14	04
Hall, Allen(Z-M)	1821	March 14	LickingCo,Oh	11	04	20
Hall, Benjamin(Y)	1831	Dec. 09	GuernseyCoOh	07	09	09
Hall, Caleb(Y)	1826	May 24	BelmontCo,Oh	07	09	09
Hall, David(Z-M)	1836	Jan. 06	KnoxCo.,Ohio	10	06	07
Hall, David(Z-M)	1836	June 17	KnoxCo.,Ohio	10	06	07
Hall, Elijah(Z)	1816	Feb. 14	KnoxCo.,Ohio	10	05	15
Hall, Henry(Z)	1815	April 20	CoshoctnCoOh	09	04	02
Hall, Isaac Senr.(Y)	1824	Feb. 09	BelmontCo,Oh	06	08	32
Hall, IsaiahPinckey(Y)	1831	July 05	BelmontCo,Oh	03	05	07
Hall, James S.(Z)	1822	Aug. 28	MonroeCo.,Oh	08	05	13
Hall, James S.(Z)	1837	May 09	WashngtnCoOh	08	05	10
Hall, James S.(Z)	1837	May 09	WashngtnCoOh	08	05	14
Hall, James Y.(Z-M)	1834	Feb. 17	BelmontCo,Oh	11	08	07
Hall, John Jr.(Y)	1829	April 27	BelmontCo,Oh	07	09	07
Hall, John(Z)	1832	Sept. 18	Morgan Co,Oh	11	12	27
Hall, John(Z)	1826	Jan. 20	Jeff.Co.,Oh.	11	11	18
Hall, John(Z-M)	1836	March 22	ZanesvilleOh	03	01	04
Hall, John(Z-M)	1836	July 11	ZanesvilleOh	04	03	21
Hall, John(Z-M)	1837	March 22	ZanesvilleOh	04	04	03
Hall, Johnson(Z-M)	1832	Nov. 24	LickingCo,Oh	10	06	13
Hall, Jordan(Z)	1831	Sept. 02	LickingCo,Oh	10	04	16
Hall, Jordan(Z-M)	1836	Jan. 11	LickingCo,Oh	11	04	20
Hall, Jordan(Z-M)	1837	March 02	LickingCo,Oh	11	04	21
Hall, Joseph(Z)	1833	May 03	WashngtnCoOh	08	05	30
Hall, Joseph(Z)	1836	June 14	WashngtnCoOh	08	05	29
Hall, Joseph(Z)	1836	Nov. 30	WashngtnCoOh	08	05	29
Hall, Lewis(Z)	1831	Dec. 07	MuskingmCoOh	12	12	07
Hall, M.(Z)	1815	June 28	MuskingmCoOh	13	09	23
Hall, Miles(Z)	1832	May 23	Morgan Co,Oh	13	09	13
Hall, Mills(Z)	1833	Dec. 20	Morgan Co,Oh	15	09	29
Hall, Nathan(Z)	1805	Jan. 11	MuskingmCoOh	15	17	28
Hall, Pierce(Z)	1836	May 23	Morgan Co,Oh	13	09	13
Hall, Solomon(Z)	1835	Nov. 17	MuskingmCoOh	11	12	22
Hall, Thomas L.(Z)	1834	Jan. 10	MuskingmCoOh	11	12	34
Hall, Thomas(Z)	1813	Dec. 10	HuntingtonPa	10	05	05
Hall, Thomas(Z)	1816	July 15	KnoxCo.,Ohio	11	05	11
Hall, William(Z)	1813	July 31	PickawayCoOh	08	05	08
Hall, William(Z)	1814	March 01	MuskingmCoOh	12	12	01
Hall, William(Z-M)	1826	Aug. 30	KnoxCo.,Ohio	11	08	14
Hall, William(Z-M)	1826	Oct. 23	HolmesCoOhio	06	09	06
Hall, William(Z-M)	1835	July 01	MuskingmCoOh	10	03	03
Hall, William(Z-M)	1838	Dec. 14	Jeff.Co.,Oh.	04	03	10
Hall, Wm. V.(Z-M)	1836	Aug. 19	LickingCo,Oh	10	04	12
Hall, Wm. V.(Z-M)	1836	Aug. 19	LickingCo,Oh	10	04	11
Haller, Jacob(Y)	1823	Nov. 03	ColumbanCoOh	05	17	21
Haller, Jacob(Y)	1823	Nov. 03	ColumbanCoOh	05	17	21
Haller, Jacob(Y)	1823	Nov. 03	ColumbanCoOh	05	17	22
Halley, John(Z)	1832	Aug. 23	Morgan Co,Oh	09	08	31
Halley, Samuel(Z)	1815	March 27	MuskingmCoOh	11	13	21
Halloway, Jacob(Y)	1824	May 19	BelmontCo,Oh	05	09	22
Halloway, Jacob(Y)	1824	May 19	BelmontCo,Oh	05	09	22
Halloway, Jacob(Y)	1824	May 19	BelmontCo,Oh	05	09	22
Halloway, Jacob(Y)	1824	May 19	BelmontCo,Oh	05	09	22
Hally, John(Z)	1833	Nov. 11	GuernseyCoOh	10	09	36
Halsel, Jacob(Y)	1824	Jan. 20	Stark Co.,Oh	07	18	30
Halsey, Silas(Z-M)	1837	April 29	CoshoctnCoOh	04	05	20
Halter, Sebastian(Y)	1834	Sept. 10	CarrollCo,Oh	07	16	04
Hama, Jacob(Y)	1822	April 24	Stark Co.,Oh	07	19	21
Hama, Jacob(Y)	1826	Sept. 06	Stark Co.,Oh	06	18	08
Hamilton, Alexander(Z)	1833	June 27	MuskingmCoOh	12	12	18
Hamilton, Alexander(Z)	1833	June 27	MuskingmCoOh	12	12	18
Hamilton, Alfred J.(Z)	1832	Dec. 01	Morgan Co,Oh	09	06	32
Hamilton, Edward(Z)	1804	Dec. 01	MuskingmCoOh	15	17	30
Hamilton, George(Y)	1828	Dec. 23	ColumbanCoOh	01	06	01
Hamilton, George(Y)	1828	Dec. 23	ColumbanCoOh	04	06	12
Hamilton, Henry(Z)	1814	Jan. 27	GuernseyCoOh	10	08	11

PURCHASER	YEAR	DATE	RESIDENCE	R	T	S
Hamilton, Henry(Z)	1816	Feb. 17	GuernseyCoOh	10	08	10
Hamilton, James(Z)	1836	March 12	GuernseyCoOh	10	09	25
Hamilton, James(Z)	1836	March 12	GuernseyCoOh	10	09	25
Hamilton, Jane(Z-M)	1824	July 07	MuskingmCoOh	09	03	21
Hamilton, John(Y)	1831	Jan. 01	TuscarwsCoOh	06	14	31
Hamilton, Joseph(Y)	1826	Feb. 20	HarrisonCoOh	07	11	13
Hamilton, Joseph(Z-M)	1838	Jan. 20	GuernseyCoOh	04	04	10
Hamilton, Joseph(Z-M)	1838	Jan. 20	GuernseyCoOh	03	04	06
Hamilton, Robert W.(Y)	1825	Aug. 17	ColumbanCoOh	07	20	03
Hamilton, Robt.(Z-M)	1824	July 07	MuskingmCoOh	09	03	21
Hamilton, Samuel W.(Z)	1833	June 11	GuernseyCoOh	08	08	36
Hamilton, Samuel W.(Z)	1833	June 11	GuernseyCoOh	08	08	35
Hamilton, Samuel(Z-M)	1830	Jan. 06	CoshoctnCoOh	05	06	05
Hamilton, Thomas(Z)	1824	Sept. 23	MuskingmCoOh	13	11	12
Hamilton, Thomas(Z)	1817	Oct. 23	Jeff.Co.,Oh.	06	07	07
Hamilton, Thomas(Z-M)	1833	Aug. 30	Jeff.Co.,Oh.	02	06	03
Hamilton, William(Y)	1832	Aug. 24	HarrisonCoOh	07	14	22
Hamilton, William(Y)	1832	Aug. 24	HarrisonCoOh	07	14	28
Hamilton, William(Z)	1805	Nov. 01	MongahlaCoVa	15	18	10
Hamilton, William(Z)	1811	June 01	MuskingmCoOh	15	18	10
Hamilton, William(Z-M)	1829	Sept. 14	CoshoctnCoOh	05	06	05
Hamilton, Wm.(Y)	1822	Nov. 04	ColumbanCoOh	02	09	21
Hamilton, Wm.(Y)	1828	June 11	Stark Co.,Oh	06	16	30
Hamilton, Wm.(Y)	1828	Aug. 07	ColumbanCoOh	02	09	21
Hamilton, Wm.(Z-M)	1824	July 07	MuskingmCoOh	09	03	21
Hamlin, Benjamin(Y)	1832	April 02	ColumbanCoOh	06	19	01
Hamlin, James(Y)	1829	Sept. 09	Stark Co.,Oh	06	19	20
Hamlin, Joshua(Y)	1827	Dec. 28	Stark Co.,Oh	06	19	15
Hamlin, Robert(Y)	1832	May 07	Jeff.Co.,Oh.	06	12	12
Hamlin, Stephen(Y)	1826	Nov. 20	Stark Co.,Oh	06	19	15
Hamm, Adam(Z-M)	1826	March 14	StarkeCo.,Oh	05	07	03
Hamm, John(Z)	1816	Feb. 26	ZanesvilleOh	14	14	11
Hamman, Esther(Z)	1828	Aug. 30	MuskingmCoOh	13	10	11
Hamman, John(Z)	1828	July 28	MuskingmCoOh	13	10	11
Hamman, John(Z)	1833	March 15	MuskingmCoOh	13	10	11
Hammel, Amelia(Z-M)	1835	March 25	TuscarwsCoOh	01	08	02
Hammel, Isaac(Z-M)	1831	April 05	Jeff.Co.,Oh.	02	06	23
Hammel, Isaac(Z-M)	1836	Jan. 27	HarrisonCoOh	02	05	02
Hammel, John(Z)	1814	Sept. 14	SomersetCoPa	10	06	22
Hammer, George(Z)	1825	June 08	Perry Co.,Oh	15	16	21
Hammer, Jacob(Z)	1805	Jan. 02	FairfeldCoOh	15	17	32
Hammerby, Adam(Z-M)	1838	June 02	HolmesCoOhio	09	08	05
Hammersley, Isaac(Z-M)	1832	June 25	GuernseyCoOh	04	04	02
Hammet, George(Z)	1806	Nov. 17	Ohio Co.,Vir	15	17	03
Hammet, James(Z)	1806	Nov. 17	Ohio Co.,Vir	15	17	13
Hammet, Joseph(Z)	1806	Nov. 17	FairfeldCoOh	15	17	04
Hammock, John(Z)	1812	March 27	HampshreCoVa	09	08	28
Hammon, Rachel(Z)	1836	Nov. 08	New York,NY.	08	05	20
Hammon, Thomas(Z)	1833	June 17	Morgan Co,Oh	11	10	04
Hammond, Benj'm. W.(Z)	1834	Feb. 03	GuernseyCoOh	10	09	24
Hammond, Benj.(Z)	1829	Dec. 31	Morgan Co,Oh	11	10	05
Hammond, D. P.(Z-M)	1832	Feb. 20	GuernseyCoOh	03	02	06
Hammond, Daniel(Z)	1815	Sept. 01	Westmr1dCoPa	05	02	24
Hammond, Daniel(Z)	1815	Oct. 04	Westmr1dCoPa	05	02	17
Hammond, Daniel(Z)	1816	April 27	MuskingmCoOh	05	02	24
Hammond, Daniel(Z)	1816	April 29	MuskingmCoOh	05	02	17
Hammond, Elizabeth(Z)	1814	Dec. 06	Brooke CoVir	08	08	11
Hammond, George(Z)	1827	Feb. 10	MuskingmCoOh	12	13	22
Hammond, George(Z)	1831	May 25	Morgan Co,Oh	12	11	25
Hammond, James(Z)	1831	July 18	Morgan Co,Oh	11	10	04
Hammond, John(Z)	1817	April 21	MuskingmCoOh	11	12	01
Hammond, John(Z-M)	1833	March 19	GuernseyCoOh	04	02	12
Hammond, John(Z-M)	1836	July 02	GuernseyCoOh	03	03	25
Hammond, Rachel(Z-M)	1838	June 15	GuernseyCoOh	10	08	19
Hammond, Sam'l.(Z-M)	1831	May 30	KnoxCo.,Ohio	10	06	19
Hammond, Sibbiann(Y)	1829	March 13	TuscarwsCoOh	07	14	26
Hammond, Stephen(Z)	1837	April 21	MuskingmCoOh	08	06	27
Hammond, Stephen(Z)	1838	Nov. 12	WindronCo,Vt	08	06	34
Hammond, William(Z)	1822	May 31	Morgan Co,Oh	11	11	30

PURCHASER	YEAR	DATE	RESIDENCE	R	T	S
Hammond, Z.(Z)	1817	Jan. 27	MuskingmCoOh	11	12	02
Hamn, Jacob(Y)	1829	March 14	Stark Co.,Oh	06	18	08
Hamp, Jacob(Z-M)	1828	Sept. 02	ColumbanCoOh	04	09	14
Hampshire, George(Z)	1805	Oct. 14	BaltimreCoMd	15	16	05
Hampton, Zachariah B.(Z)	1824	Oct. 01	LoudonCo,Vir	12	09	11
Hamrick, William(Z)	1815	March 11	MuskingmCoOh	13	12	13
Hana, Cornelius(Z)	1815	Nov. 09	N.Phila.Penn	03	10	16
Hanah, Alexander(Z)	1814	Dec. 02	BelmontCo,Oh	11	13	32
Hanby, Jno.(Z-M)	1831	Dec. 21	HarrisonCoOh	04	06	18
Hance, Benjamin(Y)	1823	Aug. 27	ColumbanCoOh	05	18	12
Hancock, George(Z)	1817	Aug. 12	MuskingmCoOh	09	03	21
Hand, Cornelius(Z-M)	1833	Aug. 26	HolmesCoOhio	06	09	24
Handel, Fiet(Y)	1824	May 25	Jeff.Co.,Oh.	04	10	18
Handel, John(Z)	1816	May 06	MuskingmCoOh	06	01	03
Handen, Isaac(Z)	1813	June 25	SomersetCoPa	10	07	15
Handen, John(Z)	1813	June 25	SomersetCoPa	10	07	16
Handle, John(Z)	1810	Dec. 14	MuskingmCoOh	06	01	04
Handle, John(Z)	1814	Nov. 21	MuskingmCoOh	06	02	16
Handy, John(Z-M)	1838	June 02	CoshoctnCoOh	04	04	03
Hanesworth, Robert(Z)	1835	Jan. 07	Morgan Co,Oh	14	12	12
Hanesworth, Robert(Z)	1836	Jan. 04	Morgan Co,Oh	13	09	30
Hanesworth, Robert(Z)	1836	Jan. 23	Morgan Co,Oh	13	09	31
Hanesworth, Robert(Z)	1836	March 05	Morgan Co,Oh	14	12	12
Haneswoth, Robert(Z)	1836	June 28	Morgan Co,Oh	13	09	32
Haney, Henry(Y)	1826	Feb. 18	ColumbanCoOh	05	17	15
Haney, Wm.(Z)	1815	March 11	WashCo.,Penn	05	01	25
Hanger, Joseph(Z)	1814	Nov. 23	KnoxCo.,Ohio	10	07	08
Hankins, John(Z)	1832	July 16	Morgan Co,Oh	11	10	34
Hankins, Philip(Z)	1829	Nov. 07	Morgan Co,Oh	09	07	22
Hankins, William(Z-M)	1832	July 05	CoshoctnCoOh	06	04	01
Hankins, William(Z-M)	1835	Aug. 10	CoshoctnCoOh	06	04	01
Hanks, Stiles(Z-M)	1828	April 30	MuskingmCoOh	06	03	25
Hann, John(Z)	1829	Jan. 12	Morgan Co,Oh	12	09	04
Hann, John(Z)	1829	Jan. 12	Morgan Co,Oh	12	09	04
Hann, Peter(Z)	1824	Feb. 14	Morgan Co,Oh	12	10	32
Hanna, Andrew(Z)	1817	Jan. 22	GuernseyCoOh	03	01	13
Hanna, James(Z)	1817	Aug. 28	KnoxCo.,Ohio	10	05	15
Hanna, James(Z-M)	1825	June 14	GuernseyCoOh	03	01	12
Hanna, John(Z)	1804	Dec. 07	BelmontCo,Oh	02	03	01
Hanna, John(Z)	1806	April 09	BelmontCo,Oh	01	03	25
Hanna, John(Z)	1806	May 13	BelmontCo,Oh	01	02	04
Hanna, John(Z)	1806	May 13	BelmontCo,Oh	01	02	05
Hanna, John(Z)	1812	Feb. 10	GuernseyCoOh	01	03	25
Hanna, John(Z)	1813	July 17	GuernseyCoOh	03	03	19
Hanna, John(Z)	1813	Aug. 17	GuernseyCoOh	10	09	07
Hanna, John(Z)	1814	June 21	GuernseyCoOh	03	03	21
Hanna, John(Z)	1814	June 21	GuernseyCoOh	01	03	25
Hanna, John(Z)	1814	Aug. 30	GuernseyCoOh	01	03	03
Hanna, John(Z)	1814	Oct. 08	GuernseyCoOh	03	01	08
Hanna, John(Z)	1815	May 04	GuernseyCoOh	01	04	25
Hanna, John(Z)	1815	June 08	ZanesvilleOh	06	01	07
Hanna, John(Z)	1815	Sept. 15	GuernseyCoOh	01	03	18
Hanna, Robert(Z)	1813	Aug. 17	GuernseyCoOh	03	04	24
Hanna, Thomas(Z)	1808	Sept. 02	MuskingmCoOh	01	02	15
Hanna, Thomas(Z)	1814	May 04	GuernseyCoOh	03	03	20
Hanna, Thomas(Z)	1814	July 21	GuernseyCoOh	01	02	06
Hanna, Thomas(Z)	1814	Aug. 30	GuernseyCoOh	01	03	17
Hanna, William(Z)	1832	May 23	LickingCo,Oh	10	04	04
Hanna, William(Z)	1811	Aug. 24	KnoxCo.,Ohio	10	05	04
Hanna, William(Z)	1815	Feb. 20	KnoxCo.,Ohio	10	05	05
Hanna, Wm.(Z)	1817	Aug. 28	KnoxCo.,Ohio	10	05	15
Hannah, Jacob(Y)	1826	June 22	Stark Co.,Oh	06	18	08
Hannah, John C.(Y)	1822	Aug. 19	WashCo.,Penn	07	11	21
Hannah, William(Z-M)	1832	Oct. 17	KnoxCo.,Ohio	10	04	04
Hannah, Wm.(Z)	1831	July 29	KnoxCo.,Ohio	10	04	04
Hannel, Geo.(Z-M)	1829	June 29	TuscarwsCoOh	02	10	16
Hannum, James(Y)	1829	Dec. 08	ColumbanCoOh	05	15	30
Hansbrough, Elijah(Z)	1838	Jan. 19	Perry Co.,Oh	15	14	31
Hansbrough, Joseph(Z-M)	1832	Nov. 22	HolmesCoOhio	07	08	01

PURCHASER	YEAR	DATE	RESIDENCE	R	T	S
Hansbrough, Joseph(Z-M)	1835	Nov. 02	HolmesCoOhio	06	09	25
Hansel, John(Z-M)	1830	Oct. 19	TuscarwsCoOh	02	08	23
Hansen, Valentine(Y)	1831	March 11	PortageCo,Oh	05	18	07
Hansley, Madison(Z)	1833	March 18	Perry Co.,Oh	14	13	26
Hanson, Joseph E.(Z)	1836	May 23	Morgan Co,Oh	09	05	35
Hanson, Joseph E.(Z)	1836	May 23	Morgan Co,Oh	09	05	35
Hansworth, Robt.(Z)	1832	March 26	Morgan Co,Oh	13	09	29
Hanum, Robert(Z)	1833	Aug. 21	GuernseyCoOh	09	08	24
Hanum, William(Z)	1833	May 29	GuernseyCoOh	09	08	13
Happer, Baptist(Z)	1817	June 07	WashCo.,Penn	11	04	17
Happer, Baptist(Z)	1817	June 07	WashCo.,Penn	11	04	17
Happer, Baptist(Z)	1817	June 07	WashCo.,Penn	11	04	18
Happer, Baptist(Z)	1817	June 07	WashCo.,Penn	11	04	24
Happer, Baptist(Z)	1817	June 07	WashCo.,Penn	11	04	25
Happer, Baptist(Z)	1817	June 07	WashCo.,Penn	11	03	04
Happer, Baptist(Z)	1817	June 07	WashCo.,Penn	11	04	18
Harah, John(Z)	1814	Nov. 21	BelmontCo,Oh	12	13	36
Haran, Alex'r.(Y)	1821	Dec. 27	Stark Co.,Oh	06	17	35
Harbaugh, Daniel(Z-M)	1832	Aug. 04	TuscarwsCoOh	02	08	13
Harbaugh, Fred'k. C.(Z)	1827	April 18	TuscarwsCoOh	01	09	06
Harbaugh, Henry(Z-M)	1829	May 19	CoshoctnCoOh	06	07	02
Harbaugh, John(Z)	1836	April 18	Perry Co.,Oh	15	14	31
Harbaugh, John(Z)	1837	Sept. 09	Perry Co.,Oh	15	14	33
Harbaugh, Peter(Z)	1816	June 10	TuscarwsCoOh	06	07	02
Harbert, Jacob(Z-M)	1832	Jan. 13	CoshoctnCoOh	09	04	05
Harble, Frederick(Y)	1831	March 04	ColumbanCoOh	07	17	25
Harden, Abraham(Z)	1813	Oct. 14	LickingCo,Oh	10	03	18
Harden, John(Z)	1816	July 30	GuernseyCoOh	01	03	11
Harden, John(Z-M)	1832	March 12	KnoxCo.,Ohio	10	07	17
Harden, Sarah(Z)	1827	March 13	MuskingmCoOh	12	11	15
Hardenbrook, W.(Z)	1816	July 04	CoshoctnCoOh	09	05	10
Hardesty, John(Z)	1816	Sept. 18	CoshoctnCoOh	09	04	19
Hardesty, John(Z)	1816	Oct. 09	CoshoctnCoOh	07	04	24
Hardesty, Thomas(Z)	1811	Aug. 13	CoshoctnCoOh	09	04	19
Harding, Hilleary(Z)	1816	Dec. 20	Jeff.Co.,Oh.	01	01	21
Harding, Jacob(Y)	1832	Jan. 10	Stark Co.,Oh	09	12	33
Harding, John(Y)	1830	Feb. 15	HarrisonCoOh	06	12	28
Harding, John(Z-M)	1833	Jan. 25	GuernseyCoOh	09	08	02
Harding, Westly(Z-M)	1838	Nov. 22	Jeff.Co.,Oh.	03	04	02
Hardinger, Philip(Z-M)	1831	Nov. 14	KnoxCo.,Ohio	10	08	08
Hardistry, John(Z)	1827	Aug. 24	MuskingmCoOh	11	13	15
Hardisty, Aquila(Z-M)	1831	Feb. 12	CoshoctnCoOh	09	04	16
Hardisty, Aquila(Z-M)	1832	Aug. 07	CoshoctnCoOh	09	04	16
Hardisty, Edmund(Z)	1811	March 28	CoshoctnCoOh	08	04	19
Hardisty, Edmund(Z)	1811	March 28	CoshoctnCoOh	08	04	19
Hardisty, Francis(Z-M)	1832	Nov. 26	KnoxCo.,Ohio	10	08	25
Hardisty, John(Z)	1805	Jan. 07	BelmontCo,Oh	08	04	22
Hardisty, John(Z)	1805	Oct. 21	MuskingmCoOh	09	03	12
Hardisty, John(Z)	1808	April 07	MuskingmCoOh	09	03	05
Hardisty, John(Z)	1817	Feb. 06	CoshoctnCoOh	08	04	11
Hardisty, John(Z-M)	1836	Jan. 13	CoshoctnCoOh	09	09	14
Hardisty, John(Z-M)	1836	April 25	HolmesCoOhio	09	09	17
Hardisty, Lewis(Z-M)	1835	June 12	GuernseyCoOh	02	04	05
Hardisty, Ralph(Z)	1806	Feb. 21	BelmontCo,Oh	05	01	09
Hardisty, Ralph(Z)	1808	Dec. 06	MuskingmCoOh	05	01	20
Hardisty, Sam'l.(Z)	1816	Oct. 04	CoshoctnCoOh	09	04	20
Hardisty, Solomon(Z-M)	1831	March 29	GuernseyCoOh	03	04	01
Hardisty, Warren M.(Z-M)	1831	Nov. 11	BelmontCo,Oh	03	04	01
Hardman, Christ'n.(Y)	1824	June 02	Stark Co.,Oh	07	18	10
Hardman, Dan'l.(Y)	1823	Oct. 23	ColumbanCoOh	06	18	26
Hardman, David(Y)	1836	May 11	Jeff.Co.,Oh.	02	08	34
Hardman, George(Y)	1823	April 07	Stark Co.,Oh	07	18	15
Hardman, Joseph(Z)	1817	Jan. 09	CoshoctnCoOh	08	05	15
Hardy, Ashford(Z)	1831	April 11	MuskingmCoOh	11	12	25
Hardy, Barnabas(Z-M)	1838	June 14	TuscarwsCoOh	03	05	17
Hardy, Benjamin(Z)	1835	March 21	Perry Co.,Oh	15	14	25
Hardy, John(Y)	1823	March 24	ColumbanCoOh	07	20	15
Hardy, Kenzie(Z)	1814	Oct. 17	BelmontCo,Oh	06	02	18
Hardy, Kenzie(Z)	1814	Oct. 17	BelmontCo,Oh	06	02	23

PURCHASER	YEAR	DATE	RESIDENCE	R	T	S
Hardy, William(Z-M)	1837	Nov. 23	Stark Co.,Oh	03	05	17
Harford, Elias(Z-M)	1829	Sept. 05	HolmesCoOhio	08	08	17
Harford, Elias(Z-M)	1829	Sept. 05	HolmesCoOhio	08	08	18
Harford, Elias(Z-M)	1833	Nov. 16	HolmesCoOhio	08	08	14
Harinan, Frederick(Z)	1814	June 24	TuscarwsCoOh	14	14	34
Haring, Conrad(Y)	1824	Aug. 06	Stark Co.,Oh	10	02	22
Haring, Conrad(Y)	1832	March 24	Stark Co.,Oh	09	12	19
Haring, Lewis(Y)	1831	Nov. 12	Stark Co.,Oh	09	12	20
Harkins, Daniel(Z)	1833	March 15	Perry Co.,Oh	15	14	15
Harkins, Philip(Z)	1835	Nov. 10	Morgan Co,Oh	09	07	15
Harkless, Henry(Y)	1828	July 26	Stark Co.,Oh	06	15	25
Harkless, William(Y)	1831	July 05	Stark Co.,Oh	07	16	02
Harkness, William(Z)	1816	April 29	PutnamCoOhio	11	13	36
Harlan, Enoch(Z)	1816	Dec. 09	MuskingmCoOh	12	12	34
Harlan, John(Z)	1817	Sept. 22	ChesterCo,Pa	12	12	26
Harless, Samuel(Y)	1833	June 01	HarrisonCoOh	06	12	18
Harman, Benj.(Z-M)	1828	Feb. 06	TuscarwsCoOh	04	08	06
Harman, Boston(Z)	1835	Oct. 15	Morgan Co,Oh	10	08	35
Harman, Conrad(Z)	1831	March 23	Morgan Co,Oh	10	08	33
Harman, George(Z-M)	1835	March 09	CoshoctnCoOh	09	04	16
Harman, George(Z-M)	1836	Jan. 25	CoshoctnCoOh	09	04	16
Harman, Jacob(Y)	1828	Aug. 19	HarrisonCoOh	06	13	03
Harman, Jacob(Y)	1832	March 05	HarrisonCoOh	05	13	21
Harman, Jacob(Z)	1827	Sept. 19	HolmesCoOhio	06	08	11
Harman, Jacob(Z)	1832	Aug. 29	Morgan Co,Oh	10	07	12
Harman, Jacob(Z)	1816	Aug. 29	GuernseyCoOh	11	11	01
Harman, Jacob(Z-M)	1826	Sept. 27	HarrisonCoOh	05	08	15
Harman, Jacob(Z-M)	1828	April 10	HolmesCoOhio	05	01	17
Harman, Jacob(Z-M)	1833	June 14	HolmesCoOhio	05	08	15
Harman, John(Y)	1828	Dec. 09	HarrisonCoOh	04	12	33
Harman, Jonas(Z-M)	1832	June 05	TuscarwsCoOh	03	09	21
Harman, Michael(Z-M)	1825	Aug. 24	HolmsCo,Ohio	04	08	05
Harman, Michael(Z-M)	1827	July 26	TuscarwsCoOh	03	10	11
Harman,Elizabeth of Michl(Z-M)	1828	July 02	TuscarwsCoOh	05	08	15
Harmon, Boston(Z)	1832	Sept. 13	Morgan Co,Oh	10	07	02
Harmon, Jonas(Y)	1825	Jan. 08	ColumbanCoOh	05	17	15
Harnel, Geo.(Z-M)	1829	June 29	TuscarwsCoOh	02	10	16
Harper, Abraham(Z)	1836	April 16	GuernseyCoOh	08	06	21
Harper, Abraham(Z-M)	1834	Feb. 13	TuscarwsCoOh	03	08	01
Harper, Alex'r.(Z)	1815	July 20	ZanesvilleOh	03	10	19
Harper, Alexander(Z)	1814	June 07	ZanesvilleOh	11	13	29
Harper, Alexander(Z)	1814	Aug. 31	ZanesvilleOh	06	04	13
Harper, Alexander(Z)	1814	Sept. 03	ZanesvilleOh	13	10	07
Harper, Daniel H.(Z)	1829	Dec. 16	Morgan Co,Oh	09	06	26
Harper, David(Z)	1837	March 13	MonroeCo.,Oh	08	06	14
Harper, Hugh(Y)	1827	Oct. 12	WashCo.,Penn	06	14	19
Harper, James(Z)	1816	Dec. 26	TuscarwsCoOh	03	08	01
Harper, James(Z-M)	1831	Sept. 22	TuscarwsCoOh	01	06	12
Harper, James(Z-M)	1834	Nov. 17	HarrisonCoOh	01	06	12
Harper, James(Z-M)	1835	June 04	HarrisonCoOh	01	06	12
Harper, James(Z-M)	1835	Nov. 05	HarrisonCoOh	01	06	12
Harper, John H.(Z)	1834	Aug. 29	Perry Co.,Oh	15	15	35
Harper, John(Z-M)	1835	June 27	CoshoctnCoOh	07	04	24
Harper, Michael(Z-M)	1835	May 26	TuscarwsCoOh	03	09	22
Harper, Samuel(Z)	1816	Sept. 09	WashCo.,Penn	04	02	16
Harper, Thomas(Z)	1825	Nov. 12	Perry Co.,Oh	15	15	21
Harper, Thomas(Z)	1825	Dec. 09	Perry Co.,Oh	15	15	21
Harper, Thomas(Z)	1834	Feb. 27	Perry Co.,Oh	15	15	27
Harper, Thomas(Z)	1814	Aug. 27	ZanesvilleOh	05	04	21
Harper, Thomas(Z)	1815	Jan. 25	ZanesvilleOh	05	04	21
Harper, William(Y)	1832	April 27	BelmontCo,Oh	06	08	19
Harper, William(Z-M)	1838	April 21	CoshoctnCoOh	05	07	24
Harret, Coonrod(Z-M)	1838	Nov. 17	MuskingmCoOh	03	04	17
Harriman, Samuel(Z-M)	1838	Aug. 25	LickingCo,Oh	11	04	13
Harrington, H.(Z)	1815	Jan. 05	LickingCo,Oh	10	03	25
Harrington, Hez'h.(Z)	1815	Aug. 25	LickingCo,Oh	10	03	16
Harrington, John(Z)	1810	Sept. 09	GreeneCo.,Pa	14	15	14
Harrington, Samuel(Z-M)	1834	Jan. 15	CarrollCo,Oh	03	08	17
Harrington, Samuel(Z-M)	1834	Jan. 15	CarrollCo,Oh	03	08	17

122

PURCHASER	YEAR	DATE	RESIDENCE	R	T	S
Harris & Galloway(Z-M)	1830	July 06	GuernseyCoOh	03	01	24
Harris, A. C.(Z-M)	1839	June 15	HarrisonCoOh	03	03	14
Harris, Abraham(Z-M)	1837	March 09	LickingCo,Oh	11	03	05
Harris, Benjamin(Z)	1812	March 04	LickingCo,Oh	15	15	05
Harris, Benjamin(Z)	1814	Sept. 05	WashngtnCoOh	11	11	30
Harris, Benjamin(Z)	1815	Dec. 11	FairfeldCoOh	14	13	17
Harris, Chris'n.(Z-M)	1830	Feb. 03	CoshoctnCoOh	08	04	08
Harris, Coley(Z)	1807	Sept. 29	BelmontCo,Oh	09	06	18
Harris, Daniel(Z-M)	1829	June 29	TuscarwsCoOh	02	10	25
Harris, David(Z-M)	1823	June 04	TuscarwsCoOh	02	10	13
Harris, David(Z-M)	1829	Sept. 11	TuscarwsCoOh	02	10	18
Harris, David(Z-M)	1831	Nov. 05	TuscarwsCoOh	02	10	25
Harris, David(Z-M)	1830	Nov. 04	TuscarwsCoOh	02	10	24
Harris, Edward(Z)	1806	March 17	FairfeldCoOh	15	18	07
Harris, Edward(Z)	1809	Nov. 27	MuskingmCoOh	15	18	18
Harris, Edward(Z)	1817	May 28	LickingCo,Oh	11	01	20
Harris, Elisha(Z)	1824	Jan. 28	Morgan Co,Oh	09	06	01
Harris, Elisha(Z)	1813	Dec. 04	BelmontCo,Oh	09	06	12
Harris, George(Z)	1835	Aug. 27	MonroeCo.,Oh	09	06	13
Harris, Henry(Z-M)	1834	Aug. 02	TuscarwsCoOh	03	08	07
Harris, Isaac(Z)	1830	June 04	Morgan Co,Oh	12	09	08
Harris, Isaac(Z)	1831	Jan. 27	LickingCo,Oh	11	03	04
Harris, Isaac(Z)	1811	Dec. 10	LickingCo,Oh	09	01	05
Harris, Isaac(Z)	1816	Dec. 05	LickingCo,Oh	11	01	21
Harris, Isaac(Z-M)	1834	July 29	LickingCo,Oh	11	03	07
Harris, Jacob(Z-M)	1839	Sept. 26	KnoxCo.,Ohio	10	08	20
Harris, James M.(Z-M)	1835	Aug. 13	MuskingmCoOh	07	08	01
Harris, James(Z)	1813	Oct. 29	FranklinCoPa	01	10	07
Harris, James(Z)	1816	April 27	Ohio Co.,Vir	08	08	13
Harris, James(Z)	1816	Dec. 05	LickingCo,Oh	12	09	10
Harris, John(Z)	1830	June 22	Morgan Co,Oh	13	08	36
Harris, John(Z)	1810	Oct. 08	LickingCo,Oh	11	01	19
Harris, John(Z)	1816	Feb. 05	LickingCo,Oh	11	03	04
Harris, John(Z)	1816	Feb. 13	LickingCo,Oh	11	03	07
Harris, John(Z)	1816	Oct. 24	LickingCo,Oh	12	09	10
Harris, John(Z)	1816	Dec. 21	LickingCo,Oh	12	09	15
Harris, John(Z-M)	1825	Sept. 29	TuscarwsCoOh	02	10	13
Harris, John(Z-M)	1829	April 08	TuscarwsCoOh	02	10	25
Harris, John(Z-M)	1831	Sept. 14	LickingCo,Oh	11	03	04
Harris, Joseph(Z)	1817	May 20	CoshoctnCoOh	08	04	14
Harris, Joseph(Z-M)	1835	Dec. 01	HolmesCoOhio	09	09	24
Harris, Josephus(Z)	1828	April 23	BelmontCo,Oh	11	10	17
Harris, Joshua(Z-M)	1835	April 20	LickingCo,Oh	11	03	08
Harris, Losson(Z-M)	1822	May 23	KnoxCo.,Ohio	11	05	20
Harris, Morgan(Z)	1829	March 04	Morgan Co,Oh	08	06	20
Harris, Morgan(Z)	1832	Aug. 25	MonroeCo.,Oh	08	06	07
Harris, Morgan(Z)	1832	Aug. 25	MonroeCo.,Oh	08	06	07
Harris, Reuben(Y)	1831	Aug. 01	ColumbanCoOh	05	15	32
Harris, Sam'l. B.(Z-M)	1832	June 07	LickingCo,Oh	11	04	06
Harris, Samuel B.(Z-M)	1837	Jan. 11	LickingCo,Oh	11	04	07
Harris, Samuel(Z-M)	1837	July 31	HarrisonCoOh	01	05	18
Harris, Stephen(Z)	1822	June 25	Morgan Co,Oh	08	06	08
Harris, Thomas(Z)	1806	April 25	FairfeldCoOh	10	01	21
Harris, Thomas(Z)	1806	Nov. 29	FairfeldCoOh	11	01	23
Harris, Thomas(Z)	1809	Feb. 20	LickingCo,Oh	15	18	18
Harris, William(Z)	1826	June 08	MuskingmCoOh	14	14	15
Harris, Wm.(Y)	1829	Oct. 12	ColumbanCoOh	05	18	30
Harrison, Benj'n.(Z-M)	1832	Feb. 28	HolmesCoOhio	06	08	08
Harrison, Benj.(Z-M)	1830	Dec. 17	HolmesCoOhio	06	08	08
Harrison, Eph'm.(Z-M)	1839	April 23	CoshoctnCoOh	08	07	04
Harrison, Ephraim(Z)	1839	March 14	CoshoctnCoOh	08	07	05
Harrison, Ephraim(Z-M)	1838	Dec. 05	Wayne Co.,Oh	08	07	03
Harrison, James(Z)	1836	Feb. 19	BelmontCo,Oh	08	08	32
Harrison, Joseph(Y)	1828	July 01	HarrisonCoOh	05	12	33
Harrison, Joshua(Y)	1825	Oct. 10	Jeff.Co.,Oh.	03	11	34
Harrison, Joshua(Y)	1825	Oct. 10	Jeff.Co.,Oh.	03	11	34
Harrison, Richard(Y)	1828	March 05	ColumbanCoOh	05	15	09
Harrison, William(Z)	1834	Dec. 03	GuernseyCoOh	09	08	13
Harriss, Esaw(Z)	1836	April 14	MonroeCo.,Oh	08	06	30

PURCHASER	YEAR	DATE	RESIDENCE	R	T	S
Harriss, Jacob(Z-M)	1834	Feb. 06	Brooke CoVir	03	04	15
Harriss, James(Z)	1835	Oct. 29	BelmontCo.,Oh	08	08	32
Harriss, James(Z-M)	1835	Oct. 16	HolmesCoOhio	09	09	01
Harriss, Joseph(Z-M)	1837	Dec. 05	HolmesCoOhio	09	09	23
Harriss, Simon(Z)	1836	Aug. 06	BelmontCo.,Oh	08	05	14
Harriss, Simon(Z)	1836	Aug. 06	BelmontCo.,Oh	08	06	32
Harriss, Stephen(Z)	1835	Nov. 23	MonroeCo.,Oh	08	06	08
Harriss, Stephen(Z)	1836	June 03	MonroeCo.,Oh	08	06	05
Harriss, Stephen(Z)	1836	June 03	MonroeCo.,Oh	08	06	08
Harriss, Stephen(Z)	1836	Sept. 09	MonroeCo.,Oh	08	06	05
Harriss, William(Z-M)	1836	April 01	MuskingmCoOh	09	03	14
Harrmann, Michael(Z-M)	1837	April 21	TuscarwsCoOh	04	07	10
Harrod, Levi(Z)	1812	Feb. 22	KnoxCo.,Ohio	11	06	23
Harrod, Levi(Z)	1814	March 03	?	11	05	08
Harrod, Michael(Z)	1813	Dec. 30	KnoxCo.,Ohio	11	06	17
Harrod, Michael(Z)	1813	Dec. 30	KnoxCo.,Ohio	11	06	24
Harrod, Michael(Z)	1814	April 23	KnoxCo.,Ohio	11	06	23
Harrod, Michael(Z)	1814	April 23	KnoxCo.,Ohio	11	06	23
Harrod, Michael(Z)	1814	April 23	KnoxCo.,Ohio	11	06	23
Harrod, Michael(Z)	1814	April 23	KnoxCo.,Ohio	11	05	03
Harrod, Michael(Z)	1815	Aug. 02	KnoxCo.,Ohio	11	06	22
Harrop, James(Z)	1826	April 19	MuskingmCoOh	13	11	28
Harrop, James(Z)	1826	May 13	MuskingmCoOh	13	11	28
Harry, Joel(Z)	1816	Oct. 09	MifflinCo,Pa	05	02	13
Harry, William(Z)	1827	Feb. 23	BelmontCo.,Oh	12	09	13
Harryman, Daniel(Z)	1824	Nov. 09	HarrisonCoOh	12	12	22
Harsh, Adam(Y)	1829	May 30	ColumbanCoOh	05	14	24
Harsh, Solomon(Y)	1823	Dec. 19	ColumbanCoOh	06	16	22
Harsh, Solomon(Y)	1824	Aug. 17	ColumbanCoOh	06	16	22
Harsh, Wm.(Y)	1822	Dec. 14	WashCo.,Penn	05	14	22
Harsha, Wm.(Z)	1831	Oct. 22	Morgan Co,Oh	13	08	27
Harshberger, Abraham(Z)	1809	June 12	FauquierCoVa	04	09	15
Harshman, George(Z-M)	1824	Oct. 25	FayetteCo,Pa	04	07	08
Harshman, Philip(Z-M)	1832	Feb. 08	CoshoctnCoOh	06	04	21
Harshman, Philip(Z-M)	1832	Feb. 21	CoshoctnCoOh	05	04	25
Harshman, Philip(Z-M)	1836	Dec. 02	CoshoctnCoOh	06	04	23
Harstin, Abraham(Z-M)	1831	Nov. 28	TuscarwsCoOh	04	07	14
Hart, Benjamin(Z-M)	1836	Jan. 25	HarrisonCoOh	01	06	23
Hart, Cyrus W.(Y)	1820	Nov. 11	ColumbanCoOh	04	13	34
Hart, Cyrus W.(Y)	1822	April 19	ColumbanCoOh	04	13	34
Hart, Cyrus W.(Y)	1829	May 28	ColumbanCoOh	04	13	29
Hart, Elijah(Z)	1806	April 22	AdamsCo,Penn	07	01	10
Hart, Howard(Z-M)	1837	May 02	MuskingmCoOh	04	03	13
Hart, Jacob(Z-M)	1831	July 06	GuernseyCoOh	03	04	07
Hart, John S.(Y)	1825	Jan. 12	ColumbanCoOh	03	12	04
Hart, Jonathan(Y)	1822	Feb. 19	Brooke CoVir	06	15	22
Hart, Jonathan(Y)	1822	Feb. 27	Brooke CoVir	06	15	15
Hart, Jonathan(Y)	1825	Dec. 22	Stark Co.,Oh	04	13	25
Hart, Jonathan(Y)	1831	Nov. 26	ColumbanCoOh	04	12	36
Hart, Joseph(Z)	1827	July 31	GuernseyCoOh	09	08	24
Hart, Joseph(Z)	1827	Aug. 29	GuernseyCoOh	09	08	14
Hart, Leonard(Z-M)	1836	Nov. 18	BelmontCo.,Oh	03	06	08
Hart, R.(Z)	1814	Feb. 14	CoshoctnCoOh	07	05	24
Hart, Reuben(Z-M)	1831	Jan. 27	CoshoctnCoOh	07	05	24
Hart, Robert(Z)	1837	Jan. 19	BelmontCo.,Oh	08	07	33
Hart, Robert(Z-M)	1835	Oct. 03	BristlCoMass	09	07	10
Hartagen, James(Z-M)	1837	Nov. 28	ZanesvilleOh	05	04	13
Hartford, Jesse(Z)	1827	Nov. 22	Morgan Co,Oh	11	10	27
Hartford, John(Z)	1815	Oct. 06	MuskingmCoOh	08	03	04
Hartford, John(Z)	1815	Oct. 07	MuskingmCoOh	08	03	04
Hartford, William(Z)	1825	Nov. 19	Brooke CoVir	11	10	25
Hartley, John(Y)	1827	April 12	GuernseyCoOh	07	09	20
Hartley, John(Z)	1833	Oct. 30	Morgan Co,Oh	09	05	19
Hartley, John(Z)	1835	Sept. 10	Morgan Co,Oh	10	06	01
Hartley, John(Z)	1816	June 11	TuscarwsCoOh	03	06	23
Hartley, John(Z-M)	1828	Sept. 12	TuscarwsCoOh	03	06	06
Hartley, John(Z-M)	1828	Sept. 12	TuscarwsCoOh	03	06	14
Hartley, Joseph(Y)	1830	May 20	BelmontCo.,Oh	07	09	19
Hartley, Martin(Y)	1836	Jan. 20	ColumbanCoOh	03	12	22

PURCHASER	YEAR	DATE	RESIDENCE	R	T	S
Hartley, Noah(Y)	1827	June 19	BelmontCo,Oh	07	09	19
Hartman, Conrad(Z)	1834	March 25	Morgan Co,Oh	10	06	03
Hartman, Dan'l.(Z-M)	1835	Dec. 29	HolmesCoOhio	06	09	24
Hartman, Daniel(Z-M)	1832	Sept. 11	HolmesCoOhio	06	09	24
Hartman, Daniel(Z-M)	1833	Sept. 11	HolmesCoOhio	06	09	24
Hartman, George(Z-M)	1828	July 22	GuernseyCoOh	04	01	20
Hartman, Henry(Z)	1821	Feb. 01	Morgan Co,Oh	10	07	28
Hartman, Henry(Z)	1833	Jan. 24	Morgan Co,Oh	10	07	22
Hartman, Jacob(Z)	1835	Dec. 17	MuskingmCoOh	10	09	25
Hartman, John Jnr.(Z)	1835	Nov. 09	GuernseyCoOh	10	09	24
Hartman, John(Z)	1835	Nov. 07	GuernseyCoOh	10	09	23
Hartman, John(Z-M)	1835	Aug. 22	Baltimore,Md	09	09	16
Hartman, Justice(Z)	1836	April 15	Morgan Co,Oh	09	05	20
Hartman, Justus(Z)	1827	Oct. 05	Morgan Co,Oh	10	07	19
Hartman, Justus(Z)	1833	June 12	Morgan Co,Oh	11	11	24
Hartman, Justus(Z)	1833	June 12	Morgan Co,Oh	11	11	25
Hartman, Michael(Z)	1815	Nov. 03	CoshoctnCoOh	06	07	13
Hartman, William(Z)	1835	Nov. 10	GuernseyCoOh	10	09	25
Hartsel, David(Z)	1836	May 14	Perry Co.,Oh	14	12	08
Hartsel, David(Z)	1836	Oct. 28	Perry Co.,Oh	14	12	08
Hartsell, Jno.(Z)	1814	Jan. 11	MuskingmCoOh	15	16	19
Hartsell, John Jr.(Z)	1833	Nov. 08	Perry Co.,Oh	14	12	05
Hartshorn, Joshua(Z-M)	1837	Oct. 27	TuscarwsCoOh	03	05	24
Hartshorn, Joshua(Z-M)	1839	Jan. 16	TuscarwsCoOh	03	05	24
Hartshorn, Norris(Y)	1823	Nov. 28	PortageCo,Oh	05	18	06
Hartshorne, Joshua(Z-M)	1825	Aug. 01	TuscarwsCoOh	02	05	18
Harttunq, Philip(Y)	1831	Nov. 09	West ?	09	12	18
Hartzal, Jacob(Y)	1821	April 05	PortageCo,Oh	05	18	10
Hartzel, Henry(Y)	1824	April 20	PortageCo,Oh	05	18	02
Hartzel, Mary(Y)	1827	June 08	PortageCo,Oh	06	18	23
Hartzel, Mary(Y)	1827	June 08	PortageCo,Oh	06	18	21
Hartzell, Geo.(Y)	1824	Aug. 17	PortageCo,Oh	05	18	05
Hartzell, Henry(Y)	1824	Jan. 07	PortageCo,Oh	05	18	02
Hartzell, Jacob(Y)	1824	March 10	PortageCo,Oh	05	18	10
Hartzell, Jonas(Y)	1826	June 13	PortageCo,Oh	05	18	04
Hartzell, Jonas(Y)	1826	Dec. 23	ColumbanCoOh	05	18	04
Hartzell, Peter(Y)	1824	Sept. 14	PortageCo,Oh	05	18	04
Harvy, David Junr.(Z)	1805	May 22	MuskingmCoOh	05	01	17
Harvy, David(Z)	1804	June 08	MuskingmCoOh	13	12	08
Harwood, Charles(Z)	1811	Nov. 09	WashngtnCoOh	10	07	08
Hassey, A.(Z)	1816	Jan. 02	WashngtnCoOh	11	11	28
Hastel, John(Z)	1815	March 01	GuernseyCoOh	01	04	18
Hastinqs, George(Z-M)	1835	June 29	GuernseyCoOh	01	05	03
Hastings, John(Z)	1837	Feb. 27	GuernseyCoOh	14	12	27
Hastings, John(Z)	1837	Feb. 27	GuernseyCoOh	14	12	22
Hastings, William(Z-M)	1835	Oct. 30	GuernseyCoOh	01	05	03
Hatch, William(Y)	1835	Nov. 06	Stark Co.,Oh	10	02	12
Hatcher, Jesse(Z)	1816	Sept. 27	Barnes'1Ohio	15	15	30
Hatcher, John(Z-M)	1832	June 05	GuernseyCoOh	03	04	01
Hatcher, John(Z-M)	1833	April 19	BelmontCo,Oh	03	04	01
Hatcher, Obadiah(Z-M)	1831	Sept. 02	BelmontCo,Oh	02	04	05
Hatcher, Wm.(Y)	1824	May 18	ColumbanCoOh	07	20	03
Hatfield, Wm.(Z)	1835	Nov. 07	GuernseyCoOh	10	09	23
Hathorn, James(Y)	1823	May 05	BelmontCo,Co	03	05	03
Hathway, Jos.(Z-M)	1831	April 10	TuscarwsCoOh	01	09	20
Hattan, Daniel(Z-M)	1837	Jan. 19	ZanesvilleOh	09	08	17
Hattan, James(Z-M)	1837	Jan. 11	ZanesvilleOh	01	06	11
Hattery, Andrew(Y)	1831	Aug. 05	ColumbanCoOh	04	13	20
Hattery, Ephraim(Z-M)	1839	April 03	TuscarwsCoOh	05	07	24
Hattery, James(Y)	1828	Aug. 29	BrookeCo,Vir	04	13	21
Hattery, James(Y)	1828	Aug. 29	BrookeCo,Vir	04	13	20
Hattery, James(Z)	1815	June 13	TuscarwsCoOh	03	08	05
Hattery, James(Z-M)	1833	Aug. 15	TuscarwsCoOh	03	08	15
Hattery, Thomas(Z-M)	1832	May 23	TuscarwsCoOh	03	08	04
Hatton, Richard(Z)	1832	March 09	MuskingmCoOh	09	06	15
Hauger, Joseph(Z)	1810	June 11	SomersetCoPa	10	07	13
Haughland, Thos.(Y)	1828	Sept. 22	HarrisonCoOh	06	12	07
Haughman, John Junr.(Z)	1833	Dec. 30	Perry Co.,Oh	15	15	24
Haughman, John Senr.(Z)	1833	Dec. 30	Perry Co.,Oh	15	15	25

PURCHASER	YEAR	DATE	RESIDENCE	R	T	S
Haughman, John(Z)	1833	Oct. 26	ZanesvilleOh	15	15	22
Haughman, Patrick(Z)	1833	Oct. 26	ZanesvilleOh	15	15	25
Haughman, William(Z)	1833	Oct. 26	ZanesvilleOh	15	15	27
Haughman, William(Z)	1834	Jan. 16	Perry Co.,Oh	15	15	26
Haughran, John Jr.(Z)	1835	Aug. 11	Perry Co.,Oh	15	15	25
Haughran, John(Z)	1836	Jan. 23	Perry Co.,Oh	15	15	22
Haughran, Thomas(Z)	1833	Oct. 29	ZanesvilleOh	15	15	25
Hauman, John(Z-M)	1836	Dec. 06	TuscarwsCoOh	03	07	14
Haun, Elizabeth(Y)	1827	Feb. 22	ColumbanCoOh	06	18	13
Haun, Jacob(Y)	1827	Aug. 27	Jeff.Co.,Oh.	05	12	28
Haus, Joseph(Z)	1815	June 09	BelmontCo,Oh	08	05	06
Hauser, David(Y)	1826	Aug. 08	Jeff.Co.,Oh.	03	11	15
Havens, Elisha(Z)	1807	Jan. 20	Jeff.Co.,Oh.	02	01	02
Haver, George W.(Z-M)	1837	Jan. 11	ZanesvilleOh	02	03	05
Haver, George W.(Z-M)	1837	Jan. 11	ZanesvilleOh	06	03	03
Haverstick, Mich'l.(Y)	1826	Dec. 22	Stark Co.,Oh	06	18	06
Haviland, Duadamia(Z-M)	1837	April 03	CoshoctnCoOh	08	07	04
Haviland, Joseph Jr.(Z-M)	1835	Dec. 23	CoshoctnCoOh	08	07	04
Haviland, Joseph Jr.(Z-M)	1837	March 29	CoshoctnCoOh	08	07	13
Haviland, Joseph(Z-M)	1835	Oct. 26	CoshoctnCoOh	08	07	03
Haviland, Joseph(Z-M)	1835	Oct. 26	CoshoctnCoOh	08	08	24
Haviland, Joseph(Z-M)	1835	Oct. 26	CoshoctnCoOh	08	08	23
Haviland, Joseph(Z-M)	1835	Dec. 16	CoshoctnCoOh	08	07	04
Haviland, Joseph(Z-M)	1836	Oct. 11	CoshoctnCoOh	08	08	24
Haviland, Lewis(Z-M)	1834	Aug. 05	CoshoctnCoOh	07	07	12
Haviland, Lewis(Z-M)	1836	Jan. 07	CoshoctnCoOh	07	07	12
Haviland, Silvanus(Z-M)	1832	Feb. 14	CoshoctnCoOh	06	07	14
Hawbeard, Thomas(Z)	1810	June 08	MuskingmCoOh	15	18	12
Hawes, Welles(Z)	1836	July 02	PutnamCoOhio	15	14	14
Hawes, Welles(Z)	1836	July 05	PutnamCoOhio	15	14	23
Hawes, Welles(Z)	1836	Aug. 19	PutnamCoOhio	09	07	24
Hawes, Welles(Z)	1836	Oct. 07	MuskingmCoOh	08	07	17
Hawes, Welles(Z)	1836	Oct. 12	MuskingmCoOh	08	07	21
Hawes, Welles(Z)	1836	Oct. 12	MuskingmCoOh	08	07	21
Hawes, Welles(Z)	1836	Oct. 18	MuskingmCoOh	08	07	29
Hawes, Welles(Z)	1836	Oct. 18	MuskingmCoOh	08	07	32
Hawes, Welles(Z)	1836	Dec. 14	PutnamCoOhio	15	14	21
Hawes, Welles(Z)	1837	Feb. 10	PutnamCoOhio	15	14	28
Hawes, Welles(Z)	1837	Feb. 15	PutnamCoOhio	15	14	31
Hawes, Welles(Z)	1837	March 01	PutnamCoOhio	08	06	10
Hawes, Welles(Z)	1837	March 04	PutnamCoOhio	15	15	25
Hawes, Welles(Z)	1837	March 09	PutnamCoOhio	14	12	13
Hawes, Welles(Z)	1837	March 11	PutnamCoOhio	08	05	28
Hawes, Welles(Z)	1837	March 11	PutnamCoOhio	15	15	24
Hawes, Welles(Z)	1837	April 25	PutnamCoOhio	14	12	08
Hawes, Welles(Z)	1837	May 06	PutnamCoOhio	08	06	35
Hawes, Welles(Z)	1837	Aug. 18	PutnamCoOhio	08	06	30
Hawes, Welles(Z)	1837	Sept. 30	PutnamCoOhio	08	06	29
Hawes, Welles(Z)	1837	Oct. 02	PutnamCoOhio	09	06	23
Hawes, Welles(Z)	1837	Oct. 17	PutnamCoOhio	08	06	28
Hawes, Welles(Z)	1838	Nov. 05	MuskingmCoOh	08	07	20
Hawes, Welles(Z-M)	1837	Feb. 13	PutnamCoOhio	10	06	05
Hawes, Welles(Z-M)	1837	Feb. 16	PutnamCoOhio	08	08	15
Hawes, Welles(Z-M)	1837	Feb. 16	PutnamCoOhio	10	08	13
Hawes, Welles(Z-M)	1837	Feb. 20	PutnamCoOhio	08	06	06
Hawes, Welles(Z-M)	1837	Feb. 27	PutnamCoOhio	05	03	10
Hawes, Welles(Z-M)	1837	Feb. 28	PutnamCoOhio	08	08	22
Hawes, Welles(Z-M)	1837	Feb. 28	PutnamCoOhio	08	08	22
Hawes, Welles(Z-M)	1837	March 03	PutnamCoOhio	10	07	21
Hawes, Welles(Z-M)	1837	March 03	PutnamCoOhio	05	07	25
Hawes, Welles(Z-M)	1837	March 03	PutnamCoOhio	09	09	17
Hawes, Welles(Z-M)	1837	March 03	PutnamCoOhio	09	09	04
Hawes, Welles(Z-M)	1837	March 21	PutnamCoOhio	09	08	24
Hawes, Welles(Z-M)	1837	April 05	PutnamCoOhio	10	04	24
Hawes, Welles(Z-M)	1837	April 14	PutnamCoOhio	08	07	03
Hawes, Welles(Z-M)	1837	April 18	PutnamCoOhio	04	04	02
Hawes, Welles(Z-M)	1837	May 06	PutnamCoOhio	08	07	03
Hawes, Welles(Z-M)	1837	May 06	PutnamCoOhio	08	07	05
Hawes, Welles(Z-M)	1837	May 06	PutnamCoOhio	09	07	19

PURCHASER	YEAR	DATE	RESIDENCE	R	T	S
Hawes, Welles(Z-M)	1837	May 06	PutnamCoOhio	09	07	20
Hawes, Welles(Z-M)	1837	May 06	PutnamCoOhio	09	07	20
Hawes, Welles(Z-M)	1837	Sept. 14	PutnamCoOhio	09	08	05
Hawes, Welles(Z-M)	1837	Sept. 14	PutnamCoOhio	09	08	05
Hawes, Welles(Z-M)	1837	Sept. 15	PutnamCoOhio	07	07	19
Hawes, Welles(Z-M)	1838	Jan. 19	PutnamCoOhio	08	08	16
Hawes, Welles(Z-M)	1838	Feb. 12	PutnamCoOhio	09	03	16
Hawes, Welles(Z-M)	1838	Feb. 12	PutnamCoOhio	10	06	06
Hawes, Welles(Z-M)	1838	Feb. 19	PutnamCoOhio	08	08	16
Hawes, Welles(Z-M)	1838	Feb. 19	PutnamCoOhio	08	08	16
Hawes, Welles(Z-M)	1838	April 21	PutnamCoOhio	08	07	13
Hawes, Welles(Z-M)	1838	June 01	PutnamCoOhio	08	08	12
Hawes, Welles(Z-M)	1838	June 05	PutnamCoOhio	09	07	21
Hawes, Welles(Z-M)	1838	June 13	PutnamCoOhio	08	07	11
Hawes, Welles(Z-M)	1838	Oct. 26	PutnamCoOhio	08	07	19
Hawes, Welles(Z-M)	1839	Jan. 28	PutnamCoOhio	09	03	16
Hawes, Welles(Z-M)	1839	Feb. 21	PutnamCoOhio	09	07	19
Hawk, Alfred(Z-M)	1831	March 09	KnoxCo.,Ohio	11	05	21
Hawk, Elijah(Z-M)	1832	Nov. 10	TuscarwsCoOh	03	10	17
Hawk, Jacob(Z)	1825	Sept. 10	Morgan Co,Oh	10	07	15
Hawk, John(Y)	1822	June 10	HarrisonCoOh	07	15	25
Hawk, John(Z-M)	1827	Feb. 13	TuscarwsCoOh	03	07	18
Hawk, John(Z-M)	1827	May 22	TuscarwsCoOh	03	07	18
Hawk, John(Z-M)	1832	July 20	TuscarwsCoOh	03	07	17
Hawk, Leonard(Z)	1826	Nov. 24	ColumbanCoOh	04	06	09
Hawk, Leonard(Z-M)	1832	Nov. 23	CoshoctnCoOh	04	06	09
Hawkins, Samuel(Z)	1816	April 19	GuernseyCoOh	01	02	07
Hawkins, Timothy(Z)	1815	Jan. 03	CoshoctnCoOh	10	06	23
Hawkins, William(Z)	1809	Sept. 27	WashngtnCoOh	02	02	21
Haws & Galloway(Z-M)	1830	July 06	GuernseyCoOh	03	01	24
Haws, Ann(Z-M)	1829	June 12	BelmontCo,Oh	03	01	25
Haws, George(Z-M)	1829	Feb. 17	HolmesCoOhio	05	08	24
Haws, John(Z)	1829	June 12	BelmontCo,Oh	10	09	03
Haws, John(Z)	1833	May 20	GuernseyCoOh	10	09	10
Hawse, Benjamin(Z-M)	1838	June 13	CoshoctnCoOh	10	07	20
Hawthorn, James(Z-M)	1829	Oct. 13	PittsburghPa	04	03	16
Hawthorn, John M.(Z-M)	1839	Feb. 18	GuernseyCoOh	04	03	16
Hawthorn, John McK.(Z-M)	1835	Dec. 11	GuernseyCoOh	04	03	16
Hawthorn, John McK.(Z-M)	1836	Dec. 17	GuernseyCoOh	04	03	16
Haxton, John(Z-M)	1826	May 22	Jeff.Co.,Oh.	06	08	22
Haxton, John(Z-M)	1828	Oct. 14	HolmesCoOhio	06	08	22
Haxton, Samuel(Z-M)	1835	Sept. 24	HolmesCoOhio	07	07	19
Haxtone, Samuel(Z-M)	1835	Sept. 17	HolmesCoOhio	07	07	22
Hay, Benjamin(Z-M)	1836	Nov. 05	HolmesCoOhio	08	08	07
Hay, Daniel(Z-M)	1833	Nov. 05	StarkeCo.,Oh	03	10	23
Hay, James(Z-M)	1831	March 01	KnoxCo.,Ohio	10	05	24
Hayden, Elijah(Y)	1834	June 10	Stark Co.,Oh	07	14	35
Hayden, Elijah(Y)	1834	June 10	Stark Co.,Oh	07	14	35
Hayes, Enoch(Z)	1836	Dec. 12	MonroeCo.,Oh	08	06	26
Hayes, Frederic(Z)	1836	Oct. 11	MonroeCo.,Oh	08	06	26
Hayes, Frederic(Z)	1836	Dec. 03	MonroeCo.,Oh	08	06	23
Hayes, James(Y)	1825	March 23	BeaverCo,Pa.	04	14	36
Hayes, James(Z-M)	1835	Sept. 29	CoshoctnCoOh	04	06	09
Hayes, John(Z)	1837	April 26	GuernseyCoOh	08	06	26
Hayes, Jos.(Z-M)	1832	Jan. 16	TuscarwsCoOh	01	09	09
Hayes, Thomas(Z-M)	1831	Oct. 27	Jeff.Co.,Oh.	04	06	01
Hayes, William(Y)	1828	Aug. 18	Stark Co.,Oh	07	16	27
Hayes, William(Z-M)	1832	Aug. 20	Jeff.Co.,Oh.	04	06	03
Hayhurst, William(Y)	1827	June 02	ColumbanCoOh	05	18	27
Haymaker, H.(Z-M)	1831	Oct. 15	MuskingmCoOh	05	03	06
Haymaker, Jno.(Z)	1834	Oct. 23	Morgan Co,Oh	11	10	24
Haymond, Abijah(Z)	1811	April 05	MuskingmCoOh	09	03	05
Hayns, James(Z-M)	1839	Feb. 12	HolmesCoOhio	10	06	05
Hays, Aaron(Y)	1834	May 31	ColumbanCoOh	03	12	11
Hays, Edmund(Y)	1825	Nov. 21	GuernseyCoOh	07	09	02
Hays, John(Z)	1837	Jan. 06	BelmontCo,Oh	15	14	02
Hays, John(Z)	1837	Jan. 06	BelmontCo,Oh	15	14	03
Hays, John(Z)	1816	Nov. 23	Brooke CoVir	13	09	34
Hays, John(Z-M)	1827	June 25	KnoxCo.,Ohio	11	08	16

PURCHASER	YEAR	DATE	RESIDENCE	R	T	S
Hays, John(Z-M)	1837	Aug. 26	BerkshirMass	09	07	12
Hays, Joseph(Z)	1813	Dec. 07	TuscarwsCoOh	01	09	09
Hays, Manly(Z)	1837	April 11	MonroeCo.,Oh	08	06	15
Hays, Michael(Z)	1817	Oct. 24	WestmrldCoPa	02	04	12
Hays, Michael(Z)	1817	Oct. 24	WestmrldCoPa	01	04	16
Hays, Thomas B.(Z-M)	1838	May 31	CoshoctnCoOh	10	04	02
Hays, Thomas(Z-M)	1834	Nov. 19	KnoxCo.,Ohio	08	08	21
Hays, Thomas(Z-M)	1834	Nov. 19	KnoxCo.,Ohio	08	08	22
Hays, Thos.(Y)	1825	May 12	GuernseyCoOh	07	09	34
Hays, William(Z-M)	1828	Oct. 27	GuernseyCoOh	02	02	07
Hays, William(Z-M)	1833	Dec. 14	CoshoctnCoOh	07	04	13
Haywood, James(Z-M)	1838	Feb. 27	KnoxCo.,Ohio	10	09	19
Haywood, James(Z-M)	1838	Feb. 27	KnoxCo.,Ohio	10	09	19
Hazel, John(Y)	1826	Aug. 28	Stark Co.,Oh	08	12	22
Hazelton, Henry(Z)	1835	Dec. 31	Perry Co.,Oh	15	14	17
Hazelton, Henry(Z)	1836	April 16	Perry Co.,Oh	15	14	30
Hazelton, Henry(Z)	1836	April 16	Perry Co.,Oh	15	14	28
Hazelton, Henry(Z)	1836	April 16	Perry Co.,Oh	15	14	33
Hazelton, Henry(Z)	1836	Dec. 17	Perry Co.,Oh	15	14	30
Hazelton, Henry(Z)	1836	Dec. 17	Perry Co.,Oh	15	14	17
Hazelton, John Jr.(Z)	1836	April 16	Perry Co.,Oh	15	14	08
Hazelton, John(Z)	1817	May 19	FayetteCo,Pa	15	14	17
Hazelton, Samuel(Z)	1817	Aug. 25	FairfeldCoOh	15	15	19
Hazen, Ahimaaz(Y)	1826	Oct. 04	PortageCo,Oh	04	17	06
Hazen, Daniel(Y)	1828	Feb. 09	PortageCo,Oh	05	18	07
Hazlet, Hugh(Z)	1810	Aug. 29	?	14	15	17
Hazlet, James(Y)	1823	May 31	Jeff.Co.,Oh.	04	10	18
Hazlet, Jo.(Y)	1822	Aug. 01	Stark Co.,Oh	07	19	15
Hazleton, John Junr.(Z)	1834	Jan. 01	Perry Co.,Oh	15	14	08
Hazleton, John(Z)	1823	Sept. 15	Perry Co.,Oh	15	14	08
Hazleton, John(Z)	1828	Aug. 15	Perry Co.,Oh	15	14	08
Hazleton, Jos.(Z)	1823	May 21	Perry Co.,Oh	15	14	19
Hazlett, Isaac(Z)	1813	Aug. 06	ZanesvilleOh	05	02	05
Hazlett, James(Z-M)	1832	Jan. 06	TuscarwsCoOh	01	09	06
Hazlett, James(Z-M)	1832	Jan. 06	TuscarwsCoOh	01	09	06
Hazlett, James(Z-M)	1832	May 12	TuscarwsCoOh	01	09	15
Hazlett, James(Z-M)	1832	May 12	TuscarwsCoOh	01	09	04
Hazlett, James(Z-M)	1831	April 09	StarkeCo.,Oh	01	09	07
Hazlett, James(Z-M)	1832	Dec. 07	TuscarwsCoOh	01	09	08
Hazlett, Jas.(Z-M)	1833	Dec. 16	StarkeCoOhio	01	09	05
Hazlett, John(Z)	1814	Nov. 16	WashCo.,Penn	01	04	23
Heacock, Nathan(Y)	1822	March 12	ColumbanCoOh	05	18	28
Headley, Carey(Z)	1832	Nov. 24	Morgan Co,Oh	09	07	15
Headley, Carey(Z)	1833	Sept. 20	Morgan Co,Oh	09	07	15
Headley, Carey(Z)	1836	Aug. 26	MonroeCo.,Oh	08	06	08
Headley, David(Z)	1833	Nov. 18	Perry Co.,Oh	15	14	06
Headley, Francis(Z)	1833	April 27	MonroeCo.,Oh	08	06	17
Headley, Francis(Z)	1836	June 03	MonroeCo.,Oh	08	06	08
Headley, Gabriel(Z-M)	1829	June 23	CoshoctnCoOh	05	06	15
Headley, Gabriel(Z-M)	1833	Feb. 20	CoshoctnCoOh	05	06	17
Headley, Gabriel(Z-M)	1833	Feb. 20	CoshoctnCoOh	05	06	17
Headley, Harrison(Z-M)	1833	Jan. 25	CoshoctnCoOh	05	06	15
Headley, Isaac(Z)	1835	Dec. 09	MonroeCo.,Oh	08	07	22
Headly, Baldwin(Z-M)	1832	March 12	CoshoctnCoOh	04	06	13
Headly, Isaac(Z-M)	1835	Dec. 28	CoshoctnCoOh	05	06	17
Headly, Samuel(Z-M)	1832	March 12	CoshoctnCoOh	04	06	13
Headly, Silas(Z-M)	1832	March 12	CoshoctnCoOh	04	06	13
Heal, William(Z)	1822	Feb. 28	MuskingmCoOh	11	12	11
Healey, James(Z-M)	1826	April 08	CoshoctnCoOh	05	06	05
Heaney, James W.(Z)	1835	Sept. 22	Morgan Co,Oh	10	07	17
Heaney, John(Z)	1834	Jan. 11	BelmontCo,Oh	10	07	18
Heans, Jacob(Z-M)	1829	Feb. 07	GuernseyCoOh	04	02	03
Hearing, Jacob(Z)	1833	Feb. 06	Perry Co.,Oh	14	13	23
Hearing, Jacob(Z)	1833	Feb. 06	Perry Co.,Oh	14	13	13
Hearing, John A.(Z)	1806	Dec. 22	MuskingmCoOh	15	17	33
Hearing, John A.(Z)	1806	Dec. 22	MuskingmCoOh	15	17	32
Hearing, John Adam(Z)	1836	Jan. 18	Perry Co.,Oh	14	13	24
Hearsman, John(Z-M)	1836	Jan. 23	CoshoctnCoOh	06	04	22
Heartly, Henry(Y)	1832	Nov. 05	ColumbanCoOh	03	12	30

PURCHASER	YEAR	DATE	RESIDENCE	R	T	S
Heastand, James(Y)	1831	Jan. 21	TuscarwsCoOh	06	13	19
Heater, George(Z-M)	1832	March 22	TuscarwsCoOh	02	07	02
Heath, Edward(Y)	1822	March 28	Jeff.Co.,Oh.	06	12	21
Heath, Edward(Y)	1822	Oct. 18	Jeff.Co.,Oh.	06	12	21
Heath, William(Z)	1812	April 20	LickingCo,Oh	15	18	02
Heaton, Isaac(Z-M)	1832	Aug. 10	CoshoctnCoOh	08	07	09
Heaton, Micajah(Z)	1817	Aug. 21	CoshoctnCoOh	09	05	11
Heavilin, Alexander(Z-M)	1834	Feb. 22	HarrisonCoOh	03	06	16
Heavilin, Samuel D.(Z-M)	1836	May 09	HarrisonCoOh	10	08	06
Hebronk, Anthony(Z)	1836	Aug. 27	Wheeling,Vir	08	06	09
Heckel, John(Z-M)	1828	Sept. 01	GuernseyCoOh	03	01	23
Hecker, James(Z)	1811	July 23	GuernseyCoOh	08	07	27
Hecker, Joseph(Z)	1811	July 23	GuernseyCoOh	08	07	27
Heckewelder, John(Z)	1808	July 30	TuscarwsCoOh	02	07	11
Heckewelder, John(Z)	1808	July 30	TuscarwsCoOh	02	07	12
Heckler, Peter(Z-M)	1836	Nov. 11	KnoxCo.,Ohio	10	08	08
Heckman, Jacob(Z)	1832	May 22	Morgan Co,Oh	10	06	14
Heckman, Jacob(Z)	1836	Feb. 23	Morgan Co,Oh	10	06	11
Heckman, Jacob(Z)	1836	Feb. 24	Morgan Co,Oh	10	06	14
Heckman, Jacob(Z)	1836	Aug. 13	Morgan Co,Oh	10	06	10
Heddington, David(Z-M)	1837	Feb. 16	HolmesCoOhio	08	08	06
Hedey, Thomas(Y)	1829	May 11	HarrisonCoOh	05	12	21
Hedge, Aaron(Z-M)	1835	Oct. 05	GuernseyCoOh	04	03	01
Hedge, Aaron(Z-M)	1835	Dec. 28	GuernseyCoOh	03	03	05
Hedge, George M.(Z-M)	1836	Dec. 27	GuernseyCoOh	03	03	05
Hedge, Israel(Z)	1836	Jan. 30	Morgan Co,Oh	13	08	33
Hedge, Israel(Z-M)	1835	Sept. 28	GuernseyCoOh	04	03	01
Hedge, Israel(Z-M)	1836	April 07	GuernseyCoOh	04	03	01
Hedge, Joseph(Z-M)	1835	Nov. 19	GuernseyCoOh	04	03	01
Hedges, Isaac 2nd.(Z)	1835	June 01	Morgan Co,Oh	10	06	28
Hedges, Isaac(Z)	1814	Sept. 14	Brooke CoVir	12	10	03
Hedges, Isaac(Z)	1814	Sept. 14	Brooke CoVir	12	10	04
Hedges, John(Z)	1816	Feb. 13	Ohio Co.,Vir	11	12	32
Hedges, Joseph(Z)	1805	Oct. 01	BerklyCo,Vir	14	15	11
Hedges, Joseph(Z)	1810	March 02	Jeff.Co.,Oh.	11	13	28
Hedges, Joseph(Z)	1810	April 16	GuernseyCoOh	04	04	11
Hedges, Joseph(Z)	1815	June 03	Brooke CoVir	12	11	36
Hedges, Samuel(Z)	1805	Oct. 01	BerklyCo,Vir	14	15	11
Hefling, Fielding(Y)	1829	March 17	HarrisonCoOh	07	12	06
Heigny, George(Z-M)	1837	March 06	CoshoctnCoOh	05	04	07
Heimbeck, Peter(Z)	1814	Aug. 20	Jeff.Co.,Oh.	05	08	11
Heindel, Leonard(Z-M)	1837	Aug. 23	CoshoctnCoOh	05	07	13
Heiny, Jacob(Y)	1829	July 25	HarrisonCoOh	06	14	04
Heishman, Jacob(Z-M)	1833	March 04	MuskingmCoOh	06	03	10
Heisor, John(Z)	1817	Oct. 31	MuskingmCoOh	13	09	05
Heister, Philip Smith(Z-M)	1835	Aug. 22	Baltimore,Md	09	09	16
Heitz, John(Y)	1822	May 29	Jeff.Co.,Oh.	07	16	15
Heldenbrand, Mich'l.(Y)	1824	Sept. 20	Stark Co.,Oh	09	11	13
Helebrant, Christoper(Z-M)	1836	Oct. 28	CoshoctnCoOh	04	05	20
Helebrant, Christoper(Z-M)	1836	Oct. 24	CoshoctnCoOh	04	05	20
Hellman, Andrew(Y)	1824	July 14	LoudenCo,Vir	05	12	24
Hellyer, Elijah(Z)	1835	Oct. 07	Morgan Co,Oh	09	08	33
Hellyer, Elijah(Z)	1836	Oct. 05	Morgan Co,Oh	09	08	33
Hellyer, John(Z-M)	1839	Jan. 16	Morgan Co,Oh	04	03	11
Hellyer, Malothi(Z)	1832	July 05	Morgan Co,Oh	09	07	15
Hellyer, Maltothi(Z)	1835	Sept. 25	Morgan Co,Oh	09	07	10
Hellyer, Robert(Z)	1833	May 03	Morgan Co,Oh	09	08	33
Hellyer, Salathiel(Z)	1832	June 12	Morgan Co,Oh	10	08	26
Hellyer, Thomas Jr.(Z)	1835	Sept. 22	Morgan Co,Oh	09	07	04
Hellyer, Thomas(Z)	1822	Aug. 16	HarrisonCoOh	09	07	09
Hellyer, Thomas(Z)	1822	Aug. 16	HarrisonCoOh	09	07	09
Hellyer, Thomas(Z)	1835	Jan. 27	Morgan Co,Oh	09	07	10
Hellyer, William(Z)	1837	Aug. 11	Morgan Co,Oh	08	06	29
Hellyer, William(Z)	1838	March 19	Morgan Co,Oh	08	05	10
Hellyer, William(Z-M)	1838	Dec. 18	Morgan Co,Oh	04	05	21
Hellyer, Wm.(Z-M)	1839	Jan. 16	Morgan Co,Oh	04	03	08
Helm, Henry(Y)	1822	June 12	Stark Co.,Oh	09	11	15
Helmick, David(Z)	1817	Aug. 06	MuskingmCoOh	13	09	06
Helmick, Joseph(Z)	1835	Dec. 15	Morgan Co,Oh	13	09	05

PURCHASER	YEAR	DATE	RESIDENCE	R	T	S
Helms, Daniel(Z-M)	1826	Oct. 16	MuskingmCoOh	07	04	24
Helms, Ebenz'r. B.(Z-M)	1838	Oct. 16	HolmesCoOhio	09	18	12
Helms, Elizabeth(Y)	1821	Oct. 01	BelmontCo,Oh	03	05	22
Helms, Michael F.(Z-M)	1835	Dec. 12	HolmesCoOhio	09	08	05
Helms, Nicholas(Z)	1815	Dec. 20	KnoxCo.,Ohio	10	08	02
Helton, Samson(Z-M)	1837	July 15	CoshoctnCoOh	07	07	23
Helurg, Samuel(Z-M)	1832	May 30	TuscarwsCoOh	04	07	20
Helwig, Benj.(Z-M)	1831	April 02	TuscarwsCoOh	04	06	09
Helwig, Benjamin(Z-M)	1823	Aug. 07	TuscarwsCoOh	04	07	21
Helwig, Benjamin(Z-M)	1823	Aug. 07	TuscarwsCoOh	04	07	20
Helwig, Benjamin(Z-M)	1823	Aug. 07	TuscarwsCoOh	04	07	20
Helwig, Samuel(Z-M)	1833	May 04	TuscarwsCoOh	04	07	20
Hemmer, Jacob(Z-M)	1837	Oct. 12	CoshoctnCoOh	08	06	01
Hemminger, George(Z)	1827	Oct. 12	TuscarwsCoOh	01	09	18
Hemminger, John(Z-M)	1830	Oct. 25	TuscarwsCoOh	01	09	14
Hemrichhouse, George(Z-M)	1835	May 23	TuscarwsCoOh	03	07	01
Hemry, Geo.(Z)	1836	May 31	CarrollCo,Oh	15	14	22
Hemry, George(Z)	1836	June 01	CarrollCo,Oh	15	14	12
Hemry, Isaac(Y)	1828	Oct. 01	HarrisonCoOh	06	13	06
Hemry, John(Z)	1836	June 20	CarrollCo,Oh	14	12	29
Hemry, John(Z)	1836	June 20	CarrollCo,Oh	14	12	29
Hemry, John(Z)	1836	June 20	CarrollCo,Oh	14	12	29
Henckle, Peter(Z-M)	1837	May 05	HolmesCoOhio	09	08	14
Henden, Joshua(Z-M)	1836	Nov. 19	Jeff.Co.,Oh.	03	04	13
Henden, Joshua(Z-M)	1836	Nov. 19	Jeff.Co.,Oh.	03	04	13
Hendershot, Caspers(Z)	1816	March 21	BelmontCo,Oh	09	07	35
Henderson, Alex.(Z)	1827	Dec. 31	MuskingmCoOh	11	10	09
Henderson, Alexander(Z)	1816	Sept. 19	HarrisonCoOh	04	02	06
Henderson, Edward(Z-M)	1826	Aug. 14	Jeff.Co.,Oh.	07	08	04
Henderson, Fred.(Z)	1831	April 12	Morgan Co,Oh	11	10	02
Henderson, George(Z)	1825	April 14	Brooke CoVir	11	10	09
Henderson, George(Z)	1828	May 07	WashCo.,Penn	11	10	03
Henderson, George(Z)	1834	July 25	Morgan Co,Oh	11	11	10
Henderson, George(Z)	1835	Nov. 13	Morgan Co,Oh	11	11	10
Henderson, Herron V.(Z)	1830	March 18	Morgan Co,Oh	11	10	10
Henderson, James(Z-M)	1823	June 03	CoshoctnCoOh	07	08	04
Henderson, Jas.(Z-M)	1835	March 16	KnoxCo.,Oh.	10	08	22
Henderson, Jno.(Y)	1826	Dec. 06	Jeff.Co.,Oh.	04	12	32
Henderson, John Junr.(Z)	1810	Oct. 25	GreenCo.,Pa.	02	03	16
Henderson, John Junr.(Z)	1810	Oct. 25	GreenCo.,Pa.	02	03	17
Henderson, John Junr.(Z)	1813	Aug. 12	GuernseyCoOh	02	03	15
Henderson, John(Y)	1828	Aug. 14	Jeff.Co.,Oh.	03	11	35
Henderson, John(Y)	1832	March 24	Jeff.Co.,Oh.	03	12	26
Henderson, John(Y)	1832	March 24	Jeff.Co.,Oh.	03	12	27
Henderson, John(Z)	1810	Oct. 25	GreenCo.,Pa.	02	03	16
Henderson, John(Z)	1810	Oct. 25	GreenCo.,Pa.	02	03	17
Henderson, John(Z)	1814	March 22	WashngtnCoOh	11	13	03
Henderson, John(Z-M)	1826	March 11	?	02	03	16
Henderson, Richard(Y)	1829	Dec. 07	PittsburghPa	03	11	36
Henderson, Richard(Y)	1829	Dec. 09	PittsburghPa	03	12	34
Henderson, Robert(Z)	1808	Aug. 23	MuskingmCoOh	14	16	18
Henderson, Robert(Z)	1810	March 29	MuskingmCoOh	15	17	14
Henderson, Robt.(Z)	1824	May 11	Brooke CoVir	11	13	22
Henderson, Samuel(Y)	1826	Oct. 07	BeaverCo.,Pa	04	13	26
Henderson, Wm. Jr.(Z-M)	1831	Nov. 14	CoshoctnCoOh	07	05	12
Henderson, Wm. Jr.(Z-M)	1831	Nov. 14	CoshoctnCoOh	07	05	13
Henderson, Wm. Jr.(Z-M)	1831	Nov. 14	CoshoctnCoOh	07	05	20
Henderson, Wm. Senr.(Z)	1816	Jan. 20	BelmontCo,Oh	09	04	03
Henderson, Wm.(Y)	1828	April 23	Jeff.Co.,Oh.	03	11	21
Henderson, Wm.(Z)	1816	Feb. 16	TuscarwsCoOh	02	08	23
Henderson, Wm.(Z-M)	1831	March 24	CoshoctnCoOh	09	04	16
Henderson, Wm.(Z-M)	1831	March 24	CoshoctnCoOh	09	04	17
Henderson, Wm.(Z-M)	1839	Feb. 21	CoshoctnCoOh	10	05	20
Hendman, Richard(Z)	1835	May 11	Morgan Co,Oh	11	10	35
Hendricks, Em'l.(Y)	1827	Aug. 02	HarrisonCoOh	05	12	32
Hendricks, Jacob Jr.(Y)	1827	April 27	HarrisonCoOh	06	14	20
Hendricks, Jacob(Y)	1827	Aug. 23	HarrisonCoOh	05	12	32
Hendricks, John(Y)	1832	May 16	HarrisonCoOh	07	15	31
Hendricks, Thomas(Y)	1832	May 08	HarrisonCoOh	07	14	36

PURCHASER	YEAR	DATE	RESIDENCE	R	T	S
Hendry, Nicholas(Z)	1837	Feb. 09	BelmontCo,Oh	08	06	25
Henery, William(Z)	1810	March 21	MuskingmCoOh	14	15	28
Heney, John(Y)	1834	Nov. 01	BeaverCo.,Pa	14	13	09
Heninger, Jacobl(Y)	1829	June 25	Stark Co.,Oh	09	12	19
Hennedey, Danial(Z-M)	1834	Jan. 03	LickingCo,Oh	10	02	24
Hennel, Henry(Z-M)	1836	May 17	CoshoctnCoOh	05	04	16
Hennel, Henry(Z-M)	1836	May 17	CoshoctnCoOh	06	04	20
Hennick, William(Z-M)	1833	Sept. 05	CoshoctnCoOh	05	07	17
Henny, Jacob(Z-M)	1832	June 02	GuernseyCoOh	03	01	06
Henny, Jacob(Z-M)	1832	June 02	GuernseyCoOh	03	01	06
Henny, Margaret(Z-M)	1834	Jan. 20	GuernseyCoOh	03	01	06
Henrey, Jane(Z)	1808	Dec. 10	LickingCo,Oh	10	01	22
Henricks, John(Z)	1805	Sept. 20	BedfordCo,Pa	15	17	17
Henricks, John(Z)	1806	Oct. 15	BedfordCo,Pa	15	17	18
Henricks, John(Z)	1811	April 25	MuskingmCoOh	15	17	18
Henry, Daniel(Z-M)	1836	Nov. 19	ColumbanCoOh	10	08	21
Henry, George Michael(Y)	1831	July 06	Stark Co.,Oh	06	16	25
Henry, Gustavus(Z-M)	1832	June 25	GuernseyCoOh	03	01	06
Henry, Harmon(Z-M)	1837	May 05	GuernseyCoOh	02	03	12
Henry, Jacob(Z-M)	1831	March 19	MuskingmCoOh	03	01	06
Henry, James(Z-M)	1829	Aug. 27	BelmontCo,Oh	02	03	25
Henry, John(Z-M)	1833	June 20	CoshoctnCoOh	07	05	05
Henry, Michael(Y)	1830	Jan. 12	HarrisonCoOh	06	16	25
Henry, Michael(Y)	1830	Jan. 12	HarrisonCoOh	06	16	25
Henry, Robert(Y)	1833	Aug. 05	SteubenvleOh	04	12	06
Henry, S. S.(Z)	1824	May 11	HolmesCoOhio	07	09	20
Henry, William(Z)	1811	Oct. 14	LickingCo,Oh	11	03	17
Henry, William(Z)	1812	Aug. 04	LickingCo,Oh	11	05	07
Hensel, James(Z-M)	1827	April 02	TuscarwsCoOh	02	07	03
Hensel, James(Z-M)	1828	April 09	TuscarwsCoOh	02	07	03
Hensel, Jno.(Z-M)	1832	Jan. 18	TuscarwsCoOh	02	07	06
Hensel, John(Z)	1824	Jan. 10	TuscarwsCoOh	02	07	06
Hensel, Joseph(Z-M)	1826	March 13	TuscarwsCoOh	03	07	11
Hensel, Joseph(Z-M)	1830	Dec. 07	TuscarwsCoOh	02	08	23
Hensel, Joseph(Z-M)	1836	Aug. 06	TuscarwsCoOh	02	07	08
Hensel, Joseph(Z-M)	1836	Oct. 27	TuscarwsCoOh	02	07	15
Hensel, Joseph(Z-M)	1836	Nov. 11	TuscarwsCoOh	03	07	01
Hensell, William(Z-M)	1835	June 23	TuscarwsCoOh	02	07	07
Henslee, Sam'l.(Z)	1805	Dec. 30	MuskingmCoOh	09	01	19
Henslee, Samuel(Z)	1811	April 16	MuskingmCoOh	09	01	15
Hensler, Christian(Z-M)	1836	Oct. 17	TuscarwsCoOh	04	08	23
Henthorn, Nathan(Z)	1808	Oct. 26	FayetteCo,Pa	15	18	05
Hepler, Caspar(Y)	1825	March 28	Stark Co.,Oh	07	18	36
Herbaugh, John(Z)	1808	Aug. 08	TuscarwsCoOh	01	10	07
Herbaugh, John(Z)	1812	May 06	TuscarwsCoOh	01	10	04
Herin, Mark(Y)	1827	Aug. 24	Harrison	07	14	29
Herin, Mark(Y)	1835	Nov. 09	TuscarwsCoOh	07	14	23
Herless, Isaac(Y)	1829	Aug. 01	HarrisonCoOh	06	12	18
Herr, Joseph(Z-M)	1839	Jan. 16	KnoxCo.,Ohio	10	06	06
Herr, Joseph(Z-M)	1839	Jan. 16	KnoxCo.,Ohio	10	06	06
Herrick, Partee(Z)	1807	June 10	MuskingmCoOh	13	12	14
Herrick, S. P.(Z-M)	1831	Oct. 18	ZanesvilleOh	09	09	16
Herricks, John(Z)	1805	Oct. 29	BedfordCo,Pa	15	17	17
Herring, Geo.(Z)	1830	Sept. 23	Morgan Co,Oh	11	11	10
Herring, George(Z)	1812	Oct. 13	BeaverCo.,Pa	11	11	09
Herring, Jacob(Z)	1831	March 23	Perry Co.,Oh	14	13	23
Herring, John A.(Z)	1815	June 09	MuskingmCoOh	15	17	03
Herrington, Sam'l.(Z)	1835	Jan. 31	MuskingmCoOh	15	14	02
Herrins, John A.(Z)	1815	Oct. 14	MuskingmCoOh	14	13	14
Herrins, John A.(Z)	1815	Oct. 19	MuskingmCoOh	14	13	12
Herrod, Levi(Z)	1810	Oct. 29	KnoxCo.,Ohio	11	05	03
Herrod, Levi(Z)	1814	March 03	?	11	05	08
Herron, Jas.(Z)	1806	Feb. 15	MuskingmCoOh	13	12	06
Herron, Levi(Z)	1810	Oct. 29	KnoxCo.,Ohio	11	05	03
Herron, Samuel(Z)	1837	Sept. 19	GuernseyCoOh	08	06	20
Herron, Samuel(Z)	1838	March 12	GuernseyCoOh	08	06	20
Herron, W.(Z)	1817	Oct. 22	WashngtnCoOh	11	13	31
Herron, William(Z)	1823	Oct. 04	MuskingmCoOh	11	12	08
Herron, William(Z)	1805	Dec. 12	FayetteCo,Pa	11	13	18

PURCHASER	YEAR	DATE	RESIDENCE	R	T	S
Herron, William(Z)	1811	Dec. 04	MuskingmCoOh	11	13	07
Herron, Wm. Jr.(Z)	1826	July 26	MuskingmCoOh	11	10	10
Herron, Wm.(Z)	1829	March 09	MuskingmCoOh	11	10	12
Herron, Wm.(Z)	1829	March 09	MuskingmCoOh	11	11	36
Hersch, John(Z)	1836	Jan. 25	Morgan Co,Oh	13	10	15
Herschberger, Henoy(Z-M)	1838	April 06	CoshoctnCoOh	03	05	25
Herschberger, Henry(Z-M)	1836	Jan. 15	CoshoctnCoOh	05	07	20
Hershberger, Christian(Y)	1830	March 18	Stark Co.,Oh	07	18	25
Hershman, George(Z-M)	1836	April 20	MuskingmCoOh	06	03	01
Hershman, Jacob(Z-M)	1832	May 22	MuskingmCoOh	06	03	10
Hershman, Philip(Z-M)	1840	Jan. 03	CoshoctnCoOh	08	06	08
Herst, Aaron(Z-M)	1835	Dec. 19	GuernseyCoOh	03	02	07
Hertzer, Fred'k.(Z-M)	1829	Nov. 16	TuscarwsCoOh	02	10	17
Herzog, P. J.(Z-M)	1837	June 13	MuskingmCoOh	06	04	20
Hesher, Jacob(Z-M)	1838	Dec. 07	ZanesvilleOh	04	04	01
Hesket, Landon(Z-M)	1831	Feb. 28	GuernseyCoOh	03	01	16
Heskett, Elam(Z-M)	1829	May 27	GuernseyCoOh	10	09	01
Heskitt, Elam(Z)	1829	June 01	GuernseyCoOh	10	09	02
Hesler, Jacob(Z)	1826	Jan. 23	Perry Co.,Oh	15	14	20
Hess, Daniel(Z-M)	1832	June 09	HarrisonCoOh	01	09	19
Hess, Henry(Y)	1829	March 25	HarrisonCoOh	05	12	34
Hess, Joseph(Z-M)	1830	June 02	KnoxCo.,Ohio	10	08	05
Hess, Joseph(Z-M)	1833	Oct. 24	KnoxCo.,Ohio	10	08	05
Hess, Thos.(Z-M)	1831	March 01	KnoxCo.,Ohio	10	05	17
Hesser, Jonathan(Y)	1832	Aug. 27	ColumbanCoOh	05	15	14
Hessey, James(Y)	1823	May 19	BelmontCo,Oh	06	09	21
Hesson, John(Z)	1836	Aug. 30	BelmontCo,Oh	08	06	20
Hesson, Samuel(Z)	1836	Sept. 07	BelmontCo,Oh	08	06	20
Hesson, Samuel(Z)	1837	July 11	MonroeCo.,Oh	08	05	01
Heuszer, Michael(Z-M)	1837	July 29	PittsburghPa	05	04	15
Hewet, Wm.(Z-M)	1837	July 11	TuscarwsCoOh	05	07	18
Hewit, John(Y)	1824	Dec. 21	WashCo.,Penn	05	14	22
Hewit, Peter(Y)	1825	March 03	ColumbanCoOh	05	15	34
Hewit, Peter(Y)	1825	Sept. 08	ColumbanCoOh	05	15	34
Hewitt, James(Y)	1824	June 24	Stark Co.,Oh	07	17	19
Hewitt, James(Y)	1825	Dec. 16	Stark Co.,Oh	07	17	19
Hewsted, Bartholomew(Z-M)	1835	Nov. 10	HolmesCoOhio	07	08	14
Heyworth, James(Z-M)	1826	Oct. 21	MuskingmCoOh	06	02	04
Hiat, Hezekiah(Z)	1811	May 02	MuskingmCoOh	12	13	24
Hiatt, Hezekiah(Z)	1826	Dec. 11	MuskingmCoOh	10	06	19
Hiatt, Hezekiah(Z)	1809	May 22	BrookCo.,Vir	11	13	18
Hiatt, Hezekiah(Z)	1811	May 02	MuskingmCoOh	12	13	24
Hiatt, William(Z-M)	1839	Dec. 02	CoshoctnCoOh	09	07	05
Hiatt, Wm.(Z-M)	1839	Nov. 19	CoshoctnCoOh	09	08	24
Hiatt, Wm.(Z-M)	1839	Nov. 19	CoshoctnCoOh	09	08	25
Hibbets, James(Z-M)	1837	March 03	KnoxCo.,Ohio	10	08	20
Hibbets, John(Z-M)	1836	May 13	KnoxCo.,Ohio	10	08	20
Hibbetts, John(Z)	1815	Jan. 07	KnoxCo.,Ohio	10	08	21
Hibbits, John(Z)	1806	Sept. 02	MuskingmCoOh	10	08	21
Hibbitts, John(Z-M)	1829	Dec. 11	HolmesCoOhio	10	08	11
Hibbitts, John(Z-M)	1833	Nov. 04	KnoxCo.,Ohio	10	08	21
Hibbitts, John(Z-M)	1829	Dec. 11	HolmesCoOhio	10	08	11
Hibbs, Abraham(Z-M)	1834	March 03	FayetteCo,Pa	02	06	19
Hibbs, Isaac(Y)	1823	April 19	RichlandCoOh	05	13	07
Hibbs, Samuel(Y)	1828	March 20	Jeff.Co.,Oh.	04	12	25
Hibbs, William(Y)	1828	Oct. 09	HarrisonCoOh	07	11	15
Hickerson, Samuel Junr.(Z-M)	1833	Jan. 12	LickingCo,Oh	10	03	09
Hickerson, Samuel(Z-M)	1832	Feb. 07	LickingCo,Oh	10	03	08
Hickey, John(Y)	1832	Sept. 26	Stark Co.,Oh	07	16	04
Hickey, Wm.(Z-M)	1836	Aug. 29	LickingCo,Oh	11	04	21
Hickle, Stephen(Z)	1834	Aug. 22	GuernseyCoOh	09	08	26
Hickman, Jacob(Z)	1834	Feb. 18	Morgan Co,Oh	10	06	11
Hickman, James(Z)	1817	April 15	FayetteCo,Pa	01	04	10
Hickman, Kimble(Z-M)	1829	April 27	CoshoctnCoOh	09	04	17
Hickman, Kimble(Z-M)	1831	March 18	CoshoctnCoOh	09	04	14
Hickman, Kimble(Z-M)	1831	March 18	CoshoctnCoOh	09	04	14
Hicks, James(Y)	1829	Nov. 06	Stark Co.,Oh	07	16	08
Hicks, James(Y)	1830	Feb. 25	Stark Co.,Oh	07	16	03
Hicks, James(Z-M)	1836	Nov. 10	CarrollCo,Oh	02	07	03

PURCHASER	YEAR	DATE	RESIDENCE	R	T	S
Hicks, Robert(Z-M)	1834	July 25	CarrollCo,Oh	03	06	06
Hicks, Solomon(Z-M)	1837	Feb. 01	TuscarwsCoOh	03	06	04
Hicks, William(Y)	1826	Feb. 16	Stark Co.,Oh	07	16	23
Hicks, William(Z-M)	1836	Aug. 30	TuscarwsCoOh	03	07	21
Hiddilston, William(Z)	1836	May 19	MonroeCo.,Oh	08	05	02
Hide, Samuel(Y)	1823	Jan. 04	HarrisonCoOh	06	13	31
Hide, Thomas(Z)	1810	March 29	WashngtnCoOh	01	02	16
Hidey, Jacob(Y)	1828	Feb. 05	HarrisonCoOh	05	12	22
Hiet, John(Z)	1816	Jan. 10	Brooke CoVir	09	07	07
Hiet, Josiah(Z-M)	1837	March 10	CoshoctnCoOh	09	07	03
Hiett, Amos(Z-M)	1831	March 31	CoshoctnCoOh	09	08	17
Higbee, Jesse(Z-M)	1832	Nov. 27	AlleghnyCoPa	04	08	22
Higbee, Jesse(Z-M)	1832	Nov. 27	AlleghnyCoPa	04	07	03
Higer, Jacob(Z-M)	1835	July 27	CoshoctnCoOh	04	05	19
Higer, Rebecca(Z-M)	1835	Oct. 20	CoshoctnCoOh	04	05	19
Higer, Rebecca(Z-M)	1836	April 06	CoshoctnCoOh	04	05	20
Higgins, Benj'n. B.(Y)	1826	July 03	ColumbanCoOh	05	15	03
Higgins, Judiah(Z)	1823	Aug. 22	Jeff.Co.,Oh.	10	07	31
Higgins, Judiah(Z)	1828	April 24	Jeff.Co.,Oh.	10	06	06
Higgs, John(Z-M)	1832	Oct. 05	LickingCo,Oh	11	04	19
Highly, Thomas(Z)	1833	Dec. 03	MuskingmCoOh	12	13	15
Highs, Jacob(Z)	1814	July 08	KnoxCo.,Ohio	10	09	19
Highshew, Enoch(Z-M)	1836	June 11	HolmesCoOhio	09	08	14
Highshew, Jacob(Z)	1815	Jan. 28	KnoxCo.,Ohio	09	08	18
Highshew, Jacob(Z-M)	1828	April 07	HolmesCoOhio	09	08	13
Hight, E. C.(Z)	1814	Feb. 09	MuskingmCoOh	10	06	29
Hildebrand, Michael(Y)	1826	Jan. 24	WashCo.,Penn	06	16	23
Hildreth, Sam'l. P.(Z)	1816	Feb. 29	MariettaOhio	13	08	12
Hildreth, Sam'l. P.(Z)	1816	Feb. 29	MariettaOhio	13	08	12
Hildreth, William(Z)	1815	Dec. 30	MuskingmCoOh	13	09	26
Hildt, John(Z-M)	1831	Aug. 19	TuscarwsCoOh	03	08	07
Hile, Andrew(Z)	1815	Sept. 02	GuernseyCoOh	01	02	12
Hile, Peter(Z)	1814	Nov. 11	SomersetCoPa	05	08	23
Hileman, Peter(Z-M)	1838	June 25	ZanesvilleOh	10	08	11
Hill, Arthur(Z-M)	1832	April 28	GuernseyCoOh	02	04	05
Hill, Christian(Y)	1827	April 14	Stark Co.,Oh	06	18	09
Hill, Isaac(Z)	1808	March 25	BelmontCo,Oh	09	06	02
Hill, Isaac(Z)	1815	July 05	BelmontCo,Oh	09	06	05
Hill, John(Z)	1836	Aug. 01	Wheeling,Vir	08	06	09
Hill, John(Z)	1836	Aug. 01	Wheeling,Vir	08	06	04
Hill, John(Z)	1836	Aug. 12	Wheeling,Vir	08	06	08
Hill, John(Z)	1836	Aug. 12	Wheeling,Vir	08	06	08
Hill, John(Z)	1837	Feb. 07	Wheeling,Vir	08	06	09
Hill, John(Z-M)	1826	March 09	GuernseyCoOh	02	02	15
Hill, Michael(Z)	1830	Nov. 11	ColumbanCoOh	14	12	10
Hill, Michael(Z)	1835	April 03	Perry Co.,Oh	14	12	10
Hill, Richard(Z-M)	1829	May 23	GuernseyCoOh	03	02	10
Hill, Robert(Y)	1824	May 22	Jeff.Co.,Oh.	01	04	31
Hill, Robert(Y)	1824	May 22	Jeff.Co.,Oh.	01	04	31
Hill, Robert(Y)	1824	June 10	Jeff.Co.,Oh.	01	04	31
Hill, Robert(Z-M)	1837	April 28	GuernseyCoOh	03	05	24
Hill, Roger(Y)	1821	Oct. 09	ColumbanCoOh	01	07	22
Hill, Samuel(Z)	1806	April 07	AdamsCo,Penn	12	13	03
Hill, William Z.(Z-M)	1835	Oct. 26	WashCo.,Penn	04	06	22
Hill, William(Z)	1813	Nov. 08	GuernseyCoOh	03	02	01
Hilleary, L. W.(Z-M)	1836	Feb. 06	LickingCo,Oh	11	04	19
Hilleary, Tilman(Z)	1827	May 01	LickingCo,Oh	09	01	06
Hilliary, Benjamin(Z)	1815	Feb. 16	LickingCo,Oh	10	01	10
Hillis, C. A.(Z)	1830	Sept. 16	Perry Co.,Oh	15	15	23
Hillyer, Thomas(Z)	1824	Oct. 12	Morgan Co,Oh	09	07	04
Hillyer, Thomas(Z)	1827	May 28	Morgan Co,Oh	09	07	04
Hilton, Richard(Z-M)	1836	Feb. 09	CoshoctnCoOh	07	04	24
Hilwig, Benjamin(Z-M)	1833	June 13	TuscarwsCoOh	04	07	19
Himminger, Joseph(Z-M)	1829	Nov. 23	TuscarwsCoOh	01	09	06
Hindall, Rob Banister(Z-M)	1832	March 10	LickingCo,Oh	11	01	20
Hindes, Moses(Z)	1815	Feb. 07	WashCo.,Penn	01	04	22
Hinds, Moses(Y)	1832	Oct. 05	TuscarwsCoOh	07	14	23
Hinebaugh, Peter(Z-M)	1832	April 23	HarrisonCoOh	05	07	19
Hinebaugh, Peter(Z-M)	1832	April 23	HarrisonCoOh	05	07	04

PURCHASER	YEAR	DATE	RESIDENCE	R	T	S
Hineline, Asa(Z)	1826	Oct. 17	GuernseyCoOh	10	09	10
Hineline, Asa(Z)	1832	Nov. 07	GuernseyCoOh	10	09	10
Hines, Alexander(Z)	1835	Nov. 30	MonroeCo.,Oh	08	06	24
Hines, John(Z-M)	1835	Oct. 14	CoshoctnCoOh	05	04	08
Hines, John(Z-M)	1835	Oct. 14	CoshoctnCoOh	05	04	13
Hines, Joseph(Y)	1829	Sept. 18	HarrisonCoOh	06	11	30
Hinkle, Christopher(Y)	1823	Aug. 15	BelmontCo,Oh	03	05	22
Hinkle, Christopher(Y)	1826	May 19	BelmontCo,Oh	03	05	20
Hinkle, John(Y)	1824	March 04	BelmontCo,Oh	03	05	22
Hinney, John(Z)	1833	Dec. 11	GuernseyCoOh	10	09	24
Hinthorn, Isaac(Z)	1816	Nov. 23	LickingCo,Oh	11	04	15
Hinton, Elizabeth(Z-M)	1835	April 08	HarrisonCoOh	07	07	22
Hinton, William(Z-M)	1831	May 06	TuscarwsCoOh	01	05	02
Hiskett, David(Y)	1827	July 16	BelmontCo,Oh	05	07	35
Hiskett, Elam(Z)	1836	Feb. 26	GuernseyCoOh	10	09	01
Hiskett, James(Z-M)	1827	March 07	GuernseyCoOh	02	04	05
Hiskett, Landon(Z-M)	1829	Jan. 14	BelmontCo,Oh	03	01	25
Hissey, James(Y)	1823	May 19	BelmontCo,Oh	06	09	21
Hitchcock, Caleb(Z)	1821	Dec. 18	Perry Co.,Oh	15	16	13
Hitchcock, Caleb(Z)	1828	Dec. 30	MuskingmCoOh	14	14	18
Hitchcock, Caleb(Z)	1831	Jan. 27	MuskingmCoOh	14	14	08
Hitchcock, Israel(Z)	1832	Nov. 26	Perry Co.,Oh	14	14	19
Hitchcock, Jefferson(Z)	1833	Feb. 01	Perry Co.,Oh	14	14	19
Hitchcock, Lucian(Z)	1833	Feb. 05	Perry Co.,Oh	14	14	18
Hitchcock, Nicholas(Z)	1827	June 18	Perry Co.,Oh	15	16	14
Hitchcock, Thomas(Z-M)	1832	March 23	HarrisonCoOh	01	06	25
Hiten, Chasles Morgan(Y)	1831	July 25	ColumbanCoOh	04	14	24
Hiten, Chasles Morgan(Y)	1831	July 25	ColumbanCoOh	04	14	24
Hites, Lewis(Z)	1832	Aug. 01	Morgan Co,Oh	13	10	35
Hizner, Sam'l.(Z)	1835	Oct. 10	Morgan Co,Oh	09	05	10
Hoagland, James Jr.(Y)	1831	May 16	HarrisonCoOh	05	11	33
Hoagland, M. Jr.(Z-M)	1836	Aug. 06	HolmesCoOhio	07	07	16
Hobart, Samuel B.(Z-M)	1833	May 06	MuskingmCoOh	10	05	24
Hobbs, James(Z-M)	1835	July 21	KnoxCo.,Ohio	10	08	17
Hobby, J.(Z)	1816	April 29	PutnamCoOhio	11	13	36
Hochstetler, John(Z-M)	1837	March 10	TuscarwsCoOh	03	08	24
Hochstetler, Moses(Z-M)	1834	Aug. 14	HolmesCoOhio	05	07	05
Hochstetter, Jeremiah(Z-M)	1832	March 16	HolmesCoOhio	05	09	13
Hochstetter, John(Z-M)	1832	Sept. 20	TuscarwsCoOh	03	08	17
Hochstetter, John(Z-M)	1832	Sept. 20	TuscarwsCoOh	03	08	16
Hochstetter, Joseph(Z-M)	1832	March 16	HolmesCoOhio	04	09	06
Hochtetler, Emanuel(Z)	1813	Nov. 12	TuscarwsCoOh	04	09	07
Hock, Dan'l.(Z)	1833	Aug. 26	MuskingmCoOh	13	11	12
Hock, Dan'l.(Z)	1833	Aug. 26	MuskingmCoOh	13	11	04
Hockinberger, Michael(Y)	1831	March 23	WayneCo.,Oh.	06	15	24
Hocksteter, Gabriel(Z-M)	1832	June 01	HolmesCoOhio	05	09	11
Hockstetler, Moses(Z-M)	1833	May 04	HolmesCoOhio	05	07	05
Hockstetter, Christian(Z-M)	1827	Jan. 18	HolmesCoOhio	05	08	10
Hockstetter, David(Z-M)	1831	April 01	HolmesCoOhio	04	09	15
Hockstetter, Jere'h.(Z-M)	1831	April 01	HolmesCoOhio	05	09	14
Hockstetter, Jos.(Z-M)	1831	March 12	HolmesCoOhio	04	09	06
Hockstetter, Wm.(Z-M)	1831	May 13	HolmesCoOhio	04	09	15
Hodge, Hugh(Z)	1835	Dec. 31	BelmontCo,Oh	09	05	15
Hodge, Israel(Z-M)	1826	April 15	GuernseyCoOh	03	04	13
Hodges, Charles(Z)	1826	June 22	Morgan Co,Oh	11	10	21
Hoey, James(Y)	1832	April 20	ColumbanCoOh	03	12	33
Hoey, Thomas(Y)	1823	March 28	AlleghnyCoPa	03	13	32
Hoff, Mary(Y)	1829	June 09	HarrisonCoOh	06	13	19
Hoffman, Abr'm.(Y)	1823	Nov. 14	BelmontCo,Oh	06	10	21
Hoffman, Adam(Y)	1826	Oct. 02	PortageCo,Oh	05	18	04
Hoffman, Christian(Z)	1833	Nov. 21	Ohio Co.,Vir	08	05	01
Hoffman, Christian(Z)	1833	Nov. 21	Ohio Co.,Vir	08	05	01
Hoffman, George(Z-M)	1833	Nov. 02	GuernseyCoOh	02	04	21
Hoffman, Jno. Senr.(Y)	1824	Jan. 30	ColumbanCoOh	06	15	05
Hoffman, Louisa(Z)	1836	May 24	WashngtnCoOh	08	05	01
Hoffman, Louisa(Z)	1836	May 24	WashngtnCoOh	08	05	01
Hoffshot, John(Y)	1823	June 14	ColumbanCoOh	01	07	15
Hofman, Wilhelmina(Z)	1836	Sept. 10	WashngtnCoOh	08	05	01
Hofman, Wilhelmina(Z)	1837	May 29	WashngtnCoOh	08	05	01

PURCHASER	YEAR	DATE	RESIDENCE	R	T	S
Hofstetler, Benj'm.(Z)	1807	June 01	SomersetCoPa	04	08	02
Hogbin, Wilson(Z-M)	1831	Oct. 26	HarrisonCoOh	06	09	25
Hogel, Lanson(Z-M)	1833	Feb. 20	CoshoctnCoOh	07	05	02
Hogeland, George(Z)	1815	Jan. 28	KnoxCo.,Ohio	09	08	18
Hogens, R. H.(Z)	1816	Dec. 05	MuskingmCoOh	06	01	01
Hogg, William(Z-M)	1832	Jan. 06	TuscarwsCoOh	01	09	06
Hogg, William(Z-M)	1831	April 09	StarkeCo.,Oh	01	09	07
Hogg, William(Z-M)	1832	Dec. 07	TuscarwsCoOh	01	09	08
Hogg, William(Z-M)	1832	Jan. 06	TuscarwsCoOh	01	09	06
Hogg, Wm.(Z-M)	1832	May 12	TuscarwsCoOh	01	09	15
Hogg, Wm.(Z-M)	1832	May 12	TuscarwsCoOh	01	09	04
Hogg, Wm.(Z-M)	1833	Dec. 16	StarkeCoOhio	01	09	05
Hogland, Isaac(Z)	1814	March 11	?	07	07	17
Hogland, Isaac(Z-M)	1835	March 11	CoshoctnCoOh	07	07	17
Hogle, Langdon(Z-M)	1835	Aug. 19	CoshoctnCoOh	07	05	03
Hogle, Leander(Z-M)	1834	Feb. 10	CoshoctnCoOh	07	07	24
Hogle, Michael(Z-M)	1832	May 22	CoshoctnCoOh	07	05	02
Hoglen, George(Z-M)	1833	Nov. 04	HolmesCoOhio	09	08	25
Hoglen, George(Z-M)	1833	Dec. 14	HolmesCoOhio	09	08	25
Hogman, Jacob(Z-M)	1827	Dec. 08	SomersetCoPa	10	06	18
Hogseed, James(Z)	1817	Oct. 21	WashCo.,Penn	05	02	11
Hogseed, John(Z)	1817	Oct. 21	WashCo.,Penn	05	02	12
Hohman, Joseph(Z)	1839	Jan. 16	MonroeCo.,Oh	08	06	10
Hohmann, Jno.(Z)	1836	Aug. 01	Wheeling,Vir	08	06	04
Hohmann, Jno.(Z)	1836	Aug. 01	Wheeling,Vir	08	06	09
Hohmann, Jno.(Z)	1836	Aug. 01	Wheeling,Vir	08	06	09
Hoit, Nicholas(Z)	1814	June 06	WashngtnCoOh	10	06	06
Holabaugh, Philip(Y)	1822	May 27	Stark Co.,Oh	07	19	21
Holabough, Philip(Y)	1826	Nov. 02	Stark Co.,Oh	07	20	06
Holcomb, Homer(Z-M)	1838	Oct. 01	MuskingmCoOh	05	03	11
Holcomb, Homer(Z-M)	1838	Sept. 22	MuskingmCoOh	05	03	11
Holcomb, Homer(Z-M)	1838	Oct. 25	MuskingmCoOh	05	03	02
Holcomb, J.(Z)	1815	Oct. 04	MuskingmCoOh	14	13	11
Holcomb, James(Z-M)	1835	Nov. 03	MuskingmCoOh	05	03	08
Holcomb, James(Z-M)	1835	Nov. 10	MuskingmCoOh	05	03	09
Holcomb, James(Z-M)	1835	Nov. 10	MuskingmCoOh	05	03	03
Holcomb, James(Z-M)	1835	Nov. 14	MuskingmCoOh	02	06	03
Holcomb, James(Z-M)	1835	Dec. 02	MuskingmCoOh	05	03	03
Holcomb, James(Z-M)	1836	Dec. 30	MuskingmCoOh	05	03	09
Holcomb, James(Z-M)	1837	Feb. 03	MuskingmCoOh	05	03	10
Holcomb, James(Z-M)	1837	Feb. 03	MuskingmCoOh	05	04	23
Holcomb, James(Z-M)	1837	Feb. 03	MuskingmCoOh	05	04	23
Holcomb, James(Z-M)	1837	Nov. 22	MuskingmCoOh	05	03	03
Holcomb, James(Z-M)	1838	Nov. 06	MuskingmCoOh	05	03	11
Holcomb, James(Z-M)	1838	Nov. 06	MuskingmCoOh	05	03	11
Holcomb, James(Z-M)	1838	Nov. 28	MuskingmCoOh	04	03	15
Holcomb, William(Z-M)	1835	Nov. 17	MuskingmCoOh	05	03	08
Holcomb, William(Z-M)	1837	Jan. 11	MuskingmCoOh	05	03	09
Holden, John(Z)	1835	Jan. 15	MonroeCo.,Oh	08	06	05
Holden, John(Z)	1836	Feb. 19	MonroeCo.,Oh	08	06	05
Holderman, Jacob(Z)	1814	May 30	TuscarwsCoOh	04	09	14
Holland, Henry(Z)	1835	Oct. 24	GuernseyCoOh	10	09	15
Holland, John(Z)	1813	April 23	MuskingmCoOh	14	16	10
Hollar, Jacob(Z-M)	1832	Nov. 21	TuscarwsCoOh	01	09	09
Hollar, Jacob(Z-M)	1832	Nov. 21	TuscarwsCoOh	01	09	08
Hollar, Mathias(Z-M)	1828	Feb. 02	CoshoctnCoOh	05	06	25
Hollenback, Chasper(Z)	1831	Sept. 19	MuskingmCoOh	11	12	27
Hollenback, Chasper(Z)	1812	Jan. 29	WashngtnCoOh	11	10	27
Hollenback, Chasper(Z)	1814	Dec. 12	WashngtnCoOh	11	12	23
Hollenback, George(Z)	1815	Oct. 09	FairfeldCoOh	15	15	29
Hollenback, Jacob(Z)	1813	March 26	FairfeldCoOh	15	16	34
Hollenbah, Chasper(Z)	1831	March 23	MuskingmCoOh	11	12	23
Hollenshead, John(Z)	1816	Oct. 24	WashngtnCoOh	13	09	07
Holler, David(Z-M)	1838	July 05	CoshoctnCoOh	08	07	10
Holler, Henry(Z-M)	1836	Aug. 09	CoshoctnCoOh	08	07	01
Holler, Jacob(Y)	1832	Aug. 06	Stark Co.,Oh	07	16	27
Holler, Jacob(Z-M)	1836	Sept. 27	CoshoctnCoOh	07	07	23
Holler, John(Z-M)	1836	March 29	CoshoctnCoOh	08	07	08
Holler, Mathias(Z-M)	1825	Oct. 04	CoshoctnCoOh	05	06	25

135

PURCHASER	YEAR	DATE	RESIDENCE	R	T	S
Hollett, John(Y)	1824	March 29	Jeff.Co.,Oh.	07	11	05
Hollingshead, Rich'd.(Z)	1817	May 12	MuskingmCoOh	13	09	06
Hollingsworth, David(Y)	1827	March 07	BelmontCo,Oh	07	12	05
Hollister, Abel(Z-M)	1834	March 17	KnoxCo.,Ohio	10	07	17
Hollister, Orange Jay(Z-M)	1836	July 19	KnoxCo.,Ohio	10	07	24
Hollister, Orange(Z-M)	1824	May 11	Mt.Vernon,Oh	10	06	04
Hollister, Orange(Z-M)	1832	Dec. 26	KnoxCo.,Ohio	10	07	24
Hollister, Orange(Z-M)	1834	Feb. 06	KnoxCo.,Ohio	10	07	24
Hollister, Orange(Z-M)	1837	Oct. 04	KnoxCo.,Ohio	10	07	24
Hollister, Orange(Z-M)	1836	July 19	KnoxCo.,Ohio	10	07	24
Hollopeter, Mathias(Y)	1824	Sept. 07	ColumbanCoOh	05	18	26
Holloway, David(Z-M)	1835	Oct. 28	KnoxCo.,Ohio	10	09	03
Holloway, David(Z-M)	1836	March 08	KnoxCo.,Ohio	10	09	18
Holloway, James(Y)	1831	July 23	HarrisonCoOh	07	12	10
Holloway, Jonas(Y)	1826	March 25	HarrisonCoOh	07	12	05
Holloway, Jonas(Y)	1830	June 14	HarrisonCoOh	07	12	05
Holly, David(Z-M)	1822	Sept. 27	CoshoctnCoOh	05	08	10
Holmes, Charles(Z-M)	1836	Feb. 05	CoshoctnCoOh	08	07	08
Holmes, Charles(Z-M)	1836	March 11	CoshoctnCoOh	08	07	09
Holmes, Isaac(Y)	1824	Feb. 03	TuscarwsCoOh	06	14	21
Holmes, Joseph Dornan(Y)	1834	June 20	Jeff.Co.,Oh.	03	11	24
Holmes, Joseph Dornan(Y)	1836	Feb. 24	Jeff.Co.,Oh.	03	11	24
Holmes, Obadiah(Z-M)	1831	April 20	TuscarwsCoOh	01	09	21
Holmes, Olin(Z-M)	1831	Aug. 24	TuscarwsCoOh	01	08	01
Holmes, William(Y)	1831	June 24	TuscarwsCoOh	07	14	33
Holmes, William(Y)	1831	July 05	TuscarwsCoOh	07	14	28
Holmes, William(Y)	1833	April 24	TuscarwsCoOh	07	14	34
Holt, Amasa(Z)	1835	Aug. 11	Morgan Co,Oh	09	06	32
Holt, James(Y)	1832	Oct. 06	GuernseyCoOh	07	09	22
Holt, James(Z)	1811	June 01	MifflinCo,Pa	01	03	23
Holt, John(Z-M)	1830	Dec. 03	CoshoctnCoOh	09	07	18
Holt, Stephen(Z-M)	1836	Sept. 23	CoshoctnCoOh	08	07	03
Holt, William(Z-M)	1833	Sept. 09	CoshoctnCoOh	07	05	08
Holtsclau, Martha(Z-M)	1834	Feb. 28	TuscarwsCoOh	03	07	22
Holtscraw, Martha(Z-M)	1833	April 16	BelmontCo,Oh	03	07	22
Holtz, George(Z-M)	1832	March 21	KnoxCo.,Ohio	10	05	12
Holtz, George(Z-M)	1831	Feb. 28	KnoxCo.,Ohio	10	05	12
Holtzman, Martin(Z-M)	1837	June 12	CarrollCo,Oh	03	07	20
Home, Martin(Z-M)	1832	Oct. 26	KnoxCo.,Ohio	10	06	12
Hommon, Philip(Z-M)	1830	March 29	Stark Co.,Oh	05	07	04
Homrighouse, John(Z)	1811	April 12	BaltimreCoMd	02	08	25
Honderick, Christian(Z-M)	1828	March 29	HolmesCoOhio	05	08	07
Hone, Henry(Z)	1836	Feb. 04	Morgan Co,Oh	13	08	09
Honeywelds, Albert(Z-M)	1837	May 30	FayetteCo,Pa	04	04	09
Honnald, Jacob(Z-M)	1829	March 27	MuskingmCoOh	07	03	21
Honnald, James(Z-M)	1829	April 21	MuskingmCoOh	05	03	06
Honnald, Noah(Z-M)	1826	Sept. 20	MuskingmCoOh	05	02	05
Honnald, Noah(Z-M)	1828	April 08	MuskingmCoOh	06	02	05
Honnald, Noah(Z-M)	1828	April 22	MuskingmCoOh	06	02	05
Honnold, Jacob(Z)	1815	July 25	GuernseyCoOh	05	02	14
Honnold, James(Z)	1815	June 03	MuskingmCoOh	05	02	15
Honnold, James(Z)	1816	May 27	MuskingmCoOh	05	02	15
Honnold, John E.(Z-M)	1827	March 30	MuskingmCoOh	06	03	15
Honnold, Richard(Z-M)	1836	Feb. 19	MuskingmCoOh	05	03	07
Honnold, Sam'l.(Z-M)	1831	Nov. 25	MuskingmCoOh	05	03	03
Honnold, Thos. C.(Z-M)	1835	Nov. 09	BelmontCo,Oh	03	06	16
Hoobler, Jacob(Y)	1829	March 17	HarrisonCoOh	05	13	08
Hoobler, Samuel(Y)	1832	Nov. 12	HarrisonCoOh	05	13	15
Hood, Robert(Z)	1814	Dec. 06	Brooke CoVir	01	01	20
Hook, Bernard T.(Z)	1829	May 27	MuskingmCoOh	12	10	25
Hook, Isaac N.(Z)	1815	Oct. 13	MuskingmCoOh	14	14	05
Hook, Joseph(Z-M)	1835	Dec. 05	CoshoctnCoOh	07	07	13
Hook, Joseph(Z-M)	1835	Dec. 23	CoshoctnCoOh	07	07	13
Hook, Joseph(Z-M)	1836	Dec. 21	CoshoctnCoOh	08	08	22
Hook, Joshua(Z-M)	1836	Aug. 03	ZanesvilleOh	10	03	04
Hook, Silvanus(Z)	1836	Nov. 29	CarrollCo,Oh	15	14	13
Hooler, William(Y)	1825	Aug. 06	Stark Co.,Oh	07	20	36
Hoon, Martin(Z)	1816	April 17	WashCo.,Penn	11	06	22
Hoon, Martin(Z)	1816	April 17	WashCo.,Penn	11	06	21

PURCHASER	YEAR	DATE	RESIDENCE	R	T	S
Hoopergerner, Geo.(Y)	1829	May 06	TuscarwsCoOh	07	15	30
Hoopes, Elisha(Y)	1823	July 02	ColumbanCoOh	05	18	26
Hoopes, Jacob(Y)	1825	March 21	BelmontCo,Oh	05	07	31
Hoopes, James(Y)	1821	Sept. 24	ColumbanCoOh	04	16	21
Hoopes, James(Y)	1821	Oct. 30	ColumbanCoOh	04	16	22
Hoopes, James(Y)	1821	Oct. 30	ColumbanCoOh	06	16	15
Hoopingarner, Daniel(Z-M)	1820	Oct. 19	TuscarwsCoOh	03	08	07
Hoopingarner, Ja.(Z)	1815	Jan. 26	WashngtnCoOh	01	08	11
Hoopingarner, Jno.(Z)	1815	Jan. 26	WashngtnCoOh	01	08	11
Hoopingarner, Jno.(Z-M)	1820	Aug. 01	TuscarwsCoOh	03	08	08
Hoopingarner, John(Z-M)	1826	March 30	TuscarwsCoOh	03	08	14
Hoopingarner, John(Z-M)	1828	June 17	TuscarwsCoOh	03	08	08
Hooten, William(Z)	1813	Nov. 08	GuernseyCoOh	03	02	01
Hootman, David(Y)	1822	Sept. 23	WashCo.,Penn	05	14	24
Hoover, Christian(Y)	1824	Nov. 15	Stark Co.,Oh	06	18	06
Hoover, Christian(Y)	1824	Nov. 15	Stark Co.,Oh	06	18	07
Hoover, Christian(Y)	1826	May 15	Stark Co.,Oh	06	18	07
Hoover, David(Y)	1826	Dec. 15	Stark Co.,Oh	07	20	36
Hoover, John(Y)	1830	Dec. 08	Jeff.Co.,Oh.	06	12	35
Hoover, John(Y)	1835	Nov. 25	TuscarwsCoOh	07	14	23
Hoover, Jonas(Z-M)	1832	Nov. 15	TuscarwsCoOh	03	10	17
Hoover, William(Y)	1828	July 05	Stark Co.,Oh	06	19	29
Hoover, Wm.(Y)	1828	April 17	Stark Co.,Oh	07	20	27
Hope, Payton(Z)	1837	Nov. 01	Perry Co.,Oh	15	14	12
Hopingarner, Daniel(Z-M)	1832	March 31	TuscarwsCoOh	03	08	07
Hopkins, Dan'l.(Z)	1832	May 22	Morgan Co,Oh	10	07	07
Hopkins, James(Z-M)	1838	July 02	CoshoctnCoOh	09	07	21
Hopkins, Nathaniel D.(Z-M)	1835	Sept. 12	HolmesCoOhio	07	08	09
Hopper, James(Z)	1835	Nov. 23	Morgan Co,Oh	09	06	30
Horn, Benjamin(Z)	1815	Nov. 28	KnoxCo.,Ohio	10	06	20
Horn, Christ'n.(Z)	1815	June 08	KnoxCo.,Ohio	10	06	25
Horn, Christian(Z)	1813	Dec. 20	Ohio Co.,Vir	10	06	24
Horn, Christian(Z-M)	1832	March 16	KnoxCo.,Ohio	10	04	03
Horn, Daniel(Z)	1817	Feb. 17	MuskingmCoOh	14	14	07
Horn, Daniel(Z)	1817	June 12	WashCo.,Penn	10	06	19
Horn, Daniel(Z)	1815	May 01	TuscarwsCoOh	03	10	19
Horn, Hardman(Z-M)	1829	Sept. 07	KnoxCo.,Ohio	10	05	23
Horn, Hartman(Z-M)	1831	Aug. 17	KnoxCo.,Ohio	10	05	11
Horn, Hartman(Z-M)	1833	March 20	KnoxCo.,Ohio	10	05	12
Horn, Jacob(Z)	1815	May 01	KnoxCo.,Ohio	10	05	02
Horn, Joseph(Z)	1815	Sept. 02	WashCo.,Penn	11	06	19
Horn, Martin(Z)	1817	July 15	WashCo.,Penn	11	06	21
Horn, Noah(Z-M)	1835	Dec. 28	KnoxCo.,Ohio	10	09	03
Horn, Noah(Z-M)	1835	Dec. 28	KnoxCo.,Ohio	10	08	03
Horn, Stephen(Z-M)	1829	Aug. 26	HarrisonCoOh	01	05	10
Horn, Thos.(Z-M)	1831	Nov. 07	HarrisonCoOh	01	05	10
Horne, Benj.(Z-M)	1828	April 21	KnoxCo.,Ohio	10	06	19
Horne, Christian(Z)	1810	Oct. 25	Ohio Co.,Vir	10	06	11
Horne, Christian(Z)	1813	Dec. 20	Ohio Co.,Vir	10	06	24
Horne, D.(Z)	1805	April 17	BelmontCo,Oh	12	13	07
Horne, D.(Z)	1805	April 23	BelmontCo,Oh	08	02	22
Horne, Daniel(Z)	1811	Sept. 05	MuskingmCoOh	15	17	36
Horne, David(Z)	1805	May 29	BelmontCo,Oh	15	17	36
Horne, Isaac V.(Z)	1816	March 18	MuskingmCoOh	13	11	21
Horne, J. T.(Z-M)	1829	Dec. 22	ZanesvilleOh	05	02	09
Horne, J. V.(Z)	1805	Aug. 27	MuskingmCoOh	02	01	21
Horne, Jacob(Z)	1810	Oct. 25	WashCo.,Penn	10	06	20
Horne, Jacob(Z-M)	1832	Nov. 10	KnoxCo.,Ohio	10	06	11
Horne, Mary(Z)	1805	April 19	BelmontCo,Oh	15	17	25
Horne, Michael(Z)	1810	Oct. 17	WashngtnCoOh	09	07	34
Horner, Adam(Z)	1814	July 26	TuscarwsCoOh	05	08	12
Horner, John(Z-M)	1836	Feb. 13	CoshoctnCoOh	05	07	13
Horner, William(Z)	1834	Feb. 21	Morgan Co,Oh	11	10	01
Horner, William(Z)	1834	Feb. 21	Morgan Co,Oh	11	10	12
Horner, Wm. Jr.(Z)	1829	Jan. 23	Morgan Co,Oh	11	10	12
Hornish, Abraham(Y)	1831	April 15	Stark Co.,Oh	07	16	06
Horst, Aaron(Z-M)	1836	Jan. 20	GuernseyCoOh	04	02	01
Horton, Daniel(Z)	1808	April 19	MuskingmCoOh	12	13	04
Horton, Daniel(Z)	1816	Oct. 07	MuskingmCoOh	09	06	21

PURCHASER	YEAR	DATE	RESIDENCE	R	T	S
Horton, Daniel(Z)	1816	Oct. 07	MuskingmCoOh	09	06	22
Horton, Daniel(Z)	1817	Jan. 30	MuskingmCoOh	09	06	19
Horton, David(Z-M)	1924	May 11	CoshoctnCoOh	09	07	18
Horton, Ezra(Z)	1806	April 30	MuskingmCoOh	08	05	06
Horton, Ezra(Z)	1807	Jan. 23	MuskingmCoOh	08	05	06
Horton, Manuel G.(Z-M)	1836	Oct. 31	HolmesCoOhio	08	08	14
Horton, Manuel J.(Z-M)	1839	March 07	HolmesCoOhio	08	08	13
Horton, Thomas(Z)	1838	March 30	MonroeCo.,Oh	08	06	36
Horton, Thomas(Z)	1816	Jan. 31	CoshoctnCoOh	09	06	12
Horton, Thomas(Z-M)	1833	March 26	CoshoctnCoOh	09	06	19
Horvy, Eveline L.(Z-M)	1839	Feb. 12	ZanesvilleOh	10	06	05
Hosack, John(Z)	1806	Nov. 08	Ohio Co.,Vir	03	03	12
Hosack, John(Z-M)	1828	Sept. 02	GuernseyCoOh	03	03	13
Hosack, John(Z-M)	1832	Dec. 08	GuernseyCoOh	03	03	19
Hosack, William(Z-M)	1824	April 01	GuernseyCoOh	03	03	01
Hosam, A.(Z)	1816	Oct. 29	ZanesvilleOh	11	11	26
Hose, Henry(Z-M)	1839	March 16	CoshoctnCoOh	09	07	20
Hosfeld, Henry(Z-M)	1838	March 22	KnoxCo.,Ohio	10	09	18
Hosfeldt, Peter(Z-M)	1837	Sept. 29	CoshoctnCoOh	04	05	22
Hosick, William(Z)	1815	Sept. 12	GuernseyCoOh	02	03	04
Hoskin, Erastus(Z)	1835	June 17	Morgan Co,Oh	10	08	26
Hoskin, Erastus(Z)	1836	Jan. 21	Morgan Co,Oh	10	08	26
Hoskin, Wait(Z)	1835	Oct. 28	Morgan Co,Oh	10	08	26
Hoskins, Erastus(Z)	1832	Feb. 15	Morgan Co,Oh	10	08	25
Hoskins, Erastus(Z)	1832	May 22	Morgan Co,Oh	10	08	26
Hoskins, Neri(Z)	1834	Jan. 10	Morgan Co,Oh	10	08	26
Hoskins, Neri(Z)	1834	Jan. 10	Morgan Co,Oh	10	08	26
Hoskins, Wait(Z)	1830	Oct. 16	Morgan Co,Oh	10	08	27
Hoskinson, Isaiah(Z)	1808	Feb. 25	MuskingmCoOh	11	01	22
Hoskinson, James(Z)	1827	Nov. 05	LickingCo,Oh	11	01	22
Hoskinson, Josiah(Z)	1813	Sept. 20	LickingCo,Pa	11	01	22
Hossler, Fred'k.(Y)	1828	June 28	Stark Co.,Oh	07	20	17
Host, Adolph(Z-M)	1839	July 02	CoshoctnCoOh	09	08	15
Host, Adolph(Z-M)	1839	July 02	CoshoctnCoOh	09	08	15
Hosterman, John(Y)	1832	March 19	HarrisonCoOh	05	13	15
Hostetler, Benj'n.(Z)	1817	May 22	TuscarwsCoOh	03	09	21
Hostetler, David(Z)	1810	Oct. 22	SomersetCoPa	04	09	06
Hostetler, David(Z)	1810	Oct. 22	SomersetCoPa	04	09	06
Hostetler, Jeremiah(Z-M)	1828	March 18	TuscarwsCoOh	05	06	18
Hostetten, Matthias(Z-M)	1839	July 02	CoshoctnCoOh	08	07	07
Hostetter, Matthias(Z-M)	1839	July 02	CoshoctnCoOh	08	07	07
Hostfeld, Henry(Z-M)	1839	March 25	KnoxCo.,Ohio	10	09	19
Hott, John(Z)	1815	Nov. 08	CoshoctnCoOh	09	07	13
Houck, John(Z)	1817	Jan. 15	ZanesvilleOh	12	12	35
Houck, Washington(Z-M)	1839	Feb. 01	KnoxCo.,Ohio	10	05	22
Hough, John(Z)	1813	Oct. 04	MuskingmCoOh	10	06	22
Hough, John(Z)	1813	Oct. 21	MuskingmCoOh	15	16	11
Houghton, John(Y)	1827	July 17	Stark Co.,Oh	08	12	15
Houghton, John(Y)	1827	July 17	Stark Co.,Oh	08	12	15
Houpelhorn, George(Z)	1815	June 05	Jeff.Co.,Oh.	05	07	22
House, Andrew Junr.(Y)	1833	April 23	CarrollCo,Oh	03	12	28
House, Andrew(Y)	1827	July 16	ColumbanCoOh	04	13	28
House, Andrew(Y)	1833	June 03	CarrollCo,Oh	03	12	28
House, Andrew(Z-M)	1837	Feb. 28	Jeff.Co.,Oh.	10	09	22
House, Eli(Z)	1815	Oct. 27	MuskingmCoOh	14	13	02
House, John(Z)	1816	Jan. 01	Ohio Co.,Vir	10	06	17
House, William(Y)	1830	July 03	HarrisonCoOh	06	12	20
House, William(Z-M)	1836	April 26	KnoxCo.,Ohio	10	09	23
Householder, Joseph(Y)	1828	Aug. 27	Jeff.Co.,Oh.	02	08	29
Householder, Peter(Y)	1836	Sept. 24	Jeff.co.,Oh.	02	08	29
Houser, Jacob(Z-M)	1834	Jan. 15	HolmesCoOhio	05	07	08
Houser, Jacob(Z-M)	1834	Jan. 15	HolmesCoOhio	05	07	13
Hout, George(Z-M)	1820	Sept. 25	TuscarwsCoOh	01	08	12
Hout, Jacob F.(Z-M)	1835	Dec. 16	TuscarwsCoOh	03	07	14
Hout, Jacob F.(Z-M)	1838	Jan. 20	TuscarwsCoOh	03	07	16
Houze, John(Y)	1822	June 07	Jeff.Co.,Oh.	07	16	15
Houze, John(Y)	1823	Oct. 08	Jeff.Co.,Oh.	07	16	15
Houze, John(Y)	1828	Dec. 03	Jeff.Co.,Oh.	07	16	19
Houze, John(Y)	1829	Nov. 09	Jeff.Co.,Oh.	07	16	19

PURCHASER	YEAR	DATE	RESIDENCE	R	T	S
Hovey, H. C.(Z)	1836	Aug. 18	WashngtnCoOh	08	05	26
Hovey, Harvey C.(Z)	1829	June 19	WashCo.,Ohio	08	05	25
Hovey, Harvey C.(Z)	1836	Feb. 11	WashngtnCoOh	08	05	05
How, Horace(Z-M)	1835	June 27	WayneCo.,Oh.	09	09	01
How, Horace(Z-M)	1837	April 07	HolmesCoOhio	07	08	07
How, J.(Z)	1815	Dec. 13	BelmontCo,Oh	13	08	03
How, Jacob Jnr.(Z-M)	1836	Jan. 04	TuscarwsCoOh	02	07	03
How, Jacob Jnr.(Z-M)	1836	Jan. 04	TuscarwsCoOh	02	07	02
How, Jacob(Z)	1812	May 30	TuscarwsCoOh	02	07	03
How, Jacob(Z)	1816	March 18	TuscarwsCoOh	02	07	04
How, Jacob(Z)	1816	March 23	KnoxCo.,Ohio	10	06	11
How, Jacob(Z-M)	1835	Oct. 27	TuscarwsCoOh	02	07	02
How, Jacob(Z-M)	1835	Nov. 02	TuscarwsCoOh	02	07	02
How, Samuel(Z-M)	1832	May 22	TuscarwsCoOh	02	07	09
How, Samuel(Z-M)	1835	Nov. 02	TuscarwsCoOh	02	07	03
Howard, Charles(Z)	1826	Jan. 30	Morgan Co,Oh	12	09	09
Howard, Charles(Z)	1830	April 12	Morgan Co,Oh	12	09	09
Howard, Charles(Z)	1810	Feb. 28	LickingCo,Oh	10	01	12
Howard, Chas.(Z)	1831	April 04	Morgan Co,Oh	12	09	05
Howard, David(Z)	1826	Feb. 13	Morgan Co,Oh	11	12	21
Howard, John(Z-M)	1836	Jan. 09	CoshoctnCoOh	07	04	01
Howard, John(Z-M)	1836	Jan. 09	CoshoctnCoOh	07	04	01
Howard, Leland(Z-M)	1838	Aug. 20	HolmesCoOhio	08	08	08
Howard, Michael(Z)	1817	July 26	MuskingmCoOh	13	09	04
Howard, Robert(Z-M)	1838	July 02	ZanesvilleOh	09	09	01
Howe, David(Z)	1814	Feb. 22	?	15	16	27
Howe, John(Z-M)	1832	June 11	CoshoctnCoOh	07	05	20
Howe, John(Z-M)	1832	Nov. 01	CoshoctnCoOh	07	05	20
Howe, William(Z-M)	1834	Feb. 15	CarrollCo,Oh	10	09	23
Howel, Phillip(Z)	1807	April 07	AlleghnyCoPa	11	13	09
Howell, Abel(Y)	1831	May 17	BelmontCo,Oh	06	10	17
Howell, Hezekiah(Z-M)	1835	March 14	BelmontCo,Oh	03	06	25
Howell, Hezekiah(Z-M)	1835	March 14	BelmontCo,Oh	03	06	25
Howell, Jeremiah(Z-M)	1830	Feb. 25	CoshoctnCoOh	04	06	03
Howell, John(Z-M)	1825	Oct. 24	CoshoctnCoOh	08	04	08
Howell, Philip(Z)	1813	Nov. 27	AlleghnyCoPa	12	13	36
Howell, William(Z)	1814	Oct. 01	AlleghnyCoPa	12	13	36
Howell, William(Z-M)	1827	March 22	CoshoctnCoOh	08	04	08
Howensthine, Jacob(Y)	1828	Oct. 23	Stark Co.,Oh	07	17	05
Howland, Charles(Z)	1814	Oct. 19	LickingCo,Oh	10	01	09
Hoyd, Joseph A.(Z-M)	1838	Nov. 03	MuskingmCoOh	05	03	11
Hoyman, Jacob(Z-M)	1828	April 22	SomersetCoPa	10	06	18
Hoyman, Jacob(Z-M)	1832	Nov. 24	KnoxCo.,Ohio	10	06	17
Hoyman, Jacob(Z-M)	1835	Jan. 06	KnoxCo.,Ohio	10	06	13
Hoyman, Jacob(Z-M)	1835	June 01	KnoxCo.,Ohio	10	06	18
Hoyt, Moses(Z-M)	1829	Sept. 07	LickingCo,Oh	11	01	01
Hoyt, Moses(Z-M)	1832	Nov. 23	LickingCo,Oh	10	03	24
Hoyt, Moses(Z-M)	1832	Nov. 23	LickingCo,Oh	10	03	25
Hoyt, Sellick(Z-M)	1827	Nov. 27	LickingCo,Oh	10	03	18
Hubble, Sharrad(Z-M)	1836	Nov. 07	LickingCo,Oh	10	04	23
Huber, Martin(Z-M)	1835	May 30	TuscarwsCoOH	02	10	24
Huber, Martin(Z-M)	1835	May 30	TuscarwsCoOH	02	10	24
Hubert, Jacob(Z-M)	1833	July 04	HolmesCoOhio	05	08	25
Hudelmeyer, John George(Y)	1830	Oct. 18	Jeff.co.,Oh.	06	16	33
Hudleston, Jas. Senr.(Y)	1829	Sept. 04	SteubenvleOh	05	13	09
Hudson, Benj'n.(Y)	1829	May 05	HarrisonCoOh	06	13	17
Hudson, Eli(Y)	1828	Dec. 24	HarrisonCoOh	07	11	24
Hudson, John(Z-M)	1826	Feb. 09	BelmontCo,Oh	02	03	12
Hudson, John(Z-M)	1836	July 12	Wayne Co.,Oh	09	09	25
Hudson, John(Z-M)	1836	July 12	Wayne Co.,Oh	09	09	25
Hudson, William(Z)	1813	June 29	WorcestrCoMd	01	05	19
Hudson, William(Z-M)	1836	May 26	CoshoctnCoOh	05	04	13
Huegel, Joseph(Y)	1832	May 31	ColumbanCoOh	03	13	19
Huegel, Louis(Y)	1832	May 31	ColumbanCoOh	03	13	19
Huet, Joseph(Y)	1824	May 17	Stark Co.,Oh	06	17	15
Huff, Geo.(Z-M)	1836	June 16	MuskingmCoOh	05	04	15
Huff, George(Z-M)	1836	Jan. 25	MuskingmCoOh	06	04	19
Huff, J.(Z)	1814	May 05	MuskingmCoOH	15	16	20
Huff, James(Z-M)	1835	Aug. 29	BelmontCo,Oh	04	06	21

139

PURCHASER	YEAR	DATE	RESIDENCE	R	T	S
Huff, James(Z-M)	1836	Sept. 07	BelmontCo,Oh	02	07	03
Huff, John(Z-M)	1829	Nov. 26	GuernseyCoOh	02	02	13
Huff, John(Z-M)	1835	Aug. 06	TuscarwsCoOh	03	05	19
Huff, Nathan(Z)	1835	Feb. 11	HarrisonCoOh	10	09	03
Huff, Nathan(Z)	1835	Dec. 21	GuernseyCoOh	10	09	03
Huff, Philip(Z)	1816	March 18	LoudonCo,Vir	02	02	12
Huff, Richard(Y)	1828	Jan. 11	HarrisonCoOh	06	13	26
Huff, Thomas J.(Z-M)	1835	Sept. 23	MuskingmCoOh	05	04	15
Huff, William J.(Z-M)	1835	April 14	TuscarwsCoOh	01	06	25
Huff, William Johnson(Z-M)	1832	March 15	TuscarwsCoOh	01	06	14
Huffman, Benjamin(Z-M)	1829	Aug. 28	GuernseyCoOh	01	03	05
Huffman, Benjamin(Z-M)	1835	Aug. 25	GuernseyCoOh	01	03	05
Huffman, Daniel(Y)	1830	March 03	Stark Co.,Oh	07	16	25
Huffman, David(Z-M)	1832	April 12	CoshoctnCoOh	09	05	16
Huffman, George(Z)	1826	April 19	BelmontCo,Oh	12	11	22
Huffman, George(Z-M)	1835	Aug. 31	GuernseyCoOh	02	03	02
Huffman, Henry(Z)	1807	Feb. 05	BelmontCo,Oh	09	03	17
Huffman, Jacob(Z-M)	1833	May 13	GuernseyCoOh	02	03	02
Huffman, Jacob(Z-M)	1835	Sept. 07	Jeff.Co.,Oh.	02	03	10
Huffman, John Jr.(Z)	1817	March 31	GuernseyCoOh	07	05	17
Huffman, John(Z)	1814	Sept. 19	GuernseyCoOh	01	04	23
Huffman, John(Z)	1817	Feb. 11	GuernseyCoOh	02	03	02
Huffman, Jonathan(Z-M)	1835	Dec. 02	CarrollCo,Oh	03	07	23
Huffman, Joseph(Z-M)	1836	July 22	CoshoctnCoOh	08	07	03
Huffman, Joseph(Z-M)	1836	July 22	CoshoctnCoOh	08	07	03
Huffman, Robt. F.(Z-M)	1836	June 01	GuernseyCoOh	02	03	10
Huffman, Solomon(Z-M)	1835	June 15	CarrolCo.,Oh	03	06	06
Huffman, Solomon(Z-M)	1835	Dec. 02	TuscarwsCoOh	03	06	06
Huffman, Solomon(Z-M)	1836	Jan. 20	CoshoctnCoOh	10	04	02
Hufford, Christian(Z)	1810	Feb. 12	WashngtnCoOh	09	01	20
Huggins, John(Z)	1835	Aug. 24	MonroeCo.,Oh	08	06	04
Huggins, John(Z)	1836	July 18	MonroeCo.,Oh	08	06	04
Huggins, John(Z)	1837	May 03	MonroeCo.,Oh	08	06	04
Huggins, John(Z)	1838	Jan. 29	MonroeCo.,Oh	08	06	04
Hughes, Aaron(Z-M)	1828	April 02	GuernseyCoOh	01	04	06
Hughes, Abraham(Z-M)	1833	Jan. 09	LickingCo,Oh	10	03	02
Hughes, Gabriel(Z)	1833	Jan. 07	Morgan Co,Oh	09	06	33
Hughes, Jonathan(Z)	1833	June 03	Morgan Co,Oh	09	06	32
Hughes, Jonathan(Z)	1814	June 13	WashngtnCoOh	09	05	18
Hughes, Marshall(Z-M)	1833	July 27	CoshoctnCoOh	10	03	02
Hughes, Samuel(Z-M)	1838	Dec. 07	CoshoctnCoOh	08	07	13
Hughes, William(Y)	1828	Dec. 25	ColumbanCoOh	05	18	32
Hughey, Robt.(Z)	1836	Aug. 17	MonroeCo.,Oh	08	06	31
Hughs, Aaron(Z)	1806	April 19	MuskingmCoOh	03	01	20
Hughs, Aaron(Z)	1806	Dec. 12	MuskingmCoOh	03	01	20
Hughs, Aaron(Z)	1813	May 21	WashngtnCoOh	09	05	09
Hughs, Amos(Z)	1834	Aug. 20	Morgan Co,Oh	09	05	09
Hughs, Amos(Z)	1836	Jan. 07	Morgan Co,Oh	09	05	19
Hughs, Amos(Z)	1836	Sept. 02	Morgan Co,Oh	09	05	19
Hughs, David(Z)	1834	Jan. 24	MuskingmCoOh	11	12	22
Hughs, Gabriel(Z)	1836	March 25	Morgan Co,Oh	09	05	22
Hughs, Gabriel(Z)	1836	March 25	Morgan Co,Oh	09	05	36
Hughs, Gabriel(Z)	1836	March 25	Morgan Co,Oh	09	05	25
Hughs, Gabriel(Z)	1836	Dec. 26	Morgan Co,Oh	09	05	25
Hughs, Gabriel(Z)	1837	Feb. 17	Morgan Co,Oh	09	05	19
Hughs, Isaac(Z)	1822	April 16	GuernseyCoOh	09	08	10
Hughs, John(Z)	1825	June 02	Morgan Co,Oh	11	10	07
Hughs, Jonathan(Z)	1809	Nov. 10	MuskingmCoOh	09	08	09
Hughs, Sara(Z-M)	1820	July 04	GreeneCo.,Pa	02	04	18
Hughs, Warne(Z)	1812	May 06	GuernseyCoOh	02	02	03
Hull, Alanson(Z-M)	1827	March 12	HolmesCoOhio	07	08	01
Hull, Benjamin(Z)	1812	Oct. 02	MuskingmCoOh	15	16	04
Hull, Benjamin(Z)	1809	June 22	MuskingmCoOh	15	16	05
Hull, Daniel(Z)	1813	Oct. 01	MuskingmCoOh	15	15	04
Hull, Ealy(Z-M)	1830	June 02	CoshoctnCoOh	08	07	18
Hull, Ealy(Z-M)	1830	June 02	CoshoctnCoOh	09	07	12
Hull, Edy(Z)	1816	Dec. 27	CoshoctnCoOh	09	06	13
Hull, Edy(Z-M)	1832	March 28	CoshoctnCoOh	08	06	09
Hull, Edy(Z-M)	1832	March 28	CoshoctnCoOh	08	07	12

140

PURCHASER	YEAR	DATE	RESIDENCE	R	T	S
Hull, Edy(Z-M)	1832	Aug. 15	CoshoctnCoOh	08	07	12
Hull, Edy(Z-M)	1833	Oct. 28	CoshoctnCoOh	08	07	12
Hull, Edy(Z-M)	1834	Feb. 11	CoshoctnCoOh	09	07	12
Hull, Edy(Z-M)	1836	May 09	CoshoctnCoOh	08	07	03
Hull, Edy(Z-M)	1836	May 09	CoshoctnCoOh	08	07	03
Hull, Garsum(Z)	1816	Dec. 17	CrawfordCoPa	04	02	15
Hull, George(Z)	1813	July 05	MuskingmCoOh	15	18	04
Hull, Henry(Y)	1830	Oct. 20	ColumbanCoOh	03	13	20
Hull, Henry(Z)	1809	Dec. 07	Ohio Co.,Vir	09	05	19
Hull, Henry(Z)	1815	Aug. 07	CoshoctnCoOh	09	05	07
Hull, Henry(Z)	1815	Oct. 27	CoshoctnCoOh	09	05	18
Hull, Jas.(Z)	1827	May 03	LickingCo,Oh	11	01	11
Hull, Jesse(Z)	1836	July 07	Perry Co.,Oh	15	15	34
Hull, John Senr.(Z)	1816	May 29	LickingCo,Oh	11	01	02
Hull, John(Y)	1822	April 01	ColumbanCoOh	03	13	15
Hull, John(Z)	1816	Jan. 19	LickingCo,Oh	11	01	09
Hull, Johnson(Z-M)	1835	Aug. 18	KnoxCo.,Ohio	10	06	13
Hull, Samuel B.(Z)	1816	Dec. 18	LickingCo,Oh	11	01	02
Hull, Samuel B.(Z-M)	1832	March 15	LickingCo,Oh	11	01	10
Hull, Samuel(Z)	1806	Nov. 05	FayetteCo,Pa	15	16	06
Hull, Samuel(Z)	1811	Dec. 28	LickingCo,Oh	11	01	08
Hull, Samuel(Z)	1812	Feb. 14	MuskingmCoOh	15	16	06
Hull, Samuel(Z)	1816	March 05	LickingCo,Oh	11	01	02
Hull, Solomon(Z-M)	1835	Dec. 11	KnoxCo.,Ohio	10	09	03
Hull, Uriah(Z-M)	1831	Feb. 23	LickingCo,Oh	11	01	10
Hull, William(Z)	1807	March 24	MuskingmCoOh	10	01	19
Hull, William(Z)	1808	Jan. 07	FairfeldCoOh	10	01	18
Hull, William(Z)	1811	Sept. 10	CoshoctnCoOh	07	08	06
Hull, William(Z)	1811	Dec. 16	CoshoctnCoOh	07	08	06
Hull, William(Z)	1813	Feb. 25	CoshoctnCoOh	10	05	06
Hull, William(Z)	1813	Sept. 18	LickingCo,Oh	03	04	24
Hull, William(Z)	1814	Jan. 04	CoshoctnCoOh	07	08	06
Hull, William(Z-M)	1821	April 26	LickingCo,Oh	11	01	10
Hull, William(Z-M)	1832	March 26	LickingCo,Oh	11	01	11
Hull, Wm.(Y)	1828	Feb. 18	ColumbanCoOh	03	13	17
Hull, Wm.(Y)	1828	May 16	ColumbanCoOh	03	13	20
Humes, John(Z-M)	1834	Oct. 23	MuskingmCoOh	07	05	12
Hummel, Jacob(Z)	1807	June 29	MuskingmCoOh	10	01	22
Hummel, John(Z-M)	1832	Dec. 28	TuscarwsCoOh	02	08	24
Hummel, John(Z-M)	1833	Nov. 23	TuscarwsCoOh	02	08	24
Hummel, Mathias(Z)	1807	June 20	MuskingmCoOh	15	17	26
Hummel, Michael(Z-M)	1832	Oct. 31	HolmesCoOhio	05	08	25
Hummel, Michael(Z-M)	1837	Feb. 24	HolmesCoOhio	06	08	11
Hummel, Thomas(Z)	1807	June 27	MuskingmCoOh	10	01	22
Hummell, Michael(Z-M)	1822	Nov. 25	CoshoctnCoOh	05	08	25
Humphrey, Benjamin(Z)	1833	Nov. 18	Perry Co.,Oh	14	14	20
Humphrey, David(Z)	1833	Nov. 18	Perry Co.,Oh	14	14	20
Humphrey, James(Z-M)	1825	Sept. 24	Jeff.Co.,Oh.	08	05	14
Humphrey, James(Z-M)	1836	Feb. 09	CoshoctnCoOh	08	06	08
Humphrey, James(Z-M)	1836	Feb. 09	CoshoctnCoOh	08	06	08
Humphrey, Jonah(Z)	1817	Oct. 10	MuskingmCoOh	11	13	24
Humphrey, William(Z)	1815	Nov. 23	CoshoctnCoOh	09	07	08
Humphreys, Royal(Z-M)	1829	March 26	MuskingmCoOh	07	03	11
Humphreys, William(Y)	1830	Feb. 17	HarrisonCoOh	06	12	04
Humphreys, William(Y)	1830	March 20	HarrisonCoOh	05	11	34
Humphrys, Mathew(Z-M)	1825	July 28	MuskingmCoOh	06	03	08
Humrichhouse, Wm.(Z-M)	1837	March 18	TuscarwsCoOh	03	08	24
Hunchberger, John(Y)	1821	Sept. 18	Stark Co.,Oh	09	12	15
Hunchberger, John(Y)	1821	Sept. 18	Stark Co.,Oh	09	12	15
Hunchberger, John(Y)	1821	Sept. 18	Stark Co.,Oh	09	12	22
Hunckberger, John(Y)	1821	March 30	Stark Co.,Oh	07	20	19
Hunt, Austin(Z)	1808	Jan. 15	MuskingmCoOh	02	03	23
Hunt, Garner(Z-M)	1829	Jan. 12	CoshoctnCoOh	03	04	09
Hunt, Horatio(Y)	1825	April 20	TuscarwsCoOh	07	15	25
Hunt, John(Z)	1835	Oct. 31	BelmontCo,Oh	08	07	13
Hunt, Seth(Z-M)	1829	Feb. 12	HolmesCoOhio	08	08	10
Hunt, Seth(Z-M)	1837	April 03	HolmesCoOhio	09	08	15
Hunt, Thomas(Z-M)	1835	April 09	WestChestrPa	01	05	01
Hunt, William Senr.(Y)	1826	May 01	ColumbanCoOh	05	18	26

PURCHASER	YEAR	DATE	RESIDENCE	R	T	S
Hunter, D.(Z-M)	1820	Sept. 16	GuernseyCoOh	02	01	06
Hunter, George(Z-M)	1832	June 12	KnoxCo.,Ohio	10	07	19
Hunter, Henry(Z)	1815	Feb. 08	WashCo.,Penn	10	08	03
Hunter, James(Z)	1816	July 27	WestmrldCoPa	06	06	01
Hunter, John(Y)	1832	Dec. 03	ColumbanCoOh	03	12	11
Hunter, John(Y)	1836	Sept. 12	ColumbanCoOh	03	12	11
Hunter, John(Z)	1812	April 21	MuskingmCoOh	13	13	04
Hunter, John(Z-M)	1831	May 17	MuskingmCoOh	04	01	19
Hunter, Joseph(Y)	1831	Oct. 17	Jeff.Co.,Oh.	07	15	20
Hunter, Robert(Y)	1827	July 18	BelmontCo,Oh	06	09	35
Hunter, Robert(Z)	1824	Sept. 04	MuskingmCoOh	12	13	02
Hunter, S.(Z)	1831	July 18	CoshoctnCoOh	08	04	23
Hunter, Samuel(Y)	1831	Dec. 07	ColumbanCoOh	03	12	12
Hunter, Samuel(Y)	1832	April 20	ColumbanCoOh	03	12	11
Hunter, Thos.(Z)	1811	May 04	MuskingmCoOh	08	04	22
Hunter, W.(Z)	1831	July 18	CoshoctnCoOh	08	04	23
Hunter, William Jnr.(Z)	1814	Dec. 01	MuskingmCoOh	11	13	10
Hunter, William Jnr.(Z)	1814	Dec. 01	MuskingmCoOh	11	13	10
Hunter, William Jr.(Z)	1815	Sept. 29	MuskingmCoOh	06	01	22
Hunter, William Jr.(Z-M)	1828	June 06	MuskingmCoOh	04	01	21
Hunter, William(Z)	1807	May 07	WashCo.,Penn	05	01	18
Hunter, William(Z)	1810	June 18	MuskingmCoOh	05	01	17
Hunter, William(Z)	1812	Aug. 10	MuskingmCoOh	11	13	09
Hunter, William(Z)	1815	Nov. 24	MuskingmCoOh	12	13	11
Hunter, William(Z-M)	1826	March 13	MuskingmCoOh	04	01	22
Hunter, William(Z-M)	1826	March 13	MuskingmCoOh	04	01	22
Hunter, William(Z-M)	1826	March 13	MuskingmCoOh	04	01	22
Hunter, William(Z-M)	1826	March 13	MuskingmCoOh	04	01	22
Hunter, William(Z-M)	1826	April 18	MuskingmCoOh	04	01	19
Hunter, Wm.(Z)	1811	May 04	MuskingmCoOh	08	04	22
Huntley, Richard P.(Z-M)	1832	July 13	KnoxCo.,Ohio	10	08	03
Huntley, Richard P.(Z-M)	1834	Nov. 20	KnoxCo.,Ohio	10	08	03
Huntsman, James(Y)	1831	Dec. 17	BelmontCo,Oh	07	12	10
Hupp, Daniel(Z)	1832	Feb. 04	MonroeCo.,Oh	08	06	21
Hupp, Daniel(Z)	1835	Dec. 24	MonroeCo.,Oh	08	06	21
Hupp, Daniel(Z)	1836	Sept. 28	MonroeCo.,Oh	08	06	21
Hupp, Ephraim(Z)	1836	Sept. 09	MonroeCo.,Oh	08	06	28
Hupp, Ephraim(Z)	1836	Sept. 10	MonroeCo.,Oh	08	06	29
Hupp, Francis Jr.(Z)	1837	Jan. 28	MonroeCo.,Oh	08	06	22
Hupp, Francis(Z)	1820	Sept. 29	Morgan Co,Oh	08	06	28
Hupp, Francis(Z)	1832	Oct. 22	MonroeCo.,Oh	08	06	28
Hupp, Francis(Z)	1835	Aug. 26	MonroeCo.,Oh	08	06	22
Hupp, Francis(Z)	1837	May 24	MonroeCo.,Oh	08	06	21
Hupp, Francis(Z)	1837	Oct. 17	MonroeCo.,Oh	08	06	28
Hupp, George(Z)	1817	April 19	WashngtnCoOh	08	05	12
Hupp, Henry(Z)	1837	June 21	WashngtnCoOh	08	05	11
Hupp, Henry(Z)	1817	Sept. 26	WashngtnCoOh	08	06	35
Hupp, Hiram(Z)	1835	Dec. 28	MonroeCo.,Oh	08	06	22
Hupp, Hiram(Z)	1836	March 05	MonroeCo.,Oh	08	06	19
Hupp, John(Z)	1836	Aug. 03	MonroeCo.,Oh	08	06	21
Hupp, John(Z)	1837	April 19	MonroeCo.,Oh	08	06	21
Hupp, John(Z)	1837	April 20	MonroeCo.,Oh	08	05	11
Hupp, John(Z)	1837	April 20	MonroeCo.,Oh	08	05	11
Hupp, Mannasseh(Z)	1836	May 30	MonroeCo.,Oh	08	06	21
Hupp, Mannasseh(Z)	1836	Aug. 24	MonroeCo.,Oh	08	06	17
Hupp, Philip(Z)	1833	May 31	MonroeCo.,Oh	08	06	07
Hupprich, John(Z-M)	1836	Oct. 06	TuscarwsCoOh	04	08	23
Hupprich, John(Z-M)	1836	Oct. 31	TuscarwsCoOh	04	08	22
Hurdle, John(Z-M)	1824	Aug. 05	BelmontCo,Oh	07	03	21
Hurlass, Samuel(Y)	1831	May 27	HarrisonCoOh	06	12	18
Hursey, Geo. Jr.(Z-M)	1831	April 11	TuscarwsCoOh	02	05	18
Hursey, George Junr.(Z-M)	1825	Jan. 20	Jeff.Co.,Oh.	02	05	18
Hursey, Robert(Z-M)	1826	Aug. 18	Jeff.Co.,Oh.	02	05	22
Hushman, Philip(Z)	1810	Nov. 15	MuskingmCoOh	06	04	22
Hushman, Philip(Z-M)	1840	Jan. 03	CoshoctnCoOh	08	06	08
Hussey, Penrose(Y)	1821	Aug. 09	Jeff.Co.,Oh.	07	15	19
Hussey, Penrose(Y)	1825	Nov. 11	Jeff.Co.,Oh.	07	15	19
Hust, Washington(Y)	1828	June 23	ColumbanCoOh	05	18	19
Hustan, John(Y)	1822	Jan. 29	BeaverCo,Pa.	06	15	22

PURCHASER	YEAR	DATE	RESIDENCE	R	T	S
Hustead, Leonard(Z-M)	1836	Jan. 19	HolmesCoOhio	07	08	17
Husted, Allen(Z-M)	1828	March 27	HolmesCoOhio	07	08	04
Husted, Asa Allen(Z-M)	1823	June 19	CoshoctnCoOh	08	08	02
Husted, Caleb(Z-M)	1824	Jan. 31	CoshoctnCoOh	08	08	19
Husted, Caleb(Z-M)	1828	April 03	HolmesCoOhio	08	08	19
Husted, Henry Purdy(Z-M)	1832	Oct. 15	HolmesCoOhio	08	08	18
Husted, Henry Senr.(Z-M)	1823	June 19	CoshoctnCoOh	08	08	11
Husted, Henry(Z-M)	1824	Jan. 31	CoshoctnCoOh	07	08	07
Husted, Leonard(Z-M)	1822	Aug. 13	CoshoctnCoOh	08	08	18
Huston, Archibald(Z)	1829	Jan. 31	Perry Co.,Oh	15	16	26
Huston, Edward(Z)	1817	June 04	MuskingmCoOh	15	15	28
Huston, Isaac(Z-M)	1833	Oct. 23	HarrisonCoOh	02	06	22
Huston, James(Y)	1829	April 24	ColumbanCoOh	05	14	02
Huston, James(Z)	1814	April 15	Brooke CoVir	11	05	23
Huston, James(Z-M)	1833	Feb. 02	KnoxCo.,Ohio	11	04	03
Huston, James(Z-M)	1833	Feb. 02	KnoxCo.,Ohio	11	04	08
Huston, Jeremiah(Y)	1826	June 05	ColumbanCoOh	01	07	35
Huston, John C.(Y)	1829	Aug. 20	HarrisonCoOh	06	14	15
Huston, John(Y)	1832	May 30	Jeff.Co.,Oh.	03	12	15
Huston, John(Y)	1832	May 31	Jeff.Co.,Oh.	03	11	11
Huston, John(Z)	1814	Jan. 14	FayetteCo,Pa	11	13	10
Huston, Robert(Y)	1825	Oct. 27	WashCo.,Penn	05	14	09
Huston, Robert(Y)	1826	Oct. 02	ColumbanCoOh	05	14	04
Huston, Robert(Z)	1816	April 16	WashCo.,Penn	11	05	18
Huston, Robert(Z)	1816	April 16	Brooke CoVir	11	05	22
Huston, Robert(Z-M)	1835	Feb. 20	KnoxCo.,Ohio	11	04	03
Huston, Samuel(Y)	1825	Oct. 27	WashCo.,Penn	05	14	09
Huston, Samuel(Y)	1829	June 19	ColumbanCoOh	04	14	25
Huston, Samuel(Y)	1829	June 19	ColumbanCoOh	04	14	25
Huston, Thomas(Z)	1814	April 15	WashCo.,Penn	11	05	23
Huston, Thomas(Z-M)	1831	Feb. 04	KnoxCo.,Ohio	11	04	03
Huston, Thomas(Z-M)	1831	Feb. 11	KnoxCo.,Ohio	11	04	03
Hutcheson, John Jr.(Z-M)	1836	Jan. 19	GuernseyCoOh	03	03	16
Hutchin, Samuel(Z)	1814	Jan. 07	FayetteCo,Pa	15	15	19
Hutchins, B.(Z)	1815	June 28	MuskingmCoOh	13	09	23
Hutchins, Bartlet(Z)	1836	March 01	Morgan Co,Oh	09	06	27
Hutchins, Bartlet(Z)	1836	Sept. 26	Morgan Co,Oh	09	06	27
Hutchins, Benjamin(Z)	1833	Jan. 05	Morgan Co,Oh	09	06	36
Hutchins, Benjamin(Z)	1836	Jan. 06	Morgan Co,Oh	09	06	35
Hutchins, Dan'l.(Z)	1817	July 12	MuskingmCoOh	09	06	36
Hutchins, David(Z)	1832	Dec. 03	Morgan Co,Oh	09	06	11
Hutchins, George(Z)	1836	Dec. 13	WashngtnCoOh	09	05	13
Hutchins, Hollis Jr.(Z)	1836	Feb. 05	Morgan Co,Oh	09	06	14
Hutchins, Hollis(Z)	1831	Dec. 09	WashCo.,Ohio	09	06	24
Hutchins, Hollis(Z)	1832	June 05	Morgan Co,Oh	09	06	24
Hutchins, Jefferson(Z)	1836	Jan. 12	Morgan Co,Oh	09	06	14
Hutchins, Jefferson(Z)	1836	Feb. 24	Morgan Co,Oh	09	06	11
Hutchins, John Jr.(Z)	1836	Aug. 17	WashngtnCoOh	09	05	13
Hutchins, John(Z)	1814	April 26	WashngtnCoOh	08	05	07
Hutchins, Joseph Jr.(Z)	1831	March 15	Morgan Co,Oh	09	06	14
Hutchins, Joseph(Z)	1814	Feb. 10	WashngtnCoOh	09	06	15
Hutchins, Shubel(Z)	1827	May 31	WashCo.,Penn	08	05	07
Hutchins, Shubel(Z)	1832	June 05	WashCo.,Ohio	08	05	06
Hutchinson, James(Y)	1829	Dec. 09	GuernseyCoOh	07	11	21
Hutchinson, James(Y)	1829	Dec. 09	GuernseyCoOh	07	11	21
Hutchinson, Wm.(Z)	1822	April 15	Morgan Co,Oh	12	11	27
Hutchison, Enoch(Z)	1838	April 20	GuernseyCoOh	08	05	22
Hutchison, Enoch(Z)	1838	Oct. 16	GuernseyCoOh	08	05	22
Hutsen, James(Y)	1829	May 28	ColumbanCoOh	04	13	29
Hyaer, Adam(Z-M)	1833	March 09	TuscarwsCoOh	03	08	16
Hyatt, David(Y)	1823	Feb. 04	ColumbanCoOh	04	15	22
Hyatt, Ezekiel(Z)	1833	March 25	MuskingmCoOh	11	12	34
Hyatt, Ezekiel(Z)	1833	March 25	MuskingmCoOh	11	12	33
Hyatt, Ezekiel(Z)	1833	March 25	MuskingmCoOh	11	12	34
Hyatt, Ezekiel(Z)	1812	June 30	BrookCo.,Vir	11	12	32
Hyatt, Ezekiel(Z)	1814	Jan. 10	BrookCo.,Vir	11	12	32
Hyatt, Ezekiel(Z)	1815	Jan. 16	Brooke CoVir	11	11	09
Hyatt, Hezekiah Jr.(Z)	1832	Jan. 13	MuskingmCoOh	11	12	28
Hyatt, Hezekiah(Z)	1809	May 22	BrookCo.,Vir	11	13	18

143

PURCHASER	YEAR	DATE	RESIDENCE	R	T	S
Hyde, Nicholas(Z-M)	1837	March 20	MuskingmCoOh	09	08	07
Hyde, Robert(Z)	1837	Feb. 07	GuernseyCoOh	08	05	15
Hyde, Thomas(Z)	1837	Feb. 07	GuernseyCoOh	08	05	15
Hyde, Thomas(Z-M)	1825	Aug. 23	GuernseyCoOh	02	02	13
Hyde, Thomas(Z-M)	1825	Dec. 07	GuernseyCoOh	02	02	13
Hyde, West(Z-M)	1832	Aug. 15	CoshoctnCoOh	06	04	09
Hyde, West(Z-M)	1832	Aug. 15	CoshoctnCoOh	06	04	09
Hyder, Adam(Z-M)	1834	March 01	TuscarwsCoOh	03	08	14
Hyer, Martin(Z)	1811	Nov. 20	CoshoctnCoOh	04	04	08
Iddings, Sam'l.(Y)	1821	Dec. 22	ColumbanCoOh	05	15	18
Iddings, Sam'l.(Y)	1821	Dec. 22	ColumbanCoOh	06	16	13
Ijams, Sarah(Z)	1817	Feb. 13	FairfeldCoOh	14	13	04
Imel, Nathaniel(Z)	1836	June 22	Perry Co.,Oh	15	14	10
Immel, John(Z)	1833	July 26	Perry Co.,Oh	15	14	10
Immel, John(Z)	1834	Jan. 09	Perry Co.,Oh	15	14	10
Imus, Horatio M.(Z-M)	1839	Sept. 30	CoshoctnCoOh	04	05	20
Ince, Thomas(Y)	1822	Dec. 31	AlleghnyCoPa	07	16	22
Infield, Joseph(Z-M)	1830	Dec. 01	HolmesCoOhio	05	08	01
Infield, Peter(Z-M)	1836	April 28	CoshoctnCoOh	05	07	01
Ingalls, Ebenezer(Z)	1811	Nov. 20	MuskingmCoOh	06	01	19
Inglehart, Adam(Z-M)	1838	Nov. 17	MuskingmCoOh	04	04	09
Inglehart, Adam(Z-M)	1838	Nov. 17	MuskingmCoOh	04	04	09
Inglehart, William(Z)	1815	July 22	GreeneCoOhio	02	02	10
Inglis, John(Z)	1816	Oct. 31	BeaverCo.,Pa	06	09	05
Inglis, John(Z)	1816	Oct. 31	BeaverCo.,Pa	06	09	04
Ingmine, Nelson(Z-M)	1832	Feb. 08	MuskingmCoOh	09	04	25
Ingmine, Snowden(Z-M)	1832	Feb. 08	MuskingmCoOh	09	04	25
Insley, Micajah(Y)	1829	Dec. 24	Stark Co.,Oh	06	12	19
Irelan, William L.(Z)	1835	Aug. 26	Morgan Co,Oh	10	06	08
Irelan, William(Z)	1835	Aug. 26	Morgan Co,Oh	10	06	08
Ireland, Thos.(Z)	1811	May 18	MuskingmCoOh	15	17	22
Irons, Thomas(Y)	1829	April 20	HarrisonCoOh	07	12	28
Irvin, Henry(Z)	1836	Feb. 19	MuskingmCoOh	11	12	34
Irvin, Henry(Z)	1836	Sept. 29	MuskingmCoOh	09	08	30
Irvin, Henry(Z)	1836	Sept. 29	MuskingmCoOh	09	08	30
Irvin, Henry(Z)	1836	Oct. 03	MuskingmCoOh	09	08	30
Irvin, Robt.(Z-M)	1831	March 29	CoshoctnCoOh	05	06	04
Irvine, John(Z-M)	1835	Oct. 26	Jeff.Co.,Oh.	07	08	08
Irvine, John(Z-M)	1835	Nov. 10	Jeff.Co.,Oh.	07	08	03
Irwin, Arthur(Z)	1827	Nov. 05	BelmontCo,Oh	12	11	26
Irwin, Arthur(Z)	1827	Nov. 05	BelmontCo,Oh	12	11	25
Irwin, David(Y)	1824	May 22	BelmontCo,Oh	04	06	10
Irwin, David(Y)	1824	May 22	BelmontCo,Oh	04	06	10
Irwin, Edward(Z)	1828	May 24	WestmrldCoPa	14	15	36
Irwin, Elisha(Z)	1833	Feb. 04	BelmontCo,Oh	13	08	20
Irwin, Elisha(Z)	1833	Feb. 04	BelmontCo,Oh	13	08	21
Irwin, Geo.(Z-M)	1821	July 05	GuernseyCoOh	02	02	14
Irwin, Guy(Z-M)	1823	Nov. 13	CoshoctnCoOh	05	07	24
Irwin, Henry(Z)	1833	Jan. 01	MuskingmCoOh	11	12	13
Irwin, James Sample(Z-M)	1833	July 22	HolmesCoOhio	05	10	04
Irwin, James(Z)	1816	Nov. 12	LickingCo,Oh	11	01	03
Irwin, Jno. A.(Z)	1834	Feb. 04	Perry Co.,Oh	14	13	29
Irwin, John A.(Z)	1836	April 04	Perry Co.,Oh	14	13	29
Irwin, John(Z-M)	1832	April 23	CoshoctnCoOh	05	07	24
Irwin, John(Z-M)	1836	March 08	CoshoctnCoOh	05	06	04
Irwin, Joseph(Y)	1823	May 12	Stark Co.,Oh	06	17	15
Irwin, William(Z)	1826	Nov. 03	Belmontco,Oh	12	11	15
Irwin, William(Z)	1833	Feb. 15	Perry Co.,Oh	14	13	20
Isely, Jacob(Z-M)	1835	July 06	TuscarwsCoOh	03	08	25
Isely, Jacob(Z-M)	1836	Feb. 06	TuscarwsCoOh	03	08	25
Israel, Robert(Z)	1837	March 16	BelmontCo,Oh	08	05	27
Israel, Sarah(Z)	1837	March 16	BelmontCo,Oh	09	05	24
Israel, Sarah(Z)	1837	March 16	BelmontCo,Oh	09	05	35
Ivory, Thomas(Z)	1828	Feb. 04	MuskingmCoOh	15	15	12
Jack, James Junr.(Z-M)	1833	Aug. 24	MuskingmCoOh	05	03	19
Jack, James S.(Z-M)	1839	March 18	MuskingmCoOh	05	03	11
Jack, James(Z)	1816	May 31	Ohio Co.,Vir	05	03	19
Jack, John(Z-M)	1835	Dec. 07	CoshoctnCoOh	07	07	13
Jackman, Edward(Y)	1831	Sept. 03	Jeff.Co.,Oh.	04	12	34

PURCHASER	YEAR	DATE	RESIDENCE	R	T	S
Jackman, Henry(Y)	1829	March 18	Jeff.Co.,Co.	05	13	04
Jackman, James(Z)	1821	Feb. 24	Perry Co.,Oh	15	16	26
Jackman, James(Z)	1821	March 02	Perry Co.,Oh	15	16	26
Jackman, Rich'd.(Y)	1821	Sept. 13	Jeff.Co.,Oh.	05	13	22
Jackman, Rich'd.(Y)	1822	Feb. 14	Jeff.Co.,Oh.	05	13	22
Jackman, William(Y)	1836	Dec. 21	CarrollCo,Oh	04	12	22
Jackman, Wm.(Y)	1824	May 27	HarrisonCoOh	04	12	21
Jackson, Benj'n.(Y)	1823	March 24	TuscarwsCoOh	04	12	30
Jackson, David(Z-M)	1827	July 21	GuernseyCoOh	04	02	10
Jackson, Dorothy(Z)	1836	July 07	MonroeCo.,Oh	08	05	02
Jackson, Elizabeth(Y)	1831	July 05	ColumbanCoOh	05	15	06
Jackson, Henry(Z)	1824	April 06	GuernseyCoOh	09	08	19
Jackson, Henry(Z)	1835	March 17	GuernseyCoOh	09	08	18
Jackson, Henry(Z)	1836	Jan. 04	GuernseyCoOh	09	08	18
Jackson, Henry(Z)	1807	Dec. 19	GreenCo.,Pa.	09	08	17
Jackson, Henry(Z)	1810	May 19	GuernseyCoOh	03	01	11
Jackson, Hesea(Z-M)	1838	Dec. 15	ZanesvilleOh	04	03	11
Jackson, Hesea(Z-M)	1838	Dec. 15	ZanesvilleOh	04	03	10
Jackson, Hosea(Z)	1838	Oct. 19	ZanesvilleOh	08	06	33
Jackson, Hosea(Z-M)	1838	Dec. 18	ZanesvilleOh	03	05	16
Jackson, J.(Z)	1807	Dec. 19	GreenCo.,Pa.	09	08	17
Jackson, John(Y)	1834	Nov. 26	CarrollCo,Oh	05	15	05
Jackson, John(Z)	1832	March 07	Morgan Co,Oh	11	11	35
Jackson, John(Z)	1832	April 16	Morgan Co,Oh	11	11	35
Jackson, Julia(Z)	1836	July 07	MonroeCo.,Oh	08	05	02
Jackson, Nathan(Z)	1815	Jan. 17	WashCo.,Penn	09	01	23
Jackson, Robert(Z)	1829	May 07	WashCo.,Ohio	08	05	28
Jackson, Robert(Z)	1835	Nov. 24	Morgan Co,Oh	10	07	34
Jackson, Samuel(Z)	1806	March 03	MuskingmCoOh	03	01	19
Jackson, Samuel(Z)	1806	April 09	MuskingmCoOh	03	01	20
Jackson, Samuel(Z)	1811	Aug. 20	GuernseyCoOh	03	01	20
Jacobs, Elizabeth(Y)	1822	Aug. 09	Jeff.Co.,Oh.	04	12	31
Jacobs, William Senr.(Z)	1833	Aug. 23	Morgan Co,Oh	09	06	32
Jacobs, William(Z)	1833	Jan. 07	Morgan Co,Oh	09	06	32
Jahrous, Fred'ck.(Z-M)	1836	Oct. 17	CuyahogaCoOh	10	09	03
James, Abner(Z)	1811	Aug. 31	MuskingmCoOh	14	15	06
James, Amos(Z)	1811	Dec. 11	LoudonCo,Vir	09	15	12
James, David(Z)	1831	April 26	MuskingmCoOh	11	12	12
James, David(Z)	1817	Sept. 26	MuskingmCoOh	11	12	01
James, Elias(Z)	1815	May 26	CoshoctnCoOh	08	05	16
James, George(Y)	1827	Nov. 12	ColumbanCoOh	04	13	20
James, George(Y)	1832	Nov. 12	ColumbanCoOh	03	12	36
James, Hollis(Z)	1815	July 04	GuernseyCoOh	09	06	14
James, Isaac(Y)	1823	March 07	ColumbanCoOh	05	18	12
James, Isaac(Z)	1816	Nov. 28	MuskingmCoOh	13	09	11
James, Isaac(Z)	1816	Nov. 28	MuskingmCoOh	13	09	11
James, Jacob(Z)	1815	Aug. 28	GreeneCo.,Oh	09	08	19
James, Jacob(Z)	1815	Aug. 28	GreeneCo.,Oh	09	08	23
James, Jacob(Z)	1815	Aug. 28	GreeneCo.,Oh	09	08	23
James, Jesse(Z)	1816	June 24	MuskingmCoOh	13	09	23
James, Jno.(Z)	1815	Aug. 28	GreeneCo.,Oh	09	08	19
James, Jno.(Z)	1815	Aug. 28	GreeneCo.,Oh	09	08	23
James, Jno.(Z)	1815	Aug. 28	GreeneCo.,Oh	09	08	23
James, John Deen(Z)	1836	March 12	GuernseyCoOh	09	05	24
James, John(Y)	1831	May 30	BelmontCo,Oh	07	15	31
James, John(Z)	1833	Nov. 27	Morgan Co,Oh	10	08	19
James, John(Z-M)	1831	Sept. 03	LickingCo,Oh	11	04	15
James, Joseph(Y)	1823	Sept. 06	ColumbanCoOh	07	20	04
James, Joseph(Y)	1823	Sept. 06	ColumbanCoOh	07	20	15
James, Joseph(Z)	1817	April 28	DelawareCoPa	13	08	14
James, Joseph(Z)	1817	April 28	DelawareCoPa	13	08	14
James, Judah(Y)	1827	July 05	GuernseyCoOh	07	09	09
James, Moses(Z)	1811	Aug. 31	MuskingmCoOh	14	16	18
James, Moses(Z)	1817	April 28	MuskingmCoOh	13	08	14
James, Moses(Z)	1817	April 28	MuskingmCoOh	13	08	23
James, Perry G.(Z)	1837	Feb. 20	CarrollCo,Oh	15	14	32
James, Robert P.(Y)	1831	May 30	BelmontCo,Oh	07	15	31
James, Thomas Jr.(Z)	1825	April 25	GuernseyCoOh	08	08	02
James, Thomas(Y)	1821	Oct. 02	TuscarwsCoOh	06	14	21

PURCHASER	YEAR	DATE	RESIDENCE	R	T	S
James, Thomas(Z)	1833	Aug. 08	GuernseyCoOh	08	08	01
James, Thomas(Z)	1811	Dec. 11	LoudonCo,Vir	08	05	16
James, Thomas(Z)	1812	April 28	MuskingmCoOh	06	03	02
James, William(Z)	1834	Jan. 04	Perry Co.,Oh	14	13	05
James, Wm.(Z)	1815	Aug. 28	GreeneCo.,Oh	09	08	19
James, Wm.(Z)	1815	Aug. 28	GreeneCo.,Oh	09	08	23
James, Wm.(Z)	1815	Aug. 28	GreeneCo.,Oh	09	08	23
Jameson, John(Z-M)	1826	Dec. 08	HolmesCoOhio	07	09	20
Jameson, Robert(Z-M)	1833	Jan. 18	HolmesCoOhio	06	09	18
Jamieson, John(Z)	1832	Dec. 17	GuernseyCoOh	10	08	21
Jamieson, John(Z)	1832	Dec. 17	GuernseyCoOh	10	08	20
Jamison, Alexander(Z)	1833	Nov. 16	GuernseyCoOh	10	08	20
Jamison, Robert(Z)	1816	Oct. 16	WashCo.,Penn	08	05	18
Jamison, Thomas(Y)	1835	Aug. 25	CarrollCo,Oh	07	14	15
Jarvis, John(Y)	1829	July 20	Jeff.Co.,Oh.	03	11	09
Jarvis, Mead(Z-M)	1839	Feb. 20	BelmontCo,Oh	03	05	25
Jay, Ann(Z)	1836	Oct. 18	Perry Co.,Oh	15	14	08
Jay, George(Z)	1814	Feb. 17	MuskingmCoOh	06	01	11
Jay, John Junr.(Z-M)	1833	July 27	MuskingmCoOh	06	03	20
Jay, John(Z)	1816	March 22	MuskingmCoOh	06	01	20
Jay, Samuel(Z)	1834	Feb. 22	MuskingmCoOh	11	12	29
Jay, William(Z)	1836	Aug. 25	Perry Co.,Oh	15	14	09
Jeffers, Robt.(Z)	1835	Dec. 18	Morgan Co,Oh	10	07	35
Jeffords, Lucinda(Z)	1817	Oct. 04	WashngtnCo ?	10	07	30
Jeffords, Nicholas(Z)	1835	Oct. 23	Morgan Co,Oh	10	06	20
Jeffreys, James(Z)	1805	July 01	MuskingmCoOh	14	16	14
Jeffries, Catharine(Y)	1828	Dec. 20	HarrisonCoOh	06	13	19
Jeffries, James(Z)	1805	Nov. 21	MuskingmCoOh	14	15	11
Jeffries, James(Z)	1805	Nov. 21	MuskingmCoOh	14	15	12
Jeffries, John S.(Z)	1833	Aug. 10	GuernseyCoOh	08	08	33
Jeffries, John S.(Z)	1833	Aug. 10	GuernseyCoOh	08	08	34
Jeffries, John S.(Z)	1833	Aug. 10	GuernseyCoOh	08	08	35
Jeffries, John S.(Z)	1833	Aug. 10	GuernseyCoOh	08	08	14
Jeffries, John S.(Z)	1833	Aug. 10	GuernseyCoOh	08	08	35
Jeffries, John(Y)	1828	Dec. 20	HarrisonCoOh	06	13	19
Jeffries, John(Z)	1833	July 26	GuernseyCoOh	08	08	26
Jeffries, William(Z)	1813	June 01	CoshoctnCoOh	05	04	23
Jeffrys, James(Z)	1810	Nov. 13	MuskingmCoOh	14	15	14
Jenkers, Jacob(Z)	1807	Jan. 20	FrederkCoVir	10	02	16
Jenkins, Arthur(Z)	1815	April 01	GuernseyCoOh	11	11	28
Jenkins, Colvin(Z)	1834	March 12	Morgan Co,Oh	13	08	09
Jenkins, Edward(Z-M)	1836	July 11	GuernseyCoOh	03	01	15
Jenkins, Eleazar(Z-M)	1835	Aug. 28	GuernseyCoOh	02	03	10
Jenkins, John M.(Z-M)	1832	Feb. 23	HarrisonCoOh	01	05	14
Jenkins, Levi(Y)	1827	March 24	Jeff.Co.,Oh.	04	11	30
Jenkins, Solomon(Y)	1823	Oct. 18	Jeff.Co.,Oh.	04	11	30
Jenkins, Thos. P.(Z-M)	1831	May 10	HarrisonCoOh	01	06	20
Jenkins, William(Z)	1836	Aug. 30	Morgan Co,Oh	13	08	06
Jenkinson, Joseph(Z)	1816	Oct. 11	WashCo.,Penn	14	15	35
Jenkinson, Thomas(Y)	1835	Oct. 13	Jeff.Co.,Oh.	03	11	23
Jennings, Benj'm.(Z)	1816	Dec. 24	MuskingmCoOh	12	09	03
Jennings, Benj.(Z)	1828	Jan. 30	Perry Co.,Oh	15	15	15
Jennings, Benjamin(Z)	1814	Sept. 19	CoshoctnCoOh	07	07	25
Jennings, David D.(Z)	1823	Sept. 02	MonongahlaVa	08	08	31
Jennings, David(Z)	1822	Feb. 21	MonongahlaVa	08	08	31
Jennings, David(Z)	1829	Sept. 26	FayetteCo,Pa	12	10	34
Jennings, David(Z)	1830	April 20	FayetteCo,Pa	12	10	23
Jennings, David(Z)	1809	April 27	MuskingmCoOh	15	18	04
Jennings, David(Z)	1814	Oct. 24	SomersetCoPa	15	15	20
Jennings, David(Z)	1816	May 14	MuskingmCoOh	12	10	28
Jennings, Gideon(Z)	1804	June 18	MuskingmCoOh	01	09	04
Jennings, Gideon(Z)	1808	Oct. 28	TuscarwsCoOh	01	09	05
Jennings, Gideon(Z)	1814	March 31	TuscarwsCoOh	03	09	05
Jennings, Isaac(Z)	1834	Jan. 03	Perry Co.,Oh	15	14	23
Jennings, Jesse(Y)	1823	June 11	ColumbanCoOh	05	18	11
Jennings, Levi(Y)	1821	Nov. 28	ColumbanCoOh	04	17	21
Jennings, Levi(Y)	1824	April 10	ColumbanCoOh	06	18	22
Jennings, Levi(Y)	1824	April 10	ColumbanCoOh	06	18	22
Jennings, Levi(Y)	1824	May 18	Stark Co.,Oh	04	16	22

PURCHASER	YEAR	DATE	RESIDENCE	R	T	S
Jennings, Levi(Y)	1825	March 14	ColumbanCoOh	06	18	22
Jennings, Levi(Y)	1828	March 24	ColumbanCoOh	05	18	30
Jennings, Mahlon(Z)	1829	May 23	MuskingmCoOh	14	14	14
Jennings, S.(Y)	1824	May 17	ColumbanCoOh	02	11	36
Jennings, S.(Y)	1824	May 17	ColumbanCoOh	02	13	07
Jennings, S.(Y)	1824	May 17	ColumbanCoOh	02	13	15
Jennings, Simeon(Y)	1824	Jan. 26	ColumbanCoOh	05	18	01
Jennings, Simeon(Y)	1824	May 17	ColumbanCoOh	02	13	07
Jennings, Simeon(Y)	1824	May 18	ColumbanCoOh	03	15	22
Jennings, Simeon(Y)	1824	May 19	ColumbanCoOh	04	16	22
Jennings, Simeon(Y)	1826	Aug. 19	ColumbanCoOh	05	17	09
Jennings, Simeon(Y)	1827	Feb. 17	ColumbanCoOh	05	18	01
Jennings, Simeon(Y)	1827	July 17	ColumbanCoOh	01	08	22
Jennings, Simeon(Y)	1827	July 17	ColumbanCoOh	01	08	22
Jennings, Simeon(Y)	1828	Feb. 18	ColumbanCoOh	05	18	30
Jennings, Simeon(Y)	1829	June 11	ColumbanCoOh	06	19	21
Jennings, Simeon(Y)	1829	Dec. 08	ColumbanCoOh	06	18	05
Jennings, Simeon(Y)	1829	Dec. 10	ColumbanCoOh	05	14	28
Jennings, Simeon(Y)	1830	July 29	ColumbanCoOh	05	18	31
Jennings, Simeon(Y)	1830	Sept. 10	ColumbanCoOh	06	19	01
Jennings, Simeon(Y)	1831	July 25	ColumbanCoOh	04	14	24
Jennings, Simeon(Y)	1831	July 25	ColumbanCoOh	04	14	24
Jennings, Simeon(Y)	1831	July 26	ColumbanCoOh	06	17	28
Jennings, Simeon(Y)	1831	July 26	ColumbanCoOh	09	12	17
Jennings, Simeon(Y)	1832	April 13	ColumbanCoOh	03	12	30
Jennings, Simeon(Y)	1832	April 13	ColumbanCoOh	05	15	04
Jew, James(Z)	1835	May 15	Perry Co.,Oh	14	12	36
Jewel, Gilbert(Y)	1823	Sept. 23	ColumbanCoOh	04	13	28
Jewell, Gilbert(Y)	1830	Dec. 18	ColumbanCoOh	04	13	19
Jewell, John(Z-M)	1825	May 30	GuernseyCoOh	01	05	09
Jewell, Jonathan(Z-M)	1836	Jan. 25	LickingCo,Oh	11	03	06
Jewell, Jonathan(Z-M)	1836	Feb. 13	LickingCo,Oh	11	03	06
Jewell, Stephen(Z-M)	1827	Dec. 07	WashCo.,Penn	10	05	25
Jewell, Zachariah(Z-M)	1834	Dec. 17	TuscarwsCoOh	01	05	09
Jewell, Zechariah(Z-M)	1836	Feb. 20	TuscarwsCoOh	01	05	10
Jewett, Barzillar(Y)	1824	Aug. 17	SteubenvleOh	01	03	29
Jewett, Samuel(Z)	1824	Aug. 02	Morgan Co,Oh	10	08	30
Jewett, Samuel(Z)	1824	Aug. 04	Morgan Co,Oh	10	08	30
Jinnings, Isaac(Z)	1835	Nov. 11	Perry Co.,Oh	15	14	26
Jinnings, Isaac(Z)	1836	Feb. 10	Perry Co.,Oh	15	14	26
Jinnins, David(Z)	1817	Feb. 15	MuskingmCoOh	13	08	25
John, Daniel(Z)	1836	Aug. 26	MonroeCo.,Oh	08	07	34
John, Hagen(Z)	1816	May 02	FayetteCo,Pa	08	08	12
John, Hiram(Z-M)	1833	Aug. 31	HarrisonCoOh	03	06	07
John, Hiram(Z-M)	1836	Aug. 17	TuscarwsCoOh	03	06	07
John, John(Z)	1831	May 25	BelmontCo,Oh	10	03	08
Johns, David(Z)	1816	Oct. 23	CoshoctnCoOh	10	05	10
Johns, John(Z)	1813	March 01	KnoxCo.,Ohio	10	06	03
Johns, John(Z-M)	1825	July 26	KnoxCo.,Ohio	10	06	04
Johns, John(Z-M)	1832	Oct. 06	KnoxCo.,Ohio	10	06	08
Johns, John(Z-M)	1836	June 28	KnoxCo.,Ohio	10	06	04
Johns, John(Z-M)	1836	June 28	KnoxCo.,Ohio	10	06	07
Johnson, Amon Shannon(Y)	1834	March 10	HarrisonCoOh	06	11	29
Johnson, Amos(Y)	1824	May 18	ColumbanCoOh	04	13	35
Johnson, Andrew(Y)	1828	Aug. 13	HarrisonCoOh	06	12	15
Johnson, Archibald(Y)	1826	April 20	BelmontCo,Oh	07	09	02
Johnson, Archibald(Y)	1831	Dec. 09	GuernseyCoOh	07	09	02
Johnson, Benjamin(Y)	1826	May 27	ColumbanCoOh	05	18	27
Johnson, Catharine(Z-M)	1833	June 04	GuernseyCoOh	02	04	07
Johnson, Charles(Y)	1820	Aug. 22	WashCo.,Penn	05	14	19
Johnson, Charles(Z-M)	1838	May 03	MuskingmCoOh	04	04	10
Johnson, Christ'n.(Y)	1824	Aug. 18	Wash'n. City	05	15	22
Johnson, Daniel(Z-M)	1834	Sept. 24	HarrisonCoOh	03	05	22
Johnson, David(Z)	1815	Aug. 23	WashngtnCoOh	11	11	18
Johnson, David(Z-M)	1833	Oct. 04	TuscarwsCoOh	03	05	01
Johnson, David(Z-M)	1836	Nov. 10	ColumbanCoOh	09	08	17
Johnson, David(Z-M)	1836	Nov. 10	ColumbanCoOh	09	08	18
Johnson, Disbury(Z-M)	1831	Sept. 24	TuscarwsCoOh	01	06	25
Johnson, Disbury(Z-M)	1833	March 09	TuscarwsCoOh	01	05	12

PURCHASER	YEAR	DATE	RESIDENCE	R	T	S
Johnson, Disbury(Z-M)	1833	Aug. 22	TuscarwsCoOh	01	05	12
Johnson, Disbury(Z-M)	1832	Feb. 14	TuscarwsCoOh	01	05	14
Johnson, Disbway(Z-M)	1829	Aug. 26	HarrisonCoOh	01	05	08
Johnson, Elijah(Y)	1822	May 02	HarrisonCoOh	06	11	21
Johnson, Elijah(Z-M)	1825	March 18	HarrisonCoOh	03	06	18
Johnson, Elijah(Z-M)	1825	June 27	HarrisonCoOh	03	06	18
Johnson, Ellis N.(Y)	1824	Nov. 16	Stark Co.,Oh	06	18	15
Johnson, Ellis N.(Y)	1826	Nov. 24	Stark Co.,Oh	06	18	02
Johnson, Ephraim(Z-M)	1831	Aug. 22	HarrisonCoOh	02	06	12
Johnson, Esop(Z)	1826	Nov. 23	TuscarwsCoOh	04	09	13
Johnson, Esop(Z-M)	1824	June 12	TuscarwsCoOh	04	09	13
Johnson, Exum(Y)	1820	Oct. 05	Stark Co.,Oh	06	19	24
Johnson, Fredrick(Z-M)	1832	April 23	MuskingmCoOh	04	01	19
Johnson, Geo.(Z-M)	1833	June 04	GuernseyCoOh	03	05	19
Johnson, George R.(Z)	1824	May 11	GuernseyCoOh	09	08	27
Johnson, George Reed(Z)	1835	June 08	GuernseyCoOh	09	08	26
Johnson, George Reed(Z)	1836	Nov. 25	GuernseyCoOh	09	08	29
Johnson, George(Z)	1827	Nov. 05	Morgan Co,Oh	12	11	35
Johnson, Henry(Z-M)	1834	Dec. 19	TuscarwsCoOh	01	06	23
Johnson, Henry(Z-M)	1836	Sept. 07	CarrollCo,Oh	09	08	25
Johnson, Henry(Z-M)	1836	Sept. 07	CarrollCo,Oh	09	08	24
Johnson, Henry(Z-M)	1836	Nov. 19	Jeff.Co.,Oh.	08	08	14
Johnson, Henry(Z-M)	1836	Nov. 19	Jeff.Co.,Oh.	08	08	14
Johnson, Jame(Z-M)	1835	Dec. 07	TuscarwsCoOh	02	06	03
Johnson, James(Z)	1805	July 03	PhladlphiaPa	08	02	08
Johnson, James(Z-M)	1829	Feb. 17	LickingCo,Oh	10	04	25
Johnson, James(Z-M)	1831	April 29	TuscarwsCoOh	01	05	07
Johnson, James(Z-M)	1831	Sept. 22	TuscarwsCoOh	01	06	25
Johnson, James(Z-M)	1833	July 02	TuscarwsCoOh	05	06	17
Johnson, James(Z-M)	1833	July 02	TuscarwsCoOh	05	06	17
Johnson, James(Z-M)	1836	March 17	CoshoctnCoOh	04	04	03
Johnson, James(Z-M)	1836	May 13	TuscarwsCoOh	02	06	11
Johnson, Jeremiah(Z)	1829	Jan. 03	Morgan Co,Oh	14	14	23
Johnson, Jesse(Z)	1827	April 03	MuskingmCoOh	13	09	15
Johnson, Jesse(Z)	1816	Sept. 23	MuskingmCoOh	14	15	36
Johnson, John W.(Z)	1815	Dec. 02	MuskingmCoOh	12	10	08
Johnson, John(Y)	1827	Aug. 29	TuscarwsCoOh	06	13	31
Johnson, John(Z)	1823	May 30	GuernseyCoOh	10	09	14
Johnson, John(Z)	1823	June 28	Morgan Co,Oh	12	11	13
Johnson, John(Z)	1823	Sept. 16	GuernseyCoOh	10	09	13
Johnson, John(Z)	1824	May 10	GuernseyCoOh	10	09	15
Johnson, John(Z)	1835	Nov. 20	GuernseyCoOh	09	08	19
Johnson, John(Z)	1835	Nov. 20	GuernseyCoOh	09	08	20
Johnson, John(Z-M)	1832	March 07	GuernseyCoOh	02	04	14
Johnson, Jonah(Y)	1824	May 17	BelmontCo,Oh	03	05	21
Johnson, Jonathan(Y)	1827	Oct. 17	ColumbanCoOh	05	18	33
Johnson, Joseph(Y)	1824	Nov. 16	Stark Co.,Oh	06	18	15
Johnson, Joseph(Y)	1828	Feb. 29	Stark Co.,Oh	06	19	28
Johnson, Luke(Z-M)	1836	March 14	HolmesCoOhio	09	08	20
Johnson, Margaret(Z)	1826	Jan. 14	GuernseyCoOh	10	09	15
Johnson, Margaret(Z-M)	1820	Sept. 15	GuernseyCoOh	04	01	22
Johnson, Mary(Z-M)	1830	Nov. 25	GuernseyCoOh	02	04	06
Johnson, Mary(Z-M)	1831	Aug. 18	TuscarwsCoOh	01	06	12
Johnson, Patrick(Z)	1808	Nov. 12	ChesterCo,Pa	13	12	08
Johnson, Paxten(Z)	1835	Aug. 28	Morgan Co,Oh	13	08	33
Johnson, Philemon(Z)	1807	Nov. 05	MuskingmCoOh	11	13	07
Johnson, Richard(Z-M)	1833	May 01	TuscarwsCoOh	03	05	19
Johnson, Robert(Z)	1824	Feb. 28	Morgan Co,Oh	10	08	18
Johnson, Robert(Z-M)	1833	Feb. 19	CoshoctnCoOh	05	04	11
Johnson, S.(Z)	1815	April 29	MuskingmCoOh	13	11	01
Johnson, Samuel(Z-M)	1837	March 13	CoshoctnCoOh	09	07	01
Johnson, Simon(Y)	1823	April 09	WashCo.,Penn	06	18	12
Johnson, Simon(Y)	1826	May 22	Stark Co.,Oh	06	18	12
Johnson, Simon(Z)	1835	Nov. 16	Morgan Co,Oh	09	06	06
Johnson, Thomas(Y)	1827	Oct. 17	ColumbanCoOh	05	18	33
Johnson, Thomas(Y)	1831	April 22	HarrisonCoOh	06	12	15
Johnson, Thomas(Z)	1810	Dec. 01	MuskingmCoOh	05	04	10
Johnson, Thomas(Z)	1811	Dec. 25	CoshoctnCoOh	04	04	05
Johnson, Thomas(Z-M)	1829	April 16	CoshoctnCoOh	05	04	09

PURCHASER	YEAR	DATE	RESIDENCE	R	T	S
Johnson, Thomas(Z-M)	1833	March 07	CoshoctnCoOh	04	04	06
Johnson, Thomas(Z-M)	1835	July 10	CoshoctnCoOh	05	04	06
Johnson, Thomas(Z-M)	1835	Aug. 04	CoshoctnCoOh	05	04	06
Johnson, Thomas(Z-M)	1835	Nov. 12	CoshoctnCoOh	05	04	07
Johnson, Thomas(Z-M)	1835	Nov. 12	CoshoctnCoOh	05	04	06
Johnson, Thomas(Z-M)	1835	Dec. 12	CoshoctnCoOh	05	04	05
Johnson, Thomas(Z-M)	1836	Dec. 21	CoshoctnCoOh	04	04	06
Johnson, Thomas(Z-M)	1836	Dec. 21	CoshoctnCoOh	05	04	02
Johnson, Thomas(Z-M)	1836	Dec. 21	CoshoctnCoOh	05	04	08
Johnson, Thomas(Z-M)	1837	June 17	GuernseyCoOh	02	04	06
Johnson, Thos.(Z-M)	1828	May 16	TuscarwsCoOh	01	05	06
Johnson, Thos.(Z-M)	1837	March 11	CoshoctnCoOh	05	04	07
Johnson, Thos.(Z-M)	1838	Oct. 15	MuskingmCoOh	03	04	17
Johnson, William Jr.(Z)	1834	Nov. 03	BelmontCo,Oh	13	08	34
Johnson, William(Z)	1832	June 20	GuernseyCoOh	10	09	11
Johnson, William(Z)	1833	Oct. 25	BelmontCo,Oh	13	08	33
Johnson, William(Z)	1833	Oct. 25	BelmontCo,Oh	13	08	33
Johnson, William(Z)	1834	Aug. 13	GuernseyCoOh	10	09	13
Johnson, William(Z)	1835	Nov. 06	GuernseyCoOh	10	09	13
Johnson, William(Z)	1812	March 27	WashngtnCoOh	05	01	15
Johnson, Wm. H.(Z-M)	1833	Nov. 04	LickingCo,Oh	11	03	07
Johnson, Wm. Junr.(Z)	1815	Sept. 23	CoshoctnCoOh	04	04	15
Johnson, Wm.(Z)	1836	Jan. 28	GuernseyCoOh	10	09	13
Johnson, Wm.(Z-M)	1832	Sept. 28	HolmesCoOhio	09	08	22
Johnson, Wm.(Z-M)	1833	Nov. 20	HolmesCoOhio	09	08	22
Johnston, A.(Z)	1815	June 22	CoshoctnCoOh	07	09	12
Johnston, A.(Z)	1815	June 22	CoshoctnCoOh	07	09	12
Johnston, Absalom(Z-M)	1831	April 06	TuscarwsCoOh	01	05	06
Johnston, Adam(Z)	1814	March 11	?	07	07	24
Johnston, Adam(Z)	1815	Jan. 17	CoshoctnCoOh	06	07	20
Johnston, Alex'r. Jr.(Y)	1824	Dec. 07	Jeff.Co.,Oh.	03	11	21
Johnston, Christopher(Y)	1824	Feb. 19	ColumbanCoOh	04	14	26
Johnston, Christopher(Y)	1834	March 13	ColumbanCoOh	04	13	14
Johnston, David(Z)	1814	July 16	TuscarwsCoOh	03	04	24
Johnston, George(Z-M)	1836	Dec. 23	WestmrldCoPa	01	08	04
Johnston, James(Y)	1827	Jan. 22	ColumbanCoOh	05	17	17
Johnston, James(Y)	1827	Jan. 22	ColumbanCoOh	05	17	17
Johnston, James(Y)	1829	July 04	ColumbanCoOh	03	13	23
Johnston, James(Z)	1817	Jan. 13	MuskingmCoOh	15	16	27
Johnston, James(Z-M)	1823	Nov. 06	GuernseyCoOh	04	02	08
Johnston, James(Z-M)	1825	April 23	Jeff.Co.,Oh.	01	05	01
Johnston, John(Y)	1821	Sept. 21	ColumbanCoOh	03	12	21
Johnston, John(Y)	1821	Sept. 21	ColumbanCoOh	03	12	21
Johnston, John(Y)	1828	April 01	ColumbanCoOh	05	18	30
Johnston, John(Y)	1828	June 11	WashCo.,Penn	05	14	19
Johnston, John(Y)	1832	Aug. 20	Jeff.Co.,Oh.	04	12	17
Johnston, John(Y)	1835	June 03	Jeff.Co.,Oh.	04	12	17
Johnston, John(Z)	1806	April 29	WestmrldCoPa	10	08	28
Johnston, John(Z)	1806	April 29	WestmrldCoPa	10	05	07
Johnston, John(Z)	1816	Nov. 22	Pittsburg,Pa	02	04	13
Johnston, John(Z-M)	1832	Sept. 18	GuernseyCoOh	02	04	14
Johnston, John(Z-M)	1832	Sept. 18	GuernseyCoOh	02	04	07
Johnston, John(Z-M)	1836	Nov. 25	TuscarwsCoOh	01	08	04
Johnston, John(Z-M)	1837	Jan. 04	TuscarwsCoOh	03	05	12
Johnston, John(Z-M)	1837	March 02	MuskingmCoOh	05	04	22
Johnston, John(Z-M)	1837	June 12	GuernseyCoOh	03	04	10
Johnston, John(Z-M)	1837	June 12	GuernseyCoOh	02	04	04
Johnston, John(Z-M)	1837	June 12	GuernseyCoOh	02	04	07
Johnston, John(Z-M)	1837	June 12	GuernseyCoOh	02	04	14
Johnston, John(Z-M)	1837	Nov. 02	GuernseyCoOh	02	04	05
Johnston, John(Z-M)	1838	Jan. 24	MuskingmCoOh	05	03	01
Johnston, Joseph(Z-M)	1828	March 21	TuscarwsCoOh	01	05	15
Johnston, Math'w.(Z)	1829	Feb. 16	HarrisonCoOh	13	08	24
Johnston, Nathaniel(Z-M)	1832	Oct. 16	KnoxCo.,Ohio	11	05	20
Johnston, Oliver(Y)	1826	Nov. 14	Stark Co.,Oh	06	19	02
Johnston, Oliver(Y)	1826	Nov. 14	Stark Co.,Oh	06	19	02
Johnston, Richard(Z)	1816	Nov. 22	Pittsburg,Pa	02	04	12
Johnston, Robert(Y)	1826	Oct. 03	ColumbanCoOh	04	14	35
Johnston, Robert(Y)	1834	Feb. 17	ColumbanCoOh	04	13	14

PURCHASER	YEAR	DATE	RESIDENCE	R	T	S
Johnston, Robert(Z)	1817	June 16	TuscarwsCoOh	01	05	11
Johnston, Robert(Z-M)	1838	April 04	CoshoctnCoOh	04	04	03
Johnston, Samuel R.(Y)	1824	May 25	SteubenvleOh	06	12	24
Johnston, Samuel R.(Y)	1824	May 25	SteubenvleOh	06	12	24
Johnston, Samuel R.(Y)	1824	May 25	SteubenvleOh	06	12	24
Johnston, Samuel R.(Y)	1824	May 25	SteubenvleOh	06	12	24
Johnston, Thomas(Y)	1829	Sept. 12	TuscarwsCoOh	06	11	30
Johnston, Thomas(Y)	1831	May 07	Jeff.Co.,Pa.	06	15	34
Johnston, Thomas(Z)	1815	June 09	CoshoctnCoOh	05	04	09
Johnston, Thomas(Z-M)	1828	Nov. 06	GuernseyCoOh	02	02	01
Johnston, Thos.(Z-M)	1831	April 06	TuscarwsCoOh	01	05	15
Johnston, William Jr.(Z)	1815	March 25	CoshoctnCoOh	04	02	15
Johnston, William(Z)	1832	Sept. 08	Morgan Co,Oh	11	10	33
Johnston, William(Z)	1832	Sept. 08	Morgan Co,Oh	11	10	28
Johnston, William(Z-M)	1838	April 04	MuskingmCoOh	05	03	01
Johnston, Wm.(Z)	1832	Sept. 14	Morgan Co,Oh	11	10	33
Johston, Robert(Y)	1831	Oct. 10	ColumbanCoOh	04	14	35
Jolley, John(Z)	1816	Dec. 20	Jeff.Co.,Oh.	01	01	20
Jolley, John(Z)	1816	Dec. 20	Jeff.Co.,Oh.	01	01	20
Jolley, Malachi(Y)	1831	May 30	HarrisonCoOh	06	13	01
Jolley, Peter(Z-M)	1834	Feb. 05	HolmesCoOhio	08	08	04
Jolley, Samuel(Y)	1821	Nov. 23	ColumbanCoOh	04	17	21
Jolly, Henry(Z-M)	1829	Feb. 19	HolmesCoOhio	07	08	05
Jolly, Henry(Z-M)	1835	Dec. 05	HolmesCoOhio	07	08	05
Jolly, Henry(Z-M)	1837	Jan. 27	HolmesCoOhio	07	08	05
Jolly, James(Z-M)	1835	Dec. 23	HolmesCoOhio	08	08	04
Jolly, Peter(Z-M)	1829	Feb. 13	HolmesCoOhio	08	08	04
Jolly, Peter(Z-M)	1832	Sept. 11	HolmesCoOhio	08	08	04
Jonas, Sam'l.(Z)	1833	Oct. 15	Perry Co.,Oh	15	14	03
Jones, Alfred(Z-M)	1832	May 30	TuscarwsCoOh	01	06	18
Jones, Anna(Y)	1836	July 04	SteubenvleOh	07	14	18
Jones, Anna(Y)	1836	Sept. 12	SteubenvleOh	03	12	22
Jones, Anthony(Z)	1832	Sept. 12	GuernseyCoOh	09	08	18
Jones, Anthony(Z)	1815	Nov. 15	GuernseyCoOh	09	07	12
Jones, Anthony(Z-M)	1832	Aug. 23	CoshoctnCoOh	10	05	20
Jones, Anthony(Z-M)	1836	Jan. 26	KnoxCo.,Ohio	10	04	02
Jones, Arch'd.(Z-M)	1835	Oct. 05	CoshoctnCoOh	05	07	01
Jones, Asbury(Z-M)	1836	Feb. 16	TuscarwsCoOh	03	05	21
Jones, Asbury(Z-M)	1837	Jan. 28	GuernseyCoOh	03	04	02
Jones, Chas. G.(Z-M)	1839	Jan. 31	GuernseyCoOh	03	04	08
Jones, Dan'l. G.(Z-M)	1832	Sept. 18	CoshoctnCoOh	06	04	09
Jones, David(Z)	1811	March 26	MuskingmCoOh	14	15	05
Jones, David(Z)	1811	Aug. 05	MuskingmCoOh	14	15	06
Jones, David(Z)	1812	June 19	MuskingmCoOh	14	15	06
Jones, Elizabeth(Z-M)	1831	Oct. 31	CoshoctnCoOh	06	04	09
Jones, Enoch(Z)	1815	Sept. 23	GuernseyCoOh	04	03	19
Jones, Enoch(Z-M)	1827	March 27	GuernseyCoOh	04	03	22
Jones, Gabriel(Z)	1815	March 27	BelmontCo,Oh	06	01	05
Jones, George A.(Z-M)	1839	Feb. 02	ZanesvilleOh	09	03	25
Jones, Henry(Y)	1830	Feb. 03	HarrisonCoOh	06	13	01
Jones, Hugh(Z-M)	1832	July 02	CoshoctnCoOh	04	03	02
Jones, Hugh(Z-M)	1836	Jan. 20	GuernseyCoOh	04	04	22
Jones, Isaac(Y)	1825	Oct. 03	HarrisonCoOh	07	12	15
Jones, Isaac(Z-M)	1836	Jan. 13	HarrisonCoOh	01	06	14
Jones, Jacob Jnr.(Z-M)	1835	Jan. 06	Jeff.Co.,Oh.	03	05	21
Jones, Jacob(Z)	1830	Nov. 18	Morgan Co,Oh	10	09	36
Jones, Jacob(Z)	1830	Nov. 18	Morgan Co,Oh	10	09	36
Jones, Jacob(Z)	1831	July 25	HolmesCoOhio	09	07	03
Jones, Jacob(Z)	1815	Feb. 06	GuernseyCoOh	09	07	02
Jones, Jacob(Z-M)	1821	April 16	CoshoctnCoOh	09	08	18
Jones, Jacob(Z-M)	1831	Nov. 14	HolmesCoOhio	09	07	03
Jones, James(Z)	1836	March 09	Perry Co.,Oh	15	14	05
Jones, James(Z)	1814	Nov. 28	CoshoctnCoOh	04	06	23
Jones, James(Z-M)	1832	June 09	GuernseyCoOh	04	03	08
Jones, Jas. L.(Z-M)	1839	Jan. 31	GuernseyCoOh	03	04	08
Jones, Jesse(Z-M)	1833	June 03	CoshoctnCoOh	04	05	21
Jones, Jno.(Z-M)	1821	April 16	CoshoctnCoOh	09	08	18
Jones, John B.(Z)	1829	Dec. 21	Morgan Co,Oh	11	10	20
Jones, John B.(Z)	1813	Nov. 13	SomersetCoPa	15	16	34

PURCHASER	YEAR	DATE	RESIDENCE	R	T	S
Jones, John Daniel(Z-M)	1836	Jan. 21	CoshoctnCoOh	03	06	16
Jones, John(Y)	1825	Nov. 05	HarrisonCoOh	07	12	36
Jones, John(Y)	1828	Nov. 26	HarrisonCoOh	07	12	30
Jones, John(Y)	1829	March 25	PittsburghPa	07	16	22
Jones, John(Z)	1827	Sept. 11	HarrisonCoOh	01	06	19
Jones, John(Z)	1827	Sept. 11	HarrisonCoOh	01	06	21
Jones, John(Z)	1827	Sept. 11	HarrisonCoOh	01	06	21
Jones, John(Z)	1827	Oct. 05	Morgan Co,Oh	10	07	19
Jones, John(Z)	1833	Dec. 27	Morgan Co,Oh	10	07	19
Jones, John(Z)	1812	Oct. 27	WashCo.,Penn	09	05	19
Jones, John(Z)	1817	Feb. 10	SteubenvleOh	03	06	13
Jones, John(Z-M)	1828	Dec. 31	HarrisonCoOh	01	05	06
Jones, John(Z-M)	1832	April 16	HarrisonCoOh	01	06	20
Jones, John(Z-M)	1833	Feb. 25	TuscarwsCoOh	01	05	14
Jones, John(Z-M)	1833	April 16	HarrisonCoOh	01	06	18
Jones, Joseph(Z)	1829	Feb. 24	BelmontCo,Oh	11	10	24
Jones, Joseph(Z)	1831	Sept. 21	Morgan Co,Oh	10	07	33
Jones, Joseph(Z)	1812	Oct. 27	WashCo.,Penn	09	05	19
Jones, Joseph(Z-M)	1839	April 13	KnoxCo.,Ohio	10	07	23
Jones, Joseph(Z-M)	1839	April 13	KnoxCo.,Ohio	10	07	22
Jones, Joshua G.(Z-M)	1827	June 30	HarrisonCoOh	01	05	08
Jones, Lewis(Z-M)	1836	Feb. 12	TuscarwsCoOh	01	05	02
Jones, Lewis(Z-M)	1837	April 20	TuscarwsCoOh	10	04	16
Jones, Lewis(Z-M)	1837	April 20	TuscarwsCoOh	10	04	24
Jones, Marshall(Z-M)	1832	Oct. 25	TuscarwsCoOh	01	06	18
Jones, Marshall(Z-M)	1837	April 08	TuscarwsCoOh	10	04	17
Jones, Marshall(Z-M)	1837	April 20	TuscarwsCoOh	10	04	17
Jones, Martin(Z-M)	1838	March 28	HolmesCoOhio	08	08	05
Jones, Robert(Y)	1826	Aug. 22	Stark Co.,Oh	07	16	22
Jones, Samuel(Z-M)	1832	Oct. 08	BelmontCo,Oh	01	06	15
Jones, Samuel(Z-M)	1832	Dec. 27	BelmontCo,Oh	01	06	15
Jones, Wellis(Z-M)	1837	April 08	TuscarwsCoOh	10	03	04
Jones, William Jnr.(Z)	1835	Dec. 04	GuernseyCoOh	10	09	24
Jones, William Senr.(Z)	1832	Oct. 13	GuernseyCoOh	10	09	13
Jones, William(Y)	1824	May 19	BelmontCo,Oh	05	09	35
Jones, William(Y)	1824	May 19	BelmontCo,Oh	06	10	17
Jones, William(Z)	1825	April 11	GuernseyCoOh	10	09	12
Jones, William(Z)	1827	Nov. 01	GreeneCoOhio	09	08	19
Jones, William(Z)	1811	Nov. 27	MuskingmCoOh	10	03	11
Jones, William(Z)	1814	Nov. 28	CoshoctnCoOh	04	06	23
Jones, William(Z)	1817	Jan. 07	GuernseyCoOh	09	08	35
Jones, William(Z-M)	1821	Dec. 14	WayneCo.,Oh.	09	08	01
Jones, William(Z-M)	1832	May 30	TuscarwsCoOh	01	06	08
Jones, William(Z-M)	1834	Jan. 03	TuscarwsCoOh	01	06	11
Jones, William(Z-M)	1836	Jan. 13	TuscarwsCoOh	01	06	18
Jones, William(Z-M)	1836	Feb. 13	TuscarwsCoOh	01	06	23
Jones, William(Z-M)	1836	Nov. 11	HolmesCoOhio	09	08	09
Jones, William(Z-M)	1837	April 10	HolmesCoOhio	09	08	03
Jones, William(Z-M)	1837	April 20	TuscarwsCoOh	10	03	06
Jones, William(Z-M)	1838	June 11	ColumbanCoOh	07	08	16
Jones, Willis(Z-M)	1836	Feb. 12	TuscarwsCoOh	01	06	22
Jones, Wm. Jr.(Z)	1831	Aug. 01	GuernseyCoOh	10	09	13
Jones, Wm.(Z)	1815	Nov. 15	GuernseyCoOh	09	07	12
Jones, Wm.(Z-M)	1830	Sept. 21	HolmesCoOhio	09	08	03
Jordan, Abraham(Z)	1832	Sept. 29	Morgan Co,Oh	09	05	18
Jordan, Adam(Z)	1815	Feb. 07	GuernseyCoOh	09	07	19
Jordan, Adam(Z)	1815	June 17	GuernseyCoOh	10	08	10
Jordan, Caleb(Z)	1817	Jan. 10	Jeff.Co.,Oh.	06	03	14
Jordan, Caleb(Z)	1817	Feb. 08	Jeff.Co.,Oh.	06	03	13
Jordan, Charles(Z)	1823	Oct. 31	MuskingmCoOh	11	12	05
Jordan, David(Z)	1832	Aug. 27	MonroeCo.,Oh	10	06	12
Jordan, David(Z-M)	1829	Sept. 05	HolmesCoOhio	07	08	09
Jordan, Isaac(Z)	1821	Nov. 20	Morgan Co,Oh	10	06	24
Jordan, Isaac(Z)	1827	Sept. 21	Morgan Co,Oh	10	06	24
Jordan, Jacob Jnr.(Z)	1835	Dec. 14	Morgan Co,Oh	09	05	17
Jordan, Jacob(Z)	1814	Jan. 27	GuernseyCoOh	10	08	14
Jordan, John(Z)	1830	Feb. 15	Morgan Co,Oh	09	05	07
Jordan, John(Z)	1835	July 06	Morgan Co,Oh	10	06	12
Jordan, Joseph(Z)	1823	April 21	MuskingmCoOh	11	12	25

PURCHASER	YEAR	DATE	RESIDENCE	R	T	S
Jordan, Peter(Z)	1824	Feb. 09	Morgan Co,Oh	10	08	11
Jordan, Samuel(Z)	1827	Nov. 05	PittsburghPa	11	12	03
Jordan, Temperence(Z)	1831	Dec. 14	MuskingmCoOh	10	06	29
Jordon, Abraham(Z)	1835	Sept. 22	Morgan Co,Oh	09	05	18
Jordon, Elijah(Z)	1834	March 10	Morgan Co,Oh	09	05	08
Jordon, Elijah(Z)	1834	March 10	Morgan Co,Oh	09	05	17
Jordon, Isaac(Z)	1833	Nov. 04	Morgan Co,Oh	10	06	24
Jordon, Jacob Jr.(Z)	1832	April 23	Morgan Co,Oh	09	05	17
Joseph, Beye N.(Z-M)	1833	July 15	CoshoctnCoOh	06	04	20
Joseph, Isaac(Y)	1820	Sept. 01	Stark Co.,Oh	06	15	34
Joseph, Isaac(Y)	1824	Dec. 03	Stark Co.,Oh	06	15	27
Joseph, Isaac(Z)	1833	Feb. 01	MuskingmCoOh	12	13	15
Joseph, Jeremiah(Z)	1810	May 17	MuskingmCoOh	12	13	02
Joseph, Jeremiah(Z)	1816	Oct. 12	MuskingmCoOh	10	03	07
Joseph, Lemuel(Z)	1806	Jan. 20	MongahlaCoVa	13	12	10
Joseph, Lemuel(Z)	1806	May 03	MuskingmCoOh	12	13	27
Joseph, Noah S.(Z)	1825	Nov. 26	MuskingmCoOh	12	13	02
Joseph, William(Z)	1814	Jan. 19	MuskingmCoOh	12	13	05
Josephs, Isaac(Y)	1830	July 12	Stark Co.,Oh	06	15	33
Journy, John(Z)	1836	Dec. 09	Perry Co.,Oh	15	14	21
Joy, Absalom(Z)	1837	Feb. 14	Morgan Co,Oh	13	08	31
Joy, Absolom(Z)	1834	Sept. 04	Morgan Co,Oh	13	08	32
Joy, James(Z-M)	1832	March 19	GuernseyCoOh	01	01	21
Joy, John Senr.(Z-M)	1832	July 31	HarrisonCoOh	06	03	19
Joy, Thomas(Z-M)	1832	June 29	HarrisonCoOh	06	03	13
Jrael, Wm.(Z-M)	1832	Feb. 04	GuernseyCoOh	02	01	19
Judkins, Carolus(?)(Y)	1824	May 19	BelmontCo,Oh	06	08	25
Judkins, Carolus(Y)	1825	Sept. 16	BelmontCo,Oh	06	08	25
Judkins, Carolus(Y)	1825	Sept. 16	BelmontCo,Oh	06	08	27
Judy, David(Z-M)	1834	Aug. 16	TuscarwsCoOh	01	08	02
Judy, David(Z-M)	1836	June 22	TuscarwsCoOh	02	07	09
Jungen, Christian(Z-M)	1837	April 03	TuscarwsCoOh	03	08	25
Juniman, Adam(Z)	1821	July 06	Morgan Co,Oh	13	09	03
Junior, John Udell(Z)	1837	May 23	AshtbulaCoOh	08	06	03
Justice, Nancy(Y)	1824	June 14	BelmontCo,Oh	04	06	31
Justice, Rebecca(Y)	1824	June 14	BelmontCo,Oh	04	06	31
Kabel, Frederick(Z-M)	1836	Dec. 14	Stark Co.,Oh	05	04	04
Kabel, Frederick(Z-M)	1837	Jan. 24	CoshoctnCoOh	05	04	07
Kackery, John(Z)	1813	June 24	FrederkCoVir	09	08	34
Kackery, John(Z)	1813	June 24	FrederkCoVir	09	08	34
Kackley, George(Z)	1833	Nov. 09	GuernseyCoOh	09	08	33
Kackley, Henry(Z)	1836	Jan. 14	GuernseyCoOh	09	08	24
Kackley, Isaac(Z)	1835	Nov. 13	GuernseyCoOh	09	08	23
Kackley, John(Z)	1813	June 24	FrederkCoVir	09	08	34
Kackley, Wm. Henry(Z)	1836	Dec. 09	GuernseyCoOh	09	08	33
Kaemmerer, Samuel(Z-M)	1832	Nov. 12	MuskingmCoOh	06	03	08
Kaesen, Daniel(Z-M)	1823	June 06	TuscarwsCoOh	04	08	15
Kaffar, Jacob(Z-M)	1836	Feb. 17	TuscarwsCoOh	03	07	11
Kahten, Jacob(Z)	1817	Aug. 20	MuskingmCoOh	12	10	01
Kail, Frederick(Z-M)	1828	Nov. 15	HarrisonCoOh	02	06	20
Kail, Henry(Z-M)	1825	June 22	TuscarwsCoOh	02	06	20
Kail, Henry(Z-M)	1825	June 22	TuscarwsCoOh	01	06	16
Kail, Henry(Z-M)	1834	Dec. 18	TuscarwsCoOh	02	06	20
Kail, Hiram(Z-M)	1833	Aug. 31	CarrollCo,Oh	03	06	07
Kail, Hiram(Z-M)	1836	Jan. 18	TuscarwsCoOh	03	06	04
Kail, Jacob(Y)	1830	Aug. 28	HarrisonCoOh	04	10	18
Kain, John(Z)	1835	April 04	Jeff.Co.,Oh.	10	07	01
Kain, John(Z)	1835	April 24	Jeff.Co.,Oh.	10	07	01
Kain, Peter(Z)	1815	July 03	TuscarwsCoOh	04	08	22
Kaiser, Isaac(Z-M)	1835	Dec. 29	TuscarwsCoOh	04	08	18
Kale, George(Y)	1826	March 22	TuscarwsCoOh	07	14	26
Kale, Jacob(Z)	1835	Dec. 30	GuernseyCoOh	09	08	15
Kamu, John(Z)	1814	March 10	?	08	04	23
Kane, Fred.(Z-M)	1831	Sept. 01	HarrisonCoOh	02	06	19
Kane, John(Z)	1833	July 15	Morgan Co,Oh	09	06	07
Kannal, Joseph(Y)	1830	March 26	ColumbanCoOh	05	15	03
Kantlebery, John(Z)	1836	Dec. 21	Perry Co.,Oh	15	14	10
Kapel, Philip(Z)	1821	May 07	Morgan Co,Oh	10	06	10
Kapel, Philip(Z)	1821	May 07	Morgan Co,Oh	10	06	11

PURCHASER	YEAR	DATE	RESIDENCE	R	T	S
Kapel, Philip(Z)	1821	May 07	Morgan Co,Oh	10	07	35
Kappel, Daniel(Z)	1836	March 30	Morgan Co,Oh	10	06	14
Kappel, George(Z)	1835	Oct. 24	Morgan Co,Oh	10	06	11
Kappel, Jacob(Z)	1834	Nov. 13	Morgan Co,Oh	10	06	03
Kappel, John(Z)	1833	July 27	Morgan Co,Oh	10	06	15
Kappel, Peter(Z)	1833	March 23	Morgan Co,Oh	10	06	10
Kappel, Peter(Z)	1835	Nov. 12	Morgan Co,Oh	10	06	10
Kapple, Daniel(Z)	1834	Feb. 18	Morgan Co,Oh	10	06	14
Karl, Henry(Z-M)	1833	May 01	TuscarwsCoOh	02	06	20
Karns, Henry(Z)	1813	Nov. 26	MuskinqmCoOh	13	12	09
Karr, James Jnr.(Z-M)	1837	Jan. 31	GuernseyCoOh	03	01	18
Karr, James Jnr.(Z-M)	1837	Jan. 28	GuernseyCoOh	03	01	18
Karr, James(Z)	1835	July 27	GuernseyCoOh	10	09	01
Karr, James(Z-M)	1821	Nov. 10	GuernseyCoOh	03	01	24
Karr, James(Z-M)	1829	April 27	GuernseyCoOh	03	01	24
Karr, James(Z-M)	1832	Dec. 07	GuernseyCoOh	03	01	17
Karr, James(Z-M)	1833	May 20	GuernseyCoOh	03	01	17
Karr, John(Z)	1835	Nov. 20	GuernseyCoOh	10	09	01
Karr, Robert(Y)	1829	June 17	Jeff.Co.,Oh.	03	11	10
Karr, Robert(Y)	1833	March 25	WashCo.,Penn	03	11	11
Kasbeer, Samuel(Z-M)	1833	Dec. 04	TuscarwsCoOh	02	08	24
Kauffman, Jacob(Z)	1811	Oct. 24	TuscarwsCoOh	09	05	19
Kaufman, George(Z-M)	1821	May 16	TuscarwsCoOh	03	08	08
Kaufman, Moses(Z-M)	1831	April 26	HolmesCoOhio	05	09	03
Kavenaugh, Rhoda(Z)	1833	May 11	Morgan Co,Oh	09	06	11
Kavr, James(Z)	1814	April 07	KnoxCo.,Ohio	11	05	06
Kay, James(Z-M)	1833	Feb. 18	CoshoctnCoOh	08	07	08
Kay, James(Z-M)	1833	Feb. 18	CoshoctnCoOh	08	07	08
Kean, John(Y)	1834	Aug. 14	Jeff.Co.,Oh.	04	12	11
Kean, John(Y)	1835	Jan. 13	Jeff.Co.,Oh.	04	12	11
Kearns, John(Z-M)	1832	June 21	GuernseyCoOh	02	03	07
Kearns, John(Z-M)	1835	Sept. 12	GuernseyCoOh	02	03	07
Keath, Benjamin(Z)	1836	Jan. 02	Morgan Co,Oh	09	05	11
Keath, Peter(Z)	1836	Jan. 08	Morgan Co,Oh	09	05	35
Keath, Peter(Z)	1836	Jan. 08	Morgan Co,Oh	09	05	35
Keckler, Abraham(Z)	1813	Sept. 15	KnoxCo.,Ohio	10	05	06
Keckley, Benjamin(Z)	1811	March 29	FredrickCo ?	09	08	09
Keefer, Frederick(Z-M)	1836	Sept. 22	KnoxCo.,Ohio	10	04	02
Keefer, Peter(Y)	1829	Dec. 22	Stark Co.,Oh	08	12	07
Keeler, Isaac(Y)	1825	Oct. 21	TuscarwsCoOh	07	15	26
Keeler, Isaac(Y)	1825	Oct. 21	TuscarwsCoOh	07	15	32
Keelor, Michael(Z)	1831	July 04	Morgan Co,Oh	09	06	09
Keen, Edward(Z-M)	1836	April 18	KnoxCo.,Ohio	10	05	22
Keen, Jesse(Z)	1836	May 30	ZanesvilleOh	15	14	01
Keen, Jesse(Z)	1836	June 25	ZanesvilleOh	08	05	20
Keen, Jesse(Z)	1836	June 25	ZanesvilleOh	08	05	19
Keen, Jesse(Z)	1836	June 28	ZanesvilleOh	08	06	31
Keen, Jesse(Z)	1836	June 28	ZanesvilleOh	08	06	32
Keen, Jesse(Z)	1836	Aug. 08	ZanesvilleOh	08	05	28
Keen, Jesse(Z)	1836	Aug. 16	ZanesvilleOh	10	06	20
Keen, Jesse(Z)	1836	Aug. 16	ZanesvilleOh	10	06	25
Keen, Jesse(Z)	1836	Dec. 13	ZanesvilleOh	08	05	29
Keen, Jesse(Z)	1837	Jan. 19	ZanesvilleOh	09	05	30
Keen, Jesse(Z)	1836	May 27	ZanesvilleOh	14	12	07
Keen, Jesse(Z-M)	1835	Dec. 12	ZanesvilleOh	02	03	10
Keen, Jesse(Z-M)	1835	Dec. 23	ZanesvilleOh	02	03	10
Keen, Jesse(Z-M)	1836	Jan. 09	ZanesvilleOh	08	09	03
Keen, Jesse(Z-M)	1836	Sept. 20	ZanesvilleOh	09	09	04
Keen, Jesse(Z-M)	1836	Oct. 13	ZanesvilleOh	08	08	04
Keen, Jesse(Z-M)	1837	Feb. 15	ZanesvilleOh	10	04	05
Keen, Jesse(Z-M)	1837	April 06	ZanesvilleOh	04	04	23
Keen, Jesse(Z-M)	1837	April 06	ZanesvilleOh	04	04	23
Keen, Jesse(Z-M)	1837	April 28	ZanesvilleOh	10	09	20
Keeran, Benj'n.(Y)	1824	Sept. 16	HarrisonCoOh	06	11	22
Keever, William(Z)	1834	Oct. 01	Jeff.Co.,Oh.	10	06	05
Keever, William(Z)	1835	Nov. 30	Morgan Co,Oh	10	06	05
Keff, Thomas(Z)	1830	April 05	Perry Co.,Oh	14	14	21
Keffer, Jacob(Z-M)	1836	Nov. 11	TuscarwsCoOh	03	07	20
Kegg, Conrad(Z)	1814	Sept. 05	TuscarwsCoOh	05	08	03

PURCHASER	YEAR	DATE	RESIDENCE	R	T	S
Keigh, Balser(Z)	1816	March 29	WashngtnCoOh	10	06	23
Keigh, Peter(Z)	1816	March 29	WashngtnCoOh	10	06	26
Keil, Adam(Y)	1830	Feb. 18	HarrisonCoOh	06	16	21
Keil, Cornelius(Z)	1833	Oct. 17	GuernseyCoOh	09	08	15
Keil, William G.(Z)	1826	July 25	ShanandhCoVa	09	08	15
Keiser, George(Z-M)	1836	Sept. 07	CoshoctnCoOh	03	05	17
Keiser, John(Z-M)	1836	March 17	TuscarwsCoOh	03	07	21
Keislar, Josiah(Y)	1834	Jan. 23	ColumbanCoOh	05	15	04
Keist, Philip(Z-M)	1832	Oct. 23	MuskingmCoOh	06	03	11
Keith, Adam(Z)	1832	Jan. 31	Morgan Co,Oh	10	06	15
Keith, Adam(Z)	1833	April 22	Morgan Co,Oh	10	06	15
Keith, Adam(Z)	1835	Dec. 14	Morgan Co,Oh	10	06	15
Keith, Adam(Z)	1816	Sept. 11	WashCo.,Penn	10	07	26
Keith, Benjamin Jr.(Z)	1836	March 11	Morgan Co,Oh	09	05	07
Keith, Benjamin Jr.(Z)	1836	March 11	Morgan Co,Oh	09	05	13
Keith, Benjamin(Z)	1827	June 21	Morgan Co,Oh	09	05	08
Keith, Benjamin(Z)	1832	May 22	Morgan Co,Oh	09	05	07
Keith, Benjamin(Z)	1832	May 22	Morgan Co,Oh	09	05	07
Keith, Benjamin(Z)	1834	Aug. 26	Morgan Co,Oh	09	05	06
Keith, Benjamin(Z)	1834	Aug. 26	Morgan Co,Oh	09	05	08
Keith, Benjamin(Z)	1835	June 03	Morgan Co,Oh	09	05	07
Keith, Benjamin(Z)	1836	Dec. 24	Morgan Co,Oh	09	05	07
Keith, Palser(Z)	1822	Sept. 25	Morgan Co,Oh	10	07	36
Keith, Peter(Z)	1826	March 31	Morgan Co,Oh	09	05	05
Keith, Peter(Z)	1833	Sept. 13	Morgan Co,Oh	09	06	32
Keith, Peter(Z)	1835	May 15	Morgan Co,Oh	09	06	32
Keith, Peter(Z)	1835	May 15	Morgan Co,Oh	09	06	32
Keith, Peter(Z)	1835	May 15	Morgan Co,Oh	09	06	32
Keith, William(Z-M)	1832	March 07	LickingCo,Oh	10	02	24
Keizer, Abraham(Z-M)	1832	May 30	TuscarwsCoOh	04	07	06
Keizer, Daniel(Z-M)	1826	April 13	TuscarwsCoOh	04	07	05
Keizer, George(Z-M)	1836	March 26	TuscarwsCoOh	04	07	06
Kell, Gustavus(Z)	1816	Sept. 28	WestmrldCoPa	14	13	24
Kell, John(Y)	1833	Aug. 28	SteubenvleOh	05	13	03
Kell, John(Z-M)	1826	Nov. 16	GuernseyCoOh	02	02	06
Kell, John(Z-M)	1829	Dec. 25	GuernseyCoOh	02	03	16
Kell, John(Z-M)	1829	Dec. 25	GuernseyCoOh	03	03	20
Kell, John(Z-M)	1834	Aug. 14	GuernseyCoOh	02	02	06
Kell, John(Z-M)	1832	Nov. 12	GuernseyCoOh	02	02	15
Kell, Robert(Z)	1833	Feb. 27	WestmrldCoPa	10	09	26
Kelland, Sam'l.(Z-M)	1840	July 28	GuernseyCoOh	04	03	15
Kelland, Sam'l.(Z-M)	1840	July 28	GuernseyCoOh	04	03	14
Kellar, John(Z)	1833	Jan. 30	Morgan Co,Oh	13	10	22
Kellar, Michael(Z)	1824	May 25	Morgan Co,Oh	09	06	10
Kellar, Michael(Z)	1833	Feb. 09	Morgan Co,Oh	09	07	15
Keller, Christian(Z-M)	1825	Sept. 19	TuscarwsCoOh	02	10	16
Keller, Fred'k.(Y)	1824	Oct. 26	ColumbanCoOh	05	18	28
Keller, Henry(Z-M)	1833	Aug. 20	TuscarwsCoOh	02	07	08
Keller, John(Z)	1829	Dec. 21	MonroeCo.,Oh	08	07	09
Keller, John(Z)	1816	Dec. 03	BelmontCo,Oh	08	07	09
Keller, Martin(Z)	1814	Aug. 19	TuscarwsCoOh	02	07	10
Keller, Michael(Z)	1835	Jan. 15	Morgan Co,Oh	09	06	15
Keller, Peter(Z)	1817	July 30	Jeff.Co.,Oh.	12	12	24
Keller, Thomas(Z-M)	1833	May 21	TuscarwsCoOh	02	07	10
Kelley, Alfred(Z-M)	1836	Dec. 29	MuskingmCoOh	03	01	05
Kelley, Daniel(Y)	1832	Nov. 26	Jeff.Co.,Oh.	02	09	25
Kelley, James(Y)	1828	Oct. 17	Stark Co.,Oh	07	17	26
Kelley, James(Z)	1817	June 21	MuskingmCoOh	14	13	09
Kelloch, Hiram(Y)	1833	Sept. 06	ColumbanCoOh	03	12	34
Kellogg, Oliver(Y)	1828	April 18	Stark Co.,Oh	07	17	27
Kelloggg, Thos.(Z-M)	1839	Feb. 25	HuronCo.Ohio	10	09	22
Kellor, John(Y)	1823	Nov. 13	ColumbanCoOh	05	18	33
Kells, Andrew(Z)	1832	March 09	GuernseyCoOh	10	09	35
Kells, Andrew(Z)	1834	Aug. 29	GuernseyCoOh	10	09	35
Kells, Andrew(Z)	1814	Oct. 17	WashngtnCoOh	08	06	26
Kelly, D. M.(Z-M)	1837	March 30	Stark Co.,Oh	04	07	12
Kelly, D. McCoy(Z-M)	1837	March 30	Stark Co.,Oh	04	07	12
Kelly, Hugh(Z)	1822	Feb. 28	AdamsCo,Penn	15	16	26
Kelly, Isaac(Y)	1829	Aug. 18	HarrisonCoOh	05	13	34

154

PURCHASER	YEAR	DATE	RESIDENCE	R	T	S
Kelly, Isaac(Z-M)	1836	Dec. 21	ColumbanCoOh	08	08	22
Kelly, John(Z)	1806	June 27	Ohio Co.,Vir	08	02	05
Kelly, John(Z)	1806	June 27	Ohio Co.,Vir	08	02	21
Kelly, John(Z)	1806	July 02	Ohio Co.,Vir	08	02	05
Kelly, John(Z-M)	1824	Jan. 16	CoshoctnCoOh	08	08	21
Kelly, Joseph(Z)	1830	Dec. 08	Perry Co.,Oh	14	14	18
Kelly, Joseph(Z)	1836	April 02	Morgan Co.,Oh	09	05	26
Kelly, Joseph(Z-M)	1825	Aug. 26	MuskingmCoOh	04	01	22
Kelly, Sarah(Z-M)	1836	Oct. 04	Jeff.Co.,Oh.	03	06	14
Kelly, Thomas(Y)	1822	Nov. 20	FayetteCo,Pa	03	10	22
Kelly, Thomas(Z)	1835	Feb. 27	ZanesvilleOh	14	12	28
Kelly, Thomas(Z)	1835	April 06	ZanesvilleOh	14	12	27
Kelly, Thomas(Z)	1805	April 29	Chmbrsbrg,Pa	07	01	09
Kelly, Thomas(Z)	1805	April 29	Chmbrsbrg,Pa	07	01	09
Kelly, William(Y)	1832	June 12	Jeff.Co.,Oh.	04	12	11
Kelly, William(Y)	1832	June 12	Jeff.Co.,Oh.	04	12	10
Kelly, Wm.(Y)	1823	June 14	HarrisonCoOh	06	14	01
Kelsey, James(Y)	1825	Nov. 25	BelmontCo,Oh	04	06	03
Kelsey, John(Y)	1825	Oct. 17	BelmontCo,Oh	04	06	08
Kelso, H.(Z)	1815	April 22	?	11	04	06
Kemble, Walter(Z)	1827	Sept. 28	HolmesCoOhio	08	08	03
Kemble, Walter(Z-M)	1825	June 06	HolmesCoOhio	08	08	08
Kemeren, John(Z)	1813	Dec. 18	KnoxCo.,Ohio	10	06	24
Kemiren, John(Z)	1813	Dec. 18	KnoxCo.,Ohio	10	06	24
Kemp, Amanda(Y)	1825	Jan. 05	HarrisonCoOh	05	11	05
Ken, George(Z-M)	1836	May 26	HolmesCoOhio	07	08	18
Kendall, Adam(Z)	1832	Dec. 27	MonroeCo.,Oh	08	07	06
Kendall, Benjamin(Z-M)	1835	Nov. 30	BelmontCo,Oh	02	06	03
Kendall, Benjamin(Z-M)	1836	May 10	BelmontCo,Oh	03	07	20
Kendall, Benjamin(Z-M)	1836	Aug. 13	BelmontCo,Oh	02	07	03
Kendell, Zebedee(Z)	1815	Feb. 24	GuernseyCoOh	02	02	22
Kendry, Nicholas(Y)	1824	Sept. 30	BelmontCo,Oh	03	05	02
Kenedy, Citizen J.(Z-M)	1827	March 30	HarrisonCoOh	03	06	08
Kenedy, John(Z)	1814	Sept. 01	FairfeldCoOh	15	15	10
Kenedy, Retun M.(Z-M)	1835	Nov. 21	TuscarwsCoOh	01	06	24
Kenedy, Return M.(Z-M)	1827	March 22	HarrisonCoOh	01	06	17
Kenison, Isaiah(Z)	1833	April 15	Morgan Co,Oh	11	10	12
Kennady, John(Y)	1827	Jan. 11	Jeff.Co.,Oh.	04	14	21
Kennard, Joseph(Z)	1825	Aug. 22	BelmontCo,Oh	12	09	17
Kennedy, Andrew(Z-M)	1838	Sept. 15	GuernseyCoOh	03	03	07
Kennedy, Citizen James(Y)	1830	March 23	HarrisonCoOh	06	11	30
Kennedy, David(Z-M)	1820	July 01	CoshoctnCoOh	06	09	14
Kennedy, Irwin(Z)	1831	Oct. 01	GuernseyCoOh	08	08	29
Kennedy, James(Z)	1832	June 26	Morgan Co,Oh	10	06	18
Kennedy, James(Z)	1833	Jan. 03	Morgan Co,Oh	10	06	07
Kennedy, James(Z)	1835	March 31	MordganCo,Oh	10	06	07
Kennedy, John L.(Z-M)	1826	Jan. 13	HarrisonCoOh	01	06	16
Kennedy, John L.(Z-M)	1827	April 03	HarrisonCoOh	01	06	17
Kennedy, John L.(Z-M)	1828	June 11	TuscarwsCoOh	01	06	16
Kennedy, M. W.(Z-M)	1837	Jan. 31	GuernseyCoOh	02	04	14
Kennedy, Martin(Z)	1831	March 15	Morgan Co,Oh	10	06	07
Kennedy, Matthew(Z-M)	1836	Jan. 25	TuscarwsCoOh	01	06	24
Kennedy, Moses W.(Z-M)	1836	Dec. 06	GuernseyCoOh	02	04	18
Kennedy, Moses Washington(Z-M)	1836	Sept. 17	GuernseyCoOh	02	04	17
Kennedy, Moses(Y)	1827	Dec. 24	Jeff.Co.,Oh.	04	14	24
Kennedy, Nap. B.(Z-M)	1831	April 02	TuscarwsCoOh	01	06	23
Kennedy, Napoleon B.(Z-M)	1826	March 27	TuscarwsCoOh	01	06	17
Kennedy, Napoleon B.(Z-M)	1828	June 05	TuscarwsCoOh	01	06	23
Kennedy, Nathaniel(Z-M)	1836	Feb. 06	MuskingmCoOh	03	01	04
Kennedy, Nathaniel(Z-M)	1836	Feb. 08	MuskingmCoOh	03	01	04
Kennedy, William C.(Z-M)	1826	Jan. 13	HarrisonCoOh	01	06	13
Kennedy, William C.(Z-M)	1832	Dec. 13	TuscarwsCoOh	01	06	13
Kennedy, William(Z)	1833	Jan. 22	WestmrldCoPa	11	12	15
Kennedy, William(Z)	1833	Jan. 22	WestmrldCoPa	11	12	14
Kennedy, Wm.(Z)	1827	April 21	BelmontCo,Oh	10	08	35
Kennedy, Wm.(Z)	1814	May 23	MuskingmCoOh	09	01	20
Kennel, Joseph(Y)	1828	Nov. 27	ColumbanCoOh	05	15	15
Kent, Isaac(Z)	1811	Oct. 26	TuscarwsCoOh	11	13	12
Kent, M.(Z)	1815	July 01	MuskingmCoOh	12	12	06

PURCHASER	YEAR	DATE	RESIDENCE	R	T	S
Kent, S. J.(Z)	1815	July 01	MuskingmCoOh	12	12	06
Kent, Wm.(Y)	1829	March 27	HarrisonCoOh	06	12	30
Keor, James(Z)	1814	April 07	KnoxCo.,Ohio	11	05	06
Kepler, Andrew(Y)	1831	Nov. 09	West ?	09	12	18
Kepler, Andrew(Y)	1833	April 12	Stark Co.,Oh	09	12	18
Kepler, Andrew(Z)	1811	Aug. 27	WestmrldCoPa	15	17	19
Kepler, David(Z)	1831	Sept. 22	Morgan Co,Oh	12	09	01
Kepler, George(Z)	1814	March 29	TuscarwsCoOh	01	08	08
Kepler, Jacob(Y)	1837	April 16	Stark Co.,Oh	10	02	13
Kepler, John Jr.(Y)	1824	Aug. 11	Stark Co.,Oh	09	12	19
Kepler, John Jr.(Y)	1824	Aug. 11	Stark Co.,Oh	09	12	19
Kepler, John(Z)	1804	June 11	MuskingmCoOh	13	12	02
Kepler, John(Z)	1806	Feb. 18	MuskingmCoOh	13	12	01
Kepler, Joseph(Z)	1811	Oct. 01	WashngtnCoMd	03	10	24
Keppel, George(Z)	1832	May 29	Morgan Co,Oh	10	06	14
Keppel, John(Z)	1836	Feb. 03	Morgan Co,Oh	10	06	09
Kepple, John(Z)	1831	April 11	Morgan Co,Oh	10	06	10
Keppler, John C.(Z-M)	1835	May 30	TuscarwsCoOh	03	10	11
Kern, John(Z-M)	1821	March 13	TuscarwsCoOh	04	08	22
Kern, John(Z-M)	1832	May 23	TuscarwsCoOh	04	08	18
Kern, John(Z-M)	1832	May 23	TuscarwsCoOh	04	08	23
Kernaghan, Samuel(Z-M)	1826	March 30	HarrisonCoOh	11	08	05
Kernahan, Sam'l.(Z-M)	1825	June 15	HarrisonCoOh	11	08	05
Kerr, James(Y)	1832	Nov. 12	ColumbanCoOh	03	12	03
Kerr, James(Y)	1832	Nov. 12	ColumbanCoOh	03	12	02
Kerr, James(Z)	1812	July 03	KnoxCo.,Ohio	11	05	05
Kerr, Jesse(Z-M)	1836	Oct. 27	HolmesCoOhio	08	08	13
Kerr, John P.(Z)	1817	May 20	FayetteCo,Pa	07	08	13
Kerr, John(Z-M)	1827	Aug. 07	HolmesCoOhio	07	08	23
Kerr, Joseph(Z)	1813	June 09	WashCo.,Penn	10	05	04
Kerr, Robert(Y)	1826	April 03	BelmontCo,Oh	04	06	27
Kerr, Robert(Y)	1827	March 08	Jeff.Co.,Oh.	03	16	22
Kerr, William(Y)	1832	May 29	ColumbanCoOh	03	12	09
Kerr, William(Y)	1835	Dec. 31	Jeff.Co.,Oh.	03	12	09
Kerr, William(Z)	1813	March 26	CoshoctnCoOh	05	04	19
Kersey, William(Z-M)	1837	March 27	MuskingmCoOh	09	07	14
Kessler, Peter(Y)	1833	Aug. 03	Stark Co.,Oh	09	11	24
Kester, Jonathan Hartley(Y)	1831	Nov. 19	GuernseyCoOh	07	09	25
Kester, William(Y)	1826	Nov. 22	GuernseyCoOh	07	09	20
Ketch, Benjamin(Z)	1813	July 27	WashngtnCoOh	09	05	08
Ketcham, George(Y)	1830	March 05	ColumbanCoOh	02	10	17
Ketchum, Holmes(Z)	1836	March 05	Perry Co.,Oh	14	12	21
Keysar, Andrew(Y)	1824	Jan. 02	BelmontCo,Oh	03	05	14
Keyser, Andrew(Z)	1835	Nov. 14	BelmontCo,Oh	10	07	25
Keyser, Andrew(Z)	1836	Jan. 30	BelmontCo,Oh	09	06	19
Keyser, Isaac(Y)	1826	May 08	BelmontCo,Oh	03	05	01
Keyser, Jacob(Y)	1827	Aug. 28	BelmontCo,Oh	03	05	09
Keyser, Oliver(Z)	1835	April 22	BelmontCo,Oh	10	07	24
Kiber, Anton(Y)	1833	Feb. 14	Stark Co.,Oh	06	16	34
Kidd, Amos(Z)	1837	Nov. 17	WashngtnCoOh	08	05	27
Kidd, Peter(Z-M)	1836	Sept. 26	HolmesCoOhio	10	08	01
Kidd, William(Y)	1823	Feb. 25	PhiladelhaPa	04	17	28
Kiefer, John(Z-M)	1835	Sept. 28	CoshoctnCoOh	06	04	21
Kieffaber, C.(Z-M)	1836	Aug. 06	TuscarwsCoOh	04	07	12
Kiehofer, Veronica(Z-M)	1828	Dec. 19	SomersetCoPa	04	09	05
Kierman, Andrew(Z)	1835	Dec. 08	Morgan Co,Oh	13	08	06
Kiernan, Andrew(Z)	1836	Aug. 15	Morgan Co,Oh	13	08	06
Kiest, Philip(Z-M)	1839	Jan. 31	MuskingmCoOh	08	07	03
Kiger, David(Z-M)	1838	May 08	HolmesCoOhio	09	08	07
Kiger, Jacob(Z-M)	1831	May 14	CoshoctnCoOh	04	04	06
Kiger, Philip(Z-M)	1837	April 05	CoshoctnCoOh	09	08	07
Kiger, William(Z-M)	1836	March 29	CoshoctnCoOh	09	07	15
Kiger, William(Z-M)	1836	July 11	CoshoctnCoOh	09	07	06
Kilbourn, Hezekiah(Z-M)	1837	March 17	LickingCo,Oh	08	07	06
Kilbourn, Hezekiah(Z-M)	1837	March 17	LickingCo,Oh	09	07	10
Kilbourn, Hezekiah(Z-M)	1837	March 17	LickingCo,Oh	09	07	11
Kilbourn, Hezekiah(Z-M)	1837	March 17	LickingCo,Oh	09	07	11
Kilbride, Michael(Z-M)	1839	Jan. 29	MuskingmCoOh	04	03	07
Kiley, Alexander(Y)	1829	Dec. 19	Jeff.Co.,Oh.	06	13	06

PURCHASER	YEAR	DATE	RESIDENCE	R	T	S
Kill, John(Z-M)	1823	March 01	GuernseyCoOh	02	02	06
Kille, Gilbert H.(Y)	1827	Aug. 25	ColumbanCoOh	06	19	15
Killer, Joseph(Y)	1829	Dec. 21	Stark Co.,Oh	07	17	17
Kilpatrick, William(Z-M)	1825	Jan. 08	HarrisonCoOh	09	04	21
Kilpatrick, Wm.(Z-M)	1835	Jan. 30	CoshoctnCoOh	08	03	05
Kimbel, Robert(Z)	1817	Feb. 11	GuernseyCoOh	01	04	15
Kimble, Adam(Z-M)	1832	March 26	GuernseyCoOh	02	03	01
Kimble, Adam(Z-M)	1833	Nov. 02	GuernseyCoOh	02	04	21
Kimble, Benjamin(Z-M)	1833	April 03	HolmesCoOhio	09	09	24
Kimble, Caleb(Z-M)	1836	Feb. 29	HolmesCoOhio	09	09	16
Kimble, Caleb(Z-M)	1836	Nov. 14	HolmesCoOhio	09	09	17
Kimble, James(Y)	1821	Sept. 25	ChesterCo,Pa	06	11	22
Kimble, Nathan(Z-M)	1835	April 04	GuernseyCoOh	09	09	24
Kimble, Thomas(Z)	1828	Oct. 07	Perry Co.,Oh	14	12	17
Kimble, Thomas(Z)	1833	Oct. 22	Perry Co.,Oh	14	12	18
Kimble, Thomas(Z)	1836	Dec. 06	Perry Co.,Oh	14	12	29
Kimble, Thomas(Z)	1836	Dec. 06	Perry Co.,Oh	14	12	29
Kimble, Thomas(Z)	1836	Dec. 06	Perry Co.,Oh	15	14	01
Kimble, Thomas(Z)	1836	Dec. 06	Perry Co.,Oh	15	14	12
Kimble, Walter(Z-M)	1822	Oct. 18	CoshoctnCoOh	08	08	08
Kimble, Walter(Z-M)	1822	Oct. 18	CoshoctnCoOh	08	08	03
Kimble, Walter(Z-M)	1822	Oct. 18	CoshoctnCoOh	08	08	02
Kimble, Washington(Z-M)	1832	Nov. 07	GuernseyCoOh	02	04	16
Kimble, Washington(Z-M)	1836	Jan. 18	GuernseyCoOh	02	04	17
Kimble, Washington(Z-M)	1837	Feb. 03	GuernseyCoOh	03	04	10
Kimble, William(Z-M)	1832	Nov. 07	GuernseyCoOh	02	04	13
Kimble, William(Z-M)	1832	Dec. 05	GuernseyCoOh	02	04	13
Kimmel, David(Y)	1828	July 30	Stark Co.,Oh	07	16	17
Kimmel, David(Y)	1830	Jan. 01	Stark Co.,Oh	07	17	18
Kimmel, Emanuel(Y)	1826	Oct. 20	Stark Co.,Oh	08	09	13
Kimmel, Emanuel(Y)	1828	Aug. 08	Stark Co.,Oh	07	17	18
Kimmel, Frederick(Z-M)	1836	April 12	HarrisonCoOh	03	07	19
Kimmel, John(Y)	1829	March 18	HarrisonCoOh	05	12	25
Kimmel, John(Z-M)	1837	March 06	Stark Co.,Oh	05	04	20
Kimmel, John(Z-M)	1837	March 06	Stark Co.,Oh	05	04	11
Kimmel, Joseph(Y)	1830	Aug. 23	Stark Co.,Oh	07	17	26
Kimmel, Leonard Jr.(Y)	1823	March 26	HarrisonCoOh	04	12	29
Kimmel, Samuel(Y)	1829	Dec. 09	Stark Co.,Oh	07	17	02
Kimmell, Joseph(Y)	1831	July 05	Stark Co.,Oh	08	12	11
Kimmersley, Isaac(Z-M)	1832	Oct. 31	GuernseyCoOh	03	03	02
Kimpton, John(Y)	1824	July 15	BelmontCo,Oh	03	05	11
Kindall, James(Z)	1836	April 12	GuernseyCoOh	08	07	31
Kinder, Adam(Y)	1825	April 26	ColumbanCoOh	04	13	33
Kinder, John(Z)	1831	Oct. 25	ColumbanCoOh	14	12	14
Kinder, Peter(Y)	1826	Nov. 18	ColumbanCoOh	04	13	29
Kinder, Peter(Z)	1836	Dec. 09	Perry Co.,Oh	14	12	10
Kinder, Samuel(Y)	1832	March 11	ColumbanCoOh	04	13	04
Kindrue, Abraham(Z)	1816	Feb. 14	TuscarwsCoOh	01	10	13
King, David(Z)	1814	March 03	SomersetCoPa	15	15	07
King, David(Z-M)	1838	Nov. 26	MedinaCoOhio	09	09	04
King, David(Z-M)	1838	Nov. 26	MedinaCoOhio	09	08	13
King, David(Z-M)	1838	Nov. 26	MedinaCoOhio	09	08	12
King, David(Z-M)	1838	Nov. 26	MedinaCoOhio	09	08	07
King, David(Z-M)	1838	Nov. 26	MedinaCoOhio	09	08	07
King, David(Z-M)	1838	Nov. 26	MedinaCoOhio	08	08	16
King, David(Z-M)	1838	Nov. 26	MedinaCoOhio	08	08	16
King, Ignatius(Y)	1832	Nov. 15	Stark Co.,Oh	08	12	23
King, Jesse(Z)	1826	Aug. 18	Perry Co.,Oh	15	15	22
King, Job S.(Z-M)	1833	Nov. 19	HarrisonCoOh	03	04	03
King, John(Y)	1825	March 05	Stark Co.,Oh	06	18	08
King, John(Y)	1826	April 03	Stark Co.,Oh	06	18	08
King, John(Z)	1832	April 23	MonroeCo.,Oh	08	07	23
King, John(Z)	1815	Nov. 23	SomersetCoPa	15	15	18
King, John(Z)	1815	Nov. 23	SomersetCoPa	15	15	07
King, Matthew(Z-M)	1836	Sept. 10	TuscarwsCoOh	03	06	07
King, Mich'l.(Z)	1815	Nov. 23	SomersetCoPa	15	15	18
King, Mich'l.(Z)	1815	Nov. 23	SomersetCoPa	15	15	07
King, Nathan(Y)	1829	Dec. 26	ColumbanCoOh	05	13	15
King, Nicholas(Z-M)	1836	Sept. 03	TuscarwsCoOh	04	07	08

PURCHASER	YEAR	DATE	RESIDENCE	R	T	S
King, Nicholas(Z-M)	1836	Sept. 03	TuscarwsCoOh	04	07	09
King, O. Wm.(Y)	1823	Aug. 04	HarrisonCoOh	06	12	22
King, Samuel D.(Z-M)	1836	Feb. 24	Newark, Ohio	11	04	19
King, Samuel(Z)	1814	Dec. 07	MuskingmCoOh	14	15	08
King, Samuel(Z)	1816	May 06	MuskingmCoOh	15	16	20
King, Thomas(Z)	1804	Dec. 18	SomersetCoPa	14	14	04
King, Thomas(Z)	1806	Nov. 25	SomersetCoPa	15	16	04
King, William(Y)	1826	May 13	YorkCo.,Penn	07	14	08
King, William(Z-M)	1828	May 14	CoshoctnCoOh	06	07	02
Kingaman, John(Z)	1808	Nov. 30	SomersetCoPa	04	08	14
Kingston, Robt.(Z)	1829	Oct. 26	MuskingmCoOh	11	12	04
Kinkead, David(Z-M)	1838	Jan. 24	GuernseyCoOh	03	03	09
Kinkead, David(Z-M)	1838	Jan. 24	GuernseyCoOh	03	03	09
Kinkead, David(Z-M)	1838	Jan. 24	GuernseyCoOh	03	03	09
Kinkead, David(Z-M)	1838	Feb. 24	GuernseyCoOh	03	03	01
Kinkead, David(Z-M)	1838	Feb. 24	GuernseyCoOh	03	03	01
Kinkead, David(Z-M)	1838	March 01	GuernseyCoOh	03	03	02
Kinkead, David(Z-M)	1838	April 07	GuernseyCoOh	03	03	01
Kinkead, David(Z-M)	1838	June 11	GuernseyCoOh	03	03	01
Kinnaird, David(Z)	1824	Aug. 10	MuskingmCoOh	11	13	21
Kinnaird, John(Z)	1825	April 11	Perry Co.,Oh	15	15	13
Kinnard, William(Z)	1822	Oct. 22	FairfildCoOh	15	15	01
Kinnard, Zebulon(Z)	1829	April 30	Perry Co.,Oh	15	15	12
Kinneer, Robert(Z-M)	1835	Aug. 21	LickingCo,Oh	11	04	22
Kinneer, Robert(Z-M)	1835	Aug. 21	LickingCo,Oh	11	04	22
Kinney, James(Z)	1813	Nov. 23	GuernseyCoOh	11	13	11
Kinney, James(Z)	1815	Feb. 18	MuskingmCoOh	11	05	23
Kinney, John(Z)	1813	Aug. 17	GuernseyCoOh	09	08	08
Kinny, Wm.(Y)	1829	April 25	Brooke CoVir	04	13	18
Kinsel, Martin(Z)	1835	Jan. 06	Perry Co.,Oh	15	15	27
Kinsey, Sam'l.(Z-M)	1836	June 18	CoshoctnCoOh	08	08	25
Kinsey, Samuel(Z-M)	1831	Sept. 09	CoshoctnCoOh	08	08	16
Kinsey, Ulysses(Z-M)	1832	June 20	HolmesCoOhio	08	08	25
Kinsley, John(Z)	1806	Dec. 17	MuskingmCoOh	03	09	19
Kintner, Christ'n.(Y)	1828	Jan. 31	Stark Co.,Oh	05	13	36
Kintner, Jacob(Z)	1806	Oct. 29	WashngtnCoVa	03	08	10
Kintner, Jacob(Z)	1806	Oct. 29	WashngtnCoVa	03	08	10
Kirby, Isaac(Y)	1824	Nov. 19	HarrisonCoOh	05	12	29
Kirby, Isaac(Y)	1828	June 23	HarrisonCoOh	05	12	29
Kirk, Charles(Z-M)	1835	Sept. 09	MuskingmCoOh	10	05	22
Kirk, John(Y)	1822	June 12	Jeff.Co.,Oh.	03	11	32
Kirk, John(Y)	1824	Dec. 22	Jeff.Co.,Oh.	03	11	32
Kirk, Robert C.(Z-M)	1835	Sept. 12	BelmontCo,Oh	04	06	11
Kirk, Robert C.(Z-M)	1835	Sept. 12	BelmontCo,Oh	04	06	11
Kirk, Samuel Senr.(Z-M)	1825	June 21	GuernseyCoOh	01	05	25
Kirk, Theophilus(Y)	1833	Feb. 18	ColumbanCoOh	02	09	25
Kirk, William(Z)	1826	Sept. 30	Jeff.Co.,Oh.	12	09	04
Kirkbride, John(Z)	1829	April 09	Morgan Co,Oh	13	08	20
Kirkbride, John(Z)	1835	Dec. 31	Morgan Co,Oh	13	08	21
Kirker & Fulton(Z)	1809	Dec. 23	MuskingmCoOh	08	02	23
Kirker, William(Z-M)	1826	Jan. 24	CoshoctnCoOh	07	05	17
Kirkland, Hugh(Z)	1836	Jan. 04	Morgan Co,Oh	10	07	22
Kirkland, William(Z)	1835	July 16	Morgan Co,Oh	10	06	23
Kirkland, William(Z)	1835	July 16	Morgan Co,Oh	10	06	14
Kirkpatrick, Andrew(Z)	1810	March 27	GuernseyCoOh	02	02	03
Kirkpatrick, David(Z-M)	1832	April 26	GuernseyCoOh	01	03	07
Kirkpatrick, Israel R.(Y)	1830	Nov. 02	HarrisonCoOh	05	11	24
Kirkpatrick, John(Z)	1816	Dec. 17	GuernseyCoOh	04	03	24
Kirkpatrick, Mary(Z)	1823	May 01	MuskingmCoOh	11	12	02
Kirkpatrick, Nathan'l.(Z)	1816	Sept. 07	LickingCo,Oh	11	04	10
Kirkpatrick, Peter(Z)	1815	May 16	LickingCo,Oh	11	04	08
Kirkpatrick, T.(Z)	1817	Oct. 22	WashngtnCoOh	11	13	31
Kirkpatrick, Thos.(Z)	1810	March 20	GuernseyCoOh	01	02	03
Kirkpatrick, William(Y)	1831	June 08	AlleghnyCoPa	06	16	29
Kirne, Nicholas(Z)	1813	Nov. 05	TuscarwsCoOh	05	09	20
Kiser, Daniel(Z-M)	1829	Oct. 26	TuscarwsCoOh	04	07	03
Kiser, George(Z-M)	1834	Feb. 19	TuscarwsCoOh	03	08	24
Kiste, Nathan(Z-M)	1836	Oct. 12	CoshoctnCoOh	05	04	14
Kiste, Nathan(Z-M)	1836	Oct. 17	CoshoctnCoOh	05	04	14

PURCHASER	YEAR	DATE	RESIDENCE	R	T	S
Kistler, Jacob(Y)	1822	June 27	Stark Co.,Oh	06	17	21
Kitch, Martin(Z)	1827	Nov. 05	TuscarwsCoOh	03	08	03
Kitchen, Wheeler(Y)	1824	Dec. 06	Stark Co.,Oh	10	01	24
Kitt, George(Y)	1828	Jan. 09	HarrisonCoOh	06	12	35
Kitt, Jacob(Y)	1822	July 22	Stark Co.,Oh	07	18	21
Kitt, Jacob(Y)	1824	May 20	Stark Co.,Oh	07	18	29
Kitt, Jacob(Y)	1824	May 20	Stark Co.,Oh	07	18	29
Kitten, Jacob(Y)	1822	May 25	ColumbanCoOh	04	13	22
Kitts, Christian(Z)	1836	Aug. 11	WashngtnCoOh	08	06	21
Kittsmiller, Jno.(Y)	1829	July 04	Stark Co.,Oh	09	11	12
Kizner, Samuel(Z)	1833	Feb. 18	GuernseyCoOh	09	05	09
Klechner, Michael(Z-M)	1832	Sept. 19	Jeff.Co.,Oh.	04	06	10
Kleckner, Frederick(Y)	1820	Aug. 05	Jeff.Co.,Oh.	06	15	14
Klein, Paul(Z-M)	1837	Sept. 01	MuskingmCoOh	09	08	05
Kleis, Jacob(Y)	1832	Sept. 07	Stark Co.,Oh	07	16	04
Klieber, Henry(Z)	1816	June 22	LickingCo,Oh	11	03	15
Kline, Godleib(Z-M)	1833	Oct. 5	MuskingmCoOh	06	03	09
Kline, Gotlieb(Z-M)	1835	Jan. 09	MuskingmCoOh	06	03	10
Kline, Henry(Y)	1827	June 18	ColumbanCoOh	06	19	02
Kline, John(Z)	1805	Nov. 04	BedfordCo,Pa	01	10	15
Kline, John(Z)	1811	Oct. 23	FayetteCo,Pa	04	09	20
Kline, John(Z)	1815	Nov. 23	TuscarwsCoOh	05	06	13
Kline, Jonas Jr.(Z-M)	1828	April 18	TuscarwsCoOh	03	10	23
Kline, Jonas(Z)	1816	May 16	TuscarwsCoOh	04	09	21
Kline, Mathew(Z-M)	1835	June 01	GuernseyCoOh	03	01	06
Kline, Michael(Z-M)	1831	March 19	HolmesCoOhio	06	09	23
Klosner, Samuel(Z-M)	1836	Oct. 01	TuscarwsCoOh	03	08	25
Knappenberger, Conrad(Z)	1814	March 03	GreensburgPa	03	09	01
Knappenberger, Philip(Z)	1815	May 31	TuscarwsCoOh	03	09	09
Knappenberger, Philip(Z-M)	1832	July 17	TuscarwsCoOh	03	09	02
Knappenberger, Philip(Z-M)	1832	July 17	TuscarwsCoOh	03	09	02
Knapperbergen, Conrad(Z)	1806	June 02	GreensburgPa	03	09	01
Knapperbergen, Conrad(Z)	1806	June 02	GreensburgPa	03	09	09
Knep, John(Z-M)	1828	June 13	TuscarwsCoOh	05	08	08
Knepper, Godfrey(Z-M)	1828	April 16	ColumbanCoOh	03	10	14
Knepper, John(Z-M)	1829	Jan. 22	ColumbanCoOh	03	10	15
Knight, John(Y)	1828	Aug. 18	HarrisonCoOh	06	11	28
Knight, John(Z-M)	1831	April 11	HarrisonCoOh	02	06	23
Knight, John(Z-M)	1831	April 11	HarrisonCoOh	02	06	22
Knight, Michael(Z-M)	1835	Nov. 19	HolmesCoOhio	09	08	16
Knight, Michael(Z-M)	1837	July 31	HolmesCoOhio	09	08	23
Knight, Michael(Z-M)	1838	Jan. 08	HolmesCoOhio	09	08	24
Knight, Sam'l. Jr.(Z-M)	1828	Dec. 30	TuscarwsCoOh	01	06	08
Knight, Samuel(Z)	1814	Dec. 12	TuscarwsCoOh	05	09	15
Knight, William(Z)	1815	March 16	KnoxCo.,Ohio	11	05	22
Knight, William(Z)	1815	June 24	KnoxCo.,Ohio	11	06	18
Knight, William(Z-M)	1836	Nov. 02	HarrisonCoOh	03	06	09
Knisely, David(Z-M)	1833	July 20	TuscarwsCoOh	01	08	03
Knisely, David(Z-M)	1833	July 22	TuscarwsCoOh	01	08	02
Knisely, David(Z-M)	1833	July 22	TuscarwsCoOh	01	08	02
Knisely, David(Z-M)	1833	July 22	TuscarwsCoOh	01	08	02
Knisely, David(Z-M)	1833	July 22	TuscarwsCoOh	01	08	02
Knisely, David(Z-M)	1833	July 22	TuscarwsCoOh	01	08	02
Knisely, David(Z-M)	1833	July 29	TuscarwsCoOh	01	08	02
Knisely, David(Z-M)	1833	Oct. 26	TuscarwsCoOh	01	08	03
Knisely, David(Z-M)	1835	Dec. 04	TuscarwsCoOh	01	08	02
Knisely, David(Z-M)	1835	Dec. 04	TuscarwsCoOh	01	08	02
Knisely, David(Z-M)	1836	Jan. 07	TuscarwsCoOh	01	08	02
Knisely, Harrison(Z-M)	1836	June 22	TuscarwsCoOh	02	07	09
Knisely, Jno. P.(Z-M)	1830	Dec. 06	TuscarwsCoOh	02	10	25
Knouff, John(Y)	1828	Nov. 06	HarrisonCoOh	05	11	22
Knouff, Mary Ann(Z)	1810	June 04	MuskingmCoOh	15	18	12
Knowles, David(Z)	1816	Jan. 16	CoshoctnCoOh	06	09	03
Knowles, Moses(Z)	1815	Aug. 07	CoshoctnCoOh	06	09	13
Knowles, Peter(Z)	1814	Nov. 25	CoshoctnCoOh	06	08	01
Knowles, Thomas(Z)	1808	Oct. 13	MuskingmCoOh	02	02	04
Knowles, Thomas(Z)	1809	July 14	MuskingmCoOh	03	01	08
Knowls, John(Z)	1816	Jan. 16	CoshoctnCoOh	06	09	05
Knox, James of David(Z-M)	1828	Dec. 26	HolmesCoOhio	07	09	20

PURCHASER	YEAR	DATE	RESIDENCE	R	T	S
Knox, John W.(Z)	1831	Oct. 12	Morgan Co,Oh	11	11	35
Knox, Levi(Z)	1828	Dec. 24	MuskingmCoOh	10	06	06
Knox, Mathew(Z)	1816	May 11	WashCo.,Penn	05	01	05
Knox, Mathew(Z)	1817	Jan. 07	WashCo.,Penn	04	02	07
Knox, Tilghman(Z)	1817	Oct. 18	MuskingmCoOh	11	11	26
Knox, William(Y)	1831	July 25	Jeff.Co.,Oh.	04	11	18
Koce, Hugh W.(Z)	1822	June 22	MuskingmCoOh	13	11	22
Kocker, David(Z-M)	1833	June 10	CoshoctnCoOh	06	07	09
Koehler, Henry(Z-M)	1837	May 08	HolmesCoOhio	09	09	25
Koffel, Jacob(Y)	1825	Aug. 29	ColumbanCoOh	07	17	01
Koffel, John D.(Y)	1824	June 30	ColumbanCoOh	06	17	15
Koffel, Samuel(Y)	1828	Aug. 13	ColumbanCoOh	03	13	15
Kohlar, Gotlieb(Z-M)	1836	July 01	CarrollCo.,Oh	03	07	24
Kohlar, Henry(Z-M)	1836	Jan. 04	HolmesCoOhio	09	09	16
Kohlar, Henry(Z-M)	1835	Dec. 17	HolmesCoOhio	09	09	15
Kohlar, Michael(Z-M)	1835	Dec. 17	HolmesCoOhio	10	09	20
Kohlar, Michael(Z-M)	1835	Dec. 17	HolmesCoOhio	10	09	21
Kohler, Henry(Z-M)	1836	May 27	HolmesCoOhio	09	09	16
Kohler, Henry(Z-M)	1837	April 07	HolmesCoOhio	10	09	20
Kohn, Bernard(Y)	1822	Aug. 28	ColumbanCoCo	05	14	21
Kollar, Adam(Z-M)	1830	Aug. 26	TuscarwsCoOh	01	09	14
Kollar, George(Z)	1813	Nov. 05	TuscarwsCoOh	01	09	09
Kollar, George(Z)	1815	Oct. 26	TuscarwsCoOh	01	09	13
Koller, George(Z)	1805	Oct. 07	Jeff.Co.,Oh.	15	17	30
Koller, George(Z)	1808	Sept. 03	Jeff.Co.,Oh.	01	09	09
Koller, Jacob(Z)	1816	July 15	TuscarwsCoOh	01	09	08
Kolp, Jacob(Z-M)	1831	June 26	HolmesCoOhio	04	09	04
Konkle, Michael(Z)	1816	March 04	KnoxCo.,Ohio	10	07	12
Konkle, Michael(Z-M)	1828	Sept. 27	KnoxCo.,Ohio	10	07	19
Konkle, Michael(Z-M)	1836	Jan. 05	KnoxCo.,Ohio	10	07	19
Koon, Jonathan(Z-M)	1833	July 22	HolmesCoOhio	05	10	04
Koons, Henry(Z)	1832	March 08	Perry Co.,Oh	14	13	18
Koons, Samuel(Z)	1833	Oct. 02	Perry Co.,Oh	14	12	20
Korbman, Geo.(Z)	1809	May 04	TuscarwsCoOh	02	07	12
Korbman, George(Z)	1808	Nov. 17	YorkCo.,Penn	02	07	13
Kore, Christopher(Z)	1806	Oct. 07	WashngtnCoMd	03	09	13
Kore, Michael(Z)	1806	Oct. 07	WashngtnCoMd	03	09	08
Kore, Michael(Z)	1806	Oct. 07	WashngtnCoMd	03	09	01
Korn, Charles(Z-M)	1833	July 22	TuscarwsCoOh	01	08	02
Korn, Charles(Z-M)	1833	July 22	TuscarwsCoOh	01	08	02
Korn, Charles(Z-M)	1833	July 29	TuscarwsCoOh	01	08	02
Kosack, William(Z)	1816	March 07	GuernseyCoOh	03	03	01
Kosser, Joseph Jr.(Z-M)	1826	Sept. 02	HolmesCoOhio	05	08	17
Kratzer, Samuel(Z)	1806	March 29	FairfeldCoOh	10	07	25
Kreamer, Henry(Y)	1837	Sept. 20	Stark Co.,Oh	08	12	23
Kregor, Jacob(Z)	1809	Oct. 27	TuscarwsCoOh	04	08	16
Kreider, Henry(Z-M)	1839	Nov. 18	GuernseyCoOh	04	04	01
Kreider, Mary(Z-M)	1838	April 17	GuernseyCoOh	04	04	01
Kreigbaum, Conrad(Z)	1816	Aug. 31	AlleghnyCoPa	03	03	21
Kreiger, Jacob(Z-M)	1820	July 03	CoshoctnCoOh	04	08	15
Kreighbaum, Jacob(Y)	1835	June 03	Stark Co.,Oh	09	12	18
Kremer, Ferdinand(Z-M)	1836	June 27	HolmesCoOhio	09	09	15
Kremer, William(Z)	1832	Nov. 28	MuskingmCoOh	11	12	13
Krepps, George(Z)	1838	June 12	HolmesCoOhio	09	08	08
Kretzer, Henry(Z)	1810	May 11	TuscarwsCoOh	03	08	08
Krigbaum, Heny(Z-M)	1836	Sept. 10	AlleghnyCoMd	10	08	25
Krighaum, Peter(Z)	1817	Jan. 18	AlleghnyCoMd	13	11	21
Krimm, John(Z)	1812	May 30	TuscarwsCoOh	02	07	03
Kritzwizer, John C.(Z-M)	1822	Sept. 13	GuernseyCoOh	01	01	22
Kritzwozer, John C.(Z-M)	1821	Aug. 09	GuernseyCoOh	01	01	22
Kromenacker, Philip(Z-M)	1832	July 02	CoshoctnCoOh	06	04	19
Kromenacker, Philip(Z-M)	1837	Feb. 15	CoshoctnCoOh	06	04	12
Krominacker, Philip(Z-M)	1832	Dec. 28	CoshoctnCoOh	06	04	20
Krontz, Henry(Z-M)	1828	Dec. 23	HolmesCoOhio	07	09	20
Krudler, John(Y)	1825	Aug. 24	Stark Co.,Oh	06	18	21
Kuhn, Jacob(Z-M)	1832	Oct. 13	TuscarwsCoOh	03	10	20
Kuhn, John G.(Z-M)	1820	Aug. 17	TuscarwsCoOh	02	08	24
Kuhn, John G.(Z-M)	1820	Aug. 17	TuscarwsCoOh	03	08	23
Kuhn, P.(Z)	1816	Aug. 20	?	02	08	16

PURCHASER	YEAR	DATE	RESIDENCE	R	T	S
Kuhn, Philip(Z)	1808	Oct. 28	YorkCo.,Penn	02	08	16
Kuhn, Philip(Z)	1808	Oct. 28	YorkCo.,Penn	02	08	25
Kuhns, Daniel Jr.(Z)	1834	Jan. 22	GuernseyCoOh	08	08	27
Kuhns, Daniel(Z)	1836	Sept. 09	GuernseyCoOh	08	06	15
Kuhns, Geo.(Z)	1833	Oct. 15	FairfeldCoOh	15	14	04
Kuhns, Susannah(Z)	1833	April 15	Morgan Co,Oh	10	07	26
Kuiser, Dan'l.(Z-M)	1822	Dec. 05	CoshoctnCoOh	04	08	18
Kuntz, Charles(Z)	1832	Sept. 10	Morgan Co,Oh	10	06	10
Kuntz, Charles(Z)	1833	April 29	Morgan Co,Oh	10	06	10
Kuntz, David(Y)	1830	Sept. 01	RichlandCoOh	07	16	23
Kuntz, Emanuel(Y)	1826	Sept. 18	ColumbanCoOh	07	17	20
Kuntz, J.(Z-M)	1830	June 11	TuscarwsCoOh	04	08	19
Kuntz, John(Z)	1825	April 08	Morgan Co,Oh	10	07	03
Kuntz, John(Z)	1829	Dec. 14	Morgan Co,Oh	10	07	03
Kuntz, Michael(Z)	1822	April 16	BelmontCo,Oh	10	07	05
Kuntz, Michael(Z)	1827	Dec. 01	Morgan Co,Oh	10	07	05
Kuntz, Michael(Z)	1836	Jan. 05	Morgan Co,Oh	10	08	35
Kuntz, Michael(Z)	1836	Feb. 06	Morgan Co,Oh	10	08	36
Kunze, Andrew(Y)	1831	Nov. 07	Stark Co.,Oh	06	18	28
Kyser, Daniel(Z)	1813	March 24	Stark Co.,Oh	04	08	13
LaFollett, James(Z)	1836	Feb. 05	GuernseyCoOh	09	08	10
Labou, Joseph(Z-M)	1832	July 19	TuscarwsCoOh	03	09	02
Lacey, Thomas(Y)	1826	Oct. 17	BelmontCo,Oh	06	18	26
Lacey, William(Z-M)	1828	Sept. 01	MuskingmCoOh	07	03	21
Lacy, William(Z-M)	1834	Dec. 03	MuskingmCoOh	07	04	17
Lacy, William(Z-M)	1836	June 21	CoshoctnCoOh	07	04	17
Ladd, Benj'n. W.(Y)	1828	Aug. 28	Jeff.Co.,Oh.	06	12	22
Ladd,Benj'n.& H.T.Crews,Tr.(Y)	1821	Sept. 24	ColumbanCoOh	06	12	21
Ladley, Joshua(Z)	1833	Nov. 06	MuskingmCoOh	14	14	20
Ladu, Oliver P.(Z-M)	1836	May 24	HolmesCoOhio	09	09	17
Ladu, Oliviver P.(Z-M)	1835	Dec. 01	HolmesCoOhio	09	09	17
Lady, Peter(Z)	1833	Sept. 05	Morgan Co,Oh	09	07	35
Laff, Geo.(Z)	1833	Feb. 26	Perry Co.,Oh	14	12	05
Laff, George(Y)	1827	April 05	ColumbanCoOh	04	13	21
Laffee, Henry(Z)	1816	July 22	TuscarwsCoOh	01	10	08
Laffer, Henry(Z)	1815	May 09	TuscarwsCoOh	01	10	07
Lafferty, Jackson(Y)	1824	Sept. 16	AlleghnyCoPa	05	15	14
Lafferty, Jas.(Y)	1824	Sept. 16	AlleghnyCoPa	05	15	14
Lafollett, James(Z)	1836	Sept. 26	GuernseyCoOh	09	08	10
Lainey, H. P.(Z-M)	1830	Nov. 19	HarrisonCoOh	01	06	13
Laird, John Jr.(Z)	1838	Nov. 30	GuernseyCoOh	08	05	26
Laird, John(Y)	1823	May 10	ColumbanCoOh	07	18	33
Laird, Mathew(Z-M)	1828	Dec. 05	Stark Co.,Oh	01	09	04
Laird, Mathew(Z-M)	1828	Dec. 05	Stark Co.,Oh	01	09	04
Laird, Matthew(Z-M)	1830	Jan. 12	TuscarwsCoOh	01	09	04
Laird, Matthew(Z-M)	1831	March 21	TuscarwsCoOh	01	09	07
Laird, Matthew(Z-M)	1831	March 21	TuscarwsCoOh	01	09	07
Laizure, Wm.(Y)	1829	April 17	HarrisonCoOh	06	11	11
Lake, John(Z-M)	1833	July 22	GuernseyCoOh	02	03	14
Lake, John(Z-M)	1837	Dec. 05	GuernseyCoOh	02	03	14
Lake, Vincent(Z-M)	1832	May 24	LickingCo,Oh	10	02	17
Lake, Vinson(Y)	1815	July 03	MuskingmCoOh	10	02	25
Lake, William(Z)	1816	June 17	MuskingmCoOh	10	02	16
Lakin, John W.(Y)	1826	Nov. 16	BedfordCo,Pa	07	12	22
Lakin, Thos. Senr.(Y)	1826	Nov. 16	HarrisonCoOh	07	12	22
Laland, James(Z-M)	1832	Sept. 15	HolmesCoOhio	07	08	24
Lalz, John(Z)	1831	Jan. 27	Perry Co.,Oh	14	13	09
Lamb, Jacob(Z)	1816	March 27	MuskingmCoOh	14	14	10
Lamberson, Tim.(Z-M)	1830	Jan. 19	TuscarwsCoOh	02	10	17
Lambrecht, John(Z)	1808	May 17	WestmrldCoPa	01	06	02
Lamey, Wm.(Z)	1815	Dec. 13	BelmontCo,Oh	13	08	03
Lammey, Andrew(Z)	1831	Jan. 27	Morgan Co,Oh	13	09	36
Lamon, Mary(Z-M)	1827	Dec. 01	TuscarwsCoOh	04	08	15
Lanam, Brooks(Z)	1836	Sept. 01	MonroeCo.,Oh	08	07	29
Lanam, George(Z)	1836	Sept. 01	MuskingmCoOh	08	07	21
Lanam, James(Z)	1832	Oct. 15	MonroeCo.,Oh	08	07	21
Lanam, James(Z)	1836	Sept. 26	MonroeCo.,Oh	08	07	21
Lanam, Jesse(Z)	1835	Nov. 30	Morgan Co,Oh	08	07	31
Lanam, Jesse(Z)	1836	Aug. 24	Morgan Co,Oh	08	07	29

161

PURCHASER	YEAR	DATE	RESIDENCE	R	T	S
Lanam, John(Z)	1836	Jan. 18	MonroeCo.,Oh	08	07	31
Lanam, Thomas(Z)	1836	Aug. 27	Morgan Co,Oh	08	07	29
Lanana, Jas.(Z)	1827	Oct. 19	MonroeCo.,Oh	08	07	21
Lanana, John(Z)	1827	Oct. 19	MonroeCo.,Oh	08	07	21
Lanbaugh, John(Z-M)	1830	Sept. 27	TuscarwsCoOh	04	08	22
Lance, Jacob(Z)	1807	Dec. 01	MuskingmCoOh	02	08	17
Land, John(Y)	1823	May 10	ColumbanCoOh	07	18	33
Landacre, Jno.(Z)	1831	Dec. 08	Morgan Co,Oh	09	05	03
Landerman, Jno.(Z)	1831	Nov. 03	Morgan Co,Oh	13	10	28
Landerman, Peter(Z)	1836	June 15	Morgan Co,Oh	13	08	19
Landerman, Peter(Z)	1817	Feb. 18	MuskingmCoOh	12	13	23
Landes, Joseph(Z-M)	1828	July 15	TuscarwsCoOh	04	09	04
Lane, Abraham Jr.(Z-M)	1831	Oct. 03	MuskingmCoOh	05	03	06
Lane, Abraham Jr.(Z-M)	1831	July 07	MuskingmCoOh	05	03	09
Lane, Abraham(Z)	1813	Oct. 23	MuskingmCoOh	05	02	04
Lane, James(Z-M)	1829	Aug. 24	FayetteCo,Pa	04	07	09
Lane, John T.(Z)	1815	Jan. 10	MuskingmCoOh	08	02	12
Lane, John T.(Z)	1816	Jan. 06	?	10	05	14
Lane, Richard(Z)	1810	Feb. 20	MuskingmCoOh	08	02	12
Lane, Thomas(Z)	1820	July 13	MuskingmCoOh	12	12	14
Lanferty, Thomas(Z)	1807	Sept. 05	MuskingmCoOh	09	08	06
Lanferty, Thomas(Z)	1807	Nov. 30	MuskingmCoOh	09	08	01
Lanfesty, Thomas(Z)	1816	April 23	GuernseyCoOh	04	03	23
Lang, Benjamin(Y)	1830	April 27	ColumbanCoOh	07	20	05
Langley, William(Z)	1806	May 21	MuskingmCoOh	13	12	03
Langlois, Peter(Z)	1822	Nov. 06	GuernseyCoOh	10	09	12
Langstaff, Benjamin Pine(Y)	1832	Aug. 24	ColumbanCoOh	06	19	21
Langstaff, Jas. H.(Z-M)	1834	Aug. 16	MuskingmCoOh	10	03	03
Langstreth, Philip(Z)	1832	Oct. 19	Morgan Co,Oh	14	12	27
Langstreth, Philip(Z)	1832	Oct. 19	Morgan Co,Oh	14	12	27
Lanhan, John H.(Z)	1832	Nov. 12	Perry Co.,Oh	15	15	14
Lanias, Jacob(Z)	1835	May 23	MuskingmCoOh	11	11	15
Laning, Isaac(Z-M)	1820	Sept. 27	GuernseyCoOh	02	03	03
Laning, Jacob(Z-M)	1828	Feb. 12	GuernseyCoOh	02	04	08
Laning, Jacob(Z-M)	1834	Jan. 13	GuernseyCoOh	04	06	20
Laning, Jacob(Z-M)	1834	Jan. 13	GuernseyCoOh	04	06	20
Laning, Jacob(Z-M)	1835	Jan. 29	CoshoctnCoOh	04	06	20
Laning, John(Z-M)	1836	March 22	GuernseyCoOh	03	04	17
Laning, Joseph(Z-M)	1828	Dec. 10	GuernseyCoOh	02	04	23
Laning, Robert H.(Z-M)	1828	Sept. 15	GuernseyCoOh	02	04	23
Lanius, Jacob(Z)	1835	May 28	MuskingmCoOh	11	11	22
Lannam, Thomas(Z)	1817	June 13	BelmontCo,Oh	08	07	27
Lanning, Cornelius(Z)	1833	April 20	Perry Co.,Oh	15	14	18
Lanning, Ezekiel(Z-M)	1825	Feb. 25	GuernseyCoOh	02	04	23
Lanning, Isaac M.(Z-M)	1831	Sept. 26	GuernseyCoOh	02	04	16
Lanning, Isaac(Z)	1816	Nov. 25	GuernseyCoOh	02	04	23
Lanning, Jacob(Z)	1814	Sept. 12	Jeff.Co.,Oh.	02	04	10
Lanning, Jacob(Z)	1816	Sept. 30	GuernseyCoOh	02	04	09
Lanning, James(Z-M)	1838	Sept. 13	GuernseyCoOh	03	04	17
Lanning, Jas.(Z-M)	1838	Sept. 17	GuernseyCoOh	03	04	17
Lanning, John 2d(Z-M)	1828	April 01	GuernseyCoOh	01	04	06
Lanning, Joseph(Z)	1833	April 20	Perry Co.,Oh	15	14	18
Lanning, Joseph(Z)	1816	Nov. 25	Jeff.Co.,Oh.	02	05	22
Lanning, Joseph(Z)	1817	June 16	MuskingmCoOh	02	05	19
Lanning, Richard(Z)	1816	Dec. 21	Jeff.Co.,Oh.	02	05	19
Lannon, James(Z)	1833	Jan. 04	Perry Co.,Oh	15	14	18
Lantz, Andrew(Z)	1807	Nov. 24	GreenCo.,Pa.	02	03	23
Lantz, George(Z)	1807	Dec. 18	MuskingmCoOh	02	03	24
Lapin, Robeson(Z)	1831	Aug. 04	BelmontCo,Oh	13	08	32
Lappin, Robinson(Z)	1833	March 30	Morgan Co,Oh	13	08	09
Large, Eliza(Z)	1829	Feb. 13	MonroeCo.,Oh	08	07	02
Large, Robert(Z)	1829	Feb. 13	MonroeCo.,Oh	08	07	02
Large, Robert(Z)	1833	Nov. 12	MonroeCo.,Oh	08	07	02
Large, Samuel(Z)	1835	Nov. 16	MonroeCo.,Oh	08	07	03
Large, Thomas(Z)	1836	Nov. 30	MonroeCo.,Oh	08	06	05
Largente, John(Z)	1831	July 18	Morgan Co,Oh	13	09	05
Largente, John(Z)	1831	July 18	Morgan Co,Oh	13	09	06
Larison, John(Z)	1804	Nov. 19	MuskingmCoOh	12	12	17
Larison, John(Z)	1804	Nov. 19	MuskingmCoOh	13	11	10

PURCHASER	YEAR	DATE	RESIDENCE	R	T	S
Larison, John(Z)	1805	Feb. 21	MuskingmCoOh	12	11	05
Larison, Thos.(Z-M)	1837	July 10	GuernseyCoOh	03	04	22
Larkins, Edward(Z)	1814	Dec. 17	FranklinCoOh	15	15	10
Larkins, Jas. W.(Z)	1838	Feb. 17	CarrollCo,Oh	15	14	35
Larow, James(Z)	1805	Feb. 11	BelmontCo,Oh	01	01	08
Larow, John(Z)	1817	March 12	BelmontCo,Oh	01	01	13
Larr, Peter(Z)	1817	July 01	CoshoctnCoOh	08	04	02
Larrick, B.(Z)	1835	Dec. 18	GuernseyCoOh	09	08	22
Larrick, Jacob(Z)	1835	Dec. 18	GuernseyCoOh	09	08	22
Larrick, Jacob(Z)	1835	Dec. 26	GurnseyCo,Oh	09	08	21
Larrick, Jacob(Z)	1836	April 02	GuernseyCoOh	09	08	22
Larrick, Jacob(Z)	1836	Aug. 20	GuernseyCoOh	09	08	22
Larrick, Jacob(Z)	1836	Aug. 20	GuernseyCoOh	09	08	23
Larrick, Joseph(Z)	1836	Jan. 28	GuernseyCoOh	09	08	15
Larrison, James Junr.(Z)	1815	Nov. 22	LickingCo,Oh	11	04	01
Larrison, James(Z-M)	1831	Nov. 17	LickingCo,Oh	11	04	01
Larrison, Johns(Z)	1805	Nov. 20	MuskingmCoOh	12	12	32
Larrou, John(Z)	1835	Oct. 29	GuernseyCoOh	15	14	21
Larrou, John(Z)	1835	Oct. 29	GuernseyCoOh	15	14	21
Larrou, John(Z)	1835	Oct. 29	GuernseyCoOh	14	12	04
Larrow, John(Z)	1836	May 02	GuernseyCoOh	15	14	21
Larrow, John(Z)	1836	May 02	GuernseyCoOh	15	14	21
Larue, David(Z)	1838	March 26	GuernseyCoOh	08	05	23
Larue, James(Z-M)	1838	March 17	GuernseyCoOh	10	01	02
Larue, John(Z)	1825	April 14	GuernseyCoOh	11	10	20
Lash, Andrew(Y)	1831	June 28	Stark Co.,Oh	06	15	24
Lash, Isaac(Y)	1827	Oct. 13	BelmontCo,Oh	04	06	19
Lash, Isaac(Z-M)	1836	Dec. 16	Stark Co.,Oh	10	08	19
Lash, Isaac(Z-M)	1836	Dec. 16	Stark Co.,Oh	10	08	22
Lashbaugh, John(Y)	1825	March 08	ColumbanCoOh	06	17	10
Lashley, Joseph(Y)	1827	Aug. 23	BelmontCo,Oh	03	05	08
Lashley, William(Z)	1805	Sept. 06	FairfeldCoOh	14	14	09
Lass, George(Y)	1822	Sept. 24	ColumbanCoPa	04	13	35
Lasure, Abraham(Z)	1809	Oct. 09	MuskingmCoOh	14	16	09
Latchshan, Jos.(Z)	1806	Oct. 17	Ohio Co.,Vir	02	02	01
Latimer, Arthur(Y)	1828	July 04	Jeff.Co.,Oh.	03	11	34
Latimer, Arthur(Y)	1829	Dec. 07	Jeff.Co.,Oh.	03	11	11
Latimer, George(Y)	1825	Oct. 10	Jeff.Co.,Oh.	03	11	34
Latimer, George(Y)	1825	Oct. 10	Jeff.Co.,Oh.	03	11	34
Latimore, Mattaw Thomas(Y)	1833	April 19	Jeff.Co.,Oh.	03	11	12
Latimore, Robert(Z)	1815	May 13	Brooke CoVir	04	02	17
Latsch, Joseph(Z-M)	1838	March 22	KnoxCo.,Ohio	10	09	18
Latta, Edward D.(Y)	1828	May 12	ColumbanCoOh	04	13	21
Latta, Edward D.(Z)	1831	Nov. 03	Perry Co.,Oh	14	12	09
Latta, George(Z)	1831	Nov. 21	Perry Co.,Oh	14	12	04
Latta, Isaac B.(Z)	1835	Dec. 30	Perry Co.,Oh	14	12	05
Latta, Isaac Burns(Z)	1835	July 13	Perry Co.,Oh	14	12	04
Latta, James(Z-M)	1828	Nov. 17	MuskingmCoOh	06	02	17
Latta, James(Z-M)	1832	Jan. 31	LickingCo,Oh	10	03	13
Latta, John(Z)	1832	June 20	Perry Co.,Oh	14	12	04
Latta, Robert(Z)	1807	March 02	BelmontCo,Oh	10	09	32
Latta, Thomas(Z)	1808	March 17	Jeff.Co.,Oh.	05	01	08
Latterson, James(Y)	1826	Jan. 23	Jeff.Co.,Oh.	02	08	33
Lau, Lovey(Z)	1832	Oct. 24	GuernseyCoOh	08	08	27
Laubaugh, Henry(Z-M)	1827	June 14	TuscarwsCoOh	04	08	19
Laubaugh, Lewis(Z)	1810	March 30	Jeff.Co.,Oh.	04	08	12
Laubaugh, Lewis(Z)	1814	May 30	TuscarwsCoOh	04	08	12
Laubaugh, Lewis(Z-M)	1834	Jan. 28	TuscarwsCoOh	04	07	03
Laubaugh, Lewis(Z-M)	1834	Feb. 19	TuscarwsCoOh	04	07	03
Laud, John(Y)	1823	May 10	ColumbanCoOh	07	18	33
Lauderman, Peter(Z)	1816	April 27	MuskingmCoOh	11	12	31
Laughbaugh, George(Z-M)	1838	April 06	TuscarwsCoOh	04	08	24
Laughead, Elisha(Z)	1832	Oct. 25	BelmontCo,Oh	08	08	09
Laugherty, John(Z)	1834	Dec. 18	Morgan Co,Oh	10	06	22
Laughery, John(Z)	1814	July 25	WashngtnCoOh	10	06	17
Laughery, Joseph(Z)	1835	Aug. 18	Morgan Co,Oh	10	06	09
Laugheud, Wm.(Z-M)	1821	Aug. 20	KnoxCo.,Ohio	10	07	19
Laughland, John(Z-M)	1826	April 17	GuernseyCoOh	02	02	23
Laughlin, Alex'r.(Y)	1824	March 06	ColumbanCoOh	05	18	05

163

PURCHASER	YEAR	DATE	RESIDENCE	R	T	S
Laughlin, Alex.(Z-M)	1828	May 22	GuernseyCoOh	02	01	09
Laughlin, David(Z-M)	1833	April 22	HarrisonCoOh	01	06	11
Laughlin, David(Z-M)	1836	Feb. 25	HarrisonCoOh	01	06	22
Laughlin, James(Z-M)	1832	Oct. 05	CoshoctnCoOh	05	04	09
Laughlin, John(Z)	1807	March 24	FayetteCo,Pa	02	01	09
Laughlin, John(Z)	1809	Dec. 29	MuskingmCoOh	02	02	22
Laughlin, John(Z)	1812	April 17	GuernseyCoOh	02	01	09
Laughlin, Joseph(Z)	1836	Jan. 13	GuernseyCoOh	09	08	23
Laughlin, Joseph(Z)	1836	Feb. 04	GuernseyCoOh	09	08	23
Laughlin, Robert(Z)	1829	May 18	MonroeCo.,Oh	13	09	09
Laughridge, Edward(Y)	1828	July 05	HarrisonCoOh	06	12	12
Laurence, Jacob(Z-M)	1836	March 22	GuernseyCoOh	04	03	02
Laurence, John(Z-M)	1833	Sept. 27	CoshoctnCoOh	04	04	03
Lauson, William(Y)	1829	March 17	ColumbanCoOh	02	09	15
Lauver, Adam(Y)	1824	Sept. 18	TuscarwsCoOh	06	13	33
Lauver, Daniel(Z-M)	1833	Sept. 25	TuscarwsCoOh	03	09	22
Lavagood, Christian(Z)	1806	Dec. 15	NrthmbldCoVa	04	08	11
Lavagood, Jacob(Z)	1810	Nov. 26	Jeff.Co.,Oh.	03	08	16
Lavengood, Geo.(Z-M)	1833	March 27	HolmesCoOhio	05	07	15
Lavengood, Geo.(Z-M)	1833	March 27	HolmesCoOhio	05	07	06
Lavengood, Jacob(Z-M)	1833	April 08	TuscarwsCoOh	05	07	16
Lavengood, Jacob(Z-M)	1833	April 08	TuscarwsCoOh	05	07	17
Lavengood, John(Z-M)	1833	March 27	HolmesCoOhio	05	07	04
Laverg, John(Z)	1827	April 19	WashCo.,Ohio	13	09	15
Law, Ada(Z)	1832	June 02	GuernseyCoOh	08	08	02
Law, Ada(Z)	1833	March 29	GuernseyCoOh	08	08	02
Law, Esther(Z-M)	1821	Nov. 21	GuernseyCoOh	05	03	21
Law, Esther(Z-M)	1829	Aug. 20	MuskingmCoOh	05	03	21
Law, Francis(Z-M)	1835	Aug. 19	GuernseyCoOh	03	06	06
Law, John Green(Z-M)	1835	Aug. 06	TuscarwsCoOh	01	05	09
Law, John Green(Z-M)	1838	Aug. 07	TuscarwsCoOh	03	05	17
Law, John(Y)	1830	July 02	HarrisonCoOh	06	13	31
Law, John(Y)	1830	July 02	HarrisonCoOh	06	13	25
Law, John(Y)	1830	Aug. 12	HarrisonCoOh	06	13	25
Law, John(Y)	1830	Sept. 28	TuscarwsCoOh	06	13	31
Law, John(Z)	1825	Feb. 19	WashCo.,Ohio	08	05	24
Law, John(Z)	1835	Oct. 28	Perry Co.,Oh	14	12	28
Law, Matthew(Y)	1828	June 11	HarrisonCoOh	05	11	34
Law, Matthew(Y)	1831	April 02	HarrisonCoOh	06	12	22
Law, Matthew(Y)	1832	June 07	HarrisonCoOh	06	12	22
Law, R.(Z)	1815	March 14	WashCo.,Penn	15	16	35
Law, Thomas(Z-M)	1838	May 17	GuernseyCoOh	03	05	17
Law, William(Z-M)	1825	Dec. 01	MuskingmCoOh	04	02	04
Lawrence, Dan(Z)	1828	June 14	Morgan Co,Oh	10	06	30
Lawrence, David(Z-M)	1831	April 23	Jeff.Co.,Oh.	02	01	06
Lawrence, Jacob(Z-M)	1831	Sept. 09	CoshoctnCoOh	04	03	02
Lawrence, Jacob(Z-M)	1836	Jan. 20	GuernseyCoOh	04	03	02
Lawrence, Sam'l.(Z-M)	1826	Dec. 15	GuernseyCoOh	01	03	07
Lawrence, Samuel(Z)	1814	June 24	GuernseyCoOh	01	02	15
Lawrence, William(Z)	1817	March 10	MuskingmCoOh	14	15	26
Layne, John D.(Z-M)	1830	May 04	GuernseyCoOh	01	01	20
Layton, Armsted(Z-M)	1829	Jan. 03	LickingCo,Oh	11	01	21
Lazear, Joseph 3d(Z)	1811	May 28	BrookCo.,Vir	15	16	03
Lazear, Joseph third(Z)	1811	May 28	BrookCo.,Vir	15	16	03
Lazeare, Francis(Z)	1824	Nov. 30	GreeneCo.,Pa	10	09	22
Lazeare, Francis(Z)	1825	Jan. 12	GreeneCo.,Pa	10	09	22
LeCirce, John(Z)	1807	Sept. 05	MuskingmCoOh	09	08	07
LeLieorc, John(Z)	1807	Sept. 05	MuskingmCoOh	09	08	07
LeRetilley, J.(Z-M)	1830	Nov. 04	CoshoctnCoOh	07	05	10
LeSerep, M. B.(Y)	1838	July 30	?	?	?	?
Lea, John(Z)	1812	June 29	MuskingmCoOh	15	17	32
Leach, Benjamin(Z-M)	1833	Feb. 16	CoshoctnCoOh	08	06	10
Leach, Benjamin(Z-M)	1836	May 06	CoshoctnCoOh	08	06	03
Leach, Edmund R.(Z)	1817	May 01	WashCo.,Penn	11	11	32
Leach, Esther(Z-M)	1837	April 12	CoshoctnCoOh	08	06	03
Leach, John Sinnard(Z-M)	1836	Sept. 09	CoshoctnCoOh	07	07	17
Leach, John Sinnard(Z-M)	1837	April 12	CoshoctnCoOh	08	06	03
Leach, Nehemiah(Z)	1813	March 15	LickingCo,Oh	10	03	25
Leach, Nehemiah(Z)	1816	March 01	LickingCo,Oh	12	10	33

PURCHASER	YEAR	DATE	RESIDENCE	R	T	S
Leamon, Reuben(Z)	1833	May 09	Morgan Co,Oh	09	05	27
Leamon, Reuben(Z-M)	1822	July 18	GuernseyCoOh	04	01	19
Lear, Conrad(Z-M)	1822	Aug. 24	AlleghnyCoPa	07	05	16
Lear, Conrad(Z-M)	1822	Aug. 24	AlleghnyCoPa	07	05	25
Lear, Henry(Z)	1807	Jan. 02	MuskingmCoOh	14	16	08
Lear, Henry(Z)	1810	June 05	MuskingmCoOh	15	18	12
Lear, Henry(Z)	1816	June 21	MuskingmCoOh	10	01	11
Lear, Henry(Z)	1816	July 15	MuskingmCoOh	09	01	06
Lear, Henry(Z-M)	1827	March 23	LickingCo,Oh	10	01	11
Leard, George(Z-M)	1834	March 05	GuernseyCoOh	02	02	06
Leary, Morgan(Z)	1821	Dec. 26	ZanesvilleOh	13	09	17
Leatherman, Peter(Y)	1830	Dec. 01	TuscarwsCoOh	07	15	25
Leavingood, John(Z-M)	1835	Aug. 17	CoshoctnCoOh	05	07	01
Lecron, Daniel(Z)	1827	April 20	TuscarwsCoOh	03	09	10
Leddy, Andrew(Z)	1835	Feb. 25	Perry Co.,Oh	14	12	24
Leddy, Andrew(Z)	1836	Oct. 22	Perry Co.,Oh	14	12	24
Lee, Ben(Z)	1816	Sept. 30	MuskingmCoOh	12	12	12
Lee, David(Y)	1826	May 01	Jeff.Co.,Oh.	02	08	35
Lee, Ezekiel(Z)	1815	April 14	SomersetCoPa	09	05	08
Lee, Hiram(Z)	1835	Oct. 28	TrumbullCoOh	10	08	35
Lee, Hugh(Z)	1814	Dec. 07	WashCo.,Penn	11	04	04
Lee, Jesse(Z-M)	1836	Aug. 30	TuscarwsCoOh	03	05	24
Lee, John(Z)	1833	Feb. 16	BelmontCo,Oh	13	08	23
Lee, John(Z-M)	1836	June 06	TuscarwsCoOh	03	05	19
Lee, Samuel(Z-M)	1831	May 28	WashCo.,Penn	04	03	24
Lee, Thomas(Y)	1835	Oct. 13	Jeff.Co.,Oh.	03	11	18
Lee, Thomas(Y)	1835	Oct. 13	Jeff.Co.,Oh.	03	11	23
Lee, William(Z)	1827	Jan. 03	BelmontCo,Oh	12	11	27
Lee, William(Z)	1815	Feb. 08	Brooke CoVir	11	04	14
Leech, Andrew(Z-M)	1833	Sept. 13	CoshoctnCoOh	04	04	03
Leech, Archibald(Z-M)	1826	Nov. 18	Jeff.Co.,Oh.	04	06	01
Leech, Archibald(Z-M)	1832	May 22	CoshoctnCoOh	04	06	10
Leech, Jno.(Y)	1824	May 17	Jeff.Co.,Oh.	03	08	15
Leech, John(Z-M)	1835	Nov. 16	KnoxCo.,Ohio	11	08	08
Leech, Thomas(Z-M)	1836	Sept. 19	MuskingmCoOh	06	04	11
Leech, Thos.(Z)	1839	Jan. 16	MuskingmCoOh	08	06	24
Leech, Thos.(Z)	1839	Jan. 16	MuskingmCoOh	08	06	25
Leech, Thos.(Z-M)	1840	June 29	Morgan Co,Oh	03	03	15
Leech, Thos.(Z-M)	1840	July 14	Morgan Co,Oh	10	08	10
Leech, Thos.(Z-M)	1840	July 15	Morgan Co,Oh	10	09	22
Leech, Wm.(Z-M)	1833	Nov. 15	Jeff.Co.,Oh.	07	07	11
Leedom, Thomas(Z)	1810	Oct. 19	WashCo.,Penn	11	13	04
Leeper, Archibald(Z)	1837	May 13	HarrisonCoOh	08	05	22
Leeper, George B.(Z-M)	1835	Dec. 16	GuernseyCoOh	03	03	09
Leeper, James(Z)	1809	Nov. 18	WashCo.,Penn	03	03	08
Leeper, James(Z-M)	1822	April 05	GuernseyCoOh	02	03	03
Leeper, John(Z-M)	1832	May 22	GuernseyCoOh	03	03	09
Leeper, William(Y)	1831	May 30	TuscarwsCoOh	07	14	23
Leeper, William(Z)	1837	April 20	HarrisonCoOh	08	05	15
Leeper, William(Z-M)	1829	April 27	GuernseyCoOh	02	03	06
Lees, John G.(Z)	1836	Feb. 01	BelmontCo,Oh	13	08	33
Lees, John G.(Z)	1836	Feb. 01	BelmontCo,Oh	13	08	33
Leffer, Henry(Z)	1834	Feb. 22	MuskingmCoOh	13	10	09
Leffer, Henry(Z)	1834	Feb. 22	MuskingmCoOh	13	10	09
Lefferts, Jonathan(Z)	1810	Aug. 07	MuskingmCoOh	14	16	06
Leffler, Henry(Z)	1832	Dec. 05	MuskingmCoOh	13	10	09
Lefler, Adam(Z)	1814	April 08	MuskingmCoOh	11	10	08
Lefler, Adam(Z)	1814	April 26	MuskingmCoOh	13	10	09
Legg, George(Z))	1832	July 04	Morgan Co,Oh	09	05	09
Legget, Thomas(Y)	1822	Nov. 16	WashCo.,Penn	07	14	22
Leggit, Jesse(Y)	1823	June 16	Stark Co.,Oh	06	15	15
Leggit, John(Y)	1822	Dec. 04	HarrisonCoOh	07	14	22
Leggit, Joshua(Y)	1832	May 31	TuscarwsCoOh	07	14	23
Leggit, Nathan(Y)	1835	Jan. 04	TuscarwsCoOh	07	14	23
Legler, Chris.(Z-M)	1830	Jan. 29	MuskingmCoOh	06	02	07
Legler, Christoph'r.(Z-M)	1824	April 29	MuskingmCoOh	06	02	06
Lehew, Moses(Z-M)	1828	Jan. 22	MuskingmCoOh	06	02	17
Lehew, William(Z)	1816	Nov. 09	ZanesvilleOh	12	11	14
Lehr, Michael(Z-M)	1835	Aug. 27	TuscarwsCoOh	02	07	01

PURCHASER	YEAR	DATE	RESIDENCE	R	T	S
Leidle, Henry(Z)	1816	July 02	WashngtnCoOh	06	07	07
Leigh, John(Z-M)	1820	Oct. 11	LickingCo,Oh	11	03	07
Leimand, Henry(Z-M)	1831	April 18	TuscarwsCoOh	01	06	17
Leinenger, George(Z)	1806	Dec. 15	YorkCo.,Penn	04	08	01
Leinenger, George(Z)	1806	Dec. 15	YorkCo.,Penn	04	08	01
Leinerd, Henry(Z-M)	1835	Nov. 21	TuscarwsCoOh	01	06	14
Leininger, G.(Z)	1815	April 03	CoshoctnCoOh	04	05	12
Leininger, Jno.(Y)	1827	Aug. 07	Stark Co.,Oh	09	11	25
Leland, James(Z-M)	1832	Dec. 31	HolmesCoOhio	07	08	24
Lellman, Morritz(Y)	1833	Aug. 03	Stark Co.,Oh	07	20	07
Leman, Thos.(Z)	1831	March 14	Morgan Co,Oh	09	07	25
Lemart, Laben(Z)	1816	Nov. 12	FauquierCoVa	09	04	25
Lemart, Laben(Z)	1816	Nov. 12	FauquierCoVa	09	03	05
Lemasters, Abraham(Y)	1832	June 02	HarrisonCoOh	07	14	35
Lemasters, Benj.(Z-M)	1826	Oct. 20	CoshoctnCoOh	06	04	03
Lemberger, Michael(Z-M)	1837	Sept. 25	MuskingmCoOh	06	04	10
Lemert, Beverly(Z-M)	1832	May 02	MuskingmCoOh	09	03	05
Lemert, Beverly(Z-M)	1830	March 22	MuskingmCoOh	09	03	05
Lemert, Beverly(Z-M)	1836	Jan. 13	MuskingmCoOh	09	03	05
Lemert, Joshua(Z-M)	1836	Feb. 09	MuskingmCoOh	09	03	17
Lemert, Leroy(Z-M)	1832	May 10	LickingCo,Oh	10	03	02
Lemert, Leroy(Z-M)	1835	Oct. 19	LickingCo,Oh	09	03	06
Lemert, William(Z-M)	1826	April 14	CoshoctnCoOh	09	03	06
Lemington, John(Z)	1834	March 07	Perry Co.,Oh	15	14	29
Lemmon, John(Z-M)	1826	Oct. 23	Jeff.Co.,Oh.	04	06	12
Lemon, Adam(Z)	1836	Jan. 21	Perry Co.,Oh	15	15	28
Lemon, William(Z-M)	1822	Feb. 11	GuernseyCoOh	04	01	20
Lemprecht, G. C.(Z-M)	1837	April 20	MuskingmCoOh	06	03	01
Lemunyon, Cornelius(Z)	1833	Sept. 16	Perry Co.,Oh	15	14	07
Lemunyon, John(Z)	1833	Sept. 16	Perry Co.,Oh	15	14	18
Lenard, Matthew(Z-M)	1836	Aug. 01	ColumbanCoOh	08	06	09
Lenfestey, Thomas(Z-M)	1832	Oct. 15	GuernseyCoOh	01	03	05
Lenhart, Christopher(Z)	1824	May 10	MuskingmCoOh	14	15	21
Lenhart, Christopher(Z)	1824	May 10	MuskingmCoOh	14	15	21
Lenhart, Christopher(Z)	1805	Dec. 11	WestmrldCoPa	15	17	10
Lenhart, Christopher(Z)	1805	Dec. 12	WestmrldCoPa	15	17	09
Lenhart, Christopher(Z)	1812	Feb. 03	MuskingmCoOh	15	17	09
Lenhart, Peter(Z)	1815	April 12	TuscarwsCoOh	03	09	19
Lenhart, Peter(Z-M)	1835	Oct. 29	CoshoctnCoOh	05	07	12
Lenhart, Peter(Z-M)	1836	Nov. 21	CoshoctnCoOh	05	07	12
Lenpesty, Thos. Senr.(Z)	1827	April 18	GuernseyCoOh	03	02	11
Lent, Ludlow(Z-M)	1834	March 05	MuskingmCoOh	04	03	13
Lent, Tobias(Z)	1805	Dec. 31	MuskingmCoOh	01	01	09
Leonard, Amos(Z)	1815	Feb. 22	KnoxCo.,Ohio	11	04	05
Leonard, Francis D.(Z-M)	1833	July 22	TuscarwsCoOh	01	08	02
Leonard, Francis D.(Z-M)	1833	July 22	TuscarwsCoOh	01	08	02
Leonard, Joseph T.(Z-M)	1834	Nov. 06	TuscarwsCoOh	01	09	22
Leonard, Reuben(Z)	1836	Jan. 25	Perry Co.,Oh	14	12	30
Leonard, Reuben(Z)	1836	April 06	Perry Co.,Oh	15	14	23
Leonard, Sam'l.(Y)	1823	Oct. 28	WashCo.,Penn	07	11	22
Leopold, Valentine Jr.(Y)	1827	June 30	Stark Co.,Oh	09	10	01
Leoud, Wm. M.(Y)	1822	May 20	Jeff.Co.,Oh.	04	12	22
Leper, Archibald(Z)	1837	Feb. 02	HarrisonCoOh	08	05	26
Lepler, Peter(Z)	1809	May 12	MuskingmCoOh	10	06	24
Lepley, George(Z-M)	1835	Dec. 28	KnoxCo.,Ohio	10	06	15
Lepley, Jacob(Z)	1815	June 10	KnoxCo.,Ohio	11	06	19
Lepley, Jacob(Z)	1815	Nov. 02	KnoxCo.,Ohio	10	06	17
Lepley, Jacob(Z-M)	1832	Aug. 25	KnoxCo.,Ohio	10	06	17
Lepley, Jacob(Z-M)	1837	March 21	KnoxCo.,Ohio	08	07	04
Lepley, Jacob(Z-M)	1838	July 02	KnoxCo.,Ohio	08	07	01
Lepley, Jno.(Z-M)	1832	Feb. 14	KnoxCo.,Ohio	11	06	20
Lepley, John(Z)	1813	March 03	KnoxCo.,Ohio	10	05	15
Lepley, John(Z-M)	1826	Jan. 02	KnoxCo.,Ohio	08	08	21
Lepley, John(Z-M)	1832	Feb. 23	KnoxCo.,Ohio	11	06	20
Lepley, Joseph(Z)	1813	Aug. 14	KnoxCo.,Ohio	11	06	11
Lepley, Joseph(Z)	1814	March 16	?	11	06	20
Lepley, Joseph(Z-M)	1834	Dec. 13	SomersetCoPa	10	06	17
Lepley, Joseph(Z-M)	1839	June 06	SomersetCoPa	10	06	14
Lepley, Peter(Z)	1813	Aug. 09	KnoxCo.,Ohio	07	08	25

PURCHASER	YEAR	DATE	RESIDENCE	R	T	S
Lepley, Peter(Z)	1813	Nov. 03	KnoxCo.,Ohio	11	06	11
Lepley, William(Z-M)	1828	April 17	KnoxCo.,Ohio	08	08	16
Lepley, William(Z-M)	1836	Feb. 22	KnoxCo.,Ohio	08	08	17
Lepley, William(Z-M)	1836	Feb. 22	KnoxCo.,Ohio	08	08	16
Lepley, William(Z-M)	1836	Nov. 17	HolmesCoOh	08	07	02
Lepley, William(Z-M)	1836	Nov. 17	HolmesCoOhio	08	08	21
Leppincott, Eliza S.(Y)	1824	Jan. 22	Stark Co.,Oh	06	19	22
Leppincott, Rebecca(Y)	1824	Jan. 22	Stark Co.,Oh	06	18	03
Lerow, William(Z)	1825	April 19	GuernseyCoOh	11	10	21
Lesean, Frank(Z-M)	1826	Oct. 25	MuskingmCoOh	06	03	12
Leslie, Adam James(Y)	1831	July 06	SteubenvleOh	07	15	04
Leslie, Joseph(Y)	1828	Sept. 25	ColumbanCoOh	06	16	26
Lett, Aquila(Z)	1830	Nov. 27	MuskingmCoOh	11	12	26
Lett, Aquilla(Z)	1826	Nov. 14	GuernseyCoOh	11	12	26
Lett, Aquilla(Z)	1834	Nov. 29	MuskingmCoOh	11	12	25
Lett, Benj'm.(Z)	1822	June 12	BelmontCo,Oh	11	12	05
Lett, Benjamin(Z)	1829	May 15	MuskingmCoOh	11	12	05
Lett, Elijah(Z)	1832	Dec. 31	Morgan Co,Oh	10	08	18
Lett, Emanuel(Z)	1833	Jan. 02	Morgan Co,Oh	11	12	10
Lett, Emmanuel(Z)	1832	Oct. 02	MuskingmCoOh	11	12	10
Lett, James(Z)	1833	Aug. 15	MuskingmCoOh	11	12	26
Lett, Othias(Z)	1834	March 04	MuskingmCoOh	11	12	23
Lett, Richard(Z-M)	1832	April 02	GuernseyCoOh	10	09	21
Lett, Samuel(Z)	1832	Nov. 15	Morgan Co,Oh	11	12	24
Lett, Solomon(Z)	1832	Sept. 29	Morgan Co,Oh	10	08	18
Lett, Solomon(Z)	1832	Nov. 24	MuskingmCoOh	11	12	14
Lett, Solomon(Z)	1832	Dec. 10	MuskingmCoOh	11	12	14
Lett, Solomon(Z)	1833	Feb. 04	Morgan Co,Oh	10	08	18
Leuman, Jno.(Z)	1831	Nov. 14	MuskingmCoOh	12	12	21
Leutes, John(Z-M)	1832	Sept. 29	CoshoctnCoOh	08	07	08
Levengood, Jacob(Z)	1808	March 05	MuskingmCoOh	06	01	12
Levengood, Magdalen(Z)	1811	June 01	MuskingmCoOh	06	01	02
Levengood, Peter(Z)	1805	Nov. 28	GreeneCo.,Pa	07	01	11
Levengood, Peter(Z)	1808	April 23	MuskingmCoOh	06	01	08
Levengood, Peter(Z)	1816	July 27	MuskingmCoOh	06	02	18
Leverage, Benjamin(Z)	1805	Dec. 19	MuskingmCoOh	01	02	21
Levergood, John(Z)	1811	Dec. 25	TuscarwsCoOh	05	08	22
Levergood, John(Z-M)	1826	Feb. 14	HolmesCoOhio	05	08	23
Leverngood, Jacob(Z-M)	1827	Dec. 13	HarrisonCoOh	04	07	22
Levingood, Jacob(Z)	1811	March 11	MuskingmCoOh	06	01	12
Levingood, John(Z)	1811	Dec. 25	TuscarwsCoOh	05	03	22
Levingood, Peter(Z)	1810	Aug. 17	?	06	01	13
Levingston, Andrew(Z)	1810	April 09	MuskingmCoOh	10	01	01
Levingston, Jacob(Z-M)	1835	Nov. 28	LickingCo,Oh	11	03	21
Levingston, Jacob(Z-M)	1836	March 28	LickingCo,Oh	11	04	21
Levingston, Tobias(Z-M)	1833	June 03	LickingCo,Oh	10	03	24
Leviston, George(Z)	1815	Jan. 21	LickingCo,Oh	11	01	01
Leviston, George(Z-M)	1832	Aug. 20	LickingCo,Oh	11	04	21
Leviston, George(Z-M)	1837	July 08	LickingCo,Oh	10	03	05
Lewis, Isaac(Z)	1824	June 11	MuskingmCoOh	14	14	17
Lewis, J.(Z)	1815	April 29	MuskingmCoOh	13	11	01
Lewis, James(Z)	1809	March 12	BaltimreCoMd	13	12	10
Lewis, James(Z)	1809	May 04	BaltimreCoMd	13	11	01
Lewis, James(Z-M)	1837	July 06	KnoxCo.,Ohio	10	06	07
Lewis, John(Y)	1821	Nov. 09	Stark Co.,Oh	06	15	15
Lewis, John(Y)	1821	Nov. 24	Stark Co.,Oh	06	15	21
Lewis, John(Y)	1823	April 29	Stark Co.,Oh	06	15	21
Lewis, John(Y)	1829	Nov. 18	ColumbanCoOh	04	14	35
Lewis, John(Z)	1828	Oct. 01	BelmontCo,Oh	12	10	25
Lewis, John(Z-M)	1836	Oct. 28	CoshoctnCoOh	05	07	14
Lewis, Jonathan(Y)	1827	April 13	Stark Co.,Oh	06	16	28
Lewis, Jonathan(Z-M)	1832	Sept. 18	GuernseyCoOh	03	04	04
Lewis, Jonathan(Z-M)	1835	Nov. 17	GuernseyCoOh	04	04	03
Lewis, Joseph(Y)	1821	May 01	Stark Co.,Oh	06	15	20
Lewis, Joseph(Y)	1826	Nov. 10	Stark Co.,Oh	06	15	26
Lewis, Morgan(Z)	1817	Jan. 06	HarrisonCoOh	01	04	07
Lewis, Samuel(Y)	1829	Dec. 21	Stark Co.,Oh	06	15	33
Lewis, Simeon(Z-M)	1837	July 06	KnoxCo.,Ohio	10	06	07
Lewis, Thomas Senr.(Z)	1817	Jan. 06	HarrisonCoOh	01	04	07

PURCHASER	YEAR	DATE	RESIDENCE	R	T	S
Lewis, Thomas(Z-M)	1831	Nov. 15	Ohio Co.,Vir	03	04	22
Lewis, Thomas(Z-M)	1837	Sept. 04	CoshoctnCoOh	04	05	22
Lewmam, William(Z)	1830	April 24	MuskingmCoOh	12	12	21
Leyde, Fred'k.(Y)	1823	Feb. 17	WarrenCo.,Pa	05	15	17
Leyde, George(Y)	1825	Feb. 10	WashCo.,Penn	05	15	29
Lichtenberger, Jno.(Y)	1827	Nov. 17	Stark Co.,Oh	09	11	35
Lickey, John(Z-M)	1833	Feb. 04	TuscarwsCoOh	02	05	11
Ligget, Alexander(Z)	1815	Jan. 20	GreeneCo.,Pa	09	01	22
Ligget, Ezra Doty(Z-M)	1837	June 08	MuskingmCoOh	08	06	08
Ligget, James Bradford(Z-M)	1836	Jan. 19	MuskingmCoOh	07	07	19
Ligget, James Bradford(Z-M)	1836	Jan. 19	MuskingmCoOh	07	07	22
Ligget, Joseph Campbell(Z-M)	1836	Jan. 19	MuskingmCoOh	07	07	22
Lightfooter, James Jr.(Z-M)	1833	Nov. 06	PerryCo,Penn	03	07	01
Lightfooter, James Jr.(Z-M)	1833	Nov. 06	PerryCo,Penn	03	07	01
Lille, Andrew(Y)	1831	June 25	TuscarwsCoOh	07	14	35
Linch, James(Z-M)	1835	Dec. 10	GuernseyCoOh	04	03	14
Linch, James(Z-M)	1835	Dec. 10	GuernseyCoOh	05	03	10
Lind, Christly(Z-M)	1834	March 25	HolmesCoOhio	06	08	20
Lindley, Davidson(Z)	1826	April 19	GuernseyCoOh	10	09	22
Lindley, Wm. D.(Z)	1831	Dec. 22	Morgan Co,Oh	10	08	09
Lindsay, James(Y)	1821	Aug. 06	BelmontCo,Oh	04	06	25
Lightfooter, James Jr.(Z-M)	1833	Nov. 06	PerryCo,Penn	03	07	02
Lightle, Levi(Z)	1812	Jan. 18	MuskingmCoOh	15	15	06
Lightle, Levi(Z)	1814	Dec. 22	MuskingmCoOh	15	16	31
Lightle, Levi(Z)	1816	Sept. 10	MuskingmCoOh	13	09	19
Linden, George(Z)	1814	June 08	MuskingmCoOh	05	02	23
Linder, George(Z)	1814	June 08	MuskingmCoOh	05	02	23
Linder, Jacob(Z)	1813	Sept. 02	WestmrldCoPa	05	02	15
Linder, James(Z)	1814	March 19	MuskingmCoOh	05	02	23
Lindsay, John(Y)	1832	Feb. 29	TuscarwsCoOh	07	15	32
Lindsay, John(Y)	1832	Oct. 29	HarrisonCoOh	06	14	27
Lindsay, William(Z)	1810	Oct. 29	WashngtnCo ?	11	06	14
Lindsey, James(Z)	1825	July 19	MuskingmCoOh	13	11	12
Lindsey, John(Z-M)	1837	June 27	GuernseyCoOh	04	03	18
Lindsey, Joseph(Z-M)	1824	June 22	BelmontCo,Oh	04	02	19
Lindsey, Wm.(Z)	1833	Nov. 13	MuskingmCoOh	13	10	18
Lindzay, Geo. W.(Z-M)	1833	Oct. 12	CoshoctnCoOh	07	07	17
Linebach, Simon(Z-M)	1836	Nov. 02	CoshoctnCoOh	08	06	05
Linebock, Sam'l.(Z-M)	1835	Dec. 18	CoshoctnCoOh	08	06	05
Ling, John(Z-M)	1823	Nov. 27	CoshoctnCoOh	07	08	03
Ling, John(Z-M)	1833	Sept. 16	HolmesCoOhio	07	08	03
Lingenfelter, Peter(Y)	1832	Sept. 03	GuernseyCoOh	07	09	32
Lininger, George(Z)	1814	Dec. 06	TuscarwsCoOh	03	05	23
Lininger, Sam'l.(Y)	1823	July 03	Stark Co.,Oh	07	19	21
Linn, Adam(Z)	1822	Feb. 23	MuskingmCoOh	12	11	27
Linn, Hugh(Y)	1829	Dec. 09	ColumbanCoOh	04	14	17
Linn, Joseph C.(Z)	1828	Dec. 11	Morgan Co,Oh	10	06	07
Linn, Joseph Clark(Z)	1835	Dec. 02	Morgan Co,Oh	10	06	08
Linn, Martha(Z-M)	1833	Feb. 05	GuernseyCoOh	06	03	09
Linn, Robert(Z)	1811	March 02	MuskingmCoOh	12	13	15
Linn, Wm.(Z)	1812	Oct. 31	Ohio Co.,Vir	11	13	03
Linsecum, Caleb(Z)	1835	Dec. 15	MonroeCo.,Oh	08	07	32
Linsey, D.(Z)	1816	Jan. 02	WashngtnCoOh	11	11	28
Linsicorn, Caleb(Z)	1834	Jan. 15	MonroeCo.,Oh	08	07	29
Linsly, Wm.(Y)	1822	Sept. 16	Jeff.Co.,Oh.	06	12	21
Linson, William T.(Z)	1816	July 09	FairfeldCoOh	09	05	03
Lint, Christian(Z-M)	1836	Feb. 26	HolmesCoOhio	07	07	19
Lint, Daniel(Z-M)	1833	Oct. 24	HolmesCoOhio	05	07	05
Lint, Henry Jr.(Z-M)	1838	Nov. 10	HolmesCoOhio	09	03	08
Lint, Henry Junr.(Z-M)	1839	July 10	HolmesCoOhio	08	08	24
Lint, Henry Sr.(Z-M)	1838	July 11	HolmesCoOhio	08	09	03
Lint, Henry(Z-M)	1832	Dec. 31	HolmesCoOhio	07	08	01
Lint, Henry(Z-M)	1836	Nov. 16	HolmesCoOhio	06	08	11
Lint, John M.(Z-M)	1837	Feb. 09	HolmesCoOhio	07	07	17
Lint, Solomon(Z-M)	1835	May 25	HolmesCoOhio	06	09	07
Lint, Solomon(Z-M)	1839	Aug. 30	HolmesCoOhio	09	04	04
Linton, Benj'm.(Z)	1836	Oct. 10	BelmontCo,Oh	08	05	10
Linton, Benj'm.(Z)	1836	Oct. 10	BelmontCo,Oh	08	05	02
Linton, Benj'm.(Z)	1836	Oct. 10	BelmontCo,Oh	08	05	03

PURCHASER	YEAR	DATE	RESIDENCE	R	T	S
Linton, Benjamin(Z)	1836	April 09	BelmontCo,Oh	08	05	10
Linton, George(Z)	1813	Dec. 13	MuskingmCoOh	08	02	20
Linton, Joseph(Z)	1826	Oct. 04	Brooke CoVir	09	08	32
Lippitt, Joseph(Z)	1820	Aug. 03	Morgan Co,Oh	10	08	24
Lirengood, John(Z-M)	1831	May 04	HolmesCoOhio	05	08	22
Lisle, Robert(Z-M)	1830	Feb. 24	HarrisonCoOh	04	02	03
Lisle, Samuel(Z-M)	1838	May 05	HolmesCoOhio	09	08	15
Lislie, Adam James(Y)	1831	July 05	SteubenvleOh	07	16	20
Liston, John(Y)	1830	Sept. 13	HarrisonCoOh	05	12	25
Liston, John(Z)	1836	Jan. 04	HarrisonCoOh	15	14	12
Littell, Thomas(Y)	1829	Dec. 10	ColumbanCoOh	04	13	17
Littell, Thomas(Y)	1833	Feb. 21	ColumbanCoOh	04	13	17
Littick, George(Z)	1810	Aug. 25	MuskingmCoOh	06	04	12
Littick, Lott(Z-M)	1832	Dec. 13	CoshoctnCoOh	06	04	12
Littick, Noah(Z-M)	1836	Jan. 06	CoshoctnCoOh	06	04	10
Littick, Reuben(Z-M)	1835	Sept. 17	CoshoctnCoOh	06	04	11
Little, Archibald(Z)	1816	Nov. 22	SteubenvleOh	02	04	19
Little, Archibald(Z)	1816	Nov. 22	SteubenvleOh	02	04	13
Little, Archibald(Z-M)	1824	Sept. 07	GuernseyCoOh	02	04	19
Little, David(Z)	1815	June 21	ZanesvilleOh	13	11	03
Little, Edward(Z-M)	1832	Sept. 27	GuernseyCoOh	02	04	12
Little, Edward(Z-M)	1836	Sept. 17	GuernseyCoOh	02	04	12
Little, Francis(Z-M)	1830	April 08	GuernseyCoOh	02	04	19
Little, Francis(Z-M)	1835	Aug. 17	GuernseyCoOh	02	04	19
Little, Francis(Z-M)	1836	Feb. 01	GuernseyCoOh	02	04	19
Little, Geo.(Z-M)	1831	April 30	ZanesvilleOh	01	06	11
Little, George(Z-M)	1830	Dec. 06	TuscarwsCoOh	01	08	09
Little, Hugh(Y)	1832	Jan. 20	TuscarwsCoOh	07	14	34
Little, James(Z-M)	1829	June 19	HarrisonCoOh	05	07	20
Little, John(Z)	1815	Feb. 21	WashCo.,Penn	04	02	25
Little, John(Z-M)	1829	June 19	GuernseyCoOh	05	07	19
Little, Lewis(Z)	1826	Jan. 20	WashCo.,Ohio	11	11	21
Little, Nicholas(Z)	1815	Feb. 21	WashCo.,Penn	04	02	16
Little, Samuel(Y)	1826	March 14	ColumbanCoOh	03	13	31
Little, Thomas(Z)	1826	Dec. 26	Morgan Co,Oh	11	10	03
Little, Thomas(Z)	1833	Sept. 11	Morgan Co,Oh	11	10	04
Little, William(Z)	1827	Nov. 24	MuskingmCoOh	11	10	09
Little, William(Z)	1816	Nov. 22	SteubenvleOh	02	04	13
Little, William(Z-M)	1824	Oct. 26	GuernseyCoOh	02	04	19
Little, William(Z-M)	1824	Oct. 26	GuernseyCoOh	02	04	19
Little, William(Z-M)	1832	May 21	GuernseyCoOh	02	03	09
Little, William(Z-M)	1832	May 21	GuernseyCoOh	02	03	09
Little, Wm.(Z-M)	1827	Dec. 07	GuernseyCoOh	02	04	14
Littzel, Dismas(Y)	1835	June 24	Stark Co.,Oh	06	15	36
Litzenberg, Simon(Z-M)	1836	May 13	KnoxCo.,Ohio	11	08	08
Livengood, Peeter(Z)	1806	Oct. 16	MuskingmCoOh	06	01	15
Livengood, Peeter(Z)	1806	Oct. 16	MuskingmCoOh	06	01	15
Livergood, George(Y)	1831	Nov. 11	Stark Co.,Oh	09	11	26
Livergood, Jacob(Z-M)	1821	Jan. 15	TuscarwsCoOh	01	05	06
Livingston, Jacob(Y)	1828	July 14	Stark Co.,Oh	08	11	19
Livingston, John(Z)	1831	March 24	LickingCo,Oh	11	04	19
Livingston, John(Z)	1815	Jan. 04	LickingCo,Oh	10	03	24
Livingston, Jacob(Z-M)	1835	April 11	LickingCo,Oh	10	03	15
Llewellyn, William(Z)	1833	March 23	MuskingmCoOh	10	09	10
Lloyd, David(Z)	1810	Jan. 06	WashngtnCoOh	12	10	11
Lloyd, David(Z)	1810	Jan. 06	WashngtnCoOh	12	10	10
Lloyd, William(Y)	1821	Sept. 22	Ross Co.,Oh.	07	16	21
Lobdell, Jane(Z)	1815	Oct. 16	MuskingmCoOh	10	05	14
Locard, Jas. Jr.(Z-M)	1827	May 15	CoshoctnCoOh	07	05	07
Locard, Jas. Sr.(Z-M)	1827	May 15	CoshoctnCoOh	07	05	07
Lock, John(Z)	1808	Nov. 17	FredrickCoMd	01	08	08
Lock, John(Z-M)	1836	Jan. 21	LickingCo,Oh	11	03	16
Lock, William(Z-M)	1832	March 02	CoshoctnCoOh	09	05	25
Lockard, And. Jr.(Z-M)	1831	June 06	CoshoctnCoOh	07	05	20
Lockard, Andrew(Z-M)	1836	Nov. 01	KnoxCo.,Ohio	10	08	08
Lockard, James(Z-M)	1826	Aug. 14	Jeff.Co.,Oh.	10	08	09
Lockard, James(Z-M)	1833	Sept. 25	KnoxCo.,Ohio	10	08	03
Lockard, Jno.(Z-M)	1831	Dec. 01	Jeff.Co.,Oh.	05	06	24
Lockard, Jno.(Z-M)	1831	Dec. 01	Jeff.Co.,Oh.	05	06	23

PURCHASER	YEAR	DATE	RESIDENCE	R	T	S
Lockard, John(Z)	1827	Nov. 05	Jeff.Co.,Oh.	05	06	08
Lockerd, Alexander(Z-M)	1833	May 17	CoshoctnCoOh	05	06	14
Lockhart, Alexander(Z-M)	1833	July 22	HolmesCoOhio	08	09	03
Lockhart, B.(Z)	1806	March 24	WashngtnCoOh	12	11	28
Lockhart, Bird(Z)	1805	April 08	WashngtnCoOh	13	09	12
Lockman, J. Jnr.(Z)	1816	Oct. 15	GuernseyCoOh	10	07	06
Loder, A.(Z-M)	1832	Jan. 26	CoshoctnCoOh	07	05	11
Loder, A.(Z-M)	1832	Jan. 26	CoshoctnCoOh	07	05	12
Loder, Aaron(Z-M)	1825	March 23	CoshoctnCoOh	07	05	13
Loder, Aaron(Z-M)	1825	March 23	CoshoctnCoOh	07	05	13
Loder, Aaron(Z-M)	1832	May 23	CoshoctnCoOh	07	05	13
Loder, John(Z-M)	1822	July 03	CoshoctnCoOh	07	05	14
Loder, Wm.(Z-M)	1832	Jan. 26	CoshoctnCoOh	07	05	11
Loder, Wm.(Z-M)	1832	Jan. 26	CoshoctnCoOh	07	05	12
Loder, Wm.(Z-M)	1832	Feb. 08	CoshoctnCoOh	07	05	12
Lodovick, John(Y)	1825	Sept. 05	ColumbanCoOh	05	17	15
Lodowick, Sam'l.(Y)	1822	Aug. 03	ColumbanCoOh	05	17	22
Lodowick, Sam'l.(Y)	1822	Aug. 03	ColumbanCoOh	05	17	22
Logan, Alex'r.(Z)	1815	Sept. 21	PickawayCoOh	01	05	23
Logan, Edward(Z-M)	1825	May 03	AlleghnyCoPa	01	04	22
Logan, James(Z-M)	1825	May 03	AlleghnyCoPa	01	04	21
Logan, Jno.(Y)	1825	April 29	AlleghnyCoPa	07	11	21
Logan, John(Z)	1828	Feb. 28	MuskingmCoOh	12	12	21
Logan, Reuben(Z-M)	1833	April 16	CoshoctnCoOh	05	04	18
Logan, Richard(Z)	1829	Oct. 26	Jeff.Co.,Oh.	11	11	22
Logan, Robert(Y)	1826	Sept. 21	Brooke CoVir	06	13	17
Logan, Thomas(Y)	1826	Aug. 04	WashCo.,Penn	06	14	20
Logan, Thomas(Y)	1829	June 22	TuscarwsCoOh	06	14	21
Logan, William(Y)	1826	Sept. 21	Brooke CoVir	06	13	11
Logan, Wm.(Y)	1825	April 29	AlleghnyCoPa	07	11	32
Logsdon, James(Z)	1817	Jan. 08	GuernseyCoOh	06	08	13
Logue, Jno.(Z-M)	1831	Dec. 29	KnoxCo.,Ohio	11	08	14
Logue, Richard(Z-M)	1832	Feb. 04	KnoxCo.,Ohio	11	08	13
Logue, Stephen(Y)	1821	Sept. 22	ColumbanCoOh	04	17	22
Logue, Stephen(Y)	1821	Sept. 22	ColumbanCoOh	04	17	22
Lomiller, John(Z)	1806	Dec. 15	JeffsnCoPenn	04	08	13
Long, Benjamin(Y)	1829	Oct. 29	Stark Co.,Oh	07	16	25
Long, Benjamin(Y)	1831	May 19	Stark Co.,Oh	07	16	25
Long, Benjamin(Y)	1832	Sept. 28	Stark Co.,Oh	07	16	19
Long, Benjamin(Y)	1832	Oct. 19	Stark Co.,Oh	07	16	25
Long, Charles(Y)	1833	March 19	WashCo.,Penn	07	14	09
Long, Charles(Z-M)	1831	June 02	GuernseyCoOh	03	04	02
Long, Daniel(Z-M)	1831	June 08	GuernseyCoOh	03	04	02
Long, David(Z)	1836	March 08	Morgan Co,Oh	09	06	21
Long, David(Z)	1836	Dec. 26	Morgan Co,Oh	09	05	25
Long, David(Z)	1836	Dec. 26	Morgan Co,Oh	09	05	24
Long, David(Z-M)	1836	Feb. 04	MuskingmCoOh	04	05	18
Long, Frederick(Z)	1813	Nov. 11	GuernseyCoOh	04	02	04
Long, George(Y)	1832	Feb. 14	TuscarwsCoOh	07	14	36
Long, Henry(Z)	1817	Jan. 04	BelmontCo,Oh	03	03	20
Long, J.(Z)	1816	Jan. 18	GuernseyCoOh	09	06	05
Long, Jacob(Z-M)	1834	Feb. 03	BeaverCo.,Pa	03	08	17
Long, Jacob(Z-M)	1836	March 22	GuernseyCoOh	03	01	03
Long, Jacob(Z-M)	1836	Sept. 26	GuernseyCoOh	03	01	03
Long, Jacob(Z-M)	1837	March 17	TuscarwsCoOh	03	08	17
Long, James(Z-M)	1828	Dec. 12	GuernseyCoOh	01	01	21
Long, John S.(Z-M)	1837	Nov. 06	TuscarwsCoOh	03	05	13
Long, John(Y)	1828	Nov. 27	WashCo.,Penn	05	14	01
Long, Michael(Z)	1832	Dec. 07	Morgan Co,Oh	13	09	03
Long, Richard(Z)	1810	Oct. 15	GreenCo.,Pa.	10	01	02
Long, S.(Z)	1816	Jan. 18	GuernseyCoOh	09	06	05
Long, Sam'l. Alex'r.(Z)	1836	Oct. 22	Morgan Co,Oh	09	07	32
Long, Sam'l.(Y)	1828	April 28	HarrisonCoOh	05	11	12
Long, William(Y)	1827	July 21	ColumbanCoOh	05	15	33
Long, William(Z-M)	1834	Feb. 03	BeaverCo.,Pa	03	08	17
Longacre, Joseph(Z)	1805	Nov. 14	FayetteCo,Pa	15	17	07
Longshore, E.(Z)	1816	Aug. 23	DelawareCoOh	08	02	20
Longsterth, Isaac(Z)	1836	April 28	Perry Co.,Oh	14	13	27
Longstreth, Barth'm.(Z)	1814	Feb. 24	MuskingmCoOh	14	14	24

PURCHASER	YEAR	DATE	RESIDENCE	R	T	S
Longstreth, Bartholomew(Z)	1833	Feb. 07	Perry Co.,Oh	14	13	03
Longstreth, Bartholomew(Z)	1833	Sept. 13	Morgan Co,Oh	14	12	22
Longstreth, Isaac(Z)	1836	Jan. 20	Perry Co.,Oh	14	12	33
Longstreth, Isaac(Z)	1836	Sept. 19	Perry Co.,Oh	14	13	27
Longstreth, James(Z-M)	1836	Nov. 07	Jeff.Co.,Oh.	03	04	06
Longstreth, M.(Z)	1835	Jan. 06	Morgan Co,Oh	13	10	18
Longstreth, Margaret(Z)	1833	Dec. 04	Morgan Co,Oh	13	10	18
Longstreth, Margaret(Z)	1836	May 09	Morgan Co,Oh	14	12	11
Longstreth, Margaret(Z)	1814	Feb. 24	MuskingmCoOh	14	14	35
Longstreth, Michael(Z)	1832	May 26	Perry Co.,Oh	14	12	33
Longstreth, Michael(Z)	1832	Nov. 29	Perry Co.,Oh	14	12	02
Longstreth, Michael(Z)	1834	Aug. 12	Morgan Co,Oh	14	13	13
Longstreth, Michael(Z)	1835	Jan. 21	Perry Co.,Oh	14	12	04
Longstreth, Michael(Z)	1835	Oct. 01	Perry Co.,Oh	14	12	04
Longstreth, Michael(Z)	1836	March 21	Perry Co.,Oh	14	12	04
Longstreth, Michael(Z)	1836	March 21	Perry Co.,Oh	14	12	10
Longstreth, Michael(Z)	1836	May 10	Perry Co.,Oh	14	12	04
Longstreth, Michael(Z)	1836	Aug. 25	Morgan Co,Oh	14	13	35
Longstreth, Michael(Z)	1836	Dec. 13	Morgan Co,Oh	14	13	36
Longstreth, Michael(Z)	1837	April 14	Perry Co.,Oh	14	12	22
Longstreth, Michael(Z)	1838	July 23	Perry Co.,Oh	14	12	02
Longstreth, Michael(Z)	1814	Feb. 24	MuskingmCoOh	14	13	01
Longstreth, Philip(Z)	1830	March 05	MuskingmCoOh	14	14	23
Longstreth, Philip(Z)	1831	Jan. 27	Morgan Co,Oh	13	10	17
Longstreth, Philip(Z)	1831	April 07	Morgan Co,Oh	14	14	13
Longstreth, Philip(Z)	1836	April 26	Morgan Co,Oh	14	13	36
Longstreth, Philip(Z)	1836	May 09	Morgan Co,Oh	14	12	11
Longstreth, Philip(Z)	1837	May 30	Morgan Co,Oh	14	12	11
Longstreth, Philip(Z)	1814	Feb. 24	MuskingmCoOh	14	14	24
Longstreth, Sarah(Z)	1835	June 02	Perry Co.,Oh	14	12	10
Longwell, Adonijah(Z)	1816	Dec. 10	MuskingmCoOh	13	08	05
Longwell, Adonijah(Z)	1816	Dec. 10	MuskingmCoOh	13	08	08
Longwile, Henry(Z)	1817	Feb. 20	MuskingmCoOh	11	10	05
Longworth, Caleb(Z-M)	1833	March 08	GuernseyCoOh	03	01	22
Longworth, John W.(Z-M)	1833	March 08	GuernseyCoOh	03	01	22
Longworth, Robert(Z)	1821	May 05	Morgan Co,Oh	12	11	29
Longworth, Robert(Z)	1815	Nov. 28	MuskingmCoOh	12	11	04
Longworth, Robt. Jr.(Z)	1831	May 03	Morgan Co,Oh	13	10	26
Longworth, Robt.(Z)	1830	March 02	Morgan Co,Oh	11	10	29
Longworth, Robt.(Z)	1830	March 02	Morgan Co,Oh	11	10	29
Lonnon, Jonathan(Z-M)	1836	April 15	HolmesCoOhio	07	07	19
Lonnon, Richard(Z-M)	1836	Oct. 20	HolmesCoOhio	07	08	17
Loper, Enoch(Z)	1816	Nov. 06	MuskingmCoOh	12	11	28
Lopp, Henry(Z-M)	1831	Nov. 07	MuskingmCoOh	06	03	19
Lorimer, Andre(Z-M)	1829	May 27	MuskingmCoOh	14	14	12
Lorimer, Andre(Z-M)	1829	May 27	MuskingmCoOh	14	14	11
Lorimer, Andrew(Z)	1814	Nov. 26	?	06	01	21
Losey, Amos(Z-M)	1829	July 02	TuscarwsCoOh	01	05	10
Losey, Stephen(Z-M)	1832	March 07	HarrisonCoOh	01	06	17
Loue, John(Z)	1832	May 22	WashCo.,Ohio	08	05	13
Loughead, Edward(Z-M)	1836	Jan. 08	CoshoctnCoOh	05	06	07
Loughery, John(Z)	1811	July 25	WashngtnCoOh	11	10	13
Loughridge, Edward(Y)	1828	Aug. 22	Jeff.Co.,Oh.	06	12	17
Loughridge, Jas.(Y)	1829	March 13	HarrisonCoOh	06	13	03
Loughridge, Matthew(Y)	1828	June 05	HarrisonCoOh	06	12	06
Loughrige, Joseph(Y)	1836	Feb. 09	HarrisonCoOh	06	12	05
Loughrige, William(Y)	1831	March 09	HarrisonCoOh	06	12	18
Love, Alexander(Z)	1816	Sept. 27	CoshoctnCoOh	05	04	09
Love, Christopher(Y)	1823	Dec. 02	WashCo.,Penn	06	16	30
Love, Christopher(Y)	1832	April 21	Stark Co.,Oh	07	17	24
Love, Henry(Z-M)	1831	Nov. 19	KnoxCo.,Ohio	11	08	23
Love, James(Y)	1821	June 12	WashCo.,Penn	03	12	07
Love, James(Z-M)	1838	July 14	CoshoctnCoOh	04	04	13
Love, James(Z-M)	1838	Aug. 29	CoshoctnCoOh	04	04	13
Love, John(Z-M)	1837	Dec. 20	CoshoctnCoOh	04	04	03
Love, Robert(Z)	1806	Jan. 06	FairfeldCoOh	15	17	30
Love, Samuel(Y)	1826	Sept. 30	Stark Co.,Oh	07	17	25
Love, Samuel(Y)	1829	June 20	Stark Co.,Oh	07	17	25
Love, Samuel(Z-M)	1833	March 05	CoshoctnCoOh	06	06	12

PURCHASER	YEAR	DATE	RESIDENCE	R	T	S
Love, William(Z)	1834	Nov. 24	BelmontCo,Oh	08	08	36
Love, William(Z)	1834	Nov. 24	BelmontCo,Oh	08	08	36
Love, William(Z)	1816	Oct. 14	ZanesvilleOh	05	04	08
Loveland, Leonard(Z)	1817	Oct. 09	GuernseyCoOh	10	08	25
Loveless, Stephen H.(Z-M)	1827	Feb. 16	Jeff.Co.,Oh.	04	06	10
Lovet, Daniel(Z)	1812	Oct. 05	MuskingmCoOh	09	03	11
Lovett, Jonas(Z)	1817	Oct. 01	AlleghnyCoMd	07	08	20
Low, Conrad(Z)	1815	Nov. 11	WestmrldCoPa	04	09	18
Low, John(Z)	1835	July 10	WashngtnCoOh	08	05	13
Low, John(Z)	1836	Sept. 20	WashngtnCoOh	08	05	24
Low, John(Z)	1809	June 16	MuskingmCoOh	01	01	02
Low, William(Y)	1832	Oct. 01	GuernseyCoOh	04	12	34
Lowden, Robert(Z-M)	1836	Dec. 12	CoshoctnCoOh	04	05	20
Lowe, Adam(Z)	1816	Sept. 24	WestmrldCoPa	06	07	04
Lowe, Charles(Z-M)	1833	Aug. 26	MuskingmCoOh	05	03	15
Lowe, Charles(Z-M)	1833	Dec. 30	MuskingmCoOh	05	03	15
Lowe, Chas.(Z-M)	1832	Oct. 31	MuskingmCoOh	06	03	20
Lowe, Conrad(Z)	1816	Oct. 28	WestmrldCoPa	06	08	18
Lowe, Conrad(Z-M)	1835	Aug. 15	HolmesCoOhio	07	08	25
Lowe, Conrad(Z-M)	1835	Sept. 04	HolmesCoOhio	07	08	25
Lowe, Conrad(Z-M)	1835	Sept. 05	HolmesCoOhio	07	08	16
Lowe, Henry(Z)	1816	Sept. 24	WestmrldCoPa	06	07	04
Lowe, Jacob(Z)	1817	May 13	WestmrldCoPa	06	07	07
Lowe, Richard(Y)	1822	Feb. 14	ColumbanCoOh	03	11	22
Lowe, Richard(Y)	1825	March 02	ColumbanCoOh	03	11	22
Lowe, Robert(Z)	1826	June 07	Morgan Co,Oh	09	06	06
Lowe, Robert(Z)	1832	Oct. 01	Morgan Co,Oh	09	07	31
Lowe, Robert(Z)	1833	May 11	Morgan Co,Oh	09	06	06
Lower, David(Y)	1822	April 23	ColumbanCoOh	07	18	02
Lower, Mathias(Y)	1826	May 24	ColumbanCoOh	06	18	15
Lower, Matthias(Y)	1823	Oct. 22	ColumbanCoOh	06	18	27
Lower, Matthias(Y)	1824	Aug. 19	ColumbanCoOh	06	18	15
Lower, Sam'l.(Z-M)	1835	April 01	CoshoctnCoOh	05	07	18
Lower, Samuel(Z-M)	1832	Oct. 05	HolmesCoOhio	05	08	22
Lower, Samuel(Z-M)	1834	Dec. 03	CoshoctnCoOh	05	07	18
Lowery, Francis(Y)	1836	Feb. 23	Jeff.Co.,Oh.	03	11	36
Lowery, James(Y)	1835	Aug. 17	Jeff.Co.,Oh.	03	11	05
Lowery, Ruth(Y)	1834	Oct. 08	Jeff.Co.,Oh.	03	11	30
Lowery, William(Y)	1833	Sept. 10	Jeff.Co.,Oh.	03	11	06
Lowman, George(Z-M)	1826	Aug. 16	CoshoctnCoOh	07	07	24
Lowny, Sam'l.(Z-M)	1832	Jan. 27	HolmesCoOhio	04	09	08
Lowrey, Robt.(Z-M)	1830	March 16	GuernseyCoOh	02	01	13
Lowry, Alexander(Y)	1835	Aug. 22	Jeff.Co.,Oh.	03	11	06
Lowry, Alexander(Y)	1835	Dec. 02	Jeff.Co.,Oh.	03	11	06
Lowry, E.(Z)	1815	Sept. 29	GuernseyCoOh	02	01	12
Lowry, Elijah(Z)	1810	Sept. 05	FayetteCo,Pa	02	01	10
Lowry, James(Y)	1830	Jan. 05	Jeff.Co.,Oh.	03	11	06
Lowry, James(Y)	1832	June 07	Jeff.Co.,Oh.	03	11	06
Lowry, James(Z)	1835	Dec. 10	Morgan Co,Oh	10	07	10
Lowry, John(Z)	1833	Feb. 01	Perry Co,Oh	14	13	19
Lowry, John(Z-M)	1826	April 06	GuernseyCoOh	02	04	17
Lowry, John(Z-M)	1832	Nov. 24	GuernseyCoOh	02	04	17
Lowry, Samuel(Z-M)	1832	Dec. 24	GuernseyCoOh	02	01	08
Lowry, William Jr.(Z)	1810	Jan. 25	FayetteCo,Pa	08	08	08
Loyd, Joshua(Y)	1823	Sept. 01	BelmontCo,Oh	06	08	26
Lucas, Adam(Y)	1822	Oct. 12	Jeff.Co.,Oh.	04	11	36
Lucas, Adam(Y)	1825	Nov. 17	Jeff.Co.,Oh.	04	11	36
Lucas, Ruth(Z)	1834	March 01	Morgan Co,Oh	10	07	14
Luccock, Naphati(Z-M)	1835	Dec. 11	GuernseyCoOh	03	03	04
Luccock, Napthati(Z-M)	1830	Oct. 26	CoshoctnCoOh	03	04	23
Luck, Jacob(Z)	1812	June 23	TuscarwsCoOh	04	09	07
Luck, Jacob(Z)	1812	Oct. 15	TuscarwsCoOh	04	09	07
Luck, Maria(Y)	1823	May 24	Stark Co,Oh	09	11	22
Luck, Thomas(Z)	1838	Sept. 22	MuskingmCoOh	08	06	36
Luck, William(Z)	1829	Oct. 08	MuskingmCoOh	12	11	09
Lucus, Elisha(Y)	1821	Nov. 19	BelmontCo,Oh	04	06	26
Lucy, Charles(Y)	1821	Sept. 12	ColumbanCoOh	04	15	22
Lucy, Edward(Z-M)	1828	Sept. 06	GuernseyCoOh	02	03	02
Lucy, Francis(Y)	1824	May 18	ColumbanCoOh	04	14	22

PURCHASER	YEAR	DATE	RESIDENCE	R	T	S
Lucy, George(Y)	1827	Dec. 18	Jeff.Co.,Oh.	04	12	36
Ludowick, Jno.(Y)	1821	Oct. 23	ColumbanCoOh	04	16	21
Ludwig, Margaret(Z)	1825	Sept. 03	Morgan Co,Oh	09	05	12
Luellen, Zadock(Z)	1836	May 20	GuernseyCoOh	09	05	32
Lugarder, Abraham(Z)	1810	March 03	GuernseyCoOh	02	02	03
Lugenbuhl, Ulric(Y)	1834	Aug. 16	CarrollCo,Oh	05	15	06
Luke, George(Z)	1810	May 17	ChesterCo,Pa	04	09	19
Luke, George(Z)	1814	April 05	TuscarwsCoOh	05	08	18
Luke, Jno.(Z)	1815	May 31	CoshoctnCoOh	05	07	21
Luke, John(Z)	1836	Oct. 25	BelmontCo,Oh	08	05	14
Luke, John(Z)	1814	April 05	TuscarwsCoOh	05	08	12
Lukens, Charles(Z)	1833	July 27	Morgan Co,Oh	10	08	12
Lukens, Jacob C.(Z)	1837	April 06	HarrisonCoOh	08	05	26
Lukens, Jacob C.(Z)	1837	April 06	HarrisonCoOh	08	05	35
Lull, James(Z-M)	1831	July 20	MuskingmCoOh	05	03	09
Lull, James(Z-M)	1835	Sept. 05	MuskingmCoOh	04	05	19
Lull, James(Z-M)	1835	Oct. 20	MuskingmCoOm	04	05	18
Lummax, James(Z)	1835	Aug. 21	MonroeCo.,Oh	08	07	03
Lummex, James(Z)	1827	June 15	MonroeCo.,Oh	08	07	12
Lummex, James(Z)	1827	June 16	MonroeCo.,Oh	08	07	12
Lummex, James(Z)	1833	June 10	MonroeCo.,Oh	08	07	03
Lummex, James(Z)	1833	June 10	MonroeCo.,Oh	08	07	11
Lummex, James(Z)	1833	June 10	MonroeCo.,Oh	08	07	03
Lummox, James(Z)	1832	Aug. 22	MonroeCo.,Oh	08	07	11
Lummox, James(Z)	1832	Aug. 22	MonroeCo.,Oh	08	07	05
Lumnox, James(Z)	1835	Jan. 21	MonroeCo.,Oh	08	07	14
Lund, Sarah A.(Z)	1829	Sept. 17	WashCo.,Ohio	08	05	07
Luntz, David(Z-M)	1822	Dec. 05	CoshoctnCoOh	05	08	09
Luntz, David(Z-M)	1828	March 29	HolmesCoOhio	05	08	09
Luper, John(Y)	1823	Oct. 15	HarrisonCoOh	06	12	10
Lutavorn, Conrad(Z-M)	1835	Aug. 31	TuscarwsCoOh	02	10	18
Lutavorn, Conrad(Z-M)	1835	Aug. 31	TuscarwsCoOh	02	10	24
Lutes, David(Z)	1817	March 26	KnoxCo.,Ohio	10	06	15
Lutes, George(Z-M)	1832	July 05	CoshoctnCoOh	08	07	10
Lutes, John(Z-M)	1832	Oct. 06	CoshoctnCoOh	08	07	08
Luts, John(Z-M)	1837	March 06	CoshoctnCoOh	08	07	08
Lutz, John(Y)	1830	Dec. 15	Stark Co.,Oh	09	11	11
Lutz, William(Y)	1829	Aug. 01	Stark Co.,Oh	07	18	25
Luzarder, Abraham(Z)	1810	March 03	GuernseyCoOh	02	02	03
Lyans, Robert(Z-M)	1834	Dec. 18	GuernseyCoOh	03	01	13
Lyans, Thomas(Z)	1829	April 24	TuscarwsCoOh	09	06	18
Lyans, Thomas(Z-M)	1826	Feb. 17	TuscarwsCoOh	01	06	21
Lydick, William(Z)	1809	March 25	SomersetCoPa	10	07	15
Lyiter, William(Z)	1820	Aug. 30	Morgan Co,Oh	14	14	01
Lyle, Robert(Z)	1832	Nov. 08	WashCo.,Penn	10	09	25
Lyle, Robert(Z)	1815	April 17	MuskingmCoOh	15	17	11
Lyman, Jacob(Y)	1831	Aug. 06	PortageCo,Oh	10	02	11
Lyman, Samuel(Y)	1833	March 23	Stark Co.,Oh	07	20	18
Lynch, Arthur(Z-M)	1836	Dec. 20	GuernseyCoOh	05	03	11
Lynch, George(Z)	1815	May 02	MuskingmCoOh	09	04	19
Lynch, James(Z-M)	1837	Sept. 04	CoshoctnCoOh	08	07	12
Lynch, John(Z-M)	1832	June 04	GuernseyCoOh	04	03	14
Lynch, John(Z-M)	1836	Feb. 01	MuskingmCoOh	05	03	11
Lyon, James(Y)	1831	Oct. 01	GuernseyCoOh	05	11	32
Lyon, Michael(Z)	1836	May 12	Morgan Co,Oh	09	06	29
Lyon, Richard(Z)	1835	Dec. 05	Morgan Co,Oh	09	06	29
Lyon, William(Z)	1816	June 19	BelmontCo,Oh	11	05	19
Lyongs, Thomas(Z)	1827	Nov. 12	TuscarwsCoOh	01	06	20
Lyons, Elijah(Z)	1835	Nov. 12	Morgan Co,Oh	09	05	22
Lyons, James(Z-M)	1824	June 16	LickingCo,Oh	11	04	01
Lyons, James(Z-M)	1829	March 05	GuernseyCoOh	04	03	22
Lyons, John(Z)	1824	Aug. 17	BelmontCo,Oh	09	04	13
Lyons, John(Z)	1832	Aug. 24	Morgan Co,Oh	09	06	06
Lyons, John(Z-M)	1826	Jan. 10	MuskingmCoOh	09	01	07
Lyons, Jonathan(Z)	1835	Aug. 20	Morgan Co,Oh	09	06	07
Lyons, Levi(Z)	1814	Jan. 10	FrederkCoVir	09	08	35
Lyons, Robert(Z-M)	1836	April 22	WashCo.,Penn	03	06	14
Lyons, Robert(Z-M)	1837	Feb. 18	Wash.Co,Penn	03	06	14
Lyons, Thomas(Z)	1822	April 23	BelmontCo,Oh	11	12	08

PURCHASER	YEAR	DATE	RESIDENCE	R	T	S
Lyons, Thomas(Z)	1835	Nov. 24	Morgan Co,Oh	09	06	07
Lyons, Thomas(Z-M)	1827	June 16	TuscarwsCoOh	01	06	21
Lyons, Thomas(Z-M)	1830	Nov. 10	HarrisonCoOh	01	06	20
Lyons, Thomas(Z-M)	1830	Nov. 10	HarrisonCoOh	01	06	19
Lyons, William(Z)	1829	Dec. 01	LickingCo,Oh	11	04	13
Lyons, William(Z)	1833	June 05	Morgan Co,Oh	09	06	06
Lyons, William(Z-M)	1836	June 02	WashCo.,Penn	03	06	04
Macdonald, Jno.(Y)	1822	March 04	ColumbanCoOh	02	10	22
Mace, Jesse(Z)	1830	Dec. 01	MuskingmCoOh	12	12	15
Machemer, George(Y)	1822	April 04	Stark Co.,Oh	08	12	22
Machemer, George(Y)	1822	April 04	Stark Co.,Oh	08	12	22
Mackall, James(Y)	1833	Feb. 22	ColumbanCoOh	01	06	01
Mackall, James(Z-M)	1836	Nov. 16	ColumbanCoOh	09	08	05
Mackey, Alex'r.(Z)	1823	Feb. 05	GuernseyCoOh	10	09	08
Mackey, Alexander(Z)	1817	Jan. 13	AlleghnyCoPa	10	09	08
Mackey, Jane(Z)	1814	Jan. 08	MuskingmCoOh	11	13	11
Mackey, John(Z)	1819	Jan. 09	MuskingmCoOh	11	13	11
Mackey, John(Z-M)	1834	Dec. 12	HolmesCoOhio	08	09	03
Mackey, Richard(Z)	1816	Dec. 18	AlleghnyCoPa	04	02	08
Mackey, Richard(Z-M)	1830	June 08	GuernseyCoOh	04	02	08
Mackey, Robert(Z-M)	1826	May 19	WashCo.,Penn	04	02	08
Mackey, Robt.(Z-M)	1829	Dec. 18	GuernseyCoOh	04	02	09
Macy, Jacob(Z-M)	1826	April 28	Jeff.Co.,Oh.	05	06	13
Madden, Jno. B.(Z)	1834	Feb. 14	Perry Co.,Oh	15	14	20
Madden, John B.(Z)	1837	Jan. 03	Perry Co.,Oh	15	14	29
Madden, John B.(Z)	1837	Jan. 03	Perry Co.,Oh	15	14	32
Madden, John(Z-M)	1836	Oct. 07	KnoxCo.,Ohio	10	07	24
Madden, John(Z-M)	1836	Oct. 07	KnoxCo.,Ohio	10	07	17
Madden, John(Z-M)	1837	April 10	KnoxCo.,Ohio	10	07	24
Maddin, Robert(Y)	1827	Oct. 25	AlleghnyCoPa	07	11	32
Magaw, William(Z-M)	1825	Feb. 02	CoshoctnCoOh	08	04	08
Magee, James(Z-M)	1833	Feb. 22	GuernseyCoOh	04	01	13
Magee, James(Z-M)	1834	Dec. 13	GuernseyCoOh	04	01	13
Magee, James(Z-M)	1833	April 13	GuernseyCoOh	03	01	13
Magee, Peter(Z)	1814	Nov. 11	KnoxCo.,Ohio	10	07	05
Magness, Mary(Z-M)	1833	Nov. 23	CoshoctnCoOh	05	04	20
Magonegal, Hugh(Z)	1824	May 11	WashCo.,Ohio	11	13	22
Mahaffy, Samuel(Z-M)	1833	April 09	GuernseyCoOh	04	02	11
Mahen, Henry(Y)	1836	Jan. 18	BrookeCo,Vir	07	14	32
Maher, Dennis(Y)	1825	Nov. 12	Stark Co.,Oh	06	16	08
Mahon, Hugh(Z-M)	1830	Jan. 25	GuernseyCoOh	08	08	11
Mahon, James(Z)	1811	Jan. 21	Jeff.Co.,Oh.	09	08	26
Mahorney, John(Z)	1836	June 09	WashngtnCoOh	10	06	20
Mains, Alex.(Z-M)	1831	June 29	TuscarwsCoOh	01	05	20
Mains, George(Z)	1835	Jan. 27	Perry Co.,Oh	14	12	33
Mains, George(Z)	1835	June 23	Perry Co.,Oh	14	12	21
Mains, George(Z)	1837	March 13	Perry Co.,Oh	14	12	27
Mairs, Alexander(Z-M)	1832	March 21	TuscarwsCoOh	01	05	19
Mairs, Alexander(Z-M)	1832	May 22	TuscarwsCoOh	01	05	12
Mairs, Jesse(Z)	1832	April 09	Morgan Co,Oh	13	08	21
Mairs, John(Z-M)	1832	March 21	TuscarwsCoOh	01	05	12
Mairs, John(Z-M)	1832	May 22	TuscarwsCoOh	01	05	11
Mairs, John(Z-M)	1833	April 27	TuscarwsCoOh	01	05	12
Mairs, Samuel(Z-M)	1825	Feb. 23	TuscarwsCoOh	01	05	18
Majors, Greeny(Z-M)	1831	Sept. 21	Jeff.Co.,Oh.	06	07	14
Maley, John(Y)	1831	Nov. 18	ColumbanCoOh	04	14	36
Malick, Jonas(Z)	1814	Nov. 01	KnoxCo.,Ohio	10	05	09
Mall, Henry(Y)	1821	Oct. 19	ColumbanCoOh	04	16	15
Mallen, Ferdinand(Z)	1834	Aug. 05	Perry Co.,Oh	14	12	13
Mallen, Ferdinard(Z)	1835	Feb. 25	Perry Co.,Oh	14	12	01
Mallen, Michael(Z)	1835	Feb. 25	Perry Co.,Oh	14	12	01
Mallen, Michael(Z)	1835	March 09	Perry Co.,Oh	14	12	01
Mallen, Michael(Z)	1837	Jan. 21	Perry Co.,Oh	14	12	13
Mallin, Ferdinand(Z)	1837	Jan. 21	Perry Co.,Oh	14	12	13
Maloy, Alford(Z-M)	1838	Dec. 13	MuskingmCoOh	04	03	06
Maloy, James(Z-M)	1838	Oct. 01	MuskingmCoOh	04	03	05
Maloy, James(Z-M)	1838	Dec. 13	MuskingmCoOh	04	03	05
Maloy, William(Z-M)	1838	Dec. 13	MuskingmCoOh	04	03	06
Man, Jacob(Z)	1836	March 16	Perry Co.,Oh	15	14	34

PURCHASER	YEAR	DATE	RESIDENCE	R	T	S
Man, Jacob(Z)	1836	March 16	Perry Co.,Oh	15	14	27
Manatt, Robert Jr.(Z-M)	1836	Aug. 19	HolmesCoOhio	07	08	08
Manatt, Robt.(Z-M)	1830	Oct. 22	HolmesCoOhio	07	08	13
Manbeck, Benj'n.(Y)	1828	Feb. 02	HarrisonCoOh	05	12	27
Manbeck, Peter(Y)	1828	Jan. 17	HarrisonCoOh	05	12	22
Manchart, A.(Z-M)	1831	Feb. 04	TuscarwsCoOh	01	05	04
Manchester, Isaac(Z-M)	1835	June 17	WashCo.,Penn	09	09	04
Manchester, Isaac(Z-M)	1835	June 17	WashCo.,Penn	09	08	01
Manett, Robert(Z-M)	1835	Sept. 05	HolmesCoOhio	07	08	08
Manett, Robert(Z-M)	1835	Nov. 10	HolmesCoOhio	07	08	14
Manfull, Stephen(Y)	1830	March 09	ColumbanCoOh	05	15	21
Manfull, Wm.(Y)	1825	March 16	ColumbanCoOh	04	14	30
Manfull, Wm.(Y)	1828	Nov. 13	ColumbanCoOh	05	15	21
Manhall, Joseph W.(Z)	1831	June 01	GuernseyCoOh	10	09	35
Manhofer, Valentine(Z-M)	1833	Aug. 22	TuscarwsCoOh	04	07	18
Manhunter, Isaac Jnr.(Z-M)	1831	Jan. 27	HolmesCoOhio	09	08	03
Manhunter, Isaac Jnr.(Z-M)	1831	Jan. 27	HolmesCoOhio	09	08	03
Manley, Jesse(Z)	1814	Feb. 21	?	16	18	14
Manley, Robert(Y)	1828	June 28	TuscarwsCoOh	06	13	19
Manly, Jesse(Z)	1814	June 29	MuskingmCoOh	15	18	14
Mann, Archibald(Z)	1827	June 29	MuskingmCoOh	13	09	36
Mann, William(Z)	1815	Feb. 11	MuskingmCoOh	14	15	35
Mansfield, Edward(Y)	1832	March 22	Stark Co.,Oh	07	16	21
Mansfield, Edward(Y)	1832	Sept. 10	Stark Co.,Oh	07	16	21
Mansfield, John(Y)	1832	May 30	Stark Co.,Oh	07	16	21
Mansfield, John(Y)	1832	Sept. 01	Stark Co.,Oh	07	14	21
Manson, Allen(Z-M)	1832	Aug. 09	Jeff.Co.,Oh.	02	06	22
Mantoriya, Isaac(Z)	1807	May 05	MuskingmCoOh	07	08	20
Manypenny, J. W.(Z-M)	1837	Feb. 17	ZanesvilleOh	04	03	02
Mapel, Aaron(Y)	1828	Nov. 27	Jeff.Co.,Oh.	03	11	14
Mapel, Benjamin(Y)	1833	April 25	Jeff.Co.,Oh.	02	08	35
Mapel, Jacob(Z-M)	1833	Sept. 16	CoshoctnCoOh	05	04	13
Mapel, James(Y)	1836	Jan. 18	Jeff.Co.,Oh.	03	12	07
Mapes, Stephen(Z)	1805	Jan. 03	MuskingmCoOh	06	01	09
Mapes, Stephen(Z)	1806	Jan. 11	MuskingmCoOh	06	01	09
Mapes, Stephen(Z)	1809	July 14	MuskingmCoOh	06	01	09
Mapes, Wm.(Z)	1815	April 26	MuskingmCoOh	06	02	20
Maple, Abraham(Z-M)	1833	June 21	GuernseyCoOh	04	04	12
Maple, Abraham(Z-M)	1833	Dec. 09	GuernseyCoOh	04	04	12
Maple, David Senr.(Z-M)	1833	Oct. 28	Jeff.Co.,Oh.	04	04	15
Maple, David(Y)	1825	April 04	HarrisonCoOh	05	14	14
Maple, Ezekiel(Y)	1829	July 04	ColumbanCoOh	04	12	30
Maple, Isaac(Z-M)	1829	May 25	GuernseyCoOh	04	03	21
Maple, Isaac(Z-M)	1832	May 22	GuernseyCoOh	04	03	21
Maple, Jacob(Z)	1826	Jan. 12	GuernseyCoOh	10	09	09
Maple, Joseph(Z-M)	1834	Aug. 04	CoshoctnCoOh	04	04	06
Maple, Thomas(Z-M)	1835	Dec. 07	CoshoctnCoOh	04	04	07
Maple, Tunis(Y)	1827	Sept. 24	ColumbanCoOh	05	14	14
Maple, William B.(Z-M)	1836	Jan. 25	CoshoctnCoOh	04	04	18
Maple, William R.(Y)	1831	April 09	Jeff.Co.,Oh.	02	08	36
Maple, William Rich(Y)	1831	Sept. 27	Jeff.Co.,Oh.	02	08	36
Maple, William(Z-M)	1835	Nov. 07	GuernseyCoOh	04	04	22
Maple, Wm.(Z)	1812	Dec. 18	GuernseyCoOh	04	04	13
March, John(Z-M)	1833	Sept. 06	TuscarwsCoOh	04	07	17
March, John(Z-M)	1833	Sept. 06	TuscarwsCoOh	04	07	17
March, John(Z-M)	1833	Sept. 06	TuscarwsCoOh	04	07	16
Marckley, Andrew(Y)	1832	May 30	TuscarwsCoOh	07	15	31
Marckley, Sevilla(Y)	1830	June 05	HarrisonCoOh	05	13	14
Mardis, Samuel(Z-M)	1833	March 30	Jeff.Co.,Oh.	03	04	07
Mardis, Samuel(Z-M)	1838	Feb. 02	TuscarwsCoOh	03	05	25
Mardis, William(Z-M)	1838	Jan. 29	GuernseyCoOh	03	04	14
Margareidge, J. D.(Z)	1830	June 10	Morgan Co,Oh	09	06	14
Margaridge, Sim'r.(Z)	1832	Jan. 10	Morgan Co,Oh	09	05	12
Maris, John(Z-M)	1825	March 09	KnoxCo.,Ohio	10	05	02
Maris, John(Z-M)	1831	April 29	TuscarwsCoOh	01	05	09
Mark, James(Z-M)	1822	April 25	KnoxCo.,Ohio	10	08	18
Markee, Henry(Z)	1835	Nov. 17	MuskingmCoOh	11	12	27
Marker, James(Z-M)	1838	Oct. 03	CoshoctnCoOh	04	03	10
Markley, Dan'l.(Y)	1823	May 05	HarrisonCoOh	05	12	15

PURCHASER	YEAR	DATE	RESIDENCE	R	T	S
Markley, Jacob(Z-M)	1832	Oct. 18	HarrisonCoOh	03	06	04
Markley, Jacob(Z-M)	1833	Jan. 12	HarrisonCoOh	03	06	04
Markley, Joseph(Z-M)	1832	May 26	TuscarwsCoOh	03	07	23
Markley, Mathias(Z-M)	1831	Oct. 13	HarrisonCoOh	03	07	17
Markley, Solomon(Y)	1827	March 23	HarrisonCoOh	05	13	10
Markley, Solomon(Y)	1827	March 23	HarrisonCoOh	05	13	10
Markley, Solomon(Y)	1827	March 23	HarrisonCoOh	05	13	10
Markley, Solomon(Y)	1830	Aug. 25	HarrisonCoOh	05	13	04
Markley, Thomas(Z-M)	1832	Oct. 18	HarrisonCoOh	03	06	06
Marks, Benj'n.(Y)	1824	Dec. 17	HarrisonCoPa	05	16	29
Marks, Jacob(Y)	1823	June 21	Stark Co.,Oh	07	19	34
Marks, Mason(Z)	1836	Aug. 10	MuskingmCoOh	09	08	30
Marks, Mason(Z)	1836	Aug. 10	MuskingmCoOh	09	08	31
Marks, Mason(Z)	1836	Aug. 10	MuskingmCoOh	09	08	31
Marlatt, Abraham(Z-M)	1836	March 28	CoshoctnCoOh	04	05	22
Marlatt, Abraham(Z-M)	1836	April 09	GuernseyCoOh	04	05	21
Marlatt, Abraham(Z-M)	1836	Sept. 26	GuernseyCoOh	04	04	02
Marlatt, David(Z-M)	1831	Dec. 16	CoshoctnCoOh	04	05	22
Marlatt, David(Z-M)	1837	Aug. 21	CoshoctnCoOh	04	05	21
Marlatt, James(Z-M)	1833	Jan. 07	CoshoctnCoOh	04	05	22
Marlatt, James(Z-M)	1836	Sept. 26	CoshoctnCoOh	04	05	22
Marlatt, James(Z-M)	1837	Nov. 13	CoshoctnCoOh	04	05	22
Marlatt, John(Z-M)	1832	Sept. 18	GuernseyCoOh	04	04	02
Marlatt, John(Z-M)	1836	Jan. 11	GuernseyCoOh	04	04	02
Marlenee, Benjamin(Z)	1836	April 04	MuskingmCoOh	09	08	30
Marlenee, John W.(Z)	1836	April 04	MuskingmCoOh	09	08	30
Marlow, Peter(Z)	1828	Aug. 19	GuernseyCoOh	02	04	08
Marlow, Peter(Z-M)	1825	July 15	GuernseyCoOh	02	04	08
Marlow, Peter(Z-M)	1833	Jan. 09	GuernseyCoOh	02	04	03
Marlow, Samuel(Z-M)	1833	Aug. 26	GuernseyCoOh	02	06	01
Marlow, Thomas(Z)	1837	March 15	GuernseyCoOh	08	07	04
Marlow, Thomas(Z)	1837	March 15	GuernseyCoOh	08	07	23
Marolf, Abraham(Y)	1826	Oct. 26	ColumbanCoOh	05	17	09
Marple, David J.(Z)	1805	Sept. 13	ZanesvilleOh	13	11	07
Marple, David J.(Z)	1805	Sept. 13	ZanesvilleOh	13	11	08
Marple, David J.(Z)	1812	July 23	MuskingmCoOh	08	04	22
Marple, David J.(Z)	1812	July 23	MuskingmCoOh	08	04	22
Marple, David J.(Z)	1805	Dec. 27	MuskingmCoOh	15	18	15
Marple, David J.(Z)	1807	July 17	MuskingmCoOh	08	08	03
Marquand, Chas.(Z-M)	1821	Aug. 13	MuskingmCoOh	05	03	04
Marquand, Chas.(Z-M)	1835	Dec. 29	MuskingmCoOh	05	03	05
Marquand, Chas.(Z-M)	1835	Dec. 29	MuskingmCoOh	05	03	05
Marquand, Geo. L.(Z-M)	1839	March 13	GuernseyCoOh	03	03	15
Marquand, John(Z-M)	1832	May 23	GuernseyCoOh	03	03	06
Marquand, John(Z-M)	1837	Jan. 09	GuernseyCoOh	03	03	15
Marquand, Solomon(Z-M)	1837	Jan. 30	MuskingmCoOh	04	04	09
Marquard, John(Z-M)	1835	Oct. 29	TuscarwsCoOh	04	07	15
Marquard, Peter(Z-M)	1835	March 25	MuskingmCoOh	05	04	17
Marquard, Peter(Z-M)	1835	March 25	MuskingmCoOh	05	04	18
Marquis, James E.(Z)	1825	Jan. 28	BelmontCo,Oh	12	10	15
Marquis, John Junr.(Z)	1833	April 02	Morgan Co,Oh	09	06	07
Marquis, Nancy(Z)	1833	Aug. 07	Morgan Co,Oh	09	06	07
Marquis, Sam'l.(Z)	1824	May 10	Morgan Co,Oh	09	06	07
Marquis, William(Z)	1815	July 06	WashngtnCo ?	10	08	10
Marriott, Daniel(Z)	1807	Aug. 15	MuskingmCoOh	03	01	21
Marriott, Homewood(Z)	1815	Nov. 22	LickingCo,Oh	11	04	02
Marriott, Homewood(Z)	1815	Nov. 22	LickingCo,Oh	11	04	09
Marriott, Homewood(Z)	1815	Nov. 22	LickingCo,Oh	11	04	02
Marriott, Homewood(Z-M)	1837	April 07	LickingCo,Oh	11	04	19
Marrison, Geo. W.(Z)	1833	Jan. 21	GuernseyCoOh	09	07	13
Marsh, Adam(Y)	1828	Nov. 19	Stark Co.,Oh	10	02	14
Marsh, Cyrus(Z)	1813	Dec. 20	CoshoctnCoOh	05	04	04
Marsh, George(Y)	1835	April 09	Stark Co.,Oh	04	12	11
Marsh, John N.(Y)	1827	March 05	Jeff.Co.,Oh.	07	12	36
Marsh, Joseph(Y)	1830	Aug. 13	GuernseyCoOh	07	09	21
Marsh, Joseph(Z)	1836	Aug. 05	GuernseyCoOh	08	06	21
Marsh, Lemuel(Z)	1813	Jan. 18	CoshoctnCoOh	05	04	03
Marshal, Elizabeth(Z)	1835	Feb. 13	WashngtnCoOh	10	09	23
Marshall, Benj'n.(Y)	1828	March 20	ColumbanCoOh	03	12	24

PURCHASER	YEAR	DATE	RESIDENCE	R	T	S
Marshall, Daniel(Z)	1835	May 20	CarrolCo.,Oh	14	12	30
Marshall, Elizabeth(Z-M)	1836	Nov. 19	CoshoctnCoOh	08	07	07
Marshall, Gideon G.(Z)	1834	Feb. 24	Morgan Co,Oh	09	06	04
Marshall, Gideon G.(Z)	1836	March 10	Morgan Co,Oh	09	06	04
Marshall, James(Z)	1822	Nov. 02	GuernseyCoOh	10	08	09
Marshall, John(Y)	1828	Dec. 15	ColumbanCoOh	03	12	32
Marshall, John(Y)	1833	Feb. 14	Brooke CoVir	04	12	17
Marshall, Jos'h.(Z)	1817	Oct. 04	HarrisonCoOh	06	06	10
Marshall, Joseph(Z-M)	1831	June 08	CoshoctnCoOh	06	06	01
Marshall, Mary(Y)	1831	March 16	ColumbanCoOh	03	12	22
Marshall, Mary(Z)	1815	Dec. 09	BelmontCo,Oh	03	02	12
Marshall, Owen(Z-M)	1830	April 22	CoshoctnCoOh	07	05	16
Marshall, Owen(Z-M)	1832	Sept. 21	CoshoctnCoOh	07	05	16
Marshall, Owen(Z-M)	1836	Nov. 19	CoshoctnCoOh	08	07	07
Marshall, Peter(Y)	1826	Nov. 09	Stark Co.,Oh	07	18	31
Marshall, Robert(Y)	1821	Oct. 02	WestmrldCoPa	04	14	22
Marshall, Robert(Y)	1824	May 11	TuscarwsCoOh	06	14	35
Marshall, Robert(Y)	1828	Feb. 21	ColumbanCoOh	03	12	24
Marshall, Robert(Y)	1831	Aug. 16	TuscarwsCoOh	06	14	35
Marshall, Robert(Z)	1816	Sept. 28	WestmrldCoPa	10	09	35
Marshall, Sam'l.(Y)	1824	March 02	GuernseyCoOh	07	09	15
Marshall, Samuel(Z)	1836	May 18	GuernseyCoOh	08	06	14
Marshall, Samuel(Z)	1836	May 18	GuernseyCoOh	08	06	14
Marshall, Sarah(Y)	1824	Aug. 10	WashCo.,Penn	03	05	34
Marshall, Thos.(Z)	1831	Dec. 27	MuskingmCoOh	11	12	11
Marshall, Thos.(Z)	1832	Jan. 30	MuskingmCoOh	11	12	15
Marshall, William(Z-M)	1827	Feb. 21	WashCo.,Penn	05	02	01
Marshall, Wm.(Y)	1824	Feb. 23	GuernseyCoOh	07	09	15
Marshel, Archibald(Z-M)	1836	Sept. 03	CoshoctnCoOh	08	07	07
Marshel, Elizabeth(Z-M)	1836	Sept. 03	CoshoctnCoOh	08	07	07
Marten, Robert(Z)	1836	Sept. 05	Morgan Co,Oh	10	07	34
Martin, Abm.(Z)	1832	Aug. 16	Perry Co.,Oh	14	14	31
Martin, Abraham(Z)	1833	Dec. 04	Perry Co.,Oh	14	14	30
Martin, Alexander(Z)	1829	April 27	Morgan Co,Oh	11	11	15
Martin, Alexander(Z)	1832	March 08	Morgan Co,Oh	11	11	10
Martin, Andrew(Z)	1835	Dec. 22	MuskingmCoOh	09	05	19
Martin, Andrew(Z)	1836	Jan. 11	MuskingmCoOh	09	05	29
Martin, Andrew(Z)	1836	Jan. 11	MuskingmCoOh	09	05	29
Martin, Andrew(Z)	1836	Feb. 16	MuskingmCoOh	09	05	30
Martin, David Sr.(Z)	1828	Nov. 11	MuskingmCoOh	13	11	23
Martin, G.(Z)	1816	Jan. 04	PutnamCoOhio	14	14	30
Martin, Geo.(Z)	1815	March 08	MuskingmCoOh	10	03	02
Martin, Geo.(Z)	1816	Jan. 16	PutnamCoOhio	14	13	20
Martin, George(Y)	1823	July 03	TuscarwsCoOh	07	15	02
Martin, Hugh(Y)	1821	Sept. 26	ColumbanCoOh	04	16	21
Martin, Hugh(Z)	1815	Nov. 03	GuernseyCoOh	05	01	04
Martin, Isaac(Z)	1821	Aug. 27	Jeff.Co.,Oh.	12	10	27
Martin, Israel(Z)	1814	Jan. 26	MuskingmCoOh	14	15	28
Martin, Jacob Senr.(Z)	1809	Aug. 11	MuskingmCoOh	15	17	03
Martin, James(Z-M)	1824	Dec. 15	TuscarwsCoOh	01	06	19
Martin, James(Z-M)	1826	Feb. 23	TuscarwsCoOh	01	06	11
Martin, James(Z-M)	1833	April 06	CarrollCo,Oh	03	06	06
Martin, James(Z-M)	1835	Sept. 07	TuscarwsCoOh	03	06	14
Martin, James(Z-M)	1836	Jan. 22	HarrisonCoOh	01	06	24
Martin, Jno.(Z-M)	1831	Nov. 18	KnoxCo.,Ohio	08	05	20
Martin, John(Y)	1821	Sept. 24	ColumbanCoOh	04	16	21
Martin, John(Y)	1825	Nov. 07	WashCo.,Penn	03	11	22
Martin, John(Y)	1829	April 23	Jeff.Co.,Oh.	03	11	21
Martin, John(Z-M)	1823	April 17	GuernseyCoOh	02	04	25
Martin, John(Z-M)	1829	May 27	GuernseyCoOh	02	03	06
Martin, John(Z-M)	1832	June 19	GuernseyCoOh	03	04	21
Martin, John(Z-M)	1833	April 04	GuernseyCoOh	02	03	05
Martin, John(Z-M)	1833	July 23	LickingCo,Oh	10	04	19
Martin, John(Z-M)	1833	July 23	LickingCo,Oh	10	04	19
Martin, John(Z-M)	1833	Dec. 16	LickingCo,Oh	10	04	19
Martin, John(Z-M)	1836	Jan. 15	LickingCo,Oh	10	04	19
Martin, John(Z-M)	1836	Feb. 23	GuernseyCoOh	03	04	21
Martin, John(Z-M)	1832	Feb. 21	GuernseyCoOh	02	03	05
Martin, Joseph(Z)	1835	Dec. 15	BelmontCo,Oh	08	06	22

PURCHASER	YEAR	DATE	RESIDENCE	R	T	S
Martin, Joseph(Z)	1837	May 11	MonroeCo.,Oh	08	06	22
Martin, Joseph(Z)	1837	July 05	MonroeCo.,Oh	08	06	22
Martin, Joshua(Y)	1824	April 15	HarrisonCoOh	05	12	24
Martin, Josiah(Z)	1827	Oct. 08	BelmontCo,Oh	13	09	24
Martin, Mahlon(Y)	1832	May 30	ColumbanCoOh	02	09	20
Martin, Mahlon(Y)	1832	May 30	ColumbanCoOh	02	09	20
Martin, Robert(Y)	1830	June 11	WashCo.,Penn	03	11	24
Martin, Robert(Y)	1830	July 03	WashCo.,Penn	03	11	24
Martin, Robert(Y)	1833	June 18	WashCo.,Penn	03	11	24
Martin, Robert(Z)	1833	March 04	GuernseyCoOh	13	08	05
Martin, Robert(Z)	1835	Aug. 06	Morgan Co,Oh	10	07	33
Martin, Samuel(Y)	1822	Aug. 19	WashCo.,Penn	07	11	34
Martin, Samuel(Y)	1822	Sept. 10	WashCo.,Penn	07	11	22
Martin, Thomas(Z)	1828	July 14	Morgan Co,Oh	11	11	33
Martin, William(Z)	1832	Sept. 10	Perry Co.,Oh	14	14	29
Martin, William(Z)	1834	Jan. 16	Morgan Co,Oh	13	08	22
Martin, William(Z)	1815	Nov. 04	MuskingmCoOh	14	14	33
Martin, Wm.(Z)	1828	Aug. 25	BelmontCo,Oh	13	08	21
Martin, Wm.(Z)	1833	Nov. 18	Perry Co.,Oh	14	14	29
Martin, Wm.(Z-M)	1831	Aug. 01	GuernseyCoOh	03	04	21
Martz, Michael(Y)	1833	Feb. 14	Stark Co.,Oh	06	16	34
Martz, Michael(Y)	1835	March 02	CarrollCo,Oh	06	16	34
Marvey, Enoch(Z)	1812	March 16	WashngtnCoOh	11	13	08
Maskimmon, John(Z)	1814	Dec. 15	CoshoctnCoOh	04	04	14
Mason, George(Y)	1826	Oct. 10	BelmontCo,Oh	03	05	02
Mason, J.(Z)	1815	Dec. 16	MuskingmCoOh	12	12	02
Mason, Jacob(Z)	1831	Feb. 26	Morgan Co,Oh	10	08	12
Massey, Enoch(Z)	1812	March 16	WashngtnCoOh	11	13	08
Massey, Richard(Z)	1828	April 23	Morgan Co,Oh	13	09	15
Massey, William(Z)	1816	Nov. 18	ChesterCo,Pa	13	09	24
Massey, William(Z)	1816	Nov. 18	ChesterCo,Pa	13	09	13
Massey, Wm.(Z)	1816	Nov. 28	ChesterCo,Pa	13	09	23
Masten, William(Z-M)	1833	April 30	CoshoctnCoOh	07	05	12
Masters, Azariah(Z-M)	1833	March 07	TuscarwsCoOh	04	07	17
Masters, Azariah(Z-M)	1833	Sept. 26	TuscarwsCoOh	04	07	17
Masters, Henry(Z-M)	1831	March 24	GuernseyCoOh	01	03	04
Masters, Henry(Z-M)	1832	Oct. 11	GuernseyCoOh	01	03	04
Masters, Isaac(Y)	1830	April 17	WestmrldCoPa	05	15	35
Masters, Joseph(Y)	1822	Dec. 31	TuscarwsCoOh	07	14	18
Masters, Joseph(Z-M)	1834	Nov. 01	TuscarwsCoOh	04	07	25
Masters, Richard(Y)	1826	May 30	GuernseyCoOh	07	10	24
Masters, Samuel(Z-M)	1834	Nov. 01	TuscarwsCoOh	04	07	25
Masters, William(Y)	1826	May 02	TuscarwsCoOh	07	15	32
Masters, William(Y)	1826	May 30	GuernseyCoOh	07	10	24
Masterson, Andrew(Z)	1837	Jan. 16	Morgan Co,Oh	14	12	12
Masterson, Charles(Z)	1836	Jan. 12	Morgan Co,Oh	13	08	05
Masterson, Patrick(Z)	1832	Sept. 13	Morgan Co,Oh	13	08	08
Masterson, Patrick(Z)	1833	Aug. 17	Morgan Co,Oh	13	08	07
Masterson, Patrick(Z)	1836	Jan. 25	Morgan Co,Oh	14	12	12
Mastin, Ann(Z-M)	1835	Dec. 22	GuernseyCoOh	02	01	14
Mastin, James(Z-M)	1836	Dec. 06	CarrollCo,Oh	03	07	22
Maston, Benjamin(Z)	1825	May 04	FayetteCo,Pa	07	05	08
Matheney, Eliab(Z)	1837	Sept. 18	MonroeCo.,Oh	08	06	29
Matheny, Andrew(Z)	1832	June 04	Morgan Co,Oh	10	07	17
Matheny, Benjamin(Z)	1836	Jan. 07	MonroeCo.,Oh	08	07	17
Matheny, Benjamin(Z)	1836	Jan. 07	MonroeCo.,Oh	08	07	18
Matheny, Cyrus(Z)	1827	June 18	Morgan Co,Oh	08	07	30
Matheou, John(Z)	1806	Feb. 07	MuskingmCoOh	14	15	01
Mather, John(Y)	1827	May 26	ColumbanCoOh	05	18	28
Mather, John(Y)	1827	May 26	ColumbanCoOh	05	18	27
Mathers, Henry(Z-M)	1833	Jan. 19	GuernseyCoOh	03	03	15
Mathers, Henry(Z-M)	1838	Oct. 27	GuernseyCoOh	03	03	16
Mathers, Samuel(Z)	1808	April 26	MuskingmCoOh	03	03	18
Mathers, William(Y)	1834	May 15	BelmontCo,Oh	07	12	35
Mathews, Christian(Z-M)	1833	April 01	LickingCo,Oh	10	03	04
Mathews, George(Z)	1804	Nov. 21	MuskingmCoOh	14	15	11
Mathews, H.(Z-M)	1831	Oct. 06	GuernseyCoOh	03	03	16
Mathews, Increase(Z)	1804	Dec. 01	MuskingmCoOh	14	15	09
Mathews, Increase(Z)	1804	Dec. 01	MuskingmCoOh	14	15	09

PURCHASER	YEAR	DATE	RESIDENCE	R	T	S
Mathews, Increase(Z)	1805	Nov. 19	MuskingmCoOh	15	16	07
Mathews, Increase(Z)	1805	Nov. 19	MuskingmCoOh	15	16	14
Mathews, Increase(Z)	1805	Nov. 19	MuskingmCoOh	14	14	03
Mathews, Increase(Z)	1811	Jan. 05	Springfield?	15	16	07
Mathews, Increase(Z)	1811	March 21	MuskingmCoOh	14	14	03
Mathews, James(Z-M)	1836	May 18	LickingCo,Oh	10	03	05
Mathews, John B.(Z)	1814	Nov. 29	MuskingmCoOh	14	15	12
Mathews, John(Z)	1804	Dec. 06	MuskingmCoOh	13	11	05
Mathews, John(Z)	1811	May 07	MuskingmCoOh	13	11	06
Mathews, John(Z)	1815	May 19	MuskingmCoOh	13	11	06
Mathews, John(Z-M)	1838	Sept. 21	RichlandCoOh	09	08	25
Mathews, Paul(Z)	1816	April 12	WashCo.,Penn	01	04	17
Mathias, Leonard(Z-M)	1832	Dec. 28	TuscarwsCoOh	02	07	13
Mathias, Leonard(Z-M)	1832	Dec. 28	TuscarwsCoOh	02	07	14
Mathias, Peter(Z-M)	1833	Jan. 25	TuscarwsCoOh	02	07	14
Matlock, Thomas(Z)	1835	March 07	BelmontCo,Oh	08	08	29
Matson, Daniel(Z)	1836	April 18	AthensCoOhio	13	08	28
Matson, Enos(Y)	1822	Sept. 21	BelmontCo,Oh	04	06	15
Matterson, Patrick(Z)	1836	Oct. 22	Morgan Co,Oh	13	08	07
Matthews, Christian(Z-M)	1832	Nov. 05	LickingCo,Oh	10	03	04
Matthews, John Jr.(Z)	1836	July 19	WashngtnCoOh	08	05	34
Matthews, John Jr.(Z)	1836	July 19	WashngtnCoOh	08	05	33
Matthews, Levi(Y)	1836	Jan. 09	SteubenvleOh	03	12	02
Mattock, Thomas(Z-M)	1827	June 23	MuskingmCoOh	11	05	21
Mattucks, Edward(Z-M)	1830	Jan. 18	HolmesCoOhio	07	07	12
Matzenbuch, John(Y)	1821	Aug. 06	WashngtnCoMd	05	17	33
Mauer, John(Z)	1814	Dec. 09	MuskingmCoOh	11	13	31
Mauk, Anthony Jr.(Z)	1836	Sept. 26	MuskingmCoOh	15	14	27
Mauk, Anthony(Z)	1837	June 26	MuskingmCoOh	14	12	34
Mauk, Anthony(Z)	1837	June 26	MuskingmCoOh	14	12	35
Mauk, F.(Z-M)	1837	July 11	TuscarwsCoOh	05	07	18
Mauk, George(Z)	1815	Jan. 30	MuskingmCoOh	14	15	32
Mauk, George(Z)	1815	Oct. 25	MuskingmCoOh	14	15	32
Mauk, Jacob(Z)	1816	Feb. 16	FrederkCoVir	14	13	13
Mauk, Jacob(Z)	1816	Feb. 16	FrederkCoVir	13	09	18
Mauk, John(Z-M)	1832	Nov. 08	TuscarwsCoOh	03	10	20
Mauk, John(Z-M)	1832	Nov. 08	TuscarwsCoOh	02	10	16
Mauk, Mathias(Z)	1830	Dec. 11	Perry Co.,Oh	14	14	19
Maurer, Jacob(Z-M)	1837	Jan. 25	TuscarwsCoOh	03	08	25
Maurer, Joseph(Z)	1832	Aug. 27	Morgan Co,Oh	13	10	21
Mavay, Enoch(Z)	1812	March 16	WashngtnCoOh	11	13	08
Mavis, Henry(Z-M)	1836	Aug. 05	CoshoctnCoOh	10	05	12
Maxfield, Emry(Z-M)	1835	Oct. 03	CoshoctnCoOh	04	06	12
Maxfield, T.(Z-M)	1829	Dec. 21	MuskingmCoOh	05	02	01
Maxon, James(Z-M)	1824	March 29	CoshoctnCoOh	07	07	23
Maxon, Nathan(Z)	1825	May 05	BelmontCo,Oh	12	09	13
Maxwell, Alex'r.(Y)	1825	March 07	Stark Co.,Oh	07	20	04
Maxwell, David(Z-M)	1832	Sept. 05	MuskingmCoOh	03	01	04
Maxwell, Henry(Y)	1829	Dec. 08	HarrisonCoOh	05	11	20
Maxwell, John(Z)	1827	Feb. 21	Morgan Co,Oh	10	08	34
Maxwell, Joseph(Z-M)	1837	Jan. 04	MuskingmCoOh	03	01	04
Maxwell, Morgan(Z)	1826	April 18	Morgan Co,Oh	10	07	30
Maxwell, Robert(Y)	1829	Dec. 11	HarrisonCoOh	05	11	27
Maxwell, Robert(Y)	1831	April 16	ColumbanCoOh	04	13	24
Maxwell, Robert(Y)	1828	Aug. 08	Jeff.Co.,Oh	01	04	25
May, Alexander(Z)	1816	April 09	WashCo.,Penn	05	02	22
May, Ezra(Z)	1806	Aug. 01	MuskingmCoOh	10	09	32
May, Ezra(Z)	1806	Oct. 03	BroomCo,N.Y.	10	09	32
May, George(Y)	1829	March 17	FayetteCo,Pa	07	12	29
May, George(Y)	1829	March 17	FayetteCo,Pa	07	12	28
May, J.(Z)	1817	June 17	WashngtnCoOh	08	06	31
May, John(Z)	1815	Dec. 13	SomersetCoPa	06	09	14
Mayhaugh, William(Z)	1832	April 14	Morgan Co,Oh	13	09	12
Mayhew, Frederick(Z)	1836	Oct. 15	Morgan Co,Oh	09	06	27
Mayhew, Frederick(Z)	1836	Oct. 15	Morgan Co,Oh	09	06	26
Mayhew, Frederick(Z)	1836	Oct. 21	Morgan Co,Oh	09	06	35
Mayhew, John(Z)	1826	Feb. 13	Jeff.Co.,Oh.	11	10	21
Mayhew, Richard(Z)	1816	Nov. 23	WashCo.,Penn	02	04	21
Mayhorne, Rebecca(Y)	1825	Aug. 18	WashCo.,Penn	02	08	18

PURCHASER	YEAR	DATE	RESIDENCE	R	T	S
Maynard, Benj'n.(Y)	1829	May 14	Jeff.Co.,Oh.	05	13	10
McAdam, Jno.(Z-M)	1831	Oct. 31	LickingCo,Oh	11	04	25
McAdam, Jno.(Z-M)	1832	Feb. 01	LickingCo,Oh	11	04	02
McAdam, John(Z-M)	1832	March 29	LickingCo,Oh	11	04	25
McAdam, John(Z-M)	1835	Dec. 11	HarrisonCoOh	11	04	25
McAdam, John(Z-M)	1835	Dec. 11	HarrisonCoOh	11	04	25
McAdoo, James(Z)	1807	June 15	MuskingmCoOh	14	15	35
McAdoo, James(Z)	1811	Sept. 30	MuskingmCoOh	14	16	11
McAffee, Henry(Z)	1816	Sept. 09	WashCo.,Penn	05	02	02
McAlhanney, John(Z-M)	1836	April 09	GuernseyCoOh	03	05	21
McAlheney, Hamilton(Z-M)	1838	Jan. 23	GuernseyCoOh	03	04	12
McAllister, Dan'l.(Y)	1826	Nov. 20	WashCo.,Penn	04	13	34
McAllister, Hector(Y)	1831	Sept. 05	ColumbanCoOh	03	12	29
McAllister, Susanna(Z)	1822	March 24	WashngtnCoOh	09	07	13
McBane, Nathan(Z-M)	1837	March 11	TuscarwsCoOh	03	05	16
McBean, Angus(Y)	1821	Oct. 11	ColumbanCoOh	02	10	21
McBean, Angus(Y)	1823	April 29	ColumbanCoOh	02	10	22
McBean, Angus(Y)	1824	Feb. 06	ColumbanCoOh	03	12	15
McBean, Angus(Y)	1824	May 18	ColumbanCoOh	03	13	15
McBean, Angus(Y)	1824	May 18	ColumbanCoOh	03	13	15
McBean, Angus(Y)	1828	July 07	ColumbanCoOh	03	12	15
McBean, Angus(Y)	1831	July 25	ColumbanCoOh	02	10	20
McBean, Angus(Y)	1832	Sept. 21	ColumbanCoOh	02	10	20
McBean, Angus(Y)	1832	Sept. 25	ColumbanCoOh	02	10	20
McBean, Charles(Y)	1835	Sept. 11	Jeff.Co.,Oh.	03	12	09
McBean, James(Y)	1832	July 16	ColumbanCoOh	02	09	31
McBean, James(Y)	1832	July 21	ColumbanCoOh	02	09	31
McBean, John(Y)	1827	April 07	ColumbanCoOh	02	10	27
McBean, John(Y)	1829	March 18	ColumbanCoOh	02	10	27
McBeath, John(Y)	1830	Nov. 26	HarrisonCoOh	06	13	25
McBeath, William(Y)	1831	March 26	HarrisonCoOh	06	12	30
McBee, James(Y)	1833	Aug. 24	Stark Co.,Oh	09	12	30
McBee, Thomas Jr.(Z-M)	1833	Sept. 24	TuscarwsCoOh	04	07	13
McBee, Thomas(Z-M)	1833	Aug. 31	StarkeCo.,Oh	04	07	12
McBee, Thomas(Z-M)	1833	Aug. 31	StarkeCo.,Oh	04	07	12
McBee, Thomas(Z-M)	1833	Sept. 24	TuscarwsCoOh	04	07	20
McBee, Thomas(Z-M)	1833	Sept. 24	TuscarwsCoOh	04	07	20
McBride, A.(Z)	1805	Aug. 13	MuskingmCoOh	14	15	18
McBride, Alex'r.(Z)	1835	Nov. 17	Morgan Co,Oh	09	08	29
McBride, And'w.(Z)	1805	July 20	MuskingmCoOh	14	16	13
McBride, And'w.(Z)	1805	July 20	MuskingmCoOh	14	15	01
McBride, Andrew(Z)	1813	July 09	HarrisonCoOh	15	17	27
McBride, Charles(Z-M)	1832	Jan. 23	CoshoctnCoOh	07	05	03
McBride, David(Z)	1815	March 25	GuernseyCoOh	09	06	12
McBride, Isaac(Z)	1805	July 02	MuskingmCoOh	14	15	02
McBride, Isaac(Z)	1810	April 16	MuskingmCoOh	14	15	12
McBride, James(Z)	1812	March 21	Jeff.Co.,Oh.	15	18	13
McBride, Jno.(Z)	1836	Aug. 12	MunroeCo.,Oh	08	06	03
McBride, John(Z)	1835	Dec. 21	MonroeCo.,Oh	08	06	01
McBride, Margaret & Heirs(Z)	1817	Sept. 19	BelmontCo,Oh	12	12	06
McBride, Michael(Z)	1836	March 28	MonroeCo.,Oh	08	06	03
McBride, Michael(Z)	1837	March 04	MonroeCo.,Oh	08	06	03
McBride, R.(Z)	1805	Aug. 13	MuskingmCoOh	14	15	18
McBride, Rich'd.(Z)	1805	July 20	MuskingmCoOh	14	16	13
McBride, Rich'd.(Z)	1805	July 20	MuskingmCoOh	14	15	01
McBride, Robt.(Z-M)	1832	Jan. 23	CoshoctnCoOh	07	05	02
McBride, Thomas(Z-M)	1832	March 29	KnoxCo.,Ohio	11	08	14
McBride, William(Z)	1832	Jan. 03	Morgan Co,Oh	10	08	15
McBride, William(Z)	1835	Sept. 19	Morgan Co,Oh	10	08	33
McBride, William(Z)	1835	Nov. 23	MonroeCo.,Oh	08	06	10
McBride, Wm.(Z)	1836	Aug. 27	MonroeCo.,Oh	08	06	10
McBride, Wm.(Z)	1836	Aug. 27	MonroeCo.,Oh	08	06	10
McBurney, John(Z-M)	1825	Nov. 26	GuernseyCoOh	01	01	12
McBurney, Joseph(Z)	1811	Nov. 20	WashCo.,Penn	01	02	17
McCabe, John(Z)	1834	Aug. 07	Morgan Co,Oh	13	08	05
McCabe, John(Z)	1834	Nov. 27	Perry Co.,Oh	15	15	31
McCabe, Simon(Z)	1836	Dec. 02	Perry Co.,Oh	14	12	13
McCaffrey, Allen(Z)	1834	Nov. 03	BelmontCo,Oh	11	11	14
McCague, James(Z)	1825	Sept. 22	WashCo.,Penn	11	13	23

PURCHASER	YEAR	DATE	RESIDENCE	R	T	S
McCain, John(Z)	1826	Aug. 12	ChesterCo,Pa	08	05	12
McCall, Barnabas(Z)	1826	April 01	HarrisonCoOh	09	06	01
McCall, Elias(Z)	1833	Aug. 27	Morgan Co,Oh	09	07	25
McCall, Elias(Z)	1835	April 14	Morgan Co,Oh	09	07	24
McCall, Elias(Z)	1836	Sept. 01	Morgan Co,Oh	09	07	25
McCallisten, James(Y)	1829	March 25	HarrisonCoOh	06	13	06
McCamet, Samuel(Z-M)	1829	Dec. 19	KnoxCo.,Ohio	10	05	19
McCammant, Sam'l.(Z-M)	1832	Aug. 23	KnoxCo.,Ohio	10	05	22
McCammant, Samuel(Z-M)	1833	Feb. 28	KnoxCo.,Ohio	10	05	19
McCammart, Andrew(Z-M)	1831	Dec. 10	KnoxCo.,Ohio	10	05	19
McCammont, Andrew(Z-M)	1835	July 07	KnoxCo.,Ohio	10	05	12
McCandless, James(Z)	1833	Nov. 15	AlleghnyCoPa	13	11	30
McCandless, John(Z)	1829	Oct. 29	WashCo.,Penn	13	11	22
McCandless, John(Z)	1830	Oct. 05	MuskingmCoOh	13	11	22
McCanement, Andrew(Z)	1816	Nov. 16	Brooke CoVir	10	05	19
McCann, R.(Z)	1815	Oct. 07	WestmrldCoPa	09	03	21
McCann, T.(Z)	1815	Oct. 07	WestmrldCoPa	09	03	21
McCann, Thomas(Z-M)	1832	June 23	GuernseyCoOh	02	01	13
McCantire, Robert(Z)	1811	May 28	BrookCo.,Vir	15	16	02
McCare, Joseph(Z-M)	1832	Sept. 29	WashCo.,Penn	04	07	24
McCarl, Jacob F.(Z)	1827	April 11	WashCo.,Penn	04	07	16
McCarl, Jacob Freeman(Z-M)	1832	April 04	TuscarwsCoOh	04	07	16
McCarl, Joseph(Z-M)	1830	Jan. 08	TuscarwsCoOh	04	07	16
McCarny, William A.(Z)	1821	Sept. 09	MuskingmCoOh	13	09	32
McCarroll, William(Y)	1832	June 07	HarrisonCoOh	06	12	11
McCarroll, Wm.(Z)	1833	Nov. 07	HarrisonCoOh	10	08	27
McCarroll, Wm.(Z)	1833	Nov. 07	HarrisonCoOh	10	08	14
McCarroll, Wm.(Z)	1833	Nov. 07	HarrisonCoOh	10	08	15
McCartney, David(Z-M)	1836	Jan. 04	GuernseyCoOh	03	04	18
McCartney, David(Z-M)	1836	Dec. 13	GuernseyCoOh	03	04	23
McCartney, Henry Jr.(Z-M)	1832	Aug. 25	GuernseyCoOh	02	04	16
McCartney, Henry Jr.(Z-M)	1836	Jan. 04	GuernseyCoOh	03	04	20
McCartney, Henry Jr.(Z-M)	1838	Nov. 08	GuernseyCoOh	03	04	20
McCartney, Henry(Z-M)	1832	Feb. 21	GuernseyCoOh	03	04	11
McCartney, Henry(Z-M)	1836	Feb. 23	GuernseyCoOh	03	04	20
McCartney, Henry(Z-M)	1836	Feb. 23	GuernseyCoOh	03	04	20
McCartney, Jas.(Z-M)	1827	July 17	GuernseyCoOh	03	03	12
McCartney, William(Z-M)	1823	Dec. 03	GuernseyCoOh	03	04	19
McCartney, William(Z-M)	1834	Nov. 01	GuernseyCoOh	03	04	19
McCartney, Wm.(Z-M)	1828	Sept. 19	GuernseyCoOh	03	04	20
McCartney, Wm.(Z-M)	1832	June 20	GuernseyCoOh	03	04	13
McCartney, Wm.(Z-M)	1832	June 20	GuernseyCoOh	03	04	19
McCartney, Wm.(Z-M)	1831	April 26	GuernseyCoOh	03	04	19
McCartor, Jonathan(Z-M)	1835	Nov. 20	MuskingmCoOh	10	04	25
McCarty, Charles(Z)	1820	Oct. 12	Jeff.Co.,Oh.	11	11	08
McCarty, Charles(Z)	1823	Oct. 05	Morgan Co,Oh	11	11	08
McCarty, Chas. Jr.(Z)	1827	Nov. 28	Morgan Co,Oh	11	10	07
McCarty, Jeremiah(Z)	1834	Dec. 03	Morgan Co,Oh	10	06	19
McCarty, Thomas R.(Z)	1832	Jan. 23	Morgan Co,Oh	11	11	17
McCarty, William(Z-M)	1837	Feb. 07	CoshoctnCoOh	08	07	19
McCarty, Wm.(Z-M)	1835	March 09	KnoxCo.,Ohio	11	04	09
McCarty, Wm.(Z-M)	1835	Dec. 26	KnoxCo.,Ohio	11	04	09
McCarty, Wm.(Z-M)	1837	March 20	CoshoctnCoOh	08	07	10
McCaskey, Geo.(Z-M)	1830	Jan. 04	CoshoctnCoOh	05	06	07
McCaskey, Hughey(Z-M)	1826	Jan. 07	Jeff.Co.,Oh.	05	06	05
McCaslin, William(Z)	1816	Oct. 31	BedfordCo.,Pa	14	14	33
McCaslin, Wm.(Z)	1832	Jan. 28	Perry Co.,Oh	15	15	11
McCastor, Jonathan(Z-M)	1835	July 20	MuskingmCoOh	10	04	24
McCauley, Patrick(Y)	1824	Aug. 18	Pittsburg,Pa	04	14	21
McCauley, Patrick(Y)	1824	Aug. 18	Pittsburg,Pa	04	14	22
McCausland, David(Z-M)	1831	Aug. 23	CoshoctnCoOh	07	07	20
McCausland, Joseph(Y)	1827	July 19	HarrisonCoOh	04	13	31
McCausland, Joseph(Y)	1830	Oct. 23	HarrisonCoOh	05	14	20
McCausland, Lindsey(Y)	1829	Sept. 24	HarrisonCoOh	05	14	02
McCavern, John(Y)	1830	June 30	ColumbanCoOh	04	13	02
McCay, Samuel(Z)	1816	Dec. 11	MuskingmCoOh	08	03	03
McClabe, Stuart(Y)	1829	Dec. 23	Jeff.Co.,Oh.	03	11	33
McClain, A.(Z)	1815	Sept. 26	CoshoctnCoOh	10	08	15
McClain, Allen(Z)	1805	Dec. 17	MuskingmCoOh	13	12	09

PURCHASER	YEAR	DATE	RESIDENCE	R	T	S
McClain, Allen(Z)	1811	Nov. 14	MuskingmCoOh	12	13	35
McClain, Andrew(Y)	1822	Nov. 30	WashCo.,Penn	04	13	30
McClain, Benjamin(Z)	1811	Aug. 26	MuskingmCoOh	14	15	32
McClain, Benjamin(Z)	1816	Jan. 19	MuskingmCoOh	14	15	35
McClain, Charles(Y)	1830	June 26	ColumbanCoOh	02	10	21
McClain, Elam(Z)	1809	Aug. 11	FranklinCoOh	08	04	10
McClain, Ephraim(Z-M)	1837	July 06	MuskingmCoOh	10	09	22
McClain, James Jr.(Y)	1824	Nov. 01	Jeff.Co.,Oh.	03	11	03
McClain, James(Z)	1815	June 09	FairfeldCoOh	12	13	09
McClain, James(Z)	1816	June 25	LickingCo,Oh	12	09	09
McClain, John Senr.(Z)	1815	Nov. 11	MercerCoPenn	05	02	25
McClain, John Senr.(Z)	1815	Nov. 11	MercerCoPenn	05	02	25
McClain, Joseph(Y)	1821	Nov. 16	WashCo.,Penn	04	13	30
McClain, Samuel Laurison(Y)	1833	Sept. 23	Jeff.Co.,Oh.	03	11	04
McClain, Samuel Lawrison(Y)	1832	Aug. 02	Jeff.Co.,Oh.	03	11	04
McClain, Samuel(Y)	1821	June 11	WashCo.,Penn	04	13	18
McClain, Seth(Z)	1811	Oct. 18	CoshoctnCoOh	05	04	09
McClain, Thomas(Z)	1813	Dec. 23	CoshoctnCoOh	08	04	09
McClain, Thomas(Z-M)	1825	Jan. 13	CoshoctnCoOh	08	05	22
McClain, Thomas(Z-M)	1825	Jan. 21	CoshoctnCoOh	08	04	02
McClain, Thomas(Z-M)	1831	Oct. 08	CoshoctnCoOh	08	05	21
McClain, William(Y)	1829	July 28	Jeff.Co.,Oh.	03	11	17
McClain, William(Y)	1837	June 10	Jeff.Co.,Oh.	03	11	11
McClanahan, David(Z)	1828	Oct. 16	BelmontCo,Oh	11	11	32
McClancy, David(Z)	1831	April 04	KnoxCo.,Ohio	11	03	03
McClane, Thomas(Z-M)	1831	Nov. 30	CoshoctnCoOh	08	04	02
McClane, William(Z)	1810	July 19	MuskingmCoOh	08	04	19
McClannahan, Alex'r.(Z)	1836	Sept. 23	Perry Co.,Oh	14	13	23
McClannahan, John(Z)	1816	May 09	CoshoctnCoOh	08	04	05
McClannahan, John(Z)	1816	May 09	CoshoctnCoOh	08	04	06
McClaray, John(Z)	1807	Nov. 03	Jeff.Co.,Oh.	01	07	02
McClare, Stuart(Y)	1825	Oct. 10	Jeff.Co.,Oh.	03	11	34
McClare, Stuart(Y)	1825	Oct. 10	Jeff.Co.,Oh.	03	11	34
McClary, Andrew(Z)	1810	June 27	GuernseyCoOh	02	02	21
McClary, Geo. Acamr.(Z-M)	1832	May 22	CoshoctnCoOh	06	04	02
McClary, Geo. Acams.(Z-M)	1832	May 22	CoshoctnCoOh	06	04	02
McClary, James(Z)	1833	Nov. 30	Brooke CoVir	11	11	13
McClashan, James(Z)	1836	Jan. 02	Morgan Co,Oh	10	07	25
McClaskey, Jos.(Z)	1836	Aug. 01	GuernseyCoOh	09	06	35
McClaughlin(Y)	1831	Sept. 28	Jeff.Co.,Oh.	04	12	30
McClean, Allen(Z)	1810	Feb. 14	MuskingmCoOh	13	12	14
McCleary, Abraham(Y)	1830	Sept. 14	ColumbanCoOh	04	13	27
McCleary, Geo. A.(Z-M)	1835	Oct. 07	CoshoctnCoOh	06	04	01
McCleary, Henry Slage(Z-M)	1832	May 22	CoshoctnCoOh	05	04	08
McCleary, James(Z)	1837	Feb. 14	BrookeCo,Vir	08	05	05
McCleary, James(Z)	1837	Feb. 14	BrookeCo,Vir	08	05	09
McCleary, Thomas(Z)	1820	Nov. 21	Morgan Co,Oh	10	08	24
McClenaehan, William(Z-M)	1833	July 04	TuscarwsCoOh	04	07	23
McClesh, Alex'r.(Y)	1828	Dec. 09	Stark co.,Oh	07	16	22
McClesh, Isaiah(Y)	1828	Dec. 09	Stark co.,Oh	07	16	23
McClintick, Geo.(Z)	1832	March 28	Morgan Co,Oh	11	11	25
McClintick, Joseph(Z)	1815	April 17	MuskingmCoOh	14	05	07
McClintick, Sam'l.(Z)	1832	May 21	Morgan Co,Oh	10	07	17
McClintick, William(Z)	1820	Oct. 23	MonroeCo.,Oh	08	07	12
McClintick, Wm.(Z)	1813	Nov. 26	MuskingmCoOh	09	03	20
McClintick, Wm.(Z)	1813	Nov. 26	MuskingmCoOh	09	03	20
McClintick, Wm.(Z)	1813	Nov. 26	MuskingmCoOh	09	03	20
McClintock, James(Y)	1823	Dec. 30	ColumbanCoOh	05	15	04
McClintock, James(Y)	1835	Feb. 03	CarrollCo,Oh	05	15	04
McClintock, John(Y)	1830	Sept. 14	HarrisonCoOh	06	12	30
McClintock, Noble W.(Y)	1822	Oct. 24	SteubenvleOh	05	11	33
McClintock, Noble W.(Y)	1825	March 04	SteubenvleOh	05	11	33
McCloskey, Charles(Z)	1834	Feb. 21	Perry Co.,Oh	15	15	31
McCloskey, Charles(Z)	1834	Feb. 21	Perry Co.,Oh	15	15	32
McCloud, Samuel(Z)	1828	March 18	MuskingmCoOh	11	11	23
McCluggage, Geo.(Z-M)	1832	Sept. 20	WashCo.,Penn	07	08	12
McClung, James(Z)	1835	May 20	Perry Co.,Oh	15	15	35
McClung, Robert Jr.(Z)	1832	May 28	Perry Co.,Oh	15	15	25
McClung, Robert Jr.(Z)	1832	May 28	Perry Co.,Oh	15	15	36

PURCHASER	YEAR	DATE	RESIDENCE	R	T	S
McClung, Robert(Z)	1833	May 16	Perry Co.,Oh	15	15	28
McClung, Robt.(Z)	1822	Oct. 16	Perry Co.,Oh	15	15	35
McClung, Thomas(Z)	1815	May 02	WashCo.,Penn	10	09	04
McClure, David(Y)	1824	Nov. 08	ColumbanCoOh	06	16	08
McClure, William(Z)	1811	May 24	MuskingmCoOh	14	16	10
McClurg, John(Z)	1836	Sept. 30	BeaverCo.,Pa	08	06	36
McCoid, James(Z)	1824	May 11	MuskingmCoOh	12	11	15
McCoid, James(Z)	1824	May 15	MuskingmCoOh	11	10	07
McCoid, James(Z)	1833	March 18	MuskingmCoOh	10	06	08
McCoid, James(Z)	1836	Jan. 01	MuskingmCoOh	13	08	32
McCoid, James(Z)	1836	Jan. 01	MuskingmCoOh	13	08	32
McCoid, James(Z)	1836	Feb. 11	MuskingmCoOh	09	05	36
McCoid, James(Z)	1816	April 20	MuskingmCoOh	12	12	14
McColaugh, Robert(Z)	1836	Jan. 15	BelmontCo,Oh	10	07	23
McCole, Condy(Y)	1834	Aug. 09	NrthmptnCoPa	04	13	07
McCollough, David(Z-M)	1835	June 03	CoshoctnCoOh	07	05	08
McCollough, Wm.(Z-M)	1832	May 22	CoshoctnCoOh	07	05	07
McCollough, Wm.(Z-M)	1832	May 22	CoshoctnCoOh	07	05	13
McCollough, Wm.(Z-M)	1832	May 22	CoshoctnCoOh	07	05	02
McCollum, Alexander(Z-M)	1826	March 09	GuernseyCoOh	02	02	07
McCollum, Byram(Z-M)	1832	Sept. 17	WashCo.,Penn	04	07	14
McCollum, Isaac(Z-M)	1826	March 09	GuernseyCoOh	02	02	07
McCollum, Jacob(Z-M)	1831	Oct. 29	WashCo.,Penn	04	07	17
McCollum, Jacob(Z-M)	1831	Oct. 29	WashCo.,Penn	04	07	17
McCollum, John(Y)	1833	Sept. 18	HarrisonCoOh	07	14	08
McCollum, John(Z-M)	1831	Oct. 29	WashCo.,Penn	04	07	25
McCollum, John(Z-M)	1832	Sept. 17	WashCo.,Penn	04	07	25
McCollum, Stephen(Z-M)	1832	Sept. 17	WashCo.,Penn	04	07	25
McComas, Daniel(Z)	1810	July 16	WashCo.,Penn	11	13	14
McComb, Hugh(Y)	1825	July 26	GuernseyCoOh	07	11	08
McComb, James(Y)	1827	Dec. 29	ColumbanCoOh	06	14	12
McCombs, William(Y)	1830	Nov. 12	ColumbanCoOh	06	12	30
McConaughy, Adams(Y)	1827	Nov. 26	Jeff.Co.,Oh.	03	11	25
McConaughy, James(Z-M)	1833	June 14	GuernseyCoOh	03	01	07
McConaughy, John(Z-M)	1835	June 04	MuskingmCoOh	03	01	04
McConaughy, William(Z-M)	1833	Aug. 06	MuskingmCoOh	03	01	08
McConkey, James(Z-M)	1838	June 15	GuernseyCoOh	04	03	17
McConn, Thos.(Z-M)	1826	June 17	WashCo.,Penn	02	02	07
McConnaughy, David P.(Z-M)	1838	Aug. 24	GuernseyCoOh	03	04	12
McConnel, Alexander(Z)	1817	June 12	MuskingmCoOh	11	10	18
McConnel, James(Y)	1831	March 08	Jeff.Co.,Oh.	06	12	18
McConnel, James(Z)	1825	April 08	GuernseyCoOh	08	08	19
McConnel, James(Z)	1814	Oct. 19	BelmontCo,Oh	08	04	18
McConnel, Matthew(Z)	1831	Sept. 13	GuernseyCoOh	08	08	20
McConnel, R.(Z)	1817	June 12	MuskingmCoOh	11	10	17
McConnel, R.(Z)	1817	June 12	MuskingmCoOh	11	10	20
McConnel, R.(Z)	1817	Aug. 30	MuskingmCoOh	11	10	07
McConnel, R.(Z)	1817	Aug. 30	MuskingmCoOh	11	10	07
McConnel, R.(Z)	1817	Aug. 30	MuskingmCoOh	12	10	12
McConnel, Robert(Z)	1806	March 22	FranklinCoPa	12	10	16
McConnel, Robert(Z)	1806	March 22	FranklinCoPa	12	10	11
McConnel, Robert(Z)	1806	March 22	FranklinCoPa	12	10	24
McConnel, Robert(Z)	1806	March 22	FranklinCoPa	12	10	13
McConnel, Robert(Z)	1806	March 22	FranklinCoPa	12	10	14
McConnel, Robert(Z)	1806	May 08	FranklinCoPa	11	10	30
McConnel, Robert(Z)	1806	May 08	FranklinCoPa	07	01	09
McConnel, Robért(Z)	1806	May 08	FranklinCoPa	07	01	01
McConnel, Robert(Z)	1806	May 08	FranklinCoPa	07	01	02
McConnel, Robert(Z)	1807	Jan. 26	MuskingmCoOh	07	01	08
McConnel, Robert(Z)	1817	June 12	MuskingmCoOh	12	10	02
McConnel, Robt.(Z)	1806	Oct. 20	MuskingmCoOh	06	01	05
McConnel, Robt.(Z)	1806	Oct. 20	MuskingmCoOh	06	01	04
McConnel, Robt.(Z)	1806	Oct. 20	MuskingmCoOh	06	01	07
McConnel, Thos.(Z)	1813	Dec. 13	Ohio Co.,Vir	13	11	25
McConnell, Alex'r.(Z)	1816	May 22	GuernseyCoOh	01	04	17
McConnell, Jane(Y)	1832	March 31	Jeff.Co.,Oh.	05	13	03
McConnell, John(Z)	1811	Dec. 17	WashngtnCoOh	12	10	13
McConnell, John(Z)	1811	Dec. 17	WashngtnCoOh	12	10	14
McConnell, Robert(Z)	1828	Sept. 12	Morgan Co,Oh	12	11	29

PURCHASER	YEAR	DATE	RESIDENCE	R	T	S
McConnell, Robert(Z)	1807	Dec. 15	MuskingmCoOh	06	01	04
McConnell, Samuel(Y)	1832	Oct. 03	Jeff.Co.,Oh.	04	12	27
McConnell, Thomas L.(Z-M)	1836	Sept. 26	CoshoctnCoOh	08	08	21
McConnell, Thomas(Z)	1816	March 16	WashngtnCoOh	02	02	18
McConnell, Thos.(Z-M)	1824	Sept. 06	CoshoctnCoOh	08	04	11
McConnell, William(Z)	1814	Nov. 04	WashCo.,Penn	11	11	08
McConnell, William(Z)	1817	Jan. 14	BelmontCo,Oh	11	04	23
McCord, Francis(Y)	1833	March 30	HarrisonCoOh	06	12	05
McCord, James(Z)	1834	Dec. 04	MuskingmCoOh	11	12	24
McCord, James(Z)	1813	Aug. 07	MuskingmCoOh	12	13	33
McCorkhill, Alex'r.(Y)	1828	Dec. 03	Jeff.Co.,Oh.	04	12	14
McCormick, Geo.(Y)	1823	Aug. 08	Stark Co.,Oh	09	11	03
McCormick, Geo.(Y)	1823	Aug. 08	Stark Co.,Oh	09	11	02
McCormick, Henry(Y)	1824	Nov. 12	ColumbanCoOh	04	14	35
McCormick, Henry(Z-M)	1828	Dec. 05	WashCo.,Penn	04	09	03
McCormick, James(Y)	1828	Aug. 27	Stark Co.,Oh	09	12	34
McCormick, James(Z-M)	1820	July 08	MuskingmCoOh	05	02	10
McCormick, John(Z)	1832	Aug. 08	Perry Co.,Oh	14	13	25
McCormick, John(Z)	1833	Aug. 27	Perry Co.,Oh	14	13	25
McCormick, John(Z-M)	1835	April 01	Stark Co.,Oh	03	07	25
McCormick, Johnston(Z-M)	1836	Jan. 22	MuskingmCoOh	05	03	12
McCormick, Robert(Y)	1826	Feb. 04	GuernseyCoOh	07	09	27
McCormick, Thomas(Z)	1833	Aug. 27	Perry Co.,Oh	14	14	31
McCormick, William(Z)	1811	May 23	MuskingmCoOh	15	16	02
McCormick, Wm.(Y)	1828	May 14	Stark Co.,Oh	09	11	03
McCormick, Wm.(Z)	1832	Aug. 08	Perry Co.,Oh	14	13	25
McCormick, Wm.(Z)	1833	Aug. 27	Perry Co.,Oh	14	13	25
McCort, James(Y)	1829	Sept. 11	HarrisonCoOh	06	14	09
McCourt, James(Y)	1821	April 03	HarrisonCoOh	06	14	04
McCourt, James(Y)	1826	April 15	HarrisonCoOh	06	14	04
McCoy, Alex'r.(Z-M)	1836	Oct. 10	CoshoctnCoOh	07	04	12
McCoy, Alexander(Z)	1806	Jan. 03	MuskingmCoOh	15	17	23
McCoy, Daniel(Z)	1833	March 06	MuskingmCoOh	13	10	07
McCoy, Dennis(Y)	1835	March 31	CarrollCo,Oh	04	13	13
McCoy, Edmund(Z-M)	1832	July 25	CoshoctnCoOh	08	07	10
McCoy, Edmund(Z-M)	1832	July 25	CoshoctnCoOh	08	07	10
McCoy, Henry(Z-M)	1829	Aug. 10	CoshoctnCoOh	07	05	23
McCoy, Henry(Z-M)	1831	Sept. 17	CoshoctnCoOh	07	05	23
McCoy, Henry(Z-M)	1836	Dec. 17	BeaverCo.,Pa	08	07	22
McCoy, Hugh(Z)	1828	Oct. 22	GuernseyCoOh	09	08	06
McCoy, Hugh(Z)	1816	Aug. 31	GuernseyCoOh	09	08	06
McCoy, Hugh(Z-M)	1832	May 11	GuernseyCoOh	03	01	19
McCoy, Hugh(Z-M)	1836	Jan. 26	HolmesCoOhio	09	09	01
McCoy, James Sephas(Z-M)	1836	Feb. 22	CoshoctnCoOh	08	07	19
McCoy, James(Y)	1827	March 12	WashCo.,Penn	06	13	18
McCoy, James(Y)	1830	Aug. 12	ColumbanCoOh	03	12	12
McCoy, John(Z)	1814	Sept. 30	BedfordCo,Pa	08	05	17
McCoy, John(Z)	1817	May 15	CoshoctnCoOh	07	04	08
McCoy, John(Z-M)	1829	Dec. 21	CoshoctnCoOh	08	07	13
McCoy, John(Z-M)	1831	Sept. 17	CoshoctnCoOh	07	04	09
McCoy, John(Z-M)	1833	June 10	CoshoctnCoOh	05	06	17
McCoy, John(Z-M)	1833	June 10	CoshoctnCoOh	05	06	17
McCoy, John(Z-M)	1837	Oct. 12	CoshoctnCoOh	08	07	12
McCoy, John(Z-M)	1837	Oct. 12	CoshoctnCoOh	08	07	13
McCoy, Joseph B.(Z-M)	1836	June 08	HolmesCoOhio	07	08	22
McCoy, Joseph B.(Z-M)	1836	Sept. 29	HolmesCoOhio	07	08	22
McCoy, Joseph Jr. (Z-M)	1830	Jan. 18	CoshoctnCoOh	07	05	23
McCoy, Joseph Jr.(Z-M)	1828	Nov. 03	CoshoctnCoOh	07	05	25
McCoy, Joseph(Z)	1806	Dec. 30	MuskingmCoOh	07	04	25
McCoy, Joseph(Z)	1814	March 02	?	08	03	07
McCoy, Robert(Z)	1827	Oct. 25	Jeff.Co.,Oh.	01	05	08
McCoy, Robert(Z-M)	1826	Nov. 21	Jeff.Co.,Oh.	01	05	08
McCoy, Robert(Z-M)	1835	June 09	TuscarwsCoOh	01	05	09
McCoy, Samuel(Y)	1830	Nov. 10	ColumbanCoOh	03	13	28
McCoy, William(Y)	1834	Jan. 21	ColumbanCoOh	03	12	24
McCracken, Robert(Z)	1812	Oct. 22	Jeff.Co.,Oh.	10	01	03
McCracken, Robert(Z)	1813	May 31	HarrisonCoOh	10	01	08
McCracken, Robert(Z-M)	1824	Aug. 11	GuernseyCoOh	04	02	15
McCracken, Robt.(Z-M)	1822	May 27	HarrisonCoOh	04	02	12

PURCHASER	YEAR	DATE	RESIDENCE	R	T	S
McCracken, Wm.(Z-M)	1830	April 28	GuernseyCoOh	02	04	17
McCrackin, Wm.(Z)	1836	Jan. 29	GuernseyCoOh	03	03	16
McCray, Edward(Z)	1816	Sept. 25	GuernseyCoOh	01	02	05
McCreaner, Morris(Y)	1830	Jan. 01	ColumbanCoOh	04	13	24
McCreary, Hugh(Z-M)	1823	Aug. 20	GuernseyCoOh	02	01	04
McCreary, James M.(Z)	1834	Jan. 28	Morgan Co,Oh	11	12	22
McCredner, Morris(Y)	1829	Sept. 28	ColumbanCoOh	04	13	29
McCrery, John(Z)	1809	Dec. 14	TuscarwsCoOh	01	09	03
McCuan, James(Z)	1832	Sept. 25	Morgan Co,Oh	08	06	07
McCue, Andrew(Y)	1831	Aug. 17	ColumbanCoOh	04	14	13
McCue, Francis(Y)	1835	Jan. 17	CarrollCo,Oh	04	13	13
McCue, James(Y)	1823	May 21	Jeff.Co.,Oh.	04	14	21
McCulley, Andrew(Y)	1829	March 18	BeaverCo.,Pa	03	12	01
McCulley, Gilbert(Z-M)	1832	May 12	GuernseyCoOh	03	03	11
McCulley, Gilbert(Z-M)	1832	May 23	GuernseyCoOh	03	03	11
McCulley, Gilbert(Z-M)	1829	Dec. 30	GuernseyCoOh	02	03	08
McCulley, Mathew(Z-M)	1832	Aug. 09	GuernseyCoOh	04	03	14
McCulley, Mathew(Z-M)	1832	Aug. 09	GuernseyCoOh	04	03	14
McCullock, Richard(Z)	1811	April 19	GuernseyCoOh	09	08	17
McCulloh, John(Z-M)	1831	Feb. 14	CoshoctnCoOh	06	04	02
McCullough, Alex'r.(Y)	1822	April 27	HarrisonCoOh	06	11	15
McCullough, Alex.(Z)	1827	Nov. 05	Jeff.Co.,Oh.	05	06	14
McCullough, Alex.(Z-M)	1827	June 16	CoshoctnCoOh	07	05	18
McCullough, Alex.(Z-M)	1830	Nov. 29	CoshoctnCoOh	07	05	18
McCullough, Alex.(Z-M)	1829	Feb. 06	CoshoctnCoOh	05	06	18
McCullough, Dan'l.(Z)	1829	Dec. 21	CoshoctnCoOh	09	05	15
McCullough, David(Z-M)	1834	Dec. 11	CoshoctnCoOh	07	05	07
McCullough, Evan(Z)	1815	May 08	GreeneCo.,Pa	11	05	04
McCullough, Jas.(Y)	1828	Dec. 29	ColumbanCoOh	03	13	21
McCullough, Jno.(Z-M)	1835	Dec. 24	GuernseyCoOh	02	03	05
McCullough, Jno.(Z-M)	1835	Dec. 25	GuernseyCoOh	02	03	05
McCullough, John(Z)	1827	Nov. 05	Jeff.Co.,Oh.	05	06	13
McCullough, John(Z)	1814	Sept. 13	GuernseyCoOh	02	03	05
McCullough, John(Z-M)	1832	Oct. 18	GuernseyCoOh	02	03	05
McCullough, John(Z-M)	1833	April 29	GuernseyCoOh	02	03	05
McCullough, Robert(Z)	1815	Dec. 30	WashCo.,Penn	02	04	24
McCullough, William(Z)	1816	May 24	AlleghnyCoPa	07	05	17
McCullough, William(Z)	1817	April 23	AlleghnyCoPa	07	05	09
McCullough, Wm.(Y)	1825	March 15	ColumbanCoOh	02	09	15
McCullough, Wm.(Z-M)	1830	Oct. 28	CoshoctnCoOh	07	05	13
McCullough, Wm.(Z-M)	1831	May 30	HarrisonCoOh	01	05	07
McCullough, Wm.(Z-M)	1831	May 30	HarrisonCoOh	01	05	05
McCullough, Wm.(Z-M)	1836	Oct. 28	TuscarwsCoOh	02	06	03
McCulluch, Phin's.(Z-M)	1839	Feb. 23	CoshoctnCoOh	07	07	02
McCune, George(Z)	1806	March 24	MuskingmCoOh	04	04	04
McCune, Hugh(Z-M)	1836	Feb. 18	HarrisonCoOh	03	04	21
McCune, James(Z)	1806	Jan. 29	MuskingmCoOh	04	04	03
McCune, James(Z)	1816	Dec. 28	WashCo.,Penn	05	03	19
McCune, James(Z-M)	1829	June 15	CoshoctnCoOh	04	04	06
McCune, James(Z-M)	1832	Sept. 15	CoshoctnCoOh	04	05	23
McCune, James(Z-M)	1834	Sept. 17	CoshoctnCoOh	03	05	15
McCune, James(Z-M)	1836	March 30	CoshoctnCoOh	04	04	03
McCune, John(Z)	1832	March 20	MuskingmCoOh	13	08	14
McCune, John(Z)	1806	March 15	MuskingmCoOh	04	04	03
McCune, John(Z-M)	1833	Dec. 12	GuernseyCoOh	03	03	11
McCune, Joseph K.(Z)	1805	Sept. 28	MuskingmCoOh	05	01	10
McCune, Joseph K.(Z)	1814	June 28	MuskingmCoOh	05	02	22
McCune, Robt.(Z)	1830	Jan. 09	Morgan Co,Oh	11	11	07
McCune, Samuel(Z)	1821	Feb. 02	Morgan Co,Oh	12	11	11
McCune, Samuel(Z)	1805	Feb. 27	MuskingmCoOh	12	10	03
McCune, Samuel(Z)	1814	Jan. 22	WashngtnCoOh	12	13	21
McCune, Samuel(Z)	1815	Nov. 11	MuskingmCoOh	12	11	03
McCune, Samuel(Z)	1815	Nov. 11	MuskingmCoOh	12	11	03
McCune, Samuel(Z)	1816	April 02	MuskingmCoOh	12	11	11
McCurdy, Daniel(Z)	1816	June 11	Jeff.Co.,Oh.	08	05	12
McCurdy, Daniel(Z)	1816	June 11	Jeff.Co.,Oh.	08	05	19
McCurdy, Daniel(Z)	1816	June 11	Jeff.Co.,Oh.	08	05	19
McCurdy, Daniel(Z)	1816	June 11	Jeff.Co.,Oh.	08	05	20
McCurdy, Daniel(Z)	1816	June 14	Jeff.Co.,Oh.	08	05	11

PURCHASER	YEAR	DATE	RESIDENCE	R	T	S
McCurdy, Daniel(Z)	1816	Oct. 14	Jeff.Co.,Oh.	08	05	18
McCurdy, Reuben(Z-M)	1836	Oct. 13	CarrollCo,Oh	01	08	04
McCurdy, William(Z)	1816	Nov. 27	CoshoctnCoOh	08	05	13
McCutchen, Samuel(Z)	1812	Feb. 09	WashCo.,Penn	11	13	06
McDaniel, Cleburgh(Z)	1834	Feb. 22	MuskingmCoOh	15	15	27
McDaniel, Cleburgh(Z)	1834	Aug. 15	MuskingmCoOh	15	15	22
McDaniel, Cleburgh(Z)	1836	Jan. 25	MuskingmCoOh	15	15	27
McDaniel, George(Y)	1831	April 23	Jeff.Co.,Oh.	04	12	27
McDaniel, Hugh(Y)	1832	June 04	Jeff.Co.,Oh.	04	12	12
McDaniel, Hugh(Y)	1834	Dec. 12	Jeff.Co.,Oh.	04	12	12
McDaniel, Reash(Y)	1829	April 08	Jeff.Co.,Oh.	04	13	05
McDaniel, William(Z-M)	1832	Oct. 06	CoshoctnCoOh	08	06	12
McDannal, Robert(Z)	1836	Nov. 02	MuskingmCoOh	15	14	26
McDannal, Robert(Z)	1836	Nov. 02	MuskingmCoOh	15	14	26
McDeeds, James(Z)	1827	March 08	MuskingmCoOh	11	12	10
McDeuit, Jno.(Y)	1828	Sept. 08	HarrisonCoOh	06	12	11
McDevit, Charles(Y)	1832	June 02	HarrisonCoOh	06	12	23
McDevit, George Jr.(Y)	1832	March 06	HarrisonCoOh	06	12	11
McDevitt, Samuel(Y)	1832	Feb. 25	TuscarwsCoOh	06	12	17
McDewit, George(Y)	1830	Feb. 17	HarrisonCoOh	05	11	36
McDivit, Charles(Y)	1824	May 18	HarrisonCoOh	06	12	17
McDivit, George Junr.(Y)	1831	July 05	HarrisonCoOh	06	12	11
McDivit, George(Y)	1832	Oct. 03	HarrisonCoOh	06	12	11
McDivit, George(Y)	1832	Oct. 03	HarrisonCoOh	06	12	17
McDonald, Dan'l.(Z-M)	1833	Sept. 30	GuernseyCoOh	03	01	05
McDonald, Elizabeth(Z-M)	1836	July 01	MuskingmCoOh	03	05	17
McDonald, James(Z)	1815	May 30	WashCo.,Penn	12	13	35
McDonald, Jas.(Z)	1831	March 15	MuskingmCoOh	12	13	34
McDonald, John(Y)	1821	Sept. 22	ColumbanCoOh	03	12	15
McDonald, John(Y)	1821	Sept. 22	ColumbanCoOh	03	12	15
McDonald, John(Z)	1825	Nov. 22	Perry Co.,Oh	14	12	15
McDonald, John(Z)	1829	Feb. 16	MuskingmCoOh	13	09	22
McDonald, John(Z)	1833	April 03	Perry Co.,Oh	14	12	29
McDonald, John(Z)	1836	April 19	Perry Co.,Oh	14	12	31
McDonald, Ronald(Z)	1811	Feb. 04	MuskingmCoOh	05	01	14
McDonald, Wm.(Z)	1836	Jan. 01	Morgan Co,Oh	10	07	35
McDonald, Wm.(Z-M)	1811	Feb. 04	MuskingmCoOh	05	01	14
McDonald, Wm.(Z-M)	1835	Dec. 16	GuernseyCoOh	04	03	07
McDonald, Wm.(Z-M)	1837	March 23	GuernseyCoOh	04	03	06
McDonald, Wm.(Z-M)	1837	March 23	GuernseyCoOh	04	03	15
McDonnel, Bartholomew(Z)	1835	May 23	ZanesvilleOh	14	12	02
McDonnel, Joseph(Y)	1833	Jan. 04	TuscarwsCoOh	07	14	09
McDonnell, John(Z-M)	1835	Feb. 23	BelmontCo,Oh	03	04	04
McDonnell, John(Z-M)	1835	Feb. 23	BelmontCo,Oh	03	04	03
McDonnell, Nath'l.(Z)	1816	March 19	WashCo.,Penn	05	03	20
McDonnell, Nathaniel(Z)	1815	March 22	WashCo.,Penn	05	01	25
McDonough, Hugh(Y)	1827	July 16	TuscarwsCoOh	07	14	26
McDougal, Andrew(Y)	1829	March 16	ColumbanCoOh	03	12	14
McDougal, Andrew(Y)	1829	March 16	ColumbanCoOh	03	12	14
McDowel, John(Z)	1816	April 22	TuscarwsCoOh	03	08	02
McDowel, Mathew(Z-M)	1835	Jan. 12	GuernseyCoOh	03	02	06
McDowell, Eph'm.(Z-M)	1840	July 28	GuernseyCoOh	04	03	15
McDowell, Eph'm.(Z-M)	1840	July 28	GuernseyCoOh	04	03	14
McDowell, James(Z)	1817	June 12	LickingCo,Oh	11	04	23
McDowell, James(Z-M)	1829	June 29	MuskingmCoOh	11	04	24
McDowell, James(Z-M)	1836	Jan. 13	HolmesCoOhio	08	08	03
McDowell, James(Z-M)	1837	May 29	HolmesCoOhio	08	08	03
McDowell, John(Z-M)	1835	Dec. 05	GuernseyCoOh	02	02	14
McDowell, Jos.(Z-M)	1828	Oct. 03	HolmesCoOhio	08	08	03
McDowell, Joseph(Z-M)	1822	June 04	CoshoctnCoOh	08	08	03
McDowell, Joseph(Z-M)	1822	June 04	CoshoctnCoOh	08	08	03
McDowell, William(Z-M)	1833	Jan. 29	LickingCo,Oh	11	03	04
McDowell, William(Z-M)	1834	Sept. 02	LickingCo,Oh	11	03	03
McDowell, Wm.(Z-M)	1835	July 06	HolmesCoOhio	07	08	02
McDowl, Mathew(Z-M)	1833	Feb. 13	GuernseyCoOh	03	02	06
McDowl, Mathew(Z-M)	1836	April 09	GuernseyCoOh	08	08	03
McDowl, Mathew(Z-M)	1836	April 09	GuernseyCoOh	08	08	04
McDownen, John(Z)	1806	Feb. 07	BelmontCo,Oh	05	01	14
McElfresh, Garrison(Z)	1834	Nov. 17	BelmontCo,Oh	13	08	26

PURCHASER	YEAR	DATE	RESIDENCE	R	T	S
McElfresh, James(Z)	1834	Nov. 17	BelmontCo,Oh	13	08	35
McElheron, Joseph(Z-M)	1836	Dec. 19	AlleghnyCoPa	04	03	11
McElivie, James(Y)	1834	Sept. 20	Jeff.Co.,Oh.	06	12	17
McElmeel, John(Z)	1836	Oct. 28	ZanesvilleOh	15	15	26
McElmeel, John(Z)	1836	Oct. 31	ZanesvilleOh	15	15	26
McElroy, Adam(Z-M)	1837	March 24	HolmesCoOhio	09	08	16
McElroy, Alexander(Z-M)	1833	Feb. 11	BeaverCo.,Pa	06	09	25
McElroy, Gillespie(Z)	1832	Jan. 18	Morgan Co,Oh	10	08	02
McElroy, John(Y)	1830	Jan. 19	GuernseyCoOh	07	11	13
McElroy, John(Z)	1831	Aug. 18	Morgan Co,Oh	10	08	08
McFadden, Elisha(Z)	1817	Oct. 16	VenangoCo,Pa	11	04	07
McFadden, Isaac(Y)	1830	June 09	HarrisonCoOh	07	15	33
McFadden, Isaac(Z-M)	1831	Aug. 08	TuscarwsCoOh	01	09	21
McFadden, James(Z)	1817	Oct. 16	VenangoCo,Pa	11	04	07
McFaddin, Charles(Z)	1817	Jan. 08	GuernseyCoOh	11	04	04
McFaddin, John M.(Z)	1836	Feb. 20	HarrisonCoOh	08	07	21
McFaddin, John(Z-M)	1828	Feb. 07	BelmontCo,Oh	02	05	19
McFadin, Joseph(Z)	1817	June 13	HarrisonCoOh	07	05	17
McFadyon, Benjamin(Z-M)	1835	June 15	CoshoctnCoOh	05	06	04
McFarlain, James(Z)	1834	Feb. 27	Perry Co.,Oh	15	15	24
McFarlan, William Jr.(Z)	1834	Dec. 18	LickingCo,Oh	15	15	24
McFarland, Armar(Z-M)	1832	May 21	CoshoctnCoOh	05	06	07
McFarland, Armar(Z-M)	1832	May 21	CoshoctnCoOh	05	06	12
McFarland, James(Z)	1833	Nov. 19	Perry Co.,Oh	15	15	13
McFarland, John(Z-M)	1830	April 08	TuscarwsCoOh	02	05	12
McFarland, John(Z-M)	1837	Jan. 10	HolmesCoOhio	08	08	25
McFarland, Moses(Z)	1824	May 11	WashCo.,Ohio	11	13	22
McFarland, Patrick(Z-M)	1832	Feb. 22	CoshoctnCoOh	07	07	22
McFarland, Patrick(Z-M)	1832	May 19	CoshoctnCoOh	05	06	24
McFarland, Patrick(Z-M)	1832	May 19	CoshoctnCoOh	05	06	04
McFarland, Robert(Y)	1836	June 28	ColumbanCoOh	01	06	01
McFarland, Robt.(Z-M)	1837	Jan. 25	HolmesCoOhio	09	08	21
McFarland, Samuel(Y)	1833	Dec. 09	Jeff.Co.,Oh.	02	08	34
McFarland, William(Z-M)	1825	March 16	BeaverCo.,Pa	06	09	17
McFarlane, Robert(Z)	1811	June 25	CoshoctnCoOh	04	06	19
McFarlane, Robert(Z)	1811	June 25	CoshoctnCoOh	04	06	12
McFarlin, James(Z)	1806	Jan. 04	MuskingmCoOh	15	17	26
McFarling, Cyrus Asa(Z)	1837	Jan. 16	Morgan Co,Oh	09	05	36
McFee, John Jnr.(Z-M)	1836	Jan. 27	TuscarwsCoOh	02	05	02
McFee, John Jr.(Z-M)	1835	Dec. 31	TuscarwsCoOh	02	05	02
McFee, Thornton(Z-M)	1831	March 21	Jeff.Co.,Oh.	01	06	24
McFerren, Samuel(Z)	1836	June 13	Morgan Co,Oh	09	07	30
McGarry, Dan'l.(Z)	1825	April 06	Morgan Co,Oh	09	06	04
McGaskan, James(Z)	1832	April 26	MuskingmCoOh	10	07	25
McGavern, John(Y)	1827	Nov. 20	ColumbanCoOh	04	13	19
McGavern, Wm.(Y)	1828	Dec. 24	ColumbanCoOh	03	12	25
McGavran, John(Y)	1827	July 04	Jeff.Co.,Oh.	04	12	35
McGee, Alex'r.(Y)	1834	April 03	TuscarwsCoOh	07	14	34
McGee, Alexander(Y)	1834	Nov. 24	TuscarwsCoOh	07	14	33
McGee, Andrew Jr.(Z)	1835	Dec. 24	Morgan Co,Oh	10	07	01
McGee, Andrew Junr.(Z)	1834	Feb. 21	Jeff.Co.,Oh.	10	07	01
McGee, Andrew Senr.(Z)	1834	Feb. 21	Jeff.Co.,Oh.	10	07	01
McGee, Richard(Z)	1815	March 22	WashCo.,Penn	05	01	17
McGee, Thomas(Y)	1831	July 25	Jeff.Co.,Oh.	04	11	18
McGee, William(Z)	1833	Feb. 28	HarrisonCoOh	10	08	23
McGiffin, William(Z)	1814	April 18	GuernseyCoOh	09	05	03
McGiffin, William(Z)	1816	Oct. 11	GuernseyCoOh	04	02	24
McGilvery, Laughlin(Y)	1832	Oct. 18	ColumbanCoOh	03	12	36
McGinnis, Hugh(Z)	1825	Dec. 02	BelmontCo,Oh	15	16	22
McGinnis, Jno.(Z)	1815	Oct. 26	AlleghnyCoPa	01	02	13
McGinnis, Wm.(Z)	1815	Oct. 26	AlleghnyCoPa	01	02	13
McGinty, Hugh(Y)	1827	Nov. 06	ColumbanCoOh	04	14	21
McGlashan, James(Z)	1832	April 26	MuskingmCoOh	10	07	25
McGlashan, Jas.(Z)	1831	July 04	MuskingmCoOh	10	07	25
McGlaughlin, Daniel(Y)	1830	April 29	ColumbanCoOh	03	12	24
McGlaughlin, James(Y)	1828	March 15	Jeff.Co.,Oh.	04	12	29
McGlauglin, Daniel*Y)	1831	Oct. 14	ColumbanCoOh	03	12	18
McGonigle, Richard(Z)	1832	Oct. 04	Perry Co.,Oh	14	13	31
McGory, John(Y)	1826	Feb. 06	ColumbanCoOh	04	14	24

PURCHASER	YEAR	DATE	RESIDENCE	R	T	S
McGouldrick, John(Z)	1833	Aug. 08	Perry Co.,Oh	14	14	31
McGouldrick, Patrick(Z)	1833	Aug. 08	Perry Co.,Oh	14	14	31
McGowan, Adam(Y)	1824	Aug. 17	PortageCo,Oh	05	18	05
McGowan, George(Z-M)	1837	March 15	GuernseyCoOh	04	03	03
McGowan, George(Z-M)	1837	April 21	GuernseyCoOh	04	03	03
McGowen, Sam'l.(Y)	1820	Sept. 27	ColumbanCoOh	05	18	04
McGowen, Sam'l.(Y)	1825	March 12	ColumbanCoOh	05	18	04
McGregor, James(Z)	1817	April 11	Ohio Co.,Vir	11	11	17
McGregor, John(Y)	1831	Nov. 21	ColumbanCoOh	02	09	27
McGrew, F. B.(Z-M)	1830	May 27	Jeff.Co.,Oh.	02	04	08
McGrew, Nathan(Z)	1809	Nov. 29	Jeff.Co.,Oh.	01	09	02
McGrew, Nathan(Z)	1815	Oct. 30	N.Phila.Penn	02	08	17
McGrew, Nathan(Z-M)	1828	Feb. 27	TuscarwsCoOh	01	09	08
McGrew, Philip(Z)	1809	Sept. 02	BelmontCo,Oh	08	04	19
McGuire, Patrick(Z-M)	1836	July 11	GuernseyCoOh	04	03	21
McGuire, Patrick(Z-M)	1836	Dec. 28	GuernseyCoOh	04	03	21
McHaffey, Robert(Z-M)	1829	Feb. 07	WashCo.,Penn	04	02	09
McHenry, Alexander(Z-M)	1832	May 23	MuskingmCoOh	05	03	18
McHenry, Alexander(Z-M)	1833	Nov. 19	MuskingmCoOh	05	03	18
McHenry, Richard(Z)	1821	July 06	MuskingmCoOh	11	12	17
McHinney, John(Y)	1836	June 11	HarrisonCoOh	07	14	35
McHugh, John(Z-M)	1833	Nov. 29	CoshoctnCoOh	07	05	07
McHugh, Peter(Y)	1832	Oct. 20	ColumbanCoOh	04	13	22
McIlrain, McLain(Y)	1825	Oct. 28	GuernseyCoOh	07	09	01
McIlroy, J.(Z)	1835	Dec. 31	BelmontCo,Oh	08	06	01
McIlroy, James(Z)	1816	May 14	GuernseyCoOh	10	08	04
McIlroy, John(Z)	1836	May 24	BelmontCo,Oh	08	06	12
McIluan, George(Z)	1832	Aug. 15	Morgan Co,Oh	08	06	06
McIluan, George(Z)	1832	Aug. 15	Morgan Co,Oh	08	06	06
McIlvain, And'w.(Z-M)	1826	May 03	BelmontCo,Oh	04	01	19
McIlvain, Gilbert(Z)	1815	Sept. 25	?	11	03	18
McIlvain, McLain(Z)	1833	July 04	GuernseyCoOh	08	08	34
McIlvain, McLain(Z)	1833	July 04	GuernseyCoOh	08	08	34
McIlvain, McLain(Z)	1833	July 04	GuernseyCoOh	08	08	34
McIlyar, Isaiah(Z-M)	1827	Aug. 08	GuernseyCoOh	04	02	11
McIlyar, William(Z-M)	1832	July 07	GuernseyCoOh	04	02	11
McIlyar, William(Z-M)	1833	Oct. 31	GuernseyCoOh	04	02	11
McInterfer, David(Y)	1827	Aug. 10	Stark Co.,Oh	06	17	30
McInterfer, John G.(Y)	1827	July 06	Stark Co.,Oh	06	17	30
McIntire, Daniel(Z)	1820	Nov. 06	MonroeCo.,Oh	08	07	11
McIntire, J.(Z)	1805	April 17	MuskingmCoOh	12	13	07
McIntire, J.(Z)	1805	April 23	MuskingmCoOh	08	02	22
McIntire, James(Y)	1826	April 18	Jeff.Co.,Oh.	04	12	35
McIntire, James(Y)	1832	Feb. 13	Jeff.Co.,Oh.	06	15	30
McIntire, Jno.(Z)	1804	June 08	MuskingmCoOh	13	11	05
McIntire, Jno.(Z)	1804	June 29	MuskingmCoOh	10	02	15
McIntire, Jno.(Z)	1804	June 29	MuskingmCoOh	10	02	14
McIntire, Jno.(Z)	1804	June 29	MuskingmCoOh	10	02	15
McIntire, Jno.(Z)	1804	Nov. 30	MuskingmCoOh	07	05	01
McIntire, Jno.(Z)	1804	Dec. 01	MuskingmCoOh	07	05	01
McIntire, Jno.(Z)	1804	Dec. 01	MuskingmCoOh	14	16	13
McIntire, Jno.(Z)	1804	Dec. 01	MuskingmCoOh	14	16	13
McIntire, John(Z)	1804	Dec. 01	MuskingmCoOh	13	11	07
McIntire, John(Z)	1804	Dec. 01	MuskingmCoOh	13	11	08
McIntire, John(Z)	1804	Dec. 01	MuskingmCoOh	15	17	20
McIntire, John(Z)	1805	Jan. 18	MuskingmCoOh	08	02	18
McIntire, John(Z)	1805	Jan. 18	MuskingmCoOh	08	02	23
McIntire, John(Z)	1805	April 23	MuskingmCoOh	08	02	19
McIntire, John(Z)	1805	Nov. 27	MuskingmCoOh	08	02	04
McIntire, John(Z)	1805	Dec. 17	MuskingmCoOh	08	02	04
McIntire, John(Z)	1805	Dec. 19	MuskingmCoOh	06	01	23
McIntire, John(Z)	1806	Jan. 16	MuskingmCoOh	08	02	08
McIntire, John(Z)	1806	June 21	ZanesvilleOh	04	02	22
McIntire, John(Z)	1806	June 21	ZanesvilleOh	10	09	27
McIntire, John(Z)	1806	June 21	ZanesvilleOh	04	02	21
McIntire, John(Z)	1806	June 21	ZanesvilleOh	10	09	28
McIntire, John(Z)	1806	July 08	MuskingmCoOh	04	02	21
McIntire, John(Z)	1810	June 09	MuskingmCoOh	12	12	29
McIntire, John(Z)	1811	Oct. 23	MuskingmCoOh	10	09	27

PURCHASER	YEAR	DATE	RESIDENCE	R	T	S
McIntire, John(Z)	1811	Oct. 23	MuskingmCoOh	04	02	22
McIntire, Robert(Z)	1810	May 28	BrookCo.,Vir	11	13	17
McIntosh, Alex'r.(Y)	1827	May 16	ColumbanCoOh	06	16	31
McIntosh, Alexander(Y)	1825	Dec. 17	ColumbanCoOh	07	16	18
McIntosh, Daniel(Y)	1831	Oct. 12	ColumbanCoOh	02	10	21
McIntosh, Donald(Y)	1821	Nov. 02	ColumbanCoOh	03	12	21
McIntosh, Evin(Y)	1821	April 16	ColumbanCoOh	03	12	09
McIntosh, Gilbert(Y)	1832	March 08	WashCo.,Penn	07	15	05
McIntosh, Wm. W.(Z)	1836	Oct. 03	WashngtnCoOh	08	05	08
McIntosh, Wm. W.(Z)	1836	Oct. 03	WashngtnCoOh	08	05	05
McIntosh, Wm. W.(Z)	1836	Oct. 03	WashngtnCoOh	08	05	05
McIntosh, Wm. Whiting(Z)	1836	June 25	WashngtnCoOh	08	05	19
McIntosh, Wm. Whiting(Z)	1836	June 25	WashngtnCoOh	08	05	19
McIntosh, Wm.(Y)	1825	Jan. 27	ColumbanCoOh	02	09	21
McJanney, John(Z)	1813	April 09	WestmrldCoPa	15	17	02
McJunnsy, John(Z)	1813	April 09	WestmrldCoPa	15	17	02
McKearn, John(Z)	1813	April 14	CoshoctnCoOh	08	05	24
McKee, Alex.(Z)	1827	Nov. 27	Morgan Co,Oh	09	07	34
McKee, Alexander(Z)	1816	March 08	KnoxCo.,Ohio	11	08	11
McKee, Andrew(Z-M)	1832	Sept. 06	HolmesCoOhio	10	08	14
McKee, Charles(Z)	1809	Nov. 07	Jeff.Co.,Oh.	10	07	07
McKee, Charles(Z)	1816	March 08	KnoxCo.,Ohio	10	08	07
McKee, Charles(Z)	1817	Sept. 08	KnoxCo.,Ohio	10	07	08
McKee, Charles(Z-M)	1832	Aug. 24	KnoxCo.,Ohio	11	08	13
McKee, Charles(Z-M)	1832	Aug. 24	KnoxCo.,Ohio	11	08	13
McKee, David(Z)	1821	Aug. 24	Pittsburg,Pa	11	12	28
McKee, David(Z)	1832	Sept. 19	Morgan Co,Oh	09	07	34
McKee, David(Z)	1811	Dec. 26	WashngtnCoOh	01	07	33
McKee, David(Z-M)	1833	June 05	GuernseyCoOh	03	01	06
McKee, Edridge(Z)	1835	Dec. 08	MonroeCo.,Oh	08	06	02
McKee, Eldridge(Z)	1835	Nov. 20	MonroeCo.,Oh	08	06	02
McKee, Ezra(Z)	1833	March 13	Morgan Co,Oh	09	07	33
McKee, James(Y)	1829	Jan. 01	Stark Co.,Oh	07	16	23
McKee, James(Z)	1820	Nov. 18	Morgan Co,Oh	10	08	25
McKee, James(Z)	1807	June 29	FayetteCo,Pa	01	09	11
McKee, James(Z)	1817	Jan. 29	TuscarwsCoOh	10	09	23
McKee, James(Z-M)	1837	April 17	GuernseyCoOh	03	04	15
McKee, Jno.(Z)	1831	Dec. 01	Morgan Co,Oh	09	07	19
McKee, John Jr.(Z-M)	1833	July 17	MuskingmCoOh	03	01	05
McKee, John(Y)	1832	Nov. 22	ColumbanCoOh	03	12	31
McKee, John(Y)	1835	Jan. 24	Jeff.Co.,Oh.	04	13	07
McKee, John(Z)	1832	Sept. 15	Morgan Co,Oh	09	07	35
McKee, John(Z)	1832	Sept. 15	Morgan Co,Oh	09	07	26
McKee, John(Z)	1836	Sept. 20	Morgan Co,Oh	09	07	34
McKee, John(Z)	1814	March 07	GuernseyCoOh	09	07	34
McKee, John(Z-M)	1836	Feb. 01	MuskingmCoOh	03	01	18
McKee, John(Z-M)	1836	Feb. 01	MuskingmCoOh	03	01	18
McKee, Jonas(Z-M)	1838	Nov. 16	GuernseyCoOh	03	04	05
McKee, L. T.(Z-M)	1830	Oct. 22	HolmesCoOhio	07	08	10
McKee, L. T.(Z-M)	1830	Oct. 22	HolmesCoOhio	07	08	10
McKee, Patrick(Z-M)	1831	April 02	CoshoctnCoOh	09	04	23
McKee, Robert(Y)	1837	March 06	ColumbanCoOh	02	09	27
McKee, Robert(Z)	1835	Dec. 18	Morgan Co,Oh	09	06	01
McKee, Robert(Z-M)	1832	Sept. 24	MuskingmCoOh	03	01	05
McKee, Robt.(Z)	1832	June 07	Morgan Co,Oh	09	07	35
McKee, Thomas(Z)	1805	May 30	AlleghnyCoPa	05	01	12
McKee, Thomas(Z)	1807	Nov. 24	WestmrldCoPa	11	13	12
McKee, Thomas(Z)	1815	Dec. 30	KnoxCo.,Ohio	09	04	20
McKee, Thomas(Z-M)	1834	Feb. 22	MuskingmCoOh	03	01	05
McKee, Thomas(Z-M)	1836	April 02	WashCo.,Penn	03	03	10
McKee, William(Z-M)	1835	Dec. 30	HolmesCoOhio	07	08	01
McKees, William(Z)	1815	Jan. 21	GuernseyCoOh	09	06	02
McKeever, Thomas(Z)	1835	Dec. 15	Perry Co.,Oh	14	14	30
McKeever, Thomas(Z-M)	1835	Nov. 19	TuscarwsCoOh	02	05	11
McKeever, Wm.(Z-M)	1832	Aug. 20	TuscarwsCoOh	02	05	11
McKein, James(Y)	1832	June 09	HarrisonCoOh	06	12	18
McKenna, Bernard(Y)	1834	March 22	ColumbanCoOh	03	12	33
McKenzie, Donald(Y)	1836	Oct. 11	Jeff.Co.,Oh.	03	12	20
McKenzie, James(Y)	1835	April 16	ColumbanCoOh	03	12	20

PURCHASER	YEAR	DATE	RESIDENCE	R	T	S
McKeown, Alex'r.(Y)	1826	Dec. 15	BelmontCo,Oh	07	11	35
McKever, T.(Z)	1815	March 14	WashCo.,Penn	15	16	35
McKever, Thomas(Z)	1833	Dec. 13	Perry Co.,Oh	14	14	30
McKever, Thomas(Z)	1815	March 14	WashCo.,Penn	14	13	04
McKever, Thomas(Z)	1815	March 14	WashCo.,Ohio	14	14	31
McKever, Thomas(Z)	1815	March 14	WashCo.,Penn	14	14	30
McKilrack, J.(Z)	1815	Dec. 25	BelmontCo,Oh	13	08	03
McKinirie, Samuel F.(Y)	1830	Jan. 19	Jeff.Co.,Oh.	07	11	27
McKinley, Dennis(Z)	1835	Aug. 28	Morgan Co,Oh	10	06	25
McKinley, Dennis(Z)	1836	April 27	Morgan Co,Oh	10	06	22
McKinley, John(Z-M)	1836	June 03	HolmesCoOhio	09	09	04
McKinney, Dan'l.(Z-M)	1831	April 11	StarkeCo.,Oh	10	10	16
McKinney, James(Z)	1811	Jan. 31	AlleghnyCoPa	05	02	21
McKinney, Robt.(Z)	1837	Jan. 30	GuernseyCoOh	08	06	25
McKinney, S. F.(Z-M)	1831	April 15	GuernseyCoOh	01	04	20
McKinney, Thomas(Z-M)	1825	Sept. 30	GuernseyCoOh	03	01	17
McKinnon, Joseph R.(Y)	1825	Jan. 17	ColumbanCoOh	01	06	35
McKister, John B.(Z-M)	1833	Aug. 24	TuscarwsCoOh	03	07	02
McKitirick, William(Z)	1814	June 13	BelmontCo,Oh	09	06	17
McKitrick, Wm.(Z)	1826	June 30	Morgan Co,Oh	13	09	34
McKitrick, Wm.(Z)	1816	April 22	BelmontCo,Oh	13	08	03
McKlintick, Joseph(Z)	1814	Nov. 09	MercerCoPenn	14	15	07
McKnight, Samuel(Z-M)	1834	Dec. 05	GuernseyCoOh	04	02	11
McKorkle, Joseph(Z)	1817	Jan. 15	Ohio Co.,Vir	04	02	09
McKown, Henry(Y)	1825	Oct. 19	ColumbanCoOh	06	18	18
McKracken, Robert(Z)	1812	Oct. 22	Jeff.Co.,Oh.	10	01	03
McKracken, Robert(Z)	1813	May 31	HarrisonCoOh	10	01	08
McKyar, William(Z-M)	1832	Nov. 13	GuernseyCoOh	04	02	20
McLain, John(Z)	1833	Dec. 27	Perry Co.,Oh	15	14	24
McLain, William(Z)	1835	Nov. 10	Jeff.Co.,Oh.	09	05	28
McLaine, John(Z)	1832	Aug. 25	Perry Co.,Oh	15	14	24
McLane, John(Z-M)	1835	July 07	CarrolCo.,Oh	03	08	14
McLane, Joseph(Z-M)	1837	Feb. 18	CoshoctnCoOh	09	07	02
McLaughlin, Alex'r.(Z)	1811	Dec. 09	ZanesvilleOh	10	02	13
McLaughlin, Alex'r.(Z)	1811	Dec. 31	MuskingmCoOh	09	03	07
McLaughlin, Alex'r.(Z)	1811	Dec. 31	MuskingmCoOh	09	03	14
McLaughlin, Alexander(Y)	1836	April 29	ColumbanCoOh	03	12	11
McLaughlin, Alexander(Z)	1811	Nov. 25	ZanesvilleOh	10	02	14
McLaughlin, Alexander(Z)	1811	Nov. 25	ZanesvilleOh	09	03	08
McLaughlin, Daniel(Y)	1830	Aug. 31	ColumbanCoOh	03	12	18
McLaughlin, Elijah(Z)	1812	May 25	FayetteCo,Pa	08	04	03
McLaughlin, Elijah(Z)	1814	June 03	CoshoctnCoOh	08	04	03
McLaughlin, Elijah(Z)	1815	Sept. 06	FayetteCo,Pa	08	04	01
McLaughlin, Elijah(Z)	1816	May 20	CoshoctnCoOh	08	04	20
McLaughlin, Elijah(Z)	1816	July 04	?	08	05	13
McLaughlin, James(Y)	1824	April 15	HarrisonCoOh	05	12	24
McLaughlin, James(Y)	1826	Oct. 17	ColumbanCoOh	02	10	07
McLaughlin, James(Y)	1826	Oct. 17	ColumbanCoOh	02	10	07
McLaughlin, James(Y)	1828	Jan. 31	ColumbanCoOh	02	09	28
McLaughlin, James(Y)	1828	Sept. 03	HarrisonCoOh	05	12	24
McLaughlin, James(Y)	1830	April 20	HarrisonCoOh	06	13	12
McLaughlin, Jno.(Z)	1831	Dec. 07	Morgan Co,Oh	10	08	18
McLaughlin, John Junr.(Z)	1833	Feb. 28	GuernseyCoOh	09	08	22
McLaughlin, John Junr.(Z)	1833	Feb. 28	GuernseyCoOh	09	08	15
McLaughlin, John(Y)	1837	May 05	PortageCo,Oh	07	20	07
McLaughlin, John(Z)	1830	Jan. 07	GuernseyCoOh	08	08	19
McLaughlin, John(Z)	1831	April 06	MuskingmCoOh	10	08	20
McLaughlin, John(Z)	1833	Feb. 28	FranklinCoNY	09	08	14
McLaughlin, John(Z)	1833	Feb. 28	FranklinCoNY	09	08	23
McLaughlin, John(Z)	1835	Jan. 12	GuernseyCoOh	08	08	18
McLaughlin, John(Z)	1811	May 09	FayetteCo,Pa	08	04	07
McLaughlin, John(Z-M)	1833	Aug. 16	Jeff.Co.,Oh.	02	06	03
McLaughlin, John(Z-M)	1833	Aug. 30	Jeff.Co.,Oh.	02	05	02
McLaughlin, Joseph(Z)	1827	May 01	BelmontCo,Oh	12	11	23
McLaughlin, Patrick(Z)	1816	Oct. 22	GuernseyCoOh	01	02	14
McLaughlin, Patrick(Z-M)	1828	Nov. 25	GuernseyCoOh	01	02	08
McLaughlin, Patrick(Z-M)	1831	April 09	GuernseyCoOh	02	04	06
McLaughlin, Robert(Z)	1815	May 31	FayetteCo,Pa	11	04	13
McLaughlin, Samuel(Z-M)	1836	Jan. 28	CoshoctnCoOh	07	05	12

PURCHASER	YEAR	DATE	RESIDENCE	R	T	S
McLaughlin, Thomas(Z)	1833	Feb. 19	Perry Co.,Oh	14	13	05
McLaughlin, Thomas(Z)	1833	March 21	Perry Co.,Oh	14	13	05
McLaughlin, Thos.(Z-M)	1836	Oct. 03	LickingCo,Oh	11	04	13
McLaughlin, Wm.(Y)	1823	Feb. 21	ColumbanCoOh	03	11	30
McLean, Allen(Y)	1830	Aug. 24	ColumbanCoOh	03	13	33
McLean, Daniel(Y)	1831	Nov. 26	ColumbanCoOh	02	10	21
McLean, John(Z)	1831	April 30	Perry Co.,Oh	15	14	24
McLean, William(Z)	1805	Nov. 14	BedfordCo,Pa	12	13	17
McLees, Joseph(Z)	1836	Oct. 31	MuskingmCoOh	15	14	36
McLees, Joseph(Z)	1836	Oct. 31	MuskingmCoOh	15	14	36
McLees, Joseph(Z)	1836	Oct. 31	MuskingmCoOh	15	14	36
McLees, Joseph(Z)	1817	May 06	MuskingmCoOh	12	12	12
McLennan, Donald(Y)	1828	Oct. 30	Jeff.Co.,Oh.	03	12	25
McLennan, Kenneth(Y)	1827	Nov. 20	Jeff.Co.,Co.	03	11	35
McLennan, Kenneth(Y)	1828	Sept. 05	Jeff.Co.,Oh.	03	12	25
McLennan, Kenneth(Y)	1828	Oct. 30	Jeff.Co.,Oh.	03	12	19
McLennon, Kenneth(Y)	1831	June 24	ColumbanCoOh	03	12	19
McLeoud, Jane(Y)	1835	Aug. 24	CarrollCo,Oh	04	12	22
McLeoud, Wm.(Y)	1829	Oct. 15	Jeff.Co.,Oh.	04	12	23
McLeoud, Wm.(Y)	1829	Oct. 15	Jeff.Co.,Oh.	04	12	22
McLoud, John Grant(Y)	1835	May 26	CarrollCo,Oh	04	12	22
McLuan, James(Z)	1832	Sept. 11	Morgan Co,Oh	08	06	06
McMahan, John(Z)	1816	June 25	CoshoctnCoOh	09	03	14
McMahon, James(Z)	1834	Feb. 21	Perry Co.,Oh	15	15	31
McMahon, James(Z-M)	1834	Oct. 31	TuscarwsCoOh	03	06	15
McMahon, John(Z)	1822	May 13	AlleghnyCoMd	15	15	31
McMan, Samuel(Z)	1805	Oct. 18	ShenandhCoVa	08	02	07
McManes, James(Y)	1824	March 26	WestmrldCoPa	07	17	05
McManes, John(Y)	1825	Jan. 20	Stark Co.,Oh	07	18	25
McManus, Patrick(Y)	1829	Nov. 18	ColumbanCoOh	03	13	23
McMaster, Jane(Y)	1835	May 05	AlleghnyCoPa	04	12	18
McMaster, John(Y)	1831	June 03	AlleghnyCoPa	04	12	18
McMaster, John(Y)	1831	June 03	AlleghnyCoPa	04	12	24
McMaster, John(Y)	1832	Aug. 10	AlleghnyCoPa	04	12	18
McMaster, John(Y)	1832	Aug. 10	?	04	12	18
McMath, David(Y)	1826	Dec. 15	HarrisonCoOh	06	11	26
McMechan, John(Z)	1836	Feb. 04	ZanesvilleOh	10	06	05
McMichael, James(Z)	1815	April 11	MuskingmCoOh	05	02	22
McMillan, Dan'l.(Y)	1825	June 13	TuscarwsCoOh	07	14	08
McMillan, Daniel(Y)	1826	May 08	TuscarwsCoOh	07	14	13
McMillan, Ephraim(Z)	1817	Feb. 08	KnoxCo.,Ohio	10	08	24
McMillan, Joseph(Z)	1816	March 08	KnoxCo.,Ohio	10	08	15
McMillan, Joseph(Z-M)	1831	April 14	KnoxCo.,Ohio	10	08	15
McMillan, Patrick(Y)	1829	Sept. 05	TuscarwsCoOh	06	13	25
McMillan, Patrick(Y)	1830	Aug. 18	TuscarwsCoOh	06	12	30
McMillan, Robt.(Z-M)	1831	Aug. 29	TuscarwsCoOh	01	06	23
McMillen, Robert(Z-M)	1832	June 30	TuscarwsCoOh	01	06	23
McMillen, William(Z-M)	1836	Sept. 23	WashngtnCoOh	03	04	10
McMillin, Joseph(Z-M)	1832	Oct. 26	GuernseyCoOh	03	03	10
McMillion, Robert(Z)	1806	Nov. 19	Jeff.Co.,Oh.	10	07	14
McMorris, Lindsey(Z-M)	1832	Nov. 19	CoshoctnCoOh	07	04	13
McMorris, Lindsey(Z-M)	1832	Dec. 28	CoshoctnCoOh	07	04	13
McMorris, Lindsey(Z-M)	1832	Dec. 28	CoshoctnCoOh	07	04	13
McMullan, Joseph(Z-M)	1836	March 21	GuernseyCoOh	03	03	10
McMullan, Joseph(Z-M)	1836	May 09	GuernseyCoOh	03	03	11
McMullen, Alex'r.(Z-M)	1835	Nov. 13	CoshoctnCoOh	07	05	07
McMullen, Alex'r.(Z-M)	1835	Nov. 13	CoshoctnCoOh	07	05	04
McMullen, James(Y)	1831	March 09	ColumbanCoOh	04	14	26
McMullen, Jesse(Z)	1829	Oct. 23	BelmontCo,Oh	13	08	21
McMullen, Jno.(Z-M)	1835	March 16	GuernseyCoOh	04	03	21
McMullen, John(Z)	1821	Sept. 18	AlleghnyCoPa	04	03	21
McMullen, John(Z-M)	1828	July 08	GuernseyCoOh	02	02	09
McMullen, John(Z-M)	1837	Feb. 14	GuernseyCoOh	04	03	21
McMullen, Joseph(Z)	1805	July 23	FairfeldCoOh	15	17	05
McMullen, Joseph(Z-M)	1823	Oct. 15	WashCo.,Penn	02	04	24
McMullen, Joseph(Z-M)	1837	Feb. 23	GuernseyCoOh	03	03	11
McMullen, Silas(Z-M)	1829	Jan. 03	LickingCo,Oh	11	01	19
McMullin, Amos(Y)	1824	May 18	ColumbanCoOh	04	14	24
McMullin, Amos(Y)	1829	March 18	ColumbanCoOh	04	14	24

PURCHASER	YEAR	DATE	RESIDENCE	R	T	S
McMullin, Archb'd.(Y)	1821	Sept. 12	ColumbanCoOh	04	14	15
McMullin, Archb'd.(Y)	1821	Sept. 12	ColumbanCoOh	04	14	15
McMullin, Enos(Y)	1831	Aug. 11	ColumbanCoOh	04	14	24
McMullin, James(Y)	1821	Oct. 24	ColumbanCoOh	04	14	21
McMullin, Patrick(Y)	1823	April 04	TuscarwsCoOh	06	13	25
McMunn, Isaac(Z)	1835	Oct. 29	BelmontCo,Oh	09	06	08
McNabb, Joseph(Z-M)	1837	March 27	CoshoctnCoOh	09	07	22
McNabb, Wm.(Z)	1827	April 19	Morgan Co,Oh	10	08	14
McNair, James(Z)	1827	Nov. 17	KnoxCo.,Ohio	11	08	12
McNair, Wm.(Z)	1827	Nov. 17	KnoxCo.,Ohio	11	08	24
McNamaree, Samuel(Z)	1816	Sept. 13	WashCo.,Penn	10	06	17
McNaughten, Neal(Z)	1805	Nov. 07	AlleghnyCoPa	11	13	29
McNaughten, Neal(Z)	1805	Nov. 07	AlleghnyCoPa	11	13	29
McNeal, Archibald(Z-M)	1833	June 10	CoshoctnCoOh	08	06	01
McNeal, Archibald(Z-M)	1836	Jan. 23	CoshoctnCoOh	08	07	20
McNeal, Henry(Z-M)	1836	Ján. 04	CoshoctnCoOh	07	07	02
McNeal, Henry(Z-M)	1836	March 17	CoshoctnCoOh	08	07	20
McNeal, John(Z)	1832	May 07	Perry Co.,Oh	14	12	22
McNeal, John(Z)	1815	Nov. 20	WashCo.,Penn	05	02	03
McNeal, Malcolm(Z-M)	1831	Nov. 12	MuskingmCoOh	05	03	22
McNeal, Malcom(Z-M)	1821	March 21	MuskingmCoOh	05	03	19
McNeal, Ross(Z)	1815	Oct. 21	WashCo.,Penn	05	02	02
McNeal, Thomas(Z-M)	1837	July 03	CoshoctnCoOh	08	07	21
McNeal, William(Z-M)	1836	Dec. 13	CoshoctnCoOh	07	07	16
McNeal, Wm.(Z-M)	1837	Feb. 21	CoshoctnCoOh	07	07	16
McNear, William(Z-M)	1831	Nov. 01	KnoxCo.,Ohio	11	08	18
McNear, Wm.(Z-M)	1828	Nov. 21	KnoxCo.,Ohio	11	08	07
McNeary, William(Z)	1817	April 08	Brooke CoVir	09	05	13
McNeely, Andrew(Z)	1817	Jan. 07	HarrisonCoOh	01	05	22
McNeely, Francis B.(Z-M)	1834	Jan. 17	GuernseyCoOh	02	04	24
McNeely, J.(Z)	1815	March 11	WashCo.,Penn	05	01	25
McNeely, John(Y)	1834	June 07	GuernseyCoOh	07	09	27
McNeely, William(Z-M)	1834	Feb. 11	CoshoctnCoOh	07	07	14
McNeen, Wm.(Z-M)	1830	June 30	KnoxCo.,Ohio	10	08	15
McNeily, Francis B.(Z-M)	1835	Jan. 06	GuernseyCoOh	04	06	20
McNelley, Thomas(Y)	1833	Feb. 14	ColumbanCoOh	04	13	01
McNelly, Jacob(Y)	1835	Feb. 10	CarrollCo,Oh	04	13	01
McNely, William(Y)	1831	July 25	ColumbanCoOh	05	16	32
McNight, Susan(Z-M)	1829	June 10	WayneCo.,Oh.	07	08	10
McNilly, John(Y)	1837	Jan. 03	Jeff.co.,Oh.	11	13	08
McNogther, Alex'r.(Z)	1815	Jan. 09	MuskingmCoOh	15	17	01
McNulty, Anthony(Z-M)	1835	Nov. 10	CoshoctnCoOh	07	05	11
McNulty, Anthony(Z-M)	1836	Jan. 15	CoshoctnCoOh	07	05	19
McNutly, Hugh(Z)	1824	Dec. 20	Perry Co.,Oh	15	16	21
McPeck, Daniel(Z)	1806	Feb. 24	BelmontCo,Oh	10	09	17
McPeck, Daniel(Z)	1806	Feb. 24	BelmontCo,Oh	10	09	17
McPeck, Rich'd.(Z)	1828	Dec. 30	Morgan Co,Oh	12	10	33
McPeck, Richard(Z)	1825	Nov. 01	Morgan Co,Oh	12	10	33
McPeek, Daniel(Z)	1817	May 06	GuernseyCoOh	01	03	12
McPeek, Philip(Z)	1831	June 30	Morgan Co,Oh	12	10	32
McPeek, Rich'd.(Z)	1828	Dec. 30	Morgan Co,Oh	12	10	33
McPherren, Richard(Z-M)	1827	March 17	Jeff.Co.,Oh.	04	06	09
McPherson, Daniel(Z)	1836	Jan. 29	GuernseyCoOh	08	06	34
McPherson, John(Z-M)	1831	Nov. 03	BelmontCo,Oh	03	06	03
McPherson, Joseph(Z)	1835	Aug. 21	Morgan Co,Oh	10	08	36
McPherson, Joseph(Z-M)	1832	June 01	BelmontCo,Oh	03	06	02
McPherson, Joseph(Z-M)	1832	June 01	BelmontCo,Oh	03	06	09
McPherson, Joseph(Z-M)	1832	Dec. 07	BelmontCo,Oh	03	06	02
McPherson, Lorenzo(Y)	1828	Feb. 28	BelmontCo,Oh	06	10	26
McPhuron, George(Z)	1816	Nov. 09	MuskingmCoOh	05	03	18
McPride, Samuel(Y)	1827	April 06	ColumbanCoOh	05	15	10
McQuaide, John(Y)	1828	Nov. 19	TuscarwsCoOh	06	13	22
McQuand, Charles(Z)	1810	June 27	MuskingmCoOh	12	13	24
McQuand, Charles(Z)	1810	June 27	MuskingmCoOh	11	13	18
McQueen, Daniel(Z)	1835	Sept. 11	AlleghnyCoPa	10	06	02
McQueen, Daniel(Z)	1835	Sept. 11	AlleghnyCoPa	10	06	02
McQueen, Minor(Z)	1829	Aug. 12	MuskingmCoOh	10	04	14
McQueen, Minor(Z-M)	1836	Jan. 07	LickingCo,Oh	10	04	17
McQueen, Minor(Z-M)	1836	Jan. 07	LickingCo,Oh	10	04	18

PURCHASER	YEAR	DATE	RESIDENCE	R	T	S
McQuin, Minor(Z-M)	1832	Nov. 06	LickingCo,Oh	10	04	13
McQuoid, Thomas(Y)	1830	Dec. 08	ColumbanCoOh	03	13	17
McQuoid, Thomas(Y)	1833	Feb. 19	ColumbanCoOh	03	13	17
McQuoid, Thos.(Y)	1828	Nov. 26	ColumbanCoOh	03	13	17
McQuoid, Thos.(Y)	1828	Nov. 26	ColumbanCoOh	03	13	17
McSand, John Grant(Y)	1832	July 11	Jeff.Co.,Oh.	04	12	22
McSenan, Kenneth(Y)	1824	Oct. 21	ColumbanCoOh	03	12	25
McTeigh, Orsemas(Z)	1830	March 02	Morgan Co,Oh	11	10	22
McTheerer, Arch.(Z-M)	1831	June 03	TuscarwsCoOh	02	05	20
McTheerer, Wm.(Z-M)	1831	June 03	TuscarwsCoOh	02	05	12
McTire, Wilson F.(Z)	1832	Dec. 17	Morgan Co,Oh	09	06	15
McVany, Moses(Z)	1817	July 18	GreeneCo.,Pa	01	09	12
McVay, Edward(Z)	1832	Dec. 01	Perry Co.,Oh	15	15	26
McVeigh, Darius(Z)	1828	Sept. 11	Morgan Co,Oh	11	10	23
McVeigh, Jos.(Z)	1828	Sept. 11	Morgan Co,Oh	11	10	23
McVelley, Thomas(Y)	1829	Nov. 28	Jeff.Co.,Oh.	04	13	01
McVey, Reason(Z-M)	1826	May 31	GuernseyCoOh	01	01	21
McVickar, Dennis(Z)	1826	Sept. 28	GuernseyCoOh	09	08	09
McVicker, Jas.(Z)	1839	Jan. 16	MonroeCo.,Oh	08	06	15
McVickers, Arch'd.(Z)	1815	Feb. 04	GuernseyCoOh	09	08	11
McWilliams, Alexander(Y)	1825	Dec. 05	BelmontCo,Oh	06	10	21
McWilliams, Dan'l.(Z-M)	1834	Oct. 15	GuernseyCoOh	02	03	05
McWilliams, Daniel(Z-M)	1835	Oct. 26	GuernseyCoOh	02	04	25
McWilliams, Hugh(Z)	1835	Oct. 16	MonroeCo.,Oh	08	07	05
McWilliams, John(Z)	1815	Oct. 20	BelmontCo,Oh	09	06	04
McWilliams, Philip(Z)	1831	Sept. 12	GuernseyCoOh	08	07	06
McWilliams, Philip(Z-M)	1826	April 14	GuernseyCoOh	02	01	07
McWilliams, Robert(Z-M)	1832	July 17	GuernseyCoOh	02	04	25
McWilliams, Robert(Z-M)	1833	Aug. 23	GuernseyCoOh	02	04	25
McWilliams, Robt.(Z-M)	1837	Dec. 05	GuernseyCoOh	02	04	25
McWilliams, Sam'l.(Z)	1815	Oct. 20	BelmontCo,Oh	09	06	06
McWilliams, Samuel(Z)	1815	Nov. 04	BelmontCo,Oh	09	06	07
MccCauley, Patrick Jr.(Y)	1826	Nov. 14	ColumbanCoOh	04	13	06
Mclain, William(Z)	1836	May 12	Morgan Co,Oh	09	05	27
MeHaffey, Samuel(Z)	1827	Nov. 01	GuernseyCoOh	04	02	09
Mealman, Jacob(Z)	1833	Nov. 25	GuernseyCoOh	08	08	26
Mealman, Jacob(Z)	1833	March 25	GuernseyCoOh	08	08	01
Means, Andrew(Z)	1833	Feb. 23	MuskingmCoOh	12	12	03
Means, Isaac(Z-M)	1839	April 06	CoshoctnCoOh	10	07	20
Medcalf, Arthur(Y)	1830	July 07	ColumbanCoOh	04	12	06
Meddles, John(Z-M)	1833	June 27	TuscarwsCoOh	01	05	03
Meddles, John(Z-M)	1836	Feb. 03	TuscarwsCoOh	01	05	03
Meddough, Ephraim(Z-M)	1836	March 29	Wayne Co.,Oh	06	09	24
Medley, Joseph(Y)	1827	July 25	BelmontCo,Oh	05	08	22
Medley, Richard(Z-M)	1835	May 21	GuernseyCoOh	03	05	19
Meek, Asa(Z-M)	1826	Nov. 18	MuskingmCoOh	09	03	07
Meek, Asa(Z-M)	1835	June 20	MuskingmCoOh	09	03	07
Meek, Daniel H.(Z-M)	1829	Sept. 01	TuscarwsCoOh	03	05	11
Meek, Daniel Hill(Z-M)	1835	July 08	TuscarwsCoOh	03	05	20
Meek, David A.(Z-M)	1837	May 06	GuernseyCoOh	09	07	01
Meek, George(Z-M)	1824	Oct. 04	CoshoctnCoOh	08	04	14
Meek, Moses(Z)	1808	April 19	LickingCo,Oh	15	18	05
Meek, Richard(Z-M)	1826	April 19	CoshoctnCoOh	09	04	25
Meek, Richard(Z-M)	1832	Dec. 28	CoshoctnCoOh	09	04	16
Meek, Richard(Z-M)	1836	Sept. 14	HolmesCoOhio	08	08	25
Meek, Robert(Y)	1831	March 29	TuscarwsCoOh	07	15	27
Meek, Thomas(Z-M)	1833	Aug. 29	Wash.Co,Penn	01	05	19
Meek, Thomas(Z-M)	1836	Dec. 09	KnoxCo.,Ohio	10	04	07
Meekley, Benjamin(Z)	1814	June 21	CoshoctnCoOh	07	07	25
Meerry, Rouse(Z)	1826	May 05	Morgan Co,Oh	09	07	36
Meese, Christopher(Y)	1831	Aug. 02	WayneCo.,Oh.	10	01	03
Meese, Jacob(Y)	1826	June 06	ColumbanCoOh	06	18	10
Megrew, Finley(Z-M)	1833	May 21	GuernseyCoOh	01	05	18
Meguyer, John(Z-M)	1832	Aug. 10	GuernseyCoOh	01	05	18
Meguyer, Thomas(Z-M)	1823	Dec. 16	GuernseyCoOh	01	05	25
Mehaffey, John(Z-M)	1826	March 28	GuernseyCoOh	04	02	18
Mehaffey, John(Z-M)	1826	July 27	GuernseyCoOh	04	02	18
Mehaffey, Robt.(Z-M)	1830	April 07	GuernseyCoOh	04	02	09
Mehaffey, Sam'l.(Z-M)	1829	Jan. 09	GuernseyCoOh	04	02	09

PURCHASER	YEAR	DATE	RESIDENCE	R	T	S
Mehaffey, Sam.(Z-M)	1830	Aug. 26	GuernseyCoOh	04	02	10
Mehaffy, S.(Z-M)	1830	Oct. 29	GuernseyCoOh	04	02	10
Meighen, John Jr.(Z)	1833	May 18	GuernseyCoOh	08	08	09
Meiser, John(Z-M)	1827	May 22	TuscarwsCoOh	04	07	21
Meiser, John(Z-M)	1827	May 22	TuscarwsCoOh	04	07	22
Meiser, John(Z-M)	1827	May 22	TuscarwsCoOh	04	06	01
Meishler, Peter(Z-M)	1827	Aug. 14	HolmesCoOhio	06	08	01
Meisinger, Adam(Z-M)	1833	Dec. 09	TuscarwsCoOh	03	08	07
Meiskimen, William(Z-M)	1826	Aug. 18	CoshoctnCoOh	04	04	08
Mekee, James(Z-M)	1838	Nov. 02	GuernseyCoOh	03	04	05
Meldrum, William(Y)	1832	March 15	Jeff.Co.,Oh.	07	12	11
Melick, A.(Z)	1816	April 24	MuskinymCoOh	15	17	21
Melick, David(Z)	1810	March 26	MuskingmCoOh	10	06	21
Melick, David(Z)	1811	Nov. 13	MuskingmCoOh	10	05	07
Melick, George(Z)	1814	April 27	KnoxCo.,Ohio	10	05	07
Melick, George(Z)	1815	Nov. 11	KnoxCo.,Ohio	10	05	08
Melick, George(Z)	1811	Nov. 13	SomersetCoPa	10	05	04
Melick, Jonas(Z)	1830	March 19	KnoxCo.,Ohio	10	05	02
Melick, N.(Z)	1816	April 24	MuskingmCoOh	15	17	21
Melick, Nathan(Z)	1824	May 10	Perry Co.,Oh	15	17	21
Melick, William(Z)	1805	Oct. 26	SomersetCoPa	14	13	03
Melick, William(Z)	1805	Oct. 26	SomersetCoPa	14	14	17
Melick, William(Z)	1813	Sept. 09	MuskingmCoOh	15	17	21
Melish, Robert(Z-M)	1831	Oct. 13	TuscarwsCoOh	01	09	21
Mellon, G.(Z)	1815	Feb. 02	WashngtnCoOh	12	11	34
Mellon, Jacob(Z)	1836	May 27	Perry Co.,Oh	15	14	10
Melon, David(Z-M)	1831	Oct. 15	BelmontCo,Oh	05	03	14
Meloy, James Jr.(Z)	1825	March 09	Morgan Co,Oh	12	11	15
Meloy, James Junr.(Z)	1825	Aug. 24	Belmontco,Oh	12	11	15
Meloy, John(Z)	1832	April 28	Morgan Co,Oh	11	11	08
Meloy, John(Z)	1834	Dec. 10	Morgan Co,Oh	11	11	03
Melvin, A.(Z)	1817	May 03	CoshoctnCoOh	09	04	07
Menaight, Wm.(Z-M)	1828	Dec. 26	WayneCo.,Oh.	07	08	10
Mendenhall, John(Z)	1833	Feb. 23	GuernseyCoOh	08	08	01
Mendenhall, Samuel(Z)	1805	Nov. 08	JeffrsnCoVir	09	03	13
Mendenhall, Samuel(Z)	1805	Nov. 08	JeffrsnCoVir	09	03	19
Mendenhall, Samuel(Z)	1805	Nov. 08	JeffrsnCoVir	09	03	18
Mendenhall, Samuel(Z)	1805	Nov. 08	JeffrsnCoVir	09	03	13
Mendenhall, Samuel(Z)	1815	Nov. 04	Jeff.Co.,Oh.	09	03	18
Mendenhall, Samuel(Z)	1815	Nov. 04	Jeff.Co.,Oh.	09	03	24
Mercer, Elizabeth(Z-M)	1820	Dec. 02	MuskingmCoOh	09	03	03
Mercer, John(Z-M)	1835	Nov. 04	LickingCo,Oh	10	04	21
Mercer, Richard(Z-M)	1836	March 30	BelmontCo,Oh	03	06	15
Mercer, Richard(Z-M)	1836	March 30	BelmontCo,Oh	03	06	15
Meredith, Isaac(Z)	1815	Oct. 18	CoshoctnCoOh	09	06	22
Meredith, Isaac(Z-M)	1833	April 24	CoshoctnCoOh	09	07	22
Meredith, Jedediah(Z-M)	1839	Feb. 09	HolmesCoOhio	08	08	12
Meredith, Jesse(Z-M)	1832	April 09	CoshoctnCoOh	09	06	19
Meredith, Job(Z)	1816	Aug. 15	CoshoctnCoOh	09	05	02
Meredith, Job(Z-M)	1832	April 09	CoshoctnCoOh	09	06	18
Meredith, Job(Z-M)	1832	June 13	CoshoctnCoOh	08	04	23
Meredith, John(Z-M)	1836	Feb. 27	TuscarwsCoOh	03	07	02
Meredith, John(Z-M)	1836	March 09	TuscarwsCoOh	03	08	25
Meredith, Nath'l. L.(Z-M)	1836	Dec. 30	CoshoctnCoOh	09	07	12
Meredith, Obed(Z)	1805	Dec. 24	MongahlaCoVa	09	06	21
Meredith, Peter(Z-M)	1833	April 24	CoshoctnCoOh	09	07	23
Meredith, Peter(Z-M)	1836	March 26	CoshoctnCoOh	09	07	22
Meredith, Robert(Z-M)	1836	Feb. 08	CoshoctnCoOh	09	07	23
Meredith, W. L.(Z-M)	1831	Oct. 05	CoshoctnCoOh	09	07	13
Merner, Jonas(Z)	1828	Feb. 27	MuskingmCoOh	12	12	03
Merrell, Mathias(Y)	1833	Sept. 18	CarrollCo,Oh	04	13	01
Merrick, Daniel(Y)	1826	Nov. 03	ColumbanCoOh	04	13	25
Merrick, Israel I.(Y)	1831	March 22	Stark Co.,Oh	06	15	31
Merrick, Israel J.(Y)	1828	April 04	ColumbanCoOh	06	15	31
Merrick, James(Y)	1832	June 02	ColumbanCoOh	03	12	20
Merrick, John(Y)	1834	June 02	Jeff.Co.,Oh.	03	12	13
Merrill, Matthias(Y)	1822	Feb. 23	ColumbanCoOh	06	16	13
Merrill, Rich.(Z-M)	1831	Sept. 03	BelmontCo,Oh	03	05	12
Merrin, Richard(Z)	1834	Feb. 28	KnoxCo.,Ohio	15	15	27

PURCHASER	YEAR	DATE	RESIDENCE	R	T	S
Merritt, Thomas(Z)	1834	Nov. 01	Morgan Co,Oh	09	05	26
Merritt, Thomas(Z)	1834	Nov. 01	Morgan Co,Oh	09	05	27
Merritt, William J.(Z)	1830	March 25	BelmontCo,Oh	10	07	22
Merritt, Wm. J.(Z)	1832	Feb. 18	Morgan Co,Oh	10	07	23
Merritt, Wm. J.(Z)	1832	Feb. 18	Morgan Co,Oh	10	07	23
Merry, Adam(Z)	1816	April 27	Brooke CoVir	09	05	06
Merry, Ambrose H.(Z)	1836	Feb. 08	MonroeCo.,Oh	08	07	30
Merry, Benson(Z)	1835	Dec. 08	Morgan Co,Oh	08	07	30
Merry, Calton(Z)	1836	Aug. 16	MonroeCo.,Oh	08	07	29
Merry, Rouse(Z)	1832	May 22	MonroeCo.,Oh	09	07	36
Merry, Rufus(Z)	1832	May 22	Morgan Co,Oh	08	07	06
Merry, Rufus(Z)	1832	May 22	Morgan Co,Oh	09	07	01
Merry, Rufus(Z)	1832	Nov. 08	Morgan Co,Oh	08	06	06
Merry, Rufus(Z)	1832	Nov. 08	Morgan Co,Oh	09	06	01
Merry, Rufus(Z)	1835	June 06	MonroeCo.,Oh	08	06	06
Meshouse, David(Z)	1816	April 22	TuscarwsCoOh	03	08	06
Meskimen, John(Z-M)	1837	Feb. 24	ZanesvilleOh	04	03	01
Messamore, Sam'l.(Y)	1823	May 12	ColumbanCoOh	06	17	15
Messer, Abraham(Z)	1805	July 27	Ohio Co.,Vir	12	13	07
Messer, Abraham(Z)	1805	July 27	Ohio Co.,Vir	12	13	07
Messer, Abraham(Z)	1805	Aug. 13	Ohio Co.,Vir	12	13	06
Messer, Abraham(Z)	1805	Aug. 13	Ohio Co.,Vir	12	13	06
Messer, Andrew(Z)	1809	Jan. 14	MuskingmCoOh	12	13	17
Messer, Francis(Y)	1829	March 18	Stark Co.,Oh	06	19	31
Messer, George(Z)	1809	Sept. 02	MuskingmCoOh	12	13	10
Messer, Henry(Z)	1836	Sept. 12	GuernseyCoOh	09	08	36
Messer, Jacob(Z)	1822	Nov. 16	MuskingmCoOh	12	12	10
Messer, Jacob(Z)	1815	Dec. 02	MuskingmCoOh	12	12	01
Messer, Jacob(Z)	1816	Dec. 26	MuskingmCoOh	12	11	14
Messer, James(Z)	1837	March 24	GuernseyCoOh	08	08	23
Messer, John(Z)	1817	Feb. 15	MuskingmCoOh	12	10	10
Metheny, Ephraim Jr.(Z)	1836	March 28	BelmontCo,Oh	08	08	34
Metheny, Joseph(Z)	1813	April 10	WashngtnCoOh	09	06	10
Metheny, Joshua(Z)	1836	March 28	BelmontCo,Oh	08	07	10
Mettelholy, Joseph(Y)	1834	Oct. 25	ColumbanCoOh	05	16	31
Metts, Peter(Z-M)	1825	April 16	HolmesCoOhio	07	09	21
Metz, Jacob(Z-M)	1832	Dec. 11	CoshoctnCoOh	05	07	04
Metz, Jacob(Z-M)	1836	Sept. 08	CoshoctnCoOh	09	08	21
Metzler, Adam(Z)	1816	July 31	MuskingmCoOh	06	08	22
Metzler, Adam(Z-M)	1832	May 15	HolmesCoOhio	05	07	05
Metzler, Frederick(Z-M)	1836	April 07	CarrollCo,Oh	01	08	03
Metzler, Paul(Z-M)	1836	March 08	HolmesCoOhio	05	07	14
Meyer, Andrew(Y)	1822	April 06	Baltimore,Md	08	10	06
Meyer, George(Z-M)	1837	May 30	HolmesCoOhio	09	09	25
Meyers, Nathaniel(Z)	1824	May 17	MuskingmCoOh	11	13	15
Michael, James W. Jr.(Z)	1817	Oct. 15	MuskingmCoOh	05	02	21
Michael, John W.(Z-M)	1822	April 05	MuskingmCoOh	04	02	13
Michael, Peter(Y)	1825	Aug. 30	Stark Co.,Oh	07	16	23
Michel, Divid(Z-M)	1836	Dec. 03	CarrollCo,Oh	05	04	04
Michler, Peter(Z-M)	1832	Nov. 02	HolmesCoOhio	06	08	01
Michler, Peter(Z-M)	1835	Nov. 17	HolmesCoOhio	06	08	01
Mick, Andrew(Y)	1829	July 25	ColumbanCoOh	04	13	20
Mick, Andrew(Y)	1833	May 03	ColumbanCoOh	04	13	14
Mickel, John(Y)	1830	June 15	Stark Co.,Oh	07	16	24
Middaugh, Jeddiah(Z-M)	1835	Dec. 12	HolmesCoOhio	08	08	19
Middleton, Benjamin(Z-M)	1825	Oct. 06	KnoxCo.,Ohio	11	08	04
Middleton, Hutchison(Z-M)	1835	Aug. 28	TuscarwsCoOh	02	06	22
Middleton, William(Y)	1830	Sept. 13	TuscarwsCoOh	07	14	09
Middleton, William(Z-M)	1834	Dec. 17	FayetteCo,Pa	02	06	23
Miers, Isaac(Z)	1834	Nov. 29	Perry Co.,Oh	14	13	31
Mifford, John H.(Z-M)	1824	Dec. 06	KnoxCo.,Ohio	10	07	04
Milbourn, David(Y)	1822	Oct. 19	ColumbanCoOh	05	15	05
Miles, Hiram(Z)	1832	May 22	Morgan Co,Oh	13	08	07
Miles, James(Z)	1816	July 05	FredrickCoMd	14	13	03
Miles, Stephen(Z-M)	1832	Sept. 17	WashCo.,Penn	04	07	13
Miles, Stephen(Z-M)	1832	Sept. 17	WashCo.,Penn	04	07	20
Miles, Stephen(Z-M)	1835	Jan. 06	LickingCo,Oh	11	04	23
Miles, Thomas(Z)	1816	July 05	FredrickCoMd	14	13	03
Miley, John(Z)	1824	Oct. 20	GuernseyCoOh	08	08	21

PURCHASER	YEAR	DATE	RESIDENCE	R	T	S
Miley, John(Z)	1831	Sept. 22	GuernseyCoOh	08	08	28
Milham, David(Z)	1820	Sept. 14	Morgan Co,Oh	12	11	09
Milhorne, John(Z)	1824	Feb. 26	GuernseyCoOh	08	08	14
Milhorne, John(Z)	1825	Oct. 13	GuernseyCoOh	08	08	15
Milhorne, John(Z)	1829	Jan. 23	GuernseyCoOh	08	08	09
Miller, Abraham(Z)	1811	May 27	WashCo.,Penn	11	13	02
Miller, Abraham(Z)	1813	Nov. 22	WashCo.,Penn	11	13	01
Miller, Abraham(Z-M)	1836	Feb. 29	HolmesCoOhio	07	08	17
Miller, Abraham(Z-M)	1837	March 29	CoshoctnCoOh	07	07	16
Miller, Abraham(Z-M)	1837	March 29	CoshoctnCoOh	07	07	16
Miller, Ada(Y)	1829	Sept. 01	HarrisonCoOh	07	12	15
Miller, Adam(Z)	1810	July 30	MuskingmCoOh	15	18	18
Miller, Adam(Z-M)	1822	Oct. 11	GuernseyCoOh	03	03	19
Miller, Adam(Z-M)	1824	Jan. 01	GuernseyCoOh	03	03	10
Miller, Adam(Z-M)	1833	Dec. 03	GuernseyCoOh	03	03	13
Miller, Alex'r.(Z-M)	1839	June 15	GuernseyCoOh	03	05	14
Miller, And'w.(Y)	1830	Oct. 11	ColumbanCoOh	05	16	31
Miller, Anthony(Z)	1807	Dec. 31	MuskingmCoOh	11	03	17
Miller, Anthony(Z)	1811	Nov. 25	HardyCo.,Vir	11	03	16
Miller, Anthony(Z-M)	1836	June 20	BelmontCo,Oh	03	07	24
Miller, Anthony(Z-M)	1836	June 20	BelmontCo,Oh	03	07	24
Miller, Asa(Y)	1829	March 17	HarrisonCoOh	07	12	15
Miller, Barney(Z-M)	1836	Aug. 30	TuscarwsCoOh	03	07	02
Miller, Barney(Z-M)	1837	April 07	TuscarwsCoOh	04	07	10
Miller, Benj'n.(Y)	1822	Jan. 29	Stark Co.,Oh	07	17	19
Miller, Bennedict(Z)	1812	July 09	AlleghnyCoPa	03	08	05
Miller, Bernard(Y)	1831	June 23	TuscarwsCoOh	07	15	31
Miller, C.(Z)	1815	June 22	CoshoctnCoOh	07	09	12
Miller, C.(Z)	1815	June 22	CoshoctnCoOh	07	09	12
Miller, Ch'o.(Z)	1815	Dec. 16	CoshoctnCoOh	06	08	10
Miller, Ch'o.(Z)	1815	Dec. 16	CoshoctnCoOh	06	08	01
Miller, Charles(Y)	1822	Sept. 14	Stark Co.,Pa	06	16	25
Miller, Charles(Z-M)	1831	May 18	CoshoctnCoOh	07	05	21
Miller, Charles(Z-M)	1834	March 22	CarrollCo.,Oh	10	09	03
Miller, Charles(Z-M)	1836	Sept. 12	CarrolCo.,Oh	10	09	23
Miller, Christopher(Y)	1828	Oct. 20	ColumbanCoOh	06	19	14
Miller, Dan'l.(Z-M)	1831	March 19	HolmesCoOhio	05	08	08
Miller, Daniel(Y)	1822	May 01	Stark Co.,Oh	10	02	33
Miller, Daniel(Y)	1828	April 16	Canton, Ohio	07	16	23
Miller, Daniel(Y)	1829	April 02	Stark Co.,Oh	07	16	23
Miller, Daniel(Z)	1826	Sept. 23	HolmesCoOhio	05	08	07
Miller, Daniel(Z)	1814	Oct. 20	TuscarwsCoOh	05	09	05
Miller, Daniel(Z-M)	1833	Sept. 26	CoshoctnCoOh	05	07	14
Miller, David D.(Z-M)	1832	March 06	HolmesCoOhio	05	08	03
Miller, David(Y)	1824	Aug. 03	HarrisonCoOh	05	12	08
Miller, David(Z)	1810	May 29	TuscarwsCoOh	01	09	12
Miller, David(Z)	1812	April 15	TuscarwsCoOh	05	09	22
Miller, David(Z)	1813	Nov. 30	FayetteCo,Pa	02	05	21
Miller, David(Z)	1814	Jan. 12	SomersetCoPa	05	09	22
Miller, David(Z)	1815	May 17	CoshoctnCoOh	05	09	08
Miller, David(Z-M)	1822	July 31	CoshoctnCoOh	04	09	24
Miller, David(Z-M)	1826	Nov. 15	HolmesCoOhio	05	08	03
Miller, David(Z-M)	1835	Sept. 17	HolmesCoOhio	05	07	13
Miller, Edward(Z)	1827	Nov. 05	Morgan Co,Oh	12	10	10
Miller, Edward(Z)	1828	Oct. 20	Morgan Co,Oh	13	08	30
Miller, Edward(Z)	1828	Oct. 20	Morgan Co,Oh	12	10	10
Miller, Edward(Z)	1829	Sept. 21	Morgan Co,Oh	12	10	04
Miller, Edward(Z)	1830	March 19	Morgan Co,Oh	12	10	04
Miller, Edward(Z)	1806	March 22	WashngtnCoOh	12	11	33
Miller, Edward(Z)	1806	March 24	WashngtnCoOh	12	11	33
Miller, Edward(Z)	1807	Jan. 31	WashngtnCoOh	11	10	31
Miller, Edward(Z)	1807	Dec. 31	WashngtnCoOh	11	10	32
Miller, Edward(Z)	1811	Aug. 20	WashngtnCoOh	12	11	33
Miller, Edward(Z)	1815	Dec. 02	WashngtnCoOh	13	08	01
Miller, Edward(Z)	1816	July 16	MuskingmCoOh	12	09	15
Miller, Edward(Z)	1816	Aug. 29	WashngtnCoOh	13	08	13
Miller, Edward(Z)	1816	Dec. 30	WashngtnCoOh	13	08	13
Miller, Edward(Z)	1816	Dec. 30	WashngtnCoOh	13	08	24
Miller, Eli(Y)	1829	March 17	HarrisonCoOh	07	12	15

PURCHASER	YEAR	DATE	RESIDENCE	R	T	S
Miller, Eli(Y)	1829	Sept. 01	HarrisonCoOh	07	12	15
Miller, Eli(Z-M)	1836	Sept. 29	CarrollCo,Oh	10	09	21
Miller, Eli(Z-M)	1836	Sept. 29	CarrollCo,Oh	10	09	21
Miller, Elias(Z-M)	1826	Sept. 23	HolmesCoOhio	05	08	14
Miller, Elizabeth(Z)	1813	Aug. 03	TuscarwsCoOh	05	09	21
Miller, Emanuel(Z)	1811	Oct. 24	TuscarwsCoOh	04	09	06
Miller, Felix(Z)	1815	Feb. 11	KnoxCo.,Ohio	10	05	14
Miller, Geo.(Z-M)	1829	Dec. 29	TuscarwsCoOh	04	07	02
Miller, Geo.(Z-M)	1831	Aug. 24	MuskingmCoOh	06	03	12
Miller, George(Y)	1830	July 09	Jeff.Co.,Oh.	03	12	25
Miller, George(Z)	1832	March 19	ColumbanCoOh	14	12	14
Miller, George(Z)	1834	Feb. 11	Perry Co.,Oh	14	13	06
Miller, George(Z)	1834	Sept. 08	Perry Co.,Oh	14	13	07
Miller, George(Z)	1836	May 02	Perry Co.,Oh	14	12	10
Miller, George(Z)	1814	Nov. 16	WashCo.,Penn	06	01	22
Miller, George(Z-M)	1826	Sept. 19	WashCo.,Penn	03	07	16
Miller, George(Z-M)	1829	May 01	LoudonCo,Vir	06	03	12
Miller, George(Z-M)	1835	May 09	TuscarwsCoOh	04	06	09
Miller, George(Z-M)	1835	May 09	TuscarwsCoOh	04	06	12
Miller, George(Z-M)	1835	Dec. 15	TuscarwsCoOh	03	07	21
Miller, George(Z-M)	1835	Dec. 15	TuscarwsCoOh	03	07	21
Miller, George(Z-M)	1836	June 09	TuscarwsCoOh	04	07	14
Miller, George(Z-M)	1836	June 23	TuscarwsCoOh	03	07	02
Miller, H.(Z)	1815	April 12	TuscarwsCoOh	04	09	14
Miller, Harrison(Z-M)	1836	June 24	HarrisonCoOh	02	06	19
Miller, Henry Junr.(Z)	1817	Jan. 08	MuskingmCoOh	13	10	29
Miller, Henry(Y)	1821	Oct. 17	TuscarwsCoOh	06	14	15
Miller, Henry(Y)	1822	May 16	TuscarwsCoOh	06	14	21
Miller, Henry(Z)	1828	Jan. 14	TuscarwsCoOh	05	09	13
Miller, Henry(Z)	1807	June 01	SomersetCoPa	04	09	22
Miller, Henry(Z)	1809	Sept. 11	SomersetCoPa	04	09	23
Miller, Henry(Z)	1810	May 30	TuscarwsCoOh	04	09	19
Miller, Henry(Z)	1810	July 20	WashCo.,Penn	11	13	11
Miller, Henry(Z)	1814	Aug. 30	TuscarwsCoOh	04	07	01
Miller, Henry(Z)	1816	March 08	KnoxCo.,Ohio	11	08	12
Miller, Henry(Z)	1816	June 24	CoshoctnCoOh	09	07	13
Miller, Henry(Z-M)	1832	May 26	TuscarwsCoOh	04	08	14
Miller, Henry(Z-M)	1831	Sept. 05	CoshoctnCoOh	05	07	20
Miller, Henry(Z-M)	1832	Dec. 08	TuscarwsCoOh	04	07	10
Miller, Henry(Z-M)	1834	Aug. 06	TuscarwsCoOh	06	08	10
Miller, Henry(Z-M)	1835	Dec. 11	TuscarwsCoOh	04	07	01
Miller, Henry(Z-M)	1836	June 23	TuscarwsCoOh	04	07	10
Miller, Henry(Z-M)	1838	Jan. 16	TuscarwsCoOh	04	07	06
Miller, Hiram(Z-M)	1836	Nov. 09	CarrollCo,Oh	10	09	12
Miller, Isaac(Z)	1822	Aug. 14	Green Co.,Pa	14	13	19
Miller, Isaac(Z)	1823	Dec. 16	GreenCo,Ohio	14	13	19
Miller, Isaac(Z)	1836	Sept. 01	WashngtnCoOH	08	05	02
Miller, Isaac(Z)	1810	Nov. 26	SomersetCoPa	05	09	12
Miller, Isaac(Z)	1816	Sept. 07	CoshoctnCoOh	06	09	16
Miller, Isaac(Z-M)	1825	April 22	HolmesCoOhio	06	09	16
Miller, Israel(Z-M)	1832	June 19	TuscarwsCoOh	04	07	03
Miller, Israel(Z-M)	1832	June 19	TuscarwsCoOh	04	07	03
Miller, Jacob H.(Z-M)	1833	Sept. 25	StarkeCo.,Oh	03	07	14
Miller, Jacob H.(Z-M)	1833	Oct. 03	StarkeCo.,Oh	03	07	13
Miller, Jacob Junr.(Y)	1827	Jan. 05	WashCo.,Penn	05	18	29
Miller, Jacob Senr.(Z)	1817	Sept. 02	TuscarwsCoOh	04	09	04
Miller, Jacob(Y)	1825	Aug. 24	Stark Co.,Oh	09	11	11
Miller, Jacob(Y)	1825	Nov. 25	WashCo.,Penn	05	18	20
Miller, Jacob(Y)	1825	Dec. 19	WashCo.,Penn	05	18	20
Miller, Jacob(Y)	1826	Aug. 07	Stark Co.,Oh	09	10	01
Miller, Jacob(Y)	1829	Dec. 08	TuscarwsCoOh	06	14	29
Miller, Jacob(Z)	1832	Sept. 14	Perry Co.,Oh	14	12	21
Miller, Jacob(Z)	1807	June 01	SomersetCoPa	04	09	21
Miller, Jacob(Z)	1810	May 30	TuscarwsCoOh	04	09	22
Miller, Jacob(Z)	1810	May 30	TuscarwsCoOh	01	09	12
Miller, Jacob(Z)	1812	July 28	TuscarwsCoOh	04	08	09
Miller, Jacob(Z)	1814	May 16	TuscarwsCoOh	04	09	19
Miller, Jacob(Z)	1815	May 17	CoshoctnCoOh	05	09	07
Miller, Jacob(Z)	1815	May 17	CoshoctnCoOh	05	08	02

PURCHASER	YEAR	DATE	RESIDENCE	R	T	S
Miller, Jacob(Z)	1816	May 31	HarrisonCoOh	01	05	22
Miller, Jacob(Z-M)	1824	July 01	MuskingmCoOh	03	03	03
Miller, Jacob(Z-M)	1827	June 02	CoshoctnCoOh	05	07	15
Miller, Jacob(Z-M)	1831	Nov. 16	TuscarwsCoOh	04	07	03
Miller, Jacob(Z-M)	1833	Feb. 09	TuscarwsCoOh	03	08	04
Miller, Jacob(Z-M)	1833	May 04	TuscarwsCoOh	04	07	03
Miller, Jacob(Z-M)	1833	June 01	LickingCo,Oh	11	03	07
Miller, Jacob(Z-M)	1834	Dec. 17	BelmontCo,Oh	02	05	20
Miller, Jacob(Z-M)	1835	Oct. 26	CoshoctnCoOh	05	04	08
Miller, Jacob(Z-M)	1836	Jan. 23	TuscarwsCoOh	04	07	10
Miller, Jacob(Z-M)	1836	May 19	LickingCo,Oh	11	03	07
Miller, Jacob(Z-M)	1836	July 06	LickingCo,Oh	11	03	13
Miller, James(Z)	1836	Sept. 09	MonroeCo.,Oh	08	06	26
Miller, James(Z)	1816	March 29	CoshoctnCoOh	08	05	03
Miller, Jno.(Z)	1815	Dec. 16	CoshoctnCoOh	06	08	10
Miller, Jno.(Z)	1815	Dec. 16	CoshoctnCoOh	06	08	01
Miller, Jno.(Z)	1816	Aug. 15	KnoxCo.,Ohio	10	05	16
Miller, John B.(Z-M)	1837	May 02	GuernseyCoOh	04	03	10
Miller, John F.(Z-M)	1836	March 10	CoshoctnCoOh	03	04	10
Miller, John F.(Z-M)	1836	March 10	CoshoctnCoOh	03	04	14
Miller, John J.(Z)	1812	Feb. 11	TuscarwsCoOh	04	09	16
Miller, John J.(Z)	1814	May 16	TuscarwsCoOh	04	09	11
Miller, John J.(Z)	1815	May 31	TuscarwsCoOh	03	09	20
Miller, John J.(Z-M)	1833	Nov. 25	StarkeCo.,Oh	06	07	10
Miller, John J.(Z-M)	1834	Jan. 28	StarkeCo.,Oh	05	07	06
Miller, John King(Z-M)	1836	Jan. 02	GuernseyCoOh	03	03	16
Miller, John P.(Y)	1829	March 14	TuscarwsCoOh	06	14	24
Miller, John(Y)	1822	Aug. 26	HarrisonCoOh	05	14	22
Miller, John(Y)	1827	Oct. 20	Jeff.Co.,Oh.	04	13	07
Miller, John(Y)	1827	Oct. 20	Jeff.Co.,Oh.	04	13	07
Miller, John(Y)	1828	March 24	ColumbanCoOh	04	13	08
Miller, John(Y)	1828	March 24	ColumbanCoOh	04	13	08
Miller, John(Y)	1828	May 23	Jeff.Co.,Oh.	04	12	12
Miller, John(Y)	1836	July 11	Jeff.Co.,Oh.	04	12	05
Miller, John(Y)*	1826	July 08	RcknghmCoVir	05	11	36
Miller, John(Z)	1830	Aug. 11	HarrisonCoOh	11	11	04
Miller, John(Z)	1832	June 25	Morgan Co,Oh	11	10	27
Miller, John(Z)	1833	Jan. 07	WashngtnCoOh	08	05	01
Miller, John(Z)	1835	Nov. 23	WashngtnCoOh	08	05	01
Miller, John(Z)	1806	Dec. 16	WashCo.,Penn	04	08	10
Miller, John(Z)	1809	June 12	FauquierCoVa	04	09	12
Miller, John(Z)	1809	Oct. 14	AlleghnyCoPa	04	09	16
Miller, John(Z)	1813	Aug. 06	TuscarwsCoOh	04	07	08
Miller, John(Z)	1815	May 17	CoshoctnCoOh	09	08	02
Miller, John(Z)	1815	June 13	CoshoctnCoOh	05	08	05
Miller, John(Z-M)	1826	Sept. 30	Stark Co.,Oh	05	08	13
Miller, John(Z-M)	1827	March 14	HolmesCoOhio	07	09	22
Miller, John(Z-M)	1828	May 20	HolmesCoOhio	07	09	21
Miller, John(Z-M)	1832	April 05	TuscarwsCoOh	01	05	22
Miller, John(Z-M)	1832	June 04	HolmesCoOhio	05	08	13
Miller, John(Z-M)	1832	Dec. 08	TuscarwsCoOh	04	07	01
Miller, John(Z-M)	1833	March 19	TuscarwsCoOh	04	07	10
Miller, John(Z-M)	1834	March 11	HolmesCoOhio	05	08	13
Miller, Jonas(Z)	1809	June 12	FauquierCoVa	04	09	16
Miller, Jonas(Z-M)	1823	June 06	TuscarwsCoOh	05	09	14
Miller, Jonas(Z-M)	1828	March 14	HolmesCoOhio	05	08	06
Miller, Jonas(Z-M)	1830	Nov. 20	HolmesCoOhio	05	08	06
Miller, Jos.(Z-M)	1822	Oct. 11	GuernseyCoOh	03	03	19
Miller, Joseph M.(Z-M)	1836	April 15	TuscarwsCoOh	04	07	14
Miller, Joseph(Z-M)	1828	Oct. 29	GuernseyCoOh	03	03	19
Miller, Joseph(Z-M)	1830	Feb. 22	TuscarwsCoOh	02	05	13
Miller, Joseph(Z-M)	1832	Dec. 17	GuernseyCoOh	03	03	19
Miller, Joseph(Z-M)	1833	Feb. 09	TuscarwsCoOh	03	08	04
Miller, Joseph(Z-M)	1834	Aug. 01	TuscarwsCoOh	03	08	04
Miller, Joseph(Z-M)	1834	Aug. 02	TuscarwsCoOh	04	07	15
Miller, Levi(Z-M)	1828	Oct. 16	TuscarwsCoOh	05	08	08
Miller, Levi(Z-M)	1830	Sept. 09	HolmesCoOhio	05	08	08
Miller, Mic.(Z-M)	1830	June 14	HolmesCoOhio	06	08	01
Miller, Michael(Z)	1833	Dec. 02	MuskingmCoOh	13	10	21

PURCHASER	YEAR	DATE	RESIDENCE	R	T	S
Miller, Michael(Z)	1811	Nov. 23	WashCo.,Penn	11	13	12
Miller, Michael(Z)	1816	April 22	TuscarwsCoOh	03	08	04
Miller, Michael(Z-M)	1830	Nov. 01	HolmesCoOhio	06	08	01
Miller, Miller(Z)	1808	Jan. 09	MuskingmCoOh	06	04	18
Miller, Nathan Jnr.(Z-M)	1836	Dec. 31	TuscarwsCoOh	02	10	23
Miller, Nathan Jnr.(Z-M)	1837	March 04	TuscarwsCoOh	03	08	24
Miller, Nathan Jnr.(Z-M)	1837	March 31	TuscarwsCoOh	03	08	23
Miller, Nathan(Z-M)	1836	July 01	TuscarwsCoOh	02	10	23
Miller, Nathan(Z-M)	1836	Nov. 15	TuscarwsCoOh	02	10	23
Miller, Peter Junr.(Z)	1816	April 22	TuscarwsCoOh	05	08	06
Miller, Peter(Y)	1822	Sept. 02	LehighCo.,Pa	09	12	15
Miller, Peter(Y)	1822	Sept. 02	LehighCo.,Pa	09	12	10
Miller, Peter(Y)	1823	June 28	Stark Co.,Oh	09	12	10
Miller, Peter(Z)	1833	July 12	Morgan Co,Oh	13	10	23
Miller, Peter(Z)	1809	Oct. 27	SomersetCoPa	04	09	25
Miller, Peter(Z)	1809	Oct. 27	SomersetCoPa	05	09	23
Miller, Philip(Z)	1811	April 22	MuskingmCoOh	15	17	34
Miller, Robert(Z-M)	1827	May 21	HolmesCoOhio	07	08	02
Miller, Robert(Z-M)	1827	May 21	HolmesCoOhio	07	08	02
Miller, Samuel(Y)	1824	May 01	PortageCo,Oh	05	18	18
Miller, Samuel(Y)	1825	March 30	PortageCo,Oh	05	18	05
Miller, Samuel(Z)	1830	June 17	WashCo.,Penn	11	11	14
Miller, Samuel(Z)	1838	April 30	GuernseyCoOh	08	06	36
Miller, Samuel(Z-M)	1835	Dec. 11	TuscarwsCoOh	03	07	02
Miller, Samuel(Z-M)	1836	March 09	BelmontCo,Oh	03	07	25
Miller, Samuel(Z-M)	1837	Jan. 21	CoshoctnCoOh	07	08	17
Miller, Simon(Z)	1815	Dec. 15	TuscarwsCoOh	05	08	03
Miller, Stephen(Y)	1829	Dec. 24	HarrisonCoOh	07	11	05
Miller, Thomas W.(Y)	1827	Nov. 12	Jeff.Co.,Oh.	04	12	06
Miller, Thomas Woods(Y)	1832	May 30	ColumbanCoOh	04	13	01
Miller, Thomas Woods(Y)	1832	May 30	ColumbanCoOh	04	13	01
Miller, Thomas(Y)	1823	Nov. 04	ColumbanCoOh	05	14	10
Miller, Thomas(Y)	1826	April 28	ColumbanCoOh	04	10	34
Miller, Thomas(Y)	1826	June 26	ColumbanCoOh	04	13	35
Miller, Thomas(Y)	1826	Aug. 10	WashCo.,Penn	06	13	24
Miller, Thomas(Y)	1826	Aug. 10	WashCo.,Penn	06	13	24
Miller, Thomas(Y)	1827	Sept. 22	Jeff.Co.,Oh.	04	12	11
Miller, Thomas(Y)	1835	June 17	Jeff.Co.,Oh.	04	12	11
Miller, Thomas(Y)	1835	Dec. 14	Jeff.Co.,Oh.	04	12	12
Miller, Thomas(Z-M)	1833	Oct. 16	KnoxCo.,Ohio	10	05	23
Miller, Thomas(of Joseph)(Y)	1825	Nov. 18	ColumbanCoOh	05	14	10
Miller, Thos. W.(Y)	1827	Nov. 20	Jeff.Co.,Oh.	04	12	06
Miller, Thos. W.(Y)	1828	Sept. 09	Jeff.Co.,Oh.	04	12	06
Miller, Thos.(Z)	1815	Feb. 11	KnoxCo.,Ohio	10	05	14
Miller, Thos.(Z)	1816	Aug. 15	KnoxCo.,Ohio	10	05	16
Miller, William(Z)	1835	Sept. 11	Jeff.Co.,Oh.	14	12	15
Miller, William(Z)	1835	Sept. 11	Jeff.Co.,Oh.	14	12	15
Miller, William(Z)	1835	Oct. 17	Jeff.Co.,Oh.	14	12	15
Miller, William(Z)	1835	Oct. 20	Jeff.Co.,Oh.	14	12	15
Miller, William(Z)	1835	Oct. 20	Jeff.Co.,Oh.	14	12	15
Miller, William(Z)	1836	March 29	Morgan Co,Oh	09	06	09
Miller, William(Z-M)	1833	Sept. 16	Jeff.Co.,Oh.	03	04	08
Miller, William(Z-M)	1835	April 24	TuscarwsCoOh	03	10	11
Miller, Wm.(Z)	1811	June 06	FairfeldCoOh	15	17	35
Miller, Wm.(Z)	1813	Nov. 03	?	15	17	34
Miller, Yost(Z)	1809	Oct. 27	SomersetCoPa	04	09	25
Miller, Yost(Z)	1814	June 28	TuscarwsCoOh	04	09	25
Miller, Yost(Z-M)	1828	March 18	CoshoctnCoOh	05	07	12
Miller, Yost(Z-M)	1831	June 14	CoshoctnCoOh	05	07	12
Miller, Yost(Z-M)	1836	Oct. 10	CoshoctnCoOh	05	07	11
Millhon, Elijah(Z)	1832	Aug. 28	GuernseyCoOh	08	08	09
Millhon, Elijah(Z)	1832	Aug. 28	GuernseyCoOh	08	08	09
Millhorn, John(Z)	1817	Jan. 08	GuernseyCoOh	08	08	05
Millhorne, John(Z)	1824	Dec. 01	GuernseyCoOh	08	08	15
Millhouse, Eliz.(Z)	1822	March 19	BelmontCo,Oh	11	10	31
Millhouse, Mary(Z)	1822	March 19	BelmontCo,Oh	11	10	31
Millhouse, Robert(Z)	1822	March 19	BelmontCo,Oh	12	10	36
Milliback, Jacob(Y)	1828	Sept. 15	TuscarwsCoOh	06	13	35
Milligan, Alexander N.(Z-M)	1833	April 04	GuernseyCoOh	02	03	05

PURCHASER	YEAR	DATE	RESIDENCE	R	T	S
Milligan, John(Y)	1821	Oct. 29	Jeff.Co.,Oh.	07	14	21
Milligan, John(Y)	1821	Nov. 03	Jeff.Co.,Oh.	07	14	21
Milligan, John(Y)	1821	Nov. 19	Jeff.Co.,Oh.	07	14	21
Milligan, John(Y)	1821	Nov. 19	Jeff.Co.,Oh.	07	14	21
Milligan, John(Y)	1821	Dec. 28	Jeff.Co.,Oh.	07	14	21
Milligan, John(Z-M)	1836	Dec. 13	GuernseyCoOh	02	03	07
Milligan, Robt.(Z-M)	1829	Oct. 21	BelmontCo,Oh	03	06	08
Milliken, Edward(Z-M)	1838	Nov. 15	GuernseyCoOh	03	03	04
Milliken, John(Z-M)	1835	Dec. 15	GreenCo.,Pa.	01	05	03
Millis, Peter(Z-M)	1838	Feb. 03	ZanesvilleOh	10	09	21
Millor, Cawood(Z)	1831	April 14	Morgan Co,Oh	12	10	14
Millor, E. O.(Z)	1831	March 04	Morgan Co,Oh	13	08	13
Millor, Edward(Z)	1831	April 06	Morgan Co,Oh	12	10	23
Millor, Edward(Z)	1831	April 06	Morgan Co,Oh	12	10	23
Millor, Gordon(Z)	1831	May 09	Morgan Co,Oh	12	10	14
Mills, Abraham(Z-M)	1837	April 10	CoshoctnCoOh	10	06	14
Mills, Anson L.(Z)	1833	June 21	Morgan Co,Oh	13	08	07
Mills, Gideon(Z)	1821	Aug. 21	Morgan Co,Oh	12	09	14
Mills, Hiram(Z)	1825	Nov. 29	Perry Co.,Oh	13	08	07
Mills, Hiram(Z)	1836	Sept. 29	Morgan Co,Oh	14	12	13
Mills, Hiram(Z)	1837	Feb. 25	Morgan Co,Oh	13	08	07
Mills, J.(Z)	1815	Aug. 19	CoshoctnCoOh	04	05	11
Mills, John Junr.(Y)	1833	March 26	Jeff.Co.,Oh.	03	12	02
Mills, John Junr.(Y)	1836	Dec. 10	Jeff.Co.,Oh.	03	11	06
Mills, John(Z)	1835	Jan. 24	GuernseyCoOh	09	08	25
Mills, John(Z)	1836	Jan. 14	GuernseyCoOh	09	08	22
Mills, Joseph(Z)	1814	March 18	?	15	16	04
Mills, Joseph(Z)	1815	March 06	MuskingmCoOh	15	16	13
Mills, Joseph(Z)	1817	Sept. 22	BedfordCo,Pa	09	05	03
Mills, Joseph(Z)	1817	Sept. 22	BedfordCo,Pa	09	05	04
Mills, Lairwood(Z)	1835	Oct. 09	AthensCoOhio	14	12	32
Mills, Marvel(Z)	1833	May 28	AthensCoOhio	14	12	32
Mills, Peter Sutton(Z-M)	1838	Aug. 14	LickingCo,Oh	11	03	18
Mills, Peter(Z)	1813	July 01	ZanesvilleOh	05	03	13
Mills, Robert(Y)	1832	March 09	Jeff.Co.,Oh.	03	11	11
Mills, Robert(Y)	1833	Dec. 11	ColumbanCoOh	03	11	05
Mills, Robert(Y)	1835	Dec. 12	Jeff.Co.,Oh.	03	11	06
Millshear, John(Z-M)	1828	Nov. 08	MuskingmCoOh	06	03	20
Milner, Edward(Z)	1806	Feb. 21	BelmontCo,Oh	01	02	16
Milner, Edward(Z)	1810	Dec. 04	MuskingmCoOh	01	03	16
Milner, Edward(Z-M)	1836	Jan. 21	GuernseyCoOh	03	05	22
Milner, Edward(Z-M)	1837	April 15	GuernseyCoOh	03	04	10
Milner, Geo.(son of Isaac)(Y)	1828	April 01	HighlandCoOh	06	18	26
Milner, George(Y)	1822	Jan. 21	Stark Co.,Oh	05	16	29
Milner, George(Y)	1823	Aug. 22	Stark Co.,Oh	05	16	29
Milner, George(Y)	1832	May 30	ColumbanCoOh	05	15	05
Milner, Jesse(Z)	1813	March 10	GuernseyCoOh	02	02	21
Milner, Jesse(Z)	1816	April 23	GuernseyCoOh	02	04	11
Milner, Thomas(Z)	1806	Feb. 21	BelmontCo,Oh	05	01	12
Milner, Thomas(Z)	1808	Nov. 04	BelmontCo,Oh	01	02	16
Milone, Barnabus(Z-M)	1831	Sept. 07	GuernseyCoOh	03	04	09
Milone, David(Z-M)	1833	Nov. 26	GuernseyCoOh	03	04	09
Milone, John(Z-M)	1831	April 22	GuernseyCoOh	03	04	09
Milsheers, John(Z-M)	1830	Sept. 14	MuskingmCoOh	06	03	20
Milton, Henry(Z)	1824	May 18	BelmontCo,Oh	12	10	22
Milton, John(Z-M)	1822	July 22	KnoxCo.,Ohio	10	08	02
Milton, John(Z-M)	1830	Dec. 09	KnoxCo.,Ohio	10	08	15
Milton, Thomas(Z)	1824	June 16	BelmontCo,Oh	12	09	14
Milton, Thomas(Z)	1824	June 16	BelmontCo,Oh	12	09	14
Minch, Michael(Z-M)	1836	Dec. 03	AlleghnyCoPa	05	04	18
Mincks, John T.(Z)	1833	Oct. 08	Morgan Co,Oh	09	05	20
Mincks, Joseph(Z)	1836	July 08	Morgan Co,Oh	09	05	19
Miner, Daniel(Z)	1813	Jan. 12	FairfeldCoOh	15	17	19
Miner, Daniel(Z)	1815	Sept. 11	MuskingmCoOh	14	13	01
Miner, Frederick(Z)	1813	Jan. 12	FairfeldCoOh	15	17	19
Miner, Frederick(Z)	1813	Nov. 22	FairfeldCoOh	15	17	33
Miner, Noah(Z)	1815	Oct. 28	MongahlaCoVa	09	05	17
Miner, Samuel(Z)	1815	Oct. 28	MongahlaCoVa	09	05	18
Mingus, William(Z)	1814	Nov. 16	MuskingmCoOh	12	13	08

PURCHASER	YEAR	DATE	RESIDENCE	R	T	S
Minick, David(Z-M)	1835	Dec. 01	MuskingmCoOh	04	05	19
Minick, David(Z-M)	1837	Feb. 23	CoshoctnCoOh	04	05	22
Minshall, Enoch(Z)	1836	April 20	Perry Co.,Oh	14	13	28
Minton, Lewis(Z)	1815	April 26	KnoxCo.,Ohio	10	06	17
MisKimin, Nelson(Z-M)	1832	June 22	GuernseyCoOh	04	03	02
Miscimen, John(Z)	1805	Dec. 28	WashngtnCoMd	04	04	07
Miser, Adam(Z-M)	1825	Feb. 07	WayneCo.,Oh.	05	07	18
Miser, Adam(Z-M)	1835	May 29	HolmesCoOhio	04	06	09
Miser, Adam(Z-M)	1835	May 29	HolmesCoOhio	04	06	08
Miser, Frederick(Z)	1815	Nov. 23	TuscarwsCoOh	06	07	01
Miser, Geo.(Z-M)	1833	March 23	TuscarwsCoOh	04	07	21
Miser, Geo.(Z-M)	1833	March 23	TuscarwsCoOh	04	07	22
Miser, George(Z-M)	1832	Dec. 08	TuscarwsCoOh	05	07	17
Miser, George(Z-M)	1833	May 02	CoshoctnCoOh	05	07	17
Miser, George(Z-M)	1835	May 29	WayneCo.,Oh.	04	06	08
Miser, George(Z-M)	1832	Dec. 05	TuscarwsCoOh	04	07	01
Miser, George(Z-M)	1836	Dec. 17	TuscarwsCoOh	04	07	01
Miser, Henry(Z-M)	1835	Jan. 06	TuscarwsCoOh	03	07	25
Miser, Jacob(Z)	1825	July 06	TuscarwsCoOh	04	07	19
Miser, Jacob(Z-M)	1825	Feb. 07	CoshoctnCoOh	05	07	21
Miser, Jacob(Z-M)	1828	March 08	TuscarwsCoOh	04	07	19
Miser, Jacob(Z-M)	1828	June 16	TuscarwsCoOh	04	07	19
Miser, Jacob(Z-M)	1832	May 25	CoshoctnCoOh	05	07	18
Miser, Jacob(Z-M)	1832	May 25	CoshoctnCoOh	05	07	19
Miser, Jacob(Z-M)	1835	Jan. 06	TuscarwsCoOh	04	07	21
Miser, Jacob(Z-M)	1835	July 08	TuscarwsCoOh	04	07	18
Miser, Jacob(Z-M)	1836	Jan. 12	TuscarwsCoOh	04	07	24
Miser, John Jnr.(Z-M)	1832	Nov. 24	TuscarwsCoOh	04	07	22
Miser, John(Z)	1835	Jan. 06	TuscarwsCoOh	03	07	16
Miser, John(Z)	1827	April 20	HolmesCoOhio	04	07	24
Miser, John(Z)	1827	April 20	HolmesCoOhio	04	07	24
Miser, John(Z-M)	1812	April 21	TuscarwsCoOh	04	08	12
Miser, John(Z-M)	1828	June 16	TuscarwsCoOh	03	07	16
Miser, John(Z-M)	1832	May 23	TuscarwsCoOh	04	07	21
Miser, Joseph(Z-M)	1835	May 12	HolmesCoOhio	04	07	18
Miser, Joseph(Z-M)	1836	March 16	CoshoctnCoOh	05	07	24
Miser, Philip(Z-M)	1834	March 18	TuscarwsCoOh	04	07	18
Miser, Sam'l.(Z-M)	1831	Dec. 20	HolmesCoOhio	04	06	01
Miser, Samuel(Z-M)	1834	Dec. 05	Wayne Co.,Oh	04	07	23
Miser, Samuel(Z-M)	1835	July 09	TuscarwsCoOh	04	07	23
Mishinims, Harvey H.(Z-M)	1835	Nov. 10	TuscarwsCoOh	03	05	17
Mishinims, Harvey H.(Z-M)	1835	Nov. 10	TuscarwsCoOh	03	05	14
Mishler, John(Y)	1823	March 27	Stark Co.,Oh	09	11	13
Mishler, John(Y)	1830	June 16	Stark Co.,Oh	09	11	13
Mishler, Moses(Z-M)	1833	April 03	HolmesCoOhio	04	08	24
Mishler, Solomon(Z-M)	1831	Aug. 16	HolmesCoOhio	06	08	10
Mishler, Valentine(Z-M)	1826	June 05	HolmesCoOhio	05	08	06
Mishler, Wm.(Y)	1826	June 12	Stark Co.,Oh	09	12	08
Miskell, Patrick(Z)	1835	Nov. 30	Perry Co.,Oh	15	15	32
Miskell, Patrick(Z)	1836	Aug. 19	Perry Co.,Oh	15	15	27
Miskemins, James(Z-M)	1837	Feb. 16	GuernseyCoOh	04	03	02
Miskile, Patrick(Z)	1833	Dec. 23	Perry Co.,Oh	15	14	15
Miskimen, Harrison(Z-M)	1838	April 24	GuernseyCoOh	04	04	12
Miskimen, James(Z)	1805	Dec. 28	WashngtnCoMd	04	04	04
Miskimen, James(Z)	1805	Dec. 28	WashngtnCoMd	05	04	19
Miskimen, James(Z)	1806	May 23	MuskingmCoOh	04	04	08
Miskimen, James(Z-M)	1822	Oct. 07	CoshoctnCoOh	04	04	08
Miskimen, James(Z-M)	1833	March 13	GuernseyCoOh	03	04	05
Miskimen, James(Z-M)	1836	Jan. 15	CoshoctnCoOh	05	04	20
Miskimen, James(Z-M)	1836	Jan. 29	CoshoctnCoOh	04	04	08
Miskimen, James(Z-M)	1836	Jan. 29	CoshoctnCoOh	05	04	18
Miskimen, James(Z-M)	1836	Jan. 29	CoshoctnCoOh	05	04	12
Miskimen, James(Z-M)	1836	Jan. 29	CoshoctnCoOh	05	04	11
Miskimen, James(Z-M)	1833	Nov. 04	GuernseyCoOh	04	04	18
Miskimen, James(Z-M)	1837	May 24	CoshoctnCoOh	04	04	08
Miskimen, James(Z-M)	1837	May 24	CoshoctnCoOh	04	04	08
Miskimen, James(Z-M)	1839	April 03	CoshoctnCoOh	04	04	01
Miskimen, Jas.(Z-M)	1826	June 03	CoshoctnCoOh	04	04	08
Miskimen, John(Z-M)	1838	April 25	ZanesvilleOh	04	04	10

PURCHASER	YEAR	DATE	RESIDENCE	R	T	S
Miskimen, William(Z)	1811	Nov. 28	CoshoctnCoOh	04	04	14
Miskimen, William(Z-M)	1822	Oct. 08	CoshoctnCoOh	04	04	13
Miskimen, William(Z-M)	1836	Jan. 09	CoshoctnCoOh	04	04	07
Miskimens, Isaac(Z-M)	1833	Aug. 03	GuernseyCoOh	03	04	05
Miskimens, Isaac(Z-M)	1833	Aug. 03	GuernseyCoOh	03	04	05
Miskimens, Isaac(Z-M)	1836	March 21	GuernseyCoOh	04	04	20
Miskimin, James(Z)	1806	June 06	MuskingmCoOh	04	04	07
Miskimin, Nelson(Z-M)	1832	May 23	GuernseyCoOh	04	03	02
Miskimins, Abraham F.(Z-M)	1836	Jan. 05	GuernseyCoOh	04	03	02
Miskimins, Hilliary(Z-M)	1832	Nov. 14	GuernseyCoOh	04	04	22
Miskomen, Hervey(Z-M)	1831	Dec. 03	CoshoctnCoOh	03	05	25
Mitchel, George(Z)	1804	Oct. 16	BelmontCo,,Oh	01	03	05
Mitchel, George(Z)	1809	Aug. 22	MuskingmCoOh	01	04	25
Mitchel, George(Z)	1812	Oct. 08	GuernseyCoOh	02	03	01
Mitchel, George(Z)	1813	June 16	GuernseyCoOh	04	04	19
Mitchel, George(Z)	1817	May 16	YorkCo.,Penn	04	03	01
Mitchel, Hance(Z-M)	1835	Dec. 14	GuernseyCoOh	03	03	04
Mitchel, Hance(Z-M)	1836	Dec. 17	CoshoctnCoOh	04	04	07
Mitchel, John(Z-M)	1835	Dec. 29	CoshoctnCoOh	09	03	05
Mitchel, Mathew(Z)	1805	Nov. 27	AlleghnyCoPa	12	13	01
Mitchel, Mathew(Z)	1805	Nov. 27	AlleghnyCoPa	05	01	01
Mitchel, William(Z-M)	1836	May 03	LickingCo,Oh	11	04	08
Mitchell, A.(Z-M)	1835	Dec. 24	GuernseyCoOh	04	04	20
Mitchell, Alexander(Z-M)	1836	May 25	GuernseyCoOh	04	04	20
Mitchell, David(Z)	1831	Oct. 21	MuskingmCoOh	11	12	10
Mitchell, Elisha(Z)	1833	Jan. 04	MuskingmCoOh	13	10	07
Mitchell, Geo. W.(Z-M)	1832	Nov. 01	GuernseyCoOh	03	03	05
Mitchell, George W.(Z-M)	1835	Sept. 19	GuernseyCoOh	04	05	18
Mitchell, George(Z-M)	1828	Oct. 29	GuernseyCoOh	04	04	12
Mitchell, George(Z-M)	1838	Jan. 10	GuernseyCoOh	04	04	10
Mitchell, Hame(Z-M)	1831	June 11	GuernseyCoOh	03	03	03
Mitchell, Hanse(Z-M)	1827	Feb. 16	GuernseyCoOh	03	04	12
Mitchell, James(Z)	1837	Jan. 06	Wheeling,Vir	08	05	13
Mitchell, James(Z)	1837	Jan. 06	Wheeling,Vir	08	05	15
Mitchell, John B.(Z-M)	1832	Nov. 01	GuernseyCoOh	03	03	05
Mitchell, John B.(Z-M)	1835	Sept. 19	GuernseyCoOh	04	05	18
Mitchell, John(Z)	1836	Oct. 22	Perry Co.,Oh	14	12	14
Mitchell, John(Z)	1815	Dec. 16	Jeff.Co.,Oh.	06	07	21
Mitchell, John(Z)	1815	Dec. 16	Jeff.Co.,Oh.	06	08	13
Mitchell, John(Z-M)	1835	Dec. 02	CoshoctnCoOh	09	03	05
Mitchell, Martin(Z)	1817	Sept. 19	WashngtnCoOh	13	09	31
Mitchell, Michael(Z)	1834	Dec. 11	Perry Co.,Oh	14	12	23
Mitchell, Thomas(Y)	1825	July 23	WashCo.,Penn	06	16	13
Mitchell, Thomas(Z)	1815	March 16	AlleghnyCoPa	11	12	29
Mitchell, Thomas(Z)	1815	April 14	AlleghnyCoPa	11	11	15
Mitchell, Thomas(Z)	1815	April 14	AlleghnyCoOh	11	12	30
Mitchell, William(Z)	1826	July 13	BelmontCo,,Oh	13	10	02
Mitchell, William(Z)	1836	Nov. 28	Perry Co.,Oh	14	12	23
Mitchell, William(Z)	1837	Feb. 07	Perry Co.,Oh	14	12	24
Mitchell, William(Z)	1837	Feb. 07	Perry Co.,Oh	14	12	23
Mittan, William(Z)	1814	Oct. 06	HarrisonCoOh	01	05	20
Mix, Amos(Z-M)	1836	Oct. 12	MuskingmCoOh	10	08	05
Mizer, Philip(Z-M)	1820	Nov. 28	TuscarwsCoOh	04	07	25
Mizer, Philip(Z-M)	1835	Dec. 29	TuscarwsCoOh	04	07	22
Moats, David(Z-M)	1834	Dec. 05	LickingCo,Oh	11	03	06
Moats, David(Z-M)	1835	Dec. 31	LickingCo,Oh	11	03	06
Moats, Henry(Z)	1815	July 12	LickingCo,Oh	11	04	14
Moats, James(Z-M)	1836	Feb. 13	LickingCo,Oh	11	03	06
Mobley, Levi(Z)	1835	Oct. 30	Morgan Co,Oh	09	06	20
Mocheman, Lewis Junr.(Y)	1827	June 05	Stark Co.,Oh	06	17	30
Mock, George(Z)	1815	Jan. 16	MuskingmCoOh	14	15	29
Mock, George(Z)	1816	Feb. 29	TuscarwsCoOh	02	10	14
Mock, John(Z)	1815	June 01	BedfordCo,Pa	02	10	14
Mock, John(Z-M)	1832	March 23	TuscarwsCoOh	02	10	16
Mock, John(Z-M)	1832	March 23	TuscarwsCoOh	02	10	17
Moeller, W. F.(Z)	1835	Oct. 28	Perry Co.,Oh	14	12	28
Moffet, Samuel(Y)	1823	Jan. 08	Jeff.Co.,Oh.	07	16	02
Moffet, Samuel(Y)	1829	March 13	Stark Co.,Oh	07	16	08
Moffet, Samuel(Y)	1830	Aug. 27	Stark Co.,Oh	07	16	02

PURCHASER	YEAR	DATE	RESIDENCE	R	T	S
Moffitt, Robert(Z)	1836	Jan. 20	Morgan Co,Oh	08	07	17
Moffitt, Robert(Z)	1836	June 08	Morgan Co,Oh	08	07	20
Moland, Isaac(Y)	1833	Oct. 26	GuernseyCoOh	07	09	15
Moland, Isaac(Y)	1835	Feb. 25	GuernseyCoOh	07	09	15
Moland, Isaac(Z)	1836	Jan. 15	GuernseyCoOh	08	06	15
Moland, Isaac(Z)	1836	Jan. 15	GuernseyCoOh	08	06	15
Moland, Isaac(Z)	1836	April 09	MonroeCo.,Oh	08	06	23
Moler, Casper(Z)	1822	Dec. 03	Morgan Co,Oh	10	07	30
Moler, Peter(Z)	1822	Nov. 22	Morgan Co,Oh	10	07	30
Moller, John(Z-M)	1830	Oct. 27	Morgan Co,Oh	10	07	30
Moller, Joseph(Z)	1834	March 25	Perry Co.,Oh	15	15	31
Moller, Joseph(Z)	1834	March 25	Perry Co.,Oh	15	15	32
Moller, Mathias(Z)	1834	Feb. 12	Perry Co.,Oh	15	14	06
Moller, Matthias(Z)	1833	April 20	Perry Co.,Oh	15	14	06
Mollett, Daniel(Y)	1833	Sept. 19	Jeff.Co.,Oh.	04	12	12
Molloy, Thos. Sr.(Z-M)	1828	Sept. 26	WashCo.,Penn	03	01	23
Monahan, John(Y)	1826	March 16	BelmontCo,Oh	03	05	17
Moncrief, John(Y)	1832	March 08	WashCo.,Penn	06	13	30
Monroe, Andrew(Z)	1814	Feb. 22	MuskingmCoOh	10	09	18
Monroe, Andrew(Z)	1815	Jan. 25	MuskingmCoOh	12	13	25
Monroe, Barnabas(Z)	1817	Oct. 30	MuskingmCoOh	13	11	16
Monroe, Joseph F.(Z)	1805	Dec. 30	MuskingmCoOh	12	12	08
Monroe, Peter(Z)	1815	March 04	MuskingmCoOh	11	13	30
Montanya, Joseph(Z)	1806	May 12	LoudonCo,Vir	13	12	03
Montgomery, Dan'l.(Z)	1826	April 20	BelmontCo,Oh	13	08	15
Montgomery, John(Y)	1830	Feb. 24	Jeff.Co.,Oh.	03	11	02
Montgomery, John(Z)	1825	Aug. 16	Perry Co.,Oh	14	13	20
Montgomery, Johnston(Y)	1826	May 26	Jeff.Co.,Oh.	03	11	23
Montgomery, Mitchel L.(Z-M)	1838	April 24	GuernseyCoOh	03	04	17
Montgomery, Robert(Y)	1824	May 18	BelmontCo,Oh	04	06	22
Montgomery, Robert(Z)	1816	Nov. 29	MuskingmCoOh	14	13	19
Montgomery, Robert(Z)	1816	Nov. 29	MuskingmCoOh	14	13	20
Montgomery, Robert(Z)	1816	Dec. 30	MuskingmCoOh	14	13	19
Montgomery, Robert(Z-M)	1829	June 01	BelmontCo,Oh	11	08	04
Montgomery, S. M.(Z)	1831	July 09	ZanesvilleOh	14	13	20
Montgomery, Silas(Z)	1833	Aug. 05	ZanesvilleOh	14	13	20
Montgomery, Wm.(Z)	1806	Feb. 15	MuskingmCoOh	13	12	06
Montre, Francis(Y)	1826	Aug. 12	Stark Co.,Oh	09	11	24
Montre, Francis(Y)	1826	Aug. 22	Stark Co.,Oh	09	11	25
Monypeny, Geo. W.(Z)	1839	Jan. 21	ZanesvilleOh	08	05	23
Moode, Richard(Z)	1817	May 20	CoshoctnCoOh	08	05	25
Moode, Richard(Z-M)	1831	Nov. 07	CoshoctnCoOh	08	05	20
Moodey, David(Y)	1828	April 10	HarrisonCoOh	04	12	35
Moodey, James Jnr.(Y)	1829	Dec. 30	Jeff.Co.,Oh.	04	12	24
Moodey, Margaret(Y)	1828	Oct. 22	Jeff.Co.,Oh.	04	12	30
Moody, D.(Z)	1816	Jan. 29	MuskingmCoOh	12	11	29
Moody, Hiram(Z)	1836	June 28	Morgan Co,Oh	14	13	36
Moody, James Weeks(Z)	1835	May 09	Morgan Co,Oh	14	13	35
Moody, Nathan(Z)	1830	Jan. 19	Morgan Co,Oh	14	14	26
Moody, Nathan(Z)	1834	July 26	Morgan Co,Oh	14	12	01
Moody, Nathan(Z)	1834	July 26	Morgan Co,Oh	14	12	01
Moody, Nathan(Z)	1835	Dec. 19	Morgan Co,Oh	14	14	26
Moody, Nathan(Z)	1836	Dec. 08	Morgan Co,Oh	14	13	34
Moody, Nathan(Z)	1836	Dec. 08	Morgan Co,Oh	14	13	34
Moody, Nathaniel(Z)	1838	Feb. 21	Morgan Co,Oh	14	13	34
Moody, Sam'l.(Z-M)	1829	May 27	Morgan Co,Oh	13	09	06
Moody, T.(Z)	1816	Jan. 29	MuskingmCoOh	12	11	29
Moody, Thomas(Z)	1828	Sept. 16	MuskingmCoOh	14	14	20
Moody, William H.(Z-M)	1833	Dec. 05	MuskingmCoOh	05	03	05
Moody, William H.(Z-M)	1833	Dec. 07	MuskingmCoOh	05	03	05
Moody, William Henry(Z-M)	1836	Jan. 15	MuskingmCoOh	06	03	10
Moody, William Henry(Z-M)	1836	Jan. 18	MuskingmCoOh	06	03	10
Moomaw, Peter(Z-M)	1836	Feb. 15	HolmesCoOhio	03	07	02
Moone, Joseph(Z)	1816	April 24	LickingCo,Oh	11	04	07
Mooney, Daniel(Z-M)	1838	June 13	LickingCo,Oh	11	03	08
Mooney, John(Z-M)	1832	Sept. 19	LickingCo,Oh	11	04	11
Moony, Jacob(Z)	1836	Oct. 15	BelmontCo,Oh	08	06	26
Moor, Littleton Jun.(Z)	1832	March 05	MuskingmCoOh	14	13	17
Moor, Sam'l. S.(Z-M)	1828	Dec. 29	GuernseyCoOh	02	04	04

PURCHASER	YEAR	DATE	RESIDENCE	R	T	S
Moore, Aaron(Z)	1834	Jan. 02	GuernseyCoOh	08	08	25
Moore, Abraham(Z)	1834	March 11	GuernseyCoOh	09	08	27
Moore, Alfred L.(Z)	1814	Dec. 26	ZanesvilleOh	14	16	04
Moore, Alfred L.(Z)	1814	Dec. 26	ZanesvilleOh	14	16	04
Moore, Allen(Y)	1821	Oct. 19	Stark Co.,Oh	06	15	15
Moore, Allen(Y)	1828	March 04	Stark Co.,Oh	07	16	01
Moore, Allen(Y)	1828	March 11	Stark Co.,Oh	07	16	02
Moore, Andrew(Z)	1807	Dec. 26	MuskingmCoOh	01	02	25
Moore, Andrew(Z)	1814	April 21	GuernseyCoOh	01	02	12
Moore, Cyrus(Y)	1828	June 06	ColumbanCoOh	04	13	03
Moore, Cyrus(Y)	1831	Feb. 01	ColumbanCoOh	04	13	04
Moore, Cyrus(Y)	1835	Nov. 27	Jeff.Co.,Oh.	03	12	25
Moore, Daniel(Z-M)	1836	Jan. 20	MuskingmCoOh	11	03	06
Moore, David of Wm.(Z)	1820	Nov. 15	Perry Co.,Oh	15	14	19
Moore, David(Z)	1813	April 29	CoshoctnCoOh	09	04	12
Moore, David(Z)	1813	Dec. 15	MuskingmCoOh	10	09	17
Moore, David(Z)	1816	Sept. 12	LickingCo,Oh	10	03	15
Moore, David(Z)	1816	Sept. 12	LickingCo,Oh	10	03	16
Moore, David(Z)	1816	Oct. 02	LickingCo,Oh	10	03	15
Moore, David(Z)	1816	Nov. 06	Newark, Ohio	10	03	16
Moore, David(Z)	1817	Feb. 18	LickingCo,Oh	11	04	07
Moore, David(Z)	1817	April 19	LickingCo,Oh	10	03	06
Moore, David(Z)	1817	April 19	LickingCo,Oh	10	03	06
Moore, David(Z-M)	1826	April 28	LickingCo,Oh	11	04	07
Moore, David(Z-M)	1829	April 08	LickingCo,Oh	11	03	24
Moore, Elias(Z)	1836	March 23	Perry Co.,Oh	14	13	23
Moore, Ellzey(Z)	1827	June 08	BelmontCo,Oh	11	10	18
Moore, Gaius(Y)	1821	Oct. 17	ChesterCo,Pa	04	17	06
Moore, George(Z)	1805	Sept. 13	FairfeldCoOh	15	17	36
Moore, George(Z)	1810	May 07	MuskingmCoOh	15	17	25
Moore, George(Z)	1814	Sept. 05	MuskingmCoOh	15	16	12
Moore, H.(Z)	1815	Jan. 09	ZanesvilleOh	12	10	25
Moore, H.(Z)	1815	Jan. 09	ZanesvilleOh	13	10	08
Moore, Henry(Z)	1828	Nov. 27	Morgan Co,Oh	13	09	01
Moore, Heziah(Z-M)	1836	Jan. 29	GuernseyCoOh	02	04	07
Moore, Isaac(Z)	1835	Dec. 14	GuernseyCoOh	10	09	23
Moore, J. D.(Z)	1830	Dec. 08	Morgan Co,Oh	11	11	11
Moore, Jacob(Z-M)	1826	Aug. 30	HolmesCoOhio	05	08	24
Moore, James Power(Z)	1832	July 05	Morgan Co,Oh	11	11	14
Moore, James Power(Z)	1832	July 05	Morgan Co,Oh	11	11	23
Moore, James(Z)	1832	May 22	Morgan Co,Oh	08	06	07
Moore, James(Z)	1832	Oct. 04	Morgan Co,Oh	09	06	13
Moore, James(Z)	1834	March 04	Perry Co.,Oh	14	13	23
Moore, James(Z)	1834	March 04	Perry Co.,Oh	14	13	23
Moore, James(Z)	1836	April 25	Morgan Co,Oh	09	06	12
Moore, James(Z)	1807	Jan. 26	FayetteCoVir	11	13	08
Moore, James(Z)	1807	Jan. 26	FayetteCoVir	11	13	05
Moore, James(Z)	1815	June 14	MuskingmCoOh	06	02	16
Moore, James(Z)	1817	Jan. 14	MuskingmCoOh	05	02	18
Moore, James(Z)	1817	Oct. 29	WashngtnCoOh	13	09	28
Moore, James(Z-M)	1833	Feb. 06	CoshoctnCoOh	09	05	25
Moore, James(Z-M)	1833	Nov. 20	HarrisonCoOh	02	07	02
Moore, James(Z-M)	1833	Nov. 20	HarrisonCoOh	02	07	02
Moore, James(Z-M)	1833	Nov. 20	HarrisonCoOh	02	07	02
Moore, James(Z-M)	1839	June 12	TuscarwsCoOh	02	07	02
Moore, James(Z-M)	1839	Nov. 19	CoshoctnCoOh	09	07	01
Moore, Jno.(Z)	1831	Dec. 02	Perry Co.,Oh	14	13	07
Moore, Jno.(Z-M)	1832	Feb. 08	LickingCo,Oh	10	03	08
Moore, John Jr.(Y)	1828	April 18	Stark Co.,Oh	06	15	27
Moore, John(Y)	1820	Aug. 31	WashCo.,Penn	06	15	20
Moore, John(Y)	1822	Sept. 23	Stark Co.,Oh	06	15	20
Moore, John(Y)	1824	Aug. 13	Stark Co.,Oh	08	12	15
Moore, John(Z)	1824	Jan. 22	GuernseyCoOh	10	09	10
Moore, John(Z)	1826	March 28	Morgan Co,Oh	11	12	31
Moore, John(Z)	1833	Aug. 02	Morgan Co,Oh	09	06	01
Moore, John(Z)	1833	Sept. 23	GuernseyCoOh	10	09	10
Moore, John(Z)	1805	Sept. 19	FairfeldCoOh	15	16	12
Moore, John(Z)	1813	Dec. 29	HarrisonCoOh	14	13	08
Moore, John(Z)	1814	Feb. 05	HarrisonCoOh	14	13	08

PURCHASER	YEAR	DATE	RESIDENCE	R	T	S
Moore, John(Z)	1815	Feb. 24	MuskingmCoOh	11	13	19
Moore, John(Z)	1815	May 15	MuskingmCoOh	06	02	16
Moore, John(Z-M)	1828	Oct. 14	HolmesCoOhio	05	08	23
Moore, John(Z-M)	1831	Dec. 30	LickingCo,Oh	10	03	07
Moore, John(Z-M)	1832	April 04	LickingCo,Oh	11	04	12
Moore, John(Z-M)	1832	April 27	LickingCo,Oh	10	03	15
Moore, John(Z-M)	1833	April 26	CoshoctnCoOh	05	07	07
Moore, John(Z-M)	1834	March 05	TuscarwsCoOh	02	07	08
Moore, John(Z-M)	1834	March 05	TuscarwsCoOh	02	07	13
Moore, John(Z-M)	1834	Aug. 26	CoshoctnCoOh	07	07	22
Moore, Jonathan E.(Z)	1827	Nov. 22	BelmontCo,Oh	11	10	07
Moore, Jos'h. Dickinson(Z)	1836	Jan. 19	Morgan Co,Oh	11	12	35
Moore, Joseph D.(Z)	1826	Sept. 30	Morgan Co,Oh	11	11	14
Moore, Joseph D.(Z)	1831	June 11	Morgan Co,Oh	11	11	11
Moore, Joseph D.(Z)	1835	March 05	Morgan Co,Oh	11	11	03
Moore, Joseph Dickinson(Z)	1835	June 23	Morgan Co,Oh	11	12	35
Moore, Joseph(Z)	1829	Aug. 13	GuernseyCoOh	09	08	21
Moore, Joseph(Z)	1807	Jan. 26	FayetteCoVir	11	13	08
Moore, Joseph(Z)	1807	Jan. 26	FayetteCoVir	11	13	05
Moore, Joseph(Z)	1808	May 02	FayetteCo,Pa	01	09	11
Moore, Joseph(Z-M)	1837	Dec. 12	MuskingmCoOh	05	03	19
Moore, Lemuel(Z)	1835	March 24	MonroeCo.,Oh	08	07	01
Moore, Littleton Jr.(Z)	1832	Feb. 13	MuskingmCoOh	14	13	17
Moore, Maurice(Y)	1823	Nov. 29	TuscarwsCoOh	06	13	31
Moore, Mordecai(Y)	1831	Aug. 04	Jeff.Co.,Oh.	04	13	15
Moore, Mordicui(Y)	1829	March 18	Jeff.Co.,Co.	03	11	33
Moore, Peter(Z-M)	1825	Nov. 30	Albany,NYork	01	04	09
Moore, Philip(Z)	1830	Dec. 07	Morgan Co,Oh	11	11	04
Moore, Philip(Z)	1831	Jan. 27	Morgan Co,Oh	11	11	04
Moore, Philip(Z)	1834	Nov. 10	Morgan Co,Oh	11	11	03
Moore, Philip(Z)	1811	April 26	FayetteCo,Pa	12	13	25
Moore, Philip(Z)	1814	May 16	MuskingmCoOh	12	13	25
Moore, Philip(Z)	1815	Feb. 14	MuskingmCoOh	11	11	04
Moore, Richard(Y)	1831	Aug. 27	AlleghnyCoPa	03	13	31
Moore, Richard(Z-M)	1832	Dec. 04	Jeff.Co.,Oh.	07	07	21
Moore, Robert(Y)	1822	Nov. 11	BelmontCo,Oh	06	09	15
Moore, Robert(Y)	1826	Nov. 06	HarrisonCoOh	06	11	02
Moore, Robert(Z)	1816	April 25	HarrisonCoOh	14	13	08
Moore, Robert(Z)	1814	Feb. 05	HarrisonCoOh	14	13	08
Moore, Robert(Z)	1814	April 27	WashCo.,Penn	14	13	17
Moore, Robert(Z)	1814	June 11	ZanesvilleOh	14	16	17
Moore, Sam'l. S.(Z-M)	1824	May 15	GuernseyCoOh	02	04	03
Moore, Samuel(Y)	1831	March 15	HarrisonCoOh	07	15	33
Moore, Samuel(Z-M)	1836	March 17	LickingCo,Oh	11	04	21
Moore, Sarah(Z-M)	1836	March 21	TuscarwsCoOh	03	06	08
Moore, Silas(Z)	1816	Sept. 30	GuernseyCoOh	02	04	09
Moore, Thomas(Y)	1829	Dec. 09	ColumbanCoOh	01	06	22
Moore, Thomas(Y)	1829	Dec. 09	ColumbanCoOh	01	06	24
Moore, Thomas(Y)	1829	Dec. 09	ColumbanCoOh	01	06	24
Moore, Thomas(Z)	1830	Feb. 11	KnoxCo.,Ohio	10	05	21
Moore, Thomas(Z)	1833	May 30	Morgan Co,Oh	10	07	19
Moore, Thomas(Z)	1833	May 30	Morgan Co,Oh	11	11	24
Moore, Thomas(Z)	1811	May 24	HardyCo.,Vir	10	09	14
Moore, Thomas(Z)	1816	March 12	HarrisonCoOh	06	07	22
Moore, Thomas(Z)	1816	April 19	WashngtnCoOh	10	08	07
Moore, Thomas(Z)	1816	Dec. 09	MuskingmCoOh	10	08	17
Moore, Thomas(Z-M)	1830	March 04	HolmesCoOhio	09	08	21
Moore, Thomas(Z-M)	1836	Feb. 05	HarrisonCoOh	03	06	08
Moore, Thos.(Z-M)	1831	Nov. 02	Morgan Co,Oh	10	08	22
Moore, Thos.(Z-M)	1830	May 30	Jeff.Co.,Oh.	02	04	07
Moore, Thos.(Z-M)	1830	May 30	Jeff.Co.,Oh.	02	04	08
Moore, Tobias(Z-M)	1829	Feb. 28	HolmesCoOhio	05	08	24
Moore, Uriah(Z)	1836	Feb. 12	Perry Co.,Oh	14	13	26
Moore, W. H.(Z)	1815	March 08	MuskingmCoOh	10	03	02
Moore, W. H.(Z)	1816	Jan. 04	PutnamCoOhio	14	14	30
Moore, W. H.(Z)	1816	Jan. 16	PutnamCoOhio	14	13	20
Moore, William(Y)	1829	June 13	HarrisonCoOh	06	12	14
Moore, William(Y)	1832	Feb. 06	ColumbanCoOh	03	12	32
Moore, William(Z)	1828	Feb. 12	BelmontCo,Oh	12	10	27

PURCHASER	YEAR	DATE	RESIDENCE	R	T	S
Moore, William(Z)	1829	Feb. 28	GuernseyCoOh	11	10	19
Moore, William(Z)	1832	Nov. 12	Perry Co.,Oh	14	12	24
Moore, William(Z)	1816	Nov. 13	GuernseyCoOh	02	03	17
Moore, William(Z-M)	1824	July 07	MuskingmCoOh	07	03	20
Moore, William(Z-M)	1830	May 26	MuskingmCoOh	07	03	20
Moore, Wm. J.(Z)	1817	April 12	WashngtnCoOh	14	13	17
Moore, Wm. Jnr.(Y)	1821	Sept. 29	BelmontCo,Oh	06	09	15
Moore, Wm.(Y)	1822	Oct. 17	Jeff.Co.,Pa.	07	14	15
Moore, Wm.(Z)	1830	Nov. 25	Morgan Co,Oh	11	12	26
Moore, Wm.(Z)	1836	June 18	Perry Co.,Oh	14	13	24
Moore, Wm.(Z)	1836	Aug. 22	Perry Co.,Oh	14	13	23
Moore, Wm.(Z)	1836	Aug. 22	Perry Co.,Oh	14	13	22
Moore, Wm.(Z)	1815	Aug. 09	GuernseyCoOh	02	03	25
Moorehead, Moses(Z-M)	1837	Feb. 25	ZanesvilleOh	05	04	24
Moorehead, Wm. M.(Z)	1831	April 06	HarrisonCoOh	10	04	22
Moores, John(Z)	1835	Dec. 19	Morgan Co,Oh	09	06	11
Moores, Thomas(Z-M)	1829	Jan. 17	Jeff.Co.,Oh.	02	04	07
Moose, Charles(Z)	1821	July 06	Morgan Co,Oh	13	09	03
Moram, Ponderous(Z-M)	1832	Nov. 01	TuscarwsCoOh	02	05	20
Moram, Thornton(Z-M)	1832	Nov. 01	TuscarwsCoOh	02	05	20
Moran, John(Z)	1836	April 04	MonroeCo.,Oh	08	06	11
Moran, Pandorus(Z-M)	1832	Nov. 12	TuscarwsCoOh	01	05	06
Morarty, Martin(Z)	1821	Feb. 24	Perry Co.,Oh	15	16	26
Morarty, Martin(Z)	1821	March 02	Perry Co.,Oh	15	16	26
Mordock, Charles(Z)	1815	March 06	GreenCo.,Pa.	09	01	19
More, John(Z)	1813	Dec. 29	HarrisonCoOh	14	18	08
More, Thomas(Z)	1811	May 24	HardyCo.,Vir	10	09	14
Moredick, David(Z)	1836	Jan. 23	MonroeCo.,Oh	08	05	11
Morehead, Alexander(Z)	1836	Jan. 11	GuernseyCoOh	08	08	07
Morehead, James(Z)	1814	Dec. 13	WashCo.,Penn	05	02	20
Morehead, T.(Z)	1816	Nov. 28	ZanesvilleOh	09	03	20
Morehead, T.(Z)	1816	Dec. 02	ZanesvilleOh	14	15	12
Morehead, T.(Z)	1816	Dec. 02	ZanesvilleOh	14	15	13
Morehead, T.(Z)	1816	Dec. 02	ZanesvilleOh	14	15	13
Morehead, Thomas(Z)	1806	May 21	MuskingmCoOh	13	12	03
Moreland, Patten(Z)	1836	Jan. 11	GuernseyCoOh	08	08	31
Morfit, John(Z-M)	1832	July 27	TuscarwsCoOh	03	09	23
Morfit, John(Z-M)	1834	Jan. 07	TuscarwsCoOh	03	09	23
Morfit, John(Z-M)	1834	Aug. 14	TuscarwsCoOh	03	09	23
Morgan, Benj'm.(Z)	1824	May 11	Perry Co.,Oh	14	12	21
Morgan, Benj.(Z)	1826	Oct. 24	Perry Co.,Oh	14	12	21
Morgan, Benj.(Z)	1831	March 01	Perry Co.,Oh	14	12	19
Morgan, Benj.(Z)	1831	March 01	Perry Co.,Oh	14	12	17
Morgan, Benjamin(Z)	1823	Aug. 07	Perry Co.,Oh	14	12	28
Morgan, Benjamin(Z)	1833	Nov. 14	Perry Co.,Oh	14	12	17
Morgan, Clement(Z)	1807	July 18	MongahlaCoVa	15	18	11
Morgan, Dan'l.(Z)	1830	Nov. 29	MuskingmCoOh	11	01	20
Morgan, Daniel(Z-M)	1832	March 06	LickingCo,Oh	11	01	20
Morgan, Eli(Y)	1827	April 09	HarrisonCoOh	06	13	05
Morgan, Eli(Z-M)	1832	March 14	HarrisonCoOh	03	07	17
Morgan, Eli(Z-M)	1833	June 14	TuscarwsCoOh	03	07	17
Morgan, Eli(Z-M)	1840	Aug. 08	TuscarwsCoOh	03	07	02
Morgan, Elijah(Z-M)	1834	Jan. 03	CarrollCo,Oh	03	07	24
Morgan, Geo.(Z)	1815	Jan. 17	MuskingmCoOh	15	18	14
Morgan, Geo.(Z)	1816	Sept. 19	MuskingmCoOh	15	18	02
Morgan, George(Z-M)	1836	Jan. 18	CarrollCo,Oh	03	07	02
Morgan, Jacob(Z-M)	1840	Aug. 08	TuscarwsCoOh	03	07	02
Morgan, Jno.(Z)	1815	Jan. 17	MuskingmCoOh	15	18	14
Morgan, Jno.(Z)	1816	Sept. 19	MuskingmCoOh	15	18	02
Morgan, John(Y)	1830	Oct. 01	HarrisonCoOh	06	13	04
Morgan, John(Y)	1831	Oct. 14	HarrisonCoOh	07	15	10
Morgan, John(Z-M)	1837	Feb. 23	CoshoctnCoOh	09	08	14
Morgan, Marks(Z-M)	1837	June 05	ZanesvilleOh	09	09	17
Morgan, Philip(Z-M)	1837	June 05	ZanesvilleOh	09	09	17
Morgan, Robt.(Z)	1832	April 04	Perry Co.,Oh	14	12	20
Morgan, Samuel(Z)	1836	March 21	Perry Co.,Oh	14	12	30
Morgan, Samuel(Z)	1836	Dec. 05	Morgan Co,Oh	14	12	29
Morgan, William(Z)	1815	Nov. 21	SomersetCoPa	09	05	05
Morgan, Wm.(Z)	1815	Dec. 06	SomersetCoPa	10	05	01

PURCHASER	YEAR	DATE	RESIDENCE	R	T	S
Morgareidge, John(Z)	1832	June 12	Morgan Co,Oh	09	06	11
Morgareidge, John(Z)	1826	Aug. 08	WashngtnOhio	08	05	06
Morgareidge, John(Z)	1833	April 05	Morgan Co,Oh	09	06	11
Morgareidge, Mardin(Z)	1832	July 30	Morgan Co,Oh	09	06	14
Morledge, John(Y)	1822	April 29	ColumbanCoOh	06	16	13
Morledge, Roger(Y)	1828	Dec. 30	ColumbanCoOh	05	15	20
Morlidge, Jno.(Y)	1821	Nov. 08	ColumbanCoOh	05	15	22
Morningstar, William(Z)	1832	May 16	KnoxCo.,Ohio	10	06	13
Morris, Aaron(Z)	1821	March 28	GuernseyCoOh	08	08	32
Morris, Aaron(Z)	1835	Dec. 09	GuernseyCoOh	08	08	31
Morris, Abraham(Z)	1833	Sept. 13	Morgan Co,Oh	09	05	14
Morris, Abraham(Z-M)	1833	Aug. 10	GuernseyCoOh	03	01	18
Morris, Abraham(Z-M)	1835	Oct. 01	GuernseyCoOh	03	01	19
Morris, Andrew(Z)	1836	Nov. 08	WashngtnCoOh	08	05	11
Morris, Andrew(Z)	1836	Nov. 08	WashngtnCoOh	08	05	11
Morris, Andrew(Z)	1837	June 26	WashngtnCoOh	08	05	11
Morris, Archibald(Z)	1811	March 09	MuskingmCoOh	08	02	22
Morris, Archibald(Z)	1814	Feb. 17	GuernseyCoOh	08	06	12
Morris, Benjamin(Z-M)	1832	April 07	TuscarwsCoOh	01	09	20
Morris, David(Z)	1832	March 03	GuernseyCoOh	08	08	20
Morris, David(Z)	1832	March 03	GuernseyCoOh	08	08	20
Morris, David(Z)	1832	Oct. 08	GuernseyCoOh	08	08	20
Morris, David(Z-M)	1828	Dec. 05	CoshoctnCoOh	09	06	19
Morris, Elisha(Z)	1825	April 11	MonroeCo.,Oh	08	07	29
Morris, Elisha(Z)	1836	Aug. 27	MonroeCo.,Oh	08	07	33
Morris, Elisha(Z-M)	1825	Feb. 09	CoshoctnCoOh	10	04	10
Morris, George(Z)	1836	Oct. 24	WashngtnCoOh	08	05	05
Morris, Henry(Z)	1823	Jan. 30	GuernseyCoOh	08	08	31
Morris, Isaac Jr.(Z-M)	1833	Aug. 10	GuernseyCoOh	03	01	18
Morris, Isaac(Z)	1831	Nov. 09	MonroeCo.,Oh	08	07	25
Morris, Isaac(Z)	1836	April 13	MonroeCo.,Oh	08	06	09
Morris, Isaac(Z)	1836	Aug. 31	MonroeCo.,Oh	08	06	09
Morris, Isaac(Z)	1812	April 08	GuernseyCoOh	08	07	36
Morris, Isaac(Z-M)	1832	Sept. 04	GuernseyCoOh	03	01	18
Morris, Isaac(Z-M)	1832	Sept. 04	GuernseyCoOh	03	01	18
Morris, James(Z)	1836	Feb. 10	WashngtnCoOh	08	05	18
Morris, James(Z)	1836	March 12	WashngtnCoOh	09	05	13
Morris, James(Z)	1836	June 16	WashngtnCoOh	08	05	18
Morris, Jesse(Z)	1831	April 12	BelmontCo,Oh	13	08	21
Morris, John(Z)	1826	Oct. 25	Jeff.Co.,Oh.	10	06	01
Morris, John(Z)	1816	June 06	BelmontCo,Oh	01	04	05
Morris, Jonathan J.(Z)	1832	Sept. 01	GuernseyCoOh	08	08	20
Morris, Jonathan J.(Z)	1833	April 02	GuernseyCoOh	08	08	20
Morris, Jonathan(Z)	1816	March 14	GreeneCo.,Pa	08	08	21
Morris, Joseph(Y)	1821	Nov. 07	BelmontCo,Oh	04	17	18
Morris, Mahlon(Y)	1829	March 17	ColumbanCoOh	07	17	25
Morris, Neal(Z)	1816	April 09	BelmontCo,Oh	01	05	16
Morris, Stephen(Z-M)	1826	Dec. 08	TuscarwsCoOh	02	05	20
Morris, Thomas(Z)	1836	July 23	Morgan Co,Oh	14	13	34
Morris, Thos.(Z)	1830	Nov. 05	Brooke CoVir	08	05	12
Morris, William(Z)	1838	Nov. 09	WashngtnCoOh	08	05	14
Morrison, Abraham(Z)	1817	Feb. 10	TuscarwsCoOh	02	07	07
Morrison, Alex'r.(Z-M)	1837	Aug. 18	MuskingmCoOh	04	04	03
Morrison, Alexander(Z)	1811	Aug. 23	Ohio Co.,Vir	06	02	24
Morrison, Alexander(Z)	1811	Aug. 23	Ohio Co.,Vir	06	02	25
Morrison, Alexander(Z)	1814	Aug. 27	MuskingmCoOh	06	02	25
Morrison, Alexander(Z-M)	1838	Aug. 13	MuskingmCoOh	04	03	03
Morrison, Alexander(Z-M)	1838	Aug. 13	MuskingmCoOh	04	03	02
Morrison, Alfred Lee(Z)	1836	Jan. 07	Morgan Co,Oh	09	07	24
Morrison, Andrew(Z)	1836	Sept. 14	Morgan Co,Oh	08	07	31
Morrison, Arthur(Z)	1828	April 18	BelmontCo,Oh	12	11	27
Morrison, Cyrus(Z)	1829	July 18	MuskingmCoOh	13	09	21
Morrison, Enoch(Z-M)	1835	Feb. 04	KnoxCo.,Ohio	10	06	06
Morrison, Eppraim(Z)	1815	Nov. 17	ChesterCo,Pa	01	05	07
Morrison, Francis(Y)	1825	Oct. 10	Jeff.Co.,Oh.	03	11	34
Morrison, Francis(Y)	1825	Oct. 10	Jeff.Co.,Oh.	03	11	34
Morrison, G. W.(Z)	1830	July 16	GuernseyCoOh	08	07	06
Morrison, Geo.(Z)	1831	Dec. 07	Morgan Co,Oh	10	07	14
Morrison, Geo.(Z)	1831	Dec. 07	Morgan Co,Oh	10	07	13

PURCHASER	YEAR	DATE	RESIDENCE	R	T	S
Morrison, Haris(Z)	1804	June 18	MuskingmCoOh	05	01	13
Morrison, James(Z)	1815	Aug. 14	?	06	02	24
Morrison, Jno.(Z)	1835	Jan. 15	CarrolCo.,Oh	10	07	24
Morrison, John Jr.(Z-M)	1837	Feb. 13	KnoxCo.,Ohio	10	06	05
Morrison, John(Y)	1832	Dec. 13	GuernseyCoOh	07	09	10
Morrison, John(Y)	1835	April 16	GuernseyCoOh	07	09	10
Morrison, John(Z)	1835	June 11	CarrolCo.,Oh	10	07	24
Morrison, John(Z)	1814	March 16	?	10	06	16
Morrison, John(Z)	1814	April 25	KnoxCo.,Ohio	10	06	16
Morrison, John(Z-M)	1832	June 20	KnoxCo.,Ohio	10	06	05
Morrison, John(Z-M)	1832	June 20	KnoxCo.,Ohio	10	06	06
Morrison, John(Z-M)	1832	Nov. 19	KnoxCo.,Ohio	10	06	05
Morrison, John(Z-M)	1832	Nov. 19	KnoxCo.,Ohio	10	06	06
Morrison, John(Z-M)	1832	.Nov. 19	KnoxCo.,Ohio	10	06	05
Morrison, John(Z-M)	1832	Nov. 19	KnoxCo.,Ohio	10	06	06
Morrison, Joseph(Z-M)	1835	Aug. 28	GuernseyCoOh	02	03	09
Morrison, Joseph(Z-M)	1835	Sept. 07	GuernseyCoOh	02	03	09
Morrison, Joseph(Z-M)	1837	June 13	GuernseyCoOh	04	04	11
Morrison, M.(Z)	1817	Oct. 10	WashngtnCoOh	08	05	23
Morrison, Michael(Z)	1821	Dec. 26	Morgan Co,Oh	09	06	17
Morrison, Michael(Z)	1836	Jan. 04	Morgan Co,Oh	10	06	08
Morrison, Morris(Z)	1837	April 07	WashngtnCoOh	08	05	23
Morrison, Nathaniel(Z)	1817	March 29	MuskingmCoOh	10	01	13
Morrison, Robert(Z)	1825	April 23	BelmontCo,Oh	11	11	32
Morrison, Robert(Z)	1816	May 10	N.CasleCoDel	13	09	34
Morrison, Samuel(Y)	1827	Oct. 26	Stark Co.,Oh	06	16	27
Morrison, Thomas(Z)	1824	Dec. 11	WashCo.,Penn	11	12	07
Morrison, Thos.(Z)	1827	Jan. 09	WashCo.,Penn	11	12	07
Morrison, W.(Z)	1815	April 20	GuernseyCoOh	08	08	09
Morrison, William(Y)	1831	Aug. 03	GuernseyCoOh	07	09	21
Morrison, William(Z)	1813	Dec. 29	CoshoctnCoOh	07	08	21
Morrison, William(Z)	1815	Nov. 17	MifflinCo,Pa	01	05	08
Morrison, William(Z)	1815	Nov. 17	MifflinCo,Pa	01	05	08
Morrison, Wm.(Z-M)	1832	Feb. 16	HolmesCoOhio	07	08	20
Morrison, Zach'r.(Z-M)	1832	Feb. 16	HolmesCoOhio	07	08	20
Morrison, Zachariah(Z-M)	1829	March 21	HolmesCoOhio	06	07	05
Morrison, Zacheriah(Z-M)	1834	Oct. 29	HolmesCoOhio	07	08	20
Morrisson, John(Y)	1820	Dec. 15	WashCo.,Penn	06	14	04
Morrisson, John(Y)	1829	July 20	HarrisonCoOh	06	14	04
Morrow, David(Z-M)	1835	Dec. 10	GuernseyCoOh	04	03	17
Morrow, James(Z-M)	1835	Dec. 10	MuskingmCoOh	04	03	15
Morrow, James(Z-M)	1838	Dec. 15	MuskingmCoOh	04	03	16
Morrow, John(Z)	1833	Aug. 03	Perry Co.,Oh	14	14	19
Morrow, Thos.(Z)	1833	Aug. 03	Perry Co.,Oh	14	14	19
Morrow, William Junr.(Y)	1833	April 15	Stark Co.,Oh	04	13	02
Morrow, William(Z-M)	1831	April 01	GuernseyCoOh	04	03	18
Morrow, William(Z-M)	1832	Aug. 28	GuernseyCoOh	04	03	14
Morrow, William(Z-M)	1837	Jan. 31	GuernseyCoOh	04	03	17
Morrow, William(Z-M)	1837	May 02	GuernseyCoOh	04	03	14
Morry, Rouse(Z)	1835	Dec. 05	MonroeCo.,Oh	08	06	06
Morse, Hiram(Z)	1835	Dec. 14	Morgan Co,Oh	09	06	11
Morse, Hiram(Z)	1835	Dec. 14	Morgan Co,Oh	09	06	11
Morse, Hiram(Z)	1836	Dec. 14	Morgan Co,Oh	09	07	27
Morse, Manly(Z)	1835	July 18	Morgan Co,Oh	09	06	11
Mortley, Ford(Z-M)	1834	Jan. 25	CoshoctnCoOh	08	06	07
Morton, Andrew(Z)	1816	May 20	ChesterCo,Pa	07	05	14
Morton, George(Y)	1836	March 14	Jeff.Co.,Oh.	04	12	12
Moser, Abraham(Z)	1827	May 04	GuernseyCoOh	08	08	21
Moser, Abraham(Z)	1837	Nov. 08	GuernseyCoOh	08	08	27
Moser, Abrahan(Z)	1828	Aug. 12	GuernseyCoOh	08	08	21
Moser, John(Z)	1821	Aug. 11	Morgan Co,Oh	11	10	24
Moser, Magdalen(Z)	1807	June 22	FayetteCo,Pa	01	09	10
Mosholder, Adam(Z)	1831	July 18	KnoxCo.,Ohio	10	04	04
Mosholder, Elijah(Z-M)	1836	Sept. 06	TuscarwsCoOh	04	07	12
Mosholder, Elijah(Z-M)	1836	Sept. 06	TuscarwsCoOh	04	07	10
Mosholder, William(Z-M)	1833	Aug. 29	TuscarwsCoOh	04	07	12
Moss, Joseph(Z)	1832	Oct. 08	Morgan Co,Oh	10	07	28
Moss, Joseph(Z)	1836	Feb. 03	Morgan Co,Oh	10	07	34
Mosshard, Christina(Z-M)	1834	Nov. 27	TuscarwsCoOh	03	08	24

PURCHASER	YEAR	DATE	RESIDENCE	R	T	S
Mossholder, Adam(Z)	1813	March 03	KnoxCo.,Ohio	10	05	03
Mossholder, Adam(Z-M)	1832	July 13	KnoxCo.,Ohio	10	05	18
Mossholder, Ascum(Z-M)	1831	March 29	KnoxCo.,Ohio	10	04	04
Mossholder, Daniel(Z)	1815	Sept. 30	CoshoctnCoOh	10	05	17
Mossholder, Geo.(Z)	1827	Nov. 05	TuscarwsCoOh	04	07	09
Mossholder, Geo.(Z-M)	1832	Feb. 14	TuscarwsCoOh	04	07	09
Mossholder, William(Z-M)	1833	Sept. 21	TuscarwsCoOh	04	07	09
Mossman, Frances(Z-M)	1829	May 12	CoshoctnCoOh	08	05	21
Mossman, James(Z-M)	1831	June 21	CoshoctnCoOh	07	05	25
Mossman, John(Z)	1808	Jan. 08	FayetteCo,Pa	08	04	12
Mossman, John(Z)	1808	Feb. 05	FayetteCo,Pa	08	04	21
Mossman, John(Z-M)	1828	Nov. 21	CoshoctnCoOh	07	05	25
Mossman, John(Z-M)	1829	April 07	CoshoctnCoOh	08	06	03
Mossman, John(Z-M)	1830	Dec. 11	CoshoctnCoOh	08	04	20
Mossman, Jos. Jr.(Z-M)	1831	Oct. 10	CoshoctnCoOh	07	04	24
Mossman, Jos. Y.(Z-M)	1827	May 11	CoshoctnCoOh	07	04	15
Mossman, Robert(Z)	1808	May 31	FayetteCo,Pa	08	04	10
Most, Joseph(Z)	1811	Oct. 24	TuscarwsCoOh	05	09	23
Mount, James(Z)	1816	March 05	CrawfordCoPa	05	03	21
Mounts, James(Z-M)	1831	Sept. 20	MuskingmCoOh	05	03	22
Mountz, Godfried(Y)	1833	June 01	ColumbanCoOh	05	16	31
Mountz, Michael(Y)	1826	Jan. 24	ColumbanCoOh	05	17	15
Mourey, Henry(Z)	1836	May 02	AthensCoOhio	13	08	18
Mouzzy, Thomas N.(Z)	1814	July 04	GuernseyCoOh	10	08	04
Mowder, William(Z-M)	1829	Sept. 05	TuscarwsCoOh	01	06	24
Mowder, William(Z-M)	1835	Nov. 09	TuscarwsCoOh	01	05	04
Mower, Lucius D.(Z-M)	1825	Oct. 08	LickingCo,Oh	11	03	18
Mower, Michael(Z)	1813	Nov. 24	TuscarwsCoOh	04	08	21
Mowery, William A.(Z)	1814	July 22	WashngtnCoOh	13	09	23
Mowl, Peter(Y)	1822	April 12	WashCo.,Penn	06	17	21
Mowrey, Henry(Y)	1823	July 05	BelmontCo,Oh	04	06	15
Mowrey, Jacob(Z-M)	1837	April 27	KnoxCo.,Ohio	10	08	18
Moyer, Adam(Y)	1832	Sept. 17	Stark Co.,Oh	09	11	26
Moyers, Frederick(Z-M)	1832	Nov. 10	TuscarwsCoOh	03	10	24
Moyers, Samuel(Z)	1810	Nov. 26	FayetteCo,Pa	04	08	02
Mubrine, John(Z)	1832	Dec. 25	GreeneCo.,Pa	08	07	10
Muchmore, Sam'l.(Z)	1830	Jan. 19	BelmontCo,Oh	11	11	33
Muckler, Godfreit(Y)	1828	June 11	Stark Co.,Oh	09	11	11
Mulkin, Isaiah(Z-M)	1836	June 15	CoshoctnCoOh	06	04	13
Mullen, Jos.(Z)	1825	Jan. 06	GuernseyCoOh	10	09	21
Mullen, Samuel(Z)	1824	Dec. 21	FayetteCo,Pa	08	08	01
Mullen, Samuel(Z-M)	1826	Feb. 24	GuernseyCoOh	01	01	20
Mullen, William(Z)	1826	Dec. 18	Perry Co.,Oh	15	15	01
Mullet, Jacob(Z-M)	1838	Jan. 05	HolmesCoOhio	07	07	02
Mullet, John(Z-M)	1838	Jan. 05	HolmesCoOhio	08	07	01
Mullin, James(Z)	1833	Nov. 04	GuernseyCoOh	10	06	09
Mullin, William(Z)	1833	Sept. 13	Perry Co.,Oh	15	15	12
Mullvain, John(Z)	1815	Feb. 11	CoshoctnCoOh	04	06	12
Mullvane, John M.(Z-M)	1836	March 01	CoshoctnCoOh	04	05	13
Mullvane, John(Z-M)	1836	March 01	TuscarwsCoOh	03	05	15
Mummah, Martin(Z-M)	1825	Nov. 12	TuscarwsCoOh	03	09	20
Mummey, J.(Z)	1815	Aug. 23	Brooke CoVir	12	11	24
Mummey, S.(Z)	1815	Aug. 23	Brooke CoVir	12	11	24
Mummey, Thomas(Z)	1832	July 03	Morgan Co,Oh	11	10	34
Munch, Philip(Z)	1809	July 14	SprngfeldCo?	15	18	10
Munger, Christian(Z-M)	1838	June 01	HolmesCoOhio	08	08	19
Munges, Abraham S.(Z-M)	1836	Aug. 15	HolmesCoOhio	08	08	13
Munro & Converse(Z)	1811	Aug. 20	ZanesvilleOh	03	02	08
Munro, Joseph A.(Z-M)	1825	Nov. 25	MuskingmCoOh	07	04	23
Munro, Joseph F.(Z)	1810	Aug. 29	MuskingmCoOh	01	02	05
Munro, Joseph F.(Z)	1810	Oct. 13	MuskingmCoOh	01	02	19
Munro, Joseph F.(Z)	1811	May 21	MuskingmCoOh	13	12	13
Munro, Joseph F.(Z)	1815	Nov. 27	MuskingmCoOh	01	02	05
Munro, Joseph F.(Z)	1817	March 19	MuskingmCoOh	05	03	05
Munro, Joseph F.(Z)	1817	July 05	MuskingmCoOh	06	04	15
Munro, Robert(Z)	1810	March 26	HampshreCoVa	11	13	14
Munroe, Daniel(Z)	1815	Jan. 18	MuskingmCoOh	12	13	24
Munroe, John(Z-M)	1830	Nov. 03	MuskingmCoOh	05	03	22
Munroe, Joseph F.(Z-M)	1828	Sept. 17	MuskingmCoOh	05	03	05

PURCHASER	YEAR	DATE	RESIDENCE	R	T	S
Munson, A.(Z)	1817	Aug. 19	LickingCo,Oh	11	03	23
Munson, J. R.(Z)	1817	Aug. 19	LickingCo,Oh	11	03	23
Munstol, Peter(Z)	1805	March 30	BelmontCo,Oh	01	03	13
Muny, Christopher(Z)	1813	Nov. 19	SomersetCoPa	15	16	17
Munyer, William(Z)	1833	Dec. 12	Perry Co.,Oh	15	14	18
Munyon, George(Z)	1833	April 19	Perry Co.,Oh	15	14	07
Munyon, John(Z)	1832	Nov. 12	Perry Co.,Oh	15	14	07
Munyon, John(Z)	1833	April 19	Perry Co.,Oh	15	14	07
Munyon, William(Z)	1833	Dec. 12	Perry Co.,Oh	15	14	18
Murdock, Jos.(Z)	1835	March 25	BelmontCo,Oh	08	05	11
Murdock, Jos.(Z)	1835	March 25	BelmontCo,Oh	08	05	14
Murdock, Joseph(Z)	1836	Oct. 06	MonroeCo.,Oh	08	06	34
Murphey, Isaac(Z)	1836	Jan. 06	Morgan Co,Oh	13	08	28
Murphey, Thomas(Z)	1836	Jan. 06	Morgan Co,Oh	13	08	21
Murphey, Thomas(Z)	1836	April 28	Morgan Co,Oh	14	13	28
Murphy, Bernard(Y)	1824	Nov. 11	ColumbanCoOh	03	13	18
Murphy, Bernard(Y)	1829	March 14	ColumbanCoOh	03	13	18
Murphy, James(Z)	1824	Sept. 13	BelmontCo,Oh	11	11	15
Murphy, James(Z)	1814	Nov. 08	GuernseyCoOh	04	02	15
Murphy, James(Z)	1817	April 24	MuskingmCoOh	13	09	25
Murphy, John(Z)	1814	Dec. 16	GuernseyCoOh	04	02	24
Murphy, Michael(Z-M)	1838	April 12	CoshoctnCoOh	04	04	03
Murphy, Philip(Z-M)	1832	Oct. 02	TuscarwsCoOh	03	09	21
Murphy, Thos.(Z)	1836	Aug. 10	Morgan Co,Oh	13	08	21
Murphy, William(Y)	1826	April 17	BelmontCo,Oh	03	05	11
Murphy, William(Z)	1810	Aug. 28	MuskingmCoOh	05	01	04
Murphy, William(Z)	1817	June 05	GuernseyCoOh	04	02	23
Murray, Caleb(Z)	1821	Sept. 11	MonongahlaVa	09	08	36
Murray, Caleb(Z)	1828	Oct. 01	GuernseyCoOh	10	08	01
Murray, John(Z)	1810	Feb. 01	WashngtnCoOh	11	10	03
Murray, John(Z)	1816	Jan. 05	MuskingmCoOh	12	13	20
Murray, John(Z)	1817	Feb. 13	MuskingmCoOh	11	10	11
Murray, Samuel(Z)	1825	July 18	Morgan Co,Oh	11	10	01
Murray, Thomas(Z)	1814	July 11	WashngtnCoOh	11	10	12
Murray, Thos.(Z)	1810	Feb. 01	WashngtnCoOh	11	10	03
Murray, William(Z)	1833	April 26	Morgan Co,Oh	11	10	01
Murry, Christopher(Z)	1813	Nov. 19	SomersetCoPa	15	16	17
Murry, James(Z)	1834	March 24	Morgan Co,Oh	09	07	27
Murry, William(Y)	1828	Aug. 28	Stark Co.,Oh	06	16	18
Murry, William(Y)	1828	Aug. 28	Stark Co.,Oh	06	16	08
Murtagh, Bryan(Z)	1835	Jan. 16	CarrolCo.,Oh	14	12	01
Murtagh, Bryan(Z)	1836	Oct. 17	Perry Co.,Oh	14	12	02
Murtz, Michael(Y)	1828	July 14	Stark Co.,Oh	08	11	19
Musgrove, Moses(Z)	1827	May 01	CoshoctnCoOh	08	05	21
Musgrove, Sam'l.(Z-M)	1831	Oct. 26	BelmontCo,Oh	02	06	11
Musgrove, Wm.(Z-M)	1832	Feb. 11	CoshoctnCoOh	08	05	19
Musser, Christopher Jur.(Z-M)	1832	Jan. 28	CoshoctnCoOh	10	06	08
Musser, Daniel(Z)	1832	Nov. 16	FairfeldCoOh	15	15	35
Musser, Daniel(Z)	1833	Jan. 22	Perry Co.,Oh	15	15	35
Mutchelknouse, Gotha(Z-M)	1820	Dec. 04	TuscarwsCoOh	04	09	17
Mutchelknouse, Mathias(Z-M)	1823	March 06	TuscarwsCoOh	04	09	17
Mutchler, Jacob(Y)	1828	July 12	Stark Co.,Oh	09	11	26
Mutchler, Sudwig(Y)	1830	July 17	Stark Co.,Oh	09	11	27
Mutshelrouse, Geo.Mich'l.(Z-M)	1832	March 21	HolmesCoOhio	04	09	14
Muzzy, Thomas N.(Z)	1836	Jan. 23	Morgan Co,Oh	10	08	21
Muzzy, Thomas N.(Z)	1816	April 27	GuernseyCoOh	10	08	04
Myer, Eli(Z-M)	1835	March 18	LickingCo,Oh	10	03	08
Myer, Eli(Z-M)	1836	April 02	LickingCo,Oh	10	03	04
Myer, Henry(Z-M)	1839	May 23	CoshoctnCoOh	10	09	11
Myer, Jacob(Z-M)	1836	July 05	HolmesCoOhio	09	09	25
Myer, Nathaniel(Y)	1830	Jan. 11	ColumbanCoOh	02	09	31
Myers, Abraham(Y)	1832	Nov. 13	Jeff.Co.,Oh.	03	12	02
Myers, Andrew Jr.(Z)	1827	Nov. 12	LickingCo,Oh	11	01	10
Myers, Andrew(Z)	1827	April 17	CoshoctnCoOh	05	07	06
Myers, Andrew(Z)	1812	May 23	LickingCo,Oh	11	01	23
Myers, Andrew(Z-M)	1823	Dec. 10	LickingCo,Oh	11	01	04
Myers, Cornelius(Z-M)	1835	May 09	TuscarwsCoOh	02	07	05
Myers, Daniel(Z)	1817	Sept. 22	GuernseyCoOh	10	06	30
Myers, David R.(Z)	1836	Dec. 28	CarrollCo.,Oh	14	12	31

PURCHASER	YEAR	DATE	RESIDENCE	R	T	S
Myers, Elizabeth B.(Z-M)	1833	May 04	TuscarwsCoOh	03	10	17
Myers, Elizabeth B.(Z-M)	1833	May 04	TuscarwsCoOh	03	10	18
Myers, Henry(Z)	1813	Sept. 21	GuernseyCoOh	01	03	25
Myers, Henry(Z)	1815	Aug. 19	GuernseyCoOh	02	05	23
Myers, Isaac(Z)	1836	July 07	Perry Co.,Oh	14	12	06
Myers, Jacob(Z)	1830	March 10	Morgan Co,Oh	13	09	15
Myers, Jacob(Z)	1816	July 09	BelmontCo,Oh	08	07	25
Myers, Jacob(Z)	1816	Aug. 16	BelmontCo,Oh	08	07	24
Myers, Jacob(Z-M)	1837	April 01	HolmesCoOhio	09	09	25
Myers, Jno.(Y)	1826	Sept. 09	Canton, Ohio	09	10	01
Myers, John(Y)	1822	Dec. 12	TrumbullCoOh	05	15	22
Myers, John(Y)	1826	March 17	Stark Co.,Oh	09	10	01
Myers, John(Z)	1811	Oct. 07	GuernseyCoOh	02	02	22
Myers, Martin(Y)	1828	Oct. 03	Jeff.Co.,Oh.	05	13	02
Myers, Samuel(Y)	1829	March 16	TuscarwsCoOh	07	12	18
Myers, William(Z-M)	1835	Oct. 14	TuscarwsCoOh	03	06	03
Mygrants, Joseph(Z-M)	1832	April 12	TuscarwsCoOh	03	08	14
Myser, Adam(Z)	1813	Oct. 30	Jeff.Co.,Oh.	04	07	01
Myser, John(Z)	1812	April 21	TuscarwsCoOh	04	08	12
Nabel, John(Z-M)	1837	Feb. 28	CoshoctnCoOh	04	07	07
Naffsker, Jacob(Y)	1828	Jan. 16	HarrisonCoOh	04	10	12
Naftel, Thomas(Z)	1807	Sept. 05	MuskingmCoOh	09	08	05
Naftsinger, Christ'n.(Z)	1815	May 31	TuscarwsCoOh	03	09	19
Nairn, William(Y)	1835	Nov. 06	ColumbanCoOh	03	13	33
Nance, William(Z)	1815	June 03	WashCo.,Penn	01	04	18
Nance, William(Z-M)	1835	June 03	GuernseyCoOh	04	06	21
Nash, John Jnr.(Z)	1821	Oct. 12	MuskingmCoOh	12	10	29
Nash, Stephen(Y)	1828	June 20	Stark Co.,Oh	06	19	20
Nash, Thomas(Z)	1816	Dec. 24	MuskingmCoOh	12	10	34
Natinger, Gotleib(Z)	1828	Feb. 04	ZanesvilleOh	12	10	27
Nattinger, Gotleib(Z)	1825	Jan. 21	Morgan Co,Oh	13	10	36
Nattinger, John(Z)	1823	Sept. 30	Morgan Co,Oh	13	10	26
Nattinger, Samuel(Z)	1829	June 11	MuskingmCoOh	13	10	26
Navnom, John(Z-M)	1833	Oct. 01	GuernseyCoOh	03	01	04
Neal, Andrew(Z)	1816	March 18	TuscarwsCoOh	06	06	08
Neal, James O.(Z-M)	1833	April 04	BrackenCo,Ky	03	06	08
Neal, Joseph(Z)	1815	June 09	TuscarwsCoOh	09	01	15
Neal, Mary(Z-M)	1829	May 06	CoshoctnCoOh	06	07	07
Nederhouser, Jacob(Y)	1826	Sept. 18	Stark Co.,Oh	09	12	19
Need, George(Z-M)	1833	June 08	Jeff.Co.,Oh.	04	07	22
Needham, John(Z)	1814	April 05	FayetteCo,Pa	02	02	19
Needler, Jacob(Z)	1827	May 03	GuernseyCoOh	09	08	14
Needler, James(Z)	1833	June 21	GuernseyCoOh	09	08	12
Needles, John(Z)	1828	March 21	GuernseyCoOh	09	08	22
Neel, George(Y)	1835	Sept. 24	CarrollCo,Oh	07	15	31
Neel, John(Z)	1838	April 17	CarrollCo,Oh	15	14	25
Neel, John(Z)	1815	Jan. 16	GuernseyCoOh	02	01	18
Neeley, Thomas(Z-M)	1828	May 28	BelmontCo,Oh	03	02	06
Neff, Adam(Z-M)	1835	Dec. 24	CoshoctnCoOh	05	08	25
Neff, Andrew(Z)	1835	Nov. 14	BelmontCo,Oh	09	05	07
Neff, Andrew(Z)	1835	Nov. 14	BelmontCo,Oh	09	06	32
Neff, Andrew(Z)	1836	March 30	BelmontCo,Oh	08	06	18
Neff, Andrew(Z)	1836	March 30	BelmontCo,Oh	08	06	19
Neff, Christian(Z)	1816	Nov. 11	Ohio Co.,Vir	11	12	33
Neff, Christian(Z)	1816	Nov. 11	Ohio Co.,Vir	11	12	31
Neff, Fielding(Z)	1833	March 06	MuskingmCoOh	12	12	07
Neff, Jacob(Z-M)	1831	June 27	TuscarwsCoOh	04	08	18
Neff, John Junr.(Z)	1814	Jan. 04	KnoxCo.,Ohio	10	08	16
Neff, John Junr.(Z)	1814	Jan. 04	KnoxCo.,Ohio	11	08	20
Neff, John(Z)	1816	May 10	TuscarwsCoOh	04	09	21
Neher, David(Y)	1830	Oct. 11	ColumbanCoOh	05	16	31
Neidlinger, Jacob(Y)	1833	June 29	Stark Co.,Oh	09	12	07
Neidlinger, Peter(Y)	1833	June 29	Stark Co.,Oh	09	12	07
Neighbarger, James(Z-M)	1833	Jan. 21	LickingCo,Oh	10	03	08
Neighbour, Jacob Jnr.(Z-M)	1837	Feb. 21	TuscarwsCoOh	03	05	14
Neighbour, Jacob Jr.(Z-M)	1836	Jan. 18	TuscarwsCoOh	03	05	14
Neighbour, Leonard(Z-M)	1837	Feb. 21	TuscarwsCoOh	03	05	16
Neil, James(Z-M)	1832	Jan. 26	GuernseyCoOh	02	04	21
Neill, Moses(Y)	1821	Oct. 11	ColumbanCoOh	04	17	15

PURCHASER	YEAR	DATE	RESIDENCE	R	T	S
Neisz, John(Z-M)	1833	July 22	Stark Co.,Oh	03	07	01
Neisz, John(Z-M)	1833	July 22	Stark Co.,Oh	03	07	02
Neisz, John(Z-M)	1833	July 29	Stark Co.,Oh	03	07	01
Neisz, John(Z-M)	1833	July 29	Stark Co.,Oh	03	07	01
Neldon, Frederick(Z)	1827	Sept. 06	CoshoctnCoOh	09	05	03
Neldon, Henry(Z)	1814	Dec. 15	CoshoctnCoOh	09	05	20
Neldon, Henry(Z)	1817	Jan. 27	CoshoctnCoOh	08	04	05
Neldon, John Senr.(Z)	1815	July 15	CoshoctnCoOh	09	05	09
Neldon, John(Z)	1812	May 22	MuskingmCoOh	09	05	09
Neldon, John(Z)	1812	May 22	CoshoctnCoOh	09	08	09
Nelson, Archibald(Z-M)	1821	Sept. 09	GuernseyCoOh	03	03	22
Nelson, Elisha(Y)	1821	Nov. 08	HarrisonCoOh	06	12	21
Nelson, Hugh B.(Z-M)	1827	June 21	HarrisonCoOh	08	05	14
Nelson, Jacob(Z-M)	1832	Feb. 13	MuskingmCoOh	06	03	20
Nelson, James(Z)	1816	Jan. 06	FairfeldCoOh	13	09	27
Nelson, Robert(Z-M)	1835	Dec. 28	GuernseyCoOh	03	01	14
Nelson, Thomas(Z-M)	1835	March 12	TuscarwsCoOh	03	06	07
Nelson, Thomas(Z-M)	1836	Feb. 27	TuscarwsCoOh	03	06	07
Neptune, Samuel L.(Z)	1835	Nov. 21	MonroeCo.,Oh	08	06	35
Neptune, Samuel S.(Z)	1836	May 02	MonroeCo.,Oh	08	06	35
Nesbit, Jonathan(Z)	1812	June 24	MuskingmCoOh	11	13	11
Nesselroad, Christopher Jr.(Z)	1836	Nov. 07	Morgan Co,Oh	09	07	32
Nesselroad, Christopher(Z)	1835	Nov. 17	Morgan Co,Oh	09	06	05
Nesselrode, Chr.(Z)	1832	July 26	Morgan Co,Oh	09	06	05
Nesselrode, John(Z)	1832	Dec. 22	Morgan Co,Oh	09	07	32
Nesselrode, John(Z)	1832	Dec. 22	Morgan Co,Oh	09	07	33
Nessly, Samuel(Y)	1829	March 17	ColumbanCoOh	02	09	20
Nevile, Jonathan(Z-M)	1835	Dec. 29	HolmesCoOhio	07	08	17
Nevill, Jonathan(Z-M)	1829	May 27	HolmesCoOhio	07	08	12
Nevill, Jonathan(Z-M)	1833	Sept. 07	HolmesCoOhio	07	08	24
Nevill, Joseph(Z-M)	1829	Feb. 04	HolmesCoOhio	07	08	19
Nevin, John D.(Z-M)	1836	Jan. 26	BelmontCo,Oh	03	01	14
Nevin, John D.(Z-M)	1836	Feb. 26	BelmontCo,Oh	03	01	04
Newburn, Thomas(Z-M)	1834	March 15	GuernseyCoOh	02	04	17
Newcomb, George(Z)	1820	Sept. 15	Morgan Co,Oh	12	10	26
Newcomb, Wm.(Z-M)	1826	Oct. 06	CoshoctnCoOh	07	05	21
Newell, Charles(Z-M)	1828	Dec. 08	GuernseyCoOh	03	03	13
Newell, Charles(Z-M)	1833	April 13	GuernseyCoOh	03	03	13
Newell, Charles(Z-M)	1837	Jan. 28	GuernseyCoOh	03	03	14
Newell, Charles(Z-M)	1838	Aug. 11	GuernseyCoOh	03	03	13
Newell, Peter(Y)	1829	April 25	TuscarwsCoOh	07	15	01
Newell, Samuel(Z)	1808	Feb. 13	BelmontCo,Oh	03	03	13
Newell, Samuel(Z)	1810	Jan. 06	MuskingmCoOh	03	04	25
Newkirk, William(Z)	1829	Sept. 14	MuskingmCoOh	12	12	09
Newland, John(Z-M)	1833	Jan. 04	GuernseyCoOh	03	01	17
Newland, Joseph(Z)	1834	Feb. 03	GuernseyCoOh	10	09	23
Newlon, Elijah(Z)	1834	Aug. 04	Morgan Co,Oh	13	09	29
Newlun, William(Z)	1833	March 11	MuskingmCoOh	11	12	34
Newman, David(Z)	1830	Feb. 15	Morgan Co,Oh	12	10	22
Newman, George(Z)	1828	Aug. 20	Morgan Co,Oh	12	10	05
Newman, John(Z)	1830	Nov. 26	MuskingmCoOh	12	10	15
Newman, Joseph(Z)	1824	Oct. 09	Morgan Co,Oh	13	09	24
Newman, William(Z)	1830	Nov. 26	MuskingmCoOh	13	09	13
Newnom, John(Z-M)	1832	Sept. 04	MuskingmCoOh	03	01	07
Newnom, John(Z-M)	1832	Sept. 24	MuskingmCoOh	03	01	07
Newport, Henry(Y)	1828	Dec. 18	Stark Co.,Oh	07	16	34
Newport, Henry(Y)	1829	July 27	TuscarwsCoOh	07	16	33
Newport, Henry(Y)	1829	July 27	TuscarwsCoOh	07	16	27
Newsom, Jordan(Z)	1821	Oct. 04	BelmontCo,Oh	12	09	01
Newsom, Jordan(Z)	1826	April 10	BelmontCo,Oh	13	08	35
Newsom, Jordan(Z)	1826	April 10	BelmontCo,Oh	13	08	36
Newsom, Jordan(Z)	1826	April 10	BelmontCo,Oh	13	08	35
Newsom, Jordan(Z)	1826	April 10	BelmontCo,Oh	13	08	26
Newson, Edwin(Z)	1832	May 05	BelmontCo,Oh	13	08	07
Newson, Edwin(Z)	1832	May 22	BelmontCo,Oh	13	08	18
Newton, Alex'r.(Z)	1835	Dec. 17	Morgan Co,Oh	10	06	25
Newton, Alexander(Z)	1833	June 20	Morgan Co,Oh	10	06	25
Newton, Alexander(Z)	1835	Aug. 28	Morgan Co,Oh	10	06	25
Newton, George(Z-M)	1836	Jan. 22	Jeff.Co.,Oh.	07	08	14

PURCHASER	YEAR	DATE	RESIDENCE	R	T	S
Newton, George(Z-M)	1836	Jan. 22	Jeff.Co.,Oh.	07	08	11
Newton, Isaac(Z)	1835	June 24	Morgan Co,Oh	10	06	26
Newton, Isaac(Z-M)	1834	Oct. 11	CarrollCo,Oh	07	08	07
Newton, James(Z)	1834	July 25	Morgan Co,Oh	13	09	29
Newton, John(Z)	1834	July 28	Morgan Co,Oh	10	06	25
Newton, John(Z)	1835	July 25	Morgan Co,Oh	10	06	25
Newton, Joseph(Z)	1823	May 05	MuskingmCoOh	11	13	33
Newton, Joseph(Z)	1827	May 14	MuskingmCoOh	11	13	27
Newton, Lambert(Z)	1833	March 13	Morgan Co,Oh	09	07	28
Newton, Lambert(Z)	1836	Jan. 22	Morgan Co,Oh	09	07	28
Newton, Lambert(Z)	1836	Jan. 22	Morgan Co,Oh	09	07	21
Newton, Nathan(Z)	1836	May 06	Morgan Co,Oh	10	06	24
Niblack, William(Y)	1830	Nov. 13	BeaverCo.,Pa	04	14	36
Nichelson, John(Z)	1836	Jan. 07	GuernseyCoOh	08	08	31
Nichelson, Thomas(Z)	1836	Jan. 07	GuernseyCoOh	09	08	26
Nicherson, Hugh(Z)	1836	Jan. 20	Morgan Co,Oh	09	07	31
Nichollson, Thomas(Z)	1834	Dec. 15	GuernseyCoOh	09	08	26
Nichols, E.(Z)	1816	July 04	CoshoctnCoOh	09	05	10
Nichols, Edward(Z)	1828	July 29	Morgan Co,Oh	12	11	22
Nichols, Elijah(Z)	1815	May 03	LickingCo,Pa	11	01	18
Nichols, Henry(Z)	1815	May 06	MuskingmCoOh	11	11	29
Nichols, Hugh(Z)	1816	March 02	Ohio Co.,Vir	12	11	10
Nichols, Israel(Z)	1836	April 07	Morgan Co,Oh	10	07	34
Nichols, James(Z-M)	1832	Oct. 11	HolmesCoOhio	06	09	24
Nichols, John Jr.(Z)	1807	Oct. 17	WestmrldCoPa	07	05	01
Nichols, John Senr.(Z)	1809	Nov. 22	WestmrldCoPa	08	02	22
Nichols, John(Z)	1807	Sept. 10	WestmrldCoPa	07	05	02
Nichols, Mathias(Z)	1817	Jan. 30	Ohio Co.,Vir	13	11	20
Nicholson, George(Z-M)	1837	April 07	TuscarwsCoOh	05	07	11
Nicholson, John(Z)	1828	June 30	GuernseyCoOh	09	08	36
Nicholson, Margaret(Z)	1833	Jan. 25	GuernseyCoOh	09	08	36
Nicholson, Margaret(Z)	1815	Feb. 24	GuernseyCoOh	08	07	18
Nicholson, Patrick(Y)	1834	Oct. 09	NrthmptnCoPa	04	13	13
Nicholson, Robert(Z-M)	1835	Jan. 06	GuernseyCoOh	03	01	03
Nicholson, Robert(Z-M)	1836	Jan. 12	GuernseyCoOh	03	01	03
Nicholson, Samuel(Z)	1832	Dec. 14	MuskingmCoOh	10	06	05
Nicholson, Samuel(Z)	1832	Dec. 14	MuskingmCoOh	10	06	06
Nicholson, Thomas(Z)	1810	Dec. 10	Jeff.Co.,Oh.	09	08	25
Nickel, Thomas(Y)	1822	Sept. 23	WashCo.,Penn	07	11	21
Nickels, George(Y)	1822	April 12	BelmontCo,Oh	06	09	15
Nickels, Wm.(Y)	1822	March 27	BelmontCo,Oh	06	10	22
Nickerson, Hugh(Z)	1834	Dec. 17	Morgan Co,Oh	10	08	36
Nickle, Samuel(Y)	1831	Nov. 10	HarrisonCoOh	07	11	22
Nickle, Thomas(Y)	1831	June 10	GuernseyCoOh	07	11	22
Nickle, William(Y)	1831	Nov. 10	GuernseyCoOh	07	11	22
Nickles, Harrison(Z)	1835	Aug. 21	Morgan Co,Oh	10	06	09
Nickols, Edward(Z)	1830	Aug. 03	Morgan Co,Oh	12	12	07
Nickols, Mounts(Z)	1830	Aug. 03	MuskingmCoOh	12	12	07
Nickols, Samuel(Z-M)	1836	Dec. 03	GuernseyCoOh	04	07	16
Nickolson, Thomas(Z)	1811	Aug. 20	GuernseyCoOh	08	08	30
Nicolson, Andrew(Z)	1812	Sept. 09	WestmrldCoPa	10	02	17
Nidey, Mathias(Z)	1809	Nov. 14	MuskingmCoOh	15	17	06
Niesz, John(Z-M)	1835	June 04	Stark Co.,Oh	03	07	02
Niesz, John(Z-M)	1835	Oct. 15	Stark Co.,Oh	03	07	02
Nighart, Conrad(Z)	1817	June 02	CoshoctnCoOh	06	08	22
Nighent, Jacob(Z-M)	1830	March 25	HolmesCoOhio	06	08	19
Niswander, John(Z)	1815	July 11	WashngtnCoOh	10	05	10
Nivin, John(Y)	1825	Jan. 24	Jeff.Co.,Oh.	05	13	28
Nixon, Andrew(Y)	1823	Feb. 11	Jeff.Co.,Oh.	03	10	18
Nixon, Hugh(Z)	1831	July 18	Morgan Co,Oh	13	09	28
Nixon, Hugh(Z)	1831	July 18	Morgan Co,Oh	13	09	28
No__, Richard Charles(Z-M)	1832	Nov. 01	KnoxCo.,Ohio	11	08	14
Noble, Andrew(Y)	1829	Nov. 06	ColumbanCoOh	02	09	20
Noble, Andrew(Y)	1831	Nov. 14	ColumbanCoOh	02	09	20
Noble, Angus(Y)	1830	Jan. 19	ColumbanCoOh	03	12	12
Noble, J.(Z)	1814	July 28	MuskingmCoOh	15	07	03
Noble, James(Z)	1814	July 21	GuernseyCoOh	09	06	18
Noble, James(Z)	1817	Feb. 13	GuernseyCoOh	09	07	11
Noble, Jas.(Z)	1822	Dec. 27	Morgan Co,Co	09	07	11

PURCHASER	YEAR	DATE	RESIDENCE	R	T	S
Noble, Jno.(Z-M)	1832	Jan. 17	CoshoctnCoOh	07	05	20
Noble, John Junr.(Z)	1824	June 22	Morgan Co,Oh	10	08	34
Noble, John(Z)	1835	Nov. 25	Morgan Co,Oh	09	07	32
Noble, John(Z)	1811	Sept. 14	WashngtnCoOh	09	07	33
Noble, John(Z-M)	1828	July 16	CoshoctnCoOh	07	05	21
Noble, Lachline(Y)	1823	April 11	ColumbanCoOh	02	10	22
Noble, Robert(Z)	1834	Jan. 03	Perry Co.,Oh	14	14	19
Noble, Samuel(Z)	1832	Oct. 26	GuernseyCoOh	09	07	27
Noble, Samuel(Z)	1834	March 13	Morgan Co,Oh	09	07	27
Noble, Thomas(Z-M)	1833	April 18	GuernseyCoOh	03	02	10
Noble, William(Z-M)	1833	Feb. 18	GuernseyCoOh	03	02	10
Noble, Wm.(Y)	1829	Sept. 26	WashCo.,Penn	04	12	26
Noel, Nicholas(Z)	1814	Nov. 17	SomersetCoPa	05	08	14
Nofsinger, John(Z-M)	1836	Feb. 01	TuscarwsCoOh	04	07	06
Nofsinger, Robert(Z-M)	1837	Nov. 15	TuscarwsCoOh	04	07	04
Noftsinger, Christian(Z-M)	1832	Nov. 12	TuscarwsCoOh	04	07	06
Noftsinger, Christian(Z-M)	1832	Nov. 12	TuscarwsCoOh	04	07	06
Noftsinger, Christian(Z-M)	1833	March 21	TuscarwsCoOh	04	07	15
Noftsinger, Christian(Z-M)	1833	May 03	TuscarwsCoOh	04	07	15
Noftsinger, Christiana(Z-M)	1833	May 03	TuscarwsCoOh	04	07	04
Noftsinger, Magdalen(Z-M)	1833	June 28	TuscarwsCoOh	04	07	06
Noftsinger, Robert(Z-M)	1833	May 03	TuscarwsCoOh	04	07	15
Nolen, Pierce(Z)	1813	Dec. 28	CoshoctnCoOh	09	04	11
Noll, John(Z-M)	1828	Jan. 03	TuscarwsCoOh	02	07	13
Noon, Charles(Z)	1828	June 14	Perry Co.,Oh	15	16	23
Noon, James(Z)	1830	April 29	Perry Co.,Oh	15	16	23
Noon, John(Z)	1828	Jan. 02	MuskingmCoOh	15	16	23
Noonan, John(Z)	1831	March 31	MuskingmCoOh	13	10	07
Noonen, John(Z)	1833	Nov. 14	MuskingmCoOh	13	10	07
Norman, Benjamin B.(Z-M)	1837	April 18	CoshoctnCoOh	04	04	09
Norman, Benjamin(Z-M)	1837	June 03	CoshoctnCoOh	09	09	23
Norman, Benjamin(Z-M)	1837	June 03	CoshoctnCoOh	09	09	18
Norman, Geo.(Z-M)	1831	April 28	HarrisonCoOh	01	05	05
Norman, George(Z)	1815	Jan. 09	MuskingmCoOh	15	18	01
Norman, Isaac(Z)	1817	Oct. 07	MuskingmCoOh	10	04	16
Norman, Samuel(Z-M)	1837	April 18	CoshoctnCoOh	04	04	02
Norman, Thomas(Z)	1814	Nov. 07	MuskingmCoOh	14	16	06
Norrick, Joseph(Y)	1829	Dec. 26	HarrisonCoOh	06	13	19
Norris, Charles(Y)	1829	June 01	FredrickCoMd	07	12	33
Norris, Chas.(Z-M)	1829	May 25	FredrickCoMd	01	05	10
Norris, Daniel(Z-M)	1832	Nov. 19	CoshoctnCoOh	07	04	12
Norris, Daniel(Z-M)	1832	Nov. 19	CoshoctnCoOh	07	04	12
Norris, Daniel(Z-M)	1833	Jan. 08	CoshoctnCoOh	07	04	17
Norris, David(Z-M)	1832	July 09	TuscarwsCoOh	03	06	15
Norris, Davis(Y)	1833	April 06	Jeff.Co.,Oh.	03	12	02
Norris, Davis(Y)	1836	Jan. 16	Jeff.Co.,Oh.	03	12	09
Norris, Gilbert Wilson(Y)	1836	Jan. 16	Jeff.Co.,Oh.	03	12	03
Norris, Jacob(Z-M)	1829	April 25	CoshoctnCoOh	04	06	11
Norris, Jacob(Z-M)	1834	Feb. 20	CoshoctnCoOh	04	06	11
Norris, Jacob(Z-M)	1835	Nov. 11	CoshoctnCoOh	04	06	11
Norris, James P.(Y)	1831	March 31	ColumbanCoOh	03	12	03
Norris, James(Z)	1831	Oct. 08	ColumbanCoOh	14	12	11
Norris, James(Z)	1836	Dec. 14	Perry Co.,Oh	14	12	10
Norris, James(Z)	1836	Dec. 14	Perry Co.,Oh	14	12	11
Norris, James(Z)	1813	Dec. 15	CoshoctnCoOh	07	04	17
Norris, Jas.(Y)	1828	Sept. 25	ColumbanCoOh	03	13	23
Norris, Jeremiah(Y)	1835	June 27	HarrisonCoOh	07	12	28
Norris, John R.(Z)	1834	Aug. 12	Perry Co.,Oh	14	12	10
Norris, John(Z-M)	1830	Jan. 09	GuernseyCoOh	04	02	08
Norris, Jon.(Z-M)	1830	April 09	CoshoctnCoOh	04	06	11
Norris, Jonathan(Z-M)	1822	Feb. 25	CoshoctnCoOh	04	06	02
Norris, Joseph(Z)	1813	Sept. 13	CoshoctnCoOh	07	04	16
Norris, Joseph(Z-M)	1837	May 19	GuernseyCoOh	04	04	12
Norris, Sam'l.(Z)	1814	March 22	CoshoctnCoOh	04	06	23
Norris, Samuel T.(Z-M)	1835	Dec. 01	HolmesCoOhio	09	08	14
Norris, Samuel(Z-M)	1832	Sept. 18	CoshoctnCoOh	07	04	13
Norris, Samuel(Z-M)	1833	Oct. 15	CoshoctnCoOh	04	06	22
Norris, Sarah(Y)	1828	Nov. 14	GreeneCo.,Pa	07	12	29
Norris, Thomas(Z)	1816	May 24	BelmontCo,Oh	08	05	07

PURCHASER	YEAR	DATE	RESIDENCE	R	T	S
Norris, Thomas(Z)	1816	May 24	BelmontCo,Oh	08	05	07
Norris, Thomas(Z-M)	1832	March 08	CoshoctnCoOh	04	06	10
Norris, Thomas(Z-M)	1832	July 02	CoshoctnCoOh	04	06	02
Norris, Thomas(Z-M)	1835	Oct. 06	CoshoctnCoOh	04	06	10
Norris, Thos.(Z-M)	1832	June 26	CoshoctnCoOh	04	06	22
Norris, William(Z)	1809	April 21	MuskingmCoOh	07	04	14
Norris, William(Z-M)	1833	Dec. 09	CoshoctnCoOh	07	04	01
Norris, Wm. D.(Y)	1828	March 03	ColumbanCoOh	02	09	28
Norris, Wm. D.(Y)	1829	May 09	ColumbanCoOh	02	09	28
Norris, Wm.(Y)	1825	Jan. 22	WashCo.,Penn	06	15	02
Norris, Wm.(Y)	1827	Sept. 08	HarrisonCoOh	06	15	02
Norris, Wm.(Z)	1814	March 22	CoshoctnCoOh	04	06	23
Norris, Wm.(Z-M)	1832	June 26	CoshoctnCoOh	04	06	22
Norris, Wm.(Z-M)	1835	Aug. 26	CoshoctnCoOh	04	06	22
Northgraves, Wm.(Z-M)	1825	Aug. 12	Jeff.Co.,Oh.	02	03	02
Northup, Henry(Z)	1813	Dec. 15	MuskingmCoOh	05	02	04
Northup, Henry(Z)	1814	Feb. 28	MuskingmCoOh	05	03	10
Northup, Henry(Z)	1814	July 04	MuskingmCoOh	05	03	09
Northup, Henry(Z)	1816	Feb. 07	MuskingmCoOh	06	03	21
Noss, Jacob(Z-M)	1834	Dec. 19	HarrisonCoOh	03	07	13
Nothdurft, Gottlieb(Y)	1829	Dec. 11	ColumbanCoOh	03	13	29
Nothdurft, Gottlieb(Y)	1830	May 06	ColumbanCoOh	03	13	29
Nowd, Richard Charles(Z-M)	1832	Nov. 01	KnoxCo.,Ohio	11	08	14
Noyes, Joseph Jr.(Z)	1833	April 13	Morgan Co,Oh	09	06	13
Noyes, Joseph Jur.(Z)	1832	May 22	Morgan Co,Oh	09	06	13
Nozinger, Christian(Z)	1807	June 01	Jeff.Co.,Oh.	03	09	18
Nugent, Patric(Z)	1833	Dec. 09	Perry Co.,Oh	14	14	30
Nugent, Patrick(Z)	1823	June 21	Perry Co.,Oh	15	16	36
Nugent, Patrick(Z)	1833	Sept. 30	Perry Co.,Oh	14	14	30
Nulton, Harrison(Z)	1828	Aug. 27	Morgan Co,Oh	13	08	36
Nulton, John(Z)	1828	Aug. 27	Morgan Co,Oh	13	08	26
Numan, Jacob(Z)	1806	June 25	ColumbanCoOh	03	10	12
Numar, Jacob(Z)	1806	June 25	ColumbanCoOh	03	10	12
Nusbaum, Daniel(Z-M)	1835	Oct. 16	CarrollCo,Oh	03	07	22
Nusbaum, Daniel(Z-M)	1835	Oct. 16	CarrollCo,Oh	03	07	19
Nusbaum, Henry(Y)	1828	July 16	Stark Co.,Oh	06	16	07
Nusbaum, Henry(Z-M)	1836	June 23	CarrollCo,Oh	03	07	23
Nutter, Erastus(Z-M)	1833	June 15	LickingCo,Oh	11	04	07
Nye, Horace(Z-M)	1826	March 20	PutnamCoOhio	09	03	22
Nye, Horace(Z-M)	1827	May 09	PutnamCo.,Oh	09	03	22
Nye, Lewis(Z)	1804	Dec. 04	MuskingmCoOh	14	15	18
Nye, Lewis(Z)	1804	Dec. 04	MuskingmCoOh	14	15	10
Nye, Lewis(Z)	1805	Oct. 28	MuskingmCoOh	09	03	19
Nye, Lewis(Z)	1805	Oct. 28	MuskingmCoOh	09	03	19
Nye, Lewis(Z)	1806	Feb. 07	MuskingmCoOh	14	15	01
Nyhart, Jacob(Z-M)	1835	Nov. 14	KnoxCo.,Ohio	10	08	03
Nyhart, Jacob(Z-M)	1835	Nov. 14	KnoxCo.,Ohio	10	09	23
O'Conner, Morris(Z)	1833	Nov. 13	ZanesvilleOh	14	14	12
O'Donnough, Barney(Y)	1835	June 01	ColumbanCoOh	04	13	13
O'Donough, Barney(Y)	1835	March 05	ColumbanCoOh	04	13	13
O'Hear, Peter(Y)	1824	May 18	ColumbanCoOh	04	14	15
O'Hear, Peter(Y)	1824	May 18	ColumbanCoOh	04	14	15
O'Neal, James(Z-M)	1833	April 04	BrackenCo,Ky	03	06	08
Oard, Peter(Z-M)	1823	Jan. 15	LickingCo,Oh	11	01	13
Oard, Peter(Z-M)	1827	March 06	LickingCo,Oh	11	01	13
Oatley, Samuel(Z)	1826	March 20	Perry Co.,Oh	15	15	15
Oatley, Samuel(Z)	1837	March 04	Perry Co.,Oh	15	15	27
Oatman, John(Z-M)	1833	June 20	LickingCo,Oh	10	02	17
Obney, John(Z-M)	1834	Oct. 16	GuernseyCoOh	03	01	06
Ocker, Jacob U.(Z-M)	1836	Jan. 23	TuscarwsCoOh	02	07	04
Ocker, Jacob U.(Z-M)	1836	Jan. 23	TuscarwsCoOh	02	07	05
Oder, Nancy(Z)	1832	Nov. 14	CoshoctnCoOh	14	13	18
Oder, Nancy(Z-M)	1830	Nov. 25	MuskingmCoOh	07	05	11
Oder, Nancy(Z-M)	1832	Nov. 03	CoshoctnCoOh	05	08	16
Odor, Jeremiah(Z-M)	1836	April 05	GuernseyCoOh	07	04	10
Officer, James(Z)	1811	Oct. 09	WashngtnCoOh	12	13	01
Officer, James(Z)	1812	May 21	WashCo.,Penn	11	13	06
Officer, John(Z)	1811	Nov. 21	WashCo.,Penn	11	13	06
Officer, Robert(Z)	1813	Dec. 15	WashngtnCoOh	12	13	12

215

PURCHASER	YEAR	DATE	RESIDENCE	R	T	S
Ogan, Evan(Z)	1817	Aug. 02	BelmontCo,Oh	11	13	24
Ogburn, Samuel(Z)	1815	June 17	HarrisonCoOh	14	13	05
Ogden, Thomas(Y)	1828	Dec. 31	FrederkCoVir	07	12	36
Ogg, Andrew(Z)	1834	Jan. 03	Perry Co.,Oh	15	14	06
Ogg, George(Z)	1817	July 11	FairfeldCoOh	15	15	01
Ogg, Rachel(Z)	1814	May 05	MuskingmCoOh	15	16	20
Ogg, Robert W.(Z)	1832	Aug. 21	BelmontCo,Oh	08	07	09
Ogg, Robert W.(Z)	1832	Aug. 20	BelmontCo,Oh	08	07	09
Ogg, Robert W.(Z)	1832	Aug. 20	BelmontCo,Oh	08	07	09
Ogg, Vachel(Z)	1814	Oct. 26	MuskingmCoOh	15	16	30
Ogg, Vachel(Z)	1816	Sept. 25	MuskingmCoOh	13	09	08
Ogier, James(Z)	1824	Jan. 07	GuernseyCoOh	10	09	11
Ogier, John(Z-M)	1833	Aug. 15	GuernseyCoOh	03	01	04
Ogier, Thomas(Z)	1822	Dec. 10	GuernseyCoOh	10	09	14
Ogier, Thomas(Z)	1822	Dec. 10	GuernseyCoOh	10	09	11
Ogier, Thomas(Z)	1823	Oct. 18	GuernseyCoOh	10	09	10
Ogier, Thomas(Z)	1826	Dec. 07	GuernseyCoOh	10	09	15
Ogilvie, George(Z-M)	1828	March 17	MuskingmCoOh	08	03	03
Ogle, Alfred(Z)	1834	Aug. 08	Morgan Co,Oh	09	06	23
Ogle, Alfred(Z)	1836	Feb. 27	Morgan Co,Oh	08	05	04
Ogle, Alfred(Z)	1837	May 17	Morgan Co,Oh	08	06	35
Ogle, Alfred(Z)	1837	Nov. 07	Morgan Co,Oh	08	06	34
Ogle, Alfred(Z)	1838	April 03	Morgan Co,Oh	08	06	34
Ogle, Henry(Y)	1832	Oct. 06	ColumbanCoOh	03	12	09
Ogle, James(Y)	1827	July 19	ColumbanCoOh	03	12	10
Ogle, William(Y)	1836	April 20	Jeff.Co.,Oh.	03	12	20
Ogle, William(Y)	1836	April 27	Jeff.Co.,Oh.	03	12	20
Ogle, William(Z)	1832	Oct. 26	Morgan Co,Oh	09	06	22
Ogle, Wm.(Y)	1823	Nov. 12	HarrisonCoOh	05	13	22
Oglevee, William(Y)	1831	April 26	HarrisonCoOh	07	11	17
Ohl, Jacob(Y)	1823	April 18	TrumbullCoOh	06	19	17
Ohleyer, George(Z-M)	1835	Oct. 20	HolmesCoOhio	10	09	20
Ohleyer, George(Z-M)	1835	Oct. 20	HolmesCoOhio	10	09	20
Ohleyer, George(Z-M)	1835	Oct. 20	HolmesCoOhio	10	09	20
Oldacres, Jesse(Z)	1805	May 30	FairfeldCoOh	15	18	07
Oldakers, Jesse(Z)	1810	Sept. 25	MuskingmCoOh	11	04	16
Oldham, Isaac(Z)	1806	June 16	MuskingmCoOh	03	02	03
Oldham, Isaac(Z)	1811	March 20	GuernseyCoOh	03	02	04
Oldham, Isaac(Z-M)	1824	March 17	GuernseyCoOh	03	03	15
Oldham, Isaac(Z-M)	1828	Jan. 19	GuernseyCoOh	03	02	05
Oldham, James(Z)	1806	Nov. 08	Ohio Co.,Vir	03	03	18
Oldham, Robert(Z-M)	1822	April 10	WashCo.,Penn	03	03	24
Oldham, Thos.(Z-M)	1828	Jan. 19	GuernseyCoOh	03	02	05
Olinger, A.(Z)	1817	May 22	TuscarwsCoOh	04	08	07
Olinger, Abraham(Z)	1814	Oct. 24	SomersetCoPa	04	08	09
Olinger, Abraham(Z-M)	1824	Sept. 11	TuscarwsCoOh	04	08	23
Olinger, C.(Z)	1817	May 22	TuscarwsCoOh	04	08	07
Olinger, Christian(Z)	1811	Aug. 20	SomersetCoPa	04	08	07
Olinger, George(Z)	1804	Dec. 06	MuskingmCoOh	15	17	20
Olinger, George(Z)	1805	Dec. 05	MuskingmCoOh	15	17	07
Olinger, Isaac(Z-M)	1835	April 23	HolmesCoOhio	05	07	05
Olinger, John(Z)	1827	Sept. 18	TuscarwsCoOh	04	07	24
Olinger, John(Z-M)	1832	May 15	TuscarwsCoOh	03	06	05
Oliphant, William(Z)	1813	May 21	WashngtnCoOh	10	06	24
Oliphant, William(Z)	1814	Aug. 15	WashngtnCoOh	10	06	13
Oliphant, William(Z)	1815	July 10	WashngtnCoOh	09	05	18
Oliver, Francis(Y)	1822	Sept. 17	Jeff.Co.,Oh.	07	14	21
Oliver, John(Z)	1835	Nov. 17	BelmontCo,Oh	10	07	26
Oliver, John(Z)	1835	Nov. 19	BelmontCo,Oh	10	07	26
Oliver, Thomas(Z-M)	1832	June 02	Jeff.Co.,Oh.	01	04	25
Oliver, Thos.(Z-M)	1831	April 06	Jeff.Co.,Oh.	01	04	25
Oliver, William(Z)	1810	Nov. 02	WashngtnCoOh	13	09	35
Oller, John(Z-M)	1834	Jan. 03	CarrollCo,Oh	03	07	12
Olliver, James(Z)	1815	Nov. 13	WashCo.,Penn	07	05	24
Olney, Silvanus(Z)	1826	Dec. 25	Morgan Co,Oh	11	10	36
Ong, Jacob Senr.(Z-M)	1822	Dec. 13	GuernseyCoOh	01	04	02
Ong, Jacob(Z-M)	1835	Oct. 26	Jeff.Co.,Oh.	07	08	08
Onstat, Henry(Z)	1815	April 03	AlleghnyCoPa	12	12	13
Onstot, Henry Jr.(Z)	1833	Nov. 16	MuskingmCoOh	11	12	27

PURCHASER	YEAR	DATE	RESIDENCE	R	T	S
Onstot, Jacob(Z)	1822	Feb. 26	MuskingmCoOh	11	12	18
Onstott, Peter(Z)	1826	June 05	MuskingmCoOh	11	12	06
Oquigley, Jno. Jr.(Z-M)	1835	Dec. 30	LickingCo,Oh	02	05	03
Organ, William(Z)	1805	Dec. 02	FairfeldCoOh	14	16	15
Orison, Jesse(Z)	1835	Oct. 09	Perry Co.,Oh	14	12	06
Orison, Jesse(Z)	1836	Feb. 03	Perry Co.,Oh	14	12	06
Orr, Andrew(Z-M)	1823	Aug. 16	MuskingmCoOh	07	03	19
Orr, Andrew(Z-M)	1827	Jan. 23	MuskingmCoOh	07	03	19
Orr, Catharine(Y)	1826	Feb. 07	ColumbanCoOh	05	17	09
Orr, John Junior(Y)	1828	March 01	HarrisonCoOh	06	11	24
Orr, John(Z-M)	1839	Feb. 19	ZanesvilleOh	04	03	08
Orr, Mathew(Z-M)	1828	April 25	GuernseyCoOh	02	04	17
Orr, Mathew(Z-M)	1832	March 30	GuernseyCoOh	02	04	07
Orr, Matthew(Z-M)	1830	March 23	GuernseyCoOh	02	04	17
Orr, Thomas(Z-M)	1833	April 16	TuscarwsCoOh	03	06	01
Orr, Thomas(Z-M)	1833	April 16	TuscarwsCoOh	03	05	12
Orr, Thomas(Z-M)	1833	April 16	TuscarwsCoOh	03	06	10
Orr, Thomas(Z-M)	1837	Jan. 04	GuernseyCoOh	03	05	12
Orr, William(Y)	1829	Aug. 26	HarrisonCoOh	06	11	24
Orr, William(Z-M)	1836	Feb. 23	BelmontCo,Oh	01	05	05
Orrison, Jesse(Z)	1836	May 27	Perry Co.,Oh	14	13	31
Orrison, Payton(Z)	1834	Jan. 30	Perry Co.,Oh	15	15	36
Orrison, Payton(Z)	1835	Dec. 17	Perry Co.,Oh	15	15	36
Orsborn, Jarred(Z)	1835	Dec. 21	Morgan Co,Oh	13	08	32
Orsborn, Levi(Z-M)	1832	Sept. 05	LickingCo,Oh	10	02	25
Osborn, George(Z)	1832	Aug. 15	Morgan Co,Oh	13	08	19
Osborn, John(Z-M)	1831	Nov. 10	MuskingmCoOh	06	04	03
Osborn, Joseph(Y)	1824	April 21	TrumbullCoOh	05	18	02
Osborn, Joseph(Y)	1824	April 30	TrumbullCoOh	05	18	01
Osborn, Joshua(Z)	1836	Jan. 01	MuskingmCoOh	13	08	32
Osborn, William(Z)	1827	Aug. 29	Monroe Co,Oh	08	07	12
Osborne, Fred'k.(Z)	1829	Feb. 07	MuskingmCoOh	12	12	22
Osborne, Joseph(Y)	1822	Aug. 19	Stark Co.,Oh	07	20	22
Osborne, Ruth(Z)	1822	Feb. 05	MonroeCo.,Oh	08	07	26
Osburn, Caleb(Z)	1836	May 18	Morgan Co,Oh	13	08	32
Osburn, George(Z)	1835	Dec. 21	Morgan Co,Oh	13	08	32
Osburn, George(Z)	1835	Dec. 21	Morgan Co,Oh	13	08	29
Osburn, George(Z)	1836	Nov. 11	Morgan Co,Oh	14	12	36
Osburn, George(Z)	1836	Nov. 24	Morgan Co,Oh	13	08	29
Osburn, George(Z)	1837	Jan. 02	Morgan Co,Oh	13	08	34
Osburn, Henry(Y)	1825	March 14	TrumbullCoOh	05	18	01
Osburn, Levi(Z-M)	1834	March 17	LickingCo,Oh	10	02	24
Oster, George(Z)	1816	Dec. 16	MuskingmCoOh	08	03	05
Ostwald, Peter(Z)	1829	Oct. 08	HolmesCoOhio	05	08	07
Oswalt, Frederick(Z-M)	1837	May 08	HolmesCoOhio	10	09	21
Oswalt, George(Z-M)	1833	April 23	·TuscarwsCoOh	03	08	01
Otis, Ezekiel(Y)	1820	Aug. 31	Stark Co.,Oh	07	17	17
Ott, John(Z-M)	1837	Oct. 09	TuscarwsCoOh	04	07	11
Ourslee, Edward(Z)	1815	Sept. 11	MuskingmCoOh	05	02	19
Oury, Jacob(Z-M)	1836	Nov. 23	KnoxCo.,Ohio	10	08	10
Out, Mathias(Z-M)	1837	Oct. 25	CoshoctnCoOh	08	07	22
Overholser, Martin(Z)	1810	June 26	TuscarwsCoOh	03	08	12
Overholts, Abraham(Z)	1810	Jan. 12	SomersetCoPa	05	08	18
Overley, John(Y)	1822	Sept. 11	GuernseyCoOh	07	09	22
Overtholtser, Barbara(Z)	1816	Aug. 28	TuscarwsCoOh	06	07	21
Owens, James(Z)	1827	April 17	MuskingmCoOh	12	12	21
Owens, James(Z)	1827	April 27	MuskingmCoOh	12	12	21
Owens, James(Z)	1828	Nov. 14	MuskingmCoOh	12	12	06
Owens, James(Z)	1828	Dec. 08	MuskingmCoOh	12	12	07
Owens, James(Z)	1829	May 16	MuskingmCoOh	13	10	23
Owens, James(Z)	1830	July 03	Morgan Co,Oh	13	10	23
Owens, James(Z)	1830	July 03	Morgan Co,Oh	13	10	23
Owens, Stephen(Z)	1810	May 14	MuskingmCoOh	14	14	04
Owens, Stephen(Z)	1813	Oct. 22	MuskingmCoOh	14	14	32
Owens, Stephen(Z)	1815	March 06	MuskingmCoOh	14	14	06
Owens, Thomas(Z)	1814	March 03	MuskingmCoOh	05	01	16
Owens, Thomas(Z-M)	1834	Dec. 18	CoshoctnCoOh	08	06	01
Owry, Adam(Z-M)	1836	Aug. 10	Stark Co.,Oh	10	08	13
Owry, Adam(Z-M)	1836	Aug. 10	Stark Co.,Oh	10	08	18

PURCHASER	YEAR	DATE	RESIDENCE	R	T	S
Oxley, John(Z-M)	1836	April 28	CoshoctnCoOh	08	07	08
Oxley, John(Z-M)	1837	March 07	CoshoctnCoOh	08	07	09
Oyler, Christ'n.(Z-M)	1832	Feb. 24	TuscarwsCoOh	02	07	09
Oyster, George(Z)	1811	June 05	MuskingmCoOh	13	10	05
Oyster, Michael(Z)	1811	June 05	MuskingmCoOh	13	10	05
Oyster, Samuel(Y)	1826	Sept. 16	ColumbanCoOh	05	18	29
Oyster, Samuel(Y)	1827	May 28	ColumbanCoOh	05	17	22
Oyster, Samuel(Y)	1827	May 28	ColumbanCoOh	05	18	30
Oyster, Samuel(Y)	1827	May 28	ColumbanCoOh	05	18	29
Oyster, Samuel(Y)	1827	June 16	ColumbanCoOh	05	17	22
PaHerson, George(Y)	1821	Aug. 10	TuscarwsCoOh	07	14	33
Pace, David Junr.(Z)	1832	Nov. 02	Perry Co.,Oh	15	15	13
Pace, David Jur.(Z)	1832	Oct. 30	Perry Co.,Oh	15	15	12
Pace, David(Z)	1832	Oct. 30	Perry Co.,Oh	15	15	12
Pace, David(Z)	1833	Jan. 23	Perry Co.,Oh	15	15	12
Pace, Jacob(Z)	1832	Jan. 26	Perry Co.,Oh	15	15	13
Packer, Hugh(Y)	1825	Dec. 06	ColumbanCoOh	05	18	27
Packer, Jno. Junr.(Y)	1821	Dec. 26	ColumbanCoOh	05	14	09
Packer, Jno. Sr.(Y)	1821	Dec. 26	ColumbanCoOh	05	14	09
Padgitt, Rich'd. B.(Z-M)	1832	Feb. 09	GuernseyCoOh	01	03	07
Paige, R. W. A.(Z-M)	1839	July 11	HolmesCoOhio	08	08	12
Paige, R. W. A.(Z-M)	1839	July 11	HolmesCoOhio	08	08	19
Painter, Enoch(Z-M)	1835	April 29	KnoxCo.,Ohio	10	04	07
Painter, Enoch(Z-M)	1835	Nov. 11	KnoxCo.,Ohio	10	04	08
Painter, George(Z)	1805	Oct. 25	MuskingmCoOh	07	03	18
Painter, Jesse(Z-M)	1836	March 07	LickingCo,Oh	10	04	15
Painter, John(Z-M)	1832	Aug. 23	LickingCo,Oh	10	04	07
Painter, Samuel(Z-M)	1832	Aug. 23	LickingCo,Oh	10	04	08
Painter, Samuel(Z-M)	1832	Dec. 28	LickingCo,Oh	10	04	02
Painter, Samuel(Z-M)	1833	Dec. 24	LickingCo,Oh	10	04	02
Painter, Samuel(Z-M)	1834	Dec. 10	LickingCo,Oh	10	04	02
Painter, Samuel(Z-M)	1836	March 07	LickingCo,Oh	10	04	03
Painter, William(Z-M)	1824	April 19	CoshoctnCoOh	07	09	22
Painter, William(Z-M)	1837	May 05	HolmesCoOhio	09	08	08
Painter, William(Z-M)	1837	May 05	HolmesCoOhio	09	08	13
Painter, William(Z-M)	1837	May 11	HolmesCoOhio	09	08	15
Painter, William(Z-M)	1837	May 11	HolmesCoOhio	09	08	15
Paisley, Cotleib(Z)	1824	Aug. 14	Morgan Co,Oh	13	10	35
Paker, George(Y)	1831	Dec. 15	HarrisonCoOh	07	12	30
Palmer, Amos(Z-M)	1831	March 23	Jeff.Co.,Oh.	07	05	23
Palmer, George(Z-M)	1836	Aug. 25	Brooke CoVir	03	04	06
Palmer, Goerge(Z-M)	1836	Aug. 25	Brooke CoVir	03	04	05
Palmer, James(Y)	1831	April 23	TuscarwsCoOh	07	14	14
Palmer, James(Z)	1832	June 07	Morgan Co,Oh	10	06	04
Palmer, James(Z-M)	1838	Nov. 20	TuscarwsCoOh	02	07	09
Palmer, John(Y)	1831	June 13	HarrisonCoOh	06	11	29
Palmer, John(Z-M)	1833	April 17	LickingCo,Oh	11	03	23
Palmer, John(Z-M)	1833	April 17	LickingCo,Oh	11	03	23
Palmer, John(Z-M)	1838	Nov. 24	GuernseyCoOh	03	04	05
Palmer, John(Z-M)	1838	Nov. 24	GuernseyCoOh	03	04	05
Palmer, Jonathan(Z-M)	1829	Sept. 30	CoshoctnCoOh	08	05	20
Palmer, Jonathan(Z-M)	1832	April 13	CoshoctnCoOh	07	05	18
Palmer, Jonathan(Z-M)	1832	April 13	CoshoctnCoOh	07	05	18
Palmer, Jonathan(Z-M)	1834	Oct. 02	CoshoctnCoOh	07	05	19
Palmer, Levick(Z)	1816	Nov. 16	HarrisonCoOh	01	04	09
Palmer, Nathaniel(Z)	1836	Dec. 13	Perry Co.,Oh	14	12	03
Palmer, Samuel(Z)	1836	Dec. 13	Perry Co.,Oh	14	12	03
Palmer, Stephen(Y)	1832	June 22	ColumbanCoOh	07	20	05
Palmer, William H.(Z)	1836	Jan. 20	WashngtnCoOh	09	05	31
Palmer, William Huston(Z)	1836	Jan. 13	WashngtnCoOh	10	06	36
Palmer, William(Z)	1836	April 28	Perry Co.,Oh	14	13	33
Palmer, William(Z)	1836	April 28	Perry Co.,Oh	14	13	33
Palmer, Wm.(Z)	1828	Oct. 03	Perry Co.,Oh	14	13	04
Pancake, Benj'n.(Y)	1824	June 12	ColumbanCoOh	01	07	22
Pancake, William(Y)	1822	March 28	ColumbanCoOh	01	07	22
Pancake, William(Z-M)	1836	June 29	ColumbanCoOh	08	06	10
Parcell, Isaac(Z)	1832	May 09	AlleghnyCoPa	10	06	15
Parcell, John(Z-M)	1832	June 28	HolmesCoOhio	09	09	16
Parcell, Lewis(Z-M)	1836	Jan. 13	HolmesCoOhio	09	09	14

218

PURCHASER	YEAR	DATE	RESIDENCE	R	T	S
Parcell, Lewis(Z-M)	1836	Jan. 13	HolmesCoOhio	09	09	17
Parcell, William(Z-M)	1837	March 03	HolmesCoOhio	09	08	01
Parish, Edward(Z)	1815	Dec. 23	BelmontCo,Oh	08	05	15
Parish, James(Z)	1834	Dec. 08	Perry Co.,Oh	15	15	24
Parish, Leonard(Y)	1825	June 13	HarrisonCoOh	07	14	20
Parish, William(Z)	1836	March 19	Morgan Co,Oh	09	05	25
Parish, William(Z-M)	1832	April 18	KnoxCo.,Ohio	11	08	14
Park, David(Z-M)	1830	Dec. 07	CoshoctnCoOh	07	05	25
Park, Jonathan D.(Z)	1835	March 02	GuernseyCoOh	09	06	19
Parke, George(Z-M)	1833	Oct. 17	CoshoctnCoOh	07	07	16
Parke, John(Z)	1832	May 22	GuernseyCoOh	08	08	15
Parke, Uriah(Z)	1831	Sept. 17	MuskingmCoOh	10	08	05
Parke, William(Z)	1833	March 08	GuernseyCoOh	08	08	15
Parke, William(Z)	1836	March 03	GuernseyCoOh	08	08	22
Parke, Zadoc(Z-M)	1838	May 11	CoshoctnCoOh	08	07	12
Parker, Alexander(Z-M)	1835	Sept. 26	TuscarwsCoOh	01	06	25
Parker, Ezekiel(Z)	1815	Dec. 22	CoshoctnCoOh	09	05	10
Parker, Farling B.(Z-M)	1831	Sept. 26	LickingCo,Oh	11	03	14
Parker, Fasting B.(Z-M)	1834	Jan. 27	LickingCo,Oh	11	03	14
Parker, Heman(Z-M)	1831	Dec. 13	HolmesCoOhio	07	08	14
Parker, J.(Z)	1816	Feb. 17	KnoxCo.,Ohio	10	07	05
Parker, James(Z)	1810	April 13	MuskingmCoOh	13	11	15
Parker, James(Z)	1817	Feb. 20	MuskingmCoOh	14	15	24
Parker, James(Z-M)	1836	Jan. 26	CoshoctnCoOh	08	07	23
Parker, James(Z-M)	1836	Dec. 01	CoshoctnCoOh	08	07	23
Parker, John(Y)	1831	July 05	HarrisonCoOh	07	12	17
Parker, John(Z)	1829	June 22	Morgan Co,Oh	13	08	06
Parker, John(Z-M)	1822	March 12	CoshoctnCoOh	06	07	02
Parker, Joseph(Z)	1815	Oct. 27	MuskingmCoOh	13	10	31
Parker, Robert(Y)	1829	Nov. 06	TuscarwsCoOh	06	14	26
Parker, S.(Z)	1805	March 05	MuskingmCoOh	13	12	09
Parker, Samuel(Z)	1831	Nov. 17	Perry Co.,Oh	14	14	34
Parker, Samuel(Z)	1836	Jan. 19	MonroeCo.,Oh	08	06	32
Parker, Samuel(Z)	1816	Jan. 27	MuskingmCoOh	11	11	05
Parker, Solomon(Z)	1811	April 11	MuskingmCoOh	13	11	15
Parker, Sylvanus(Z-M)	1832	Sept. 28	HolmesCoOhio	08	08	17
Parker, Sylvanus(Z-M)	1832	Sept. 28	HolmesCoOhio	08	08	17
Parker, William H.(Z)	1836	May 19	Morgan Co,Oh	09	05	34
Parker, Wm. H.(Z)	1833	Sept. 26	Morgan Co,Oh	09	05	33
Parker, Wm. H.(Z)	1835	Dec. 26	Morgan Co,Oh	09	05	33
Parkes, John(Z-M)	1832	July 10	TuscarwsCoOh	01	05	03
Parkhason, John(Z)	1812	Jan. 18	MuskingmCoOh	15	15	06
Parkhill, John(Z)	1806	Nov. 17	FranklinCoPa	04	02	25
Parkinson, Jno.(Z)	1816	Oct. 30	MuskingmCoOh	15	15	06
Parkinson, John(Z)	1805	Nov. 27	MuskingmCoOh	13	12	08
Parkinson, Thomas(Z)	1817	Sept. 29	HarrisonCoOh	02	02	05
Parks, David(Y)	1832	Sept. 28	BelmontCo,Oh	06	10	35
Parks, David(Y)	1833	March 29	BelmontCo,Oh	06	10	35
Parks, David(Z-M)	1837	Nov. 28	HolmesCoOhio	08	08	04
Parks, Hugh(Y)	1824	May 19	BelmontCo,Oh	06	09	21
Parks, Hugh(Y)	1824	May 19	BelmontCo,Oh	06	09	21
Parks, James(Z)	1815	Jan. 11	BeaverCo.,Pa	11	06	21
Parks, John(Z)	1830	Oct. 28	BelmontCo,Oh	11	12	30
Parks, Jos.(Z-M)	1831	Nov. 14	CoshoctnCoOh	07	05	09
Parks, Joseph(Z-M)	1831	March 14	CoshoctnCoOh	07	05	25
Parks, Robert(Y)	1826	April 13	HarrisonCoOh	07	12	03
Parks, Uriah(Z)	1831	April 26	ZanesvilleOh	10	08	05
Parmer, Jesse(Y)	1837	Jan. 03	Jeff.co.,Oh.	04	12	05
Parminter, John D.(Z)	1830	April 30	Morgan Co,Oh	11	11	34
Parmitco, John D.(Z)	1830	April 30	Morgan Co,Oh	11	11	34
Parnel, John(Z-M)	1833	Nov. 14	LickingCo,Oh	10	04	24
Parnel, Stephen(Z-M)	1832	Oct. 01	LickingCo,Oh	10	04	25
Parnell, John(Z-M)	1835	Nov. 23	LickingCo,Oh	10	04	24
Parnell, Richard(Z-M)	1829	June 08	HolmesCoOhio	09	09	15
Parnell, Stephen(Z-M)	1835	Nov. 23	LickingCo,Oh	10	03	06
Parr, Samuel(Z-M)	1829	Dec. 21	LickingCo,Oh	11	01	21
Parr, Samuel(Z-M)	1829	Dec. 30	LickingCo,Oh	11	01	21
Parr, Samuel(Z-M)	1831	Sept. 06	LickingCo,Oh	11	01	19
Parrish, Edward E.(Z)	1828	July 02	GuernseyCoOh	10	09	25

PURCHASER	YEAR	DATE	RESIDENCE	R	T	S
Parrish, Enoch(Z)	1816	Jan. 31	KnoxCo.,Ohio	11	08	22
Parrish, Evans(Z)	1831	Aug. 27	GuernseyCoOh	10	09	36
Parrish, Evans(Z)	1835	Sept. 05	GuernseyCoOh	10	09	25
Parrish, Isaac(Z)	1835	July 13	Morgan Co,Oh	10	08	26
Parrish, Jarett(Z-M)	1824	Dec. 14	HarrisonCoOh	08	05	23
Parrish, John(Z-M)	1836	May 13	TuscarwsCoOh	02	06	03
Parrish, Joseph(Z)	1816	April 27	BelmontCo,Oh	08	05	03
Parrish, Joseph(Z)	1816	April 27	BelmontCo,Oh	08	05	04
Parrish, Joshua(Z-M)	1832	Jan. 07	BelmontCo,Oh	02	06	11
Parrish, Joshua(Z-M)	1833	May 16	CoshoctnCoOh	08	06	10
Parrish, Peter(Z-M)	1825	April 14	CoshoctnCoOh	08	05	19
Parrish, Samuel(Z-M)	1832	Nov. 16	BelmontCo,Oh	02	06	18
Parrish, Samuel(Z-M)	1833	March 13	BelmontCo,Oh	02	06	19
Parrish, Solomon(Z-M)	1832	Aug. 23	BelmontCo,Oh	02	06	19
Parrish, Solomon(Z-M)	1832	Aug. 23	BelmontCo,Oh	02	06	19
Parrish, William(Z-M)	1833	Jan. 04	KnoxCo.,Ohio	11	08	14
Parrish, William(Z-M)	1833	July 30	TuscarwsCoOh	02	06	03
Parry, Gibbons(Z-M)	1833	July 22	HarrisonCoOh	02	06	03
Parse, Ambrose(Z-M)	1837	Feb. 03	TuscarwsCoOh	03	05	15
Parse, Isaac(Z-M)	1835	Dec. 31	CoshoctnCoOh	04	05	20
Parse, Isaac(Z-M)	1837	Feb. 16	CoshoctnCoOh	04	05	20
Parse, Zachariah(Z-M)	1836	Jan. 15	TuscarwsCoOh	03	05	15
Parsons, Isaac(Z-M)	1831	Nov. 28	HolmesCoOhio	09	09	18
Parsons, Isaac(Z-M)	1833	Sept. 17	HolmesCoOhio	09	09	18
Passmore, Joseph(Z)	1806	April 14	MuskingmCoOh	06	01	11
Passmore, Joseph(Z)	1809	Nov. 27	MuskingmCoOh	06	01	10
Paterson, John(Z)	1807	Nov. 11	GreenCo.,Pa.	03	04	24
Patrick, James(Z-M)	1833	Aug. 05	TuscarwsCoOh	01	08	02
Patrick, James(Z-M)	1833	Aug. 05	TuscarwsCoOh	01	08	02
Patrick, James(Z-M)	1835	Sept. 28	TuscarwsCoOh	01	08	02
Patrick, John(Z-M)	1832	May 23	GuernseyCoOh	04	03	19
Patrick, John(Z-M)	1833	Feb. 05	GuernseyCoOh	04	03	13
Patrick, John(Z-M)	1836	Feb. 25	GuernseyCoOh	04	03	12
Patrick, Thos.(Z-M)	1838	Sept. 25	CoshoctnCoOh	05	04	12
Patridge, Alib'e.(Z)	1815	Dec. 29	LickingCo,Oh	11	01	20
Patten, James(Z)	1817	April 07	Pittsburg,Pa	09	04	14
Patterson, Aaron(Z)	1810	June 12	TuscarwsCoOh	03	10	25
Patterson, Abijah(Z)	1835	Sept. 12	MuskingmCoOh	10	09	25
Patterson, Clark(Z)	1828	Aug. 09	BelmontCo,Oh	13	09	21
Patterson, Clark(Z)	1828	Aug. 09	BelmontCo,Oh	13	09	21
Patterson, Clark(Z)	1829	Dec. 28	Morgan Co,Oh	13	09	21
Patterson, Clark(Z)	1830	Feb. 15	Morgan Co,Oh	13	09	21
Patterson, Daniel(Z)	1808	Feb. 10	GreenCo.,Pa.	02	02	04
Patterson, Elias(Z-M)	1836	Feb. 04	GuernseyCoOh	03	03	14
Patterson, Elias(Z-M)	1837	Jan. 28	GuernseyCoOh	03	03	14
Patterson, Geo.(Z-M)	1833	March 14	GuernseyCoOh	02	04	25
Patterson, George(Y)	1821	Aug. 10	TuscarwsCoOh	07	14	33
Patterson, George(Y)	1832	March 17	TuscarwsCoOh	07	14	33
Patterson, George(Z-M)	1833	April 04	GuernseyCoOh	02	04	25
Patterson, Henry(Z-M)	1832	Aug. 04	MuskingmCoOh	05	02	10
Patterson, James H.(Z)	1817	June 06	FayetteCo,Pa	10	04	06
Patterson, James(Y)	1826	Feb. 23	SteubenvleOh	03	10	07
Patterson, James(Z)	1821	Jan. 27	Morgan Co,Oh	11	11	34
Patterson, James(Z)	1825	Nov. 26	Perry Co.,Oh	15	15	20
Patterson, James(Z)	1835	Oct. 06	Perry Co.,Oh	15	15	24
Patterson, James(Z)	1814	Nov. 21	WashCo.,Penn	04	02	01
Patterson, James(Z)	1815	Nov. 04	Brooke CoVir	09	03	24
Patterson, James(Z-M)	1833	Aug. 12	GuernseyCoOh	02	02	06
Patterson, Jno.(Z-M)	1832	Jan. 26	WashCo.,Penn	06	07	14
Patterson, John(Y)	1826	Feb. 23	SteubenvleOh	03	10	07
Patterson, John(Y)	1829	Nov. 07	HarrisonCoOh	05	13	34
Patterson, John(Z)	1817	Oct. 20	BaltimreColld	12	12	25
Patterson, John(Z)	1817	Oct. 20	BaltimreCoMd	12	13	36
Patterson, John(Z-M)	1835	Sept. 21	GuernseyCoOh	03	04	21
Patterson, John(Z-M)	1832	June 21	GuernseyCoOh	03	04	21
Patterson, Joseph(Z)	1815	June 15	AlleghnyCoPa	04	02	01
Patterson, Joseph(Z)	1817	Feb. 17	HarrisonCoOh	02	02	05
Patterson, Laban B.(Z)	1825	Oct. 17	BelmontCo,Oh	12	10	27
Patterson, Robert M.(Z-M)	1835	Aug. 31	GuernseyCoOh	03	03	03

PURCHASER	YEAR	DATE	RESIDENCE	R	T	S
Patterson, Sam'l.(Y)	1827	Nov. 29	HarrisonCoOh	06	13	31
Patterson, Samuel(Z-M)	1838	Jan. 20	GuernseyCoOh	03	04	22
Patterson, Stout(Z-M)	1833	Feb. 20	GuernseyCoOh	02	02	06
Patterson, Stout(Z-M)	1833	April 10	GuernseyCoOh	02	02	06
Patterson, Stout(Z-M)	1835	Dec. 15	GuernseyCoOh	02	02	06
Patterson, William(Y)	1833	Oct. 03	HarrisonCoOh	07	14	32
Patterson, William(Z)	1832	July 09	Morgan Co,Oh	11	10	12
Patterson, William(Z)	1832	July 09	Morgan Co,Oh	11	10	12
Patterson, Wm.(Y)	1829	Aug. 01	HarrisonCoOh	07	14	01
Pattison, Daniel(Z-M)	1838	Aug. 18	GuernseyCoOh	02	04	16
Pattison, Daniel(Z-M)	1838	Aug. 18	GuernseyCoOh	02	04	16
Patton, James(Z-M)	1831	March 14	CoshoctnCoOh	09	04	14
Patton, Smith(Z)	1833	Jan. 18	BelmontCo,Oh	08	07	06
Paul, George(Z)	1810	Feb. 16	MuskingmCoOh	02	02	10
Paul, George(Z)	1815	Nov. 22	StClrsvlOhio	09	06	05
Paul, Henry(Y)	1831	March 30	ColumbanCoOh	03	12	11
Paul, Jacob(Z)	1822	July 24	Morgan Co,Oh	11	12	36
Paulson, John(Y)	1822	April 30	FredrickCoMd	06	11	15
Pautsch, George(Y)	1824	Feb. 25	Stark Co.,Oh	09	11	22
Paxon, Heston Camby(Y)	1834	Aug. 26	ColumbanCoOh	05	15	04
Paxson, Joseph(Z)	1833	June 26	MuskingmCoOh	12	12	03
Paxson, William Magell(Y)	1834	Nov. 24	ColumbanCoOh	05	15	04
Paxton, John(Z)	1804	Dec. 07	BelmontCo,Oh	02	03	10
Paxton, John(Z)	1806	Oct. 25	FayetteCo,Pa	02	03	01
Paxton, M. F. F.(Z)	1830	Sept. 10	GuernseyCoOh	10	09	15
Paxton, M. F. F.(Z)	1830	Sept. 10	GuernseyCoOh	10	09	14
Paxton, Nath'l.(Z)	1827	Nov. 05	GuernseyCoOh	04	02	14
Paxton, Sam'l.(Z)	1831	June 06	MuskingmCoOh	10	08	18
Paxton, Sam'l.(Z-M)	1821	Sept. 13	MuskingmCoOh	04	01	21
Paxton, Samuel(Z)	1822	Dec. 26	MuskingmCoOh	11	12	12
Paxton, Samuel(Z)	1828	June 18	MuskingmCoOh	11	12	11
Paxton, Samuel(Z)	1831	Dec. 28	MuskingmCoOh	11	12	12
Paxton, Samuel(Z)	1832	Jan. 31	MuskingmCoOh	11	12	10
Paxton, Samuel(Z)	1835	Sept. 12	GuernseyCoOh	10	06	01
Paxton, Samuel(Z)	1836	March 19	GuernseyCoOh	10	09	25
Paxton, Samuel(Z)	1836	May 30	Perry Co.,Oh	15	14	15
Paxton, Samuel(Z)	1837	April 06	Perry Co.,Oh	15	14	08
Paxton, Samuel(Z-M)	1820	July 01	GuernseyCoOh	02	04	24
Paxton, Thomas(Z)	1826	March 16	GuernseyCoOh	10	09	15
Paxton, Thomas(Z-M)	1829	Jan. 07	GuernseyCoOh	03	01	24
Payne, Aaron(Z)	1836	Aug. 24	WashngtnCoOh	08	05	25
Payne, George(Z-M)	1835	Nov. 11	KnoxCo.,Ohio	11	08	17
Payne, George(Z-M)	1836	Oct. 28	KnoxCo.,Ohio	11	08	17
Payne, Jason(Z)	1820	Sept. 19	Morgan Co,Oh	10	06	11
Payne, Jason(Z)	1836	May 18	Morgan Co,Oh	10	06	13
Payne, Jason(Z)	1836	June 11	Morgan Co,Oh	10	06	11
Payne, Jesse(Y)	1825	May 17	BelmontCo,Oh	04	06	31
Payne, Jesse(Y)	1825	Dec. 07	BelmontCo,Oh	04	06	27
Payne, Vincent(Z-M)	1832	Sept. 07	WashngtnCoOh	08	05	24
Peabody, Benj'n.(Y)	1825	Jan. 13	ColumbanCoOh	01	07	15
Peach, John(Z)	1838	Nov. 02	AleganaCo,Pa	04	04	10
Peach, Joseph(Z)	1816	Dec. 21	MuskingmCoOh	14	15	26
Peacock, Eli(Y)	1827	Sept. 06	HarrisonCoOh	06	11	14
Peadan, James(Z)	1816	Oct. 01	GuernseyCoOh	02	02	09
Peadan, James(Z)	1817	Jan. 06	GuernseyCoOh	02	02	02
Peairs, David(Z)	1828	Dec. 19	MuskingmCoOh	12	13	15
Peairs, Elisha(Z)	1815	Oct. 13	AlleghnyCoPa	12	11	02
Peairs, Elisha(Z)	1815	Oct. 13	AlleghnyCoPa	12	11	04
Peairs, Thomas(Z)	1817	Jan. 24	HarrisonCoOh	01	05	25
Pearce, James(Z)	1812	May 18	FairfeldCoOh	09	03	17
Pearch, Coneard(Y)	1821	Oct. 24	TuscarwsCoOh	07	15	21
Pearson, Jesse(Z)	1830	Aug. 17	BelmontCo,Oh	11	11	02
Pearson, Jesse(Z)	1830	Aug. 17	BelmontCo,Oh	11	12	35
Pearson, Jesse(Z)	1830	Oct. 27	BelmontCo,Oh	11	12	35
Pearson, William(Z)	1833	Jan. 30	Morgan Co,Oh	11	11	03
Pearson, Wm.(Z)	1830	Aug. 17	BelmontCo,Oh	11	11	03
Peatt, Thos.(Z)	1806	Feb. 24	BelmontCo,Oh	10	09	17
Peck, Chas.(Z-M)	1828	Aug. 11	MuskingmCoOh	06	03	25
Peck, Rich'd. M.(Z)	1828	Dec. 30	Morgan Co,Oh	12	10	33

PURCHASER	YEAR	DATE	RESIDENCE	R	T	S
Peck, Sally(Z-M)	1828	Aug. 11	MuskingmCoOh	06	03	25
Peck, William B.(Z)	1807	Nov. 12	FairfeldCoOh	13	09	26
Peckham, Charles(Y)	1831	June 01	ColumbanCoOh	04	13	10
Peckham, Eason C.(Z-M)	1837	Aug. 07	KnoxCo.,Ohio	10	08	20
Peckham, Eason C.(Z-M)	1837	April 07	KnoxCo.,Ohio	10	09	21
Peckham, Sarah(Z)	1831	May 12	KnoxCo.,Ohio	10	08	18
Peden, William(Y)	1833	Aug. 27	ColumbanCoOh	03	12	36
Pedvin, Nicholas L.(Z)	1828	June 30	GuernseyCoOh	10	09	11
Pedwin, Nicholas(Z-M)	1832	May 22	GuernseyCoOh	03	01	25
Peek, William B.(Z)	1807	Dec. 23	FairfeldCoOh	13	09	26
Peerson, Alex'r.(Z)	1837	Dec. 20	Morgan Co,Oh	08	05	08
Peerson, Alexander(Z)	1835	Sept. 01	Morgan Co,Oh	10	07	34
Peffle, David(Z-M)	1836	June 02	TuscarwsCoOh	03	08	24
Peirce, Nicholas(Z)	1826	Feb. 10	MuskingmCoOh	13	09	36
Peittit, George(Z-M)	1836	Jan. 26	CoshoctnCoOh	08	07	20
Peittit, George(Z-M)	1836	Jan. 26	CoshoctnCoOh	08	07	21
Pence, Henry(Z)	1810	Nov. 14	SomersetCoPa	02	08	15
Pene, Lewis(Z)	1806	July 30	AlleghnyCoPa	11	13	20
Pengo, Isaac(Y)	1831	Jan. 14	GuernseyCoOh	07	09	09
Penicks, Jacob(Y)	1829	Aug. 05	Jeff.Co.,Oh.	07	15	27
Pennell, Lewis(Z)	1828	Sept. 22	Morgan Co,Oh	12	10	08
Pennick, John(Z-M)	1831	Oct. 06	TuscarwsCoOh	01	08	10
Pennington, Joshua(Z-M)	1836	Nov. 30	BelmontCo,Oh	03	06	03
Pennington, Joshua(Z-M)	1838	Oct. 02	GuernseyCoOh	03	05	13
Pennock, Enoch(Y)	1828	Sept. 06	ColumbanCoOh	05	15	07
Pennock, George(Y)	1829	June 12	ColumbanCoOh	05	15	11
Pennock, Joshua(Y)	1828	July 31	Stark Co.,Oh	06	16	05
Pennock, Joshua(Y)	1830	Aug. 21	Stark Co.,Oh	06	17	32
Pennock, Joshua(Y)	1830	Aug. 21	Stark Co.,Oh	06	16	05
Pennock, Nathaniel(Y)	1825	Aug. 16	ColumbanCoOh	05	15	11
Penrod, Peter(Z-M)	1830	May 06	HolmesCoOhio	04	09	08
Penrod, Samuel(Z)	1829	April 30	Perry Co.,Oh	14	13	07
Penrod, Samuel(Z)	1834	Jan. 09	Perry Co.,Oh	14	13	07
Penrose, Abraham(Y)	1822	Sept. 03	BelmontCo,Oh	03	05	15
Penrose, Richard(Z)	1828	Aug. 22	Jeff.Co.,Oh.	12	09	11
Penrot, John(Z-M)	1822	Nov. 29	TuscarwsCoOh	04	08	21
Penrot, John(Z-M)	1832	Feb. 29	TuscarwsCoOh	04	07	01
Penrot, John(Z-M)	1836	March 17	TuscarwsCoOh	04	08	21
Peokham, Eason C.(Z-M)	1836	March 30	KnoxCo.,Ohio	10	08	02
Peoples, William Jones(Z-M)	1836	Jan. 14	GuernseyCoOh	03	05	22
Peoples, Wm. J.(Z-M)	1829	March 07	GuernseyCoOh	01	04	16
Peper, Sylvanus(Z)	1817	July 08	WashngtnCoOh	11	10	18
Peper, Sylvanus(Z)	1817	July 08	WashngtnCoOh	12	10	20
Peper, Sylvanus(Z)	1817	July 08	WashngtnCoOh	12	10	22
Perdew, John(Z)	1816	Nov. 15	CoshoctnCoOh	09	05	18
Perdew, Jonathan(Z)	1816	Dec. 12	HarrisonCoOh	01	04	02
Perdew, Laban(Z)	1817	June 25	BedfordCo,Pa	08	05	07
Perdew, Laban(Z)	1817	June 25	BedfordCo,Pa	08	05	07
Perdew, Laban(Z)	1817	Sept. 12	BedfordCo,Pa	08	05	08
Perdew, Laban(Z-M)	1828	April 03	HolmesCoOhio	08	08	05
Perdew, Laban(Z-M)	1835	April 10	HolmesCoOhio	08	08	06
Perdew, William(Z)	1816	Nov. 11	CoshoctnCoOh	08	11	05
Perdue, Jacob Hols(Y)	1832	May 01	ColumbanCoOh	05	16	33
Perdue, William(Z-M)	1835	Dec. 30	GuernseyCoOh	02	06	03
Peredo, Isaac(Y)	1826	March 06	GuernseyCoOh	07	09	10
Peredo, James Senr.(Y)	1826	March 14	GuernseyCoOh	07	09	22
Perkins, Amasa(Y)	1824	Oct. 13	PortageCo,Oh	06	19	15
Perkins, Anthony(Z)	1810	Aug. 20	WashngtnCoOh	09	06	26
Perkins, Fielder(Z-M)	1834	Nov. 08	BelmontCo,Oh	01	05	12
Perkins, J.(Z)	1836	Aug. 11	WashngtnCoOh	08	05	19
Perkins, James(Z-M)	1836	Jan. 01	CoshoctnCoOh	07	04	17
Perkins, John(Z)	1815	Dec. 18	CoshoctnCoOh	09	04	02
Perkins, John(Z)	1816	Feb. 17	CoshoctnCoOh	09	04	11
Perkins, Samuel(Z)	1815	Dec. 18	CoshoctnCoOh	09	04	01
Perkins, Z.(Z)	1830	Dec. 13	BelmontCo,Oh	08	06	20
Permar, John(Y)	1826	June 19	Jeff.Co.,Oh.	05	14	06
Permar, John(Y)	1826	Sept. 02	Jeff.Co.,Oh.	05	14	06
Permar, Nathan(Y)	1822	April 09	Jeff.Co.,Oh.	05	14	05
Permar, Nathan(Y)	1826	Sept. 20	ColumbanCoOh	05	14	06

PURCHASER	YEAR	DATE	RESIDENCE	R	T	S
Permar, Nathan(Y)	1828	Jan. 31	ColumbanCoOh	05	14	06
Perrin, Edward Jr.(Z)	1834	Jan. 22	Wash.Co,Penn	11	11	12
Perrolla, Lewis(Y)	1833	March 29	Jeff.Co.,Oh.	06	15	24
Perry, John(Z)	1815	July 05	WashCo.,Penn	10	06	26
Perry, Thomas(Z)	1836	April 20	HolmesCoOhio	09	08	02
Perry, W.(Z)	1815	Nov. 23	GuernseyCoOh	11	10	25
Perry, W.(Z)	1815	Nov. 23	GuernseyCoOh	11	10	25
Perry, Walter G.(Z)	1836	Dec. 17	GuernseyCoOh	09	08	30
Perry, Walter Gibbons(Z)	1832	Oct. 09	GuernseyCoOh	10	09	13
Perry, William(Z)	1833	April 16	BelmontCo,Oh	13	08	27
Peterman, Jacob(Z)	1816	Dec. 02	TuscarwsCoOh	04	08	21
Peterman, Jacob(Z-M)	1821	March 10	TuscarwsCoOh	04	09	07
Peterman, Jacob(Z-M)	1830	June 01	CoshoctnCoOh	04	09	07
Peters, Abraham(Z-M)	1826	April 17	GuernseyCoOh	02	01	07
Peters, Adam(Z)	1817	Feb. 19	ZanesvilleOh	09	04	23
Peters, Daniel(Z-M)	1832	April 11	GuernseyCoOh	02	01	07
Peters, John(Z-M)	1831	Nov. 02	HarrisonCoOh	02	06	20
Peters, John(Z-M)	1836	Aug. 02	MuskingmCoOh	10	03	05
Peters, John(Z-M)	1838	July 21	MuskingmCoOh	08	06	08
Peterson, James(Y)	1837	April 11	Jeff.Co.,Oh.	04	12	05
Peterson, John(Y)	1825	Oct. 10	Jeff.Co.,Oh.	03	11	34
Peterson, John(Y)	1830	Oct. 11	Stark Co.,Oh	06	15	34
Pettay, Dan'l.(Z)	1822	March 12	Morgan Co,Oh	12	11	13
Pettay, Daniel(Z)	1832	March 19	MonroeCo.,Oh	08	07	07
Pettay, Daniel(Z)	1833	March 14	MonroeCo.,Oh	08	07	05
Pettay, Daniel(Z)	1833	March 14	MonroeCo.,Oh	08	07	05
Pettay, Daniel(Z)	1836	Feb. 26	MonroeCo.,Oh	08	07	08
Pettay, Daniel(Z)	1836	Feb. 26	MonroeCo.,Oh	08	07	08
Pettay, Daniel(Z-M)	1834	Nov. 26	Morgan Co,Oh	10	08	16
Pettay, Daniel(Z-M)	1835	Oct. 05	MonroeCo.,Oh	10	09	03
Petteey, Francis(Z)	1836	Jan. 01	Morgan Co,Oh	09	07	24
Pettet, Daniel(Z)	1836	April 16	Perry Co.,Oh	14	13	26
Pettet, David(Z-M)	1832	April 21	TuscarwsCoOh	04	07	25
Pettet, Emanuel(Z)	1837	June 12	Morgan Co,Oh	14	12	02
Pettet, Josiah W.(Z-M)	1837	Sept. 11	CoshoctnCoOh	08	06	09
Pettey, Francis(Z)	1822	Oct. 19	BelmontCo,Oh	10	07	18
Petticord, Dorsey(Z)	1832	June 16	GuernseyCoOh	11	11	14
Petticord, Thomas(Z)	1833	Dec. 12	Morgan Co,Oh	11	11	14
Pettis, Robert(Y)	1826	Dec. 30	TuscarwsCoOh	06	12	32
Pettit, Barthol'm.(Z)	1815	Oct. 30	MuskingmCoOh	11	11	06
Pettit, Emanuel(Z)	1836	April 20	Morgan Co,Oh	14	13	28
Pettit, Job(Z)	1833	April 22	Morgan Co,Oh	13	08	19
Pettit, Job(Z)	1836	Jan. 12	Morgan Co,Oh	13	08	28
Pettit, John(Z)	1828	Aug. 14	Morgan Co,Oh	12	10	15
Pettit, Joseph(Z)	1816	Jan. 12	WashngtnCoOh	14	13	10
Pettit, Joseph(Z)	1816	Sept. 20	WashngtnCoOh	10	09	07
Pettit, Joseph(Z-M)	1823	Oct. 11	CoshoctnCoOh	08	06	02
Pettit, Joseph(Z-M)	1836	July 16	CoshoctnCoOh	08	06	02
Pettit, Josiah W.(Z-M)	1836	Oct. 27	CoshoctnCoOh	08	06	08
Pettit, Samuel(Z)	1816	May 29	MuskingmCoOh	13	09	14
Pettit, Samuel(Z)	1816	May 29	MuskingmCoOh	13	09	10
Pettit, Thomas(Z)	1815	Dec. 07	MuskingmCoOh	12	17	10
Pettit, Wm.(Z)	1833	Nov. 12	Perry Co.,Oh	14	13	24
Pettit, Wm.(Z)	1833	Nov. 12	Perry Co.,Oh	14	13	25
Petty, Edward(Z)	1836	Jan. 16	Morgan Co,Oh	10	06	22
Petty, Francis(Z)	1832	Nov. 27	Morgan Co,Oh	09	07	23
Petty, Leroy(Y)	1830	Sept. 04	HarrisonCoOh	06	12	15
Petty, Rodem(Y)	1829	Nov. 04	HarrisonCoOh	06	11	11
Peugh, Wm. H.(Z)	1829	Dec. 12	Morgan Co,Oh	13	08	35
Pfaifer, Francis(Z-M)	1835	March 05	TuscarwsCoOh	02	07	02
Pfaifer, Francis(Z-M)	1835	March 05	TuscarwsCoOh	02	07	09
Pfautz, Jacob(Y)	1829	Oct. 26	HarrisonCoOh	06	13	13
Pfautz, John(Y)	1828	Dec. 24	HarrisonCoOh	06	11	23
Pfautz, Jonathan(Y)	1827	April 03	HarrisonCoOh	06	12	23
Pfautz, Mich'l.(Y)	1824	June 24	HarrisonCoOh	06	13	13
Pfersich, Frederick C.(Z-M)	1829	May 11	TuscarwsCoOh	01	10	14
Pfersick, F. C.(Z-M)	1837	Feb. 18	TuscarwsCoOh	02	10	24
Pfersick, F. C.(Z-M)	1837	Feb. 18	TuscarwsCoOh	03	08	24
Pfoutz, Michael(Y)	1831	Feb. 04	TuscarwsCoOh	06	13	20

PURCHASER	YEAR	DATE	RESIDENCE	R	T	S
Phelps, Richard(Z-M)	1836	Sept. 10	HarrisonCoOh	02	06	13
Pherson, George(Z)	1815	Nov. 07	MuskingmCoOh	15	16	29
Pherson, Patton(Z)	1815	Sept. 14	FairfeldCoOh	?	?	17
Philips, David(Y)	1825	March 07	AlleghnyCoPa	06	15	11
Philips, James(Z)	1832	Nov. 12	Morgan Co,Oh	13	09	02
Philips, Joseph(Z-M)	1839	July 02	CoshoctnCoOh	09	08	24
Philips, Joseph(Z-M)	1839	July 02	CoshoctnCoOh	09	08	24
Philips, Peorge(Y)	1832	Dec. 03	ColumbanCoOh	04	13	06
Philips, William(Z-M)	1830	April 12	GuernseyCoOh	01	01	11
Philips, Zachariah(Z)	1810	Oct. 15	MuskingmCoOh	14	15	22
Philips, Zephaniah L.(Z-M)	1833	March 16	GuernseyCoOh	02	04	24
Philkie, John(Z)	1824	May 26	MuskingmCoOh	11	10	15
Phillips, Benj.(Z-M)	1830	March 18	CoshoctnCoOh	09	07	05
Phillips, George(Z-M)	1838	Feb. 01	CoshoctnCoOh	04	04	03
Phillips, John Senr.(Z-M)	1827	Feb. 16	GuernseyCoOh	03	04	10
Phillips, John Sr.(Z-M)	1828	Sept. 22	GuernseyCoOh	03	04	11
Phillips, John(Y)	1829	March 13	HarrisonCoOh	05	12	28
Phillips, John(Z)	1814	Nov. 30	GuernseyCoOh	03	03	14
Phillips, John(Z-M)	1829	Dec. 14	TuscarwsCoOh	01	09	07
Phillips, John(Z-M)	1832	May 28	GuernseyCoOh	03	03	14
Phillips, Joseph(Y)	1828	Dec. 13	Jeff.Co.,Oh.	07	12	21
Phillips, Moses(Z-M)	1836	Jan. 02	CoshoctnCoOh	09	05	25
Phillips, Richard(Y)	1829	June 10	HarrisonCoOh	07	12	21
Phillips, T.(Z)	1814	Feb. 14	CoshoctnCoOh	07	05	24
Phillips, Thomas(Z)	1835	Nov. 07	ZanesvilleOh	10	06	29
Phillips, Thomas(Z)	1835	Nov. 07	ZanesvilleOh	10	06	29
Phillips, Thomas(Z)	1836	June 01	ZanesvilleOh	10	09	26
Phillips, Thomas(Z)	1836	Sept. 09	ZanesvilleOh	08	06	08
Phillips, Thomas(Z-M)	1835	Nov. 10	ZanesvilleOh	08	09	03
Phillips, Thomas(Z-M)	1835	Nov. 19	ZanesvilleOh	11	08	18
Phillips, Thomas(Z-M)	1835	Dec. 11	ZanesvilleOh	03	03	03
Phillips, Thomas(Z-M)	1836	Nov. 14	ZanesvilleOh	10	08	02
Phillips, Thomas(Z-M)	1837	Feb. 23	ZanesvilleOh	10	08	12
Phillips, Thomas(Z-M)	1837	March 28	ZanesvilleOh	10	07	01
Phillips, Thomas(Z-M)	1837	March 31	ZanesvilleOh	10	09	13
Phillips, Thos.(Z)	1836	June 18	ZanesvilleOh	10	06	29
Phillips, Thos.(Z)	1836	Aug. 22	ZanesvilleOh	08	06	22
Phillips, William(Z-M)	1831	Dec. 29	CoshoctnCoOh	09	07	04
Phillips, William(Z-M)	1831	Dec. 29	CoshoctnCoOh	09	07	04
Phillips, Wm.(Z-M)	1831	Jan. 31	CoshoctnCoOh	09	07	04
Phillips, Wm.(Z-M)	1831	Feb. 14	CoshoctnCoOh	09	07	07
Phillis, Charles(Z-M)	1829	Jan. 14	WashCo.,Penn	05	03	06
Phillis, Henry(Z)	1828	Feb. 13	Morgan Co,Oh	10	06	04
Phillis, Henry(Z)	1833	March 18	Morgan Co,Oh	10	06	09
Phillis, Henry(Z)	1835	March 28	Morgan Co,Oh	10	06	03
Phillis, Henry(Z)	1835	Oct. 03	Morgan Co,Oh	10	06	09
Phillis, Henry(Z)	1836	Jan. 26	Morgan Co,Oh	10	06	10
Phillis, Henry(Z)	1836	Jan. 26	Morgan Co,Oh	10	06	10
Phillis, Henry(Z)	1836	March 14	Morgan Co,Oh	10	06	09
Phillis, James(Z)	1835	Sept. 25	Morgan Co,Oh	10	07	34
Phillis, John B.(Z)	1833	June 24	Morgan Co,Oh	10	06	10
Phillis, John Jr.(Z)	1836	Feb. 22	Morgan Co,Oh	10	06	11
Phillis, John(Z)	1833	June 24	Morgan Co,Oh	10	06	01
Phillis, John(Z)	1835	Aug. 29	Morgan Co,Oh	10	06	02
Phillis, John(Z)	1835	Sept. 03	Morgan Co,Oh	10	06	11
Phillis, John(Z)	1836	Nov. 24	Morgan Co,Oh	10	06	11
Phillis, Joseph(Z)	1834	Feb. 17	Morgan Co,Oh	10	06	14
Phillis, Joseph(Z)	1835	June 27	Morgan Co,Oh	10	06	02
Phillis, Joseph(Z)	1836	Feb. 16	Morgan Co,Oh	10	06	14
Phillis, Joseph(Z)	1836	Feb. 16	Morgan Co,Oh	10	06	11
Philpot, William(Z)	1832	April 26	MonroeCo.,Oh	08	07	01
Philpot, William(Z)	1816	Oct. 09	BelmontCo,Oh	08	07	26
Philps, Richard(Z-M)	1833	April 02	HarrisonCoOh	02	06	23
Philson, Elizabeth(Y)	1822	March 01	Stark Co.,Oh	08	09	24
Philson, William(Y)	1820	Dec. 30	Stark Co.,Oh	08	09	24
Picken, Alexander(Y)	1835	Jan. 20	HarrisonCoOh	05	11	35
Picken, Matthew(Y)	1829	April 01	HarrisonCoOh	05	11	34
Picken, Matthew(Y)	1831	Feb. 22	HarrisonCoOh	05	11	35
Picken, Matthew(Y)	1832	March 06	HarrisonCoOh	05	11	34

PURCHASER	YEAR	DATE	RESIDENCE	R	T	S
Pickenpaugh, Peter(Z)	1832	Feb. 04	Morgan Co,Oh	10	07	12
Pickens, L.(Z)	1815	Aug. 23	GuernseyCoOh	02	01	23
Pickering, Abel(Z-M)	1826	March 29	HarrisonCoOh	01	06	17
Pickering, Abel(Z-M)	1826	March 29	HarrisonCoOh	01	06	17
Pickering, Abel(Z-M)	1826	March 29	HarrisonCoOh	01	06	16
Pickering, Greenberg(Z-M)	1833	March 23	GuernseyCoOh	02	03	07
Pickering, Greenbery(Z-M)	1832	Sept. 22	GuernseyCoOh	02	03	07
Pickering, Hiram(Y)	1833	Feb. 14	HarrisonCoOh	07	11	05
Pickering, Jonathan(Y)	1826	Feb. 01	BelmontCo,Oh	07	12	11
Pickering, Lot(Z-M)	1834	Jan. 27	GuernseyCoOh	02	03	07
Picket, Martin(Z-M)	1836	Dec. 12	KnoxCo.,Ohio	10	08	11
Picket, Moses(Z)	1824	March 24	BelmontCo,Oh	12	09	14
Picket, Moses(Z)	1824	May 18	BelmontCo,Oh	12	10	22
Pickingpaugh, John(Z)	1826	Aug. 01	Morgan Co,Oh	10	07	12
Pickingpaugh, Peter(Z)	1833	March 06	Morgan Co,Oh	10	07	01
Pickingpaugh, Peter(Z)	1826	Aug. 01	Morgan Co,Oh	10	07	01
Pickle, John(Y)	1829	April 28	ColumbanCoOh	07	16	18
Pickley, Jacob(Y)	1831	July 01	Stark Co.,Oh	09	12	18
Pidcock, John(Z)	1828	Nov. 27	Morgan Co,Oh	09	07	35
Pidcock, John(Z)	1832	July 26	Morgan Co,Oh	09	07	35
Pidcock, John(Z)	1833	March 21	Morgan Co,Oh	09	07	32
Pidcock, John(Z)	1836	March 01	Morgan Co,Oh	09	07	32
Pidcock, John(Z)	1837	April 28	Morgan Co,Oh	15	14	33
Pierce, Andrew(Z)	1816	Jan. 31	Jeff.Co.,Oh.	11	13	33
Pierce, Dean(Z-M)	1836	Nov. 29	Wayne Co.,Oh	09	09	17
Pierce, Jonathan(Z)	1815	May 03	MuskingmCoOh	11	12	06
Pierce, Joseph(Z)	1805	March 16	AlleghnyCoPa	12	13	17
Pierce, Joseph(Z)	1805	March 16	AlleghnyCoPa	12	13	17
Pierce, Joseph(Z)	1805	March 16	AlleghnyCoPa	12	13	18
Pierce, Joseph(Z)	1805	March 16	AlleghnyCoPa	12	13	08
Pierce, Lazarus Jnr.(Z)	1837	Feb. 01	Morgan Co,Oh	13	08	17
Pierce, Lazarus(Z)	1816	Dec. 19	MuskingmCoOh	13	08	08
Pierce, Lazarus(Z)	1816	Dec. 19	MuskingmCoOh	13	08	17
Pierce, Lewellen(Z)	1814	April 02	?	11	13	20
Pierce, Lewis(Z)	1805	Oct. 02	AlleghnyCoPa	11	13	19
Pierce, Lewis(Z)	1805	Nov. 07	AlleghnyCoPa	11	13	20
Pierce, Lewis(Z)	1805	Nov. 07	AlleghnyCoPa	11	13	20
Pierce, Sam'l. W.(Z)	1817	May 10	N.Haven,Conn	09	03	07
Pierce, Thomas L.(Z)	1829	Oct. 08	MuskingmCoOh	12	11	09
Pierpoint, Jon'th.(Z)	1824	April 30	ColumbanCoOh	12	09	11
Pierpoint, Jon'th.(Z)	1824	April 30	ColumbanCoOh	12	09	02
Pierpoint, Jonathan(Z)	1824	Oct. 16	ColumbanCoOh	12	09	01
Pierpoint, Jonathan(Z)	1824	Oct. 16	ColumbanCoOh	12	09	14
Piggott, Nathan H.(Z)	1825	Nov. 28	BelmontCo,Oh	12	10	21
Pigman, John G.(Z)	1814	Dec. 15	CoshoctnCoOh	06	04	02
Pigman, Joseph W.(Z)	1816	May 02	CoshoctnCoOh	09	05	12
Pigman, Nathaniel(Z-M)	1832	Nov. 06	KnoxCo.,Ohio	10	05	19
Pilcher, Thomas Jr.(Z-M)	1835	Sept. 04	BelmontCo,Oh	04	06	19
Piles, James(Z)	1832	Aug. 27	GuernseyCoOh	08	08	26
Pilkington, R.(Z)	1835	Dec. 30	Morgan Co,Oh	10	06	19
Pillingham, Thomas(Y)	1832	Dec. 21	ColumbanCoOh	03	12	01
Pilliod, Tawbell(Y)	1828	Sept. 09	Stark Co.,Oh	09	11	23
Pindell, Thomas(Z)	1817	March 03	MuskingmCoOh	10	04	14
Pinicks, Jacob(Y)	1829	Sept. 05	WashCo.,Penn	04	13	13
Pinkerton, Wm.(Z)	1831	Sept. 03	Brooke CoVir	10	07	25
Pinkington, Row'd.(Z)	1831	Aug. 29	Morgan Co,Oh	10	06	19
Piper, Daniel(Z)	1812	Jan. 21	WashngtnCoMd	03	10	14
Piper, Daniel(Z)	1812	May 06	WashngtnCoVa	03	08	06
Piper, Henry(Z-M)	1833	April 05	CoshoctnCoOh	05	04	16
Piper, Jesse O.(Z)	1835	Dec. 25	Perry Co.,Oh	15	15	14
Piper, Jonathan(Z)	1831	Jan. 27	GuernseyCoOh	09	08	33
Piper, Silvanus(Z)	1815	Sept. 18	WashngtnCoOh	13	09	36
Piper, Sylvanus(Z)	1817	July 08	WashngtnCoOh	11	10	18
Piper, Sylvanus(Z)	1817	July 08	WashngtnCoOh	12	10	20
Piper, Sylvanus(Z)	1817	July 08	WashngtnCoOh	12	10	22
Pitney, James(Z)	1814	July 06	KnoxCo.,Ohio	11	05	24
Pittinger, Samuel(Y)	1826	Jan. 27	HarrisonCoOh	06	14	21
Pitzar, Baltzar(Y)	1821	Dec. 05	AdamsCo,Penn	02	11	22
Plank, Peter(Z-M)	1828	Dec. 19	HolmesCoOhio	05	09	03

PURCHASER	YEAR	DATE	RESIDENCE	R	T	S
Plansix, Andrew(Z)	1814	March 17	?	10	06	04
Platt, Amelia(Z)	1812	Dec. 01	KnoxCo.,Ohio	11	05	25
Platt, Ezekiah(Z-M)	1826	June 05	LickingCo,Oh	11	08	15
Platt, John(Z-M)	1831	Feb. 01	TuscarwsCoOh	02	05	21
Platt, Thomas(Z-M)	1835	Oct. 26	CoshoctnCoOh	05	04	08
Platt, Thomas(Z-M)	1837	Oct. 05	CoshoctnCoOh	04	05	21
Platz, David(Y)	1828	Sept. 29	Stark Co.,Oh	06	17	32
Platz, David(Y)	1829	Oct. 02	Stark Co.,Oh	06	17	32
Platz, David(Y)	1830	July 29	Stark Co.,Oh	06	17	32
Platz, David(Y)	1830	Sept. 29	Stark Co.,Oh	06	17	31
Pleacher, Henry(Z)	1815	Sept. 12	LoudonCo,Vir	14	14	24
Pleacher, Henry(Z)	1815	Sept. 12	LoudonCo,Vir	13	10	19
Pleacher, Henry(Z)	1815	Sept. 12	LoudonCo,Vir	13	10	19
Pleacher, Henry(Z)	1815	Sept. 12	LoudonCo,Vir	13	10	30
Pleacher, Henry(Z)	1815	Sept. 12	LoudonCo,Vir	13	10	31
Pleacher, Henry(Z)	1817	April 17	LoudonCo,Vir	14	14	13
Pleacher, Henry(Z)	1817	April 17	LoudonCo,Vir	13	10	32
Pleacher, Henry(Z)	1817	April 17	LoudonCo,Vir	13	10	19
Pleacher, Henry(Z)	1817	Oct. 04	MuskingmCoOh	13	10	20
Plecher, John(Joiner)(Y)	1827	April 14	NewLisbon,Oh	05	17	04
Pletcher, Henry(Z)	1828	Jan. 26	Morgan Co,Oh	14	14	15
Pletcher, Jacob(Z)	1830	Dec. 20	Morgan Co,Oh	13	10	34
Pletcher, John(Z)	1826	Sept. 26	Morgan Co,Oh	13	10	21
Pletcher, John(Z)	1829	Aug. 03	Morgan Co,Oh	13	10	20
Pletcher, John(Z)	1830	Dec. 01	Morgan Co,Oh	13	10	20
Pletcher, John(Z)	1831	June 26	Morgan Co,Oh	13	10	18
Pletcher, John(Z)	1831	June 26	Morgan Co,Oh	13	10	20
Pletcher, John(Z)	1834	Aug. 29	Morgan Co,Oh	14	14	13
Plummer, Casander(Z)	1810	Aug. 20	BrookCo.,Vir	15	17	33
Plummer, Eli(Z)	1810	Aug. 20	BrookCo.,Vir	15	17	33
Plummer, Jerome(Z)	1810	Aug. 20	?	15	17	33
Plummer, John(Z)	1815	Sept. 06	?	12	10	17
Plummer, John(Z)	1816	March 25	BelmontCo,Oh	12	10	28
Plummer, John(Z)	1816	March 25	BelmontCo,Oh	12	10	34
Plummer, John(Z)	1816	March 25	BelmontCo,Oh	12	10	27
Plummer, John(Z)	1816	March 29	BelmontCo,Oh	12	10	27
Plummer, John(Z)	1816	March 29	BelmontCo,Oh	12	10	35
Plummer, John(Z-M)	1828	March 24	LickingCo,Oh	10	02	25
Plummer, John(Z-M)	1833	Jan. 08	LickingCo,Oh	10	02	16
Plummer, Jorum(Z)	1810	Aug. 04	MuskingmCoOh	15	17	34
Plummer, Jorum(Z)	1812	June 01	MuskingmCoOh	15	16	03
Plummer, Joshua(Z)	1810	Aug. 04	MuskingmCoOh	15	17	34
Plummer, Moses(Z)	1814	July 23	MuskingmCoOh	15	16	13
Plummor, John(Z)	1820	Aug. 10	Morgan Co,Oh	12	10	34
Plyston, John(Z)	1815	Aug. 17	Jeff.Co.,Oh.	02	04	09
Plyston, John(Z)	1815	Aug. 17	Jeff.Co.,Oh.	02	04	02
Poe, Benj. D.(Z)	1830	March 20	Perry Co.,Oh	14	14	21
Poff, George(Y)	1822	Oct. 28	ColumbanCoOh	05	16	32
Poff, George(Y)	1822	Oct. 28	ColumbanCoOh	05	16	32
Poff, George(Y)	1826	Sept. 15	ColumbanCoOh	06	18	14
Poff, George(Y)	1827	Feb. 21	Stark Co.,Oh	06	18	13
Pogue, Jane(Z-M)	1836	Aug. 16	LickingCo,Oh	10	04	17
Pogue, Samuel(Z)	1809	March 18	BrookCo.,Vir	10	01	20
Polan, Nathaniel Junr.(Y)	1833	March 12	HarrisonCoOh	05	13	15
Poland, Jas.(Z-M)	1831	Oct. 14	HarrisonCoOh	04	06	08
Poland, Martin(Y)	1826	Aug. 29	ColumbanCoOh	06	16	08
Poland, Wm. H.(Z-M)	1831	May 09	HarrisonCoOh	03	04	08
Poland, Wm. H.(Z-M)	1836	Feb. 05	GuernseyCoOh	03	04	08
Polen, Elias(Y)	1833	April 06	HarrisonCoOh	07	14	14
Polen, George(Y)	1836	July 04	HarrisonCoOh	07	14	28
Pollock, Abraham(Z)	1815	May 04	GuernseyCoOh	11	13	01
Pollock, James(Z)	1815	Jan. 16	BelmontCo,Oh	11	05	17
Pollock, James(Z)	1815	Jan. 16	BelmontCo,Oh	11	05	17
Pollock, James(Z)	1815	Feb. 10	BelmontCo,Oh	11	05	16
Pollock, John(Z)	1810	Jan. 16	LickingCo,Oh	10	01	11
Pollock, Samuel(Z)	1815	April 20	GuernseyCoOh	11	13	01
Pollock, Samuel(Z)	1816	June 19	GuernseyCoOh	05	02	08
Polmer, John(Y)	1830	Aug. 27	ColumbanCoOh	07	20	05
Polmer, John(Y)	1831	July 25	Stark Co.,Oh	07	20	05

PURCHASER	YEAR	DATE	RESIDENCE	R	T	S
Ponce, Peter(Y)	1825	Oct. 24	ColumbanCoOh	05	17	04
Ponish, Daniel(Z-M)	1836	Jan. 20	ZanesvilleOh	09	06	11
Pontius, Nich's.(Y)	1824	June 28	Stark Co.,Oh	08	12	18
Pool, John(Y)	1824	July 03	BelmontCo,Oh	03	05	21
Pool, John(Y)	1824	July 03	BelmontCo,Oh	03	05	15
Pool, Samuel(Z)	1831	Oct. 21	BelmontCo,Oh	11	08	03
Pool, Samuel(Z-M)	1833	Feb. 06	BelmontCo,Oh	11	08	04
Pool, Thomas(Y)	1827	Oct. 19	Brooke CoVir	07	17	08
Pool, William(Z)	1816	July 26	BelmontCo,Oh	08	08	02
Poole, Phillip(Y)	1833	Feb. 22	BelmontCo,Oh	03	05	03
Poole, Robert V.(Z-M)	1826	Sept. 28	BelmontCo,Oh	04	01	12
Porst, Warren G.(Z)	1831	Nov. 15	ColumbanCoOh	14	12	23
Porter, Alexander(Y)	1831	April 20	BrookeCo,Vir	07	14	12
Porter, Arthur(Z)	1835	Nov. 13	MonroeCo.,Oh	08	07	23
Porter, Arthur(Z)	1835	Dec. 02	MonroeCo.,Oh	08	07	23
Porter, Arthur(Z)	1836	March 30	MonroeCo.,Oh	08	07	22
Porter, Arthur(Z)	1836	Dec. 20	MonroeCo.,Oh	08	06	11
Porter, Arthur(Z)	1836	Dec. 20	MonroeCo.,Oh	08	07	15
Porter, Arthur(Z)	1837	Sept. 30	MonroeCo.,Oh	08	06	14
Porter, Charles(Z-M)	1836	Oct. 25	CarrollCo,Oh	08	08	23
Porter, Charles(Z-M)	1836	Oct. 25	CarrollCo,Oh	08	08	18
Porter, Elizabeth(Z-M)	1831	June 17	HarrisonCoOh	01	05	18
Porter, Irum(Z)	1837	March 03	WashngtnCoOh	08	05	27
Porter, Isaac(Z-M)	1836	Nov. 16	KnoxCo.,Ohio	11	08	13
Porter, Jacob(Z-M)	1835	Sept. 03	BelmontCo,Oh	03	06	25
Porter, James M.(Z)	1835	Sept. 16	Jeff.Co.,Oh.	14	13	32
Porter, James(Z)	1829	June 08	Jeff.Co.,Oh.	11	10	26
Porter, James(Z)	1836	Dec. 05	MonroeCo.,Oh	15	14	03
Porter, James(Z)	1805	Sept. 06	FairfeldCoOh	14	15	33
Porter, James(Z)	1813	June 05	ChesterCo,Pa	15	17	26
Porter, James(Z)	1816	Nov. 26	FayetteCo,Pa	11	05	19
Porter, Jas. L.(Z)	1830	June 29	Morgan Co,Oh	13	08	15
Porter, Jaum(Z)	1838	April 20	WashngtnCoOh	08	05	27
Porter, John(Z)	1824	May 10	MuskingmCoOh	14	14	21
Porter, John(Z)	1824	May 11	MuskingmCoOh	15	17	15
Porter, John(Z)	1824	May 22	MuskingmCoOh	14	14	21
Porter, John(Z)	1832	July 09	Jeff.Co.,Oh.	14	13	24
Porter, John(Z)	1836	Dec. 29	MonroeCo.,Oh	08	07	23
Porter, John(Z)	1805	Sept. 19	FairfeldCoOh	15	16	01
Porter, John(Z)	1805	Sept. 19	FairfeldCoOh	15	17	23
Porter, John(Z)	1811	Dec. 17	MuskingmCoOh	14	14	06
Porter, John(Z)	1813	April 13	FayetteCo,Pa	03	03	03
Porter, John(Z)	1814	Jan. 24	MuskingmCoOh	15	17	22
Porter, John(Z)	1814	Aug. 18	MuskingmCoOh	15	17	22
Porter, John(Z)	1815	Feb. 10	MuskingmCoOh	15	16	11
Porter, John(Z)	1815	Oct. 07	MuskingmCoOh	14	14	06
Porter, John(Z)	1816	Dec. 07	HarrisonCoOh	08	04	01
Porter, John(Z)	1816	Dec. 16	MuskingmCoOh	15	17	14
Porter, John(Z-M)	1829	Jan. 28	KnoxCo.,Ohio	11	08	22
Porter, Jon'n.(Z)	1817	June 30	ZanesvilleOh	12	10	09
Porter, Joseph(Z-M)	1834	Jan. 27	LickingCo,Oh	10	04	08
Porter, Joum(Z)	1838	April 20	WashngtnCoOh	08	05	27
Porter, Mary(Z)	1807	June 15	MuskingmCoOh	14	14	10
Porter, Moses(Z)	1816	Nov. 26	FayetteCo,Pa	02	02	19
Porter, Otho(Z-M)	1832	Oct. 08	HarrisonCoOh	01	05	14
Porter, Philip(Z)	1811	Jan. 22	MuskingmCoOh	08	02	08
Porter, Richard(Y)	1831	April 02	BrookeCo,Vir	06	14	20
Porter, Robert(Z)	1833	Feb. 21	Perry Co.,Oh	14	13	18
Porter, Samuel(Z)	1832	July 06	Perry Co.,Oh	15	15	34
Porter, Samuel(Z)	1832	July 06	Perry Co.,Oh	15	15	35
Porter, Samuel(Z-M)	1836	Oct. 25	CarrollCo,Oh	08	08	18
Porter, Samuel(Z-M)	1836	Oct. 25	CarrollCo,Oh	08	08	23
Porter, Sarah(Z)	1807	June 15	MuskingmCoOh	14	14	10
Porter, Steward(Z-M)	1827	Dec. 01	GuernseyCoOh	01	03	12
Porter, Stewart(Z-M)	1830	Sept. 22	GuernseyCoOh	02	03	11
Porter, Thomas(Z)	1833	Feb. 21	Perry Co.,Oh	14	13	18
Porter, William(Z-M)	1835	April 24	KnoxCo.,Ohio	11	08	17
Porter, William(Z-M)	1835	Nov. 07	MuskingmCoOh	11	04	21
Porterfield, James(Z-M)	1831	Oct. 15	LickingCo,Oh	11	04	24

PURCHASER	YEAR	DATE	RESIDENCE	R	T	S
Porterfield, John(Y)	1825	Dec. 10	BelmontCo,Oh	04	06	26
Porterfield, S. C.(Z-M)	1835	Dec. 24	KnoxCo.,Ohio	10	05	24
Ports, Absalom(Z-M)	1827	Feb. 13	TuscarwsCoOh	01	08	10
Ports, Absalom(Z-M)	1833	June 10	TuscarwsCoOh	01	08	09
Ports, Philip(Z)	1811	Dec. 07	TuscarwsCoOh	01	09	13
Post, Henry(Y)	1825	Oct. 29	ColumbanCoOh	04	13	22
Post, Jared(Z)	1831	Nov. 21	Perry Co.,Oh	14	12	26
Post, Jared(Z)	1831	Nov. 21	Perry Co.,Oh	14	12	27
Post, Jared(Z)	1836	March 29	Perry Co.,Oh	14	12	27
Potter, Daniel(Z-M)	1837	Sept. 12	CoshoctnCoOh	03	05	14
Potter, David(Z-M)	1838	Sept. 10	TuscarwsCoOh	03	05	14
Potter, Henry(Z)	1814	Dec. 09	MuskingmCoOh	15	17	01
Potter, Horace(Y)	1821	Dec. 21	ColumbanCoOh	06	17	35
Potter, Horace(Y)	1822	Jan. 24	NewLisbon,Oh	06	16	01
Potter, Horace(Y)	1822	Jan. 31	NewLisbon,Oh	08	09	15
Potter, Horace(Y)	1824	May 18	NewLisbon,Oh	04	14	07
Potter, Horace(Y)	1824	May 20	NewListon,Oh	06	17	35
Potter, Horace(Y)	1824	May 20	NewLisbon,Oh	06	17	35
Potter, Horace(Y)	1824	Aug. 11	NewLisbon,Oh	08	09	15
Potter, Leonard(Z-M)	1833	Feb. 15	HolmesCoOhio	08	08	20
Potter, Leonard(Z-M)	1836	Nov. 14	HolmesCoOhio	08	08	20
Potter, Relita(Z)	1835	Jan. 12	Ohio Co.,Vir	14	12	18
Potter, William(Z)	1836	March 28	Ohio Co.,Vir	14	12	30
Pottorf, Andrew(Y)	1822	May 15	Stark Co.,Oh	06	15	24
Potts, David(Y)	1832	Feb. 08	ColumbanCoOh	05	13	04
Potts, Erastus(Z-M)	1837	Sept. 20	MuskingmCoOh	05	03	04
Potts, Harrison(Y)	1835	Dec. 24	CarrollCo,Oh	03	12	26
Potts, James(Y)	1829	May 15	ColumbanCoOh	04	13	19
Potts, John(Y)	1826	April 05	ColumbanCoOh	04	13	26
Potts, John(Z)	1831	Oct. 21	ColumbanCoOh	14	12	26
Potts, Jonathan(Y)	1824	Aug. 24	SteubenvleOh	04	13	03
Potts, Jonathan(Y)	1829	Aug. 31	SteubenvleOh	04	13	03
Potts, Jonathan(Y)	1829	Aug. 31	SteubenvleOh	04	13	04
Potts, Jonathan(Y)	1829	Sept. 03	SteubenvleOh	04	13	03
Potts, Martin(Z-M)	1837	Sept. 20	MuskingmCoOh	05	03	04
Potts, Thomas(Z)	1835	Sept. 02	CarrollCo,Oh	14	12	23
Potts, Thomas(Z)	1835	Sept. 02	CarrollCo,Oh	14	12	26
Potts, William(Y)	1830	Nov. 06	ColumbanCoOh	04	13	05
Potts, William(Z)	1832	Sept. 18	GuernseyCoOh	09	06	30
Potts, William(Z)	1833	March 07	GuernseyCoOh	09	06	30
Potts, William(Z)	1835	Nov. 16	Morgan Co,Oh	10	07	25
Poulson, John(Y)	1822	May 01	FredrickCoMd	06	11	15
Poulson, Nelson(Y)	1827	May 30	HarrisonCoOh	06	11	15
Pounds, Samuel(Z-M)	1825	May 10	GuernseyCoOh	01	03	04
Pounds, William(Z-M)	1833	Aug. 26	GuernseyCoOh	01	03	07
Powel, Isaac(Z)	1835	Nov. 16	MonroeCo.,Oh	08	06	18
Powel, Isaac(Z)	1836	Sept. 07	MonroeCo.,Oh	08	06	18
Powel, James(Z)	1836	June 06	Morgan Co,Oh	13	08	18
Powel, Michael(Z-M)	1838	April 09	MuskingmCoOh	09	09	25
Powel, Samuel(Z)	1835	Nov. 27	MonroeCo.,Oh	08	06	07
Powel, Samuel(Z)	1835	Nov. 27	MonroeCo.,Oh	08	06	07
Powell, Abel(Z-M)	1827	Feb. 03	GuernseyCoOh	01	04	02
Powell, Empson(Z)	1832	June 20	Perry Co.,Oh	14	12	09
Powell, Isaac(Z)	1824	Jan. 10	MonroeCo.,Oh	08	06	18
Powell, Isaac(Z)	1832	May 22	MonroeCo.,Oh	08	06	18
Powell, Isaac(Z)	1833	June 13	MonroeCo.,Oh	08	06	18
Powell, Isaac(Z)	1836	Aug. 02	BelmontCo,Oh	09	07	24
Powell, James(Z)	1824	May 10	MonroeCo.,Oh	08	06	18
Powell, James(Z)	1832	Aug. 27	Morgan Co,Oh	13	08	17
Powell, Jesse(Z)	1836	Sept. 07	BelmontCo,Oh	08	07	29
Powell, John(Z)	1826	March 01	Morgan Co,Oh	13	08	15
Powell, Michael(Z-M)	1837	Aug. 19	KnoxCo.,Ohio	10	08	09
Powell, Michael(Z-M)	1837	Aug. 19	KnoxCo.,Ohio	10	08	10
Powell, Samuel(Z)	1822	Aug. 13	MonroeCo.,Oh	08	06	07
Powell, Stephen(Z)	1833	March 01	Perry Co.,Oh	15	15	26
Powell, Stephen(Z)	1834	Feb. 04	Perry Co.,Oh	15	15	36
Powell, William(Y)	1833	Feb. 15	ColumbanCoOh	03	12	34
Powell, William(Y)	1833	Nov. 19	ColumbanCoOh	03	12	28
Powell, William(Z)	1836	Dec. 14	Perry Co.,Oh	14	12	10

228

PURCHASER	YEAR	DATE	RESIDENCE	R	T	S
Powell, Willis(Y)	1827	June 01	Stark Co.,Oh	06	19	22
Powelson, Abraham(Z-M)	1835	Dec. 12	CoshoctnCoOh	09	07	08
Powelson, Conrad(Z)	1812	May 15	CoshoctnCoOh	05	04	18
Powelson, Conrad(Z)	1813	Oct. 09	CoshoctnCoOh	05	04	19
Powelson, Conrad(Z-M)	1829	April 25	CoshoctnCoOh	05	04	22
Powelson, Conrad(Z-M)	1829	Aug. 01	CoshoctnCoOh	05	04	22
Powelson, Conrad(Z-M)	1832	May 22	CoshoctnCoOh	05	04	18
Powelson, Conrad(Z-M)	1832	May 22	CoshoctnCoOh	05	04	22
Powelson, Conrad(Z-M)	1835	Nov. 07	CoshoctnCoOh	05	04	14
Powelson, Conrad(Z-M)	1837	April 07	CoshoctnCoOh	05	04	13
Powelson, Conrad(Z-M)	1838	Nov. 03	CoshoctnCoOh	05	04	23
Powelson, Morgan(Z-M)	1836	Dec. 12	CoshoctnCoOh	05	04	22
Powelson, Rencar(Z-M)	1832	May 22	CoshoctnCoOh	06	04	02
Powelson, Rinear(Z-M)	1832	Aug. 11	CoshoctnCoOh	06	04	02
Powelson, Valentine(Z-M)	1835	Sept. 12	CoshoctnCoOh	05	04	22
Powelson,Valentine Johnson(Z-M	1836	Jan. 16	CoshoctnCoOh	05	04	14
Powers, John N.(Z-M)	1837	July 08	MuskingmCoOh	10	02	24
Prather, John(Y)	1822	Aug. 22	HarrisonCoOh	06	12	14
Pratt, Rufus(Z-M)	1820	Dec. 09	GuernseyCoOh	01	01	12
Preist, Jno.(Z)	1817	Oct. 07	MuskingmCoOh	10	04	16
Prescot, James T.(Y)	1824	June 12	ColumbanCoOh	01	07	22
Prescot, James T.(Y)	1824	June 12	ColumbanCoOh	01	07	22
Prescot, James T.(Y)	1825	May 03	ColumbanCoOh	01	07	22
Presgraves, George(Z)	1817	Sept. 17	MuskingmCoOh	11	10	08
Presley, Joseph(Z-M)	1836	March 23	GuernseyCoOh	03	04	21
Presley, William Junr.(Z-M)	1833	April 12	GuernseyCoOh	03	03	02
Prestley, Joseph(Z-M)	1835	Sept. 12	GuernseyCoOh	03	04	21
Preston, Henry(Z-M)	1833	Jan. 22	CoshoctnCoOh	05	06	24
Preston, Henry(Z-M)	1833	Jan. 22	CoshoctnCoOh	05	06	24
Preston, Oliver(Z-M)	1836	Feb. 02	KnoxCo.,Ohio	10	08	25
Price, Abigail(Y)	1827	June 26	Jeff.Co.,Oh.	05	13	33
Price, Absalom(Y)	1826	Jan. 11	TuscarwsCoOh	06	12	17
Price, Benjamin(Z-M)	1832	April 09	TuscarwsCoOh	01	08	01
Price, Edward(Z-M)	1835	Sept. 03	CarrolCo.,Oh	04	07	20
Price, Gerard(Z)	1830	Jan. 29	Morgan Co,Oh	10	07	21
Price, Gerard(Z)	1837	March 22	Morgan Co,Oh	08	05	09
Price, J.(Z)	1816	March 20	FayetteCo,Pa	01	05	20
Price, Jacob R.(Z)	1828	Dec. 30	Morgan Co,Oh	12	11	34
Price, Jeffery(Z)	1814	Jan. 26	ZanesvilleOh	14	15	08
Price, Jeffry(Z)	1810	Nov. 02	ZanesvilleOh	12	13	04
Price, Jeffry(Z)	1810	Nov. 02	ZanesvilleOh	12	13	04
Price, Jeffry(Z)	1812	March 07	MuskingmCoOh	09	01	22
Price, John D.(Y)	1824	Jan. 06	BelmontCo,Oh	06	08	32
Price, John D.(Y)	1824	Sept. 28	BelmontCo,Oh	06	08	25
Price, John D.(Y)	1825	Nov. 24	BelmontCo,Oh	06	08	32
Price, John(Y)	1828	Jan. 05	Jeff.Co.,Oh.	05	13	33
Price, John(Y)	1831	Oct. 21	Stark Co.,Oh	06	16	30
Price, John(Z)	1824	May 11	Morgan Co,Oh	13	09	22
Price, John(Z)	1826	April 08	Morgan Co,Oh	13	09	22
Price, John(Z)	1816	Nov. 30	MuskingmCoOh	13	09	27
Price, John(Z)	1816	Nov. 30	MuskingmCoOh	11	10	17
Price, John(Z)	1816	Nov. 30	MuskingmCoOh	12	10	05
Price, John(Z)	1817	Jan. 03	MuskingmCoOh	13	09	22
Price, John(Z)	1817	Jan. 06	MuskingmCoOh	13	09	24
Price, John(Z-M)	1835	Nov. 20	MuskingmCoOh	09	03	15
Price, Josiah(Y)	1829	Dec. 09	Stark Co.,Oh	08	09	25
Price, Peter(Z-M)	1833	July 22	HolmesCoOhio	07	10	03
Price, Robert(Y)	1824	Aug. 04	BelmontCo,Oh	06	08	33
Price, Samuel M.(Z)	1836	March 19	Morgan Co,Oh	09	07	25
Price, William(Z)	1824	Nov. 10	MuskingmCoOh	15	17	15
Price, William(Z)	1828	Jan. 07	MuskingmCoOh	13	10	11
Price, William(Z)	1829	March 30	Morgan Co,Oh	13	08	04
Price, William(Z)	1833	Dec. 07	Morgan Co,Oh	13	10	11
Prier, James(Z-M)	1834	Aug. 02	MuskingmCoOh	09	03	06
Prier, James(Z-M)	1837	Nov. 06	MuskingmCoOh	09	03	16
Priest, George(Z-M)	1836	Nov. 07	LickingCo,Oh	10	04	17
Priest, Hansfield(Z-M)	1833	Oct. 26	MuskingmCoOh	10	03	03
Priest, Hansfield(Z-M)	1835	July 13	LickingCo,Oh	10	03	03
Priest, Henry(Z)	1832	Aug. 18	Morgan Co,Oh	13	08	30

PURCHASER	YEAR	DATE	RESIDENCE	R	T	S
Priest, Jacob(Z-M)	1836	Aug. 13	LickingCo,Oh	10	04	08
Priest, James(Z-M)	1828	June 28	LickingCo,Oh	10	03	03
Priest, James(Z-M)	1833	Feb. 06	LickingCo,Oh	10	03	03
Priest, Jno. Junr.(Z)	1814	July 11	MuskingCoOh	09	01	21
Priest, John(Z)	1832	Oct. 04	Morgan Co,Oh	13	08	18
Priest, John(Z-M)	1837	Oct. 07	LickingCo,Oh	10	04	03
Priest, Lee Roy(Z-M)	1826	Aug. 26	LickingCo,Oh	10	04	14
Priest, Levi(Z)	1814	July 11	MuskingCoOh	09	02	21
Priest, Levi(Z-M)	1834	Feb. 13	HolmesCoOhio	09	08	12
Priest, Milford(Z-M)	1831	Nov. 05	MuskingCoOh	10	03	04
Priest, Moses(Z-M)	1827	Dec. 15	LickingCo,Oh	10	04	13
Priest, Moses(Z-M)	1835	Nov. 03	LickingCo,Oh	10	04	08
Priest, Moses(Z-M)	1836	Sept. 22	LickingCo,Oh	10	04	15
Priest, Presley(Z-M)	1835	Sept. 16	LickingCo,Oh	10	03	07
Priest, Presley(Z-M)	1835	Sept. 16	LickingCo,Oh	10	11	07
Priest, Prestley(Z-M)	1833	Nov. 14	LickingCo,Oh	10	03	07
Priest, Russell(Z-M)	1834	Aug. 29	LickingCo,Oh	11	04	12
Priest, Sanford(Z-M)	1836	Jan. 25	LickingCo,Oh	10	03	04
Priest, Solomon(Z-M)	1828	Feb. 06	LickingCo,Oh	10	04	14
Priest, Solomon(Z-M)	1832	Nov. 06	LickingCo,Oh	10	04	18
Priest, Solomon(Z-M)	1833	Dec. 16	LickingCo,Oh	10	04	18
Priest, Solomon(Z-M)	1833	Dec. 16	LickingCo,Oh	10	04	23
Priest, Susannah(Z)	1827	Oct. 08	Morgan Co,Oh	11	11	06
Priest, Susannah(Z)	1833	April 22	Morgan Co,Oh	13	08	18
Priest, William(Z-M)	1833	Oct. 26	MuskingmCoOh	10	03	08
Priest, William(Z-M)	1833	Oct. 29	MuskingmCoOh	10	03	08
Priest, William(Z-M)	1835	Sept. 28	LickingCo,Oh	10	03	04
Primrose, R. H.(Z)	1836	June 03	MuskingmCoOh	15	14	29
Pringle, Henry(Z)	1816	June 10	MuskingmCoOh	05	02	25
Pringle, Henry(Z)	1816	June 10	MuskingmCoOh	05	02	25
Pringle, Henry(Z)	1816	June 20	MuskingmCoOh	12	11	11
Prior, Barbara(Z)	1806	Jan. 29	MuskingmCoOh	08	02	15
Prior, Barbara(Z)	1807	Jan. 13	MuskingmCoOh	08	02	15
Prior, Frederick(Z)	1814	Feb. 17	MuskingmCoOh	08	03	06
Prior, Isaac Junr.(Z)	1813	March 30	?	12	13	01
Prior, Jeremiah(Y)	1828	April 03	Jeff.Co.,Oh.	06	12	12
Prior, Jesse(Z)	1814	Feb. 26	?	12	13	01
Prior, Jno.(Z)	1814	Feb. 26	?	12	13	01
Prior, John(Z)	1811	June 14	GreeneCo.,Pa	15	18	09
Prior, John(Z)	1813	March 30	?	12	13	01
Prior, Joseph(Z)	1817	March 07	MuskingmCoOh	14	12	19
Prior, William(Z)	1816	April 27	PortageCo,Oh	11	12	11
Prior, William(Z-M)	1832	March 07	MuskingCoOh	08	03	14
Prior, William(Z-M)	1831	Aug. 31	BelmontCo,Oh	11	08	03
Pritchard, John(Z)	1806	Dec. 08	BrookCo.,Vir	09	05	10
Pritchard, John(Z)	1806	Dec. 08	BrookCo.,Vir	09	05	10
Pritchard, John(Z)	1807	Jan. 14	BrookCo.,Vir	09	06	22
Proby, John(Z)	1836	Jan. 27	Perry Co.,Oh	14	14	19
Proudfoot, David(Z)	1815	Sept. 15	FayetteCo,Pa	05	03	22
Proudfoot, David(Z)	1815	Nov. 24	FayetteCo,Pa	05	03	23
Prouty, Russel Jnr.(Z)	1837	Nov. 30	Morgan Co,Oh	08	06	32
Prouty, Russel Jnr.(Z)	1838	Jan. 23	Morgan Co,Oh	08	06	33
Prouty, Russel Jnr.(Z)	1838	Jan. 24	Morgan Co,Oh	08	06	33
Prouty, Russel Jr.(Z)	1836	Jan. 26	Morgan Co,Oh	10	08	20
Prouty, Russel Jr.(Z)	1838	April 05	Morgan Co,Oh	08	06	33
Prouty, Russel(Z)	1835	Aug. 05	Morgan Co,Oh	11	12	13
Prouty, Russel(Z)	1835	Aug. 05	Morgan Co,Oh	11	12	13
Prouty, Russel(Z)	1837	Feb. 02	Morgan Co,Oh	08	06	29
Prouty, Russel(Z)	1837	Feb. 02	Morgan Co,Oh	08	06	30
Prouty, Russel(Z)	1837	Feb. 02	Morgan Co,Oh	08	06	30
Prouty, Russel(Z)	1817	Jan. 07	WashngtnCoOh	10	08	08
Prouty, Russel(Z)	1817	May 05	GuernseyCoOh	10	07	18
Prouty, Russel(Z)	1817	May 05	GuernseyCoOh	10	07	17
Prouty, Russell(Z)	1835	Jan. 19	Morgan Co,Oh	10	08	20
Prouty, Russell(Z)	1835	Jan. 19	Morgan Co,Oh	10	08	28
Prouty, Russell(Z)	1835	Jan. 19	Morgan Co,Oh	10	08	21
Prouty, Russell(Z)	1835	Jan. 19	Morgan Co,Oh	10	08	21
Prouty, William(Z)	1838	Jan. 23	Morgan Co,Oh	08	05	25
Prouty, William(Z)	1838	Jan. 24	Morgan Co,Oh	08	05	25

PURCHASER	YEAR	DATE	RESIDENCE	R	T	S
Provens, Thornton(Z-M)	1833	April 27	MuskingmCoOh	05	04	23
Pruellmayr, George(Z-M)	1836	Oct. 29	ColumbanCoOh	05	04	16
Pruellmays, George(Z-M)	1836	Sept. 26	ColumbanCoOh	05	04	16
Pruellmays, George(Z-M)	1836	Sept. 26	ColumbanCoOh	05	04	16
Pugh, Daniel(Y)	1827	Sept. 03	Stark Co.,Oh	06	15	36
Pugh, John(Z)	1835	Nov. 27	GuernseyCoOh	09	05	28
Pugh, William(Y)	1834	March 10	CarrollCo,Oh	04	13	14
Pulley, Adam(Y)	1822	March 06	GuernseyCoOh	07	10	22
Pulley, Henson(Z-M)	1832	Dec. 31	GuernseyCoOh	02	03	11
Pumphery, Beal(Z-M)	1835	Nov. 13	Brooke CoVir	03	05	16
Pumphery, Beal(Z-M)	1836	Feb. 16	Brooke CoVir	03	05	25
Pumphrey, Beal(Y)	1824	Jan. 20	Brooke CoVir	06	09	06
Pumphrey, Beal(Y)	1825	Nov. 01	BrookeCo,Vir	05	08	36
Pumphrey, Beal(Y)	1826	May 13	Brooke CoVir	06	14	21
Pumphrey, John(Y)	1825	Dec. 14	HarrisonCoOh	06	10	34
Pumphrey, John(Z-M)	1831	Sept. 29	GuernseyCoOh	03	06	15
Pumphrey, John(Z-M)	1832	July 09	TuscarwsCoOh	03	06	13
Pumphrey, John(Z-M)	1832	July 09	TuscarwsCoOh	03	06	18
Pumphrey, John(Z-M)	1832	July 09	TuscarwsCoOh	03	06	23
Pumphrey, Reason(Y)	1827	June 23	Brooke CoVir	06	12	33
Pumphrey, Reason(Y)	1827	Aug. 16	Brooke CoVir	07	14	13
Pumphrey, Reason(Y)	1827	Aug. 16	Brooke CoVir	07	14	13
Pumphrey, Reason(Y)	1831	May 13	TuscarwsCoOh	06	12	33
Pumphrey, Reason(Y)	1831	May 31	TuscarwsCoOh	06	12	33
Pumphrey, William Ridgeley(Y)	1833	Jan. 03	ColumbanCoOh	03	12	02
Purdum, Levi B.(Y)	1826	Aug. 25	BelmontCo,Oh	06	10	15
Purdy, Aaron(Z-M)	1831	Dec. 26	CoshoctnCoOh	07	08	24
Purdy, Abner(Z-M)	1828	Feb. 05	HolmesCoOhio	07	08	08
Purdy, Abner(Z-M)	1828	Feb. 05	HolmesCoOhio	07	08	08
Purdy, Amos(Z)	1816	Sept. 27	Wayne Co.,Pa	06	07	13
Purdy, Amos(Z-M)	1830	March 09	CoshoctnCoOh	06	07	13
Purdy, Charles(Z-M)	1822	July 24	CoshoctnCoOh	08	08	11
Purdy, Charles(Z-M)	1822	July 24	CoshoctnCoOh	08	08	11
Purdy, Ebenezer(Z-M)	1832	June 20	HolmesCoOhio	08	08	17
Purdy, Horatio(Z-M)	1827	June 14	HolmesCoOhio	08	08	18
Purdy, Nathaniel(Z-M)	1826	Jan. 07	HolmesCoOhio	08	08	12
Purdy, Nathaniel(Z-M)	1836	Jan. 26	HolmesCoOhio	08	08	12
Purdy, Nathaniel(Z-M)	1839	July 04	HolmesCoOhio	08	08	19
Purdy, Sylvenus(Z-M)	1829	Sept. 05	HolmesCoOhio	08	08	17
Purdy, Sylvenus(Z-M)	1829	Sept. 05	HolmesCoOhio	08	08	17
Purdy, Wm. Junr.(Z-M)	1823	Jan. 18	CoshoctnCoOh	07	08	06
Purkey, Jacob(Z)	1834	Aug. 18	Morgan Co,Oh	10	07	24
Purkey, Jacob(Z)	1835	Dec. 10	Morgan Co,Oh	10	07	12
Purkey, Jacob(Z)	1835	July 15	Morgan Co,Oh	10	07	24
Purkey, Levi(Z)	1836	Feb. 03	Morgan Co,Oh	10	07	23
Purky, Levi(Z)	1835	July 10	Morgan Co,Oh	09	06	19
Purviance, David(Z)	1815	May 29	Jeff.Co.,Oh.	01	04	07
Purviance, David(Z)	1815	May 29	Jeff.Co.,Oh.	01	04	05
Purviance, David(Z)	1815	May 29	Jeff.Co.,Oh.	01	04	06
Purviance, David(Z)	1815	June 07	Jeff.Co.,Oh.	01	04	15
Purviance, David(Z)	1815	Oct. 16	Jeff.Co.,Oh.	01	04	11
Purviance, David(Z)	1815	Dec. 25	Jeff.Co.,Oh.	01	04	11
Purviance, David(Z)	1816	April 08	GuernseyCoOh	01	04	13
Puskey, Jacob(Z)	1832	Oct. 31	Morgan Co,Oh	10	07	24
Putman, John(Z)	1817	Oct. 17	FredrickCoMd	08	05	16
Putman, Sam'l.(Z)	1817	Oct. 17	FredrickCoMd	08	05	14
Putnam, Wm. R.(Z)	1807	July 16	WashngtnCoOh	09	08	08
Putt, Daniel(Z-M)	1836	Nov. 11	TuscarwsCoOh	03	08	04
Putt, Francis(Z-M)	1831	April 02	TuscarwsCoOh	03	08	23
Putt, Francis(Z-M)	1831	April 02	TuscarwsCoOh	03	07	18
Putt, Francis(Z-M)	1832	Aug. 06	TuscarwsCoOh	03	07	19
Putt, Francis(Z-M)	1830	March 22	TuscarwsCoOh	03	07	19
Putt, John(Z-M)	1832	May 30	TuscarwsCoOh	03	08	24
Putt, Louis(Z-M)	1832	May 30	TuscarwsCoOh	04	07	21
Pyle, Isaac(Z-M)	1836	June 14	CarrollCo,Oh	03	07	18
Pyle, Isaac(Z-M)	1836	June 14	CarrollCo,Oh	03	07	23
Pyle, Samuel(Z)	1816	Nov. 29	KnoxCo.,Ohio	11	08	22
Queen, John(Y)	1822	March 02	ColumbanCoOh	04	14	35
Queen, Minoreu(Z-M)	1830	Jan. 26	LickingCo,Oh	10	04	14

PURCHASER	YEAR	DATE	RESIDENCE	R	T	S
Queen, Sam'l.(Y)	1828	Aug. 16	ColumbanCoOh	04	13	11
Queen, Samuel(Y)	1827	June 23	ColumbanCoOh	04	13	11
Queen, Samuel(Y)	1829	Nov. 09	ColumbanCoOh	04	13	11
Quier, David(Z-M)	1836	Nov. 16	HolmesCoOhio	04	07	04
Quigley, James H.(Z-M)	1835	May 12	TuscarwsCoOh	02	05	03
Quigley, James H.(Z-M)	1835	May 12	TuscarwsCoOh	02	05	03
Quigley, James Henry(Z-M)	1835	July 03	TuscarwsCoOh	02	05	03
Quigley, John(Z)	1811	Oct. 15	WashngtnCoOh	13	08	12
Quill, Adam(Z-M)	1830	May 20	HarrisonCoOh	01	05	06
Quillin, Elihu(Y)	1827	Aug. 27	HarrisonCoOh	07	12	32
Quin, John(Y)	1828	Dec. 15	ColumbanCoOh	04	14	36
Quin, William(Y)	1826	April 12	ColumbanCoOh	06	18	23
Quinn, Luke(Y)	1831	July 09	TuscarwsCoOh	07	14	29
Quinn, Luke(Y)	1832	June 29	TuscarwsCoOh	07	14	29
Quinn, Luke(Y)	1832	June 29	TuscarwsCoOh	07	14	35
Quinn, Michael Heirs of(Y)	1825	Dec. 10	TuscarwsCoOh	07	14	22
Quinn, Paul(Y)	1835	Aug. 22	TuscarwsCoOh	07	14	22
Rabbel, Joseph(Y)	1831	Oct. 13	Brooke CoVir	06	15	18
Racey, Landon(Z)	1826	Aug. 04	HarrisonCoOh	09	07	30
Rackstraw, Kimbel(Z)	1816	April 19	MuskingmCoOh	09	04	17
Radcliff, John(Z)	1832	May 23	Morgan Co,Oh	09	06	21
Radcliff, John(Z)	1807	April 13	FairfeldCoOh	10	02	17
Radcliff, Wm.(Z)	1835	Jan. 16	Morgan Co,Oh	09	06	20
Radcliff, Wm.(Z)	1835	Jan. 16	Morgan Co,Oh	09	06	21
Raffar, Jacob(Z-M)	1836	Feb. 17	TuscarwsCoOh	03	07	11
Rager, Conrad(Z-M)	1829	Aug. 05	TuscarwsCoOh	04	08	19
Rager, Conrad(Z-M)	1833	July 26	TuscarwsCoOh	04	08	19
Rager, Jacob Jur.(Z-M)	1834	March 19	TuscarwsCoOh	05	06	17
Raginauld, A.(Z-M)	1832	April 06	HarrisonCoOh	05	08	11
Rainsbaugh, Adam(Z-M)	1828	Dec. 24	TuscarwsCoOh	01	09	23
Rainsbaugh, Jacob(Z-M)	1828	Dec. 24	TuscarwsCoOh	01	09	23
Rakestraw, Levi(Y)	1823	Dec. 20	ColumbanCoOh	05	18	13
Ralston, James(Z)	1813	Sept. 25	WashCo.,Penn	04	02	19
Rambo, Andrew(Z)	1826	April 22	Perry Co.,Oh	15	14	18
Rambo, Moses(Z)	1806	June 14	MuskingmCoOh	15	17	12
Rambo, Moses(Z)	1812	May 11	MuskingmCoOh	15	17	02
Rambo, Peter(Z)	1814	Nov. 07	MercerCoPenn	05	04	11
Rambo, Solomon(Z)	1837	Aug. 24	Perry Co.,Oh	15	14	27
Rambo, Thomas(Z)	1814	Nov. 11	MuskingmCoOh	04	04	06
Rambo, Thomas(Z)	1815	Sept. 15	FayetteCo,Pa	05	02	19
Rambo, William(Z-M)	1822	Aug. 10	KnoxCo.,Ohio	11	03	07
Rambo, William(Z-M)	1822	Aug. 10	KnoxCo.,Ohio	11	03	07
Ramey, Samuel(Z)	1810	May 14	MuskingmCoOh	15	17	21
Ramey, Thomas(Z)	1810	May 14	MuskingmCoOh	15	17	21
Ramsay, Eunice(Z-M)	1836	Dec. 02	CoshoctnCoOh	08	07	11
Ramsay, Mary(Z-M)	1836	Dec. 02	CoshoctnCoOh	08	07	11
Ramsay, Robert(Z-M)	1833	Feb. 25	TuscarwsCoOh	03	10	24
Ramsay, Sam'l.(Y)	1824	Dec. 17	BelmontCo,Oh	04	06	01
Ramsay, Sarah M.(Y)	1830	Jan. 23	WashCo.,Penn	03	12	31
Ramsay, William(Z-M)	1837	April 10	CoshoctnCoOh	08	08	25
Ramsay, William(Z-M)	1837	April 10	CoshoctnCoOh	09	08	20
Ramsbottom, Obadiah(Y)	1823	May 19	HarrisonCoOh	05	12	21
Ramsey, James(Y)	1833	Nov. 11	Jeff.Co.,Oh.	02	09	27
Ramsey, James(Z)	1812	Dec. 03	FairfeldCoOh	15	15	18
Ramsey, John(Z)	1812	Dec. 03	FairfeldCoOh	15	15	18
Ramsey, Robert(Z-M)	1828	Dec. 25	TuscarwsCoOh	03	10	24
Ramsey, Sennet(Z)	1829	Jan. 03	Morgan Co,Oh	12	11	20
Ramsperger, Jacob(Z-M)	1831	Nov. 14	TuscarwsCoOh	05	08	07
Ramy, Alexander(Z)	1810	July 11	MuskingmCoOh	01	09	29
Ramy, John Junr.(Z)	1815	Nov. 18	MuskingmCoOh	13	12	12
Ramy, John(Z)	1811	March 21	MuskingmCoOh	13	12	12
Ramy, Samuel(Z)	1810	May 14	MuskingmCoOh	15	17	21
Ramy, Thomas(Z)	1810	May 14	MuskingmCoOh	15	17	21
Randall, Annarrias(Z)	1814	Nov. 07	GuernseyCoOh	05	04	01
Randall, Annarrias(Z)	1814	Nov. 07	GuernseyCoOh	02	05	21
Randall, Annarrias(Z)	1814	Nov. 07	GuernseyCoOh	02	05	22
Randall, Leander(Y)	1827	March 26	ColumbanCoOh	05	14	04
Randels, Wm.(Y)	1823	June 14	ColumbanCoOh	01	07	15
Randles, A.(Z-M)	1835	March 16	CoshoctnCoOh	07	05	08

PURCHASER	YEAR	DATE	RESIDENCE	R	T	S
Randles, Abr'm.(Z)	1816	Dec. 09	CoshoctnCoOh	07	05	05
Randles, Abraham(Z-M)	1836	Feb. 11	CoshoctnCoOh	07	05	02
Randles, Abraham(Z-M)	1832	May 23	CoshoctnCoOh	07	05	08
Randles, Isaac(Z-M)	1832	June 04	CoshoctnCoOh	07	05	03
Randles, Isaac(Z-M)	1835	Feb. 10	CoshoctnCoOh	07	05	03
Randles, John(Z-M)	1835	Sept. 28	CoshoctnCoOh	07	05	04
Randles, Jonas(Z)	1816	Dec. 09	CoshoctnCoOh	07	05	05
Randles, William(Z-M)	1838	Dec. 05	HarrisonCoOh	09	07	03
Randolph, John Junr.(Y)	1835	May 18	ColumbanCoOh	04	13	04
Randolph, John(Y)	1833	Feb. 14	ColumbanCoOh	04	13	04
Randolph, Nathaniel(Y)	1832	Sept. 20	BeaverCo.,Pa	03	12	26
Rankin, Davis(Z-M)	1827	July 26	LickingCo,Oh	10	03	15
Rankin, James(Z-M)	1834	Feb. 03	MuskingmCoOh	04	03	07
Rankin, James(Z-M)	1835	Dec. 29	GuernseyCoOh	04	03	07
Rankin, James(Z-M)	1836	March 30	GuernseyCoOh	04	03	07
Rankin, Jas.(Z)	1835	Jan. 16	BelmontCo,Oh	09	05	23
Rankin, Jas.(Z)	1835	Jan. 16	BelmontCo,Oh	09	05	14
Rankin, Jas.(Z)	1835	Jan. 16	BelmontCo,Oh	09	05	14
Rankin, John(Y)	1824	May 27	BelmontCo,Oh	04	06	21
Rankin, John(Z)	1834	Dec. 10	BelmontCo,Oh	09	05	15
Rankin, Thomas(Z-M)	1833	Aug. 30	HarrisonCoOh	01	06	17
Rankin, Wm.(Y)	1825	Feb. 26	MontgmryCoPa	04	06	21
Rannees, David(Z)	1832	Feb. 08	GuernseyCoOh	10	09	26
Rannelds, Abraham(Z-M)	1823	Sept. 18	CoshoctnCoOh	07	05	04
Rannelds, Jonas(Z-M)	1823	Sept. 18	CoshoctnCoOh	07	05	04
Rannels, Joseph(Z)	1812	June 23	GuernseyCoOh	10	09	34
Rannels, Joseph(Z)	1817	June 04	GuernseyCoOh	10	09	34
Rannels, William(Z)	1810	April 05	WashCo.,Penn	10	08	05
Rasennaugh, Robt.(Z)	1830	Feb. 22	MuskingmCoOh	11	12	30
Rasor, John(Z)	1835	June 15	GuernseyCoOh	08	08	33
Ratcliff, David(Z)	1833	Aug. 29	Morgan Co,Oh	09	06	21
Ratcliff, Hannah(Z)	1813	Sept. 22	FairfeldCoOh	10	02	17
Ratcliff, John B.(Z)	1826	Nov. 25	Perry Co.,Oh	15	15	13
Ratcliff, Stephen(Z)	1833	Feb. 25	Perry Co.,Oh	15	15	24
Ratliff, David(Z)	1830	Dec. 03	Morgan Co,Oh	09	06	21
Ratliff, David(Z)	1836	March 04	Morgan Co,Oh	09	06	21
Ratliff, David(Z)	1836	March 21	Morgan Co,Oh	09	06	21
Ratliff, John(Z)	1836	March 04	Morgan Co,Oh	09	06	13
Ratliff, John(Z)	1836	March 21	Morgan Co,Oh	08	06	19
Ratliff, John(Z)	1836	March 21	Morgan Co,Oh	08	06	19
Ratliff, William(Z)	1836	May 26	Morgan Co,Oh	08	06	06
Ratliff, Wm.(Z)	1836	June 01	Morgan Co,Oh	08	06	19
Ratliff, Wm.(Z)	1836	June 01	Morgan Co,Oh	08	06	30
Rauenyahn, Abraham(Y)	1833	Aug. 27	Stark Co.,Oh	09	12	33
Raush, Godfrey(Y)	1826	Nov. 17	Stark Co.,Oh	09	12	33
Rave, Stephen(Z)	1814	April 09	MuskingmCoOh	12	13	15
Rawden, William(Z)	1815	Sept. 11	CoshoctnCoOh	10	05	08
Rawls, John(Y)	1823	Sept. 04	Stark Co.,Oh	06	19	24
Ray, Charles(Y)	1829	April 18	ColumbanCoOh	05	14	15
Ray, Michael(Z-M)	1832	Sept. 05	HolmesCoOhio	07	08	22
Ray, Thomas(Y)	1827	Aug. 02	ColumbanCoOh	05	14	23
Ray, Thomas(Z)	1833	April 16	Brooke CoVir	11	11	23
Ray, Thomas(Z-M)	1828	Oct. 16	Ohio Co.,Vir	03	04	12
Ray, Thomas(Z-M)	1835	Nov. 20	GuernseyCoOh	04	04	20
Rayley, William L.(Z)	1834	Aug. 08	WashngtnCoOh	08	05	17
Raymond, Enoch S.(Z-M)	1837	March 03	HolmesCoOhio	09	09	01
Raymond, Enoch S.(Z-M)	1837	March 03	HolmesCoOhio	09	09	17
Raymond, Enoch Sears(Z-M)	1836	Jan. 13	HolmesCoOhio	09	09	17
Raynolds, John(Z)	1810	June 18	MuskingmCoOh	11	13	09
Raynolds, John(Z)	1815	March 17	?	05	02	08
Raynolds, John(Z)	1816	May 28	MuskingmCoOh	05	02	16
Raynolds, William(Z)	1808	April 22	WestmrldCoPa	10	09	18
Raynolds, William(Z)	1808	April 22	WestmrldCoPa	10	09	07
Raynolds, William(Z)	1808	April 22	WestmrldCoPa	11	13	10
Raynolds, Wm.(Y)	1822	July 01	Stark Co.,Oh	09	11	15
Raynolds, Wm.(Y)	1822	July 02	Stark Co.,Oh	09	11	22
Raynolds, Wm.(Y)	1822	Aug. 01	Stark Co.,Oh	07	19	15
Rayot, Fred'k.(Y)	1829	May 04	Stark Co.,Oh	06	19	31
Rea, Henry(Z)	1814	July 26	TuscarwsCoOh	05	08	23

PURCHASER	YEAR	DATE	RESIDENCE	R	T	S
Rea, James(Z-M)	1835	July 02	GuernseyCoOh	03	03	01
Rea, William(Z-M)	1837	April 22	GuernseyCoOh	03	03	05
Read, John(Y)	1827	Feb. 09	TuscarwsCoOh	07	14	32
Reading, Michael(Z)	1832	Oct. 23	Perry Co.,Oh	15	16	24
Reading, Patrick(Z)	1834	Nov. 13	Perry Co.,Oh	15	16	24
Reager, John(Z)	1815	Oct. 26	MuskingmCoOh	10	04	22
Reagh, Thomas(Z)	1810	Sept. 10	BelmontCo,Oh	11	05	07
Reagle, George(Z)	1815	Dec. 07	HarrisonCoOh	05	07	16
Reagle, George(Z)	1816	Dec. 07	Jeff.Co.,Oh.	05	07	15
Reagle, Jacob(Z)	1814	Dec. 28	UnionCo,Penn	05	08	22
Reagle, Michael(Z-M)	1828	Nov. 27	CoshoctnCoOh	04	06	01
Ream, Jacob(Z)	1805	June 08	MuskingmCoOh	14	15	27
Ream, S.(Z)	1815	April 01	MuskingmCoOh	15	16	26
Ream, Sam'l.(Z)	1805	June 08	MuskingmCoOh	14	15	27
Ream, Samuel(Z)	1804	Dec. 18	SomersetCoPa	15	17	31
Ream, Samuel(Z)	1806	Feb. 04	MuskingmCoOh	15	17	31
Ream, Samuel(Z)	1812	Oct. 08	MuskingmCoOh	15	15	08
Ream, Samuel(Z)	1814	Aug. 29	MuskingmCoOh	15	16	15
Reaman, George(Z)	1815	Nov. 15	SomersetCoPa	06	09	13
Reamen, George(Z)	1816	Nov. 13	SomersetCoPa	06	08	22
Reamer, George(Z)	1816	Nov. 13	SomersetCoPa	06	08	22
Reamy, Elias(Z)	1828	Jan. 02	Morgan Co,Oh	09	05	08
Rear, Nicholas(Z)	1833	May 18	Morgan Co,Oh	13	10	21
Reares, Hallowell(Z-M)	1838	Nov. 22	GuernseyCoOh	03	04	09
Rearnan, Charles(Z)	1815	Dec. 13	SomersetCoPa	06	09	14
Reasoner, George(Z)	1815	Feb. 06	SomersetCoPa	03	09	19
Reasoner, Henry(Z)	1807	Sept. 22	MuskingmCoOh	05	01	03
Reasoner, Henry(Z)	1814	July 11	MuskingmCoOh	05	01	03
Reasoner, John(Z)	1814	Dec. 15	GuernseyCoOh	04	02	25
Reasoner, John(Z)	1816	Nov. 09	GuernseyCoOh	10	09	35
Reasoner, Joseph(Z-M)	1822	Nov. 01	MuskingmCoOh	11	12	14
Reasoner, Sol'n.(Z)	1817	May 22	MuskingmCoOh	04	01	18
Reasoner, William(Z)	1815	Dec. 21	GuernseyCoOh	04	02	23
Reaves, Hallowell(Z-M)	1838	Nov. 22	GuernseyCoOh	03	04	09
Rece, Jacob(Z)	1807	March 18	MuskingmCoOh	14	16	15
Rece, Jacob(Z)	1807	April 23	MuskingmCoOh	14	16	18
Rece, Jacob(Z)	1807	April 23	MuskingmCoOh	13	11	26
Rechner, John(Z-M)	1836	Dec. 13	TuscarwsCoOh	02	07	09
Rechner, John(Z-M)	1838	Aug. 27	TuscarwsCoOh	02	07	01
Reck, John Benj'm.(Z-M)	1836	Nov. 05	TuscarwsCoOh	04	08	23
Reck, John Benj'm.(Z-M)	1836	Nov. 05	TuscarwsCoOh	05	07	20
Redd, Peter(Z)	1816	Nov. 16	WashCo.,Penn	10	09	17
Redd, Peter(Z)	1816	Nov. 16	WashCo.,Penn	10	09	18
Redd, Peter(Z)	1817	Feb. 14	WashCo.,Penn	10	09	08
Reddick, John(Z)	1805	Aug. 19	FredrickCoMd	14	15	18
Reddick, John(Z)	1813	Dec. 20	MuskingmCoOh	15	17	35
Redenour, David(Y)	1833	June 08	Jeff.Co.,Oh.	03	11	17
Redman, Beday(Z-M)	1837	April 04	MuskingmCoOh	10	03	04
Redman, Jesse(Z)	1817	Sept. 04	MuskingmCoOh	09	01	13
Redman, John(Z)	1813	Nov. 29	MuskingmCoOh	15	16	10
Redman, Robert(Z-M)	1836	Feb. 17	CarrollCo,Oh	02	04	05
Redman, Robert(Z-M)	1836	Feb. 17	CarrollCo,Oh	03	05	01
Redman, Thomas(Z)	1817	Oct. 28	MuskingmCoOh	09	01	14
Redmond, Isreal(Z)	1829	Dec. 21	PerryCo.,Oh.	12	10	15
Reece, Bailey(Z)	1824	July 27	MuskingmCoOh	13	11	19
Reece, Jacob(Z)	1807	March 18	MuskingmCoOh	14	16	15
Reece, Jacob(Z)	1813	Aug. 17	MuskingmCoOh	13	11	26
Reece, Rinherd(Z)	1814	May 04	GreeneCo.,Pa	11	05	25
Reece, Rinherd(Z)	1814	May 04	GreeneCo.,Pa	11	06	25
Reece, Rinherd(Z)	1814	Nov. 30	KnoxCo.,Ohio	11	05	16
Reed, Abraham(Z-M)	1826	April 28	WashCo.,Penn	05	07	21
Reed, Benjamin(Z)	1836	March 01	Morgan Co,Oh	09	07	32
Reed, Benjamin(Z)	1836	March 25	Morgan Co,Oh	09	05	35
Reed, Benjamin(Z)	1836	March 25	Morgan Co,Oh	09	05	36
Reed, Bonam(Z)	1836	March 31	Morgan Co,Oh	09	05	24
Reed, Bonam(Z)	1836	March 31	Morgan Co,Oh	09	05	25
Reed, David(Z)	1822	May 09	MuskingmCoOh	11	12	17
Reed, Geo.(Z)	1832	Feb. 29	Perry Co.,Oh	14	13	15
Reed, George(Y)	1827	April 10	Jeff.Co.,Oh.	07	14	32

PURCHASER	YEAR	DATE	RESIDENCE	R	T	S
Reed, George(Z)	1824	Dec. 23	Perry Co.,Oh	14	13	22
Reed, George(Z)	1826	June 30	Perry Co.,Oh	14	13	22
Reed, George(Z)	1829	Dec. 02	Perry Co.,Oh	14	13	15
Reed, George(Z)	1831	July 08	Perry Co.,Oh	14	13	09
Reed, George(Z)	1831	July 21	Perry Co.,Oh	14	13	21
Reed, George(Z)	1836	April 27	Perry Co.,Oh	14	13	23
Reed, George(Z)	1836	Sept. 20	Perry Co.,Oh	14	13	22
Reed, George(Z)	1814	Sept. 26	MuskingmCoOh	15	14	09
Reed, George(Z)	1815	Sept. 15	MuskingmCoOh	14	13	14
Reed, George(Z)	1815	Sept. 15	MuskingmCoOh	14	13	11
Reed, Hezekiah Bm.(Z-M)	1836	Jan. 07	GuernseyCoOh	02	01	05
Reed, Horace(Z)	1814	Nov. 29	SpringfeldOh	07	07	25
Reed, Hugh(Y)	1821	Nov. 26	ColumbanCoOh	03	13	15
Reed, J.(Z)	1817	Jan. 08	PutnamCoOhio	13	09	09
Reed, James A.(Z)	1835	Jan. 28	Perry Co.,Oh	15	14	04
Reed, James(Z)	1824	Dec. 08	Morgan Co,Oh	09	07	15
Reed, James(Z)	1826	June 15	Morgan Co,Oh	09	07	29
Reed, James(Z)	1832	Dec. 20	Morgan Co,Oh	10	06	05
Reed, James(Z)	1811	Nov. 23	WashngtnCoOh	09	07	28
Reed, Jeremiah(Z)	1810	Jan. 27	SomersetCoPa	14	14	32
Reed, Jeremiah(Z)	1814	Oct. 15	SomersetCoPa	14	14	29
Reed, Jno.(Z)	1817	Oct. 10	MuskingmCoOh	11	13	24
Reed, John H.(Z-M)	1836	Aug. 29	CoshoctnCoOh	08	06	08
Reed, John Junr.(Y)	1829	July 01	Stark Co.,Oh	06	16	19
Reed, John Myer(Z-M)	1838	April 21	CoshoctnCoOh	08	07	20
Reed, John(Y)	1825	Feb. 03	Stark Co.,Oh	07	20	22
Reed, John(Y)	1831	June 02	Stark Co.,Oh	06	16	29
Reed, John(Z)	1824	Sept. 01	BelmontCo,Oh	12	11	01
Reed, John(Z)	1833	Oct. 05	Brooke CoVir	11	12	36
Reed, John(Z)	1834	March 13	Perry Co.,Oh	14	14	32
Reed, John(Z)	1811	Oct. 15	WashngtnCoOh	09	07	29
Reed, John(Z)	1813	Aug. 17	WashngtnCoOh	09	07	20
Reed, John(Z)	1816	Aug. 17	HarrisonCoOh	01	04	04
Reed, John(Z-M)	1831	Feb. 01	GuernseyCoOh	01	04	03
Reed, Jonathan(Z-M)	1836	April 22	MuskingmCoOh	06	04	22
Reed, Joseph(Z)	1811	Oct. 15	WashngtnCoOh	09	07	20
Reed, Leonard W.(Y)	1823	May 03	ColumbanCoOh	05	18	13
Reed, Mathew(Z)	1815	April 22	MuskingmCoOh	12	13	12
Reed, Robert(Y)	1831	June 02	Stark Co.,Oh	06	16	29
Reed, Robert(Z)	1827	Sept. 19	PittsburghPa	01	04	21
Reed, Robert(Z-M)	1833	Sept. 11	MuskingmCoOh	07	07	21
Reed, Stephen(Z)	1814	April 14	GuernseyCoOh	02	01	06
Reed, Thomas(Z-M)	1833	April 09	CoshoctnCoOh	07	07	21
Reed, William(Z-M)	1829	Sept. 24	CoshoctnCoOh	03	06	14
Reed, William(Z-M)	1832	June 01	TuscarwsCoOh	03	06	15
Reed, William(Z-M)	1836	Jan. 01	GuernseyCoOh	04	04	21
Reed, William(Z-M)	1836	Feb. 24	TuscarwsCoOh	03	06	14
Reed, William(Z-M)	1836	Feb. 24	TuscarwsCoOh	03	06	14
Reed, William(Z-M)	1837	Feb. 11	GuernseyCoOh	04	03	09
Reem, Peter(Z-M)	1836	Feb. 29	CoshoctnCoOh	05	07	15
Reeosoner, Henry(Z)	1814	Oct. 13	MuskingmCoOh	05	01	03
Rees, Bailey(Z)	1824	May 22	MuskingmCoOh	13	11	19
Rees, Chas. L.(Z)	1822	May 02	Morgan Co,Oh	12	10	09
Rees, James(Z)	1834	Feb. 03	MuskingmCoOh	13	08	31
Rees, Thomas(Z)	1824	May 22	MuskingmCoOh	13	11	13
Rees, William(Z)	1835	Jan. 13	Morgan Co,Oh	11	12	24
Reese, Benjamin(Z)	1812	May 01	GuernseyCoOh	08	08	05
Reese, Dan'l.(Y)	1823	July 26	Stark Co.,Oh	06	17	33
Reese, Emeline(Z)	1836	Oct. 04	Perry Co.,Oh	14	12	25
Reese, George(Y)	1824	June 08	Stark Co.,Oh	06	18	34
Reese, George(Z)	1835	July 14	Perry Co.,Oh	14	12	36
Reese, John Jr.(Y)	1824	May 21	Stark Co.,Oh	09	12	22
Reese, John Jr.(Y)	1824	May 21	Stark Co.,Oh	09	12	22
Reese, John(Y)	1823	April 21	Stark Co.,Oh	07	19	22
Reese, John(Y)	1824	Nov. 22	Stark Co.,Oh	09	12	19
Reese, John(Y)	1824	Nov. 22	Stark Co.,Oh	09	12	19
Reeve, Aaaron(Z)	1813	Nov. 27	TuscarwsCoOh	01	09	04
Reeve, Aaron(Z)	1813	Nov. 27	TuscarwsCoOh	01	09	04
Reeve, John(Z)	1836	Jan. 26	Perry Co.,Oh	15	14	23

235

PURCHASER	YEAR	DATE	RESIDENCE	R	T	S
Reeve, John(Z)	1836	June 23	Perry Co.,Oh	15	14	23
Reeve, Stephen(Z)	1831	Oct. 03	MuskingmCoOh	08	08	10
Reeve, Stephen(Z)	1832	June 04	MuskingmCoOh	12	13	22
Reeve, William(Z)	1825	July 20	GuernseyCoOh	08	08	10
Reeves, J.(Z)	1805	April 29	MuskingmCoOh	08	08	10
Reeves, Joseph(Z)	1831	April 28	GuernseyCoOh	08	08	02
Reeves, Joseph(Z)	1831	April 28	GuernseyCoOh	08	08	03
Reeves, Joseph(Z)	1806	Jan. 30	MuskingmCoOh	08	08	10
Reeves, M.(Z-M)	1830	Aug. 12	GuernseyCoOh	03	02	10
Reeves, Stephen(Z)	1810	Dec. 12	MuskingmCoOh	12	13	21
Regel, Jacob(Z-M)	1836	March 09	CoshoctnCoOh	05	07	15
Regester, Thomas(Y)	1823	Dec. 17	WashCo.,Penn	05	16	33
Register, Robert(Y)	1831	Jan. 12	ColumbanCoOh	05	15	03
Register, Robert(Z)	1833	April 11	Perry Co.,Oh	15	14	09
Register, Thomas(Y)	1826	Sept. 08	ColumbanCoOh	05	16	33
Regle, Peter(Z-M)	1835	Dec. 22	CoshoctnCoOh	05	07	16
Regle, Peter(Z-M)	1838	Sept. 08	CoshoctnCoOh	05	07	16
Regnier, Alfred(Z)	1836	Aug. 15	WashngtnCoOh	08	05	08
Regula, Adam(Z-M)	1834	Sept. 09	HolmesCoOhio	04	07	17
Reh, Henry(Z)	1815	Sept. 19	CoshoctnCoOh	05	06	07
Reid, George(Z)	1833	Nov. 04	Perry Co.,Oh	15	14	04
Reid, George(Z)	1833	Aug. 09	Perry Co.,Oh	15	14	04
Reid, James(Z)	1831	Oct. 05	ColumbanCoOh	14	12	04
Reid, John(Z)	1824	July 05	Morgan Co,Oh	09	07	21
Reid, Mathew(Z)	1812	Feb. 15	WashCo.,Penn	11	13	04
Reid, Noah(Z-M)	1835	Jan. 29	LickingCo,Oh	10	03	03
Reid, Robert(Y)	1832	Sept. 21	TuscarwsCoOh	07	14	34
Reider, Stephen(Y)	1835	June 15	Jeff.Co.,Oh.	04	13	07
Reigal, George(Y)	1824	July 06	Jeff.Co.,Oh.	05	13	14
Reigal, George(Y)	1824	July 06	Jeff.Co.,Oh.	05	13	13
Reigal, George(Y)	1826	April 17	Jeff.Co.,Oh.	05	13	14
Reignier, John B.(Z)	1816	Sept. 04	WashngtnCoOh	08	05	08
Reilley, John(Z)	1832	Aug. 25	Perry Co.,Oh	15	15	23
Reilley, John(Z)	1832	Oct. 22	Perry Co.,Oh	15	15	23
Reinenger, George(Y)	1835	Sept. 04	Stark Co.,Oh	09	12	33
Reinenger, George(Y)	1835	Sept. 04	Stark Co.,Oh	09	12	33
Reinhart, Joseph(Z)	1836	Jan. 19	GuernseyCoOh	08	07	17
Reisacher, Xaveri(Z)	1837	Sept. 08	MuskingmCoOh	14	12	24
Remdles, Enoch(Z-M)	1830	Dec. 08	CoshoctnCoOh	07	05	04
Remey, Elias(Z)	1830	Feb. 12	Morgan Co,Oh	11	10	15
Remf, Jacob(Z-M)	1827	Nov. 28	HolmesCoOhio	05	06	15
Remington, Oliver M.(Z-M)	1836	May 21	HolmesCoOhio	09	08	23
Remington, Sally(Z-M)	1826	Dec. 30	CoshoctnCoOh	09	07	07
Remington, Sally(Z-M)	1833	Aug. 15	HolmesCoOhio	09	08	18
Remsberger, Jacob(Z-M)	1826	Oct. 03	HolmesCoOhio	05	08	17
Remy, Lewis(Z)	1824	Dec. 03	Morgan Co,Oh	11	10	15
Rendels, William(Z-M)	1836	Jan. 08	CoshoctnCoOh	05	04	20
Renfew, James(Z-M)	1829	Feb. 04	CoshoctnCoOh	05	07	03
Renfrew, James(Z)	1810	May 15	ChesterCo,Pa	03	04	25
Renfrew, James(Z)	1810	May 15	ChesterCo,Pa	03	04	25
Renfrew, James(Z)	1810	Oct. 25	ChesterCo,Pa	04	04	22
Renfrew, William(Z)	1810	Sept. 21	ChesterCo,Pa	04	04	21
Renfrew, William(Z-M)	1833	Aug. 08	CoshoctnCoOh	08	05	11
Rennia, Stephen(Y)	1829	March 21	TuscarwsCoOh	07	16	28
Reno, Sam'l. P.(Y)	1826	Aug. 14	BeaverCo.,Pa	05	18	17
Rensselear, Sanders Van(Y)	1833	Oct. 15	Stark Co.,Oh	08	12	14
Rensselear, Sanders Van(Y)	1833	Nov. 01	Stark Co.,Oh	08	12	14
Rerick, John(Y)	1828	Aug. 26	Jeff.Co.,Oh.	06	14	11
Rese, Rudolph(Y)	1830	Sept. 30	Stark Co.,Oh	10	02	11
Resener, Henry(Z)	1806	March 10	MuskingmCoOh	05	01	08
Reshley, David(Z-M)	1832	Dec. 15	TuscarwsCoOh	03	10	23
Reshley, David(Z-M)	1833	Feb. 27	TuscarwsCoOh	03	10	24
Resoner, Benjamin(Z)	1805	Jan. 11	MuskingmCoOh	05	01	11
Resoner, Henry(Z)	1814	Oct. 13	MuskingmCoOh	05	01	03
Resoner, John(Z)	1804	Dec. 04	MuskingmCoOh	05	01	01
Resoner, Soloman(Z)	1805	June 29	MuskingmCoOh	05	01	10
Ressler, Hennry(Y)	1832	Dec. 14	Stark Co.,Oh	09	12	30
Reuleder, Gottlieb(Z-M)	1837	July 05	CoshoctnCoOh	08	06	03
Rex, Geo. A.(Y)	1824	April 16	Stark Co.,Oh	10	02	01

PURCHASER	YEAR	DATE	RESIDENCE	R	T	S
Rex, George Adam(Y)	1832	July 07	Stark Co.,Oh	10	02	12
Rex, George Adam(Y)	1832	July 07	Stark Co.,Oh	10	02	12
Rex, George Adam(Y)	1832	July 07	Stark Co.,Oh	10	02	12
Rex, Jacob(Y)	1826	Sept. 25	Stark Co.,Oh	10	02	11
Rex, Jonathan(Z)	1825	Dec. 22	Morgan Co,Oh	11	12	36
Rex, Jonathan(Z)	1831	Jan. 27	Morgan Co,Oh	10	07	18
Rex, Jonathan(Z)	1831	May 31	Morgan Co,Oh	11	11	12
Rex, Jonathan(Z)	1831	June 02	Morgan Co,Oh	11	11	12
Rex, Jonathan(Z)	1834	Sept. 04	Morgan Co,Oh	10	07	07
Rex, Joseph(Y)	1830	May 07	Stark Co.,Oh	10	02	11
Rex, Rudolph(Y)	1830	May 07	Stark Co.,Oh	10	02	11
Rex, Stephen(Y)	1826	Dec. 11	Stark Co.,Oh	05	18	32
Rex, Stephen(Y)	1826	Dec. 11	Stark Co.,Oh	05	18	32
Reynolds, Abia(Z)	1835	Nov. 14	BelmontCo,Oh	08	06	26
Reynolds, Caleb F.(Z)	1836	Oct. 04	WashngtnCoOh	08	05	29
Reynolds, Caleb F.(Z)	1836	Oct. 04	WashngtnCoOh	08	05	32
Reynolds, Caleb F.(Z)	1836	Oct. 04	WashngtnCoOh	08	05	32
Reynolds, Caleb F.(Z)	1836	Oct. 04	WashngtnCoOh	08	05	33
Reynolds, Ebenezer(Z)	1825	Nov. 21	Perry Co.,Oh	15	15	20
Reynolds, Ebenezer(Z)	1825	Nov. 21	Perry Co.,Oh	15	15	21
Reynolds, James(Z-M)	1835	Oct. 26	HolmesCoOhio	09	08	11
Reynolds, Jas.(Z-M)	1823	May 17	CoshoctnCoOh	09	08	13
Reynolds, Jeremiah(Z-M)	1833	Dec. 09	FayetteCo,Pa	01	05	01
Reynolds, Joseph Jr.(Y)	1823	Nov. 17	BelmontCoOh	06	09	24
Reynolds, Lewis(Z-M)	1823	May 17	CoshoctnCoOh	09	08	13
Reynolds, William(Z)	1807	Nov. 24	WestmrldCoPa	11	13	02
Rhamy, Richard(Z-M)	1837	April 12	CoshoctnCoOh	09	08	25
Rhamy, Richard(Z-M)	1837	Nov. 11	HolmesCoOhio	09	07	05
Rhodes, Anny(Z-M)	1838	May 15	HolmesCoOhio	09	08	02
Rhodes, Dudley W.(Z)	1836	Dec. 02	ZanesvilleOh	14	12	32
Rhodes, Ebenezer(Z)	1804	Dec. 25	MuskingmCoOh	14	15	10
Rhodes, Nimrod(Y)	1827	Aug. 31	ColumbanCoOh	03	12	15
Rhodes, Nimrod(Y)	1829	July 10	ColumbanCoOh	03	12	17
Rhodes, William Waters(Z)	1836	Sept. 02	GuernseyCoOh	09	07	01
Rhodes, Wm. Waters(Z)	1836	Sept. 08	GuernseyCoOh	09	08	36
Rible, Nicholas(Z)	1811	June 06	FairfeldCoOh	15	17	35
Rible, Nicholas(Z)	1813	Nov. 03	?	15	17	34
Rice, Frederick(Z-M)	1831	Oct. 21	KnoxCo.,Ohio	10	08	08
Rice, Frederick(Z-M)	1831	Oct. 21	KnoxCo.,Ohio	10	08	13
Rice, George(Z-M)	1831	May 03	KnoxCo.,Ohio	10	08	17
Rice, George(Z-M)	1835	Jan. 06	KnoxCo.,Ohio	10	08	16
Rice, George(Z-M)	1835	Jan. 06	KnoxCo.,Ohio	10	08	13
Rice, Isaac(Z-M)	1830	Nov. 11	KnoxCo.,Ohio	10	08	14
Rice, Isaac(Z-M)	1832	Nov. 12	KnoxCo.,Ohio	10	08	12
Rice, Isaac(Z-M)	1832	Nov. 12	KnoxCo.,Ohio	10	08	12
Rice, James(Z)	1810	Aug. 28	MuskingmCoOh	14	15	05
Rice, John(Y)	1829	Jan. 01	Jeff.Co.,Oh.	04	12	30
Rice, John(Z)	1810	Aug. 28	MuskingmCoOh	14	15	05
Rice, John(Z-M)	1832	June 26	TuscarwsCoOh	02	07	15
Rice, John(Z-M)	1835	Nov. 03	KnoxCo.,Ohio	10	04	24
Rice, John(Z-M)	1835	Nov. 03	KnoxCo.,Ohio	10	04	24
Rice, Sampson(Y)	1832	March 03	Stark Co.,Oh	07	17	25
Rice, William(Z)	1834	Aug. 01	Perry Co.,Oh	14	13	32
Rich, Abraham(Z)	1821	Sept. 04	GuernseyCoOh	08	08	31
Rich, Abraham(Z)	1822	Nov. 16	GuernseyCoOh	08	08	31
Rich, Arbraham(Z)	1836	Jan. 19	GuernseyCoOh	09	08	36
Rich, Daniel(Z)	1832	Sept. 26	GuernseyCoOh	08	08	31
Rich, George(Z)	1811	Aug. 09	Jeff.Co.,Oh.	09	08	35
Rich, George(Z)	1814	Aug. 11	GuernseyCoOh	08	08	30
Rich, George(Z)	1815	Aug. 23	GuernseyCoOh	09	08	35
Rich, Jacob(Z)	1832	Aug. 11	GuernseyCoOh	08	08	02
Rich, John(Z)	1811	Aug. 09	GuernseyCoOh	09	08	25
Richard, Frederick(Z)	1810	Nov. 09	AlleghnyCoPa	05	08	11
Richard, Frederick(Z)	1810	Nov. 09	AlleghnyCoPa	05	08	11
Richard, George(Y)	1833	Aug. 10	Stark Co.,Oh	07	20	06
Richards, Benjamin(Z)	1815	April 04	MuskingmCoOh	09	06	19
Richards, David(Y)	1827	Nov. 28	HarrisonCoOh	05	13	10
Richards, Henry(Z-M)	1824	Jan. 08	CoshoctnCoOh	09	05	03
Richards, James(Z)	1810	Jan. 19	MuskingmCoOh	09	01	21

PURCHASER	YEAR	DATE	RESIDENCE	R	T	S
Richards, James(Z-M)	1833	Oct. 01	HolmesCoOhio	09	08	12
Richards, James(Z-M)	1837	March 14	HolmesCoOhio	09	08	25
Richards, John(Y)	1824	Dec. 22	Stark Co.,Oh	06	16	30
Richards, John(Z-M)	1836	Aug. 26	CoshoctnCoOh	07	04	01
Richards, John(Z-M)	1837	March 14	HolmesCoOhio	09	08	10
Richards, Josiah(Z-M)	1832	March 01	CoshoctnCoOh	07	05	12
Richards, Josiah(Z-M)	1836	Sept. 23	CoshoctnCoOh	07	04	12
Richards, Josiah(Z-M)	1836	Sept. 23	CoshoctnCoOh	07	04	10
Richards, Michael(Z-M)	1834	Feb. 01	TuscarwsCoOh	01	09	05
Richards, Thomas(Z)	1812	May 01	MuskingmCoOh	09	01	20
Richards, Thomas(Z)	1815	June 15	MuskingmCoOh	10	02	17
Richards, Tounson(Y)	1835	May 30	ColumbanCoOh	05	16	32
Richards, William(Z)	1816	May 02	CoshoctnCoOh	08	05	17
Richardson, ? (Z)	1815	Dec. 18	GuernseyCoOh	10	08	07
Richardson, Alpheus(Z-M)	1832	May 22	MuskingmCoOh	05	03	10
Richardson, Benj'm.(Z)	1824	Sept. 16	Morgan Co,Oh	11	10	05
Richardson, D.(Z)	1816	April 29	MuskingmCoOh	05	03	09
Richardson, David(Z-M)	1837	Nov. 22	MuskingmCoOh	05	03	02
Richardson, Edward(Y)	1831	Sept. 21	HarrisonCoOh	07	15	21
Richardson, Elijah(Z-M)	1831	July 30	CoshoctnCoOh	08	06	13
Richardson, Elijah(Z-M)	1838	June 08	CoshoctnCoOh	08	06	08
Richardson, Geo. W.(Z-M)	1828	Nov. 21	LickingCo,Oh	10	04	25
Richardson, Geo.(Z)	1815	Feb. 20	TuscarwsCoOh	04	09	18
Richardson, George(Z)	1808	Aug. 08	FayetteCo,Pa	04	09	23
Richardson, J.(Z)	1814	April 25	TuscarwsCoOh	04	09	18
Richardson, James(Z)	1808	Nov. 16	FayetteCo,Pa	04	08	03
Richardson, James(Z)	1809	Feb. 08	TuscarwsCoOh	04	09	23
Richardson, James(Z)	1810	Jan. 12	TuscarwsCoOh	04	09	23
Richardson, James(Z)	1815	Feb. 20	TuscarwsCoOh	04	09	18
Richardson, Jesse(Z-M)	1836	Jan. 12	MuskingmCoOh	05	03	10
Richardson, Jno.(Y)	1828	April 16	HarrisonCoOh	05	12	35
Richardson, John(Z)	1836	Nov. 29	CarrollCo,Oh	14	12	26
Richardson, Jos.(Z-M)	1832	Jan. 16	CoshoctnCoOh	07	05	04
Richardson, Joseph(Z)	1827	Nov. 05	LancastrCoPa	12	10	23
Richardson, Joseph(Z-M)	1825	April 01	LickingCo,Oh	10	04	25
Richardson, Joseph(Z-M)	1832	Oct. 01	LickingCo,Oh	10	04	25
Richardson, Joseph(Z-M)	1832	Oct. 22	LickingCo,Oh	10	04	16
Richardson, Joseph(Z-M)	1835	Aug. 18	CoshoctnCoOh	07	05	03
Richardson, Joseph(Z-M)	1835	Aug. 18	CoshoctnCoOh	07	05	03
Richardson, Martin(Z-M)	1835	May 09	MuskingmCoOh	05	03	09
Richardson, Martin(Z-M)	1837	Jan. 13	MuskingmCoOh	05	03	10
Richardson, Martin(Z-M)	1838	May 23	MuskingmCoOh	05	03	10
Richardson, R.(Z)	1816	April 29	MuskingmCoOh	05	03	09
Richardson, Sam'l.(Z)	1828	July 03	Morgan Co,Oh	12	10	23
Richardson, Thoma(Z-M)	1821	May 09	TuscarwsCoOh	04	09	14
Richardson, William(Z)	1834	Sept. 16	MuskingmCoOh	14	14	20
Richardson, William(Z)	1811	Aug. 08	MuskingmCoOh	05	01	24
Richarees, Thomas(Z)	1808	Feb. 29	FayetteCo,Pa	10	08	06
Richart, Philip(Y)	1826	Sept. 15	Stark Co.,Oh	09	11	25
Richcreek, Humphrey(Z-M)	1832	April 25	MuskingmCoOh	07	05	08
Richcreek, Jefferson(Z-M)	1831	Nov. 25	MuskingmCoOh	07	05	20
Richcreek, Jefferson(Z-M)	1831	Nov. 28	CoshoctnCoOh	07	05	20
Richcreek, Jefferson(Z-M)	1833	April 30	MuskingmCoOh	07	05	18
Richcreek, John(Z-M)	1832	April 25	MuskingmCoOh	07	05	08
Riche, Jacob(Y)	1826	Dec. 05	Stark Co.,Oh	06	18	17
Richerson, John(Z-M)	1836	Aug. 18	CoshoctnCoOh	08	07	07
Richeson, William(Z-M)	1832	Dec. 15	GuernseyCoOh	01	01	20
Richey, George(Z)	1811	Oct. 19	GuernseyCoOh	14	14	28
Richey, George(Z)	1815	April 24	MuskingmCoOh	12	13	12
Richey, J.(Z)	1814	June 28	MuskingmCoOh	14	16	03
Richey, John(Z)	1827	Dec. 07	HarrisonCoOh	11	10	28
Richey, Thomas(Z)	1810	March 01	GuernseyCoOh	08	08	07
Richey, Thos.(Z)	1831	June 03	GuernseyCoOh	08	08	06
Richie, Thomas(Z)	1810	March 01	GuernseyCoOh	08	08	07
Richman, John(Z-?)	1838	June 13	TuscarwsCoOh	?	?	?
Richy, J.(Z)	1814	April 12	ZanesvilleOh	14	16	03
Rickabaugh, David(Z-M)	1824	June 07	HolmesCoOhio	06	09	14
Rickart, George(Z-M)	1832	Nov. 06	TuscarwsCoOh	03	09	02
Rickebaugh, David(Z-M)	1829	Feb. 12	HolmesCoOhio	06	09	14

PURCHASER	YEAR	DATE	RESIDENCE	R	T	S
Ricker, Elipha(Z)	1817	Jan. 15	ZanesvilleOh	15	17	02
Ricker, Wentworth(Z)	1811	Nov. 21	WashngtnCoOh	08	05	07
Ricket, Gasper(Z-M)	1834	Sept. 20	CarrollCo,Oh	08	07	22
Ricket, Gasper(Z-M)	1834	Sept. 20	CarrollCo,Oh	08	06	09
Rickets, Philemon(Z-M)	1828	Aug. 05	TuscarwsCoOh	01	09	19
Ricketts, John(Z-M)	1832	June 04	CoshoctnCoOh	04	06	22
Ricketts, Philemon(Z-M)	1827	July 04	TuscarwsCoOh	01	09	19
Rickey, Benj.(Z)	1830	Dec. 16	Morgan Co,Oh	10	06	07
Rickey, Benjamin(Z)	1836	Jan. 28	Morgan Co,Oh	10	06	08
Rickey, Brice(Z-M)	1836	Jan. 07	HarrisonCoOh	03	05	13
Rickey, George(Z)	1812	Nov. 23	MuskingmCoOh	05	01	04
Rickey, George(Z)	1812	Nov. 23	MuskingmCoOh	05	01	07
Rickey, Henry(Z-M)	1834	July 28	CoshoctnCoOh	07	05	10
Rickey, John(Z)	1830	April 15	BelmontCo,Oh	11	10	12
Rickey, John(Z)	1835	Sept. 11	Morgan Co,Oh	10	06	07
Rickey, John(Z)	1836	Jan. 07	Morgan Co,Oh	10	07	15
Rickey, John(Z)	1836	Jan. 28	Morgan Co,Oh	10	07	10
Riddle, George(Z)	1837	April 03	Morgan Co,Oh	08	06	33
Riddle, George(Z)	1837	April 03	Morgan Co,Oh	08	06	33
Riddle, George(Z)	1837	April 03	Morgan Co,Oh	08	06	28
Riddle, Michael(Z)	1836	Nov. 24	HolmesCoOhio	08	07	32
Riddle, Moses(Z)	1837	April 07	MonroeCo.,Oh	08	06	10
Ridenbaugh, George(Y)	1827	Oct. 23	Jeff.Co.,Oh.	05	13	13
Ridenour, David(Z-M)	1833	March 16	TuscarwsCoOh	04	07	23
Ridenour, David(Z-M)	1835	May 04	TuscarwsCoOh	04	07	23
Rider, Adam(Z)	1825	Oct. 05	MuskingmCoOh	14	14	22
Rider, Adam(Z)	1825	Oct. 05	MuskingmCoOh	14	14	22
Rider, Adam(Z)	1832	Oct. 16	MuskingmCoOh	14	14	21
Rider, Adam(Z)	1816	March 05	MuskingmCoOh	14	14	14
Rider, Adam(Z)	1817	Aug. 07	MuskingmCoOh	14	14	11
Ridge, Joseph(Z-M)	1827	Oct. 20	FayetteCo,Pa	01	06	19
Ridgeley, Charles(Z)	1814	Nov. 22	MuskingmCoOh	15	16	23
Ridgely, A.(Z)	1815	May 12	Brooke CoVir	11	11	19
Ridgely, A.(Z)	1816	Feb. 17	Ohio Co.,Vir	12	11	25
Ridgeway, Bazil(Z-M)	1829	Oct. 12	BelmontCo,Oh	06	03	21
Ridgeway, Bazil(Z-M)	1829	Oct. 12	BelmontCo,Oh	06	03	22
Ridgway, Jonathan(Z-M)	1836	Aug. 29	BelmontCo,Oh	03	07	02
Ridgway, Jonathan(Z-M)	1836	Aug. 29	BelmontCo,Oh	03	07	02
Ridinger, Michael(Z)	1812	Oct. 15	YorkCo.,Penn	02	08	17
Ridinour, Daniel(Z-M)	1826	Nov. 07	HarrisonCoOh	03	07	18
Riegal, Benj'n.(Y)	1823	Jan. 13	TrumbullCoOh	04	17	10
Rig, Gilbert(Z-M)	1825	July 11	LickingCo,Oh	10	04	12
Rigby, Aaron(Y)	1821	Dec. 11	ColumbanCoOh	04	15	22
Rigby, Augustus(Y)	1829	Oct. 19	HarrisonCoOh	06	14	03
Rigden, John F.(Z-M)	1838	Nov. 12	GuernseyCoOh	04	03	06
Rigdon, Stephen(Z)	1817	Oct. 24	GuernseyCoOh	10	09	08
Rigel, Jacob Jr.(Y)	1821	Aug. 03	HarrisonCoOh	07	15	31
Riggal, Jacob(Y)	1830	Sept. 14	HarrisonCoOh	06	12	29
Riggle, Adam(Z-M)	1827	Feb. 01	TuscarwsCoOh	01	08	01
Riggle, Daniel(Z-M)	1831	April 01	TuscarwsCoOh	01	09	21
Riggle, David(Z-M)	1824	April 24	TuscarwsCoOh	01	08	01
Riggle, David(Z-M)	1827	Nov. 28	TuscarwsCoOh	01	08	01
Riggle, Geo.(Z-M)	1833	March 11	CoshoctnCoOh	05	07	25
Riggle, George(Z-M)	1832	Dec. 17	CoshoctnCoOh	05	07	24
Riggle, Michael(Z-M)	1831	Oct. 10	CoshoctnCoOh	04	06	01
Riggle, Michael(Z-M)	1832	June 08	CoshoctnCoOh	04	06	01
Riggle, Michael(Z-M)	1835	April 01	CoshoctnCoOh	04	06	01
Riggle, Philip(Y)	1829	April 02	TuscarwsCoOh	07	15	32
Riggle, Philip(Z)	1827	March 08	TuscarwsCoOh	01	08	10
Riggle, Philip(Z-M)	1831	July 06	TuscarwsCoOh	01	08	10
Riggs, Daniel(Z)	1836	Jan. 08	GuernseyCoOh	09	08	12
Riggs, Evan(Z-M)	1836	Dec. 02	GuernseyCoOh	02	01	05
Riggs, John L.(Z-M)	1836	March 15	HolmesCoOhio	09	09	13
Riggs, John Levi(Z-M)	1835	Dec. 01	HolmesCoOhio	09	09	18
Riggs, John Levi(Z-M)	1835	Dec. 01	HolmesCoOhio	09	09	14
Riggs, Joseph T.(Z-M)	1828	Feb. 07	GuernseyCoOh	02	01	12
Rightmire, James(Z)	1807	June 25	MuskingmCoOh	10	07	24
Rightmire, William(Z-M)	1836	Oct. 04	KnoxCo.,Ohio	10	07	17
Rihie, Geo.(Z)	1808	April 25	Jeff.Co.,Oh.	08	08	06

PURCHASER	YEAR	DATE	RESIDENCE	R	T	S
Rihie, Geo.(Z)	1808	April 25	Jeff.Co.,Oh.	08	08	06
Rihie, Jno.(Z)	1808	April 25	Jeff.Co.,Oh.	08	08	06
Rihie, Jno.(Z)	1808	April 25	Jeff.Co.,Oh.	08	08	06
Rikey, Benj'm.(Z)	1835	Aug. 14	Morgan Co,Oh	10	06	07
Rile, James(Z)	1815	Aug. 26	BelmontCo,Oh	09	06	08
Riley, Alexander(Y)	1829	Dec. 19	Jeff.Co.,Oh.	06	13	06
Riley, Frederick(Z)	1836	Sept. 14	Morgan Co,Oh	15	14	30
Riley, Hugh(Z)	1815	Oct. 19	SomersetCoPa	13	09	17
Riley, James M. B.(Z)	1836	Sept. 20	Morgan Co,Oh	15	14	31
Riley, Job(Z-M)	1840	July 07	WarwickCoRIs	09	07	11
Riley, John(Y)	1826	March 29	Jeff.Co.,Oh.	06	14	03
Riley, John(Y)	1827	April 04	Jeff.Co.,Oh.	06	14	03
Riley, John(Z)	1831	May 17	Perry Co.,Oh	15	15	31
Riley, John(Z)	1832	Nov. 12	Perry Co.,Oh	15	15	30
Riley, John(Z)	1834	Feb. 17	Perry Co.,Oh	15	15	30
Riley, Moses(Y)	1826	May 01	HarrisonCoOh	07	12	36
Riley, Nathan(Z)	1826	Jan. 13	GuernseyCoOh	09	07	24
Riley, Reuben(Z)	1836	Sept. 14	Morgan Co,Oh	15	14	30
Riley, Reubin(Z)	1836	Sept. 19	Morgan Co,Oh	15	14	31
Riley, Ric'd.(Z)	1836	June 18	Morgan Co,Oh	13	09	31
Riley, Richard(Z)	1833	June 25	Morgan Co,Oh	13	09	31
Riley, Richard(Z-M)	1828	Oct. 23	CoshoctnCoOh	09	04	07
Riley, Richard(Z-M)	1832	March 22	CoshoctnCoOh	10	04	11
Riley, Smith(Z)	1833	Sept. 05	Perry Co.,Oh	15	15	22
Riley, Thomas Junr.(Y)	1828	Feb. 06	Jeff.Co.,Oh.	05	13	07
Riley, Wm.(Z-M)	1836	Sept. 10	HarrisonCoOh	02	06	13
Rine, Henry(Z)	1815	Dec. 04	BedfordCo,Pa	08	05	25
Rine, Henry(Z)	1815	Dec. 04	BedfordCo,Pa	08	05	25
Rine, William(Z-M)	1830	March 01	CoshoctnCoOh	09	05	17
Rinehard, David(Z)	1813	Nov. 24	TuscarwsCoOh	04	08	20
Rinehard, Michael(Z)	1813	Nov. 24	TuscarwsCoOh	04	08	11
Rinehard, Philip(Z)	1813	Nov. 24	TuscarwsCoOh	04	08	11
Rinehard, Philip(Z)	1813	Nov. 24	TuscarwsCoOh	04	08	20
Rinehardt, Philip(Z-M)	1829	June 17	TuscarwsCoOh	03	08	24
Rinehart, Enos(Z)	1832	Nov. 10	MonroeCo.,Oh	08	08	09
Rinehart, John(Z-M)	1835	Nov. 16	TuscarwsCoOh	05	07	01
Rinehart, Michael(Z-M)	1832	Oct. 15	TuscarwsCoOh	03	08	10
Riney, Simon(Z-M)	1822	Dec. 13	OnondagoCoNY	07	07	17
Ringle, Abraham(Y)	1830	Nov. 16	Stark Co.,Oh	06	17	32
Ringle, Adam(Y)	1825	March 28	Stark Co.,Oh	07	17	02
Ringle, David(Y)	1826	April 06	Stark Co.,Oh	07	18	36
Ringlr, David(Y)	1830	Feb. 23	Stark Co.,Oh	06	15	21
Rinker, William(Z)	1836	March 22	Perry Co.,Oh	15	14	32
Ripley, A. S.(Z-M)	1831	Aug. 25	HarrisonCoOh	01	05	22
Ripley, Jacob(Z-M)	1826	Jan. 11	HarrisonCoOh	01	06	19
Ripley, Jacob(Z-M)	1827	Dec. 05	HarrisonCoOh	01	06	19
Ripley, Jacob(Z-M)	1832	June 07	TuscarwsCoOh	01	06	18
Ripley, John Jr.(Z-M)	1826	Feb. 14	GuernseyCoOh	01	06	18
Ripley, Wm. Labden(Z-M)	1832	May 22	GuernseyCoOh	01	05	18
Riplogle, John(Z-M)	1836	Sept. 21	HolmesCoOhio	07	08	15
Riseng, B. F.(Z-M)	1838	March 10	CoshoctnCoOh	09	07	19
Riser, Christian(Z)	1816	April 08	SomersetCoPa	02	07	06
Risher, Abm.(Z-M)	1832	Sept. 03	GuernseyCoOh	02	04	03
Risher, Abm.(Z-M)	1832	Sept. 03	GuernseyCoOh	02	04	03
Risher, Abraham(Z-M)	1831	Oct. 19	GuernseyCoOh	02	04	02
Risher, Henry(Z)	1838	June 28	TuscarwsCoOh	03	05	01
Risher, Henry(Z-M)	1830	Feb. 23	GuernseyCoOh	02	05	20
Risher, Henry(Z-M)	1835	Oct. 02	TuscarwsCoOh	03	05	12
Risher, Henry(Z-M)	1835	Oct. 02	TuscarwsCoOh	03	05	19
Risher, Manasses(Z-M)	1833	May 01	TuscarwsCoOh	02	06	11
Rishstine, Geo.(Z)	1831	Sept. 06	Morgan Co,Oh	11	11	05
Rising, B. F.(Z-M)	1838	March 10	CoshoctnCoOh	09	07	19
Rising, Benj. F.(Z-M)	1838	June 27	CoshoctnCoOh	08	07	19
Rison, John(Z)	1813	Sept. 11	FairfeldCoOh	13	09	26
Rison, Thomas(Z)	1815	April 18	WashngtnCoOh	13	09	24
Rissler, Frederick(Y)	1830	Dec. 15	Stark Co.,Oh	10	01	03
Rissler, Henry(Y)	1833	Feb. 15	Stark Co.,Oh	07	17	25
Rist, Jacob(Z)	1836	June 01	Perry Co.,Oh	15	14	09
Ritcher, John(Z)	1833	July 30	Perry Co.,Oh	14	12	18

PURCHASER	YEAR	DATE	RESIDENCE	R	T	S
Ritcher, John(Z)	1833	July 30	Perry Co.,Oh	14	12	18
Ritchey, J.(Z)	1815	March 21	MuskingmCoOh	13	09	02
Ritchey, John(Y)	1824	Sept. 18	ColumbanCoOh	05	17	15
Ritchey, Welsh(Z)	1814	Feb. 18	MuskingmCoOh	14	16	04
Ritchie, Geo.(Z)	1808	April 25	Jeff.Co.,Oh.	08	08	06
Ritchie, Geo.(Z)	1808	April 25	Jeff.Co.,Oh.	08	08	06
Ritchie, Thos.(Z)	1808	April 25	Jeff.Co.,Oh.	08	08	06
Ritchie, Thos.(Z)	1808	April 25	Jeff.Co.,Oh.	08	08	06
Ritenhour, David(Z-M)	1829	May 16	TuscarwsCoOh	04	07	23
Ritter, Abraham(Y)	1832	April 05	TuscarwsCoOh	07	16	09
Ritter, Abraham(Y)	1833	Feb. 14	CarrollCo,Oh	07	16	19
Ritter, Jacob Senr.(Y)	1824	Dec. 13	MontgmryCoPa	03	12	21
Ritter, Jacob Senr.(Y)	1824	Dec. 13	MontgmryCoPa	04	13	04
Rizer, Henry(Z)	1836	June 06	Perry Co.,Oh	15	14	13
Rizin, Jacob(Z)	1810	April 14	KnoxCo.,Ohio	10	07	04
Rlussel, John(Y)	1834	Sept. 01	Jeff.Co.,Oh.	03	11	12
Roach, Daniel(Z)	1835	Oct. 02	Morgan Co,Oh	09	05	34
Roach, Frederick(Z)	1835	June 27	GuernseyCoOh	08	07	13
Roach, Hambleton(Z)	1836	May 12	Morgan Co,Oh	09	05	34
Roach, John(Y)	1832	Sept. 03	Jeff.Co.,Oh.	03	11	17
Roach, William(Y)	1833	Nov. 18	CarrollCo,Oh	03	11	17
Roach, William(Z)	1834	Sept. 22	Morgan Co,Oh	09	05	27
Roach, William(Z)	1836	Jan. 06	Morgan Co,Oh	09	05	34
Roach, William(Z)	1836	May 12	Morgan Co,Oh	09	05	34
Roach, Wm.(Z)	1831	July 18	Morgan Co,Oh	09	05	34
Road, George(Y)	1829	May 19	Stark Co.,Oh	09	12	30
Road, George(Y)	1829	June 15	Stark Co.,Oh	10	02	36
Road, George(Y)	1829	June 29	Stark Co.,Oh	09	11	04
Road, George(Y)	1830	July 13	Stark Co.,Oh	10	02	36
Roads, Geo. T.(Z)	1832	June 23	Morgan Co,Oh	09	07	01
Roatch, Laurence(Y)	1828	Sept. 10	ColumbanCoOh	04	13	28
Robart, John(Z-M)	1833	April 12	TuscarwsCoOh	03	09	22
Robb, And'w.(Z-M)	1821	June 11	GuernseyCoOh	03	02	01
Robb, Andrew(Z-M)	1821	Sept. 09	GuernseyCoOh	03	02	01
Robb, Daniel(Z)	1814	June 21	GuernseyCoOh	01	02	17
Robb, Hamilton(Z)	1816	Dec. 30	BeaverCo.,Pa	05	02	20
Robb, James(Z-M)	1828	Nov. 27	GuernseyCoOh	03	04	16
Robb, John(Z)	1815	Oct. 19	AlleghnyCoPa	04	02	06
Robb, Joshua(Z)	1816	Feb. 03	GuernseyCoOh	01	02	16
Robb, William(Z)	1804	Dec. 31	WestmrldCoPa	14	15	10
Robbins, Jno.(Z-M)	1832	Feb. 22	HolmesCoOhio	07	08	06
Robbins, John(Z)	1828	Feb. 05	GuernseyCoOh	10	09	11
Robbins, John(Z-M)	1830	July 30	GuernseyCoOh	03	01	23
Robbins, Joseph(Y)	1824	June 04	ColumbanCoOh	04	12	30
Robe, David(Z-M)	1829	Dec. 16	GuernseyCoOh	02	01	19
Robe, Josiah(Z)	1807	May 07	MuskingmCoOh	01	02	02
Robert, Benjamin(Z)	1834	Feb. 18	Morgan Co,Oh	09	07	29
Robert, Lewis(Z-M)	1836	Jan. 25	GuernseyCoOh	03	03	07
Robert, Paul(Z-M)	1822	March 04	GuernseyCoOh	03	02	04
Robert, Paul(Z-M)	1823	Dec. 27	GuernseyCoOh	03	02	07
Robert, Paul(Z-M)	1834	March 17	GuernseyCoOh	03	01	01
Robert, Paul(Z-M)	1834	March 17	GuernseyCoOh	03	01	01
Roberts, Abner(Z)	1834	Aug. 20	MuskingmCoOh	13	10	03
Roberts, Abraham(Z)	1831	Nov. 16	Perry Co.,Oh	15	14	06
Roberts, Abraham(Z)	1832	Sept. 28	Perry Co.,Oh	15	14	06
Roberts, Amos(Z)	1815	May 31.	DelawareCoPa	15	16	27
Roberts, Benjamin(Z)	1833	Aug. 20	Morgan Co,Oh	09	07	29
Roberts, Charles(Z)	1815	Aug. 05	ZanesvilleOh	06	02	23
Roberts, Charles(Z)	1815	Aug. 05	ZanesvilleOh	06	02	17
Roberts, Charles(Z)	1815	Aug. 16	ZanesvilleOh	06	02	11
Roberts, Charles(Z)	1815	Aug. 16	ZanesvilleOh	06	02	11
Roberts, Charles(Z)	1816	Aug. 31	ZanesvilleOh	12	12	32
Roberts, David J.(Z)	1835	March 12	Morgan Co,Oh	10	06	28
Roberts, David Jones(Z)	1836	Jan. 11	Morgan Co,Oh	10	06	28
Roberts, Ephraim(Z)	1835	Aug. 13	Morgan Co,Oh	11	10	26
Roberts, Ephraim(Z)	1835	Aug. 20	Morgan Co,Ob	11	10	35
Roberts, Ephraim(Z)	1816	Dec. 03	Brooke CoVir	12	12	25
Roberts, Henry(Z)	1836	May 27	MuskingmCoOh	14	13	36
Roberts, Isaac N.(Z-M)	1830	Jan. 15	FayetteCo,Pa	01	05	08

PURCHASER	YEAR	DATE	RESIDENCE	R	T	S
Roberts, John Jr.(Z)	1825	Oct. 29	MonroeCo.,Oh	08	07	28
Roberts, John Jr.(Z)	1833	Nov. 30	WashngtnCoOh	08	05	02
Roberts, John(Z)	1833	April 09	MonroeCo.,Oh	08	07	15
Roberts, John(Z)	1833	Nov. 30	MonroeCo.,Oh	08	07	15
Roberts, John(Z)	1817	July 08	MuskingmCoOh	14	14	08
Roberts, Jonathan(Z-M)	1835	Jan. 12	TuscarwsCoOh	02	06	03
Roberts, Joseph(Z)	1828	Nov. 18	Morgan Co,Oh	13	09	14
Roberts, Rebecca(Z)	1820	July 04	MuskingmCoOh	13	11	22
Roberts, Sam'l. S.(Z)	1817	Oct. 17	Cambridge,Oh	13	09	35
Roberts, William(Z)	1834	Feb. 04	Perry Co.,Oh	14	13	20
Roberts, William(Z)	1836	Dec. 13	Perry Co.,Oh	14	12	03
Roberts, William(Z)	1805	Aug. 13	MuskingmCoOh	05	01	10
Robertson, Daniel(Z)	1836	April 02	GuernseyCoOh	08	07	09
Robertson, Denny(Y)	1824	May 20	Stark Co.,Oh	07	17	07
Robertson, Denny(Y)	1824	May 20	Stark Co.,Oh	07	17	07
Robertson, Denny(Y)	1824	May 20	Stark Co.,Oh	07	07	18
Robertson, James(Y)	1831	June 24	Stark Co.,Oh	07	17	23
Robertson, James(Y)	1831	Oct. 07	Stark Co.,Oh	07	17	12
Robertson, John(Y)	1831	March 12	Stark Co.,Oh	07	17	24
Robertson, John(Y)	1831	March 12	Stark Co.,Oh	07	17	26
Robertson, John(Y)	1832	May 10	Stark Co.,Oh	07	16	18
Robertson, John(Z-M)	1828	Nov. 17	GuernseyCoOh	04	03	11
Robertson, Joseph(Z-M)	1837	Oct. 03	ZanesvilleOh	04	03	09
Robertson, Sal.(Z-M)	1836	Aug. 19	GuernseyCoOh	03	03	06
Robertson, Sam'l.(Z-M)	1828	Dec. 01	GuernseyCoOh	03	04	16
Robertson, Sam'l.(Z-M)	1831	Oct. 18	GuernseyCoOh	03	03	20
Robertson, Sam'l.(Z-M)	1831	Dec. 28	GuernseyCoOh	03	02	20
Robertson, William(Y)	1826	Jan. 25	Stark Co.,Oh	07	17	24
Robertson, William(Y)	1830	Sept. 18	Stark Co.,Oh	07	17	24
Robertson, William(Z)	1810	March 19	Jeff.Co.,Oh.	10	07	06
Robertson, William(Z)	1815	April 26	CoshoctnCoOh	04	06	18
Robertson, William(Z)	1816	Jan. 22	MuskingmCoOh	11	13	28
Robertson, William(Z)	1816	Jan. 22	MuskingmCoOh	11	13	28
Robertson, Wm.(Z-M)	1830	June 10	GuernseyCoOh	01	05	22
Robertson, Wm.(Z-M)	1830	June 10	GuernseyCoOh	01	05	23
Robeson, John W.(Z-M)	1836	Jan. 13	KnoxCo.,Ohio	10	07	17
Robinett, Abijah(Z-M)	1829	Jan. 01	TuscarwsCoOh	01	06	09
Robinett, Joseph Jr.(Z)	1834	Sept. 05	Perry Co.,Oh	14	13	26
Robinett, Joseph(Z)	1836	Feb. 23	Perry Co.,Oh	14	13	26
Robins, Abraham(Y)	1829	April 16	ColumbanCoOh	05	15	02
Robins, Clayton(Y)	1834	May 12	CarrollCo,Oh	05	15	04
Robins, John Thos.(Z)	1836	Feb. 03	GuernseyCoOh	09	08	19
Robins, John Thos.(Z)	1836	Feb. 03	GuernseyCoOh	09	08	30
Robins, John(Y)	1832	Jan. 23	Jeff.Co.,Oh.	05	13	05
Robins, John(Z)	1821	Jan. 16	GuernseyCoOh	10	09	12
Robins, John(Z)	1822	Nov. 06	GuernseyCoOh	10	09	12
Robins, John(Z)	1824	Sept. 29	GuernseyCoOh	10	09	12
Robins, John(Z)	1827	Aug. 01	GuernseyCoOh	10	09	11
Robins, John(Z)	1827	Aug. 01	GuernseyCoOh	10	09	11
Robins, John(Z)	1829	March 02	GuernseyCoOh	10	09	02
Robins, John(Z)	1832	April 05	GuernseyCoOh	09	08	18
Robins, John(Z)	1831	July 06	GuernseyCoOh	10	09	02
Robins, John(Z)	1831	Aug. 31	GuernseyCoOh	10	09	02
Robins, John(Z)	1833	Aug. 09	GuernseyCoOh	10	09	13
Robins, John(Z)	1834	Oct. 27	GuernseyCoOh	10	09	10
Robins, John(Z)	1835	Jan. 06	GuernseyCoOh	10	09	13
Robins, John(Z)	1836	Jan. 20	GuernseyCoOh	10	09	01
Robins, John(Z)	1835	Sept. 04	GuernseyCoOh	10	09	01
Robins, John(Z)	1836	June 23	GuernseyCoOh	10	09	02
Robins, John(Z)	1807	Dec. 24	MuskingmCoOh	09	08	07
Robins, John(Z-M)	1835	Sept. 04	GuernseyCoOh	03	01	23
Robins, Peter Daniel(Z)	1835	Dec. 14	GuernseyCoOh	09	08	20
Robinson, Aaron(Y)	1828	Aug. 26	HarrisonCoOh	06	11	05
Robinson, Adam(Y)	1830	March 20	Stark Co.,Oh	06	16	33
Robinson, Alexander(Z)	1815	May 24	Brooke CoVir	01	03	24
Robinson, Arthur S.(Z)	1832	July 20	ZanesvilleOh	14	14	18
Robinson, Arthur S.(Z)	1832	July 20	ZanesvilleOh	14	14	18
Robinson, B.(Z)	1816	Nov. 11	CoshoctnCoOh	09	05	13
Robinson, Benj.(Z-M)	1827	Jan. 09	LickingCo,Oh	11	01	10

PURCHASER	YEAR	DATE	RESIDENCE	R	T	S
Robinson, Benjamin(Z)	1806	Jan. 13	HarrisonCoVa	09	03	25
Robinson, Benjamin(Z)	1806	Jan. 13	HarrisonCoVa	09	03	25
Robinson, Benjamin(Z)	1810	Sept. 09	MuskingmCoOh	06	04	08
Robinson, Caleb(Z)	1836	July 13	BelmontCo,Oh	08	05	24
Robinson, Caleb(Z)	1836	Oct. 01	BelmontCo,Oh	08	05	24
Robinson, Caleb(Z)	1839	Aug. 16	WashngtnCoOh	08	05	23
Robinson, David(Y)	1822	Oct. 01	ColumbanCoOh	05	14	12
Robinson, David(Y)	1822	Dec. 18	ColumbanCoOh	04	13	18
Robinson, David(Y)	1827	April 16	ColumbanCoOh	04	13	17
Robinson, David(Y)	1828	June 02	ColumbanCoOh	04	13	23
Robinson, Henry(Z-M)	1825	Aug. 23	GuernseyCoOh	02	01	03
Robinson, Israel(Z)	1809	March 13	BrookCo.,Vir	11	13	17
Robinson, Israel(Z)	1810	Dec. 13	MuskingmCoOh	11	13	08
Robinson, Israel(Z)	1814	March 02	?	11	13	08
Robinson, Jacob(Z)	1811	Jan. 02	KnoxCo.,Ohio	10	07	14
Robinson, Jacob(Z-M)	1836	June 29	ColumbanCoOh	08	06	10
Robinson, Jacob(Z-M)	1836	June 29	ColumbanCoOh	08	06	09
Robinson, Jacob(Z-M)	1836	June 29	ColumbanCoOh	08	06	09
Robinson, Jacob(Z-M)	1836	Aug. 01	ColumbanCoOh	08	06	11
Robinson, James(Y)	1823	Jan. 01	TrumbullCoOh	04	13	25
Robinson, James(Y)	1823	April 28	ColumbanCoOh	04	13	25
Robinson, James(Y)	1828	May 01	ColumbanCoOh	04	13	25
Robinson, James(Y)	1831	Aug. 26	ColumbanCoOh	04	13	20
Robinson, James(Y)	1833	Aug. 29	TuscarwsCoOh	07	14	29
Robinson, James(Y)	1833	Aug. 29	TuscarwsCoOh	07	11	28
Robinson, James(Z)	1824	Aug. 28	Morgan Co,Oh	11	13	21
Robinson, James(Z)	1825	Sept. 10	Morgan Co,Oh	10	09	21
Robinson, James(Z)	1828	June 21	Morgan Co,Oh	10	06	06
Robinson, James(Z)	1815	March 15	WashCo.,Penn	02	02	23
Robinson, James(Z-M)	1827	Jan. 17	GuernseyCoOh	02	03	06
Robinson, James(Z-M)	1832	May 26	GuernseyCoOh	02	03	07
Robinson, James(Z-M)	1832	Nov. 12	CoshoctnCoOh	06	04	10
Robinson, James(Z-M)	1832	Nov. 26	CoshoctnCoOh	06	04	09
Robinson, James(Z-M)	1835	Aug. 21	GuernseyCoOh	02	03	07
Robinson, John(Y)	1831	Aug. 26	ColumbanCoOh	04	13	20
Robinson, John(Z)	1811	May 13	MuskingmCoOh	06	01	05
Robinson, John(Z-M)	1832	March 22	GuernseyCoOh	02	01	07
Robinson, Joseph(Z-M)	1833	Jan. 12	HarrisonCoOh	03	07	17
Robinson, Joseph(Z-M)	1833	Oct. 04	KnoxCo.,Ohio	11	08	19
Robinson, Lucy(Z-M)	1838	April 24	CoshoctnCoOh	08	07	15
Robinson, Robert(Z-M)	1835	Oct. 03	BristlCoMass	08	07	06
Robinson, Robert(Z-M)	1835	Oct. 03	BristlCoMass	08	07	15
Robinson, Robt. Sulliven(Z-M)	1836	Sept. 21	HolmesCoOhio	07	08	22
Robinson, Samuel(Z)	1808	Oct. 12	AlleghnyCoPa	14	15	08
Robinson, Sol'm.(Z)	1815	Jan. 13	KnoxCo.,Ohio	10	07	15
Robinson, Solomon(Z)	1810	Sept. 05	KnoxCo.,Ohio	10	07	06
Robinson, Thomp'n. A.(Z)	1832	Jan. 26	CoshoctnCoOh	10	08	17
Robinson, Will'm. Junr.(Z)	1815	Dec. 25	MuskingmCoOh	14	14	17
Robinson, William(Y)	1832	June 08	HarrisonCoOh	05	11	27
Robinson, William(Z)	1805	Aug. 13	MuskingmCoOh	05	04	24
Robinson, William(Z)	1807	March 27	MuskingmCoOh	06	04	13
Robinson, William(Z)	1807	March 27	MuskingmCoOh	06	04	08
Robinson, William(Z)	1807	March 27	MuskingmCoOh	06	04	03
Robinson, William(Z)	1811	Dec. 26	CoshoctnCoOh	06	04	02
Robinson, William(Z)	1813	May 01	CoshoctnCoOh	05	04	20
Robinson, William(Z)	1815	Feb. 15	CoshoctnCoOh	06	04	02
Robinson, William(Z)	1815	Feb. 15	CoshoctnCoOh	06	04	02
Robinson, William(Z)	1815	March 15	WashCo.,Penn	02	02	19
Robinson, William(Z)	1816	June 06	LickingCo,Oh	11	04	10
Robinson, Wm. D.(Z)	1832	July 20	ZanesvilleOh	14	14	18
Robinson, Wm. D.(Z)	1832	July 20	ZanesvilleOh	14	14	18
Robinson, Wm.(Z)	1833	Oct. 05	MuskingmCoOh	11	12	10
Robinson, Wm.(Z)	1815	Jan. 13	KnoxCo.,Ohio	10	07	15
Robinson, Wm.(Z-M)	1840	July 07	BrisleCoMass	07	07	11
Robinson, Wm.(Z-M)	1840	July 07	BrisleCoMass	09	07	11
Robinson, Wm.(Z-M)	1840	July 07	BrisleCoMass	08	07	15
Robison, Job(Y)	1828	Aug. 25	HarrisonCoOh	06	11	36
Robison, Joseph(Z-M)	1835	March 09	KnoxCo.,Ohio	11	08	20
Robison, Thomas(Z)	1822	June 08	WashCo.,Penn	11	10	11

PURCHASER	YEAR	DATE	RESIDENCE	R	T	S
Robison, Thomas(Z)	1822	June 08	WashCo.,Penn	11	10	11
Robison, Thomas(Z)	1822	June 08	WashCo.,Penn	11	10	01
Roblins, John(Z)	1808	Feb. 01	MuskingmCoOh	10	09	12
Roby, Hanson Walker(Y)	1834	Feb. 07	TuscarwsCoOh	07	14	30
Roby, James(Y)	1821	Aug. 06	RuscarwsCoOh	07	14	30
Roby, John(Z)	1838	Nov. 20	BelmontCo,Oh	08	06	20
Roby, John(Z)	1838	Nov. 20	BelmontCo,Oh	08	06	21
Roby, Joseph(Y)	1832	Feb. 06	Jeff.Co.,Oh.	07	14	01
Roby, Leonard(Y)	1832	Feb. 06	TuscarwsCoOh	07	14	07
Roby, William(Y)	1832	Jan. 23	HarrisonCoOh	06	12	35
Rockhill, Samuel(Y)	1822	April 13	ColumbanCoOh	06	19	34
Rockhille, David(Y)	1820	Nov. 16	Stark Co.,Oh	06	19	26
Rodeback, Smith(Z-M)	1833	Feb. 05	LickingCo,Oh	11	03	23
Rodecker, Morres(Z-M)	1837	Sept. 13	ZanesvilleOh	06	04	23
Roder, Jno. M.(Z-M)	1835	Dec. 23	TuscarwsCoOh	01	06	22
Roder, John Adam(Z-M)	1832	Aug. 20	BelmontCo,Oh	01	06	22
Roder, John M.(Z-M)	1833	Aug. 19	TuscarwsCoOh	01	06	23
Rodereck, Lewis(Z-M)	1826	Aug. 25	CoshoctnCoOh	05	04	23
Roderick, John(Z-M)	1833	June 04	TuscarwsCoOh	02	06	13
Roderick, Lewis A.(Z-M)	1833	Aug. 06	CoshoctnCoOh	06	04	12
Roderick, Zale(Z-M)	1825	Sept. 19	CoshoctnCoOh	06	04	19
Rodgers, James(Y)	1829	March 17	ColumbanCoOh	03	13	19
Rodgers, John(Z)	1836	March 21	Perry Co.,Oh	14	12	29
Rodgers, John(Z)	1836	June 28	Perry Co.,Oh	14	12	32
Rodgers, John(Z-M)	1838	Jan. 11	GuernseyCoOh	03	04	07
Rodgers, John(Z-M)	1838	Jan. 11	GuernseyCoOh	03	04	07
Rodgers, John(Z-M)	1838	Feb. 02	GuernseyCoOh	03	04	06
Rodgers, Joseph Jnr.(Z)	1836	Nov. 30	Perry Co.,Oh	15	14	12
Rodgers, Joseph(Z)	1830	Nov. 17	Perry Co.,Oh	14	12	18
Rodgers, Joseph(Z)	1835	Jan. 12	AthensCoOhio	15	14	13
Rodgers, Joseph(Z)	1835	Jan. 12	AthensCoOhio	14	12	18
Rodgers, Joseph(Z)	1836	Dec. 05	Perry Co.,Oh	15	14	12
Rodgers, Mich'l.(Y)	1824	Aug. 03	BelmontCo,Oh	04	06	19
Rodgers, William(Y)	1825	Aug. 27	ColumbanCoOh	06	18	18
Rodinghouse, David(Y)	1829	Aug. 24	Jeff.Co.,Oh.	04	12	18
Rodman, Joseph(Z-M)	1824	May 11	MuskingmCoOh	09	01	18
Rodney, John(Z-M)	1831	Sept. 14	CoshoctnCoOh	04	06	19
Rodney, John(Z-M)	1835	Sept. 12	CoshoctnCoOh	04	06	19
Roe, David S.(Z)	1836	June 17	MonroeCo.,Oh	08	06	02
Roe, David(Z)	1835	Dec. 31	MonroeCo.,Oh	08	06	02
Roe, Jesse(Z-M)	1821	Jan. 02	MuskingmCoOh	06	03	14
Roe, Jesse(Z-M)	1821	Feb. 14	MuskingmCoOh	06	03	14
Rogan, James(Z)	1832	Dec. 28	MuskingmCoOh	15	15	26
Rogan, James(Z)	1832	Dec. 28	MuskingmCoOh	15	15	26
Rogers, Edward(Y)	1824	Dec. 02	WashCo.,Penn	03	13	19
Rogers, Jacob(Z)	1832	April 04	Morgan Co,Oh	12	09	12
Rogers, John(Y)	1828	Aug. 13	ColumbanCoOh	03	13	31
Rogers, John(Y)	1828	Sept. 29	Stark Co.,Oh	06	16	31
Rogers, John(Z)	1816	July 22	MuskingmCoOh	12	10	08
Rogers, Joseph(Y)	1831	July 05	ColumbanCoOh	03	13	30
Rogers, Lewis(Z)	1832	Oct. 05	Perry Co.,Oh	15	15	22
Rogers, Susannah(Z)	1815	Nov. 21	MuskingmCoOh	12	10	08
Rogers, William(Z)	1815	Dec. 19	LickingCo,Oh	11	01	09
Rogers, Wm.(Y)	1824	May 17	ColumbanCoOh	01	08	21
Rogers, Wm.(Y)	1824	May 17	ColumbanCoOh	01	08	21
Rogers, Wm.(Y)	1824	May 18	ColumbanCoOh	04	15	22
Rohan, John(Z)	1824	May 10	Perry Co.,Oh	14	14	30
Rohrbaugh, Christian(Y)	1830	March 27	Stark Co.,Oh	10	02	13
Roider, Adam(Z)	1810	Jan. 16	MuskingmCoOh	14	14	10
Rokely, Samuel(Y)	1824	May 19	SteubenvleOh	05	07	02
Rokely, Samuel(Y)	1824	May 19	SteubenvleOh	05	07	02
Rolen, Conrad(Z)	1817	April 18	LoudonCo,Vir	06	03	19
Rolen, Frederick(Z)	1817	April 18	LoudonCo,Vir	06	03	22
Rolen, John(Z)	1817	April 19	LoudonCo,Vir	06	03	21
Rolingson, John(Z-M)	1833	Sept. 12	AlleganyCoPa	02	03	18
Rollings, Thomas(Z-M)	1836	Feb. 02	MuskingmCoOh	06	03	11
Rollins, Geo. W.(Z-M)	1833	Jan. 14	CoshoctnCoOh	07	04	17
Rollins, Jonathan(Z-M)	1828	Sept. 10	BelmontCo,Oh	03	02	06
Rollins, Thos.(Z-M)	1832	Oct. 31	MuskingmCoOh	06	03	20

PURCHASER	YEAR	DATE	RESIDENCE	R	T	S
Rollins, William K.(Z-M)	1827	Aug. 27	CoshoctnCoOh	06	04	23
Rollins, Wm. K.(Z-M)	1831	July 26	CoshoctnCoOh	06	04	03
Rolsten, David(Z-M)	1833	Dec. 23	MuskingmCoOh	06	03	09
Rolston, David(Z-M)	1834	Dec. 16	MuskingmCoOh	06	03	09
Rolston, David(Z-M)	1836	March 14	MuskingmCoOh	06	03	12
Romaine, Marr(Z-M)	1831	Aug. 20	MuskingmCoOh	10	03	15
Romans, Robt.(Z-M)	1832	June 06	HarrisonCoOh	01	05	05
Roof, Jacob Junr.(Z-M)	1824	Sept. 29	KnoxCo.,Ohio	11	08	12
Roof, Jacob(Z-M)	1832	Nov. 07	KnoxCo.,Ohio	11	08	19
Roop, Jacob(Z)	1815	May 31	CoshoctnCoOh	05	07	21
Roop, Jacob(Z)	1816	Jan. 08	CoshoctnCoOh	05	07	04
Roop, Jacob(Z-M)	1828	March 19	CoshoctnCoOh	05	06	25
Roop, Michael(Y)	1830	Nov. 18	Stark Co.,Oh	07	16	08
Roos, Thomas(Z)	1822	May 02	Morgan Co,Oh	12	10	09
Roose, Elisha(Z)	1828	March 12	Morgan Co,Oh	10	06	13
Roose, Elisha(Z)	1816	Dec. 18	GuernseyCoOh	10	09	04
Roose, Frederick Jnr.(Y)	1825	Nov. 16	ColumbanCoOh	06	18	04
Root, Laurel L.(Z-M)	1840	April 02	CoshoctnCoOh	08	07	03
Rooze, Elisha(Z)	1832	Sept. 01	GuernseyCoOh	10	09	04
Rorar, Daniel(Z-M)	1833	Sept. 04	FairfeldCoOh	08	08	02
Rorer, Daniel(Z-M)	1835	Dec. 11	HolmesCoOhio	08	08	24
Rorer, Daniel(Z-M)	1836	Dec. 29	HolmesCoOhio	08	08	24
Rose, Alvah B.(Z)	1836	Jan. 20	Perry Co.,Oh	14	13	22
Rose, Christopher(Z)	1833	Jan. 19	Jeff.Co.,Oh.	11	11	02
Rose, Christopher(Z)	1833	Jan. 19	Jeff.Co.,Oh.	11	11	02
Rose, Daniel(Z)	1829	Aug. 03	MuskingmCoOh	12	13	23
Rose, David(Y)	1829	March 14	ColumbanCoOh	03	13	29
Rose, Elisha(Z)	1816	Dec. 18	GuernseyCoOh	10	09	04
Rose, Ezekiel(Z)	1831	June 16	Perry Co.,Oh	14	13	23
Rose, Ezekiel(Z)	1835	Feb. 11	Perry Co.,Oh	14	13	35
Rose, Ezekiel(Z)	1836	Jan. 20	Perry Co.,Oh	14	13	35
Rose, Ezekiel(Z)	1805	March 25	MuskingmCoOh	14	14	03
Rose, Ezekiel(Z)	1814	Dec. 15	MuskingmCoOh	14	14	03
Rose, Ezekiel(Z)	1816	Sept. 18	MuskingmCoOh	13	09	08
Rose, Ezekiel(Z)	1817	Jan. 09	MuskingmCoOh	14	13	10
Rose, Ezekiel(Z)	1817	Jan. 09	MuskingmCoOh	15	14	24
Rose, Jeremiah(Z)	1815	July 28	MuskingmCoOh	14	14	05
Rose, John T.(Z)	1831	March 23	Perry Co.,Oh	14	13	15
Rose, John Thrap(Z)	1833	Jan. 30	Perry Co.,Oh	14	13	15
Rose, John Thrap(Z)	1836	April 25	Perry Co.,Oh	15	14	27
Rose, John Thrap(Z)	1836	April 25	Perry Co.,Oh	15	14	27
Rose, John(Y)	1832	Oct. 06	GuernseyCoOh	07	09	27
Rose, John(Z-M)	1826	Dec. 07	GuernseyCoOh	04	02	09
Rose, John(Z-M)	1833	April 20	GuernseyCoOh	03	04	14
Rose, John(Z-M)	1835	Dec. 21	GuernseyCoOh	03	04	14
Rose, John(Z-M)	1839	Aug. 22	TuscarwsCoOh	03	05	17
Rose, Robert(Y)	1826	Sept. 01	HarrisonCoOh	06	11	28
Rose, Samuel(Z)	1816	May 02	BedfordCo,Pa	08	05	06
Rose, Thompson(Z-M)	1832	Oct. 15	GuernseyCoOh	03	04	18
Rose, Thompson(Z-M)	1832	Oct. 15	GuernseyCoOh	03	04	13
Rose, William(Z)	1833	April 15	Perry Co.,Oh	14	14	30
Rose, William(Z)	1835	July 04	Perry Co.,Oh	14	13	23
Rose, Wm.(Z)	1835	March 30	Perry Co.,Oh	14	13	23
Rosen, Henry B.(Z-M)	1836	Aug. 29	CoshoctnCoOh	09	07	05
Ross, Benj'n. of Sarah(Z-M)	1832	March 29	WashCo.,Penn	04	07	25
Ross, Caleb(Z-M)	1834	Sept. 16	HarrisonCoOh	03	06	01
Ross, Caleb(Z-M)	1835	March 31	HarrisonCoOh	03	07	22
Ross, Caleb(Z-M)	1835	Oct. 08	HarrisonCoOh	03	07	22
Ross, Caleb(Z-M)	1836	March 17	HarrisonCoOh	03	06	01
Ross, Conard(Z-M)	1836	Feb. 04	LickingCo,Oh	10	04	05
Ross, Daniel Senr.(Z)	1836	Sept. 05	MonroeCo.,Oh	08	05	28
Ross, Daniel(Z-M)	1825	March 28	MuskingmCoOh	06	03	24
Ross, David(Z-M)	1833	Nov. 27	MuskingmCoOh	06	03	10
Ross, David(Z-M)	1835	Nov. 04	MuskingmCoOh	06	03	10
Ross, David(Z-M)	1836	Jan. 13	MuskingmCoOh	06	04	09
Ross, E.(Z)	1815	Jan. 09	FairfeldCoOh	12	10	25
Ross, E.(Z)	1815	Jan. 09	FairfeldCoOh	13	10	08
Ross, Fred.(Z-M)	1831	May 12	TuscarwsCoOh	02	10	15
Ross, George(Z)	1832	Oct. 24	MonroeCo.,Oh	08	07	03

PURCHASER	YEAR	DATE	RESIDENCE	R	T	S
Ross, George(Z)	1833	Dec. 09	MonroeCo.,Oh	08	08	25
Ross, George(Z-M)	1830	May 04	HarrisonCoOh	02	06	12
Ross, George(Z-M)	1830	Sept. 14	HarrisonCoOh	02	06	12
Ross, George(Z-M)	1833	March 22	TuscarwsCoOh	02	06	19
Ross, Gilbert(Z-M)	1835	Nov. 09	MuskingmCoOh	06	03	10
Ross, Israel(Z)	1825	Nov. 11	Morgan Co,Oh	10	06	17
Ross, J.(Z)	1836	June 17	WashngtnCoOh	10	06	29
Ross, James(Z-M)	1827	June 25	GuernseyCoOh	02	04	02
Ross, James(Z-M)	1829	July 31	HolmesCoOhio	07	08	01
Ross, James(Z-M)	1833	Jan. 04	HolmesCoOhio	07	08	01
Ross, James(Z-M)	1833	Jan. 04	HolmesCoOhio	07	08	01
Ross, Jas.(Y)	1828	April 18	Stark Co.,Oh	07	17	27
Ross, John(Y)	1827	July 17	Stark Co.,Oh	07	17	27
Ross, John(Y)	1829	March 17	Stark Co.,Oh	07	17	23
Ross, John(Y)	1831	Nov. 15	Stark Co.,Oh	07	17	23
Ross, John(Z)	1828	Oct. 10	MuskingmCoOh	01	12	22
Ross, John(Z-M)	1832	March 05	GuernseyCoOh	02	04	03
Ross, John(Z-M)	1832	Dec. 17	PutnamCoOhio	08	07	21
Ross, John(Z-M)	1835	Dec. 15	MuskingmCoOh	06	04	09
Ross, John(Z-M)	1835	Dec. 15	MuskingmCoOh	06	04	09
Ross, John(Z-M)	1835	Dec. 16	WashCo.,Penn	05	07	24
Ross, Lyman(Z)	1817	April 16	MuskingmCoOh	06	02	03
Ross, Peter(Y)	1824	May 17	ColumbanCoOh	02	09	27
Ross, Peter(Y)	1829	March 18	ColumbanCoOh	02	09	27
Ross, Peter(Y)	1831	Nov. 17	ColumbanCoOh	02	09	27
Ross, Philemon Jnr.(Z-M)	1837	Jan. 10	HolmesCoOhio	08	08	13
Ross, R.(Z)	1836	June 17	WashngtnCoOh	10	06	29
Ross, Rich'd.(Z)	1825	Nov. 11	Morgan Co,Oh	10	06	17
Ross, Robert(Z)	1814	March 24	?	14	14	34
Ross, Samuel Davis(Z-M)	1832	Oct. 03	KnoxCo.,Ohio	10	05	25
Ross, Samuel(Z-M)	1829	Sept. 19	CoshoctnCoOh	06	06	09
Ross, Samuel(Z-M)	1832	May 29	MuskingmCoOh	06	03	08
Ross, Samuel(Z-M)	1831	Aug. 23	MuskingmCoOh	06	03	08
Ross, Samuel(Z-M)	1835	April 04	KnoxCo.,Ohio	10	05	24
Ross, Samuel(Z-M)	1836	March 11	KnoxCo.,Ohio	10	05	24
Ross, Timothy(Y)	1822	Aug. 19	GreeneCo.,Pa	06	15	18
Ross, Timothy(Z)	1813	Sept. 16	?	11	06	24
Ross, William Jr.(Z-M)	1836	June 06	TuscarwsCoOh	02	07	03
Ross, William(Y)	1824	May 25	HarrisonCoOh	05	11	21
Ross, William(Y)	1834	April 02	ColumbanCoOh	03	12	20
Ross, William(Y)	1834	April 02	ColumbanCoOh	03	12	20
Ross, William(Z)	1816	Aug. 14	TuscarwsCoOh	02	08	17
Ross, William(Z-M)	1832	April 09	KnoxCo.,Ohio	10	05	21
Ross, William(Z-M)	1832	May 26	TuscarwsCoOh	03	05	20
Ross, William(Z-M)	1833	Jan. 15	TuscarwsCoOh	03	05	20
Ross, Wm.(Z-M)	1831	Jan. 27	TuscarwsCoOh	01	05	24
Ross, Wm.(Z-M)	1831	Jan. 27	TuscarwsCoOh	01	05	24
Rossenberger, John(Z-M)	1838	June 02	CoshoctnCoOh	09	08	15
Rosser, Sarah(Z)	1829	Dec. 23	MuskingmCoOh	14	14	01
Rosseter, Thomas(Z)	1828	Nov. 28	GuernseyCoOh	08	08	03
Rotch, Thos.(Y)	1821	Sept. 14	Kend1StkCoOh	09	10	02
Roth, Conrad(Z)	1814	May 21	TuscarwsCoOh	03	10	20
Roth, Conrad(Z)	1814	June 11	TuscarwsCoOh	03	10	11
Roth, Conrad(Z)	1814	June 11	TuscarwsCoOh	03	10	21
Rouanzoun, Sol'n.(Z)	1817	Oct. 21	FredrickCoMd	12	09	09
Roudebugh, Abraham(Y)	1830	Oct. 28	ColumbanCoOh	05	14	03
Roudebugh, Jesse(Y)	1830	Dec. 14	ColumbanCoOh	05	14	15
Roudebush, Tobias(Y)	1821	March 29	ColumbanCoOh	05	14	03
Roudebush, Tobias(Y)	1821	Nov. 14	ColumbanCoOh	05	14	15
Roudebush, Tobias(Y)	1824	Nov. 26	ColumbanCoOh	05	14	15
Roup, Jacob(Z)	1814	April 05	TuscarwsCoOh	05	08	21
Roup, Jacob(Z-M)	1828	April 03	CoshoctnCoOh	05	07	14
Rouse, George(Z-M)	1823	May 12	CoshoctnCoOh	05	07	06
Rouse, Smith(Z)	1817	May 24	MuskingmCoOh	05	03	12
Rouse, Smith(Z-M)	1833	Aug. 27	MuskingmCoOh	05	03	12
Rouse, Smith(Z-M)	1833	Sept. 20	MuskingmCoOh	05	03	12
Router, Thomas(Z)	1816	Jan. 01	GuernseyCoOh	01	01	22
Row, Andrew(Z-M)	1836	July 07	HolmesCoOhio	05	08	22
Row, David(Z-M)	1836	Feb. 18	TuscarwsCoOh	05	07	17

PURCHASER	YEAR	DATE	RESIDENCE	R	T	S
Row, Francis(Y)	1832	July 12	Stark Co.,Oh	09	11	24
Row, George S. Jr.(Z-M)	1836	Jan. 18	HolmesCoOhio	05	07	06
Row, John(Z)	1836	March 21	HolmesCoOhio	05	07	07
Row, John(Z-M)	1835	Nov. 06	HolmesCoOhio	05	07	07
Row, John(Z-M)	1836	Aug. 30	HolmesCoOhio	05	07	07
Row, Lewis(Z-M)	1826	Feb. 07	CoshoctnCoOh	04	07	05
Row, Nich'l.(Z)	1814	April 25	TuscarwsCoOh	05	08	21
Row, Samuel(Z-M)	1833	June 27	HolmesCoOhio	05	07	07
Rowe, George(Z)	1827	May 08	HolmesCoOhio	05	08	22
Rowe, George(Z-M)	1832	May 22	HolmesCoOhio	05	08	22
Rowen, Robert(Z-M)	1822	April 02	GuernseyCoOh	02	02	12
Rowland, Henry(Z)	1815	May 05	MuskingmCoOh	10	01	12
Rowland, Jacob(Y)	1825	Nov. 08	Stark Co.,Oh	09	11	03
Rowland, Robert(Z)	1824	May 11	Morgan Co,Oh	11	11	22
Rowland, Robt.(Z)	1824	Aug. 13	Morgan Co,Oh	11	11	22
Rowland, William(Z)	1829	Dec. 23	Morgan Co,Oh	11	11	05
Rowland, William(Z)	1813	June 07	AlleghnyCoPa	11	11	04
Rowland, Wm.(Z)	1831	April 16	Morgan Co,Oh	11	11	09
Rowlands, Edw.(Z)	1832	Jan. 14	WashCo.,Ohio	09	05	12
Rowlands, James(Z)	1836	June 20	MonroeCo.,Oh	08	05	19
Rowlands, James(Z)	1836	June 21	MonroeCo.,Oh	08	05	19
Rowlands, James(Z)	1836	July 05	MonroeCo.,Oh	08	05	19
Rowlands, James(Z)	1836	July 05	MonroeCo.,Oh	08	05	19
Rowlands, James(Z)	1836	July 05	MonroeCo.,Oh	08	05	19
Rowlands, James(Z)	1836	Aug. 11	MonroeCo.,Oh	08	05	19
Rowlands, James(Z)	1836	Aug. 17	MonroeCo.,Oh	09	05	13
Rowlands, William(Z)	1833	April 13	WashngtnCoOh	08	05	18
Rowlands, William(Z)	1836	Sept. 07	WashngtnCoOh	08	05	18
Rowlands, Wm.(Z)	1836	Feb. 17	WashngtnCoOh	08	05	18
Rowlands, Wm.(Z)	1836	July 05	WashngtnCoOh	08	05	18
Rownd, James M.(Z)	1836	Oct. 11	Morgan Co,Oh	08	07	20
Royer, Christian(Z)	1813	Aug. 03	SomersetCoPa	04	07	02
Royer, Elizabeth(Z-M)	1832	Feb. 15	TuscarwsCoOh	04	07	07
Royer, Michael(Z-M)	1832	April 23	TuscarwsCoOh	04	07	08
Royer, Sam'l.(Z-M)	1831	April 13	TuscarwsCoOh	04	07	07
Royer, Samuel(Z-M)	1833	March 19	TuscarwsCoOh	04	07	07
Rozer, Henry(Z)	1836	June 06	Perry Co.,Oh	15	14	13
Rubad, Vincent(Z-M)	1820	Sept. 07	GuernseyCoOh	04	04	22
Rubel, James(Z-M)	1836	March 12	HolmesCoOhio	08	08	05
Ruble, Abraham(Z)	1817	Feb. 05	LickingCo,Oh	14	13	07
Ruble, David(Z)	1807	May 07	MuskingmCoOh	01	02	19
Ruby, Isaac(Z-M)	1836	March 14	HolmesCoOhio	08	08	02
Ruby, John Mash(Z-M)	1832	Aug. 23	KnoxCo.,Ohio	11	08	04
Ruchley, Henry(Z-M)	1820	Aug. 08	TuscarwsCoOh	04	09	08
Rucker, Julius(Z)	1836	Jan. 19	GuernseyCoOh	08	08	23
Rucker, Julius(Z)	1836	March 24	GuernseyCoOh	08	08	23
Ruckle, Thos. R.(Z-M)	1835	Oct. 22	MuskingmCoOh	09	03	25
Ruckle, Thos. R.(Z-M)	1836	Feb. 18	MuskingmCoOh	09	03	25
Rud, Joseph(Z)	1834	Feb. 11	Morgan Co,Oh	11	12	36
Ruder, David(Z)	1833	Nov. 11	FairfeldCoOh	15	14	09
Rudy, Christian(Z)	1816	April 13	LancastrCoPa	01	06	01
Rudy, Rudolph(Z)	1820	July 17	MuskingmCoOh	13	10	35
Rudy, Rudolph(Z)	1824	Dec. 02	MuskingmCoOh	15	16	22
Ruetschey, Samuel(Z-M)	1836	Nov. 08	TuscarwsCoOh	04	07	06
Rugg, John(Z-M)	1829	March 07	WayneCo.,Oh.	07	08	09
Ruhl, John(Y)	1821	Oct. 31	ColumbanCoOh	05	16	15
Ruhl, John(Y)	1821	Dec. 06	ColumbanCoOh	05	16	15
Rule, John(Y)	1821	March 30	HarrisonCoOh	06	12	35
Rummell, Catharine(Z-M)	1833	July 22	TuscarwsCoOh	01	08	02
Rummell, Frederick(Z-M)	1835	Aug. 27	TuscarwsCoOh	01	08	02
Rummerfield, John(Y)	1836	March 24	HarrisonCoOh	07	11	17
Rumpf, Peter(Y)	1834	Dec. 17	CarrollCo,Oh	05	15	05
Rumpf, Peter(Y)	1834	Dec. 17	CarrollCo,Oh	05	15	06
Rundle, Rich'd. A.(Z)	1834	Feb. 14	Perry Co.,Oh	15	14	06
Runyon, David(Y)	1827	Nov. 06	Jeff.Co.,Oh.	02	09	21
Ruper, William(Z-M)	1834	Feb. 28	BelmontCo,Oh	03	07	22
Rupert, Andrew R.(Y)	1827	Oct. 16	ColumbanCoOh	07	17	02
Ruppart, Bemken(Z)	1809	May 04	TuscarwsCoOh	02	07	12
Ruppert, Bemken(Z)	1809	May 04	TuscarwsCoOh	02	07	12

PURCHASER	YEAR	DATE	RESIDENCE	R	T	S
Ruppert, John(Z-M)	1838	March 31	CoshoctnCoOh	08	07	01
Rush, Admiral N.(Z)	1837	April 24	Perry Co.,Oh	15	14	19
Rush, Ezekiel(Z)	1834	Feb. 11	Perry Co.,Oh	15	14	06
Rush, Isaiah(Z)	1831	Nov. 25	Perry Co.,Oh	15	15	32
Rush, Isaiah(Z)	1832	Nov. 23	Perry Co.,Oh	15	15	32
Rush, Isaiah(Z)	1834	Feb. 11	Perry Co.,Oh	15	14	05
Rush, Isaiah(Z)	1839	Oct. 30	Perry Co.,Oh	15	14	09
Rush, Isaiah(Z)	1816	April 29	FairfeldCoOh	15	16	29
Rush, Jacob(Z)	1805	June 24	MuskingmCoOh	14	14	04
Rush, John(Z)	1804	Dec. 29	MuskingmCoOh	05	01	09
Rush, Nathaniel(Z)	1816	April 05	WashngtnCoOh	15	14	08
Rush, Samuel(Z)	1826	Nov. 22	Perry Co.,Oh	15	15	23
Rush, Samuel(Z)	1831	Sept. 22	Perry Co.,Oh	15	15	21
Rush, Samuel(Z)	1833	April 11	Perry Co.,Oh	15	15	21
Rush, Samuel(Z)	1813	Oct. 21	FayetteCo,Pa	15	15	17
Rush, William(Z)	1813	Sept. 25	MuskingmCoOh	15	15	09
Rush, William(Z)	1816	May 01	FairfeldCoOh	15	14	06
Rush, William(Z-M)	1832	Sept. 17	KnoxCo.,Ohio	10	05	24
Rusk, Daniel(Z)	1836	Jan. 14	Morgan Co,Oh	14	13	25
Rusk, Enoch(Z)	1816	Jan. 12	GuernseyCoOh	04	02	17
Rusk, Humphrey(Z)	1817	Oct. 25	BelmontCo,Oh	13	08	10
Rusk, Isaiah(Z)	1813	Dec. 09	MuskingmCoOh	15	15	17
Rusk, James(Z)	1834	Dec. 19	Morgan Co,Oh	14	13	24
Rusk, James(Z)	1805	Dec. 14	MuskingmCoOh	05	01	08
Rusk, James(Z)	1817	Oct. 25	BelmontCo,Oh	13	08	10
Rusk, James(Z)	1817	Oct. 25	BelmontCo,Oh	13	08	23
Rusk, John M.(Z)	1834	Aug. 30	Morgan Co,Oh	13	08	35
Rusk, John(Z)	1821	Oct. 10	Perry Co.,Oh	12	09	08
Rusk, John(Z)	1833	June 20	Morgan Co,Oh	14	13	24
Rusk, John(Z)	1836	Jan. 27	Perry Co.,Oh	14	13	24
Rusk, John(Z)	1816	Jan. 24	BelmontCo,Oh	13	08	03
Rusk, Nathaniel(Z-M)	1832	June 27	CoshoctnCoOh	08	07	09
Rusorl, Robert(Y)	1830	Jan. 25	ColumbanCoOh	03	12	13
Russel, Arthur(Y)	1837	Feb. 22	Jeff.Co.,Oh.	03	12	07
Russel, Charles(Z-M)	1836	Sept. 22	CoshoctnCoOh	05	07	16
Russel, Jas.(Y)	1830	March 01	Jeff.Co.,Oh.	03	11	12
Russel, John(Y)	1836	Jan. 11	Jeff.Co.,Oh.	03	11	12
Russel, Joseph(Y)	1827	Dec. 24	ColumbanCoOh	03	12	19
Russel, Joseph(Y)	1828	April 03	Jeff.Co.,Oh.	03	12	26
Russel, Joseph(Y)	1828	April 07	Jeff.Co.,Oh.	03	12	20
Russel, Joseph(Y)	1829	March 14	Jeff.Co.,Oh.	03	12	26
Russel, Joseph(Y)	1832	May 14	Jeff.Co.,Oh.	03	11	18
Russel, Joseph(Y)	1836	Jan. 11	Jeff.Co.,Oh.	03	12	19
Russel, Robert(Y)	1828	Sept. 15	ColumbanCoOh	03	12	13
Russel, Robert(Y)	1832	Feb. 17	Jeff.Co.,Oh.	03	11	17
Russel, Robert(Y)	1832	May 31	Jeff.Co.,Oh.	03	11	18
Russel, Robert(Y)	1832	May 31	Jeff.Co.,Oh.	03	11	18
Russel, Robert(Y)	1832	June 11	ColumbanCoOh	03	12	13
Russel, Robert(Y)	1836	Jan. 02	Jeff.Co.,Oh.	03	12	13
Russel, Robert(Y)	1836	Jan. 02	Jeff.Co.,Oh.	03	12	07
Russel, Shubail(Z)	1816	Nov. 21	MuskingmCoOh	13	09	25
Russell, Alexander(Y)	1827	June 30	BelmontCo,Oh	03	11	21
Russell, Alfred(Z-M)	1832	Feb. 08	BelmontCo,Oh	01	05	23
Russell, Andrew(Z)	1816	Sept. 09	WashCo.,Penn	05	02	16
Russell, Andrew(Z)	1816	Sept. 09	WashCo.,Penn	05	03	09
Russell, Arthur(Y)	1826	May 02	PhladlhaCoPa	03	11	24
Russell, Henry(Y)	1824	Nov. 06	Jeff.Co.,Oh.	02	08	33
Russell, Hugh(Z)	1815	Aug. 14	StarkeCo.,Oh	01	10	04
Russell, Isaac B.(Z-M)	1833	Oct. 17	KnoxCo.,Ohio	10	05	25
Russell, James(Y)	1837	March 02	Jeff.Co.,Oh.	03	12	14
Russell, James(Z)	1832	Sept. 15	MuskingmCoOh	10	07	14
Russell, James(Z-M)	1832	Oct. 03	KnoxCo.,Ohio	10	05	25
Russell, Jas.(Y)	1824	Nov. 06	Jeff.Co.,Oh.	02	08	33
Russell, John(Z)	1827	Oct. 01	MuskingmCoOh	10	08	14
Russell, John(Z)	1835	Sept. 29	GuernseyCoOh	09	07	10
Russell, John(Z)	1813	July 09	MuskingmCoOh	14	15	04
Russell, John(Z)	1816	Dec. 16	PutnamCoOhio	13	09	27
Russell, Joseph(Y)	1826	June 24	Jeff.Co.,Oh.	04	13	01
Russell, Joseph(Y)	1828	Feb. 25	ColumbanCoOh	03	12	19

248

PURCHASER	YEAR	DATE	RESIDENCE	R	T	S
Russell, Joseph(Y)	1839	May 18	Jeff.Co.,Oh.	03	11	18
Russell, Joseph(Z)	1833	Jan. 18	GuernseyCoOh	09	08	27
Russell, Joseph(Z)	1836	Jan. 14	GuernseyCoOh	09	08	27
Russell, Reuben(Z)	1832	Nov. 08	GuernseyCoOh	09	08	26
Russell, Richard(Z)	1816	March 19	MuskingmCoOh	15	15	25
Russell, Robert(Y)	1826	March 08	Jeff.Co.,Oh.	03	11	11
Russell, Robt.(Y)	1824	Jan. 14	Jeff.Co.,Oh.	03	11	18
Russell, Sam'l.(Z-M)	1833	Oct. 08	KnoxCo.,Ohio	10	05	25
Russell, Samuel(Z)	1832	April 03	BelmontCo,Oh	10	09	03
Russell, Thomas(Z)	1816	May 27	MuskingmCoOh	09	13	23
Russell, Thomas(Z-M)	1832	Nov. 06	GuernseyCoOh	03	01	23
Russell, William(Z)	1814	Dec. 20	MuskingmCoOh	14	15	06
Russell, William(Z-M)	1833	Feb. 08	BelmontCo,Oh	04	07	23
Russill, John W.(Y)	1830	Oct. 06	Stark Co.,Oh	07	17	25
Russle, Ann(Y)	1830	June 19	TuscarwsCoOh	07	14	14
Rust, Samuel(Z)	1838	Nov. 24	GuernseyCoOh	08	05	27
Rutan, Daniel(Y)	1827	March 28	HarrisonCoOh	05	12	22
Rutan, Daniel(Y)	1830	Sept. 17	HarrisonCoOh	05	12	21
Rutan, John(Y)	1825	June 06	HarrisonCoOh	05	12	22
Rutledge, Archer(Y)	1831	May 20	TuscarwsCoOh	07	14	29
Rutledge, Edward(Z-M)	1836	March 03	CarrollCo,Oh	03	07	02
Rutledge, George(Y)	1831	May 17	HarrisonCoOh	07	14	28
Rutledge, James(Z-M)	1824	Nov. 01	WashCo.,Penn	04	03	18
Rutledge, John D.(Y)	1817	Jan. 13	Brooke CoVir	11	10	06
Rutledge, John E.(Z)	1828	Dec. 30	MuskingmCoOh	14	14	18
Rutledge, John E.(Z)	1837	March 10	MuskingmCoOh	15	15	34
Rutledge, Peter(Z-M)	1829	June 15	CoshoctnCoOh	08	07	23
Rutledge, Robert(Z-M)	1836	March 10	CarrollCo,Oh	03	07	02
Rutledge, Robert(Z-M)	1836	March 10	CarrollCo,Oh	03	07	02
Rutledge, Thomas(Z-M)	1827	July 21	GuernseyCoOh	04	03	22
Rutledge, Thos.(Z-M)	1832	Sept. 18	CoshoctnCoOh	09	06	19
Rutledge, William(Y)	1831	May 20	TuscarwsCoOh	07	14	28
Rutledge, William(Z)	1811	April 16	Ohio Co.,Vir	15	18	08
Rutter, John(Z)	1834	March 19	Morgan Co,Oh	13	08	19
Rutter, Joseph(Y)	1829	April 08	TuscarwsCoOh	06	14	25
Ryan, Eben'r.(Z)	1806	April 24	MuskingmCoOh	08	02	05
Ryan, Ebenezer(Z)	1806	Sept. 08	MuskingmCoOh	08	02	19
Ryan, John(Z)	1817	Sept. 09	ZanesvilleOh	09	07	19
Ryan, John(Z-M)	1831	Sept. 08	BelmontCo,Oh	01	03	20
Ryan, Timothy(Z)	1837	Oct. 12	Morgan Co,Oh	14	12	02
Ryian, Ebenezer(Z)	1805	April 29	MuskingmCoOh	08	02	19
Ryian, Ebenezer(Z)	1805	April 29	MuskingmCoOh	08	02	19
Ryland, Fredus(Z)	1816	Oct. 09	MifflinCo,Pa	05	02	05
Saburien, Urban(Y)	1825	Sept. 01	Stark Co.,Oh	08	11	30
Sackman, Mary(Z)	1815	Dec. 14	GuernseyCoOh	01	03	19
Sackman, William(Y)	1824	May 18	HarrisonCoOh	04	12	21
Sadler, Jacob(Y)	1828	Jan. 10	HarrisonCoOh	05	13	27
Sadler, Jacob(Z)	1806	Dec. 15	Jeff.Co.,Oh.	04	08	12
Sadler, Jacob(Z-M)	1835	April 03	CarrolCo.,Oh	03	07	02
Sadler, William(Z-M)	1832	June 15	HarrisonCoOh	03	07	12
Sadler, William(Z-M)	1832	June 28	HarrisonCoOh	03	07	13
Sadler, Wm. S.(Z-M)	1833	July 26	TuscarwsCoOh	02	05	20
Saffell, Amos(Z)	1832	June 25	Perry Co.,Oh	15	15	22
Saffell, Amos(Z)	1837	Feb. 04	Perry Co.,Oh	15	15	34
Saffell, Amos(Z)	1837	Feb. 04	Perry Co.,Oh	15	15	33
Saffell, Edmund(Z)	1837	Jan. 18	Perry Co.,Oh	15	15	24
Saffell, Thomas(Z-M)	1833	Aug. 20	MuskingmCoOh	06	03	09
Saffell, Thomas(Z-M)	1833	Aug. 20	MuskingmCoOh	06	03	10
Safford, Harry(Z)	1827	Jan. 26	PutnamCoOhio	13	10	10
Saib, Andrew(Z-M)	1822	Dec. 05	CoshoctnCoOh	05	08	09
Sailor, Samuel Jr.(Z)	1834	Feb. 17	Morgan Co,Oh	10	06	01
Sailor, Samuel Jr.(Z)	1834	March 19	Morgan Co,Oh	10	06	01
Sailor, Samuel(Z)	1815	Feb. 20	GuernseyCoOh	10	07	23
Sailov, William(Z)	1832	June 30	MuskingmCoOh	10	07	26
Sailov, William(Z)	1832	June 30	MuskingmCoOh	10	07	26
Sain, William(Z)	1815	Sept. 25	FairfeldCoOh	11	01	03
Sain, William(Z)	1816	Dec. 18	LickingCo,Oh	11	01	02
Sainer, George(Y)	1828	July 31	ColumbanCoOh	07	18	25
Saling, John(Z)	1838	May 21	MonroeCo.,Oh	08	06	22

PURCHASER	YEAR	DATE	RESIDENCE	R	T	S
Salladay, Elias(Z)	1836	Feb. 03	GuernseyCoOh	09	08	36
Sallman, James(Y)	1833	Dec. 11	Jeff.Co.,Oh.	03	11	11
Salmon, Edward(Y)	1832	Dec. 31	Jeff.Co.,Oh.	07	14	29
Salmon, Frederick(Z)	1810	March 08	FredrickCoMd	01	09	01
Salmon, Jno.(Z-M)	1831	Dec. 23	CoshoctnCoOh	07	05	10
Salmon, John(Z)	1810	Sept. 15	TuscarwsCoOh	02	08	18
Salsberry, Peter(Z)	1815	May 12	Jeff.Co.,Oh.	05	07	18
Salsberry, Peter(Z)	1815	June 05	HarrisonCoOh	05	07	24
Salsbury, Christopher(Y)	1829	May 04	HarrisonCoOh	05	13	10
Salsbury, William(Y)	1832	Aug. 23	HarrisonCoOh	07	14	32
Saltman, John(Y)	1836	March 07	Jeff.co.,Oh.	03	11	11
Saltman, Philip Joshua(Y)	1832	Oct. 05	ColumbanCoOh	04	13	13
Saltman, Philip Joshua(Y)	1835	May 12	CarrollCo,Oh	04	13	13
Saltoman, Martin(Y)	1832	Oct. 27	Jeff.Co.,Oh.	02	08	34
Saltsgiver, Casper(Z)	1813	Sept. 16	GuernseyCoOh	01	03	23
Saltsgiver, Peter(Z)	1808	April 25	MuskingmCoOh	02	02	11
Saltsgiver, Peter(Z)	1812	March 09	MuskingmCoOh	02	02	10
Saltsgiver, Peter(Z)	1812	Sept. 17	GuernseyCoOh	01	02	04
Saltsman, Daniel(Y)	1832	Nov. 05	Jeff.Co.,Oh.	03	11	17
Saltsman, John(Y)	1828	Dec. 15	Jeff.Co.,Oh.	03	11	11
Saltsman, John(Y)	1828	Dec. 15	Jeff.Co.,Oh.	03	11	11
Saltsman, Martin Junr.(Y)	1835	Dec. 27	Jeff.Co.,Oh.	03	11	36
Samford, Wm.(Z)	1831	Feb. 22	WashngtnCoOh	08	06	32
Sampsel, Daniel(Z-M)	1837	June 28	HolmesCoOhio	08	07	19
Sampsel, Henry(Z-M)	1833	March 28	CoshoctnCoOh	05	07	07
Sampsel, Jacob(Z-M)	1837	June 28	HolmesCoOhio	08	07	19
Sampson, Francis(Y)	1832	Sept. 10	HarrisonCoOh	07	14	28
Sampson, John(Y)	1827	Nov. 01	HarrisonCoOh	06	12	22
Samuel Crawford(Y)	1830	Sept. 01	ColumbanCoOh	03	13	20
Samuel, Smith(Z)	1807	July 18	MuskingmCoOh	15	18	03
Sandel, Volentine(Z-M)	1835	Jan. 12	MuskingmCoOh	06	03	09
Sander, George(Y)	1826	June 06	ColumbanCoOh	06	18	11
Sanders, Benj'm.(Z-M)	1837	Aug. 25	KnoxCo.,Ohio	10	06	15
Sanders, Benj'm.(Z-M)	1837	Aug. 25	KnoxCo.,Ohio	10	06	15
Sanders, Dennis(Z)	1833	July 22	MuskingmCoOh	11	12	36
Sanders, Jacob(Y)	1824	July 15	PhladlhaCoPa	04	14	06
Sanders, Jacob(Y)	1824	July 15	PhladlhaCoPa	04	14	06
Sanders, Jesse(Z)	1837	March 16	Perry Co.,Oh	14	12	28
Sanders, John Jun.(Z)	1832	March 06	Perry Co.,Oh	15	15	01
Sandford, Robin'n.(Z)	1817	June 17	WashngtnCoOh	08	06	31
Sandford, Robinson(Z)	1833	May 03	MonroeCo.,Oh	08	06	32
Sandle, Jacob(Z-M)	1835	Sept. 08	CoshoctnCoOh	06	04	21
Sandle, Jacob(Z-M)	1835	Sept. 08	CoshoctnCoOh	06	04	20
Sands, Wm.(Z-M)	1835	Jan. 22	WashCo.,Penn	03	06	14
Sanford, D. F.(Z)	1837	Feb. 20	MonroeCo.,Oh	08	06	32
Sanford, R.(Z)	1833	May 03	MonroeCo.,Oh	08	06	31
Sanford, Wm. H.(Z)	1836	Aug. 11	MonroeCo.,Oh	08	06	31
Sanford, Wm. H.(Z)	1837	Sept. 30	MonroeCo.,Oh	08	06	31
Sanker, Clark(Z-M)	1838	Aug. 28	TuscarwsCoOh	08	07	20
Santee, Thomas(Y)	1824	Dec. 16	ColumbanCoOh	05	18	11
Sapp, Adam D.(Z-M)	1832	Nov. 27	KnoxCo.,Ohio	10	08	17
Sapp, Adam D.(Z-M)	1836	Oct. 07	KnoxCo.,Ohio	10	08	23
Sapp, Adam(Z-M)	1831	Jan. 28	KnoxCo.,Ohio	11	08	19
Sapp, Benj'm.(Z-M)	1836	Oct. 07	KnoxCo.,Ohio	10	08	23
Sapp, Benjamine(Z-M)	1836	Oct. 27	KnoxCo.,Ohio	10	08	23
Sapp, Charles(Z-M)	1832	Aug. 03	KnoxCo.,Ohio	10	08	16
Sapp, Daniel(Z)	1809	Dec. 05	KnoxCo.,Ohio	10	07	04
Sapp, Daniel(Z-M)	1833	Jan. 04	KnoxCo.,Ohio	11	08	13
Sapp, Daniel(Z-M)	1833	Jan. 04	KnoxCo.,Ohio	11	08	13
Sapp, Geo.(Z)	1816	Feb. 17	KnoxCo.,Ohio	10	07	05
Sapp, George(Z)	1808	Jan. 23	FairfeldCoOh	10	07	05
Sapp, George(Z)	1813	Oct. 14	KnoxCo.,Ohio	10	07	06
Sapp, George(Z)	1807	Sept. 12	FairfeldCoOh	10	07	06
Sapp, George(Z-M)	1826	Dec. 14	KnoxCo.,Ohio	11	08	23
Sapp, George(Z-M)	1832	Dec. 15	KnoxCo.,Ohio	11	08	19
Sapp, George(Z-M)	1832	Dec. 15	KnoxCo.,Ohio	11	08	23
Sapp, Henry(Z)	1833	June 14	MuskingmCoOh	13	11	11
Sapp, John(Z-M)	1826	March 22	KnoxCo.,Ohio	10	07	04
Sapp, John(Z-M)	1832	Oct. 19	KnoxCo.,Ohio	10	08	17

PURCHASER	YEAR	DATE	RESIDENCE	R	T	S
Sapp, John(Z-M)	1833	Nov. 11	KnoxCo.,Ohio	10	08	25
Sapp, Jonth'n. A.(Z-M)	1831	Nov. 12	KnoxCo.,Ohio	11	08	22
Sapp, Joseph Jnr.(Z-M)	1821	July 25	KnoxCo.,Ohio	10	08	15
Sapp, Joseph Jr.(Z-M)	1836	Nov. 09	KnoxCo.,Ohio	10	08	04
Sapp, Joseph M.(Z-M)	1833	Sept. 20	KnoxCo.,Ohio	11	08	19
Sapp, Samuel(Z-M)	1832	June 11	KnoxCo.,Ohio	10	08	25
Sapp, Samuel(Z-M)	1832	Nov. 29	KnoxCo.,Ohio	10	08	17
Sapp, Simon H.(Z-M)	1836	May 03	KnoxCo.,Ohio	11	08	12
Sapp, Simona H.(Z-M)	1835	Dec. 14	KnoxCo.,Ohio	11	08	20
Sapp, William R.(Z-M)	1833	Dec. 23	KnoxCo.,Ohio	10	08	24
Sappington, Thomas(Z)	1813	Sept. 24	Stark Co.,Oh	03	09	09
Sarchet, David(Z-M)	1833	Feb. 19	GuernseyCoOh	03	03	15
Sarchet, Moses(Z-M)	1833	Feb. 19	GuernseyCoOh	03	03	15
Sarchet, Nicholas(Z)	1807	Feb. 02	MuskingmCoOh	09	08	05
Sarchet, Peter B.(Z-M)	1833	Feb. 19	GuernseyCoOh	03	03	15
Sarchet, Peter Sr.(Z-M)	1828	Oct. 22	GuernseyCoOh	03	03	19
Sarchet, Thomas(Z)	1806	Aug. 16	MuskingmCoOh	03	03	23
Sarchet, Thomas(Z)	1806	Aug. 16	MuskingmCoOh	03	03	24
Sarchet, Thomas(Z)	1806	Aug. 16	MuskingmCoOh	03	03	24
Sarchet, Thomas(Z)	1806	Aug. 16	MuskingmCoOh	03	03	23
Sarchet, Thomas(Z)	1806	Aug. 16	MuskingmCoOh	03	03	23
Sarchett, Peter Senr.(Z-M)	1827	Feb. 17	GuernseyCoOh	03	03	19
Sarchett, Peter(Z)	1815	April 27	MuskingmCoOh	12	13	23
Sarge, Thomas(Z)	1833	Aug. 01	MonroeCo.,Oh	08	07	02
Sargent & English(Z-M)	1837	Oct. 10	TuscarwsCoOh	04	05	20
Sargent, John(Z)	1824	Oct. 07	Morgan Co,Oh	12	11	15
Sargent, Laurence(Z-M)	1836	June 16	TuscarwsCoOh	02	07	01
Sargent, Moses(Z)	1824	Sept. 29	Morgan Co,Oh	12	11	15
Sargent, Thomas(Z-M)	1833	July 31	TuscarwsCoOh	01	08	02
Sason, Martin(Z-M))	1833	June 04	TuscarwsCoOh	02	06	19
Satterthwait, Thomas(Z)	1811	June 22	GuernseyCoOh	02	01	11
Satterthwaite, Joseph W.(Z)	1805	Aug. 20	BelmontCo,Oh	01	01	09
Satterthwaite, Joseph W.(Z)	1805	Aug. 20	BelmontCo,Oh	01	01	10
Satterthwaite, Joseph W.(Z)	1805	Aug. 20	BelmontCo,Oh	01	01	09
Satterthwaite, Joseph W.(Z)	1805	Oct. 28	BelmontCo,Oh	09	08	03
Satterthwaite, Joseph W.(Z)	1805	Oct. 28	BelmontCo,Oh	09	08	04
Satterthwaite, Joseph W.(Z)	1805	Oct. 28	BelmontCo,Oh	03	01	21
Satterthwaite, Joshua W.(Z)	1805	Oct. 18	BurlngtnCoNJ	02	01	21
Satterthwaite, Joshua W.(Z)	1805	Oct. 18	BurlngtnCoNJ	01	01	22
Satterthwaite, Joshua W.(Z)	1805	Oct. 18	BurlngtnCoNJ	09	08	01
Satterthwaite, Joshua W.(Z)	1805	Oct. 18	BurlngtnCoNJ	09	08	02
Satterthwaite, Joshua W.(Z)	1805	Oct. 28	BurlngtnCoNJ	09	08	03
Satterthwaite, Joshua W.(Z)	1805	Oct. 28	BurlngtnCoNJ	09	08	03
Satterthwaite, Joshua W.(Z)	1805	Oct. 28	BurlngtnCoNJ	09	08	04
Satterthwaite, Joshua W.(Z)	1805	Oct. 28	BurlngtnCoNJ	09	08	04
Satterthwaite, Joshua W.(Z)	1805	Oct. 28	BurlngtnCoNJ	09	08	02
Satterthwaite, Joshua W.(Z)	1805	Oct. 28	BurlngtnCoNJ	03	01	21
Sauder, Henry(Z-M)	1823	Dec. 29	TuscarwsCoOh	05	08	01
Saunder, Wm.(Z)	1805	March 05	MuskingmCoOh	13	12	09
Saunders, Jesse(Z)	1829	March 16	Morgan Co,Oh	14	12	19
Saunders, Nathan(Z-M)	1824	Feb. 12	CoshoctnCoOh	06	03	24
Saunders, Thomas(Z-M)	1832	Oct. 08	GuernseyCoOh	01	05	18
Savage, Towner(Z-M)	1828	Aug. 05	HolmesCoOhio	07	08	18
Savely, George(Z-M)	1832	March 09	BelmontCo,Oh	03	01	24
Savely, John(Z-M)	1832	Dec. 05	GuernseyCoOh	03	01	17
Saviers, John(Z-M)	1829	June 08	GuernseyCoOh	02	04	21
Sawyer, Samuel Jr.(Z-M)	1836	Oct. 08	CarrollCo,Oh	03	07	17
Sawyer, Samuel Jr.(Z-M)	1836	Oct. 08	CarrollCo,Oh	03	07	14
Sayers, Ephraim(Z)	1806	May 13	GreeneCo.,Pa	11	10	30
Sayre, David(Z-M)	1831	March 18	GuernseyCoOh	01	01	19
Sayre, Lewis(Z)	1821	Aug. 21	Morgan Co,Oh	10	08	23
Sayre, Mark A.(Z-M)	1839	July 23	KnoxCo.,Ohio	10	09	11
Scales, John(Y)	1832	Feb. 16	BelmontCo,Oh	03	05	33
Scales, Thomas(Y)	1828	June 24	BelmontCo,Oh	03	05	33
Scammahorne, Isaac(Z)	1810	Nov. 02	MuskingmCoOh	05	04	24
Scarff, Andrew(Z-M)	1825	Nov. 18	MuskingmCoOh	05	02	07
Scarlett, Rich'd.(Y)	1827	Oct. 29	Jeff.Co.,Oh.	04	12	26
Scarlett, Richard(Y)	1826	Sept. 13	Jeff.Co.,Oh.	04	12	26
Scarlett, Richard(Y)	1828	Feb. 22	Jeff.Co.,Oh.	04	12	25

PURCHASER	YEAR	DATE	RESIDENCE	R	T	S
Scarlett, William(Y)	1831	Nov. 21	Jeff.Co.,Oh.	04	12	27
Scarlott, William(Y)	1836	Sept. 12	CarrollCo,Oh	04	12	27
Scarlott, Wm.(Y)	1829	April 04	Jeff.Co.,Oh.	04	12	26
Scattergood, David(Y)	1831	Dec. 26	ColumbanCoOh	03	12	17
Scattergood, David(Y)	1832	Nov. 27	ColumbanCoOh	03	13	28
Schaal, Augustus(Z-M)	1836	Oct. 29	MuskingmCoOh	06	04	09
Schaal, Augustus(Z-M)	1836	Oct. 29	MuskingmCoOh	06	04	09
Schaal, Augustus(Z-M)	1836	Oct. 29	MuskingmCoOh	06	04	12
Schafer, George(Y)	1824	Jan. 28	ColumbanCoOh	07	20	17
Scharking, Jacob(Y)	1824	Feb. 05	Stark Co.,Oh	07	19	34
Schaul, Augustus(Z-M)	1833	Oct. 16	MuskingmCoOh	06	03	03
Scheer, John(Y)	1832	Aug. 01	Stark Co.,Oh	07	15	30
Scheetz, John(Z)	1835	June 23	Jeff.Co.,Oh.	11	10	28
Schelling, John(Y)	1824	May 28	Stark Co.,Oh	07	19	15
Scherrer, Jacob(Z-M)	1836	July 06	PittsburghPa	05	04	17
Scherrer, Jacob(Z-M)	1836	Nov. 16	CoshoctnCoOh	05	04	14
Scherrer, Jacob(Z-M)	1836	Nov. 16	CoshoctnCoOh	05	04	17
Schieber, Ignatius(Y)	1832	May 31	ColumbanCoOh	04	14	36
Schieber, Ignatius(Y)	1832	May 31	ColumbanCoOh	03	13	31
Schield, Daniel(Z-M)	1832	Nov. 05	HolmesCoOhio	07	08	05
Schield, Henry(Z-M)	1835	March 30	HolmesCoOhio	09	08	11
Schimpf, Francis(Z-M)	1836	Dec. 03	AlleghnyCoPa	05	04	18
Schimpf, John(Z-M)	1836	Dec. 03	AlleghnyCoPa	05	04	07
Schleiff, Henry(Z)	1808	May 30	WestmrldCoPa	04	09	20
Schleiff, Henry(Z)	1808	May 30	WestmrldCoPa	04	09	22
Schlibach(Y)	1826	Sept. 27	TrumbullCoOh	06	19	31
Schneider, Gottlieb(Y)	1824	June 15	Stark Co.,Oh	07	19	22
Schnided, Adam(Z)	1807	July 27	WashngtnCoOh	03	09	21
Schnider, Jacob(Y)	1827	April 20	Stark Co.,Oh	06	18	03
Schock, Stephen(Z)	1810	Jan. 29	MuskingmCoOh	06	01	09
Schoenenberger, Martin(Z-M)	1838	May 24	HolmesCoOhio	09	08	08
Schoff, Philip(Z)	1808	Nov. 16	Jeff.Co.,Oh.	04	04	19
Schofield, William(Z)	1815	June 10	MuskingmCoOh	14	15	15
Scholfield, Elizabeth(Z)	1807	Nov. 17	MuskingmCoOh	15	17	24
Scholfield, Wm.(Z)	1815	June 12	MuskingmCoOh	14	15	15
Schooler, John(Z)	1814	Sept. 10	BeaverCo.,Pa	11	06	22
Schooler, Joseph(Z-M)	1838	Dec. 13	KnoxCo.,Ohio	10	04	04
Schooler, William(Z-M)	1832	Nov. 05	LickingCo,Oh	10	04	04
Schooler, Wm.(Z-M)	1836	March 28	LickingCo,Oh	10	04	03
Schoolers, Joseph(Z-M)	1838	Dec. 10	KnoxCo.,Ohio	10	04	05
Schooley, Joseph(Z-M)	1829	Oct. 27	GuernseyCoOh	01	04	02
Schooley, Samuel(Z)	1817	April 26	Jeff.Co.,Oh.	01	05	24
Schooley, Samuel(Z-M)	1825	Nov. 28	TuscarwsCoOh	01	05	07
Schooley, Samuel(Z-M)	1833	Aug. 13	TuscarwsCoOh	01	05	05
Schouman, Touissaint(Z)	1807	Jan. 03	WashngtnCoOh	11	11	27
Schoutz, Henry(Y)	1822	Sept. 02	ArmstrngCoPa	07	19	21
Schraier, John(Y)	1828	Jan. 26	Stark Co.,Oh	07	16	24
Schranz, John(Z-M)	1836	Sept. 21	Stark Co.,Oh	03	08	17
Schriber, Ignatius(Y)	1832	Jan. 14	Pittsburg,Pa	04	14	36
Schrock, Jacob(Z-M)	1828	March 28	HolmesCoOhio	05	08	01
Schrog, David(Z)	1810	Nov. 26	SomersetCoPa	05	09	11
Schults, Jacob(Z)	1814	Nov. 07	KnoxCo.,Ohio	?	07	07
Schultz, Jacob(Z-M)	1836	April 05	KnoxCo.,Ohio	10	08	04
Schultz, Mic'l. M.(Z-M)	1835	Oct. 16	TuscarwsCoOh	05	07	01
Schwartz, George(Z-M)	1837	Jan. 11	KnoxCo.,Ohio	10	07	12
Schwevzen, Valentine(Z-M)	1836	Oct. 22	TuscarwsCoOh	04	07	18
Schwyhart, Jacob(Z-M)	1837	Jan. 11	BelmontCo,Oh	03	03	01
Schwyhart, Joseph(Z-M)	1837	Jan. 11	BelmontCo,Oh	03	04	17
Scoffield, E.(Z)	1804	June 29	FairfeldCoOh	10	02	15
Scoffield, E.(Z)	1804	June 29	FairfeldCoOh	10	02	15
Scoffield, E.(Z)	1804	June 29	FairfeldCoOh	10	02	15
Scoffield, E.(Z)	1804	Dec. 04	Lancaster,Oh	10	06	33
Scoles, Henry(Z-M)	1826	June 05	KnoxCo.,Ohio	11	08	15
Scott, Abraham(Z)	1814	Nov. 30	Jeff.Co.,Oh.	01	04	17
Scott, Abraham(Z)	1815	April 22	Jeff.Co.,Oh.	01	04	14
Scott, Abraham(Z-M)	1828	Aug. 07	GuernseyCoOh	02	03	16
Scott, Abraham(Z-M)	1828	Sept. 11	GuernseyCoOh	02	03	16
Scott, Alexander(Z-M)	1833	Dec. 12	CoshoctnCoOh	10	05	20
Scott, Alexander(Z-M)	1834	Jan. 23	CoshoctnCoOh	10	05	20

PURCHASER	YEAR	DATE	RESIDENCE	R	T	S
Scott, And'w.(Z)	1816	Nov. 14	MuskingmCoOh	13	08	02
Scott, Andrew(Z)	1829	June 08	Jeff.Co.,Oh.	11	10	18
Scott, Andrew(Z-M)	1821	July 03	Jeff.Co.,Oh.	05	06	07
Scott, Archibald(Z)	1829	Dec. 15	Morgan Co,Oh	13	08	10
Scott, Charles(Y)	1820	Dec. 02	WashCo.,Penn	06	15	26
Scott, Charles(Y)	1831	April 28	Jeff.Co.,Oh.	06	12	32
Scott, Charles(Z)	1816	June 21	Ohio Co.,Vir	04	03	23
Scott, David(Y)	1824	May 18	ColumbanCoOh	04	15	22
Scott, David(Z)	1816	Nov. 14	MuskingmCoOh	13	08	01
Scott, Francis(Z)	1828	Sept. 13	Morgan Co,Oh	10	08	15
Scott, Francis(Z)	1832	July 16	Morgan Co,Oh	10	08	22
Scott, Francis(Z)	1832	July 16	Morgan Co,Oh	10	08	15
Scott, Francis(Z)	1832	July 16	Morgan Co,Oh	10	08	14
Scott, Francis(Z)	1825	March 18	Morgan Co,Oh	10	08	15
Scott, Francis(Z-M)	1832	Aug. 20	GuernseyCoOh	04	03	22
Scott, Francis(Z-M)	1833	March 19	GuernseyCoOh	04	02	12
Scott, Hamilton(Y)	1827	May 05	TuscarwsCoOh	07	15	30
Scott, Hugh(Z)	1834	Jan. 28	GuernseyCoOh	10	09	01
Scott, Humphrey(Z-M)	1834	Nov. 24	CoshoctnCoOh	10	05	11
Scott, James(Y)	1827	Oct. 06	WashCo.,Penn	04	13	31
Scott, James(Z)	1823	Aug. 27	Jeff.Co.,Oh.	10	09	02
Scott, James(Z)	1828	March 13	GuernseyCoOh	10	09	02
Scott, James(Z)	1832	Aug. 03	GuernseyCoOh	10	09	02
Scott, James(Z)	1833	Oct. 09	Morgan Co,Oh	10	07	13
Scott, James(Z)	1835	Nov. 20	Morgan Co,Oh	10	07	13
Scott, James(Z-M)	1834	Aug. 12	BelmontCo,Oh	03	06	16
Scott, James(Z-M)	1835	March 09	BelmontCo,Oh	04	06	22
Scott, James(Z-M)	1836	Feb. 24	BelmontCo,Oh	04	06	20
Scott, James(Z-M)	1836	Feb. 24	BelmontCo,Oh	03	06	17
Scott, James(Z-M)	1836	Feb. 24	BelmontCo,Oh	03	06	24
Scott, James(Z-M)	1835	March 09	BelmontCo,Oh	03	06	15
Scott, James(Z-M)	1837	March 07	BelmontCo,Oh	03	06	01
Scott, James(Z-M)	1837	March 07	BelmontCo,Oh	03	07	20
Scott, James(Z-M)	1837	March 07	BelmontCo,Oh	02	07	03
Scott, Jesse(Y)	1832	May 17	GuernseyCoOh	07	09	25
Scott, John A.(Z-M)	1831	Sept. 05	BelmontCo,Oh	03	06	17
Scott, John(Y)	1830	Aug. 27	ColumbanCoOh	04	13	33
Scott, John(Y)	1831	March 23	HarrisonCoOh	06	12	32
Scott, John(Z)	1821	Aug. 10	MuskingmCoOh	12	10	35
Scott, John(Z)	1822	Oct. 08	Morgan Co,Oh	12	10	35
Scott, John(Z)	1808	March 11	MuskingmCoOh	01	02	20
Scott, John(Z)	1814	Sept. 17	WashngtnCoOh	11	10	19
Scott, John(Z)	1814	Oct. 13	WashngtnCoOh	10	06	31
Scott, John(Z)	1814	Oct. 13	WashngtnCoOh	10	06	32
Scott, John(Z)	1815	May 15	WashCo.,Penn	09	05	05
Scott, John(Z-M)	1820	Nov. 22	CoshoctnCoOh	05	06	07
Scott, John(Z-M)	1822	Aug. 05	CoshoctnCoOh	08	05	08
Scott, John(Z-M)	1825	March 16	Jeff.Co.,Oh.	09	04	21
Scott, John(Z-M)	1831	Aug. 17	TuscarwsCoOh	01	05	24
Scott, John(Z-M)	1833	July 19	TuscarwsCoOh	03	06	16
Scott, Joseph(Y)	1835	June 03	Stark Co.,Oh	09	11	25
Scott, Josiah(Y)	1828	Feb. 01	WashCo.,Penn	05	13	14
Scott, Matthew(Y)	1821	Sept. 25	TuscarwsCoOh	07	15	15
Scott, Sam'l. P.(Z-M)	1829	Jan. 14	MuskingmCoOh	05	03	06
Scott, Samuel(Z)	1815	May 30	Jeff.Co.,Oh.	15	16	22
Scott, Samuel(Z-M)	1836	Feb. 27	WashCo.,Penn	04	03	24
Scott, Theodore(Z)	1833	Sept. 13	WashngtnCoOh	08	05	08
Scott, Thomas Ansley(Z)	1836	June 24	WashngtnCoOh	08	05	08
Scott, Thomas M.(Y)	1831	March 28	Stark Co.,Oh	07	17	26
Scott, Thomas(Y)	1828	Oct. 21	WashCo.,Penn	07	14	15
Scott, Thomas(Y)	1828	Oct. 21	WashCo.,Penn	07	14	15
Scott, Thomas(Z-M)	1830	Jan. 15	KnoxCo.,Ohio	10	06	18
Scott, Thomas(Z-M)	1831	Sept. 13	GuernseyCoOh	03	01	23
Scott, Thomas(Z-M)	1833	Aug. 13	GuernseyCoOh	03	01	23
Scott, W.(Z-M)	1829	June 10	WayneCo.,Oh.	07	08	10
Scott, William(Y)	1822	Feb. 27	Jeff.Co.,Oh.	04	12	32
Scott, William(Z)	1837	May 20	Morgan Co,Oh	08	06	28
Scott, William(Z)	1817	July 30	LickingCo,Oh	10	04	07
Scott, William(Z-M)	1825	Aug. 29	CoshoctnCoOh	10	05	11

253

PURCHASER	YEAR	DATE	RESIDENCE	R	T	S
Scott, William(Z-M)	1829	May 05	GuernseyCoOh	04	03	17
Scott, William(Z-M)	1831	Oct. 12	LickingCo,Oh	10	04	04
Scott, William(Z-M)	1831	Oct. 17	LickingCo,Oh	10	04	07
Scott, William(Z-M)	1830	March 25	LickingCo,Oh	10	04	07
Scott, William(Z-M)	1830	Sept. 07	KnoxCo.,Ohio	10	05	11
Scott, William(Z-M)	1832	Sept. 21	CoshoctnCoOh	07	08	10
Scott, William(Z-M)	1832	Oct. 05	LickingCo,Oh	10	04	15
Scott, William(Z-M)	1833	March 05	KnoxCo.,Ohio	10	05	20
Scott, William(Z-M)	1836	March 02	KnoxCo.,Ohio	10	05	20
Scott, William(Z-M)	1838	Jan. 24	HolmesCoOhio	08	08	05
Scroggen, William(Z)	1815	Dec. 02	GuernseyCoOh	09	06	18
Seagly, Philip Jacob(Y)	1830	Oct. 28	PortageCo,Oh	07	20	18
Seagly, Philip Jacob(Y)	1831	June 28	Stark Co.,Oh	07	20	17
Sealmahorn, Sol'm.(Z)	1816	April 29	Jeff.Co.,Oh.	10	08	09
Sealock, Thomas(Z)	1833	Feb. 02	Morgan Co,Oh	10	06	29
Sealock, Thos.(Z)	1831	Sept. 05	MuskingmCoOh	10	06	29
Seamans, Benj. B.(Z)	1829	Jan. 20	MuskingmCoOh	11	12	10
Seares, John M.(Z)	1834	March 17	Morgan Co,Oh	10	07	17
Searf, Andrew(Z)	1817	Sept. 26	MuskingmCoOh	11	10	09
Searf, Ruth(Z)	1817	Sept. 26	MuskingmCoOh	11	10	09
Sears, Caleb J.(Z)	1832	June 07	MuskingmCoOh	11	11	01
Sears, Enoch(Y)	1826	Sept. 06	TuscarwsCoOh	07	12	26
Sears, Enoch(Z-M)	1829	April 08	TuscarwsCoOh	02	06	21
Sears, Ephraim(Z)	1815	Aug. 16	HarrisonCoOh	01	05	14
Sears, John(Z)	1832	June 07	Morgan Co,Oh	10	07	17
Sears, Wm. A.(Z)	1831	Feb. 02	Morgan Co,Oh	11	11	01
Sears, Wm. Alf'd.(Z)	1832	June 07	Morgan Co,Oh	11	11	01
Seavin, Margaret(Z)	1832	June 18	MuskingmCoOh	15	15	12
Seaward, Eli(Z)	1815	Dec. 19	MuskingmCoOh	09	04	05
Seaward, William B.(Z-M)	1836	April 02	CoshoctnCoOh	09	04	05
Seaward, Wm. B.(Z-M)	1837	Nov. 22	CoshoctnCoOh	09	04	05
Seawell, Benjamin(Z-M)	1833	June 27	CoshoctnCoOh	07	05	11
Sebrell, Joseph(Y)	1824	Jan. 05	ColumbanCoOh	06	19	10
Secor, Joshua(Z)	1815	Sept. 18	GreeneCo.,Pa	08	05	16
Secrest, Henry(Z)	1836	June 16	GuernseyCoOh	09	08	24
Secrest, Isaac(Z)	1836	Jan. 06	GuernseyCoOh	09	08	21
Secrest, Jacob Jr.(Z)	1836	Jan. 06	GuernseyCoOh	09	08	15
Secrest, Jacob Jr.(Z)	1836	Jan. 19	GuernseyCoOh	09	08	15
Secrest, Joseph(Z)	1836	Jan. 01	GuernseyCoOh	08	08	18
Secrest, Nathan(Z)	1836	Jan. 09	GuernseyCoOh	09	08	21
Secrist, Andrew(Z)	1822	April 03	GuernseyCoOh	08	07	19
Secrist, Frederick(Z)	1810	June 11	HampshreCoVa	09	08	09
Secrist, Henry(Z)	1826	Feb. 07	GuernseyCoOh	09	08	24
Secrist, Isaac(Z)	1826	Jan. 04	GuernseyCoOh	09	08	21
Secrist, J.(Z)	1815	Aug. 23	GuernseyCoOh	02	01	23
Secrist, Jacob(Z)	1814	Nov. 01	GuernseyCoOh	09	08	21
Secrist, James(Z)	1834	March 24	GuernseyCoOh	09	08	21
Secrist, John(Z)	1832	Feb. 28	GuernseyCoOh	09	08	09
Secton, Samuel(Y)	1831	Nov. 15	Jeff.Co.,Oh.	04	12	15
Seeley, John H.(Z)	1830	Jan. 30	WashngtnCoOh	10	06	28
Seely, Thomas(Z)	1817	Jan. 21	WashngtnCoOh	10	06	28
Sees, Christian(Z)	1811	Oct. 24	TuscarwsCoOh	04	09	22
Sees, George(Z-M)	1832	Aug. 28	TuscarwsCoOh	03	10	17
Sees, George(Z-M)	1832	Nov. 10	TuscarwsCoOh	03	10	18
Seever, Robert(Z-M)	1838	May 15	CoshoctnCoOh	10	04	10
Seggit, Levi(Y)	1831	Sept. 22	WashCo.,Penn	07	14	22
Sehirer, Jacob(Z)	1814	Jan. 12	MuskingmCoOh	05	02	05
Sehus, George(Z-M)	1837	June 26	CoshoctnCoOh	06	04	20
Seib, Andrew(Z-M)	1828	June 25	HolmesCoOhio	05	08	09
Seidle, Henry(Z-M)	1833	April 19	CoshoctnCoOh	06	07	11
Selby, Eli(Z)	1815	Feb. 28	MuskingmCoOh	15	15	01
Selby, Eli(Z)	1815	Feb. 28	MuskingmCoOh	15	15	01
Selby, Eli(Z)	1815	Feb. 28	MuskingmCoOh	15	16	36
Selders, Henry(Z-M)	1836	Dec. 10	GuernseyCoOh	03	01	05
Self, John(Z)	1805	June 06	FrederkCoVir	05	01	06
Self, John(Z)	1805	June 06	FrederkCoVir	05	01	06
Self, John(Z)	1805	June 06	FrederkCoVir	05	01	15
Self, John(Z)	1805	June 06	FrederkCoVir	05	01	15
Self, Thomas(Z)	1806	June 16	MuskingmCoOh	13	12	02

PURCHASER	YEAR	DATE	RESIDENCE	R	T	S
Self, Thomas(Z)	1806	June 23	?	13	12	02
Selix, D.(Z)	1815	Dec. 02	MuskingmCoOh	12	12	01
Sell, Anthony(Y)	1828	April 07	HarrisonCoOh	05	12	36
Sell, Anthony(Y)	1829	March 16	HarrisonCoOh	05	12	36
Sell, John(Z)	1809	Sept. 11	Jeff.Co.,Oh.	01	09	02
Sell, Peter(Y)	1821	April 19	TuscarwsCoOh	07	16	28
Sell, Peter(Y)	1828	Dec. 15	Stark Co.,Oh	07	16	34
Sell, Peter(Y)	1828	Dec. 20	Stark Co.,Oh	07	16	34
Sell, Peter(Y)	1829	March 17	Stark Co.,Oh	07	16	27
Sellars, Henry(Z)	1816	Sept. 18	MuskingmCoOh	15	16	33
Sellars, Isaac(Z)	1811	April 15	MuskingmCoOh	15	16	05
Sellars, Wm.(Z)	1811	April 15	MuskingmCoOh	15	16	05
Sellers, Henry(Z)	1808	Feb. 06	FairfeldCoOh	15	16	08
Sellers, Isaac(Z)	1807	Dec. 26	MuskingmCoOh	15	16	06
Sellers, John Junr.(Z)	1814	Feb. 16	MuskingmCoOh	15	16	17
Sellers, John(Z)	1807	Dec. 26	MuskingmCoOh	15	16	03
Sellman, Morrits(Y)	1839	May 06	Stark Co.,Oh	07	20	07
Sells, David(Z-M)	1935	Dec. 18	GuernseyCoOh	03	04	22
Sells, Henry(Z-M)	1835	Dec. 18	GuernseyCoOh	03	04	18
Seltenright, David(Z-M)	1823	Jan. 14	TuscarwsCoOh	04	09	04
Seltenright, David(Z-M)	1832	Dec. 25	TuscarwsCoOh	04	07	04
Seltenright, David(Z-M)	1832	Dec. 25	TuscarwsCoOh	04	07	04
Seltenwright, David Senr.(Z)	1817	Jan. 06	TuscarwsCoOh	04	07	16
Seltenwright, David(Z)	1814	May 30	TuscarwsCoOh	04	08	18
Seltle, Gaden(Z)	1834	Jan. 24	Perry Co.,Oh	14	14	20
Semmy, John(Z-M)	1831	Sept. 15	HolmesCoOhio	07	08	09
Semple, Edward(Z)	1827	Nov. 13	GuernseyCoOh	03	04	13
Senerson, Benj.(Z-M)	1830	Dec. 08	TuscarwsCoOh	03	05	11
Senerson, John(Z-M)	1830	Dec. 08	TuscarwsCoOh	03	05	20
Sennart, Philip(Y)	1823	May 06	Stark Co.,Oh	07	17	08
Senofenck, John(Z)	1808	June 15	MuskingmCoOh	04	02	23
Sensten, Abraham(Z-M)	1838	March 31	TuscarwsCoOh	08	08	15
Sergent, Thos.(Z-M)	1834	Jan. 16	TuscarwsCoOh	03	09	10
Sergent, Thos.(Z-M)	1834	Jan. 16	TuscarwsCoOh	01	08	04
Seright, Jas.of And'w.(Z)	1828	Nov. 14	MuskingmCoOh	11	12	08
Settewright, Samuel(Z-M)	1834	March 22	TuscarwsCoOh	04	08	23
Settle, Gaden(Z)	1834	Jan. 24	Perry Co.,Oh	14	14	20
Sevall, John(Z)	1827	July 06	Morgan Co,Oh	12	11	01
Sevall, John(Z)	1828	Sept. 09	Morgan Co,Oh	11	11	06
Sevan, Edward E.(Z-M)	1835	April 10	HolmesCoOhio	08	08	05
Severance, Daniel(Z-M)	1824	Feb. 10	CoshoctnCoOh	08	06	14
Severance, Rodney(Z)	1822	April 15	Morgan Co,Oh	10	08	13
Severance, Rodney(Z)	1822	May 01	Morgan Co,Oh	10	08	13
Severance, Silas(Z)	1835	Dec. 10	MonroeCo.,Oh	08	06	27
Severance, Silas(Z)	1836	Sept. 10	MonroeCo.,Oh	08	06	29
Severance, Silas(Z)	1836	Oct. 06	MonroeCo.,Oh	08	06	28
Severance, Silas(Z)	1837	May 10	MonroeCo.,Oh	08	06	21
Severns, Daniel(Z-M)	1834	Jan. 08	CoshoctnCoOh	08	06	02
Severns, Daniel(Z-M)	1835	Sept. 08	CoshoctnCoOh	08	06	06
Severns, Daniel(Z-M)	1836	Feb. 01	CoshoctnCoOh	08	06	02
Severns, Daniel(Z-M)	1836	Sept. 06	CoshoctnCoOh	08	06	07
Severns, James(Z-M)	1836	Aug. 15	CoshoctnCoOh	08	06	02
Severns, James(Z-M)	1836	Aug. 15	CoshoctnCoOh	08	07	22
Severns, John S.(Z-M)	1836	May 23	CoshoctnCoOh	08	06	03
Severns, John S.(Z-M)	1837	June 12	CoshoctnCoOh	08	06	08
Severns, Joseph(Z)	1811	Feb. 07	CoshoctnCoOh	09	06	20
Severns, Joseph(Z)	1815	Sept. 25	CoshoctnCoOh	09	06	11
Severns, Joseph(Z)	1816	March 08	CoshoctnCoOh	09	06	23
Severson, Benjamin(Z-M)	1833	June 05	TuscarwsCoOh	03	05	20
Sewall, John B.(Z-M)	1829	March 11	TuscarwsCoOh	01	05	15
Seward, Ebenezer(Z-M)	1829	July 20	CoshoctnCoOh	09	04	07
Seward, Eli(Z)	1815	Dec. 13	MuskingmCoOh	09	04	06
Seward, Elijah(Y)	1829	Dec. 24	HarrisonCoOh	07	11	05
Seward, Elijah(Z)	1836	April 22	Morgan Co,Oh	09	07	24
Seward, James E.(Z-M)	1828	May 12	CoshoctnCoOh	09	04	05
Sewell, Andrew(Y)	1831	July 05	TuscarwsCoOh	07	12	30
Sewell, John B.(Z-M)	1835	Sept. 26	TuscarwsCoOh	01	05	06
Sewell, William(Z-M)	1832	March 22	TuscarwsCoOh	02	06	21
Sewell, William(Z-M)	1836	May 23	TuscarwsCoOh	02	06	03

PURCHASER	YEAR	DATE	RESIDENCE	R	T	S
Sewerd, Elija(Y)	1833	Oct. 07	HarrisonCoOh	07	11	05
Sexton, William(Z)	1835	Oct. 09	Perry Co.,Oh	14	13	28
Sexton, William(Z)	1836	Feb. 02	Perry Co.,Oh	14	13	21
Shackler, M.(Z)	1836	Aug. 01	Wheeling,Vir	08	06	04
Shackler, M.(Z)	1836	Aug. 01	Wheeling,Vir	08	06	05
Shade, Samuel(Y)	1825	Aug. 13	ColumbanCoOh	05	17	10
Shaeffer, J.(Z-M)	1830	Nov. 08	TuscarwsCoOh	04	07	08
Shaeffer, P.(Z-M)	1830	Nov. 08	TuscarwsCoOh	04	07	08
Shafer, Frederick(Y)	1822	June 25	Stark Co.,Oh	09	11	27
Shafer, George(Z)	1836	Jan. 14	GuernseyCoOh	08	08	33
Shafer, George(Z-M)	1832	Oct. 05	HolmesCoOhio	08	08	02
Shafer, Henry(Y)	1831	July 26	Stark Co.,Oh	06	17	28
Shafer, Henry(Z)	1815	Oct. 19	SomersetCoPa	02	07	03
Shafer, Henry(Z)	1815	Oct. 19	SomersetCoPa	02	07	07
Shafer, Henry(Z)	1815	Oct. 19	SomersetCoPa	02	07	04
Shafer, Henry(Z-M)	1833	May 04	TuscarwsCoOh	03	07	25
Shafer, Jacob(Z-M)	1832	Oct. 27	TuscarwsCoOh	03	07	25
Shafer, Jacob(Z-M)	1832	Oct. 27	TuscarwsCoOh	03	07	25
Shafer, John F.(Z-M)	1836	May 11	TuscarwsCoOh	03	07	17
Shafer, John(Y)	1837	April 06	Stark Co.,Oh	07	20	07
Shafer, John(Z)	1825	May 23	WashCo.,Penn	11	10	14
Shafer, John(Z-M)	1832	Oct. 05	HolmesCoOhio	08	08	09
Shafer, Nathan(Z-M)	1832	Oct. 11	HolmesCoOhio	07	08	11
Shafer, Nicholas(Z-M)	1832	Oct. 17	HolmesCoOhio	07	08	09
Shafer, Nicholas(Z-M)	1832	Oct. 17	HolmesCoOhio	07	08	09
Shafer, Peter(Z-M)	1833	Sept. 24	KnoxCo.,Ohio	11	08	12
Shafer, Peter(Z-M)	1835	Dec. 28	KnoxCo.,Ohio	11	08	13
Shafer, Samuel(Z)	1835	Sept. 23	GuernseyCoOh	09	05	10
Shafer, Samuel(Z)	1836	March 28	GuernseyCoOh	09	05	25
Shafer, Wm.(Z)	1835	March 13	GuernseyCoOh	08	08	27
Shafer, Wm.(Z)	1836	Jan. 28	GuernseyCoOh	08	08	27
Shaff, Philip(Z-M)	1838	Oct. 17	GuernseyCoOh	03	04	03
Shaff, Philip(Z-M)	1838	Oct. 17	GuernseyCoOh	03	04	03
Shaffer, Abraham(Y)	1832	Oct. 16	AdamsCo,Penn	04	13	14
Shaffer, Ch'sph.(Z-M)	1837	Sept. 27	CoshoctnCoOh	04	04	02
Shaffer, David(Y)	1826	Feb. 06	Stark Co.,Oh	07	16	17
Shaffer, Jacob Jr.(Z-M)	1833	Aug. 17	TuscarwsCoOh	04	07	13
Shaffer, Jacob(Y)	1823	May 15	TuscarwsCoOh	07	16	01
Shaffer, Jacob(Z-M)	1831	Nov. 14	FayetteCo,Pa	04	07	13
Shaffer, James(Y)	1828	Aug. 21	ColumbanCoOh	04	13	17
Shaffer, Peter(Y)	1826	Oct. 16	Stark Co.,Oh	07	16	17
Shaffer, Philip(Z-M)	1822	Dec. 06	MuskingmCoOh	11	08	15
Shaffer, Sam'l.(Z-M)	1832	Jan. 19	CoshoctnCoOh	06	04	01
Shaffer, Sam'l.(Z-M)	1837	Sept. 27	CoshoctnCoOh	04	04	02
Shaffer, Samuel(Z-M)	1837	Feb. 01	CoshoctnCoOh	05	04	23
Shaffer, Samuel(Z-M)	1837	Sept. 30	CoshoctnCoOh	04	04	02
Shaffer, William(Y)	1826	May 15	Stark Co.,Oh	06	18	10
Shaffer, William(Y)	1826	Oct. 09	Stark Co.,Oh	06	18	11
Shaffer, William(Z-M)	1836	Nov. 23	HolmesCoOhio	09	08	17
Shaffer, Wm.(H)	1823	June 27	Stark Co.,Oh	06	18	27
Shaffer, Wm.(Y)	1823	June 20	Stark Co.,Oh	06	18	10
Shaffer, Wm.(Y)	1823	June 20	Stark Co.,Oh	06	18	10
Shaffer, Wm.(Y)	1824	Feb. 20	Stark Co.,Oh	06	18	10
Shafor, Conrad(Z)	1832	Sept. 06	GuernseyCoOh	08	08	28
Shaklee, Peter Jr.(Z)	1827	May 24	Morgan Co,Oh	10	07	35
Shaklee, William H.(Z)	1835	Dec. 14	Morgan Co,Oh	09	05	21
Shaklee, Wm. Hardy(Z)	1835	Nov. 09	Morgan Co,Oh	09	05	21
Shakler, William Hardy(Z)	1832	Oct. 19	Morgan Co,Oh	09	05	15
Shalock, John(Z)	1831	Feb. 26	Morgan Co,Oh	10	06	07
Shambaugh, Isaac(Z-M)	1833	Nov. 27	CoshoctnCoOh	06	04	13
Shambaugh, Jno.(Y)	1825	May 24	HarrisonCoOh	05	12	35
Shamee, John(Z-M)	1832	May 29	TuscarwsCoOh	02	06	19
Shanan, Henry(Z-M)	1830	Oct. 19	TuscarwsCoOh	02	08	23
Shane, A.(Z)	1814	Oct. 10	TuscarwsCoOh	04	09	24
Shane, Abraham(Z)	1807	May 30	MuskingmCoOh	03	10	18
Shane, Abraham(Z)	1814	June 11	TuscarwsCoOh	04	08	03
Shane, Abraham(Z-M)	1833	July 22	TuscarwsCoOh	04	10	01
Shaner, Henry(Z)	1834	Dec. 02	AthensCoOhio	14	12	32
Shaner, Henry(Z)	1834	Dec. 02	AthensCoOhio	14	12	32

PURCHASER	YEAR	DATE	RESIDENCE	R	T	S
Shaner, Henry(Z-M)	1831	Feb. 21	TuscarwsCoOh	03	07	11
Shank, Christopher(Z-M)	1832	July 03	FayetteCo,Pa	04	07	09
Shank, Christopher(Z-M)	1832	July 03	FayetteCo,Pa	04	07	12
Shank, Henry(Z-M)	1831	Nov. 14	FayetteCo,Pa	04	07	09
Shankland, Robt.(Z-M)	1832	Feb. 18	CoshoctnCoOh	09	04	14
Shanklin, Robt.(Z-M)	1829	Feb. 14	Jeff.Co.,Oh.	09	04	15
Shanks, David(Z-M)	1836	Nov. 02	TuscarwsCoOh	03	07	25
Shanks, Frederick(Z)	1837	Jan. 28	WashngtnCoOh	08	06	33
Shanks, Frederick(Z)	1837	Jan. 28	WashngtnCoOh	08	06	34
Shanks, James(Z-M)	1833	June 06	TuscarwsCoOh	04	07	19
Shanks, James(Z-M)	1836	Dec. 10	TuscarwsCoOh	03	06	01
Shannifelt, David(Z-M)	1832	Dec. 05	MuskingmCoOh	05	03	15
Shannon, Aaron(Z)	1817	Jan. 23	WashCo.,Penn	01	05	07
Shannon, Amon(Z)	1817	May 17	WashCo.,Penn	02	04	20
Shannon, Amon(Z-M)	1830	Feb. 26	TuscarwsCoOh	01	09	07
Shannon, Benj.(Z)	1830	April 07	Morgan Co,Oh	11	11	24
Shannon, Enos(Z-M)	1828	July 30	TuscarwsCoOh	02	06	21
Shannon, Enos(Z-M)	1836	April 07	TuscarwsCoOh	02	05	01
Shannon, Isaac(Z-M)	1830	March 05	CoshoctnCoOh	07	07	20
Shannon, Isaac(Z-M)	1832	July 06	CoshoctnCoOh	07	07	20
Shannon, Isaac(Z-M)	1836	May 24	CoshoctnCoOh	07	07	20
Shannon, James(Z)	1834	July 28	Morgan Co,Oh	11	11	15
Shannon, James(Z-M)	1836	Feb. 19	LickingCo,Oh	11	04	13
Shannon, Jno.(Z-M)	1831	Nov. 21	LickingCo,Oh	11	04	13
Shannon, John(Z)	1815	May 17	LickingCo,Oh	11	04	08
Shannon, Joseph(Z-M)	1836	Nov. 11	TuscarwsCoOh	03	06	10
Shannon, Owen(Z)	1837	Oct. 12	Morgan Co,Oh	14	12	13
Shannon, Owen(Z)	1837	Oct. 12	Morgan Co,Oh	14	12	24
Shannon, Owen(Z)	1837	Dec. 28	Morgan Co,Oh	13	08	09
Shannon, Philip(Z)	1837	Oct. 12	Morgan Co,Oh	14	12	02
Shannon, Thomas(Z)	1815	March 13	HarrisonCoOh	01	05	17
Shannon, William(Z-M)	1831	Oct. 28	LickingCo,Oh	11	04	08
Shannon, Wm.(Z-M)	1836	Feb. 19	LickingCo,Oh	11	04	08
Shanock, James(Z)	1805	Nov. 19	MuskingmCoOh	01	02	21
Sharan, William(Z)	1816	Oct. 21	Jeff.Co.,Oh.	01	05	16
Sharit, Joseph Lake(Z-M)	1832	July 31	CoshoctnCoOh	09	07	06
Sharitt, Joseph L.(Z-M)	1832	June 13	CoshoctnCoOh	09	07	07
Sharkey, Wm. W.(Z)	1834	Jan. 28	Perry Co.,Oh	15	15	25
Sharklee, William Hardy(Z)	1832	Oct. 19	Morgan Co,Oh	09	05	22
Sharp, Arch'd.(Z)	1831	Jan. 27	Perry Co.,Oh	15	14	24
Sharp, Benjamin(Y)	1825	Sept. 28	HarrisonCoOh	05	12	23
Sharp, David(Z)	1835	Aug. 20	BelmontCo,Oh	10	09	36
Sharp, Elias(Y)	1826	Nov. 03	HarrisonCoOh	05	12	24
Sharp, Ethelbert(Y)	1827	March 28	ColumbanCoOh	03	12	18
Sharp, John(Z)	1825	June 15	Morgan Co,Oh	10	06	26
Sharp, John(Z)	1827	Nov. 23	Morgan Co,Oh	10	06	26
Sharp, John(Z)	1815	Dec. 27	BelmontCo,Oh	12	11.	26
Sharp, Michael(Z-M)	1836	May 02	Wayne Co.,Oh	08	08	12
Sharp, Pearley(Y)	1826	Feb. 09	Ohio Co.,Vir	03	05	01
Sharp, Pearley(Y)	1826	March 13	Ohio Co.,Vir	03	05	02
Sharp, Pearley(Y)	1826	March 13	Ohio Co.,Vir	03	05	02
Sharp, Robt.(Y)	1827	March 28	ColumbanCoOh	03	12	18
Sharrock, Benjamin(Z)	1816	June 13	GuernseyCoOh	06	02	05
Sharrock, Benjamin(Z)	1816	Sept. 21	GuernseyCoOh	04	02	14
Sharrock, Everuret(Z)	1816	Sept. 21	GuernseyCoOh	04	03	22
Sharrock, James(Z)	1806	Jan. 23	MuskingmCoOh	01	01	10
Sharrow, Christian(Z)	1836	Jan. 05	Morgan Co,Oh	09	06	30
Shatto, Nicholas(Z)	1832	Oct. 25	GuernseyCoOh	08	08	28
Shatts, Joseph(Z)	1835	Aug. 12	MonroeCo.,Oh	08	07	05
Shaver, Henry(Z)	1815	Oct. 19	SomersetCoPa	02	07	04
Shaver, Henry(Z)	1816	June 29	SomersetCoPa	02	07	07
Shaver, Henry(Z-M)	1833	July 15	TuscarwsCoOh	02	07	07
Shaver, Henry(Z-M)	1835	June 22	TuscarwsCoOh	02	07	05
Shaver, Jonas(Z)	1829	Sept. 09	MuskingmCoOh	12	12	15
Shaver, Jonas(Z)	1832	March 05	MuskingmCoOh	12	12	09
Shaver, Jonas(Z)	1836	Feb. 11	MuskingmCoOh	09	05	26
Shaver, Jonas(Z)	1815	Aug. 26	MuskingmCoOh	12	13	26
Shaver, Samuel(Z)	1816	Oct. 09	MuskingmCoOh	13	11	16
Shaw, Alexander(Z)	1814	Feb. 15	FairfeldCoOh	10	01	13

PURCHASER	YEAR	DATE	RESIDENCE	R	T	S
Shaw, Austin(Z-M)	1835	Sept. 23	NewYork,N.Y.	05	03	01
Shaw, Charles(Z-M)	1832	April 23	LickingCo,Oh	11	04	25
Shaw, George(Z-M)	1833	Feb. 07	KnoxCo.,Ohio	10	07	25
Shaw, James(Z-M)	1822	Aug. 30	CoshoctnCoOh	07	05	04
Shaw, James(Z-M)	1833	Sept. 26	CoshoctnCoOh	07	05	04
Shaw, Jesse(Z-M)	1836	March 23	CoshoctnCoOh	08	06	10
Shaw, Joel(Z)	1836	Jan. 25	Perry Co.,Oh	15	14	22
Shaw, Joel(Z)	1836	Aug. 30	Perry Co.,Oh	15	14	27
Shaw, Joseph(Z)	1805	Dec. 02	MuskingmCoOh	02	02	03
Shaw, Latimer R.(Z-M)	1833	Nov. 13	NewYork,N.Y.	05	03	01
Shaw, Margaret(Z-M)	1836	Jan. 07	CoshoctnCoOh	06	04	09
Shaw, N.(Z)	1817	June 21	MuskingmCoOh	14	13	09
Shaw, Nathan(Z)	1824	July 06	MuskingmCoOh	15	16	21
Shaw, Z.(Z)	1816	March 30	LickingCo,Oh	12	09	17
Shaw, Zachariah(Z)	1813	Nov. 11	Lickingco,Oh	10	01	12
Shay, David Jr.(Z-M)	1834	Feb. 07	CoshoctnCoOh	05	04	16
Shay, David Junr.(Z)	1833	March 30	?	?	?	?
Shay, David(Z)	1833	March 30	?	?	?	?
Shay, David(Z-M)	1833	Sept. 27	CoshoctnCoOh	05	04	17
Shay, John(Z-M)	1832	Dec. 11	CoshoctnCoOh	04	06	11
Shay, John(Z-M)	1836	April 15	CoshoctnCoOh	04	07	25
Sheehan, Corn's. Jr.(Y)	1824	March 25	ColumbanCoOh	03	13	22
Sheehan, Cornelius(Y)	1831	Aug. 24	ColumbanCoOh	03	13	22
Sheeley, Christian(Z-M)	1835	Nov. 16	GuernseyCoOh	03	04	16
Sheelin, David(Y)	1826	Feb. 15	WashCo.,Penn	05	15	07
Sheely, Christian(Z)	1814	June 08	HarrisonCoOh	04	03	09
Sheely, Christian(Z)	1814	June 08	HarrisonCoOh	04	04	20
Sheely, Christian(Z)	1814	June 08	HarrisonCoOh	03	04	15
Sheely, Christian(Z)	1814	June 08	HarrisonCoOh	03	04	15
Sheely, John(Z)	1814	June 08	HarrisonCoOh	04	04	11
Sheely, Joseph(Z)	1816	April 25	GuernseyCoOh	06	09	04
Sheely, Joseph(Z-M)	1828	Sept. 02	HolmesCoOhio	06	09	17
Sheenan, James(Z)	1832	May 22	Perry Co.,Oh	15	15	23
Sheeran, James(Z)	1833	March 25	Perry Co.,Oh	15	15	23
Sheeran, James(Z)	1836	Dec. 03	Perry Co.,Oh	15	15	23
Sheerer, Adam(Y)	1827	July 17	Stark Co.,Oh	07	17	02
Sheerer, Jacob(Y)	1822	June 11	Stark Co.,Oh	06	16	36
Sheets, George(Y)	1821	Nov. 09	ColumbanCoOh	04	16	15
Sheets, George(Z-M)	1836	Oct. 19	HolmesCoOhio	09	08	16
Sheets, George(Z-M)	1836	Oct. 19	HolmesCoOhio	09	08	14
Sheets, Samuel(Z-M)	1835	Sept. 08	HolmesCoOhio	09	09	01
Sheets, William(Z-M)	1831	June 29	TuscarwsCoOh	01	09	08
Sheir, Michael Jr.(Z-M)	1838	June 05	CoshoctnCoOh	09	07	21
Shelden, David(Z-M)	1836	March 31	BelmontCo,Oh	03	06	13
Shelden, Thomas(Z-M)	1836	June 06	HolmesCoOhio	09	08	21
Shelden, William(Z)	1837	Jan. 21	Morgan Co,Oh	09	06	22
Sheldon, William(Z)	1833	March 19	Morgan Co,Oh	09	06	22
Sheldorn, James(Z)	1836	Nov. 01	WashngtnCoOh	09	07	09
Sheline, Mich'l.(Y)	1828	April 18	HarrisonCoOh	06	15	36
Shellenbarger, Abraham(Z-M)	1837	May 31	KnoxCo.,Ohio	10	08	04
Shellenberger, Abraham(Z-M)	1833	Oct. 18	KnoxCo.,Ohio	10	09	03
Shellenberger, Abraham(Z-M)	1836	Sept. 03	KnoxCo.,Ohio	10	09	03
Shellenberger, Jno.(Z-M)	1831	Nov. 14	KnoxCo.,Ohio	10	08	03
Shellenberger, Sam'l.(Z-M)	1831	Oct. 25	KnoxCo.,Ohio	10	08	04
Shelt, Henry(Z-M)	1831	Oct. 26	HolmesCoOhio	07	08	05
Sheneman, Benjamin(Z-M)	1836	Jan. 21	HolmesCoOhio	06	08	20
Sheneman, Christian(Z-M)	1826	March 24	HolmesCoOhio	05	08	25
Sheneman, Ferdinand(Z-M)	1829	Feb. 17	HolmesCoOhio	06	08	20
Sheneman, Henry(Z)	1815	Nov. 23	TuscarwsCoOh	05	08	25
Sheneman, Henry(Z-M)	1836	March 29	HolmesCoOhio	08	06	11
Sheneman, Henry(Z-M)	1836	Nov. 24	HolmesCoOhio	05	08	25
Sheneman, Jonathan(Z-M)	1829	Feb. 17	HolmesCoOhio	06	08	20
Sheneman, Jonathan(Z-M)	1833	Feb. 16	HolmesCoOhio	06	08	20
Shenneman, Henry(Z-M)	1833	April 26	HolmesCoOhio	05	08	25
Shenock, James(Z)	1805	Dec. 02	MuskingmCoOh	01	02	22
Shepard, Henry(Z)	1833	Oct. 19	Morgan Co,Oh	10	06	28
Sheperd, Benj.(Z)	1831	March 12	Morgan Co,Oh	13	08	20
Sheperd, Henry(Z)	1830	Jan. 13	Morgan Co,Oh	10	06	28
Sheperd, Isaiah(Z)	1838	Dec. 20	Morgan Co,Oh	13	08	21

PURCHASER	YEAR	DATE	RESIDENCE	R	T	S
Sheperdson, Jacob(Z)	1816	Feb. 21	MuskingmCoOh	05	03	09
Shephard, Michael(Z)	1833	Aug. 13	Morgan Co,Oh	09	06	20
Shepherd, Absalon B.(Z)	1832	April 12	MuskingmCoOh	14	13	32
Shepherd, Arnold(Z)	1833	Dec. 20	Morgan Co,Oh	09	06	20
Shepherd, James(Y)	1825	April 04	Jeff.Co.,Oh.	02	09	15
Shepherd, James(Y)	1827	March 01	HarrisonCoOh	05	13	02
Shepherd, James(Y)	1828	Jan. 14	PittsburghPa	02	09	15
Shepherd, James(Y)	1828	Jan. 30	HarrisonCoOh	05	13	02
Shepherd, James(Y)	1828	Nov. 07	PittsburghPa	02	09	15
Shepherd, John(Y)	1827	Dec. 29	Jeff.Co.,Co.	04	12	14
Shepherd, John(Y)	1832	Feb. 27	Jeff.Co.,Oh.	04	12	14
Shepherd, John(Y)	1834	June 11	Jeff.Co.,Oh.	04	12	15
Shepherd, John(Z)	1833	April 18	Morgan Co,Oh	13	08	17
Shepherd, John(Z)	1837	Jan. 11	Morgan Co,Oh	13	08	17
Shepherd, Nathaniel(Z)	1823	Aug. 27	Morgan Co,Oh	12	10	29
Shepherd, Peter(Y)	1825	Oct. 24	Jeff.Co.,Oh.	04	12	34
Shepherd, Peter(Y)	1827	Oct. 10	Jeff.Co.,Oh.	04	12	34
Shepherd, Peter(Z)	1827	May 22	MuskingmCoOh	13	11	19
Shepherd, Richard(Y)	1827	Aug. 29	BelmontCo,Oh	04	06	15
Shepherd, Thomas(Z)	1824	May 11	WashCo.,Penn	11	13	22
Shepler, Henry(Z)	1807	Nov. 02	WashCo.,Penn	11	13	13
Shepler, Henry(Z)	1807	Nov. 02	WashCo.,Penn	11	13	13
Sheppard, Geo.(Z)	1833	Nov. 15	BelmontCo,Oh	09	06	20
Sheppard, Michael(Z)	1835	Oct. 21	Morgan Co,Oh	09	06	20
Sheppard, Nathan(Z-M)	1837	Nov. 23	BelmontCo,Oh	02	05	01
Sheppard, Timothy(Z-M)	1836	Jan. 13	CoshoctnCoOh	09	05	16
Shepperd, Lenox(Z)	1816	Oct. 16	WestmrldCoPa	09	04	10
Sherar, George W.(Z-M)	1837	Aug. 15	MuskingmCoOh	04	03	04
Sherer, John(Y)	1823	Sept. 22	Stark Co.,Oh	07	18	26
Sherlock, John(Z)	1835	April 11	Morgan Co,Oh	10	06	18
Sherlock, Martin(Z)	1830	June 16	Morgan Co,Oh	10	06	18
Sherlock, Martin(Z)	1835	April 11	Morgan Co,Oh	10	06	18
Sherlock, Patrick(Z)	1831	Oct. 17	Morgan Co,Oh	10	06	19
Sherlock, Patrick(Z)	1831	Aug. 19	Morgan Co,Oh	10	06	17
Sherlock, Patrick(Z)	1835	March 27	Morgan Co,Oh	10	06	18
Sherlock, Patrick(Z)	1835	Sept. 23	Morgan Co,Oh	10	06	18
Sherman, Caleb(Y)	1830	March 24	HarrisonCoOh	05	12	34
Sherman, Eli(Z)	1815	March 04	MuskingmCoOh	12	13	27
Sherman, Ferd.(Z-M)	1832	Jan. 30	HolmesCoOhio	06	08	11
Sherman, Josiah(Z)	1827	Nov. 05	MuskingmCoOh	12	13	27
Sherman, Moses(Z)	1815	Sept. 02	GuernseyCoOh	01	03	20
Sherman, William(Z)	1814	Aug. 19	GuernseyCoOh	10	07	08
Sherod, Amos(Y)	1831	April 04	TuscarwsCoOh	07	14	18
Sherod, Charles M.(Y)	1829	Aug. 03	TuscarwsCoOh	07	15	26
Sherod, George(Z-M)	1835	Feb. 17	CarrolCo.,Oh	04	07	21
Sherod, John Green(Y)	1831	Dec. 10	TuscarwsCoOh	07	14	18
Sherod, Joseph(Y)	1832	Oct. 02	TuscarwsCoOh	07	14	24
Sherod, Wm.(Y)	1829	March 18	TuscarwsCoOh	07	15	07
Sheron, Patrick(Z)	1837	April 26	MuskingmCoOh	14	12	23
Sheron, Patrick(Z)	1837	April 28	MuskingmCoOh	14	12	14
Sherrard, Robert A.(Z)	1816	May 24	Jeff.Co.,Oh.	04	02	24
Sherrard, Wm.(Z-M)	1831	Oct. 11	GuernseyCoOh	04	02	10
Sherrard, Wm.(Z-M)	1831	March 11	GuernseyCoOh	04	02	10
Sherwood, Asa(Z)	1814	Nov. 28	LickingCo,Oh	06	02	14
Shick, John(Z)	1817	Jan. 20	Jeff.Co.,Oh.	03	02	10
Shidler, David(Y)	1824	Dec. 13	WashCo.,Penn	06	18	21
Shield, Daniel(Z-M)	1833	Sept. 05	HolmesCoOhio	07	08	05
Shield, Daniel(Z-M)	1833	Sept. 16	HolmesCoOhio	07	08	05
Shield, Daniel(Z-M)	1833	Feb. 01	HolmesCoOhio	07	08	05
Shield, Henry(Z-M)	1834	Sept. 02	HolmesCoOhio	08	08	15
Shields, Hugh(Z)	1835	Sept. 24	BelmontCo,Oh	10	07	13
Shields, Joseph(Z)	1809	Nov. 07	AlleghnyCoPa	11	13	17
Shields, Joshua(Z)	1832	Nov. 06	Perry Co.,Oh	15	15	31
Shields, William(Z)	1833	Feb. 04	GuernseyCoOh	08	07	06
Shields, William(Z)	1836	Jan. 30	BelmontCo,Oh	10	07	36
Shilling, Amos(Z)	1816	May 02	MuskingmCoOh	12	12	34
Shilling, Jacob(Y)	1827	March 10	HarrisonCoOh	05	13	27
Shilling, Jacob(Y)	1828	May 22	ColumbanCoOH	06	19	01
Shilling, Wm.(Z)	1828	March 19	MuskingmCoOh	12	12	03

PURCHASER	YEAR	DATE	RESIDENCE	R	T	S
Shiltz, John(Z-M)	1832	May 18	TuscarwsCoOh	01	09	22
Shimpler, Abraham(Z-M)	1832	March 16	HolmesCoOhio	07	08	15
Shimpler, Abraham(Z-M)	1832	March 16	HolmesCoOhio	08	08	01
Shince, Wm.(Z)	1831	June 07	Morgan Co,Oh	11	11	06
Shineman, Fred(Z-M)	1832	May 16	HolmesCoOhio	06	08	20
Shineman, Jonathan(Z-M)	1835	Sept. 07	HolmesCoOhio	06	08	20
Shinn, Levi(Z)	1810	May 29	MuskingmCoOh	15	18	08
Shinn, Samuel(Z)	1835	Nov. 27	GuernseyCoOh	09	05	29
Shinn, Samuel(Z)	1835	Nov. 27	GuernseyCoOh	09	05	20
Shinnifield, John(Z)	1827	Nov. 17	MuskingmCoOh	06	03	12
Shipler, Henry(Z)	1807	Dec. 17	WashCo.,Penn	11	13	14
Shipley, Amon(Z)	1833	Jan. 25	GuernseyCoOh	13	10	03
Shipley, Amon(Z)	1835	Aug. 18	GuernseyCoOh	13	10	03
Shipley, Amon(Z-M)	1831	Feb. 21	GuernseyCoOh	01	04	21
Shipley, Chas.(Z)	1836	Aug. 11	MuskingmCoOh	14	12	32
Shipley, George(Z)	1835	Sept. 22	GuernseyCoOh	09	05	03
Shipley, George(Z)	1833	Nov. 04	GuernseyCoOh	09	06	32
Shipley, James(Z)	1816	Dec. 24	GuernseyCoOh	04	06	19
Shipley, Jesse(Z)	1835	Oct. 28	Perry Co.,Oh	14	12	34
Shipley, Jesse(Z)	1836	July 02	Perry Co.,Oh	14	12	34
Shipley, Nicholas(Z)	1831	Aug. 16	MuskingmCoOh	12	12	21
Shipley, Rachel(Z)	1833	April 13	GuernseyCoOh	14	12	33
Shipley, Simon(Z-M)	1836	Sept. 20	HolmesCoOhio	09	08	09
Shipman, Jacob(Z)	1832	June 29	Morgan Co,Oh	10	07	10
Ships, Nathan(Z)	1815	Jan. 06	LickingCo,Oh	11	01	09
Shipton, Wm.(Y)	1828	Feb. 19	HarrisonCoOh	05	11	20
Shirck, Christian(Z)	1831	Nov. 18	Morgan Co,Oh	13	09	03
Shirck, Christian(Z)	1816	Dec. 16	MuskingmCoOh	13	10	29
Shire, Jacob(Z)	1815	Sept. 07	TuscarwsCoOh	01	10	15
Shirek, John(Z)	1817	May 06	MuskingmCoOh	13	10	33
Shirembrand, Jacob(Z)	1832	Oct. 15	Morgan Co,Oh	13	10	28
Shirer, Dave(Z-M)	1828	Aug. 23	MuskingmCoOh	06	03	25
Shirer, Jacob(Z-M)	1825	May 23	MuskingmCoOh	06	03	16
Shirer, Jacob(Z-M)	1825	May 23	MuskingmCoOh	06	03	25
Shirer, Peter(Z)	1814	Sept. 28	MuskingmCoOh	07	03	20
Shirer, Peter(Z)	1816	May 10	MuskingmCoOh	05	02	06
Shires, Valentine(Z)	1810	Feb. 19	MuskingmCoOh	07	03	23
Shirey, Valentine(Z)	1816	Oct. 14	MuskingmCoOh	06	03	16
Shirey, Valentine(Z)	1817	April 30	MuskingmCoOh	06	03	15
Shirlar, John(Z-M)	1832	Oct. 04	TuscarwsCoOh	03	10	15
Shirley, John(Z)	1816	Jan. 20	WashngtnCoOh	09	06	29
Shirley, Joseph(Z)	1832	Dec. 07	Morgan Co,Oh	10	06	22
Shirley, Peter(Z)	1833	July 30	Morgan Co,Oh	10	06	23
Shirur, Isaac(Z)	1813	Dec. 27	MuskingmCoOh	06	01	13
Shively, Christ'n.(Y)	1823	Jan. 14	Stark Co.,Oh	07	18	15
Shively, Isaac(Y)	1824	May 20	Stark Co.,Oh	07	18	14
Shiver, David(Z-M)	1829	Dec. 21	MuskingmCoOh	07	03	22
Shiver, Jacob(Z)	1814	Jan. 12	MuskingmCoOh	05	02	05
Shivers, Samuel(Y)	1826	Oct. 02	ColumbanCoOh	02	10	07
Shmyer, William(Z)	1806	July 01	MuskingmCoOh	03	10	20
Shnyer, William(Z)	1806	July 21	MuskingmCoOh	03	10	20
Shock, Jacob(Z-M)	1833	May 06	KnoxCo.,Ohio	10	07	18
Shock, Peter(Z-M)	1837	June 06	CoshoctnCoOh	05	07	07
Shockley, Nathan(Z)	1837	March 02	Morgan Co,Oh	08	06	33
Shockly, Nathan(Z)	1836	April 07	Morgan Co,Oh	09	05	23
Shoe, Jacob(Y)	1828	Sept. 26	Stark Co.,Oh	06	15	34
Shoemaker, Barnard(Z)	1831	Nov. 18	Morgan Co,Oh	13	10	28
Shoemaker, David(Y)	1827	Feb. 20	ColumbanCoOh	05	17	21
Shoff, John(Z-M)	1835	Oct. 23	GuernseyCoOh	04	05	23
Shoff, John(Z-M)	1835	Nov. 09	GuernseyCoOh	04	05	18
Shoff, Philip(Z-M)	1831	Sept. 19	GuernseyCoOh	03	01	12
Shoff, Philip(Z-M)	1834	March 03	GuernseyCoOh	04	04	20
Shoff, Washington(Z-M)	1836	Jan. 06	GuernseyCoOh	04	04	20
Shoin, James(Z-M)	1822	April 20	GuernseyCoOh	02	04	18
Sholl, John(Z)	1807	April 24	SomersetCoPa	02	18	16
Sholl, John(Z)	1810	Nov. 14	TuscarwsCoOh	02	08	16
Shook, John(Z-M)	1833	Nov. 14	HarrisonCoOh	03	07	12
Shore, Jeremiah(Z-M)	1833	Feb. 05	BelmontCo,Oh	03	07	24
Shore, Jeremiah(Z-M)	1833	Feb. 05	BelmontCo,Oh	03	07	24

PURCHASER	YEAR	DATE	RESIDENCE	R	T	S
Shores, James(Z-M)	1833	Feb. 04	BelmontCo,Oh	03	06	09
Shores, James(Z-M)	1837	Jan. 11	CoshoctnCoOh	07	05	05
Shores, Joseph(Z-M)	1835	May 16	BelmontCo,Oh	03	06	08
Shores, Richard(Z-M)	1831	Sept. 16	TuscarwsCoOh	03	06	08
Shores, Richard(Z-M)	1831	Sept. 16	TuscarwsCoOh	03	06	08
Short, Peter(Z-M)	1833	Aug. 24	TuscarwsCoOh	03	07	02
Shott, Philip(Z)	1807	Oct. 26	WashngtnCoMd	04	08	12
Shotwell, Hugh(Y)	1829	May 18	HarrisonCoOh	07	12	15
Shotwell, John(Y)	1822	April 24	FayetteCo,Pa	07	12	15
Shotwell, John(Z)	1816	Sept. 05	FayetteCo,Pa	01	05	09
Shotwell, Jonathan(Y)	1832	July 10	HarrisonCoOh	07	14	36
Shoup, Frederick(Z)	1814	June 23	TuscarwsCoOh	03	09	12
Shoup, George(Y)	1836	Sept. 17	Stark Co.,Oh	07	20	18
Shoup, Jacob(Z)	1810	June 09	TuscarwsCoOh	03	08	09
Shoup, Jonathan(Y)	1826	Aug. 09	ColumbanCoOh	07	19	22
Shouse, Bernard(Y)	1826	Nov. 07	ColumbanCoOh	04	13	21
Shouse, John(Y)	1833	Aug. 22	CarrollCo,Oh	04	13	22
Showaker, William(Z)	1836	March 30	MonroeCo.,Oh	08	07	14
Showalter, Henry(Z)	1812	June 01	WestmrldCoPa	04	09	03
Showalter, J.(Z)	1814	April 25	TuscarwsCoOh	04	09	18
Showalter, Peter(Z)	1814	July 26	TuscarwsCoOh	04	09	04
Shrack, David(Z)	1816	Aug. 29	CoshoctnCoOh	04	09	17
Shrader, Dutrick(Z)	1834	Feb. 05	MuskingmCoOh	13	10	08
Shrake, Frederick(Z)	1814	Nov. 10	BelmontCo,Pa	09	05	23
Shrake, Geo.(Z-M)	1833	March 07	CoshoctnCoOh	09	05	16
Shrake, George(Z-M)	1836	March 24	CoshoctnCoOh	10	05	20
Shreve, James Jr.(Z)	1833	Oct. 02	Perry Co.,Oh	14	12	21
Shreve, James(Z)	1828	Sept. 03	Perry Co.,Oh	14	12	15
Shreve, William(Z)	1829	Jan. 20	Perry Co.,Oh	14	12	19
Shreve, William(Z)	1833	Oct. 25	Perry Co.,Oh	14	12	18
Shreve, William(Z)	1836	March 09	Perry Co.,Oh	14	12	18
Shrimfein, Abraham(Z-M)	1834	Oct. 20	HolmesCoOhio	08	08	10
Shrimpein, Abraham(Z-M)	1834	Oct. 20	HolmesCoOhio	08	08	10
Shrimplen, Oliver(Z-M)	1835	Nov. 25	HolmesCoOhio	08	08	10
Shrimplin, Abra'm.(Z)	1815	Sept. 29	CoshoctnCoOh	08	08	01
Shrimplin, Abraham(Z)	1812	June 06	CoshoctnCoOh	08	08	10
Shrimplin, Abraham(Z)	1814	Dec. 31	CoshoctnCoOh	08	08	01
Shrimplin, Abraham(Z-M)	1835	Sept. 29	HolmesCoOhio	07	08	05
Shrimplin, John(Z-M)	1836	Jan. 13	HolmesCoOhio	08	08	09
Shrimplin, John(Z-M)	1836	Jan. 13	HolmesCoOhio	08	08	12
Shrimplin, Samuel(Z)	1812	March 06	CoshoctnCoOh	08	08	10
Shrimplin, Samuel(Z-M)	1832	Oct. 06	HolmesCoOhio	08	08	07
Shrimplin, William(Z-M)	1832	Oct. 06	HolmesCoOhio	08	08	09
Shrimplin, William(Z-M)	1835	Nov. 21	HolmesCoOhio	08	08	10
Shrive, Caleb(Z)	1824	Dec. 11	MuskingmCoOh	15	16	21
Shrive, Caleb(Z)	1813	April 08	MuskingmCoOh	15	16	32
Shrive, James(Z)	1814	Jan. 17	MuskingmCoOh	15	16	28
Shrive, James(Z)	1814	April 14	FairfeldCoOh	15	16	28
Shriver, Adam(Z)	1814	Jan. 03	GuernseyCoOh	03	01	17
Shriver, Adam(Z-M)	1832	May 23	GuernseyCoOh	03	01	19
Shriver, Elias(Y)	1827	Aug. 13	Stark Co.,Oh	07	20	19
Shriver, Elijah(Z)	1814	Jan. 03	GuernseyCoOh	03	01	17
Shriver, Jacob(Z)	1824	May 11	GuernseyCoOh	10	09	22
Shriver, Jacob(Z)	1834	Feb. 17	GuernseyCoOh	10	09	13
Shriver, Jacob(Z)	1834	Feb. 17	GuernseyCoOh	09	08	18
Shriver, Jacob(Z)	1834	Nov. 15	GuernseyCoOh	10	09	24
Shriver, Jacob(Z)	1836	Jan. 06	GuernseyCoOh	09	08	33
Shriver, Jacob(Z)	1836	Feb. 09	GuernseyCoOh	09	08	33
Shriver, Jacob(Z)	1836	Feb. 09	GuernseyCoOh	09	08	18
Shriver, Jacob(Z)	1824	May 10	GuernseyCoOh	10	09	22
Shriver, Jacob(Z)	1811	Aug. 27	GreenCo.,Pa.	09	08	19
Shriver, Jacob(Z-M)	1833	Feb. 07	GuernseyCoOh	03	01	13
Shriver, Jacob(Z-M)	1835	Dec. 22	GuernseyCoOh	03	01	13
Shriver, James P.(Z)	1834	Nov. 24	GuernseyCoOh	10	09	13
Shriver, John(Z)	1816	Dec. 16	GreeneCo.,Pa	10	06	12
Shriver, Michael(Z)	1831	Aug. 22	Morgan Co,Oh	09	06	33
Shriver, Michael(Z)	1815	Dec. 26	GreeneCo.,Pa	09	06	33
Shrock, David(Z-M)	1832	March 26	HolmesCoOhio	04	09	14
Shrock, J.(Z)	1815	April 12	TuscarwsCoOh	04	09	14

261

PURCHASER	YEAR	DATE	RESIDENCE	R	T	S
Shrock, John(Z)	1814	Aug. 04	TuscarwsCoOh	05	09	20
Shroger, Christian(Z-M)	1829	Feb. 17	MuskingmCoOh	05	02	05
Shrok, Jacob(Z)	1813	Nov. 05	TuscarwsCoOh	04	09	24
Shrok, John(Z)	1814	June 23	TuscarwsCoOh	04	09	24
Shrop, Henry(Z)	1813	Nov. 05	TuscarwsCoOh	04	08	17
Shrop, Hervey(Z)	1813	Nov. 05	TuscarwsCoOh	04	08	17
Shrory, John(Z)	1815	Oct. 27	WashngtnCoMd	03	09	03
Shrott, Joseph(Z)	1807	Sept. 09	FayetteCo,Pa	01	02	25
Shroy, Jacob(Z-M)	1832	Aug. 28	TuscarwsCoOh	03	10	13
Shroy, Jacob(Z-M)	1834	Feb. 22	TuscarwsCoOh	03	09	03
Shroyer, Christian(Z-M)	1829	Feb. 17	MuskingmCoOh	05	02	05
Shroyer, Christian(Z-M)	1837	April 11	MuskingmCoOh	05	04	06
Shroyer, Jacob(Z-M)	1833	Aug. 21	MuskingmCoOh	06	03	12
Shroyer, William(Z-M)	1836	Oct. 24	MuskingmCoOh	06	04	10
Shrum, Hannah(Z-M)	1833	June 04	MuskingmCoOh	08	07	19
Shryock, Eli O. H.(Z-M)	1834	Aug. 02	CoshoctnCoOh	04	04	15
Shryock, John(Z-M)	1834	Aug. 02	CoshoctnCoOh	04	04	15
Shuck, Jacob(Y)	1824	April 23	HarrisonCoOh	06	14	03
Shugart, Worley C.(Z)	1829	Jan. 12	Morgan Co,Oh	12	11	34
Shuler, John(Z-M)	1832	March 29	KnoxCo.,Ohio	11	03	05
Shull, Frederick(Z)	1811	April 08	TuscarwsCoOh	02	08	25
Shull, John(Z-M)	1837	July 15	MuskingmCoOh	08	07	22
Shull, Samuel(Z-M)	1836	Feb. 03	TuscarwsCoOh	01	09	06
Shults, George(Z-M)	1835	Aug. 17	CoshoctnCoOh	05	07	04
Shultz, Emanuel(Z-M)	1836	March 22	KnoxCo.,Ohio	10	08	03
Shultz, John(Z-M)	1835	Nov. 14	KnoxCo.,Ohio	10	07	18
Shultz, Mich'l.(Z)	1831	Nov. 08	GuernseyCoOh	08	08	19
Shuly, Christian(Z-M)	1822	June 29	GuernseyCoOh	04	04	12
Shumaker, Christian(Z-M)	1837	Oct. 12	CoshoctnCoOh	08	06	01
Shuman, Curtis(Z)	1814	Feb. 19	WashngtnCoOh	11	11	30
Shuman, Daniel(Z)	1836	April 06	CarrollCo,Oh	15	14	13
Shuman, Daniel(Z)	1837	April 22	Perry Co.,Oh	15	14	11
Shuman, Fred'k.(Y)	1825	Feb. 17	HarrisonCoOh	06	14	01
Shuman, Henry(Z)	1837	March 20	Morgan Co,Oh	08	06	32
Shuman, John Jr.(Z)	1835	Feb. 25	GuernseyCoOh	10	07	25
Shuman, John(Z)	1807	March 27	BelmontCo,Oh	01	02	23
Shumon, Henry(Z)	1838	Dec. 05	Morgan Co,Oh	08	06	29
Shunk, Isaac(Z-M)	1832	Nov. 12	LickingCo,Oh	10	04	07
Shurman, Wm.(Z)	1816	Oct. 15	GuernseyCoOh	10	07	06
Shurts, John(Z)	1817	May 30	MuskingmCoOh	06	02	05
Shurtz, Henry(Z)	1816	April 26	LickingCo,Oh	07	03	22
Shurtz, John(Z)	1815	Aug. 17	MuskingmCoOh	06	03	21
Shurtz, Samuel(Z)	1816	Oct. 16	MuskingmCoOh	06	02	05
Shuster, Abraham(Z)	1832	Oct. 05	Morgan Co,Oh	10	07	15
Shuster, George(Z)	1832	March 08	Morgan Co,Oh	10	07	21
Shuster, Isaac(Z)	1835	Sept. 07	Morgan Co,Oh	10	07	15
Shuster, John(Z)	1823	Sept. 12	Morgan Co,Oh	10	07	27
Shutt, John(Z)	1827	June 13	Morgan Co,Oh	13	09	09
Shutt, Peter(Z)	1807	Oct. 26	FredrickCoMd	04	08	04
Shutt, Peter(Z)	1807	Oct. 26	FredrickCoMd	04	08	04
Shutt, Peter(Z)	1814	April 02	TuscarwsCoOh	03	10	22
Shutt, Peter(Z)	1814	April 16	TuscarwsCoOh	03	09	02
Shutts, Wm.(Z)	1835	March 09	BelmontCo,Oh	08	06	05
Shuttz, Jacob(Z-M)	1833	Sept. 24	KnoxCo.,Ohio	10	08	18
Shuttz, John(Z-M)	1833	Sept. 24	KnoxCo.,Ohio	10	08	18
Shuttz, Michael M.(Z-M)	1839	May 08	TuscarwsCoOh	09	07	01
Sibe, Christian(Z-M)	1822	Dec. 30	CoshoctnCoOh	05	08	01
Sickel, Levi Van(Z-M)	1836	June 20	HarrisonCoOh	04	05	19
Sickle, Elias(Y)	1827	April 20	HarrisonCoOh	05	12	28
Sickle, Isaac(Y)	1829	June 19	HarrisonCoOh	04	13	04
Sickles, Benj'm.(Z-M)	1832	Jan. 12	KnoxCo.,Ohio	10	05	19
Sickles, Benjamin(Z-M)	1829	June 12	KnoxCo.,Ohio	10	05	18
Sickly, Jacob(Y)	1826	June 23	Stark Co.,Oh	09	12	28
Sidwell, Eli(Z)	1815	May 29	Jeff.Co.,Oh.	01	04	04
Sidwell, Nathan(Z)	1816	March 25	BelmontCo,Oh	12	10	20
Sidwell, Nathan(Z)	1816	July 31	BelmontCo,Oh	12	09	12
Sidwell, Nathan(Z)	1816	July 31	BelmontCo,Oh	12	09	11
Sidwell, Nathan(Z)	1816	Aug. 12	BelmontCo,Oh	12	09	12
Sidwell, Nathan(Z)	1816	Aug. 12	BelmontCo,Oh	12	09	02

PURCHASER	YEAR	DATE	RESIDENCE	R	T	S
Sidwell, Nathan(Z)	1817	Aug. 14	WashngtnCoOh	12	09	11
Sidwell, Nathan(Z)	1817	Oct. 20	WashngtnCoOh	12	09	13
Sidwell, Nathan(Z)	1815	Sept. 06	?	12	10	17
Sieffert, Michael(Z-M)	1837	July 11	ZanesvilleOh	03	05	18
Sieffert, Michael(Z-M)	1837	July 11	ZanesvilleOh	03	05	18
Sieton, Robert(Y)	1827	March 27	Jeff.Co.,Oh.	04	12	20
Sieton, Robert(Y)	1827	April 09	Jeff.Co.,Oh.	04	12	20
Sieton, Wm.(Y)	1827	March 27	Jeff.Co.,Oh.	04	12	20
Sights, Casper(Z-M)	1839	Feb. 11	GuernseyCoOh	03	03	15
Sights, David(Z-M)	1828	Feb. 04	Cambridge,Oh	03	03	15
Siglar, Philip(Z)	1817	April 10	LickingCo,Oh	11	01	11
Sigler, John(Z)	1836	Dec. 14	Morgan Co,Oh	10	06	01
Sigler, John(Z)	1836	Dec. 14	Morgan Co,Oh	09	06	09
Sigler, John(Z)	1808	Feb. 23	FairfeldCoOh	11	01	12
Sigler, John(Z)	1808	Feb. 23	FairfeldCoOh	11	01	08
Sigman, Jno.(Z-M)	1832	Feb. 17	GuernseyCoOh	02	01	05
Silbaugh, Isaac(Z)	1837	Dec. 26	Perry Co.,Oh	15	14	35
Silbaugh, Isaac(Z)	1837	Dec. 26	Perry Co.,Oh	15	14	36
Silbaugh, Philip(Z)	1836	Aug. 23	CoshoctnCoOh	15	14	26
Silders, John(Z)	1817	Oct. 21	GuernseyCoOh	04	02	17
Sillhinson, Charles(Z)	1807	Sept. 14	FayetteCo,Oh	10	09	31
Sillhison, Charles(Z)	1807	Sept. 14	FayetteCo,Oh	10	09	31
Sills, Jonathan(Z-M)	1836	Jan. 05	GuernseyCoOh	03	04	18
Silous, Isaac(Z)	1835	June 20	WashngtnCoOh	10	06	22
Silvey, Ada(Y)	1826	May 05	ColumbanCoOh	05	18	29
Silvey, Robert(Z)	1836	Nov. 15	MuskingmCoOh	12	12	18
Silvey, Robert(Z)	1836	Nov. 15	MuskingmCoOh	13	10	11
Silvey, Robert(Z)	1836	Nov. 19	MuskingmCoOh	13	10	14
Silvey, William(Z)	1827	March 07	Morgan Co,Oh	13	10	24
Silvey, William(Z)	1828	March 13	Morgan Co,Oh	12	12	31
Silvey, William(Z)	1828	March 15	Morgan Co,Oh	12	12	31
Silvey, William(Z)	1828	March 15	Morgan Co,Oh	13	10	14
Silvey, William(Z)	1828	March 15	Morgan Co,Oh	12	12	31
Silvey, William(Z)	1828	April 22	Morgan Co,Oh	13	10	14
Silvey, William(Z)	1830	April 12	PutnamCoOhio	12	10	29
Silvus, Isaac(Z)	1835	June 25	WashngtnCoOh	10	06	22
Sim, D.(Z)	1817	Jan. 27	MuskingmCoOh	11	12	02
Sim, David(Z)	1823	Feb. 06	MuskingmCoOh	11	12	17
Sim, David(Z)	1824	Jan. 08	MuskingmCoOh	11	12	08
Simafrank, Jacob(Z-M)	1830	March 18	GuernseyCoOh	04	02	20
Simerl, Jesse(Z)	1836	Jan. 16	Perry Co.,Oh	14	13	35
Simerl, Malissa(Z)	1835	Sept. 30	Perry Co.,Oh	13	08	27
Simerl, Sam'l. Dare.(Z)	1836	Jan. 07	Morgan Co,Oh	13	08	27
Simerl, Samuel Davi(Z)	1835	May 26	Morgan Co,Oh	13	08	27
Simkins, Amon(Z-M)	1831	Sept. 07	GreeneCo.,Pa	03	04	03
Simmerman, Jacob(Z-M)	1831	Sept. 12	WashCo.,Penn	02	05	20
Simmerman, Jacob(Z-M)	1829	Nov. 18	WashCo.,Penn	02	05	20
Simmerman, John(Z-M)	1837	April 28	GuernseyCoOh	04	03	01
Simmers, Daniel(Z-M)	1836	June 04	TuscarwsCoOh	02	07	03
Simmons, Benjamin(Z-M)	1832	March 29	CoshoctnCoOh	09	07	08
Simmons, Chas.(Z-M)	1833	Nov. 23	ZanesvilleOh	05	03	19
Simmons, Joshua(Z-M)	1833	Jan. 01	TuscarwsCoOh	03	07	20
Simmons, Joshua(Z-M)	1833	April 11	TuscarwsCoOh	02	07	09
Simmons, Joshua(Z-M)	1836	June 20	TuscarwsCoOh	02	07	01
Simmons, Joshua(Z-M)	1836	Sept. 01	TuscarwsCoOh	02	07	01
Simmons, Peter(Y)	1830	Dec. 06	Stark Co.,Oh	06	16	28
Simmons, Wm. H.(Z-M)	1836	March 18	CoshoctnCoOh	08	06	12
Simmons, Wm. H.(Z-M)	1836	March 18	CoshoctnCoOh	08	06	12
Simon, Christian(Z)	1835	April 18	Morgan Co,Oh	09	06	12
Simon, Nimrod(Z)	1836	March 08	Morgan Co,Oh	09	06	12
Simpkinson, Chas.(Z-M)	1837	July 18	CarrollCo,Oh	08	08	22
Simpson, Alex.(Z)	1829	Dec. 11	Morgan Co,Oh	12	11	20
Simpson, Alexander(Y)	1831	April 25	HarrisonCoOh	06	12	10
Simpson, Alexander(Y)	1832	June 14	HarrisonCoOh	06	12	17
Simpson, David(Z)	1829	Dec. 11	Morgan Co,Oh	13	08	36
Simpson, John(Z)	1825	Dec. 08	Morgan Co,Oh	12	09	09
Simpson, John(Z)	1827	Sept. 19	Morgan Co,Oh	12	09	05
Simpson, John(Z)	1828	May 19	Morgan Co,Oh	12	09	08
Simpson, Joseph(Z-M)	1833	May 31	GuernseyCoOh	04	02	11

| --- | --- | --- | --- | --- | --- | --- |
Simpson, Robert(Y)	1829	May 04	HarrisonCoOh	06	12	36
Simpson, Robert(Y)	1830	April 14	HarrisonCoOh	06	12	09
Simpson, Robert(Y)	1831	July 05	HarrisonCoOh	06	12	15
Simpson, Robert(Z-M)	1836	July 04	MuskingmCoOh	01	05	05
Simpson, Robt. Jnr.(Z-M)	1835	March 25	Brooke CoVir	03	06	07
Simpson, Turner(Z)	1833	March 02	MuskingmCoOh	11	12	23
Simpson, Turner(Z)	1833	Nov. 27	MuskingmCoOh	11	12	23
Simpson, W.(Z)	1815	Nov. 23	WashCo.,Penn	05	02	11
Simrall, James(Z)	1816	Nov. 13	Jeff.Co.,Oh.	02	02	04
Simrel, Jesse(Z)	1810	Nov. 02	MuskingmCoOh	14	13	12
Sims, Mahlon(Z-M)	1832	Oct. 06	MuskingmCoOh	10	04	18
Sims, Mahlon(Z-M)	1832	Oct. 06	MuskingmCoOh	10	04	18
Sims, Simon(Z)	1810	Feb. 26	MuskingmCoOh	15	18	03
Sinclair, George(Z)	1816	Jan. 25	WashCo.,Penn	11	13	32
Sinclair, James(Z)	1807	Nov. 02	WashCo.,Penn	11	13	23
Sinclair, Samuel(Z)	1815	May 17	MuskingmCoOh	11	13	23
Sinclair, Thomas(Z)	1834	Sept. 25	MuskingmCoOh	11	12	24
Sinclair, Thompson(Y)	1831	Dec. 01	BelmontCo,Oh	07	12	04
Sinclair, William(Z)	1816	Jan. 25	WashCo.,Penn	11	13	33
Sinclear, John P.(Z)	1833	March 04	AshtbulaCoOh	11	11	14
Sines, Absalom(Z)	1835	Nov. 10	GuernseyCoOh	10	09	25
Sines, Henry(Z)	1827	Dec. 07	MuskingmCoOh	11	12	08
Singer, Christ'n. F.(Z-M)	1829	Feb. 09	Jeff.Co.,Oh.	02	10	16
Singer, Christ'r. F.(Z-M)	1829	Feb. 09	Jeff.Co.,Oh.	02	10	16
Sinmons, Joshua(Z-M)	1833	Aug. 03	TuscarwsCoOh	01	08	02
Sintclair, James(Z)	1807	Nov. 02	WashCo.,Penn	11	13	23
Siston, John(Y)	1830	July 06	HarrisonCoOh	05	12	34
Sivard, J. A.(Z)	1836	June 17	Morgan Co,Oh	10	06	25
Sivard, John A.(Z)	1833	Nov. 13	Morgan Co,Oh	10	07	31
Sivard, John A.(Z)	1836	April 20	Morgan Co,Oh	10	06	24
Six, Conrad(Z)	1835	Dec. 28	Morgan Co,Oh	09	05	29
Six, Convou(Z)	1838	Oct. 15	Morgan Co,Oh	08	05	23
Skannem, Pat(Z)	1830	Oct. 15	Morgan Co,Oh	13	08	07
Skeels, Nicholas(Y)	1823	Aug. 29	Jeff.Co.,Oh.	07	15	19
Skeels, Nicholas(Z-M)	1834	Jan. 20	CarrollCo,Oh	01	08	04
Skeonton, J.(Z)	1816	Feb. 03	ZanesvilleOh	13	11	06
Skinin, Thomas(Z)	1835	May 23	Morgan Co,Oh	14	12	02
Skinnan, John(Z)	1837	March 15	Morgan Co,Oh	14	12	02
Skinner, Asa W.(Z-M)	1830	Jan. 18	LickingCo,Oh	10	02	24
Skinner, Asa W.(Z-M)	1835	Aug. 27	LickingCo,Oh	10	01	02
Skinner, Cornelius(Z)	1824	Nov. 26	Perry Co.,Oh	15	15	21
Skinner, Cornelius(Z)	1811	Oct. 14	MuskingmCoOh	15	16	30
Skinner, Cortlin(Z)	1828	March 04	Morgan Co,Oh	09	07	03
Skinner, Elias(Z-M)	1826	Jan. 09	MuskingmCoOh	06	03	22
Skinner, George(Z)	1808	Jan. 12	FairfeldCoOh	15	16	19
Skinner, Jabez(Z)	1826	March 01	Perry Co.,Oh	15	14	03
Skinner, James Senr.(Z)	1832	April 23	Perry Co.,Oh	15	15	32
Skinner, James(Z)	1831	July 18	Perry Co.,Oh	15	14	05
Skinner, James(Z)	1833	April 20	Perry Co.,Oh	15	15	32
Skinner, James(Z)	1835	June 12	Perry Co.,Oh	14	13	35
Skinner, James(Z)	1835	June 12	Perry Co.,Oh	14	13	35
Skinner, James(Z)	1835	Nov. 27	BelmontCo,Oh	15	15	22
Skinner, James(Z)	1835	Nov. 27	BelmontCo,Oh	15	15	21
Skinner, James(Z)	1836	Nov. 24	Perry Co.,Oh	14	13	35
Skinner, Jas.(Z)	1831	Jan. 31	Perry Co.,Oh	15	15	21
Skinner, John C.(Z-M)	1828	June 16	MuskingmCoOh	07	03	22
Skinner, John(Z)	1833	April 12	Perry Co.,Oh	15	14	07
Skinner, John(Z)	1816	June 06	SomersetCoPa	15	14	07
Skinner, Nath'l.(Z)	1814	March 29	FayetteCo,Pa	15	16	29
Skinner, Nath'l.(Z)	1814	March 29	FayetteCo,Pa	15	16	32
Skinner, Nathaniel(Z)	1833	Dec. 30	Perry Co.,Oh	15	14	05
Skinner, Peter(Z)	1836	Oct. 27	LoudounCoVir	14	12	01
Skinner, Peter(Z)	1836	Nov. 28	LoudounCoVir	14	12	01
Skinner, Reuben(Z)	1825	Feb. 05	Perry Co.,Oh	15	14	03
Skinner, Reuben(Z)	1833	July 24	Perry Co.,Oh	15	14	04
Skinner, Richard(Z)	1833	Nov. 30	Perry Co.,Oh	15	14	18
Skinner, Sam'l.(Z)	1816	June 06	SomersetCoPa	15	14	07
Skinner, Samuel(Z)	1813	Oct. 21	FayetteCo,Pa	15	15	17
Skinner, Wm.(Z)	1804	Nov. 29	MariettaOhio	12	12	20

PURCHASER	YEAR	DATE	RESIDENCE	R	T	S
Skinner, Wm.(Z)	1804	Dec. 04	MariettaOhio	10	06	33
Skinnin, Patrick(Z)	1835	Dec. 09	Morgan Co,Oh	14	12	12
Skinnin, Patrick(Z)	1836	Oct. 03	Morgan Co,Oh	13	08	06
Skiving, Polly(Z)	1831	May 31	Morgan Co,Oh	11	11	13
Slack, Abel(Z)	1812	Nov. 03	MuskingmCoOh	06	02	08
Slack, Benjamin(Z)	1815	April 22	GuernseyCoOh	09	08	30
Slagel, Christian(Z-M)	1837	Sept. 14	HolmesCoOhio	08	08	14
Slagel, Christian(Z-M)	1837	Sept. 14	HolmesCoOhio	08	08	15
Slagel, Christian(Z-M)	1837	Sept. 14	HolmesCoOhio	08	08	17
Slasor, George(Z-M)	1825	July 27	GuernseyCoOh	02	02	12
Slater, Anthony(Z-M)	1825	Dec. 06	MuskingmCoOh	06	03	20
Slater, Daniel(Z)	1835	Aug. 28	Morgan Co,Oh	10	06	13
Slater, David(Z)	1806	Feb. 21	BelmontCo,Oh	01	02	14
Slater, David(Z)	1810	June 08	GuernseyCoOh	02	02	13
Slater, David(Z)	1815	July 12	BelmontCo,Oh	01	02	07
Slater, Ellis(Z)	1836	June 01	Morgan Co,Oh	10	06	13
Slater, Jacob(Z-M)	1826	July 25	GuernseyCoOh	03	01	22
Slater, James(Z)	1813	Oct. 11	FayetteCo,Pa	10	09	05
Slater, John(Z)	1825	April 16	GuernseyCoOh	09	08	14
Slater, Linnvill(Z)	1836	June 22	Perry Co.,Oh	15	14	20
Slates, Conrad(Y)	1828	Sept. 01	HarrisonCoOh	05	13	01
Slates, Conrad(Y)	1830	Nov. 17	HarrisonCoOh	05	13	01
Slatzer, Martin(Z)	1836	March 28	Perry Co.,Oh	15	14	20
Slaughter, Frederick(Z)	1814	July 27	GuernseyCoOh	01	02	18
Slaughter, Henry Jr.(Z-M)	1834	Jan. 27	CoshoctnCoOh	07	04	17
Slaughter, Henry(Z)	1813	Nov. 13	CoshoctnCoOh	07	04	08
Slaughter, Henry(Z)	1816	Oct. 18	CoshoctnCoOh	07	04	03
Slaughter, Joseph(Z-M)	1835	Nov. 17	CoshoctnCoOh	07	04	18
Slaven, George(Y)	1825	Aug. 30	TrumbullCoOh	05	18	10
Slaven, George(Y)	1825	Sept. 13	TrumbullCoOh	05	18	10
Slavin, Margaret(Z)	1832	Dec. 03	MuskingmCoOh	15	15	12
Slavin, Owen(Z)	1838	Aug. 24	Perry Co.,Oh	15	14	34
Sleeth, David(Z-M)	1836	July 02	GuernseyCoOh	03	03	25
Sleiele, John(Z)	1835	March 04	BelmontCo,Oh	10	07	36
Slemons, James(Z)	1816	June 06	Jeff.Co.,Oh.	01	05	23
Slemons, James(Z)	1816	June 06	Jeff.Co.,Oh.	01	05	23
Slenger, J.(Z)	1817	Jan. 08	PutnamCoOhio	13	09	09
Slingluff,Deardorff & Bohon(Z)	1806	Sept. 08	MuskingmCoOh	03	08	01
Slingluff,Deardorff & Bohon(Z)	1806	Sept. 22	MuskingmCoOh	03	08	03
Slingluff,Deardorff & Bohon(Z)	1806	Sept. 08	MuskingmCoOh	03	08	01
Slingluff,Deardorff & Bohon(Z)	1806	Sept. 08	MuskingmCoOh	03	08	02
Slinker, Andrew(Z)	1805	May 23	YorkCo.,Penn	12	13	04
Sloan, James(Y)	1829	March 16	ColumbanCoOh	03	12	17
Slurman, James(Z-M)	1837	Jan. 13	CoshoctnCoOh	05	04	20
Slutz, John(Z-M)	1829	Nov. 23	TuscarwsCoOh	01	09	05
Smails, Jno.(Z-M)	1834	Jan. 13	OtsegoCoNYrk	07	05	01
Smails, Robt.(Z-M)	1834	Jan. 13	OtsegoCoNYrk	07	05	01
Small, John(Z)	1826	Dec. 19	Perry Co.,Oh	15	15	15
Small, John(Z)	1835	June 09	AthensCoOhio	15	14	21
Smalley, James(Z)	1830	Jan. 12	KnoxCo.,Ohio	10	05	13
Smels, Martin(Y)	1829	June 01	HarrisonCoOh	05	13	30
Smetherst, James(Z)	1834	Nov. 13	Morgan Co,Oh	11	10	29
Smiley, George(Z)	1811	May 14	TuscarwsCoOh	04	09	11
Smith, Aaron(Z-M)	1832	June 08	GuernseyCoOh	01	04	02
Smith, Abraham(Z)	1832	May 22	Morgan Co,Oh	10	07	30
Smith, Adam(Y)	1839	Feb. 02	Stark Co.,Oh	10	02	12
Smith, Adam(Z)	1832	July 30	Brooke CoVir	08	08	29
Smith, Adam(Z)	1832	July 30	Brooke CoVir	08	08	32
Smith, Adam(Z)	1835	Dec. 09	GuernseyCoOh	08	08	29
Smith, Adam(Z)	1807	April 16	ShanandhCoVa	10	01	22
Smith, Adam(Z)	1807	April 16	ShanandhCoVa	10	01	21
Smith, Adam(Z)	1807	April 16	ShanandhCoVa	10	01	19
Smith, Adam(Z)	1807	April 16	ShanandhCoVa	10	01	19
Smith, Alexander(Z)	1827	March 26	BelmontCo,Oh	11	11	07
Smith, Alexander(Z)	1816	Oct. 21	WashCo.,Penn	04	02	06
Smith, Alexander(Z-M)	1824	Feb. 16	KnoxCo.,Ohio	10	08	14
Smith, Andrew(Z-M)	1831	Sept. 09	CoshoctnCoOh	09	07	03
Smith, Andrew(Z-M)	1837	May 25	KnoxCo.,Ohio	10	06	14
Smith, Anthony(Z)	1836	Nov. 07	Morgan Co,Oh	08	06	30

PURCHASER	YEAR	DATE	RESIDENCE	R	T	S
Smith, Archebald(Z)	1827	May 01	CoshoctnCoOh	09	04	23
Smith, Archibald(Z-M)	1826	March 16	CoshoctnCoOh	09	04	23
Smith, Bartho'l.(Z-M)	1827	May 22	WashCo.,Penn	04	07	18
Smith, Bartholomew(Z-M)	1837	March 03	TuscarwsCoOh	04	07	18
Smith, Benj'n.(Z-M)	1832	Feb. 18	CoshoctnCoOh	09	04	14
Smith, Benjamin(Z)	1817	Jan. 20	MuskingmCoOh	09	06	20
Smith, Charles(Y)	1827	April 16	ColumbanCoOh	05	18	27
Smith, Christopher(Z-M)	1836	March 12	HolmesCoOhio	08	08	06
Smith, Christopher(Z-M)	1836	Oct. 13	HolmesCoOhio	08	08	04
Smith, Christopher(Z-M)	1838	March 31	HolmesCoOhio	09	07	02
Smith, Daniel(Y)	1824	May 20	HarrisonCoOh	06	12	15
Smith, Daniel(Y)	1827	Aug. 15	HarrisonCoOh	07	14	13
Smith, Daniel(Y)	1829	Dec. 07	ColumbanCoOh	02	10	22
Smith, Daniel(Y)	1831	Oct. 25	ColumbanCoOh	03	12	21
Smith, Daniel(Y)	1833	June 14	Stark Co.,Oh	09	12	07
Smith, Daniel(Y)	1835	Oct. 27	Jeff.Co.,Oh.	03	12	20
Smith, Darnall(Z)	1829	Jan. 12	HarrisonCoOh	12	09	08
Smith, David(Z)	1814	May 21	Lancaster,Oh	14	13	30
Smith, David(Z)	1814	March 23	ZanesvilleOh	12	13	29
Smith, David(Z-M)	1814	May 21	MuskingmCoOh	05	03	01
Smith, Ebenzer(Z-M)	1836	Jan. 11	WayneCo.,Oh.	05	07	24
Smith, Edward(Z)	1831	July 07	GuernseyCoOh	03	03	03
Smith, Edward(Z)	1836	June 09	Brooke CoVir	10	06	23
Smith, Edward(Z)	1815	Aug. 07	MuskingmCoOh	15	18	02
Smith, Edward(Z)	1815	Nov. 06	Cadiz, Ohio	08	05	11
Smith, Ely(Y)	1826	Oct. 16	HarrisonCoOh	07	12	11
Smith, Frederick(Y)	1829	Sept. 25	ColumbanCoOh	06	19	24
Smith, George(Y)	1823	March 12	ColumbanCoOh	04	14	34
Smith, George(Y)	1823	May 10	ColumbanCoOh	02	09	21
Smith, George(Y)	1824	April 12	ColumbanCoOh	04	14	34
Smith, George(Y)	1827	June 01	Stark Co.,Oh	07	20	26
Smith, George(Y)	1829	March 14	HarrisonCoOh	05	12	27
Smith, George(Y)	1829	June 29	ColumbanCoOh	04	13	06
Smith, George(Z)	1825	Nov. 11	WashCo.,Penn	12	11	22
Smith, George(Z)	1825	Nov. 11	WashCo.,Penn	12	11	22
Smith, George(Z)	1812	Nov. 04	MuskingmCoOh	13	11	16
Smith, George(Z)	1814	Oct. 01	MuskingmCoOh	13	10	30
Smith, George(Z-M)	1828	June 16	CoshoctnCoOh	04	07	23
Smith, Henry W.(Y)	1828	Jan. 05	TuscarwsCoOh	07	14	18
Smith, Henry(Z)	1833	March 23	MuskingmCoOh	10	08	27
Smith, Henry(Z)	1836	July 20	MuskingmCoOh	14	13	27
Smith, Henry(Z)	1837	May 20	Morgan Co,Oh	08	06	28
Smith, Henry(Z-M)	1832	Sept. 14	RichlandCoOh	10	08	13
Smith, Henry(Z-M)	1833	Sept. 10	MuskingmCoOh	05	03	12
Smith, Henry(Z-M)	1835	Feb. 28	GuernseyCoOh	02	01	14
Smith, Henry(Z-M)	1836	March 17	KnoxCo.,Ohio	10	08	13
Smith, Henry(Z-M)	1837	June 22	KnoxCo.,Ohio	10	08	13
Smith, Henry(Z-M)	1837	Sept. 27	TuscarwsCoOh	03	05	17
Smith, Henry(Z-M)	1838	Sept. 13	KnoxCo.,Ohio	10	08	09
Smith, Hiram(Z)	1835	May 15	Morgan Co,Oh	10	06	01
Smith, Hiram(Z)	1835	Oct. 13	Morgan Co,Oh	10	07	36
Smith, Isaac(Z)	1834	Sept. 11	Morgan Co,Oh	13	08	24
Smith, J. C.(Z)	1814	May 21	Lancaster,Oh	14	13	30
Smith, Jacob M.(Z)	1828	Oct. 14	Morgan Co,Oh	12	09	04
Smith, Jacob M.(Z-M)	1836	April 14	LickingCo,Oh	10	04	01
Smith, Jacob(Y)	1827	Nov. 07	Jeff.Co.,Oh.	04	11	24
Smith, Jacob(Z)	1836	Nov. 08	Morgan Co,Oh	10	07	35
Smith, Jacob(Z)	1805	April 20	MuskingmCoOh	14	15	02
Smith, Jacob(Z)	1807	May 04	MuskingmCoOh	14	15	27
Smith, Jacob(Z)	1814	Aug. 27	ZanesvilleOh	05	04	21
Smith, Jacob(Z)	1814	Nov. 16	KnoxCo.,Ohio	11	05	16
Smith, Jacob(Z)	1815	May 08	ZanesvilleOh	14	15	25
Smith, Jacob(Z)	1817	Jan. 22	MuskingmCoOh	14	15	14
Smith, Jacob(Z)	1817	Jan. 29	MuskingmCoOh	14	15	24
Smith, Jacob(Z)	1817	Aug. 19	NrthumldCoPa	11	01	22
Smith, Jacob(Z-M)	1825	July 06	CoshoctnCoOh	05	07	18
Smith, Jacob(Z-M)	1832	June 12	TuscarwsCoOh	13	08	15
Smith, Jacob(Z-M)	1836	Aug. 10	CoshoctnCoOh	08	07	08
Smith, Jacob(Z-M)	1838	March 23	GuernseyCoOh	04	04	09

PURCHASER	YEAR	DATE	RESIDENCE	R	T	S
Smith, James A.(Z)	1836	Nov. 23	Morgan Co,Oh	10	07	36
Smith, James Catlet(Z-M)	1832	Oct. 04	CoshoctnCoOh	08	04	23
Smith, James E.(Z-M)	1833	July 22	TuscarwsCoOh	02	07	04
Smith, James Russell(Y)	1831	Aug. 22	TuscarwsCoOh	07	14	30
Smith, James(Y)	1821	Oct. 13	HarrisonCoOh	07	12	11
Smith, James(Z)	1828	July 03	Morgan Co,Oh	12	10	22
Smith, James(Z)	1831	March 24	BelmontCo,Oh	10	07	15
Smith, James(Z)	1837	May 05	MonroeCo.,Oh	08	06	24
Smith, James(Z)	1811	Dec. 09	BelmontCo,Oh	15	18	18
Smith, James(Z)	1812	Feb. 14	CoshoctnCoOh	05	04	11
Smith, James(Z)	1812	Aug. 10	MuskingmCoOh	10	01	10
Smith, James(Z)	1813	June 25	MuskingmCoOh	15	17	06
Smith, James(Z)	1815	March 18	LickingCo,Oh	10	01	12
Smith, James(Z-M)	1821	Aug. 27	CoshoctnCoOh	03	05	23
Smith, James(Z-M)	1830	Jan. 04	LickingCo,Oh	10	02	17
Smith, James(Z-M)	1831	Sept. 10	LickingCo,Oh	10	02	16
Smith, James(Z-M)	1832	Aug. 08	LickingCo,Oh	10	02	16
Smith, James(Z-M)	1833	Jan. 23	GuernseyCoOh	03	04	08
Smith, James(Z-M)	1833	Dec. 27	CoshoctnCoOh	09	06	21
Smith, James(Z-M)	1836	May 21	GuernseyCoOh	02	04	17
Smith, Jas. Madison(Z-M)	1832	June 18	GuernseyCoOh	01	03	05
Smith, Jas. N.(Z-M)	1839	March 21	CoshoctnCoOh	08	07	02
Smith, Jesse(Y)	1835	Jan. 24	Stark Co.,Oh	09	12	18
Smith, Jesse(Z-M)	1831	March 10	GuernseyCoOh	01	04	08
Smith, Jno.(Z-M)	1831	Oct. 05	CoshoctnCoOh	05	04	05
Smith, Job. G.(Z)	1829	Jan. 12	HarrisonCoOh	12	09	05
Smith, John Beckup(Z-M)	1836	Nov. 14	LickingCo,Oh	10	03	04
Smith, John H.(Y)	1830	March 10	BelmontCo,Oh	04	06	26
Smith, John H.(Z-M)	1827	Aug. 25	HolmesCoOhio	07	08	25
Smith, John H.(Z-M)	1835	Dec. 29	HolmesCoOhio	08	07	01
Smith, John Hugh(Z-M)	1834	Sept. 27	HolmesCoOhio	07	08	17
Smith, John J.(Y)	1823	March 24	BelmontCo,Oh	06	10	15
Smith, John J.(Z)	1833	Aug. 07	Morgan Co,Oh	09	07	36
Smith, John N.(Z)	1833	Aug. 21	MonroeCo.,Oh	08	06	12
Smith, John Wesley(Z-M)	1837	Jan. 16	ColumbanCoOh	08	07	19
Smith, John(Y)	1825	March 29	ColumbanCoOh	03	12	30
Smith, John(Y)	1826	Feb. 16	Stark Co.,Oh	06	18	07
Smith, John(Y)	1827	Jan. 12	Stark Co.,Oh	06	18	07
Smith, John(Y)	1831	May 21	Stark Co.,Oh	07	20	07
Smith, John(Y)	1832	June 18	Stark Co.,Oh	09	11	23
Smith, John(Y)	1839	Oct. 04	Stark Co.,Oh	08	12	23
Smith, John(Z)	1815	March 13	Jeff.Co.,Oh.	05	07	23
Smith, John(Z)	1815	Oct. 31	WashCo.,Penn	01	03	22
Smith, John(Z-M)	1829	Nov. 26	CoshoctnCoOh	04	07	18
Smith, John(Z-M)	1829	Nov. 26	CoshoctnCoOh	05	07	14
Smith, John(Z-M)	1831	Oct. 26	BelmontCo,Oh	02	03	15
Smith, John(Z-M)	1832	May 22	CoshoctnCoOh	05	04	05
Smith, John(Z-M)	1830	Feb. 26	Jeff.Co.,Oh.	02	04	08
Smith, John(Z-M)	1830	Feb. 26	Jeff.Co.,Oh.	02	04	08
Smith, John(Z-M)	1830	Nov. 19	CoshoctnCoOh	05	07	13
Smith, John(Z-M)	1831	Jan. 27	CoshoctnCoOh	05	04	04
Smith, John(Z-M)	1831	March 14	TuscarwsCoOh	01	08	02
Smith, John(Z-M)	1834	Jan. 24	LickingCo,Oh	11	03	03
Smith, John(Z-M)	1836	Feb. 01	LickingCo,Oh	11	03	03
Smith, John(Z-M)	1836	Dec. 30	CoshoctnCoOh	05	04	05
Smith, John(Z-M)	1837	Feb. 28	KnoxCo.,Ohio	10	07	23
Smith, John(Z-M)	1837	Feb. 28	KnoxCo.,Ohio	10	07	18
Smith, John(Z-M)	1836	Sept. 23	GuernseyCoOh	03	07	21
Smith, Jonathan J.(Z-M)	1837	March 02	Wayne Co.,Oh	08	08	20
Smith, Jonathan(Z-M)	1836	Oct. 17	HolmesCoOhio	10	09	19
Smith, Jonathan(Z-M)	1837	March 22	KnoxCo.,Ohio	10	09	19
Smith, Jos. J.(Z)	1832	Jan. 06	Morgan Co,Oh	09	06	25
Smith, Jos. Junior(Z)	1832	March 06	Morgan Co,Oh	09	07	26
Smith, Jos. R.(Z-M)	1831	July 11	GuernseyCoOh	01	04	08
Smith, Joseph B.(Z-M)	1836	April 12	GuernseyCoOh	03	04	09
Smith, Joseph(Z)	1828	Aug. 26	BelmontCo,Oh	11	11	06
Smith, Joseph(Z)	1829	Aug. 15	BelmontCo,Oh	11	11	06
Smith, Joseph(Z)	1836	March 08	Morgan Co,Oh	08	06	19
Smith, Joseph(Z)	1804	June 29	MuskingmCoOh	01	02	19

PURCHASER	YEAR	DATE	RESIDENCE	R	T	S
Smith, Joseph(Z)	1804	June 29	MuskingmCoOh	02	01	15
Smith, Joseph(Z)	1805	Feb. 26	MuskingmCoOh	01	01	02
Smith, Joseph(Z)	1805	Dec. 03	MuskingmCoOh	01	02	12
Smith, Joseph(Z)	1811	Jan. 26	GuernseyCoOh	01	02	20
Smith, Joseph(Z)	1816	April 01	MuskingmCoOh	01	02	08
Smith, Joseph(Z)	1817	Jan. 07	LickingCo,Oh	12	09	15
Smith, Joseph(Z-M)	1836	June 13	HolmesCoOhio	08	08	22
Smith, Josiah(Z-M)	1836	Dec. 10	TuscarwsCoOh	02	07	15
Smith, Lachlan(Y)	1828	Jan. 23	ColumbanCoOh	02	09	28
Smith, Lewis(Y)	1824	Nov. 19	ColumbanCoOh	04	13	18
Smith, Lewis(Y)	1833	Sept. 25	Stark Co.,Oh	08	12	14
Smith, Ludwick(Y)	1828	June 26	Stark Co.,Oh	06	15	33
Smith, Mahlon Senr.(Z)	1820	Dec. 11	Morgan Co,Oh	12	10	29
Smith, Martin(Z-M)	1837	June 09	CoshoctnCoOh	05	07	17
Smith, Mary A.(Z)	1833	Aug. 07	Morgan Co,Oh	09	07	36
Smith, Mary(Z-M)	1835	April 22	GuernseyCoOh	02	01	13
Smith, Mary(Z-M)	1836	Jan. 13	MuskingmCoOh	07	04	23
Smith, Mathew P.(Z)	1832	May 07	Morgan Co,Oh	10	08	19
Smith, Michael Junr.(Y)	1830	Sept. 11	Jeff.Co.,Oh.	05	13	08
Smith, Michael(Z)	1814	Aug. 04	TuscarwsCoOh	01	08	12
Smith, Mordecai(Z)	1835	Jan. 06	GuernseyCoOh	08	08	35
Smith, Morris V.(Z)	1821	Feb. 13	Perry Co.,Oh	15	16	26
Smith, Morris(Y)	1824	Sept. 29	WashCo.,Penn	05	14	01
Smith, Nath'l.(Z)	1816	Jan. 29	KnoxCo.,Ohio	11	05	18
Smith, Nathan(Z)	1821	Feb. 10	Morgan Co,Oh	12	11	14
Smith, Nathan(Z)	1826	April 08	Morgan Co,Oh	12	12	10
Smith, Nathaniel(Z-M)	1835	Aug. 18	GuernseyCoOh	03	04	02
Smith, Nathaniel(Z-M)	1835	Aug. 18	GuernseyCoOh	03	04	09
Smith, Nathaniel(Z-M)	1835	Sept. 04	GuernseyCoOh	03	04	02
Smith, Nathaniel(Z-M)	1837	April 11	HarrisonCoOh	03	04	08
Smith, Newman(Z-M)	1832	June 06	CoshoctnCoOh	07	04	02
Smith, Newman(Z-M)	1832	June 06	CoshoctnCoOh	07	04	09
Smith, Patrick(Z)	1833	June 19	Perry Co.,Oh	14	14	31
Smith, Peter(Y)	1823	Jan. 31	HarrisonCoOh	05	13	27
Smith, Peter(Y)	1823	Jan. 31	HarrisonCoOh	05	13	33
Smith, Peter(Y)	1825	July 13	TuscarwsCoOh	06	13	22
Smith, Peter(Z)	1825	March 18	Perry Co.,Oh	15	16	22
Smith, Peter(Z)	1810	Sept. 20	TuscarwsCoOh	03	09	12
Smith, Peter(Z-M)	1839	Jan. 16	HolmesCoOhio	07	07	02
Smith, Rachel(Z)	1833	Aug. 07	Morgan Co,Oh	09	07	36
Smith, Ransom(Z)	1832	April 03	BelmontCo,Oh	10	09	03
Smith, Robert(Y)	1829	March 31	HarrisonCoOh	06	13	17
Smith, Robert(Y)	1829	Dec. 08	HarrisonCoOh	06	13	15
Smith, Robert(Y)	1830	March 27	GuernseyCoOh	07	09	07
Smith, Robert(Y)	1831	Sept. 27	HarrisonCoOh	06	12	30
Smith, Robert(Z)	1833	Nov. 25	Perry Co.,Oh	15	14	24
Smith, Robt.(Z)	1831	Oct. 20	BelmontCo,Oh	10	07	35
Smith, Robt.(Z)	1833	April 18	Perry Co.,Oh	15	14	24
Smith, Robt.(Z)	1817	Sept. 19	ZanesvilleOh	14	14	02
Smith, Samuel A.(Z)	1836	Sept. 19	WashngtnCoOh	08	05	24
Smith, Samuel Anderson(Z)	1836	July 23	WashngtnCoOh	08	05	24
Smith, Samuel H.(Z)	1808	March 08	Clinton,Ohio	09	08	06
Smith, Samuel(Z)	1807	Jan. 23	ColumbanCoOh	03	10	12
Smith, Samuel(Z)	1807	March 28	ColumbanCoOh	03	11	13
Smith, Samuel(Z)	1807	July 18	MuskingmCoOh	15	18	03
Smith, Samuel(Z)	1808	Aug. 22	TuscarwsCoOh	03	10	19
Smith, Samuel(Z)	1816	March 05	GuernseyCoOh	15	15	29
Smith, Serrens(Z-M)	1831	March 12	TuscarwsCoOh	01	06	10
Smith, Shubal(Z)	1829	Dec. 21	Morgan Co,Oh	09	06	34
Smith, Thomas(Z)	1809	Nov. 03	MuskingmCoOh	12	13	03
Smith, Thomas(Z)	1814	Oct. 19	HarrisonCoOh	15	17	08
Smith, Thomas(Z)	1816	Feb. 21	GuernseyCoOh	01	03	18
Smith, Thomas(Z-M)	1835	Nov. 04	CoshoctnCoOh	10	04	01
Smith, Thomas(Z-M)	1836	Nov. 25	LickingCo,Oh	09	04	05
Smith, Valentine(Z-M)	1832	Aug. 29	TuscarwsCoOh	01	09	14
Smith, Vincent(Z)	1836	March 30	MonroeCo.,Oh	08	06	13
Smith, Vincent(Z)	1838	Aug. 25	MonroeCo.,Oh	08	06	13
Smith, Walter(Z)	1821	Oct. 01	Morgan Co,Oh	10	06	19
Smith, William A.(Z)	1805	Nov. 18	MuskingmCoOh	12	13	18

PURCHASER	YEAR	DATE	RESIDENCE	R	T	S
Smith, William C.(Z-M)	1836	Oct. 12	CoshoctnCoOh	04	04	03
Smith, William J.(Z-M)	1831	Oct. 28	HolmesCoOhio	08	08	23
Smith, William J.(Z-M)	1836	March 14	KnoxCo.,Ohio	10	06	05
Smith, William J.(Z-M)	1836	Nov. 19	HolmesCoOhio	08	07	01
Smith, William N.(Z-M)	1836	April 14	GuernseyCoOh	02	04	14
Smith, William Neal(Z-M)	1836	Oct. 12	CoshoctnCoOh	04	04	10
Smith, William S.(Z)	1814	June 15	GuernseyCoOh	02	02	03
Smith, William(Y)	1825	Aug. 16	BelmontCo,Oh	07	09	22
Smith, William(Y)	1825	Aug. 16	BelmontCo,Oh	07	09	22
Smith, William(Y)	1829	Dec. 07	Pittsburg,Pa	04	10	12
Smith, William(Y)	1831	Oct. 11	HarrisonCoOh	06	12	17
Smith, William(Y)	1832	March 30	Jeff.Co.,Oh.	03	11	33
Smith, William(Y)	1832	Aug. 27	Jeff.Co.,Oh.	03	12	26
Smith, William(Z)	1824	Oct. 02	Morgan Co,Oh	09	07	04
Smith, William(Z)	1826	Nov. 15	BelmontCo,Oh	12	09	10
Smith, William(Z)	1833	Aug. 21	MonroeCo.,Oh	08	06	12
Smith, William(Z)	1836	April 12	GuernseyCoOh	08	07	30
Smith, William(Z)	1805	Sept. 25	RockbrdgCoVa	15	17	05
Smith, William(Z)	1805	Sept. 25	RockbrdgCoVa	15	18	06
Smith, William(Z)	1805	Sept. 30	RockbrdgCoVa	15	18	06
Smith, William(Z)	1805	Sept. 30	RockbrdgCoVa	15	18	06
Smith, William(Z)	1810	Oct. 29	AlleghnyCoPa	11	06	18
Smith, William(Z)	1811	July 30	Jeff.Co.,Oh.	15	17	14
Smith, William(Z)	1811	Dec. 26	BelmontCo,Oh	13	12	11
Smith, William(Z)	1813	June 18	GuernseyCoOh	02	02	09
Smith, William(Z)	1815	April 14	WashCo.,Penn	09	08	08
Smith, William(Z)	1815	Dec. 04	BelmontCo,Oh	12	12	24
Smith, William(Z)	1815	Dec. 04	BelmontCo,Oh	12	12	24
Smith, William(Z-M)	1829	June 09	TuscarwsCoOh	04	07	11
Smith, William(Z-M)	1832	March 03	GuernseyCoOh	01	04	02
Smith, William(Z-M)	1832	Oct. 06	Jeff.Co.,Oh.	03	10	15
Smith, William(Z-M)	1833	Feb. 05	MonroeCo.,Oh	08	06	12
Smith, William(Z-M)	1835	Oct. 06	CoshoctnCoOh	04	07	11
Smith, William(Z-M)	1836	Feb. 22	HolmesCoOhio	10	09	12
Smith, William(Z-M)	1839	May 17	CarrollCo,Oh	08	06	07
Smith, William(Z-M)	1840	April 25	HolmesCoOhio	09	08	23
Smith, Wilson(Z-M)	1833	Sept. 23	GuernseyCoOh	03	04	07
Smith, Wm. A.(Z)	1805	Oct. 18	MuskingmCoOh	14	15	14
Smith, Wm. J.(Z-M)	1837	March 29	HolmesCoOhio	08	07	02
Smith, Wm. L.(Z)	1831	Sept. 12	MuskingmCoOh	11	12	30
Smith, Wm. N.(Z-M)	1832	Feb. 10	GuernseyCoOh	02	04	14
Smith, Wm. N.(Z-M)	1831	March 25	GuernseyCoOh	02	04	15
Smith, Wm.(Z)	1832	May 16	Morgan Co,Oh	10	08	28
Smithson, John(Z)	1834	Aug. 07	WashngtnCoOh	08	05	20
Smithson, John(Z)	1836	Aug. 09	WashngtnCoOh	08	05	08
Smoot, Daniel(Z-M)	1830	Jan. 20	MuskingmCoOh	06	03	10
Smoot, John(Z)	1833	July 24	Morgan Co,Oh	09	06	07
Smootz, Joseph(Z-M)	1824	June 21	CoshoctnCoOh	07	07	07
Smur, Solomon(Z-M)	1833	Sept. 20	HolmesCoOhio	06	09	25
Smur, Wm. F.(Z-M)	1833	Sept. 23	HolmesCoOhio	06	08	02
Smutts, Jacob(Z)	1817	Feb. 10	TuscarwsCoOh	03	08	01
Sneary, H. S.(Y)	1830	Feb. 23	HarrisonCoOh	06	13	10
Sneary, Jacob Jr.(Y)	1830	Feb. 23	HarrisonCoOh	06	13	10
Sneary, John(Y)	1829	Nov. 18	HarrisonCoOh	07	16	03
Sneary, John(Y)	1829	Nov. 18	HarrisonCoOh	06	15	33
Snedecker, Peter(Z)	1827	Nov. 17	KnoxCo.,Ohio	11	08	25
Snedecker, Peter(Z-M)	1825	Dec. 21	BelmontCo,Oh	11	08	25
Snedeker, Garret(Z-M)	1822	Dec. 06	BelmontCo,Oh	11	08	06
Snedeker, Jacob(Z-M)	1830	May 12	KnoxCo.,Ohio	11	08	14
Snedeker, Jacob(Z-M)	1830	May 12	KnoxCo.,Ohio	11	08	14
Snedeker, John A.(Z)	1833	March 26	BelmontCo,Oh	11	12	10
Snedeker, Pet.(Z)	1830	June 07	BelmontCo,Oh	10	07	15
Snedeker, Peter(Z-M)	1832	June 15	KnoxCo.,Ohio	11	08	17
Snedeker, Peter(Z-M)	1835	July 08	KnoxCo.,Ohio	11	08	07
Snediker, Garret(Z-M)	1832	June 06	KnoxCo.,Ohio	11	08	06
Snellenberger, Adam(Z-M)	1836	Feb. 27	HolmesCoOhio	05	07	15
Snellenberger, Fred'k.(Z-M)	1828	May 23	ColumbanCoOh	04	08	24
Snellenberger, Frederick(Z-M)	1836	Feb. 06	TuscarwsCoOh	04	07	04
Snider, Asa B.(Z)	1812	May 04	LickingCo,Oh	09	03	23

PURCHASER	YEAR	DATE	RESIDENCE	R	T	S
Snider, Benj'n.(Y)	1825	June 14	TrumbullCoOh	06	19	01
Snider, Benj'n.(Y)	1828	March 25	Stark Co.,Oh	06	19	01
Snider, Benjamin(Z)	1836	Feb. 22	BelmontCo,Oh	14	12	07
Snider, Benjamin(Z)	1836	Feb. 22	BelmontCo,Oh	14	12	05
Snider, Benjamin(Z)	1836	Aug. 17	BelmontCo,Oh	14	12	05
Snider, David(Y)	1834	May 12	WashngtnCoOh	07	14	08
Snider, Frederick(Z)	1826	Dec. 22	MonroeCo.,Oh	08	07	24
Snider, George(Y)	1830	Oct. 29	Stark Co.,Oh	06	16	27
Snider, George(Y)	1834	Nov. 28	Stark Co.,Oh	07	20	07
Snider, George(Z)	1816	March 26	BelmontCo,Oh	09	05	17
Snider, Jacob(Z)	1825	Oct. 10	Perry Co.,Oh	15	16	22
Snider, John C.(Z-M)	1837	Aug. 28	CoshoctnCoOh	08	07	10
Snider, John(Y)	1831	March 09	HarrisonCoOh	06	12	18
Snider, John(Z)	1812	May 04	LickingCo,Oh	09	03	23
Snider, John(Z)	1816	Nov. 08	MuskingmCoOh	09	04	09
Snider, Nicholas(Z)	1823	June 02	Perry Co.,Oh	13	10	27
Snider, Philip(Z)	1837	Feb. 07	Wheeling,Vir	08	06	03
Snider, Philip(Z)	1837	Feb. 07	Wheeling,Vir	08	06	04
Snider, Samuel(Z-M)	1838	Feb. 28	HolmesCoOhio	04	05	19
Sniff, John Junr.(Z)	1816	Nov. 09	MuskingmCoOh	13	09	28
Sniff, John Senr.(Z)	1816	Nov. 09	MuskingmCoOh	13	09	32
Sniff, John Senr.(Z)	1817	Jan. 04	MuskingmCoOh	13	09	10
Sniff, William(Z)	1821	Oct. 02	MuskingmCoOh	13	09	20
Snode, Isaac(Y)	1824	March 04	ColumbanCoOh	05	18	14
Snode, Isaac(Y)	1829	March 13	ColumbanCoOh	05	18	15
Snode, Joseph(Y)	1824	Aug. 25	ColumbanCoOh	05	18	11
Snodgrass, James(Z-M)	1838	Feb. 22	MuskingmCoOh	04	03	06
Snoots, Henry(Z-M)	1832	Sept. 12	MuskingmCoOh	06	03	20
Snoots, Henry(Z-M)	1832	Sept. 24	MuskingmCoOh	06	03	11
Snoufer, Frederick(Z-M)	1832	Nov. 03	TuscarwsCoOh	03	08	13
Snow, Alonzo(Z-M)	1836	Jan. 23	CoshoctnCoOh	08	07	19
Snow, Alonzo(Z-M)	1837	July 03	CoshoctnCoOh	08	07	19
Snow, Darius(Z-M)	1836	Jan. 14	CoshoctnCoOh	07	07	15
Snow, Simeon(Z-M)	1836	Oct. 07	HolmesCoOhio	08	08	24
Snow, Simeon(Z-M)	1836	Oct. 07	HolmesCoOhio	08	08	24
Snyder, Frederick(Z-M)	1831	Oct. 13	TuscarwsCoOh	02	10	18
Snyder, Frederick(Z-M)	1831	Oct. 13	TuscarwsCoOh	02	10	18
Snyder, Frederick(Z-M)	1833	March 05	TuscarwsCoOh	03	10	13
Snyder, Frederick(Z-M)	1833	March 05	TuscarwsCoOh	03	10	13
Snyder, Frederick(Z-M)	1833	March 05	TuscarwsCoOh	02	10	24
Snyder, Geo.(Z-M)	1832	Feb. 25	CoshoctnCoOh	05	07	08
Snyder, George(Z-M)	1830	Feb. 25	CoshoctnCoOh	05	07	19
Snyder, George(Z-M)	1835	May 25	TuscarwsCoOh	02	10	24
Snyder, Henry(Z-M)	1835	May 26	TuscarwsCoOh	03	09	22
Snyder, Jacob(Y)	1821	April 30	AlleghnyCoMd	05	14	05
Snyder, Jacob(Z)	1830	Feb. 17	Morgan Co,Oh	13	10	35
Snyder, Jacob(Z-M)	1833	March 05	TuscarwsCoOh	03	10	17
Snyder, Jacob(Z-M)	1833	March 05	TuscarwsCoOh	03	10	23
Snyder, Michael(Z)	1806	Sept. 15	MuskingmCoOh	15	17	01
Snyder, Samuel(Y)	1826	Oct. 17	HarrisonCoOh	06	12	24
Snyder, Samuel(Y)	1828	Jan. 09	HarrisonCoOh	06	12	29
Sockman, John Junr.(Z)	1816	June 03	MuskingmCoOh	10	07	06
Solinger, James(Z-M)	1839	Feb. 08	ZanesvilleOh	04	03	11
Solinger, James(Z-M)	1839	Feb. 08	ZanesvilleOh	04	03	20
Somers, Jacob(Z-M)	1832	April 23	TuscarwsCoOh	04	07	18
Somerville, Robt.(Z-M)	1831	March 17	HolmesCoOhio	06	09	06
Sonafrank, John(Z)	1813	Aug. 28	MuskingmCoOh	04	02	23
Sondel, Dorothy(Z-M)	1833	Dec. 14	CoshoctnCoOh	05	06	18
Sondels, Jacob(Z-M)	1837	Nov. 09	RiclandCo,Oh	08	07	02
Song, Peter(Y)	1832	June 26	Stark Co.,Oh	10	01	03
Sorg, Henry(Z-M)	1832	Nov. 01	CoshoctnCoOh	05	07	15
Sorg, Michael(Z-M)	1832	Sept. 08	CoshoctnCoOh	06	07	11
Sorrence, Joseph(Z)	1831	Jan. 28	MuskingmCoOh	11	13	34
Sorrick, Adam(Y)	1824	May 21	Stark Co.,Oh	10	02	23
Sorrick, Adam(Y)	1824	May 21	Stark Co.,Oh	10	02	23
Sorrick, John(Y)	1824	Jan. 20	Stark Co.,Oh	10	02	13
Souls, John(Z-M)	1837	Feb. 28	KnoxCo.,Ohio	10	07	23
Southard, Francis H.(Z)	1817	May 20	LickingCo,Oh	10	03	17
Southard, Isaiah(Z-M)	1829	Aug. 18	AdamsCo,Ohio	10	03	18

PURCHASER	YEAR	DATE	RESIDENCE	R	T	S
Southard, Joseph(Z-M)	1836	Sept. 01	LickingCo,Oh	10	04	17
Southard, Silvester F.(Z-M)	1835	Nov. 10	LickingCo,Oh	10	03	07
Sovereigns, Benj.(Z-M)	1838	June 23	KnoxCo.,Ohio	10	09	19
Sowards, Jacob(Z-M)	1831	Dec. 09	RichlandCoOh	07	08	11
Sowder, Jacob(Z)	1824	May 11	Morgan Co,Oh	13	10	21
Sowder, Jacob(Z)	1829	Dec. 24	Morgan Co,Oh	13	10	20
Sowers, Acquilla(Z)	1826	Aug. 23	MuskingmCoOh	14	14	12
Sowers, Bassel(Z)	1833	June 07	Morgan Co,Oh	14	13	06
Sowers, George(Z)	1827	March 14	MuskingmCoOh	14	14	15
Sowers, John(Z)	1831	Jan. 27	Morgan Co,Oh	14	13	08
Sowers, Joshua(Z)	1831	Nov. 12	Morgan Co,Oh	14	14	15
Sowers, Joshua(Z)	1831	Nov. 12	Morgan Co,Oh	14	14	22
Sowers, Joshua(Z)	1831	Nov. 12	Morgan Co,Oh	14	14	22
Sowers, Wm.(Z)	1831	June 17	MuskingmCoOh	14	14	13
Spaear, Benedict(Z-M)	1838	Jan. 15	HolmesCoOhio	08	06	01
Spaear, Benedict(Z-M)	1838	Jan. 15	HolmesCoOhio	08	06	02
Spaer, Benedict(Z-M)	1832	May 28	HolmesCoOhio	05	08	15
Spaid, Frederick(Z-M)	1836	April 02	HolmesCoOhio	08	08	06
Spaid, Michael(Z)	1836	Jan. 15	GuernseyCoOh	09	08	09
Spaid, Michael(Z)	1836	Dec. 26	GuernseyCoOh	09	08	15
Spaid, William(Z)	1836	Jan. 13	GuernseyCoOh	09	08	09
Spangler, C.(Z)	1815	Dec. 04	ZanesvilleOh	06	02	22
Spangler, Christian(Z)	1810	Oct. 13	MuskingmCoOh	13	11	17
Spangler, D.(Z)	1815	Dec. 04	ZanesvilleOh	06	02	22
Spangler, Daniel(Z)	1829	Oct. 29	WashCo.,Penn	13	11	19
Spangler, David(Z)	1816	Oct. 04	ZanesvilleOh	08	03	14
Spangler, David(Z)	1816	Nov. 13	ZanesvilleOh	12	13	33
Spangler, George C. Jr.(Z)	1810	June 12	NrthmbldCo ?	05	08	19
Spangler, George C. Senr.(Z)	1810	June 12	NrthmbldCo ?	05	08	19
Spangler, George C. Senr.(Z)	1810	June 12	NrthmbldCo ?	04	08	16
Spangler, John Jacob(Z)	1810	June 12	NrthmbldCo ?	05	08	19
Spangler, John(Y)	1828	June 19	Stark Co.,Oh	09	10	11
Spangler, John(Z)	1810	June 12	NrthmbldCo ?	05	08	19
Spangler, John(Z-M)	1836	Feb. 03	TuscarwsCoOh	04	07	11
Spangler, Jonathan(Z-M)	1829	July 02	TuscarwsCoOh	04	07	19
Spangler, Mathias(Z)	1813	Aug. 28	MuskingmCoOh	13	11	02
Spangler, Peter(Z)	1814	April 16	TuscarwsCoOh	02	08	14
Spangler, Rudolph(Z)	1807	June 15	MuskingmCoOh	15	18	11
Sparks, Eli(Z-M)	1837	Oct. 09	GuernseyCoOh	04	04	01
Sparks, Isaac(Z)	1807	June 29	FayetteCo,Pa	01	09	01
Sparks, John B.(Z-M)	1836	Dec. 30	LickingCo,Oh	10	04	04
Sparks, Robert(Z-M)	1823	Sept. 08	TuscarwsCoOh	01	08	01
Sparks, Sidney(Z-M)	1834	Jan. 09	MuskingmCoOh	10	04	04
Sparks, William B.(Y)	1830	Jan. 19	HarrisonCoOh	05	13	21
Speakman, Amos(Z)	1817	Aug. 05	ChesterCo,Pa	12	12	35
Spear, David(Z-M)	1835	July 08	TuscarwsCoOh	04	06	20
Spear, James(Z-M)	1835	Jan. 29	GuernseyCoOh	04	06	21
Spear, Jane(Z-M)	1835	July 08	TuscarwsCoOh	04	06	21
Spear, Nehemiah(Z)	1836	March 19	Morgan Co,Oh	08	06	19
Spear, Robert(Z)	1804	June 12	MuskingmCoOh	04	02	21
Spear, Robert(Z)	1804	June 12	MuskingmCoOh	05	01	01
Spear, Robert(Z)	1804	Oct. 29	MuskingmCoOh	05	01	01
Spears, Thomas(Z)	1804	Nov. 03	MuskingmCoOh	01	02	19
Speck, John(Z-M)	1833	May 21	GuernseyCoOh	01	05	17
Speer, Alexander(Z)	1806	Dec. 17	WashCo.,Penn	04	02	22
Speer, James(Z-M)	1830	March 11	HolmesCoOhio	03	10	25
Speer, Jas.(Z-M)	1831	Nov. 02	HolmesCoOhio	03	10	25
Speer, Robert(Z)	1806	June 13	MuskingmCoOh	04	02	21
Speer, Stewart(Z)	1808	Jan. 19	MuskingmCoOh	04	02	18
Speer, Stuart(Z)	1807	Jan. 12	AdamsCo.,Vir	04	02	22
Speer, Thomas(Z)	1811	May 25	MuskingmCoOh	05	01	10
Speer, Thos.(Z)	1806	April 07	MuskingmCoOh	05	01	10
Speers, Robt.(Z-M)	1833	April 18	GuernseyCoOh	02	03	13
Spence, Charles(Y)	1824	June 28	AlleghnyCoPa	04	14	33
Spence, Charles(Z)	1815	Sept. 21	WashCo.,Penn	05	01	16
Spence, Chas.(Y)	1824	June 02	AlleghnyCoPa	04	14	33
Spencer, Amos Lyons(Z)	1836	Nov. 15	MonroeCo.,Oh	08	06	35
Spencer, Elisha(Z)	1817	Sept. 17	WashngtnCoOh	09	06	30
Spencer, Foreman(Z)	1811	Sept. 19	MuskingmCoOh	08	02	05

PURCHASER	YEAR	DATE	RESIDENCE	R	T	S
Spencer, Geo.(Z)	1815	June 16	FairfeldCoOh	15	15	20
Spencer, George(Z)	1813	March 22	MuskingmCoOh	15	15	05
Spencer, Israel(Z)	1833	Feb. 11	Morgan Co,Oh	09	06	34
Spencer, James(Z)	1828	Feb. 25	BelmontCo,Oh	11	10	18
Spencer, James(Z)	1807	Oct. 06	FairfeldCoOh	15	16	07
Spencer, James(Z)	1813	March 22	MuskingmCoOh	15	15	05
Spencer, James(Z)	1815	June 16	FairfeldCoOh	15	15	20
Spencer, John W.(Z)	1816	April 24	HarrisonCoOh	01	04	01
Spencer, John W.(Z)	1816	April 24	HarrisonCoOh	01	04	01
Spencer, Judith(Z-M)	1835	Dec. 23	MuskingmCoOh	06	04	10
Spencer, Nathan(Z)	1829	Sept. 19	BelmontCo,Oh	11	10	18
Spencer, Nathan(Z)	1831	Aug. 17	BelmontCo,Oh	11	10	20
Spencer, Nathan(Z-M)	1828	March 25	MuskingmCoOh	04	01	21
Spencer, Nathan(Z-M)	1829	April 07	GuernseyCoOh	04	01	21
Spencer, S. C.(Z-M)	1831	March 23	TuscarwsCoOh	03	05	22
Spencer, Samuel(Z)	1829	March 09	BelmontCo,Oh	11	10	17
Spencer, Thomas(Z)	1813	April 28	FairfeldCoOh	15	16	14
Spencer, William(Z)	1813	Oct. 18	MuskingmCoOh	08	03	15
Spencer, William(Z-M)	1833	Dec. 11	MuskingmCoOh	06	02	07
Sperreer, E.(Z)	1837	April 28	Morgan Co,Oh	15	14	33
Sperreer, W. G.(Z)	1837	April 28	Morgan Co,Oh	15	14	33
Spicer, Benjamin(Z-M)	1835	Oct. 19	MuskingmCoOh	11	04	12
Spicer, Daniel(Z)	1816	Jan. 06	MuskingmCoOh	06	02	20
Spicer, David(Z)	1815	Dec. 02	MuskingmCoOh	06	02	20
Spicer, John(Z)	1815	June 08	ButlerCoPenn	06	02	23
Spicer, John(Z)	1816	April 23	SomersetCoPa	04	08	19
Spicer, Jonathan(Z)	1817	Sept. 12	MuskingmCoOh	08	03	05
Spicer, Joseph(Z-M)	1832	Nov. 28	GuernseyCoOh	01	04	02
Spidle, Jacob(Y)	1824	June 24	Stark Co.,Oh	09	11	14
Spidle, Michael(Y)	1829	March 13	Stark Co.,Oh	08	12	15
Spiker, Christopher(Z)	1832	Aug. 15	Morgan Co,Oh	10	08	24
Spiker, Isaac(Y)	1832	Feb. 15	HarrisonCoOh	06	12	23
Spilman, James(Z)	1825	Oct. 04	Morgan Co,Oh	10	09	21
Spinifield, David(Z-M)	1825	Dec. 06	MuskingmCoOh	06	03	20
Sponslar, Jacob(Z)	1824	May 29	Perry Co.,Oh	14	14	21
Sponslar, Jacob(Z)	1833	April 01	Perry Co.,Oh	15	14	07
Spoon, Martin(Z-M)	1832	Jan. 30	TuscarwsCoOh	02	06	12
Spooner, Ebenezer(Z)	1816	May 28	GuernseyCoOh	10	08	03
Spooner, Elisha(Z-M)	1829	March 25	TuscarwsCoOh	01	05	17
Spoonie, Ebenezer(Z)	1816	May 28	GuernseyCoOh	10	08	03
Spotz, Ludwig(Y)	1826	June 02	Stark Co.,Oh	09	12	28
Spragg, Benajah(Z-M)	1833	Nov. 22	MuskingmCoOh	05	03	07
Spragg, Benajah(Z-M)	1833	Nov. 22	MuskingmCoOh	05	03	07
Spragg, Benijah Jr.(Z-M)	1835	Jan. 06	MuskingmCoOh	05	03	04
Sprague J.(Z-M)	1830	May 12	MuskingmCoOh	05	03	07
Sprague, Abrm.(Z-M)	1838	Oct. 25	KnoxCo.,Ohio	10	07	21
Sprague, Elias(Z-M)	1832	May 22	MuskingmCoOh	05	03	04
Sprague, Elijah(Z-M)	1832	Sept. 22	MuskingmCoOh	05	03	04
Sprague, Elijah(Z-M)	1838	Oct. 27	MuskingmCoOh	05	03	03
Sprague, James(Z)	1806	March 19	MuskingmCoOh	07	03	19
Sprague, James(Z)	1814	Sept. 15	MuskingmCoOh	05	03	13
Sprague, Jonathan(Z)	1838	June 02	MuskingmCoOh	04	03	05
Sprague, Jonathan(Z-M)	1835	Dec. 23	MuskingmCoOh	04	03	06
Sprague, Jonathon(Z-M)	1838	May 26	MuskingmCoOh	05	03	11
Sprague, Jotham(Z)	1824	July 22	Morgan Co,Oh	10	08	03
Sprague, Nath'l. W.(Z)	1823	July 30	MuskingmCoOh	13	10	36
Sprague, Nath'l. W.(Z)	1828	Feb. 02	Morgan Co,Oh	13	09	01
Sprague, S.(Z)	1816	Oct. 15	GuernseyCoOh	10	07	06
Sprague, S.(Z-M)	1830	May 12	MuskingmCoOh	05	03	07
Sprague, Samuel(Z)	1806	Feb. 26	WashngtnCoOh	10	07	05
Sprague, Samuel(Z)	1815	Feb. 18	GuernseyCoOh	?	07	06
Sprague, Samuel(Z)	1815	April 25	GuernseyCoOh	10	07	29
Sprague, Solomon(Z)	1828	Nov. 06	Morgan Co,Oh	10	07	27
Sprague, Stephen(Z)	1836	April 12	Morgan Co,Oh	10	06	01
Sprague, Wilber(Z)	1814	April 18	WashngtnCoOh	09	05	08
Sprang, Philip G.(Z-M)	1837	May 30	HolmesCoOhio	09	09	25
Spratt, Andrew(Y)	1832	June 12	Stark Co.,Oh	07	17	25
Spratt, James(Z)	1826	July 18	MuskingmCoOh	11	13	22
Spring, Jacob(Z)	1805	June 05	MuskingmCoOh	15	17	25

PURCHASER	YEAR	DATE	RESIDENCE	R	T	S
Spring, John(Z-M)	1832	April 05	HarrisonCoOh	02	06	11
Springer, Cornelius(Z)	1810	April 25	MuskingmCoOh	14	16	09
Springer, Daniel(Z)	1836	Jan. 13	HarrisonCoOh	15	14	13
Springer, James(Z-M)	1831	Sept. 26	HolmesCoOhio	08	08	14
Springer, John(Y)	1828	Oct. 31	ColumbanCoOh	02	10	17
Springer, John(Y)	1829	Aug. 03	HarrisonCoOh	06	12	35
Springer, John(Z)	1805	July 03	Ohio Co.,Vir	18	16	18
Springer, John(Z)	1806	Aug. 30	MuskingmCoOh	13	10	05
Springer, John(Z)	1816	May 10	MuskingmCoOh	13	09	28
Springer, John(Z)	1816	Nov. 27	MuskingmCoOh	13	08	04
Springer, John(Z)	1806	Aug. 30	MuskingmCoOh	13	11	24
Springer, Levi(Z)	1805	Nov. 14	FayetteCo,Pa	14	14	32
Springer, Levi(Z)	1805	Nov. 14	FayetteCo,Pa	14	14	09
Springer, Levi(Z)	1805	Nov. 14	FayetteCo,Pa	13	12	08
Springg, Samuel(Y)	1824	May 22	Ohio Co.,Vir	03	05	02
Sprinkle, Peter(Z)	1809	June 23	MuskingmCoOh	03	03	12
Sprinkle, Peter(Z)	1809	July 14	MuskingmCoOh	03	03	12
Sproal, James(Z-M)	1832	April 25	HolmesCoOhio	07	08	03
Sproal, James(Z-M)	1832	Sept. 10	HolmesCoOhio	07	08	02
Sproal, James(Z-M)	1832	Oct. 08	HolmesCoOhio	07	08	02
Sproal, James(Z-M)	1833	Jan. 07	HolmesCoOhio	07	08	02
Sproat, Richard(Y)	1825	Dec. 19	Wash.Co.,Pen	05	18	17
Sproat, Samuel(Z)	1810	Oct. 23	FayetteCo,Pa	08	08	04
Sproat, Samuel(Z)	1810	Oct. 23	FayetteCo,Pa	08	08	04
Sproul, John(Y)	1830	Jan. 16	HarrisonCoOh	06	12	12
Sproul, William(Y)	1831	March 10	HarrisonCoOh	05	11	36
Sprowls, John(Z)	1833	Feb. 11	WashngtnCoOh	10	08	22
Spry, Samuel(Z-M)	1837	March 21	KnoxCo.,Ohio	10	08	12
Spurgen, George(Z-M)	1833	Jan. 08	KnoxCo.,Ohio	10	07	25
Spurgen, Wm.(Z-M)	1835	Aug. 27	KnoxCo.,Ohio	10	09	12
Spurgeon, Nathaniel(Z)	1805	May 22	MuskingmCoOh	10	06	03
Spurgin, George(Z-M)	1833	April 02	KnoxCo.,Ohio	10	07	21
Spurgin, George(Z-M)	1833	April 02	KnoxCo.,Ohio	10	07	21
Spurgin, James(Z-M)	1832	Sept. 03	HolmesCoOhio	08	08	07
Spurgin, James(Z-M)	1832	Sept. 03	HolmesCoOhio	08	08	08
Spurgin, Nathaniel(Z)	1809	July 14	KnoxCo.,Ohio	10	07	07
Spurgin, Wm.(Z-M)	1822	Feb. 09	CoshoctnCoOh	08	08	07
Spurgin, Wm.(Z-M)	1836	June 03	HolmesCoOhio	08	08	07
Spurirer, Warner(Z)	1829	June 20	Morgan Co,Oh	12	09	03
Spurrier, John(Z)	1828	Oct. 22	Jeff.Co.,Oh.	11	11	07
Squier, Abiram(Y)	1820	Nov. 28	TrumbullCoOh	03	16	12
Squier, Benjamin(Y)	1821	Sept. 11	TrumbullCoOh	03	16	22
Squier, Benjamin(Y)	1821	Sept. 11	TrumbullCoOh	03	16	22
Squier, Jehiel(Y)	1820	Nov. 28	TrumbullCoOh	03	16	12
Squier, Jehiel(Y)	1821	Sept. 11	ColumbanCoOh	02	13	07
Squier, Miriam(Y)	1822	March 15	TrumbullCoOh	02	13	07
Squire, Bradly(Z-M)	1832	Oct. 02	CoshoctnCoOh	07	05	22
Squire, Chas.(Z-M)	1831	Feb. 28	CoshoctnCoOh	07	05	25
Squire, Samuel(Z-M)	1831	Nov. 01	CoshoctnCoOh	07	05	19
Squire, Samuel(Z-M)	1831	Sept. 14	CoshoctnCoOh	07	05	19
Squire, Samuel(Z-M)	1831	Sept. 27	CoshoctnCoOh	07	05	19
Squires, Bradly(Z-M)	1831	Sept. 27	CoshoctnCoOh	07	05	22
Squires, Bradly(Z-M)	1831	Sept. 27	CoshoctnCoOh	07	05	19
Squires, Bradly(Z-M)	1831	Sept. 27	CoshoctnCoOh	07	05	22
Squires, John(Z-M)	1836	Feb. 20	MuskingmCoOh	09	03	17
Srins, Wm.(Z-M)	1831	April 11	GuernseyCoOh	03	01	15
St. Clair, John(Z)	1814	Dec. 17	MuskingmCoOh	11	13	23
St. Clair, John(Z)	1814	Dec. 17	MuskingmCoOh	10	09	19
St. Clair, John(Z)	1817	June 30	GuernseyCoOh	10	09	17
St. John, Russel(Z)	1836	Aug. 26	WashngtnCoOh	08	05	22
St. John, Russel(Z)	1836	Aug. 26	WashngtnCoOh	08	05	22
StClair, John(Z)	1816	March 15	GuernseyCoOh	10	09	19
Stacey, James(Z-M)	1832	Aug. 03	TuscarwsCoOh	01	05	18
Staddon, Hiram(Z-M)	1834	Dec. 17	TuscarwsCoOh	01	05	10
Stafford, Aaron(Z)	1817	Feb. 04	TuscarwsCoOh	03	06	17
Stafford, Francis A.(Z)	1816	March 23	CoshoctnCoOh	08	04	13
Stafford, Francis A.(Z-M)	1824	July 21	CoshoctnCoOh	08	04	09
Stafford, Francis H.(Z)	1809	Sept. 27	MuskingmCoOh	08	04	20
Stafford, Richard A.(Z)	1812	Aug. 25	CoshoctnCoOh	08	04	14

273

PURCHASER	YEAR	DATE	RESIDENCE	R	T	S
Stafford, Robert(Z)	1817	Feb. 04	TuscarwsCoOh	03	06	18
Staggs, Franklin(Z-M)	1837	Jan. 07	BelmontCo,Oh	03	06	01
Stain, Gotlieb(Z-M)	1835	Oct. 13	CoshoctnCoOh	05	07	04
Stainbrook, Ab'm.(Z)	1828	July 30	MuskingmCoOh	13	10	17
Stainbrook, Abraham(Z)	1833	March 19	MuskingmCoOh	13	10	17
Stainbrook, Abraham(Z)	1836	Feb. 09	MuskingmCoOh	13	10	17
Stainbrook, Henry 2nd.(Z)	1837	Jan. 26	MuskingmCoOh	13	10	10
Stainbrook, Henry(Z)	1831	Sept. 05	MuskingmCoOh	13	11	12
Stainbrook, Henry(Z)	1815	May 08	CrawfordCoPa	13	10	08
Stainbrook, Henry(Z)	1815	May 08	CrawfordCoPa	13	10	05
Stainbrook, Peter(Z)	1834	Feb. 22	MuskingmCoOh	13	10	17
Stainbrook, Sarah(Z)	1830	May 29	MuskingmCoOh	13	10	22
Stainbrook, Sarah(Z)	1830	April 28	MuskingmCoOh	13	10	22
Stainer, Jacob(Z-M)	1836	May 06	TuscarwsCoOh	03	08	25
Staley, Joel(Z)	1833	Feb. 21	Perry Co.,Oh	15	14	05
Stall, Joshua(Z-M)	1835	Sept. 05	KnoxCo.,Ohio	10	08	04
Shambaugh, Isaac(Z-M)	1836	March 12	CoshoctnCoOh	06	04	13
Stanberry, Jonas(Z)	1829	May 04	ZanesvilleOh	12	12	06
Stanberry, Jonas(Z)	1831	Oct. 22	ZanesvilleOh	10	08	31
Stanberry, Jonas(Z)	1832	Jan. 14	ZanesvilleOh	10	07	11
Stanberry, Jonas(Z-M)	1832	Jan. 19	ZanesvilleOh	06	04	01
Stanberry, Jonas(Z-M)	1832	May 16	ZanesvilleOh	07	08	05
Stanberry, Robt. H.(Z)	1825	April 06	Morgan Co,Oh	13	09	15
Stall, Wm.(Z)	1815	May 12	Jeff.Co.,Oh.	03	07	29
Stallard, James(Z-M)	1837	April 10	MuskingmCoOh	05	04	20
Stallings, D.(Z)	1814	Dec. 08	MuskingmCoOh	15	15	10
Stamer, William(Z)	1811	Aug. 07	KnoxCo.,Ohio	11	05	21
Stanbery, Charles(Z)	1836	Sept. 17	ZanesvilleOh	09	06	24
Stanbery, Charles(Z)	1836	Oct. 17	ZanesvilleOh	08	06	23
Stanbery, Charles(Z-M)	1833	Aug. 15	ZanesvilleOh	01	08	02
Stanbery, Chas.(Z)	1836	Sept. 09	ZanesvilleOh	08	06	02
Stanbery, Chas.(Z-M)	1836	Sept. 08	ZanesvilleOh	09	08	21
Stanbery, Henry(Z)	1828	Sept. 20	FairfeldCoOh	12	11	26
Stanbery, Henry(Z-M)	1836	Aug. 20	ZanesvilleOh	07	04	01
Stanbery, Howard(Z)	1835	April 27	ZanesvilleOh	13	09	05
Stanbery, Howard(Z)	1836	Jan. 09	ZanesvilleOh	08	07	19
Stanbery, Howard(Z)	1836	March 08	ZanesvilleOh	08	08	18
Stanbery, Howard(Z)	1836	May 12	ZanesvilleOh	08	06	06
Stanbery, Howard(Z)	1836	Sept. 02	ZanesvilleOh	15	14	09
Stanbery, Howard(Z)	1836	Sept. 08	ZanesvilleOh	09	07	25
Stanbery, Howard(Z)	1836	Sept. 09	ZanesvilleOh	08	05	20
Stanbery, Howard(Z)	1836	Sept. 30	ZanesvilleOh	08	06	36
Stanbery, Howard(Z)	1837	Jan. 10	ZanesvilleOh	09	06	25
Stanbery, Howard(Z)	1837	Jan. 11	ZanesvilleOh	09	08	13
Stanbery, Howard(Z)	1837	Sept. 04	ZanesvilleOh	08	06	23
Stanbery, Howard(Z)	1837	Oct. 17	ZanesvilleOh	08	06	23
Stanbery, Howard(Z)	1837	Nov. 07	ZanesvilleOh	14	13	32
Stanbery, Howard(Z)	1838	Jan. 30	ZanesvilleOh	08	06	09
Stanbery, Howard(Z)	1838	Feb. 05	ZanesvilleOh	08	06	03
Stanbery, Howard(Z)	1838	Oct. 11	ZanesvilleOh	08	06	13
Stanbery, Howard(Z)	1838	Oct. 11	ZanesvilleOh	08	06	24
Stanbery, Howard(Z)	1839	Jan. 18	ZanesvilleOh	08	06	22
Stanbery, Howard(Z)	1839	Jan. 24	ZanesvilleOh	08	06	32
Stanbery, Howard(Z)	1839	Jan. 24	ZanesvilleOh	08	06	31
Stanbery, Howard(Z)	1839	Jan. 24	ZanesvilleOh	08	06	32
Stanbery, Howard(Z-M)	1835	Dec. 12	ZanesvilleOh	10	04	16
Stanbery, Howard(Z-M)	1836	June 15	ZanesvilleOh	06	04	13
Stanbery, Howard(Z-M)	1836	Sept. 02	ZanesvilleOh	04	03	08
Stanbery, Howard(Z-M)	1836	Sept. 05	ZanesvilleOh	04	06	11
Stanbery, Howard(Z-M)	1836	Sept. 20	ZanesvilleOh	10	03	03
Stanbery, Howard(Z-M)	1836	Sept. 28	ZanesvilleOh	07	08	22
Stanbery, Howard(Z-M)	1836	Dec. 20	ZanesvilleOh	03	04	18
Stanbery, Howard(Z-M)	1836	Oct. 10	ZanesvilleOh	10	04	17
Stanbery, Howard(Z-M)	1837	Jan. 09	ZanesvilleOh	11	04	09
Stanbery, Howard(Z-M)	1837	May 17	ZanesvilleOh	03	07	20
Stanbery, Howard(Z-M)	1837	May 17	ZanesvilleOh	03	07	20
Stanbery, Howard(Z-M)	1838	Jan. 01	ZanesvilleOh	11	03	03
Stanbery, Howard(Z-M)	1838	Feb. 12	ZanesvilleOh	03	04	05
Stanbery, Howard(Z-M)	1838	March 01	ZanesvilleOh	03	03	02

PURCHASER	YEAR	DATE	RESIDENCE	R	T	S
Stanbery, Howard(Z-M)	1838	March 03	ZanesvilleOh	09	08	04
Stanbery, Howard(Z-M)	1838	March 03	ZanesvilleOh	09	08	05
Stanbery, Howard(Z-M)	1838	March 31	ZanesvilleOh	08	07	22
Stanbery, Howard(Z-M)	1838	April 25	ZanesvilleOh	04	04	09
Stanbery, Howard(Z-M)	1838	May 29	ZanesvilleOh	08	08	13
Stanbery, Howard(Z-M)	1838	Aug. 25	ZanesvilleOh	04	03	02
Stanbery, Howard(Z-M)	1838	Nov. 21	ZanesvilleOh	08	08	08
Stanbery, Howard(Z-M)	1838	Dec. 15	ZanesvilleOh	04	03	17
Stanbery, Howard(Z-M)	1839	Jan. 25	ZanesvilleOh	04	03	13
Stanbery, Howard(Z-M)	1839	Feb. 01	ZanesvilleOh	08	06	07
Stanbery, Howard(Z-M)	1839	Feb. 14	ZanesvilleOh	04	04	09
Stanbery, Howard(Z-M)	1839	April 15	ZanesvilleOh	08	07	02
Stanbery, Howard(Z-M)	1839	Nov. 28	ZanesvilleOh	10	08	10
Stanbery, Jacob W.(Z)	1829	March 03	Morgan Co,Oh	13	09	02
Stanbery, Jonas(Z)	1824	May 11	ZanesvilleOh	08	05	15
Stanbery, Jonas(Z)	1824	May 11	ZanesvilleOh	08	05	35
Stanbery, Jonas(Z)	1824	May 11	ZanesvilleOh	13	11	13
Stanbery, Jonas(Z)	1825	Jan. 09	ZanesvilleOh	13	11	13
Stanbery, Jonas(Z)	1828	Sept. 04	ZanesvilleOh	14	12	14
Stanbery, Jonas(Z)	1832	Jan. 14	ZanesvilleOh	10	08	22
Stanbery, Jonas(Z)	1835	Feb. 02	ZanesvilleOh	09	07	10
Stanbery, Jonas(Z)	1835	Feb. 07	ZanesvilleOh	11	11	01
Stanbery, Jonas(Z)	1835	Feb. 19	ZanesvilleOh	09	06	20
Stanbery, Jonas(Z)	1835	Feb. 19	ZanesvilleOh	09	06	17
Stanbery, Jonas(Z)	1835	March 16	ZanesvilleOh	10	06	15
Stanbery, Jonas(Z)	1835	May 19	ZanesvilleOh	11	12	13
Stanbery, Jonas(Z)	1835	May 25	ZanesvilleOh	09	05	23
Stanbery, Jonas(Z)	1835	June 12	ZanesvilleOh	09	07	10
Stanbery, Jonas(Z)	1835	June 22	ZanesvilleOh	08	08	07
Stanbery, Jonas(Z)	1835	July 10	ZanesvilleOh	14	13	13
Stanbery, Jonas(Z)	1835	July 13	ZanesvilleOh	10	08	26
Stanbery, Jonas(Z)	1835	July 17	ZanesvilleOh	11	11	01
Stanbery, Jonas(Z)	1835	July 23	ZanesvilleOh	11	11	03
Stanbery, Jonas(Z)	1835	July 28	ZanesvilleOh	09	08	06
Stanbery, Jonas(Z)	1835	Aug. 14	ZanesvilleOh	09	06	29
Stanbery, Jonas(Z)	1835	Aug. 15	ZanesvilleOh	12	13	22
Stanbery, Jonas(Z)	1835	Aug. 31	ZanesvilleOh	10	09	36
Stanbery, Jonas(Z)	1835	Sept. 01	ZanesvilleOh	13	10	11
Stanbery, Jonas(Z)	1835	Sept. 07	ZanesvilleOh	10	08	30
Stanbery, Jonas(Z)	1835	Sept. 11	ZanesvilleOh	10	06	22
Stanbery, Jonas(Z)	1835	Sept. 12	ZanesvilleOh	10	06	01
Stanbery, Jonas(Z)	1835	Sept. 26	ZanesvilleOh	10	06	10
Stanbery, Jonas(Z)	1835	Oct. 06	ZanesvilleOh	09	07	22
Stanbery, Jonas(Z)	1835	Oct. 21	ZanesvilleOh	09	06	20
Stanbery, Jonas(Z)	1835	Oct. 31	ZanesvilleOh	10	07	12
Stanbery, Jonas(Z)	1835	Nov. 12	ZanesvilleOh	09	07	32
Stanbery, Jonas(Z)	1835	Nov. 30	ZanesvilleOh	09	07	36
Stanbery, Jonas(Z)	1835	Dec. 09	ZanesvilleOh	08	07	22
Stanbery, Jonas(Z)	1836	Jan. 20	ZanesvilleOh	10	08	36
Stanbery, Jonas(Z)	1836	Feb. 01	ZanesvilleOh	08	07	17
Stanbery, Jonas(Z)	1836	Feb. 12	ZanesvilleOh	08	08	33
Stanbery, Jonas(Z)	1836	Feb. 17	ZanesvilleOh	13	10	03
Stanbery, Jonas(Z)	1836	Feb. 20	ZanesvilleOh	09	07	31
Stanbery, Jonas(Z)	1836	Feb. 29	ZanesvilleOh	13	08	33
Stanbery, Jonas(Z)	1836	March 02	ZanesvilleOh	08	07	01
Stanbery, Jonas(Z)	1836	March 02	ZanesvilleOh	08	07	03
Stanbery, Jonas(Z)	1836	March 02	ZanesvilleOh	08	07	01
Stanbery, Jonas(Z)	1836	March 05	ZanesvilleOh	08	07	04
Stanbery, Jonas(Z)	1836	March 12	ZanesvilleOh	08	08	36
Stanbery, Jonas(Z)	1836	March 12	ZanesvilleOh	08	08	22
Stanbery, Jonas(Z)	1836	March 17	ZanesvilleOh	09	05	29
Stanbery, Jonas(Z)	1830	April 19	ZanesvilleOh	12	12	03
Stanbery, Jonas(Z)	1836	March 19	ZanesvilleOh	09	06	13
Stanbery, Jonas(Z)	1836	March 21	ZanesvilleOh	14	13	32
Stanbery, Jonas(Z)	1836	March 25	ZanesvilleOh	08	08	23
Stanbery, Jonas(Z)	1836	March 25	ZanesvilleOh	08	08	22
Stanbery, Jonas(Z)	1836	March 29	ZanesvilleOh	09	05	12
Stanbery, Jonas(Z)	1836	April 01	ZanesvilleOh	08	06	12
Stanbery, Jonas(Z)	1836	April 02	ZanesvilleOh	08	07	09

PURCHASER	YEAR	DATE	RESIDENCE	R	T	S
Stanbery, Jonas(Z)	1836	April 06	ZanesvilleOh	08	08	27
Stanbery, Jonas(Z)	1836	April 07	ZanesvilleOh	08	07	35
Stanbery, Jonas(Z)	1836	April 14	ZanesvilleOh	12	12	18
Stanbery, Jonas(Z)	1836	April 26	ZanesvilleOh	14	13	32
Stanbery, Jonas(Z)	1836	May 30	ZanesvilleOh	08	06	07
Stanbery, Jonas(Z)	1836	June 03	ZanesvilleOh	08	06	18
Stanbery, Jonas(Z)	1836	June 06	ZanesvilleOh	09	07	15
Stanbery, Jonas(Z)	1836	June 06	ZanesvilleOh	09	07	15
Stanbery, Jonas(Z)	1836	June 13	ZanesvilleOh	09	07	08
Stanbery, Jonas(Z)	1836	June 15	ZanesvilleOh	08	07	29
Stanbery, Jonas(Z)	1836	June 15	ZanesvilleOh	13	09	32
Stanbery, Jonas(Z)	1836	June 16	ZanesvilleOh	09	08	24
Stanbery, Jonas(Z)	1836	June 18	ZanesvilleOh	08	08	22
Stanbery, Jonas(Z)	1836	June 23	ZanesvilleOh	10	09	36
Stanbery, Jonas(Z)	1836	June 23	ZanesvilleOh	09	08	31
Stanbery, Jonas(Z)	1836	June 27	ZanesvilleOh	10	09	23
Stanbery, Jonas(Z)	1836	June 29	ZanesvilleOh	09	08	12
Stanbery, Jonas(Z)	1836	July 04	ZanesvilleOh	08	05	06
Stanbery, Jonas(Z)	1836	July 04	ZanesvilleOh	08	06	31
Stanbery, Jonas(Z)	1836	July 09	ZanesvilleOh	08	05	02
Stanbery, Jonas(Z)	1836	July 12	ZanesvilleOh	13	08	21
Stanbery, Jonas(Z)	1836	July 19	ZanesvilleOh	08	07	05
Stanbery, Jonas(Z)	1836	Aug. 03	ZanesvilleOh	08	06	22
Stanbery, Jonas(Z)	1836	Aug. 04	ZanesvilleOh	08	07	20
Stanbery, Jonas(Z)	1836	Aug. 11	ZanesvilleOh	08	05	01
Stanbery, Jonas(Z)	1836	Aug. 11	ZanesvilleOh	08	06	18
Stanbery, Jonas(Z)	1836	Aug. 15	ZanesvilleOh	10	06	22
Stanbery, Jonas(Z)	1836	Aug. 17	ZanesvilleOh	08	06	17
Stanbery, Jonas(Z)	1836	Aug. 17	ZanesvilleOh	09	08	15
Stanbery, Jonas(Z)	1836	Aug. 18	ZanesvilleOh	08	06	17
Stanbery, Jonas(Z)	1836	Aug. 20	ZanesvilleOh	09	07	24
Stanbery, Jonas(Z)	1836	Aug. 22	ZanesvilleOh	09	06	35
Stanbery, Jonas(Z)	1836	Aug. 25	ZanesvilleOh	10	06	08
Stanbery, Jonas(Z)	1836	Aug. 26	ZanesvilleOh	08	07	29
Stanbery, Jonas(Z)	1836	Oct. 27	ZanesvilleOh	09	06	25
Stanbery, Jonas(Z)	1836	Nov. 11	ZanesvilleOh	14	13	06
Stanbery, Jonas(Z)	1836	Nov. 29	ZanesvilleOh	15	14	13
Stanbery, Jonas(Z)	1836	Dec. 17	ZanesvilleOh	14	12	24
Stanbery, Jonas(Z)	1836	Dec. 17	ZanesvilleOh	15	14	14
Stanbery, Jonas(Z)	1836	Dec. 28	ZanesvilleOh	14	12	28
Stanbery, Jonas(Z)	1836	Dec. 29	ZanesvilleOh	09	05	27
Stanbery, Jonas(Z)	1837	Jan. 11	ZanesvilleOh	08	06	30
Stanbery, Jonas(Z)	1837	Jan. 24	ZanesvilleOh	09	07	05
Stanbery, Jonas(Z)	1837	Feb. 01	ZanesvilleOh	08	07	09
Stanbery, Jonas(Z)	1837	Feb. 18	ZanesvilleOh	08	05	24
Stanbery, Jonas(Z)	1837	March 06	ZanesvilleOh	08	06	23
Stanbery, Jonas(Z)	1837	March 28	ZanesvilleOh	08	06	03
Stanbery, Jonas(Z)	1837	April 06	ZanesvilleOh	15	14	05
Stanbery, Jonas(Z)	1837	April 14	ZanesvilleOh	08	06	25
Stanbery, Jonas(Z)	1837	Aug. 14	ZanesvilleOh	08	05	02
Stanbery, Jonas(Z)	1837	Sept. 18	ZanesvilleOh	14	12	11
Stanbery, Jonas(Z)	1837	Sept. 18	ZanesvilleOh	14	12	14
Stanbery, Jonas(Z)	1838	Jan. 30	ZanesvilleOh	08	06	13
Stanbery, Jonas(Z)	1838	Dec. 20	ZanesvilleOh	08	06	25
Stanbery, Jonas(Z)	1839	Jan. 18	ZanesvilleOh	08	05	26
Stanbery, Jonas(Z-M)	1832	Jan. 12	ZanesvilleOh	07	05	20
Stanbery, Jonas(Z-M)	1831	Dec. 31	ZanesvilleOh	07	08	24
Stanbery, Jonas(Z-M)	1833	March 30	ZanesvilleOh	11	03	03
Stanbery, Jonas(Z-M)	1833	July 22	ZanesvilleOh	11	09	03
Stanbery, Jonas(Z-M)	1833	July 22	ZanesvilleOh	11	09	03
Stanbery, Jonas(Z-M)	1833	July 22	ZanesvilleOh	11	09	03
Stanbery, Jonas(Z-M)	1833	July 22	ZanesvilleOh	10	09	01
Stanbery, Jonas(Z-M)	1833	Aug. 26	ZanesvilleOh	11	09	04
Stanbery, Jonas(Z-M)	1833	Oct. 02	ZanesvilleOh	01	05	11
Stanbery, Jonas(Z-M)	1835	Feb. 11	ZanesvilleOh	07	04	13
Stanbery, Jonas(Z-M)	1835	March 12	ZanesvilleOh	11	04	23
Stanbery, Jonas(Z-M)	1835	March 16	ZanesvilleOh	11	08	19
Stanbery, Jonas(Z-M)	1835	March 21	ZanesvilleOh	02	06	03
Stanbery, Jonas(Z-M)	1835	March 26	ZanesvilleOh	07	07	11

PURCHASER	YEAR	DATE	RESIDENCE	R	T	S
Stanbery, Jonas(Z-M)	1835	April 06	ZanesvilleOh	03	08	04
Stanbery, Jonas(Z-M)	1835	April 06	ZanesvilleOh	03	08	04
Stanbery, Jonas(Z-M)	1835	May 02	ZanesvilleOh	06	03	10
Stanbery, Jonas(Z-M)	1835	May 18	ZanesvilleOh	03	07	20
Stanbery, Jonas(Z-M)	1835	July 08	ZanesvilleOh	03	05	20
Stanbery, Jonas(Z-M)	1835	July 09	ZanesvilleOh	07	04	09
Stanbery, Jonas(Z-M)	1835	July 24	ZanesvilleOh	02	05	02
Stanbery, Jonas(Z-M)	1835	Aug. 10	ZanesvilleOh	06	03	12
Stanbery, Jonas(Z-M)	1835	Aug. 15	ZanesvilleOh	02	05	02
Stanbery, Jonas(Z-M)	1835	Aug. 15	ZanesvilleOh	07	08	25
Stanbery, Jonas(Z-M)	1835	Aug. 20	ZanesvilleOh	04	04	03
Stanbery, Jonas(Z-M)	1835	Aug. 27	ZanesvilleOh	11	08	14
Stanbery, Jonas(Z-M)	1835	Aug. 27	ZanesvilleOh	11	08	07
Stanbery, Jonas(Z-M)	1835	Sept. 12	ZanesvilleOh	03	08	04
Stanbery, Jonas(Z-M)	1835	Oct. 22	ZanesvilleOh	09	09	24
Stanbery, Jonas(Z-M)	1835	Oct. 26	ZanesvilleOh	09	08	11
Stanbery, Jonas(Z-M)	1835	Oct. 26	ZanesvilleOh	09	08	11
Stanbery, Jonas(Z-M)	1835	Oct. 31	ZanesvilleOh	03	01	15
Stanbery, Jonas(Z-M)	1835	Dec. 28	ZanesvilleOh	07	05	09
Stanbery, Jonas(Z-M)	1836	Jan. 12	ZanesvilleOh	07	08	04
Stanbery, Jonas(Z-M)	1836	Jan. 18	ZanesvilleOh	03	01	07
Stanbery, Jonas(Z-M)	1836	Jan. 20	ZanesvilleOh	07	04	10
Stanbery, Jonas(Z-M)	1836	Jan. 25	ZanesvilleOh	11	04	22
Stanbery, Jonas(Z-M)	1836	Jan. 26	ZanesvilleOh	04	06	10
Stanbery, Jonas(Z-M)	1836	Feb. 09	ZanesvilleOh	09	03	17
Stanbery, Jonas(Z-M)	1836	Feb. 11	ZanesvilleOh	03	01	06
Stanbery, Jonas(Z-M)	1836	Feb. 11	ZanesvilleOh	03	01	15
Stanbery, Jonas(Z-M)	1836	March 08	ZanesvilleOh	08	06	10
Stanbery, Jonas(Z-M)	1836	March 09	ZanesvilleOh	10	08	02
Stanbery, Jonas(Z-M)	1836	March 09	ZanesvilleOh	10	08	13
Stanbery, Jonas(Z-M)	1836	March 11	ZanesvilleOh	10	05	25
Stanbery, Jonas(Z-M)	1836	March 15	ZanesvilleOh	09	09	18
Stanbery, Jonas(Z-M)	1836	March 15	ZanesvilleOh	09	09	13
Stanbery, Jonas(Z-M)	1836	March 07	ZanesvilleOh	10	04	23
Stanbery, Jonas(Z-M)	1836	March 22	ZanesvilleOh	10	08	03
Stanbery, Jonas(Z-M)	1836	March 23	ZanesvilleOh	09	09	01
Stanbery, Jonas(Z-M)	1836	March 24	ZanesvilleOh	05	07	20
Stanbery, Jonas(Z-M)	1836	March 25	ZanesvilleOh	03	10	24
Stanbery, Jonas(Z-M)	1836	March 25	ZanesvilleOh	03	07	21
Stanbery, Jonas(Z-M)	1836	March 28	ZanesvilleOh	07	08	08
Stanbery, Jonas(Z-M)	1836	March 28	ZanesvilleOh	11	04	03
Stanbery, Jonas(Z-M)	1836	March 29	ZanesvilleOh	03	01	13
Stanbery, Jonas(Z-M)	1836	April 05	ZanesvilleOh	07	04	09
Stanbery, Jonas(Z-M)	1836	April 08	ZanesvilleOh	07	08	18
Stanbery, Jonas(Z-M)	1836	April 20	ZanesvilleOh	10	04	02
Stanbery, Jonas(Z-M)	1836	April 22	ZanesvilleOh	07	08	22
Stanbery, Jonas(Z-M)	1836	April 26	ZanesvilleOh	10	09	23
Stanbery, Jonas(Z-M)	1836	April 29	ZanesvilleOh	03	03	16
Stanbery, Jonas(Z-M)	1836	May 06	ZanesvilleOh	09	08	01
Stanbery, Jonas(Z-M)	1836	May 24	ZanesvilleOh	09	09	04
Stanbery, Jonas(Z-M)	1836	May 27	ZanesvilleOh	07	05	24
Stanbery, Jonas(Z-M)	1836	May 30	ZanesvilleOh	09	03	14
Stanbery, Jonas(Z-M)	1836	June 06	ZanesvilleOh	10	08	08
Stanbery, Jonas(Z-M)	1836	June 06	ZanesvilleOh	10	08	03
Stanbery, Jonas(Z-M)	1836	June 09	ZanesvilleOh	06	03	02
Stanbery, Jonas(Z-M)	1836	June 09	ZanesvilleOh	06	03	02
Stanbery, Jonas(Z-M)	1836	June 11	ZanesvilleOh	10	08	23
Stanbery, Jonas(Z-M)	1836	June 18	ZanesvilleOh	07	08	13
Stanbery, Jonas(Z-M)	1836	June 20	ZanesvilleOh	04	05	18
Stanbery, Jonas(Z-M)	1836	June 27	ZanesvilleOh	04	05	20
Stanbery, Jonas(Z-M)	1836	June 27	ZanesvilleOh	09	09	02
Stanbery, Jonas(Z-M)	1836	June 27	ZanesvilleOh	07	04	01
Stanbery, Jonas(Z-M)	1836	June 28	ZanesvilleOh	08	06	02
Stanbery, Jonas(Z-M)	1836	July 04	ZanesvilleOh	04	05	23
Stanbery, Jonas(Z-M)	1836	July 04	ZanesvilleOh	05	06	15
Stanbery, Jonas(Z-M)	1836	July 07	ZanesvilleOh	04	04	02
Stanbery, Jonas(Z-M)	1836	Aug. 03	ZanesvilleOh	03	05	20
Stanbery, Jonas(Z-M)	1836	Aug. 03	ZanesvilleOh	03	07	02
Stanbery, Jonas(Z-M)	1836	Aug. 09	ZanesvilleOh	10	09	03

PURCHASER	YEAR	DATE	RESIDENCE	R	T	S
Stanbery, Jonas(Z-M)	1836	Aug. 09	ZanesvilleOh	10	04	11
Stanbery, Jonas(Z-M)	1836	Aug. 12	ZanesvilleOh	11	04	22
Stanbery, Jonas(Z-M)	1836	Aug. 19	ZanesvilleOh	07	08	14
Stanbery, Jonas(Z-M)	1836	Aug. 22	ZanesvilleOh	08	07	03
Stanbery, Jonas(Z-M)	1836	Aug. 26	ZanesvilleOh	08	08	15
Stanbery, Jonas(Z-M)	1836	Aug. 26	ZanesvilleOh	09	08	22
Stanbery, Jonas(Z-M)	1836	Oct. 07	ZanesvilleOh	08	08	24
Stanbery, Jonas(Z-M)	1836	Oct. 07	ZanesvilleOh	08	08	24
Stanbery, Jonas(Z-M)	1836	Oct. 17	ZanesvilleOh	08	07	03
Stanbery, Jonas(Z-M)	1836	Oct. 19	ZanesvilleOh	08	08	09
Stanbery, Jonas(Z-M)	1836	Oct. 26	ZanesvilleOh	10	04	18
Stanbery, Jonas(Z-M)	1836	Nov. 03	ZanesvilleOh	09	08	10
Stanbery, Jonas(Z-M)	1836	Nov. 09	ZanesvilleOh	11	08	17
Stanbery, Jonas(Z-M)	1836	Dec. 21	ZanesvilleOh	08	08	22
Stanbery, Jonas(Z-M)	1836	Dec. 27	ZanesvilleOh	09	07	08
Stanbery, Jonas(Z-M)	1837	Jan. 13	ZanesvilleOh	05	03	10
Stanbery, Jonas(Z-M)	1837	Jan. 17	ZanesvilleOh	10	08	22
Stanbery, Jonas(Z-M)	1837	Jan. 21	ZanesvilleOh	10	08	22
Stanbery, Jonas(Z-M)	1837	Jan. 21	ZanesvilleOh	08	08	25
Stanbery, Jonas(Z-M)	1837	Jan. 26	ZanesvilleOh	09	07	03
Stanbery, Jonas(Z-M)	1837	Jan. 27	ZanesvilleOh	11	08	20
Stanbery, Jonas(Z-M)	1837	Jan. 28	ZanesvilleOh	09	07	04
Stanbery, Jonas(Z-M)	1837	Jan. 30	ZanesvilleOh	09	07	06
Stanbery, Jonas(Z-M)	1837	Jan. 30	ZanesvilleOh	09	04	05
Stanbery, Jonas(Z-M)	1837	Feb. 03	ZanesvilleOh	04	04	09
Stanbery, Jonas(Z-M)	1837	Feb. 11	ZanesvilleOh	08	08	12
Stanbery, Jonas(Z-M)	1837	Feb. 16	ZanesvilleOh	08	07	06
Stanbery, Jonas(Z-M)	1837	Feb. 23	ZanesvilleOh	09	08	16
Stanbery, Jonas(Z-M)	1837	Feb. 24	ZanesvilleOh	09	08	02
Stanbery, Jonas(Z-M)	1837	Feb. 24	ZanesvilleOh	09	08	02
Stanbery, Jonas(Z-M)	1837	Feb. 25	ZanesvilleOh	09	08	18
Stanbery, Jonas(Z-M)	1837	Feb. 25	ZanesvilleOh	08	07	05
Stanbery, Jonas(Z-M)	1837	March 02	ZanesvilleOh	09	08	14
Stanbery, Jonas(Z-M)	1837	March 02	ZanesvilleOh	09	08	13
Stanbery, Jonas(Z-M)	1837	March 02	ZanesvilleOh	09	08	15
Stanbery, Jonas(Z-M)	1837	March 04	ZanesvilleOh	01	06	15
Stanbery, Jonas(Z-M)	1837	March 10	ZanesvilleOh	09	08	07
Stanbery, Jonas(Z-M)	1837	March 14	ZanesvilleOh	09	08	14
Stanbery, Jonas(Z-M)	1837	March 14	ZanesvilleOh	11	04	20
Stanbery, Jonas(Z-M)	1837	March 18	ZanesvilleOh	08	09	03
Stanbery, Jonas(Z-M)	1837	March 24	ZanesvilleOh	09	08	14
Stanbery, Jonas(Z-M)	1837	March 24	ZanesvilleOh	09	08	07
Stanbery, Jonas(Z-M)	1837	March 24	ZanesvilleOh	09	08	14
Stanbery, Jonas(Z-M)	1837	March 27	ZanesvilleOh	08	07	06
Stanbery, Jonas(Z-M)	1837	March 27	ZanesvilleOh	09	07	03
Stanbery, Jonas(Z-M)	1837	March 27	ZanesvilleOh	09	07	03
Stanbery, Jonas(Z-M)	1837	March 28	ZanesvilleOh	03	08	13
Stanbery, Jonas(Z-M)	1837	March 30	ZanesvilleOh	09	08	01
Stanbery, Jonas(Z-M)	1837	March 31	ZanesvilleOh	09	09	04
Stanbery, Jonas(Z-M)	1837	April 03	ZanesvilleOh	04	03	03
Stanbery, Jonas(Z-M)	1837	April 03	ZanesvilleOh	10	08	19
Stanbery, Jonas(Z-M)	1837	April 07	ZanesvilleOh	10	09	20
Stanbery, Jonas(Z-M)	1837	April 07	ZanesvilleOh	10	09	21
Stanbery, Jonas(Z-M)	1837	April 07	ZanesvilleOh	10	09	21
Stanbery, Jonas(Z-M)	1837	April 07	ZanesvilleOh	05	04	22
Stanbery, Jonas(Z-M)	1837	April 11	ZanesvilleOh	03	04	16
Stanbery, Jonas(Z-M)	1837	April 11	ZanesvilleOh	03	04	16
Stanbery, Jonas(Z-M)	1837	April 13	ZanesvilleOh	04	03	14
Stanbery, Jonas(Z-M)	1837	May 06	ZanesvilleOh	09	08	16
Stanbery, Jonas(Z-M)	1837	May 06	ZanesvilleOh	09	08	16
Stanbery, Jonas(Z-M)	1837	July 31	ZanesvilleOh	10	04	23
Stanbery, Jonas(Z-M)	1837	Sept. 04	ZanesvilleOh	08	07	03
Stanbery, Jonas(Z-M)	1837	Oct. 02	ZanesvilleOh	03	05	23
Stanbery, Jonas(Z-M)	1837	Nov. 29	ZanesvilleOh	05	03	01
Stanbery, Jonas(Z-M)	1837	Dec. 04	ZanesvilleOh	09	08	07
Stanbery, Jonas(Z-M)	1837	Dec. 05	ZanesvilleOh	08	08	04
Stanbery, Jonas(Z-M)	1838	Jan. 10	ZanesvilleOh	04	04	11
Stanbery, Jonas(Z-M)	1838	Jan. 13	ZanesvilleOh	07	08	14
Stanbery, Jonas(Z-M)	1838	Jan. 19	ZanesvilleOh	08	08	16

PURCHASER	YEAR	DATE	RESIDENCE	R	T	S
Stanbery, Jonas(Z-M)	1838	Jan. 19	ZanesvilleOh	08	08	06
Stanbery, Jonas(Z-M)	1838	Jan. 30	ZanesvilleOh	09	09	04
Stanbery, Jonas(Z-M)	1838	Jan. 30	ZanesvilleOh	09	08	01
Stanbery, Jonas(Z-M)	1838	Feb. 24	ZanesvilleOh	08	08	05
Stanbery, Jonas(Z-M)	1838	March 05	ZanesvilleOh	04	04	12
Stanbery, Jonas(Z-M)	1838	March 05	ZanesvilleOh	04	04	12
Stanbery, Jonas(Z-M)	1838	March 06	ZanesvilleOh	09	08	10
Stanbery, Jonas(Z-M)	1838	March 08	ZanesvilleOh	10	07	19
Stanbery, Jonas(Z-M)	1838	March 09	ZanesvilleOh	10	08	14
Stanbery, Jonas(Z-M)	1838	April 06	ZanesvilleOh	04	04	03
Stanbery, Jonas(Z-M)	1838	April 07	ZanesvilleOh	09	07	09
Stanbery, Jonas(Z-M)	1838	May 29	ZanesvilleOh	08	08	17
Stanbery, Jonas(Z-M)	1838	Sept. 01	ZanesvilleOh	09	08	10
Stanbery, Jonas(Z-M)	1838	Sept. 15	ZanesvilleOh	03	04	16
Stanbery, Jonas(Z-M)	1838	Sept. 21	ZanesvilleOh	08	08	03
Stanbery, Jonas(Z-M)	1838	Sept. 25	ZanesvilleOh	08	08	09
Stanbery, Jonas(Z-M)	1838	Sept. 27	ZanesvilleOh	05	04	12
Stanbery, Jonas(Z-M)	1838	Nov. 16	ZanesvilleOh	02	04	15
Stanbery, Jonas(Z-M)	1838	Nov. 16	ZanesvilleOh	02	04	15
Stanbery, Jonas(Z-M)	1838	Nov. 26	ZanesvilleOh	03	05	15
Stanbery, Jonas(Z-M)	1838	Dec. 01	ZanesvilleOh	09	07	09
Stanbery, Jonas(Z-M)	1838	Dec. 01	ZanesvilleOh	08	08	03
Stanbery, Jonas(Z-M)	1838	Dec. 05	ZanesvilleOh	08	08	18
Stanbery, Jonas(Z-M)	1838	Dec. 05	ZanesvilleOh	08	08	18
Stanbery, Jonas(Z-M)	1838	Dec. 05	ZanesvilleOh	08	08	18
Stanbery, Jonas(Z-M)	1838	Dec. 15	ZanesvilleOh	03	04	04
Stanbery, Jonas(Z-M)	1838	Dec. 20	ZanesvilleOh	10	04	02
Stanbery, Jonas(Z-M)	1839	Jan. 17	ZanesvilleOh	03	04	06
Stanbery, Jonas(Z-M)	1839	Jan. 17	ZanesvilleOh	03	04	05
Stanbery, Jonas(Z-M)	1839	June 25	ZanesvilleOh	04	03	11
Stanbery, Jonas(Z-M)	1839	July 19	ZanesvilleOh	05	04	21
Stanbery, Jonas(Z-M)	1839	July 27	ZanesvilleOh	09	08	16
Stanbery, Jonas(Z-M)	1836	June 09	ZanesvilleOh	10	05	24
Stanbery, Jonas(Z-M)	1836	June 22	ZanesvilleOh	10	04	19
Stanbey, Howard(Z)	1835	April 21	ZanesvilleOh	11	10	01
Stanbey, Jacob W.(Z)	1835	Aug. 24	Morgan Co,Oh	13	09	03
Stanburg, Luther M.(Z)	1833	May 10	Morgan Co,Oh	10	08	31
Stanbury, J.(Z-M)	1829	Dec. 21	MuskingmCoOh	05	02	01
Stanbury, J.(Z-M)	1829	Dec. 22	ZanesvilleOh	05	02	09
Stanbury, Jonas(Z)	1829	Dec. 21	ZanesvilleOh	13	11	12
Stanbury, Jonas(Z)	1830	Sept. 06	ZanesvilleOh	08	07	19
Stanbury, Jonas(Z)	1831	July 25	ZanesvilleOh	11	12	21
Stanbury, Jonas(Z)	1835	Jan. 30	ZanesvilleOh	11	11	03
Stanbury, Jonas(Z-M)	1829	June 25	ZanesvilleOh	05	06	06
Stanbury, Jonas(Z-M)	1829	June 27	ZanesvilleOh	12	10	36
Stanbury, Jonas(Z-M)	1832	March 14	ZanesvilleOh	08	07	18
Stanbury, Jonas(Z-M)	1829	Dec. 21	ZanesvilleOh	05	03	18
Stanbury, Jonas(Z-M)	1830	Feb. 20	MuskingmCoOh	10	04	13
Stanbury, Jonas(Z-M)	1830	May 11	ZanesvilleOh	05	03	07
Stanbury, Jonas(Z-M)	1834	Jan. 17	ZanesvilleOh	08	08	23
Stanbury, Jonas(Z-M)	1831	April 12	ZanesvilleOh	04	03	18
Stanbury, Luthur M.(Z)	1833	May 10	Morgan Co,Oh	10	08	31
Stance, Benjamin(Z-M)	1832	Nov. 09	CoshoctnCoOh	05	07	11
Stance, Magdeline(Z-M)	1832	Nov. 09	CoshoctnCoOh	05	07	11
Standiford, John(Z)	1817	May 01	BaltimreCoMd	12	11	36
Standiford, William(Z)	1832	Oct. 01	Perry Co.,Oh	14	12	26
Standiford, William(Z)	1815	Oct. 21	Baltimore,Md	14	12	35
Standiford, William(Z)	1815	Oct. 21	Baltimore,Md	14	12	35
Stanford, Oliver Jr.(Y)	1823	July 03	TrumbullCoOh	07	20	13
Stanley, Andrew(Y)	1821	Sept. 19	ColumbanCoOh	04	16	15
Stanley, Francis R.(Z)	1826	Feb. 24	WashngtnOhio	08	05	25
Stanley, Francis R.(Z)	1817	March 18	WashngtnCoOh	08	05	17
Stanley, Garland(Y)	1827	April 06	ColumbanCoOh	05	18	15
Stanley, Garland(Y)	1827	April 12	ColumbanCoOh	05	18	15
Stanley, Isaac(Y)	1827	Jan. 29	ColumbanCoOh	05	18	26
Stanley, Moses(Y)	1821	Sept. 24	ColumbanCoOh	04	16	15
Stanley, Thomas(Y)	1823	Sept. 06	ColumbanCoOh	05	18	26
Stanley, Waddy(Y)	1827	July 04	ColumbanCoOh	05	18	27
Stannus, George(Y)	1824	Sept. 23	BelmontCo,Oh	03	05	14

279

PURCHASER	YEAR	DATE	RESIDENCE	R	T	S
Stansbury, Christian(Z-M)	1834	Nov. 15	TuscarwsCoOh	04	07	15
Stansbury, Jonas(Z-M)	1834	Sept. 13	ZanesvilleOh	09	07	03
Stark, G.(Z)	1815	Aug. 19	CoshoctnCoOh	04	05	11
Starkey, Caleb(Y)	1832	Oct. 01	ColumbanCoOh	05	15	04
Starkey, Charles(Y)	1833	Oct. 01	Jeff.Co.,Oh.	03	12	13
Starkey, Charles(Y)	1834	Aug. 14	Jeff.Co.,Oh.	03	12	20
Starkey, David(Z-M)	1833	March 20	GuernseyCoOh	02	03	09
Starkey, David(Z-M)	1833	April 24	GuernseyCoOh	02	03	13
Starkey, David(Z-M)	1833	April 24	GuernseyCoOh	02	03	09
Starkey, Effy(Z-M)	1827	March 05	CoshoctnCoOh	09	06	12
Starkey, George(Z-M)	1827	March 05	CoshoctnCoOh	09	06	12
Starkey, Jonathan(Z-M)	1821	March 17	MuskingmCoOh	06	03	22
Starkey, Jonathan(Z-M)	1821	Oct. 23	MuskingmCoOh	06	03	22
Starkey, Levi(Y)	1824	Dec. 22	ColumbanCoOh	03	12	14
Starkweather, David A.(Y)	1833	Oct. 26	Stark Co.,Oh	09	11	23
Starling, David(Y)	1830	May 27	TuscarwsCoOh	07	14	01
Starling, Launcelot(Z)	1811	March 21	FairfeldCoOh	15	17	18
Starner, Daniel(Z-M)	1832	Sept. 29	HolmesCoOhio	09	09	24
Starner, Daniel(Z-M)	1836	Aug. 31	HolmesCoOhio	09	09	23
Starner, George(Z)	1836	Dec. 10	MuskingmCoOh	15	14	34
Starner, John(Z)	1811	Dec. 11	MuskingmCoOh	01	12	01
Starner, William Junr.(Z)	1815	June 13	KnoxCo.,Ohio	10	08	25
Starner, William(Z-M)	1834	March 03	HolmesCoOhio	09	09	24
Starner, William(Z-M)	1836	Sept. 26	HolmesCoOhio	09	08	07
Starold, Peter(Y)	1825	June 13	Stark Co.,Oh	06	17	30
Starrat, Adam(Z)	1810	Nov. 12	MuskingmCoOh	15	17	26
Starrat, Adam(Z)	1811	Nov. 10	MuskingmCoOh	17	16	02
Starrett, Joseph(Z)	1827	June 04	MuskingmCoOh	11	12	05
Starrett, Joseph(Z)	1831	Feb. 24	MuskingmCoOh	11	13	30
Starrus, Jacob(Y)	1825	July 26	Stark Co.,Oh	07	19	15
Statler, Michael(Z)	1816	Jan. 16	LickingCo,Oh	10	02	23
Stats, Frederick(Z)	1817	Jan. 20	LoudonCo,Vir	03	02	09
Stats, Frederick(Z)	1817	Jan. 20	LoudonCo,Vir	03	02	09
Stats, Jno.(Z)	1817	Jan. 15	Jeff.Co.,Oh.	03	02	06
Stats, Jno.(Z)	1817	Jan. 20	Jeff.Co.,Oh.	03	02	12
Staubaugh, John(Z)	1827	Sept. 26	HolmesCoOhio	06	09	23
Steal, George(Z)	1816	June 11	TuscarwsCoOh	05	08	16
Stebbens, Silas(Z)	1827	Feb. 07	Morgan Co,Oh	12	12	32
Stedman, Isaac T.(Z)	1837	April 01	MuskingmCoOh	14	12	13
Stedman, Isaac Thos.(Z)	1837	March 28	MuskingmCoOh	13	08	18
Stedman, Isaac Thos.(Z)	1838	March 29	Morgan Co,Oh	13	08	19
Stedman, John(Z)	1837	Aug. 31	Morgan Co,Oh	14	12	24
Steel, David(Z-M)	1832	Aug. 22	SomersetCoPa	05	08	17
Steel, Elias(Z-M)	1829	Nov. 28	HolmesCoOhio	05	08	15
Steel, Elias(Z-M)	1833	April 13	HolmesCoOhio	05	08	15
Steel, George(Z-M)	1830	Sept. 02	HolmesCoOhio	05	08	17
Steel, George(Z-M)	1832	Dec. 21	HolmesCoOhio	05	08	25
Steel, Harvey B.(Z-M)	1837	March 17	LickingCo,Oh	09	07	01
Steel, John(Z)	1814	Oct. 26	FayetteCo,Pa	04	02	01
Steel, John(Z)	1814	Oct. 26	FayetteCo,Pa	04	02	02
Steel, William(Z)	1814	Oct. 26	FayetteCo,Pa	04	02	03
Steel, William(Z)	1814	Oct. 27	FayetteCo,Pa	05	02	24
Steele, James(Z-M)	1824	Aug. 21	GuernseyCoOh	04	01	20
Steele, James(Z-M)	1830	May 14	GuernseyCoOh	04	01	20
Steely, John Jr.(Z-M)	1831	Feb. 24	TuscarwsCoOh	02	10	17
Steen, Abner(Y)	1829	May 02	WashCo.,Penn	06	14	06
Steen, Robert(Z)	1817	June 03	WashngtnCoOh	10	07	24
Steenrod, Daniel(Z)	1805	Nov. 22	Ohio Co.,Vir	05	01	17
Steenrod, Lewis(Z)	1810	Sept. 18	MuskingmCoOh	06	01	18
Steenrod, Lewis(Z)	1814	April 26	MuskingmCoOh	06	01	03
Steepy, Godleib(Z-M)	1833	Oct. 19	TuscarwsCoOh	04	07	03
Steeves, William(Y)	1832	Oct. 08	HarrisonCoOh	07	15	31
Steffler, David 3rd.(Z-M)	1832	Nov. 23	TuscarwsCoOh	01	08	03
Steffler, David(Z-M)	1833	Aug. 03	TuscarwsCoOh	01	08	02
Steffy, George(Y)	1828	March 01	HarrisonCoOh	05	13	21
Steffy, John(Z)	1836	May 12	Morgan Co,Oh	09	06	12
Stegman, Adam(Z-M)	1837	Dec. 22	CoshoctnCoOh	05	04	13
Steiner, John A.(Z-M)	1833	Jan. 05	Morgan Co,Oh	13	09	05
Steinman, Jacob(Z-M)	1833	Sept. 27	TuscarwsCoOh	02	07	05

PURCHASER	YEAR	DATE	RESIDENCE	R	T	S
Steinman, Jacob(Z-M)	1837	April 21	TuscarwsCoOh	03	07	02
Stelgenbauer, Jacob(Z-M)	1836	April 15	TuscarwsCoOh	04	07	07
Stemlen, Lewis(Z-M)	1839	July 01	CoshoctnCoOh	10	09	11
Stemler, Lewis(Z-M)	1839	July 01	CoshoctnCoOh	10	09	11
Stenger, Jacob(Z-M)	1839	June 15	ZanesvilleOh	10	08	11
Stennenat, Robt.(Z-M)	1831	Sept. 24	LickingCo,Oh	11	03	07
Stephan, Adam(Z-M)	1837	Oct. 18	HolmesCoOhio	09	09	23
Stephens, Benj.(Z-M)	1831	April 06	FayetteCo,Pa	07	05	17
Stephens, David(Z)	1810	Sept. 19	MuskingmCoOh	11	12	09
Stephens, David(Z)	1811	Jan. 25	MuskingmCoOh	11	11	36
Stephens, John(Z-M)	1829	Feb. 05	BelmontCo,Oh	03	01	24
Stephens, John(Z-M)	1833	Oct. 11	GuernseyCoOh	03	01	18
Stephens, Joseph(Z)	1836	Dec. 24	Morgan Co,Oh	09	05	07
Stephens, Nathan(Z)	1836	April 29	Morgan Co,Oh	10	06	10
Stephens, Wm.(Z-M)	1831	March 31	FayetteCo,Pa	08	04	02
Stephenson, George(Z-M)	1823	Dec. 30	KnoxCo.,Ohio	10	05	15
Stephenson, Jno.(Z)	1814	Feb. 23	WashCo.,Penn	11	05	24
Stepher, Elijah(Z)	1807	March 02	BelmontCo,Oh	10	09	33
Stermer, Adam(Z-M)	1833	July 29	TuscarwsCoOh	02	07	08
Steuart, Francis(Z)	1836	March 03	GuernseyCoOh	09	08	15
Stevens, Abraham(Z)	1815	Feb. 03	WashngtnCoOh	10	06	07
Stevens, Abraham(Z)	1815	April 15	WashngtnCoOh	10	06	27
Stevens, Benjamin(Y)	1829	Aug. 29	ColumbanCoOh	04	13	15
Stevens, Benjamin(Z-M)	1836	Dec. 17	ColumbanCoOh	08	07	22
Stevens, Benjamin(Z-M)	1837	Jan. 11	ColumbanCoOh	08	07	22
Stevens, Charles A.(Z-M)	1826	Jan. 27	BelmontCo,Oh	04	01	22
Stevens, David(Z)	1834	March 24	Morgan Co,Oh	10	07	31
Stevens, Elijah(Z)	1833	Oct. 15	Morgan Co,Oh	11	11	23
Stevens, Elijah(Z)	1833	Oct. 15	Morgan Co,Oh	11	11	24
Stevens, Elijah(Z)	1834	Nov. 03	Morgan Co,Oh	11	11	23
Stevens, Elijah(Z-M)	1833	Jan. 30	GuernseyCoOh	03	01	18
Stevens, James(Z)	1831	June 28	GuernseyCoOh	08	08	19
Stevens, James(Z)	1834	Dec. 15	GuernseyCoOh	09	08	24
Stevens, Jno.(Z-M)	1831	Nov. 14	GuernseyCoOh	03	01	24
Stevens, John(Z)	1814	Oct. 07	GuernseyCoOh	01	03	20
Stevens, Joseph(Z)	1832	Sept. 29	Morgan Co,Oh	09	05	07
Stevens, Vernon(Z)	1836	Dec. 21	Morgan Co,Oh	09	05	25
Stevens, W.(Z)	1815	Sept. 26	CoshoctnCoOh	10	08	15
Stevens, William(Z)	1832	Nov. 26	GuernseyCoOh	10	09	04
Stevens, William(Z)	1834	March 19	Morgan Co,Oh	10	06	03
Stevens, William(Z)	1834	Aug. 25	Morgan Co,Oh	10	06	03
Stevenson, Edward(Z)	1817	June 10	FairfeldCoOh	15	16	23
Stevenson, George(Z-M)	1827	March 30	WashCo.,Penn	04	02	15
Stevenson, James(Z)	1836	Nov. 30	MonroeCo.,Oh	08	07	33
Stevenson, Robert(Z)	1815	Jan. 13	WestmrldCoPa	06	07	22
Stevenson, Robert(Z)	1815	Feb. 06	WestmrldCoPa	06	07	22
Stevenson, Robert(Z)	1815	Jan. 13	WestmrldCoPa	06	07	23
Stevenson, Thos.(Z-M)	1821	Sept. 10	MuskingmCoOh	05	01	25
Stevins, Almon(Z)	1835	Dec. 12	Morgan Co,Oh	10	06	07
Stevison, Isaac V.(Z-M)	1837	March 30	BelmontCo,Oh	04	07	11
Stevison, Isaac V.(Z-M)	1837	March 30	BelmontCo,Oh	04	07	12
Steward, James(Y)	1827	March 02	ColumbanCoOh	05	18	17
Steward, James(Y)	1835	Aug. 25	Jeff.Co.,Oh.	03	11	29
Stewart, David(Z-M)	1836	Aug. 15	LickingCo,Oh	11	03	14
Stewart, Ebzen(Z-M)	1836	Dec. 06	CarrollCo,Oh	03	07	22
Stewart, Ebzen(Z-M)	1836	Dec. 06	CarrollCo,Oh	03	07	23
Stewart, Edie(Z-M)	1836	May 27	GuernseyCoOh	03	03	09
Stewart, Eliz'th.(Z)	1817	Jan. 13	Brooke CoVir	11	10	05
Stewart, Elizabeth(Z)	1824	May 31	MuskingmCoOh	11	10	07
Stewart, Francis(Z)	1815	Dec. 01	Cambridge,Oh	03	01	21
Stewart, Francis(Z)	1815	Dec. 01	Cambridge,Oh	03	01	16
Stewart, Francis(Z)	1815	Dec. 01	Cambridge,Oh	03	01	19
Stewart, George(Z)	1826	June 08	MuskingmCoOh	11	13	26
Stewart, George(Z-M)	1829	Sept. 13	LickingCo,Oh	11	03	15
Stewart, James W.(Z-M)	1836	Feb. 11	GuernseyCoOh	03	03	14
Stewart, James W.(Z-M)	1838	Jan. 02	GuernseyCoOh	03	03	14
Stewart, James junior(Y)	1836	March 21	Jeff.co.,Oh.	03	11	29
Stewart, James(Y)	1826	March 24	ColumbanCoOh	05	18	08
Stewart, James(Y)	1833	Feb. 19	PortageCo,Oh	03	13	17

PURCHASER	YEAR	DATE	RESIDENCE	R	T	S
Stewart, James(Y)	1835	May 27	PortageCo,Oh	03	13	17
Stewart, James(Z)	1823	Nov. 27	YorkCo.,Penn	10	07	14
Stewart, James(Z)	1824	June 03	Morgan Co,Oh	10	07	14
Stewart, James(Z)	1833	July 25	Morgan Co,Oh	12	10	32
Stewart, James(Z-M)	1821	March 14	GuernseyCoOh	03	03	11
Stewart, James(Z-M)	1822	Feb. 06	GuernseyCoOh	03	03	07
Stewart, James(Z-M)	1824	Feb. 28	GuernseyCoOh	03	03	07
Stewart, James(Z-M)	1828	Dec. 24	MuskingmCoOh	06	03	13
Stewart, James(Z-M)	1832	May 22	GuernseyCoOh	03	03	07
Stewart, James(Z-M)	1832	Nov. 27	GuernseyCoOh	03	02	10
Stewart, James(Z-M)	1833	April 08	GuernseyCoOh	03	02	10
Stewart, James(Z-M)	1835	Nov. 19	GuernseyCoOh	03	03	07
Stewart, James(Z-M)	1837	Jan. 10	GuernseyCoOh	02	03	14
Stewart, John(Y)	1825	Feb. 18	ColumbanCoOh	02	10	21
Stewart, John(Z)	1806	Dec. 06	WashCo.,Penn	01	03	14
Stewart, John(Z-M)	1824	Feb. 26	KnoxCo.,Ohio	11	08	05
Stewart, John(Z-M)	1831	Oct. 15	TuscarwsCoOh	03	05	21
Stewart, John(Z-M)	1831	Oct. 15	TuscarwsCoOh	03	05	21
Stewart, John(Z-M)	1832	May 29	MuskingmCoOh	06	03	12
Stewart, John(Z-M)	1831	Aug. 18	MuskingmCoOh	06	03	12
Stewart, John(Z-M)	1835	Aug. 03	MuskingmCoOh	06	03	10
Stewart, John(Z-M)	1835	Nov. 19	GuernseyCoOh	03	04	19
Stewart, Joseph(Z)	1815	Nov. 06	WashCo.,Penn	11	13	30
Stewart, Mahlon(Z-M)	1836	June 17	CarrollCo,Oh	04	07	23
Stewart, Robert(Z)	1836	Oct. 25	ZanesvilleOh	08	07	31
Stewart, Robert(Z)	1811	April 24	WashCo.,Penn	01	02	21
Stewart, Robert(Z)	1811	Oct. 11	LickingCo,Oh	11	03	15
Stewart, Robert(Z)	1815	Feb. 06	LickingCo,Oh	11	03	16
Stewart, Robert(Z-M)	1826	March 28	ZanesvilleOh	11	03	24
Stewart, Samuel W.(Z-M)	1837	Jan. 28	GuernseyCoOh	03	03	07
Stewart, Samuel(Y)	1825	April 19	ColumbanCoOh	05	18	20
Stewart, Samuel(Z)	1811	Oct. 01	LickingCo,Oh	11	03	14
Stewart, Thomas H.(Z-M)	1835	Oct. 31	GuernseyCoOh	03	01	15
Stewart, Thomas(Y)	1827	June 22	HarrisonCoOh	06	14	12
Stewart, Thomas(Z)	1817	Jan. 06	ZanesvilleOh	06	02	24
Stewart, Washing'n.(Z)	1829	Dec. 28	Morgan Co,Oh	10	07	03
Stewart, Washington(Z)	1829	July 31	Morgan Co,Oh	10	07	03
Stewart, Washington(Z)	1836	Jan. 05	Morgan Co,Oh	10	08	35
Stewart, Washington(Z)	1836	Feb. 04	Morgan Co,Oh	10	08	35
Stewart, William(Y)	1833	April 24	ColumbanCoOh	03	13	17
Stewart, William(Z-M)	1837	Feb. 20	GuernseyCoOh	03	03	10
Stewart, Wm.(Z)	1811	April 24	WashCo.,Penn	01	02	21
Stiager, John G.(Y)	1828	Sept. 25	ColumbanCoOh	06	19	29
Stichler, George(Y)	1834	April 02	Stark Co.,Oh	08	12	23
Stickler, Michael(Y)	1826	June 01	Stark Co.,Oh	08	12	23
Stickler, Peter(Y)	1829	Jan. 02	Stark Co.,Oh	10	01	03
Stierman, Richard(Z-M)	1833	Feb. 07	LickingCo,Oh	10	03	09
Stiers, John(Z)	1833	Aug. 22	GuernseyCoOh	09	08	31
Stiers, Sam'l.(Z-M)	1828	March 11	GuernseyCoOh	01	01	11
Stiers, Samuel Sr.(Z-M)	1828	Dec. 08	GuernseyCoOh	01	01	11
Stigler, Benj.(Z-M)	1830	March 06	GuernseyCoOh	01	01	18
Stile, Ebenezer(Z)	1837	March 09	Morgan Co,Oh	08	05	27
Stiles, John(Z)	1836	March 24	Perry Co.,Oh	15	14	27
Stiles, Jonathan(Z)	1807	Dec. 18	MuskingmCoOh	02	03	17
Stiles, Jonathan(Z)	1815	July 01	GuernseyCoOh	02	03	09
Stiles, Jonathan(Z-M)	1836	March 07	GuernseyCoOh	02	03	14
Stiles, Simon(Z-M)	1832	July 25	GuernseyCoOh	02	03	18
Stiles, Thomas(Z-M)	1836	March 17	GuernseyCoOh	02	03	14
Still, John(Z)	1835	Dec. 18	Morgan Co,Oh	09	06	01
Stillinger, John(Z-M)	1833	July 22	KnoxCo.,Ohio	10	07	01
Stillinger, Philip(Z)	1833	June 22	KnoxCo.,Ohio	10	07	11
Stillinger, Philip(Z-M)	1837	Nov. 16	KnoxCo.,Ohio	10	07	11
Stillwell, Asher(Z-M)	1836	Aug. 20	LickingCo,Oh	09	03	21
Stillwell, Asher(Z-M)	1837	Feb. 13	HolmesCoOhio	09	08	21
Stillwell, Asher(Z-M)	1837	Feb. 25	HolmesCoOhio	08	07	05
Stillwell, Asher(Z-M)	1839	Dec. 05	HolmesCoOhio	08	08	25
Stillwell, Daniel(Z-M)	1836	April 01	MuskingmCoOh	07	04	23
Stilwell, Stephen(Z)	1817	April 28	CoshoctnCoOh	09	05	15
Stince, Henry(Z)	1816	April 22	TuscarwsCoOh	04	08	14

PURCHASER	YEAR	DATE	RESIDENCE	R	T	S
Stine, John(Y)	1829	March 13	HarrisonCoOh	05	12	11
Stine, John(Z)	1824	May 11	Perry Co.,Oh	15	16	15
Stine, Samuel(Z)	1836	May 06	Perry Co.,Oh	15	14	28
Stine, Samuel(Z)	1836	May 06	Perry Co.,Oh	15	14	21
Stine, Solomon(Y)	1823	Aug. 01	HarrisonCoOh	04	11	30
Stiner, Nicholas(Z-M)	1827	Feb. 27	GuernseyCoOh	03	04	14
Stinges, Solomon(Z)	1830	May 28	PutnamCoOhio	12	12	19
Stingess, S.(Z)	1830	July 14	PutnamCoOhio	12	09	03
Stingess, Solomon(Z)	1830	Feb. 12	PutnamCoOhio	13	09	21
Stingess, Solomon(Z)	1830	Feb. 12	PutnamCoOhio	14	14	27
Stinson, William(Z)	1817	Feb. 13	MuskingmCoOh	12	11	35
Stires, Benjamin(Z)	1812	July 04	FairfeldCoOh	15	15	02
Stires, John(Z)	1811	Sept. 30	GuernseyCoOh	01	01	10
Stires, Joseph(Z)	1811	April 15	GuernseyCoOh	02	01	11
Stires, Joseph(Z)	1815	June 03	GuernseyCoOh	06	02	08
Stires, Samuel(Z)	1805	Dec. 17	BelmontCo,Oh	01	01	10
Stites, Simon(Z-M)	1832	July 25	GuernseyCoOh	02	03	18
Stitevell, Stephen(Z-M)	1821	Sept. 24	CoshoctnCoOh	06	04	19
Stittinger, Philip(Z-M)	1839	Aug. 31	KnoxCo.,Ohio	10	07	11
Stoakes, Wm. Jr.(Y)	1829	April 20	Jeff.Co.,Oh.	02	08	36
Stober, Daniel(Z-M)	1834	Sept. 02	HolmesCoOhio	08	08	12
Stockdale, James(Z-M)	1831	April 05	GuernseyCoOh	01	03	11
Stockdale, Jno. Jr.(Y)	1828	May 24	GuernseyCoOh	07	11	31
Stockdale, John(Z-M)	1835	May 13	MuskingmCoOh	10	05	19
Stockdale, John(Z-M)	1835	June 15	MuskingmCoOh	10	05	18
Stockdale, John(Z-M)	1836	Jan. 14	MuskingmCoOh	10	05	23
Stockdale, John(Z-M)	1837	Dec. 06	MuskingmCoOh	10	04	03
Stockdale, Joseph(Y)	1834	April 29	ColumbanCoOh	01	06	12
Stockdale, Robert(Z-M)	1837	Feb. 14	GuernseyCoOh	02	03	12
Stockdale, Robert(Z-M)	1837	Feb. 14	GuernseyCoOh	02	03	13
Stockdale, William(Z)	1816	Dec. 09	ZanesvilleOh	13	11	26
Stocker, Andrew(Z)	1817	Oct. 22	TuscarwsCoOh	03	06	10
Stocker, Andrew(Z-M)	1837	March 08	TuscarwsCoOh	03	06	10
Stocker, Christian(Z-M)	1837	March 08	TuscarwsCoOh	03	06	10
Stofer, Jacob(Y)	1826	Nov. 09	ColumbanCoOh	05	17	18
Stokely, David(Z)	1804	Oct. 15	MuskingmCoOh	14	15	34
Stokely, David(Z)	1814	Feb. 19	MuskingmCoOh	14	15	33
Stokely, Elizabeth Alicia(Y)	1837	April 24	SteubenvleOh	05	13	04
Stokely, Elizabeth Alicia(Y)	1837	May 30	SteubenvleOh	02	09	25
Stokely, Jane(Y)	1837	July 14	SteubenvleOh	02	09	31
Stokely, Jane(Y)	1837	Aug. 03	SteubenvleOh	05	11	12
Stokely, Mountford(Y)	1837	Oct. 20	SteubenvleOh	03	12	19
Stokely, Mountford(Y)	1838	June 30	SteubenvleOh	02	09	31
Stokely, S.(Y)	1827	Sept. 03	SteubenvleOh	07	17	21
Stokely, Sam'l.(Y)	1824	Aug. 03	SteubenvleOh	04	06	19
Stokely, Sam'l.(Y)	1827	July 16	Jeff.Co.,Oh.	01	03	29
Stokely, Sam'l.(Y)	1827	Aug. 02	SteubenvleOh	07	17	21
Stokely, Samuel(Y)	1825	Oct. 04	SteubenvleOh	04	06	21
Stokely, Samuel(Y)	1827	March 24	SteubenvleOh	07	12	29
Stokely, Samuel(Y)	1827	April 13	SteubenvleOh	03	12	03
Stokely, Samuel(Y)	1827	May 22	SteubenvleOh	07	12	35
Stokely, Samuel(Y)	1827	July 18	SteubenvleOh	07	12	35
Stokely, Samuel(Y)	1828	Oct. 01	SteubenvleOh	07	17	29
Stokely, Samuel(Y)	1829	Dec. 08	SteubenvleOh	06	15	22
Stokely, Samuel(Y)	1829	Dec. 09	SteubenvleOh	05	13	24
Stokely, Samuel(Y)	1831	April 02	SteubenvleOh	07	12	22
Stokely, Samuel(Y)	1831	April 28	SteubenvleOh	07	12	05
Stokely, Samuel(Y)	1831	May 02	SteubenvleOh	07	12	28
Stokely, Samuel(Y)	1831	May 11	SteubenvleOh	07	12	34
Stokely, Samuel(Y)	1831	June 02	SteubenvleOh	07	16	30
Stokely, Samuel(Y)	1831	July 02	SteubenvleOh	07	14	07
Stokely, Samuel(Y)	1831	July 05	SteubenvleOh	07	14	14
Stokely, Samuel(Y)	1831	July 06	SteubenvleOh	07	14	34
Stokely, Samuel(Y)	1831	July 25	SteubenvleOh	02	10	20
Stokely, Samuel(Y)	1831	July 26	SteubenvleOh	06	07	28
Stokely, Samuel(Y)	1831	July 26	SteubenvleOh	07	11	30
Stokely, Samuel(Y)	1831	July 26	SteubenvleOh	07	11	30
Stokely, Samuel(Y)	1831	Oct. 14	SteubenvleOh	07	12	04
Stokely, Samuel(Y)	1831	Oct. 31	SteubenvleOh	03	12	22

PURCHASER	YEAR	DATE	RESIDENCE	R	T	S
Stokely, Samuel(Y)	1831	Dec. 17	SteubenvleOh	07	12	22
Stokely, Samuel(Y)	1831	Dec. 17	SteubenvleOh	06	12	33
Stokely, Samuel(Y)	1832	Jan. 13	SteubenvleOh	04	12	35
Stokely, Samuel(Y)	1832	Jan. 16	SteubenvleOh	04	10	08
Stokely, Samuel(Y)	1832	Jan. 18	SteubenvleOh	04	12	23
Stokely, Samuel(Y)	1832	Jan. 18	SteubenvleOh	04	12	29
Stokely, Samuel(Y)	1832	Jan. 18	SteubenvleOh	04	12	23
Stokely, Samuel(Y)	1832	Jan. 19	SteubenvleOh	04	12	09
Stokely, Samuel(Y)	1832	Jan. 23	SteubenvleOh	04	12	02
Stokely, Samuel(Y)	1832	Feb. 16	SteubenvleOh	04	13	10
Stokely, Samuel(Y)	1832	May 01	SteubenvleOh	04	12	02
Stokely, Samuel(Y)	1832	May 01	SteubenvleOh	04	12	24
Stokely, Samuel(Y)	1832	June 20	SteubenvleOh	07	17	26
Stokely, Samuel(Y)	1832	Aug. 11	SteubenvleOh	04	12	17
Stokely, Samuel(Y)	1832	Sept. 01	SteubenvleOh	07	12	34
Stokely, Samuel(Y)	1832	Sept. 03	SteubenvleOh	04	13	19
Stokely, Samuel(Y)	1832	Sept. 20	SteubenvleOh	05	13	15
Stokely, Samuel(Y)	1833	Jan. 04	SteubenvleOh	07	16	20
Stokely, Samuel(Y)	1833	Jan. 04	SteubenvleOh	07	12	22
Stokely, Samuel(Y)	1833	Feb. 14	SteubenvleOh	04	12	15
Stokely, Samuel(Y)	1833	Feb. 14	SteubenvleOh	05	13	04
Stokely, Samuel(Y)	1833	Feb. 15	SteubenvleOh	07	14	08
Stokely, Samuel(Y)	1833	April 05	Jeff.Co.,Oh.	03	13	15
Stokely, Samuel(Y)	1833	June 01	SteubenvleOh	04	13	04
Stokely, Samuel(Y)	1833	June 06	SteubenvleOh	05	13	03
Stokely, Samuel(Y)	1833	Sept. 16	SteubenvleOh	04	12	15
Stokely, Samuel(Y)	1833	Dec. 09	SteubenvleOh	03	12	22
Stokely, Samuel(Y)	1834	Jan. 03	SteubenvleOh	04	12	17
Stokely, Samuel(Y)	1834	Feb. 08	SteubenvleOh	07	14	30
Stokely, Samuel(Y)	1834	May 09	SteubenvleOh	04	12	15
Stokely, Samuel(Y)	1834	June 23	SteubenvleOh	04	13	19
Stokely, Samuel(Y)	1834	Sept. 30	SteubenvleOh	05	13	09
Stokely, Samuel(Y)	1834	Dec. 03	SteubenvleOh	03	12	31
Stokely, Samuel(Y)	1834	Dec. 22	SteubenvleOh	04	13	04
Stokely, Samuel(Y)	1834	Dec. 25	SteubenvleOh	03	12	28
Stokely, Samuel(Y)	1835	Jan. 20	SteubenvleOh	07	14	33
Stokely, Samuel(Y)	1835	June 09	SteubenvleOh	07	14	14
Stokely, Samuel(Y)	1835	June 15	SteubenvleOh	03	11	17
Stokely, Samuel(Y)	1835	July 10	SteubenvleOh	07	14	15
Stokely, Samuel(Y)	1835	Aug. 31	SteubenvleOh	07	14	23
Stokely, Samuel(Y)	1835	Sept. 07	SteubenvleOh	03	11	05
Stokely, Samuel(Y)	1835	Sept. 19	SteubenvleOh	03	11	12
Stokely, Samuel(Y)	1835	Oct. 14	SteubenvleOh	03	12	22
Stokely, Samuel(Y)	1835	Dec. 14	SteubenvleOh	03	11	18
Stokely, Samuel(Y)	1836	March 01	SteubenvleOh	04	12	05
Stokely, Samuel(Y)	1836	April 08	SteubenvleOh	03	11	24
Stokely, Samuel(Y)	1836	June 20	SteubenvleOh	02	08	35
Stokely, Samuel(Y)	1836	July 04	SteubenvleOh	02	09	31
Stokely, Samuel(Y)	1836	July 06	SteubenvleOh	03	11	24
Stokely, Samuel(Y)	1836	July 11	SteubenvleOh	04	12	03
Stokely, Samuel(Y)	1836	Dec. 14	SteubenvleOh	03	11	30
Stokely, Samuel(Y)	1836	Dec. 22	SteubenvleOh	03	11	06
Stokely, Samuel(Y)	1838	June 02	SteubenvleOh	03	12	14
Stokely, Samuel(Y)	1838	June 30	SteubenvleOh	03	12	13
Stokely, Samuel(Z-M)	1835	Dec. 08	SteubenvleOh	01	08	04
Stokely, Samuel(Z-M)	1836	April 29	SteubenvleOh	01	08	04
Stokely, Samuel(©)	1831	June 01	SteubenvleOh	02	09	32
Stokum, Christopher(Z-M)	1837	Nov. 07	CoshoctnCoOh	05	04	07
Stone, Albert(Z)	1834	Feb. 26	Morgan Co,Oh	09	07	27
Stone, Charles(Z-M)	1838	May 14	CoshoctnCoOh	04	07	16
Stone, Jno. B.(Z)	1828	Dec. 16	Morgan Co,Oh	12	10	02
Stone, John R.(Z)	1825	Nov. 07	MonroeCo.,Oh	08	07	15
Stone, John Rice(Z)	1832	June 15	MonroeCo.,Oh	08	07	15
Stone, John Rice(Z)	1834	Jan. 16	MonroeCo.,Oh	08	07	15
Stone, John(Y)	1823	Nov. 25	HarrisonCoOh	05	12	23
Stone, Lemuel(Z)	1835	March 20	HarrisonCoOh	10	07	12
Stone, Noyce(Z)	1810	Oct. 01	ZanesvilleOh	02	01	03
Stonebraker, Joseph(Z-M)	1835	Nov. 17	BelmontCo,Oh	03	06	02
Stonebrook, Daniel(Z-M)	1837	Feb. 15	TuscarwsCoOh	03	06	03

284

PURCHASER	YEAR	DATE	RESIDENCE	R	T	S
Stonebrook, Frederick(Z-M)	1835	June 11	CarrolCo.,Oh	03	07	23
Stonebrook, John(Z-M)	1835	Aug. 28	CarrollCo,Oh	03	06	04
Stoneburner, Freder'k.(Z)	1815	Sept. 16	LoudonCo,Vir	14	15	31
Stoneburner, M.(Z)	1830	Dec. 02	Morgan Co,Oh	13	09	04
Stoneburner, Peter(Z)	1824	June 25	MuskingmCoOh	13	10	18
Stoneburner, Philip(Z)	1815	Sept. 16	MuskingmCoOh	14	14	07
Stoneburner, Sam'l.(Z)	1836	Aug. 29	Perry Co.,Oh	15	15	34
Stoneburner, Samuel(Z)	1835	July 21	Perry Co.,Oh	15	14	04
Stoneburner, Samuel(Z)	1836	Jan. 15	Perry Co.,Oh	15	15	34
Stonehocker, Jacob(Z)	1812	June 18	TuscarwsCoOh	04	08	20
Stonehocker, John(Z)	1815	June 16	TuscarwsCoOh	06	07	19
Stonehocker, Mich'l.(Z)	1815	March 27	CoshoctnCoOh	06	07	18
Stoneking, Elijah(Z)	1832	Nov. 26	Morgan Co,Oh	10	08	22
Stoneking, Elijah(Z)	1835	Feb. 02	Morgan Co,Oh	10	08	26
Stoneking, Jno.(Z)	1831	Dec. 21	Morgan Co,Oh	10	08	23
Stoner, George(Z)	1817	Feb. 19	MuskingmCoOh	06	02	04
Stoner, George(Z)	1817	Feb. 19	MuskingmCoOh	06	03	24
Stoner, Jacob(Y)	1830	Jan. 06	Stark Co.,Oh	07	15	30
Stoner, Jacob(Z-M)	1832	Sept. 03	MuskingmCoOh	06	03	03
Stoner, Jacob(Z-M)	1832	Sept. 08	MuskingmCoOh	06	03	02
Stoner, Jacob(Z-M)	1833	Oct. 19	TuscarwsCoOh	03	08	25
Stoner, Nicholas(Z)	1814	Oct. 21	GuernseyCoOh	01	03	19
Stonevoker, Jacob(Z)	1812	June 18	TuscarwsCoOh	04	08	20
Storey, George P.(Z)	1834	July 30	Perry Co.,Oh	15	14	03
Storey, George P.(Z)	1834	July 30	Perry Co.,Oh	15	14	02
Storey, Isaac C.(Z)	1835	March 23	MuskingmCoOh	15	14	21
Storm, George(Z-M)	1834	Dec. 09	CoshoctnCoOh	05	07	17
Storm, George(Z-M)	1837	May 23	CoshoctnCoOh	05	07	17
Storm, John(Z)	1816	Aug. 02	WestmrldCoPa	06	07	10
Storts, Daniel(Z)	1832	Feb. 14	Perry Co.,Oh	15	15	14
Story, G.(Z)	1829	Nov. 23	Morgan Co,Oh	13	10	36
Story, Michael(Z)	1836	July 05	WashngtnCoOh	09	05	29
Story, Michael(Z)	1836	July 05	WashngtnCoOh	09	05	28
Story, Palmer(Z)	1827	Sept. 12	Morgan Co,Oh	13	10	22
Story, Palmer(Z)	1828	March 15	Morgan Co,Oh	13	10	23
Story, Palmer(Z)	1829	July 21	Morgan Co,Oh	13	09	01
Story, William(Z)	1835	Aug. 24	MuskingmCoOh	15	15	34
Stosoner, John(Z)	1809	March 24	MuskingmCoOh	07	03	23
Stotler, Mathias(Z-M)	1826	Aug. 03	KnoxCo.,Ohio	10	08	25
Stottar, John(Z-M)	1836	March 12	BelmontCo,Oh	01	05	05
Stotts, Daniel(Z)	1817	Feb. 05	LickingCo,Oh	14	13	07
Stotts, Jacob(Z)	1829	April 30	Perry Co.,Oh	15	15	13
Stotts, Jacob(Z)	1832	Oct. 31	Perry Co.,Oh	14	13	18
Stotts, Jacob(Z-M)	1829	Dec. 21	MuskingmCoOh	06	02	04
Stotts, Yennis(Z)	1832	June 13	GuernseyCoOh	08	08	35
Stoughton, Jane(Z)	1831	Nov. 09	MuskingmCoOh	12	12	06
Stout, John(Z)	1825	March 21	BelmontCo,Oh	10	07	02
Stout, John(Z)	1825	March 21	BelmontCo,Oh	10	07	02
Stout, Jonathan(Z)	1834	March 03	Morgan Co,Oh	10	07	01
Stout, Philip(Z)	1825	Sept. 23	Morgan Co,Oh	13	09	21
Stout, William(Z-M)	1837	Feb. 04	LickingCo,Oh	09	08	16
Stover, Matthias D.(Z-M)	1839	Aug. 30	CoshoctnCoOh	08	07	21
Stover, Michael(Z-M)	1824	Jan. 22	CoshoctnCoOh	08	07	19
Stover, Michael(Z-M)	1834	Feb. 03	CoshoctnCoOh	08	07	19
Stover, Michael(Z-M)	1834	Feb. 03	CoshoctnCoOh	08	07	18
Stover, Sam'l.(Z)	1831	Nov. 10	MuskingmCoOh	14	14	03
Stover, Samuel(Z)	1813	Jan. 11	FairfeldCoOh	13	10	06
Stover, Samuel(Z)	1814	June 08	MuskingmCoOh	13	11	25
Stovner, John(Z)	1809	March 24	MuskingmCoOh	07	03	23
Stowner, George(Z)	1813	Sept. 22	MuskingmCoOh	05	03	13
Stowner, John(Z)	1806	June 02	SomersetCoPa	07	03	19
Stradley, Eares(Z)	1814	Feb. 21	MuskingmCoOh	10	04	20
Stradley, Eares(Z)	1816	Oct. 01	MuskingmCoOh	09	04	10
Straer, John(Y)	1825	May 28	Jeff.Co.,Oh.	05	14	21
Strahe, David(Z-M)	1832	Aug. 01	BelmontCo,Oh	03	01	25
Strahl, David(Z-M)	1833	Feb. 01	BelmontCo,Oh	03	01	20
Strahl, James(Z)	1827	Sept. 12	Morgan Co,Oh	11	11	18
Strahl, Samuel(Z)	1833	April 10	BelmontCo,Oh	13	08	28
Strahl, Stacy(Z)	1830	May 06	Morgan Co,Oh	13	08	36

PURCHASER	YEAR	DATE	RESIDENCE	R	T	S
Strahl, William(Z)	1832	April 03	BelmontCo,Oh	10	09	03
Straight, Jacob(Z)	1814	March 29	FayetteCo,Pa	15	16	29
Straight, Peter(Z)	1816	May 07	FairfeldCoOh	15	15	29
Strait, Benjamin(Z)	1836	Dec. 20	Perry Co.,Oh	15	14	33
Strait, Jacob(Z)	1833	June 28	Perry Co.,Oh	14	12	07
Strait, Jacob(Z)	1833	June 28	Perry Co.,Oh	14	12	07
Strait, Jacob(Z)	1833	June 28	Perry Co.,Oh	14	12	08
Strait, Jacob(Z)	1833	Oct. 12	Perry Co.,Oh	14	12	17
Strait, Jacob(Z)	1815	Feb. 08	LickingCo,Oh	15	15	06
Strait, Nathaniel(Z)	1836	May 25	Perry Co.,Oh	15	14	12
Strait, Peter(Z)	1831	Sept. 09	Perry Co.,Oh	15	14	30
Strait, Samuel(Z)	1832	Oct. 23	Perry Co.,Oh	15	14	30
Strait, Samuel(Z)	1833	Feb. 06	Perry Co.,Oh	15	14	30
Straite, Jacob(Z)	1825	Nov. 22	Perry Co.,Oh	14	12	17
Strakacker, Isaac(Y)	1832	March 27	Stark Co.,Oh	09	12	34
Stranahan, James(Z)	1825	Nov. 01	GuernseyCoOh	08	07	17
Stranahan, Wm.(Z)	1817	June 19	BelmontCo,Oh	09	08	13
Stranathan, Isaac(Z)	1828	April 25	GuernseyCoOh	10	08	15
Stranathan, Thomas(Z)	1836	Jan. 18	GuernseyCoOh	09	08	26
Stranthan, Thomas(Z)	1835	Nov. 09	GuernseyCoOh	09	08	13
Stratton, Joshua(Y)	1821	Dec. 10	ColumbanCoOh	04	17	15
Stratton, Stacey(Y)	1822	Aug. 19	ColumbanCoOh	04	17	10
Straun, John Thos.(Z)	1836	Feb. 04	Perry Co.,Oh	15	15	31
Strawn, Jacob(Z)	1824	Jan. 28	LickingCo,Oh	11	04	16
Strawn, Jacob(Z-M)	1831	April 06	TuscarwsCoOh	01	09	21
Strawn, Thomas(Z)	1814	Jan. 22	FairfeldCoOh	15	15	17
Streachbary, Joshua(Z)	1833	Dec. 24	MonroeCo.,Oh	08	07	06
Streachbary, William(Z)	1835	Nov. 17	MonroeCo.,Oh	08	07	30
Streachbery, Joshua(Z)	1836	Feb. 11	MonroeCo.,Oh	08	07	19
Strean, Joseph(Y)	1830	March 26	ColumbanCoOh	03	12	11
Strebe, John Jr.(Z-M)	1825	Aug. 31	TuscarwsCoOh	02	10	17
Streeby, William(Z-M)	1832	Aug. 23	TuscarwsCoOh	03	10	20
Street, Benjamin(Z)	1833	Jan. 12	MonroeCo.,Oh	08	07	04
Street, Benjamin(Z-M)	1835	Oct. 05	MonroeCo.,Oh	10	09	03
Street, Jeremiah(Z)	1833	Dec. 07	Perry Co.,Oh	14	13	33
Street, Jeremiah(Z)	1836	June 17	Perry Co.,Oh	14	13	33
Street, John(Y)	1825	June 22	ColumbanCoOh	05	18	12
Street, John(Z)	1833	April 23	Perry Co.,Oh	14	13	28
Street, John(Z)	1835	Dec. 01	Perry Co.,Oh	14	13	28
Street, John(Z-M)	1835	Nov. 09	MonroeCo.,Oh	10	09	03
Street, Robert(Y)	1831	Jan. 04	BelmontCo,Oh	04	06	19
Stretchbary, Bony(Z)	1833	Feb. 18	GuernseyCoOh	08	08	31
Stricker, Daniel(Z)	1815	July 11	KnoxCo.,Ohio	10	06	24
Stricker, Daniel(Z)	1815	July 11	KnoxCo.,Ohio	10	05	01
Stricker, Daniel(Z-M)	1833	Feb. 25	KnoxCo.,Ohio	10	06	11
Stricker, Jacob Jur.(Z-M)	1832	Oct. 29	KnoxCo.,Ohio	10	06	19
Stricker, Jacob(Z)	1815	Oct. 31	WashCo.,Penn	10	05	01
Stricker, William(Z)	1815	Oct. 31	WashCo.,Penn	10	05	13
Stricker, William(Z)	1815	Oct. 31	WashCo.,Penn	10	05	13
Stricker, William(Z)	1815	Oct. 31	WashCo.,Penn	10	05	10
Striebig, Michael(Z-M)	1836	Dec. 03	AlleghnyCoPa	05	04	13
Stringer, George(Z)	1810	Aug. 24	MuskingmCoOh	05	04	01
Stringer, George(Z)	1813	April 09	CoshoctnCoOh	03	02	05
Stringer, George(Z)	1814	Nov. 28	CoshoctnCoOh	06	04	22
Stringfellow, Pierce(Z-M)	1837	March 21	HolmesCoohio	09	07	09
Strong, Albert(Z)	1833	June 10	GuernseyCoOh	08	08	05
Strong, Alexander(Z)	1832	Nov. 28	Morgan Co,Oh	11	11	36
Strong, Alexander(Z)	1832	Nov. 28	Morgan Co,Oh	11	11	36
Strong, Christena(Z)	1834	Nov. 05	Jeff.Co.,Oh.	11	11	13
Strong, James(Z)	1829	Oct. 13	HarrisonCoOh	11	11	35
Strong, James(Z)	1831	Sept. 19	HarrisonCoOh	11	11	35
Strong, Orasha(Z)	1808	Feb. 27	GalliaCoOh	09	07	20
Strong, Thomas Fulton(Z)	1832	March 19	GuernseyCoOh	09	08	14
Strong, Thos. F.(Z)	1833	Aug. 02	GuernseyCoOh	09	08	12
Strosnider, Adam(Z)	1835	March 23	CoshoctnCoOh	09	06	21
Stroub, John Christian(Y)	1826	May 13	YorkCo.,Penn	07	14	08
Stroub, Wm.(Y)	1826	Aug. 15	ColumbanCoOh	05	17	07
Stroub, Wm.(Y)	1826	Aug. 15	ColumbanCoOh	05	17	18
Stroup, John Christian(Z-M)	1832	Aug. 15	HolmesCoOhio	05	08	22

PURCHASER	YEAR	DATE	RESIDENCE	R	T	S
Stroup, John(Z-M)	1835	June 22	ColumbanCoOh	05	06	17
Stroup, William(Z-M)	1832	June 27	CoshoctnCoOh	05	06	24
Stroup, Wm.(Y)	1822	Sept. 18	ColumbanCoOh	05	17	21
Strouse, George(Z-M)	1836	June 24	CoshoctnCoOh	09	07	06
Strows, Jacob(Z-M)	1833	Jan. 02	TuscarwsCoOh	02	07	15
Struthers, Alex'r.(Z)	1816	Aug. 31	MuskingmCoOh	07	03	22
Struthers, Andrew(Z)	1815	Nov. 24	MuskingmCoOh	07	03	22
Stuart, Charles(Z-M)	1830	April 05	GuernseyCoOh	02	01	08
Stuart, Charles(Z-M)	1836	Jan. 23	GuernseyCoOh	02	01	08
Stuart, Jno.(Z)	1831	Dec. 15	Morgan Co,Oh	09	07	01
Stubbs, Iddo(Z)	1821	Sept. 24	Morgan Co,Oh	12	10	26
Stuber, Daniel(Z-M)	1836	Oct. 08	HolmesCoOhio	08	08	20
Stucker, Dan'l.(Z-M)	1825	Aug. 31	TuscarwsCoOh	03	06	11
Stuckey, John(Y)	1826	April 01	ColumbanCoOh	05	17	09
Studsman, Jacob(Z)	1813	Nov. 05	TuscarwsCoOh	05	03	02
Studsman, Jacob(Z)	1814	March 03	TuscarwsCoOh	04	08	20
Studsman, Jacob(Z)	1814	May 16	TuscarwsCoOh	05	08	20
Studsman, Jacob(Z)	1814	June 28	TuscarwsCoOh	04	08	25
Studsman, Jacob(Z)	1815	June 06	CoshoctnCoOh	05	08	05
Study, George(Y)	1831	July 05	TuscarwsCoOh	07	15	33
Studybaker, Dan'l.(Y)	1823	June 19	Stark Co.,Oh	07	18	15
Stufflebeeny, Jacob(Z)	1829	Sept. 09	MuskingmCoOh	13	10	15
Stull, Henry(Z)	1815	July 17	GuernseyCoOh	02	02	07
Stull, John(Z)	1815	July 04	HarrisonCoOh	06	07	20
Stull, John(Z)	1816	March 05	HarrisonCoOh	06	07	09
Stull, John(Z)	1816	March 05	HarrisonCoOh	06	07	10
Stull, John(Z-M)	1832	Sept. 13	GuernseyCoOh	02	03	17
Stull, Michael(Z-M)	1826	May 20	CoshoctnCoOh	04	06	09
Stults, John(Y)	1832	Dec. 13	Stark Co.,Oh	06	15	24
Stultz, Harman(Y)	1827	Aug. 20	Stark Co.,Oh	08	09	03
Stultz, John(Y)	1831	June 07	Stark Co.,Oh	06	15	24
Stump, David(Z)	1816	Feb. 24	LickingCo,Oh	10	01	10
Stump, J.(Z)	1816	Feb. 29	MuskingmCoOh	10	04	23
Stump, J.(Z)	1816	Feb. 29	MuskingmCoOh	10	04	23
Stump, Jacob(Y)	1822	Dec. 24	Stark Co.,Oh	06	18	11
Stump, John(Y)	1827	March 05	ColumbanCoOh	06	18	22
Stump, Joseph(Z)	1810	June 18	LickingCo,Oh	10	01	01
Stump, Joseph(Z)	1814	June 29	LickingCo,Oh	10	01	01
Stump, Leonard(Z)	1808	April 01	MuskingmCoOh	09	03	19
Stump, Leonard(Z)	1808	April 18	MuskingmCoOh	09	03	11
Sturdy, Michael(Z-M)	1828	July 19	GuernseyCoOh	07	03	11
Sturgeon, Robert(Z)	1814	Sept. 29	FairfeldCoOh	15	16	11
Sturgeon, Samuel(Z-M)	1837	March 20	CoshoctnCoOh	08	06	04
Sturges, Hezekiah(Z)	1836	Dec. 05	PutnamCoOhio	13	08	06
Sturges, Hezekiah(Z)	1836	Dec. 06	PutnamCoOhio	15	14	30
Sturges, Hezekiah(Z)	1836	Dec. 06	PutnamCoOhio	15	14	32
Sturges, Hezekiah(Z)	1836	Dec. 06	PutnamCoOhio	13	08	08
Sturges, Hezekiah(Z-M)	1836	Dec. 05	PutnamCoOhio	03	04	04
Sturges, S.(Z)	1836	July 30	PutnamCoOhio	15	15	33
Sturges, Sol.(Z)	1836	Aug. 11	PutnamCoOhio	14	12	31
Sturges, Sol.(Z)	1836	Aug. 11	PutnamCoOhio	15	15	25
Sturges, Sol.(Z)	1836	Aug. 11	PutnamCoOhio	14	12	32
Sturges, Sol.(Z)	1836	Aug. 11	PutnamCoOhio	14	12	32
Sturges, Sol.(Z)	1836	Aug. 11	PutnamCoOhio	15	14	15
Sturges, Solomon J.(Z)	1833	Nov. 27	PutnamCoOhio	14	13	06
Sturges, Solomon(Z)	1824	May 18	PutnamCoOhio	14	12	25
Sturges, Solomon(Z)	1824	June 09	PutnamCoOhio	12	11	04
Sturges, Solomon(Z)	1829	Aug. 22	PutnamCoOhio	13	10	24
Sturges, Solomon(Z)	1832	Feb. 15	PutnamCoOhio	13	10	14
Sturges, Solomon(Z)	1833	Oct. 31	PutnamCoOhio	14	13	18
Sturges, Solomon(Z)	1833	Oct. 31	PutnamCoOhio	15	15	34
Sturges, Solomon(Z)	1833	Nov. 01	PutnamCoOhio	15	14	06
Sturges, Solomon(Z)	1833	Nov. 12	PutnamCoOhio	14	14	20
Sturges, Solomon(Z)	1833	Nov. 13	PutnamCoOhio	14	14	19
Sturges, Solomon(Z)	1833	Nov. 19	PutnamCoOhio	14	12	19
Sturges, Solomon(Z)	1833	Nov. 21	PutnamCoOhio	14	13	29
Sturges, Solomon(Z)	1833	Dec. 12	PutnamCoOhio	15	14	07
Sturges, Solomon(Z)	1833	Dec. 30	PutnamCoOhio	08	08	35
Sturges, Solomon(Z)	1833	Dec. 30	PutnamCoOhio	15	14	05

PURCHASER	YEAR	DATE	RESIDENCE	R	T	S
Sturges, Solomon(Z)	1834	Jan. 02	PutnamCoOhio	10	07	12
Sturges, Solomon(Z)	1834	Jan. 04	PutnamCoOhio	15	14	03
Sturges, Solomon(Z)	1834	Jan. 08	PutnamCoOhio	15	15	26
Sturges, Solomon(Z)	1836	April 28	PutnamCoOhio	13	08	27
Sturges, Solomon(Z)	1836	April 30	PutnamCoOhio	10	09	25
Sturges, Solomon(Z)	1836	April 30	PutnamCoOhio	14	13	28
Sturges, Solomon(Z)	1836	May 02	PutnamCoOhio	14	13	28
Sturges, Solomon(Z)	1836	May 02	PutnamCoOhio	14	13	28
Sturges, Solomon(Z)	1836	May 24	PutnamCoOhio	15	15	36
Sturges, Solomon(Z)	1836	May 24	PutnamCoOhio	15	15	36
Sturges, Solomon(Z)	1836	May 24	PutnamCoOhio	15	15	36
Sturges, Solomon(Z)	1836	May 24	PutnamCoOhio	15	15	35
Sturges, Solomon(Z)	1836	May 27	PutnamCoOhio	15	14	03
Sturges, Solomon(Z)	1836	May 28	PutnamCoOhio	14	13	29
Sturges, Solomon(Z)	1836	May 30	PutnamCoOhio	14	14	20
Sturges, Solomon(Z)	1836	May 30	PutnamCoOhio	14	13	31
Sturges, Solomon(Z)	1836	June 01	PutnamCoOhio	15	14	11
Sturges, Solomon(Z)	1836	June 01	PutnamCoOhio	15	14	11
Sturges, Solomon(Z)	1836	June 06	PutnamCoOhio	10	06	30
Sturges, Solomon(Z)	1836	June 08	PutnamCoOhio	15	14	11
Sturges, Solomon(Z)	1836	June 14	PutnamCoOhio	15	14	15
Sturges, Solomon(Z)	1836	June 14	PutnamCoOhio	15	15	33
Sturges, Solomon(Z)	1836	June 20	PutnamCoOhio	14	12	25
Sturges, Solomon(Z)	1836	June 20	PutnamCoOhio	15	14	11
Sturges, Solomon(Z)	1836	June 22	PutnamCoOhio	15	14	15
Sturges, Solomon(Z)	1836	June 24	PutnamCoOhio	15	15	33
Sturges, Solomon(Z)	1836	June 29	PutnamCoOhio	15	14	23
Sturges, Solomon(Z)	1836	July 01	PutnamCoOhio	15	15	24
Sturges, Solomon(Z)	1836	July 02	PutnamCoOhio	14	12	34
Sturges, Solomon(Z)	1836	July 02	PutnamCoOhio	14	12	29
Sturges, Solomon(Z)	1836	July 02	PutnamCoOhio	14	12	34
Sturges, Solomon(Z)	1836	July 02	PutnamCoOhio	15	14	14
Sturges, Solomon(Z)	1836	July 02	PutnamCoOhio	15	14	11
Sturges, Solomon(Z)	1836	July 05	PutnamCoOhio	15	14	23
Sturges, Solomon(Z)	1836	July 05	PutnamCoOhio	15	14	22
Sturges, Solomon(Z)	1836	July 05	PutnamCoOhio	15	14	25
Sturges, Solomon(Z)	1836	July 05	PutnamCoOhio	15	14	14
Sturges, Solomon(Z)	1836	July 07	PutnamCoOhio	14	12	06
Sturges, Solomon(Z)	1836	July 07	PutnamCoOhio	14	12	05
Sturges, Solomon(Z)	1836	July 07	PutnamCoOhio	14	13	32
Sturges, Solomon(Z)	1836	July 18	PutnamCoOhio	14	13	30
Sturges, Solomon(Z)	1836	July 18	PutnamCoOhio	14	12	30
Sturges, Solomon(Z)	1836	July 18	PutnamCoOhio	14	12	30
Sturges, Solomon(Z)	1836	July 18	PutnamCoOhio	14	12	18
Sturges, Solomon(Z)	1836	July 18	PutnamCoOhio	15	14	25
Sturges, Solomon(Z)	1836	July 18	PutnamCoOhio	15	14	25
Sturges, Solomon(Z)	1836	July 18	PutnamCoOhio	15	14	26
Sturges, Solomon(Z)	1836	July 20	PutnamCoOhio	14	12	17
Sturges, Solomon(Z)	1836	July 26	PutnamCoOhio	14	14	13
Sturges, Solomon(Z)	1836	July 28	PutnamCoOhio	15	14	26
Sturges, Solomon(Z)	1836	Aug. 10	PutnamCoOhio	13	08	22
Sturges, Solomon(Z)	1836	Aug. 10	PutnamCoOhio	08	06	17
Sturges, Solomon(Z)	1836	Aug. 15	PutnamCoOhio	08	07	21
Sturges, Solomon(Z)	1836	Aug. 16	PutnamCoOhio	08	07	30
Sturges, Solomon(Z)	1836	Aug. 19	PutnamCoOhio	15	15	27
Sturges, Solomon(Z)	1836	Aug. 19	PutnamCoOhio	15	15	28
Sturges, Solomon(Z)	1836	Aug. 20	PutnamCoOhio	09	07	24
Sturges, Solomon(Z)	1836	Sept. 27	PutnamCoOhio	14	12	06
Sturges, Solomon(Z)	1836	Nov. 30	PutnamCoOhio	14	13	28
Sturges, Solomon(Z)	1836	Dec. 21	PutnamCoOhio	13	08	18
Sturges, Solomon(Z)	1836	Dec. 21	PutnamCoOhio	13	08	18
Sturges, Solomon(Z)	1836	Dec. 24	PutnamCoOhio	15	14	23
Sturges, Solomon(Z)	1836	Dec. 26	PutnamCoOhio	15	14	20
Sturges, Solomon(Z)	1838	Jan. 17	PutnamCoOhio	15	14	33
Sturges, Solomon(Z)	1838	Jan. 22	PutnamCoOhio	15	14	31
Sturges, Solomon(Z)	1838	Feb. 06	PutnamCoOhio	08	06	03
Sturges, Solomon(Z)	1838	March 01	PutnamCoOhio	15	14	08
Sturges, Solomon(Z)	1838	April 07	PutnamCoOhio	08	06	33

PURCHASER	YEAR	DATE	RESIDENCE	R	T	S
Sturges, Solomon(Z)	1838	April 12	PutnamCoOhio	08	06	29
Sturges, Solomon(Z)	1838	April 13	PutnamCoOhio	15	14	12
Sturges, Solomon(Z)	1838	April 18	PutnamCoOhio	08	05	10
Sturges, Solomon(Z)	1838	May 24	PutnamCoOhio	15	14	36
Sturges, Solomon(Z)	1838	May 26	PutnamCoOhio	13	08	07
Sturges, Solomon(Z)	1838	June 11	PutnamCoOhio	10	08	19
Sturges, Solomon(Z)	1838	June 22	PutnamCoOhio	14	12	22
Sturges, Solomon(Z)	1838	June 28	PutnamCoOhio	04	03	01
Sturges, Solomon(Z)	1838	Aug. 25	PutnamCoOhio	08	06	34
Sturges, Solomon(Z)	1838	Aug. 25	PutnamCoOhio	08	06	34
Sturges, Solomon(Z)	1838	Sept. 21	PutnamCoOhio	08	05	01
Sturges, Solomon(Z)	1838	Oct. 01	PutnamCoOhio	13	08	31
Sturges, Solomon(Z)	1838	Nov. 03	PutnamCoOhio	14	12	36
Sturges, Solomon(Z)	1838	Nov. 24	PutnamCoOhio	08	05	26
Sturges, Solomon(Z)	1838	Nov. 24	PutnamCoOhio	08	05	22
Sturges, Solomon(Z)	1838	Dec. 11	PutnamCoOhio	15	14	35
Sturges, Solomon(Z)	1838	Dec. 12	PutnamCoOhio	08	05	02
Sturges, Solomon(Z)	1838	Dec. 20	PutnamCoOhio	13	08	17
Sturges, Solomon(Z)	1839	Jan. 18	PutnamCoOhio	08	06	13
Sturges, Solomon(Z)	1839	Jan. 18	PutnamCoOhio	08	06	29
Sturges, Solomon(Z)	1839	Jan. 18	PutnamCoOhio	08	05	22
Sturges, Solomon(Z)	1839	Jan. 18	PutnamCoOhio	08	05	01
Sturges, Solomon(Z)	1839	Jan. 28	PutnamCoOhio	08	06	35
Sturges, Solomon(Z)	1839	Feb. 09	PutnamCoOhio	08	05	08
Sturges, Solomon(Z)	1839	Feb. 09	PutnamCoOhio	08	05	09
Sturges, Solomon(Z)	1839	Feb. 09	PutnamCoOhio	08	05	09
Sturges, Solomon(Z)	1839	Feb. 09	PutnamCoOhio	08	05	10
Sturges, Solomon(Z)	1839	Feb. 09	PutnamCoOhio	08	05	22
Sturges, Solomon(Z)	1839	March 29	PutnamCoOhio	08	05	36
Sturges, Solomon(Z)	1839	March 29	PutnamCoOhio	08	05	25
Sturges, Solomon(Z)	1838	May 24	PutnamCoOhio	15	14	35
Sturges, Solomon(Z)	1838	June 11	PutnamCoOhio	10	08	19
Sturges, Solomon(Z-M)	1832	Feb. 11	MuskingmCoOh	10	02	07
Sturges, Solomon(Z-M)	1832	April 16	MuskingmCoOh	07	07	23
Sturges, Solomon(Z-M)	1832	April 30	PutnamCoOhio	05	04	09
Sturges, Solomon(Z-M)	1833	Dec. 30	PutnamCoOhio	03	06	05
Sturges, Solomon(Z-M)	1834	Feb. 18	PutnamCoOhio	11	03	23
Sturges, Solomon(Z-M)	1836	May 16	PutnamCoOhio	06	04	19
Sturges, Solomon(Z-M)	1836	June 18	PutnamCoOhio	02	04	25
Sturges, Solomon(Z-M)	1836	July 12	PutnamCoOhio	02	04	25
Sturges, Solomon(Z-M)	1836	Aug. 17	PutnamCoOhio	04	07	11
Sturges, Solomon(Z-M)	1836	Aug. 17	PutnamCoOhio	08	06	01
Sturges, Solomon(Z-M)	1836	Aug. 19	PutnamCoOhio	08	06	02
Sturges, Solomon(Z-M)	1836	Dec. 16	PutnamCoOhio	10	09	03
Sturges, Solomon(Z-M)	1836	Dec. 16	PutnamCoOhio	10	09	03
Sturges, Solomon(Z-M)	1838	Feb. 27	PutnamCoOhio	10	08	01
Sturges, Solomon(Z-M)	1838	April 27	PutnamCoOhio	08	07	11
Sturges, Solomon(Z-M)	1838	April 27	PutnamCoOhio	08	07	12
Sturges, Solomon(Z-M)	1838	April 30	PutnamCoOhio	09	08	24
Sturges, Solomon(Z-M)	1838	July 03	PutnamCoOhio	09	07	21
Sturges, Solomon(Z-M)	1838	Aug. 21	PutnamCoOhio	08	09	03
Sturges, Solomon(Z-M)	1838	Aug. 25	PutnamCoOhio	11	03	18
Sturges, Solomon(Z-M)	1838	Sept. 06	PutnamCoOhio	02	04	16
Sturges, Solomon(Z-M)	1838	Sept. 06	PutnamCoOhio	02	04	25
Sturges, Solomon(Z-M)	1838	Sept. 15	PutnamCoOhio	10	08	21
Sturges, Solomon(Z-M)	1838	Sept. 18	PutnamCoOhio	10	08	09
Sturges, Solomon(Z-M)	1838	Sept. 20	PutnamCoOhio	08	09	03
Sturges, Solomon(Z-M)	1838	Oct. 13	PutnamCoOhio	08	07	20
Sturges, Solomon(Z-M)	1838	Oct. 15	PutnamCoOhio	10	04	03
Sturges, Solomon(Z-M)	1838	Nov. 03	PutnamCoOhio	08	07	13
Sturges, Solomon(Z-M)	1838	Nov. 14	PutnamCoOhio	03	04	06
Sturges, Solomon(Z-M)	1838	Nov. 21	PutnamCoOhio	03	04	22
Sturges, Solomon(Z-M)	1838	Nov. 29	PutnamCoOhio	08	08	12
Sturges, Solomon(Z-M)	1838	Dec. 18	PutnamCoOhio	04	05	21
Sturges, Solomon(Z-M)	1838	Dec. 18	PutnamCoOhio	04	05	21
Sturges, Solomon(Z-M)	1839	Jan. 16	PutnamCoOhio	08	07	03
Sturges, Solomon(Z-M)	1839	Jan. 16	PutnamCoOhio	03	04	18
Sturges, Solomon(Z-M)	1839	Jan. 17	PutnamCoOhio	03	04	04
Sturges, Solomon(Z-M)	1839	Jan. 17	PutnamCoOhio	03	04	07

PURCHASER	YEAR	DATE	RESIDENCE	R	T	S
Sturges, Solomon(Z-M)	1839	Jan. 17	PutnamCoOhio	03	04	03
Sturges, Solomon(Z-M)	1839	Jan. 17	PutnamCoOhio	03	04	05
Sturges, Solomon(Z-M)	1839	Jan. 17	PutnamCoOhio	03	04	03
Sturges, Solomon(Z-M)	1839	Jan. 25	PutnamCoOhio	04	03	13
Sturges, Solomon(Z-M)	1839	Jan. 25	PutnamCoOhio	04	03	17
Sturges, Solomon(Z-M)	1839	Jan. 25	PutnamCoOhio	04	03	17
Sturges, Solomon(Z-M)	1839	Jan. 31	PutnamCoOhio	08	07	03
Sturges, Solomon(Z-M)	1839	Jan. 31	PutnamCoOhio	03	04	12
Sturges, Solomon(Z-M)	1839	Feb. 04	PutnamCoOhio	04	04	10
Sturges, Solomon(Z-M)	1839	Feb. 04	PutnamCoOhio	03	04	08
Sturges, Solomon(Z-M)	1839	Feb. 04	PutnamCoOhio	03	04	17
Sturges, Solomon(Z-M)	1839	Feb. 04	PutnamCoOhio	03	04	16
Sturges, Solomon(Z-M)	1839	Feb. 04	PutnamCoOhio	03	04	06
Sturges, Solomon(Z-M)	1839	Feb. 04	PutnamCoOhio	03	04	06
Sturges, Solomon(Z-M)	1839	Feb. 04	PutnamCoOhio	03	04	06
Sturges, Solomon(Z-M)	1839	Feb. 09	PutnamCoOhio	02	05	01
Sturges, Solomon(Z-M)	1839	March 02	PutnamCoOhio	04	04	09
Sturges, Solomon(Z-M)	1839	March 02	PutnamCoOhio	04	04	10
Sturges, Solomon(Z-M)	1839	March 02	PutnamCoOhio	04	04	10
Sturges, Solomon(Z-M)	1839	March 02	PutnamCoOhio	04	05	21
Sturges, Solomon(Z-M)	1839	March 02	PutnamCoOhio	04	04	01
Sturges, Solomon(Z-M)	1839	March 02	PutnamCoOhio	04	04	12
Sturges, Solomon(Z-M)	1839	March 02	PutnamCoOhio	04	04	10
Sturges, Solomon(Z-M)	1839	March 26	PutnamCoOhio	08	07	21
Sturges, Solomon(Z-M)	1839	April 02	PutnamCoOhio	10	08	02
Sturges, Solomon(Z-M)	1839	April 06	PutnamCoOhio	10	06	07
Sturges, Solomon(Z-M)	1839	April 06	PutnamCoOhio	10	06	13
Sturges, Solomon(Z-M)	1839	April 06	PutnamCoOhio	09	07	03
Sturges, Solomon(Z-M)	1839	April 06	PutnamCoOhio	09	07	32
Sturges, Solomon(Z-M)	1839	April 06	PutnamCoOhio	10	06	13
Sturges, Solomon(Z-M)	1839	April 08	PutnamCoOhio	10	06	07
Sturges, Solomon(Z-M)	1839	April 11	PutnamCoOhio	03	04	03
Sturges, Solomon(Z-M)	1839	April 22	PutnamCoOhio	10	06	07
Sturges, Solomon(Z-M)	1839	April 25	PutnamCoOhio	10	06	14
Sturges, Solomon(Z-M)	1839	May 14	PutnamCoOhio	07	07	15
Sturges, Solomon(Z-M)	1839	June 10	PutnamCoOhio	08	07	21
Sturges, Solomon(Z-M)	1839	July 08	PutnamCoOhio	10	09	12
Sturges, Solomon(Z-M)	1839	July 27	PutnamCoOhio	10	09	11
Sturges, Solomon(Z-M)	1839	Nov. 15	PutnamCoOhio	05	04	09
Sturges, Solomon(Z-M)	1836	July 16	PutnamCoOhio	11	04	13
Sturges, Solomon(Z-M)	1838	April 17	PutnamCoOhio	09	08	09
Sturgess, Solomon(Z)	1829	Nov. 30	PutnamCoOhio	12	11	04
Sturgess, Solomon(Z)	1829	Dec. 16	PutnamCoOhio	13	10	23
Sturgess, Solomon(Z-M)	1825	Nov. 13	PutnamCoOhio	10	02	18
Sturgs, Solomon(Z)	1833	Nov. 25	PutnamCoOhio	14	13	21
Sturman, James(Z-M)	1835	Nov. 21	CoshoctnCoOh	05	04	20
Sturman, James(Z-M)	1836	Jan. 13	CoshoctnCoOh	05	04	20
Stuter, Jacob(Z-M)	1835	Aug. 24	CoshoctnCoOh	06	04	21
Stuts, Joseph(Z)	1837	May 18	GuernseyCoOh	08	06	10
Stutsman, Chris'ph.(Z)	1815	Dec. 15	CoshoctnCoOh	05	09	14
Stutsman, Jacob(Z)	1809	Oct. 06	SomersetCoPa	05	09	20
Stutsman, Jacob(Z)	1815	Dec. 15	CoshoctnCoOh	06	09	08
Stutsman, Jonas(Z)	1809	Oct. 06	SomersetCoPa	05	09	21
Stutsman, Jonas(Z)	1815	Dec. 15	CoshoctnCoOh	06	08	10
Stutt, Henry(Z)	1808	March 28	MuskingmCoOh	02	03	18
Stutts, Jacob(Z-M)	1832	Sept. 24	KnoxCo.,Ohio	11	03	04
Stutts, William(Z)	1811	June 01	TuscarwsCoOh	01	09	03
Stuttsman, Christian(Z)	1810	Oct. 22	SomersetCoPa	05	09	11
Stuttsman, Jacob Jr.(Z-M)	1823	June 06	CoshoctnCoOh	05	09	19
Stuttsman, Jacob(Z)	1811	Oct. 24	TuscarwsCoOh	05	09	21
Styett, David(Y)	1829	April 10	ColumbanCoOh	05	15	22
Suadner, Jacob(Y)	1825	Sept. 24	ColumbanCoOh	05	17	10
Suit, Philip C.(Z-M)	1835	Oct. 29	GuernseyCoOh	04	02	20
Suitor, Philip(Y)	1831	Jan. 24	TuscarwsCoOh	07	15	30
Sullivan, Cornelius(Z)	1814	Jan. 03	FairfeldCoOh	15	17	20
Sullivant, Charles(Z)	1807	Sept. 14	FayetteCo,Pa	10	08	06
Summany, Samuel(Z-M)	1833	April 08	HolmesCoOhio	07	08	10
Summer, David(Y)	1822	June 17	ColumbanCoOh	05	17	22
Summer, David(Y)	1822	June 17	ColumbanCoOh	05	17	22

PURCHASER	YEAR	DATE	RESIDENCE	R	T	S
Summer, David(Y)	1823	Oct. 28	ColumbanCoOh	05	17	23
Summer, David(Y)	1826	Dec. 19	ColumbanCoOh	05	17	10
Summer, David(Y)	1827	Feb. 20	ColumbanCoOh	05	17	21
Summer, David(Y)	1827	Feb. 20	ColumbanCoOh	05	18	32
Summers, John(Y)	1825	Feb. 12	Stark Co.,Oh	06	16	28
Summers, William(Z-M)	1834	March 21	TuscarwsCoOh	03	05	21
Summerville, James(Z)	1811	Jan. 31	LickingCo,Oh	10	03	23
Summerville, Sam'l.(Z)	1825	Oct. 25	LickingCo,Oh	10	03	07
Summory, Sam'l.(Z-M)	1832	June 06	HolmesCoOhio	07	08	10
Susaman, George(Z)	1815	March 22	BelmontCo,Oh	09	05	12
Susaman, George(Z)	1816	March 26	BelmontCo,Oh	09	05	15
Susaman, George(Z-M)	1834	March 18	CoshoctnCoOh	09	05	15
Suter, John(Z)	1816	Oct. 15	WestmrldCoPa	06	07	03
Suter, John(Z)	1816	Oct. 15	WestmrldCoPa	06	08	23
Sutherland, John Town(Y)	1836	July 16	SteubenvleOh	03	01	23
Suton, Abraham(Z-M)	1822	May 06	WestmrldCoPa	06	07	01
Suttles, Bennet(Z)	1809	March 25	MuskingmCoOh	14	15	08
Sutton, David(Z)	1817	Oct. 08	GuernseyCoOh	08	07	24
Sutton, Elisha(Z-M)	1833	Nov. 16	GuernseyCoOh	04	05	23
Sutton, Elisha(Z-M)	1837	Oct. 12	CoshoctnCoOh	04	05	21
Sutton, Jacob(Z-M)	1832	April 16	GuernseyCoOh	01	03	22
Sutton, Jeremiah(Z)	1815	Feb. 24	AlleghnyCoPa	11	12	19
Sutton, John(Z)	1816	Nov. 07	WestmrldCoPa	10	04	10
Sutton, Lewis(Z)	1816	Nov. 07	WestmrldCoPa	10	04	10
Sutton, Thomas(Z-M)	1832	Oct. 13	WashCo.,Penn	04	07	24
Sutton, Wm.(Z)	1817	Oct. 08	GuernseyCoOh	08	07	24
Sutton, Zachariah(Y)	1822	May 08	BelmontCo,Oh	06	09	24
Suttsgiver, Jacob(Z)	1805	May 30	MuskingmCoOh	01	02	04
Suver, Robert(Z-M)	1838	May 15	CoshoctnCoOh	10	04	10
Swaim, Matthias Murphy(Z-M)	1837	April 03	Jeff.Co.,Oh.	03	04	07
Swaim, Matthias Murphy(Z-M)	1837	April 03	Jeff.Co.,Oh.	03	04	14
Swaney, James(Z)	1813	Oct. 29	FredrickCoMd	01	10	14
Swaney, John(Y)	1832	April 18	BeaverCo.,Pa	03	12	32
Swank, Christian(Z)	1812	May 01	TuscarwsCoOh	01	10	05
Swank, George Junr.(Z)	1816	Sept. 03	FayetteCo,Pa	05	08	25
Swank, John(Z)	1834	Sept. 11	Morgan Co,Oh	10	07	04
Swank, Peter(Z-M)	1831	Feb. 14	TuscarwsCoOh	02	10	16
Swank, Philip(Z)	1815	July 05	DelmontCo,Oh	09	04	04
Swank, William(Z)	1832	Jan. 13	Morgan Co,Oh	10	07	10
Swank, William(Z)	1833	Sept. 13	Morgan Co,Oh	10	07	10
Swank, William(Z)	1834	Nov. 18	Morgan Co,Oh	10	07	10
Swany, Thomas(Z)	1836	Oct. 17	Perry Co.,Oh	14	12	23
Swart, Gilbert(Z)	1833	Jan. 04	MuskingmCoOh	13	08	11
Swart, William(Z)	1833	Jan. 04	MuskingmCoOh	13	08	11
Swarts, Jacob(Z-M)	1836	Aug. 24	AlleghnyCoPa	10	08	19
Swarts, James(Z)	1833	Feb. 01	Perry Co.,Oh	14	13	19
Swartz, Martin(Y)	1822	July 09	ColumbanCoOh	06	19	17
Swayze, William(Y)	1821	Jan. 05	PortageCo,Oh	05	18	05
Sweany, Albert G.(Z)	1832	Dec. 03	GuernseyCoOh	10	08	19
Sweany, Albert G.(Z)	1833	April 29	Morgan Co,Oh	10	08	19
Sweany, Jacob(Y)	1832	Nov. 03	Stark co.,Oh	07	16	34
Swearingen, Thomas(Z)	1812	Aug. 22	WashngtnCoOh	08	02	06
Swearingen, Thomas(Z-M)	1837	March 15	CarrollCo,Oh	04	04	23
Swearingen, Thomas(Z-M)	1837	March 15	CarrollCo,Oh	04	04	23
Sweeney, Nathaniel E.(Z)	1834	Dec. 01	MuskingmCoOh	11	12	23
Sweeney, Nathaniel E.(Z)	1834	Dec. 01	MuskingmCoOh	11	12	25
Swenay, Daniel(Y)	1828	May 29	Stark Co.,Oh	07	16	33
Sweney, John Kean(Y)	1831	Sept. 12	Jeff.Co.,Oh.	04	12	17
Sweny, Edw'd.(Y)	1826	Aug. 16	ColumbanCoOh	04	14	30
Swigart, Jacob(Z-M)	1827	March 21	MuskingmCoOh	10	08	06
Swigart, John(Z)	1815	Jan. 14	HarrisonCoOh	05	09	15
Swigert, Cath.(Z-M)	1831	July 26	CoshoctnCoOh	05	06	04
Swigert, John(Z)	1831	Oct. 04	Stark co.,Oh	10	03	13
Swihert, John(Y)	1830	Nov. 10	Stark Co.,Oh	10	01	03
Swikart, Andrew(Z-M)	1826	Jan. 14	TuscarwsCoOh	03	09	20
Swikurt, Andrew(Z-M)	1820	Oct. 04	TuscarwsCoOh	03	09	20
Swindel, William(Z-M)	1837	Feb. 25	LickingCo,Oh	11	04	19
Swindel, William(Z-M)	1837	Feb. 25	LickingCo,Oh	11	04	22
Swindle, Wm.(Z)	1831	July 13	MuskingmCoOh	13	11	23

PURCHASER	YEAR	DATE	RESIDENCE	R	T	S
Swinehart, Frederick(Z)	1806	Oct. 29	WashngtnCoVa	03	08	09
Swinehart, Frederick(Z)	1806	Oct. 29	WashngtnCoVa	03	09	11
Swinehart, Frederick(Z)	1810	Nov. 07	TuscarwsCoOh	03	08	09
Swinehart, Geo.(Z-M)	1833	Feb. 23	Jeff.Co.,Oh.	03	08	11
Swinehart, George(Z-M)	1835	Aug. 27	TuscarwsCoOh	03	08	11
Swinehart, Jacob(Z-M)	1831	March 16	TuscarwsCoOh	03	08	04
Swinehart, John(Y)	1828	Oct. 10	Jeff.Co.,Oh.	02	08	35
Swinehart, John(Y)	1832	May 28	Jeff.Co.,Oh.	02	08	29
Swinehart, William(Z-M)	1836	March 23	TuscarwsCoOh	03	08	07
Swineheart, Thad.(Z-M)	1831	April 13	TuscarwsCoOh	03	08	03
Swingle, George Junr.(Z)	1833	Aug. 24	MuskingmCoOh	13	10	18
Swingle, Henry(Z)	1811	Dec. 11	ZanesvilleOh	12	13	09
Swingle, Henry(Z)	1815	Feb. 24	ZanesvilleOh	13	12	13
Swingle, Jacob(Z)	1833	Jan. 22	MuskingmCoOh	13	10	08
Swingle, John(Z)	1833	Jan. 22	MuskingmCoOh	13	10	17
Swingle, N.(Z)	1831	Feb. 28	Morgan Co,Oh	13	10	04
Swingle, Samuel(Z)	1834	March 11	MuskingmCoOh	13	10	04
Swingle, William(Z)	1826	Oct. 16	MuskingmCoOh	13	11	24
Swingle, William(Z)	1830	Feb. 24	MuskingmCoOh	12	12	07
Swingle, Wm.(Z)	1821	Nov. 07	Morgan Co,Oh	13	11	29
Swingle, Wm.(Z)	1830	Dec. 18	MuskingmCoOh	13	11	30
Swingle, Wm.(Z)	1831	Feb. 28	MuskingmCoOh	13	10	04
Swisher, Stephen(Z-M)	1838	Jan. 01	GuernseyCoOh	03	03	05
Switchfield, Benj'n.(Y)	1823	Aug. 26	BelmontCo,Oh	03	05	22
Switzer, Daniel(Y)	1824	Jan. 30	Stark Co.,Oh	06	18	26
Switzer, Daniel(Y)	1826	Nov. 21	Stark Co.,Oh	06	18	26
Switzer, Jacob(Y)	1824	May 24	ColumbanCoOh	06	18	09
Switzer, Jacob(Y)	1824	May 24	ColumbanCoOh	06	18	09
Switzer, Jacob(Y)	1824	May 24	ColumbanCoOh	06	18	05
Switzer, Jacob(Y)	1825	Nov. 16	ColumbanCoOh	06	18	04
Switzer, Martin(Y)	1823	May 26	ColumbanCoOh	02	11	34
Switzer, Martin(Y)	1828	April 02	ColumbanCoOh	02	11	34
Swob, Jacob(Z)	1836	April 05	Morgan Co,Oh	13	10	26
Swollie, John(Z)	1817	Oct. 31	MuskingmCoOh	13	09	05
Swolveland, Jacob(Z)	1817	Oct. 16	TuscarwsCoOh	05	09	13
Swoneland, Michael(Z)	1815	Dec. 13	CoshoctnCoOh	05	09	06
Swope, J.(Z)	1815	Sept. 11	MuskingmCoOh	13	10	30
Swope, J.(Z)	1815	Sept. 11	MuskingmCoOh	13	10	19
Swope, Jacob(Z)	1832	Feb. 08	MuskingmCoOh	13	10	22
Swundy, George(Z)	1833	Aug. 29	MonroeCo.,Oh	08	06	12
Swyhart, Jos.(Z-M)	1839	April 22	GuernseyCoOh	03	03	14
Sycks, John(Z)	1833	April 23	GreenCo.,Pa.	15	15	34
Sycks, John(Z)	1833	April 23	GreenCo.,Pa.	15	15	34
Syles, Elias(Z)	1817	Oct. 29	WashngtnCoOh	08	05	23
Sylvers, George(Z)	1832	Oct. 17	Morgan Co,Oh	13	10	35
Taber, Margaret(Z-M)	1838	July 05	CoshoctnCoOh	09	07	21
Table, Catharine(Z-M)	1836	June 30	HolmesCoOhio	04	07	11
Tackaberry, Robt.(Z)	1817	Oct. 08	PittsburghPa	08	07	13
Tadrow, John(Z)	1806	June 09	MuskingmCoOh	14	15	07
Tagert, Joseph(Z)	1811	Nov. 25	ZanesvilleOh	10	02	14
Tagert, Joseph(Z)	1811	Nov. 25	ZanesvilleOh	09	03	08
Tagert, Joseph(Z)	1811	Dec. 09	ZanesvilleOh	10	02	13
Tagert, Joseph(Z)	1811	Dec. 31	MuskingmCoOh	09	03	07
Tagert, Joseph(Z)	1811	Dec. 31	MuskingmCoOh	09	03	14
Taggert, Arthur(Z-M)	1830	Feb. 27	LickingCo,Oh	11	01	21
Taggert, Arthur(Z-M)	1830	Feb. 27	LickingCo,Oh	11	01	19
Talbot, Allen Fouts(Z)	1834	Sept. 20	Morgan Co,Oh	11	11	15
Talbot, Jos.(Z)	1827	Oct. 19	HarrisonCoOh	11	10	28
Talbot, Jos.(Z)	1827	Oct. 19	HarrisonCoOh	11	10	27
Talbot, Rich'd.(Z)	1827	Oct. 19	HarrisonCoOh	11	10	28
Talbot, Rich'd.(Z)	1827	Oct. 19	HarrisonCoOh	11	10	27
Talbot, S.(Z)	1806	April 07	MuskingmCoOh	05	01	10
Talbott, George W.(Z)	1834	Aug. 26	Baltimore,Md	14	12	25
Talbott, Richard L.(Z)	1834	July 28	Brooke CoVir	10	07	19
Talbott, Richard L.(Z)	1834	July 28	Brooke CoVir	10	07	20
Talbott, Wm. A.(Y)	1823	Dec. 10	Jeff.Co.,Oh.	05	14	04
Tallmadge, Jos.(Z-M)	1831	Oct. 29	CoshoctnCoOh	08	07	19
Tallmadge, Joseph(Z-M)	1829	March 26	CoshoctnCoOh	07	04	03
Tallmadge, Joseph(Z-M)	1829	July 01	CoshoctnCoOh	07	04	03

PURCHASER	YEAR	DATE	RESIDENCE	R	T	S
Tallmadge, Joseph(Z-M)	1829	Nov. 28	CoshoctnCoOh	07	05	18
Talmage, Joseph(Z-M)	1836	Dec. 12	CoshoctnCoOh	08	07	23
Talmage, Joseph(Z-M)	1837	Dec. 04	CoshoctnCoOh	08	07	08
Tanner, John(Z)	1836	Jan. 20	Morgan Co,Oh	13	08	11
Tanner, John(Z)	1811	July 23	MuskingmCoOh	14	15	28
Tanner, John(Z)	1816	Feb. 09	MuskingmCoOh	13	08	11
Tanner, John(Z)	1816	Feb. 09	MuskingmCoOh	13	08	02
Tanney, James(Z-M)	1839	July 01	CoshoctnCoOh	09	07	20
Tarney, Solomon(Z-M)	1834	March 11	HarrisonCoOh	03	06	16
Tatman, Bartholomew(Z)	1832	Oct. 04	Perry Co.,Oh	14	13	22
Tatman, Bartholomew(Z)	1833	Feb. 06	Perry Co.,Oh	14	13	22
Tatman, Benjamin Junr.(Z)	1833	Dec. 10	Perry Co.,Oh	14	13	27
Tatman, Benjamin Junr.(Z)	1833	Dec. 10	Perry Co.,Oh	14	13	27
Tatman, Benjamin(Z)	1836	Feb. 12	Perry Co.,Oh	14	13	21
Tatman, Cyrenius(Z)	1836	Dec. 03	Perry Co.,Oh	14	13	34
Tatman, Joseph(Z)	1836	April 25	Perry Co.,Oh	14	13	34
Tatman, Joseph(Z)	1836	Dec. 03	Perry Co.,Oh	14	13	27
Tatman, Levi(Z-M)	1838	April 12	TrumbullCoOh	08	07	07
Tatman, Lewis(Z)	1833	Nov. 05	Perry Co.,Oh	14	13	22
Tatman, Obadiah(Z)	1833	Dec. 02	Perry Co.,Oh	14	13	21
Tatman, Obadiah(Z)	1833	Dec. 02	Perry Co.,Oh	14	13	28
Tatman, Syrenius(Z)	1836	April 18	Perry Co.,Oh	14	13	33
Tatman, Thomas(Z)	1832	Nov. 12	Perry Co.,Oh	14	13	27
Tayler, Alexander(Y)	1831	July 25	HarrisonCoOh	06	12	09
Tayler, George(Y)	1831	July 21	Jeff.Co.,Oh.	05	13	34
Tayler, Jacob(Y)	1832	March 31	ColumbanCoOh	05	16	32
Tayler, William(Y)	1834	Feb. 06	Jeff.Co.,Oh.	03	11	24
Taylor, Alexander(Y)	1828	Jan. 16	BelmontCo,Oh	06	16	01
Taylor, Ann(Y)	1825	Aug. 22	WashCo.,Penn	03	11	15
Taylor, Ann(Y)	1826	Dec. 16	Jeff.Co.,Oh.	03	11	09
Taylor, Benj.(Z-M)	1839	Oct. 05	WarrenCo,N.J	08	06	04
Taylor, Benjamin(Y)	1826	Jan. 17	BelmontCo,Oh	04	06	01
Taylor, Benjamin(Z-M)	1834	Jan. 31	CoshoctnCoOh	09	04	17
Taylor, David(Z)	1836	May 04	MonroeCo.,Oh	08	06	27
Taylor, E.(Z)	1816	Dec. 05	CoshoctnCoOh	11	05	18
Taylor, Edward(Y)	1824	Dec. 02	Jeff.Co.,Oh.	03	11	02
Taylor, Frazeur(Y)	1824	Aug. 09	BelmontCo,Oh	03	05	31
Taylor, George(Z-M)	1835	Aug. 28	GuernseyCoOh	01	03	06
Taylor, Henry(Z-M)	1836	Jan. 11	TuscarwsCoOh	03	05	20
Taylor, Henry(Z-M)	1837	April 10	TuscarwsCoOh	04	08	21
Taylor, Hiram(Y)	1826	June 02	PortageCo,Oh	05	18	29
Taylor, Isaac(Y)	1821	May 03	ColumbanCoOh	05	18	35
Taylor, Isaac(Y)	1826	Nov. 01	Jeff.Co.,Oh.	04	12	32
Taylor, Isaac(Y)	1828	Oct. 25	ColumbanCoOh	05	18	35
Taylor, Isaac(Y)	1835	Aug. 13	Jeff.Co.,Oh.	04	12	10
Taylor, James(Y)	1822	Jan. 29	Jeff.Co.,Oh.	03	11	15
Taylor, James(Y)	1828	May 13	Jeff.Co.,Oh.	03	11	14
Taylor, James(Z)	1828	July 17	MuskingmCoOh	13	11	02
Taylor, James(Z)	1831	April 28	Morgan Co,Oh	11	11	26
Taylor, James(Z)	1835	April 08	Morgan Co,Oh	09	05	28
Taylor, James(Z)	1836	Jan. 06	Morgan Co,Oh	09	05	28
Taylor, James(Z)	1836	Jan. 08	Morgan Co,Oh	09	05	33
Taylor, James(Z)	1805	Jan. 18	MuskingmCoOh	08	02	18
Taylor, James(Z)	1805	Jan. 18	MuskingmCoOh	08	02	13
Taylor, James(Z)	1806	Jan. 25	MuskingmCoOh	08	02	07
Taylor, James(Z)	1806	April 03	MuskingmCoOh	08	02	04
Taylor, James(Z)	1806	Oct. 07	MuskingmCoOh	08	04	22
Taylor, James(Z)	1806	Oct. 07	MuskingmCoOh	08	04	22
Taylor, James(Z)	1806	Oct. 20	MuskingmCoOh	06	01	05
Taylor, James(Z)	1806	Oct. 20	MuskingmCoOh	06	01	04
Taylor, James(Z)	1806	Oct. 20	MuskingmCoOh	06	01	07
Taylor, James(Z)	1815	June 21	ZanesvilleOh	13	11	02
Taylor, James(Z-M)	1829	June 17	TuscarwsCoOh	02	05	13
Taylor, James(Z-M)	1832	June 05	TuscarwsCoOh	02	05	18
Taylor, Jas.,Mercht.(Z)	1827	Nov. 10	MuskingmCoOh	12	11	10
Taylor, Jesse(Y)	1825	April 16	BelmontCo,Oh	04	06	01
Taylor, Jno.(Z)	1835	Dec. 28	Morgan Co,Oh	09	05	15
Taylor, Jno.(Z)	1817	Aug. 01	MariettaOhio	09	05	15
Taylor, Jno.(Z-M)	1832	Feb. 08	CoshoctnCoOh	09	05	25

PURCHASER	YEAR	DATE	RESIDENCE	R	T	S
Taylor, John B.(Z)	1830	Jan. 05	HarrisonCoOh	11	12	30
Taylor, John C.(Z-M)	1839	Aug. 17	Wayne Co.,Oh	09	09	24
Taylor, John C.(Z-M)	1839	Aug. 17	Wayne Co.,Oh	09	08	02
Taylor, John Junr.(Z)	1833	June 27	Morgan Co,Oh	09	05	27
Taylor, John Senr.(Z)	1815	Dec. 13	MuskingmCoOh	09	04	04
Taylor, John Senr.(Z)	1816	Aug. 02	MuskingmCoOh	09	04	04
Taylor, John W.(Z-M)	1833	July 22	TuscarwsCoOh	01	08	02
Taylor, John W.(Z-M)	1833	July 22	TuscarwsCoOh	01	08	02
Taylor, John W.(Z-M)	1833	July 22	TuscarwsCoOh	01	08	02
Taylor, John W.(Z-M)	1833	July 22	TuscarwsCoOh	01	08	02
Taylor, John(Y)	1828	April 18	ColumbanCoOh	04	13	17
Taylor, John(Z)	1823	Nov. 29	Morgan Co,Oh	09	05	10
Taylor, John(Z)	1826	March 25	Morgan Co,Oh	09	05	22
Taylor, John(Z)	1832	Sept. 10	Morgan Co,Oh	11	11	10
Taylor, John(Z)	1832	Sept. 10	Morgan Co,Oh	11	11	10
Taylor, John(Z)	1832	Oct. 05	Morgan Co,Oh	09	05	22
Taylor, John(Z)	1833	May 03	Morgan Co,Oh	09	05	27
Taylor, John(Z)	1834	Jan. 10	Morgan Co,Oh	11	11	10
Taylor, John(Z)	1835	Oct. 26	Morgan Co,Oh	09	05	22
Taylor, John(Z)	1836	April 12	Morgan Co,Oh	09	05	22
Taylor, John(Z)	1837	March 22	Morgan Co,Oh	08	05	09
Taylor, John(Z)	1811	Dec. 02	BelmontCo,Oh	11	05	06
Taylor, John(Z)	1812	Dec. 11	KnoxCo.,Ohio	09	05	13
Taylor, John(Z)	1815	Aug. 19	Ohio Co.,Vir	10	06	21
Taylor, John(Z-M)	1836	Dec. 29	MuskingmCoOh	03	01	05
Taylor, John(Z-M)	1837	April 10	CarrollCo,Oh	10	08	02
Taylor, John(Z-M)	1837	April 10	CarrollCo,Oh	10	08	02
Taylor, Johnsey(Z-M)	1837	Feb. 25	TuscarwsCoOh	03	05	12
Taylor, Joseph Jr.(Z-M)	1830	Dec. 17	Jeff.Co.,Oh.	02	04	04
Taylor, Joseph Jr.(Z-M)	1836	March 02	Jeff.Co.,Oh.	03	05	19
Taylor, Joseph(Y)	1822	Dec. 09	Stark Co.,Oh	07	20	03
Taylor, Joseph(Z)	1815	June 07	MuskingmCoOh	11	12	01
Taylor, Joshua(Z-M)	1832	Oct. 17	CoshoctnCoOh	09	05	25
Taylor, Joshua(Z-M)	1833	Nov. 28	KnoxCo.,Ohio	10	05	21
Taylor, Lewis(Z-M)	1835	Oct. 13	GuernseyCoOh	03	05	24
Taylor, Lewis(Z-M)	1835	Oct. 13	GuernseyCoOh	03	05	20
Taylor, Perry A. W.et al(Z-M)	1832	April 03	LickingCo,Oh	02	10	17
Taylor, Peter(Z)	1823	Nov. 29	Morgan Co,Oh	09	05	10
Taylor, Peter(Z)	1832	April 30	Morgan Co,Oh	09	05	33
Taylor, Peter(Z)	1835	Dec. 28	Morgan Co,Oh	09	05	15
Taylor, Peter(Z)	1817	Aug. 01	MariettaOhio	09	05	15
Taylor, Robert(Y)	1828	April 17	ColumbanCoOh	05	18	17
Taylor, Robt.(Z)	1811	Nov. 25	ZanesvilleOh	10	02	14
Taylor, Robt.(Z)	1811	Nov. 25	ZanesvilleOh	09	03	08
Taylor, Robt.(Z)	1811	Dec. 09	ZanesvilleOh	10	02	13
Taylor, Robt.(Z)	1811	Dec. 31	MuskingmCoOh	09	03	07
Taylor, Robt.(Z)	1811	Dec. 31	MuskingmCoOh	09	03	14
Taylor, Robt.(Z-M)	1831	June 29	TuscarwsCoOh	02	06	18
Taylor, Samuel(Y)	1836	Nov. 28	Jeff.Co.,Oh.	04	12	03
Taylor, Samuel(Z)	1830	Aug. 30	MuskingmCoOh	14	13	09
Taylor, Samuel(Z)	1809	Nov. 10	WestmrldCoPa	08	02	24
Taylor, Samuel(Z)	1815	May 30	WashCo.,Penn	11	13	11
Taylor, Samuel(Z-M)	1833	Feb. 04	GuernseyCoOh	02	03	13
Taylor, Samuel(Z-M)	1835	Jan. 27	GuernseyCoOh	02	03	13
Taylor, Samuel(Z-M)	1838	July 09	CoshoctnCoOh	03	04	16
Taylor, Thomas Holliday(Y)	1834	April 23	Jeff.Co.,Oh.	03	12	20
Taylor, Thomas Jr.(Z)	1836	Jan. 08	Morgan Co,Oh	09	05	35
Taylor, Thomas Jr.(Z)	1836	Jan. 08	Morgan Co,Oh	09	05	34
Taylor, Will'm.(Z)	1817	June 03	GreeneCo.,Pa	07	08	22
Taylor, William Jr.(Z-M)	1836	June 20	HolmesCoOhio	07	08	24
Taylor, William(Y)	1832	Oct. 12	Jeff.Co.,Oh.	04	12	03
Taylor, William(Y)	1833	May 10	Jeff.Co.,Oh.	04	12	03
Taylor, William(Y)	1836	Feb. 23	Jeff.Co.,Oh.	05	11	34
Taylor, William(Y)	1836	June 23	Jeff.Co.,Oh.	04	12	03
Taylor, William(Z)	1835	July 24	Morgan Co,Oh	09	05	13
Taylor, William(Z)	1836	April 09	Morgan Co,Oh	09	05	10
Taylor, Wm.(Y)	1827	Dec. 19	Jeff.Co.,Oh.	04	12	03
Teal, Lloyd(Z)	1813	Dec. 23	FairfeldCoOh	14	13	05
Teal, Lloyd(Z)	1813	Dec. 23	FairfeldCoOh	14	13	05

PURCHASER	YEAR	DATE	RESIDENCE	R	T	S
Teal, Loyd(Z)	1813	Dec. 23	FairfeldCoOh	14	13	05
Teal, Loyd(Z)	1813	Dec. 23	FairfeldCoOh	14	13	05
Teal, Walter(Z)	1817	Feb. 13	FairfeldCoOh	14	13	04
Teaters, John(Z)	1828	Aug. 25	Morgan Co,Oh	10	07	21
Teatsorth, Isaac Senr.(Y)	1828	Nov. 24	HarrisonCoOh	06	13	10
Teegarden, Geo.(Y)	1826	Nov. 10	ColumbanCoOh	05	17	06
Teegarden, George(Y)	1826	April 19	ColumbanCoOh	05	17	06
Teegarden, William Jnr.(Y)	1826	April 24	ColumbanCoOh	05	17	06
Teegarden, Wm. Jr.(Y)	1826	Oct. 28	ColumbanCoOh	05	18	31
Teegarden, Wm. Jr.(Y)	1827	Jan. 06	ColumbanCoOh	05	17	06
Teel, Edward(Z)	1833	June 13	Perry Co.,Oh	14	13	06
Teel, Losson(Z)	1822	March 24	Perry Co.,Oh	14	13	09
Teeling, Eleanor(Z-M)	1825	March 17	HolmesCoOhio	07	08	24
Teeling, William(Z-M)	1826	Aug. 25	HolmesCoOhio	07	08	24
Teeling, William(Z-M)	1832	May 23	HolmesCoOhio	07	08	24
Teetars, John(Y)	1826	Sept. 21	ColumbanCoOh	06	19	22
Teetars, John(Y)	1826	Sept. 21	ColumbanCoOh	06	19	22
Teetars, John(Y)	1826	Sept. 21	ColumbanCoOh	06	19	22
Teetars, John(Y)	1826	Sept. 21	ColumbanCoOh	06	19	22
Teetars, John(Y)	1826	Sept. 21	ColumbanCoOh	06	19	20
Teeters, Jonathan(Y)	1826	July 17	Stark Co.,Oh	06	19	24
Teeters, Jonathan(Y)	1829	April 22	ColumbanCoOh	06	19	21
Teetors, John(Y)	1826	Nov. 08	ColumbanCoOh	07	20	22
Teetors, John(Y)	1826	Nov. 08	ColumbanCoOh	06	19	17
Templeman, Willis H.(Z)	1835	April 15	Perry Co.,Oh	15	14	02
Templeton, William(Z)	1814	July 14	GuernseyCoOh	01	03	23
Tennant, John(Y)	1837	July 19	SteubenvleCh	04	12	22
Tennant, John(Y)	1837	July 19	SteubenvleCh	04	12	22
Tenor, Henry(Z)	1832	Jan. 10	Morgan Co,Oh	10	08	15
Tenox, John(Y)	1831	July 25	FauquierCoVa	04	11	18
Tenox, John(Y)	1831	July 25	FauquierCoVa	04	11	18
Terrel, Calvin(Z-M)	1837	Feb. 09	MarshallCoVa	03	04	15
Tesling, William(Z-M)	1834	Sept. 11	HolmesCoOhio	07	08	17
Teter, Henry Senr.(Z)	1821	Feb. 13	Morgan Co,Oh	10	07	03
Teter, Henry(Z)	1833	Jan. 08	Morgan Co,Oh	10	07	02
Teter, Henry(Z)	1332	March 02	Morgan Co,Oh	10	08	34
Teter, Samuel(Z)	1828	Dec. 26	Morgan Co,Oh	10	07	04
Teter, Samuel(Z)	1832	Dec. 18	Morgan Co,Oh	10	07	12
Teterick, Nicholas(Z)	1813	May 21	MuskingmCoOh	13	11	17
Teters, John(Z)	1834	Aug. 06	Morgan Co,Oh	10	07	01
Tetirick, Adam(Z-M)	1835	Aug. 07	GuernseyCoOh	02	03	11
Tetrick, Balser(Z)	1806	Sept. 16	MuskingmCoOh	13	11	27
Tetro, Andrew(Z)	1812	May 12	TuscarwsCoOh	01	09	03
Tetter, Henry(Z)	1836	Jan. 11	Morgan Co,Oh	10	07	02
Thachley, Geo.(Z)	1831	July 18	GuernseyCoOh	09	08	33
Thachley, Henry(Z)	1831	Sept. 23	GuernseyCoOh	09	08	24
Tharer, Jonas(Z)	1834	Feb. 17	MuskingmCoOh	10	07	18
Tharp, A.(Z)	1815	Jan. 16	MuskingmCoOh	09	01	22
Tharp, Archibald(Z)	1836	July 18	Perry Co.,Oh	15	14	25
Tharp, David(Z)	1835	July 06	Perry Co.,Oh	15	14	24
Tharp, James(Z-M)	1835	April 21	MuskingmCoOh	03	01	15
Tharp, Jesse(Z)	1834	Feb. 20	Perry Co.,Oh	15	14	25
Tharp, Jesse(Z)	1836	July 05	Perry Co.,Oh	15	14	25
Tharp, Job(Z)	1833	Oct. 16	Perry Co.,Oh	14	13	29
Tharp, Job(Z)	1836	Oct. 04	Perry Co.,Oh	14	12	09
Tharp, John W.(Z)	1835	Nov. 28	Perry Co.,Oh	14	13	31
Tharp, John W.(Z)	1836	Jan. 25	Perry Co.,Oh	14	12	30
Tharp, John Wallace(Z)	1836	Jan. 18	Perry Co.,Oh	14	12	30
Tharp, Leonard(Z)	1833	March 19	Perry Co.,Oh	15	14	23
Tharp, Leonard(Z)	1836	June 24	Perry Co.,Oh	15	14	11
Tharp, Reuben(Z)	1834	Jan. 02	Perry Co.,Oh	15	14	24
Tharp, Reuben(Z)	1835	Nov. 19	FayetteCo,Pa	14	13	31
Tharp, Reuben(Z)	1835	Dec. 10	FayetteCo,Pa	14	12	09
Thatcher, Aaron(Y)	1821	Oct. 04	Stark Co.,Oh	06	16	32
Thatcher, Aaron(Y)	1821	Oct. 04	Stark Co.,Oh	06	15	25
Thatcher, Isaac(Y)	1829	April 07	ColumbanCoOh	06	16	31
Thatcher, Isaac(Z-M)	1823	July 14	CoshoctnCoOh	09	07	03
Thatcher, Isaac(Z-M)	1832	Feb. 29	CoshoctnCoOh	09	07	15
Thatcher, Stephen(Z)	1816	Sept. 25	CoshoctnCoOh	09	07	03

PURCHASER	YEAR	DATE	RESIDENCE	R	T	S
Thayer, Ephraim(Z)	1833	July 09	CoshoctnCoOh	08	08	10
Thayer, Ephraim(Z)	1816	Feb. 14	MuskingmCoOh	06	03	23
Theisz, Peter(Z)	1832	Aug. 18	Morgan Co,Oh	13	10	22
Thempen, Samuel(Z)	1805	Oct. 02	WashCo.,Penn	15	16	05
Thinsby, William(Y)	1831	July 26	Stark Co.,Oh	09	12	17
Thissel, Ezra(Z)	1828	Oct. 14	Morgan Co,Oh	12	11	20
Thissel, Ezra(Z)	1828	Oct. 14	Morgan Co,Oh	12	11	20
Thomas, Benjamin(Z-M)	1833	June 20	GuernseyCoOh	02	01	06
Thomas, Charles(Z)	1817	Aug. 11	WashngtnCoOh	09	05	34
Thomas, Daniel(Z-M)	1835	Nov. 20	HolmesCoOhio	03	09	22
Thomas, Daniel(Z-M)	1836	Sept. 02	TuscarwsCoOh	04	07	13
Thomas, Daniel(Z-M)	1836	Sept. 02	TuscarwsCoOh	04	07	13
Thomas, Enoch(Z)	1814	Jan. 13	GuernseyCoOh	02	01	10
Thomas, Enoch(Z-M)	1825	Jan. 01	GuernseyCoOh	02	01	04
Thomas, Enoch(Z-M)	1828	Aug. 13	GuernseyCoOh	02	01	14
Thomas, George(Z)	1815	Nov. 08	SomersetCoPa	04	07	05
Thomas, George(Z-M)	1828	Oct. 16	SomersetCoPa	05	08	06
Thomas, Henry(Z)	1806	Oct. 07	WashngtnCoMd	03	09	18
Thomas, Henry(Z)	1806	Oct. 07	WashngtnCoMd	03	09	01
Thomas, Isaac(Z)	1810	Aug. 21	TuscarwsCoOh	03	08	10
Thomas, Isaac(Z)	1816	Aug. 26	TuscarwsCoOh	03	08	10
Thomas, Jacob(Z)	1807	May 25	BelmontCo,Oh	02	01	01
Thomas, Jacob(Z)	1807	Oct. 26	WashngtnCoMd	04	08	01
Thomas, Jacob(Z)	1807	Oct. 26	WashngtnCoMd	04	08	09
Thomas, Jacob(Z)	1813	Dec. 28	KnoxCo.,Ohio	11	06	15
Thomas, James(Z)	1828	Oct. 29	GuernseyCoOh	12	09	04
Thomas, James(Z-M)	1831	April 01	CoshoctnCoOh	08	04	09
Thomas, John Junr.(Z)	1833	Nov. 25	Perry Co.,Oh	14	14	19
Thomas, John(Y)	1829	March 25	Stark Co.,Oh	06	16	28
Thomas, John(Z)	1807	Nov. 24	WestmrldCoPa	11	13	12
Thomas, John(Z)	1807	Nov. 24	WestmrldCoPa	11	13	12
Thomas, John(Z-M)	1834	Dec. 03	CoshoctnCoOh	05	07	01
Thomas, Jonathan(Y)	1824	July 10	HarrisonCoOh	07	11	21
Thomas, Jonathan(Z-M)	1824	May 28	HarrisonCoOh	05	02	10
Thomas, Josiah Jr.(Y)	1830	March 11	GuernseyCoOh	07	09	21
Thomas, Levi(Z)	1832	March 24	MuskingmCoOh	11	12	27
Thomas, Levi(Z)	1834	Sept. 27	MuskingmCoOh	11	12	34
Thomas, Philip(Y)	1824	June 22	BelmontCo,Oh	06	08	17
Thomas, Samuel(Z-M)	1832	May 23	GuernseyCoOh	02	03	10
Thomas, Samuel(Z-M)	1836	June 29	BeaverCo.,Pa	08	06	02
Thomas, Samuel(Z-M)	1836	June 29	BeaverCo.,Pa	08	06	02
Thomas, Solomon(Z)	1817	May 10	LoudonCo,Vir	05	02	06
Thomas, William(Z)	1805	Aug. 16	MuskingmCoOh	01	01	01
Thomas, William(Z)	1814	June 24	TuscarwsCoOh	11	05	24
Thomas, William(Z)	1817	Jan. 04	KnoxCo.,Ohio	11	04	04
Thompon, Samuel(Z)	1805	Oct. 02	WashCo.,Penn	15	16	05
Thompson, Ab.(Z-M)	1830	Oct. 05	GuernseyCoOh	02	04	07
Thompson, Abraham(Z)	1836	Jan. 01	GuernseyCoOh	09	08	29
Thompson, Abraham(Z)	1816	Dec. 10	GuernseyCoOh	09	08	28
Thompson, Abraham(Z-M)	1832	April 13	GuernseyCoOh	03	04	13
Thompson, Abraham(Z-M)	1832	May 22	GuernseyCoOh	02	04	15
Thompson, Andrew(Z)	1806	March 31	BelmontCo,Oh	08	08	08
Thompson, Andrew(Z)	1808	Aug. 27	LancastrCoPa	06	01	20
Thompson, Ann(Y)	1832	Feb. 21	HarrisonCoOh	06	12	11
Thompson, Bradway(Z)	1816	June 21	HarrisonCoOh	01	04	19
Thompson, David(Y)	1823	July 30	BelmontCo,Oh	07	09	21
Thompson, David(Y)	1823	Sept. 20	BelmontCo,Oh	07	09	21
Thompson, David(Y)	1824	Oct. 23	ColumbanCoOh	07	20	27
Thompson, David(Z)	1816	July 15	MuskingmCoOh	04	02	16
Thompson, David(Z-M)	1831	May 28	GuernseyCoOh	02	01	08
Thompson, Eli'u.(Y)	1830	Sept. 25	HarrisonCoOh	06	14	35
Thompson, Elijah(Z)	1811	Jan. 18	GuernseyCoOh	09	08	20
Thompson, Elijah(Z)	1811	Jan. 18	GuernseyCoOh	09	08	17
Thompson, Elijah(Z)	1815	April 20	GuernseyCoOh	09	08	20
Thompson, George(Z)	1834	Aug. 07	Perry Co.,Oh	14	12	11
Thompson, George(Z)	1836	Feb. 10	Perry Co.,Oh	14	12	11
Thompson, Hugh(Y)	1828	Dec. 06	ColumbanCoOh	04	14	25
Thompson, Hugh(Y)	1829	March 17	ColumbanCoOh	04	14	35
Thompson, Hugh(Y)	1829	Dec. 07	ColumbanCoOh	04	13	09

PURCHASER	YEAR	DATE	RESIDENCE	R	T	S
Thompson, Hugh(Y)	1831	Oct. 19	ColumbanCoOh	04	13	06
Thompson, Hugh(Z)	1823	July 01	BelmontCo,Oh	13	08	35
Thompson, J.(Z)	1815	April 20	GuernseyCoOh	08	08	09
Thompson, Jacob(Z)	1825	Oct. 21	GuernseyCoOh	08	08	15
Thompson, Jacob(Z)	1832	Nov. 28	GuernseyCoOh	08	08	18
Thompson, Jacob(Z)	1811	Jan. 18	FayetteCo,Pa	09	08	27
Thompson, Jacob(Z)	1811	April 20	GuernseyCoOh	08	08	17
Thompson, James(Z)	1824	Sept. 29	GuernseyCoOh	09	08	10
Thompson, James(Z)	1810	May 26	FayetteCo,Pa	09	03	11
Thompson, James(Z)	1813	April 29	CoshoctnCoOh	09	04	12
Thompson, Jno.(Y)	1822	Nov. 19	HarrisonCoOh	06	12	10
Thompson, John Junr.(Y)	1831	June 03	BelmontCo,Oh	03	05	01
Thompson, John Sen.(Z-M)	1836	Oct. 18	Jeff.Co.,Oh.	03	04	10
Thompson, John(Y)	1831	March 09	ColumbanCoOh	04	13	06
Thompson, John(Y)	1833	April 01	Jeff.Co.,Oh.	04	12	36
Thompson, John(Y)	1834	Dec. 30	CarrollCo,Oh	04	13	14
Thompson, John(Z)	1823	July 01	BelmontCo,Oh	13	08	36
Thompson, John(Z)	1832	Dec. 27	Morgan Co,Oh	09	07	13
Thompson, John(Z)	1835	Oct. 22	Morgan Co,Oh	13	08	36
Thompson, John(Z)	1811	Jan. 18	GuernseyCoOh	09	08	28
Thompson, John(Z)	1811	Jan. 18	GuernseyCoOh	09	08	28
Thompson, John(Z)	1812	May 04	MuskingmCoOh	15	17	32
Thompson, John(Z)	1813	Aug. 19	MuskingmCoOh	15	15	08
Thompson, John(Z)	1815	Aug. 26	MuskingmCoOh	14	13	01
Thompson, John(Z)	1815	Nov. 24	MuskingmCoOh	14	13	11
Thompson, John(Z-M)	1824	Sept. 06	CoshoctnCoOh	08	04	11
Thompson, John(Z-M)	1829	Feb. 14	MuskingmCoOh	06	02	24
Thompson, John(Z-M)	1832	April 03	GuernseyCoOh	03	04	09
Thompson, John(Z-M)	1830	June 25	HarrisonCoOh	01	06	11
Thompson, John(Z-M)	1833	April 19	BelmontCo,Oh	03	04	01
Thompson, John(Z-M)	1833	June 12	GuernseyCoOh	03	04	09
Thompson, John(Z-M)	1833	June 12	GuernseyCoOh	03	04	12
Thompson, John(Z-M)	1837	Aug. 12	GuernseyCoOh	03	04	10
Thompson, John(Z-M)	1839	June 06	TuscarwsCoOh	03	05	23
Thompson, John(Z-M)	1839	June 13	TuscarwsCoOh	03	05	23
Thompson, Johnston(Z)	1804	Nov. 24	WestmrldCoPa	14	15	10
Thompson, Johnston(Z)	1805	May 04	WestmrldCoPa	14	15	04
Thompson, Johnston(Z)	1816	Nov. 11	MuskingmCoOh	13	09	14
Thompson, Johnston(Z)	1816	Nov. 11	MuskingmCoOh	13	09	14
Thompson, Johnston(Z)	1816	Nov. 12	MuskingmCoOh	12	10	05
Thompson, Johnston(Z)	1816	Nov. 12	MuskingmCoOh	13	09	25
Thompson, Jos. L.(Z)	1831	April 15	Morgan Co,Oh	11	11	15
Thompson, Josias(Y)	1828	Dec. 22	HarrisonCoOh	05	12	29
Thompson, Martin(Z-M)	1834	Oct. 09	Jeff.Co.,Oh.	03	04	10
Thompson, Moses(Z)	1815	Oct. 17	CoshoctnCoOh	06	07	22
Thompson, Pierce C.(Y)	1825	Aug. 25	ColumbanCoOh	07	20	04
Thompson, Rob't.(Y)	1828	April 18	Stark Co.,Oh	07	17	12
Thompson, Robert(Y)	1830	Nov. 29	Stark Co.,Oh	07	17	12
Thompson, Robert(Z)	1811	Aug. 23	GuernseyCoOh	08	08	06
Thompson, Robert(Z)	1813	July 08	BelmontCo,Oh	01	02	14
Thompson, Sam'l.(Z-M)	1831	March 05	KnoxCo.,Ohio	11	05	20
Thompson, Samuel(Y)	1828	March 21	ColumbanCoOh	02	10	31
Thompson, Samuel(Z)	1806	July 01	MuskingmCoOh	15	16	18
Thompson, Samuel(Z)	1810	Nov. 02	ZanesvilleOh	05	01	17
Thompson, Samuel(Z)	1811	Jan. 23	MuskingmCoOh	15	17	05
Thompson, Samuel(Z)	1811	April 16	ZanesvilleOh	08	08	11
Thompson, Samuel(Z)	1811	May 22	MuskingmCoOh	01	02	07
Thompson, Samuel(Z)	1813	May 26	ZanesvilleOh	14	16	10
Thompson, Samuel(Z)	1816	Dec. 10	ZanesvilleOh	01	02	07
Thompson, Samuel(Z)	1817	Jan. 18	ZanesvilleOh	06	02	04
Thompson, Thomas(Z-M)	1836	May 18	CarrollCo,Oh	03	07	15
Thompson, Thomas(Z-M)	1836	May 27	CarrollCo,Oh	03	07	16
Thompson, Will'm.(Z)	1816	June 20	MuskingmCoOh	13	10	27
Thompson, William(Z)	1804	Dec. 31	WestmrldCoPa	14	15	11
Thompson, William(Z)	1810	May 26	FayetteCo,Pa	08	08	07
Thompson, William(Z)	1812	Feb. 15	MuskingmCoOh	05	03	05
Thompson, William(Z)	1816	Nov. 23	WashCo.,Penn	02	01	04
Thompson, William(Z-M)	1833	March 18	CoshoctnCoOh	07	05	04
Thompson, Wm.(Y)	1827	June 05	Jeff.Co.,Oh.	04	12	19

PURCHASER	YEAR	DATE	RESIDENCE	R	T	S
Thompson, Wm.(Z)	1811	Dec. 26	MuskingmCoOh	05	03	05
Thompson, Wm.(Z-M)	1829	Feb. 14	MuskingmCoOh	06	02	24
Thorla, Benjamin(Z)	1825	May 16	Morgan Co,Oh	09	07	21
Thorla, Richard(Z)	1836	Jan. 25	Morgan Co,Oh	10	08	27
Thornburg, Absalom(Z-M)	1834	Feb. 11	KnoxCo.,Ohio	10	05	22
Thornburgh, B.(Z-M)	1831	Feb. 16	HarrisonCoOh	01	06	09
Thornburgh, Benjamin(Z-M)	1836	May 02	TuscarwsCoOh	01	06	08
Thornbury, Lewis(Z)	1836	Aug. 03	WashngtnCoOh	08	05	14
Thorne, Michael(Z)	1807	March 04	FairfeldCoOh	10	02	16
Thorne, Michael(Z)	1813	Aug. 17	LickingCo,Oh	10	02	16
Thornton, James(Z)	1836	Aug. 03	Morgan Co,Oh	10	07	10
Thornton, Samuel(Y)	1834	Dec. 12	Stark Co.,Oh	09	12	33
Thorp, Abner(Z)	1836	May 30	Perry Co.,Oh	14	12	05
Thorp, James(Z)	1832	Nov. 09	Perry Co.,Oh	15	14	24
Thorp, James(Z)	1832	Nov. 12	Perry Co.,Oh	15	14	24
Thorp, John W.(Z)	1833	April 16	Perry Co.,Oh	14	13	32
Thorp, John(Y)	1823	May 14	PhladlhaCoPa	05	18	13
Thorp, Reuben(Z)	1833	April 23	Perry Co.,Oh	14	12	19
Thrailkile, Taliver(Z-M)	1836	Sept. 27	MuskingmCoOh	10	04	18
Thrailkill, T.(Z)	1815	Jan. 16	MuskingmCoOh	09	01	22
Thrap, David(Z)	1834	Jan. 03	Perry Co.,Oh	15	14	24
Throush, Casper(Z-M)	1835	Oct. 30	CoshoctnCoOh	06	04	20
Thrush, Jno.(Z)	1817	Sept. 19	ZanesvilleOh	14	14	02
Thrush, John W.(Z)	1833	March 11	Morgan Co,Oh	14	14	34
Thrush, John(Z)	1829	Feb. 18	MuskingmCoOh	14	14	27
Thurla, Daniel(Z)	1835	Dec. 18	MarionCoOhio	08	06	07
Thurld, Daniel(Z)	1834	Jan. 04	Morgan Co,Oh	09	06	13
Thurlo, Daniel(Z)	1833	April 15	Morgan Co,Oh	09	06	13
Thurlo, John(Z)	1826	April 19	Morgan Co,Oh	09	07	36
Thurlo, Rhoda(Z)	1833	March 30	Morgan Co,Oh	09	06	11
Thurlo, Silas(Z)	1814	Aug. 29	GuernseyCoOh	09	06	02
Thurlow, John(Z)	1823	June 07	Morgan Co,Oh	10	08	26
Thursh, John W.(Z)	1833	Jan. 23	Morgan Co,Oh	14	14	34
Thustin, Jacob(Y)	1822	Sept. 12	BeaverCo,Pa.	01	07	22
Tichner, Aaron(Z)	1836	Aug. 20	MonroeCo.,Oh	08	07	20
Tidball, Brownhill(Z-M)	1827	Aug. 25	AlleghnyCoPa	07	09	20
Tidball, Wm. B.(Z-M)	1833	Aug. 02	HolmesCoOhio	06	09	24
Tidball, Wm. B.(Z-M)	1837	Sept. 26	HolmesCoOhio	09	09	04
Tidball, Wm. B.(Z-M)	1837	Sept. 26	HolmesCoOhio	09	08	01
Tilden, Jason(Z)	1827	Jan. 09	Morgan Co,Oh	10	08	07
Tilton, Alden D.(Z)	1834	Aug. 01	Morgan Co,Oh	09	06	27
Tilton, Alden(Z)	1836	Feb. 29	Morgan Co,Oh	09	06	27
Tilton, Elijah Jr.(Z-M)	1836	Aug. 09	KnoxCo.,Ohio	10	08	04
Tilton, Elijah Jun.(Z-M)	1832	March 02	CoshoctnCoOh	07	04	18
Tilton, Elijah Jun.(Z-M)	1832	March 02	CoshoctnCoOh	10	08	06
Tilton, Elijah Jun.(Z-M)	1832	March 01	CoshoctnCoOh	10	08	05
Tilton, Elijah(Z)	1816	March 09	CoshoctnCoOh	10	05	01
Tilton, Elijah(Z-M)	1828	Sept. 22	KnoxCo.,Ohio	10	05	17
Tilton, Hebron(Z)	1832	May 23	Morgan Co,Oh	09	06	27
Tilton, Hebron(Z)	1832	May 23	Morgan Co,Oh	09	06	28
Tilton, Hebron(Z)	1836	Oct. 21	Morgan Co,Oh	09	06	35
Tilton, Hebron(Z)	1836	Oct. 21	Morgan Co,Oh	09	06	35
Tilton, John Perkins(Z-M)	1836	Sept. 09	CoshoctnCoOh	07	04	11
Tilton, John(Z)	1811	April 17	WashngtnCoOh	11	05	04
Tilton, John(Z)	1814	Nov. 22	WashCo.,Penn	11	05	07
Tilton, Joseph W.(Z)	1836	July 01	Morgan Co,Oh	09	06	27
Tilton, Josephus(Z-M)	1836	April 12	KnoxCo.,Ohio	10	08	05
Tilton, Matthew(Z)	1834	Aug. 01	Morgan Co,Oh	09	06	27
Tilton, Matthew(Z)	1836	Feb. 29	Morgan Co,Oh	09	06	22
Tilton, Rich'd.(Z-M)	1831	Nov. 03	CoshoctnCoOh	07	04	17
Tilton, Richard(Z)	1805	Aug. 21	MuskingmCoOh	07	04	16
Tilton, Richard(Z)	1814	Feb. 24	?	07	04	16
Tilton, William C.(Z-M)	1835	July 16	KnoxCo.,Ohio	10	08	04
Tilton, Wm.of Elijah(Z-M)	1828	Sept. 22	KnoxCo.,Ohio	10	05	24
Timmerman, Henry(Z-M)	1833	March 11	Jeff.Co.,Oh.	01	05	04
Timmerman, John(Y)	1831	July 05	Stark Co.,Oh	07	18	13
Timony, D.(Z)	1814	Nov. 28	GuernseyCoOh	08	08	20
Timony, Patrick(Z)	1814	Jan. 28	GuernseyCoOh	08	08	09
Timony, Peter(Z)	1814	Nov. 28	GuernseyCoOh	08	08	20

PURCHASER	YEAR	DATE	RESIDENCE	R	T	S
Tingle, George R.(Z)	1814	Feb. 21	Cambridge,Oh	03	02	03
Tingle, George R.(Z)	1815	Oct. 12	Cambridge,Oh	03	01	11
Tingle, John(Z)	1816	Aug. 12	GuernseyCoOh	03	01	14
Tingle, John(Z-M)	1824	Feb. 10	GuernseyCoOh	03	01	18
Tingley, William(Y)	1831	May 14	Cadiz, Ohio	06	11	30
Tingley, Wm.(Y)	1825	Jan. 27	HarrisonCoOh	06	11	23
Tinker, Alex'r.(Z)	1836	Oct. 31	Perry Co.,Oh	14	12	25
Tinker, Alex'r.(Z)	1836	Oct. 31	Perry Co.,Oh	14	12	26
Tinker, Alex'r.(Z)	1836	Oct. 31	Perry Co.,Oh	14	12	26
Tiptin, Samuel(Y)	1829	March 23	HarrisonCoOh	06	12	20
Tipton, Absalom(Z)	1811	April 22	BelmontCo,Oh	04	04	07
Tipton, Absalom(Z)	1816	May 31	CoshoctnCoOh	09	05	01
Tipton, Absolam(Z)	1811	May 18	MuskingmCoOh	15	17	22
Tipton, Absolam(Z)	1813	May 25	MuskingmCoOh	15	17	33
Tipton, Jonathan(Z-M)	1833	Sept. 10	TuscarwsCoOh	03	06	07
Tipton, Jonathan(Z-M)	1835	Dec. 01	HolmesCoOhio	09	09	17
Tipton, Jonathan(Z-M)	1835	Dec. 01	HolmesCoOhio	09	09	16
Tipton, Jonathan(Z-M)	1836	Aug. 10	HolmesCoOhio	09	09	25
Tipton, Luke Junr.(Z-M)	1823	April 28	CoshoctnCoOh	07	08	04
Tipton, Luke Senr.(Z)	1816	Aug. 15	Jeff.Co.,Oh.	06	07	08
Tipton, Luke Senr.(Z)	1816	Sept. 30	CoshoctnCoOh	05	06	16
Tipton, Samuel(Z-M)	1836	March 31	TuscarwsCoOh	09	09	24
Tipton, Solomon(Z)	1813	Aug. 19	CoshoctnCoOh	08	05	15
Tipton, Sylverton(Y)	1823	April 28	HarrisonCoOh	04	10	18
Tipton, Thomas(Z)	1815	Oct. 28	BelmontCo,Oh	08	05	05
Tipton, William(Z-M)	1823	May 10	CoshoctnCoOh	07	08	03
Tipton, William(Z-M)	1824	Aug. 02	CoshoctnCoOh	07	09	20
Tison, John(Z)	1816	Nov. 13	WashngtnCoOh	11	11	34
Tison, Zephaniah(Z)	1810	Sept. 20	BelmontCo,Oh	11	10	02
Titareck, Balser(Z)	1807	May 04	MuskingmCoOh	13	11	27
Titareck, Balser(Z)	1807	May 04	MuskingmCoOh	13	11	24
Titareck, Balser(Z)	1807	May 04	MuskingmCoOh	13	11	17
Titareck, Balser(Z)	1807	May 04	MuskingmCoOh	14	16	14
Titareck, Nicholas(Z)	1807	May 04	MuskingmCoOh	13	11	27
Titarick, Balser(Z)	1806	May 24	MuskingmCoOh	14	16	11
Titerick, Jacob Senr.(Z)	1811	July 30	GuernseyCoOh	01	03	15
Titerick, Jacob(Z)	1814	June 13	GuernseyCoOh	01	03	19
Titerick, John Junr.(Z)	1811	April 19	GuernseyCoOh	01	03	14
Titerick, Michael(Z)	1814	June 13	GuernseyCoOh	01	03	23
Titirick, Michael(Z)	1814	Aug. 11	GuernseyCoOh	01	03	06
Titirik, Balser(Z)	1815	Nov. 20	MuskingmCoOh	13	11	27
Titrack, Balser(Z)	1807	June 15	MuskingmCoOh	15	18	11
Titrick, Balser(Z)	1806	May 06	MuskingmCoOh	14	16	11
Titrick, Jacob(Z)	1805	Sept. 23	BelmontCo,Oh	01	03	15
Tittrick, John(Z)	1814	June 28	GuernseyCoOh	01	03	16
Titus, Rachel(Y)	1831	July 14	HarrisonCoOh	06	11	28
Tobin, Isaac(Z-M)	1833	June 04	GuernseyCoOh	02	04	14
Tobin, John(Z-M)	1836	Sept. 24	GuernseyCoOh	03	04	12
Tobin, Nathaniel(Z-M)	1836	Oct. 28	GuernseyCoOh	03	04	09
Todd, Edward(Z-M)	1835	March 06	KnoxCo.,Ohio	11	04	09
Todd, John(Y)	1833	Dec. 12	ColumbanCoOh	03	12	14
Todd, John(Z)	1807	June 23	Ohio Co.,Vir	15	18	08
Todd, John(Z)	1817	Feb. 17	MuskingmCoOh	11	10	06
Todd, Joshua(Y)	1821	May 03	ColumbanCoOh	03	12	07
Todd, Joshua(Y)	1833	March 12	ColumbanCoOh	01	06	01
Todd, Lot(Y)	1823	Nov. 17	ColumbanCoOh	03	13	21
Todd, Thomas W.(Z-M)	1833	Jan. 25	CoshoctnCoOh	09	04	17
Todd, Thomas(Y)	1833	June 27	BeaverCo.,Pa	01	06	01
Todd, Thomas(Z-M)	1837	Feb. 20	BeaverCo.,Pa	08	07	22
Todel, John(Z)	1807	Oct. 16	Ohio Co.,Vir	15	18	05
Toffin, Robert(Z)	1827	Oct. 22	GreeneCoOhio	01	06	22
Toland, Benjamin(Y)	1828	May 17	HarrisonCoOh	05	12	29
Toland, James(Y)	1826	May 13	Beaver Co,Pa	04	13	28
Toland, James(Y)	1826	June 09	BeaverCo.,Pa	04	13	22
Toland, John(Z)	1816	June 03	Jeff.Co.,Oh.	01	03	04
Toland, William(Y)	1831	May 26	ColumbanCoOh	04	13	28
Tolbert, Benjamin(Z)	1813	Nov. 20	BrookCo.,Vir	11	11	29
Tolbot, Eskridge H.(Z)	1833	Dec. 13	Morgan Co,Oh	13	08	24
Toles, Lewis(Z-M)	1835	Feb. 28	MuskingmCoOh	09	03	14

PURCHASER	YEAR	DATE	RESIDENCE	R	T	S
Toles, Lewis(Z-M)	1835	Sept. 05	MuskingmCoOh	09	03	14
Tolman, Chester(Z)	1836	July 21	WashngtnCoOh	08	05	27
Tomer, John(Z-M)	1829	Jan. 06	TuscarwsCoOh	02	10	15
Tomkins, Jonah(Z-M)	1836	March 14	CoshoctnCoOh	07	05	07
Tomlinson, Phineas(Z-M)	1833	March 15	MuskingmCoOh	06	03	22
Tomlinson, Thomas(Y)	1831	June 08	HarrisonCoOh	05	12	26
Tomlinson, Thomas(Z)	1816	March 16	WashngtnCoOh	14	13	02
Tomlinson, Thos.(Z)	1831	July 01	ZanesvilleOh	12	12	04
Tompkin, Gerard(Z)	1808	Nov. 16	BaltimreCoMd	05	01	09
Toner, Charles(Z-M)	1823	Nov. 03	WashCo.,Penn	04	02	14
Toner, Charles(Z-M)	1826	May 11	GuernseyCoOh	04	02	14
Tonner, John(Z-M)	1835	April 04	HarrisonCoOh	03	05	21
Toohey, Patrick(Z)	1835	March 31	MordganCo,Oh	10	06	18
Tool, John(Z-M)	1834	Feb. 18	HarrisonCoOh	03	04	01
Tool, John(Z-M)	1834	March 22	HarrisonCoOh	03	05	21
Toot, George(Y)	1824	Oct. 13	Jeff.Co.,Oh.	05	13	28
Toothman, Michael(Z-M)	1832	Aug. 31	KnoxCo.,Ohio	10	04	09
Tope, Henry(Y)	1827	May 01	Jeff.Co.,Oh.	06	14	02
Tope, Jacob(Y)	1832	Feb. 10	HarrisonCoOh	06	14	27
Tope, John(Z)	1832	Oct. 09	Morgan Co,Oh	11	11	02
Tope, John(Z)	1834	Dec. 12	Morgan Co,Oh	10	08	31
Tope, Levi(Z-M)	1828	April 03	HolmesCoOhio	05	08	08
Tope, Susan'ah.(Z-M)	1828	April 03	HolmesCoOhio	05	08	08
Torode, Jno.(Z)	1817	Oct. 17	Cambridge,Oh	13	09	35
Torode, John(Z-M)	1836	April 27	GuernseyCoOh	03	01	04
Torppy, Wm.(Z-M)	1839	April 20	ColumbanCoOh	08	07	03
Torppy, Wm.(Z-M)	1839	April 20	ColumbanCoOh	08	07	03
Torrence, Joseph(Z)	1811	Oct. 14	FayetteCo,Pa	09	08	13
Tossel, Daniel(Y)	1831	July 25	TuscarwsCoOh	07	15	30
Totten, Samuel(Y)	1827	Sept. 13	ColumbanCoOh	06	16	05
Tounsley, Joseph R.(Z-M)	1838	Aug. 01	CoshoctnCoOh	05	07	24
Townsend, David(Z)	1816	June 17	HarrisonCoOh	01	05	21
Townsend, John(Y)	1824	March 12	GuernseyCoOh	07	09	07
Townsend, Talbot/(Y)	1832	March 26	Jeff.Co.,Oh.	02	09	20
Townshend, Robert(Z-M)	1834	March 12	GuernseyCoOh	03	01	06
Trace, Mathias(Z)	1815	May 13	WashCo.,Penn	05	02	11
Trace, Matthias(Z-M)	1835	March 25	MuskingmCoOh	04	03	17
Tracey, Andrew(Z)	1827	Nov. 01	BelmontCo,Oh	11	11	33
Track, Adam(Z)	1835	May 18	Morgan Co,Oh	09	06	29
Track, Adam(Z)	1835	Sept. 22	Morgan Co,Oh	09	06	29
Tracy, Andrew(Z)	1831	May 25	Morgan Co,Oh	11	10	11
Tracy, Andw.(Z)	1828	Dec. 13	BelmontCo,Oh	11	11	33
Tracy, Basil(Z)	1813	April 17	LickingCo,Oh	11	01	18
Trainer, John(Z)	1832	Dec. 12	BelmontCo,Oh	10	07	27
Traner, John(Z)	1828	Oct. 24	Jeff.Co.,Oh.	12	10	10
Travis, John S.(Z-M)	1834	July 28	TuscarwsCoOh	04	07	03
Travis, Robert(Y)	1832	Feb. 15	ColumbanCoOh	03	13	24
Trefts, George(Y)	1830	June 19	ColumbanCoOh	06	19	21
Trego, Daniel(Y)	1824	June 23	ColumbanCoOh	05	18	22
Trenner, Henry(Z)	1821	June 16	GuernseyCoOh	09	08	31
Trenner, Michael(Z)	1833	Nov. 15	Morgan Co,Oh	09	07	06
Tresslen, Michael(Y)	1827	Nov. 23	Stark Co.,Oh	07	17	19
Treux, Richard(Z)	1834	Feb. 05	Perry Co,.Oh	15	14	28
Trible, George(Y)	1831	Nov. 15	HarrisonCoOh	05	11	34
Trimble, Hugh(Z-M)	1836	Jan. 16	MuskingmCoOh	05	03	03
Trimble, James(Z-M)	1828	Feb. 25	MuskingmCoOh	05	03	14
Trimble, James(Z-M)	1828	May 06	MuskingmCoOh	05	03	14
Trimble, John(Z)	1815	May 15	WashCo.,Penn	09	05	06
Trimble, John(Z)	1815	Nov. 17	?	09	05	05
Trimmer, Anthony Jr.(Z-M)	1836	Nov. 01	WashCo.,Penn	03	07	16
Trinner, Michael(Z)	1824	May 10	GuernseyCoOh	09	07	06
Trioh, John(Y)	1835	Jan. 06	Stark Co.,Oh	07	16	05
Triplett, Joel(Z)	1827	March 19	MuskingmCoOh	13	11	19
Triplett, Phebe(Z)	1826	Jan. 24	MuskingmCoOh	13	11	28
Tripp, Caleb(Y)	1826	Oct. 04	WashCo.,Penn	06	13	24
Tripp, David(Y)	1829	May 28	WashCo.,Penn	06	13	24
Tripp, Joseph(Y)	1822	June 05	WashCo.,Penn	07	11	22
Tripp, Sylvester(Y)	1826	Sept. 30	WashCo.,Penn	06	13	24
Trippeer, John(Z-M)	1832	June 19	LickingCo,Oh	11	03	15

PURCHASER	YEAR	DATE	RESIDENCE	R	T	S
Trippeer, John(Z-M)	1836	Jan. 25	LickingCo,Oh	11	03	05
Trippy, George(Y)	1831	Nov. 08	ColumbanCoOh	04	14	36
Trisch, Henry(Y)	1824	Oct. 20	Stark Co.,Oh	09	11	17
Trish, Christian(Y)	1830	July 08	Stark Co.,Oh	09	11	11
Troger, Joseph(Z-M)	1829	Jan. 28	HolmesCoOhio	05	09	03
Tronor, Michael(Z)	1832	Aug. 15	Morgan Co,Oh	09	08	31
Trott, John(Z-M)	1832	April 03	BelmontCo,Oh	01	03	19
Troup, Jacob(Y)	1824	June 09	Canton, Ohio	09	11	25
Trout, Casper(Z)	1831	March 30	Morgan Co,Oh	14	13	13
Trout, Henry(Y)	1824	June 23	Canton, Ohio	09	11	26
Trout, Noah(Z)	1816	Oct. 15	RcknghmCoVir	11	01	12
Trowbridge, Caleb(Z)	1835	Sept. 28	Morgan Co,Oh	09	05	36
Trowbridge, Caleb(Z)	1835	Sept. 28	Morgan Co,Oh	09	05	25
Trowbridge, Walter(Z)	1833	Sept. 10	Morgan Co,Oh	09	05	25
Trowbridge, Walter(Z)	1833	Sept. 10	Morgan Co,Oh	09	05	36
Troyer, David(Z)	1816	June 11	CoshoctnCoOh	05	08	03
Troyer, David(Z-M)	1830	Oct. 22	HolmesCoOhio	05	08	06
Troyer, Jonathan(Z-M)	1835	March 07	HolmesCoOhio	05	08	15
Troyer, Joseph(Z)	1814	Jan. 12	SomersetCoPa	05	09	06
Troyer, Joseph(Z)	1815	June 06	CoshoctnCoOh	05	08	04
Troyer, Joseph(Z-M)	1828	July 23	HolmesCoOhio	05	09	03
Troyer, Joseph(Z-M)	1833	July 22	HolmesCoOhio	05	10	04
Troyer, Michael(Z)	1817	May 15	TuscarwsCoOh	05	08	09
Troyer, Michael(Z)	1816	Dec. 18	TuscarwsCoOh	04	08	06
Troyer, Michael(Z-M)	1832	March 08	HolmesCoOhio	05	08	08
True, Moses(Z)	1835	Jan. 08	WashngtnCoOh	08	05	36
True, Moses(Z)	1836	Aug. 20	WashngtnCoOh	08	05	24
True, Thomas(Y)	1820	July 03	BelmontCo,Oh	07	15	19
True, William(Y)	1832	Oct. 24	TuscarwsCoOh	07	14	24
Trueman, Benjamin(Y)	1831	May 30	BelmontCo,Oh	07	15	31
Trueman, Robert P.(Y)	1831	May 30	BelmontCo,Oh	07	15	31
Truex, Henry(Z)	1836	March 01	Perry Co.,Oh	15	14	29
Truex, Joseph(Z)	1836	March 10	Perry Co.,Oh	15	14	29
Truex, Joseph(Z)	1825	Oct. 04	Perry Co.,Oh	15	14	29
Truex, Thomas(Y)	1831	May 30	TuscarwsCoOh	07	15	19
Trumbley, Josiah(Z)	1816	Jan. 29	KnoxCo.,Ohio	10	08	22
Trumlo, Mathias(Z)	1805	Oct. 28	FairfeldCoOh	11	01	13
Trump, Jacob(Z-M)	1836	Nov. 09	HolmesCoOhio	05	07	01
Trumpt, Jacob(Z)	1816	Sept. 30	KnoxCo.,Ohio	11	05	19
Tschramer, Jno.(Y)	1827	Aug. 29	Stark Co.,Oh	06	16	03
Tschramer, Jno.(Y)	1827	Aug. 29	Stark Co.,Oh	06	16	03
Tucker, John W.(Z)	1833	Nov. 09	Perry Co.,Oh	14	14	31
Tucker, Jones(Z-M)	1836	Oct. 31	KnoxCo.,Ohio	10	08	20
Tucker, Obadiah(Z-M)	1836	Nov. 02	KnoxCo.,Ohio	10	08	20
Tucker, William(Z)	1816	Jan. 12	KnoxCo.,Ohio	10	08	20
Tucker, William(Z-M)	1836	Nov. 28	KnoxCo.,Ohio	09	08	15
Tucker, William(Z-M)	1836	Nov. 28	KnoxCo.,Ohio	09	08	14
Tucker, William(Z-M)	1836	Dec. 14	KnoxCo.,Ohio	09	08	15
Tudor, William(Z)	1815	May 09	MuskingmCoOh	09	01	11
Tunis, Henry(Z-M)	1832	Dec. 17	MuskingmCoOh	09	03	17
Tunis, Henry(Z-M)	1832	Dec. 17	MuskingmCoOh	09	03	16
Tunis, Henry(Z-M)	1836	March 10	MuskingmCoOh	09	03	16
Tunis, Juliana(Z-M)	1833	June 15	MuskingmCoOh	09	03	16
Turkle, John(Y)	1821	Oct. 23	BelmontCo,Oh	07	10	15
Turkle, Joseph(Y)	1821	Oct. 24	GuernseyCoOh	07	10	15
Turnbull, Robert(Y)	1823	Oct. 10	TrumbullCoOh	04	17	09
Turner, Benjamin(Z)	1806	Oct. 21	FairfeldCoOh	14	15	17
Turner, Henry(Z-M)	1832	Oct. 01	HolmesCoOhio	09	08	17
Turner, Isaac(Z)	1813	Oct. 02	MuskingmCoOh	14	15	04
Turner, James(Z-M)	1835	Oct. 31	HarrisonCoOh	01	06	10
Turner, Jane(Z)	1816	April 05	PutnamCoOhio	14	15	25
Turner, Joseph(Z)	1807	Jan. 31	FairfeldCoOh	14	16	14
Turner, Thomp'sn.(Z-M)	1831	Dec. 14	TuscarwsCoOh	01	08	02
Turner, Walter(Z-M)	1832	Sept. 25	CoshoctnCoOh	09	07	23
Turner, Wm.(Y)	1829	March 25	TuscarwsCoOh	07	12	27
Turney, Solomon(Z-M)	1834	March 07	HarrisonCoOh	03	06	16
Tuttle, Church B.(Z)	1835	April 24	MonroeCo.,Oh	08	07	06
Tuttle, Daniel(Z)	1836	June 20	Morgan Co,Oh	09	06	29
Tuttle, Joel(Z)	1836	Sept. 02	Morgan Co,Oh	09	06	27

PURCHASER	YEAR	DATE	RESIDENCE	R	T	S
Twaddle, Alexander(Y)	1836	April 26	CarrollCo,Oh	04	12	12
Twaddle, Philip(Y)	1831	Aug. 24	Jeff.Co.,Oh.	04	12	17
Twaddle, William(Y)	1835	July 10	Jeff.Co.,Oh.	04	12	12
Twadle, William(Y)	1834	Sept. 02	Jeff.Co.,Oh.	04	12	12
Twig, Jesse(Z)	1836	Dec. 07	Perry Co.,Oh	14	12	02
Twig, William(Z)	1836	Dec. 06	Perry Co.,Oh	14	13	27
Twig, William(Z)	1836	Dec. 06	Perry Co.,Oh	14	13	22
Twigg, Robert(Z-M)	1832	June 15	HarrisonCoOh	01	06	22
Tye, Peter(Z)	1816	April 23	TuscarwsCoOh	05	08	14
Udell, John Junior(Z)	1837	May 23	AshtbulaCoOh	08	06	03
Uhl, Charles(Z)	1811	July 04	AlleghnyCoPa	07	09	19
Uhl, Charles(Z)	1811	July 04	AlleghnyCoOh	07	09	23
Uhl, Charles(Z)	1817	Oct. 03	AlleghnyCoMd	07	08	20
Uhl, Charles(Z)	1817	Oct. 03	AlleghnyCoMd	07	08	11
Uhrich, John(Z-M)	1828	April 23	TuscarwsCoOh	01	06	16
Uhrich, John(Z-M)	1828	April 23	TuscarwsCoOh	01	06	16
Uhrich, John(Z-M)	1828	April 23	TuscarwsCoOh	01	06	16
Uian, William(Z-M)	1839	Feb. 25	KnoxCo.,Ohio	10	08	10
Uion, Frederick Jr.(Z)	1836	Nov. 28	MuskingmCoOh	15	14	36
Ulrg, John(Z)	1815	June 13	GreeneCo.,Pa	11	06	22
Umbaugh, Jno.(Y)	1823	Dec. 15	Stark Co.,Oh	06	15	05
Umbaugh, John(Y)	1830	Aug. 26	Stark Co.,Oh	06	16	35
Umbenhower, Abraham(Z-M)	1834	Aug. 09	MuskingmCoOh	10	03	04
Umberhower, Abraham(Z-M)	1835	Sept. 18	LickingCo,Oh	10	03	03
Umstot, Abraham(Z)	1810	Dec. 04	GuernseyCoOh	01	02	05
Umstot, Peter(Z)	1806	Aug. 19	MuskingmCoOh	02	02	18
Umstot, Peter(Z)	1815	June 20	GuernseyCoOh	01	03	24
Underhile, Thomas(Y)	1830	Aug. 27	HarrisonCoOh	06	12	35
Underhill, John(Z)	1834	Aug. 12	GuernseyCoOh	14	13	25
Underhill, Samuel(Z-M)	1833	April 13	GuernseyCoOh	03	02	06
Underhill, Thomas(Y)	1831	April 18	HarrisonCoOh	06	12	35
Underwood, Amos(Y)	1833	Sept. 10	ColumbanCoOh	07	20	05
Underwood, Benj.(Z)	1828	Jan. 30	ZanesvilleOh	14	14	15
Underwood, Wm.(Z)	1828	April 05	MuskingmCoOh	14	14	15
Underwood, Wm.(Z-M)	1826	Sept. 23	WashCo.,Penn	09	05	16
Unselt, Gottlieb(Z-M)	1837	Jan. 20	HolmesCoOhio	04	07	11
Updegraff, James(Y)	1820	Oct. 02	Jeff.Co.,Oh.	06	13	04
Updegraff, Jesse(Z-M)	1835	May 07	CarrolCo.,Oh	02	05	03
Updike, Abraham(Z-M)	1833	June 18	CoshoctnCoOh	07	07	25
Upmayer, Michael(Z)	1836	May 07	GuernseyCoOh	08	08	35
Urfer, John(Z-M)	1833	Sept. 27	TuscarwsCoOh	03	08	24
Urice, David(Z)	1816	May 22	GuernseyCoOh	01	04	13
Urie, David(Z)	1816	Sept. 11	GuernseyCoOh	01	04	15
Urie, David(Z)	1817	Feb. 03	GuernseyCoOh	02	03	09
Urion, Frederick Jr.(Z)	1836	Nov. 28	MuskingmCoOh	15	14	36
Va, John(Z)	1815	March 27	GuernseyCoOh	08	08	10
Vail, Alsop Junr.(Z)	1810	April 18	MuskingmCoOh	15	18	17
Vail, Lewis(Y)	1830	Sept. 11	Stark Co.,Oh	06	16	29
Vail, Lewis(Z)	1816	Aug. 27	CoshoctnCoOh	04	04	03
Valkert, Peter(Z-M)	1838	Nov. 17	MuskingmCoOh	03	04	18
Vambrah, Abraham(Z-M)	1831	Aug. 02	TuscarwsCoOh	01	06	11
Van Dyke, Arthur(Z)	1817	Sept. 04	WashCo.,Penn	08	08	02
Van Horn, Pearson(Z-M)	1836	March 24	CoshoctnCoOh	05	07	16
Van Horne, Amasa(Z)	1817	Oct. 01	ZanesvilleOh	11	13	11
Van Horne, Isaac(Z)	1831	May 03	ZanesvilleOh	10	08	20
Van Horne, Isaac(Z)	1831	May 04	ZanesvilleOh	11	11	15
Van Horne, Isaac(Z)	1831	Sept. 09	ZanesvilleOh	10	09	03
Van Horne, Isaac(Z)	1805	June 29	MuskingmCoOh	14	15	03
Van Horne, Isaac(Z-M)	1831	March 02	ZanesvilleOh	06	07	14
Van Lehn, Henry(Z-M)	1823	March 13	TuscarwsCoOh	02	07	01
Van Pelt, Jno.(Z)	1817	Oct. 08	MuskingmCoOh	10	09	09
Van Rensselear, Sanders(Y)	1833	Oct. 18	Stark Co.,Oh	08	12	14
Van Rensselear, Sanders(Y)	1833	Nov. 01	Stark Co.,Oh	08	12	14
VanCampen, John(Z-M)	1836	Oct. 03	WashngtnCoOh	02	03	12
VanFossen, John(Z-M)	1837	March 01	TuscarwsCoOh	03	05	01
VanHorn, Pearson(Z-M)	1836	Oct. 18	CoshoctnCoOh	05	07	16
VanLehn, Henry(Z-M)	1823	March 13	TuscarwsCoOh	02	07	01
VanSickel, Levi(Z-M)	1836	June 20	HarrisonCoOh	04	05	19
Vanatta, James(Z)	1834	Jan. 04	Perry Co.,Oh	14	12	33

PURCHASER	YEAR	DATE	RESIDENCE	R	T	S
Vanatta, James(Z)	1837	Jan. 06	Perry Co.,Oh	14	12	31
Vanausdale, John(Z-M)	1832	July 12	HolmesCoOhio	08	08	19
Vanausdall, John(Z-M)	1832	Oct. 03	CoshoctnCoOh	08	08	19
Vanbuskirk, Laur'ce.Jr.(Y)	1822	Feb. 14	GreeneCo.,Pa	07	15	21
Vanbuskirk, Laurance(Y)	1821	Sept. 27	TuscarwsCoOh	07	15	21
Vance, John(Z)	1814	Oct. 30	WashCo.,Penn	01	05	17
Vance, William(Z)	1815	June 03	WashCo.,Penn	01	04	18
Vancuren, Cornelius(Z-M)	1832	Oct. 02	GuernseyCoOh	03	01	12
Vancusen, Cornelius(Z-M)	1832	Oct. 22	GuernseyCoOh	03	01	12
Vandebarak, David(Z)	1816	Oct. 07	MuskingmCoOh	09	04	17
Vandebarak, David(Z)	1816	Oct. 07	MuskingmCoOh	09	04	17
Vandebarak, David(Z)	1816	Oct. 09	MuskingmCoOh	09	04	16
Vandeberg, David(Z)	1813	Nov. 13	MuskingmCoOh	03	03	06
Vandeberg, David(Z)	1813	Nov. 13	MuskingmCoOh	03	03	06
Vandeberg, David(Z)	1813	Nov. 13	MuskingmCoOh	08	03	07
Vandeberg, David(Z)	1814	April 01	?	09	04	06
Vandeberg, David(Z)	1815	July 11	MuskingmCoOh	09	04	06
Vanderort, Jas.(Z)	1831	March 10	MuskingmCoOh	11	05	26
Vandervort, John(Z)	1828	April 15	MuskingmCoOh	11	12	17
Vandevort, Barnet(Z)	1831	June 09	MuskingmCoOh	11	12	25
Vandevort, Barnet(Z)	1810	March 20	AlleghnyCoPa	03	01	23
Vandevort, John(Z)	1824	May 11	MuskingmCoOh	11	13	22
Vandine, Charles(Y)	1831	Nov. 07	ColumbanCoOh	03	12	01
Vandine, Charles(Z)	1836	March 28	Jeff.Co.,Oh.	14	12	09
Vandine, Charles(Z)	1836	March 28	Jeff.Co.,Oh.	14	12	09
Vandine, Charles(Z)	1836	May 09	Jeff.Co.,Oh.	14	12	09
Vandvort, Barnat(Z)	1824	Dec. 24	MuskingmCoOh	10	09	08
Vanfesser, George(Y)	1829	April 20	BelmontCo,Oh	06	10	25
Vanfleet, Jeremiah(Z)	1833	June 14	Morgan Co,Oh	09	06	13
Vanfossan, Arnold(Y)	1830	May 21	ColumbanCoOh	02	10	21
Vanfossen, John(Z-M)	1834	Feb. 28	BelmontCo,Oh	02	05	18
Vanfossen, William(Z-M)	1834	March 11	TuscarwsCoOh	02	05	03
Vanfossen, Wm.(Z-M)	1835	Oct. 05	TuscarwsCoOh	02	05	01
Vanhock, William(Z-M)	1835	July 09	CoshoctnCoOh	07	04	11
Vanhock, William(Z-M)	1835	July 09	CoshoctnCoOh	07	04	10
Vanhorn, Amasa(Z)	1816	Oct. 09	MuskingmCoOh	14	14	35
Vanhorn, David(Z)	1814	June 04	MuskingmCoOh	15	18	13
Vanhorn, Peirson(Z)	1827	Nov. 16	HarrisonCoOh	05	07	16
Vanhorne, Isaac Jr.(Z)	1806	Jan. 16	MuskingmCoOh	07	01	12
Vanhorne, Isaac Jr.(Z)	1810	Nov. 02	ZanesvilleOh	12	13	04
Vanhorne, Isaac(Z-M)	1832	March 09	ZanesvilleOh	09	07	04
Vanhorne, J. Junr.(Z)	1812	March 07	MuskingmCoOh	09	01	22
Vanhorne, John(Z)	1805	Dec. 27	MuskingmCoOh	13	12	14
Vanhorne, John(Z)	1806	March 24	MuskingmCoOh	15	18	04
Vanhorne, John(Z)	1806	March 24	MuskingmCoOh	15	18	09
Vanhorne, John(Z)	1806	May 17	MuskingmCoOh	02	01	21
Vanhorne, Mary(Z)	1806	Nov. 12	MuskingmCoOh	07	01	08
Vanhorne, Sarah(Z)	1806	Aug. 26	MuskingmCoOh	14	16	08
Vanivey, Aaron(Z)	1833	March 19	Perry Co.,Oh	14	13	29
Vanlahn, Henry(Z-M)	1838	July 16	TuscarwsCoOh	02	07	09
Vanmater, Morgan(Y)	1828	Nov. 01	Stark Co.,Oh	07	16	28
Vanmatre, Jesse(Y)	1822	Jan. 07	ColumbanCoOh	05	16	22
Vannorstran, Fred'k.(Y)	1828	Dec. 10	Stark Co.,Oh	07	17	26
Vannorstrone, Samuel(Z)	1833	Feb. 06	MuskingmCoOh	11	12	28
Vanpelt, Daniel(Z-M)	1832	June 22	GuernseyCoOh	02	03	07
Vanpelt, John(Z)	1816	July 09	MuskingmCoOh	10	09	05
Vansant, Elizabeth(Z)	1812	Nov. 30	MuskingmCoOh	15	18	01
Vansant, John(Z)	1806	July 07	MuskingmCoOh	14	16	07
Vansant, John(Z)	1812	Nov. 30	MuskingmCoOh	14	16	06
Vanscoyae, Jonathan(Z)	1810	May 30	ColumbanCoOh	01	10	08
Vansickle, Isaac(Z)	1832	June 04	HarrisonCoOh	14	12	18
Vansickle, Isaac(Z)	1832	June 04	HarrisonCoOh	14	12	17
Vansickle, Peter A.(Z)	1816	Oct. 30	MuskingmCoOh	15	15	06
Vanvlerah, Sam'l.(Z-M)	1833	Nov. 30	TuscarwsCoOh	01	06	10
Vanvoorhis, John(Z)	1817	Feb. 11	MuskingmCoOh	10	04	14
Vanvoorhis, John(Z)	1817	March 22	MuskingmCoOh	10	04	14
Vanwinkle, Jas.(Z-M)	1831	Dec. 10	LickingCo,Oh	10	04	10
Vanwinkle, Moses Junr.(Z-M)	1833	March 14	LickingCo,Oh	10	04	18
Vanwinkle, Moses(Z)	1806	Jan. 06	MuskingmCoOh	08	02	03

PURCHASER	YEAR	DATE	RESIDENCE	R	T	S
Vanwinkle, Moses(Z)	1815	July 10	MuskingmCoOh	10	04	01
Vanwinkle, Moses(Z)	1815	July 10	MuskingmCoOh	10	04	01
Vanwinkle, Moses(Z)	1816	April 02	MuskingmCoOh	10	04	01
Vanwinkle, Moses(Z-M)	1833	March 22	LickingCo,Oh	10	04	01
Varnar, Martin(Z)	1814	Jan. 28	MuskingmCoOh	09	01	05
Varner, Jacob(Z-M)	1823	Sept. 27	LickingCo,Oh	10	04	12
Varner, Jacob(Z-M)	1825	July 11	LickingCo,Oh	10	04	12
Varner, Sam'l.(Z-M)	1831	Dec. 06	LickingCo,Oh	10	04	13
Varner, Samuel(Z)	1831	Sept. 12	Morgan Co,Oh	13	09	14
Varner, Samuel(Z)	1815	Jan. 02	LickingCo,Oh	09	01	06
Varner, Samuel(Z-M)	1835	Aug. 08	LickingCo,Oh	10	04	13
Varnum, Moses(Z)	1813	Dec. 25	WashngtnCoOh	11	11	28
Vaugan, James(Z)	1814	Feb. 15	TuscarwsCoOh	03	01	23
Vaughan, Ely(Z)	1836	June 14	WashngtnCoOh	09	05	36
Vaughan, Ely(Z)	1836	Nov. 30	WashngtnCoOh	08	05	29
Vaughn, Eli(Z)	1823	April 11	WashCo.,Ohio	08	05	31
Vaughn, James(Z)	1816	Feb. 13	MuskingmCoOh	11	11	34
Veatch, Nathan(Z)	1813	Oct. 13	GreeneCo.,Pa	11	05	05
Veatch, Nathan(Z)	1813	Oct. 13	GreeneCo.,Pa	11	06	25
Veatch, Nathan(Z)	1814	Oct. 21	Greene Co,Pa	11	05	12
Veatch, Peter(Z)	1813	Oct. 09	GreenCo.,Pa.	11	05	05
Veidick, Abraham(Y)	1822	April 13	ColumbanCoOh	06	17	21
Venable, Joel(Y)	1821	Nov. 23	ColumbanCoOh	04	17	15
Venderberg, David(Z)	1810	Jan. 16	MuskingmCoOh	08	02	06
Vendumeuk, Charach(Z)	1815	Jan. 02	MuskingmCoOh	04	01	23
Venne, George(Y)	1830	Nov. 29	HarrisonCoOh	05	13	09
Vernon, Amos(Z)	1814	March 05	MuskingmCoOh	06	02	24
Vernon, Isaac(Z)	1810	June 12	MuskingmCoOh	06	01	12
Vernon, Isaac(Z)	1813	April 19	MuskingmCoOh	05	01	06
Vernon, John(Z)	1810	June 13	MuskingmCoOh	06	01	03
Vernon, John(Z)	1815	May 17	MuskingmCoOh	06	02	04
Vernon, Joseph(Z)	1804	Nov. 12	GreeneCo.,Pa	07	01	11
Vernon, Joseph(Z)	1805	May 18	MuskingmCoOh	07	01	10
Vernon, Joseph(Z)	1810	June 13	MuskingmCoOh	06	01	05
Vernon, Peter(Z)	1817	Jan. 31	MuskingmCoOh	10	03	13
Vernon, Samuel(Z)	1811	Feb. 27	MuskingmCoOh	06	02	25
Vernon, Samuel(Z)	1815	May 13	MuskingmCoOh	06	02	15
Vernon, William C.(Z-M)	1835	Oct. 24	KnoxCo.,Ohio	10	08	04
Vernon, Wm. C.(Z-M)	1832	April 14	KnoxCo.,Ohio	10	08	04
Vernors, Isaac(Z)	1830	June 04	Morgan Co,Oh	12	10	33
Vickers, James(Z)	1817	Feb. 19	MuskingmCoOh	14	14	02
Vickers, James(Z)	1817	Feb. 19	MuskingmCoOh	14	14	14
Vickers, James(Z)	1816	March 26	MuskingmCoOh	12	13	21
Vickers, John(Y)	1822	Sept. 16	Jeff.Co.,Oh.	06	12	26
Vickers, John(Y)	1830	April 20	Jeff.Co.,Oh.	06	12	26
Villiod, Jacob(Y)	1831	March 11	Stark Co.,Oh	09	11	26
Vincent, Geo. A.(Z)	1831	Aug. 05	Morgan Co,Oh	11	10	23
Vincent, George A.(Z)	1829	April 04	Brooke CoVir	11	10	23
Vincent, Thomas(Z)	1827	Oct. 23	HarrisonCoOh	11	10	27
Vincent, Thomas(Z)	1827	Oct. 23	HarrisonCoOh	11	10	27
Virtue, Archibald(Y)	1830	Dec. 10	HarrisonCoOh	06	12	05
Voellnagle, M.(Y)	1824	May 17	ColumbanCoOh	02	13	15
Volbrecht, Henry L.(Z-M)	1838	Jan. 26	CoshoctnCoOh	10	07	11
VonLehir, Casper H.(Z)	1815	May 25	TuscarwsCoOh	02	07	10
Vonsickle, Samuel(Z-M)	1839	March 01	GuernseyCoOh	03	03	15
Voohers, Albert(Z-M)	1833	Dec. 14	TuscarwsCoOh	01	05	13
Voorhees, Albert(Z)	1828	Dec. 15	BelmontCo,Oh	11	10	22
Voorhes, John(Z-M)	1834	Jan. 01	Jeff.Co.,Oh.	04	03	22
Voorhes, Robert(Z-M)	1837	March 20	GuernseyCoOh	04	03	19
Vorheis, Daniel(Z)	1832	Jan. 02	GuernseyCoOh	08	08	22
Vorheis, Daniel(Z)	1836	Jan. 26	GuernseyCoOh	08	08	22
Vorheis, Ephraim(Z)	1833	May 31	GuernseyCoOh	08	08	33
Vorheis, Ephraim(Z)	1836	Feb. 19	GuernseyCoOh	08	08	32
Vorheis, Isaac(Z)	1833	March 14	GuernseyCoOh	08	08	15
Vorheis, J.(Z)	1805	April 29	MuskingmCoOh	08	08	10
Vorheis, John(Z)	1832	March 12	GuernseyCoOh	08	08	22
Vorhes, Robert(Z-M)	1833	Oct. 24	Jeff.Co.,Oh.	04	02	02
Vorhies, Aaron(Z)	1833	Dec. 12	GuernseyCoOh	08	08	27
Vorhies, Aaron(Z)	1835	June 03	GuernseyCoOh	08	08	28

PURCHASER	YEAR	DATE	RESIDENCE	R	T	S
Vorhies, Aaron(Z)	1836	Feb. 23	GuernseyCoOh	08	08	27
Vorhies, Ephraim(Z)	1826	Sept. 09	GuernseyCoOh	08	08	33
Vorhies, Ephraim(Z)	1827	March 08	GuernseyCoOh	08	08	33
Vorhies, Isaac(Z)	1828	April 26	GuernseyCoOh	08	08	10
Vorhis, Aaron(Z)	1814	Nov. 02	GuernseyCoOh	08	08	28
Votaw, Benjamin(of Isaac)(Y)	1826	March 13	ColumbanCoOh	05	18	21
Votaw, Thomas(Y)	1829	March 13	ColumbanCoOh	05	10	22
Votaw, Thos.(Y)	1826	Nov. 13	ColumbanCoOh	04	17	06
Votestine, Peter(Y)	1827	Aug. 22	HarrisonCoOh	05	12	18
Vulgamot, Jacob(Z)	1816	Oct. 12	CoshoctnCoOh	06	09	07
Vulgamot, John(Z)	1809	Oct. 04	MuskingmCoOh	03	03	08
Waber, John George(Z-M)	1836	March 26	TuscarwsCoOh	02	10	23
Wachly, John(Y)	1820	Dec. 23	ColumbanCoOh	06	16	27
Waddell, James(Z)	1816	Dec. 04	GuernseyCoOh	11	08	24
Waddle, Abm.(Z)	1815	Dec. 18	GuernseyCoOh	11	08	24
Waddle, D. Brooke(Z-M)	1831	Oct. 27	KnoxCo.,Ohio	11	08	18
Waddle, David(Z-M)	1833	Feb. 05	KnoxCo.,Ohio	11	08	17
Waddle, David(Z-M)	1833	Sept. 20	KnoxCo.,Ohio	11	08	17
Waddle, George(Z)	1815	Dec. 18	GuernseyCoOh	11	08	24
Wade, John Senr.(Z)	1812	May 06	WashngtnCoMd	03	09	13
Wade, John(Z)	1809	Nov. 01	TuscarwsCoOh	03	10	18
Wade, Joseph(Z-M)	1832	March 21	GuernseyCoOh	03	04	19
Wade, Joseph(Z-M)	1836	Oct. 04	GuernseyCoOh	03	04	13
Waden, Hillery(Z-M)	1833	Nov. 05	BelmontCo,Oh	02	05	19
Waer, William W.(Z-M)	1836	Aug. 31	HolmesCoOhio	08	08	10
Waerly, John(Y)	1827	April 23	HarrisonCoOh	06	19	32
Wagers, Richard(Y)	1829	April 15	HarrisonCoOh	06	12	23
Wagers, Wm.(Z-M)	1828	Oct. 25	Baltimore,Md	06	08	09
Waggoner, George(Y)	1821	May 08	Stark Co.,Oh	10	02	14
Waggoner, Jacob(Z-M)	1835	Aug. 05	CoshoctnCoOh	04	05	19
Waggoner, Jacob(Z-M)	1835	Oct. 28	CoshoctnCoOh	04	05	20
Waggoner, Jacob(Z-M)	1835	Oct. 28	CoshoctnCoOh	04	05	19
Waggoner, Jno.(Y)	1821	Sept. 26	Stark Co.,Oh	07	16	11
Waggoner, John(Z)	1808	Aug. 25	FairfeldCoOh	14	14	09
Waggoner, John(Z)	1813	Dec. 13	CoshoctnCoOh	04	05	12
Waggoner, John(Z)	1814	June 27	FairfeldCoOh	15	15	07
Waggoner, Mathias(Y)	1826	Dec. 09	Stark Co.,Oh	06	16	30
Waggoner, Matthias(Y)	1830	March 05	TuscarwsCoOh	07	14	34
Waggoner, Matthias(Y)	1831	May 09	TuscarwsCoOh	07	14	34
Waggoner, Philip(Z)	1808	Dec. 05	TuscarwsCoOh	04	05	11
Waggoner, Philip(Z)	1810	Oct. 15	MuskingmCoOh	05	04	01
Waggoner, William(Z-M)	1836	Jan. 22	CoshoctnCoOh	04	05	20
Wagner, Andrew(Z-M)	1834	Nov. 01	CarrollCo,Oh	10	09	18
Wagner, Andrew(Z-M)	1836	Dec. 21	KnoxCo.,Ohio	10	09	18
Wagner, Anthony(Z-M)	1836	March 17	PittsburghPa	05	04	15
Wagner, Anthony(Z-M)	1836	March 17	PittsburghPa	05	04	15
Wagner, George(Y)	1825	Feb. 02	HarrisonCoOh	05	13	22
Wagner, James(Z)	1836	Feb. 19	Morgan Co,Oh	09	06	22
Wagner, John Senr.(Y)	1824	Dec. 03	HarrisonCoOh	05	13	32
Wagner, John(Z)	1832	May 23	Morgan Co,Oh	09	06	28
Wagner, Joseph(Z)	1835	Sept. 01	Morgan Co,Oh	09	05	20
Wagner, Joseph(Z)	1835	Nov. 05	Morgan Co,Oh	09	05	20
Wagner, Joseph(Z-M)	1836	March 17	PittsburghPa	05	04	15
Wagner, Michael(Z-M)	1836	March 17	PittsburghPa	05	04	07
Wagner, Michael(Z-M)	1836	March 17	PittsburghPa	06	04	20
Wagner, Peter(Z)	1835	Nov. 17	LickingCo,Oh	09	05	30
Wagner, Peter(Z)	1835	Nov. 17	LickingCo,Oh	09	05	30
Wagner, Peter(Z)	1836	May 23	Morgan Co,Oh	09	05	30
Wagoner, John(Z-M)	1833	Jan. 15	GuernseyCoOh	02	04	03
Wagoner, Phillip(Z-M)	1838	June 27	CoshoctnCoOh	09	07	20
Wagors, John(Y)	1829	July 30	HarrisonCoOh	06	12	23
Wagstaff, James(Z-M)	1826	Feb. 09	AlleghnyCoPa	04	03	11
Wagstaff, James(Z-M)	1832	Nov. 08	GuernseyCoOh	04	03	11
Wagstaff, James(Z-M)	1838	July 24	GuernseyCoOh	04	03	11
Wagstaff, John(Z-M)	1829	April 11	HarrisonCoOh	04	03	20
Wagstaff, Jos.(Z-M)	1835	March 25	GuernseyCoOh	04	03	10
Wagstaff, Joseph(Y)	1828	Oct. 22	HarrisonCoOh	05	11	21
Wagstaff, Robt.(Z-M)	1836	Aug. 19	GuernseyCoOh	04	03	10
Waldher, Frederick(Z-M)	1836	Nov. 03	TuscarwsCoOh	02	07	05

PURCHASER	YEAR	DATE	RESIDENCE	R	T	S
Waldorf, Joseph(Z-M)	1835	June 06	HolmesCoOhio	07	08	02
Walgamot, Joseph(Z)	1838	Oct. 25	RichlandCoOh	06	09	18
Walgamot, Joseph(Z-M)	1829	June 18	HolmesCoOhio	06	09	18
Walgamott, David(Z-M)	1833	June 17	GuernseyCoOh	03	04	16
Walgamott, John(Z-M)	1832	Dec. 27	GuernseyCoOh	03	04	16
Walgamott, John.(Z-M)	1831	April 22	GuernseyCoOh	04	04	20
Walker, Alex.(Z-M)	1828	May 08	MuskingmCoOh	09	03	21
Walker, Christian(Y)	1822	May 02	ColumbanCoOh	05	14	21
Walker, Eleanor(Z)	1815	Aug. 29	MuskingmCoOh	14	14	17
Walker, Eli(Z-M)	1833	May 04	TuscarwsCoOh	03	08	25
Walker, George B.(Z)	1817	Oct. 29	MontgmryCoMd	13	11	22
Walker, George L. B.(Z)	1815	July 13	GreeneCoOhio	01	04	12
Walker, George L. B.(Z)	1815	July 13	GreeneCoOhio	01	04	12
Walker, George L. B.(Z)	1815	July 13	GreeneCoOhio	01	04	11
Walker, George L. B.(Z)	1815	July 13	GreeneCoOhio	01	04	12
Walker, George L. B.(Z)	1815	July 13	GreeneCoOhio	01	04	12
Walker, George L. B.(Z)	1815	July 13	GreeneCoOhio	01	04	13
Walker, George L. B.(Z)	1816	April 08	GuernseyCoOh	01	04	09
Walker, Hamilton(Y)	1833	April 08	Jeff.Co.,Oh.	03	11	36
Walker, James(Y)	1828	Aug. 11	HarrisonCoOh	05	11	32
Walker, James(Z)	1829	Feb. 02	AlleghnyCoPa	03	03	21
Walker, James(Z-M)	1832	Sept. 28	BelmontCo,Oh	01	03	06
Walker, James(Z-M)	1832	Sept. 28	BelmontCo,Oh	01	03	06
Walker, Jesse(Z-M)	1830	Sept. 30	BelmontCo,Oh	08	04	09
Walker, Jno.(Y)	1823	May 27	Brooke CoVir	02	09	21
Walker, Joel(Z)	1830	June 14	Morgan Co,Oh	13	08	11
Walker, Joel(Z)	1834	Oct. 21	Morgan Co,Oh	13	08	11
Walker, John(Z)	1828	Sept. 23	Morgan Co,Oh	13	09	25
Walker, John(Z)	1831	Jan. 27	MuskingmCoOh	07	03	21
Walker, Joseph(Y)	1833	May 28	Jeff.Co.,Oh.	03	11	36
Walker, Joseph(Y)	1836	March 15	Jeff.Co.,Oh.	03	11	36
Walker, Joseph(Z)	1815	Nov. 08	CoshoctnCoOh	09	07	07
Walker, Joseph(Z-M)	1833	April 02	CoshoctnCoOh	09	07	14
Walker, Meshach(Z-M)	1835	July 06	MuskingmCoOh	10	04	24
Walker, N.(Z-M)	1830	Sept. 25	CoshoctnCoOh	05	06	07
Walker, Nathan(Z)	1817	Oct. 23	Jeff.Co.,Oh.	04	02	18
Walker, Nathan(Z)	1817	Oct. 23	Jeff.Co.,Oh.	13	11	20
Walker, Robert(Z)	1807	May 08	WashCo.,Penn	05	01	16
Walker, Robert(Z)	1815	May 11	KnoxCo.,Ohio	09	08	19
Walker, Silas(Z-M)	1829	April 30	TuscarwsCoOh	04	07	09
Wallace, Alex'r.(Z-M)	1832	May 28	GuernseyCoOh	03	01	03
Wallace, Alex'r.(Z-M)	1835	Dec. 28	GuernseyCoOh	03	01	03
Wallace, Catharine(Z-M)	1826	April 22	HarrisonCoOh	11	08	05
Wallace, Drusilla(Y)	1828	July 25	WashCo.,Penn	06	13	06
Wallace, Gayan(Y)	1831	April 06	ColumbanCoOh	04	13	26
Wallace, Isaac(Z)	1814	Oct. 20	MuskingmCoOh	15	16	13
Wallace, James C.(Z)	1835	April 07	Perry Co.,Oh	14	14	20
Wallace, James(Z)	1829	Feb. 19	MuskingmCoOh	12	12	22
Wallace, John(Y)	1828	Oct. 04	Brooke CoVir	02	08	33
Wallace, John(Z)	1825	Oct. 17	MuskingmCoOh	12	12	15
Wallace, John(Z)	1815	May 17	AlleghnyCoPa	05	02	02
Wallace, R.(Y)	1824	May 17	ColumbanCoOh	02	11	36
Wallace, Robert(Y)	1826	June 26	ColumbanCoOh	03	13	17
Wallace, Robert(Y)	1831	March 14	ColumbanCoOh	04	13	20
Wallace, Robinson(Z-M)	1836	April 06	KnoxCo.,Ohio	11	08	04
Wallace, Stewart(Z)	1836	Nov. 03	AllengnyCoPa	08	05	14
Wallace, Stewart(Z)	1836	Nov. 03	AlleghnyCoPa	08	05	14
Wallace, Stewart(Z)	1836	Nov. 03	AlleghnyCoPa	08	05	14
Wallace, William(Y)	1827	March 14	Jeff.Co.,Oh.	04	12	12
Wallace, William(Y)	1834	Jan. 22	Jeff.Co.,Oh.	11	12	18
Waller, David(Z)	1828	March 26	Morgan Co,Oh	09	05	34
Waller, Jesse Jr.(Z)	1833	Aug. 31	Morgan Co,Oh	09	05	26
Waller, Josep(Z-M)	1832	Oct. 06	GuernseyCoOh	04	01	20
Waller, L. C.(Z)	1835	Dec. 30	Morgan Co,Oh	09	05	10
Waller, Lewis C.(Z)	1836	April 02	Morgan Co,Oh	09	05	14
Waller, Margaret(Z-M)	1833	Sept. 28	GuernseyCoOh	03	01	04
Waller, Saml.(Z-M)	1831	Feb. 02	GuernseyCoOh	03	01	04
Waller, William(Z)	1827	Oct. 13	GuernseyCoOh	04	01	11
Waller, William(Z)	1815	July 14	GuernseyCoOh	04	01	11

PURCHASER	YEAR	DATE	RESIDENCE	R	T	S
Waller, William(Z-M)	1832	June 06	GuernseyCoOh	04	01	20
Wallers, Lewis C.(Z)	1836	April 22	Morgan Co,Oh	09	05	13
Wallick, Andrew(Z-M)	1834	Oct. 20	HolmesCoOhio	07	08	04
Wallick, Benjamin(Z)	1816	Nov. 06	TuscarwsCoOh	04	09	13
Wallick, George(Z)	1816	Feb. 16	TuscarwsCoOh	03	10	18
Wallick, Henry(Z-M)	1828	Sept. 20	HolmesCoOhio	07	08	07
Wallick, Philip(Z)	1816	Feb. 24	BedfordCo,Pa	08	06	08
Walling, Thomas(Z-M)	1826	Jan. 06	UnionCo,Penn	06	09	24
Wallon, Benjamin(Y)	1835	Nov. 11	CarrollCo,Oh	05	13	04
Walls, Eli(Z)	1817	Jan. 15	MuskingmCoOh	14	14	14
Walls, Eli(Z)	1816	July 15	MuskingmCoOh	12	11	10
Walls, Eliza(Z)	1815	Oct. 06	MuskingmCoOh	13	10	30
Walls, Elza(Z)	1815	Nov. 21	MuskingmCoOh	14	14	23
Walls, Ezra(Z)	1814	Jan. 17	MuskingmCoOh	14	14	36
Walls, Jonathan(Z)	1836	May 24	Morgan Co,Oh	14	13	21
Walls, Jonathan(Z)	1805	Dec. 26	MuskingmCoOh	14	16	10
Walls, Nathan(Z)	1831	Jan. 27	BelmontCo,Oh	13	08	28
Walls, Richard(Z)	1815	July 06	MuskingmCoOh	14	14	26
Walls, Thos.(Z)	1816	July 15	MuskingmCoOh	12	11	10
Walpole, John(Z)	1834	Nov. 24	Morgan Co,Oh	13	08	05
Walpole, Luke(Z)	1815	Nov. 27	PutnamCoOhio	14	14	21
Walpole, Luke(Z)	1815	Dec. 06	PutnamCoOhio	14	15	21
Walpole, Luke(Z)	1816	Oct. 07	PutnamCoOhio	14	15	21
Walpole, Luke(Z)	1817	Jan. 20	PutnamCoOhio	13	09	33
Walpole, Martin(Z)	1830	Jan. 06	Morgan Co,Oh	13	09	34
Walpole, Martin(Z)	1831	July 18	Morgan Co,Oh	13	09	06
Walpole, Martin(Z)	1834	July 28	Morgan Co,Oh	13	09	32
Walpole, Martin(Z)	1834	July 28	Morgan Co,Oh	13	08	05
Walpole, Martin(Z)	1836	March 12	Morgan Co,Oh	13	08	28
Walpole, Martin(Z)	1836	Aug. 11	Morgan Co,Oh	13	08	05
Walpole, Patrick(Z)	1836	Feb. 22	Morgan Co,Oh	14	12	27
Walraven, Wm.(Z-M)	1825	April 15	CoshoctnCoOh	08	04	09
Walser, Robert(Y)	1830	Jan. 06	ColumbanCoOh	07	16	10
Walsh, David(Z)	1835	Feb. 04	LickingCo,Oh	14	12	32
Walsh, David(Z)	1835	Feb. 04	LickingCo,Oh	14	12	32
Walta, Catherine(Z-M)	1831	March 19	TuscarwsCoOh	03	08	11
Walter, Henry Jr.(Y)	1826	Dec. 09	ColumbanCoOh	02	11	36
Walter, Jacob(Y)	1834	Dec. 15	Jeff.Co.,Oh.	04	13	07
Walter, Jesse(Z)	1816	Dec. 28	GuernseyCoOh	09	05	27
Walter, John(Z)	1833	June 11	Morgan Co,Oh	09	07	26
Walter, John(Z-M)	1825	April 06	GuernseyCoOh	04	01	19
Walter, Joseph(Z-M)	1824	Sept. 23	GuernseyCoOh	03	01	25
Walter, Martin(Z-M)	1835	July 13	TuscarwsCoOh	01	08	13
Walters, Allen(Y)	1830	Sept. 29	HarrisonCoOh	06	12	21
Walters, Allen(Z-M)	1832	April 18	HarrisonCoOh	07	08	20
Walters, David(Z-M)	1835	Aug. 10	TuscarwsCoOh	01	08	02
Walters, George(Z-M)	1829	Aug. 19	HarrisonCoOh	01	08	09
Walters, Henry(Y)	1829	Dec. 29	HarrisonCoOh	05	12	30
Walters, Jacob(Z)	1806	Feb. 06	GreeneCo.,Pa	07	01	09
Walters, Jacob(Z)	1806	Feb. 06	GreeneCo.,Pa	07	01	02
Walters, Jacob(Z-M)	1829	Oct. 19	TuscarwsCoOh	01	08	09
Walters, John(Z)	1812	June 01	WestmrldCoPa	04	09	12
Walters, John(Z-M)	1828	Dec. 20	TuscarwsCoOh	01	08	09
Walters, Jonah(Z)	1828	June 04	BelmontCo,Oh	10	07	15
Walters, Jonah(Z)	1832	May 30	Morgan Co,Oh	10	07	15
Walters, Jonah(Z)	1830	Dec. 02	Morgan Co,Oh	10	07	22
Walters, Jonah(Z)	1835	Feb. 18	Morgan Co,Oh	10	07	15
Walters, Joseph(Z-M)	1836	Jan. 13	CarrollCo,Oh	02	04	04
Walters, Joseph(Z-M)	1836	Feb. 17	CarrollCo,Oh	02	04	04
Walters, Martin(Z-M)	1832	June 01	TuscarwsCoOh	01	08	10
Walters, Peter(Z)	1823	Jan. 13	GuernseyCoOh	10	07	11
Walters, Peter(Z)	1832	Feb. 24	Morgan Co,Oh	10	07	11
Walters, S.(Z)	1814	April 25	TuscarwsCoOh	05	08	21
Walters, Sam'l.(Z-M)	1828	Dec. 20	TuscarwsCoOh	01	08	02
Walters, Samuel(Z-M)	1835	Dec. 03	TuscarwsCoOh	04	08	23
Walters, Solomon(Y)	1834	Jan. 24	HarrisonCoOh	07	14	35
Walters, William(Z-M)	1836	April 15	HolmesCoOhio	09	09	24
Walton, Benjamin(Y)	1833	June 11	ColumbanCoOh	05	16	31
Walton, Benjamin(Y)	1835	May 24	ColumbanCoOh	05	16	31

PURCHASER	YEAR	DATE	RESIDENCE	R	T	S
Walton, John Jnr.(Z-M)	1837	Dec. 02	CoshoctnCoOh	08	07	14
Walton, John(Y)	1833	June 11	CarrollCo,Oh	05	16	32
Walton, John(Z-M)	1834	Aug. 19	CoshoctnCoOh	08	07	15
Walton, John(Z-M)	1834	Aug. 19	CoshoctnCoOh	08	07	06
Walton, John(Z-M)	1835	Oct. 03	CoshoctnCoOh	08	07	15
Walton, John(Z-M)	1837	Aug. 01	CoshoctnCoOh	08	07	14
Walton, Nich's.(Z-M)	1835	Oct. 02	TuscarwsCoOh	02	06	19
Walton, Nicholas(Z-M)	1835	Sept. 26	TuscarwsCoOh	02	06	13
Walton, Wm.(Y)	1825	May 18	ColumbanCoOh	05	15	15
Waltz, Daniel(Z-M)	1835	April 22	TuscarwsCoOh	01	08	02
Waltz, Sam'l.(Z-M)	1831	April 06	TuscarwsCoOh	01	09	22
Waltz, Samuel(Z-M)	1828	March 22	TuscarwsCoOh	01	09	19
Waltz, Samuel(Z-M)	1828	March 22	TuscarwsCoOh	01	09	22
Wame, Abraham(Z)	1805	Oct. 02	AlleghnyCoPa	11	13	19
Wandling, Jacob(Y)	1822	Sept. 14	ColumbanCoOh	04	14	21
Wandling, Jacob(Y)	1824	July 05	ColumbanCoOh	04	13	17
Wandling, Jacob(Z)	1836	April 22	Morgan Co,Oh	09	05	21
Wanen, Jas. C.(Z-M)	1839	March 23	MuskingmCoOh	08	06	06
Wank, George(Y)	1830	Sept. 22	PittsburghPa	07	17	18
Ward, Abijah(Z-M)	1837	July 28	KnoxCo.,Ohio	10	08	01
Ward, Abraham(Z)	1833	Oct. 12	Morgan Co,Oh	13	08	31
Ward, Abraham(Z)	1833	Oct. 12	Morgan Co,Oh	13	08	30
Ward, Andrew(Z-M)	1836	Oct. 31	KnoxCo.,Ohio	10	08	01
Ward, Cornelius(Y)	1830	July 17	ColumbanCoOh	04	13	21
Ward, Cornelius(Z-M)	1833	April 19	HolmesCoOhio	08	08	05
Ward, Cornelius(Z-M)	1836	April 05	KnoxCo.,Ohio	10	09	21
Ward, Cornelius(Z-M)	1837	July 28	KnoxCo.,Ohio	10	08	02
Ward, David(Z)	1838	June 15	GuernseyCoOh	08	05	02
Ward, Edward(Z)	1807	June 17	MuskingmCoOh	08	08	03
Ward, Edward(Z)	1807	Nov. 03	AlleghnyCoPa	15	17	07
Ward, Edward(Z)	1812	Dec. 01	MuskingmCoOh	15	17	17
Ward, Hiram(Z)	1835	Sept. 08	Perry Co.,Oh	14	12	26
Ward, Hiram(Z)	1836	Jan. 18	MuskingmCoOh	14	12	26
Ward, John(Z)	1833	March 25	Perry Co.,Oh	15	16	24
Ward, Nelson(Z)	1837	March 18	ColumbanCoOh	08	06	15
Ward, Patrick(Y)	1827	Oct. 27	ColumbanCoOh	04	14	32
Ward, Robert(Y)	1830	Jan. 12	ColumbanCoOh	02	09	27
Ward, Samuel(Y)	1828	Sept. 18	ColumbanCoOh	04	13	27
Ward, Samuel(Z-M)	1830	Jan. 09	GuernseyCoOh	04	02	11
Ward, Samuel(Z-M)	1837	Aug. 07	KnoxCo.,Ohio	09	08	05
Ward, Sutton(Z)	1836	April 15	WashngtnCoOh	08	05	04
Ward, Sutton(Z)	1837	Feb. 10	WashngtnCoOh	08	05	05
Ward, Thomas(Y)	1824	May 17	ColumbanCoOh	02	10	15
Ward, Thomas(Y)	1824	May 17	ColumbanCoOh	02	10	15
Ward, Thomas(Y)	1826	June 26	Stark Co.,Oh	09	11	24
Ward, Thomas(Y)	1832	July 09	ColumbanCoOh	03	12	24
Ward, William(Z)	1824	Nov. 09	Perry Co.,Oh	13	08	30
Ward, William(Z)	1833	Aug. 24	Perry Co.,Oh	15	15	26
Ward, William(Z)	1836	Jan. 04	Morgan Co,Oh	13	08	30
Ward, Wm.(Y)	1822	June 20	Stark Co.,Oh	06	15	34
Ward, Wm.(Z)	1822	Jan. 11	GuernseyCoOh	08	08	03
Ward, Wm.(Z)	1822	Jan. 11	GuernseyCoOh	08	08	03
Wardan, Isaac(Z-M)	1837	Feb. 10	GuernseyCoOh	03	03	07
Warden, David M.(Z-M)	1828	Dec. 30	GuernseyCoOh	04	03	22
Warden, Hamilton(Z-M)	1836	Aug. 16	GuernseyCoOh	03	03	17
Warden, Hamilton(Z-M)	1836	Aug. 16	GuernseyCoOh	03	03	17
Warden, Isaac J.(Z-M)	1833	Jan. 21	GuernseyCoOh	02	01	12
Warden, Isaac Jr.(Z-M)	1832	May 24	GuernseyCoOh	03	03	17
Warden, Isaac(Z)	1812	Feb. 29	GuernseyCoOh	03	03	17
Warden, Isaac(Z)	1816	March 13	GuernseyCoOh	03	03	17
Warden, Isaac(Z-M)	1823	March 10	GuernseyCoOh	03	03	07
Warden, Isaac(Z-M)	1835	Feb. 26	GuernseyCoOh	03	03	07
Warden, Isaac(Z-M)	1839	Feb. 22	GuernseyCoOh	03	03	15
Warden, Jane(Z-M)	1828	Dec. 30	GuernseyCoOh	04	03	22
Warden, John S.(Z-M)	1837	Feb. 18	GuernseyCoOh	04	03	23
Warden, Sam'l.(Z-M)	1828	Sept. 30	GuernseyCoOh	03	03	04
Warden, Samson(Z-M)	1824	July 02	CoshoctnCoOh	08	04	02
Warden, Samuel(Z-M)	1835	Aug. 24	GuernseyCoOh	03	03	04
Warden, Samuel(Z-M)	1836	Dec. 13	GuernseyCoOh	03	03	04

PURCHASER	YEAR	DATE	RESIDENCE	R	T	S
Warden, Samuel(Z-M)	1838	Sept. 07	GuernseyCoOh	03	03	04
Ware, Amos(Y)	1823	Dec. 15	ColumbanCoOh	05	18	12
Warfield, Wm.(Z-M)	1835	Feb. 02	HolmesCoOhio	07	08	10
Warford, John(Y)	1826	April 21	TuscarwsCoOh	07	15	27
Warne, Abraham(Z)	1814	Oct. 28	MuskingmCoOh	11	13	19
Warner, Adam Jr.(Y)	1828	Jan. 05	Stark Co.,Oh	08	12	02
Warner, Casper(Z)	1812	July 07	TuscarwsCoOh	01	06	02
Warner, John(Y)	1832	Jan. 12	TuscarwsCoOh	07	14	02
Warner, Paul(Z-M)	1836	April 22	CarrollCo,Oh	10	07	11
Warner, T.(Z)	1816	March 20	WashCo.,Penn	07	09	20
Warner, T.(Z)	1816	March 20	WashCo.,Penn	08	08	01
Warnick, James(Z)	1816	March 28	GuernseyCoOh	02	04	02
Warnick, Jno.(Z-M)	1833	June 13	GuernseyCoOh	02	04	07
Warnick, Jno.(Z-M)	1833	June 13	GuernseyCoOh	02	04	07
Warnick, John(Z-M)	1837	Nov. 23	GuernseyCoOh	02	04	07
Warrack, James(Z)	1804	Dec. 06	BelmontCo,Oh	01	03	14
Warren, Ai(Z)	1835	June 10	Morgan Co,Oh	09	06	25
Warren, Ai(Z)	1835	June 10	Morgan Co,Oh	09	06	25
Warren, George(Z)	1817	Sept. 30	GuernseyCoOh	02	03	24
Warren, James S.(Z)	1835	May 28	Morgan Co,Oh	09	06	25
Warren, James S.(Z)	1836	April 12	Morgan Co,Oh	08	06	31
Warren, James S.(ZM)	1826	June 16	Morgan Co,Oh	09	06	22
Warren, John(Y)	1829	March 16	Stark Co.,Oh	06	16	29
Warrick, Isaac(Z-M)	1836	Nov. 24	ColumbanCoOh	09	07	04
Warrick, Isaac(Z-M)	1836	Nov. 24	ColumbanCoOh	09	07	05
Warrington, Ab'm. Jr.(Y)	1827	April 12	ColumbanCoOh	05	18	22
Warrington, Abm.(Y)	1826	Sept. 01	ColumbanCoOh	05	18	22
Warrington, Enoch(Y)	1835	May 28	ColumbanCoOh	05	16	32
Wartenbe, Francis(Z)	1815	June 20	Brooke CoVir	10	08	12
Wartenbe, William(Z)	1815	March 27	Brooke CoVir	10	08	11
Wartenbe, William(Z)	1815	April 03	Brooke CoVir	09	07	06
Wartenbe, William(Z)	1815	April 03	Brooke CoVir	09	07	06
Wartenbe, William(Z)	1815	June 20	Brooke CoVir	09	07	06
Wartenbee, Isaac(Z)	1827	June 22	MuskingmCoOh	12	13	15
Wartenbee, Isaac(Z)	1829	Jan. 10	MuskingmCoOh	12	13	21
Washington, Lach'l. D.(Y)	1823	July 04	ColumbanCoOh	07	20	22
Wason, George(Y)	1822	Aug. 26	Jeff.Co.,Oh.	06	16	18
Wass, Samuel(Y)	1821	Nov. 24	ColumbanCoOh	06	16	21
Waterman, A.(Z)	1814	Feb. 09	MuskingmCoOh	10	06	29
Waterman, Reuben R.(Z)	1835	May 25	Morgan Co,Oh	10	06	28
Waterman, Reuben R.(Z)	1835	Nov. 07	Morgan Co,Oh	10	06	29
Watermire, John(Z)	1805	Oct. 23	MuskingmCoOh	14	15	26
Waters, Allen(Z-M)	1832	Dec. 29	HarrisonCoOh	07	07	19
Waters, John(Z)	1816	Feb. 29	GuernseyCoOh	01	03	13
Waters, John(Z-M)	1838	Sept. 08	HarrisonCoOh	04	03	09
Waters, Richard A.(Z-M)	1835	Sept. 25	MuskingmCoOh	05	03	12
Waters, Samuel(Z-M)	1838	Oct. 09	MuskingmCoOh	05	03	12
Waters, Timothy(Z)	1817	Aug. 06	MuskingmCoOh	05	03	02
Watkins, Benjamin(Z)	1833	Oct. 18	GuernseyCoOh	10	06	08
Watkins, Denton(Z-M)	1836	Sept. 07	BelmontCo,Oh	03	08	13
Watkins, Denton(Z-M)	1836	Sept. 07	BelmontCo,Oh	03	08	13
Watkins, Rezin(Z-M)	1833	May 23	TuscarwsCoOh	01	08	02
Watkins, Ryin(Z-M)	1830	Sept. 03	TuscarwsCoOh	01	08	02
Watkins, William(Y)	1832	May 22	TuscarwsCoOh	07	14	09
Watkins, William(Z-M)	1836	Feb. 08	TuscarwsCoOh	03	08	13
Watkins, Wm.(Y)	1824	Sept. 13	BelmontCo,Oh	04	06	21
Watrons, Samuel(Z-M)	1832	May 22	MuskingmCoOh	05	03	10
Watrous, Samuel(Z-M)	1832	June 18	MuskingmCoOh	05	03	07
Watson, Alexander(Z)	1815	Feb. 14	CumberldCoPa	01	03	07
Watson, Daniel(Z-M)	1835	Sept. 22	TuscarwsCoOh	01	06	24
Watson, G.(Z)	1815	April 26	MuskingmCoOh	06	02	20
Watson, Gabriel(Z-M)	1833	Nov. 08	TuscarwsCoOh	01	06	15
Watson, Gabriel(Z-M)	1834	Feb. 27	TuscarwsCoOh	01	06	15
Watson, Geo.(Z-M)	1831	Nov. 14	KnoxCo.,Ohio	10	08	06
Watson, George(Z)	1815	April 21	MuskingmCoOh	12	13	27
Watson, George(Z)	1817	April 06	MuskingmCoOh	06	02	21
Watson, Isaac(Z)	1816	Dec. 16	LickingCo,Oh	11	03	04
Watson, Jacob Yoho(Z)	1836	April 30	MonroeCo.,Oh	08	07	04
Watson, James(Y)	1831	Oct. 19	ColumbanCoOh	05	15	10

PURCHASER	YEAR	DATE	RESIDENCE	R	T	S
Watson, James(Y)	1833	Feb. 14	ColumbanCoOh	05	15	10
Watson, James(Z)	1823	Jan. 21	GuernseyCoOh	08	07	04
Watson, James(Z)	1833	April 22	MonroeCo.,Oh	08	07	04
Watson, James(Z)	1836	April 30	MonroeCo.,Oh	08	07	04
Watson, Jno.(Z)	1834	Oct. 25	Morgan Co,Oh	10	06	19
Watson, John Jr.(Z-M)	1831	April 27	HarrisonCoOh	02	06	22
Watson, John(Z)	1831	Feb. 01	Morgan Co,Oh	10	06	19
Watson, Joseph(Y)	1823	June 10	ColumbanCoOh	05	15	15
Watson, Mathew(Y)	1826	May 04	ColumbanCoOh	04	13	17
Watson, Matthew(Y)	1830	May 24	ColumbanCoOh	06	13	19
Watson, Robert(Z)	1833	April 06	Morgan Co,Oh	10	06	19
Watson, Robert(Z-M)	1839	March 04	TuscarwsCoOh	08	07	22
Watson, Robert(Z-M)	1839	May 09	TuscarwsCoOh	08	07	21
Watson, Robt.(Z)	1834	Oct. 25	Morgan Co,Oh	10	06	19
Watson, Robt.(Z-M)	1839	March 14	TuscarwsCoOh	08	07	22
Watson, William(Z-M)	1832	Dec. 31	CoshoctnCoOh	09	04	15
Watt, Jacob(Z)	1808	June 09	TuscarwsCoOh	15	15	03
Watt, Samuel(Z)	1806	Jan. 18	MuskingmCoOh	14	14	28
Watta, John(Y)	1835	Jan. 19	CarrollCo,Oh	06	16	34
Watter, Jacob(Z)	1807	June 01	WestmrldCoPa	04	09	12
Watters, George(Z)	1835	Dec. 17	Morgan Co,Oh	10	07	02
Watters, Jacob(Z)	1807	June 01	WestmrldCoPa	04	09	12
Watters, Jonah(Z)	1836	Jan. 25	Morgan Co,Oh	10	07	22
Watters, Jonah(Z)	1836	Jan. 25	Morgan Co,Oh	10	07	15
Watters, Joseph(Y)	1825	Nov. 26	HarrisonCoOh	05	12	35
Watters, Wm. W.(Z)	1831	March 28	Morgan Co,Oh	13	08	28
Wattman, John(Z-M)	1833	April 26	HolmesCoOhio	07	08	04
Watts, Mountzion(Z-M)	1833	July 30	MuskingmCoOh	06	03	11
Watts, Mountzion(Z-M)	1835	Sept. 19	MuskingmCoOh	06	03	11
Way, Coventon(Z-M)	1829	Aug. 20	HolmesCoOhio	08	08	02
Way, Coventon(Z-M)	1835	Dec. 05	HolmesCoOhio	08	08	02
Way, Edward(Z)	1834	July 26	Morgan Co,Oh	09	05	14
Way, Edward(Z)	1836	Jan. 07	Morgan Co,Oh	09	05	14
Way, Elias(Z-M)	1833	April 08	CoshoctnCoOh	07	04	01
Way, Elias(Z-M)	1836	Jan. 19	CoshoctnCoOh	07	04	10
Way, Elias(Z-M)	1836	Jan. 19	CoshoctnCoOh	07	04	01
Way, John B.(Y)	1827	June 02	ColumbanCoOh	07	20	12
Wean, John(Y)	1824	Feb. 06	TrumbullCoOh	05	18	02
Weand, Michael(Z-M)	1835	Jan. 06	TuscarwsCoOh	04	07	21
Wear, David(Z)	1836	Jan. 19	GuernseyCoOh	08	07	20
Weatherbee, Paul(Z-M)	1836	Jan. 07	TuscarwsCoOh	03	06	10
Weatherbee, Paul(Z-M)	1836	Jan. 07	TuscarwsCoOh	03	06	10
Weatherwax, Adam(Z-M)	1836	Oct. 11	CoshoctnCoOh	07	07	02
Weatherwax, Adam(Z-M)	1836	Oct. 11	CoshoctnCoOh	08	07	11
Weatherwax, Adam(Z-M)	1836	Dec. 13	CoshoctnCoOh	08	07	11
Weatherwax, Andrew(Z-M)	1833	Feb. 04	CoshoctnCoOh	07	07	25
Weatherwax, Andrew(Z-M)	1835	Aug. 01	CoshoctnCoOh	07	07	24
Weatherwax, Andrew(Z-M)	1836	Jan. 27	CoshoctnCoOh	08	07	21
Weatherwax, Andrew(Z-M)	1836	Jan. 27	CoshoctnCoOh	07	07	21
Weatherwax, Andrew(Z-M)	1837	Nov. 18	CoshoctnCoOh	07	07	02
Weatherwax, George(Z-M)	1834	March 14	HolmesCoOhio	07	08	22
Weatherwax, Leonard(Z-M)	1834	Feb. 10	CoshoctnCoOh	07	07	14
Weatherwax, Leonard(Z-M)	1836	Jan. 13	CoshoctnCoOh	07	07	17
Weatherwax, Leonard(Z-M)	1837	March 18	CoshoctnCoOh	07	07	14
Weatherwax, Leonard(Z-M)	1837	April 12	CoshoctnCoOh	07	07	13
Weatherwax, Leonard(Z-M)	1837	Nov. 18	CoshoctnCoOh	07	07	15
Weatherwax, Leonard(Z-M)	1837	Nov. 18	CoshoctnCoOh	07	07	02
Weaver, Benj. F.(Z-M)	1831	Jan. 28	TuscarwsCoOh	01	10	03
Weaver, David(Y)	1826	May 01	Stark Co.,Oh	06	16	27
Weaver, Deloss(Z-M)	1831	Feb. 19	TuscarwsCoOh	01	10	15
Weaver, Deloss(Z-M)	1831	Feb. 19	TuscarwsCoOh	01	10	04
Weaver, F.(Z-M)	1830	June 11	TuscarwsCoOh	04	08	19
Weaver, Fred'k.(Y)	1829	Nov. 16	TuscarwsCoOh	07	15	26
Weaver, Jacob(Z-M)	1828	March 01	HolmesCoOhio	06	07	10
Weaver, John(Z-M)	1832	Feb. 23	TuscarwsCoOh	01	09	18
Weaver, Joseph(Z-M)	1838	Nov. 21	HolmesCoOhio	08	08	14
Weaver, Nich's.(Y)	1825	April 11	Stark Co.,Oh	06	16	35
Weaver, Peter(Z)	1837	June 02	MuskingmCoOh	13	10	17
Weaver, Samuel(Z-M)	1838	May 29	HolmesCoOhio	08	08	14

PURCHASER	YEAR	DATE	RESIDENCE	R	T	S
Webb, John(Y)	1821	Sept. 12	ColumbanCoOh	04	17	21
Webb, John(Y)	1821	Sept. 12	ColumbanCoOh	04	17	21
Webb, Thomas(Y)	1823	Oct. 06	ColumbanCoOh	03	16	09
Webb, Thomas(Y)	1827	Oct. 17	ColumbanCoOh	06	19	24
Webber, Eunis(Z)	1832	Jan. 13	Morgan Co,Oh	09	06	35
Webber, James(Z)	1834	March 06	Morgan Co,Oh	08	06	19
Webber, James(Z)	1836	Feb. 09	Morgan Co,Oh	09	06	35
Webber, James(Z)	1836	Feb. 24	Morgan Co,Oh	09	06	35
Webber, Nathaniel(Z)	1832	Aug. 15	Morgan Co,Oh	09	06	35
Webber, Nathaniel(Z)	1836	Feb. 23	Morgan Co,Oh	08	06	30
Webber, Nathaniel(Z)	1836	April 12	Morgan Co,Oh	08	06	30
Weber, David(Z)	1811	March 21	TuscarwsCoOh	04	08	15
Weber, Valentine(Z)	1836	July 18	Ohio Co.,Vir	08	06	09
Weber, Valentine(Z)	1836	July 18	Ohio Co.,Vir	08	06	04
Webster, Charles Pigeon(Y)	1836	Feb. 03	GuernseyCoOh	07	09	25
Webster, John(Y)	1826	Jan. 12	GuernseyCoOh	07	09	13
Webster, Joseph(Y)	1832	Nov. 19	GuernseyCoOh	07	09	25
Wederwole, Joseph(Z)	1832	June 01	Perry Co.,Oh	15	16	10
Wederwole, Joseph(Z)	1837	Jan. 13	Perry Co.,Oh	15	14	10
Weeden, George(Z)	1826	Oct. 27	Jeff.Co.,Oh.	11	10	22
Weekley, Benj.(Z)	1836	Aug. 31	Morgan Co,Oh	09	06	01
Weekley, Benjamin(Z)	1836	Jan. 30	Morgan Co,Oh	09	06	01
Weekley, Benjamin(Z)	1836	Sept. 03	Morgan Co,Oh	08	06	07
Weekley, Nathan(Z-M)	1832	June 16	LickingCo,Oh	10	04	12
Weekley, William(Z)	1835	Nov. 30	Morgan Co,Oh	08	06	07
Weekly, Elias(Z-M)	1835	Dec. 28	LickingCo,Oh	10	04	16
Weekly, Nathan(Z-M)	1835	Dec. 28	LickingCo,Oh	10	04	12
Weekly, Reuben(Y)	1826	July 18	BelmontCo,Oh	04	06	26
Weekly, Reuben(Z)	1835	Oct. 20	BelmontCo,Oh	08	06	19
Weekly, Robinson(Z)	1837	Feb. 07	MonroeCo.,Oh	08	06	19
Weibel, William(Z-M)	1835	Aug. 27	TuscarwsCoOh	03	08	04
Weimar, Valentine(Y)	1827	Aug. 27	Stark Co.,Oh	06	15	34
Weir, Andrew(Z)	1833	March 18	Morgan Co,Oh	10	06	04
Weir, Joseph(Z-M)	1838	Nov. 28	GuernseyCoOh	04	03	15
Weir, Joseph(Z-M)	1839	March 25	GuernseyCoOh	04	03	15
Weir, Thomas(Z-M)	1830	July 31	GuernseyCoOh	04	03	03
Weir, Thomas(Z-M)	1832	Nov. 28	GuernseyCoOh	04	03	03
Weiss, Christian(Z-M)	1836	Aug. 13	TuscarwsCoOh	03	08	14
Weisz, George(Z)	1829	Aug. 12	FairfeldCoOh	15	14	34
Welch, Andrew(Z)	1816	Sept. 24	GuernseyCoOh	11	10	24
Welch, Jacob(Y)	1826	Dec. 05	ColumbanCoOh	02	10	22
Welch, Jacob(Y)	1827	Feb. 23	ColumbanCoOh	02	10	22
Welch, John(Z)	1817	Jan. 15	MuskingmCoOh	09	04	23
Welch, Lewis(Y)	1822	March 29	ColumbanCoOh	02	10	15
Welch, Rezen H.(Z)	1835	Feb. 04	Perry Co.,Oh	14	12	09
Welch, Rezen H.(Z)	1835	Feb. 04	Perry Co.,Oh	14	12	04
Welch, Samuel(Y)	1822	March 08	TrumbullCoOh	07	20	13
Welch, Samuel(Y)	1827	Aug. 03	HarrisonCoOh	05	11	28
Welch, William(Z)	1806	Jan. 09	MuskingmCoOh	01	03	08
Welch, William(Z)	1806	Aug. 26	MuskingmCoOh	01	04	25
Welch///////////, Lewis(Y)	1822	March 15	ColumbanCoOh	02	10	15
Welker, Abraham(Z)	1812	Dec. 19	KnoxCo.,Ohio	10	07	16
Welker, Abraham(Z)	1815	May 03	KnoxCo.,Ohio	09	08	12
Welker, David(Z-M)	1836	Sept. 06	KnoxCo.,Ohio	04	04	03
Welker, Henry(Y)	1827	June 27	Stark Co.,Oh	07	17	08
Welker, Jno.(Z)	1814	Dec. 12	KnoxCo.,Ohio	10	07	15
Welker, Mich'l.(Y)	1824	Aug. 14	Stark Co.,Oh	08	09	01
Welker, Samuel(Z-M)	1826	Dec. 12	KnoxCo.,Ohio	10	07	17
Welker, Solomon(Z)	1813	Aug. 30	KnoxCo.,Ohio	10	07	05
Welker, Wm.(Z)	1814	Dec. 12	KnoxCo.,Ohio	10	07	15
Weller, Henry(Z)	1831	March 12	Morgan Co,Oh	13	10	29
Weller, Henry(Z)	1807	May 26	MuskingmCoOh	14	15	26
Weller, Peter(Z)	1812	Oct. 12	GuernseyCoOh	01	02	14
Wellhelm, George(Z)	1806	Nov. 24	WashCo.,Penn	02	07	11
Welling, Henry(Z)	1824	May 26	Morgan Co,Oh	12	11	34
Welling, Henry(Z-M)	1824	Dec. 28	CoshoctnCoOh	08	05	13
Welling, Thomas(Z-M)	1824	June 14	HarrisonCoOh	08	05	14
Wellis, William(Z)	1815	May 12	TuscarwsCoOh	06	07	12
Wellis, William(Z)	1815	May 12	TuscarwsCoOh	06	06	02

311

PURCHASER	YEAR	DATE	RESIDENCE	R	T	S
Wells, Abraham(Z)	1817	Oct. 18	GreeneCo.,Pa	11	13	36
Wells, Alexander(Y)	1827	May 01	SteubenvleOh	09	10	02
Wells, Alexander(Y)	1828	Aug. 19	SteubenvleOh	09	10	01
Wells, Alexander(Y)	1828	Aug. 19	SteubenvleOh	09	10	02
Wells, Alexander(Y)	1828	Aug. 19	SteubenvleOh	05	13	09
Wells, Alexander(Y)	1828	Aug. 19	SteubenvleOh	05	13	15
Wells, Alexander(Y)	1826	May 05	SteubenvleOh	09	11	35
Wells, Amon(Z)	1832	Sept. 13	Morgan Co,Oh	11	11	23
Wells, Asa(Z)	1826	Dec. 16	MuskingmCoOh	13	11	23
Wells, Asa(Z)	1827	Feb. 13	MuskingmCoOh	13	11	22
Wells, B.(Y)	1825	April 07	SteubenvleOh	09	11	35
Wells, Barton(Z)	1823	June 09	WashCo.,Ohio	08	05	26
Wells, Barton(Z)	1836	July 04	MonroeCo.,Oh	08	06	35
Wells, Benj'm.(Z)	1834	Feb. 12	Perry Co.,Oh	15	14	07
Wells, Benjamin(Z)	1827	Dec. 20	Morgan Co,Oh	12	11	10
Wells, Benjamin(Z)	1833	Nov. 02	Perry Co.,Oh	15	14	07
Wells, Bezaleel(Y)	1824	June 03	SteubenvleOh	09	11	35
Wells, Claudius C.(Z)	1836	Feb. 02	MonroeCo.,Oh	08	07	32
Wells, Claudius C.(Z)	1836	Feb. 09	WashngtnCoOh	09	06	24
Wells, David(Y)	1827	Jan. 05	Jeff.Co.,Oh.	04	12	29
Wells, David(Y)	1827	April 17	Jeff.Co.,Oh.	04	12	35
Wells, Isaac(Z)	1827	May 14	BelmontCo,Oh	12	10	21
Wells, Isaac(Z)	1815	Jan. 31	HarrisonCoOh	01	05	21
Wells, Jesse(Y)	1831	Feb. 14	YorkCo.,Penn	06	19	21
Wells, John(Z)	1836	April 15	Morgan Co,Oh	09	05	20
Wells, John(Z)	1813	Nov. 03	MuskingmCoOh	08	03	15
Wells, John(Z-M)	1835	May 23	CoshoctnCoOh	05	04	06
Wells, Levi G.(Z)	1830	Jan. 13	Morgan Co,Oh	12	10	21
Wells, Levi(Y)	1822	Feb. 27	BelmontCo,Oh	07	10	15
Wells, Peter(Z)	1815	Dec. 16	MuskingmCoOh	12	12	02
Wells, Randal S.(Z)	1836	Oct. 04	MonroeCo.,Oh	08	06	34
Wells, Randall L.(Z)	1836	April 05	MonroeCo.,Oh	08	06	27
Wells, Rice B.(Y)	1823	July 03	TrumbullCoOh	07	20	15
Wells, Samuel(Z-M)	1836	Jan. 01	AlleghnyCoPa	04	02	02
Wells, Troy(Z)	1829	Dec. 19	MuskingmCoOh	13	11	29
Wells, William(Y)	1832	April 11	ColumbanCoOh	03	12	21
Wells, William(Z)	1824	June 22	Jeff.Co.,Oh.	12	10	21
Wells, William(Z)	1824	Aug. 14	Jeff.Co.,Oh.	12	10	21
Welsh, Henry(Y)	1829	March 13	ColumbanCoOh	04	13	10
Welsh, John(Y)	1821	Oct. 09	WashCo.,Penn	05	11	21
Welsh, Michael(Z)	1836	May 05	HarrisonCoOh	14	12	07
Welsh, Michael(Z)	1836	June 14	HarrisonCoOh	14	12	06
Welsh, Michael(Z)	1836	June 14	HarrisonCoOh	14	12	07
Welsh, Robert(Z)	1817	May 22	Ohio Co.,Vir	11	10	23
Welsh, Sam'l.(Y)	1822	Jan. 10	HarrisonCoOh	05	11	22
Welsh, Sam'l.(Y)	1824	Aug. 20	Stark Co.,Oh	05	11	27
Welsh, Samuel(Y)	1822	Dec. 13	HarrisonCoOh	05	11	27
Welsh, Samuel(Y)	1831	March 16	HarrisonCoOh	05	11	22
Welty, Abraham(Z)	1812	June 03	TuscarwsCoOh	03	08	25
Welty, Abraham(Z)	1814	July 20	TuscarwsCoOh	03	09	21
Welty, Christian(Y)	1830	Jan. 27	Stark Co.,Oh	06	17	34
Welty, Jacob(Z)	1815	Nov. 27	WashngtnCoMd	03	09	20
Welty, John(Z)	1810	April 23	TuscarwsCoOh	03	08	13
Welty, John(Z)	1812	July 28	TuscarwsCoOh	04	08	10
Welty, John(Z)	1815	Nov. 27	WashngtnCoMd	03	09	20
Welty, Joseph C.(Y)	1826	June 10	Stark Co.,Oh	09	12	35
Welty, Peter(Z-M)	1828	Dec. 19	TuscarwsCoOh	04	09	05
Welty, Samuel(Z-M)	1831	May 26	TuscarwsCoOh	03	08	14
Welty, Samuel(Z-M)	1832	Nov. 26	TuscarwsCoOh	03	08	14
Weltz, David(Z-M)	1825	Dec. 05	TuscarwsCoOh	03	08	13
Wenner, Benedick(Y)	1824	Nov. 23	Jeff.Co.,Oh.	05	13	20
Wenss, James A.(Z)	1806	Dec. 29	FayetteCo,Pa	15	17	14
Wenzell, Lewis(Z-M)	1837	April 28	Morgan Co,Oh	08	07	22
Wepler, Martin(Z-M)	1837	Sept. 15	ZanesvilleOh	09	08	06
Wepler, Martin(Z-M)	1837	Sept. 15	ZanesvilleOh	09	08	06
Werden, Isaac(Z-M)	1836	Jan. 08	GuernseyCoOh	03	03	06
Wergele, Hartman(Z-M)	1836	Nov. 03	TuscarwsCoOh	02	07	05
Werhley, Henry Jr.(Z-M)	1832	Aug. 29	HarrisonCoOh	03	07	13
Werhley, Henry(Z-M)	1832	June 28	HarrisonCoOh	03	07	13

PURCHASER	YEAR	DATE	RESIDENCE	R	T	S
Werhley, Henry(Z-M)	1832	June 28	HarrisonCoOh	03	07	12
Werhley, Henry(Z-M)	1832	Oct. 01	TuscarwsCoOh	03	07	18
Werhley, Henry(Z-M)	1832	June 28	HarrisonCoOh	03	07	19
Werhley, Michael(Z-M)	1832	Aug. 07	TuscarwsCoOh	03	07	24
Werhly, Michael(Z-M)	1836	March 25	TuscarwsCoOh	03	07	24
Werner, George(Z)	1817	Oct. 24	TuscarwsCoOh	01	06	10
Werner, John(Z)	1838	May 21	MonroeCo.,Oh	08	06	22
Wert, John(Y)	1824	June 04	HarrisonCoOh	05	12	21
Wert, John(Y)	1824	June 04	HarrisonCoOh	05	12	21
Wert, John(Y)	1828	June 12	HarrisonCoOh	05	11	12
Wert, Wm.(Y)	1829	Nov. 16	TuscarwsCoOh	06	14	19
Wertman, Lot(Z)	1813	Dec. 20	WestmrldCoPa	05	02	16
Werts, Peter(Z-M)	1833	Aug. 26	MuskingmCoOh	05	04	05
Wesscot, John(Z-M)	1831	March 22	HolmesCoOh	09	08	02
Wesscot, John(Z-M)	1833	Dec. 20	HolmesCoOhio	09	08	22
West, Ann(Z)	1836	June 13	Morgan Co,Oh	10	06	04
West, Eber(Z-M)	1833	March 06	GuernseyCoOh	02	02	01
West, Eli(Z-M)	1838	May 16	MuskingmCoOh	08	07	11
West, Eli(Z-M)	1838	June 13	CoshoctnCoOh	08	07	11
West, Isaac(Y)	1832	June 05	ColumbanCoOh	06	15	36
West, Isaac(Y)	1832	June 05	ColumbanCoOh	06	15	36
West, John(Y)	1827	June 01	TuscarwsCoOh	06	14	26
West, Nathan(Z)	1833	June 20	GuernseyCoOh	10	09	27
West, Nathan(Z)	1834	Aug. 01	GuernseyCoOh	10	09	35
West, Robert(Z-M)	1832	Sept. 27	HarrisonCoOh	05	04	05
West, Stephen(Y)	1825	March 08	ColumbanCoOh	06	16	26
West, Thomas J.(Z)	1836	Jan. 20	GuernseyCoOh	10	06	14
West, William(Z)	1812	Dec. 26	BelmontCo,Oh	11	13	09
West, William(Z-M)	1832	Oct. 29	TuscarwsCoOh	05	04	05
West, William(Z-M)	1832	Nov. 09	TuscarwsCoOh	05	04	04
West, Wm.(Z)	1830	Oct. 18	ZanesvilleOh	11	12	17
West, Wm.(Z-M)	1832	Jan. 28	TuscarwsCoOh	04	07	09
Westbay, William(Y)	1820	Aug. 22	WashCo.,Penn	06	15	34
Westbrook, Martin(Z)	1825	Nov. 01	Morgan Co,Oh	10	08	02
Westcott, Christopher(Z)	1832	June 20	Morgan Co,Oh	10	08	13
Westcott, Christopher(Z)	1833	March 26	Morgan Co,Oh	09	07	19
Westcott, Christopher(Z)	1834	Nov. 25	Morgan Co,Oh	09	07	19
Westcott, Christopher(Z)	1835	Dec. 14	Morgan Co,Oh	10	08	13
Westcott, Christopher(Z)	1816	Aug. 09	WashngtnCoOh	10	08	24
Westcott, Joel Jr.(Z-M)	1833	Nov. 16	HolmesCoOhio	09	08	22
Westcott, Sylvester(Z)	1816	Aug. 22	WashngtnCoOh	09	07	20
Westlake, George(Z-M)	1824	Dec. 27	CoshoctnCoOh	08	05	16
Westleoafer, Conrad(Z)	1815	June 21	TuscarwsCoOh	01	06	02
Weston, James(Z-M)	1837	March 10	Wayne Co.,Oh	07	07	16
Weston, Jeremy(Z)	1817	Oct. 08	WashngtnCo ?	13	09	31
Westover, Enos(Z)	1815	Dec. 13	MuskingmCoOh	10	04	11
Wetherwax, George(Z-M)	1832	May 25	HolmesCoOhio	07	08	22
Wetherwax, Leonard(Z-M)	1833	Oct. 28	CoshoctnCoOh	07	07	15
Wetherwax, Leonard(Z-M)	1833	Oct. 28	CoshoctnCoOh	07	07	14
Wetty, Michael(Z-M)	1825	Jan. 31	TuscarwsCoOh	03	09	20
Wetzel, John(Z)	1806	May 24	MuskingmCoOh	13	12	10
Weven, Jas. C.(Z-M)	1839	March 23	MuskingmCoOh	08	06	06
Weyandt, Jn.(Y)	1826	Oct. 20	TuscarwsCoOh	06	13	26
Weyandt, John(Y)	1827	Nov. 22	TuscarwsCoOh	07	14	02
Weyandt, John(Y)	1827	Nov. 22	TuscarwsCoOh	07	14	02
Weyandt, John(Y)	1830	Aug. 24	TuscarwsCoOh	07	14	02
Weyandt, John(Y)	1832	April 04	TuscarwsCoOh	07	14	02
Weyer, Anthony(Z)	1813	Oct. 29	GuernseyCoOh	01	03	24
Weyer, James(Z)	1818	Oct. 06	GuernseyCoOh	01	03	24
Weylie, John(Z)	1832	Nov. 12	Perry Co.,Oh	14	14	30
Weylie, Joseph(Z)	1808	Dec. 13	MuskingmCoOh	14	15	32
Weylie, William(Z)	1808	March 05	FairfeldCoOh	15	17	14
Weymer, Godfrey(Z)	1805	Aug. 28	SomersetCoPa	14	16	14
Weymer, Hannah(Z)	1816	March 02	KnoxCo.,Ohio	10	07	17
Weyrick, John(Z)	1808	March 03	BelmontCo,Oh	03	03	08
Weyrick, Peter(Z)	1809	Oct. 24	MuskingmCoOh	03	03	02
Weyrick, Peter(Z-M)	1835	Dec. 12	TuscarwsCoOh	03	05	17
Whaley, Levi(Z)	1834	Feb. 14	Morgan Co,Oh	11	11	36
Wharton, Andrew(Z)	1825	Jan. 14	Morgan Co,Oh	10	09	22

PURCHASER	YEAR	DATE	RESIDENCE	R	T	S
Wharton, Andrew(Z)	1813	March 15	GuernseyCoOh	10	08	08
Wharton, Henry(Z)	1817	Jan. 07	WashCo.,Penn	11	12	03
Wharton, Jacob(Z)	1823	Sept. 17	Morgan Co,Oh	10	08	29
Wharton, Jacob(Z)	1824	Aug. 30	Morgan Co,Oh	11	12	21
Wharton, John(Z)	1824	Nov. 25	GuernseyCoOh	10	09	21
Wharton, Robert(Z)	1826	Nov. 22	GuernseyCoOh	10	08	19
Wheatley, George(Z)	1832	June 28	Brooke CoVir	11	10	26
Wheatly, Geo.(Z)	1833	May 30	Brooke CoVir	11	10	26
Wheeler, Eliphalet(Z)	1827	Aug. 27	Morgan Co,Oh	09	07	21
Wheeler, Eliphalet(Z)	1835	Dec. 22	Morgan Co,Oh	09	07	34
Wheeler, Eliphalet(Z)	1835	Dec. 22	Morgan Co,Oh	09	07	27
Wheeler, Eliphalet(Z)	1836	Jan. 28	Morgan Co,Oh	09	07	34
Wheeler, Eliphalet(Z)	1835	Dec. 22	Morgan Co,Oh	09	07	34
Wheeler, Europe(Z)	1833	March 26	Morgan Co,Oh	09	06	17
Wheeler, Geo. W.(Z)	1831	Oct. 18	KnoxCo.,Ohio	10	05	24
Wheeler, George(Z)	1815	Nov. 21	MuskingmCoOh	07	03	19
Wheeler, Hanson(Z-M)	1829	Dec. 31	Brooke CoVir	05	03	18
Wheeler, Hanson(Z-M)	1831	March 01	MuskingmCoOh	05	03	19
Wheeler, Henry(Z-M)	1826	Oct. 14	MuskingmCoOh	05	02	06
Wheeler, Henson(Z-M)	1836	Jan. 02	MuskingmCoOh	05	03	05
Wheeler, Ignatious(Z)	1836	Oct. 22	Morgan Co,Oh	08	05	10
Wheeler, John(Z)	1834	Nov. 27	Morgan Co,Oh	09	06	01
Wheeler, John(Z)	1836	Feb. 16	Morgan Co,Oh	09	06	25
Wheeler, John(Z-M)	1829	Dec. 29	KnoxCo.,Ohio	10	05	14
Wheeler, Nehemiah(Z-M)	1834	Feb. 22	LickingCo,Oh	11	04	25
Wheeler, Regin(Z-M)	1831	June 06	Jeff.Co.,Oh.	03	04	02
Wheeler, Samuel(Z)	1813	Feb. 23	LickingCo,Oh	10	05	05
Wheeler, Samuel(Z)	1813	Feb. 24	LickingCo,Oh	05	05	06
Wheeler, Timothy(Z)	1806	May 24	MuskingmCoOh	15	16	14
Wheeler, William(Z)	1816	April 20	MuskingmCoOh	06	03	16
Wheeler, William(Z-M)	1837	March 10	TuscarwsCoOh	05	04	07
Wheeler, Wm.(Y)	1823	June 18	Brooke CoVir	04	13	26
Wheelirs, George(Z-M)	1829	Dec. 21	MuskingmCoOh	07	03	20
Whelan, Fred'k.(Y)	1824	May 18	ColumbanCoOh	03	15	22
Whetstone, Daniel(Z)	1808	June 18	BelmontCo,Oh	01	02	22
Whetstone, John(Z)	1832	Nov. 06	Perry Co.,Oh	15	15	31
Whetstone, John(Z)	1833	Nov. 11	Perry Co.,Oh	15	15	31
Whihen, William(Y)	1831	June 01	HarrisonCoOh	06	12	32
While, Jacob(Z-M)	1838	May 01	CoshoctnCoOh	08	07	12
Whils, Adam(Z)	1831	July 05	GuernseyCoOh	08	08	28
Whiney, Limri(Y)	1826	May 04	ColumbanCoOh	05	18	15
Whip, Ezekiel(Z)	1831	April 01	Perry Co.,Oh	15	14	01
Whips, Ezekiel(Z)	1832	Dec. 01	Perry Co.,Oh	14	12	06
Whips, Ezekiel(Z)	1833	April 30	Perry Co.,Oh	15	14	02
Whips, John(Z)	1831	Oct. 22	Perry Co.,Oh	15	14	02
Whips, Lloyd(Z)	1833	Nov. 05	Perry Co.,Oh	15	14	02
Whips, Lloyd(Z)	1836	Dec. 09	Perry Co.,Oh	14	13	31
Whips, Mathias(Z)	1832	Jan. 06	Perry Co.,Oh	15	15	14
Whips, William Aug(Z)	1832	Dec. 18	Perry Co.,Oh	14	13	31
Whitacre, Edward Thomas(Y)	1833	March 11	ColumbanCoOh	05	15	04
Whitacre, Thomas(Y)	1832	Nov. 21	ColumbanCoOh	05	15	05
Whitacre, Thos.(Y)	1829	April 16	ColumbanCoOh	05	16	33
Whitacre, William(Y)	1831	Feb. 10	ColumbanCoOh	05	16	33
Whitaker, Geo. W.(Z-M)	1833	Nov. 20	GuernseyCoOh	02	03	01
Whitaker, James(Z)	1806	June 28	MuskingmCoOh	14	16	17
Whitaker, Joseph(Z-M)	1834	Jan. 24	GuernseyCoOh	03	06	16
Whitaker, Lewis(Z)	1811	May 18	MuskingmCoOh	13	11	24
Whitaker, Obed(Z)	1814	Aug. 27	Jeff.Co.,Oh.	02	04	22
Whitaker, Obed(Z-M)	1824	April 26	GuernseyCoOh	02	04	22
Whitaker, Wm.(Z-M)	1829	April 24	GuernseyCoOh	02	04	21
Whitcraft, George(Y)	1826	Oct. 03	TuscarwsCoOh	06	14	17
Whitcraft, James(Y)	1823	June 07	GuernseyCoOh	07	09	22
Whitcraft, James(Y)	1823	June 07	GuernseyCoOh	07	09	21
Whitcraft, James(Y)	1831	July 01	GuernseyCoOh	07	09	21
White, Alexander(Z-M)	1829	March 03	MuskingmCoOh	07	03	22
White, Ann(Z)	1835	Sept. 01	GuernseyCoOh	09	06	30
White, Anthony(Z)	1836	Aug. 27	Wheeling,Vir	08	06	09
White, Anthony(Z-M)	1826	Nov. 01	KnoxCo.,Ohio	11	08	19
White, Augustus(Z)	1816	Jan. 02	FauquierCoVa	09	04	09

PURCHASER	YEAR	DATE	RESIDENCE	R	T	S
White, Augustus(Z)	1816	April 01	FauquierCoVa	09	04	09
White, Benj.(Z-M)	1829	Nov. 20	MuskingmCoOh	04	02	13
White, Benjamin(Z-M)	1832	May 22	MuskingmCoOh	05	02	10
White, Benjamin(Z-M)	1834	Dec. 17	CoshoctnCoOh	07	07	12
White, Benjamin(Z-M)	1835	April 23	CoshoctnCoOh	07	07	12
White, Bennet(Y)	1828	Feb. 15	Brooke CoVir	03	11	36
White, Bennet(Y)	1828	Feb. 15	Brooke CoVir	03	12	31
White, Bennet(Y)	1832	May 12	ColumbanCoOh	04	12	06
White, Benoni(Z-M)	1833	June 01	TuscarwsCoOh	01	06	13
White, Catharine(Y)	1830	Jan. 15	ColumbanCoOh	03	13	22
White, Charles(Y)	1827	Nov. 30	HarrisonCoOh	06	11	11
White, Dileworth(Z)	1834	March 25	Morgan Co,Oh	10	06	03
White, Dilworth(Z)	1835	Aug. 12	Morgan Co,Oh	10	06	03
White, Elihu(Y)	1827	Oct. 19	FayetteCo,Pa	07	11	28
White, Elihu(Z-M)	1836	Feb. 18	MuskingmCoOh	02	04	05
White, George(Z-M)	1837	Sept. 18	AlleghnyCoPa	04	04	11
White, Israel(Z)	1829	April 09	BelmontCo,Oh	13	08	27
White, Israel(Z)	1829	Dec. 21	Morgan Co,Oh	13	08	28
White, James M.(Y)	1825	Aug. 29	WashCo.,Penn	05	12	23
White, John(Z)	1832	Dec. 28	MuskingmCoOh	11	12	15
White, John(Z)	1833	Nov. 25	MuskingmCoOh	11	12	22
White, John(Z)	1834	Aug. 02	MuskingmCoOh	11	12	26
White, John(Z-M)	1832	July 17	MuskingmCoOh	10	03	03
White, John(Z-M)	1833	Dec. 12	LickingCo,Oh	10	08	02
White, Joseph(Z)	1814	Dec. 31	WashCo.,Penn	05	02	20
White, Joseph(Z-M)	1824	June 02	BelmontCo,Oh	09	05	13
White, Josiah(Z-M)	1836	Nov. 11	CoshoctnCoOh	07	07	19
White, Lewis(Y)	1827	Jan. 26	Stark Co.,Oh	07	20	12
White, Loyed(Z-M)	1835	Oct. 07	LickingCo,Oh	09	03	06
White, Loyed(Z-M)	1836	Feb. 06	LickingCo,Oh	09	03	06
White, Thomas(Z)	1813	Dec. 18	KnoxCo.,Ohio	10	07	18
White, Thomas(Z-M)	1824	Oct. 07	KnoxCo.,Ohio	11	08	19
White, Thomas(Z-M)	1825	Aug. 31	MuskingmCoOh	05	02	19
White, Thomas(Z-M)	1829	Oct. 21	TuscarwsCoOh	11	08	19
White, Thomas(Z-M)	1833	Sept. 24	KnoxCo.,Ohio	11	08	19
White, Timothy(Y)	1832	Oct. 08	BrookeCo,Vir	03	11	36
White, Timothy(Y)	1832	Oct. 08	BrookeCo,Vir	03	11	36
White, Wells(Z)	1829	Dec. 18	Morgan Co,Oh	12	09	14
White, William(Y)	1831	July 05	Jeff.Co.,Oh.	04	12	28
Whitehill, Thomas Jr.(Z-M)	1823	Oct. 20	GuernseyCoOh	02	03	06
Whitehill, Thomas Senr.(Z-M)	1823	Oct. 20	GuernseyCoOh	02	03	06
Whitehurste, Jahew(Z-M)	1837	Sept. 04	TuscarwsCoOh	03	05	24
Whitehurste, Jahew(Z-M)	1837	Sept. 04	TuscarwsCoOh	03	05	25
Whiteraft, James(Y)	1826	March 16	GuernseyCoOh	07	09	22
Whitesell, John(Z-M)	1838	Oct. 13	CoshoctnCoOh	08	07	20
Whitman, George(Z-M)	1836	Dec. 30	HolmesCoOhio	05	07	07
Whitmon, John(Z)	1834	Jan. 03	Perry Co.,Oh	15	14	06
Whitmore, Geo.(Z-M)	1831	March 19	TuscarwsCoOh	03	08	08
Whitmore, James(Z)	1835	Jan. 24	BelmontCo,Oh	09	06	34
Whitmore, James(Z)	1836	April 09	WashngtnCoOh	08	05	11
Whitmore, Peter(Z)	1835	April 29	Perry Co.,Oh	15	15	31
Whitmore, Samuel(Z)	1815	Dec. 09	HarrisonCoOh	09	04	03
Whitmyer, Philip(Y)	1824	Dec. 06	Stark Co.,Oh	09	12	30
Whitney, Ephraim Jr.(Z-M)	1835	Oct. 01	HarrisonCoOh	01	06	22
Whittaker, James(Y)	1828	Dec. 23	HarrisonCoOh	05	11	30
Whittatch, John(Z)	1836	June 10	AthensCoOhio	15	14	34
Whitten, Sarah(Z-M)	1825	June 07	GuernseyCoOh	02	01	06
Whitten, Sarah(Z-M)	1826	Dec. 07	GuernseyCoOh	03	01	15
Whitten, Thomas(Z)	1811	Oct. 01	GuernseyCoOh	09	08	19
Whitten, Wm.(Y)	1828	Jan. 14	Jeff.Co.,Oh.	06	12	26
Whittenton, Wm.(H)	1823	Dec. 18	HarrisonCoOh	07	11	22
Whittle, Daniel(Y)	1826	Sept. 26	BelmontCo,Oh	05	18	08
Whittle, Daniel(Y)	1826	Sept. 26	BelmontCo,Oh	05	18	18
Whittle, Daniel(Y)	1826	Sept. 26	BelmontCo,Oh	05	18	08
Whittle, Daniel(Y)	1826	Sept. 26	BelmontCo,Oh	05	18	07
Whittle, Daniel(Y)	1826	Sept. 26	BelmontCo,Oh	05	18	07
Whittle, Daniel(Y)	1826	Sept. 26	BelmontCo,Oh	05	18	18
Whittle, Daniel(Y)	1826	Sept. 26	BelmontCo,Oh	05	18	18
Whittle, Daniel(Y)	1826	Oct. 05	BelmontCo,Oh	05	18	08

PURCHASER	YEAR	DATE	RESIDENCE	R	T	S
Whittle, Daniel(Y)	1826	Oct. 05	BelmontCo,Oh	05	18	08
Whittle, Daniel(Y)	1826	Oct. 05	BelmontCo,Oh	05	18	08
Whittle, Daniel(Y)	1826	Oct. 05	BelmontCo,Oh	05	18	08
Whittle, Daniel(Y)	1826	Oct. 05	BelmontCo,Oh	05	18	07
Whittle, Daniel(Y)	1826	Oct. 05	BelmontCo,Oh	05	18	07
Whittle, Daniel(Y)	1826	Oct. 05	BelmontCo,Oh	05	18	19
Whittle, Daniel(Y)	1826	Oct. 05	BelmontCo,Oh	06	19	13
Whittle, Daniel(Y)	1826	Oct. 05	BelmontCo,Oh	06	19	25
Whittle, Daniel(Y)	1826	Oct. 05	BelmontCo,Oh	05	18	19
Wiand, John Senr.(Y)	1823	Oct. 27	HarrisonCoOh	05	13	20
Wiand, John Senr.(Y)	1824	Nov. 23	HarrisonCoOh	05	13	20
Wiand, John(Y)	1829	March 14	HarrisonCoOh	05	13	21
Wiand, John(Y)	1831	Aug. 31	HarrisonCoOh	05	13	22
Wiand, Mary(Y)	1832	June 01	HarrisonCoOh	05	13	21
Wiandt, Adam(Z-M)	1836	April 02	TuscarwsCoOh	03	07	16
Wiandt, Adam(Z-M)	1836	April 02	TuscarwsCoOh	03	07	15
Wiandt, Adam(Z-M)	1836	April 02	TuscarwsCoOh	03	07	16
Wiandt, Daniel(Z-M)	1836	Nov. 02	TuscarwsCoOh	04	07	12
Wianett, Michael(Z-M)	1832	Nov. 28	TuscarwsCoOh	04	07	21
Wiant, Jacob(Z-M)	1835	Sept. 03	TuscarwsCoOh	03	07	25
Wibble, Jacob(Z)	1814	July 20	TuscarwsCoOh	03	09	08
Wibel, Solomon(Z-M)	1838	July 03	KnoxCo.,Ohio	10	06	14
Wible, George(Y)	1831	July 05	HarrisonCoOh	05	11	34
Wickam, Samuel(Z)	1816	March 18	WashngtnCoOh	11	10	25
Wickens, George(Z)	1836	April 01	WashngtnCoOh	08	05	30
Wickens, George(Z)	1836	July 05	WashngtnCoOh	08	05	30
Wickens, George(Z)	1836	Oct. 12	WashngtnCoOh	08	05	29
Wickerd, Jno.(Y)	1821	Dec. 31	ColumbanCoOh	06	17	21
Wickham, Anson(Z)	1836	June 15	MonroeCo.,Oh	08	07	32
Wickham, Asahal M.(Z)	1835	Dec. 10	MuskingmCoOh	08	07	32
Wickham, Asahel M.(Z)	1835	Dec. 10	MuskingmCoOh	08	06	05
Wickham, Ebenezer(Z)	1836	Feb. 19	MuskingmCoOh	08	07	33
Wickham, Jeremiah(Z)	1836	Jan. 18	MonroeCo.,Oh	08	06	06
Wickham, Jeremiah(Z-M)	1833	Aug. 02	MonroeCo.,Oh	08	07	30
Wickham, John Junr.(Z)	1817	July 08	ColumbanCoOh	09	06	01
Wickham, Nath'h. Robins(Z-M)	1838	Dec. 03	TuscarwsCoOh	03	05	18
Wickham, Nathan R.(Z-M)	1836	Feb. 01	TuscarwsCoOh	03	05	11
Wickham, Nathan R.(Z-M)	1836	Feb. 01	TuscarwsCoOh	03	05	11
Wickham, Nathan(Z)	1826	May 05	Morgan Co,Oh	09	07	36
Wickham, Nathan(Z)	1833	April 15	MonroeCo.,Oh	08	07	30
Wickham, Nathan(Z)	1836	Jan. 18	MonroeCo.,Oh	08	07	32
Wickham, Rosetta(Z)	1833	June 04	Morgan Co,Oh	11	10	26
Wickham, Salathiel(Z)	1835	Dec. 09	Morgan Co,Oh	08	07	33
Wickham, Salathiel(Z)	1835	Dec. 09	Morgan Co,Oh	08	06	04
Wickham, Thomas(Z)	1810	Nov. 12	MuskingmCoOh	05	04	18
Wickins, Geo. Jur.(Z)	1832	June 05	WashCo.,Ohio	08	05	11
Wickiser, Abraham(Z)	1812	June 29	MuskingmCoOh	14	16	05
Wicklaser, Abraham(Z)	1812	June 29	MuskingmCoOh	14	16	05
Wicoff, John(Z-M)	1835	July 16	WayneCo.,Oh.	07	08	07
Wier, John(Z)	1835	Aug. 17	Morgan Co,Oh	10	06	09
Wier, John(Z)	1835	Sept. 23	Morgan Co,Oh	10	06	09
Wier, William(Z-M)	1823	Oct. 27	GuernseyCoOh	04	03	15
Wier, William(Z-M)	1835	Dec. 05	GuernseyCoOh	04	03	15
Wiers, Benjamin(Z-M)	1832	Sept. 12	GuernseyCoOh	03	01	14
Wiggins, Edward(Z)	1807	Jan. 19	BrookCo.,Vir	05	04	11
Wiggins, Edward(Z)	1812	April 21	CoshoctnCoOh	05	03	01
Wiggins, Edward(Z)	1814	Dec. 19	CoshoctnCoOh	05	04	02
Wiggins, Edward(Z-M)	1835	Oct. 26	CoshoctnCoOh	05	04	12
Wiggins, Isaac(Y)	1820	Oct. 20	SteubenvleOH	04	13	31
Wiggins, Isaac(Y)	1830	May 05	ColumbanCoOh	04	13	25
Wiggins, Isaac(Y)	1830	Oct. 27	ColumbanCoOh	05	13	10
Wiggins, Isaac(Y)	1832	Feb. 08	ColumbanCoOh	05	13	10
Wiggins, John(Z-M)	1833	Feb. 19	CoshoctnCoOh	05	04	11
Wiggins, John(Z-M)	1835	Oct. 24	CoshoctnCoOh	05	04	12
Wilbur, Thomas(Z-M)	1823	Oct. 08	LickingCo,Oh	11	01	11
Wilcox, Chas.(Z-M)	1835	Dec. 24	MuskingmCoOh	06	03	03
Wilcox, James(Z)	1833	Jan. 16	MuskingmCoOh	13	10	07
Wilcox, James(Z)	1811	Nov. 12	MuskingmCoOh	06	03	02
Wilcox, Wm.(Z-M)	1836	Jan. 28	MuskingmCoOh	06	03	02

316

PURCHASER	YEAR	DATE	RESIDENCE	R	T	S
Wilcox, Wm.(Z-M)	1835	Dec. 24	MuskingmCoOh	06	03	03
Wilcoxon, Anthony(Y)	1830	March 15	Stark Co.,Oh	06	05	27
Wildes, James(Z)	1837	April 14	ColumbanCoOh	15	14	35
Wildman, George(Z)	1836	March 03	Morgan Co,Oh	14	13	26
Wildy, James(Z)	1836	Nov. 09	ColumbanCoOh	15	14	35
Wile, John George(Y)	1833	June 04	Jeff.Co.,Oh.	03	11	17
Wilex, James(Z)	1811	Nov. 12	MuskingmCoOh	06	03	02
Wiley, David(Y)	1822	June 24	ColumbanCoOh	05	18	13
Wiley, David(Z)	1833	April 08	Morgan Co,Oh	09	06	04
Wiley, Hans(Z-M)	1831	Sept. 01	GuernseyCoOh	02	03	06
Wiley, James(Z)	1830	March 12	Ohio Co.,Vir	11	11	05
Wiley, James(Z)	1833	June 04	Morgan Co,Oh	09	07	31
Wiley, James(Z)	1836	Jan. 21	Morgan Co,Oh	09	07	31
Wiley, John(Z)	1830	May 12	Morgan Co,Oh	09	06	04
Wiley, John(Z)	1833	April 08	Morgan Co,Oh	09	06	09
Wiley, John(Z)	1812	Sept. 01	GuernseyCoOh	09	06	03
Wiley, John(Z)	1815	Sept. 28	BelmontCo,Oh	09	06	08
Wiley, T.(Z)	1815	Aug. 26	BelmontCo,Oh	09	06	08
Wiley, Thomas(Z)	1834	Oct. 16	Morgan Co,Oh	09	06	04
Wiley, William Jnr.(Z-M)	1836	Dec. 16	GuernseyCoOh	02	01	14
Wiley, William(Z)	1815	Nov. 23	GuernseyCoOh	09	06	06
Wilhelm, George(Z)	1806	Nov. 24	WashCo.,Penn	02	07	11
Wilkey, Samuel(Y)	1826	Sept. 14	Stark Co.,Oh	06	16	08
Wilkin, Henry(Z)	1808	Oct. 28	HardyCo.,Vir	04	03	17
Wilkin, James(Y)	1830	Feb. 25	TuscarwsCoOh	06	16	30
Wilkin, John(Y)	1825	Aug. 20	WashCo.,Penn	07	11	13
Wilkin, Mathew(Z-M)	1825	June 08	HarrisonCoOh	07	08	12
Wilkin, Robert(Z-M)	1827	March 01	HolmesCoOhio	08	08	13
Wilkin, Robert(Z-M)	1831	Feb. 12	HolmesCoOhio	07	08	12
Wilkin, Thomas(Y)	1827	July 16	GuernseyCoOh	07	11	14
Wilkins, D.(Z)	1814	Feb. 17	MuskingmCoOh	08	03	06
Wilkins, Francis(Z)	1810	March 29	WashngtnCoOh	13	11	03
Wilkins, Francis(Z)	1810	May 05	WashCo.,Penn	01	02	15
Wilkinson, Thos. P.(Z)	1838	Feb. 06	MonroeCo.,Oh	08	06	36
Wilkinson, Thos.(Z-M)	1826	Nov. 14	GuernseyCoOh	02	01	02
Wilkison, William(Z-M)	1834	Oct. 23	CoshoctnCoOh	05	06	15
Wilkison, William(Z-M)	1834	Oct. 23	CoshoctnCoOh	05	06	15
Wilks, Ira(Z)	1832	Nov. 27	Morgan Co,Oh	11	11	22
Willard, Henry(Z)	1811	July 31	GuernseyCoOh	03	10	19
Willcox, James(Z-M)	1831	Oct. 10	MuskingmCoOh	06	03	02
Willert, John(Y)	1822	Sept. 02	ArmstrngCoPa	07	19	21
Willet, Fleming(Z-M)	1838	June 18	KnoxCo.,Ohio	10	05	21
Willey, Absalom(Z)	1833	Feb. 09	Morgan Co,Oh	09	07	19
Willey, Geo.(Z)	1836	June 16	Morgan Co,Oh	09	07	30
Willey, Levi(Z)	1836	Dec. 12	Morgan Co,Oh	09	05	25
Willey, Levi(Z)	1836	Dec. 12	Morgan Co,Oh	09	05	36
Willey, Thomas(Z-M)	1833	Oct. 28	TuscarwsCoOh	03	08	13
Willey, Wm. P.(Z)	1831	Dec. 13	Morgan Co,Oh	09	07	20
Willey, Wm. P.(Z)	1831	Jan. 27	Morgan Co,Oh	09	07	20
Willhelm, S. A.(Z-M)	1836	Feb. 12	CoshoctnCoOh	05	06	23
Willhelm, S. J. W.(Z-M)	1836	Feb. 12	CoshoctnCoOh	05	06	23
Williams, Ab'm.(Y)	1828	Sept. 25	ColumbanCoOh	04	13	24
Williams, Abel(Z)	1807	Feb. 12	GreeneCo.Vir	01	09	10
Williams, Able(Z-M)	1833	Jan. 10	TuscarwsCoOh	01	09	12
Williams, Abraham(Z)	1835	Oct. 29	Perry Co.,Oh	15	14	22
Williams, Abraham(Z)	1835	Oct. 29	Perry Co.,Oh	15	14	15
Williams, Abraham(Z)	1806	June 04	MuskingmCoOh	01	02	21
Williams, Anthony(Z-M)	1829	Jan. 01	GuernseyCoOh	01	01	19
Williams, Benj'm.(Z)	1814	July 02	CoshoctnCoOh	05	04	12
Williams, Benj'm.(Z-M)	1836	Aug. 18	CoshoctnCoOh	08	06	07
Williams, Benj'm.(Z-M)	1836	Aug. 29	CoshoctnCoOh	08	06	03
Williams, Benj'm.(Z-M)	1836	Aug. 29	CoshoctnCoOh	08	07	03
Williams, Benjamin(Z)	1813	Dec. 28	TuscarwsCoOh	01	09	11
Williams, Benjamin(Z-M)	1833	Jan. 10	TuscarwsCoOh	01	09	12
Williams, Benjamin(Z-M)	1836	Sept. 16	CoshoctnCoOh	08	07	03
Williams, Benjamin(Z-M)	1836	Sept. 16	CoshoctnCoOh	08	06	06
Williams, Billingsley(Y)	1833	Dec. 21	Jeff.Co.,Oh.	04	13	15
Williams, Charles(Z)	1814	Jan. 10	CoshoctnCoOh	07	08	21
Williams, Charles(Z)	1814	Jan. 31	CoshoctnCoOh	07	07	16

PURCHASER	YEAR	DATE	RESIDENCE	R	T	S
Williams, Chester(Z)	1831	Aug. 18	Morgan Co,Oh	10	06	27
Williams, Christ'n.(Y)	1829	March 17	ColumbanCoOh	03	13	15
Williams, Collins(Z)	1829	July 02	Morgan Co,Oh	10	06	27
Williams, Collins(Z)	1833	Sept. 09	Morgan Co,Oh	10	06	22
Williams, Cyrus(Z)	1836	June 23	GuernseyCoOh	09	05	31
Williams, David(Z-M)	1824	March 12	GuernseyCoOh	03	01	08
Williams, David(Z-M)	1833	Oct. 28	GuernseyCoOh	03	01	08
Williams, George(Y)	1832	July 11	Stark Co.,Oh	10	02	33
Williams, George(Z-M)	1831	Nov. 19	Perry Co.,Oh	04	06	13
Williams, George(Z-M)	1835	Nov. 03	CoshoctnCoOh	04	06	12
Williams, Isaac(Y)	1825	Oct. 11	Stark Co.,Oh	07	19	15
Williams, Isaac(Z)	1832	May 29	Morgan Co,Oh	13	08	20
Williams, J.(Z)	1816	Dec. 05	CoshoctnCoOh	11	05	18
Williams, Jackson (Z-M)	1833	Nov. 19	TuscarwsCoOh	03	05	18
Williams, James Senr.(Z-M)	1821	Oct. 17	TuscarwsCoOh	04	07	22
Williams, James(Z)	1828	Nov. 22	BelmontCo,Oh	13	08	20
Williams, James(Z)	1835	Nov. 10	BelmontCo,Oh	09	07	22
Williams, James(Z)	1811	April 18	CoshoctnCoOh	08	04	10
Williams, James(Z)	1814	Oct. 25	KnoxCo.,Ohio	11	05	15
Williams, James(Z)	1815	Oct. 06	CoshoctnCoOh	06	03	03
Williams, James(Z-M)	1835	Nov. 09	CoshoctnCoOh	05	04	25
Williams, James(Z-M)	1835	Nov. 09	CoshoctnCoOh	06	04	21
Williams, Jas. B.(Z-M)	1827	July 17	CoshoctnCoOh	05	04	25
Williams, Jeremiah(Z-M)	1837	Sept. 01	CoshoctnCoOh	08	06	04
Williams, Jeremiah(Z-M)	1837	Sept. 01	CoshoctnCoOh	08	06	07
Williams, Jeremiah(Z-M)	1838	Sept. 03	CoshoctnCoOh	08	06	03
Williams, Jeremiah(Z-M)	1838	Sept. 03	CoshoctnCoOh	08	06	03
Williams, Jeremiah(Z-M)	1836	Sept. 16	CoshoctnCoOh	08	07	03
Williams, Jesse(Z)	1810	Sept. 19	MuskingmCoOh	06	02	15
Williams, Jesse(Z)	1816	Feb. 13	MuskingmCoOh	06	02	13
Williams, Joel(Z)	1836	Aug. 19	Morgan Co,Oh	09	05	30
Williams, Joel(Z)	1810	April 17	GuernseyCoOh	08	08	04
Williams, Joel(Z)	1810	April 17	GuernseyCoOh	08	08	04
Williams, John R.(Z-M)	1835	Nov. 14	CoshoctnCoOh	05	04	13
Williams, John R.(Z-M)	1835	Nov. 14	CoshoctnCoOh	05	04	12
Williams, John R.(Z-M)	1838	Sept. 27	CoshoctnCoOh	05	04	13
Williams, John Senr.(Z)	1827	March 22	Morgan Co,Oh	13	08	12
Williams, John Senr.(Z)	1815	Jan. 17	CoshoctnCoOh	06	07	19
Williams, John Senr.(Z)	1815	Jan. 17	CoshoctnCoOh	06	06	03
Williams, John(Y)	1828	June 20	ColumbanCoOh	04	13	15
Williams, John(Y)	1829	Oct. 08	ColumbanCoOh	04	13	15
Williams, John(Y)	1833	Feb. 14	ColumbanCoOh	04	13	15
Williams, John(Z)	1830	July 01	Morgan Co,Oh	13	08	12
Williams, John(Z)	1835	Oct. 05	Morgan Co,Oh	09	07	05
Williams, John(Z)	1835	Nov. 04	BelmontCo,Oh	10	06	20
Williams, John(Z)	1835	Nov. 04	BelmontCo,Oh	10	06	20
Williams, John(Z)	1805	June 14	MuskingmCoOh	01	02	17
Williams, John(Z)	1805	July 26	MuskingmCoOh	14	15	03
Williams, John(Z)	1812	March 26	MuskingmCoOh	15	17	01
Williams, John(Z)	1814	May 05	GuernseyCoOh	03	02	09
Williams, John(Z)	1814	July 06	TuscarwsCoOh	04	08	14
Williams, John(Z-M)	1825	April 04	HolmesCoOhio	07	08	02
Williams, John(Z-M)	1832	April 04	HolmesCoOhio	05	09	08
Williams, John(Z-M)	1830	Nov. 18	TuscarwsCoOh	01	09	22
Williams, John(Z-M)	1830	Nov. 18	TuscarwsCoOh	01	09	19
Williams, John(Z-M)	1833	Feb. 07	LickingCo,Oh	11	04	22
Williams, John(Z-M)	1834	Oct. 10	BelmontCo,Oh	03	02	11
Williams, John(Z-M)	1836	Jan. 16	CoshoctnCoOh	04	04	03
Williams, Jonathan(Z)	1835	June 05	GuernseyCoOh	08	08	18
Williams, Joseph Jr.(Z)	1836	Jan. 22	GuernseyCoOh	09	05	30
Williams, Joseph Jr.(Z)	1836	Jan. 25	GuernseyCoOh	09	05	30
Williams, Joseph(Y)	1832	Dec. 17	ColumbanCoOh	03	12	34
Williams, Joseph(Y)	1833	June 21	ColumbanCoOh	03	12	34
Williams, Joseph(Z)	1836	Jan. 22	GuernseyCoOh	09	05	31
Williams, Joseph(Z)	1805	Jan. 18	BelmontCo,Oh	01	01	01
Williams, Joseph(Z)	1806	Nov. 14	MuskingmCoOh	07	03	20
Williams, Joseph(Z)	1816	May 30	ZanesvilleOh	06	02	14
Williams, Joseph(Z)	1816	Aug. 02	GuernseyCoOh	01	01	22
Williams, Joseph(Z-M)	1837	March 07	CoshoctnCoOh	07	07	16

318

PURCHASER	YEAR	DATE	RESIDENCE	R	T	S
Williams, Levi(Z)	1814	Sept. 10	GuernseyCoOh	01	04	24
Williams, Lewis(Z)	1812	Nov. 14	ChesterCo,Pa	06	02	22
Williams, Michael F.(Z)	1817	Aug. 22	MuskingmCoOh	15	14	10
Williams, Nathaniel(Z-M)	1836	Jan. 08	HolmesCoOhio	09	09	25
Williams, Nathaniel(Z-M)	1836	Aug. 13	CoshoctnCoOh	09	07	20
Williams, Nathaniel(Z-M)	1837	April 17	CoshoctnCoOh	09	07	19
Williams, Nehemiah(Z-M)	1833	Jan. 08	GuernseyCoOh	03	01	03
Williams, Nimrod(Z)	1835	Aug. 15	GuernseyCoOh	09	05	31
Williams, Nimrod(Z)	1835	Nov. 05	GuernseyCoOh	09	05	31
Williams, Philip(Z)	1835	Nov. 27	GuernseyCoOh	09	08	33
Williams, Rich'd.(Z-M)	1836	Oct. 17	HolmesCoOhio	09	08	08
Williams, Richard(Z)	1828	Nov. 22	BelmontCo,Oh	13	08	20
Williams, Richard(Z)	1833	Aug. 28	Perry Co.,Oh	14	12	20
Williams, Richard(Z)	1812	May 21	CoshoctnCoOh	05	04	24
Williams, Richard(Z-M)	1835	Nov. 04	CoshoctnCoOh	05	04	16
Williams, Robt.(Z)	1831	March 24	KnoxCo.,Ohio	10	07	25
Williams, S. L.(Z)	1814	Oct. 12	MuskingmCoOh	15	18	01
Williams, Sam'l.(Z)	1831	March 01	Perry Co.,Oh	14	12	19
Williams, Sam'l.(Z-M)	1833	Dec. 09	CoshoctnCoOh	04	04	08
Williams, Samuel(Z)	1811	June 10	MuskingmCoOh	15	18	04
Williams, Samuel(Z)	1813	May 01	MuskingmCoOh	15	18	05
Williams, Samuel(Z-M)	1835	Nov. 19	CoshoctnCoOh	04	04	02
Williams, Samuel(Z-M)	1836	Jan. 29	CoshoctnCoOh	07	05	03
Williams, Sarah(Z)	1816	Sept. 17	Jeff.Co.,Oh.	01	04	19
Williams, Silas(Z-M)	1829	Jan. 19	TuscarwsCoOh	01	09	19
Williams, Susannah(Z-M)	1835	Sept. 28	CoshoctnCoOh	07	05	08
Williams, T.(Z)	1814	Oct. 12	MuskingmCoOh	15	18	01
Williams, Thomas R.(Z-M)	1834	March 04	CoshoctnCoOh	07	05	05
Williams, Thomas(Z-M)	1836	April 20	CoshoctnCoOh	05	04	24
Williams, Thos.(Z-M)	1831	July 06	TuscarwsCoOh	01	09	08
Williams, Wash'n.(Z-M)	1835	Nov. 30	HolmesCoOhio	08	08	24
Williams, Washington(Z-M)	1836	Sept. 26	HolmesCoOhio	08	08	24
Williams, William(Z)	1830	Jan. 08	GuernseyCoOh	08	08	25
Williams, Wm. M.(Z)	1814	Dec. 01	BelmontCo,Oh	11	05	13
Williams, Wm. M.(Z)	1814	Dec. 01	BelmontCo,Oh	11	05	14
Williams, Wm. M.(Z)	1814	Dec. 01	BelmontCo,Oh	11	05	06
Williams, Wm.(Z)	1821	June 16	GuernseyCoOh	09	08	32
Williams, Wm.(Z)	1814	July 02	CoshoctnCoOh	05	04	12
Williamson, George(Y)	1834	Oct. 07	Stark Co.,Oh	09	12	33
Williamson, Joseph(Z)	1814	Dec. 21	MuskingmCoOh	05	02	24
Williamson, Piatt(Z-M)	1836	Jan. 13	CoshoctnCoOh	07	07	17
Williamson, Piatt(Z-M)	1837	March 04	CoshoctnCoOh	07	07	16
Williamson, Pieatt(Z-M)	1822	Dec. 23	CoshoctnCoOh	07	07	17
Williman, Jacob(Y)	1828	Jan. 29	Stark Co.,Oh	07	17	01
Willis, Daniel(Z)	1835	Nov. 28	MuskingmCoOh	13	10	17
Willis, Edward(Z-M)	1831	July 09	GuernseyCoOh	02	03	02
Willis, Henry(Z-M)	1835	Oct. 22	CoshoctnCoOh	05	07	14
Willis, Isaac(Z-M)	1832	Oct. 26	GuernseyCoOh	02	03	10
Willis, James(Y)	1822	Dec. 23	GreeneCo.,Pa	05	16	21
Willis, James(Y)	1822	Dec. 23	GreeneCo.,Pa	05	16	21
Willis, James(Z-M)	1824	May 11	GuernseyCoOh	02	03	02
Willis, Joseph(Y)	1822	June 13	GreeneCo.,Pa	05	16	21
Willis, L. P.(Z)	1831	March 19	Perry Co.,Oh	14	14	19
Willis, Richard(Z-M)	1832	Sept. 29	CoshoctnCoOh	08	06	12
Willis, Robert(Z)	1835	Dec. 19	Morgan Co,Oh	13	08	22
Willis, Stephen(Z-M)	1836	March 18	CoshoctnCoOh	08	06	09
Willis, Stephen(Z-M)	1838	June 08	CoshoctnCoOh	08	06	08
Willis, William(Z-M)	1833	June 26	CoshoctnCoOh	05	07	17
Willison, Egbert Benson(Z-M)	1832	Aug. 24	CoshoctnCoOh	09	08	11
Willison, Egbert Benson(Z-M)	1832	Aug. 24	CoshoctnCoOh	09	08	11
Willison, John(Z)	1836	Nov. 30	Perry Co.,Oh	14	13	21
Wills, Amon(Z)	1828	March 29	Morgan Co,Oh	12	11	34
Wills, Amon(Z)	1833	Feb. 11	Morgan Co,Oh	11	10	13
Wills, Robert(Z)	1813	May 05	MuskingmCoOh	10	02	23
Wills, William(Z)	1811	Nov. 27	FairfeldCoOh	10	01	02
Willson, David(Z)	1835	April 02	Morgan Co,Oh	09	05	31
Willson, Gilman(Z)	1821	Sept. 11	Morgan Co,Oh	12	10	29
Willson, James(Z-M)	1837	March 03	MuskingmCoOh	03	01	15
Willson, John(Z)	1836	March 24	Morgan Co,Oh	10	06	11

PURCHASER	YEAR	DATE	RESIDENCE	R	T	S
Willson, Joseph(Z-M)	1834	Dec. 18	HarrisonCoOh	02	06	20
Willson, William(Z)	1832	Jan. 16	GuernseyCoOh	08	08	26
Willson, William(Z-M)	1829	June 29	LickingCo,Oh	10	04	09
Willson, William(Z-M)	1835	Nov. 19	GuernseyCoOh	03	04	19
Wilson, Ann(Z)	1820	July 17	MuskingmCoOh	13	10	35
Wilson, Charles(Z)	1832	Jan. 16	WashCo.,Ohio	09	06	31
Wilson, Daniel G.(Z)	1832	Jan. 16	WashCo.,Ohio	09	06	30
Wilson, Daniel G.(Z)	1833	May 16	WashngtnCoOh	09	06	30
Wilson, David(Y)	1829	May 05	ColumbanCoOh	01	06	01
Wilson, David(Z)	1827	Dec. 06	Morgan Co,Oh	10	07	28
Wilson, David(Z)	1832	Jan. 17	Morgan Co,Oh	10	07	21
Wilson, David(Z)	1832	Oct. 27	Morgan Co,Oh	13	08	19
Wilson, David(Z)	1834	Feb. 19	Morgan Co,Oh	13	08	19
Wilson, David(Z-M)	1815	July 10	GuernseyCoOh	09	05	17
Wilson, David(Z-M)	1835	Nov. 23	GuernseyCoOh	03	05	24
Wilson, David(Z-M)	1836	Oct. 14	GuernseyCoOh	03	04	07
Wilson, Edward(Z)	1806	June 14	ShanandhCoVa	09	01	13
Wilson, Edward(Z)	1806	July 10	MuskingmCoOh	09	01	22
Wilson, Edward(Z-M)	1832	Aug. 18	GuernseyCoOh	04	03	09
Wilson, Edward(Z-M)	1837	Dec. 08	GuernseyCoOh	04	03	08
Wilson, Eliza(Y)	1828	Aug. 28	Jeff.Co.,Oh.	04	11	17
Wilson, Geo. Layport(Z-M)	1838	Nov. 26	TuscarwsCoOh	03	05	16
Wilson, George(Z)	1835	Dec. 14	Morgan Co,Oh	10	06	25
Wilson, George(Z-M)	1824	Aug. 21	KnoxCo.,Ohio	10	08	06
Wilson, Hannah(Y)	1824	Dec. 28	WashCo.,Penn	03	11	15
Wilson, Hans(Y)	1824	May 18	SteubenvleOh	03	10	15
Wilson, Hans(Y)	1824	May 18	SteubenvleOh	03	10	21
Wilson, Hans(Y)	1826	Feb. 09	SteubenvleOh	03	11	05
Wilson, Hans(Y)	1826	Feb. 20	SteubenvleOh	03	11	03
Wilson, Hans(Y)	1827	July 17	SteubenvleOh	02	08	36
Wilson, Hans(Y)	1828	March 03	SteubenvleOh	04	12	30
Wilson, Hans(Y)	1829	Dec. 07	SteubenvleOh	03	10	21
Wilson, Hans(Y)	1829	Dec. 09	SteubenvleOh	04	13	01
Wilson, Hans(Y)	1831	July 22	SteubenvleOh	06	15	12
Wilson, Hans(Y)	1832	March 31	SteubenvleOh	07	14	07
Wilson, Henry(Z)	1815	June 07	MuskingmCoOh	09	01	18
Wilson, Henry(Z-M)	1831	Oct. 28	GuernseyCoOh	04	04	12
Wilson, Henry(Z-M)	1833	Aug. 28	GuernseyCoOh	04	04	12
Wilson, Isaac(Z-M)	1829	July 02	GuernseyCoOh	03	01	16
Wilson, Isaac(Z-M)	1831	Nov. 09	GuernseyCoOh	03	01	16
Wilson, Isaac(Z-M)	1836	Aug. 17	GuernseyCoOh	03	01	15
Wilson, J.(Z)	1815	Feb. 20	MuskingmCoOh	11	13	02
Wilson, Jacob(Y)	1827	Sept. 06	WashCo.,Penn	03	05	33
Wilson, James(Y)	1821	Aug. 10	TuscarwsCoOh	07	14	33
Wilson, James(Z)	1824	Dec. 09	Perry Co.,Oh	15	16	21
Wilson, James(Z)	1824	Dec. 09	Perry Co.,Oh	15	16	21
Wilson, James(Z)	1825	Oct. 25	Perry Co.,Oh	15	16	21
Wilson, James(Z)	1836	Dec. 29	MuskingmCoOh	10	06	14
Wilson, James(Z)	1805	May 30	AlleghnyCoPa	05	01	11
Wilson, James(Z)	1805	Dec. 31	AlleghnyCoMd	15	16	08
Wilson, James(Z)	1810	May 30	WashCo.,Penn	11	13	05
Wilson, James(Z)	1815	Nov. 23	AlleghnyCoPa	03	02	04
Wilson, James(Z-M)	1838	Jan. 17	MuskingmCoOh	03	03	06
Wilson, James(Z-M)	1838	Jan. 17	MuskingmCoOh	04	03	01
Wilson, Jas.(Z)	1805	Dec. 30	MuskingmCoOh	09	01	19
Wilson, Jeremiah(Z)	1836	June 29	WashngtnCoOh	10	06	36
Wilson, Jesse(Z-M)	1834	Aug. 05	GuernseyCoOh	03	01	15
Wilson, John Jr.(Z-M)	1835	Feb. 16	Delaware ?	10	04	12
Wilson, John Jr.(Z-M)	1835	Feb. 16	Delaware ?	10	04	19
Wilson, John Junr.(Z)	1809	Dec. 30	HardyCo.,Vir	11	03	17
Wilson, John Potter(Z-M)	1836	Jan. 13	CoshoctnCoOh	05	07	17
Wilson, John Potter(Z-M)	1836	Jan. 23	CoshoctnCoOh	05	07	25
Wilson, John S.(Z)	1831	March 19	MuskingmCoOh	11	12	17
Wilson, John(Y)	1824	June 01	Jeff.Co.,Oh.	04	10	12
Wilson, John(Y)	1825	July 06	ColumbanCoOh	06	16	32
Wilson, John(Y)	1828	Jan. 14	ColumbanCoOh	06	16	32
Wilson, John(Y)	1838	March 19	Jeff.Co.,Oh.	03	12	15
Wilson, John(Z)	1834	Feb. 21	Morgan Co,Oh	11	10	01
Wilson, John(Z)	1834	Oct. 09	HockingCo,Oh	15	14	21

PURCHASER	YEAR	DATE	RESIDENCE	R	T	S
Wilson, John(Z)	1810	Nov. 28	FayetteCo,Pa	08	08	03
Wilson, John(Z)	1815	June 12	CoshoctnCoOh	06	07	21
Wilson, John(Z)	1817	Oct. 28	TuscarwsCoOh	01	05	19
Wilson, John(Z-M)	1830	Nov. 26	TuscarwsCoOh	01	05	25
Wilson, Jonathan(Z)	1817	June 21	Jeff.Co.,Oh.	01	04	10
Wilson, Joseph(Z)	1836	Jan. 11	Morgan Co,Oh	09	05	23
Wilson, Josiah(Z)	1816	Feb. 14	WashCo.,Penn	03	02	05
Wilson, Mahlon(Z)	1824	Dec. 08	Morgan Co,Oh	10	07	21
Wilson, Margaret(Z)	1816	Oct. 12	FayetteCo,Pa	02	01	19
Wilson, Margret(ZZ)	1807	Sept. 09	FayetteCo,Pa	01	02	18
Wilson, Mary M.(Z)	1814	Feb. 10	Newark ?	11	03	25
Wilson, Mathew(Z)	1821	Oct. 12	Morgan Co,Oh	11	11	07
Wilson, Michael(Z)	1833	Nov. 21	Perry Co.,Oh	15	14	19
Wilson, Michael(Z)	1812	June 03	FairfeldCoOh	15	15	05
Wilson, Michael(Z)	1814	Feb. 03	FairfeldCoOh	15	15	19
Wilson, Michael(Z)	1815	Nov. 22	FairfeldCoOh	15	15	19
Wilson, Michael(Z)	1815	Dec. 23	FairfeldCoOh	15	15	18
Wilson, Michael(Z)	1816	May 27	FairfeldCoOh	15	15	30
Wilson, Nathan(Z)	1807	July 11	MuskingmCoOh	09	01	08
Wilson, Nathan(Z)	1810	Aug. 14	MuskingmCoOh	09	01	23
Wilson, Robert(Y)	1829	Nov. 06	TuscarwsCoOh	06	14	26
Wilson, Robert(Z)	1833	March 21	Perry Co.,Oh	14	13	30
Wilson, Robert(Z)	1833	Nov. 01	MuskingmCoOh	11	12	22
Wilson, Robert(Z)	1834	Jan. 28	Perry Co.,Oh	14	13	30
Wilson, Robert(Z)	1835	Jan. 06	Morgan Co,Oh	10	06	20
Wilson, Robert(Z)	1836	Jan. 18	Morgan Co,Oh	10	06	19
Wilson, Robert(Z)	1811	Dec. 02	MuskingmCoOh	15	18	03
Wilson, Robert(Z)	1815	Nov. 25	WashCo.,Penn	08	03	05
Wilson, Robert(Z-M)	1832	Jan. 05	TuscarwsCoOh	01	05	19
Wilson, Robt.(Z-M)	1830	July 14	CoshoctnCoOh	06	07	09
Wilson, Sam'l. Dole(Z-M)	1836	Oct. 21	CarrollCo,Oh	03	05	16
Wilson, Sam'l. McDole(Z-M)	1833	Oct. 19	GuernseyCoOh	03	04	04
Wilson, Sam'l.(Z)	1822	Nov. 18	Brooke CoVir	11	12	07
Wilson, Scott(Z)	1830	Dec. 10	MuskingmCoOh	11	12	14
Wilson, T.(Z)	1815	March 21	MuskingmCoOh	13	09	02
Wilson, Thomas H.(Y)	1822	March 29	WashCo.,Penn	06	09	21
Wilson, Thomas Stokely(Y)	1836	April 06	SteubenvleOh	03	11	17
Wilson, Thomas Stokely(Y)	1836	July 16	SteubenvleOh	03	01	23
Wilson, Thomas(Y)	1834	Sept. 06	TuscarwsCoOh	07	14	33
Wilson, Thomas(Z)	1810	April 26	FayetteCo,Pa	09	08	10
Wilson, Thomas(Z)	1813	Sept. 22	SomersetCoPa	15	15	08
Wilson, Thomas(Z)	1817	June 07	GuernseyCoOh	09	08	13
Wilson, Thomas(Z-M)	1824	Aug. 17	GuernseyCoOh	03	03	03
Wilson, Thomas(Z-M)	1832	Oct. 05	GuernseyCoOh	03	01	12
Wilson, William H.(Z)	1834	March 05	MuskingmCoOh	11	12	22
Wilson, William(Z)	1826	Feb. 07	FairfeldCoOh	15	15	24
Wilson, William(Z)	1828	Jan. 03	MuskingmCoOh	11	12	18
Wilson, William(Z)	1828	May 29	MuskingmCoOh	11	12	17
Wilson, William(Z)	1828	Dec. 26	MuskingmCoOh	11	12	09
Wilson, William(Z)	1832	May 23	MonroeCo.,Oh	08	07	23
Wilson, William(Z)	1835	Nov. 13	MonroeCo.,Oh	08	07	01
Wilson, William(Z)	1835	Nov. 13	MonroeCo.,Oh	08	07	01
Wilson, William(Z)	1836	Jan. 18	Morgan Co,Oh	10	06	20
Wilson, William(Z)	1832	May 23	MonroeCo.,Oh	08	07	23
Wilson, William(Z)	1805	June 17	FairfeldCoOh	15	17	29
Wilson, William(Z)	1805	June 17	FairfeldCoOh	15	17	31
Wilson, William(Z)	1805	Aug. 17	FairfeldCoOh	15	16	01
Wilson, William(Z)	1811	Jan. 19	Newark ?	11	03	25
Wilson, William(Z)	1811	Feb. 11	Newark ?	11	03	25
Wilson, William(Z)	1813	Nov. 20	SomersetCoPa	10	05	09
Wilson, William(Z)	1815	March 23	MuskingmCoOh	10	04	09
Wilson, Wm. M.(Z-M)	1838	Feb. 09	GuernseyCoOh	03	04	04
Wilson, Wm.(Z)	1830	Dec. 20	MonroeCo.,Oh	08	08	26
Wilson, Wm.(Z)	1830	Dec. 20	MonroeCo.,Oh	08	08	26
Wimer, Michael(Y)	1823	Aug. 13	Stark Co.,Oh	07	18	15
Wimmer, Anthony(Z-M)	1836	June 03	CoshoctnCoOh	06	04	20
Wimmer, John(Z)	1813	Sept. 07	FairfeldCoOh	15	15	02
Winberinger, Barnet(Z)	1827	Sept. 27	KnoxCo.,Ohio	10	07	18
Winberinger, Thos.(Z)	1827	Sept. 27	KnoxCo.,Ohio	10	07	18

PURCHASER	YEAR	DATE	RESIDENCE	R	T	S
Wince, Philip(Z-M)	1837	Feb. 15	MuskingmCoOh	10	04	24
Wince, Samuel(Z-M)	1835	Oct. 24	MuskingmCoOh	10	04	24
Wince, William(Z-M)	1837	Jan. 05	MuskingmCoOh	10	04	24
Wincklebleck, Jacob(Z)	1809	Sept. 20	Jeff.Co.,Oh.	04	09	19
Wincklebleck, Philip(Z)	1810	Jan. 12	TuscarwsCoOh	05	09	18
Winckleblick, Adam(Z)	1815	June 09	Jeff.Co.,Oh.	05	06	03
Winckleblick, Christ'n.(Z)	1815	April 12	TuscarwsCoOh	05	06	03
Winckleblick, Jacob(Z)	1814	June 27	TuscarwsCoOh	05	08	21
Winckleblick, Jacob(Z)	1815	April 12	TuscarwsCoOh	05	06	08
Winder, Benjamin(Y)	1823	March 05	ColumbanCoOh	04	14	06
Winders, Thomas(Z)	1816	Aug. 28	CoshoctnCoOh	07	04	02
Winders, Thomas(Z)	1816	Dec. 16	CoshoctnCoOh	07	04	15
Windstandley, Peter(Z)	1832	Jan. 23	Morgan Co,Oh	09	05	11
Wine, George(Z-M)	1831	March 16	GuernseyCoOh	01	03	06
Wine, George(Z-M)	1832	Nov. 28	GuernseyCoOh	01	03	06
Wine, George(Z-M)	1835	June 01	GuernseyCoOh	01	03	06
Wineburner, William(Y)	1832	Sept. 10	GuernseyCoOh	07	09	22
Wingardner, John(Z)	1814	Aug. 07	LickingCo,Oh	15	18	08
Wingate, Elihu(Z-M)	1823	May 03	TuscarwsCoOh	01	09	05
Wingate, Henry Jr.(Y)	1829	June 22	TuscarwsCoOh	07	16	27
Winings, Jacob(Y)	1829	Sept. 09	HarrisonCoOh	05	13	02
Winings, Jacob(Y)	1830	Jan. 04	HarrisonCoOh	05	13	02
Winings, John Junr.(Y)	1831	March 14	HarrisonCoOh	05	13	14
Winings, John(Y)	1832	Feb. 15	HarrisonCoOh	05	13	09
Winings, John(Y)	1832	Feb. 15	HarrisonCoOh	05	13	15
Winklebleck, Christian(Z)	1808	May 02	Jeff.Co.,Oh.	09	09	21
Winklebleck, James(Z-M)	1832	Aug. 06	TuscarwsCoOh	03	09	22
Winklebleck, Philip(Z)	1812	June 18	MuskingmCoOh	04	08	21
Winklebleek, Jas.(Z-M)	1830	Jan. 08	CoshoctnCoOh	05	07	22
Winkleblut, Christian(Z-M)	1831	April 26	TuscarwsCoOh	05	07	22
Winklepleck, James(Z-M)	1836	Oct. 17	TuscarwsCoOh	04	08	22
Winn, Patrick(Z)	1834	July 25	Perry Co.,Oh	14	14	32
Winn, Patrick(Z)	1834	Sept. 23	Perry Co.,Oh	14	14	31
Winn, Richard(Z-M)	1825	Jan. 20	CoshoctnCoOh	08	04	02
Winn, Thomas(Z)	1829	Dec. 31	MuskingmCoOh	13	11	21
Winn, Thos.(Z)	1830	Dec. 18	MuskingmCoOh	13	11	21
Winn, William(Z)	1835	Sept. 08	MuskingmCoOh	10	09	36
Winn, William(Z)	1836	Aug. 19	MuskingmCoOh	09	08	31
Winne, Thos.(Z)	1835	Dec. 25	MuskingmCoOh	12	12	18
Winner, John(Y)	1828	Nov. 21	Stark Co.,Oh	06	19	01
Winstandley, Peter(Z)	1832	Feb. 20	Morgan Co,Oh	09	05	11
Winstandly, Peter(Z)	1835	Jan. 28	Morgan Co,Oh	09	05	11
Winter, Jacob(Z)	1806	April 30	RcknghmCoVir	14	15	33
Winteringer, James(Z-M)	1832	Sept. 13	KnoxCo.,Ohio	10	07	12
Winteringer, Jesse(Z)	1807	March 14	JeffsnCoPenn	10	07	13
Winteringer, Nathan(Z)	1807	March 14	JeffsnCoPenn	10	07	13
Winterringer, James(Z-M)	1831	Oct. 26	KnoxCo.,Ohio	10	07	19
Winterringer, Jesse(Z)	1832	Feb. 24	KnoxCo.,Ohio	10	07	17
Winterringer, Thomas(Z-M)	1832	Feb. 01	KnoxCo.,Ohio	10	07	20
Winteunger, James(Z-M)	1833	April 03	KnoxCo.,Ohio	10	07	18
Winton, Lewis(Z-M)	1832	May 05	MuskingmCoOh	06	03	01
Wirebaugh, Henry(Y)	1826	April 03	ColumbanCoOh	04	13	12
Wirebaugh, John(Y)	1830	May 03	ColumbanCoOh	04	13	12
Wirebaugh, Nicholas Jr.(Z-M)	1837	May 23	CarrollCo,Oh	09	08	05
Wirick, Obediah G.(Z-M)	1836	Feb. 15	GuernseyCoOh	02	02	01
Wirick, Peter(Z)	1805	July 09	BelmontCo,Oh	01	02	15
Wirts, John(Z-M)	1835	Aug. 08	MuskingmCoOh	05	04	05
Wirts, Peter(Z-M)	1833	March 28	MuskingmCoOh	06	04	01
Wirts, Peter(Z-M)	1835	June 16	MuskingmCoOh	05	04	06
Wirts, Peter(Z-M)	1835	June 16	MuskingmCoOh	05	04	06
Wirts, Peter(Z-M)	1835	Nov. 17	MuskingmCoOh	06	04	10
Wirts, Peter(Z-M)	1835	Nov. 17	MuskingmCoOh	06	04	10
Wirtz, Peter(Z)	1816	July 30	MuskingmCoOh	05	02	07
Wise, Elizabeth(Y)	1824	Dec. 18	BelmontCo,Oh	03	05	14
Wise, George(Z-M)	1836	Aug. 26	LickingCo,Oh	10	04	18
Wise, Jacob(Z-M)	1836	April 07	LickingCo,Oh	10	03	02
Wise, Jacob(Z-M)	1836	Aug. 18	LickingCo,Oh	10	04	18
Wise, Jeremiah(Z)	1817	June 02	MuskingmCoOh	14	13	10
Wise, Martin(Y)	1830	Sept. 29	Stark Co.,Oh	09	11	13

PURCHASER	YEAR	DATE	RESIDENCE	R	T	S
Wise, Samuel(Y)	1823	Sept. 13	BelmontCo,Oh	03	05	15
Wise, Silas(Y)	1829	March 18	ColumbanCoOh	06	16	25
Wise, William(Z)	1828	Dec. 08	Morgan Co,Oh	14	14	34
Wisecarver, Abraham W.(Z-M)	1831	Nov. 05	MuskingmCoOh	06	03	12
Wisecarver, Abraham(Z)	1815	May 18	CoshoctnCoOh	06	03	18
Wisecarver, Jacob(Z)	1814	March 26	MuskingmCoOh	06	02	17
Wisecarver, John(Z)	1825	May 05	MuskingmCoOh	09	06	31
Wisecarver, John(Z)	1814	May 23	Greene Co,Pa	06	02	18
Wisecarver, Truslers(Z-M)	1837	Sept. 01	MuskingmCoOh	04	03	04
Wisecarver, Truslers(Z-M)	1837	Sept. 01	MuskingmCoOh	04	03	05
Wisecarver, Truslers(Z-M)	1837	Sept. 01	MuskingmCoOh	04	03	07
Wisecarver, Truslers(Z-M)	1837	Sept. 01	MuskingmCoOh	04	03	07
Wisecarver, Truslers(Z-M)	1837	Sept. 01	MuskingmCoOh	04	03	06
Wiseman, John(Y)	1829	July 07	ColumbanCoOh	05	15	11
Wiseman, M.(Z)	1831	Feb. 04	Morgan Co,Oh	12	10	09
Wiseman, Peter(Y)	1820	July 03	ColumbanCoOh	06	16	14
Wiseman, Peter(Y)	1826	Sept. 02	Stark Co.,Oh	06	16	14
Wiskominz, Harvey(Z-M)	1831	Oct. 27	CoshoctnCoOh	03	05	25
Wiston, Jeremy(Z)	1817	Sept. 19	WashngtnCoOh	13	09	31
Wite, John George(Y)	1835	Jan. 27	Jeff.Co.,Oh.	03	11	17
Witherwax, Andrew(Z-M)	1823	Oct. 11	CoshoctnCoOh	07	07	24
Withrow, Charles(Z-M)	1835	Jan. 28	HolmesCoOhio	07	08	11
Withrow, Hugh(Z-M)	1832	Jan. 30	HolmesCoOhio	07	09	22
Withrow, James(Y)	1829	Nov. 25	ColumbanCoOh	04	13	23
Withrow, James(Z-M)	1836	Sept. 17	CarrollCo,Oh	10	08	03
Withrow, James(Z-M)	1837	April 18	KnoxCo.,Ohio	10	09	22
Withrow, Sam'l.(Z-M)	1826	June 08	HolmesCoOhio	07	09	22
Withrow, Samuel(Z)	1817	April 30	Jeff.Co.,Oh.	09	04	04
Withrow, Samuel(Z)	1817	April 30	Jeff.Co.,Oh.	09	04	08
Withrow, Samuel(Z)	1817	May 01	Jeff.Co.,Oh.	09	04	08
Withrow, Wm.(Y)	1828	Feb. 08	ColumbanCoOh	04	13	18
Witstone, Jno.(Y)	1821	Oct. 08	Stark Co.,Oh	07	20	28
Witterberry, Christ'n.(Z)	1815	Aug. 30	MuskingmCoOh	06	03	17
Witterberry, Christ'n.(Z)	1815	Aug. 30	MuskingmCoOh	06	03	17
Wittleton, Edmund(Z-M)	1837	Dec. 01	CoshoctnCoOh	08	07	06
Wiyrick, Peter Jr.(Z-M)	1836	Feb. 15	CoshoctnCoOh	03	03	02
Wockman, Benjamin(Z)	1810	March 27	WestmrldCoPa	05	01	07
Wocksell, Abm.(Y)	1822	March 26	Stark Co.,Oh	07	20	21
Wold, James(Z-M)	1824	June 08	CoshoctnCoOh	08	05	24
Wolf, Eli(Z)	1832	Feb. 15	Jeff.Co.,Oh.	12	09	17
Wolf, George(Z)	1813	April 16	CoshoctnCoOh	10	05	08
Wolf, George(Z)	1815	Aug. 29	GreeneCo.,Pa	11	01	01
Wolf, George(Z)	1816	Nov. 15	GreeneCo.,Pa	13	09	33
Wolf, George(Z)	1816	Nov. 15	GreeneCo.,Pa	13	09	29
Wolf, George(Z)	1816	Nov. 15	GreeneCo.,Pa	13	09	29
Wolf, John(Z)	1834	March 03	LickingCo,Oh	13	08	36
Wolf, John(Z)	1810	Sept. 06	CumberldCo ?	05	04	10
Wolf, John(Z)	1814	Feb. 03	CoshoctnCoOh	10	06	23
Wolf, John(Z-M)	1834	Oct. 15	CarrollCo,Oh	02	07	05
Wolf, Joshua(Z-M)	1832	May 29	GreenCo,Ohio	10	04	21
Wolf, Margaret(Z-M)	1831	July 18	CoshoctnCoOh	04	05	13
Wolf, Margaret(Z-M)	1833	Jan. 08	CoshoctnCoOh	04	05	13
Wolf, Mary Eve(Z)	1833	July 15	Perry Co.,Oh	15	14	06
Wolf, Michael(Z)	1836	March 23	TuscarwsCoOh	02	07	04
Wolf, Michael(Z-M)	1836	March 23	TuscarwsCoOh	02	07	05
Wolf, P.(Z)	1815	April 03	CoshoctnCoOh	04	05	12
Wolf, Peter(Z)	1814	Nov. 14	Ohio Co.,Vir	10	06	25
Wolf, Peter(Z)	1816	Jan. 22	KnoxCo.,Ohio	10	06	25
Wolf, Peter(Z)	1817	May 02	AlleghnyCoPa	01	09	07
Wolf, Peter(Z-M)	1831	Nov. 26	KnoxCo.,Ohio	10	06	25
Wolf, Philip(Z)	1814	Dec. 06	CoshoctnCoOh	04	05	13
Wolf, Philip(Z)	1815	Oct. 23	CoshoctnCoOh	03	05	23
Wolf, Solomon(Z)	1833	Aug. 21	MonroeCo.,Oh	08	07	23
Wolf, William(Z)	1807	March 09	BedfordCo,Pa	03	09	11
Wolf, William(Z-M)	1836	June 17	TuscarwsCoOh	03	07	20
Wolfle, Frederick(Z-M)	1839	June 03	TuscarwsCoOh	02	07	02
Wolford, Andrew(Z-M)	1831	Aug. 31	MuskingmCoOh	06	03	09
Wolford, David(Z-M)	1821	June 12	GuernseyCoOh	01	01	11
Wolford, David(Z-M)	1832	Feb. 09	GuernseyCoOh	01	01	11

PURCHASER	YEAR	DATE	RESIDENCE	R	T	S
Wolford, Frederick(Z)	1810	June 19	MuskingmCoOh	05	01	06
Wolford, Frederick(Z)	1811	March 27	MuskingmCoOh	06	02	19
Wolford, Isaac(Z)	1834	Jan. 14	GuernseyCoOh	09	05	14
Wolford, J.(Z)	1817	Feb. 18	CoshoctnCoOh	08	05	23
Wolford, John(Z)	1836	May 02	Morgan Co,Oh	08	05	03
Wolford, John(Z)	1838	June 14	WashngtnCoOh	08	05	04
Wolford, John(Z)	1807	May 09	BelmontCo,Oh	09	03	04
Wolford, John(Z)	1810	Sept. 24	BelmontCo,Oh	08	05	18
Wolford, John(Z-M)	1828	Aug. 19	MuskingmCoOh	06	03	24
Wolford, M.(Z)	1817	Feb. 18	CoshoctnCoOh	08	05	23
Wolford, Moses(Z)	1810	Oct. 09	BelmontCo,Oh	08	05	24
Wolford, Peter(Z)	1813	Dec. 15	MuskingmCoOh	06	02	19
Wolford, William(Z-M)	1836	Jan. 25	CoshoctnCoOh	07	04	01
Wolford, William(Z-M)	1836	Jan. 25	CoshoctnCoOh	07	04	02
Wolford, William(Z-M)	1836	July 14	CoshoctnCoOh	07	04	02
Wolford, William(Z-M)	1836	July 14	CoshoctnCoOh	07	04	01
Wolgamot, Henry(Z)	1811	Oct. 01	CoshoctnCoOh	07	09	19
Wolgamot, Henry(Z)	1811	Oct. 01	CoshoctnCoOh	03	10	16
Wolgamot, Henry(Z)	1817	Jan. 20	CoshoctnCoOh	06	09	06
Wolgamott, David(Z-M)	1837	Feb. 27	GuernseyCoOh	03	04	16
Wollam, Archibald(Y)	1828	March 18	ColumbanCoOh	04	13	06
Wollam, Archibald(Y)	1831	Oct. 26	ColumbanCoOh	04	13	05
Wollam, John Jur.(Y)	1826	Dec. 05	ColumbanCoOh	01	06	23
Wollam, Peter(Y)	1829	March 13	ColumbanCoOh	03	13	29
Wollihan, John Jr.(Y)	1827	June 21	ColumbanCoOh	06	18	02
Wollihan, John(Y)	1825	June 02	ColumbanCoOh	07	20	04
Wolper, John F.(Z)	1823	Nov. 01	Morgan Co,Oh	13	10	26
Wolpert, J. F.(Z)	1837	Jan. 20	Morgan Co,Oh	13	09	03
Wolpert, John J.(Z)	1830	Feb. 04	MuskingmCoOh	13	10	36
Womer, Mathias(Z-M)	1828	July 02	MuskingmCoOh	06	02	05
Wonsetler, Matthias(Y)	1829	Sept. 10	Stark Co.,Oh	06	19	02
Wood, Aaron(Z)	1829	April 09	BelmontCo,Oh	13	08	27
Wood, Frederick(Z)	1833	June 14	Morgan Co,Oh	11	11	01
Wood, Frederick(Z)	1833	Dec. 13	Morgan Co,Oh	11	11	01
Wood, Israel(Y)	1824	Feb. 04	MonroeCo.,Oh	07	09	01
Wood, Israel(Z)	1825	Oct. 24	MonroeCo.,Oh	13	08	22
Wood, John(Y)	1822	Nov. 07	FayetteCo,Pa	06	19	27
Wood, John(Y)	1822	Nov. 07	FayetteCo,Pa	06	18	03
Wood, John(Y)	1822	Nov. 07	FayetteCo,Pa	06	18	02
Wood, John(Y)	1831	Sept. 02	HarrisonCoOh	07	11	28
Wood, John(Y)	1831	Dec. 03	HarrisonCoOh	07	11	17
Wood, Jonathan(Z)	1811	April 29	MuskingmCoOh	09	03	25
Wood, Jonathan(Z)	1812	Oct. 31	MuskingmCoOh	09	03	25
Wood, Jonathan(Z)	1817	April 28	MuskingmCoOh	10	04	05
Wood, Jonathan(Z)	1817	Sept. 03	MuskingmCoOh	09	03	17
Wood, Joseph(Z)	1829	Dec. 21	Morgan Co,Oh	12	10	29
Wood, Josephus(Z-M)	1834	Jan. 20	MuskingmCoOh	09	03	15
Wood, Joshua(Z-M)	1831	Oct. 15	CoshoctnCoOh	04	06	08
Wood, Lewis(Z)	1832	March 06	BelmontCo,Oh	13	08	29
Wood, Lewis(Z)	1832	March 06	BelmontCo,Oh	13	08	20
Wood, Lewis(Z)	1832	March 06	BelmontCo,Oh	13	08	20
Wood, Mathew(Z)	1820	Dec. 16	MonroeCo.,Oh	08	07	25
Wood, Nathan(Y)	1822	Nov. 02	FayetteCo,Pa	06	19	34
Wood, Nathan(Y)	1822	Nov. 02	FayetteCo,Pa	06	19	34
Wood, Richard Jr.(Z-M)	1826	Feb. 17	LickingCo,Oh	10	03	13
Wood, Stephen(Z)	1814	Oct. 15	WashngtnCoOh	02	03	04
Wood, Stephen(Z)	1814	Nov. 22	WashngtnCoOh	03	03	10
Wood, Thomas(Y)	1827	Nov. 30	Stark Co.,Oh	06	19	15
Wood, Zachariah(Z)	1825	Dec. 01	BelmontCo,Oh	13	08	15
Woodard, James(Z)	1828	Sept. 30	Morgan Co,Oh	09	06	15
Woodard, Joseph(Z)	1835	April 18	Morgan Co,Oh	13	09	12
Woodbridge, William(Z)	1806	Feb. 07	MariettaOhio	08	04	13
Woodbridge, William(Z)	1806	Feb. 07	MariettaOhio	08	04	18
Woodcock, Bernard B.(Z-M)	1837	July 10	LickingCo,Oh	10	02	24
Woodford, Andrew A.(Z)	1835	Feb. 28	Morgan Co,Oh	09	06	08
Woodford, Andrew A.(Z)	1835	Jan. 10	Morgan Co,Oh	09	06	09
Woodford, Aranda(Z)	1833	Aug. 24	Morgan Co,Oh	09	06	21
Woodford, Aranda(Z)	1834	Sept. 01	Morgan Co,Oh	09	06	21
Woodget, Jared(Y)	1826	Dec. 13	BelmontCo,Oh	07	10	12

PURCHASER	YEAR	DATE	RESIDENCE	R	T	S
Woodrow, Henry(Z-M)	1823	June 20	GuernseyCoOh	03	01	19
Woodruff, Meker(Z)	1815	April 20	GreeneCo.,Pa	11	05	20
Woodruff, Nathan F.(Z-M)	1833	March 05	TuscarwsCoOh	02	08	13
Woodruff, Solomon(Z-M)	1834	Oct. 27	HolmesCoOhio	06	09	25
Woodruff, Solomon(Z-M)	1835	Jan. 08	HolmesCoOhio	06	09	25
Woods, Abm. H.(Z)	1810	Aug. 29	?	14	15	17
Woods, Abraham H.(Z)	1811	Sept. 28	ZanesvilleOh	11	11	36
Woods, Archibald(Y)	1826	April 07	Brooke CoVir	03	11	04
Woods, Archibald(Z)	1805	Dec. 17	Ohio Co.,Vir	08	08	11
Woods, Archibald(Z)	1805	Dec. 17	Ohio Co.,Vir	08	08	12
Woods, Archibald(Z)	1806	Jan. 13	Ohio Co.,Vir	08	08	12
Woods, Archibald(Z)	1806	Jan. 13	Ohio Co.,Vir	08	08	13
Woods, George(Y)	1828	May 17	Jeff.Co.,Oh.	04	12	09
Woods, George(Y)	1835	Feb. 06	CarrollCo,Oh	06	15	36
Woods, Robert(Y)	1829	March 14	Stark co.,Oh	06	15	36
Woods, Samuel(Z-M)	1835	Jan. 26	GuernseyCoOh	03	04	14
Woods, Thomas(Z)	1836	June 01	GuernseyCoOh	10	06	13
Woods, William(Y)	1822	Aug. 03	Morgan Co,Oh	06	09	21
Woods, William(Y)	1825	Aug. 31	HarrisonCoOh	06	15	35
Woods, William(Y)	1832	June 05	Stark Co.,Oh	07	16	04
Woods, William(Y)	1832	Aug. 21	Stark Co.,Oh	06	15	35
Woods, William(Y)	1834	Aug. 14	CarrollCo,Oh	06	15	36
Woods, William(Z-M)	1822	June 12	GuernseyCoOh	02	02	12
Woods, Wm.(Y)	1829	June 12	Stark Co.,Oh	07	17	26
Woodward, John Fordyce(Z)	1832	Oct. 20	Morgan Co,Oh	13	09	02
Woodward, William(Z)	1813	Nov. 03	MuskingmCoOh	09	06	36
Wooley, J.(Z)	1815	Oct. 04	MuskingmCoOh	14	13	11
Woolf, Samuel(Y)	1823	Nov. 25	Stark Co.,Oh	07	19	21
Woolf, William(Z)	1815	May 08	TuscarwsCoOh	02	07	14
Woolford, Jacob(Z-M)	1833	Oct. 16	MuskingmCoOh	05	03	04
Woolford, John(Z)	1833	Jan. 24	GuernseyCoOh	09	05	10
Woolford, John(Z)	1833	Jan. 25	GuernseyCoOh	09	05	10
Woolley, Elijah(Z)	1833	Nov. 14	Perry Co.,Oh	14	12	08
Woolman, Aaron A.(Y)	1827	April 12	ColumbanCoOh	05	18	21
Work, John J.(Z)	1831	June 10	Morgan Co,Oh	12	09	02
Work, Robert J.(Z)	1831	Nov. 25	Morgan Co,Oh	12	09	02
Work, Samuel(Z)	1833	Aug. 15	BelmontCo,Oh	09	05	26
Work, Samuel(Z)	1835	Jan. 16	BelmontCo,Oh	09	05	23
Work, Samuel(Z)	1836	April 15	BelmontCo,Oh	09	05	23
Work, Samuel(Z)	1836	April 15	BelmontCo,Oh	09	05	26
Work, Samuel(Z)	1836	April 15	BelmontCo,Oh	09	05	23
Work, Samuel(Z)	1836	April 15	BelmontCo,Oh	09	05	35
Working, Jacob(Z-M)	1834	Sept. 08	TuscarwsCoOh	04	07	19
Workman, Ab'm.(Y)	1822	Dec. 27	BelmontCo,Oh	03	05	22
Workman, Abraham(Z-M)	1823	June 10	CoshoctnCoOh	09	07	06
Workman, Abraham(Z-M)	1833	April 02	CoshoctnCoOh	09	07	04
Workman, Abraham(Z-M)	1833	Nov. 02	HolmesCoOhio	09	08	24
Workman, Abraham(Z-M)	1837	March 10	CoshoctnCoOh	09	07	05
Workman, Amos C.(Z-M)	1836	April 15	CoshoctnCoOh	09	07	09
Workman, Benjamin(Z)	1183	Aug. 17	Morgan Co,Oh	11	11	25
Workman, Benjamin(Z)	1833	Dec. 12	MuskingmCoOh	11	11	25
Workman, Benjamin(Z)	1833	Dec. 12	MuskingmCoOh	11	11	25
Workman, David(Y)	1824	Oct. 25	Jeff.Co.,Oh.	05	12	25
Workman, Elias(Z-M)	1829	Oct. 17	HolmesCoOhio	09	08	11
Workman, Isaac A.(Z-M)	1832	Oct. 25	KnoxCo.,Ohio	10	08	08
Workman, Isaac(Z-M)	1832	Feb. 23	KnoxCo.,Ohio	10	08	07
Workman, Isaac(Z-M)	1832	Feb. 23	KnoxCo.,Ohio	10	08	08
Workman, Isaac(Z-M)	1832	June 09	KnoxCo.,Ohio	10	08	07
Workman, Isaac(Z-M)	1833	Dec. 14	KnoxCo.,Ohio	10	08	03
Workman, Isaac(Z-M)	1836	Nov. 14	KnoxCo.,Ohio	10	08	02
Workman, Isaac(Z-M)	1836	Nov. 14	KnoxCo.,Ohio	10	08	03
Workman, James(Z-M)	1836	Jan. 11	CoshoctnCoOh	09	08	24
Workman, Jesse(Z-M)	1831	Nov. 12	KnoxCo.,Ohio	09	07	04
Workman, Jesse(Z-M)	1833	Dec. 09	HolmesCoOhio	09	08	22
Workman, Jesse(Z-M)	1835	Dec. 30	HolmesCoOhio	09	08	25
Workman, Jesse(Z-M)	1836	Nov. 02	CoshoctnCoOh	09	08	16
Workman, Jesse(Z-M)	1837	April 08	CoshoctnCoOh	09	08	25
Workman, Jno. G.(Z-M)	1832	Feb. 06	KnoxCo.,Ohio	10	07	12
Workman, John(Z-M)	1832	Sept. 01	HolmesCoOhio	09	08	14

PURCHASER	YEAR	DATE	RESIDENCE	R	T	S
Workman, John(Z-M)	1834	Oct. 07	HolmesCoOhio	09	08	07
Workman, Jos. Depew(Z-M)	1836	Jan. 18	CoshoctnCoOh	05	04	08
Workman, Joseph D.(Z-M)	1832	Aug. 29	CoshoctnCoOh	05	04	12
Workman, Nancy(Z-M)	1834	Oct. 16	HolmesCoOhio	09	08	07
Workman, Nancy(Z-M)	1834	Oct. 16	HolmesCoOhio	09	08	07
Workman, Sol.(Z-M)	1828	July 14	CoshoctnCoOh	10	08	15
Workman, Stephen(Z-M)	1832	Aug. 16	KnoxCo.,Ohio	10	08	14
Worley, Jonathan(Y)	1831	April 30	Stark Co.,Oh	07	16	04
Worley, Joseph(Y)	1828	June 07	Stark Co.,Oh	06	16	31
Worley, Ruth(Z)	1830	Dec. 01	Perry Co.,Oh	14	12	17
Worley, Samuel(Z)	1833	Dec. 02	Perry Co.,Oh	14	12	08
Worley, Samuel(Z)	1836	Nov. 19	Perry Co.,Oh	14	12	17
Worrall, Benj.(Z)	1826	Aug. 21	HarrisonCoOh	12	09	10
Worrall, George(Z)	1829	March 09	Morgan Co,Oh	12	10	26
Worstal, John(Z)	1827	June 11	MuskingmCoOh	13	11	13
Worth, Richard(Z)	1814	Oct. 13	TuscarwsCoOh	03	06	24
Worthey, James F.(Z-M)	1835	Jan. 06	BelmontCo,Oh	07	04	09
Worthey, James Fox(Z-M)	1835	June 01	CoshoctnCoOh	07	04	09
Worthington, Amy(Z)	1825	June 13	BucksCo,Penn	12	12	23
Worthington, Wm.(Z)	1828	Aug. 19	MuskingmCoOh	12	12	28
Wortman, Benjamin Jr.(Z)	1832	Feb. 21	MuskingmCoOh	11	11	25
Wortman, Benjamin Jr.(Z)	1834	Oct. 08	Morgan Co,Oh	11	11	25
Wortman, Benjamin Jr.(Z)	1834	Oct. 08	Morgan Co,Oh	11	11	26
Wortman, Benjamin(Z)	1824	July 14	MuskingmCoOh	11	11	25
Wortman, Benjamin(Z)	1826	July 24	MuskingmCoOh	11	11	25
Wortman, Jacob(Z)	1814	Dec. 31	MuskingmCoOh	05	02	17
Wortman, James(Z-M)	1836	March 11	MuskingmCoOh	05	03	03
Wortman, James(Z-M)	1836	Aug. 24	MuskingmCoOh	05	03	03
Wortman, John(Z)	1814	May 25	WestmrldCoPa	05	02	16
Wortman, John(Z-M)	1838	May 10	MuskingmCoOh	05	03	02
Wortman, Lot(Z)	1813	Dec. 20	WestmrldCoPa	05	02	16
Wrey, George(Z-M)	1832	Oct. 27	Jeff.Co.,Oh.	05	06	17
Wrey, James(Z-M)	1836	Jan. 04	CoshoctnCoOh	05	06	18
Wright, Andrew(Z)	1811	Dec. 05	MuskingmCoOh	15	15	02
Wright, Andrew(Z)	1815	June 10	FairfeldCoOh	15	15	11
Wright, Bloyse(Z)	1811	Nov. 25	MuskingmCoOh	10	01	23
Wright, Hiram(Z-M)	1833	Oct. 25	KnoxCo.,Ohio	09	07	15
Wright, J.(Z)	1817	Aug. 21	MuskingmCoOh	13	09	06
Wright, James(Z-M)	1829	Aug. 21	TuscarwsCoOh	01	05	04
Wright, John(Z)	1837	May 30	AthensCoOhio	13	08	34
Wright, John(Z)	1815	June 10	FairfeldCoOh	15	15	32
Wright, John(Z-M)	1834	Nov. 14	TuscarwsCoOh	05	07	08
Wright, John(Z-M)	1835	Feb. 19	TuscarwsCoOh	05	07	08
Wright, Jos.(Z-M)	1831	Nov. 03	CoshoctnCoOh	07	05	19
Wright, Jos.(Z-M)	1831	Nov. 03	CoshoctnCoOh	07	05	22
Wright, Jos.(Z-M)	1836	Aug. 08	HarrisonCoOh	03	05	13
Wright, Joseph Jr.(Y)	1824	June 22	ColumbanCoOh	05	18	20
Wright, Joseph Jr.(Y)	1824	June 22	ColumbanCoOh	05	18	17
Wright, Joseph Jr.(Z-M)	1834	Nov. 10	CoshoctnCoOh	07	04	09
Wright, Joseph Junr.(Y)	1822	May 17	ColumbanCoOh	05	18	14
Wright, Joseph(Y)	1822	Dec. 28	ColumbanCoOh	04	17	03
Wright, Joseph(Z-M)	1832	March 06	CoshoctnCoOh	07	05	19
Wright, Joseph(Z-M)	1832	March 13	CoshoctnCoOh	07	05	21
Wright, Joseph(Z-M)	1835	Dec. 03	CoshoctnCoOh	07	04	10
Wright, Joshua(Y)	1827	Feb. 27	Jeff.Co.,Oh.	03	10	17
Wright, Josiah(Z)	1817	Aug. 21	MuskingmCoOh	13	09	08
Wright, Lloyd(Z-M)	1831	Nov. 25	CoshoctnCoOh	07	04	18
Wright, Loyd(Z-M)	1832	Oct. 04	CoshoctnCoOh	07	04	18
Wright, Moses(Z)	1815	April 28	CoshoctnCoOh	09	05	23
Wright, Nathan(Z)	1814	July 26	CoshoctnCoOh	09	05	21
Wright, Nathan(Z)	1814	Nov. 02	CoshoctnCoOh	08	05	25
Wright, Robert(Y)	1828	Nov. 03	ColumbanCoOh	02	10	17
Wright, Robert(Y)	1831	May 03	ColumbanCoOh	02	10	20
Wright, Robert(Y)	1832	April 20	ColumbanCoOh	02	10	20
Wright, Sam'l.(Z-M)	1831	Sept. 22	TuscarwsCoOh	01	08	12
Wright, Samuel(Y)	1831	May 09	Jeff.Co.,Oh.	03	12	01
Wright, Samuel(Z-M)	1827	Jan. 18	Jeff.Co.,Oh.	01	08	09
Wright, Thomas Washington(Y)	1832	Sept. 01	HarrisonCoOh	06	11	29
Wright, Thomas(Y)	1826	Feb. 20	ColumbanCoOh	05	18	20

PURCHASER	YEAR	DATE	RESIDENCE	R	T	S
Wright, Thomas(Y)	1826	March 15	ColumbanCoOh	05	18	15
Wright, Thomas(Z)	1806	Oct. 24	MuskingmCoOh	15	16	07
Wright, Thomas(Z)	1815	June 06	FairfeldCoOh	15	15	11
Wright, William(Y)	1832	Sept. 18	Jeff.Co.,Oh.	06	11	29
Wright, William(Y)	1833	April 13	Jeff.Co.,Oh.	06	11	29
Wright, William(Z)	1815	Nov. 01	AlleghnyCoMd	06	07	12
Wright, William(Z)	1815	Nov. 02	AlleghnyCoMd	06	07	12
Wright, William(Z)	1816	Nov. 18	CoshoctnCoOh	09	04	22
Wright, Willis(Z-M)	1831	April 09	CoshoctnCoOh	07	04	02
Wright, Willis(Z-M)	1834	March 17	CoshoctnCoOh	07	04	10
Wright, Wm.(Y)	1822	Feb. 15	HarrisonCoOh	06	12	21
Wyand, Barget(Y)	1829	May 06	HarrisonCoOh	05	13	27
Wyand, Jacob(Y)	1830	April 03	HarrisonCoOh	07	16	19
Wyand, Peter(Y)	1830	March 06	HarrisonCoOh	07	15	05
Wyandt, George(Y)	1828	March 17	Jeff.Co.,Oh.	06	14	11
Wyant, Daniel(Z-M)	1835	Nov. 25	TuscarwsCoOh	04	07	11
Wyant, Fr.(Z)	1816	Sept. 30	MuskingmCoOh	12	12	12
Wyant, Fred'k.(Z)	1815	Oct. 20	MuskingmCoOh	12	12	12
Wyant, Fred.(Z)	1830	May 18	MuskingmCoOh	11	12	08
Wyant, Frederick(Z)	1811	Dec. 09	MuskingmCoOh	12	13	35
Wyant, Jacob(Z-M)	1828	June 16	TuscarwsCoOh	03	07	25
Wyant, Jacob(Z-M)	1832	May 26	TuscarwsCoOh	03	07	25
Wyate, James(Y)	1835	May 11	Jeff.Co.,Oh.	03	11	30
Wyatt, David(Z)	1817	May 13	ZanesvilleOh	11	11	20
Wyatt, James(Y)	1834	Sept. 27	Jeff.Co.,Oh.	03	11	30
Wybrant, Hugh(Z)	1825	June 20	PittsburghPa	08	07	15
Wybrant, Hugh(Z)	1835	Jan. 21	MonroeCo.,Oh	08	07	15
Wybrant, John(Z)	1826	Dec. 18	PittsburghPa	08	07	14
Wybrant, John(Z)	1832	Aug. 22	MonroeCo.,Oh	08	07	11
Wybrant, John(Z)	1832	Aug. 22	MonroeCo.,Oh	08	07	14
Wyckoff, James(Y)	1823	July 23	TuscarwsCoOh	07	15	04
Wycoff, John(Z)	1815	Oct. 13	AlleghnyCoPa	12	11	03
Wykoff, Cornelius(Y)	1824	July 27	Brooke CoVir	13	11	20
Wykuff, Henry(Y)	1835	Oct. 06	CarrollCo,Oh	03	12	27
Wylie, John(Z)	1806	Sept. 13	AlleghnyCoPa	05	01	14
Wylie, John(Z)	1806	Sept. 13	AlleghnyCoPa	05	01	15
Wylie, John(Z)	1806	Sept. 13	AlleghnyCoPa	05	01	02
Wylie, John(Z)	1806	Sept. 13	AlleghnyCoPa	05	01	02
Wylie, Joseph(Z)	1810	April 27	MuskingmCoOh	14	14	08
Wylie, Joseph(Z)	1815	Sept. 07	MuskingmCoOh	14	14	05
Wylie, Samuel(Z)	1806	Oct. 27	AlleghnyCoVa	05	01	02
Wylie, Samuel(Z)	1806	Oct. 27	AlleghnyCoVa	10	09	31
Wylly, John(Z)	1805	Nov. 28	MongahlaCoVa	13	12	07
Wymer, Geo.(Z)	1814	July 30	MuskingmCoOh	06	02	21
Wymer, John(Z)	1831	March 22	Morgan Co,Oh	11	11	11
Wymer, Peter(Z-M)	1825	Jan. 07	TuscarwsCoOh	03	09	19
Wymm, William(Z)	1811	June 18	MuskingmCoOh	06	01	09
Wynn, William(Z)	1805	Dec. 07	LoudonCo,Vir	07	01	10
Wyrick, Andrew(Z-M)	1838	Aug. 20	TuscarwsCoOh	03	05	14
Yangue, William(Z)	1814	Nov. 29	AlleghnyCoPa	11	12	20
Yant, Anthony(Z-M)	1832	May 31	TuscarwsCoOh	02	10	15
Yant, Anthony(Z-M)	1832	July 27	TuscarwsCoOh	02	10	15
Yant, David(Z-M)	1832	May 31	TuscarwsCoOh	01	20	15
Yant, Dd.(Z-M)	1832	July 27	TuscarwsCoOh	02	10	15
Yant, John(Y)	1827	Aug. 24	Stark Co.,Oh	06	16	22
Yant, John(Y)	1827	Aug. 24	Stark Co.,Oh	08	09	01
Yantiss, Jacob(Z-M)	1831	Jan. 27	TuscarwsCoOh	01	05	11
Yarger, George(Z)	1834	Jan. 20	Perry Co.,Oh	15	14	21
Yarger, George(Z)	1835	Dec. 21	Perry Co.,Oh	15	14	21
Yarger, John(Z)	1811	Nov. 18	MuskingmCoOh	15	16	21
Yarigg, Robert(Z-M)	1832	June 15	HarrisonCoOh	01	06	22
Yarnall, Benjamin(Z)	1833	Oct. 28	GuernseyCoOh	09	05	04
Yarnall, Eli(Z)	1836	Jan. 15	GuernseyCoOh	08	07	10
Yarnall, Eli(Z)	1837	June 05	MonroeCo.,Oh	08	06	25
Yarnall, Eli(Z)	1837	Sept. 04	MonroeCo.,Oh	08	06	25
Yarnall, Jefferson(Z)	1834	Nov. 12	BelmontCo,Oh	09	05	10
Yarnall, Mordecai(Z-M)	1827	June 18	CoshoctnCoOh	08	04	02
Yarnel, David(Z-M)	1832	Oct. 15	GuernseyCoOh	02	03	14
Yates, Gabriel(Z)	1833	Dec. 30	Perry Co.,Oh	15	15	22

PURCHASER	YEAR	DATE	RESIDENCE	R	T	S
Yates, James(Y)	1826	March 13	ColumbanCoOh	05	18	21
Yates, William(Y)	1826	March 13	ColumbanCoOh	05	18	28
Yauger, William(Z)	1833	Sept. 09	MuskingmCoOh	11	12	29
Ychne, George(Y)	1832	Feb. 17	HarrisonCoOh	?	?	?
Yeakly, Christian(Z-M)	1837	May 06	TuscarwsCoOh	04	07	10
Yeats, Pliny B.(Z)	1836	June 10	Morgan Co,Oh	09	05	32
Yeats, Pliny Britt(Z)	1835	Aug. 15	GuernseyCoOh	09	05	19
Yenan, Henry(Z)	1835	Oct. 24	Morgan Co,Oh	10	06	14
Yerean, Frederick(Z-M)	1833	Feb. 05	MuskingmCoOh	06	02	07
Yerean, Jacob(Z)	1828	Dec. 17	MuskingmCoOh	09	06	31
Yerian, Henry(Z)	1836	Feb. 29	Morgan Co,Oh	10	06	14
Yerian, William(Z)	1835	Dec. 05	Morgan Co,Oh	09	05	11
Yerian, William(Z)	1836	Dec. 26	Morgan Co,Oh	09	05	27
Yerion, Frederick(Z)	1806	Aug. 18	BelmontCo,Oh	10	09	07
Yingling, Henry(Y)	1826	April 08	HarrisonCoOh	04	11	22
Yingling, John(Z-M)	1835	Nov. 17	CarrollCo,Oh	03	07	18
Yingling, John(Z-M)	1836	June 23	CarrollCo,Oh	03	07	18
Yoder, Ab. Jr.(Z-M)	1831	July 13	HolmesCoOhio	05	09	07
Yoder, Ab. Jr.(Z-M)	1831	July 13	HolmesCoOhio	06	08	02
Yoder, Daniel(Z)	1816	April 23	TuscarwsCoOh	05	08	15
Yoder, David(Z)	1815	Nov. 15	TuscarwsCoOh	06	08	02
Yoder, Henry(Z)	1815	Dec. 30	SomersetCoPa	05	08	04
Yoder, Henry(Z)	1816	May 09	Tuscarora?Pa	05	08	04
Yoder, Jacob(Z)	1815	Nov. 15	SomersetCoPa	06	08	03
Yoder, Jacob(Z-M)	1836	April 01	HolmesCoOhio	04	07	04
Yoder, John(Z)	1815	June 06	TuscarwsCoOh	05	08	05
Yoder, Yost(Z-M)	1829	Jan. 26	HolmesCoOhio	06	08	02
Yoho, Jacob(Z)	1814	Dec. 28	GuernseyCoOh	08	08	12
Yoler, Adam(Z)	1831	Dec. 31	Morgan Co,Oh	09	07	21
Yoler, John(Z)	1831	Dec. 31	Morgan Co,Oh	09	07	21
Yonkin, Simon(Z)	1816	Aug. 29	MuskingmCoOh	09	06	12
Yonkin, Simon(Z)	1816	Aug. 29	MuskingmCoOh	09	06	19
Yorter, John(Z-M)	1830	March 17	HolmesCoOhio	05	08	02
Yost, Anastatius(Z-M)	1833	July 01	TuscarwsCoOh	05	07	08
Yost, Anastatius(Z-M)	1835	April 28	CoshoctnCoOh	05	07	08
Yotter, Abraham(Z-M)	1826	Oct. 16	HolmesCoOhio	05	09	07
Yotter, Christian(Z)	1809	Oct. 06	SomersetCoPa	05	09	22
Yotter, Christian(Z)	1810	Nov. 26	TuscarwsCoOh	05	09	19
Yotter, Christian(Z)	1814	Oct. 20	TuscarwsCoOh	05	09	04
Yotter, Henry(Z)	1809	Oct. 06	SomersetCoPa	05	09	19
Yotter, Henry(Z)	1811	May 28	SomersetCoPa	05	09	22
Yotter, Isaac(Z-M)	1826	Aug. 01	WayneCo.,Oh.	05	09	19
Yotter, Jacob(Z)	1814	Oct. 20	TuscarwsCoOh	05	09	07
Yotter, John(Z)	1807	June 01	SomersetCoPa	04	08	02
Yotter, John(Z)	1807	June 01	SomersetCoPa	04	08	08
Yotter, Stephen(Z)	1814	Jan. 19	TuscarwsCoOh	04	09	08
Youger, Philip(Z)	1816	Oct. 16	MuskingmCoOh	11	12	20
Youkey, Christian(Y)	1826	Oct. 07	Stark Co.,Oh	06	16	08
Young, Alexander(Z)	1837	Feb. 27	GuernseyCoOh	14	12	22
Young, Alexander(Z)	1837	Feb. 27	GuernseyCoOh	14	12	27
Young, Alexander(Z)	1815	June 24	GuernseyCoOh	01	03	21
Young, Alexander(Z)	1815	June 24	GuernseyCoOh	01	01	03
Young, Cornelius(Z-M)	1832	Oct. 24	KnoxCo.,Ohio	10	06	12
Young, Cornelius(Z-M)	1832	Nov. 01	KnoxCo.,Ohio	10	06	12
Young, Ephraim(Z)	1814	Feb. 12	MuskingmCoOh	10	06	22
Young, Ephraim(Z)	1816	Nov. 26	KnoxCo.,Ohio	10	05	02
Young, Ephrain(Z-M)	1832	Oct. 24	KnoxCo.,Ohio	10	06	19
Young, Fred'k.(Y)	1828	April 15	Stark Co.,Oh	09	11	17
Young, Frederick(Z)	1805	May 23	YorkCo.,Penn	12	13	04
Young, Frederick(Z)	1805	May 23	YorkCo.,Penn	12	13	04
Young, George(Y)	1828	Jan. 28	Stark Co.,Oh	07	16	29
Young, George(Z)	1815	Aug. 23	StarkeCo.,Oh	05	08	16
Young, J.(Z)	1816	Feb. 03	ZanesvilleOh	13	11	06
Young, Jacob(Y)	1821	Sept. 19	ColumbanCoOh	01	07	22
Young, Jacob(Y)	1821	Sept. 19	ColumbanCoOh	01	07	15
Young, Jacob(Y)	1821	Sept. 19	ColumbanCoOh	01	07	15
Young, Jacob(Y)	1823	Jan. 04	ColumbanCoOh	01	07	15
Young, Jacob(Y)	1824	Aug. 16	ColumbanCoOh	01	07	24
Young, Jacob(Y)	1825	April 18	ColumbanCoOh	01	07	15

PURCHASER	YEAR	DATE	RESIDENCE	R	T	S
Young, Jacob(Y)	1829	April 06	ColumbanCoOh	01	07	24
Young, James(Y)	1830	March 18	BelmontCo,Oh	07	09	02
Young, Jesse(Z)	1813	Dec. 28	MuskingmCoOh	09	04	09
Young, John(Z-M)	1834	Oct. 10	HolmesCoOhio	09	09	04
Young, John(Z-M)	1836	Jan. 22	MuskingmCoOh	06	03	03
Young, John(Z-M)	1840	June 03	HolmesCoOhio	09	08	20
Young, McKinzie(Z-M)	1829	April 10	HarrisonCoOh	01	05	15
Young, Michael(Z)	1835	Sept. 24	GuernseyCoOh	09	08	14
Young, Michael(Z-M)	1836	Jan. 13	TuscarwsCoOh	02	07	08
Young, Robert(Z-M)	1834	Dec. 15	Ohio Co.,Vir	02	03	07
Young, Samuel(Z-M)	1821	May 12	TuscarwsCoOh	03	08	03
Young, Theobald(Z)	1833	Aug. 26	MuskingmCoOh	13	11	12
Young, Theobald(Z)	1833	Aug. 26	MuskingmCoOh	13	11	04
Young, Thomas(Z)	1835	Nov. 26	MonroeCo.,Oh	08	07	15
Young, William B.(Z)	1816	Oct. 03	ZanesvilleOh	12	10	10
Young, William Jnr.(Z)	1836	April 14	MonroeCo.,Oh	08	07	23
Young, William Jr.(Z)	1835	Sept. 23	MonroeCo.,Oh	08	07	23
Young, William(Z)	1825	Nov. 07	MonroeCo.,Oh	08	07	26
Young, William(Z)	1825	Nov. 07	MonroeCo.,Oh	08	07	22
Young, William(Z)	1825	Nov. 12	MonroeCo.,Oh	08	07	27
Young, William(Z)	1825	Dec. 06	MonroeCo.,Oh	08	07	28
Young, William(Z)	1825	Dec. 12	MonroeCo.,Oh	08	07	29
Young, William(Z)	1830	April 14	ZanesvilleOh	11	12	04
Young, William(Z)	1830	May 04	ZanesvilleOh	11	12	05
Young, William(Z)	1830	May 10	ZanesvilleOh	11	12	09
Young, William(Z)	1831	Aug. 17	BelmontCo,Oh	11	10	24
Young, William(Z)	1836	Aug. 17	MonroeCo.,Oh	08	06	17
Young, William(Z)	1836	Aug. 17	MonroeCo.,Oh	08	06	11
Young, William(Z-M)	1824	Dec. 01	AlleghnyCoPa	04	03	24
Young, William(Z-M)	1834	Feb. 19	HolmesCoOhio	08	08	02
Young, Wm.(Z)	1836	May 30	Perry Co.,Oh	08	06	20
Young, Wm.(Z)	1837	Feb. 27	GuernseyCoOh	14	12	21
Young, Wm.(Z)	1837	Feb. 27	GuernseyCoOh	14	12	22
Younger, Wm.(Z)	1830	Oct. 26	MuskingmCoOh	11	12	20
Youngker, Isaac(Y)	1833	Feb. 14	Stark Co.,Oh	06	16	27
Youngker, John(Y)	1828	Dec. 26	Stark Co.,Oh	06	16	27
Younker, Peter(Z-M)	1836	March 29	CoshoctnCoOh	08	06	06
Younker, Peter(Z-M)	1836	March 29	CoshoctnCoOh	08	08	06
Younker, Peter(Z-M)	1836	April 21	CoshoctnCoOh	08	06	06
Younker, Peter(Z-M)	1836	May 07	CoshoctnCoOh	08	06	06
Younker, Simon(Z-M)	1831	Sept. 13	CoshoctnCoOh	09	06	19
Younkin, H.(Z)	1816	June 01	LoudonCo,Vir	14	13	14
Younkin, H.(Z)	1816	June 01	LoudonCo,Vir	14	13	11
Younkin, Isaac(Z-M)	1835	Aug. 26	TuscarwsCoOh	01	08	02
Younkin, J.(Z)	1816	June 01	LoudonCo,Vir	14	13	14
Younkin, J.(Z)	1816	June 01	LoudonCo,Vir	14	13	11
Younkin, Samuel(Z)	1828	Jan. 08	Perry Co.,Oh	14	13	22
Younkin, Samuel(Z)	1833	Nov. 18	Perry Co.,Oh	14	13	15
Younkins, Wm.(Z)	1835	March 16	WestmrldCoPa	10	06	14
Yullough, William(Z)	1836	Sept. 26	MuskingmCoOh	10	09	24
Yullough, William(Z)	1836	Sept. 26	MuskingmCoOh	10	09	24
Yunker, Henry(Z-M)	1836	June 23	CoshoctnCoOh	09	07	22
Yunker, John(Z-M)	1832	Sept. 28	CoshoctnCoOh	09	04	07
Yunker, Simon(Z-M)	1832	Oct. 22	CoshoctnCoOh	09	07	21
Yunker, Simon(Z-M)	1832	Nov. 16	CoshoctnCoOh	09	07	22
Zane, Asa(Z)	1805	June 11	MuskingmCoOh	12	16	17
Zane, I.(Z)	1814	April 12	ZanesvilleOh	14	16	03
Zane, Isaac(Z)	1805	April 17	MuskingmCoOh	14	16	11
Zane, Isaac(Z)	1806	June 28	MuskingmCoOh	14	16	17
Zane, Isaac(Z)	1810	June 09	MuskingmCoOh	12	12	29
Zane, J.(Z)	1814	June 28	MuskingmCoOh	14	16	03
Zane, Jno.(Z)	1804	June 06	Ohio Co.,Vir	01	02	11
Zane, Jno.(Z)	1804	Nov. 29	Ohio Co.,Vir	02	02	11
Zane, Joel(Z)	1805	Oct. 16	MuskingmCoOh	08	02	22
Zane, Joel(Z)	1806	Jan. 13	Ohio Co.,Vir	08	02	21
Zane, Joel(Z)	1806	June 27	Ohio Co.,Vir	08	02	22
Zane, Joel(Z)	1806	June 27	Ohio Co.,Vir	08	02	06
Zane, Joel(Z)	1806	July 02	Ohio Co.,Vir	08	02	05
Zane, John(Z)	1804	June 01	Ohio Co.,Vir	12	10	24

PURCHASER	YEAR	DATE	RESIDENCE	R	T	S
Zane, John(Z)	1804	June 01	Ohio Co.,Vir	12	10	25
Zane, John(Z)	1804	Nov. 29	Ohio Co.,Vir	15	17	17
Zane, John(Z)	1804	Nov. 29	Wheeling,Vir	12	12	20
Zane, John(Z)	1804	Nov. 30	Ohio Co.,Vir	14	16	02
Zane, John(Z)	1804	Nov. 30	Ohio Co.,Vir	14	16	02
Zane, John(Z)	1804	Nov. 30	Ohio Co.,Vir	13	12	15
Zane, Noah(Z)	1806	Jan. 16	Ohio Co.,Vir	08	02	08
Zane, Noah(Z)	1806	April 24	Wheeling,Vir	08	02	05
Zane, Noah(Z)	1806	June 21	Wheeling,Vir	04	02	22
Zane, Noah(Z)	1806	June 21	Wheeling,Vir	10	09	27
Zane, Noah(Z)	1806	June 21	Wheeling,Vir	04	02	21
Zane, Noah(Z)	1806	June 21	Wheeling,Vir	10	09	28
Zane, Noah(Z)	1806	July 08	Ohio Co.,Vir	04	02	21
Zane, Noah(Z)	1806	Sept. 08	Wheeling,Vir	08	02	19
Zane, Noah(Z)	1811	Oct. 23	MuskingmCoOh	10	09	27
Zane, Noah(Z)	1811	Oct. 23	ZanesvilleOh	04	02	22
Zane, Silas(Z)	1805	Oct. 16	MuskingmCoOh	08	02	22
Zane, Silas(Z)	1806	Jan. 13	Ohio Co.,Vir	08	02	21
Zane, Silas(Z)	1806	June 27	Ohio Co.,Vir	08	02	22
Zane, Silas(Z)	1806	June 27	Ohio Co.,Vir	08	02	06
Zane, Silas(Z)	1806	July 02	Ohio Co.,Vir	08	02	05
Zane, Thomas(Z)	1832	Sept. 28	Perry Co.,Oh	14	13	26
Zegler, Jos.(Z)	1836	Aug. 12	Wheeling,Vir	08	06	05
Zeigler, Andrew(Z)	1806	May 24	MuskingmCoOh	14	16	11
Zeigler, Henry(Z-M)	1826	Sept. 05	TuscarwsCoOh	03	09	02
Zeller, Christian(Z-M)	1829	Feb. 24	TuscarwsCoOh	01	08	13
Zeller, Frederick(Z-M)	1835	Nov. 02	TuscarwsCoOh	03	07	14
Ziglar, A.(Z)	1815	Sept. 11	MuskingmCoOh	13	10	19
Ziglar, A.(Z)	1815	Sept. 11	MuskingmCoOh	13	10	30
Ziglar, Andrew(Z)	1807	March 28	MuskingmCoOh	14	15	23
Zigler, Daniel(Z-M)	1832	Aug. 28	TuscarwsCoOh	03	10	24
Zigler, Daniel(Z-M)	1832	Aug. 28	TuscarwsCoOh	03	10	24
Ziler, George(Z)	1831	May 09	Morgan Co,Oh	10	08	29
Ziler, George(Z)	1831	May 09	Morgan Co,Oh	18	08	28
Zimerman, Christian(Z-M)	1835	Oct. 26	TuscarwsCoOh	04	08	23
Zimerman, John(Z-M)	1835	Nov. 20	TuscarwsCoOh	04	08	22
Zimmer, Michael(Z-M)	1830	Aug. 28	MuskingmCoOh	06	03	24
Zimmer, Michael(Z-M)	1837	Jan. 03	AlleghnyCoPa	06	04	22
Zimmer, Michael(Z-M)	1837	Jan. 03	AlleghnyCoPa	06	04	19
Zimmer, Val.(Z-M)	1830	Aug. 07	ZanesvilleOh	06	03	24
Zimmer, Val.(Z-M)	1831	July 18	MuskingmCoOh	06	02	05
Zimmerman, Casper(Z)	1831	Dec. 08	Morgan Co,Oh	13	09	11
Zimmerman, Casper(Z)	1831	Dec. 12	Morgan Co,Oh	13	09	11
Zimmerman, Christian(Z-M)	1832	March 30	TuscarwsCoOh	04	07	14
Zimmerman, D. C.(Z-M)	1836	Aug. 31	CoshoctnCoOh	10	06	04
Zimmerman, David(Y)	1827	May 22	Stark Co.,Oh	06	18	22
Zimmerman, Henry(Z)	1805	Nov. 22	FairfeldCoOh	14	15	02
Zimmerman, J.(Z-M)	1835	Dec. 19	Jeff.Co.,Oh.	01	05	04
Zimmerman, Jacob(Y)	1825	Nov. 19	FranklinCoPa	09	11	04
Zimmerman, Jacob(Z-M)	1838	June 18	KnoxCo.,Ohio	10	08	13
Zimmerman, John(Y)	1831	May 09	Stark Co.,Oh	07	18	13
Zimmerman, John(Z-M)	1837	June 07	Jeff.Co.,Oh.	04	03	19
Zimmerman, John(Z-M)	1839	Aug. 30	GuernseyCoOh	04	03	10
Zimmerman, John(Z-M)	1839	Sept. 03	GuernseyCoOh	04	03	10
Zobb, Isaac(Z)	1804	Nov. 21	WestmrldCoPa	14	15	08
Zollars, David(Z-M)	1836	March 24	CoshoctnCoOh	05	07	11
Zollars, Fredrick(Z-M)	1832	June 01	CoshoctnCoOh	10	04	11
Zollars, Jacob(Z-M)	1837	Sept. 14	HarrisonCoOh	08	08	16
Zollars, Zephenia(Z-M)	1836	Sept. 26	HarrisonCoOh	09	08	17
Zwiegbrucker, Joseph(Z-M)	1836	March 17	PittsburghPa	05	04	14